To David Driggs and Dave Crow who brought water and fire.

Jess Lederman

To my parents.

Robert Klein

Table of Contents

Preface

As the editors of numerous books on the financial markets, many of which deal with state-of-the-art strategies and innovative new products, we are not easily excited by new publishing projects. However, working on *The Handbook of Derivatives and Synthetics* was a thrilling experience, because we quickly realized that a new classic was being born. It is the most comprehensive book ever assembled on the hottest, fastest growing sector of the financial markets. Novices will find that all of the basics are at their fingertips, while experts can access a wealth of information on the latest product innovations and trading tactics, including topics such as exotic options, emerging market derivatives, and advanced derivatives technology.

We would like to acknowledge the book's real heroes: the 54 chapter authors, men and women from around the world, all of whom are leaders in their field. They worked closely with us over the past year, taking time from hectic schedules to produce this invaluable handbook, and we thank them for a job superbly done. Thanks is also owed to the editorial staff of Probus Publishing, which recognized the importance of this project, and to the production staff, which was able to get this book out into the marketplace in record time.

Jess Lederman and Robert Klein

Contributing Authors

Jan Aaseth
Currency Broker
Den norske Bank

Until 1994, Mr. Aaseth was a trading floor official for the options and futures market at the Oslo Stock Exchange. He was also responsible for the marketing of the derivatives market at the exchange. Mr. Aaseth holds a bachelor of commerce degree in finance from the University of British Columbia in Vancouver, Canada.

J. Marc Allaire
Director
The Options Institute

The Options Institute is the educational arm of the Chicago Board Options Exchange. Mr. Allaire teaches classes on options strategies, futures, and portfolio management. In addition, he is the editor and a contributor to the second edition of *Options: Essential Concepts and Trading Strategies*.

Mr. Allaire holds an undergraduate degree from the University of Ottawa and a M.B.A. degree from McGill University in Montreal.

Prior to joining the Chicago Board Options Exchange, Mr. Allaire was Vice President and Options Manager with Richardson Greenshields of Canada Limited. His primary focus was on the retail side of the business, where he concentrated on broker education, strategy development, and sales support. Mr. Allaire also has traded futures and options for a regional brokerage firm in Montreal and had responsibility for options marketing for the Montreal Exchange.

Vincent M. Aquilino
Partner
Chapman and Cutler

Mr. Aquilino is chair of the firm's *Derivative Products Group* and is the senior partner in its Tax Department. He and Steven Conlon are the principal authors and co-editors of the book *Tax-Exempt Derivatives: A Guide to Legal Considerations for Lawyers, Finance Professionals and Municipal Issuers* (American Bar Association, 1994). He has chaired recent seminars on tax-exempt derivatives and has served as a panelist or speaker at a number of seminars dealing with the legal issues relating to a variety of financial products. He has submitted comments and has testified on a number of recent Internal Revenue Service regulations projects dealing with financial transactions. He has worked extensively in the leveraged lease and corporate finance areas, including international financing transactions such as off-shore financing projects and cross-border leasing. His professional activities have also included teaching law school federal income tax courses. Mr. Aquilino received his B.A. *summa cum laude* and M.B.A. from DePaul University and his J.D. from Northwestern University School of Law.

Steven A. Babus
Vice President and
Head of International Management Consulting
Union Bank of Switzerland North America Region

Prior to joining the bank, Mr. Babus spent a number of years providing external consulting services to the financial industry as a Managing Associate with Coopers and Lybrand.

Mr. Babus has a broad range of operations improvement and technology experience including: the design and implementation of trading and operational systems, strategic technology planning, and the design and evaluation of technical architecture's. He has also both evaluated package software, and designed and implemented custom software to support the derivatives business. In addition, he has conducted derivative market entry studies, assisted derivative start ups in establishing operations, and conducted risk management studies for financial institutions. Earlier in his career, he assisted in the development of the first generation of listed stock index futures.

Prior to Coopers & Lybrand, Mr. Babus was employed at Merrill Lynch Capital Markets and the Securities Industry Automation Corporation (SIAC). He has a Masters in Planning from the University of Pennsylvania.

Eileen Baecher
Financial Consultant

Eileen Baecher is a financial consultant. Formerly, Ms. Baecher was a Vice President in the Fixed Income Research Department at Goldman, Sachs & Co. Prior to assuming this position, she worked as an options trader at Citibank and in derivatives sales at

Goldman Sachs. She holds a BA from Yale University and an MBA from Columbia University.

Sheila C. Bair
Commissioner
Commodity Futures Trading Commission

Ms. Bair was nominated to serve as a CFTC Commissioner by President Bush in April 1991. After confirmation by the Senate, she was sworn in on May 29, 1991. She was appointed Chairman of the Financial Products Advisory Committee on December 20, 1991.

Prior to her appointment to the Commission, Ms. Bair was Legislative Counsel to the New York Stock Exchange (NYSE) in Washington beginning in 1988. She left this position in January 1990 to run for the House of Representatives from her home district in Kansas. Ms. Bair ran a highly-respected grassroots campaign, narrowly losing by 1 percent in the GOP primary. She returned to the NYSE after the campaign was over.

Ms. Bair, a native of Independence, Kansas, received her B.A. degree from the University of Kansas in 1975 and her J.D. from the University of Kansas School of Law in 1978. Based on her law school academic achievements, she was awarded a teaching fellowship at the University of Arkansas Law School. Ms. Bair is on the Board of Governors of the University of Kansas School of Law. Her published articles include "Why 'Offshore' Doesn't Mean 'Off-limits,'" *Futures Magazine* (Jan. 1992); "Is There a 'Future' in Swaps," *Mortgage Banking* (Sept. 1992); and "The Worst of Arkansas Best," *University of Kansas Law Review* (to be published Spring 1993).

William J. Barclay
Vice President, Strategic Planning and International Development
Chicago Board Options Exchange

Dr. Barclay's primary responsibilities include the development and implementation of CBOE's competitive strategy, managing CBOE's FLEX Option product, directing CBOE's Technical Assistance Program for emerging derivative markets, establishing relationships between the CBOE and major non-U.S. exchanges and regulators, coordination of the joint venture between the CBOE and Chicago Board of Trade, and policy development on regulatory issues governing the interaction of cash and derivative markets.

After joining the Exchange in 1986, Dr. Barclay became Assistant Vice President, Department of Operations Planning in 1987. Previously he was employed at the Chicago Board of Trade and the MidAmerica Commodity Exchange.

Dr. Barclay received his Ph.D. from Michigan State University in 1975, his M.A. from Cornell University in 1969, and his B.A. from the University of North Carolina in 1967. He attended public schools in Raleigh, North Carolina where his parents reside. He is active in community affairs and is a former board member and Chair of Prairie State Canoeists.

Brandon Becker
Director, Division of Market Regulation
Securities and Exchange Commission

The Division is responsible primarily for administering the SEC's programs for the oversight of securities markets and securities professionals. These duties include, among other matters, oversight of broker-dealers, transfer agents, the stock and options exchanges, the National Association of Securities Dealers, Inc., the Municipal Securities Rulemaking Board, and clearing agencies; as well as trading practices in connection with the issuance of securities.

In addition, Mr. Becker has taught a variety of securities regulation courses at Georgetown University Law Center, American University and George Mason University and published widely in the field of securities regulations. Following graduation from the Universities of Minnesota (B.A., 1974) and San Diego (J.D., 1977), Mr. Becker was an Associate-in-Law at Columbia Law School where he obtained his LL.M. degree (1979).

Tanya Styblo Beder
President
Capital Market Advisors, Inc.

Capital Market Advisors, Inc. specializes in financial institutions, capital markets, and derivatives. Prior to founding a consulting firm in 1987, Ms. Beder was a Vice President of The First Boston Corporation, where she worked over a 10-year period in a variety of areas, including Mergers and Acquisitions, Capital Markets, Derivative Products, and Fixed Income Research. Previously, she was a consultant in the financial institutions practice at McKinsey & Company. Ms. Beder is on the Board of Directors of the International Association of Financial Engineers, and is a Management Fellow on the faculty of the Yale School of Management. Her articles on derivatives have been published in books and professional magazines, including the *Harvard Business Review* and *The Journal of Financial Engineering*. She received a B.A. in mathematics from Yale University and an M.B.A. from the Harvard Business School.

Brian R. Bruce
Vice President
State Street Bank and Trust Company

Mr. Bruce joined Asset Management in May 1990 with eleven years experience in investment management. His unit is responsible for asset allocation, balanced fund management, active equity portfolio management and research and development.

Prior to joining State Street, Mr. Bruce worked eight years for Northern Investment Management Co. where he was Director of International Equity. At Northern, he managed global portfolios and co-developed a tactical asset allocation model with Roger Ibbotson. Mr. Bruce currently serves as Editor-in-Chief of Institutional Investor's Journal of Investing and has authored and edited four books on investing including "Global Portfolios" (Business One-Irwin, 1991) and "Quantitative International Investing" (Probus, 1990).

Mr. Bruce received a BS from Illinois State University, an MS in Computer Science from DePaul University, and an MBA in Finance from the University of Chicago where he won the prestigious CEO award.

Jeffrey P. Burns
Associate
Gordon Altman Butowsky Weitzen Shalov & Wein

Prior to joining the firm, which specializes in securities regulation, Mr. Burns was an attorney in the Branch of Derivatives Regulations, Office of Self-Regulatory Oversight (OSRO), Division of Market Regulation (Division) of the Securities and Exchange Commission (SEC). The Branch of Derivatives Regulation is responsible for reviewing derivative product proposals from the national securities exchanges, the NASD, and broker-dealers for compliance with the federal securities laws, the Commodity Exchange Act, and self-regulatory organization rules. In addition, the Branch also coordinates with the Commodity Futures Trading Commission regarding the relationship between futures and securities.

Mr. Burns is a graduate of John Carroll University (B.S. Economics, 1984), Cleveland-Marshall College of Law (J.D., 1988), Cleveland State University (M.B.A., 1988), and Georgetown University Law Center (LL.M. Securities Regulation, 1994).

DiAnne Calabrisotto
Assistant Vice President
Williams Financial Markets, a division of Jefferies & Company

Ms. Calabrisotto joined WFM in 1992. She has nine years experience in securities operations and clearance, office management/administration, and accounting having held similar positions at Prudential Bache Securities, Wolff Investment Group, Inc., and Maria Ramirez Capital Consultants.

Joseph B. Cole
Managing Director
Centre Financial Products Limited

Centre Financial Products Limited is a risk management firm that specializes in derivative market applications for the development of new products and new markets. Dr. Cole's responsibilities include product and account development and the marketing of structured financial instruments, with special emphasis on risk management and yield enhancement. These duties currently include new product development in the emerging markets for insurance futures and options and environmental trading.

Dr. Cole has spoken at numerous seminars and conferences on financial futures and options trading, commodity and oil-related hedging, asset-liability management, SO_2 allowance trading, and insurance futures. He has also served as a consultant to several exchanges and financial institutions in the development and analysis of new products, pension fund management, hedge design, and bank holding company asset-liability and futures trading programs.

In addition to a B.S. in Mathematics from Briar Cliff College and an M.B.A. from the University of South Dakota, Dr. Cole holds a Ph.D. in business administration from the University of Iowa.

Steven D. Conlon
Associate
Chapman and Cutler

Mr. Conlon is an associate in the Chicago office of the law firm of Chapman and Cutler. He advises a number of major mutual fund sponsors and investment banks on the development and evaluation of new financial products. Mr. Conlon is incoming chair of the Financial Transactions Committee of the Tax Section of the American Bar Association and chair of the Complex Financial Products Task Force of the Regulated Investment Companies Committee. Mr. Conlon and Vincent M. Aquilino are the principal authors and co-editors of the book *Tax-Exempt Derivatives: A Guide to Legal Considerations for Lawyers, Finance Professionals and Municipal Issuers* (American Bar Association, 1994). Mr. Conlon has co-authored a number of articles on the taxation of financial products in tax journals such as *The Journal of Taxation, TAXES Magazine, Tax Law Review,* and *Tax Notes.* He is also an adjunct professor at Illinois Institute of Technology Chicago Kent College of Law and teaches *Taxation of Financial Service Entities* in the Financial Services Law L.L.M. Program. He received his B.B.A. *summa cum laude* and his J.D. *cum laude* from Loyola University of Chicago.

David Courtney
Marketing Director
OMLX, The London Securities and Derivatives Exchange

Mr. Courtney read Business Studies at Lady Spencer Churchill College, Oxford before coming to work in the City of London in 1983. He has specialized in the derivatives markets ever since and has worked as a practitioner both within the brokerage and market-making communities with interests in the financial, energy and commodity markets.

Having direct experience of many European and Far East markets, including a period of secondment to Tokyo where he set up Credit Lyonnais' derivatives brokerage operation, he has gained widespread knowledge of many of the world's rapidly growing exchanges. He has written 3 books on the derivatives markets to date, the last, 'Derivatives Trading in Europe' seeks to map out the shape of the derivatives industry in Europe given moves towards economic and monetary union.

Richard A. Crowell
President and Chief Investment Officer
PanAgora Asset Management, Inc.

PanAgora Asset Management, Inc. was The Boston Company's Structured Investment Products Group. Since joining The Boston Company in 1964, he has been a leading contributor to quantitative product development and investment management activities. He founded the Investment Technology Group and managed the investment activities of the company's mutual funds. He served as an advisor to major public and corporate pension funds on investment objectives and asset allocation. Dr. Crowell is a graduate of Massachusetts Institute of Technology and holds an M.S. and Ph.D. from the M.I.T. Sloan School of Management. He is the author of *Stock Market Strategy,* (McGraw-Hill, 1977) and numerous articles in professional journals.

Patrick Cusatis
Associate
Lehman Brothers

Dr. Cusatis assisted in the development of several new municipal derivative products including RIBS/SAVRS and Bond Payment Obligations. In addition, Dr. Cusatis has developed a computer valuation model for the municipal market that values municipal bond components including caps, floors, call options, and swaps.

Dr. Cusatis received a B.S. and Ph.D. in Finance from the Pennsylvania State University. His academic work includes publications in *Journal of Financial Economics, Journal of Applied Corporate Finance,* and *Municipal Finance Journal.*

Kosrow Dehnad
Vice President
Chase Securities, Inc.

Dr. Dehnad works in the Derivative Origination and Structuring Group, responsible for new product development.

Prior to joining Chase in 1990, Dr. Dehnad worked for AT&T Bell Laboratories where he researched mathematical foundations of Robust Design as well as consulted on several major quality improvement projects. Dr. Dehnad has been published in various technical journals and is the author of the book entitled *Quality Control, Robust Design, and the Taguchi Method.* He has been adjunct professor at San Jose State University, Rutgers University and is presently in the Department of Operations Research at Columbia University.

Dr. Dehnad received a Doctorate in Applied Statistics from Stanford University. He received a second Doctorate in Mathematics from the University of California at Berkeley where he also received a Master of Arts in Statistics and Mathematics. Dr. Dehnad received his Bachelor of Science with First Class Honors in Mathematics from the Victoria University of Manchester, England.

Ron S. Dembo
President
Algorithmics Incorporated

Algorithmics Incorporated is a firm that specializes in state-of-the-art mathematical finance services and software. Dr. Dembo is also an Adjunct Professor of Operations Research at the University of Toronto. Before starting Algorithmics, Dr. Dembo was a Professor of Operations Research and Computer Science at Yale University. Dr. Dembo is the author of a patent on portfolio replication, and has written over 40 scientific publications on large-scale optimization. He has consulted extensively on financial risk exposure management, portfolio optimization, and hedging to major corporations and to the financial industry.

Anne B. Eisenberg
Vice President
State Street Bank and Trust Company

Ms. Eisenberg is responsible for directing and implementing quantitative applications in derivatives investment management. Ms. Eisenberg has over eight years experience in managing synthetic index funds and is responsible for the management of State Street Global Advisors' commingled futures fund (SPIFF) as well as numerous stock index portfolios—including SSGA's & P500 Flagship Index Fund.

Most recently Ms. Eisenberg worked on the development on SSGA's global synthetic index fund, International Stock Performance Index Futures Fund (ISPIFF) and the Enhanced SPIFF Fund.

Ms. Eisenberg received her BS from Tufts University and her MBA from Boston University.

Jörg Franke
Chief Executive Officer
DTB Deutsche Terminbörse

Dr. Franke was appointed Chief Executive Officer of DTB Deutsche Terminbörse GmbH, Frankfurt, in August 1988. He was General Manager of the Berlin Stock Exchange from late 1984 until the end of 1988. Also he was a member of the Executive Board of the Berliner Kassenverein A-Wertpapiersammelbank until the end of 1989.

Dr. Franke passed law school in 1966, and obtained his doctorate in 1971. In 1970, he joined the Westdeutsche Landesbank Girozentrale in Dusseldorf. In 1974, he was granted the power of attorney and in 1978, he was appointed vice president of the new issue department.

He wrote and published numerous articles on securities and the stock exchange and he is co-author of several books with the same topic, which were published between 1987 and 1990.

Charles J. Freifeld
Vice President, Senior Quantitative Analyst
The Boston Company

Mr. Freifeld joined the Fixed Income Management Group of The Boston Company in 1992. He is responsible for the design and implementation of quantitative investment strategies, as well as the analysis of structured investment products containing options and derivative-linked payoffs. Before joining The Boston Company, he was President of Advanced Algorithms, Inc., a Commodity Trading Advisor and Commodity Pool Operator.

Mr. Freifeld has managed portfolios in the commodity, currency and financial futures markets for over twenty-three years. He has used computerized, mathematical portfolio management systems for the last twelve years. In addition, he has written articles on portfolio management, spoken at industry conferences and served as an arbitrator for the National Futures Association.

Mr. Freifeld graduated summa cum laude in mathematics from Columbia College in New York and received an M.A. in 1964 and a Ph.D. in 1968, in mathematics, from Harvard University.

Adam W. Glass
Partner
Orrick, Herrington & Sutcliffe

Mr. Glass' areas of expertise are in asset securitization and municipal derivative products. He has practiced corporate and securities law since 1982, with an emphasis on mortgage- and asset-backed securities since 1985. He is an active member of the ABA Asset Securitization Subcommittee and the ABA Structured Finance Task Force, was the draftsman of the ABA's comment letter on risk-based capital standards applicable to senior-subordinated transactions, and, more recently, participated in drafting the ABA comment letter on Rule 3A-7. He is a frequent speaker and panelist on the federal securities regulation of municipal derivative products.

Mr. Glass is a graduate of Stanford Law School, where he was editor-in-chief of the Law Review. He obtained his undergraduate degree from Harvard College.

Varun Gosain
Head of Emerging Market Fixed-Income Derivatives
Paribas Capital Markets

Mr. Gosain joined the group in 1991. Prior to that he was a member of the Product Development and Emerging Market Debt Trading groups at Chemical Bank. He has an M.B.A. from the Indian Institute of Management and has completed all requirements except dissertation for a Ph.D. in Finance from the Wharton School of the University of Pennsylvania.

Gary Gray
Managing Director
Lehman Brothers

Dr. Gray has worked in municipal finance since 1972 and has been responsible for a number of innovative financial products including: tax-exempt zero coupon bonds and capital appreciation bonds; agricultural revenue bonds; tender option crossover refunding bonds; secondary market programs for tax-exempts and preferred stock including Multiple Option Municipal Securities and a variety of Unit Investment Trust products.

Most recently, Dr. Gray has been involved int he development of the RIBS/SAVRS program as well as a number of other municipal derivative products, including Premium Municipal Bond Receipts, Bond Payment Obligations ("BPO"), tender option bonds and a secondary market version of RIBS/SAVRS employing a custodial arrangement.

Dr. Gray received a B.S. in Electrical Engineering, and both an M.B.A. and a Ph.D. in Finance from the Pennsylvania State University. He currently teaches a course in investment banking and financial innovation to M.B.A. students at the Pennsylvania State University.

Peter Harris
Editorial Director
Waters Information Services

At Waters Information Services, a newspaper publisher, Mr. Harris has editorial responsibility for *Dealing with Technology, Derivatives Engineering & Technology,* and *FX Week.*

Before becoming a journalist in 1988, Mr. Harris was a computer systems developer and software manager. He spent over ten years working for financial organizations, including the *Financial Times,* Knight-Ridder Financial, and the London Stock Exchange.

Gary A. Herrmann
Partner
Orrick, Herrington & Sutcliffe

Mr. Herrmann is a partner with expertise in a broad spectrum of federal and state tax issues. His practice includes corporate finance and reorganizations, partnerships, investment companies, executive and employee compensation, exempt organizations, project finance, and real estate.

Mr. Herrmann served as the principal tax lawyer to CP National Corporation on its acquisition by Alltel Corporation and has advised Lucky Stores, Inc., with respect to major asset dispositions, including its Eagle Food Centers and Hash n' Karry divisions. He advises several investment companies, including Fidelity California Tax-Free Fund, Ballard Biehl & Kaiser Funds, and Bergstrom Capital Corporation.

Mr. Herrmann has advised numerous syndicated partnerships whose activities have ranged from real estate to computer software to aircraft to restaurants. He has advised many corporations, ranging from start-up companies to major public companies such as Transamerica Corporation, Lucky Stores, CP National Corporation, and Safeway as to stock option and other executive compensation issues.

He received his B.A., magna cum laude, in 1976 from Yale University and his J.D., magna cum laude, in 1979 from Harvard Law School. He served as a law clerk for the Hon. Irving L. Goldberg of the U.S. Court of Appeals for the Fifth Circuit and joined Orrick, Herrington & Sutcliffe in 1982.

Robert H. Herz
Partner
Coopers & Lybrand

At Coopers & Lybrand in New York, Mr. Herz is the firm's associate national director of accounting and SEC Services. He has served as the audit partner on a number of his firm's major clients in the financial services industry, including several derivatives products dealers. Mr. Herz also heads Coopers and Lybrand's Financial Transactions Advisory Group, which advises investment bankers and corporate clients on the accounting and tax aspects of financial instruments, mergers and acquisitions, project financing, and hedging transactions. He has authored numerous publications, including the firm's monographs, *Foreign Currency Translation—An Implementation Guide* and Coopers & Lybrand's *Guide to Financial Instruments* as well as numerous other publications and articles on derivatives and other financial instruments. Mr. Herz is both a U.S. CPA and an English Chartered Accountant.

Ming Jiao Hsia
Vice President
Williams Financial Markets, a division of Jefferies & Company

Dr. Hsia joined WFM in 1992. He specialized in the quantitative analysis of structured corporate and mortgage-backed fixed-income securities. Dr. Hsia received his Ph.D. in physics in 1992, masters degrees in mathematics and physics in 1988, and a masters of philosophy in 1989 from Columbia University. He also received his bachelor of arts degree in mathematics and physics graduating with highest honors from Columbia University in 1986. Dr. Hsia's coursework has also included graduate level corporate finance, debt markets, options and interest rate theory.

Michael Keppler
President
Keppler Asset Management, Inc.

Mr. Keppler is the founder of Keppler Asset Management, Inc. The firm specializes in the development of value-oriented integrated portfolio approaches, which focus on sophisticated asset allocation as well as market, sector, and stock selection strategies designed to exploit market inefficiencies.

Mr. Keppler is Vice Chairman of the investment committee of Graf Lambsdorff Money Management AG in St. Gallen, Switzerland, a leading money management firm, and serves on the board of directors of the Luxembourg equity mutual fund family *Global Advantage Funds* of State Street Bank and Trust Company, Boston.

Previously, Mr. Keppler served in various capacities in the securities business with one of the largest German banks in both Frankfurt and New York. Between 1983 and 1985, he received special training at leading New York investment banks, e.g., Morgan Stanley and Donaldson, Lufkin & Jenrette. From 1987 through 1992, he headed the global investment strategy, portfolio management and institutional sales departments of a New York investment bank as first vice president.

Mr. Keppler, who holds an M.B.A. from the University of Regensburg, has been an active contributor to numerous investment conferences, and has published in leading investment journals both here and in Germany.

Juan-Antonio Ketterer
Deputy General Manager
MEFF Renta Fija

Dr. Ketterer received his Ph.D. in Economics (1982) from the University of Minnesota, and has received several awards for his work in that field. He has worked in International Finance for the World Bank, and as Professor of Finance at the Business Schools of Northwestern University and Carnegie Mellon University.

In his current position, he is the second highest ranking executive at the Spanish Financial Futures and Options Exchange.

Roger Kristiansen
Director of Derivatives Securities
Oslo Stock Exchange

Mr. Kristiansen joined the exchange in 1989, and has been responsible for developing a derivatives market at the exchange. Mr. Kristiansen came to the exchange from a position as head of options and futures at Alfred Berg Norway, a part of the brokerfirm Alfred Berg Group. Mr. Kristiansen holds an MBA in finance from the University of Denver. He also holds a securities broker exam from Norway.

R. McFall Lamm, Jr.
Vice President and Chief Economist
Coffee, Sugar & Cocoa Exchange

Mr. Lamm, Vice President and Chief Economist with The Coffee, Sugar & Cocoa Exchange, previously held the same position with COMEX. He received a Ph.D. in agricultural economics and operations research from the Virginia Polytechnic Institute and is the author of numerous articles.

Jeff Landle
Managing Director
Twenty-First Securities Corporation

Twenty-First Securities Corp. in New York is a broker-dealer and money management firm that specializes in hedged and arbitrage strategies. Mr. Landle directs the firm's quantitative efforts and is involved with the implementation of a number of hedged investment programs. His background includes positions as an equity analyst, portfolio strategist, quantitative analyst, and portfolio manager. Mr. Landle has a B.S. in finance from St. John's University and an M.B.A. in finance from New York University's Stern School of Business. He is a Chartered Financial Analyst, and lectures at seminars and conferences on advanced investment strategies.

Hasan Latif
Senior Vice President
Williams Financial Markets, a division of Jefferies & Company

Mr. Latif joined WFM after nine years at Lehman Brothers, where he most recently was a Vice President and Senior Structuring/Trading Specialist in the swap and financial products department. Having previously held positions in the fixed income research and futures departments, Mr. Latif is experienced in interest rate, currency and commodity derivative markets. Mr. Latif received a Master's degree in Industrial Administration for Carnegie-Mellon University and a Bachelor's degree in Commerce from the University of Bombay.

Robert M. Mark
Partner
Coopers & Lybrand

Dr. Mark heads the Financial Risk Management consulting practice at Coopers & Lybrand (C&L), based in New York. The risk management practice advises clients on financial risk management issues and is directed toward financial institutions and multinational corporations. He is also chairperson of the National Asset Liability Management Association (NALMA), and an adjunct professor at NYU's Stern Graduate School of Business.

Prior to his current position at C&L, he was a Managing Director in the Asia, Europe, and Capital Markets Group (AECM) at Chemical Bank. He was a Senior Officer at Marine Midland Bank/Hong Kong Shanghai Bank Group, where he headed the technical analysis group within the capital markets sector. Earlier, he was Director of a systems profit center at American Express.

Dr. Mark earned his Ph.D. with a dissertation in options pricing from New York University's Graduate School of Engineering and Science, graduating first in his class. He subsequently received an Advanced Professional Certificate (APC) in accounting from NYU's Graduate School of Business.

Scott McDermott
Vice President
Goldman, Sachs & Co.

Mr. McDermott is a Vice President in the Fixed Income Research Department at Goldman, Sachs & Co., where he is responsible for market research in fixed income derivative products, including the futures, options, and swaps markets. He holds an SB and a Ph.D. in Physics from the Massachusetts Institute of Technology.

Jacob Navon
Senior Vice President
The Boston Company Asset Management Inc.

Mr. Navon joined The Boston Company Asset Management Inc. in 1990, specializing in the investment research of cash and short-term securities. He is the chairman of the reserve asset strategy committee. Previously, Mr. Navon worked for Durkee Capital Advisors Inc. as a Managing Director and Portfolio Manager. Earlier, he was a Senior Fixed-Income Specialist at Mabon Nugent & Co. From 1984 to 1989, he worked at Salomon Brothers in fixed-income sales and research. He has expertise in futures, options, dollar and nondollar foreign bonds as well as mortgage-backed bonds and their derivatives. Mr. Navon graduated from Harvard Business School, earning an M.B.A. with distinction, and was awarded both B.A. and M.A. degrees in natural sciences, with honors, from the University of Cambridge.

Andrew Parry
Assistant Manager/Public Relations
Sydney Futures Exchange Limited

Mr. Parry has worked for the SFE for the past 14 months. Previously he was a finance journalist with *Australian Business Magazine* and *Australian Business Monthly* (since 1989).

Lois B. Peltz
Managing Editor and Vice President
Managed Account Reports Inc

Ms. Peltz joined Managed Account Reports Inc in March 1992, and is responsible for the editorial content of MAR publications, including *Managed Account Reports* and *Quarterly Performance Report*, and MAR conference programs. She was formerly Vice President and Manager of Marketing Services/CTA Selection at ML Futures Investment Partners Inc, where she was responsible for advisor analysis, alternative fund structures, the review of all current funds, and marketing support for futures funds and pools at Merrill Lynch's managed futures subsidiary.

Ms. Peltz graduated Phi Beta Kappa from Vassar College and holds an M.A. in international affairs from Columbia University and an M.B.A. from New York University.

Gérard Pfauwadel
Chairman
MATIF

Mr. Pfauwadel also holds the position of Chairman of the Banque Centrale de Compensacion, B.C.C., (Commodities Futures Clearing House), and Chairman of F.M.A. (or O.M.F.). Mr. Pfauwadel graduated from the Ecole Polytechnique and the Ecole Nationale d'Administration (E.N.A.). He served in the French Treasury from 1976 to 1988.

Leslie Lynn Rahl
President
Leslie Rahl Associates

Leslie Rahl Associates is a consulting firm specializing in swaps, options, and derivative products. Ms. Rahl is a pioneer in the swaps and derivatives business. She was the founder of the interest rate cap, collar and floor business. She has managed all facets of this business including trading, risk management, financial engineering, origination, research, documentation and legal. Her expertise includes both swap and option products in US dollars, foreign currencies, equities and municipals.

For nine years, Ms. Rahl led the pre-eminent Citibank swaps and derivatives team of 45 traders, 30 originators/financial engineers and 10 researchers. Her team was rated #1 by both Euromoney and Greenwich.

Ms. Rahl received her undergraduate degree in Computer Science from MIT and an MBA from the Sloan School of Management at MIT. She attended a special program, "Marketing Management: A Strategic Perspective" at Stanford University.

Lisa M. Raiti
Managing Director
Centre Financial Products Limited

Ms. Raiti's responsibilities at Centre Financial Products Limited include marketing a turnkey product—the creation of 'AAA' rated derivative subsidiaries for banks, insurance companies and brokerage houses. She also focuses her efforts on the development and securitization of credit enhanced securities that bridge the gap between insurance and the capital markets.

Formerly, Ms. Raiti held a position at Standard & Poor's Corporation as Director of the Derivative Product Companies Group—a group she headed since its inception—which rates the creditworthiness of standalone 'AAA' subsidiaries set up to do business in over-the-counter derivative markets. Ms. Raiti spearheaded the development of criteria for rating these innovative companies, and has lectured extensively on this cutting edge area of financial products.

Ms. Raiti holds an M.B.A. in finance and accounting from New York University, and a B.S. in civil engineering from Columbia University.

Jeff Reckseit
Director/Institutional Sales
Campbell & Company

Mr. Reckseit became interested in the commodities futures markets in 1975, trading for his own account. He then went to the "sell side" working for one of the large wire-houses for ten years. In 1989, he returned to the "buy-side" with one of the oldest and largest commodity futures trading advisors in existence, Campbell & Company. Mr. Reckseit travels extensively, representing the managed futures industry to employee benefit retirement plan sponsors. He attended Cornell University in Ithaca, NY, and Emerson College in Boston.

Joseph S. Rizzello
Senior Vice President of Marketing and New Product Development
Philadelphia Stock Exchange

Mr. Rizzello is directly responsible for the marketing of all current PHLX products, development of new products, and operation of the Exchange's office in London. Since joining the PHLX in 1985, Mr. Rizzello's primary responsibility has been the marketing of products and services offered by the Exchange, including stocks, equity options, index options, currency options, and the Exchange's automated trade execution systems, known as "PACE" for equities and "AUTOM" equity and index options.

Prior to joining the PHLX, Mr. Rizzello was Vice President and Branch Manager for Thomson McKinnon Securities, Inc., in Philadelphia.

Mr. Rizzello has presented lectures on a variety of subjects that include the Exchange's business in equities, equity options and, specifically, foreign exchange risk management for private and public sector institutions in North America, the Pacific Rim, Europe, and the Middle East. He is a personal guest speaker of universities and business schools such as INSEAD in Foutainbleu, France, and the Wharton School of the University of Pennsylvania.

Richard L. Sandor
Chairman and Chief Executive Officer
Centre Financial Products Limited

Centre Financial Products Limited is an affiliate of Centre Reinsurance Company, a Bermuda-based subsidiary of the Zurich Insurance Group, an international insurance company with $49 billion in assets. For more than three years, Dr. Sandor was Vice President and Chief Economist at the Chicago Board of Trade, during which time he earned the reputation as the "principal architect of interest rate futures markets."

In 1991, Dr. Sandor was elected as a nonresident Director of the Chicago Board of Trade. He concurrently serves as an industry governor of the Chicago Mercantile Exchange. Dr. Sandor is a Distinguished Adjunct Professor at Columbia University Graduate School of Business.

Dr. Sandor received his B.A. degree from City University of New York, Brooklyn College, and earned his Ph.D. in Economics from the University of Minnesota in 1967. Dr. Sandor was formerly a member of the board of directors of the Lincoln Park Zoological Society and is currently a member of the board of governors of the School of the Art Institute of Chicago and is a Major Benefactor of the Art Institute of Chicago.

Wendy Seward
Numerical Analyst
Algorithmics Incorporated

Dr. Seward is responsible for the implementation of pricing methods for financial instruments at Algorithmics, as well as for the design and implementation of numerical methods. She has extensive research experience in numerical analysis and has worked in application areas ranging from mathematical biology to semiconductor device simulation. Dr. Seward is the author of a number of papers in mathematical journals. Before joining Algorithmics in January 1993, she was an Assistant Professor at the University of Waterloo. Dr. Seward holds M.Sc. and Ph.D. degrees in Computer Science from the University of Toronto.

Jay J. Shartsis
Director of Options Trading
R.F. Lafferty & Co., Inc.

R. F. Lafferty & Co., Inc., is a New York brokerage firm specializing in option trading. For more than a decade, Mr. Shartsis has been writing *Shartsis on Charts*, a technical market letter focusing on chart formations, put/call ratios, divergences, and option premium studies.

A 30 year veteran of the stock market wars, Mr. Shartsis is frequently consulted by the financial press. He has authored "The Striking Price," *Barron's Magazine's* option column several times.

Colin Southall
Senior Consultant
BRAXXON Technology, Limited

BRAXXON Technology, Limited is a systems and management consultancy based in London that provides IT services to City financial institutions. Mr. Southall has over 15 years' experience of real-time systems development and has worked in the City for the past eight years.

He has carried out consultancy and project management assignments for clients, primarily international banks, in the areas of risk management, systems architecture, dealing room technology, development methods, and operations.

Prior to joining BRAXXON, Mr. Southall worked for the London Stock Exchange, where he managed the development of information distribution systems for the domestic and international markets.

Thomas A. Szczesny
Senior Vice President and Manager
Investment Technology Division
The Bank of New York

Mr. Szczesny is responsible for providing performance, analytic, and consulting services to institutional investors. He has over 20 years of experience in investment strategy and policy formulation, product development, and capital markets analysis.

Mr. Szczesny holds B.A. and M.A. degrees in mathematics from the State University of New York, Buffalo. He has completed all requirements but the dissertation for a Ph.D. in operations research from the Polytechnic Institute of New York in Brooklyn.

Melinda M. Twomey
Senior Vice President
Williams Financial Markets, a division of Jefferies & Company

Ms. Twomey joined WFM after six years at Lehman Brothers where she was most recently a Senior Vice President and Senior Marketer in the Swap and Financial Products Department. She brings to WFM substantial derivative product knowledge and extensive experience in advising a variety of clients, including banks, thrifts, money managers and insurance companies with regard to derivative product applications. Prior to joining Lehman, Ms. Twomey spent two years at Chase Manhattan Bank in the corporate finance and swap groups. Ms. Twomey received a Masters degree in International Affairs form Columbia University and a B.A. degree from Smith College.

Bruce M. Usher
Senior Vice President
Williams Financial Markets, a division of Jefferies & Company

Mr. Usher joined WFM after almost four years at Lehman Brothers in the Derivatives Products group, both in New York and Tokyo, most recently as a Vice President and trader on the Structured Product desk. Specifically, he has created notes indexed to a wide variety of interest rates and currencies, which have been tailored to meet the specific requirements of domestic and international investors. In addition, Mr. Usher has made dozens of presentations to both investors and regional dealers on the intricacies of the structured note market. Prior to joining Lehman, Mr. Usher spent several years trading swaps at the Canadian Imperial Bank of Commerce and the Chuo Trust & Banking Company, both in Tokyo. Mr. Usher holds a Master of Business Administration degree from Harvard Business School and an Honors Bachelor of Commerce from Queen's University.

Christopher J. Williams
Managing Principal
Williams Financial Markets, a division of Jefferies & Company

Mr. Williams formed WFM in 1992 after an eight year career with Lehman Brothers in New York, where he was a Senior Vice President responsible for origination and trading of structured investments. In addition to derivatives expertise, Mr. Williams has extensive knowledge of the public and private investment grade fixed income markets. Mr. Williams is experienced in advising institutional investors and borrowers with regard to derivative products as well as transacting a variety of hedge strategies. Mr. Williams holds a Master of Business Administration Degree form the Amos Tuck School of Business Administration at Dartmouth College and a Bachelor of Architecture from Howard University.

George G. Wolf
Partner
Orrick, Herrington & Sutcliffe

Mr. Wolf is a partner who specializes in corporate finance and public finance tax matters. Leader of the firm's Corporate Tax Group, he handles nearly all aspects of federal and state tax planning, including those for investment companies, financial transactions, equipment leasing, limited partnership financing, real estate transactions, tax-exempt organizations, and unrelated business income tax issues, tax-exempt bonds, structured and securitized financings, and foreign financing transactions.

He is a member of the Financial Transactions Committee of the Taxation Section of the American Bar Association and has served as Chairman of the Distribution Subcommittee of the Corporate Tax Committee. He lectures on a variety of tax and financial topics.

Mr. Wolf received his B.A. degree in 1970 from Fresno State College and his J.D. degree in 1973 from the University of California, Davis, where he was a member of the Order of the Coif. He served in the Tax Division of the Department of Justice, Appellate Section, from 1973 to 1977 and joined Orrick, Herrington & Sutcliffe in 1977.

INTRODUCTION

The Development and Evolution of Derivative Products

Joseph S. Rizzello
Senior Vice President of Marketing
and New Product Development
Philadelphia Stock Exchange

THE ORIGINS AND IMPORTANCE OF THE
DERIVATIVE PRODUCT REVOLUTION

Few developments in the history of finance have created more new and efficient investment strategies than the class of instruments called "derivatives."

On a typical day, derivatives departments at major money center banks, investment banks, and other institutional investors are being called upon to price mortgages, new bond offerings, and equity issuances and to manage reinsurance and currency risk. Almost unknown just a decade ago, these new instruments are now fully integrated into modern treasury and investment practice. Their flexibility and ability to cope with changing market conditions has become so renowned that this class of instruments is being used in boardrooms to help discover new financing alternatives and to provide protection against adverse price movements. An example may illustrate the range of solutions offered by derivatives.

Take the case of what a treasurer in a billion-dollar multinational U.S. corporation faces on a daily basis. With operations on four continents, the company faces a variety of financial and commodity price exposures. To monitor these variables, the corporation establishes a financial division specifically designed to better manage its hedging operations and make its operating units more efficient. Teams of traders in Melbourne, London, and Cleveland trade currencies, bonds, and petroleum in the cash, futures, and options markets 24 hours a day. Information is passed along continuously. With operations in over 70 countries, the corporation faces many currency exposures, but its core risk is in dollar/sterling rates. Because its revenues are dollar-based, all of its accounting is done in dollars. But as a non-U.S. corporation, its dividends are paid in the local currency. That requires a separate currency management approach.

With over half of its debt in short- and long-term paper, the corporation issues its own commercial paper and Eurobonds in the Euromarkets and in the U.S. To be strategically positioned, half of its short-term debt is kept on hand for acquisitions; the other half is used for operations. As a crude oil company, there is also an active degree of swap trading going six months to two years into the future. Counterparties may be other oil companies or banks. Most of the swaps are done on a monthly cash settlement basis, some are tied to interest payments, others are held to expiration. Hedging is also done in the futures markets, and the corporation then manages the risk between spot and future prices.

What is going on? Nothing less than a quantum leap in financial management, most of it made possible through the use of a new class of products called derivative instruments.

DERIVATIVES DEFINED

As the name implies, derivative instruments derive their value from the cash markets in stocks, bonds, currencies, and commodities. Accordingly, the cash market drives both the mechanics—cash flows, physical delivery of assets, timing of the delivery process—and most importantly, the pricing of all derivative instruments. These instruments are used today in a variety of ways: to hedge against adverse price risk, or exposures to the underlying asset's price movements, or to provide alternative delivery mechanisms.

Derivative instruments exist in two forms: exchange-listed, and over-the-counter (OTC). Exchange-listed products usually are composed of futures and options. A futures contract is a binding agreement to buy or sell an underlying asset at a future date at a predetermined price. Organized futures markets were created as substitutes for the underlying cash market. Long options contracts provide the right, but not the obligation, to buy or sell an underlying asset at a specified price (the exercise price) within a specific time frame. An option with the right to buy is a call and an option with the right to sell is a put.

One key distinction between these two instruments is the payoff structure. Options partition the payoff for buyers and sellers of call and put options. A call buyer, for instance, benefits from price appreciation, but is protected from price declines. Futures are primarily used as a substitute for the underlying cash market instrument and have a more straight-line payoff structure. Over-the-counter products address the development and implementation of financial instruments designed to meet a customized financial problem. In many cases, OTC products incorporate solutions to a variety of financial risks under the umbrella of providing a "structured" product. This could include the use of futures and options, in addition to non-exchange-listed products.

While these delineations seem strict, in practice many corporations move fluidly between markets to find appropriate solutions. For example, when a corporation seeks to raise capital, it issues stocks or bonds. Derivatives can be used by both the issuer and equity holder to create new types of ownership with different risk-reward payoffs and by investors seeking to speculate on ownership prices or to hedge existing holdings against adverse price fluctuations.

In all instances, the value of derivatives is dependent on the assets upon whose price the derivative is based. Corporate equities, for instance, provide the pricing basis for exchange-traded options and all other variations of equity instruments. The price activity of currencies, commodities, and almost any other tradable asset likewise drives their respective derivative instrument prices.

The size and frequency of transactions in the cash markets are key indicators of a market's commercial health and financial viability. This same barometer also can determine any subsequent level of financial activity, such as hedging strategies, which can be sustained on an ongoing commercial basis. Hedging is an important first step in determining the marketplace's ultimate demand for new derivative instruments. If there is not sufficient trading activity in a corporation's bonds, for instance, issuers do not have the adequate volume or liquidity to initiate a cost-effective hedging strategy. Indeed, it is the high frequency of hedging strategies that has provided the primary impetus for developing many derivative product instruments.

In addition to hedging, the other activity that has propelled advances in derivative practice is arbitrage. Arbitrage, in its broadest definition, is a purchase or sale simultaneously in two or more markets done with the intent of profiting from any price discrepancies that may exist. While arbitrage is often considered a "riskless" transaction, it is better to think of this activity as a low-risk venture seeking to profit from temporary market inefficiencies. There are also many different types of arbitrage, which have spawned new types or combinations of instruments that deliver the properties without holding the actual instrument itself. This type of exposure is obtained synthetically, that is, by re-creating the real instrument's or asset's cash flow characteristics or other desired properties from another set of instruments.

This is possible because of the advances in understanding hedging, options, and arbitrage theories. This understanding, combined with the computer technology that is needed to break down basic risk-reward payoff and cash flows, has enabled financial engineers to create a synthetic derivative, or synthetic cash instrument.

Arbitrage is one of the oldest trading strategies and is often initiated in various ways: between buying and selling similar instruments on different exchanges; within different delivery months; among the same futures contract (spreading); and between buying and selling different cash market instruments.

The story of this financial product evolution has many beginnings: in the origin of key financial theories, in the maturation of exchanges, and in the rising level of financial assets. But one focal point provides a great demonstration of how powerful market forces converged to create something that is now integral to modern money management. That story begins with the foreign exchange markets.

HEDGING INTANGIBLES: CURRENCY FUTURES

Like most great inventions, financial derivatives began with a simple need: a group of Chicago commodity traders wanted to speculate in the British pound. But when they were told the currency could be purchased only in the interbank market in $1 million denominations, the denial transformed itself into a challenge. Within a few years, currency futures were trading on a Chicago futures exchange.

The conditions that created currency futures trading were in place since the unwinding of the Bretton Woods Agreement in 1971. The International Monetary

Fund, which was established after the Bretton Woods Conference of 1944 and which included most of the world's major countries, had adopted the Bretton Woods system calling for the close monitoring of foreign exchange rates. Under the agreement, the U.S. dollar was fixed at 1/35 of an ounce of gold. The dollar was also the mainstay currency by which all other currencies were traded. In practice, this meant that other nations were obliged to buy or sell their own currencies against the dollar and limit any market fluctuations to 1 percent above or below par. If a government failed to maintain its own currency, it could revalue and then seek to stabilize it at the new rate.

The system worked well until the late 1960s, when U.S. inflation, fueled by the Vietnam War and the Great Society domestic program, was combined with a large balance-of-payments deficit. Other countries saw the dangers this inflationary scenario could produce and, in an effort to protect themselves, began selling large quantities of dollars on the international market. Against this changing international backdrop, the U.S. revalued the dollar in August 1971 by raising the price of gold and simultaneously ending convertibility. In December 1971, the U.S. moved to expand the fluctuation band for IMF currencies to 2 1/4 percent above or below par.

A second revaluation of the U.S. dollar in February 1973 marked the beginning of floating currency rates. After that, central bank interventions notwithstanding, volatility was to become a permanent feature in world currency markets.

Prior to the unraveling of the Bretton Woods Agreement, trading had begun in seven currencies at the Chicago Mercantile Exchange (CME). Dominated by the huge interbank market, which routinely conducts trading in spot and forward sales and swaps, futures initially were a small adjunct to foreign exchange risk management.

The start of currency futures trading in May 1972 has been followed by waves of breakthrough products, not only in new categories, such as options, but in new methods of settlement and clearing.

One of the better examples of the far-reaching effects of new products occurred in April 1973 when the first equity options exchange was created as an offshoot of the Chicago Board of Trade (CBOT). When trading began on the Chicago Board Options Exchange (CBOE) in April 1973 on a restricted list of call options (put options were not part of the original experiment), it opened the way for other exchanges to expand their product lines. Options began trading on the American Stock Exchange in 1973 and in 1975 on the Philadelphia Stock Exchange (PHLX).

Today, entire new categories of exchange-listed and customized products are available for trading by the largest groups of investors and traders in history (see Exhibit 1). There are now over 54 organized futures and options exchanges worldwide that list products ranging from Eurodollars and precious metals to currencies, dried cocoons, stock indexes, and bonds. Countries with equity exchanges are also considering options trading as an additional way to provide liquidity to their current equity and treasury bond trading.

All of these activities have developed in conjunction with the $28 trillion global cash market. In the worldwide cash markets, there is $1 trillion a day in activity in foreign exchange (see Exhibit 2). The markets in non-U.S. equities, non-U.S. bonds, and in U.S government securities also number in the billions. In each of these capital markets, the existence of derivatives has been credited with making it easier to conduct business with less risk.

Exhibit 1. Futures and Options Trading Volume on U.S. Futures and Securities Exchanges

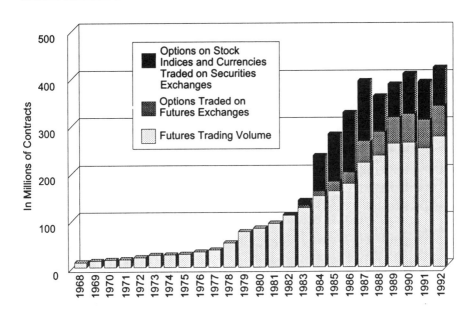

	Jan. 1992	Jan. 1993	% Change
Interest Rates	18,827,999	16,818,008	(10.68%)
Energy Products	4,293,690	4,632,129	7.88%
Ag. Commodities	5,574,166	4,598,781	(17.50%)
For. Currency/Index	3,569,609	2,823,478	(20.90%)
Equity Indices	1,489,396	1,279,649	(17.08%)
Precious Metals	1,426,679	842,018	(40.98%)
Nonprecious Metals	157,076	162,898	3.71%
Other	22,915	34,801	51.87%
TOTAL	35,361,530	31,191,762	(11.79%)

Source: Futures Industry

To accommodate the transfer of financial information and clearing, worldwide data and settlement networks were created to clear and report multilateral, multicurrency trades. Similarly, large systems were developed to handle custodian and equity trade processing functions for mutual funds and institutional equity trading accounts. Creating and assembling the needed technology to provide these essential trading

Exhibit 2. Total Gross Reported FX Turnover

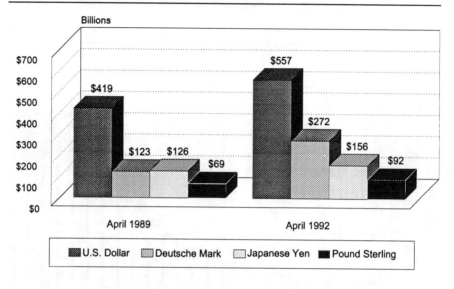

Source: Bank for International Settlements 1992 Survey

services ranks as one of the private sector's greatest, and less publicly acknowledged, achievements. Indeed, were it not for the computational horsepower, data transmission speed, and price information streams needed for the exacting demands of derivatives clearing and settlement, modern trading would not exist.

The democratizing effect of making these massive informational and capital flows available to more investors than at any other time in history has caused major changes in the way financial services are developed, delivered, and regulated.

Indeed, aside from the well-acknowledged effect technology has had on product development and strategy implementation, technology has also had an inordinate impact on international government regulation. In his book, *The Troubled Money Business,* William Sihler, professor at the Darden School of Management, notes that rigid regulatory structures often cannot adapt quickly enough to accommodate the changing capital flows and strategies that are facilitated by technological change.

As a case in point, Professor Sihler cites the October 1987 stock market crash in which technology's role clashed with a more rigid regulatory trading structure. In 1992, the currency markets were also assaulted as central banks moved to support the value of their declining currencies in the face of massive selling precipitated by traders and fueled by rapid-fire trade execution systems powered by streams of international data on currency movements.

In both cases, information and trading technologies worked together to help alter capital flows into essential markets. But the regulatory framework, which in the case of the U.S. dates back to the 1930s, has failed to keep pace with the actualities present in today's marketplace.

WHAT THE REVOLUTION PRODUCED

This confluence of advances in market usage and technology helped produce an assortment of over-the-counter and new exchange-traded instruments to meet changing customer demands. To help manage the risks of these complex trades once they were booked, the broker-dealers who created these OTC positions often looked to listed exchanges. This relationship helps explain how the volume in many exchange-listed products has paralleled the proportional growth in similar OTC-related products.

While exchanges are frequently taking the initiative and developing new products to meet member and customer needs, the creation and introduction of new products is a daunting task. During the 1970s and 1980s, market demands helped produce an array of revolutionary new products that profoundly changed the way exchanges operate.

Through successful new product introductions, exchanges not only became the trading arena for hedging and speculative strategies, but also the focal point for new customers who never used listed exchanges before.

Options represent one of the greatest developments of modern finance because they allow investors to systematically increase or decrease the amount of risk an investor is able to accept. By contouring risk to an acceptable level, the seller or grantor of an option forgoes the opportunity for additional appreciation in the value of the owned asset in return for a payment of an option premium, which reduces the amount of loss if the asset's value drops. Alternately, through leverage, a call option buyer is able to control a larger asset value than would be possible if the asset were purchased outright. Option buyers benefit when the asset's value increases; potential losses are limited to the amount of the option premium.

The beginning of options trading initiated four major changes in the industry. First, the industry opted to standardize strike prices and expiration dates. Second, it allowed the transfer of options contracts between anonymous buyers and sellers. Third, by centralizing trading and clearing in one organization (i.e., The Options Clearing Corporation issues, clears, and settles equity, index, and currency options traded on U.S. securities exchanges), net transaction costs were lowered for all trading parties. Finally, the centralized exchange also made it easier to monitor, regulate, and if needed, prosecute any violation of exchange rules and regulations.

By combining call and put options, investors can construct numerous strategies that yield flexible risk-reward boundaries, and protect against adverse price movements. The challenge is to know which strategy is most appropriate to a given circumstance at any time.

While options and futures each provide unique forms of price protection, options were designed to incorporate the price differential between the underlying stock's trading price and the option's strike price. To get this same structure, futures traders had to construct arbitrage and spreading strategies.

This is accomplished by examining the distinct price relationship between the cash and futures markets known as "basis," which is defined as the arithmetic difference between cash market and futures prices. Basis provides the fundamental link between the two markets.

Futures prices are determined, in part, by future interest rates. Since the instruments in most underlying futures positions are financed, interest payments over the course of the contract's holding period are incorporated into the market price. Because futures markets do not trade in a vacuum independent of interest rates, it is possible to calculate a futures contract's price, given a specific cash price and cost of funds, by incorporating such variables as cash price adjusted for yield to maturity; current yield on a cash instrument; cost of funds and days until delivery. While hedging does not eliminate price risk, it does reduce it by substituting the price differential between the cash and futures prices (basis risk) for the less manageable and predictable price risk.

Inherent in determining basis risk is the cost of carry. This cost includes interest rates, storage and assay costs, inflation, and in the case of stock index futures, dividend income on the basket of stocks.

Because of these established price relationships, arbitrageurs constantly monitor the price relationships between separate markets and instruments to determine when a discrepancy in the price relationship occurs. When futures prices are too high, for example, traders will sell the futures and simultaneously buy the underlying cash market instrument in an attempt to profit from the price discrepancy. When futures prices inaccurately reflect the cost of carry, arbitrageurs will buy futures and in some cases accept delivery, in the hope of selling the cash instrument in the market at a better price.

The practice of arbitrage advanced to a higher level as a result of trading stock index futures. Because of the institutional size of the equities market, the popularity of indexation, and readily available technology, stock index arbitrage emerged as a powerful display of how derivatives can be used to link new technology with a proven trading strategy. This practice also showed how other instruments, such as convertible securities or options, could be substituted for investment in the cash stocks to achieve the same equity market exposure.

The popularity of stock index arbitrage also indicated how institutionalized the marketplace for derivatives had become. While financial institutions began entering the derivatives marketplace in the early to mid-1970s, it was not until the early 1980s that institutions began to purchase clearinghouse memberships.

Needless to say, the presence of large institutions produced some fundamental changes in the way the marketplace operates. New concerns over market liquidity, risk aversion, price volatility, the role of technology, and staying abreast of market advances have helped push investment managers into considering investing as a more comprehensive process. To make an investment decision today, managers must include not only the risk-reward potential of the trade itself, but also other factors, such as agency costs and tax and accounting ramifications.

THE CASH MARKETS: SIZE AND USER DEMANDS

It is becoming increasingly evident that international capital flows are being facilitated by improving central bank structures, buttressed by sophisticated clearing, trading, and settlement technology.

Exhibit 3. Global Investment Market by Asset Class— $28.3 Trillion Market

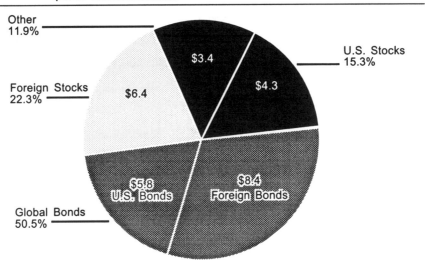

Other 11.9%

U.S. Stocks 15.3%

Foreign Stocks 22.3%

$6.4

$3.4

$4.3

$5.8 U.S. Bonds

$8.4 Foreign Bonds

Global Bonds 50.5%

Source: Brinson Partners

While the discussion thus far has centered on new trading products and technology, these advances are occurring within a fertile and ever expanding global capital investment market. The size of global asset classes has fueled the growth in new products and trading strategies to meet investor demands.

As of 1992, the global investment market was $28.3 trillion and was composed of 50.5 percent global bonds. Of that amount, $8.4 trillion was in foreign bonds and $5.8 trillion was in U.S. bonds. Foreign stocks accounted for 22.3 percent of this market, or $6.4 trillion, while U.S. stocks comprised 15.3 percent, or $4.3 trillion in value. The remaining 11.9 percent was in other asset classes such as precious metals and real estate, according to a study by Brinson Partners of Chicago (see Exhibit 3).

The reality of global investing has produced the need for global risk management. As a result, this has produced the need for products that provide a customized solution using longer-dated OTC options to provide commodity and currency floors over the life of an asset's price exposure.

COMPARING CASH, FUTURES, AND SYNTHETICS

Any discussion of the similarities and differences between the world of cash, derivative, and synthetic instruments is an admittedly ambitious task, well beyond the scope of this introductory chapter. Still, there are basic characteristics shared by these instruments that can at least establish a framework in which to make comparisons. By making these comparisons, it is easier to get an overall understanding about how each group of instruments developed, and what is propelling their development today.

The first step in looking at this genre of risk management tools is to examine why they were created and what risks they were designed to mitigate. Both futures and forward contracts are legal agreements that provide for predetermined prices on instruments that are to be settled or delivered at some future date. While futures and options can be highly standardized instruments, they can also be customized instruments, often created by dealer banks. Because of their ability to be customized, over-the-counter markets have served to create a wider range of products, most notably swaps.

Since their introduction in 1979, swaps have become extremely popular methods of reducing financing costs while providing a variety of hedging purposes. A swap can be defined as a binding agreement between two parties, one of whom agrees to pay a fixed price for a quantity of assets to a second party who in return agrees to pay a floating price to the first party. As in most other hedging situations, this agreement is predicated on both parties achieving mutually beneficial goals: hedging protection in exchange for a desirable cash flow.

Swaps are widely used to hedge and reduce financing costs because they are extremely flexible instruments that cut across traditional product boundaries. Today, there are swaps on currencies, interest rates, municipal bonds, equities, and commodities, as well as hybrids that provide solutions to multiple-risk exposures.

Swaps can also be used at different periods in the interest rate cycle. When recessionary pressures reduce loan demands, for example, many banks seek to maintain or extend the wide net interest margins (the spread between low-interest borrowing costs and high-interest returns derived from loans and investments) through yield-enhancing products, such as CMOs or other mortgage-backed securities.

Swaps allow counterparties to alter cash flow payoffs over time and at different risk levels to provide benefits to both swap issuers and buyers. Commercial banks and other liability sensitive institutions can change their portfolios via swaps to either reduce interest rate sensitivity or seek higher yielding instruments. The common element in all swap transactions is the exchange of a quantity of underlying assets (called the notional amount) between two parties to the transaction, called counterparties. While swaps are highly customized, the key variable that is most often manipulated in any swap transaction is the exchange pattern, or payment terms, of the notional amount.

Because swaps are cash market creations, the key concern between involved parties is their mutual creditworthiness. It is for this reason that the first swap occurred between two counterparties with solid financial standing: the World Bank and IBM, which entered into a currency swap in 1981 brokered by Salomon Brothers. Because swaps are ideally suited to alter a portfolio's interest rate profile, their next major use was by the Student Loan Marketing Association, which exchanged fixed for floating interest rates in 1981.

Structurally, the common intermediary between the two swap parties is the dealer or broker who facilitates the trade by making the market in the bid-ask spread priced into the swap coupon (see Exhibit 4).

Today, the creativity being applied to new types of swaps is being expanded on an almost daily basis. Indeed, it is this flexibility that has become one of the most attractive features of swap activity. Almost every key variable in a swap transaction

Exhibit 4

Swap: Initial Exchange of Notionals (optional)

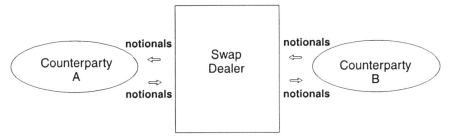

Swap: Periodic Usage or Purchase Payments (required)

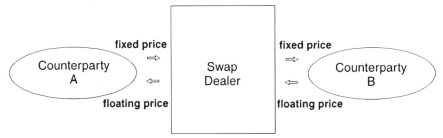

Swap: Reexchange of Notionals (optional)

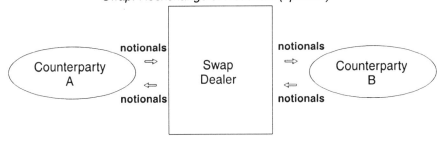

is negotiable. Notional amounts, for example, need not be transferred or re-exchanged in all cases. What must remain intact are the cash flows between the two counterparties.

Swap activity in U.S. dollar interest rates by banks alone grew from $121 billion in 1987 to $229 billion by 1991, according to the International Swaps and Derivatives Association. Interest rate swaps are most commonly used to reorient an issuer's or bank's asset-liability exposure. Swap activity has become more popular for variable-rate exposures, such as that found in credit cards and mortgages, where banks seek to lock in higher rates before a downturn. In many cases, the bank would enter into a

Exhibit 5

Interest Rate Swap with Cash Market Transactions (initial borrowing of principals)

CASH MARKET TRANSACTIONS

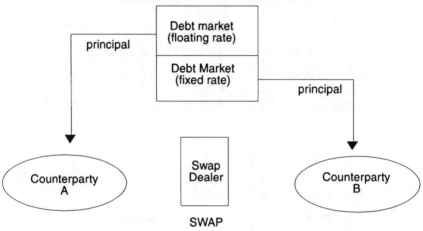

Interest Rate Swap with Cash Market Transactions (debt service with swap payments)

CASH MARKET TRANSACTIONS

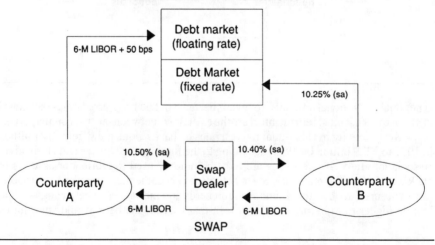

short-term swap, with the bank paying a floating rate and obtaining a fixed rate in return (see Exhibit 5).

In a rising interest rate scenario, the bank could either let existing swaps mature or go neutral and not engage in any more swaps. This allows the bank to readjust its loans at a higher rate faster as rates increase. By keeping the portfolio's time frame in check, swaps would not necessarily have to be bought back unless there is an extreme interest rate move. While these activities are helpful to regional banks with variable-rate exposures, commercial banks facing a flattening yield curve have also used swaps to minimize borrowing costs.

Swaps also have a role in reorienting the basis risk between different lending benchmarks, such as LIBOR (London Interbank Offered Rate) and the prime rates. Since most U.S. consumer, business, and home loans are prime-based, while overall bank funding costs are based on LIBOR, this spread relationship impacts bank profit margins. If rates rise, the Prime-LIBOR spread narrows, thus reducing bank profits. While swaps (with the bank paying prime and receiving LIBOR) work well when the spreads are within historical ranges, embedded options can reduce costs. In this scenario, the bank receives LIBOR, but limits the interest rate rise (through the embedded option). Swaps costs are reduced because the bank receives an up-front premium in exchange for receiving a higher yield. The premium acts to reduce the swap cost.

Aside from the flexibility inherent in these instruments, swaps have also grown in conjunction with their use on listed futures exchanges. As shown, swap activity does not exist in a vacuum, but grows as a function of the other markets. When these uses intersect and result in a new instrument whose behavior replicates that of an existing one, a synthetic product has been created.

SYNTHETIC INSTRUMENTS

While modern financial engineers can be accused of being too creative, they cannot be called magicians who use sleight of hand to create illusions. But by re-creating many of the strategies noted earlier in this chapter, financial engineers can create a new instrument that presents similar features, such as risk exposure coverage or cash flows, to a cash instrument. When this occurs, it results in the creation of a synthetic security.

Synthetic instruments are used for a variety of reasons. These can range from legal and tax benefit issues to execution considerations. In some cases, synthetic positions also may be cheaper to create due to the lower transaction and market impact costs in the derivative markets.

Synthetic exposures can be created in the cash market or via listed futures and options. Because option combinations can produce a variety of risk and profit exposures, they are ideally suited as the core element in producing substitutes for taking actual cash positions. Further, these trades can be initiated on an exchange at competitive prices and commission rates.

Exhibit 6 shows the synthetic positions which can be produced using a combination of futures and options. Again, exchange-listed synthetic positions are created for many of the same reasons as their cash market counterparts, while also providing many of the benefits of trading on a listed exchange.

Exhibit 6. Synthetic Positions

The following combinations of futures and options positions can produce specific exposures. These strategies are often used in arbitrage or in conjunction with more complex options positions on listed exchanges.

> Long call = long put + long futures
> Short call = short put + short futures
> Long put = long call + short futures
> Short put = short call + long futures
> Long futures = short put + long call
> Short futures = short call + long put

The classic benefits of trading exchange-listed derivatives can be summarized as follows:

- Public price disclosure and efficiency. Since bids and offers are displayed in a public forum and competitively bid, derivatives offer a price efficiency often not found in other environments.

- Lower transaction costs, due to standardization, competitive commissions, and other cost efficiencies shared by exchange members and the clearinghouse.

- Digression—executing through brokers.

- Ease in initiating and liquidating both long and short trading positions due to the market's structure and regulation.

- Reduces counterparty credit risk because a clearinghouse becomes the intermediary in every trade.

WHY DO SOME PRODUCTS FAIL? A CASE HISTORY

One of the essential points of product creation, whether it be in the consumer or financial industries, is market acceptance. Too often, products are created only to fail in their application. This is true for both OTC and exchange-listed products. The traditional product introduction cycle for exchange-listed products has some of the same stages as that of any retail or consumer product: a need is detected; market research is conducted; the product is designed and sold to the appropriate potential audiences; and then the product is launched.

Among exchange-listed products, this cycle has produced a high degree of failure: probably 75 percent of all listed futures and options fail to reach critical trading mass after six months. After that, these products may languish or face being delisted by the exchange.

Why do some products fail while others succeed? In many cases, the best answer is simple: market forces of supply and demand failed to produce a critical trading mass.

In other cases, the answer may range from a diminished need for the new product to the fact that the new product and its risk/reward profile can be more efficiently created elsewhere, such as on the OTC market. Product failures can also be tied to restrictive federal regulations, which have failed to keep pace with current market developments.

One of the better examples of this regulatory impediment was in the creation of Cash Index Participation contracts (CIPs) in 1988 by the Philadelphia Stock Exchange, and their eventual delisting. CIPs were designed to provide investors the price exposure and dividends contained in two indexes: the Standard & Poor's 500 Index and the Blue Chip CIP, which was based on a price-weighted index of 25 stocks designed to correlate with the Dow-Jones Industrial Average.

CIPs allowed investors to participate in the overall market movements of these two indexes without any continuous management fee (as in load mutual funds) or margin payments. Because they were listed as any other traditional equity on a stock exchange, CIPs could be sold short, pay dividends, be bought on margin, and day-traded at the prevailing stock market price. For tax purposes, CIPs were treated similarly to any other individual stock and would have been cleared and settled by the Options Clearing Corporation, which issues, guarantees, and clears all option trades at the Philadelphia Stock Exchange.

From a strategic point of view, CIPs, as cash index products, acted as the missing link between the stock and the stock index futures markets. Because of this synthesis, the creation of a cash index product would have provided the structural bridge between stock index options and futures and cash equity trading. But while a coherent argument could be made from the market perspective, federal regulators at the Commodity Futures Trading Commission (CFTC) and the Securities and Exchange Commission (SEC) faced a different set of problems. The futures industry contended that, because of certain trading characteristics, CIPs were a futures contract and therefore should fall under the jurisdiction of the CFTC. In August 1989, the U.S. Court of Appeals for the Seventh Circuit agreed and ordered that trading in CIPs cease.

Since this decision was rendered, similar stock index basket products have begun trading on equity exchanges under the SEC regulatory umbrella. Among the more popular of these products are Standard & Poor's Depository Receipts (SPDRs) and SuperTrust, both basket-variant products that are traded on the American Stock Exchange.

SPDRs and SuperTrust represent the new types of equity products that have been designed to provide features of both cash market instruments and listed exchange trading. SPDRs are designed to provide investors with an interest in a unit investment trust that holds a portfolio of common stocks designed to track the S&P 500 Index. As part of this new category of securities under the concept of Portfolio Depository Receipts, SPDRs represent ownership of an underlying cash portfolio (similar to actual cash possession), which provides dividends, short-selling opportunities, and continuous pricing. For institutional investors, SPDRs provide the ability to exchange specified baskets of the underlying stocks with the SPDR Trust.

While this product is an early application of the concept, Portfolio Depository Receipts may represent the way to deliver the benefits of an underlying instrument with investors in an open, continuously trading marketplace. Conceptually, any underlying basket of stocks or Treasury instruments could be placed into a unit investment trust framework and traded.

While it is too early to declare the success of SPDRs and SuperTrust, both represent important advances in both product design and trading. These products also indicate how the once-distinct boundaries between markets—cash and exchange-listed derivatives—has blurred.

Similar changes have been occurring in the way currencies are traded. Listed exchanges, such as the Philadelphia Stock Exchange, have refined their contract specifications to resemble a customized contract more closely, and thus meet the demands of institutional hedgers, who are currently very familiar with the mechanics and customs of interbank currency trading.

Furthermore, to communicate the benefits of exchange-listed FX trading, the PHLX addressed some of the key concerns of OTC traders in an effort to expand their trading opportunities. To do this, the Exchange examined issues ranging from the very important question of determining counterparty risk and market liquidity, to more mechanical questions, such as the length of the exchange's trading day. Certainly, one of the most important potential problems facing swap market participants is the risk that the borrower will fail to make timely payments of interest or principal on the debt outstanding. Most debt issuers have their credit rated by outside agencies, such as Moody's or Standard & Poor's. Unrated issuers face a difficult, if not impossible, task of getting their debt issued without these appropriate ratings.

But in February 1993, The Options Clearing Corporation (OCC) received a triple-A credit rating from Standard & Poor's Corporation. Because this is the agency's highest rating, it enables all OCC exchange members to issue a quality guarantee for all options transactions occurring on an OCC member exchange. Under its current rules, the OCC accepts cash, marginable securities, and irrevocable letters of credit as acceptable margin for all positions it holds.

This guarantee came at a time when adequate credit ratings in the interbank market were becoming more scarce. As a result, it enhanced the position of exchange-traded equity and currency options by making their credit veracity more readily available to investors.

By customizing options characteristics, exchange-listed options also have come to more closely resemble their OTC counterparts. Options trading, for example, now extends out to longer dated maturities (i.e., 24 months from the date of issuance), in addition to trading in the near term with weekly, and in some instances, daily expirations. Similarly, the interval in option strike prices is continually being refined and minimized to make the options coincide with spot levels. More recently, custom-ized exchange-listed options have been developed at the Chicago Board Options Exchange (CBOE) in their FLEX options and the Philadelphia Stock Exchange has endeavored to bridge the listed and OTC markets with an evolving marketplace that offers total customization for currency options.

Finally, because trading in some products is truly an international activity, the trading day has been expanded to cover other time zones. Electronic trading systems will also make the 24-hour trading day available to all investors, not just global trading banks.

THE IMPORTANCE OF A FAVORABLE REGULATORY ENVIRONMENT

One of the most commonly cited factors in any product or investment strategy's success is the regulatory conditions under which it is introduced.

For many years, some countries (as an example, Germany) considered commodity trading a form of gambling. As a result, the courts held that a trader's inability to meet a margin call incurred as a result of trading was a gambling debt and was not enforceable. Understandably, many international brokerage firms were reluctant to do business with traders domiciled in Germany.

Similarly, a government's action on tax, accounting, and enforcement practices may create a form of regulatory arbitrage among countries that have different trade regulatory practices. One of the most commonly cited reasons for the growth in offshore futures trading pools and funds is that the filing and reporting process is less stringent than in the U.S., which therefore reduces ongoing fund expenses. This may account for the fact that there is over $20 million in offshore trading funds outstanding.

Unfavorable changes in the tax law also have eliminated many popular trading strategies. One of the most popular was rolling a futures contract's open interest into the first expiration cycle of the new year in order to postpone the realization of capital gains. When the Economic Recovery Tax Act of 1981 virtually eliminated the tax advantage of spreading between delivery months, futures trading gains were realized in the year in which they occurred. Similarly, as illustrated in the case of the CIPs contracts, we have already seen how a jurisdictional dispute between U.S. federal regulatory agencies can be resolved in favor of one industry at the expense of another.

Accounting regulations have also produced a greater interest in derivatives. Traditionally, banks have recorded their assets as cost, thus making them immune to any interest rate increases. Gains and losses would be realized upon the sale of the asset. When rates declined, banks often sold appreciated assets and realized the gains, but kept securities in the portfolio, which had lost value.

But with the adoption of the Financial Accounting Standards Board (FASB) statement 115, banks must now value their assets according to how their sale will impact shareholder equity. Under the new standards, banks must create three separate categories of assets:

- If a bank intends to sell assets for profit, they are held in trading accounts and valued on a mark-to-market basis;

- Assets held for investment purposes with the intention of being "held to maturity" are valued at the lower of cost or market value;

- Assets judged to be "available for sale" will be marked to market.

By revaluing assets, banks will also be forced to restructure their balance sheets and put assets into the three categories. Banks may then move assets into different parts of the yield curve, which can be better controlled with off-balance-sheet instruments such as swaps.

In the U.S., overlapping jurisdictions and reporting requirements, combined with everyday difficulties, such as having dual-licensed brokers who offer both futures and securities-regulated products, has helped prompt calls for a unified U.S. securities and futures industry regulatory body. Under one proposal, a new agency combining the "functional" elements of the CFTC and SEC would be created to regulate along product lines, as opposed to traditional administrative or jurisdictional boundaries. Proponents of the proposal contend it would ease the dangers of systemic risk to the entire U.S. financial system by providing for a common clearing and settlement framework that would be applied to all markets.

Today, the federal agencies that are responsible for overseeing the financial services industry include parts or all of the Office of the Comptroller of the Currency; Office of Thrift Supervision; Federal Deposit Insurance Corporation; Commodity Futures Trading Commission; Securities and Exchange Commission; Securities Investor Protection Corporation; and the Pension Benefit Guaranty Corporation. Regulatory functions relating to the financial services industry are also provided by departments in the Federal Reserve Board and the Department of Labor.

The rationale for creating and maintaining a competitive and functional regulatory framework is tied to the daily function of the financial marketplace. When the marketplace changes, it may strain portions of the system. The greatest challenge facing the financial industry is to make regulation as flexible as the products and services under its jurisdiction, while also delivering the regulator's mandate and fostering global competition. Given the fact that many of today's federal agencies supervising the financial services industry date back to the 1930s, it may be necessary to update this structure to reflect new product development, advances in telecommunications, and the need to compete internationally.

LOOKING AHEAD:
EXPANDING THE APPEAL OF DERIVATIVES

The dramatic impact of derivatives is evident in the proliferation of new strategic alliances that have been created to capture this business. A good example of this occurred in the acquisition of CRT, a Chicago proprietary trading firm, by NationsBank. This acquisition provides an interesting case study in how a proprietary listed options and futures trading firm evolved into an OTC product arbitrage trading operation.

CRT began by developing its own analytics and technology, which allowed it to trade U.S. Treasury bonds, currencies, stock index futures, and energy futures. With its options modeling and other proprietary trading models in place, it developed an aggressive arbitrage business in exchange-listed options. But as the spreads began to diminish in exchange-listed instruments, CRT sought to expand into longer-dated OTC and other customized options. Often, the construction of these strategies required not only the advanced modeling techniques, which CRT had developed, but also greater lines of capital and credit.

Because of this strategic relationship with NationsBank, CRT is now in a better position to create more advanced products, which can be sold through an established bank network. Conversely, the bank gets access to selected pieces of the firm's advanced risk management software and its exchange and desk personnel, plus a primary dealer division, CRT Government Securities.

While this key acquisition has merit as a case history in strategic management, it also represents a definite trend in forging intellectual and marketing relationships between diversified financial services companies or dealers and specialty managers. Similar acquisitions have occurred among managed futures firms, which specialize in trading specific markets, or other bond or equity boutiques.

These developments will drive derivatives and synthetics into an increasingly wider range of applications. While the true test of any product is how well it weathers various market cycles, it is clear that despite their youth, origins, and stigma, derivatives have found their way into the mainstream of modern finance.

The remaining chapters in this book go into detail about the innovations, operation, and mechanics of individual products and strategies in the synthetic and derivative markets. Part One examines many of the most innovative products that have been developed. Part Two demonstrates how derivatives and synthetics are used in institutional investing, trading, and risk management. Part Three looks at risk analysis and management, and in Part Four the book turns from the U.S. to global markets. Technology is the subject of Part Five, while the legal and regulatory issues that govern how this entire genre of instruments is traded are covered in Part Six. The book concludes with tax and accounting issues in Part Seven.

PART ONE

INNOVATIONS IN THE SYNTHETIC AND DERIVATIVE MARKETS

CHAPTER 1

Index Options: Fundamental Concepts and Strategies

J. Marc Allaire
Director
The Options Institute

This chapter is an introduction to index options. This initiation to index options will be divided into three parts. "What are Index Options?" will give the basic definitions, look at pricing considerations, and briefly examine the effects of cash settlement. "Passive Portfolio Hedging" will look at one use of index options while covering the variables that are part of the hedging decision-making process. The last section, "LEAPS®, CAPS®, End-of-Quarter Options, and FLEX Options™,"[1] will go beyond the standard listed options to give an overview of the new products that have been listed for trading over the past few years.

WHAT ARE INDEX OPTIONS?

A look at any definition of an option will yield a variation on the following: "An option gives its holder (buyer) the right to buy (in the case of a call option) or to sell (in the case of a put option) an underlying security at a given price (the exercise or strike price) over a specified period of time (until the option's expiration date)." It is a straightforward definition, but it runs into a problem when applied to index options: The underlying value, an index, is just a number, and a number can neither be bought nor sold. An index option turns out to be an option on an intangible, an entity that cannot be bought, sold, or held.

---

1 "Standard & Poor's," "S&P," "S&P 100," "100," "S&P 500," and "500" are trademarks of Standard & Poor's Corporation; "The Russell 2000" is a registered trademark of Frank Russell Company; "LEAPS," "Long-term Equity AnticiPation Securities," and "OEX" are registered trademarks; "SPX," and "CAPS" are trademarks of the Chicago Board Options Exchange, Inc.

Of course the component stocks of an index can be traded, but one of the first things that must be pointed out about index options is that index options are not options on the component stocks. The standard option definition is thus inadequate, and we would like to suggest the following revision:

> An index option will let its holder (buyer) participate in the rise of an index (in the case of a call option) or the fall of an index (in the case of a put option) from a specified index level (the exercise price of the option) onwards over a given period of time (until the option's expiration date).

The right to buy or sell has been replaced by the notion of participation. This is due to the cash settlement feature of index options, to which we will return shortly.

When the holder of an equity option exercises the same, the overall bias of this holder's position does not necessarily change. For example, an investor or a speculator who holds a long call position has a position with a bullish bias: The long call will gain in value if the price of the underlying rises far enough, fast enough. If the holder of the call exercises this option, the resulting position is one of long stock. This position also has a bullish bias: The stock position will become profitable if the price of the stock rises. The risk/reward profile of the position has been changed through exercise, i.e., the long call position had a much smaller potential loss than the long stock position, and the amount of capital committed may be significantly higher, but the bullish bias remains the same.

This holds true of equity option positions that are combined with other options or with the underlying security, insofar as the option's exercise does not eliminate all of the investor's exposure to the underlying. An example of a position where exercise eliminates an investor's position is a long stock, long put position. When the put is exercised, the position as a whole collapses and is converted into cash. The point being made is that an equity option position can be structured so that if the option or options that are part of this position are exercised and/or assigned, the bias of the overall position will remain unchanged.

This is not the case with index options. The exercise or assignment of an index option will never result in a position in the underlying; the settlement is effected in cash, thereby eliminating the bias of the exercised/assigned position. The holder of an index call who exercises this option will no longer have a position with a bullish bias, but will be credited with the in-the-money amount of this call option. Anyone with a long index option position can therefore choose to collapse this position through exercise. However, the writer of an index option is assuming a position where, if the index options are of the American type, an unexpected early assignment could result in the bias of the position being completely changed through the conversion of an option position to cash. We will address this problem later when we discuss the American and European types of index options.

So let us return to the notion of participation that is part of our revised definition of index options. The holder of an index option obtains the right, not to purchase or sell a security or a basket of securities, but to receive a cash settlement, which will be based on the level of the underlying index relative to the exercise price of the index option. This first major difference between index and equity options will result in a different use of the product when strategies are implemented. For example, an equity option can be used to initiate a position in the underlying; the writer of put options agrees to purchase the underlying if assigned. By writing equity puts an investor could end up with an actual position in the underlying. The writer of index puts, on the other hand, cannot end up with a position in the underlying unless an independent series of transactions is undertaken and the component stocks of the index are purchased. The writer of index puts may be called upon to pay a cash settlement equal to the difference between the closing level of the index on the day the puts were exercised and the strike price of the option.

Although both positions, short equity puts and short index puts, have a bullish bias, assignment maintains the bullish position created by writing the equity puts, whereas assignment completely eliminates the position of the index put writer. This is no minor difference and must be well understood when transposing known equity option strategies to index options.

Buyers of index options can control the point at which an index option position is collapsed. Not so with index option writers. This is where the distinction between the American and European option types is pivotal.

American-type options can be exercised by their holders at any point in time. All equity and some index options are American-type. Writers of American-type options run the risk of early assignment. Depending on the circumstances, early exercise can be seen as a curse or a blessing. The covered call writer will generally look upon early assignment as a positive: The stock is sold at an earlier date, making funds available for reinvestment now rather than later, and the overall return from the covered write strategy is realized over a shorter period of time. But when earlier assignment signifies that the covered writer will not be receiving a dividend that had been included in the strategy's potential return, it then becomes a mixed blessing: Funds are available at an earlier time, but they have been reduced by the forgone dividend.

With index options, early assignment on American-type options usually results in a complete unwinding of the position (for strategies that involve only one series of options) or in a position with a risk/reward profile totally different than the one originally intended (for strategies involving more than one series of options). An example of the latter situation is spreads. A spread involves the purchase of one option and the sale of another. Spreads, such as bull or bear spreads, are usually entered into to limit or reduce the risk of the overall position. When the short option of an index spread is assigned, the resulting position is usually a "naked" long position whose outright risk is greater than that of the spread. Also, because an assignment notice is received in the morning and the settlement value of the short option will be based on the previous business day's close, investors are subject to overnight risk. The market may open at a level significantly different from the previous day's closing, which may play in favor of or against the remaining long option position.

This is where the value of European-type options come in. Unlike American-type options, these can be exercised only on their expiration date. The holder of a European-type index option cannot exercise it until its expiration date, although there are no restrictions in liquidating such an option in the secondary market. What may appear as a disadvantage for the option holder is an obvious advantage to the option writer: The risk of early assignment has been completely eliminated.

Would the buyer of an index option give up the possibility of exercising it early without asking for any compensation in return? In all likelihood not. Observation has shown that an American-type option is more likely to trade at a higher premium than a similar European-type option. One understands why intuitively. To benefit from the possibility of exercising an option at any point in time, buyers will have to pay a slight premium. And to be compensated for the risk of early assignment, option writers will demand a somewhat higher option premium.

In addition to having a choice between American- and European-type options, investors must decide if they prefer a.m. or p.m.-settled options. When first listed, index options settled based on the closing price of the index, usually that of the third Friday of the expiration month. As the markets have evolved, some index options have gone to an a.m. settlement. This does not mean that the options settle on the opening value of the index, which is usually a value close to the previous day's closing price and usually represents the first recalculation of the value of the index for that trading day. The process is slightly more complicated.

The settlement value of a.m. settled options is obtained by taking all of the individual opening prices of the component stocks of the index and calculating the value of the index using these opening prices. Because it is virtually impossible for all the component stocks of an index to open contemporaneously, this method of settling index options has a few twists and turns that need to be highlighted.

First, the settlement value may not be available for a relatively long time after the market's opening. Because all of the component stocks must be open for the settlement value to be calculated, any trading halt at the beginning of the trading day will delay the availability of the settlement value. In other cases, such as that of the Russell 2000® index, which comprises up to 2000 low capitalization stocks, there have been situations where one or more component stocks did not trade on a given expiration day. In these instances, the previous day's closing prices of those stocks that did not trade are used in determining the settlement value of the options, but this can be done only after the close of trading, since a stock could open minutes prior to the close.

A second phenomenon that has occurred is a settlement value outside the day's index range. Assume heavy selling pressure in the component stocks of an index at the opening; each stock opens at a price below yesterday's close. But if the selling pressure quickly abates and the stocks rally back to their previous level or to a higher one, and if the stocks open over a sufficiently protracted period of time such that the overall level of the index never fully reflects the relatively low opening prices of all the component stocks, the settlement value of the index could actually be lower than the daily "low" of the index. The possibility also exists that the settlement value of the index is higher than that day's "high" for the index. This phenomenon is not common, but it is not unknown.

Lastly in this first section, we want to take a brief look at some of the pricing considerations that are particular to index options. It is a well-known fact that the components used in determining the theoretical value of an option are: The price of the underlying, the strike price of the option, the time remaining to the option's expiration, the cost of carry (i.e., the risk-free rate of interest less the dividend yield of the underlying), and the underlying's volatility. Three of these inputs merit some remarks as far as index options are concerned.

The most easily understood factor affecting the price of an option is the price of the underlying. For equity options there is a very straightforward relationship between the underlying and the option's price. For index options the relationship is not as evident as might at first appear. The price of the underlying is important, as it determines the option's intrinsic value, and for out-of-the-money options what kind of a move the underlying must make to become in-the-money. The price of the underlying is also very important for arbitrage and hedging purposes. Professional market makers and specialists will usually quote the price of an option based on their ability to trade the underlying at a known price in order to hedge some of their risk. As mentioned above, an index is nothing but a number, and it cannot be bought or sold. Of course, it is possible to buy and sell the component stocks of any index, but the operation is much more complicated than trading the one stock underlying an equity option. Some firms have the technical and logistical capability of trading baskets of stocks quickly and at little cost, but this alternative is not available to all index option market makers and specialists.

There exists an alternative way to hedge a position in index options: Index futures contracts. The purchase or sale of an index futures contract will, in one transaction, replicate the purchase or sale of the component stocks of the index. Market makers and specialists need not trade baskets of stocks; index futures are a viable alternative.

But then the question arises of which is most important in valuing an option: The price of the underlying index (the cash index), or the price of the futures contract on the underlying index. There is no clear-cut answer to this question. A firm engaged in the business of pricing index options will monitor both hedging possibilities: The actual stocks underlying the index and the futures contract on the same. When determining which hedge it should use to reduce or eliminate risk from a given option position, such a firm would use the hedge with the lowest cost. The costs of hedging with futures contracts are determined by the price of the said contract, margin requirements, and expected slippage when the hedge is entered into. (Slippage is the effect that buying or selling futures contracts will have on the price of the futures. For example, if the hedge requires the firm to purchase a large number of contracts, this purchase could actually push up the price of the futures, thereby increasing the cost of the hedge.)

When hedging with the actual underlying stocks, the factors that will determine the cost of the hedge are the prices of the underlying stocks (i.e., the bid prices if selling stocks is the appropriate action, and the asked price if stocks must be purchased), the slippage that will result, and the firm's net cost of carry if it is buying stocks or how profitably it can invest funds if stocks are being sold short.

We have just referred to a firm's net cost of carry. Let us elaborate. If the hedge to an option position involves the purchase of a basket of stocks, the firm doing this operation must know what its carrying cost will be. This is its cost of holding the stocks, usually using borrowed funds, less any dividends that are expected from the underlying stocks over the period of time the position is expected to be held. It is important to note that different firms will have different costs of funds: Firm A may be able to borrow at 4 percent, whereas Firm B must pay 4.125 percent. The same is true for the rates at which firms will be able to invest funds when putting on a hedge that generates funds, either through the sale or the short sale of stocks. The firm able to generate the higher returns on the funds generated will have the lowest cost hedge.

One final note on hedging with the actual stocks. The feasibility of the trade must be considered. If the hedge dictates that the firm sell stock baskets short, then the limitations of the up-tick rule must be taken into account. In a rapidly falling market shorting stocks can be difficult or impossible, so that the theoretical hedge will not be feasible.

Why is the above discussion of importance in pricing index options? Because the first factor that goes into option pricing models is "the price of the underlying." For index options, this may not necessarily be the price of the underlying cash index. Rather, it is the least expensive hedge available to a given market participant.

The second pricing variable that merits our attention is the cost of carry. For equity options, this represents the risk-free interest rate less any dividends paid by the underlying stock over the option's life. When looking at index options, the "dividends paid over the life of the option" part of the equation becomes somewhat more complicated.

Stocks usually pay dividends on a quarterly basis, at fairly set intervals, so that calculating the present value of a stock's dividend stream over the next three or six months is a fairly straightforward operation. When pricing index options, one must take into account the dividends paid by all of the component stocks, and which of these dividends will be paid during the option's life. Take the Standard & Poor's 100 index as an example. One hundred component stocks mean a potential 100 ex-dividend dates every quarter, an average of more than one per trading day. A relatively unsophisticated way of calculating the theoretical value of index options would be to assume a constant, even flow of dividends throughout the quarter. But this assumption is obviously false; the dividend rates of the component stocks are not equal, and there are periods during the quarter of "heavy dividends" during which a disproportionately high number of the component stocks go ex-dividend.

Calculating the present value of the dividend stream over the life of an index option becomes a much more involved process. One must determine which stocks will go ex, on which dates, and by which amounts. What one must calculate is therefore the yield of the index from today to a specific option's expiration date. This yield will not be the same for the different expiration dates, and will have to be recalculated each trading day to exclude stocks that have gone ex on the previous day. Although "cost of carry" as defined cannot be calculated exactly if only the risk-free rate and the dividend yield of the underlying index are known, this can serve as a first approximation for most traders. Those involved in the finer aspects of index option trading, such as market making or arbitrage, will need to go one step further and fine-tune their numbers by dissecting all of the available dividend data of an index's component stocks.

Finally, a few words on volatility. The volatility used in option pricing models is the underlying's expected volatility over the life of the option. Of course, no one knows with certainty what the future volatility of an index will be, but a combination of past volatility and educated guesswork can furnish one with a reasonable estimate.

Now answer the following two questions: (1) Give dates when the overall market dropped 20 percent or more in one day, and (2) Give dates when the overall market rose 20 percent or more in one day. The first question probably caused you no problems, while the second one . . . . An important point is being made here: Large downside moves in the market have, in the past, been of a larger magnitude than large upside moves. In expectation that the future will resemble the past, some option professionals believe that the pricing of calls and puts should be done using two different volatilities, with the higher volatility reserved for the puts. Of course we do not know what the future will bring, but this argument helps explain some empirical observations: At times puts have traded with higher implied volatilities than the corresponding call options.

Could the same argument be made for equity options? This question is more difficult to answer. There have been occasions when the prices of individual stocks have shot up as a result of corporate developments or takeovers, actual or rumored. Nevertheless, this dichotomy, as it applies to index options, helps explain why using one volatility to price index options can at times lead to the conclusion that the calls are inexpensive and the puts overvalued.

A final note on pricing considerations: We have already underscored the difference between American- and European-type options, and how for similar options the American-type option should be worth the same or somewhat more than the equivalent European-type option. Special notice must be taken of deep in-the-money European-type put options. Observation reveals that deep in-the-money European puts trade at a discount to their intrinsic value. For example, assume a given index's level is 150, short-term rates are 4 percent, the component stocks of the index pay no dividends, and a three-month put option with a strike price of 200 is listed for trading. What is the fair value of this put?

If the option were an American-type option, the answer would be $50, its intrinsic value. The early exercise feature of this option means that an investor could always exercise to obtain the option's full intrinsic value. But with a European-type option, early exercise is not possible, and the question of fair value is not as easily answered. Consider the following: If the index is at the 150 level, and the put has a strike price of 200, how can an investor who owns this put and cannot exercise it lock in its intrinsic value if there is no secondary market for this option? The answer: By purchasing the component stocks of the index at prices reflecting the 150 level. The investor who purchases the component stocks "locks in" the put's 50-point intrinsic value, since the combined stocks and option will be worth a minimum of $50 no matter at what level the index is trading three months hence.

What is the problem with this hedging strategy? It ties up the investor's capital for a three-month period: $150 is now invested in stocks, and $50 in the option. As we assumed 4 percent interest rates, this represents a financing cost of $2 for the three-month period. This $2 financing cost would be reflected in the put option's price in the secondary market, and its fair value can then be said to be $48.

The discount at which deep in-the-money European put options trade in the marketplace reflects the cost of carrying the hedged position until the option's expiration date. It does not reflect market sentiment or an "unfair" price.

PASSIVE PORTFOLIO HEDGING

In this second section, we want to elaborate on the various facets of one of the more basic option strategies: The purchase of puts as insurance. Our goal is to explain the strategy, using an example where the various components are examined one at a time.

This section is based on an example that is usually classified as passive hedging. This represents a position that is most often entered into with the intention of carrying it for a good length of time without making any adjustments. This contrasts with dynamic hedging, of which portfolio insurance is one of the better-known subsets. These strategies are beyond the scope of this chapter and will not be covered.

Passive hedging is something most individuals do without realizing it. They purchase various forms of insurance for their car, their house, their belongings. The insurance is purchased on an annual or semiannual basis, and very seldom are adjustments made to the terms of these policies while they are in effect. This is passive hedging, our topic of discussion.

Consider an equity portfolio manager who owns all of the component stocks of our Fictitious Index (FIK):

C. Eleven AirLines (CXI):	$45
Boring Utilities (BOR):	$55
DNA-RNA (BIO):	$30
High-Low Technologies (RAM):	$20
Foundry Manufacturing (OLD):	$85
Video Pizza (VCR):	$15
Fictitious Index (FIK):	$250

There are only six stocks in the FIK, and the value of the index is computed by simply adding up the prices of the component stocks. If a manager is looking to insure these holdings, the first question that may come up is "Why use index options, and not equity options?" This is a very valid question, and is usually answered: "Because index options are less expensive." The following table gives values for three-month at-the-money put options for all of the component stocks and for FIK. The option prices have been computed using the volatilities indicated, and assuming that none of the component stocks pay any dividend.

	Volatility	Put Price
CXI	35%	2 7/8
BOR	12%	1 1/16
BIO	61%	3 1/2
RAM	44%	1 5/8
OLD	23%	3 1/2
VCR	39%	1 1/16
FIK	15%	6 1/4

The volatility of the index is lower than that of all of the stocks but one. This is because of the portfolio effect; an index will tend to be less volatile than its component stocks, since not all stocks will move in the same direction at once. This principle would not be as true of a six-stock portfolio, but this example is only meant as an illustration.

Insuring the whole portfolio using equity puts (and assuming 100 shares of each component stock are being held), would cost a total of $1,362.50; purchasing one FIK put option would cost only $625. Index options are less expensive! So if our market is an efficient one, why is there such a discrepancy between the cost of insuring with index options and with equity options? This question is best answered by looking at what may happen if the above portfolio is insured with equity puts and with index puts.

Let us look first at the results of the insurance strategy when after three months, the overall level of the index has remained unchanged. The first observation is that if the overall index remains unchanged, it does not necessarily follow that the component stocks will be at the same level. So let us envision three scenarios: (1) FIK is unchanged, and all of the component stocks are also unchanged; (2) FIK is unchanged, and the component stocks have fluctuated within a 5 percent band of their initial prices; (3) FIK is unchanged, but the component stocks have moved substantially from their initial prices. Table 1 gives possible stock prices for these three scenarios and the value of the at-the-money options at expiration.

Table 1.   Three Scenarios

	Scenario 1		Scenario 2		Scenario 3	
	Stock Price	Put Price	Stock Price	Put Price	Stock Price	Put Price
CXI	45	0	47	0	56	0
BOR	55	0	52	3	49	6
BIO	30	0	31	0	24	6
RAM	20	0	19	1	29	0
OLD	85	0	86	0	81	4
VCR	15	0	15	0	11	4
Total	250	0	250	4	250	20
FIK	250	0	250	0	250	0

In Scenario 1 in Table 1, none of the component stock prices fluctuated and all of the equity puts expired worthless. The cost of insuring the portfolio turned out to be $1,362.50 versus $625 for insuring with index puts.

In Scenario 3, where stock prices fluctuated strongly but the overall index was unchanged, the put options had a final total value of $20, generating a profit of 6 3/8 ($637.50). This scenario holds the key to why equity puts are more expensive than index puts: They offer more protection.

If portfolio managers are concerned only with the overall value of their holdings, then they need only purchase index options to insure them. But if they are looking to hedge against the possible price decline of individual securities, then equity puts will be more appropriate. But it should come as no surprise that the higher degree of protection offered by the equity puts will come at a higher cost.

The first decision, described above, was which type of risk to insure: Systematic—i.e., portfolio risk, in which case index options are adequate—or unsystematic risk, in which case equity puts are required. Once the decision to hedge using index options has been made, another set of decisions must be made: The period of coverage, the level of coverage, and the amount of coverage. We will now turn to these decisions.

One element inherent in purchasing insurance is that there is a cost involved. But because of the dynamics of options, the cost of an option is not always directly proportional to the amount of time covered by the option. Table 2 gives the cost of at-the-money put options for our Fictitious Index. The pricing of these options assumes a 15 percent volatility and no dividend yield. The cost of the insurance also is given

Table 2.   Cost of At-the-Money Put Options

	Option Premium	Option Premium as % of Index	"Annualized" Cost of Insurance
1 month	3 7/8	1.55%	18.6%
2 months	5 1/4	2.10%	12.6%
3 months	6 1/4	2.50%	10.0%
6 months	8 1/8	3.25%	6.50%
9 months	9 1/4	3.70%	4.93%
12 months	10 1/8	4.05%	4.05%
24 months	11 3/8	4.55%	2.28%

as a percentage of the index value and as an annualized cost.

What quickly becomes obvious from Table 2 is that the annualized cost of insurance when at-the-money options are used decreases as the option's time to expiration increases. This does not mean that one should never buy short-term at-the-money options, but that if one does, one should fully recognize the cost involved.[2]

Does this relationship between the annualized cost of an option and its time to expiration hold for all options? Things are not quite that simple. Table 3 recalculates the option prices for puts that are 10 percent out-of-the-money. With our index at 250, we are therefore pricing 225 puts, once again assuming a 15 percent volatility and no dividend yield.

We now get a completely different relationship between the annualized cost of insurance and the options' expiration dates. Whereas for the at-the-money options the annualized cost of insurance got gradually lower as the time to expiration increased, for the out-of-the money options the annualized cost at first increases and then decreases. It must also be noted that for options ranging from 3 to 24 months, the annualized cost of insurance varies little, around 1 percent. A final note of caution on the above numbers: The values of the shorter-term options are low absolute numbers. Because of the discrete nature of option pricing (i.e., in increments of 1/16 below $3),

---

2 Another way to interpret Table 2 is that a series of 24 one-month options costs more than one 24-month option because the former offers more protection. This increased protection would take the form of purchasing put options with higher strike prices after market rallies.

Table 3.   Option Prices for 10% Out-of-the-Money Puts

	Option Premium	Option Premium as % of Index	"Annualized" Cost of Insurance
1 month	–	–	–
2 months	3/16	0.08%	0.45%
3 months	7/16	0.18%	0.70%
6 months	1 3/8	0.55%	1.10%
9 months	2 1/4	0.90%	1.20%
12 months	2 7/8	1.15%	1.15%
24 months	4 3/8	1.75%	0.88%

purchasing the two-month option at 1/4 instead of 3/16 would increase the annualized cost of insurance to 0.60 percent from 0.45 percent.

The above analysis of the relationship between an option's annualized cost and its time to expiration brings us to the next variable: The level of coverage desired. We have given two possibilities: A 250 at-the-money strike price, which insures the portfolio against any market decline, and a 225 out-of-the-money strike price, which offers protection only if the market falls more than 10 percent. In insurance terms, these two options are said to have, respectively, a zero deductible, and a 10 percent deductible. In the marketplace, the investor will be faced with an even greater choice of strike prices. With FIK at 250, the following strikes for three-month options are possible, with prices as indicated (calculated assuming a volatility of 15 percent and no dividend yield):

Strike	Premium
225	7/16
230	7/8
235	1 5/8
240	2 11/16
245	4 1/4
250	6 1/4
255	8 3/4
260	11 7/8

Which strike should a portfolio manager choose? The question is akin to which deductible should a driver choose when purchasing car insurance. There is no single correct answer. Driver will select the deductible on their car insurance based on their risk aversion and on theirwillingness to pay the higher premium required by the policy with the lower deductible. Investment managers are virtually in the same position: Their risk tolerance will be considered (there is a good chance that the manager of a fully funded pension fund will be more risk averse than the manager of a relatively aggressive equity mutual fund) as will their willingness to pay up for the higher strike prices (the latter being a function of their market expectations and their level of confidence in these). If a large downward move is given a high probability of occurring, then purchasing more of the lower-priced options will offer more leverage than fewer of the more highly priced options.

If a fund manager is truly looking to hedge a position in the underlying stocks, his or her approach should be that of an insurance buyer: At what point does a market pullback become unacceptable, and is the cost of the desired protection acceptable? Analyzing the purchase of protective puts through the leverage offered by various option series means that the manager has moved from insuring a portfolio to using options to speculate on a down move of the market.

Related to the choice of strike price is the amount of coverage desired. Individuals tend to insure all of their personal belongings, whereas portfolio managers seldom protect their entire holdings; they will purchase puts to insure a part of their holdings, adding or subtracting to this coverage as the market reaches certain levels. Once again, there is no set proportion of a portfolio that should be insured; a manager's risk aversion given the prevailing market conditions will remain a major factor.

Once the amount of coverage desired has been set, the relationship existing between the portfolio and the index underlying the options should be determined. Very seldom will options be listed on an index that replicates the portfolio to be hedged. In most cases, the manager will have to decide which of the available listed options most closely approximates the stocks to hedge. Through regression analysis, it is possible to determine the beta of a portfolio relative to various indices and the coefficient of correlation between the two.

Consider the following example. A manager holds a portfolio of mostly blue chip higher capitalization stocks. She is unsure whether options on the Standard & Poor's 100 or the Standard & Poor's 500 index represent the better hedge. Regression analysis of her portfolio versus these two indices gives the following results:

	Beta	R^2
Versus S&P 100	1.05	0.80
Versus S&P 500	1.10	0.75

The above numbers should be interpreted as follows: For every 1 percent move in the S&P 100, this portfolio is expected to fluctuate 1.05 percent. For every 1 percent move in the S&P 500, this portfolio is expected to fluctuate 1.10 percent. The coefficient of correlation (R^2) indicates that there is a stronger relationship between the portfolio and the S&P 100. (An R^2 of 1.00 would indicate a perfect correlation between the two; an R^2 of 0.00 would indicate no correlation at all, and an R^2 of -1.00 would indicate perfect negative correlation, i.e., when the index moves up, the portfolio moves down, and vice versa). The higher R^2 versus the S&P 100 would make this the preferred hedge. Of course it should be remembered that regression analysis tells us how the portfolio has tracked the index in the past; things could be different in the future.

Now, if the decision has been made to use the S&P 100 options, the beta of the portfolio has to be considered. The portfolio being hedged is slightly more volatile than the S&P 100 index. If we assume a total portfolio value of $100 million and a desired coverage of 25 percent, or $25 million, then the manager would need to purchase put options on $26.25 million of the underlying index to obtain the level of coverage desired. Because the portfolio is slightly more risky than the options' underlying index, additional protection is required. If the portfolio were less risky than the index chosen, i.e., if the beta were less than 1.00, then less protection would be needed and fewer contracts required.

Finally, the following question must be answered: At what cost insurance? This section has looked at the variables that come into play once the decision has been made to insure a portfolio using index options. But a final (or maybe initial) question must be asked: How expensive is insurance at this point?

We do not believe that some option series are less expensive than others for the same underlying index as measured by implied volatility. When these situations exist, they are quickly arbitraged away. The question that interests us is that of the overall level of option premium, or implied volatility.

The volatility number used in pricing options is of great interest. It is the only true unknown in the equation, as it represents expected future volatility. But it can also be a number that lets market participants take the pulse of the market. Implied volatility reflects the global estimate as to how risky the market is at a given point in time. Some historical perspective may be of help here. Exhibit 1 represents the implied volatility of options on the Standard & Poor's 100 index (OEX) for the years 1986 through 1993 as measured by the VIX index. The VIX index is the weighted average implied

Exhibit 1.   VIX: Historical Levels
1986–1993

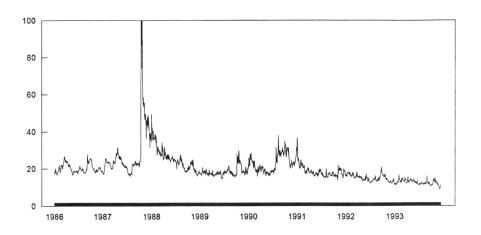

volatility of eight different OEX series: Four calls and four puts, two from each of the two first expirations.[3] The strike prices chosen are those that bracket the current level of the index.

The VIX lets market participants gauge the level of option premiums of the most actively traded index option class. Past history has shown that the level of other broad index options will closely parallel that of OEX options.

One observation from Exhibit 1 is that index options are most expensive immediately following major market moves: 100 percent+ implied volatility after the crash of October 1987, 35 percent+ when Iraq invaded Kuwait in August of 1990, 30 percent when the market corrected in August of 1989. Not surprisingly, insurance is most expensive when demand hits a peak.

LEAPS®, CAPS®, END-OF-QUARTER OPTIONS, AND FLEX OPTIONS

Since the listing of call options on 16 stocks in 1973, exchanges have multiplied manyfold the number and type of listed option products. In addition to these, the over-the-counter market provides the added flexibility of designing options that meet very specific needs. This section looks at four of the exchange-listed products that do not fall under the plain vanilla index option umbrella.

LEAPS®

Index LEAPS® (Long-term Equity AnticiPation Securities) can summarily be defined as long-term or long-dated options. Although this quick definition is somewhat accurate, it does not encompass the reduced value indices, and on another plane, pays no consideration to pricing issues that differentiate shorter- and longer-term options. We will return to these in a few paragraphs.

First the issue of reduced value indices. In order to maintain premium levels at an "acceptable" level, exchanges have listed some index LEAPS® on reduced value indexes. For example, with an S&P 100 level of 450, the reduced index level is set at one-tenth the actual index, or 45. Index LEAPS® trade off this reduced level, and investors would find options listed with strike prices of 42 1/2, 45, and 47 1/2. It is important to keep in mind that it takes ten reduced value options to equate to one short-term index option. This is important when calculating the underlying value of each index LEAPS® option, for example, when using puts to insure a portfolio or when establishing spreads between shorter- and longer-term options.

As of the date of this writing, reduced value index LEAPS options were listed on the following indices: Standard & Poor's 100 (OEX), Standard & Poor's 500 (SPX), Major Market Index (XMI), Russell 2000 (RUT), CBOE BioTech Index (BGX), Amex Biotechnology Index (BTK), Value Line Index (VLE), Amex Pharmaceutical Index (DRG).

---

3 During the week immediately preceding expiration Saturday, the expiring options are taken out of the index to avoid distortion.

Index LEAPS® are also listed on the full value of the Standard & Poor's 500 index, the Institutional Index (XII), and the Japan Index (JPN). Should investors have a preference as to which they trade, full value or reduced value LEAPS®? The options will fluctuate in the same way and should trade with similar implied volatilities, but an investor who is looking to purchase or sell a relatively large number of contracts should remember that the reduced value options will multiply the bid-ask spread and the commissions paid.

In the second section above, the importance of volatility in pricing index options was underscored. But when the expiration date of an option is pushed further and further back, volatility becomes relatively less important. In the following paragraphs we will illustrate how the relative importance of three of the factors that affect index option prices change as the time to expiration increases. These three factors are: Volatility, interest rates, and dividend yield.

Table 4 gives theoretical index call option values based on the following assumptions: Index level of 200; option strike price of 200; interest rate of 5 percent; dividend yield of 2 percent; times to expiration of 3, 12, and 24 months; and volatilities from 11 percent to 18 percent.

Table 4. Theoretical Index Call Option Values

	3-month option		12-month option		24-month option	
Volatility	Value	% Chg.	Value	% Chg.	Value	% Chg.
11%	5 1/8	–	11 7/8	–	18 3/4	–
12%	5 1/2	7.31%	12 5/8	6.31%	19 3/4	5.33%
13%	6	9.09%	13 1/2	6.93%	20 3/4	5.06%
14%	6 3/8	6.25%	14 1/4	5.55%	21 7/8	5.42%
15%	6 3/4	5.88%	15	5.26%	22 7/8	4.57%
16%	7 1/8	5.55%	15 3/4	5.00%	23 7/8	4.37%
17%	7 1/2	5.26%	16 1/2	4.76%	25	4/71%
18%	7 7/8	5.00%	17 1/4	4.54%	26	4.00%

The percent change column calculates the increase in the option's theoretical value when the volatility is increased by 1 percent. Fox example, the price of the three-month call option rises by 7.31 percent when the volatility used to calculate its value goes from 11 percent to 12 percent.

What Table 4 shows is the decreasing incremental effect of volatility for longer-dated options; as the expiration date is set further and further into the future, a 1 percent increase in the volatility assumption will have a smaller and smaller effect on the percentage change in the price of an option.

The second pricing variable we want to look at is the interest rate assumption. In pricing options, the interest rate is usually the risk-free rate that is expected over the life of the option. A first difficulty arises with longer-dated options when one tries to determine what the risk-free rate will be over the next two years. One may be quite confident in one's interest rate assumption in pricing a three-month option, but when the time horizon is pushed back, the level of one's confidence in making an interest rate assumption diminishes. This uncertainty is compounded by the increasing importance of the interest rate assumption, as illustrated in Table 5. This table shows theoretical index call option prices calculated using the following assumptions: An index level of 200; option strike price of 200; volatility of 15 percent; index dividend yield of 2 percent; times to expiration of 3, 12, and 24 months; and interest rate assumptions from 2 percent to 9 percent.

Table 5 tells a totally different story than Table 4, where the effect of volatility was shown. Changes in interest rates have the most marked effect on the longer-dated options. In fact, for the 12- and 24-month options, a 1 percent rise in the risk-free rate has a greater effect on the options' prices than a 1 percent increase in the volatility assumption, whereas the reverse is true for the three-month option.

Table 5.   Theoretical Index Call Option Prices

Risk-Free	3-month option		12-month option		24-month option	
	Value	% Chg.	Value	% Chg.	Value	% Chg.
2%	6	–	12	–	16 7/8	–
3%	6 1/4	4.17%	12 7/8	7.29%	18 3/4	11.11%
4%	6 1/2	4.00%	13 7/8	7.77%	20 3/4	10.67%
5%	6 3/4	3.85%	15	8.11%	22 7/8	10.24%
6%	7	3.70%	16	6.67%	25 1/8	9.83%
7%	7 1/4	3.57%	17 1/8	7.03%	27 3/8	8.96%
8%	7 1/2	3.45%	18 3/8	7.30%	29 3/4	8.76%
9%	7 7/8	5.00%	19 1/2	6.12%	32 1/8	7.98%

The last pricing variable we want to consider is the dividend yield of the underlying index. Table 6 gives theoretical index call prices based on the following assumptions: An index level of 200; strike price of 200; volatility of 15 percent; interest rate of 5 percent; times to expiration of 3, 12, and 24 months; and dividend yields from 0 percent to 5 percent.

Note that in Table 6 the far left-hand column shows the yield on the underlying index decreasing, not increasing. Compare the numbers in this table to the numbers in Table 5 for the rates from 2 percent to 7 percent. The numbers are identical. The reason is that interest rates and dividend yield are but two components of the same pricing variable: Cost of carry. A one-percent drop in the yield of the index will have the same effect on the theoretical prices as a one-percent rise in the risk-free rate, as either of these would raise the cost of carry by one percent.

This somewhat long-winded discussion on pricing considerations leads us to a rather succinct conclusion: Changes in the cost of carry will have a relatively more marked effect on longer-dated options than changes in the volatility assumption. This contrasts with shorter-term options, where the reverse holds.

Table 6.   Theoretical Index Call Option Prices

Yield	3-month option		12-month option		24-month option	
	Value	% Chg.	Value	% Chg.	Value	% Chg.
5%	6	–	12	–	16 7/8	–
4%	6 1/4	4.17%	12 7/8	7.29%	18 3/4	11.11%
3%	6 1/2	4.00%	13 7/8	7.77%	20 3/4	10.67%
2%	6 3/4	3.85%	15	8.11%	22 7/8	10.24%
1%	7	3.70%	16	6.67%	25 1/8	9.83%
0%	7 1/4	3.57%	17 1/8	7.03%	27 3/8	8.96%

CAPS®

The simplest way to think of capped index options is as prepackaged bull and bear spreads. But as we will see, although this quick definition is fairly accurate, there are marked differences between CAPS® options and index bull and bear spreads.

First, let us consider some similarities. there are both call and put index CAPS®. The purchase of a call CAPS® is similar to the purchase of a bull call spread; the sale of a call CAPS® is similar to a bear call spread. The purchase of a put CAPS® approximates the purchase of a bear put spread, and the sale of a put CAPS®, a bull put spread.

We will take as an example the purchase of a call CAPS® option, and compare it to a bull call spread in order to highlight the similarities and differences. The payoff from these two strategies **at expiration** will be identical if the strike prices chosen are the same. A bull call spread consists of the purchase of a call option and sale of a second call option having the same expiration but a higher strike price. For example, buy an OEX December 400 call and sell an OEX December 430 call. In this example, a 30-point interval between the two strike prices was chosen to simplify comparison with a capped option.

The analogous strategy to the 400–430 bull call spread would be to purchase the 400/430 call CAPS® option. It should be noted that the number of different capped options listed is much more restricted than the different strike prices available with standard index options. It should also be noted that as of the time of this writing, CAPS® were available for trading on the Standard & Poor's 100 index (OEX), the Standard & Poor's 500 index (SPX), the Institutional Index (XII), and the Major Market Index (XMI), and in the case of the OEX capped options, were only available with a 30-point differential between the lower exercise price and the capped price.

Keeping the above limitations in mind, let's compare the 400–430 bull call spread and the 400/430 CAPS® call. Both positions are established for an initial debit and this debit represents the maximum potential loss to the call spread purchaser and the CAPS® call buyer. Both positions will have intrinsic value as long as the underlying index is at any level above 400. Both positions can only return a fixed maximum profit, attained if the underlying index is at 430 or higher.

So where are the differences? The differences reside in the exercise features of the options. Options on the Standard & Poor's 100 index can be exercised at any time from the moment they are purchased. This means that the holder of the 400–430 bull call spread may exercise the long 400 call at any time. But this means that there is the risk of early assignment on the short 430 call position. This is one of the special risks associated with spreads; should the short option be assigned, the investor is left with only the long 400 call. This option can be exercised to eliminate the position completely, but if the short 430 call was exercised by its holder on, say, a Wednesday, the holder of the bull call spread would receive an assignment notice on the following business day, in this case the Thursday morning. Exercising the long 400 call on the Thursday would expose the investor to what is known as overnight risk: The cash settlement of the short 430 call would be calculated based on the closing value of the index on the Wednesday but the settlement resulting from the exercise of the long 400 call would be calculated based on the closing value of the index on the Thursday. The odds are that the Wednesday and Thursday closing prices will be different, exposing the investor to any fluctuations in the index on the Thursday.

(An alternative to exercising the long leg of a spread when the short option has been assigned is to sell it. In our example, this would mean selling the option on the opening on Thursday. The risk remains that the index will open at a level different from the previous day's close.)

Capped options, on the other hand, cannot be exercised until their last trading day, unless the underlying index closes at or above the cap price, which is 430 in our example. This means there is no possibility to exercise a CAPS® option before expiration, but there is also no risk of early assignment. However, the European exercise feature of CAPS® only holds as long as the underlying index does not close at or above the upper strike price of the CAPS® option. When the underlying index closes at or above the upper strike price, the CAPS® is **automatically** exercised and its holder receives the maximum value of $30.

This automatic exercise feature at the capped price is to the CAPS® holder's advantage. Spreads created using standard index options usually reach their maximum value only if both legs of the spread are deep in-the-money, or if the short option is slightly in-the-money **and** there is little time left to expiration. CAPS® options will reach their maximum value on the first day that the underlying index closes at or above the higher strike. This means that in all cases a capped option will be as valuable as the equivalent spread, and in a lot of cases will be more valuable. Past trading has shown CAPS® trading at a premium to the equivalent spread in the corresponding index options.

End-of-Quarter Options

For the most part, listed options expire on the Saturday immediately following the third Friday of the expiration month. This convention, now taken for granted by market participants, has the distinct disadvantage of not corresponding to most investors' accounting periods. A vast majority of pension and mutual funds for example, report their results at the end of each calendar quarter. A fund manager who is hedging a portfolio through the purchase of put options for the fiscal year-end is left with the following dilemma: Whether to purchase December index options (which may have an expiration date ranging from December 16 to December 22) or to purchase January index options (which will also have an expiration date ranging from the 16th to the 22nd). The first alternative leaves the manager unhedged for a period of up to 15 days. The second choice introduces other variables such as the volatility that will be used by the marketplace to price these options in early January, when the hedge will more than likely be taken off.

End-of-quarter options are index options designed to address this problem. At the time of this writing, end-of-quarter options were available only on the Standard & Poor's 500 index (SPX), the Major Market Index (XMI) the Institutional Index (XII) and the Mid-Cap Index (MID). They differ from their corresponding options in the following ways: Their expiration dates are set as the business day that immediately follows March 31, June 30, September 30, and December 31; their settlement value is determined based on the closing level of the relevant index on the options' last trading day. The settlement value of "regular" SPX options, for example, is calculated based on the opening prices of the component stocks of the index on the trading day immediately preceding the expiration date.

End-of-quarter options are of European exercise style, and usually the next four quarterly expiration dates are listed for trading.

FLEX Options

FLEX options (FLexible EXchange options) are an attempt by the option exchanges to recapture part of the business that has migrated to the over-the-counter market. The major advantage of over-the-counter options over the listed variety is the nonstandardized terms: Expiration dates, strike prices, and method of settlement can be tailored to fit a user's specific needs. The flip side of this coin is the lack of price discovery. Trades in over-the-counter options are not reported and a user or potential user may have a more difficult time gauging the current price level of those options that he or she may have an interest in purchasing or writing.

FLEX options were designed to provide users with some of the flexibility of over-the-counter options while maintaining the price discovery mechanism of listed options. In addition, FLEX options address the increasingly important issue of counterparty risk.

As of this writing, FLEX options were listed on only three indexes: The Standard & Poor's 100 (OEX), the Standard & Poor's 500 (SPX), and the Russell 2000. The product is aimed squarely at the institutional market, as the size of an opening trade must have a minimum of ten million dollars underlying value, currently equivalent to approximately 250 OEX or SPX contracts or to approximately 450 RUT contracts. Despite having only three indexes as possible underlying values, FLEX options let their users set all of the following contract terms: Exercise price; expiration date (to a maximum of 5 years); American, European, or capped exercise; and settlement value (based on the opening or the closing value or an average of the two, or based on the day's high or low prices or an average of the two, or based on the average of the opening, closing, high and low).

Because FLEX options are exchange-traded, the terms of each transaction, including the options' premium, are reported, helping in the price discovery mechanism. FLEX options are also cleared and guaranteed by the Options Clearing Corporation (OCC), eliminating counterparty risk. When an institution purchases an over-the-counter option, it is accepting what is known as counterparty risk, i.e., the risk that the writer of the option will not be able to perform when the option expires or is exercised by its holder. In the case of longer-term options, this risk can be significant and not so easily quantifiable. FLEX options address this issue.

Like all standardized option contracts, FLEX options are cleared and guaranteed by the OCC. An option buyer is therefore not concerned with who has taken the opposite side of the trade because the OCC automatically acts as the seller to every buyer and the buyer to every seller.

In early 1993, the OCC obtained a AAA credit rating from Standard & Poor's Corporation, thereby quantifying the counterparty risk associated with an exchange-traded option.

CHAPTER 2

FLEX Options: A New Generation of Derivatives

William Barclay
Vice President, Strategic Planning
and International Development
Chicago Board Options Exchange (CBOE)

On February 26, 1993, the Chicago Board Options Exchange (CBOE) initiated trading in FLexible EXchange (FLEX) Options. In less than four months of trading, FLEX surpassed $5 billion in notional value. The FLEX market attracted interest and involvement from a wide array of market participants, and FLEX established itself as perhaps the most important innovation from a U.S. derivative market during the past five years.

FLEX is not simply a new product. It is as much or more a new way of providing markets, designed to meet the needs of institutional portfolio managers, an important and growing segment of the derivative market users. Thus, the decision to develop FLEX was the result of a strategic analysis of the evolution of the derivative market and the assessment of an appropriate exchange response. Before describing FLEX and FLEX trading in detail, it is useful to consider the strategic analysis that guided the creation of FLEX.

EXCHANGE AND OTC MARKETS: SYMBIOSIS AND INNOVATION

Exchange and over-the-counter (OTC) option markets are frequently described as competitors; with almost equal frequency it is argued that these markets are complementary. In reality, the relationship between the exchange-listed and the OTC option markets has been a symbiotic one from the beginning. Both markets have benefited

---

The opinions and conclusions presented in this paper are those of the author and do not represent the policy or beliefs of the Chicago Board Options Exchange.

from and competed with each other in the development of new products and the expansion of option usage by new segments of market participants.

Prior to the creation in 1973 of the CBOE, the first listed options market, members of the Put and Call Brokers and Dealers Association traded options in an OTC market, responding to customer requests for option quotes, and providing tailored expirations, strikes, and sizes. Beginning in April 1973, the CBOE standardized all contract terms and provided a central clearinghouse for equity options. Within two years CBOE achieved volume levels more than 50 times that of the Association. Standardization, transparency, competitive open outcry, and centralized clearing responded to the needs of a largely retail option customer base and caused a rapid expansion of the market.

For the next 12 to 15 years, the CBOE and other U.S. option markets accounted for virtually all option trading and led in the development of new option products. The most important new product developed during this time was the index option (see Chapter 1). Although all U.S. option markets trade one or more index option products, by the 1987 market crash the CBOE's S&P 100 and S&P 500 index options accounted for over 80 percent of total index option market share; in the post-crash period the CBOE products have captured more than 90 percent of the exchange-listed option market.

Index options account for less than half the contracts traded on U.S. exchanges; however, these products generate almost 60 percent of the total premium for equity and index options and represent a notional value several times that of equity options. Of greater importance is the appeal of index options to institutions seeking to manage and hedge market risk. Index options dramatically expanded the customer base of the listed option market by providing a risk management tool that could not be economically replicated using the existing options on individual stocks. These new customers accounted for much of the growth of the listed option market after the early 1980s. Although an almost limitless number of option strategies have been developed by market participants, institutional participants in the index option market have three primary goals for uses of the product: managing market risk, implementing asset allocation programs, and seeking to enhance returns through timing of market entry and exit.

During the past few years, however, the exchange-listed option market has not been the entire story. A new OTC index option market has emerged. This new OTC market has a very different cast of participants with needs and goals that also differ from those characteristic of the pre-1973 OTC option market. Rather than individual investors seeking options on specific stocks, the new OTC players are the large institutional investors that dominate trading in the underlying stock market and are the primary users of index options—pension funds, mutual funds, banks, and insurance companies. These institutional investors hold diversified portfolios of stocks valued in the hundreds of millions or even billions of dollars.

STRATEGIC ANALYSIS: COMPARING EXCHANGE AND OTC MARKETS

Why did a new OTC options market develop and what has been the exchange response to that new market? The answers to these questions illuminate the strategic rationale for CBOE's FLEX, and the similar products being developed on other domestic as well as foreign exchanges.

Table 1 summarizes the features of the OTC and exchange option marketplace. Even a cursory examination of the table reveals significant differences between exchange and OTC option markets on a variety of dimensions. What is most striking, however, is the degree to which nonstandardized contract terms are characteristic of OTC transactions. A major historic rationale of derivative exchanges—options or futures—has been the standardization of contract terms, allowing market participants to "trade with strangers." In turn, contract standardization made possible centralized clearing and facilitated the creation of liquid secondary markets. In contrast, the OTC

Table 1.   Exchange and OTC Option Markets: A Comparison

	Exchange	*OTC Market*
Contract Terms		
(1) Maturities	listed expiration dates only	customized
(2) Transaction Size	standard (contract size)	variable
(3) Strikes	listed, regular point intervals	any value
Trading Environment		
(1) Price Discovery	transparent	opaque
(2) Market Type	retail: immediacy	wholesale: liquidity in depth
(3) Secondary Market Liquidity	good	very limited
(4) Regulatory Oversight	extensive: position limits, disclosure	none
Product Distribution		
(1) Target	individuals and institutions	institutions
(2) Distribution Channel	broker-dealers	large broker-dealers and investment banks
Clearing and Settlement		
(1) Settlement Terms	daily mark-to-market	negotiated
(2) Clearing	clearinghouse	counterparty credit
(3) Counterparty	centralized clearinghouse	large broker-dealers and investment banks

option market allows time to expiration, size, and strike to be established on a transaction-by-transaction basis. There is a very limited secondary market for OTC trades. In many respects OTC index option transactions resemble a forward cash market rather than an option (or futures) market.

The customization characteristic of the OTC index option market appeals to institutional participants. As institutional portfolio managers have become more familiar and comfortable with options (and other derivative products) and, at the same time, performance measurement has become both widespread and more exacting, many portfolio managers have become concerned with the imprecision that is a necessary concomitant of standardized exchange-based contracts. Portfolio performance is evaluated at the end of a fiscal or calendar quarter or year, not at the close or open of business on the third Friday, the date on which conventional exchange-listed options stop trading. Similarly, the market risk of diversified portfolios can be more precisely managed by selecting an exact index value rather than using the five-index-point strike price intervals characteristic of exchange-traded index option products. In addition, because exchange market making is based on concentration of a large volume of transactions into a single contract or a few contracts, these contracts are of necessity, relatively elementary in design, allowing only for simple puts and calls or option positions that can be readily created by use of different standardized "legs."[1]

These differences in contract terms result in quite different trading environments in the OTC and exchange option marketplaces. Exchanges specialize in centralizing the price discovery process and providing immediacy. Market participants seeking to transact may do so in a very short time frame, confident that their order is exposed to several competing bids (offers) and therefore assured of a best price that reflects current market valuation. In contrast, OTC markets are decentralized and bids (offers) may be compared only by contacting multiple dealers, a time-consuming process. The OTC market is not a day trader's locale.

The centralization of bids and offers found on an exchange also facilitates the creation of a liquid secondary market, allowing market participants to change their minds and have their new market outlook implemented almost immediately. Finally, exchange markets, because they are readily accessible to the investing public, are highly regulated. This regulation extends both to the nature of the information that must be disclosed to an investor in advance of a transaction and to the nature and size of the transactions that investors with differing financial status and investment experience may be allowed to execute. These regulatory restrictions are absent from the OTC market.

The final difference between exchange and OTC markets is the process of clearing and guaranteeing the transaction. Exchange transactions are guaranteed by a clearinghouse with financial resources greater than those available to any single counterparty to a trade. The security of OTC transactions is based on the financial integrity of the counterparty and is therefore subject to change as the fortunes of business vary.

---

1 Although this concern with complexity is often cited as a major reason for institutional use of OTC index options, I do not believe it is the primary motivation to date. Most portfolio managers have relatively little use for the more exotic option strategies such as binaries, lookbacks, hydras, etc.

Clearly, the two markets have significant differences in structure and trading environment and meet different needs. However, the markets are not insulated from each other. Trades on one market (frequently the OTC) may generate activity on the other. Of much greater importance, however, is the fact that the participants in the two markets are not distinct. Many exchange member firms are active in both the exchange and OTC option market—and, as noted above, institutional users of exchange-listed products may also make use of OTC markets. In recent years they have done so increasingly. Managers of institutional portfolios have thus emerged as the primary source of volume growth in both exchange and OTC index option markets. At the same time, the primary distribution system for exchange-listed products, the member firm, is also the distribution system for OTC products. In the latter case it is the institutional sales force that has product marketing responsibility.

To complete an understanding of the strategic analysis behind FLEX it is necessary to assess the relative size and growth of the exchange and OTC index option markets. In the case of the exchange market this is quite easy: The transparency and centralized clearing features of exchange markets facilitate ready measurement of both volume and open interest. Unfortunately, the opacity of the OTC market makes exact comparison difficult. If the focus is market size, the exchange market clearly dwarfs the OTC market. In the U.S. the notional value of exchange index option trading is in excess of $4 trillion annually and open interest at any time is more than $150 billion. In contrast, our analysis of the OTC index option market estimated trading value in notional terms of $150 to $200 billion and open positions valued at approximately $60 to $70 billion.[2] In early 1993 the International Swap Dealers Association (ISDA) conducted its first survey to determine notional value of OTC index option positions outstanding. The reported total was $59 billion.

Based on the foregoing comparison, it is clear that OTC open interest is much more significant relative to exchange open interest than is OTC volume. However, by all accounts OTC index option volume has been growing rapidly; the same is not true for exchange index option volume. Thus, the CBOE concluded that the OTC market was capturing an increasing share of institutional business, the market segment essential to continued exchange volume growth. The CBOE's strategic analysis suggested that the symbiosis of OTC and exchange markets was again urging the necessity of innovative product development efforts by the exchange to retain the business of a key group of market participants. The CBOE responded by returning to its roots: seeking to combine the benefits of exchange trading with the product innovation demand emanating from an OTC market.

FLEX: WEDDING OTC AND EXCHANGE MARKETS

But what are the benefits of exchange trading if standardization is not desirable? And how could these benefits be combined with the tailored contract terms and liquidity

---

2 This assessment of relative market size and growth is a very condensed summary of many interviews and discussions with both OTC and exchange market participants. The comparative numbers for the OTC and exchange markets are certainly subject to debate; the assessment of relative growth and the contribution of institutional market participants to that growth is a reflection of an almost unanimous opinion among participants in both markets.

of OTC trading? How extensive a menu of customized products should the CBOE seek to offer? These questions, along with those of trading procedures, were the focus of CBOE's FLEX development project.

The Exchange determined that there existed a complexity curve of OTC transactions and that the degree of complexity is inversely related to the number of transactions (although perhaps directly related to amount of financial media coverage and number of conference presentations). Put another way, most OTC transactions appear to differ from those executed on an exchange on only a limited number of dimensions.

The CBOE concluded that the competitive advantages of exchange-traded options over those of the OTC market resided in four market features: fungibility, centralization of price discovery through the competitive auction process, the credit quality of the clearinghouse, and transparency.[3]

Based on this analysis of the OTC market the CBOE decided to initially offer customization along four key dimensions of an option contract: strike price, time to expiration, exercise style, and expiry value determination. In addition, above a specified minimum size, the exchange imposed no minimum size increments. At the same time, CBOE applied several dimensions of standardization to FLEX options: a minimum transaction size, predefined classes, transparency, settlement and clearing, trading hours, and competitive auction. Table 2 lists the dimensions of standardization and customization for CBOE's FLEX options.

The first strategic decision regarding standardization was the choice of classes. Our analysis of the OTC index option market indicated that the bulk of OTC index transactions involving exposure to the U.S. equity market were based on the S&P 500 index. Thus, the CBOE determined to initiate FLEX trading by listing only predefined classes, that is, not to allow trading in baskets defined at the time of the transaction. This decision also reflected the existing limits on the ability of the clearing corporation to settle and margin customized baskets and the limited experience that most CBOE market makers have had with pricing these baskets.

The choice of a minimum transaction size was also driven by our analysis of OTC index options market practices and was designed to accomplish several goals. The Exchange wanted a transaction size large enough to assure that FLEX would draw institutional business. At the same time, as a new participant in the customized index option market, we believed that the transaction size had to be small enough to encourage an institution with OTC experience to try the CBOE market with at least a

---

3 Not all market participants would agree that transparency is a competitive advantage. Some participants in the OTC market argue that the opacity of the market is positive, preventing other market participants from learning of transactions in size. While this may be true (although perhaps overstated) from the perspective of the individual institutional user of risk-management markets, the application of this principal to all users of these markets would produce less efficient pricing and greater volatility. A major advantage of transparent markets, aside from the benefits of equitable pricing, is the ability of market participants to gauge the demand for risk management at various price levels and respond accordingly. Absent the information available from transparent exchange-based transactions, financial markets would be subject to rumor and surmise, with the likely result being an increase in volatility and a reduction in pricing efficiency.

Table 2. CBOE's FLEX Options: Dimensions of Standardization and Customization

Dimensions of Standardization	
Classes Available:	S&P 100; S&P 500; Russell 2000
Minimum Transaction Size	$10 million notional for new series ($1 million in secondary trading)
Transparency:	Request for quote, quote, and last sale dissemination
Settlement/Clearing:	Clearinghouse guarantee; standard margins; position offsets; daily mark-to-market
Trading Hours:	9:00–3:15 Central time

Dimensions of Customization	
Strike Price:	Any index value to one decimal
Expiration Date:	Any business day up to five years; however, expiration Friday and two business days on either side are excluded
Exercise Style:	European, American, capped
Expiry Value:	Open, close, averages

portion of their desired transaction. Finally, the minimum transaction size was also established at a level that well-capitalized CBOE market makers could price efficiently and competitively. The result of these at times conflicting goals was the choice of a $10 million minimum for transactions that open a new FLEX series.

In addition to the rationale noted previously, the requirement that FLEX be a transparent marketplace is intended to elicit interest from off-floor as well as from CBOE traders. All requests for quote (RFQs) are immediately diseminated, allowing upstairs desks to contact their customers or to respond on behalf of their proprietary trading account. The use of the Options Clearing Corporation (OCC) as the settlement and guarantee mechanism provides a AAA credit for each transaction, effectively eliminating counterparty credit risk. In addition, OCC provides offsets against other index option positions established in conventional listed products, marks the value of each FLEX position daily, and accepts market index option escrow receipts for qualifying FLEX positions. Customized transactions are "converted" into standardized positions and receive many of the benefits that accrue to the latter.

The customization features embodied in FLEX are essential to: (1) the CBOE strategy of attracting transactions from the "plain vanilla" end of the OTC complexity curve; and (2) expanding the universe of institutional users of customized derivative products. Prior to FLEX, some institutions were not able to execute customized transactions, either because of mandate limitations that prevented use of OTC products or because of concern regarding the financial integrity of such transactions. FLEX thus extends the benefits of customized transactions to new participants.

The first two dimensions of customization offered by FLEX, choice of strike price and choice of expiration date, allow a user to match precisely the size of the portfolio through strike price selection and to establish a risk-management position for a duration that reflects market outlook. These customization features are readily adaptable to the creation of various structured products, for example, a market-linked CD with part or all of the returns tied to the performance of the S&P 500 or S&P 100. Collars may be established for any period of time and at any net debit or credit sought by the portfolio manager.

The FLEX transactor may also specify the style of exercise, choosing to eliminate the risk of early exercise (European) or to reserve to the option purchaser that possibility (American). Lastly, by providing a choice in determination of the index value to which the FLEX position will be marked at expiry, portfolio managers whose performance is normally evaluated through the close of business are not exposed to the risk of a large intraday price movement after the FLEX position expires. Although opening price settlement of index options is popular with certain regulatory agencies and various members of Congress, banks and the IRS value portfolios basis the close of business. The disjuncture between the political pressures that have imposed opening settlement on an increasing number of exchange-listed index option products and the realities of financial market operation and evaluation has acted to push transactions away from the regulated exchange markets to the largely unregulated OTC market.[4]

THE FLEX TRADING PROCESS

OTC trading differs from that characteristic of an exchange market. As noted in Table 1, the latter market specializes in immediacy; the former, in depth liquidity with fewer concerns about the time required to transact. Many OTC trades may be priced several times over a period of days before the actual transaction occurs. However, this difference between the OTC and exchange trading process is less marked in large, institutional-sized transactions, where there is frequently some period of price and size negotiation even in an active trading post such as that of the S&P 500 and S&P 100 index options. CBOE designed FLEX to integrate the exchange and OTC markets, with the emphasis on the provision of the in-depth liquidity that is characteristic of the OTC index option market.

FLEX is a request-for-quote market, and the transactions occur with less immediacy and more negotiation than is the case elsewhere on the CBOE trading floor. The request-for-quote (RFQ) process allows the submitting member to specify the nature of the transaction sought along the customization dimensions discussed previously. The RFQ is then transmitted both to the trading floor and to the outside world,

---

4 Although there is not enough space to discuss the evidence here, it has not been demonstrated that use of closing settlement prices for expiry values of index options has generated any significant amount of market volatility or that moves to opening price settlement have eliminated or reduced any such volatility. Indeed, use of opening prices often results in marks that are outside the trading range for the day. The bulk of FLEX users have selected closing price settlement.

in the latter case through vendors with the capability of handling nonstandardized transactions.[5]

To insure liquidity, the CBOE recruited Appointed Market Makers (AMMs) who would commit to respond to all RFQs. The responsive bid (offer) must be in at least the minimum transaction size of $10 million notional value. In addition, other CBOE market makers may respond if they meet the financial requirements for trading in FLEX. Finally, the dissemination of FLEX RFQs and the interval allowed for quote response provides the opportunity for off-floor market participants to bid or offer in response to RFQs also.

If the sequence of quote request and response resembles that of the OTC market, the actual trading resembles that of the CBOE floor. After the specified time for quote response has elapsed, the AMMs and other interested parties assemble at the FLEX post and an Exchange employee (Order Book Official) conducts an open outcry auction. The price and time priorities applicable to the FLEX trading process are similar to those found on the rest of the floor and are designed to centralize the price discovery process by providing a market considerably more transparent than the existing OTC market. Matching of FLEX trades is done on a real-time basis. All parties to the transaction are required to sign the trade confirmation before the trade is submitted to the OCC for clearing.

FLEX TRADING: A WINDOW INTO THE OTC MARKET

Although there have been several official studies that included the OTC equity index market in their coverage and countless articles discussing trading in this market, there is almost no hard data regarding actual numbers or types of transactions, size of trades, etc. Media articles and conference presentations are necessarily selective and tend to emphasize the complex, the exotic, and the new products being developed. FLEX transaction statistics, therefore, provide an almost unique window into the OTC index option market, covering a wide range of transactions entered into by a broad array of participants. The only other available data, and a useful source for comparison, is that from the 1993 ISDA survey cited previously.

Table 3 provides summary statistics on trading in FLEX through the first year of trading. Table 3A reproduces ISDA index option open position data for year-end 1992 by country of market exposure. The absolute amount of FLEX transactions to date indicates significant acceptance of the product in the marketplace. More importantly, comparing Tables 3 and 3A provides strong evidence that FLEX has established itself as a viable format for conducting transactions that offer many of the same features as the traditional OTC index option market. During a period in which the price range on the S&P 500 index was only slightly in excess of 40 points (slightly over 320 DJIA points), FLEX notional value exceeded $11 billion. Open interest has been consistently in the range of $4 to $5.5 billion, and average transaction size has been over to $25 million.

---

5 I am omitting a discussion of the significant operational difficulties that were confronted by the CBOE in the creation of a dissemination system for FLEX. Issues such as symbols, quote vendor programming capabilities, internal capture of quotes, and last sales for audit and clearing purposes, etc., required considerable efforts on the part of CBOE, OCC, and vendor staff.

Table 3.   FLEX Transactions, Feb. 26–Feb. 18, 1994

Total Volume	368,300 contracts
Notional Principal Transacted	$16.7 billion
Total RFQs	1,744
Total Transactions	656
No. of Open Series	133
Contracts/Transaction	561
Notional Principal/Transaction	$25.4 million
Open Interest	$5.25 billion

Table 3A.   SDA: Notional Value Outstanding (12/31/92) (billions of U.S. dollars)

Index Options (by country of market exposure)	Dealer/Dealer	Dealer/End User	Total
U.S.	3	8	11
Japan	11	9	20
U.K.	6	5	11
Germany	4	2	6
France	3	2	5
Other	2	2	4

As the CBOE expected, most FLEX trading has occurred in the S&P 500, with considerably less interest in the S&P 100 and the Russell 2000.[6] The S&P 500 is the benchmark for many portfolio managers in the U.S. and is the most active product in OTC trading. Although the majority of FLEX trading during the initial eight months has been in shorter-dated options, the average maturity has increased over the past half year. In addition, there have been a significant number of transactions with maturities in excess of two years (the longest exchange-listed option), amounting to almost $7 billion notional value.

The OTC window offered by FLEX is not limited to the amount and size of transactions; the type of transactions is also of interest. Although it is not always possible to ascertain the motivations of FLEX customers by simply looking at the trade, many FLEX participants have been willing to talk, in general terms, about their use of FLEX. Most FLEX transactions to date may be characterized as overwriting, collars, or structured products.

As noted above, FLEX was launched during a period of relatively low market volatility. Many option strategies do not work well during such periods; however, overwriting does. A large number of the short-term (less than 90 days) positions

---

6 The Russell 2000 was not listed for trading in FLEX until August 6, 1993.

established in FLEX have been by overwriters seeking to enhance the returns to portfolios under management. This strategy has been executed with different approaches. Some overwriters have sold deep out-of-the-money calls, increasing their returns by a few basis points but providing very little protection against any downward market move, although allowing for gains if the market advances. Another approach has been the use of in-the-money calls, resulting in increased premium collected, again enhancing portfolio returns but with strikes that have frequently expired in-the-money.

During the first year of trading, the largest FLEX transactions have been collars. This is true despite the limited market movement that has occurred not only since FLEX was launched but also for the entire year of 1993. Although some of the collars have been done on a zero-cost basis, customers have also sought to establish collars at small net credits, providing for superior portfolio returns over a wide range of market movement. Collar expirations have not always coincided with end of quarter or end of year time frames, indicating an interest in benefiting from the expiration date customization feature of FLEX.

A final use of FLEX that should be mentioned is the creation of structured products. FLEX transactions have been used as a part of market-linked CDs as well as a means of hedging products issued prior to the opening of trading in FLEX. This use of FLEX should grow over time.

THE FUTURE OF FLEX: CBOE AND BEYOND

The CBOE has already added one product to FLEX, the Russell 2000 index option. In addition, the CBOE has submitted rule filings to the SEC that will allow trading of equity indexes denominated in currencies other than U.S. dollars and to include non-U.S. equity index products in FLEX. The Exchange also has other products under consideration for inclusion in the FLEX trading format.

Perhaps even more striking is the intense interest generated by FLEX among other exchanges, both in the U.S. and abroad. After examining CBOE's FLEX filing, the American Stock Exchange developed a similar filing for its own index products and launched its own FLEX indices in September 1993. At least two other U.S. derivative markets are actively considering the establishment of a FLEX-type capability. Staff from several European and Asian exchanges have discussed FLEX extensively with the CBOE and many have visited the CBOE to view FLEX trading.

Clearly the FLEX concept is adaptable to other than the equity index products that were launched by the CBOE in February 1993. The benefits of FLEX—competitive price discovery, fungibility, transparency of price discovery, and the elimination of trading counterparty credit risk—are attractive to participants in a wide variety of OTC markets. Although FLEX is still a quite recent product innovation, the concept has already successfully reemphasized the benefits of exchange markets. In the larger dynamic of exchange and OTC market innovation and response, FLEX has pointed the way toward a new generation of exchange-traded derivative products.

CHAPTER 3

Exotic Options in Action

Kosrow Dehnad
Vice President
Chase Securities, Inc.

INTRODUCTION

Exotic options first appeared as purely academic exercises and were treated by practitioners as an attempt to answer questions that nobody asked. Putting it in less friendly terms, they were referred to as errors of the third kind—"answering the wrong question incorrectly." Users of derivative products also viewed exotics as whimsical and novel products ahead of their time. They also expressed concern about liquidity and the cost of unwinding such trades before their maturity. This point was expressed succinctly by a customer, who said, "Whenever I hear 'exotic options,' I reach for my wallet." But exotic options have come a long way; what began as an arcane academic exercise has become a legitimate product. Yesterday's exotics are today's "plain vanillas." They have been imbedded in structures to create powerful and efficient means of monetizing a view, tailor-made to the risk appetite, and budget of the user. The rate and economic environments of the early 90s have also helped, as historically low interest rates have sent investors hunting for "yield pickup." And exotic options have been used in many creative ways to achieve this and other goals. On the liability side, the historically steep yield curve and the large spread between the long- and short-term rates "negative carry" have made moving up the yield curve painful. Here also, exotic options have come to the rescue and have enabled users to fix their debt without being unduly penalized for the steepness of the yield curve. This chapter attempts to illustrate these points through actual examples. It starts by classifying exotic options into broad categories. Next it uses actual cases, based on trades at Chase Securities, to illustrate how exotic options are used to solve real-life problems. When appropriate, pricing and hedging issues are also discussed. It should be emphasized that the most natural way to market an exotic option is to embed it in a structure, rather than marketing it as a stand-alone product—very similar to a transistor, where customers' demand is for usable gadgets like a TV and not for a transistor by itself. The crucial issue is packaging.

WHAT ARE EXOTIC OPTIONS?

There is no clear-cut answer to this question because the field is vast and still evolving. New products and structures are introduced to the market almost every day, and an exotic product today is "plain vanilla" tomorrow. From a practical viewpoint, however, an exotic option can be defined as an option that relaxes one or more assumptions of a standard call or put, or has some additional parameters. Additional parameters and looser assumptions are the main reasons why exotic options provide better and more precise tools for risk management than standard options. Take a two-year standard interest rate cap on three-month LIBOR with a strike of 4 percent on $10,000,000, which costs $90,000 (90 basis points). All the parameters of this structure are known at the time of trade, namely:

Type = Cap (call on LIBOR)

Underlying Instrument = 3-month LIBOR

Premium = 90 basis points

Payoff = Max (LIBOR-4, 0)

Size = $10,000,000

Maturity = Two years

Strike = 4.0 %

By relaxing one or more of the above parameters, we arrive at different classes of exotic options. In the case of *Chooser Options*, the type of the option is determined sometime in the future at the discretion of the buyer. For *Better-of-Two* or *Rainbow Options* the underlying instrument is not unique and is the best performing of two or more assets. The option premium that the buyer of a *Self-Funding Cap* ends up paying is not known beforehand and depends on the number of times that the cap goes in-the-money. Unlike a standard cap, the payoff of a *Digital Cap* is fixed irrespective of how deep in-the-money the option is. On the other hand, the payoff of a *LIBOR Squared Cap* increases quadratically, the deeper in-the-money the option is. The principal of the trade in the *Indexed Principal Swap (IPS)* changes during the life of the trade, depending on the path that the index takes. In the case of *Barrier Options* the option *knocks in* should the index hit a certain barrier, which renders the maturity of the deal unknown at the time of the trade. Finally, in the case of *Periodic Caps*, the strike of the caplets is not known beforehand and depends on the path that the interest rate takes. The last three examples were from the class of *Path-Dependent* options, where certain parameters of the option are not known beforehand and depend on the path along which a certain index evolves. These classes of options enable us to achieve various financial goals with ease and precision, as shown below. In each section we pose a problem and solve it with a structure that involves an exotic option, and later we describe the way the structure was constructed.

SEMI-FIXED SWAPS (NONLINEAR PAYOFF)

Problem: An issuer desires five-year funding in U.S. dollars. An investor has a view that the dollar will appreciate against the French franc (FRF), specifically, he thinks that the FRF/$ exchange rate will be above 5.75. He requires a dollar-linked payoff and wants to limit his downside should he prove wrong.

Solution: A semi-fixed note with FX trigger. The issuer borrows at, say, 5.35 percent (semiannual bond), which is the five-year Treasury rate plus his borrowing spread. The investor will receive the above-market rate of 6 percent during the periods when FRF/$ > = 5.75, and 4.15 percent when FRF/$ < 5.75 (see Exhibit 1).

Exhibit 1. Semi-Fixed Note with FX Trigger

• *Solution:*

Maturity: Five Years

Note pays: 6% if FRF/$ > 5.75
4% if FRF/$ < 5.75

Problem: In order to expand its operations, a mining company borrows at the floating rate of L(3) plus its borrowing spread. The company is worried about an increase in interest rates and is thinking of swapping its floating-rate liability into fixed (see Exhibit 2). The steep yield curve, however, makes the swap very unattractive

---

Exhibit 2

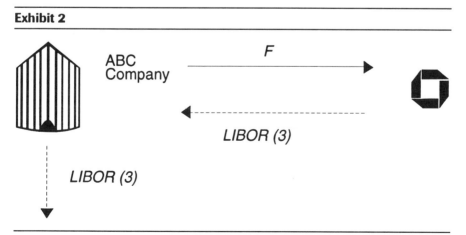

because of the huge initial negative carry—particularly at the start of the project. Specifically, the three-month LIBOR rate of 3.5 and the swap rate of 6 percent (quarterly money market rate) translate into an initial negative carry of 6-3.5 = 250 bp. On the other hand, the company has a natural exposure to gold and should the price of gold rise, it will be in a favorable position to service its debt.

Solution: A semi-fixed swap with gold trigger. This structure lets the company pay a below-market swap rate when the price of gold is low and it is in need of some relief from its interest payments. In return, the company will pay a higher rate when the price of gold is above a certain level and it is in a better financial position (see Exhibit 3).

Exhibit 3.   Semi-Fixed Swap with Gold Trigger

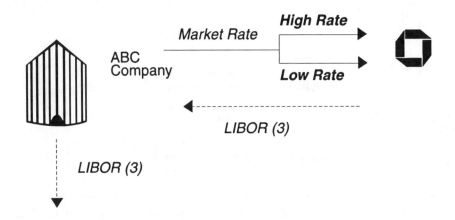

ABC Company pays low rate if Gold Price < Trigger
ABC Company pays high rate if Gold Price ≥ Trigger

Both structures are the combination of a standard swap and a digital option. A digital call with strike of K has one of two payoffs: nothing if the option is out-of-the-money, and a fixed amount if the option is in-the-money, irrespective of how deep in-the-money the option might be (see Exhibit 4). In the first case, the investor sells a digital option on FRF/$ exchange rate. He receives the premium in terms of higher yield (see Exhibit 5). For those periods when the option is in-the-money and the investor has to make a payment, he receives a lower coupon. The difference between the higher and lower coupons is equal to the digital call payoff that the investor has sold.

In the case of the mining company, the digital call is on gold and the premium from the sale of the option is received by the company in terms of a lower swap rate.

Exhibit 4.   Comparison of a Standard Call and a Digital Call

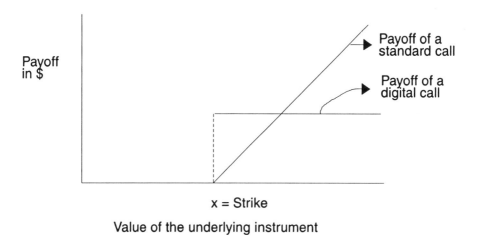

x = Strike

Value of the underlying instrument

Exhibit 5.   Construction of Semi-Fixed Note with FX Trigger

i)

II) Investor sells a digital option on FRF/$ with strike of 5.75

Exhibit 6.   Construction of Semi-Fixed Note with FX Trigger

---

iii) Possible payoff of the note

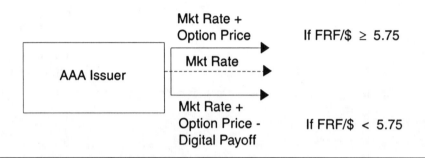

In those periods that gold is above the strike, the option would be in-the-money and the company has to make a fixed (digital) payoff. This is accomplished by the company paying a higher rate during these periods (see Exhibit 6).

The flexibility of the semi-fixed swap stems from the fact that it has more parameters than the standard swap, namely: the higher rate, the lower rate, and the trigger level for digital option. These parameters enable us to tailor the semi-fixed swap to a particular economic view, risk appetite, and budget. In general, given two of the above factors, the third one can be determined. For example, given one of the rates and the trigger level of the digital option, the other rate can be determined. Similarly, given the two rates, the trigger level can be determined. In fact, the standard swap can be viewed as a special case of the semi-fixed swap when the trigger level of the digital option is set in such a way to render it worthless. Another source of the flexibility of the semi-fixed swap is that the underlying instrument of the swap can be different from that of the digital option, which could be an interest rate index like LIBOR, the price of a commodity like gold, the foreign exchange rate of FRF, etc. This provides the semi-fixed swap with the flexibility of being able to meet certain financial goals, like a lower swap rate, by taking into account certain views, like strengthening of the dollar versus a certain currency, or some other factor, like a natural exposure to gold by a counterparty.

BASKET OPTIONS (MULTI-ASSETS AND CORRELATION)

Problem: A fixed-income investor has investments in foreign bonds: 20 percent Germany (Bund), 50 percent U.K. (Gilts), and 30 percent France (OATS). She is concerned about her FX exposure and would like to hedge some of it. Microhedging and buying options on each currency separately is expensive.

Solution: Buy an option on the value of the portfolio. This option will be less expensive, and it provides a cleaner and more accurate hedge than buying a basket of options. For example, in 1993, the premium for three months option with the strike set at-the-money forward rates was

FRF put / USD call	2.73% of USD notional amount
DEM put / USD call	2.68% of USD notional amount
GBP put / USD call	2.85% of USD notional amount

Cost of the basket of options (weighted sum): 2.73 percent of USD notional amount
Cost of the option on the basket: 2.39 percent of USD notional amount

Problem: A manufacturer, on a quarterly basis, services his debt and purchases aluminum for his operation. He is concerned about inflation and higher interest rates and wants to hedge his aluminum and interest rate exposures. Buying separate caps on aluminum and interest rates is expensive.

Solution: Since the true exposure of the manufacturer is to the total cost of purchasing aluminum and servicing his debt, an integrated hedge is a more precise and cost-effective approach than buying separate caps. The manufacturer will buy a cap on the total cost of purchasing aluminum and interest payments. Should this combined expense exceed the strike of the cap, he will be compensated for the difference.

Both structures are based on the fact that "a basket of options" is more expensive than an "option on a basket" because a basket of options overinsures the basket and ignores the advantages of correlation among the elements of the basket. For illustration, consider a bond portfolio consisting of German (Bund) and French (OATS) bonds. Hedging each FX exposure separately through the purchase of FRF and DM puts will result in overinsurance, as illustrated in Exhibit 7. The equivalue line is the combination of rates for which the portfolio has the same value. The overinsurance areas are combinations of FX rates for which the gain on one currency more than compensates for the loss on the other, thus rendering insurance unnecessary. Moreover, microhedging ignores the correlation among the elements of the basket. Exhibits 8 and 9 show the probability density functions of two instruments with positive and negative correlation, respectively. The movements of two positively correlated instruments are often in the same direction, and for the negatively correlated instruments the movements are in opposite directions. Since for two instruments that are negatively correlated, a loss on one is often accompanied by a gain on the other, the impact of

---

Exhibit 7

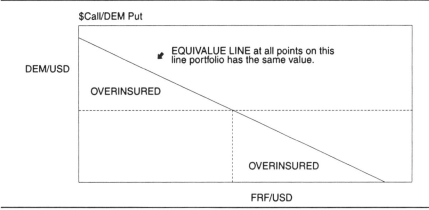

Exhibit 8. Positive Correlation between Two Instruments

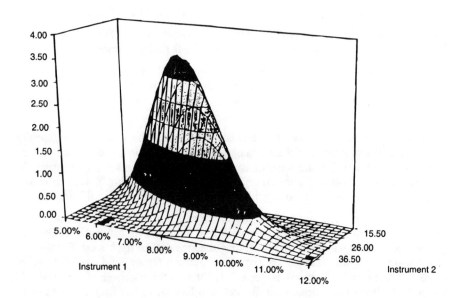

Exhibit 9. Negative Correlation between Two Instruments

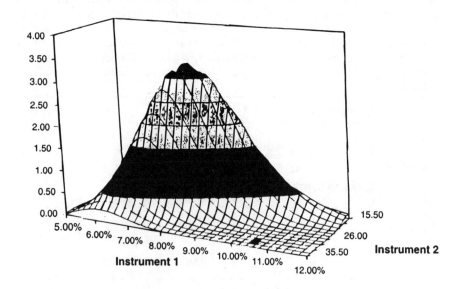

Exhibit 10

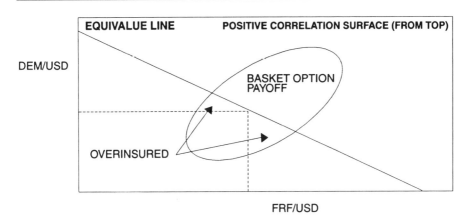

overinsurance is accentuated in such cases. On the other hand, if two instruments are highly correlated, then the impact of overinsurance is less severe. In fact if two instrument are perfectly correlated, they are the same instruments except for the scale and there will be no overinsurance. To illustrate these points, suppose DM and FRF rates are positively correlated, and the ellipse in Exhibit 10 contains the most probable combinations of DM and FRF. In this case, the magnitude of overinsurance is not considerable. On the other hand, suppose these two rates are negatively correlated, then as shown in Exhibit 11, the overinsurance can be significant, and considerable savings can be realized by using basket options and integrated hedges.

Exhibit 11

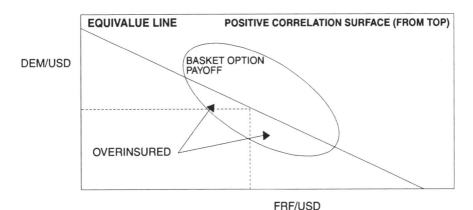

Thus, the option on a basket is cheaper than the basket of options.

BARRIER OPTIONS

Problem: An investor is prepared to realize some yield pickup by selling interest rate caps in the current low-rate, low inflation environment. Her main concern is, however, the possibility of rising rates should the recovery change from being anemic to robust. She believes that gold and inflation are highly correlated.

Solution: A leveraged capped floater with gold knock-out. The investor buys a floater and sells 6 percent caps with four times the notional amount of the floater with the provision that should the price of gold go above the barrier of $450/oz, the cap would disappear. The final structure is

> Issuer: A finance company
>
> Maturity: Three years
>
> Structure: Minimum of zero or
>
> > a) LIBOR plus 60 basis points or
> >
> > b) 24.6 - 3 LIBOR
>
> Plus gold knock-out feature

If at any time prior to maturity the price of gold breaks the barrier of $450/oz, the structure converts to a LIBOR + 60 basis points floater.

Problem: A project finance has made the purchase of interest rate protection a requirement of lending. Caps are expensive because of the steep yield curve and high market volatility. Further, the borrowers do not foresee a rise in the rates and are concerned that the cap will expire out-of-the-money and the substantial cap premium will be wasted.

Solution: A premium knock-in cap. This structure provides the buyer with a standard cap and requires no upfront premium. In fact, payment for the cap does not start until the rates break a predetermined barrier. Should this happen, from then until the maturity of the cap the buyer will make regular periodic payments. The barrier and size of the payments are all determined at the time of the trade. Consequently, if the rates do not break the barrier, the buyer will never make any payments, or if they do so near the maturity, very few payments have to be made and the buyer will still be better off than if he had bought a standard cap. On the other hand, if rates break the barrier in the early part of the life of the cap, the buyer could end up paying considerably more than the price of the standard cap.

Barrier options come in a number of flavors: knock-in, knock-out, up-and-in, up-and-out, down-and-in, down-and-out, one touch, or more complex conditions, such as if an index breaks a certain barrier and stays above it for a number of days. The index that is used to determine the event can be interest rate, commodity, or any tradable instrument or something highly correlated with it. Barrier options use conditioning to achieve certain objectives that cannot be achieved using standard options.

SPREAD OPTIONS

Problem: An investor has a strong view that the yield curve will flatten and the spread between CMT(30) and CMT(2) will shrink. However, he does not want to take a risk on the direction of the flattening. Buying CMT(2) caps and selling CMT(30) caps is a valid strategy provided the yield curve does not shift downward and the flattening is due to a rise in the front end of the curve. On the other hand, a steepening of the curve due to a rise in CMT(30) yield could be painful. The payoff of this strategy is shown in Exhibit 12. Similarly, selling CMT(2) floors and buying CMT(30) floors is a valid strategy, provided the yield curve does not shift upward and the flattening is due to a fall in the far end of the curve. A steepening of the curve where the front end of the curve falls can be costly. The payoff of this strategy is shown in Exhibit 13.

Exhibit 12. Payoff Profile for Long CMT (2) Cap and Short CMT (30) Cap

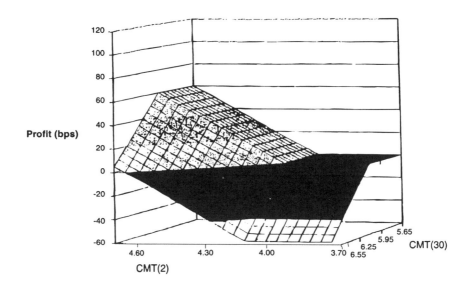

Solution: An option on the spread between CMT(30) and CMT(2). Since the investor does not want to take directional risk, buying a floor on the spread between CMT(30) and CMT(2) will achieve this goal. The payoff of this strategy is shown in Exhibit 14.

An alternative would be to sell caps on this spread or enter into a zero-cost collar, where the investor buys the cap and sells the floor. In all the above strategies, the investor is not taking a view on the absolute level of rates or the direction of flattening.

Exhibit 13. Payoff Profile for Long CMT (30) Floor and Short CMT (2) Floor

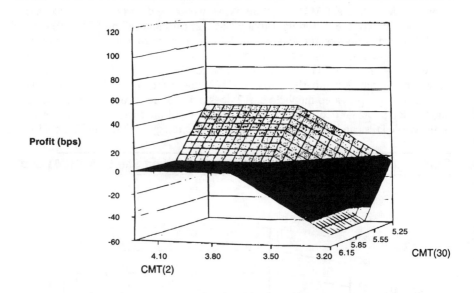

Exhibit 14. Payoff Profile for Long CMT (2) Cap and Short CMT (30) Cap

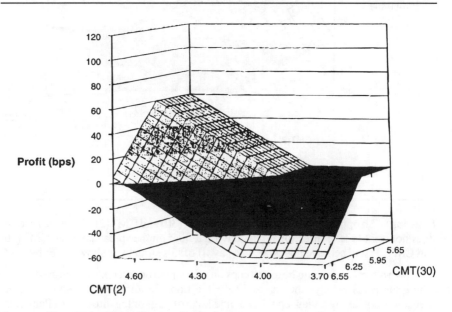

Source: The 1993 Institutional Investor Conference

Problem: A finance company has assets whose return is tied to the prime rate. The company finances itself through the issuing of commercial paper (CP). The spread between these two rates is at a historical high, and the company is concerned that the spread will shrink. The company can buy CP caps to limit its liability and finance this through the sale of prime caps. This strategy assumes no downward shift in the rate and implies a directional view on rates. An alternative would be to buy prime floors to insure the return on the company's assets and finance that through the sale of CP floor. This strategy assumes no upward shift in rates and implies a directional view of rates.

Solution: An option on prime-CP spread. The company can buy a floor on the spread between Prime and CP. Alternatively, the company can enter into a zero-cost collar on the Prime-CP spread, where it sells a cap and buys a floor.

Spread options are members of the so-called correlation family, where the correlation or co-movement of the two assets enters into the pricing of the options. Another member of this family is differential swaps, where one party receives, say, DM LIBOR and the other party receives US LIBOR, all paid (quantized) in U.S. dollars. These correlation products have been very popular because they can provide the exact risk exposure that an investor is seeking or trying to hedge, as shown in the above examples.

INDEXED PRINCIPAL SWAP (IPS)

Problem: A fixed-income investor in search of higher yields is prepared to invest in mortgage-backed securities and bear the prepayment risk. Her main concern is that the prepayment of the cash instruments, apart from the level of interest rates, depends on other factors, such as the overall state of the economy, type of the mortgages in the pool (e.g., FHA, Jumbo), the regional economy from which the mortgages in the pool have come, etc. Among all the factors affecting mortgage prepayment, she is willing to take the interest rate risk but does not have the expertise and willingness to have exposure to other factors.

Solution: An indexed principal swap. The investor enters into a swap where she receives the fixed rate and pays LIBOR. After a lock-out period, the notional amount of the swap amortizes based on the LIBOR setting and an amortization schedule. Often, there is a provision that the swap will disappear if the notional amount falls below a clean-up level.

Following is an example of an IPS.

Maturity = three years

Lock-out Period = one year

Initial Notional Amount = $100 million

Floating Index = 6-month LIBOR

Amortization Schedule

LIBOR	Percent Amortization	Amortization Multiplier
5	100%	0.0
6	40%	0.6
8	0%	1.0

Linear Interpolation for Intermediate Values

Suppose that after the lock-out period, $L(6)$ is set at 7 percent. Since this number is halfway between 6 percent and 8 percent, the amortization is the linear interpolation between 40 percent and 0 percent—that is, 20 percent. Since the notional amount for the next period = previous notional amount * amortization multiplier, the notional amount for the third period would be $80 million = $100 million * 0.8.

IPSs come in various forms. The amortization index can be LIBOR, CMT, or even FX rates. The amortization schedule can be discrete as opposed to continuous. For instance, in the above example the notional amount could amortize by 40 percent for all the LIBOR settings between 6 and 8. The amortization can be based on the original amount or the remaining amount.

Problem: A company has a fixed-rate obligation. It wants to take advantage of prevailing low interest rate environment by swapping that into fixed rate. The main concern is about a rise in the rates, which would make the original fixed-rate obligation more attractive.

Solution: A reverse indexed principal swap. The company enters into a reverse indexed principal swap, where it receives LIBOR and pays a fixed rate. The notional amount of the swap, however, will amortize should the rates rise. Effectively, the obligation of the company is a mix of fixed and floating, with the mix to be fully floating after the swap. As rates rise, the weight of the fixed component of the mix increases until it becomes fully fixed should rates rise significantly (see Exhibit 15).

Index principal swaps are another example of path-dependent structures. They are effective tools for generating synthetic assets with properties similar to mortgage-backed securities.

PERIODIC CAPS

Problem: An investor has a view at variance with the quarterly increases of more than 25 basis points in the future spot rates implied by the steep yield curve. These increases imply a number of tightening moves by the Federal Reserve incompatible with an anemic recovery. The investor wants to monetize this view without taking directional risk.

Solution: The investor buys a floating-rate note and sells a periodic cap. The note will pay the floating rate plus the spread with the condition that the coupon cannot increase by more than 25 basis points from one period to the other.

Exhibit 15. Reverse Indexed Principal Swaps

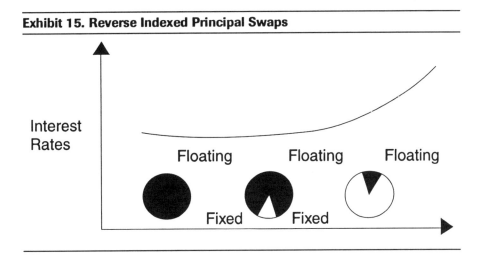

Problem: A fixed-rate borrower does not believe that future spot rates will increase by more than 25 basis points every quarter for the next two years, as indicated by the steep yield curve. He wants to monetize this view to reduce his cost of borrowing.

Solution: The borrower sells a path-dependent cap that pays the buyer Max (0, LIBOR – Previous LIBOR – 25 bp). He uses the option premium to reduce his cost of borrowing. For the next two years he will make a payment to the buyer of the cap only during those periods when LIBOR rises by more than 25 basis points.

WHERE ARE EXOTICS HEADING?

Where users want them. The examples cited above demonstrate the problem-solving power of exotic options. The topics that we have covered are only the tip of the iceberg. Differential swaps, options on differential swaps, look-back options, ladders, percentage caps, indexed premium caps, options of basket of equities, LIBOR squared caps, quadratic swaps, cumulative caps, and velocity options are but additional examples of exotics. The field is expanding very rapidly, and sophisticated users are demanding more such products. Currently, exotic options are applied to new areas of risk management such as real estate, economic cycles, and insurance.

Exotic options are in general more complicated to price and hedge (see Chapter 19), which affects, to a certain extent, the liquidity of these products. This situation is, however, improving with the increased acceptability of exotics as legitimate and powerful tools for risk management.

CHAPTER 4

A Survey of Spread Options for Fixed-Income Investors

Scott McDermott
Vice President
Goldman, Sachs & Co.

INTRODUCTION

In the late 1980s, Goldman, Sachs & Co. began trading a new family of fixed-income derivative products that are options on the spreads between different fixed-income asset classes. These new products include: SYCURVE^{SM} options, which are put and call options on the slope of a yield curve; MOTTO^{SM} options, which are put and call options on the spread between mortgage and Treasury securities; ISO^{SM} options, which are put and call options on the spread between foreign fixed-income securities and other foreign fixed-income securities or U.S. Treasury securities; CROSS^{SM} options, which are put and call options on fixed-income securities in which the option's strike price is established in a currency other than the currency in which the underlying securities are denominated; and finally, SPREAD-LOCK options, which are put and call options on interest rate swap spreads.[1]

These new fixed-income derivative products were introduced in response to a growing client need for hedges against different types of spread exposure. For reasons that we will examine below, it is difficult to hedge against spread exposure using only over-the-counter (or listed) put or call options on individual fixed-income securities. In fact, there is no way to replicate an option on a spread merely by purchasing and holding combinations of options on individual securities. As a result, the growth of the market for over-the-counter options on spreads has been quite rapid. This chapter presents a summary statement of the spread options market, surveying the available products and giving examples of their use.

---

1 SYCURVE, MOTTO, ISO, and CROSS are service marks of Goldman, Sachs & Co.

Copyright 1992 by Goldman Sachs.

For spread options, there are two ways in which the in-the-money value of the option is realized on exercise: (1) through a change in ownership of the securities underlying the option contract, or (2) through a cash payment equal to the in-the-money value. By their nature, spread options can have two or more underlying securities, which makes settlement through a change in ownership particularly complex. For convenience, some investors prefer to settle the intrinsic value of spread options with a cash payment (cash settlement) and without a change in ownership of the underlying securities. The cash payment usually takes place on the business day following the expiration or exercise date of the spread option.

Other investors, however, prefer options that involve a physical exchange of securities, and for these investors we have developed the DUOP^{SM} structure.[2] Any spread option can be structured as a DUOP. For example, SYCURVE-DUOP options are put and call options on the slope of the yield curve that—if the options expire in-the-money or are exercised—involve the purchase of Treasury securities in one maturity sector and the simultaneous sale of Treasury securities in another maturity sector at a strike price spread. In our experience, the majority of MOTTO and CROSS options have DUOP structures, while a majority of SYCURVE, ISO, and SPREAD-LOCK options are cash-settled. This chapter contains examples of both cash-settled options and spread options with the DUOP structure.

Before we describe each of the spread options individually, it is important to emphasize that over-the-counter spread options carry special risks. The value of any spread option, for example, will be determined by the changing relationship (the spread) between prices or yields of the securities underlying the spread option's contract, and not necessarily by changes in prices or yields of any individual security. Accordingly, there is no theoretical limit on the amount of the spread and on the liability of the party that is short the spread option. In certain instances, a performance assurance deposit may be required. Over-the-counter spread options are individual agreements between a buyer and a seller, and each counterparty must evaluate the credit risks involved. In general, these agreements cannot be transferred or assigned without the consent of both counterparties, so over-the-counter spread options may lack liquidity. These special risks are inherent in the over-the-counter spread options market; they are in addition to the risks—exchange-rate risk, for example—normally found in the market for the spread option's underlying securities.

SYCURVE OPTIONS

Movements in the shape of yield curves around the world, and uncertainty as to their future course, have left many market participants looking for efficient ways either to take positions with respect to the future shape of a yield curve or to reduce the risk to their existing portfolios associated with yield curve movements. SYCURVE (slope-of-the-yield-curve) options meet this need, offering the opportunity to "buy" (call options) or "sell" (put options) the yield curve. In our terminology, buying the yield curve means buying the shorter-maturity instrument and simultaneously selling a duration-matched amount of the longer-maturity instrument. Selling the yield curve

---

2 DUOP is a service mark of Goldman, Sachs & Co.

**Exhibit 1. The U.S. Treasury Yield Curve
(For Settlement August 16, 1991)**

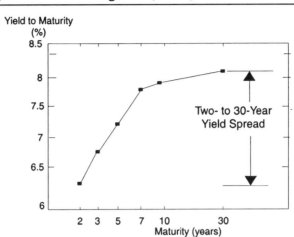

is the reverse strategy. Thus, SYCURVE call options increase in value as the yield curve steepens (or becomes less inverted), while SYCURVE put options increase in value as the yield curve flattens (or becomes more inverted).

Goldman, Sachs & Co. first introduced SYCURVE options in mid-1989.[3] We have found that the most commonly traded SYCURVE options are on the U.S. Treasury yield curve and, more specifically, on either the 2- to 10-year yield spread or the 2- to 30-year yield spread (see Exhibit 1). Accordingly, the examples that follow are drawn from the U.S. Treasury market. However, SYCURVE options can also be structured on most foreign yield curves, and investor interest in SYCURVE options on the Japanese and Canadian yield curves is especially strong.

Definition of Terms

Before we give specific examples of the uses of SYCURVE options, let us first consider the terms of the SYCURVE option contract. As with most over-the-counter options, the strike spread level, expiration date, and underlying securities can be tailored to meet an individual client's needs. In what follows, we review the most common structures.

SYCURVE options may be either European, which can be exercised only on the expiration date, at any hour before the close of trading, or American, which can be exercised at any time prior to (or on) the expiration date. Because American options give the owner of the option more flexibility, the option premium for an American

---

3 See *SYCURVE^{SM} Options: Puts and Calls on the Slope of the Yield Curve*, Goldman, Sachs & Co., November 1989.

option is usually larger than the premium for a European option. Typically, clients prefer European options, and all of the examples that follow will assume European exercise.

The strike price of a SYCURVE option is quoted as a yield spread, in basis points, between two underlying fixed-income securities that are specified at the trade date. SYCURVE options are cash-settled, based on bid-side yields for both underlying instruments. The spread that determines the SYCURVE option's payoff will be the yield spread between the two specific securities.[4] Typically, for example, a SYCURVE call option on the yield spread between the 30-year Treasury bond and 2-year Treasury note is based on the on-the-run 2-year note issue and the on-the-run 30-year bond issue that are outstanding at the trade date, even though new 2-year notes or 30-year bonds may be issued prior to the option's expiration date.

The SYCURVE option's payoff at expiration depends only on the yield *spread* between the two underlying securities, not upon whether general yield *levels* have increased or decreased during the term of the option. As the payoff is not affected by changes in market rates, the duration and convexity of SYCURVE put and call options are approximately zero.[5]

For example, assume that an investor has purchased a SYCURVE put option based upon the yield spread between the 30-year Treasury bond and 2-year Treasury note, with a strike spread of 150 bp, one month until expiration, and European exercise. Assuming a trade date of August 15, 1991, the underlying securities would be the 6 7/8s of July 31, 1993, and the 8 1/8s of August 15, 2021, and the option would expire on September 15, 1991. We would say that the investor is long a SYCURVE 2/30 put at 150 bp.[6]

The SYCURVE option will expire in-the-money if the yield spread between the 8 1/8s of August 2021 and the 6 7/8s of July 1993 is less than 150 bp on the expiration date. Otherwise, the option will expire worthless. SYCURVE options that are in-the-money will be exercised automatically on expiration.

If the option expires in-the-money or an in-the-money option is exercised, the holder of a SYCURVE option with a notional principal amount of $1 million is entitled to receive a payoff equal to the difference in basis points between the strike yield spread and the actual yield spread at expiration, multiplied by $10,000. (We use a convention of $10,000 per basis point per $1 million notional principal amount of SYCURVE option contracts.) The notional principal amount of a SYCURVE option is always specified at the trade date. Assuming our investor is long a SYCURVE 2/30 put at 150

---

4 SYCURVE-DUOP options would settle by a physical exchange of the underlying securities at the exercise date or expiration date of an in-the-money option. The payoff of SYCURVE-DUOP options is based on a price spread between two underlying fixed-income securities that are specified on the trade date. We describe SYCURVE-DUOP structures beginning on page 81 of this chapter.

5 A parallel shift in the forward yield curve (the expected yield curve at the option expiration date) will not affect SYCURVE option values. But a parallel shift in today's yield curve does not necessarily imply a parallel shift in the forward yield curve. Especially if today's yield curve is steeply upward sloping or inverted, parallel changes in today's yield curve may imply small changes in the slope of the forward yield curve. So, strictly speaking, and prior to the expiration date, SYCURVE put and call options do retain a small exposure to yield levels.

6 We present this example, and all other examples in this chapter, for illustrative purposes only. Examples are not meant to reflect actual market conditions.

bp with a notional principal amount of $1 million, and assuming the yield spread at expiration is 130 bp, the SYCURVE option's payoff at expiration would be:

Strike yield spread of SYCURVE 2/30 put option	150 bp
Less: Yield spread at the expiration date	130 bp
In-the-money amount	20 bp
Multiply by: Payoff per $1 million SYCURVE contract	× $10,000 per bp
Dollar payoff per $1MM SYCURVE contract	$200,000
Notional principal amount of SYCURVE 2/30 put at 150 bp	$1 [million]
Multiply by: Dollar payoff per $1 million SYCURVE contract	× 200,000
Net option payoff at the expiration date	$200,000

We calculate the premium on a SYCURVE option in a similar fashion. A SYCURVE option premium is quoted in units of basis points, with a dollar cost equal to $10,000 per $1 million notional principal amount per basis point of quoted premium. For example, if the premium on the SYCURVE 2/30 put option was quoted as 12 bp, then the dollar cost for the investor to buy $1 million notional principal amount of the option would be $120,000.

We have intentionally chosen to quote the SYCURVE option premium in the same units as the strike yield spread, so that the break-even yield spread at expiration is easy to calculate. For the investor who paid a 12 bp premium for a SYCURVE put at 150 bp, the break-even yield spread is:

Strike yield spread of SYCURVE 2/30 put option	150 bp
Less: Quoted option premium	−12 bp
Break-even yield spread at the expiration date	138 bp

The SYCURVE Option's Equivalent Portfolio

Suppose we formed the following model portfolio of 30-year U.S. Treasury bonds and 2-year Treasury notes: long $8.9 million face amount of the 8 1/8s of August 15, 2021, and short $54.8 million of the 6 7/8s of July 31, 1993. This portfolio has a dollar duration of zero, meaning that it is insensitive to parallel movements in the yield curve.[7] However, the portfolio is very sensitive to the yield spread between the 30-year bonds held long and 2-year notes held short. When the 2- to 30-year yield spread narrows, the portfolio gains $10,000 per basis point decrease in the yield spread. For comparison, our investor's $1 million notional principal amount SYCURVE 2/30 put

---

7 Dollar duration is defined as the change in dollar value of a security per unit face amount of that security per unit change in the security's yield. For the 6 7/8s of July 31, 1993, we assume a dollar duration of $182.60 per $1 million face amount per basis point. And for the 8 1/8s of August 15, 2021, we assume a dollar duration of $1,123.78 per $1 million face amount per basis point. In the illustration, the portfolio dollar duration and dollar sensitivity of the portfolio to changes in yield curve slope have been rounded to the nearest $100 per basis point.

option also gains $10,000 per basis point decrease, assuming the put option expires in-the-money.

In fact, we could use our model portfolio to reproduce synthetically the returns from a SYCURVE 2/30 put option. At the expiration date, we would want to own our model portfolio if the SYCURVE 2/30 put option expired in-the-money. Otherwise, we would not want to own our model portfolio at all. Prior to the expiration date, we would want to own only a fraction of our model portfolio, with the fraction roughly corresponding to the probability that the SYCURVE 2/30 put option will finish in-the-money. In practice, we would want to own a fraction of the model portfolio equal to the hedge ratio (the delta) of the SYCURVE 2/30 put option.[8] For example, if the SYCURVE 2/30 put option had a delta equal to 0.5, we would want to hold only half of our model portfolio: long $4.45 million face amount of the 8 1/8s of August 2021 and short $27.4 million face amount of the 6 7/8s of July 1993. By continuously adjusting the amount of our model portfolio that we own, we could synthetically reproduce the returns from the SYCURVE 2/30 put struck at 150 bp.

In practice, most investors would find such dynamic hedging extremely tedious, expensive, and difficult to reproduce. These investors use over-the-counter SYCURVE options as a simple and convenient substitute.

Pricing SYCURVE Options

To value a SYCURVE option, we first determine the forward yield spread (the expected yield spread at the expiration date) between the two securities underlying the SYCURVE option. Then, using an estimate, perhaps the historical level, of the volatility of the yield spread, we estimate the probability that the SYCURVE option will finish in-the-money. This gives us the expected in-the-money portion of the option, the amount of the equivalent portfolio we need to own (the hedge ratio), and therefore, the option value.[9]

Notice that the SYCURVE option's price is based on the forward yield spread between the option's underlying securities. The forward date is the option's expiration date. The forward yield spread will usually differ from the yield spread at the trade date (termed the spot yield spread) and can differ by a large amount in a steeply sloping yield curve environment. A steeply sloping yield curve, such as that occurring in the U.S. Treasury market throughout much of 1991, reflects expectations of both a rapid rise in yield levels and a narrowing of yield spreads between long- and short-maturity securities (i.e., a yield curve flattening).[10]

---

8   Strictly speaking, an option's delta is defined as the change in dollar value of the option per unit change in dollar value of the underlying security, and is not necessarily equal to the probability that the option will finish in-the-money. We present an analytic formula for the delta of European SYCURVE put and call options in the Appendix to this chapter.

9   In the Appendix to this chapter, we derive an analytic formula for the value of European SYCURVE put and call options.

10 Technically speaking, in a steeply sloping yield curve environment, implied forward yields are above spot yields at all maturities. And the difference between implied forward yields of short-maturity securities and their spot yields is much larger than the difference between implied forward yields of long-maturity securities and their spot yields. In sum, when the yield curve is steep, implied forward yield spreads between long- and short-maturity securities are narrower than spot yield spreads.

Therefore, in a steeply sloping yield curve environment, SYCURVE put options with a strike yield spread equal to the spot yield spread tend to be deeply in-the-money on a forward basis and hence command a high premium. Conversely, SYCURVE call options with a strike yield spread equal to the spot yield spread in a steeply sloping yield curve environment tend to be out-of-the-money on a forward basis and hence carry a much lower premium.

Investors who believe that the yield curve will remain steep for a long period (longer than implied by forward rates) will be natural sellers of SYCURVE put options and buyers of SYCURVE call options. Investors who believe that the yield curve is likely to flatten very soon (sooner than implied by forward rates) will be natural sellers of SYCURVE call options and buyers of SYCURVE put options.

The implied forward yield is usually determined by a combination of the security's yield on the trade date, the security's repo rate between the trade date and the forward date, and the volatility of those rates. Note that repo rates are important, since they help to determine forward yields. Therefore, SYCURVE option values prior to the expiration date are sensitive to the level of repo rates (all else held constant), while the option's payoff depends only on yield spreads at the expiration date.

An Application of SYCURVE Options

SYCURVE options can be used by portfolio managers whose performance is measured against the performance of a bond market benchmark index. Suppose a portfolio manager is measured against an index of 10-year maturity Treasury notes, with a duration of approximately seven years. The manager anticipates a yield curve flattening and, accordingly, has positioned the portfolio to be long 30-year Treasury bonds and short Treasury note futures contracts to achieve the target 7-year duration.

The manager estimates that the portfolio will outperform the index by $1,100,000 if the 10- to 30-year yield spread narrows by 10 bp over the next three months but will underperform the index by $1,100,000 if the yield spread widens by 10 bp over that period. Suppose that the spot 10- to 30-year yield spread is 25 bp.

In the discussion that follows, we will give three examples of how this investor could use SYCURVE options in his or her portfolio. These examples are not meant to be trading recommendations, but rather serve to show how investors can use SYCURVE options to either increase or reduce their exposure to changes in yield spreads.

Very Bullish Strategy

Suppose that a manager anticipates a yield curve flattening and believes that, at worst, the 10- to 30-year yield spread could widen by no more than 3-5 bp in the next three months. In that case, the manager might be willing to increase his or her exposure to yield spreads still further, and could sell $11 million notional principal amount of SYCURVE 10/30 calls at a strike of 20 bp. Exhibit 2 illustrates this "very bullish" slope-of-the-yield-curve strategy.

Let's assume that SYCURVE 10/30 call options are priced at 7.9 bp, so that $11 million notional principal amount SYCURVE 10/30 call options would be valued at $869,000 (the premium that the manager receives). If these options expire 10 bp in-the-money, their payoff would be $1,100,000. We chose the notional principal

Exhibit 2.   Very Bullish Slope-of-the-Yield-Curve Strategy

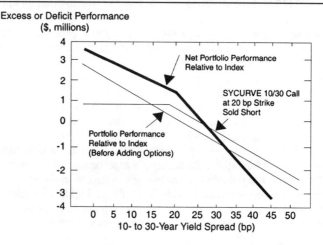

amount of $11 million in this example so that the manager's portfolio and the
SYCURVE 10/30 call options would have equal dollar sensitivity to changes in yield
curve slope. Under these circumstances, if the 10- to 30-year yield spread is 27.9 bp
after three months and the SYCURVE options expire 7.9 bp in-the-money, the
portfolio manager breaks even on the option position. If the yield spread is between
20 and 27.9 bp, then the manager profits on the SYCURVE call option position,
because the option finishes in-the-money by less than the option premium received.

  If the portfolio manager's view is correct, and the yield spread is less than 20
bp after three months, then the manager will profit both because (1) the portfolio will
outperform the benchmark index and (2) the SYCURVE call option will expire
worthless and the entire option premium may be retained. By selling the SYCURVE
10/30 call option, the manager increases his or her performance in a yield curve
flattening. However, if the 10- to 30-year yield spread is wider than 27.9 bp after three
months, the manager risks dramatically underperforming the benchmark index.

Bullish Strategy

Alternatively, suppose that the manager anticipates a yield curve flattening but is not
willing to risk dramatically underperforming the benchmark index. In that case, the
manager could follow a "bullish" slope-of-the-yield-curve strategy (Exhibit 3) and sell
$11 million notional principal amount of SYCURVE 10/30 puts at a strike of 20 bp,
effectively guaranteeing that the portfolio will modestly outperform the benchmark
index over a wide range of yield spreads. Suppose these options are also priced at 7.9
bp ($869,000). Again, notice that we chose the notional principal amount of $11
million so that the manager's portfolio and the SYCURVE 10/30 put options would
have equal dollar sensitivity to changes in yield curve slope.

  Under these circumstances, if the 10- to 30-year yield spread is less than 32.9
bp after three months, then the manager's portfolio will have outperformed the

---

Exhibit 3. Bullish Slope-of-the-Yield-Curve Strategy

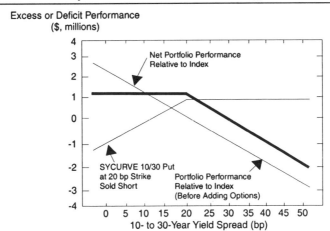

benchmark index. If the yield spread is less than or equal to 20 bp after three months, the manager will have outperformed the benchmark index by a constant dollar amount equal to the sum of the SYCURVE put option's premium plus $550,000. If the 10- to 30-year yield spread is wider than 32.9 bp after three months, the manager's portfolio will have underperformed the benchmark index, but by less than what would have occurred had the manager not sold the SYCURVE put options.

Conservative Strategy

Finally, in a "conservative" slope-of-the-yield-curve strategy (Exhibit 4), a manager could buy $11 million notional principal amount of SYCURVE 10/30 call options at 20 bp to eliminate the risk of dramatically underperforming the benchmark index in the event that yield spreads widen. In this case, the portfolio's performance would equal that of the benchmark index if the 10- to 30-year yield spread fell to 17.1 bp after three months. If the yield spread narrowed to less than 17.1 bp, the manager would outperform the benchmark index. If the 10- to 30-year yield spread were between 17.1 bp and 20 bp, the manager would modestly underperform the benchmark index (by $319,000 at worst). If the 10- to 30-year yield spread were greater than 20 bp, the manager would underperform the benchmark index by a constant $319,000.

Compare this to the manager's original position, where his or her underperformance versus the index would be greater than $319,000 if the 10- to 30-year yield spread were to widen substantially. In this example, the manager has used SYCURVE 10/30 call options to limit losses in the event that his or her views turned out to be incorrect.

Portfolio managers are not the only users of SYCURVE options. Financial institutions, for example, can also face yield curve risk even when their assets are duration-matched to their liabilities. These institutions could use SYCURVE options

Exhibit 4.   Conservative Slope-of-the-Yield-Curve Strategy

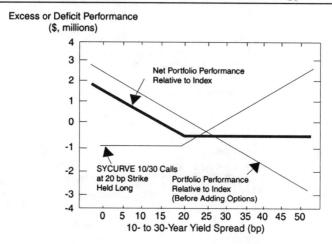

to maintain the integrity of their balance sheets by protecting against losses caused by changes in the slope of the yield curve.

Does a SYCURVE Option Equal a Portfolio of Options on Individual Securities?

Before the development of the SYCURVE option, an investor seeking an option on the yield spread between the 30-year Treasury bond and 2-year Treasury note might have bought the following portfolio of over-the-counter options expiring on September 15, 1991: long call options on $8.9 million face amount of the 8 1/8s of August 15, 2021, with a strike price of 100; and long put options on $54.8 million face amount of the 6 7/8s of July 31, 1993, with a strike price of 100 14/32. We have chosen the strike prices so that the 2- to 30-year yield spread is approximately 150 bp if both options are at-the-money on the expiration date. If both options expire in-the-money, the net payoff at expiration is equal to approximately $10,000 per basis point decrease in the yield spread. Therefore, the investor has bought a portfolio that has option-like payoffs—with losses limited to the premiums paid to purchase the options therein— and that is sensitive to changes in the slope of the yield curve. Nevertheless, this portfolio is not the same as a SYCURVE option, as we shall show below.

Even though the portfolio of options appears to provide the same $10,000 payoff per basis point decrease in the 2- to 30-year yield spread, as does the $1 million notional principal amount SYCURVE 2/30 put option, the two are not identical substitutes for each other. For one thing, the owner of the portfolio of options has more flexibility than the owner of a SYCURVE 2/30 put option. The owner of the portfolio, for example, can choose to exercise one of the options while letting the other option expire worthless. This added flexibility means that the portfolio of options is more valuable than the SYCURVE 2/30 put option, and that is reflected in the option premiums paid.

Typically, such a portfolio of options would be three to four times more expensive than a SYCURVE 2/30 put option.

To see why the portfolio of options is not equivalent to a SYCURVE 2/30 put option, consider the dollar duration of each: By construction, the SYCURVE option's payoff is insensitive to the overall level of Treasury yields (only yield spreads matter) and its dollar duration is zero. The portfolio of options is insensitive to the overall level of Treasury yields only when both the put and call option expire in-the-money. If either of the two options in the portfolio were to expire out-of-the-money while the remaining option expired in-the-money, then the payoff of the portfolio would depend only on the overall level of rates (in particular, it would depend on the yield of the underlying security of the in-the-money option) and not on the yield spread. The dollar duration of the portfolio of options is therefore not zero.

For example, assume that neither the SYCURVE option nor any option in the portfolio of individual put and call options is in-the-money, and consider what would happen after a very large market move. For convenience, assume that the very large market move occurred just before the options' expiration date. Assume that the market move did not change the slope of the yield curve but did change the overall level of rates dramatically. In this case, the SYCURVE option's payoff would be unchanged, and it would expire worthless—since we have assumed that it was out-of-the-money before the market move and that the market move did not affect yield spreads. With the portfolio of options, however, assuming the market move is very large, it is certain that either the call option or the put option, but not both, would be deep in-the-money at expiration.

The only time in which a portfolio of options on individual securities will behave like a SYCURVE option over a wide range of market conditions is when all of the options in the portfolio must be exercised together—even if one of them is out-of-the-money—or not at all. Such contingent exercise structures have become popular, and we have given them a special name, the DUOP.

SYCURVE-DUOP OPTIONS

A DUOP (dual-exercise option) structure is a portfolio of a put option and a call option on two different underlying securities, linked by a contingent exercise provision that requires that both options be exercised together, or not at all. A SYCURVE-DUOP structure is very similar to a cash-settled SYCURVE option, except that a SYCURVE-DUOP put or call option has a payoff based upon the price spread between the two underlying securities and requires a physical exchange of the underlying securities at the strike price spread if the SYCURVE-DUOP option expires in-the-money.[11]

In two cases, the SYCURVE-DUOP structure is superior to cash-settled SY-CURVE options: (1) when the spread option must have strike levels based on prices, rather than yields, because the yield of the underlying securities is ambiguous or

---

11 Strictly speaking, because the DUOP structure's payoff is dependent upon a price spread while the SYCURVE option's payoff is dependent upon a yield spread, the payoff from a DUOP structure will usually differ from the payoff of a SYCURVE option because of the convexity of the underlying securities. Only when the underlying securities have approximately equal convexities will the DUOP structure's payoff approximately equal the SYCURVE option's payoff.

difficult to measure; and (2) when an investor prefers to settle by physical delivery. An example of the first case occurs in the Japanese market when an investor wishes to take a position on the spread between 90-day Euroyen time deposits and 10-year Japanese government bonds, and prefers a DUOP structure based on futures contract prices for which yield is not well-defined. An example of the second case occurs when a portfolio manager, rather than receiving a SYCURVE option's cash payoff, wishes to physically swap out of one sector of the yield curve and into another sector at a target price spread.

Let us return to the example of an option on the spread between a 30-year Treasury bond and a 2-year Treasury note. Suppose an investor has purchased a SYCURVE-DUOP structure containing the following portfolio of options expiring on September 15, 1991: long call options on $8.9 million face amount of the 8 1/8s of August 15, 2021, with a strike price of 100; and long put options on $54.8 million face amount of the 6 7/8s of July 31, 1993, with a strike price of 100 14/32, with the provision that both options must be exercised together, or not at all. We would say that the investor is long a SYCURVE-DUOP 2/30 put.

The mechanics of calculating the strike price spread, break-even price spread, and SYCURVE-DUOP payoff at expiration are straightforward but more complex than in the case of a SYCURVE option. For example, the SYCURVE-DUOP 2/30 put has the following strike price spread:

Flat price of $54.8MM 2-year notes at 100 14/32	$55,039,750
Less: Flat price of $8.9MM 30-year bonds at 100	−8,900,000
Strike price spread	$46,139,750

The strike price spread represents the cash that the owner of the SYCURVE-DUOP 2/30 put would receive if the SYCURVE-DUOP put were exercised and $54.8 million face amount of 2-year Treasury notes were exchanged for $8.9 million face amount of 30-year Treasury bonds.

If the flat price of $54.8 million face amount of the 6 7/8s of July 1993 minus the flat price of $8.9 million face amount of the 8 1/8s of August 2021 is less than $46,139,750 at the expiration date, then the SYCURVE-DUOP 2/30 put is in-the-money and both of the options in the DUOP structure should be exercised.[12] Otherwise, the SYCURVE-DUOP 2/30 put will be out-of-the-money and should be allowed to expire worthless. Note that if the owner exercised the SYCURVE-DUOP 2/30 put, he or she would be buying 30-year bonds at 100 and selling 2-year notes at 100 14/32. That is, the DUOP would settle through a physical exchange of cash and securities. The DUOP structure is in-the-money when such a physical exchange of securities can occur at a net cost less (net cash received greater) than the market value of the exchange on the expiration date.

---

12 We require the price spread to be less than the break-even price spread only because we have structured the DUOP portfolio as a 2/30 put option. If the DUOP portfolio were composed of a put option on the 8 1/8s of August 2021 with a strike price of 100 and a call option on the 6 7/8s of July 1993 with a strike price of 100 14/32, then we would have formed a DUOP 2/30 call that would be in-the-money if the price spread was greater than the break-even price spread on the expiration date.

The contingent exercise provision means that the option premium paid for the SYCURVE-DUOP 2/30 put is less than the cost of the two options purchased separately. The SYCURVE-DUOP 2/30 put has a payoff that is nearly identical to the payoff of the $1 million notional principal amount SYCURVE 2/30 put at 150 bp. Neglecting convexity (see footnote 11), we would expect the SYCURVE-DUOP 2/30 put to have the same $120,000 premium as the SYCURVE 2/30 put at 150 bp. The premium of the DUOP structure would be quoted in price units. In this case, the SYCURVE-DUOP 2/30 put would be quoted at a price of 1 21/64 per $100 face amount of the 30-year bonds. (We have rounded the price to the nearest 1/64.)

One type of DUOP structure that is particularly popular is an option on the spread between mortgage securities and U.S. Treasury securities. In fact, we have assigned this structure a separate name, the MOTTO option.

MOTTO OPTIONS

MOTTO (mortgage over Treasury) spread options are designed to allow investors to profit from—or control the risk of—changes in the spread between mortgage and Treasury securities. Many investors seek efficient ways either to take a position on the future direction of the spread or to hedge their mortgage portfolios against possible future spread changes. The owner of a MOTTO call option benefits when mortgage-backed securities (MBSs) outperform Treasury securities, while the owner of a MOTTO put option benefits when MBSs underperform Treasury securities.

Structuring MOTTO Put and Call Options

MOTTO options are more complex to structure than SYCURVE options because the conversion from price to yield, and vice versa, is more complex in the mortgage securities market than in the U.S. Treasury market. For most Treasury notes and bonds, the future cash flows to the owner of the security are known with certainty.[13] The owner of $1 million face amount of the 6s of November 15, 1994, for example, can expect to receive an interest payment of $30,000 on the 15th day of May and November in each of the years 1992 through 1994, as well as a principal payment of $1 million on November 15, 1994. If this security were priced at 100-18 for settlement on December 2, 1991, it would carry a yield of 5.789 percent. (The yield is the discount rate that would equate the security's price with the discounted present value of the future cash flows.)

For such securities, there is a one-to-one correspondence between price and yield. This one-to-one correspondence is the reason why SYCURVE put and call

---

13 The exceptions are 25- or 30-year Treasury bonds originally issued in the 1970s and early 1980s that are callable at par on any coupon payment date within five years of the maturity date. The 10 3/8s of November 15, 2012, for example, originally issued in 1982, are callable at par on any coupon payment date on or after November 15, 2007. We cannot know with certainty whether these bonds will be called or not, and the yield on these bonds could be the yield to maturity, the yield to the first call date, or somewhere in between. When such bonds are among the underlying securities in a SYCURVE put or call option, the option agreement will explicitly specify either yield to maturity or yield to first call date.

options can be based either on yield spreads or, in a DUOP structure with a nearly identical payoff, on price spreads between the underlying securities.

Unfortunately, in the mortgage securities market there is no one-to-one correspondence between the price of a mortgage security and its yield, for the reason that the future cash flows of a mortgage security are not known with certainty. We cannot know the future cash flows from a mortgage security principally because we do not know, with certainty, the prepayment rates of the individual mortgages backing the security (the mortgages in the pool). Government National Mortgage Association 9 percent coupon mortgage pass-through securities (GNMA 9s), for example, trading for settlement on December 17, 1991, were quoted at a price of 104-06 on November 29, 1991. Even though we know the price of these securities, the yield is ambiguous, since it depends upon the prepayment rate of the underlying mortgages.

Most investors use a mortgage prepayment model to estimate the future mortgage prepayments, cash flows, and therefore the yield on an MBS.[14] A mortgage prepayment model will combine the weighted average coupon rate (WAC) of the mortgages in the pool, the weighted average loan age (WALA) in the pool, the average time since each mortgage in the pool was issued, current and prior period levels of mortgage financing rates, seasonal adjustments, and house prices to estimate future mortgage prepayment rates. Unfortunately, unlike the standard calculations that specify the relationship between price and yield for a Treasury note or bond, there is no mortgage prepayment model that has been accepted industry-wide. The Public Securities Association (PSA) model, which was originally intended to be an industry-wide standard prepayment model, does not explicitly account for the effect of differences between the current mortgage financing rate and the WAC of the mortgage pool.

The PSA model is now used by market participants as a reference point rather than as an industry standard. High coupon MBSs, for example, whose underlying mortgages were issued in a much higher interest rate environment and could be profitably refinanced today, would be expected to prepay more rapidly than the PSA model would suggest. Low coupon mortgages, whose underlying mortgages were issued in a much lower interest rate environment—so that those homeowners are now paying below-market rates of interest—would be expected to prepay more slowly than the PSA model would suggest.

While many broker/dealers have proprietary mortgage prepayment models that are improvements on the PSA model, there is no consensus about which model is the best and therefore no consensus about the yield of an MBS. For example, returning to the GNMA 9s priced at 104-06 on November 29, 1991, for settlement on December 17, 1991, the Goldman Sachs mortgage prepayment model would estimate the yield on these securities as 8.308 percent, equivalent to a prepayment speed of 142 percent PSA. This is also equivalent to an annualized conditional prepayment rate (CPR) of 8.35 percent, or a constant monthly prepayment rate (CMP) of 0.72 percent. By way of comparison, other broker/dealers' mortgage prepayment models generate estimates

---

14 See Scott Pinkus, Susan Mara Hunter, and Richard Roll, *An Introduction to the Mortgage Market and Mortgage Analysis*, Goldman, Sachs & Co., February 1987; Scott F. Richard and Richard Roll, *Modeling Prepayments on Fixed Rate Mortgage-Backed Securities*, Goldman, Sachs & Co., September 1988; and Scott F. Richard, *Housing Prices and Prepayments for Fixed Rate Mortgage-Backed Securities*, Goldman, Sachs & Co., October 1991.

of the prepayment rates on these same GNMA 9s that range between 130 percent and 227 percent PSA, corresponding to yields of 8.340 percent to 8.075 percent.

What is more important, the prepayment rate will change with changes in the overall level of interest rates. If interest rates were to rise, the prepayment rate of the mortgage pool underlying the GNMA 9s would be expected to decrease. Conversely, if interest rates were to fall, the prepayment rate of the mortgage pool underlying the GNMA 9s would be expected to increase. While broker/dealers' proprietary mortgage prepayment models do recognize this effect, there is no consensus as to exactly how much prepayment rates rise when interest rates fall and vice versa.

For all of these reasons, it is difficult to structure a MOTTO option based on the yield spread between MBSs and U.S. Treasury securities. We would have to agree in advance on a mortgage prepayment model to use when calculating prepayment rates, future cash flows, and therefore the yield on the MBS. For a start, we would have to agree on what prepayment rate to use at every level of U.S. Treasury yields and, indeed, for every possible shape of the U.S. Treasury yield curve. Clearly, this is not feasible.

Accordingly, a MOTTO put or call option is always formed as a DUOP structure. A MOTTO call option would permit the owner to buy a predetermined amount of MBSs and sell a predetermined amount of Treasury securities at a predetermined (strike) price spread. Similarly, a MOTTO put option would permit the owner to sell MBSs and buy Treasury securities at a strike price spread. Prices have the advantage of being unambiguous: GNMA 9s can trade in the market at 104-06, meaning that market participants agree on the value of the security, even though some market participants believe the GNMA 9s yield 8.340 percent at 130 percent PSA while others believe the GNMA 9s yield 8.075 percent at 227 percent PSA.

Choosing the Underlying Treasury and Mortgage-Backed Securities

When comparing the price performance of MBSs to that of Treasury securities, and therefore when choosing the underlying securities for MOTTO put and call options, it is important to choose securities that are "comparable." In theory, an MBS should be compared with the U.S. Treasury security whose dollar duration is closest to the dollar duration of the MBS. In practice, only on-the-run Treasury securities are used as benchmarks. Estimates of the dollar duration of MBSs require a mortgage prepayment model and are therefore uncertain, but fortunately, this uncertainty is small enough that the appropriate Treasury benchmark can be assigned with confidence.

Typically, new-issue current coupon mortgages (MBSs trading at or near par value) have dollar durations similar to the dollar duration of seven-year Treasury notes. When first traded, MOTTO put and call options were often based on price spreads either between GNMA 9s and seven-year Treasury notes or between GNMA 9 1/2s and five-year Treasury notes. Today, when GNMA 7 1/2s are considered the current coupon issue, MOTTO put and call options are often based on price spreads either between GNMA 7 1/2s and seven-year Treasury notes or between GNMA 8s and five-year Treasury notes. In practice, an investor is free to choose the MBS and Treasury security that will underlie a MOTTO put or call option; those referred to above are merely the more frequent combinations.

When MBSs outperform Treasury securities, MBS prices rise relative to comparable-duration Treasury prices. Similarly, when MBSs underperform Treasury securities, MBS prices fall relative to comparable-duration Treasury prices.

Typically, the ratio of the face amount of MBSs to the face amount of Treasury securities underlying a MOTTO put or call option is one-for-one. On the expiration date of the option, the owner of $10 million face amount MOTTO put options on GNMA 9s versus five-year Treasury notes, for example, would have the right, but not the obligation, to sell $10 million face amount of GNMA 9s and buy $10 million face amount of five-year Treasury notes at the strike price spread. Because the face amounts of both underlying securities are equal, the payoff from a MOTTO option depends only on the price spread (when quoted for settlement on the same forward date) between the underlying MBS and Treasury security.

The MOTTO option can be structured to cash-settle or to require physical delivery. In the former case, when a MOTTO put or call option expires in-the-money or is exercised, the owner of the option receives a cash payment equal to the option's in-the-money value. In the latter case, the owner of a MOTTO put option has the right, but not the obligation, to exchange an MBS for an equal face amount of a Treasury security on a designated forward settlement date. Conversely, the owner of a MOTTO call option settled by physical delivery has the right, but not the obligation, to exchange a Treasury security for an equal face amount of an MBS on a designated forward settlement date. At the trade date, the Treasury security, MBS, strike price spread, source of price quotes, expiration date, and forward settlement date are all specified uniquely.

A MOTTO Option Example

Trades in the MBS markets settle at designated forward dates. GNMA pass-through securities carrying coupons of 9 1/2 or less, for example, are classified as Class B securities and settle on a specific day each month. In September 1991, Class B securities settled on September 17, while in August 1991, Class B securities settled on August 20. The expiration date of MOTTO put and call options is usually set at five business days prior to the mortgage settlement date, to allow for a delivery notice on the MBSs. And the settlement date of the MOTTO options is usually set to coincide with the mortgage settlement date. With MOTTO options, it is important to pay close attention to trade dates, expiration dates, and settlement dates.

Suppose, for example, that an investor has purchased a MOTTO call option expiring on August 13, 1991, and settling on August 20, 1991, with a strike price spread of 30/32nds. Suppose further that the underlying securities are GNMA 9s and seven-year U.S. Treasury notes (the 7 7/8s of April 15, 1998). We say that the investor is long an August MOTTO call at 0-30.

Exhibit 5 shows recent price spreads. On July 2, 1991, the 7 7/8s of April 1998 were quoted at 98 17/32 for settlement on July 3, 1991. GNMA 9s were quoted at 99 14/32 for settlement on July 16, 1991. The price spread of 29/32nds (equal to 99 14/32 less 98 17/32) is not meaningful to the holder of the August MOTTO call at 0-30, since neither the GNMA 9s nor the seven-year Treasury note have been priced for settlement on the MOTTO call option's August 20, 1991, settlement date. The investor needs to ask for forward prices.

Exhibit 5. Price Spread: GNMA 9s versus Seven-Year U.S. Treasury (GNMA 9s and Treasury 7 7/8s of 1998, quoted for settlement on August 20, 1991)

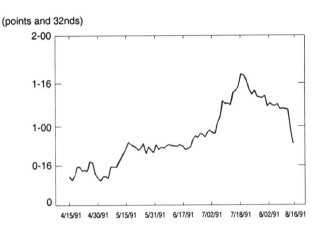

(points and 32nds)

The forward price of the GNMA 9s is 99 6/32 for settlement on August 20, 1991. And the forward price of the 7 7/8s of April 1998 is 98 8/32 for settlement on August 20, 1991. Therefore, the forward price spread is 30/32nds at the option settlement date. Note that the MOTTO call option's strike price spread is at-the-money on a forward basis.

The investor's MOTTO call option will finish in-the-money if the price of GNMA 9s for August delivery is more than 30/32nds higher than the forward price of the 7 7/8s of April 1998 on the expiration date, August 13, 1991. Assuming that on the expiration date, GNMA 9s were quoted at 100 13/32 and the 7 7/8s of April 1998 were quoted at 99 5/32, both for settlement on August 20, 1991, then the August MOTTO call at 0-30 will finish in-the-money by 10/32nds. Assuming the investor had purchased $10 million face amount of August MOTTO calls at 0-30, then the payoff value would be equal to:

GNMA 9s over seven-year notes price spread at expiration (32nds)	40
Less: Strike price spread of August MOTTO call option (32nds)	−30
In-the-money amount (32nds)	10
Notional principal amount of August MOTTO call at 0-30	$10,000,000
Multiply by: In-the-money amount (decimal)	× 0.003125
Net option value at the expiration date	$31,250

If the investor purchased the $10 million notional principal amount August MOTTO call at 0-30 on a cash-settled basis, the investor would be entitled to receive the net option value in cash. If the investor purchased the MOTTO call on a physical-delivery basis, the investor would be entitled to sell $10 million face amount of the 7 7/8s of April 1998 and simultaneously purchase an equal face amount of GNMA 9s at a net cost of 30/32nds, at a time when the market price of such an exchange is 40/32nds.

The premium for a MOTTO put or call option is quoted in 1/32nds, which is the same unit in which the price spread between the underlying MBS and Treasury security is denominated. Therefore, the break-even price spread at expiration is easy to calculate. In this case, the August MOTTO call at 0-30 was quoted at a 7/32nds premium, and the break-even price spread is:

Strike price spread of MOTTO call option (32nds)	30
Add: Quoted option premium (32nds)	+7
Break-even price spread at the expiration date (32nds)	37

In this example, the investor made a net profit of 3/32nds on the MOTTO call option, equal to a dollar profit of $9,375 on a $10 million notional principal amount.

As with the SYCURVE option, the MOTTO option's premium will be based on the forward price spread between the option's underlying securities, where the forward date is the option's expiration date. The forward price spread will usually differ from the quoted price spread at the trade date, if only because U.S. Treasury security prices are normally quoted for next-day settlement rather than for forward settlement. Investors will form their opinions by studying forward price spreads. Investors who believe that MBSs will underperform Treasury securities will be natural buyers of MOTTO put options and sellers of MOTTO call options. Conversely, investors who believe that MBSs will outperform Treasury securities will be natural buyers of MOTTO call options and sellers of MOTTO put options.

The payoff from MOTTO put and call options depends directly upon the price spread between the underlying MBS and Treasury security at the expiration date, and only indirectly upon overall market levels.[15] Like SYCURVE options, MOTTO put and call options can be synthetically reproduced by dynamic hedging of an equivalent portfolio. In the case of a MOTTO call option, the equivalent portfolio consists of MBSs purchased forward combined with Treasury securities sold forward, and the notional amount of the equivalent portfolio owned would have to be continuously adjusted to match changes in the MOTTO call option's hedge ratio (the option's delta). Most investors would find such dynamic hedging tedious, expensive, and difficult to reproduce in practice. These investors prefer over-the-counter MOTTO options when hedging a mortgage portfolio's spread exposure or establishing a position that will profit in the event of spread widening or narrowing.

---

15 The MBS and Treasury security underlying a MOTTO put or call option are chosen to have approximately equal dollar durations, so the dollar duration of the MOTTO option itself is approximately zero. However, the two underlying securities will not have equal dollar convexity, so the convexity of a MOTTO option is nonzero. In this sense, MOTTO put and call options retain an exposure to overall market levels. MOTTO call options have negative convexity, while MOTTO put options have positive convexity.

ISO OPTIONS

Virtually all international investors closely monitor yield spreads between different government bond markets. For the international fund manager, yield spreads are often the primary criterion for asset allocation decisions. For the arbitrager, international yield spreads have historically been a significant source of trading profits. The ISO (international spread option) provides investors with a flexible way to alter a portfolio's exposure to international markets, hedge that exposure, and take a position in international yield spreads that will profit when spreads change.

ISOs are similar to SYCURVE options in that both are options on the yield spread between two specific bonds. But the bonds that underlie ISO put and call options are drawn from two different government bond markets and are denominated in different currencies. Typically, each bond's yield is quoted according to the convention that applies in its domestic market, with the exception that Japanese government bond yields are typically quoted on a semiannually compounded basis. ISO call options represent the right to "buy" the yield spread, and they increase in value when the yield spread increases. ISO put options represent the right to "sell" the yield spread, and they increase in value when yield spreads decrease. Goldman, Sachs & Co. first introduced ISOs in mid-1990.[16]

Like SYCURVE options, ISO put and call options are typically cash-settled. The currency in which the owner of the option is paid when the option expires in-the-money is specified in advance, and that is the currency in which the option is said to be denominated. Since each of the underlying bonds is denominated in a different currency, the ISO option is typically denominated in one or the other, whichever the investor prefers. Alternatively, the ISO option can be denominated in a third currency, which is usually the domestic currency in which the investor's performance is measured. At the trade date, the underlying bonds, yield convention, strike yield spread, source of yield quotes, expiration date, settlement date, currency of denomination, and notional principal amount of an ISO put or call option are all specified uniquely.

Also like SYCURVE options, ISO put and call options can be formed as a DUOP structure that would settle through a physical exchange of securities. ISO-DUOP structures, for example, would allow international portfolio managers to physically reallocate their portfolios between different international bond markets at target price spreads.

As of the close of trading on August 9, 1991, the French government OAT 8 1/2s of March 28, 2000, were quoted at a price of 96.25 (decimal) to yield 9.132 percent, and the German government Bund 9s of October 20, 2000, were quoted at 102.12 (decimal) to yield 8.647 percent (see Exhibit 6). The spot OAT versus Bund yield spread is therefore 48.5 bp. Suppose an investor has purchased F1 million notional principal amount of ISO put options on the yield spread between the OAT 8 1/2s of March 2000 and the Bund 9s of October 2000. Suppose the options have a strike yield spread of 45 bp. We would say the investor is long F1 million ISO OAT/Bund puts at 45 bp.

---

16 See Richard Thomasson, "International Spread Options," *The International Fixed-Income Analyst,* Goldman, Sachs & Co., November 16, 1990.

**Exhibit 6. International Yield Curves
(Based on Quoted Prices as of August 9, 1991)**

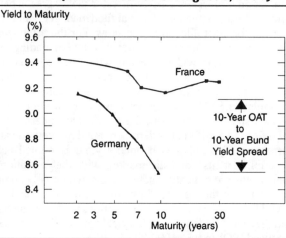

In this example, we have chosen to denominate the ISO put options in French francs, but the ISO put options could just as easily have been denominated in German marks or even, if the investor was a U.S.-based portfolio manager, in U.S. dollars. As with SYCURVE options, the premiums and payoffs of ISO put and call options are quoted in basis points, with each basis point representing 1 percent of the notional principal amount of the option. For example, if an ISO OAT/Bund put at 45 bp was quoted at a premium of 10 bp, the net cost to the investor to purchase F1 million notional principal amount of ISO OAT/Bund puts at 45 bp would be calculated as follows:

Quoted premium of ISO OAT/Bund put at 45 bp	10 bp
Multiply by: Cost per F1 notional principal per bp	× 0.01 per bp
French franc cost per F1 notional principal	0.10
Notional principal amount of ISO OAT/Bund put at 45 bp	F1 million
Multiply by: French franc cost per F1 notional principal	× 0.10
Net option cost at the trade date	F100,000

We have intentionally chosen to quote the ISO option premium in the same units as the strike yield spread, so that the break-even yield spread at expiration is easy to calculate. Note that the break-even yield spread does not depend upon the currency in which the ISO put or call option is denominated. For the investor who paid a 10 bp premium for an ISO OAT/Bund put at 45 bp, the break-even yield spread is:

Strike yield spread of ISO OAT/Bund put option	45 bp
Less: Quoted option premium	−10 bp
Break-even yield spread at the expiration date	35 bp

The ISO OAT/Bund put at 45 bp will finish in-the-money if the yield at the quoted price of the OAT 8 1/2s of March 2000 minus the yield at the quoted price of the Bund 9s of October 2000 is less than 45 bp on the option's expiration date. The ISO OAT/Bund put therefore increases in value when the French government bond market outperforms the German government bond market. Assuming that the yield spread at the expiration date is 30 bp, the owner of F1 million ISO OAT/Bund puts at 45 bp would receive a payoff equal to:

Strike yield spread of ISO OAT/Bund put option	45 bp
Less: Yield spread at the expiration date	−30 bp
In-the-money amount	15 bp
Multiply by: Payoff per F1 notional principal per bp	× 0.01 per bp
French franc payoff per F1 notional principal	0.15
Notional principal amount of ISO OAT/Bund put at 45 bp	F1 million
Multiply by: French franc payoff per F1 notional principal	× 0.15
Net option payoff at the expiration date	F150,000

In this case, the investor has paid a F100,000 premium for the option and received a F150,000 payoff at the option expiration date for a net profit of F50,000.

The ISO Option's Equivalent Portfolio

An ISO put option on the OAT/Bund yield spread increases in value as the French government bond market outperforms the German government bond market. The ISO OAT/Bund put at 45 bp is at-the-money at the expiration date when the yield at the quoted price of the OAT 8 1/2s of March 2000 minus the yield at the quoted price of the Bund 9s of October 2000 is equal to 45 bp. For each basis point that the yield spread at the expiration date is below 45 bp, then F1 million notional principal amount of the ISO OAT/Bund put at 45 bp will increase in value by F10,000.

Suppose that we form the following model portfolio on August 9, 1991: long F17.7 million face amount of the OAT 8 1/2s of March 2000, and short DM 5.05 million face amount of the Bund 9s of October 2000. Assuming an August 9, 1991, French franc versus deutsche mark cross rate of 3.4015, this portfolio increases in value by F10,000 per each basis point that the yield spread between the OAT 8 1/2s of March 2000 and the Bund 9s of October 2000 decreases. Notice that, if the yield of the OAT 8 1/2s of March 2000 and yield of the Bund 9s of October 2000 both increased or decreased by the same amount, so that the yield spread did not change, and if the French franc versus deutsche mark cross rate did not change, then the value of the model portfolio would not change.[17]

---

17 For the OAT 8 1/2s of March 2000, we assume a French franc duration of F565.80 per F1 million face amount per basis point. And for the Bund 9s of October 2000 we assume a deutsche mark duration of DM 582.59 per DM 1 million face amount per basis point. In the example, the portfolio French franc sensitivity to changes in yield spread has been rounded to the nearest F100.

We can use this model portfolio to reproduce synthetically the returns from an ISO OAT/Bund put option at 45 bp. At the expiration date, we would want to own the model portfolio if the yield spread between the OAT 8 1/2s of March 2000 and the Bund 9s of October 2000 were less than 45 bp. Otherwise, the put option will be out-of-the-money and we would not want to own the model portfolio at all.

Prior to the expiration date, we would want to own only a fraction of the model portfolio. In fact, we would want to own a fraction of the model portfolio equal to the hedge ratio (the delta) of the ISO OAT/Bund put option at 45 bp. If the delta of the put option was 0.20, we would want to own only a fifth of the model portfolio: long F3.54 million face amount of the OAT 8 1/2s of March 2000, and short DM 1.01 million face amount of the Bund 9s of October 2000. By continuously adjusting the amount of the model portfolio that we own, and by continuously rebalancing the portfolio to keep the portfolio's exposure to yield spread changes at F10,000 per basis point, we can synthetically reproduce the returns from an ISO OAT/Bund put option at 45 bp.

Most investors would find such dynamic hedging tedious, expensive, and difficult to reproduce in practice. These investors would prefer over-the-counter ISO put and call options as a simple and convenient substitute.

Applications of ISO Put and Call Options

An international portfolio manager is bullish on French government bonds and bearish on German government bonds. As a result, the manager's portfolio is overweighted in OATs and underweighted in Bunds. As we have seen, on August 9, 1991, the yield spread between the OAT 8 1/2s of March 2000 and the Bund 9s of October 2000 is 48.5 bp. Suppose the manager's performance is measured against the returns from an international government bond index. If the yield spread between French government bonds and Bunds tightens to 45 bp, the manager intends to return to a neutral weighting relative to the index by selling approximately F18 million in French government bonds and buying DM 5 million in Bunds.

The portfolio manager might choose to hedge his or her investment view by writing an ISO-DUOP OAT/Bund put at 45 bp. The portfolio manager prefers the DUOP structure since, if the yield spread between French government bonds and Bunds tightens to less than 40 bp and the put option expires in-the-money, then the manager will automatically be swapped out of French government bonds into Bunds, and therefore into a neutral weighting relative to the index.

Suppose that on the trade date of August 9, 1991, an ISO-DUOP OAT/Bund put at 45 bp could be sold at a premium of 10 bp. In order to swap out of approximately F18 million face amount of OATs into approximately DM 5 million face amount of Bunds, the portfolio manager would sell short F1 million notional principal amount of ISO-DUOP OAT/Bund puts at 45 bp and receive a premium of F100,000.

Now consider what happens at the expiration date: If the portfolio manager's view is correct, and the yield spread between the OAT 8 1/2s of March 2000 and the Bund 9s of October 2000 were less than 45 bp on the expiration date, then the ISO-DUOP put at 45 bp will be in-the-money. The manager's portfolio will have benefited from the 3.5 bp narrowing of the yield spread to 45 bp. And the manager's portfolio will have benefited from the F100,000 option premium received. Finally, when the ISO-DUOP put option was exercised, the manager would have been swapped out of F17.7 million face amount of the OAT 8 1/2s of March 2000, and into DM 5.05 million face amount of the Bund 9s of October 2000, returning the manager's portfolio to a neutral weighting with respect to the index. In effect, the manager would have swapped out of French government bonds and into German government bonds at a yield spread of 35 bp.

Otherwise, if the yield spread between the OAT 8 1/2s and the Bund 9s were greater than 45 bp on the expiration date, then the ISO-DUOP put at 45 bp would be out-of-the-money and expire worthless. The manager's portfolio would still benefit from the F100,000 premium received on the ISO-DUOP OAT/Bund puts at 45 bp sold short.

In summary, ISO put and call options offer portfolio managers a convenient way to alter a portfolio's exposure to international markets. ISO put and call options on the OAT versus Bund, U.K. gilt versus Bund, Japanese government bond versus U.S. Treasury, and Canadian government bond versus U.S. Treasury spreads have been particularly popular.

CROSS OPTIONS

CROSS put and call options are options on bonds in which the premium, strike price, and payoff are denominated in a currency different from the currency in which the bonds' coupons and principal are paid. We include CROSS put and call options in this chapter because they share an important characteristic with the spread options that we described earlier. The payoff from a CROSS put or call option is dependent upon two (risky) market prices: bond prices and currency exchange rates.

Managers of international fixed-income portfolios have used CROSS put and call options to hedge risks or achieve market exposures that cannot be hedged or achieved efficiently using traditional option products. International portfolio managers are inevitably judged on the basis of their portfolio's total returns when measured in the managers' domestic currency. These managers are exposed to a combination of both foreign interest rate risk and exchange-rate risk. CROSS put and call options help investors manage this risk.

CROSS put and call options were first used by Japanese insurance companies that held U.S. Treasury notes and bonds in yen-based portfolios. These investors wanted either (1) to buy put options to protect the yen value of their portfolios, or (2) to sell call options in buy-write programs. Traditional, dollar-denominated put and call options could not meet their needs. If these investors sold dollar-denominated call options against their Treasury bond portfolios in a buy-write program, for example, they risked a loss if U.S. Treasury bond prices rose while the dollar simultaneously fell sharply against the yen.

Suppose, for example, that a Japanese investor purchased $1 million face amount of U.S. Treasury bonds (the 7 7/8s of February 15, 2021) at 97, and paid ¥135 per dollar for the dollars required to buy the bond (see Exhibit 7).[18] The cost basis for the

---

18 The Japanese investor would also be required to pay accrued interest, if any, in dollars at the purchase date and would receive coupons in dollars and accrued interest, if any, in dollars when the bond was sold. Since a bond's coupon dates are known and its accrued interest at each date can be determined exactly in advance, the Japanese investor could hedge this dollar exposure with such traditional instruments as currency options, futures, and forward contracts.

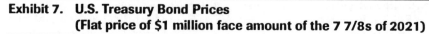

**Exhibit 7. U.S. Treasury Bond Prices
(Flat price of $1 million face amount of the 7 7/8s of 2021)**

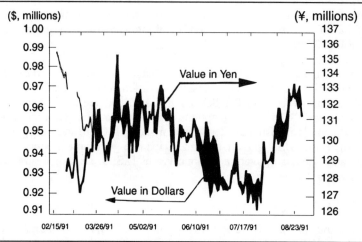

Japanese investor is therefore ¥13,095 per $100 face amount of bonds owned, for a total of ¥130.95 million. Suppose the Japanese investor pursues a buy-write strategy and sells traditional, dollar-denominated call options with a strike price of 98 on the entire $1 million face amount of bonds owned. Note that when sold, the call options were one point out-of-the-money.

For a U.S.-based investor, such a strategy would effectively guarantee a capital gain in the event that the call option expired in-the-money. The calculation below shows the net capital gain or loss on this buy-write strategy if the call option sold short expires in-the-money and the call option is exercised. In this case, the dollar-based investor will always realize a capital gain.

Sale price of 7 7/8s of February 2021 (option strike price)	$980,000
Less: Purchase price of 7 7/8s of February 2021	970,000
Net capital gain at the option expiration date	$10,000

If the call options expire out-of-the-money, and therefore worthless, the U.S.-based investor would not be required to sell the bonds to the option holder. The investor would retain the bonds, though with an unrealized gain or loss. In any case, the investor retains the call option premium and accrued interest on the bonds between the purchase date and the option expiration date. Thus, an investor might pursue a buy-write strategy in order to enhance the current income from his or her portfolio. A buy-write strategy can be very successful, in particular, whenever actual market volatility over the term of the option is less than the call option's implied volatility on the date the option is sold short.

In contrast to the U.S.-based investor, a Japanese investor pursuing a buy-write strategy would be exposed to currency risk. If the call option expired in-the-money and the call option was exercised, the Japanese investor could realize either a capital gain or loss, depending upon the yen-dollar exchange rate in effect on the option expiration date. If the exchange rate was unchanged at ¥135 per dollar, then the Japanese investor's capital gain would be a simple multiple of the U.S.-based investors's capital gain. In this example, it would be ¥1.35 million. Unfortunately, foreign exchange rates are quite volatile, and even modest changes in the exchange rate could turn the Japanese investor's capital gain into a capital loss.

As we show in the following calculation, if the exchange rate at the option expiration date had increased to ¥140 per dollar, the Japanese investor would realize a capital gain of ¥6.25 million. If the exchange rate at the option expiration date had decreased to ¥130 per dollar, the Japanese investor would face a capital loss of ¥3.55 million.

In the latter case, even when the bonds appreciated so that the U.S.-based investor realized a capital gain of $10,000, the fall in the value of the dollar against the yen caused the Japanese investor to realize a substantial capital loss. Because of this uncertainty, the Japanese investor faces difficulty in using a buy-write strategy with traditional option products to enhance the portfolio's current income.

Sale price of 7 7/8s of February 2021 (option strike price)	$980,000	$980,000
Multiply by: Exchange rate (yen per dollar)	× 140	× 130
Net yen received (millions of yen)	137.20	127.40
Less: Purchase price (millions of yen at ¥135 per dollar)	−130.95	−130.95
Net capital gain or (loss) (millions of yen)	6.25	(3.55)

Suppose instead that the Japanese investor had sold CROSS call options on $1 million face amount of the 7 7/8s of February 2021 at a strike price of ¥13,230 per $100 face amount. We would say the investor is short $1 million face amount CROSS call options on the 7 7/8s of February 2021 at ¥13,230.

By selling yen-denominated CROSS call options instead of traditional dollar-denominated options, the Japanese investor is effectively guaranteed a capital gain in the event that the call options expire in-the-money. The calculations below show the net capital gain or loss on a CROSS option buy-write strategy if the CROSS call options sold short expires in-the-money and the options are exercised. Like the dollar-based investor selling dollar-denominated call options, a Japanese investor selling yen-denominated CROSS call options will always realize a capital gain.

Sale price of 7 7/8s of February 2021 (CROSS option strike price)	¥132,300,000
Less: Purchase price (at ¥135 per dollar)	−¥130,950,000
Net capital gain at the option expiration date	¥1,350,000

Just as with the U.S.-based investor, if the call options sold short expired out-of-the-money and therefore worthless, the Japanese investor would not be required to sell the bonds to the option holder. The Japanese investor would retain the bonds, though with an unrealized gain or loss. The investor would also retain the call option premium and accrued interest on the bonds between the purchase date and the option expiration date.

In this example, a Japanese investor used CROSS call options to execute a buy-write strategy on U.S. Treasury securities. The Japanese investor chose CROSS options because they minimize the strategy's exposure to currency fluctuations. By using CROSS put and call options, portfolio managers can invest in foreign securities and pursue the same option strategies open to them in their domestic markets, while minimizing currency risk and exchange-rate exposures.

Does a Portfolio of Options Equal a CROSS Option?

The Japanese investor pursuing a buy-write strategy with dollar-denominated options could try to hedge the strategy's currency risk by using currency options. Suppose that a Japanese investor purchases $1 million face amount of U.S. Treasury bonds (the 7 7/8s of February 2021) at 97, and pays ¥135 per dollar for the dollars required to buy the bonds. Suppose, again, that the Japanese investor pursues a buy-write strategy and sells dollar-denominated call options with a strike price of 98 on the entire $1 million face amount of bonds owned.

We saw earlier that this strategy leaves the Japanese investor exposed to currency risk. Suppose the Japanese investor tries to hedge that currency risk by purchasing a currency option giving the Japanese investor the right, but not the obligation, to buy $980,000 worth of yen at an exchange rate of ¥135 per dollar. Now, the Japanese investor has a portfolio of options: short a dollar-denominated call option on $1 million face amount of the 7 7/8s of February 2021 at 98, and long an option to buy $980,000 worth of yen at an exchange rate of ¥135 per dollar. Both options expire on the same date.

With this portfolio, the Japanese investor is effectively guaranteed a gain in the event that the call option on the 7 7/8s of February 2021 expires in-the-money. For example, if the exchange rate at the call option expiration date has increased to ¥140 per dollar, the Japanese investor would realize a capital gain of ¥6.25 million (though the currency option held long would expire worthless). But if the exchange rate at the option expiration date has decreased to ¥130 per dollar, the Japanese investor would choose to exercise the currency option and purchase yen at an exchange rate of ¥135 per dollar, leading to a net gain of ¥1.35 million.

Sale price of 7 7/8s of February 2021 (CROSS option strike price)	$980,000	$980,000
Multiply by: Exchange rate, yen per dollar (higher of market rate or ¥135 per dollar option strike)	× 140	× 135
Net yen received (millions of yen)	137.20	132.30
Less: Purchase price (millions of yen at ¥135/$)	−130.95	−130.95
Net capital gain or (loss) (millions of yen)	6.25	1.35

In the event that the call option on the 7 7/8s of February 2021 expires in-the-money, the currency option protects the Japanese investor from a capital loss.

However, the portfolio of options—the call option sold short and currency option held long—are not equivalent to a CROSS option sold short. For one thing, the portfolio of options gives the Japanese investor more flexibility than the CROSS option. In particular, the options in the portfolio can be exercised independently of each other. The call option sold short, for example, could expire worthless, while the currency option held long could expire in-the-money. This added flexibility means that the portfolio of options is more valuable than the CROSS option, and that is reflected in the portfolio's cost.

The portfolio of options—the call option on the 7 7/8s of February 2021 sold short and the currency option held long—will behave like a CROSS call option when, and only when, all of the options in the portfolio are exercised simultaneously (even when one of the options is out-of-the-money) or not at all. If the portfolio of options contained a contingent exercise provision—requiring that all of the options be exercised together or not at all—only then would the portfolio be equivalent to a CROSS option.

It is easy to see why an investor pursuing a buy-write strategy would prefer to use CROSS options. If the CROSS option expired out-of-the-money, a Japanese investor pursuing a buy-write strategy with CROSS options would retain the entire option premium. The option premium would enhance the portfolio's current income. In contrast, a Japanese investor pursuing a buy-write strategy with traditional dollar-denominated options would spend a substantial portion of the option premium to purchase the currency options needed to hedge the portfolio against the possibility of a capital loss. In this example, a Japanese investor could use CROSS options to eliminate exchange-rate risk without reducing the premium income received.

SPREAD-LOCK OPTIONS

No survey of spread options would be complete without a description of over-the-counter options on interest rate swap spreads. Interest rate swaps are normally quoted in terms of a spread over the comparable maturity U.S. Treasury security (see Exhibit 8), so options on swap spreads are a natural extension of the interest rate swap market. On the option's expiration date, the owner of a SPREAD-LOCK call option has the right, but not the obligation, to buy an interest rate swap (receive a fixed rate and pay a floating rate) at a predetermined swap spread. Conversely, the owner of a SPREAD-LOCK put option has the right, but not the obligation, to sell an interest rate swap (pay fixed and receive floating) at a predetermined swap spread. SPREAD-LOCK call options increase in value as swap spreads decrease, while SPREAD-LOCK put options increase in value as swap spreads increase.

SPREAD-LOCK put and call options are different from more-traditional options contracts in the interest rate swap market, such as swaptions, caps, and floors. The latter options are all options on interest rate levels rather than on interest rate spreads. For example, on the option's expiration date, the owner of a call swaption has the right, but not the obligation, to buy an interest rate swap at a predetermined swap rate.

Note that swaptions specify the entire fixed-rate side of the swap in advance, while SPREAD-LOCK put and call options only specify the swap spread in advance. For SPREAD-LOCK put and call options, the fixed-rate side of the swap is equal to

**Exhibit 8.   Interest Rate Swap Spreads
(Pay fixed, receive six-month LIBOR floating)**

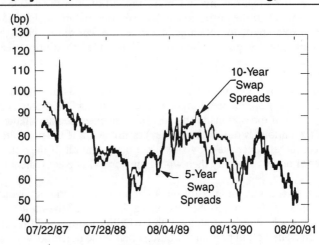

a sum of the prespecified swap spread plus the yield, as of the exercise date of the option, of the comparable-maturity U.S. Treasury security.

Suppose, for example, that on August 21, 1991, an investor had purchased a SPREAD-LOCK put option on a five-year interest rate swap (fixed versus six-month LIBOR floating) at a strike swap spread of 55 bp. The SPREAD-LOCK put option expires on September 21, 1991. We say that the investor is long a five-year SPREAD-LOCK put at 55 bp. On the expiration date, the investor has the right, but not the obligation, to sell a five-year interest rate swap (pay fixed and receive six-month LIBOR floating). The fixed-rate side of the swap would equal the sum of 55 bp plus the yield, on the expiration date, of the outstanding five-year U.S. Treasury note.

Consistent with the conventions used in the interest rate swap market itself, the underlying U.S. Treasury security is not usually identified in advance. For example, with the five-year SPREAD-LOCK put at 55 bp, the fixed-rate side of the underlying swap would equal the sum of 55 bp plus the yield, on the expiration date, of the outstanding five-year U.S. Treasury note, even though that Treasury note may have been issued after the SPREAD-LOCK option's trade date.

The premium of SPREAD-LOCK put and call options is quoted in basis points, which represent a decimal fraction of the notional principal amount of the swap. For example, suppose the investor has purchased $100 million notional principal amount of the five-year SPREAD-LOCK puts at 55 bp for a premium of 9 bp. The dollar cost to the investor would be $90,000.

Notional principal amount of five-year SPREAD-LOCK put at 55 bp	$100 million
Multiply by: Option premium in basis points (decimal)	× 0.0009
Dollar Cost of the option	$90,000

The five-year SPREAD-LOCK put option will be in-the-money if, on the expiration date, the five-year swap rate (fixed versus six-month LIBOR floating) is greater than 55 bp. Suppose that on the expiration date, the five-year swap rate is quoted in the market at 65 bp. In that case the five-year SPREAD-LOCK put option will be 10 bp in-the-money. The owner of the SPREAD-LOCK option would be entitled to sell a five-year swap (pay fixed and receive six-month LIBOR floating), paying a fixed rate of 55 bp over the yield on the outstanding five-year U.S. Treasury note, at a time when the market swap rate is 65 bp over the yield on the outstanding five-year U.S. Treasury note.

The SPREAD-LOCK put option's break-even swap rate can be estimated from the dollar duration of the underlying interest rate swap contract. For example, the $100 million notional amount, five-year SPREAD-LOCK put at 55 bp has a break-even swap spread of approximately 57.2 bp.[19]

Dollar cost of $100 million five-year SPREAD-LOCK put at 55 bp	$90,000
Divide by: Dollar duration of $100 million five-year swap	÷ $41,500 per bp
Break-even in-the-money amount	2.2 bp
Add: SPREAD-LOCK strike spread	+55.0 bp
Break-even swap spread on the expiration date	57.2 bp

In the example shown above, the SPREAD-LOCK put option was structured for physical settlement: the owner of the SPREAD-LOCK option had the right, but not the obligation, to sell a five-year swap contract (pay fixed and receive six-month LIBOR floating). Alternatively, SPREAD-LOCK options can be structured to cash-settle. For example, the investor could have purchased $100 million notional principal amount of five-year SPREAD-LOCK put options at a strike spread of 55 bp and strike dollar duration of $415 per $1 million notional principal amount per basis point. In this case, the investor would be entitled to receive $41,500 for each basis point that the five-year swap spread exceeds 55 bp on the option expiration date. If the swap rate is 65 bp on the option expiration date, the investor would be entitled to receive a cash payment of $415,000.

Five-year swap spread on the option expiration date	65 bp
Less: SPREAD-LOCK strike swap spread	−55 bp
In-the-money amount	10 bp
Multiply by: SPREAD-LOCK strike dollar duration	× $41,500 per bp
Dollar payoff at the option expiration date	$415,000

---

19 We assume that the five-year swap has a dollar duration of $415 per $1 million notional principal amount per bp.

Applications of SPREAD-LOCK Put and Call Options

Portfolio managers and institutions use SPREAD-LOCK put and call options to ensure a favorable asset-liability balance. A financial institution, for example, may own a portfolio of mortgage assets yielding approximately 90 bp over seven-year U.S. Treasury notes and having a dollar duration approximately equal to that of the Treasury notes. Assuming the financial institution can fund at LIBOR flat, and assuming servicing and operating costs are 25 bp, this financial institution can be profitable if it can swap LIBOR-based floating-rate liabilities into fixed-rate liabilities at a spread of less than 65 bp over seven-year Treasury notes.

The financial institution anticipates purchasing an additional $100 million in assets and wants to ensure that these assets can be funded profitably. The financial institution plans to raise capital, with a floating-rate issue, in one month. Assume that seven-year interest rate swap spreads are quoted at 57 bp. If the floating-rate issue and asset purchase occurred today, the financial institution would be profitable, and its profit margin, after operating and servicing costs, would be 8 bp. Since the financial institution intends to raise funding and purchase assets one month from now, it can hedge against a possible widening of swap spreads by purchasing a seven-year SPREAD-LOCK put option expiring in one month.

SUMMARY OF SPREAD OPTIONS FOR FIXED-INCOME INVESTORS

This chapter has described a wide variety of over-the-counter options on interest rate spreads between different fixed-income classes:

- SYCURVE options, which are put and call options on the slope of the yield curve;

- MOTTO options, which are put and call options on the spread between the mortgage and Treasury markets;

- ISO options, which are put and call options on the spread between foreign fixed-income markets and other foreign fixed-income markets or the U.S. Treasury market;

- CROSS options, which are put and call options on fixed-income securities in which the option's strike price is established in a currency that is different from the currency in which the fixed-income security itself is denominated; and finally,

- SPREAD-LOCK options, which are put and call options on interest rate swap spreads.

These option products allow investors (1) to alter a portfolio's exposure to interest rate spreads, (2) to hedge interest rate spread exposures, and (3) to profit from changes in interest rate spreads. These options can be structured either for a cash settlement or for the physical exchange of securities. With a cash-settled structure, the owner of the spread option receives a cash payment equal to the in-the-money value when the option expires or is exercised. Alternatively, he can use a DUOP structure, which involves the physical exchange of the underlying securities if the options expire in-the-money or are exercised.

Merely purchasing and holding a portfolio of options on individual securities does not replicate the payoff from an option on interest rate spreads. Moreover, a portfolio of options on individual securities that minimally meets an investor's hedging requirements is often more expensive (the investor is overhedged) than the alternative of a single, over-the-counter spread option. Over-the-counter interest rate spread options can be simple, convenient, and well-matched to investors' needs.

APPENDIX

An Analytic Formula for Valuing European SYCURVE Put and Call Options

In this chapter, we intentionally did not include a detailed description of how to calculate the dollar value of SYCURVE put and call options, nor did we describe how to determine an option's hedge ratio (the option's delta). Such a description is complex and may not be of interest to all readers. Rather than place such calculations in the body of the text, we develop in this Appendix the formulas required to value SYCURVE put and call options. Throughout the discussion that follows, we will assume that the SYCURVE options are European and can be exercised only on the option's expiration date.

Determinants of Value

On the trade date, the value of SYCURVE put and call options is determined by a combination of at least five ingredients: (1) the strike yield spread, (2) the expiration date, (3) the discount factor between the trade date and the expiration date, (4) the forward yield spread between the SYCURVE option's two underlying securities, and (5) the volatility of the forward yield spread. Before developing the option pricing formulas, we will briefly examine each of these components.

The Strike Yield Spread and Expiration Date

The strike yield spread and option expiration date are easy to determine, as they are always specified on the trade date. Option premiums are settled on the business day following the trade date. And if the option buyer elects to exercise the option and the option is cash-settled, the option's payoff settles on the business day following the option's expiration date.

The Discount Factor

The value of a SYCURVE put or call option is determined by the expected value of the payoff on the option's expiration date, discounted to the trade date. Normally, we use the financing cost of the underlying securities (either the repo rate, LIBOR, or spread over LIBOR, as appropriate) to determine the discount factor.

The Forward Yield Spread

The payoff from SYCURVE put and call options is based on the forward yield spread—the difference in yield between the two underlying securities—where the forward date is the option's expiration date. For each of the two underlying securities, we can obtain an estimate of the forward price, based on the security's price today, coupon rate, and repo rate until the forward date. Given the expected forward price for each security, the expected forward yield follows. And the difference between the expected forward yields is the expected forward yield spread.[20]

Assume, for example, that on September 17, 1991, we wish to determine the expected forward yield spread to an October 17, 1991, option expiration date (an October 18, 1991, forward settlement date) between the 8 1/8s of May 15, 2021 (a 30-year bond), and the 6 7/8s of July 31, 1993 (a 2-year note). Assume that the 30-year bond and 2-year note are trading at prices of 101 31/32 and 101 7+/32nds, respectively, for settlement on September 18, 1991. Finally, assume that both securities can be financed at a term repo rate of 5.40 percent.

Exhibit 9 shows our calculation of forward prices and forward yields for both the 30-year bond and 2-year note. We find the expected forward yield spread to be 178.0 bp.[21] Note that the expected forward yield spread is less than the 179.1 bp yield spread between the 30-year bond and 2-year note on the trade date. This is typical of an upward sloping yield curve environment (see footnote 10).

Exhibit 9.   Forward Yield Spreads (30-Year Bond versus 2-Year Note)

		For Settlement on September 18, 1991			For Forward Settlement on October 18, 1991	
Coupon Rate	Maturity Date	Quoted Price (decimal)	Yield (%)	Term Financing Rate (%)	Forward Price (decimal)	Yield at the Forward Price (%)
8.125	05/15/21	101.96875	7.950	5.400	101.77776	7.967
6.875	07/31/93	101.234375	6.159	5.400	101.13359	6.187
Expected forward yield spread (bp)						178.0

The Volatility of the Yield Spread

We use the word *volatility* as a shorthand notation for variability—in this case the likely variability of the forward yield spread between the underlying securities from the trade date until the expiration date of the option. The volatility is important because of its effect on option values: the larger the volatility, the higher the probability that a put or call option will finish in-the-money, and therefore the more valuable the option.

At first glance, the volatility of the forward yield spread seems difficult to determine. Going back to our earlier example, since the forward yield spread is the difference between the forward yield of the 30-year bond and the forward yield of the 2-year note, the volatility of the forward yield spread could in principle be found from

---

20 Strictly speaking, the expected forward yield is not exactly equal to the security's yield at the forward price if the security has a nonzero convexity. Fortunately, however, the difference is small for short-dated options, so we neglect it in the example that follows.

21 In this example, the correction to the forward yield spread due to the nonzero convexity of the underlying securities (see footnote 20) is approximately 0.4 bp.

the volatility of 30-year bond yields, the volatility of 2-year note yields, and the correlation between the two. Fortunately, there is an easier approach.

In the discussion that follows, we assume that the forward yield spread itself is a volatile security. SYCURVE put and call options can then be thought of as put and call options on a single security, rather than (complex) options on the spread between two independently volatile (risky) securities. However, if we use the former approach, we need to recognize that the way in which changes in yield spreads behave is not the same as the way in which note and bond yields change.

We usually assume that note and bond yields are lognormally distributed, meaning that the quantity $\ln(y_{t+\Delta t}/y_t)$ is assumed to be normally distributed, where yt is the note's or bond's yield today and $y_{t+\Delta t}$ is the note's or bond's yield at some future date. The yield volatility, then, would be the (annualized) standard deviation of the quantity $\ln(y_{t+\Delta t}/y_t)$. The forward yield spread, however, has a different property.

For example, Exhibit 10 shows a histogram of month-to-month changes in the yield spread between the on-the-run 30-year bond and the on-the-run 2-year note from January 31, 1985, through September 13, 1991. As the chart shows, changes in the yield spread are, to a good approximation, normally distributed. Over this period, the volatility of the yield spread was 70.1 bp per year. This means that changes in forward yield spreads, $S_{t+\Delta t} - St$, are normally distributed, where St is the forward yield spread today and $St+Dt$ is the forward yield spread at some future date. The volatility of the yield spread, then, is the (annualized) standard deviation of the quantity $S_{t+\Delta t} - S_t$.

Exhibit 10. Histogram of 2- to 30-Year Yield Spread (1,694 trading days, 21 trading days per month, January 31, 1985, through September 13, 1991)

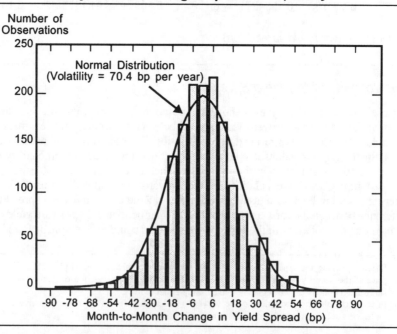

Returning to the yield spread between the 8 1/8s of May 2021 and the 6 7/8s of July 1993, we show in Exhibit 11 a history of the yield of each security and a history of the yield spread from July 31, 1991, when the 2-year note was issued, through September 17, 1991. During this period, the historical yield spread volatility was 69.6 bp.

Exhibit 11 also shows an alternative way of estimating the yield spread volatility, namely

$$\sigma \simeq \sqrt{(\sigma_2 y_2)^2 + (\sigma_{30} y_{30})^2 - 2\rho_{2,30}\, \sigma_2 y_2\, \sigma_{30} y_{30}} \tag{1}$$

where σ is the volatility of the yield spread between the 30-year bond and 2-year note, y_{30} is the 30-year bond yield, σ_{30} is the volatility of the 30-year bond yield, y_2 is the 2-year note yield, σ_2 is the volatility of the 2-year note yield, and $\rho_{2,30}$ is the correlation coefficient. The estimated yield spread volatility, found by using Equation 1 and the historical yield volatilities, average yields, and the historical correlation coefficient, is 70.2 bp (see Exhibit 11).

In Exhibits 10 and 11, we have used historical changes in the yield spread as a proxy for changes in the forward yield spread, and historical yield spread volatility as a proxy for expected future yield spread volatility. This is a good approximation only when future market behavior is expected to closely resemble past market behavior. In practice, this is rarely the case. Often, an option will trade in the market at an implied volatility (an expected future volatility implied by the option's price) different from the historical volatility of the underlying security. Moreover, an option's implied volatility may differ for different option expiration dates (there is a term structure of volatility). This does not mean that the option is mispriced. Instead, it means that market participants expect future conditions to differ from those of the immediate past.

We can use Equation 1 to approximate the estimated future volatility of the yield spread by using the implied volatility of options on individual securities. For example, on September 17, 1991, the 8 1/8s of May 2021 were priced to yield 7.950 percent and the 6 7/8s of July 1993 were priced to yield 6.159 percent (see Exhibit 11). On the same date, one-month put and call options on the 30-year bond were trading at an implied volatility of approximately 9.0 percent, and one-month put and call options on the 2-year note were trading at an implied volatility of approximately 16.5 percent. Using Equation 1 and assuming a correlation coefficient of 70 percent, we find that the expected future volatility of the yield spread between the 30-year bond and 2-year note would be approximately 72.6 bp.

So far, we have used four different methods to determine the expected future volatility of the yield spread between the 8 1/8s of May 2021 and the 6 7/8s of July 1993: (1) the historical volatility, 70.4 bp, of the yield spread between on-the-run 30-year bonds and on-the-run 2-year notes; (2) the historical volatility, 69.6 bp, of the yield spread between the 8 1/8s of May 2021 and the 6 7/8s of July 1993, specifically; (3) the estimated yield spread volatility, 70.2 bp, based on the average yield of each security, the historical yield volatility of each security, and the historical correlation coefficient; and (4) an estimate of the expected future yield spread volatility, 72.6 bp, based on the actual yield of each security on the trade date, the implied yield volatility of put and call options on each security on the trade date, and an estimate of the expected future correlation coefficient. All of these estimates of the expected future

Exhibit 11. Yield Spread Volatility

	8 1/8s of 5/15/21 30-Year Treasury Bond		6 7/8s of 7/31/93 Two-Year Treasury Note		2/30 Yield Spread	
Date	Yield (%)	Log Change	Yield (%)	Log Change	Spread (%)	Change (%)
07/30/91	8.384%	–	6.832%	–	1.552%	–
07/31/91	8.352%	−0.0039	6.798%	−0.0050	1.554%	0.002%
08/01/91	8.378%	0.0031	6.849%	0.0074	1.529%	−0.024%
08/02/91	8.248%	−0.0157	6.687%	−0.0240	1.561%	0.032%
08/05/91	8.233%	−0.0017	6.678%	−0.0013	1.556%	−0.005%
08/06/91	8.171%	−0.0076	6.566%	−0.0168	1.605%	0.049%
08/07/91	8.171%	0.0000	6.532%	−0.0053	1.639%	0.035%
08/08/91	8.222%	0.0062	6.489%	−0.0066	1.733%	0.094%
08/09/91	8.242%	0.0024	6.470%	−0.0029	1.772%	0.039%
08/12/91	8.222%	−0.0024	6.469%	−0.0001	1.753%	−0.019%
08/13/91	8.188%	−0.0042	6.460%	−0.0014	1.728%	−0.025%
08/14/91	8.092%	−0.0117	6.356%	−0.0161	1.736%	0.008%
08/15/91	8.123%	0.0038	6.321%	−0.0055	1.802%	0.066%
08/16/91	8.118%	−0.0007	6.284%	−0.0059	1.833%	0.031%
08/19/91	8.132%	0.0017	6.206%	−0.0125	1.925%	0.092%
08/20/91	8.120%	−0.0014	6.137%	−0.0113	1.984%	0.058%
08/21/91	8.095%	−0.0031	6.247%	0.0179	1.848%	−0.136%
08/22/91	8.079%	−0.0021	6.246%	−0.0002	1.832%	−0.016%
08/23/91	8.163%	0.0103	6.408%	0.0256	1.754%	−0.078%
08/26/91	8.182%	0.0024	6.442%	0.0053	1.740%	−0.014%
08/27/91	8.163%	−0.0024	6.398%	−0.0069	1.765%	0.024%
08/28/91	8.087%	−0.0093	6.293%	−0.0166	1.794%	0.030%
08/29/91	8.021%	−0.0082	6.240%	−0.0085	1.781%	−0.013%
08/30/91	8.087%	0.0082	6.323%	0.0133	1.764%	−0.017%
09/03/91	8.079%	−0.0010	6.305%	−0.0029	1.774%	0.010%
09/04/91	8.090%	0.0014	6.287%	−0.0029	1.803%	0.030%
09/05/91	8.115%	0.0031	6.295%	0.0013	1.820%	0.017%
09/06/91	8.045%	−0.0086	6.230%	−0.0103	1.815%	−0.005%
09/09/91	8.029%	−0.0021	6.212%	−0.0030	1.817%	0.002%
09/10/91	8.040%	0.0014	6.202%	−0.0016	1.838%	0.021%
09/11/91	8.048%	0.0010	6.218%	0.0027	1.830%	−0.008%
09/12/91	7.980%	−0.0086	6.182%	−0.0059	1.798%	−0.032%
09/13/91	7.985%	0.0007	6.170%	−0.0019	1.815%	0.017%
09/16/91	7.961%	−0.0031	6.160%	−0.0016	1.800%	−0.015%
09/17/91	7.950%	−0.0038	6.159%	−0.0002	1.791%	−0.010%
Average	8.124%		6.362%		1.762%	
Historical Yield Volatility		9.114%		15.980%		
Historical Covariance			1.054%			
Historical Correlation Coefficient			72.4%			
Estimatied Yield Spread Volatility			0.702%			
Historical Yield Spread Volatility						0.696%

yield spread volatility are very close to each other, though that may not be true in general. They can be used to value—or to establish a range of values for—SYCURVE put and call options.

Now that we have developed estimates of all of the elements that determine the value of SYCURVE put or call options, we can proceed to calculate an option's value using an option pricing formula. Unfortunately, because changes in the forward yield spread are not lognormally distributed, we cannot use the usual option pricing tools, such as the Black-Scholes model, to value SYCURVE put and call options. Instead, we need to develop an entirely new option pricing model for securities whose changes follow a normal distribution.

The SYCURVE Option Pricing Formula

To value a SYCURVE put or call option, we assume that forward yield spreads obey the following process:

$$S_{t+\Delta t} = S_t + \sigma \sqrt{\Delta t}\, Z, \tag{2}$$

where: S_t = forward yield spread at time t,

              $S_{t+\Delta t}$ = forward yield spread at time t+Δt,

              σ = standard deviation of the yield spread per unit time, and

              Z = standard normal random variable with mean = 0 and standard deviation = 1.

The standard normal random variable, Z, will probably look more familiar to readers when it is operated on by the probability operator, Prob$\{\cdots\}$. For example:

$$\text{Prob}\{x \le Z \le x + dx\} = \frac{1}{\sqrt{2\pi}}\, e^{-x^2/2}\, dx$$

$$= N'(x)\, dx,$$

$$\text{Prob}\{Z \le y\} = \frac{1}{\sqrt{2\pi}} \int_{-\infty}^{y} e^{-x^2/2}\, dx$$

$$= N(y),$$

$$\text{Prob}\{Z \ge y\} = \text{Prob}\{Z \le -y\}$$

$$= N(-y)$$

$$= 1 - N(y),$$

and it follows that E$\{Z\} = 0$, Var$\{Z\} = 1$, and E$\{Z^2\} = 1$, where E$\{\cdots\}$ is the expected value operator and Var$\{\cdots\}$ is the variance operator.

Based on Equation 2 and the properties of the standard normal random variable, we find the expected value and variance of the forward yield spread to be

$$E\{S_{t+\Delta\tau}\} = S_t, \text{ and}$$
$$\text{Var}\{S_{t+\Delta t}\} = \sigma^2\, \Delta t.$$

This means that the expected value of the forward yield spread is, sensibly, the forward yield spread itself, and that changes in the forward yield spread are normally distributed.

Now suppose that we wish to know the value at time t (today) of a European SYCURVE call option on the yield spread with a strike yield spread K. And suppose that the call option expires at time T (the option's expiration date). In this case, C_t is the value of the SYCURVE call option and S_t is the expected value, at time t, of the forward yield spread. At expiration, the SYCURVE call option will have a value C_T = Max(0, $S_T - K$), where S_T is the yield spread on the option expiration date, and the operator Max($\cdots$) selects the largest item in the list. The value of the SYCURVE call option today is equal to the expected value of C_T discounted to today, namely

$$C_t = e^{-r\tau}\, E\{Max(0, S_T - K)\} \tag{3}$$

where $\tau = T - t$ is the time to expiration of the option and $e^{-r\tau}$ is the discount factor between today and the option's expiration date.[22]

If $p = Prob\{S_T > K\}$ is the probability that the SYCURVE call option expires in-the-money, and if $E\{S_T | S_T > K\}$ is the expected value of the yield spread given that the SYCURVE call option expires in-the-money, then Equation 3 becomes

$$C_t = (1 - p)e^{-r\tau}\,(0) + pe^{-r\tau}\,(E\{S_T | S_T > K\} - K)$$

$$= e^{-r\tau}\,(pE\{S_T | S_T > K\} - K) \tag{4}$$

Step 1: Evaluation of p

$$p = Prob\{S_T > K\}$$
$$= Prob\{S_t + \sigma\sqrt{\tau}\,Z > K\}$$
$$= Prob\left\{Z > \frac{1}{\sigma\sqrt{\tau}}(K - S_t)\right\}$$
$$= Prob\left\{Z < \frac{1}{\sigma\sqrt{\tau}}(S_t - K)\right\}$$
$$= N(h)$$

$$\text{where } h = \frac{1}{\sigma\sqrt{\tau}}(S_t - K)\,.$$

---

22 Here, r is the continuously compounded risk-free rate. Normally, we would use LIBOR or the repo rate, R, as a proxy for the risk-free rate and make the substitution

$$e^{-r\tau} \rightarrow \left[1 + R\frac{\tau}{360}\right]^{-1}.$$

Step 2: Evaluation of $pE\{ST \mid ST > K\}$

$$pE\{S_T \mid S_T > K\} = \frac{1}{\sqrt{2\pi}} \int_{S_T > K} S_T e^{-x^2/2} \, dx$$

$$= \frac{1}{\sqrt{2\pi}} \int_{S_t + \sigma\sqrt{\tau}\,x > K} (S_t + \sigma\sqrt{\tau}\,x) e^{-x^2/2} \, dx$$

$$= \frac{1}{\sqrt{2\pi}} \int_{x > \frac{1}{\sigma\sqrt{\tau}}(K - S_t)} (S_t + \sigma\sqrt{\tau}\,x) \, e^{-x^2/2} \, dx$$

$$= S_t \frac{1}{\sqrt{2\pi}} \int_{x = \frac{1}{\sigma\sqrt{\tau}}(K - S_t)}^{+\infty} e^{-x^2/2} \, dx + \sigma\sqrt{\tau} \frac{1}{\sqrt{2\pi}} \int_{x = \frac{1}{\sigma\sqrt{\tau}}(K - S_t)}^{+\infty} x e^{-x^2/2} \, dx$$

$$= S_t \frac{1}{\sqrt{2\pi}} \int_{-\infty}^{x = \frac{1}{\sigma\sqrt{\tau}}(S_t - K)} e^{-x^2/2} \, dx + \sigma\sqrt{\tau} \frac{1}{\sqrt{2\pi}} \int_{y = \frac{1}{2}\left[\frac{1}{\sigma\sqrt{\tau}}(S_t - K)\right]^2}^{+\infty} e^{-y} \, dy$$

$$= S_t N(h) - \sigma\sqrt{\tau} \frac{1}{\sqrt{2\pi}} \left[e^{-y}\right]_{y = h^2/2}^{+\infty}$$

$$= S_t N(h) + \sigma\sqrt{\tau} \frac{1}{\sqrt{2\pi}} e^{-h^2/2}$$

$$= S_t N(h) + \sigma\sqrt{\tau} \, N'(h) .$$

Substituting these results into Equation 4 gives the formula for the value of a SYCURVE call option

$$C_t = e^{-r\tau}[(S_t - K) N(h) + \sigma\sqrt{\tau} N'(h)] \tag{5}$$

where $h = \dfrac{1}{\sigma\sqrt{\tau}}(S_t - K)$.

This completes our derivation of the SYCURVE call option formula. The only other formula that may be of interest is the hedge ratio (the delta, Δ_C) of the SYCURVE call option. The delta is equal to the sensitivity of the SYCURVE call option value to changes in the forward yield spread. In particular,

$$\Delta_C = \frac{\partial C_t}{\partial S_t} \tag{6}$$

$$= e^{-r\tau} N(h).$$

Most spreadsheet programs and hand-held calculators do not have the ability to solve directly for the standard normal distribution, $N(h)$. Fortunately, there is a reasonably accurate polynomial approximation of $N(h)$ valid for h 0, which is:[23]

$$N(h) = 1 - N'(h)\,(b_1 z + b_2 z^2 + b_3 z^3 + b_4 z^4 + b_5 z^5)$$

where: $z = \dfrac{1}{1 + ah}$,

          $a = 0.2316419,$
          $b_1 = 0.319381530,$
          $b_2 = -0.356563782,$
          $b_3 = 1.781477937,$
          $b_4 = -1.821255978,$ and
          $b_5 = 1.330274429.$

For $h < 0$, we invoke the identity $N(h) = 1 - N(-h)$ and use the above polynomial approximation to solve for $N(-h)$.

Though we will not reproduce the derivation here, we can use put-call parity to find the formula for a SYCURVE put option, P_t,

$$P_t = e^{r\tau}\Big[(K - S_t)(1 - N(h)) + \sigma\sqrt{\tau}\,N'(h)\Big] \tag{7}$$

where, again, $h = \dfrac{1}{\sigma\sqrt{\tau}}\,(S_t - K).$

Finally, the hedge ratio (the delta, Δ_p) of a SYCURVE put option is equal to

$$\Delta_p = \frac{\partial P_t}{\partial S_t} \tag{8}$$

$$= e^{-r\tau}\,(N(h) - 1).$$

Example: Value of a 30-Day SYCURVE 2/30 Call Option

Now, at last, we are able to value a SYCURVE call option on the yield spread between the 8 1/8s of May 2021 and the 6 7/8s of July 1993. Suppose, on September 17, 1991, we wish to determine the value of a SYCURVE call option expiring on October 17, 1991. We saw earlier that the forward yield spread is 178.0 bp. Suppose we choose the strike yield spread also to be 178.0 bp (we say the option is at-the-money on a forward basis) and suppose we use 72.6 bp as the (annualized) expected future volatility of the forward yield spread over the life of the option. To review,

23 Milton Abramowitz and Irene A. Stegun, Handbook of Mathematical Functions (Washington: National Bureau of Standards, 1972), Equation 26.2.17.

$$
\begin{aligned}
\text{Trade Date, } t &= \text{September 17, 1991,} \\
\text{Expiration Date, } T &= \text{October 17, 1991,} \\
\tau &= \text{30 calendar days} \\
&= \text{23 trading days} \\
&= \text{0.08984375 years,} \\
\sigma &= \text{72.6 bp,} \\
S_t &= \text{178.0 bp,} \\
K &= \text{178.0 bp,}
\end{aligned}
$$

and therefore

$$
\begin{aligned}
e^{-r\tau} &= 0.99552016, \\
h &= 0, \\
N'(h) &= 0.3989422804, \text{ and} \\
N(h) &= 0.5,
\end{aligned}
$$

where we have assumed a (continuously compounded) risk-free rate of 4.9975 percent, equivalent to a term repo rate of 5.40 percent (see footnote 21). After substituting these factors into Equation 5, we find that the value of a 30-day SYCURVE 2/30 call option is

$$
\begin{aligned}
C_t &= 8.6425 \text{ bp} \\
&\cong 9 \text{ bp,}
\end{aligned}
$$

where we have rounded the result to the nearest basis point. In dollar terms, SYCURVE put and call options are priced at \$10,000 per basis point per \$1 million notional principal amount. If we assume a notional principal amount of \$1 million, the premium of the 30-day SYCURVE 2/30 call at 178 bp would be \$90,000. Exhibit 12 displays a graph of the value of the SYCURVE call option for several values of the forward yield spread.

Exhibit 12. Value of 30-Day SYCURVE 2/30 Call Option

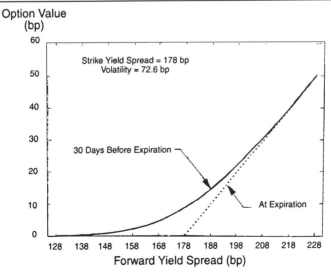

CHAPTER 5

Swaps and the Derivative Markets

Eileen Baecher
Financial Consultant

INTRODUCTION

Over the last several years, the derivative products available in the capital markets have increased in number and complexity. The traditional interest rate swap market has expanded to include a variety of swaps and other hedge products with option characteristics. These products can be tailored to reflect almost any interest rate or currency outlook and create an appropriate risk exposure. There are now three broad groups of uses for the derivative products. The traditional use has been in *liability hedging,* where, for example, an issuer might be able to obtain more favorable funding rates by issuing floating-rate debt (if that is the market in which it has a comparative advantage) and then swapping the floating-rate payments for fixed-rate payments. Swaps and caps have also been used to alter the structure of existing liabilities for purposes of *balance sheet management.* For example, an outstanding fixed-rate liability can readily be swapped into floating, or vice versa, to adjust for term or basis exposure. Additionally, swaps and caps are "off-balance-sheet" transactions, and as such, they may be particularly useful for certain applications. Finally, derivative products are more frequently being used in *asset hedging.* This category includes the packaging of any type of underlying financial asset with a derivative to create a relatively more attractive synthetic security, in terms of its yield, credit quality, or some other criterion.

In this chapter, we explain the structural details of the derivative products and markets. We include many examples of how the products are being combined in complex structures for the purposes of creating specific risk profiles. We also provide a list of criteria that can be used for choosing among the many available alternatives.

I am grateful to Dave Boren, Sam Collins, Erol Hakanoglu, Tom Macirowski, Tom Montag, Bruce Petersen, Scott Pinkus, and John Tormondsen for their helpful comments on earlier drafts of this paper.

The appendixes include more-detailed information on a variety of topics, including credit risk; a comparison of future to swap markets; bond math; and some legal, accounting, and tax issues that are important in the practical use of the products but are not necessary for a basic understanding.

THE DERIVATIVE PRODUCTS

There are four broad categories of capital market derivative products: swaps, swaptions, warrants, and caps. We will consider each of them separately.

Swaps

A swap is a contractual agreement in which two counterparties agree to exchange streams of payments over time. The two main types are *interest rate swaps* and *currency swaps*.

Interest Rate Swaps

In an interest rate swap, the counterparties exchange interest payment streams of differing character on an underlying notional principal amount. No principal is exchanged. The two main types are *coupon swaps* (fixed rate exchanged for floating rate) and *basis swaps* (floating against one reference rate to floating against another reference rate.) We illustrate a standard coupon swap involving Goldman Sachs Capital Markets (GSCM) in Exhibit 1.

The standard "vanilla" structure of a coupon swap is the exchange of six-month LIBOR (London Interbank Offered Rate) versus a fixed rate. Payments are exchanged semiannually, and the notional principal amount remains constant over the life of the swap.[1] Swap maturities or terms are generally from 2 to 10 years, although there are occasionally terms of up to 20 years. The notional sizes of swaps range from $5 million to $500 million, with an average of $25–50 million.

Swaps are priced in terms of the fixed-rate payment level, which is quoted as a spread over the U.S. Treasury note with a maturity corresponding to the maturity of the swap.[2] For example, a standard five-year swap might exchange six-month LIBOR (flat) for the five-year Treasury yield plus 50 bp. The LIBOR rate will float and is reset at the beginning of each period. The Treasury yield is set only once at the beginning of the swap and remains fixed over the life of the swap. The payments in a standard swap are exchanged every six months, corresponding to the term of the floating-rate index. This is, of course, subject to negotiation in the structuring of the swap agreement, and the exchange frequency can be longer, shorter, or the same as the term of the floating-rate index.

---

1 The floating rate is usually set at the beginning of the payment period, although the actual payment is exchanged at the end of the period, much like the accrual on a floating-rate bond.

2 In nondollar markets, where typically there are no benchmark issues throughout the 2- to 20-year maturity range, the swaps are quoted as the all-in fixed rate, rather than as a spread to a comparable-maturity government issue.

Exhibit 1. Standard Coupon Swap

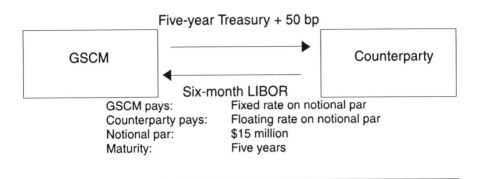

Five-year Treasury + 50 bp

GSCM → Counterparty

Six-month LIBOR

GSCM pays:	Fixed rate on notional par
Counterparty pays:	Floating rate on notional par
Notional par:	$15 million
Maturity:	Five years

There can be many other variations on this theme. The floating rate can be a spread off of LIBOR, such as six-month LIBOR plus 20 bp. Note that this can be translated into an adjustment to the fixed-rate spread over Treasuries, although the 20 bp must be converted from a money market basis to a corporate bond-equivalent yield (BEY) basis to accurately determine the net fixed-rate expense. The net fixed rate defines the all-in cost of the swap, which allows the easy comparison of swaps of varying structures and cash market alternatives. Alternatively, the floating rate could be some other short-term rate, such as Treasury bill, cost-of-funds index (COFI), commercial paper, or tax-exempt. Regardless of which rate is used, it is very important to recognize the different quoting conventions and compounding frequencies among markets when calculating the all-in costs (see Appendix C to this chapter for detailed information).

Another alternative to the standard swap is exchanging the floating six-month LIBOR for another floating short-term rate, such as three-month LIBOR, Treasury bills, or commercial paper. In Exhibit 2, we illustrate this structure, known as a basis

Exhibit 2. Basis Swap

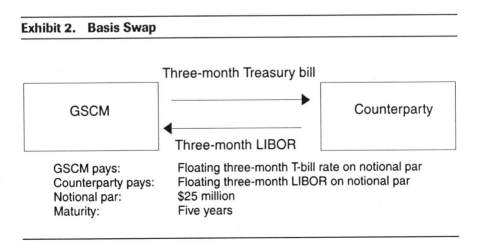

Three-month Treasury bill

GSCM → Counterparty

Three-month LIBOR

GSCM pays:	Floating three-month T-bill rate on notional par
Counterparty pays:	Floating three-month LIBOR on notional par
Notional par:	$25 million
Maturity:	Five years

swap, with an exchange of two floating-rate indexes: three-month Treasury bills and three-month LIBOR. Basis swaps can have maturities of up to 10 years, although shorter maturities are much more common. There are few standards for quoting conventions because there is so much flexibility in the choice of interest rate indexes. The two floating indexes do not have to be exchanged flat as in our example, nor do the terms of the rates need to be equal. For example, one fairly common basis swap structure is to exchange one-month commercial paper for three-month LIBOR plus a spread in basis points.

Currency Swaps

In a currency swap, the counterparties exchange specific amounts of two different currencies at the outset and repay over time according to a predetermined rule that reflects both interest payments and amortization of principal. There are two general types of currency swaps: traditional *fixed/fixed currency swaps* and *cross-currency interest rate swaps*. A traditional fixed/fixed currency swap involves fixed interest rates in each currency. Exchange of principal may or may not be part of the transaction. If the principal is exchanged, the fixed/fixed currency swap essentially transforms a fixed coupon bond denominated in one currency into a fixed coupon bond in the other currency, as shown in Exhibit 3.

A cross-currency interest rate swap involves the exchange of fixed and floating payment streams as well as payments in different currencies. These arrangements are sometimes combined as a single transaction while at other times the currency and interest rate components are separated. Typically, this type of swap involves the

---

Exhibit 3.   Currency Swap

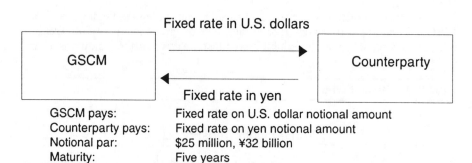

Fixed rate in U.S. dollars

| GSCM | | Counterparty |

Fixed rate in yen

GSCM pays: Fixed rate on U.S. dollar notional amount
Counterparty pays: Fixed rate on yen notional amount
Notional par: $25 million, ¥32 billion
Maturity: Five years

If principal is exchanged:

GSCM would pay ¥32 billion and receive $25 million at commencement date. On final reset date, GSCM would receive ¥32 billion and pay $25 million. These principal payments assume that rates are market levels at commencement; i.e., there is no discount or premium in the rates.

Exhibit 4.   Cross-Currency Interest Rate Swap

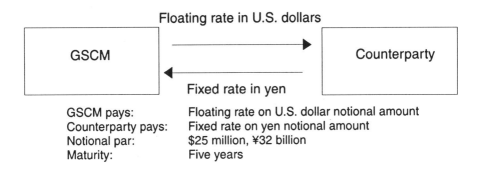

Floating rate in U.S. dollars

GSCM → Counterparty

Fixed rate in yen

GSCM pays:	Floating rate on U.S. dollar notional amount
Counterparty pays:	Fixed rate on yen notional amount
Notional par:	$25 million, ¥32 billion
Maturity:	Five years

exchange of nondollar fixed-rate interest payments for dollar floating rate interest payments, as illustrated in Exhibit 4.

General Swap Variations

There are many variations on the basic swap structures discussed so far. The following list includes the primary variations:

- *Amortizing Swap:* A swap with a variable notional balance, e.g., balances that match the expected cash flows of a financing project or the prepayment schedule of a mortgage asset or liability. The amortization schedule may be determined either *a priori* or by actual prepayment experience over the swap term.

- *Forward Swap:* A swap that does not begin until a designated future date. The fixed-rate level is established at spot market rates, and the swap must be carried out on the specified date.

- *Step UP/Down:* A swap in which the fixed-rate payment level varies—either increasing or decreasing for some portion of the swap term. For example, the fixed rate might be set below the market for the first two years, with an above-market rate for the remainder of the term.

Commodity Swaps

In a commodity swap, the counterparties agree to exchange payments based on the value of a particular physical commodity, e.g., gold or oil. One party pays a fixed price for the commodity and receives the spot price of the commodity on that reset date. This market is only beginning to develop but may have particular value to commodity fund managers or to entities that need to hedge the pricing of commodities for inventory purposes. Maturities for these swaps are generally short—two or three years—but are available for terms up to seven years. The short-dated swaps are analogous to strips of futures contracts and will therefore be priced similarly.

Two products that also may be of interest to commodity swap users are *indexed medium-term notes* and *indexed commercial paper*. The indexing structure is the same for both products, although the terms of the two products differ: two to five years for the notes and up to 270 days for commercial paper. The products link the return on a fixed income security to the relative performance of the commodity or currency. The commodity exposure can be built into either the coupon payment or the principal repayment. For example, for a coupon-indexed note, if the price of gold increases by $20, the coupon payment for that period might increase to 11 percent from 10 percent. On a principal-indexed note, the principal repaid at maturity may be more or less than par to reflect an increase or decrease in the commodity value.

The indexed note market is flexible; an investor can negotiate issue specifications with the issuer, which might be a highly rated corporation or government agency. Currency-indexed notes have recently become popular among investors. In particular, indexing the dollar (or other low-yielding currency) versus a basket of high-yielding currencies has been attractive for many fixed-income asset managers as a means of diversifying their portfolio risk without having to invest directly in foreign markets.

Indexed Return Swaps

One of the newer innovations in the swaps market is the linking of one of the payments to the total return of a market portfolio. This return can be exchanged for a payment stream based on either a fixed rate, such as the five-year Treasury +50 bp, or a floating rate such as LIBOR. The indexed portfolio can be an equity basket, such as the S&P 500, or a fixed-income index. These structures may be particularly useful for investing in foreign markets, where the costs of execution and portfolio management may be higher than domestic costs.[3] Foreign indexed swaps may be either currency hedged, to capture relative performance of security types (e.g., U.S. equities versus German equities), or unhedged for a complete foreign investment.

For example, assume that an investor owns a three-year floating-rate note yielding LIBOR plus 25 bp. The investor wants to be exposed to Japanese government bonds (JGBs) but is unable to trade the securities directly and to manage the yen/dollar risk. The investor can enter into a swap whereby he or she receives the dollar equivalent of the monthly JGB returns and pays LIBOR, giving a total exposure of the JGB bond return plus 25 bp. Using a swap rather than trading the underlying securities has the additional benefit of allowing the investor complete freedom to trade the underlying floater.

Swaps can be indexed against a number of markets, including the government bonds of various countries—such as Britain, Germany, or Japan—and can be further broken down to specific maturity sectors. Corporate bond indexes are also logical candidates, segregated by credit or maturity characteristics or both. Options and swaptions on these and other indexes are also possible.

---

3 For example, taxes can be applied differently for dealers versus foreign investors. The dealer's relative advantage can be priced in the swap, making the swap a more attractive investment.

Mortgage Swaps

An increasing number of swaps are structured to replicate all or a portion of the yield or return characteristics of mortgage securities. In the most straightforward structure, a mortgage yield is exchanged for a floating-rate return, and the notional balance on which the payments are based amortizes according to either a specific prepayment assumption or the actual prepayment experience of the underlying pool(s). A more complex structure exchanges the total return of a mortgage security against a floating-rate payment stream. The underlying mortgage may be a particular pool (or pools), or a specific mortgage derivative, such as a CMO tranche. In these swaps, the principal amortization generally is based on the actual prepayment experiences of the underlying security.

The most recent innovation in mortgage-based swaps is an *indexed amortization swap*. A fixed-rate payment is exchanged for a floating-rate payment, but the notional balance amortizes according to a triggered schedule. For example, the schedule may be based on movements in the yield of the current coupon GNMA. If the current coupon falls by no less than one percentage point but no more than two points, then the balance will amortize by 5 percent over the period. If the current coupon falls by at least two points but no more than three points, then the balance amortizes by 10 percent, and so on. The benefit of the indexed amortization structure is the greater predictability of the cash flows, because the prepayment options of this synthetic mortgage will be economically exercised.

Swap Pricing

Long-Term Interest Rate Swaps—Early swap pricing was driven by the desire to exploit a specific arbitrage by each of two counterparties (such as the need of BBB-rated U.S. corporate issuers to raise fixed-rate funds and Japanese banks to raise floating-rate funds), and the dynamics of pricing were simple. Swap pricing took advantage of the comparative advantage each party had in different capital markets, and the agreed-upon price was simply what each individual transaction could stand while making economic sense for both parties. However, as the users of swaps have multiplied, so have the influences on pricing. Counterparties use swaps for vastly different applications, and they compete with each other on a price basis for the same basic product. Additionally, the market now has a significant number of market makers or swap traders who are continually positioning in anticipation of future market changes. This professional market trading has gradually established a commodity price level for the product. Such trading has eliminated or reduced the returns of many arbitrages.

The price of a swap is generally quoted as the all-in fixed rate that will be exchanged, and the fixed-rate levels will reflect the general level of corporate borrowing rates. The major influences on the commodity price therefore include:

- The absolute level of base (Treasury) interest rates,

- The shape of the yield curve,

- Hedging costs, and

■ The level of new issue spreads in corporate bond markets (domestic and Eurodollar).

The "commodity" price will apply to a standard swap, while the pricing of any particular swap will depend on how much it varies from the standard format. When variations are incorporated to suit one counterparty (and the other counterparty is relatively indifferent), there may be a significant price advantage to be gained by the counterparty willing to be accommodative.

Once a swap is established, its performance and value in the market are quantified in the same way as those of a fixed-rate coupon bond. The fixed-rate payment yield is used as a coupon equivalent, and for purposes of calculating a yield to maturity, the notional value is considered to be paid at the onset of the swap and repaid at the maturity of the swap. The floating-rate payment may be viewed as the financing cost of the principal. This essentially makes the risk of the swap position equivalent to that of a financed bond purchase.

Interestingly, the relative creditworthiness of different counterparties is seldom a major influence on the price of a swap—in stark contrast to most fixed interest markets. The primary reason is that the exposure of the counterparties is limited to the difference between the interest rate levels being exchanged; no principal is at risk. We outline additional reasons in Appendix A to this chapter. Suffice it to say here that the usual price variation between a swap quoted to a double-A as opposed to a triple-B credit is frequently less than 5 bp per annum.

Short-Term Interest Rate Swaps—The arbitrage and pricing of interest rate swaps with maturities of up to three years is directly related to the pricing of futures contracts in Eurodollar deposits. This is because a strip of futures contracts—i.e., the purchase or sale of a series of consecutive maturity futures contracts—replicates the risk of an interest rate swap between three-month LIBOR and the fixed rate of the full strip. While there is a mismatch between the terms of the floating-rate indexes—three-month LIBOR versus six-month LIBOR—the use of strips to hedge short-dated vanilla swaps is accurate enough to keep their relative pricing within a few basis points (see Appendix B to this chapter for a more complete description of the pricing of Eurodollar strips).

Swaptions

Options are more and more frequently being combined with interest rate and currency swaps to create a variety of interest rate risk profiles. These combinations are grouped under the label "swaptions." Before we describe the specifics of swaptions, it will be useful to briefly review the terminology of interest rate options in general.

A *call* option gives the *holder* (buyer) of the option the right, but not the obligation, to purchase a security at a specific price, known as the option *strike*. The holder pays the *writer* (seller) of the option a *premium* for this right. The holder will *exercise* this right if interest rates fall and the market price of the security rises above the strike. A *put* option gives the holder of the option the right, but not the obligation, to sell a security at a strike. The holder will exercise the put—i.e., sell it to the option writer, if the strike price is greater than the bid in the general market by the time the option *expires.*

The *swaption* market includes any options that give the buyer the right, but not the obligation, to enter into a swap on a future date. It also includes any options that allow an existing swap to be terminated or extended by one of the counterparties. These structures are also called cancelable, callable, or puttable swaps. Swaptions can be either *American,* exercisable at any point during the option term, or *European,* exercisable only on the last day of the option term. Swaptions that establish swaps when exercised may be puts or calls. In both cases, the fixed rate that will be exchanged is established when the swaption is purchased. The term of the swap is also specified. If a call swaption is exercised, the option holder will enter a swap to receive the fixed rate and pay a floating rate in exchange. The exercise of a put would entitle the option holder to pay fixed and receive floating. Note that the call/put terminology makes sense if you think in price terms. Calls become more valuable when prices rise and rates fall. The option holder will exercise a call swaption when rates have fallen from the strike level. The put swaption will be exercised when market rates rise above the fixed rate the option holder can pay (i.e., prices have fallen).

Swaptions generally are long-dated, with terms comparable to those of embedded options in the corporate bond market. For example, a European 7/3 put swaption allows the option buyer to pay a fixed rate and receive LIBOR in a four-year swap that can begin in three years. Swaptions can also be very short-dated, such as a three-month option to enter a ten-year swap.

Swaptions that allow the holder to either terminate or extend an existing swap are directly comparable to callable and putable corporate debt in their structures, and are therefore frequently referred to as callable or putable swaps. Because there is an existing swap in place during the option period, there is a choice on how to manage the premium payments. The premium can be paid up front or it can be built into the fixed-rate payment used to make the periodic interest rate exchanges. Premiums are quoted as a percentage of the notional amount. For example, an up-front premium of 25 bp on a $100 million call swaption would require a payment of $250,000. Exhibits 5 and 6 illustrate the dynamics of both types of swaptions.

The swaption holder is exposed to changes in the level of general corporate borrowing rates and to a change in the shape of the borrowing curve. In addition, a change in the implied volatility that the market is using to price swaptions will affect the value of the swaption. Specifically, the swaption is a call or put on the forward rate between the exercise date and the maturity of the swap. If rates were to rise or the curve were to flatten, a swaption that allowed the holder to pay fixed would become more valuable.

When combined with callable, putable, and straight bonds, swaptions can be used to create various synthetic fixed- and floating-rate structures that provide savings for issuers or increased yields for investors. For example, a borrower could issue a callable bond at a wider spread over Treasuries than the spread for a bullet bond. He or she could then combine this callable bond with the sale of a call swaption, and the all-in rate might end up below the rate on a bullet bond. This arbitrage opportunity exists when the swaption market values the call option embedded in debt securities

---

Exhibit 5.   European Callable Swap

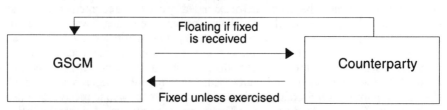

On settlement date:
  GSCM receives: Option premium
  GSCM pays: Floating rate, e.g., LIBOR
  Counterparty pays: Fixed rate in U.S. dollars
  Notional par: $25 million
  Maturity: Four years, or seven years if not exercised

On exercise date in year 4:
  Swap can be terminated, no additional payments

Exhibit 6.   Call Swaption

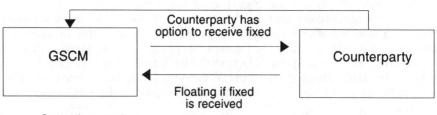

On settlement date:
  GSCM receives: Option premium

If option is exercised in year 3, a four-year swap begins in which:
  GSCM pays: Fixed rate in U.S. dollars on notional par
  Counterparty pays: Floating rate, e.g., LIBOR on notional par
  Notional par: $25 million
  Maturity: Four years from exercise date

more highly than the investor market does. Conversely, if the swaption market is valuing the call option at a lower level, this provides an asset buyer with an opportunity.

Warrants

A close corollary to a swaption is a warrant on a particular bond. Warrants give the purchaser the right, but not the obligation, to purchase or sell the bond of a particular issuer at a specific price at some future date. Warrants generally have terms of several years, and the underlying security also tends to be fairly long-dated—typically ten years or more to maturity.

There are two significant differences between a swaption and a warrant. First, the swaption is sensitive to the level of general corporate rates, as reflected in the swap pricing curve, while the warrant is sensitive to the new issue rate levels of a particular issuer. Second, if the buyer exercises the swaption, he or she is long only the difference between the fixed rate and the floating rate. There is actually no need to have an underlying principal investment. To exercise the warrant, however, the buyer must actually purchase the bond, and he or she is net long a fixed-rate asset. These differences contribute to the much greater liquidity available in the swaption market in comparison with the warrant market.[4] But for those willing to take on the credit exposure of a particular issuer, the warrant market can provide an excellent means of acquiring relatively inexpensive long-term volatility.

Caps/Collars

Although the cap market has been in existence for almost as long as the swap market, it has remained relatively small. Within the last several years, however, it has seen a marked increase in activity and liquidity. The cap market is an option market. Strikes are set at particular interest rate levels, although the convention for put/call terminology is based on price levels. For example, a cap is simply considered to be a series of consecutive expiration puts on a short-term interest rate. When rates rise and prices fall, the puts become more valuable. The standard vanilla cap uses three-month LIBOR as the underlying rate, and all of the individual cap resets are struck at the same rate level. The buyer pays a premium at the beginning of the cap period to the cap writer. In return, the writer of the cap has the obligation to make payments to the buyer in an amount equal to the greater of zero or the difference of the spot market rate minus the strike rate of the cap on each reset date. Premiums are quoted as a percentage of the notional amount. For example, a premium of 10 bp or a $100 million cap would require a payment of $100,000. Exhibit 7 illustrates a standard cap.

The cap market has developed as many derivatives and customizations as those seen in the swap and standard option markets combined. The underlying rate can be something other than three-month LIBOR. It might be for a different term, such as one- or six-month LIBOR, or even a completely different rate, such as prime or commercial paper. Amortizing balances, mixed strike levels, and in particular, com-

---

4 Once the warrant is exercised, of course, the position has the liquidity of the underlying corporate note issue.

Exhibit 7. Standard Cap

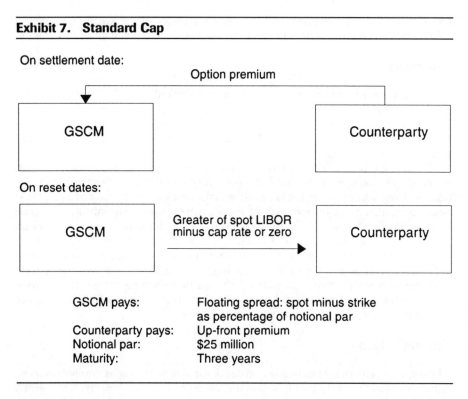

On settlement date:

Option premium

GSCM

Counterparty

On reset dates:

GSCM

Greater of spot LIBOR
minus cap rate or zero

Counterparty

GSCM pays:	Floating spread: spot minus strike as percentage of notional par
Counterparty pays:	Up-front premium
Notional par:	$25 million
Maturity:	Three years

binations of purchases and sales of options are all fairly common. The most common variations include:

- *Floors.* The buyer purchases a series of consecutive expiration calls on a short-term rate. (Again, note that the terminology relates to prices although the strikes are expressed as interest rates.) The writer receives a premium and is obligated to pay the greater of zero or the difference between the strike rate minus the spot market rate at the expiration date of the periodic option.

- *Collars.* To offset the expense of purchasing a cap, the buyer sells a floor on the same underlying rate. Typically, the cap strike is higher than the floor strike.

- *Corridors.* To offset the expense of purchasing a cap, the buyer sells another cap with a strike rate above that of the long cap, e.g., long a 10 percent cap on three-month LIBOR and short a 13 percent cap on three-month LIBOR. The same could be done with a floor, except that the floor sold would be struck at a lower rate than the floor purchased.

The sizes of cap transactions vary from $5 million to $500 million, with an average range of $25 million to $50 million. Maturities range from 3 months to 12 years. For the shorter maturity caps, there is a direct comparison with strips of exchange-traded options on Eurodollar futures, which are traded on the Chicago Mercantile Exchange. Liquidity in the options is not as great as in the futures, however,

Exhibit 8.   Summary of Terminology

Product	Buy	Sell
Fixed/Floating Swap	Pay fixed. Receive floating.	Pay floating. Receive fixed.
Cap	Pay premium. Receive greater of zero or market minus strike.	Receive premium Pay greater of zero or market minus strike.
Floor	Pay premium. Receive greater of zero or strike minus market.	Receive premium. Pay greater of zero or strike minus market.
Put Swaption	Pay premium. Option to pay fixed and receive floating.	Receive premium. If exercised, receive fixed and pay floating.
Call Swaption	Pay premium. Option to receive fixed and pay floating.	Receive premium. If exercised, pay fixed and receive floating.
Put Warrant	Pay premium. Option to issue bond.	Receive premium. If exercised, buy fixed-rate bond.
Call Warrant	Pay premium. Option to purchase bond.	Receive premium. If exercised, issue fixed-rate bond.

so the pricing difference between exchange-traded options and over-the-counter (OTC) caps will be wider than the difference between strips[5] and swaps.

Terminology

The nomenclature listed in Exhibit 8 is generally accepted, although not all traders bother using the bid/offered terms. Many prefer simply to state the desired position—for example: "The customer wants to pay fixed and receive floating." Being specific helps to reduce the communication problems that can arise, particularly with complex structures.

---

5 A series of consecutive-maturity futures contracts.

DERIVATIVE COMBINATIONS

Swaps, caps, and options can be applied in a wide variety of situations. This section presents a selection of applications that, while in no way complete, provides a representative sample of the myriad uses of these products for such purposes as financing, investing, liability management, hedging, or pure speculation. Some of the examples cited are applicable to more than one of the categories.

Synthetic Floater

Many money managers and banks are interested in acquiring floating-rate assets that have a positive spread to LIBOR. Synthetic floaters can be created to provide LIBOR plus 15 bp or more, depending on the level of credit risk the customer is willing to accept. Banks in particular are very willing buyers at levels of LIBOR plus 20 bp for a two- to three-year issue of a double-A credit. Naturally, these synthetic assets should be compared with original issue floaters to determine their relative value.

The first step in creating a synthetic floater is to purchase a fixed-rate asset with the desired maturity. The cleanest structures could use a corporate note or a credit card asset-backed security. These securities have fixed coupon levels and no prepayment risks, although credit is still an issue. A swap is then arranged in which the customer would pay fixed and receive floating, e.g., the three-year Treasury rate plus 50 bp versus six-month LIBOR. Again, in order to have the cleanest arbitrage, the reset dates of the swap should match the coupon dates of the fixed-rate asset.

Synthetic Fixed Rate

Another fairly straightforward use of a swap is the reverse of the above transaction: A floating-rate asset is combined with a swap in which the customer pays floating and receives fixed. The transaction can be used to hedge a decline in floating rates or as an arbitrage to achieve a higher fixed-rate return than might be available in the underlying markets.

Yield Curve Positions

In a yield curve swap, the payment exchange on each reset date is based on two floating rates within the same market: for example, a short-term rate such as the three-month Treasury bill yield and a long-term rate such as the yield to maturity of the then-current 10-year Treasury note. Because both rates are floating and the notional amount underlying each of the yields is set to equalize dollar duration, only spread risk exists in this position; there is no exposure to changes in the general level of interest rates. One counterparty pays the yield spread as of the reset date. The other counterparty pays a fixed yield spread. Options on the shape of the yield curve can also be built into caps and floors, for either a single period or multiple reset periods. There also is no reason why the yield spread must be between two securities of the same market. For example, the yield spread between benchmark 10-year issues in two government bond markets could also serve as the basis for a swap, cap, or option. Yield spread derivatives may be very useful for asset allocations that define target yield spreads triggering a swap between markets.

Embedded Option Structures

The combination of swaptions with securities containing embedded options probably provides greater opportunities for picking up additional value than do the straight swap arbitrages that have been used for many years. This is true because the swaption market has not yet become a commodity market—and it seems unlikely to become one, since the valuation of long-dated options involves numerous assumptions. Issuers in particular have been fairly aggressive in using the swaption market to achieve lower costs of funding than would otherwise be available. This has worked in both directions, fostering the creation of synthetic bullets as well as synthetic callable and putable bonds.

Exhibit 9 illustrates a synthetic bullet issuance, created by combining a callable bond issue with the sale of a call swaption.

Exhibit 9.   Synthetic Bullet Issuance

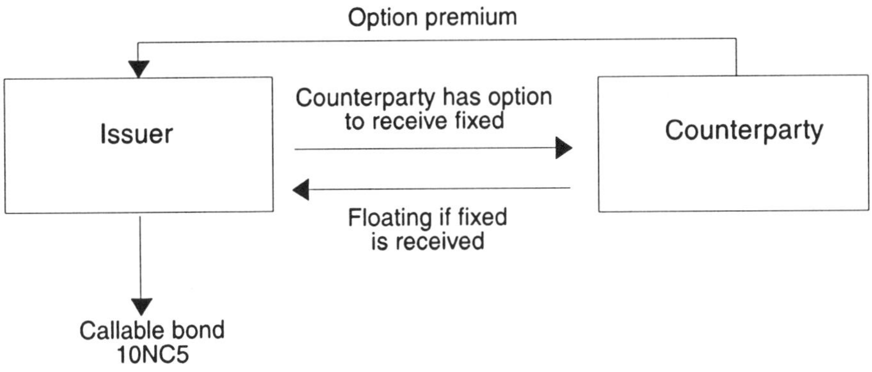

```
On settlement date:
    Issuer receives:        Option premium
                            Proceeds of callable bond issue

If rates rise, the swaption will not be exercised:
    Issuer pays:            Callable bond coupon

If rates fall, the swaption will be exercised:
    Issuer:                 Borrows at floating to call bond
                            Pays fixed in swap
    Counterparty:           Floating rate, e.g., LIBOR
    Notional par:           $25 million
    Maturity:               Five years from exercise date,
                            Ten years from settlement
```

Another possibility arises because the long-dated options embedded in corporate bonds are frequently priced to relatively low levels of implied volatility compared with the implied volatilities found in the liquid capital markets. This suggests a trading opportunity for those with the capacity to take on and manage the option exposures. For example, consider the following situation:

Putable Bond
        Term: 30-year with put to the issuer in year 7
        Coupon: 9.35% fixed
        Credit Spread: 7-year Treasury plus 89 bp = 9.35%
Bullet Credit Spreads
        7-year: Treasury plus 112 bp = 9.59%
        30-year: Treasury plus 142 bp = 9.84%.

Empirical Option Value
        9.35% coupon, 7-year discounted at Treasury plus 112 = 98.84
        1.16 for call
        9.35% coupon, 30-year discounted at Treasury plus 142 = 95.40
        4.60 for put

Using the above pricing as inputs, Goldman Sachs's option valuation model calculates implied volatilities in the 6.5 percent to 7.0 percent range for this embedded option. The same option, if offered outright in, for example, a put swaption, would probably be priced with an implied volatility of 9.0 percent. This difference in volatilities affords an excellent relative value opportunity for investors.

WHICH PRODUCT FITS?

The products illustrated above provide a variety of opportunities to the sophisticated investor or issuer. The choice of which product to use will be based primarily on the specific risk profile that the product supplies: fixed or floating, asymmetric versus symmetric interest rate exposure, etc. Additionally, there are several other criteria that can and should influence the choice. We outline the major issues below.

Liquidity

For the long-term investor, liquidity is not going to be a significant consideration. But for a short-term trader who is taking a position on the direction of rates, there is clearly a reason to consider bid-asked spreads on the various instruments. The most liquid instrument is the vanilla swap, with a bid-asked spread of 6 bp. In the cap market, the bid-asked spread varies with the term of the cap, from 6 bp for 2 years to 20 bp for 5 years and 35 bp for 10 years. For both instruments, the more customized are the payment specifications, the less liquid will be the secondary market. Swaptions have roughly the same liquidity as other OTC options of comparable maturity. By contrast, warrants are very illiquid and should be used only with a long-term horizon.

A swap, swaption, or cap can be reversed in any of three ways. The first is to assign the contract. This means that the counterparty that wants to close the contract must locate a replacement for itself that will meet the existing counterparty's credit and pricing requirements. The second way is to reverse the contract with the original counterparty. Both of these techniques would allow the contract to be removed from this counterparty's books, eliminating both price and credit exposure.

The third method is to enter into a new contract with a different counterparty that offsets the initial contract's price risk. The initial counterparty does not need to be involved in the process. There are two drawbacks to this method: Credit exposures are increased, and the contracts must still be managed, logistically and on the books.

Documentation

Swap documentation for both interest rate and currency swaps is relatively simple, typically consisting of two parts. Initially, one counterparty sends a confirmation to the other for acknowledgement (usually sent by telex or fax), outlining the rate and payment terms of the swap. This is followed by a complete 10-12 page contract containing all of the more detailed provisions of the swap. This may be either a deal-specific contract or a master agreement that allows the two parties to do multiple swap transactions off the same master document simply by using confirmations for each individual swap.

The swap contract usually contains the following provisions: rate and payment terms; the representations and warranties of the parties; a specification of events of default and termination events; and various mechanical matters, such as assignability and governing law. In addition, the contract may contain a guarantee whereby the credit of a counterparty is supported by some other entity, typically its parent. Also, some counterparties with weaker credits may be required to document any collateralization of their obligations.

In mid-1985, the International Swap Dealers Association (ISDA) published a "Code of Standard Wording, Assumptions, and Provisions for Swaps," with the intention of standardizing interest rate swap contracts used by different counterparties. The code covers the definition of cash flow and the calculation of amounts payable at early termination. Credit-related issues are left to parties to negotiate among themselves. The code comes in two forms, one applying to interest rate swaps, the other to currency swaps.

APPENDIX A

Credit Exposure

Swaps

Matching or hedging the price risk of swap positions does not reduce either counter-party's exposure to credit risk. Credit exposure depends on the joint probability of an adverse move in interest rates and a performance failure by the swap counterparty. Moreover, because swap contracts are usually medium-term and do not normally provide for voluntary early termination, the credit risk involved is essentially medium-term in nature.

It is important to note that the amount at risk under a swap is not the principal amount of the swap. The potential loss is the cost of reestablishing a contract with the swap's interest and currency flows at current market rates, i.e., the difference in the swap contract's market value at the initial and the current interest rates. The value of the contract to the party receiving fixed-rate payments is the difference between the present values of the fixed-rate payments and the floating-rate payments.

Alternatively, the potential loss could be considered as the cost of reestablishing the swap payments by borrowing and investing in other markets. The counterparty could reestablish its floating-rate payments by issuing a floating-rate note with a coupon of LIBOR. Its fixed-rate receipts can be reestablished by purchasing a security or group of securities yielding payments identical to those on the swap. The potential loss is the difference between the discounted value of the two securities plus any issue costs.

In practice, the credit risk in swaps is small, not only because of the nature of the swap but because of the quality of counterparties. In general, corporations entering into swap transactions will be expected to contract only with high credit quality counterparties—typically prime banks. Even when two exactly matching transactions are identified, a bank will generally act as principal to both transactions. That is, it will "intermediate" the transaction to eliminate credit risk for the ultimate counterparties, to maintain confidentiality, and sometimes to facilitate cross-border payment flows. It is interesting to note that target returns for such intermediation—and the price differentiation of intermediary fees for differing credit qualities—are quite small. This suggests that banks consider their credit risk on swap transactions to be very low.

Swaptions, Caps, and Collars

For any option structure, the credit exposure is fairly insignificant for the writer of the option. The only cash inflow that the writer expects is the premium, and since this is generally received at the onset of the option period, the credit risk is limited. In cases where the premium payment is made over time the risk clearly increases but is still limited to the replacement cost of the position.

For the option buyer, the exchange of the premium is only the beginning of the credit exposure. However, the exposure can be valued in much the same way as in the case of a swap. The notional amount of the option is not at risk. The exposure is limited to the cost of reestablishing the cash flows of the position, which will be equivalent to the change in the present value of the payments that would be received under the current interest rate structures and those that were used in initially pricing the option.

APPENDIX B

Eurodollar Strips versus Swaps

Contract Definition

Two types of Eurodollar futures are traded on the Chicago Mercantile Exchange. The original (and most liquid) contract is based on the interest level of three-month LIBOR. The second contract, introduced in April 1990, is based on one-month LIBOR. We will focus on the three-month contract, which is the one used most frequently for swap hedging and pricing. The nominal size of this contract is $1 million; the purchaser of the contract is buying an interest rate level for a forward three-month period. The forward period covered by the contract begins two days after the final trading day of the contract and ends 90 days later. The interest rate is equal to the price of the future subtracted from 100. For example, a purchase price of 91.00 reflects an annual simple interest rate of 9.0 percent. The minimum change in the futures price is essentially 1 bp[6] of simple interest yield; 90.00 to 90.01 is equivalent to a yield change from 10.0 percent to 9.99 percent.

Note that only an interest rate level is purchased—there is no actual investment purchase. This is because the contract is settled with cash and does not require physical delivery. The cash settlement procedure is just a continuation of the daily *marking to market* procedure used in all futures markets. Each day the difference between that day's closing price and the previous day's closing price (or the trade price if the position was established during the day) is matched with a cash payment. Money is paid to the clearinghouse if the trade is down or is received from the clearinghouse if the trade is profitable. The interest rate that the buyer of the future "locked in" is realized through the combination of the net margin payments plus the interest earned on an actual three-month investment purchased on the last trading day of the contract at the settlement LIBOR rate. For example:

Purchase one June 1990 three-month LIBOR future @ 91.50
$\quad$ 100 − 91.50 = 8.50 = simple annual LIBOR rate.

Final settlement price on June 18,1990 @ 92.00
$\qquad$ Cumulative margin payments

$\qquad\quad$ 50 × .0001 × 1,000,000 × 90/360	$1,250
$\qquad$ Cash investment @ 8.0%	
$\qquad\quad$ $1,000,000 × .08 × 90/360	$20,000
$\qquad$ Total dollar return	$21,250
$\qquad\quad$ $21,250/$1,000,000 × 360/90	8.50%

Another way to think about the futures contract is to recognize that it is itself a forward three-month swap. The buyer of the contract is essentially receiving the fixed rate implied by the futures purchase price and paying the floating LIBOR available at

---

6 One basis point equals 1/100 of 1 percent, i.e., 0.01 percent or 0.0001.

the final settlement of the future. If rates fall, the buyer will have a net credit from the margin flows. If rates rise, there is a net debit.

Each future covers a three-month period.[7] By purchasing a consecutive series of contracts, the buyer can fix a longer-term rate. For example, buying one contract each in June 1990, September 1990, December 1990, and March 1991 would have fixed a rate for the period from June 1990 to June 1991 on $1 million. The effective rate would be the compounded rate of the individual futures rates, as we illustrate in the following example:

Purchase one June 1990 three-month LIBOR future @ 91.50		8.50%
Purchase one Sept. 1990 three-month LIBOR future @ 91.40		8.60%
Purchase one Dec. 1990 three-month LIBOR future @ 91.20		8.80%
Purchase one March 1990 three-month LIBOR future @ 91.00		9.00%

Compounded strip rate:

$(1 + .085 \times 90/360)(1 + .086 \times 90/360)(1 + .088 \times 90/360)$
$(1 + .09 \times 90/360)$ 9.01%

(Note that the compounded rate is expressed as an annual simple interest rate and may need to be converted to semiannual bond-equivalent yield.)

Hedge Ratios

The transaction outlined above is a simplistic representation of the construction of a futures strip to replicate a long-term asset. In practice, the dollar duration of the strip must match the dollar duration[8] of the target asset in order to have an accurate hedge or synthetic security. If the target asset is a coupon-bearing note or an interest rate swap, this means that the face value of the strip will be different from the face value of the note or swap, although the contract months used would generally closely match the calendar period covered by the note. The example below is an illustration of the comparison between a Eurodollar futures strip and a two-year swap in transforming a floating-rate asset into a fixed-rate asset.

An Example

An investor currently has $100 million dollars invested in a three-month LIBOR floater but is concerned about a possible decline in interest rates and wants to fix his asset yield for two years. The investor can enter a swap to pay floating and receive a fixed rate at some spread over the two-year U.S. Treasury note yield. Alternatively,

---

7 This is true for the original contract. The newer one-month Eurodollar future covers a one-month period.
8 Dollar duration quantifies the change in the present value of a security resulting from a unit change in yield. The unit change can be a percentage point or a basis point; the magnitude of the change is significant only in that the change must be consistent among all the securities being evaluated. Dollar duration per basis point change is the same measure as the "dollar value of an 01."

the sale of a strip will offset the floating-rate exposure and effectively fix the asset yield. In both cases the investor continues to hold the LIBOR floater.

Trade date: September 18, 1990
Swap terms: Pay six-month LIBOR and receive two-year
                  Treasury yield plus 45 bp = 8.55%

                  Notional amount $100,000,000

                  Dollar duration (per basis point) at 8.55%
                  equals 0.01806% × $100,000,000, or $18,060

Strip: $100 million three-month LIBOR investment
                  plus 89 each of December 1990 to June 1992

                  Spot plus strip dollar duration equals $25 × 100
                  plus $25 × 89 × 7, or $18,075

The strip has a term yield equal to the compounded rate of the individual contracts. If we assume the following structure of prices:

Spot	=	92.00	Sep 91	=	91.60
Dec 90	=	91.90	Dec 91	=	91.50
Mar 91	=	91.80	Mar 92	=	91.40
Jun 91	=	91.70	June 92	=	91.30

The term rate is calculated as:

$$[1 + 0.08\,(90/360)][1 + 0.081\,(90/360)][1 + 0.082\,(90/360)][1 + 0.083\,(90/360)] \times$$
$$[1 + 0.084\,(90/360)][1 + 0.085\,(90/360)][1 + 0.086\,(90/360)][1 + 0.087\,(90/360)] =$$
$$1.18$$

The total compound return for the two years is 18 percent. Note that this is an estimate and is not locked in, owing to the need to adjust the number of futures contracts to match the duration of the swap.

To express the total compound return as a semiannual bond equivalent:

$$\left(1.18^{\left(\frac{365}{2 \times 720}\right)} - 1\right) \times 2 = 8.56\%$$

This strip structure is not the only possibility. As long as the overall dollar duration of the futures or futures and cash positions are equivalent, then the swap will be price-hedged for parallel shifts in the yield curve. One frequently used variation of the strip is a *stack,* in which the contracts are not spread evenly over the maturity spectrum but are executed all in one, or a few, specific forward periods. For example, rather than use 89 contracts in each of the first seven futures, the hedger could use a stack of 623 December 1990 contracts. This has the same dollar duration but adds an exposure to a nonparallel shift in the yield curve.

The fixed rates available from the swap and strip alternatives are essentially the same: 8.55 percent versus 8.56 percent. The choice between the two will therefore depend on such secondary considerations as (1) whether the floating-rate asset resets quarterly (strip) or semiannually (swap); (2) liquidity preference, which would generally favor the futures markets; (3) an ability or a desire on the investor's part to actively manage a futures position that requires cash margining; and (4) tax and accounting treatments—these vary, and one may be preferable.

APPENDIX C

Yield/Price Formulas

Unless otherwise noted, yield formulas are annualized rates. The abbreviations used are:

$$
\begin{array}{rcl}
d & = & \text{Discount yield} \\
i & = & \text{Simple interest yield} \\
y & = & \text{Bond-equivalent yield} \\
t & = & \text{Days from settlement to maturity} \\
C & = & \text{Annual coupon rate} \\
F & = & \text{Face or par value of security} \\
PV & = & \text{Present value} \\
P & = & \text{Price ex-accrued} \\
A & = & \text{Accrued interest} \\
IRR & = & \text{Internal rate of return}
\end{array}
$$

Yields

Simple Interest

$$
i = \frac{\text{income}}{\text{cash invested}} \times \frac{360}{t}
$$

Discount Interest

$$
d = \frac{\text{income}}{\text{face value}} \times \frac{360}{t}
$$

U.S. Bond-Equivalent Yield

$y = $ coupon period internal rate of return $\times 2$

$$
P + A = PV = \frac{0.5C}{(1 + IRR)^{n_1}} + \frac{0.5C}{(1 + IRR)^{n_2}} + \cdots + \frac{100}{(1 + IRR)^{n_m}}
$$

where n equals the days from settlement to cash flow date expressed in semiannual periods and C equals the coupon rate multiplied by 100. Price plus accrued interest is the spot market full price (present value) for the bond.

Accrued Interest Calculations

Note that the calculation of accrued interest is different for Treasury bonds and corporate bonds. Treasury accrued is calculated by multiplying one-half the coupon rate by a ratio of the actual days from the last coupon to the actual days in that coupon period. For example, assume a coupon rate of 8.0 percent payable May 15 and November 15 annually. We calculate the accrued interest on a trade that settles on September 15, 1990, as:

$$A = F \times 0.04 \times \frac{123}{184}$$

Accrued interest for corporate bonds is calculated based on a 30/360-day calendar. That is, we assume that each month has 30 days, and a full year therefore has only 360 days. Assuming the same coupon rate and payment dates as in the Treasury calculation, the accrued interest is:

$$A = F \times 0.04 \times \frac{15 + 30 + 30 + 30 + 15}{180}$$

Conversions

Simple to Bond-Equivalent

$$y = \left(1 + \left(i \times \frac{t}{360}\right)^{\left(\frac{365}{2 \times t}\right)} - 1\right) \times 2$$

Discount to Bond-Equivalent

If maturiy is less than six months:

$$y = \frac{365 \times d}{360 - (d \times t)}$$

If maturity is greater than six months:

$$y = \left(1 - \left(d \times \frac{t}{360}\right)^{-\left(\frac{1}{2 \times \frac{t}{365}}\right)} - 1\right) \times 2$$

Annual to Bond-Equivalent

$$y = \left[(1 + A)^{0.5} - 1\right] \times 2$$

APPENDIX D

Legal and Regulatory Issues

Swap documentation was developed through a combination of contract law and standard loan documentation. In legal terms, swaps are relatively straightforward contracts and are governed by the contract law of whatever jurisdiction the parties specify, typically either New York or British law. The ISDA has removed a significant hurdle to swap execution by creating a standardized documentation process that is widely used by the dealer community. The two major issues that are covered in the documentation are the responsibilities of the counterparties in the events of default and early termination of swaps. Standard documentation is not currently available for the other derivative products.

Default

As in standard loan documentation, the events of default usually include:

- nonpayment, although in most cases there is a grace period;
- failure to perform covenants other than promises to pay;
- making of representations and warranties that are incorrect in any material aspect;
- mergers involving the defaulting party in which it is not the surviving entity or in which the surviving entity does not pick up the contract; and
- lapse of a credit support document.

In addition, some contracts include a cross-default clause that ties performance on the swap contract to performance on all other swap contracts or debt outstanding with that counterparty.

Other circumstances are usually specified in which the swap may be terminated without either counterparty being in default. These include optional terminations agreed to by both parties, material credit decline as a result of merger when no available alternative is present, terminations in the event of the imposition of withholding taxes (in cross-border swaps),[9] and terminations due to supervening illegality—that is, when changes in laws, regulations, or treaties make payments under the swap illegal.

Early Termination

The ISDA Code provides three different options for settlement in the event of early termination:

---

9 Other contracts require the payer to bear the costs in the event that withholding taxes are imposed and the counterparty had misrepresented the tax situation. The payer adjusts payments such that the net amount actually received by both parties free and clear of taxes is equal to the amount that the party would have received had no such taxes been withheld.

- ■ "Agreement value" fixes the profit or loss on the basis of quotations from market makers at the price of a replacement swap that would generate the same payment streams as the swap being terminated.

- ■ "Formula" calculates profit or loss on the basis of hypothetical alternative borrowings and investments available on the early termination date. Adjustments for an element of fault or differences in creditworthiness of the parties may be made by specifying spreads above or below the relevant borrowing and investment rates.

- ■ "Indemnification" allows the parties to calculate damages on the basis of a general indemnity.

Swap contracts typically are written on a "no-fault" basis and use two-way payment procedures in cases of early termination. Regardless of which, if either, of the counterparties causes the default, whichever suffers the greater loss is compensated by the other. A few contracts do stipulate that payments are to be made on a "fault" basis. In this case, the party suffering the greater loss recovers only if it cannot be held accountable for the event that caused the early termination.

Bankruptcy

Recently enacted legislation has significantly improved the protection afforded to nondefaulting swap participants in the event of the bankruptcy or receivership of a defaulting counterparty. Under the U.S. Bankruptcy Code and U.S. banking laws, a nondefaulting party may exercise its contractual right to terminate a swap agreement and set off its claims against the defaulting party's obligations and collateral. In addition, prepetition transfers related to the swap agreement are protected from avoidance attack. The definition of swap agreement is broad under both statutes and includes master agreements.

Exchange Controls and Withholding Taxes

In international swap transactions, exchange controls and withholding taxes may be a consideration. Exchange controls in one party's country may place limitations on the ability to make swap payments. Participants should take account of this prior to entering into any swap transaction.

Governments sometimes impose withholding taxes on payments (typically under loans) made out of one country to a resident of another. Where such taxes apply to payments by a swap counterparty, the swap contract typically includes gross-up provisions.

APPENDIX E

Tax and Accounting Considerations

Tax Treatment

To accurately compare the costs of various derivative products, the user must consider the relevant tax and accounting treatment. From a tax perspective, there are two issues to be considered: whether the gain or loss will be considered as capital or ordinary, and when the gain or loss will be recognized.

The capital or ordinary designation is based on the presence of a formal sale or exchange of securities. If securities are exchanged, as in a future contract or forward sale, then the transaction receives capital gain treatment. The only firm exception to this is in the case of a hedge of inventory, i.e., property held for sale to customers in the ordinary course of business. (Refer to *Arkansas Best Corporation v. Commissioner,* U.S. Supreme Court, March 1988.) A swap ordinarily does not involve the exchange of any principal, and consequently, the cash flows on the swap are treated as ordinary income or expense and are deductible (includable) in the year in which they accrue. When a swap is closed, any gain or loss is recognized at that time and is also treated as ordinary income or expense. Caps, collars, and floors are treated in a similar manner. The option premium is treated as ordinary income or expense and amortized over the option life. A call or put swaption is likely to receive this treatment, but there has been no definitive statement.

With respect to the timing of income recognition, the gain or loss from a future, which is marked to market, is recognized upon termination or at the close of the taxable year, whichever is earlier. The exception to this occurs when the futures are part of a hedge of inventory, in which case the gain or loss is treated as ordinary income. A forward is treated slightly differently: the capital gain or loss is generally recognized when the hedge is lifted.

Accounting Treatment

For swaps, the net amount due to or from a counterparty for a particular financial reporting period should be accrued and included in the determination of net income. Any gain or loss on termination of a swap used to hedge a liability (or asset) is deferred and amortized over the remaining term of the liability (or asset) or over the remaining term of the original swap, whichever is shorter.

The accounting treatment of futures is outlined in FASB Statement 80. This requires that a change in the market value of an open futures contract be recognized in the income statement as a gain or loss in the period of the change, unless the contract qualifies as a hedge under the hedge criteria specified in Statement 80. If these criteria are met, a change in the market value of the futures contract is usually reported as an adjustment of the carrying amount of the hedged item. Most accountants believe that if a forward contract meets the Statement 80 hedge criteria, then it also should be carried at market, with gains or losses deferred and recognized as an adjustment to the carrying amount of the anticipated debt.

This appendix is intended only to give an overview of the important tax and accounting considerations involved when evaluating the derivative products. It is neither comprehensive nor definitive, and customers should consult with their own experts in these fields for authoritative opinions.

APPENDIX F

Glossary

Accreting Swap: A swap in which the notional principal amount increases over the life of the swap in a specified manner.

Amortizing Swap: A swap in which the notional principal amount diminishes over the life of the swap in a specified manner.

Asset Swap: A swap arranged to create a synthetic asset.

Basis Point: One-hundredth of a percentage point, i.e., 0.01 percent.

Buyout: The assignment (i.e., sale) of an existing swap. This will usually involve an up-front payment, as it would be a coincidence if the existing swap were priced exactly at current market rates.

Call: An option that gives the holder the right, but not the obligation, to purchase an asset at the strike price.

Close: Agree to terms. Closing is not the same as commencement, completion of documentation, etc. Closing virtually always takes place on the telephone to be followed by a telex, telefax, or letter confirmation of the main terms. Documentation is negotiated and executed subsequently and often is not completed until after commencement.

Commencement Date: The date on which the accruals on the swap commence.

Confirm: Confirmation telex or letter. Usually sent immediately after closing, it includes the basic commercial terms of the agreed-upon transaction.

Collar: The combination of a short (long) cap and long (short) floor with a lower strike.

Corridor: The combination of a short (long) cap and a long (short) cap with a higher strike. Also, the combination of a long (short) put and a lower-strike short (long) put.

Deferred Coupon Swap: A swap in which the fixed payments are deferred and paid in the form of a higher coupon on the later dates.

Delay: The period between the time of execution and the commencement of accruals of payments.

Delayed Reset Swap: The exchange of the same base floating rate, such as six-month LIBOR, with one payment set as of the current reset date and the other payment set at the rate available on the previous reset date. Essentially, it is a means of trading the short-term yield curve movements with an exposure to rate changes.

Exchange Names: When a swap is close to being executed, the parties will exchange names, i.e., confirm the identity of the entity that will be acting as principal to the transaction. This is done to avoid possible problems after both sides are committed to terms. However, swaps are also executed subject to name approval.

Forward Swap: A swap with a commencement date more than six weeks forward. Up to six weeks is a common delay because of the number of swaps linked to Eurobond new issues, which close up to six weeks after launch.

Initial Exchange: Under a currency swap, principal is often exchanged between the counterparties on the commencement date. It flows in the opposite direction from the future interest payments, e.g., a payer of DM will receive DM on the initial exchange. The existence or absence of an initial exchange should always be specified.

Intermediary: A principal to two matching swap contracts. When two counterparties are both nonbank entities, an intermediary bank will often act as principal to both counterparties. An intermediary takes a spread for its services by entering into the two swaps at slightly different rates. A counterparty's contract stops with the intermediary, i.e., it cannot "look through" the intermediary to the ultimate counterparty.

ISDA: International Swap Dealers Association. An association of investment and commercial banks that are active in the swap markets. It was established in 1985 and has produced standardized contracts for interest rate and currency swaps.

LIBOR: London Interbank Offered Rate. Other quoted rates are the interbank bid rate, LIBID, and the average of the bid and asked rates, LIMEAN.

Marked to Market: The process by which the daily gains and losses on exchange-traded futures are recognized in cash payments to and from the exchange clearing-house.

Match Dates: To arrange a swap with specific floating-rate reset dates or fixed-maturity date, so as to match either an existing swap or a cash market obligation or investment. For instance, it is sometimes important to match dates to fix the interest costs on a floating-rate note.

Payer: The swap counterparty that pays the fixed rate and receives the floating rate.

Premium: The fee paid by the purchaser of an option to the seller of the option. Generally, premiums are paid at the beginning of the option period, but they may be built into coupon levels or into other annuity streams in a linked transaction.

Put: An option that gives the holder the right, but not the obligation, to sell an asset at the strike price.

Rate Setting: Establishing a floating rate for a particular period under a swap (also, the date for doing so).

Receiver: The swap counterparty that receives the fixed rate and pays the floating rate.

Reversal: A new swap entered into to exactly neutralize the effects of an existing swap; or an outright assignment (i.e., sale) of an existing swap.

Seasonal Swap: A swap in which the notional amount is adjusted to meet certain needs resulting from seasonal fluctuations in cash flows.

Spot: Strictly, a swap on which the first LIBOR fixing is immediate, and accruals commence in two business days. Generally, a swap with a commencement date less than one week ahead.

Spread: Strictly, the difference between two prices or yields. Generally, it refers to the difference between the fixed rate payable on a swap and the bond-equivalent yield on the appropriate U.S. Treasury note at the time of execution. It is often used as the bid or asked (offered) price for a swap.

Spread Lock: A swap where only the fixed-rate swap spread over the appropriate U.S. Treasury yield is agreed to at the present time. One counterparty will have the right to elect when that underlying Treasury rate is set in order to establish the absolute cost of the swap. This counterparty must set the rate during a specified period, and the swap must be entered or offset explicitly; this is not an option to enter a swap.

Step Up/Down: A swap with multiple fixed-rate payment levels. The levels are not subject to market movements and are therefore not floating, but are agreed to at the time the swap is established.

Strike: The price or yield at which a purchase or sale of an asset will occur if an option is exercised.

Subject to Name: A swap or offer of a swap in which all the terms are agreed to except the identity of the counterparty. An entity entering into a swap subject to name has the right to cancel the agreement if for some reason (e.g., credit) it is not able to contract with the entity concerned.

Synthetic/Synthetic Asset: A combination of a cash market security and swap to convert the income from the security into another form or currency.

Trigger Swap: A swap in which the fixed-rate payer does not make a payment during a period unless a predetermined condition is met. For example, the fixed payment is made only if the Treasury note yield at the reset date exceeds 10 percent.

Up-Front Payment: A payment made by one counterparty to the other, usually on the commencement date, when the ongoing fixed and floating cash flows are off spot market levels. It is agreed to at the time of execution.

Zero Coupon Swap: A swap in which the floating-rate payment is made on a current basis against the notional amount and the fixed-rate payment is made on a discount basis.

95 Off: Swap quote indicating a fixed rate of 0.95 percent per annum above the bond-equivalent yield of the appropriate U.S. Treasury note.

CHAPTER 6

Municipal Derivative Securities

Gary Gray
Managing Director
Patrick Cusatis
Associate

Lehman Brothers

INTRODUCTION

Beginning in March 1990 with the creation of Residual Interest Bonds (RIBS®)[1] by Lehman Brothers, numerous new municipal bonds with embedded contingent interest payment components have been introduced into the market. The interest rates associated with these bonds are dependent, to some extent, on future unknown levels of interest rates. This chapter describes, in a very simple manner, how to analyze and value these contingent interest securities.

The authors of this chapter are investment bankers specializing in new product development in the tax-exempt market and are acutely aware of the current confusion among market participants regarding municipal derivative securities. Most market participants are not familiar with assumptions underlying *expectational analysis.* Many participants hope that inverse floaters, embedded swaps and caps, and all the various acronyms would just go away. Others, however, are determined to take the time and invest the energy to understand derivative securities. It is for those brave participants who are willing to learn new skills that we have written this chapter.

---

1 Registered Trademark of Lehman Brothers, Inc.

The valuation of the bonds that we examine herein is dependent on what we call *expectational analysis*. By expectational analysis we mean that the cash flow and valuation of an asset are not found simply by discounting a known cash flow on a *Monroe* bond trader, but are dependent upon expectations of future levels of interest rates and the volatility of those rates. Therefore, it is crucially important to understand how the interest rate setting mechanism of the bond works and how the expectations of future interest rates are incorporated into valuation models.

The chapter begins with an attempt to define municipal derivative securities and explains how the yield curve quantifies, to some degree, expectations of future uncertain rates. To that end, we guide the reader through the mathematics underlying expectational analysis: full-coupon yield curve → implied zero yield curve → implied forward rates → implied tax-exempt forward rates.

The approach used in this chapter is to take a complex security like an inverse floater or a BEAR floater (BEARS[SM]),[2] analytically divide it into more simple securities or building blocks,[3] and sum and value the underlying components using a Derivative Asset Pricing (DAP) approach.[4]

The DAP approach is easily applied when dealing with "derivative" securities. Derivative securities are financial instruments whose value is derived from or based on the value of another security or on the level of an index. For example, the value of a stock option is dependent on, among other things, the value of the underlying share of common stock. The value of a Kenny-based interest rate swap, cap, or floor is dependent on the present and expected, as embodied in the yield curve, future levels of the Kenny Index when compared to a contractual fixed interest rate.

It is possible for financial engineers to build, model, and value complex derivative securities with optionlike features by analyzing them as combinations of the simpler underlying financial building blocks (e.g., fixed-rate bonds, zero-coupon bonds, swaps and forward contracts, and option contracts). This type of approach, which is common in the corporate finance market, is relatively new to municipal finance.

In successful derivative products, like CMOs in the mortgage market, CATS and TIGRS in the Treasury market, and inverse floaters in the municipal market, combinations of unique cash-flow streams may be created that are more highly valued by investors than a simple aggregate of the underlying streams. Investors may be willing to discount these unique streams at a lower rate, thereby paying a higher price. Or structural aspects of the transaction may enhance the tax characteristics of the cash flows, thereby increasing the value of a derivative security. Hence, until arbitrage activity, if it can be done, takes these advantages away, successful derivative products will have a positive *structure value* wherein the asset will have a value greater than the sum of its parts.

---

2 Service Mark of Shearson Lehman Brothers.
3 See Smithson, C.W., "A LEGO Approach to Financial Engineering: An Introduction to Forwards, Futures, Swaps and Options," *Midland Corporate Journal*, vol. 4 (no. 4, 1987), pp. 16–28.
4 See Gray, G., and K. Engebretson, "Residual Interest Bonds (RIBS)," *Municipal Finance Journal*, vol. 13 (no. 1, Spring 1992), pp. 1–29. They refer to their approach as a "Synthetic Asset Pricing Model."

The remainder of this chapter is arranged in the following manner. In the next section the yield curve is examined and the mathematics underlying expectational analysis is explained. Then we describe the building blocks of derivative securities, what they are and how they should be valued. Next we examine and value three complex municipal securities that currently exist in the municipal market—an inverse floater, a cap bond, and a BEAR floater. The last section is the conclusion. Valuation models are included in the exhibits that follow.

THE YIELD CURVE AND EXPECTATIONAL ANALYSIS

Theories of the Yield Curve

The valuation of a security whose cash flows depend on unknown future interest rates is a problem that has been addressed in the corporate derivatives market. Since the introduction of interest rate swaps in the early 1980s, and the recent trading of interest rate cap and floor options based on interest rate indexes, market participants have had to develop valuation models that attempt to project levels of future interest rates. As a basis for these projections, these models generally incorporate the term structure of interest rates.

In examining the yield curve, it is important that securities represented on a given curve differ only by duration or maturity and not by other factors, particularly risk of default. Typically, the shape of the taxable yield curve is determined by noncallable, riskless, liquid U.S. Treasury securities. Several hypotheses exist concerning the term structure of interest rates. The three most common explanations of the yield curve are the Pure Expectations Hypothesis, the Preferred Habitat Hypothesis, and the Liquidity Preference Hypothesis. Each of these hypotheses is briefly outlined below.

Pure Expectations Hypothesis

The *Pure Expectations Hypothesis* explains the yield curve as a function of expected forward rates. As such, the yield curve can be decomposed into a series of expected future short-term rates, which will adjust in such a way that investors receive equivalent holding period returns. The *traditional* form of this hypothesis implies that the expected average annual return on a long-term bond is the geometric mean of the expected short-term rates. For example, the two-period spot rate can be thought of as the one-year spot rate and the one-year rate expected to prevail one year hence. Under this theory, an upward sloping yield curve means investors expect higher future short-term rates; whereas an inverted yield curve implies expectations of lower future short-term rates. Since expected short-term rates are implied in the yield curve, an investor is indifferent between holding a twenty-year investment, a series of twenty consecutive one-year investments, or two consecutive ten-year investments. The more *modern* continuous-time version of the pure expectations hypothesis posits that, regardless of maturity, the expected one-year holding period return on all bonds is the same as a one-year bond. Under the pure expectations hypothesis, investors are assumed to be risk-neutral. This theory implies a flat yield curve when investors expect that short-term rates will remain constant.

Liquidity Preference Hypothesis

The *Liquidity Preference Hypothesis* is an extension of the pure expectations hypothesis. It states that long-term rates are composed of expected short-term rates plus a liquidity premium. The theory posits that most investors prefer to hold short-term maturities. In order to induce investors to hold bonds of longer maturities, they must be paid a liquidity premium. For example, an investor who prefers a bond with a two-year maturity can purchase a bond with a three-year maturity and sell the bond after two years; however, this incurs additional risk. The liquidity premium is risk compensation for investors who would otherwise invest in shorter maturities. The risk premium increases with time to maturity. For investors who prefer longer maturities, the risk premium represents additional compensation. The liquidity preference theory assumes that investors are risk-averse. This theory implies an upward sloping yield curve even when investors expect that short-term rates will remain constant.

Preferred Habitat Hypothesis

The *Preferred Habitat Hypothesis* recognizes that the market is composed of diverse investors with differing investment requirements. Some investors, such as corporations, prefer bonds at the short end of the yield curve while others, such as insurance companies and pension funds, require bonds with longer maturities. All investors prefer to invest so that the life of their assets matches that of their liabilities. In order to induce investors to move away from their preferred position on the yield curve, they must be paid a premium. For this reason, the preferred habitat hypothesis predicts that any maturities that do not have a balance of supply and demand will sell at a premium or discount to their expected yields.

The Mathematics of Expectational Analysis

In an effort to objectively value these contingent interest securities, continuous-time models have been developed that describe the yield curve in terms of one variable—the short-term, risk-free interest rate (the spot rate). Therefore, any long-term bond yield may be described by the current spot rate and a series of expected future spot rates. Most of the models used by practitioners, in order to present an objective valuation without regard to individual risk preferences, incorporate the *pure expectations* theory of the yield curve.

The sections that follow provide a simple description of the theory and mathematics underlying the projections associated with the models. The example that follows uses a full-coupon yield curve to calculate future forward interest rates that act as the basis to value-contingent interest securities—forwards, swaps, and options.

Implied Zero Rates

The implied zero rate is the discount rate that equates the cash flows of a full-coupon bearing bond to those of a comparable maturity zero-coupon bond. Since a zero-coupon bond makes no interest payments until maturity, the theoretical zero rate adjusts the full-coupon rate for the loss or gain associated with the periodic reinvestment of the semiannual interest payments.

Assume that a full-coupon bond makes a payment of $\$C_t$ (e.g., \$2.25), for time periods $t = 1, 2, 3, \ldots, n$. At time n, the full-coupon bond also pays the \$100 face value. Using Equation (1) below, we can directly derive a zero-coupon curve from a full-coupon curve. The zero discount rate, r_t, is the rate such that:

$$100 = \left[\sum_{t=1}^{n-1} \frac{C_t}{(1 + r_t)^t} \right] + \frac{100 + C_n}{(1 + r_n)^n} \tag{1}$$

Columns 3 and 4 of Table 1 represent a sample full-coupon annual and semiannual yield curve. As a starting point, the zero-coupon rate for the first time period is equal to the spot rate of 0.0220. This follows because a six-month, semiannual pay, coupon bond is equivalent to a six-month zero-discount bond. To calculate the *one-year* implied zero, we discount the known semiannual coupon payments (\$2.25) over one year by the known (six-month) zero rate (r_1) and solve for the remaining (one-year) zero rate (r_2) as follows:

$$100 = \frac{2.25}{1.022} + \frac{102.25}{(1 + r_2)^2}$$

Solving for r_2 gives us an implied one-year zero rate of 0.022505. Similarly, using the implied one-year zero rate from above, we now can solve for the 1.5 year implied zero rate (r_3) as follows:

$$100 = \frac{2.30}{1.022} + \frac{2.30}{(1.022505)^2} + \frac{102.30}{(1 + r_3)^3}$$

The zero rate (r_3) that solves this equation is 0.023015. In this manner, we continually solve for the zero rate (r_n) and use the results to calculate the next implied zero rate. Column 5 of Table 1 summarizes the implied zero-coupon yield curve for three years (six semiannual periods).

Table 1

Period (t)	Years	Annual Full-Coupon Rates	Semiannual Full-Coupon Rates	Implied Zero Rates (r_t)
1	0.5	4.400	2.200	2.200
2	1.0	4.500	2.250	2.251
3	1.5	4.600	2.300	2.302
4	2.0	4.800	2.400	2.402
5	2.5	4.900	2.450	2.454
6	3.0	5.000	2.500	2.507

Implied Forward Rates

Implied forward rates represent the expected short-term spot interest rate at some time in the future. For example, assuming semiannual rates, the 2-year forward rate is equal to the expected six-month rate two years hence. Using the pure expectations model, forward rates can be easily calculated from the zero-coupon yield curve derived in the previous section.

The forward rate for period 1, f_1, is equal to the zero rate, r_1. In general, the forward rate, f_t, for period t is calculated as:[5]

$$f_t = [(1 + r_t)^t / (1 + f_1)(1 + f_2) \ldots (1 + f_{t-1})] - 1 \qquad (2)$$

where r_t represents the zero-coupon rate for period t.

For example, using the zero-coupon curve from Table 2, we can derive forward rates as follows:

.5-year forward rate = 0.0220
1.0-year forward rate = $[(1.022505)^2 / (1.0220)]-1 = 0.02301$
1.5-year forward rate = $[(1.023015)^3 / (1.0220)(1.02301)]-1 = 0.02405$
2.0-year forward rate = $[(1.024017)^4 / (1.0220)(1.02301)(1.02405)]-1 = 0.02702$

Table 2 summarizes sample forward rates for the full-coupon yield curve presented and the implied zero-coupon curve derived in the previous section.

Table 2

Period (t)	Years	Annual Full-Coupon Rates	Semiannual Full-Coupon Rates	Implied Zero Rates (r_t)	Implied Forward Rate (f_t)
1	0.5	4.400	2.200	2.200	2.200
2	1.0	4.500	2.250	2.251	2.301
3	1.5	4.600	2.300	2.302	2.405
4	2.0	4.800	2.400	2.402	2.702
5	2.5	4.900	2.450	2.454	2.662
6	3.0	5.000	2.500	2.507	2.772

Implied Tax-Exempt Forward Rates

The previous sections addressed how to theoretically derive the expected future short-term taxable interest rates from a full-coupon taxable yield curve. This section

---

5 See Francis, J.C., *Investments—Analysis and Management* (New York: McGraw-Hill, 1991), p. 362.

addresses the valuation of contingent interest tax-exempt securities. Our focus is on how to introduce expectations of future short-term *tax-exempt* rates.

The exemption from federal and certain state and local income taxation of interest on tax-exempt bonds is a key investment feature for investors. All else equal, we expect the tax-exempt yield curve to be related to the Treasury yield curve as adjusted for taxes. However, because of the great diversity of issues, credit risk, and redemption features, the tax-exempt yield curve is not as *pure* as the Treasury yield curve is in forecasting future expected interest rates. Compared with Treasury securities, tax-exempt bonds have higher default risk, less liquidity, and embedded redemption features, creating an increased uncertainty of future cash flows.

Because of the uncertainties inherent in the municipal yield curve, participants in the municipal securities market generally have used taxable yield curves (e.g., LIBOR or Treasury) to predict future short-term taxable rates and by multiplying by a conversion ratio (e.g., 70 percent to 74 percent), convert them to tax-exempt equivalent rates. Gray and Engebretson[6] compared short-term Treasury yields (91-day Treasury bill) with short-term municipal yields (J.J. Kenny high-grade index) on a bond-equivalent yield basis for the period of September 1981 to August 1991. They found that the J.J. Kenny Index averaged 74 percent of the short-term Treasury rate. In the valuation analysis presented later in this chapter, the Treasury yield curve will be used to derive expected taxable short-term forward rates, f_t, and will be converted to tax-exempt forward rates by multiplying by 74 percent. *The implied tax-exempt forward rates are the crucial inputs that are used in the valuation procedures for the hedging and option components described in this chapter.*

THE BUILDING BLOCKS FOR MUNICIPAL DERIVATIVES

Complex derivative securities usually can be analyzed as a package of simpler securities or building blocks, whose value is dependent upon the sum of the underlying components. For the purposes of valuing municipal derivative securities, these building blocks can be broadly grouped into three categories:

1. *Debt or credit extension components*—fixed-rate bonds, zero-coupon bonds, and mortgage-style level amortizing debt.

2. *Hedging or price-fixing components*—interest rate forward contracts and interest rate swap contracts.

3. *Option or price insurance components*—interest rate floor and interest rate cap options.

The sections that follow describe each of the instruments, their payment characteristics, and their valuation procedures. We focus on municipal related instruments and applications and all of the hedging and option contracts are based on a municipal inde: The J.J. Kenny Short-Term Index (the "Kenny Index"). Special attention is given to the valuation of the hedging and option instruments and the influence of the expected short-term rate as implied by the yield curve.

---

6 See supra, note 3.

Debt Components

Definition and Use

The debt components of municipal derivative securities consist of the cash-flow obligations that may be thought of as the repayment of the principal portion of the security and the "normal" payment or accretion of interest on the security. In this chapter we consider three types of debt components:

1. A fixed-rate bond component that has a semiannual payment of interest at a fixed interest rate and the repayment of principal at maturity or redemption.

2. A zero-coupon bond component which has a semiannual accretion of interest at a fixed interest rate and the actual payment of accreted interest and the repayment of principal at maturity or redemption.

3. A level amortizing bond component which has a semiannual payment of both principal and interest, calculated at a fixed interest rate, such that the payments are equal.

Valuation

The valuation of debt components is familiar to many market participants. The fixed-rate bond component is valued like any fixed-rate municipal bond with semiannual cash flows. Similarly, the zero-coupon bond component simply is the discounted present value of a single expected future cash flow. The level amortizing bond component is similar to a semiannual pay mortgage and is simply valued by discounting expected future cash flows.

A similar characteristic for all of the debt components is that the present value of the debt component will decrease as the discount rate increases. Likewise, its value will increase as the relevant discount rate decreases (see Exhibit 1).

Exhibit 1. Present Value of Debt Component

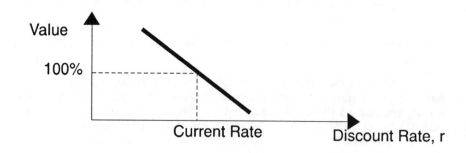

Hedging Components

Definition and Use

The hedging components of municipal derivative securities consist of interest obligations whose payment and valuation are dependent on future levels of interest rates or an index. In this chapter, we focus on contracts that are based on a formula that is dependent on the Kenny Index. The two types of hedging components that we consider are interest rate forward contracts and interest rate swap contracts.

An *interest rate forward contract* is an obligation under which two parties, a "floating-rate payer," and a "fixed-rate payer" agree to receive or make a net payment at a future point in time. This net payment is based on a "notional principal amount" (e.g., $1,000), the level of an interest index (e.g., Kenny) versus a prespecified fixed "reference rate" (e.g., 5.0 percent), and the number of days in the period (e.g., 1/2 year). For example, if the Kenny Index averaged 6.0 percent over the 1/2-year period and the reference rate equaled 5.0 percent, the fixed-rate payer would receive from the floating-rate payer the following amount:

$$\begin{pmatrix} \text{Notional} \\ \text{Amount} \end{pmatrix} \times \begin{pmatrix} \text{Period} \\ \text{Length} \end{pmatrix} \times \begin{pmatrix} \text{Kenny} \\ \text{Index} \end{pmatrix} - \begin{pmatrix} \text{Reference} \\ \text{Rate} \end{pmatrix} = \text{Forward Payment} \qquad (3)$$

$$(\$1000) \times (1/2 \text{ year}) \times (6.00\% - 5.00\%) = \$5.00$$

An *interest rate swap contract* is simply a series of forward contracts that have payoffs on a series of specified future dates. For example, assume that there are two parties to a three-year, semiannual payment Kenny swap with a reference rate of 5.00 percent and a notional amount of $1000. During any period in which Kenny averages greater than 5.00 percent, the floating-rate payer will make a payment to the fixed-rate payer in accordance with Equation (3), above. Conversely, when Kenny averages less than 5.00 percent, the fixed-rate payer will make a payment to the floating-rate payer as calculated by Equation (3). In general, when we analyze complex municipal derivative securities that have embedded interest components that perform similarly to Equation (3), we value them like interest rate swaps.

Valuation

The valuation of hedging instruments is more complex than the valuation of the debt components described above. Like any financial instrument, the present value of an interest rate forward or interest rate swap contract is equal to the discounted value of its anticipated future cash flows. Depending on current swap rates and expected forward rates, forward and swap contracts may have positive, zero, or *negative* present values.

As expected forward interest rates, f_t, rise, the value of an interest rate forward or swap contract to a fixed-rate payer rises. Conversely, as f_t falls, the value of forward

---

Exhibit 2.   Payoff Profile of Swaps and Forwards

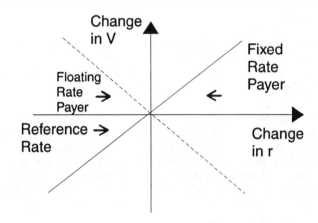

and swap contracts to floating-rate payers rises. For a payoff profile of forwards and swaps see Exhibit 2.

Derivative market participants value forwards and swaps based on the present value, discounted at the relevant zero-coupon discount rate, of the expected future cash flows associated with the instrument. This is the valuation technique underlying expectational analysis. For illustrative purposes, we use the yield curve shown in Table 2 to value a three-year, semiannual payment, Kenny interest rate swap with a reference rate of 3.60 percent—1.80 percent semiannually. We assume that the conversion ratio to convert from taxable forward rates to tax-exempt forward rates is 74.0 percent. From the standpoint of a fixed-rate payer, we develop Table 3:

Table 3.   Net Present Value of Swap to Fixed-Rate Payer

Period (t)	Year	Implied Zero Rates (r_t)	Implied Taxable Forward Rate (f_t)	Implied Tax-Exempt Forward Rate (74.0%)	Reference Rate	Difference	Present Value Difference
1	0.5	2.200	2.200	1.628	1.800	(0.172)	(0.168)
2	1.0	2.251	2.301	1.703	1.800	(0.097)	(0.092)
3	1.5	2.302	2.405	1.780	1.800	(0.020)	(0.019)
4	2.0	2.402	2.702	1.999	1.800	0.199	0.183
5	2.5	2.454	2.662	1.970	1.800	0.170	0.151
6	3.0	2.507	2.772	2.051	1.800	0.251	0.216

Exhibit 3.   Yield Curve (Semiannual Basis)

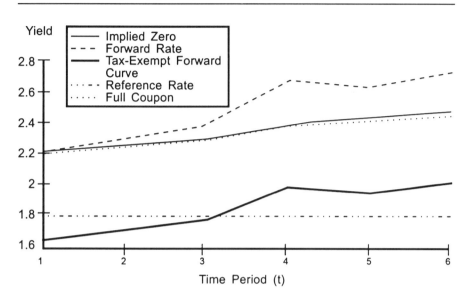

Exhibit 3 shows a graph of the taxable full-coupon curve, the taxable implied-zero curve (r_t), the taxable forward curve (f_t), and the tax-exempt forward curve, all on a semiannual basis. In the hypothetical interest rate environment shown above, the fixed-rate payer expects to make payments in periods 1 through 3 and receive payments in periods 4 through 6. The net present value of these payments discounted at the relevant zero-coupon rates is equal to 0.271.

Option Components

Definition and Use

The option or price insurance components of municipal derivative securities also consist of contingent interest obligations whose payment characteristics and value depend on unknown future levels and also on the volatility of the Kenny Index. The two types of option components on which we focus are interest rate cap and interest rate floor contracts.

An *interest rate cap* is an obligation designed to provide insurance against the rate of interest, in our case the Kenny Index, going above a specified level or Cap Rate, C. It is a contract between two parties, the "cap writer" and the "cap owner." The cap writer, in consideration of an up-front payment, agrees to make periodic payments to the cap owner in the event that the Kenny Index exceeds C (e.g., 5.0 percent) for a period of time. The payment is the greater of $0 and the product of a notional amount (e.g., $1,000), times the excess of the average Kenny Index above C, times the number of days in the period (e.g., 0.5 year). For example, if the Kenny Index averaged 5.0

percent or less during the period, the cap owner would receive $0. If the Kenny Index averaged 6.0 percent during the period, the cap owner would receive the following amount from the cap writer:

$$\begin{pmatrix} \text{Notional} \\ \text{Amount} \end{pmatrix} \times \begin{pmatrix} \text{Period} \\ \text{Length} \end{pmatrix} \times MAX \begin{pmatrix} \text{Kenny} \\ \text{Index} \end{pmatrix} - \begin{matrix} \text{Cap} \\ \text{Rate, 0} \end{matrix} \end{pmatrix} = \text{Payment to Cap Owner} \qquad (4)$$

$$(\$1000) \times (1/2 \text{ year}) \times MAX\,(6.00\% - 5.00\%,\, 0) = \$5.00$$

An *interest rate floor* is an obligation designed to provide insurance against the Kenny Index going below a specified level or Floor Rate, F. The floor writer, in consideration of an up-front payment, agrees to make periodic payments to the floor owner in the event that the Kenny Index is below F (e.g., 5.0 percent) for a period of time. Its payment profile is opposite to a cap in that the floor owner receives zero if the Kenny Index averages greater than or equal to F during the period. If the Kenny Index averages 4.0 percent during the period, the floor owner receives the following amount from the floor writer:

$$\begin{pmatrix} \text{Notional} \\ \text{Amount} \end{pmatrix} \times \begin{pmatrix} \text{Period} \\ \text{Length} \end{pmatrix} \times MAX \begin{pmatrix} \text{Floor} \\ \text{Rate} \end{pmatrix} - \begin{matrix} \text{Kenny} \\ \text{Index, 0} \end{matrix} \end{pmatrix} = \text{Payment to Floor Owner} \qquad (5)$$

$$(\$1000) \times (1/2 \text{ year}) \times MAX\,(5.00\% - 4.00\%,\, 0) = \$5.00$$

Valuation

The valuation of option instruments is even more complex than that of hedging instruments described above. Not only are the option values dependent on expectations or future interest rates inherent in the forward curves, but they are also dependent on the volatility of interest rates.

The payoff profiles for a cap owner and a cap writer are shown in Exhibit 4. It is assumed that the cap owner pays the cap premium to the cap writer as consideration for making the contingent interest payments as described in Equation (4). If the Kenny Index exceeds C, the cap owner will receive payments in accordance with Exhibit 4.

The payoff profiles for a floor owner and a floor writer are shown in Exhibit 5, and payments are made as described in Equation (5). If the Kenny Index is less than F, the floor owner will receive payments from the floor writer.

From the perspective of the cap and floor owners, a single payment is made, the cap premium or floor premium, for the purchase of interest rate insurance, and a stream of future cash flows will be received that is dependent on unknown future levels of the Kenny Index. The value of the cap and floor options are dependent on the expectations of future Kenny Index levels and the volatility of the Index. Below we briefly describe the process of cap and floor option valuation.

Like the other valuation methods discussed in this chapter, valuing cap and floor options involves estimating uncertain future cash flows. Since the cap and floor rates are fixed throughout the life of the option, option pricing concentrates on estimating the probabilities that the underlying index, in our case the Kenny Index, will exceed

Exhibit 4.   Payoff Profile of Cap Option

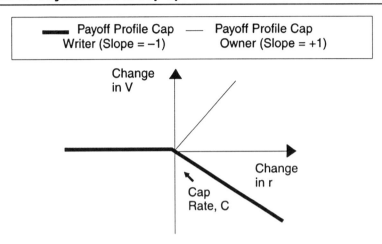

Exhibit 5.   Payoff Profile of Floor Option

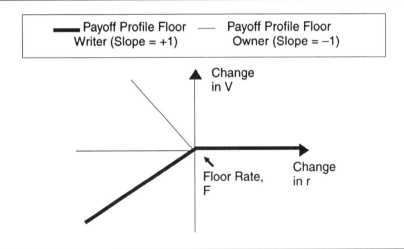

the cap or floor rate. Inputs to a typical option pricing model are the volatility of the Kenny Index, the time to maturity of the option, the specified level of the cap or floor option, and a risk-free rate of interest with which to discount cash flows (see Schedules 2.2, 3.1, and 4.2 in Appendix I of this chapter).

The volatility is used to estimate how extreme movements in the Index will be in the future. If the volatility is low over the length of the option, the Kenny Index is not expected to diverge much from the expectations of tax-exempt forward rates implied in the yield curve, and the value of the option decreases. The value of a cap

or floor option increases as volatility increases because it increases the probability that
the Kenny Index will move away from the implied forward rates. For the valuation of
interest rate caps and floors in the next section, we use a volatility estimate of 8.0
percent.

To arrive at values for the various cap and floor options described in the next
section, we use Black's model[7] for valuing interest rate options:

$$P_c = \sum_{t=1}^{T} \frac{\tau}{1 + \tau F_t} \, e^{-rt} \, [F_t N(d_1) - C N(d_2)] \tag{6}$$

where:

$$d_1 = \frac{\ln (F_t / C) + \sigma_F^2 \, t / 2}{\sigma_F \sqrt{t}} \tag{7}$$

$$d_2 = d_1 - \sigma \sqrt{t} \tag{8}$$

In Equation (6) above, the price of the cap, P_C is derived as a portfolio of 0.5-year
(τ-period) options, the last of which matures at time T; (F_t) represents the tax-exempt
forward rate in each period and C represents the cap rate. The cash flows are discounted
by the various zero-coupon risk-free rates of interest, r. $N(\cdot)$ represents the cumulative
standard normal density function. In (7) and (8), σ^2 is the volatility of the tax-exempt
forward rate.

Expected Kenny Rates (F_t) derived from the yield curve, and the implied zero
discount rates (r) are used to discount the expected cash flows. The discounted cash
flows are then adjusted for the probability distributions ($N(\cdot)$).

THE VALUATION PROCEDURE

The Derivative Asset Pricing Model

Gray and Engebretson,[8] in an analysis of residual interest bonds, used a derivative
asset pricing (DAP) model to analyze a complex security such as RIBs, by separating
it into its various underlying simpler components and valuing each component. Smith[9]
and Woolridge[10] have also used the DAP approach to value taxable inverse floaters.

Inherent to the DAP approach is the ability to assign a positive *structure value*
to cash flows, which enhances the value of the derivative security to a level that is
greater than the sum of the underlying parts. This enhanced value may be due to the
unique tax characteristics of the resulting cash flows, which increase the value of a
derivative security. The cash-flow characteristics of inverse floaters can be created

---

7 See Hull, J., *Introduction to Futures and Options* (Englewood Cliffs, NJ: Prentice-Hall, 1991), pp.
   350–351.
8 See supra, note 3.
9 Smith, D.J., "The Arithmetic of Financial Engineering," *The Journal of Applied Corporate Finance*
   (Winter 1989), pp. 49–58.
10 Woolridge, J.R., "An Economic Analysis of Residual Interest Bonds (RIBS)," Unpublished
   manuscript commissioned by Shearson Lehman Hutton, Inc., (February 1990).

synthetically by owning a fixed-rate bond and writing a fixed to floating interest rate swap that contains an interest rate cap. However, all of the interest associated with inverse floaters has been tax-exempt, while the interest associated with BEAR floaters, which have embedded interest rate swaps, has similarly been tax-exempt income. Therefore, tax-exempt inverse floaters and BEAR floaters, because of this tax treatment, have structural value in excess of the sum of their underlying components.

Valuation of the Securities

To say that there is a degree of uncertainty among traders, underwriters, and investors in the valuation of complex municipal derivative securities would be an understatement. With this in mind, we will now take the expectational analysis approach detailed earlier to project future levels of interest rates, layer in the building block components described, and couple them with the DAP model to provide a *theoretical* value for three specific municipal derivative securities: an inverse floater, a cap bond, and a BEAR floater. These valuations are theoretical and are not meant to be a market valuation of a specific issue. The capital markets frequently assign market values to securities that differ significantly from theoretical values.

For each of the valuations that follow, we assume a valuation date of November 2, 1992, and we use the Treasury yield curve at the close of business on that day as a basis for valuation of contingent interest payments (see Schedule 1 in Appendix I and Exhibit 6).

Exhibit 6.   Yield Curve as of 11/2/1992

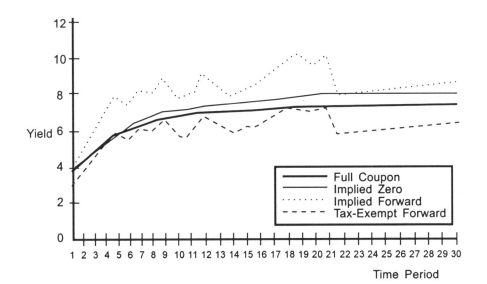

Valuation of an Inverse Floater

We now value AA-rated hospital revenue bonds that mature on February 15, 2012, and are subject to optional redemption on August 15, 2002 at a price of 102 percent, declining to 100 percent on August 15, 2004 (the "inverse floaters"). Assume that the inverse floaters pay interest prior to August 15, 1999, semiannually on August 15 and February 15, at a rate of 6.15 percent + (4.70 percent – Kenny Index), and thereafter at 6.15 percent per annum. Also assume that a "plain vanilla" 20-year comparable bond with similar call protection would currently yield 6.70 percent. What is the value of this municipal security?

The first order of business is to divide this complex security into a combination of simpler underlying securities. We start with an examination of the interest rate setting mechanism, in terms of the building block components discussed earlier. Graphically, the inverse floater rate versus the Kenny Index is shown below in Exhibit 7.

Exhibit 7.   Inverse Floater Interest Rate Profile

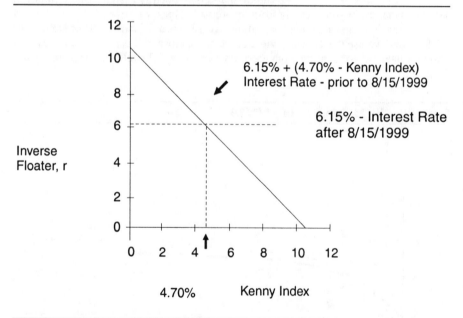

$$r = (6.15\%) + (4.70\% - \text{Kenny Index})\text{—prior to } 8/15/99$$

$$r = 6.15\%\text{—after } 8/15/99$$

The *debt component* of this inverse floater can be valued as a 6.15 percent fixed-rate bond with a maturity of 8/15/2012. The inverse floater also has a *hedging component* of the form (4.70 percent – Kenny Index) and a term of 8/15/99 that can be valued as an interest rate swap that expires on 8/15/99, under which the investor is the floating-rate payer and the issuer is a 4.70 percent fixed-rate payer. There is also an *option component* embedded in this transaction. During the period prior to 8/15/99, the interest rate formula does not allow the inverse floater rate to be less than zero for any interest period. This gives the inverse floater owner an embedded Kenny-based interest rate cap of 10.85 percent. Based on the above, the theoretical DAP value of the inverse floater may be expressed as:

$$\text{DAP Price}\begin{pmatrix}\text{Inverse}\\\text{Floater}\end{pmatrix} = \text{Price}\left[\begin{pmatrix}\text{Fixed}\\\text{Rate}\\\text{Bond}\end{pmatrix} + \begin{pmatrix}\text{Fixed-to}\\\text{Floating}\\\text{Swap}\end{pmatrix} + \begin{pmatrix}\text{Interest}\\\text{Rate}\\\text{Cap}\end{pmatrix}\right]$$

Valuation of Debt Component—The valuation of the 6.15 percent fixed-rate bond component is straightforward. One simply discounts, at the market discount rate of 6.70 percent, the cash flows of a plain vanilla 6.15 percent bond with a maturity of 8/15/2012 to get a debt component value of 94.007 percent.

Valuation of Hedging Component—The present value of the swap component is equal to the discounted value of its anticipated future cash flows. The Treasury yield curve of 11/2/92 gives implied zero-coupon, implied taxable forward rates, and tax-exempt forward rates shown in Schedule 1 in the Appendix. The present value swap rate, which represents expectations of the weighted-average short-term, tax-exempt rate over the swap period, for an interest rate swap maturing in 1999 is 4.878 percent (see Schedule 2.1 in Appendix). This results in a swap value for the 4.70 percent fixed- and pay-floating swap to be –0.579 percent.

Valuation of the Option Component—The present value of the interest rate cap option component, with a cap rate of 10.85 percent, a cap expiration date of 8/15/99, and an interest rate volatility assumption of 8.0 percent, calculated in accordance with Black's model, is 0.01 percent (see Schedule 2.2 in Appendix).

Valuation Summary—Combining the values of the three components (without structure value) of the valuation model, using the assumptions described above, gives the following DAP model valuation of the inverse floater:

DAP Price = 94.007% + (–0.579%) + 0.01% = 93.438%
(No Structure Value—see Schedule 2.3 in Appendix)

If we believe that the structure value inherent in the inverse floater is worth 15 basis points, we would discount the debt component cash flow at 6.55 percent rather than 6.70 percent and would have a value equal to:

DAP Price = 95.587% + (–0.579%) + 0.01% = 95.018%
(15 bp Structure Value—see Schedule 2.4 in Appendix)

Valuation of a Cap Bond

The next security that we value is a Baa1 general obligation bond that matures on October 1, 2016, and is subject to optional redemption on October 1, 2002, at a price of 101.5 percent, declining to par on October 1, 2004 (the "Cap Bond"). Assume that the Cap Bonds pay semiannual interest, prior to October 1, 1997, according to the formula 6.60 percent + max [0, Kenny Index – 3.50 percent], and thereafter at 6.60 percent per annum. Graphically, the interest rate on the Cap Bond versus the Kenny Index is shown in Exhibit 8. Also assume that a "plain vanilla" comparable bond with similar call protection would currently yield 7.15 percent: What is the value of the Cap Bond?

Exhibit 8. Cap Bond Interest Rate Profile

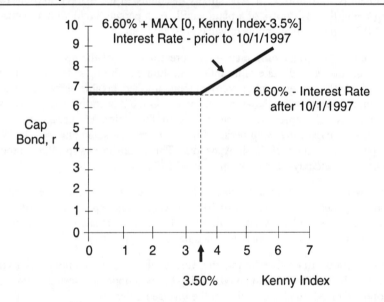

The *debt component* of the Cap Bond can be valued as a 6.60 percent fixed-rate bond with a maturity of 10/1/2016. The Cap Bond has an *option component* of the form + max [0, Kenny Index – 3.5 percent], which is equivalent to owning a 3.5 percent Kenny-based interest rate cap that expires on 10/1/1997. A Cap Bond also has tax-related structural value to an investor. Generally, interest on an interest rate cap held in isolation has been treated by recipients as taxable income, while all of the interest associated with tax-exempt cap bonds has been, in the opinion of bond counsel, exempt from taxation.

Valuation of the Debt Component—Discounting, at a market discount rate of 7.15 percent, the 6.60 percent fixed-rate debt component associated with the Cap Bond with a maturity of 10/1/2016 gives us a debt component of 93.733 percent.

Valuation of Option Component—Our model's theoretical value, based on the Treasury yield curve of 11/2/1992, of a 3.50 percent Kenny-based interest rate cap that expires on 10/1/1997, is 4.886 percent (see Schedule 3.1 in Appendix).

Valuation Summary

$$\text{DAP Price} = \text{Price}\left[\left(\begin{array}{c}\text{Fixed--Rate}\\ \text{Bond}\end{array}\right) + \left(\begin{array}{c}\text{Cap}\\ \text{Value}\end{array}\right)\right]$$

DAP Price = 93.733% + 4.886% = 98.619%
(No Structure Value—see Schedule 3.2 in Appendix)

DAP Price = 95.380 + 4.886% = 100.266%
(15 bp Structure Value—see Schedule 3.3 in Appendix)

Valuation of a BEAR Floater

We will now value insured AAA-rated hospital revenue bonds that mature on August 15, 2022, and are subject to optional redemption on August 15, 2002, at a price of 102 percent declining to 100 percent on August 15, 2004 (the "BEAR floaters"). Assume that the BEAR floaters pay semiannual interest prior to August 15, 2002, at a rate of 6.10 percent + 2 × (Kenny Index − 5 percent), subject to a minimum rate of 4 percent and a maximum rate of 8.20 percent. On and after August 15, 2002, the BEAR floater rate equals 6.10 percent. Graphically, the interest rate on the BEAR floater versus the Kenny Index is shown in Exhibit 9. Also assume that a plain vanilla similar 30-year bond currently yields 6.60 percent. What is the value of the BEAR floater?

Exhibit 9.   BEAR Floater Interest Rate Profile

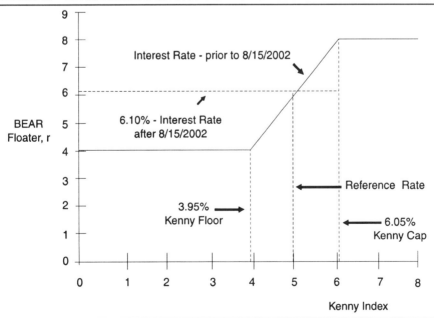

We will now divide the BEAR floater into its simpler underlying component. We can think of the *debt component* of the BEAR floater as a 6.10 percent fixed-rate bond with a maturity of 8/15/2022. The BEAR floater has a *hedging component* of the form 2 × (Kenny Index – 5 percent) that can be valued as two interest rate swaps that expire on 8/15/2002, under which the BEAR floater investor is the 5 percent fixed-rate payer and the issuer is the floating-rate payer. The *option components* embedded in the BEAR floater are due to the constraints that the interest rate, prior to August 15, 2002, will not go above 8.20 percent or below 4.00 percent. These constraints are equivalent to a BEAR floater investor being a cap writer for two Kenny interest rate caps at 6.05 percent and being a floor owner of two Kenny interest rate floors of 3.95 percent.

Valuation of the Debt Component—Discounting, at a market discount rate of 6.60 percent, the 6.10 percent debt component associated with the BEAR floater with a maturity of 8/15/2022 gives us a debt component value of 93.507 percent.

Valuation of the Hedging Component—The present value swap rate from our model for an interest rate swap that expires on 8/15/2002 in accordance with the Treasury yield curve of 11/2/1992 (see Schedule 4.1 in Appendix) is 5.185 percent. This results in a swap value to the BEAR floater investor for two swaps in which the investor receives Kenny and pays 5 percent fixed to be 1.654 percent.

Valuation of the Option Components—The theoretical values, according to our model, of a 6.05 percent Kenny cap option and a 3.95 percent Kenny floor option, which both expire on 8/15/2002, are 1.990 percent and 1.333 percent, respectively (see Schedule 4.2 in Appendix). The present value to the BEAR floater investor, who may be viewed as the floor owner of the two embedded 3.95 percent interest rate floor options, is 2.666 percent. Conversely, since the BEAR floater investor can be viewed as being a cap writer, the present value cost of the two embedded 6.05 percent interest rate caps is (3.980) percent.

Valuation Summary

$$\text{DAP Price} = \text{Price}\left[\begin{pmatrix}\text{Fixed-}\\\text{Rate}\\\text{Bond}\end{pmatrix} + \begin{pmatrix}\text{Floating-}\\\text{to-Fixed}\\\text{Swaps}\end{pmatrix} + \begin{pmatrix}\text{Floor}\\\text{Values}\end{pmatrix} - \begin{pmatrix}\text{Cap}\\\text{Values}\end{pmatrix}\right]$$

DAP Price = 93.507% + 1.654% + 2.666 – (3.980) = 93.847%
(No Structure Value—see Schedule 4.3 in Appendix)

DAP Price = 95.380% + 1.654% + 2.666 – (3.980) = 95.720%
(15 bp Structure Value—see Schedule 4.4 in Appendix)

CONCLUSION

The authors have attempted to introduce to participants in the municipal marketplace the fundamental aspects underlying the understanding and valuation of derivative securities. The first essential step in this process is to understand the mathematics underlying expectational analysis. To introduce this concept, we guide the reader through a sample full-coupon Treasury yield curve, show how an implied zero curve is iteratively calculated, show how implied forward rates are determined, and derive implied tax-exempt forward rates. The implied tax-exempt forward rates are the crucial inputs that are used in the valuation procedures in the chapter.

We then examine the building blocks of municipal derivatives: the debt or bond components; the hedging components of forwards and swaps; and the option components of caps and floors. Once an understanding of the valuation process of these is achieved, we use these instruments to value complex derivative municipal securities; securities that currently exist in the marketplace: an inverse floater, a cap bond, and a BEAR floater.

We hope that we have collected into this chapter and adequately explained all of the varied aspects that allow the practitioner to begin to intelligently understand and value municipal derivative securities. An understanding of this process by practitioners is important to the success of and expansion of the municipal derivative marketplace.

APPENDIX I

List of Schedules

1   Yield Curve—11/2/1992

Inverse Floater

2.1   Yield Curve—11/2/1992 (7-Year Swap Value of 4.878%)
2.2   Option Pricing Schedule—11/2/1992 (10.85% Cap Value of 0.01%)
2.3   Inverse Floater Valuation—No Structure Value Assumption—
         6.70% Discount Rate
2.4   Inverse Floater Valuation—15 Basis Point Structure Value
         Assumption—6.55% Discount Rate

Cap Bond

3.1   Option Pricing Schedule—11/2/1992 (3.5% Cap Value of 4.886%)
3.2   Cap Bond Valuation—No Structure Value Assumption—
         7.15% Discount Rate
3.3   Cap Bond Valuation—15 Basis Point Structure Value Assumption—
         7.00% Discount Rate

BEAR Floater

4.1   Yield Curve—11/2/1992 (10-Year Swap Value of 5.185%)
4.2   Option Pricing Schedule—11/2/1992 (3.95% Floor Value of 1.333%,
         6.05% Cap Value of 1.990%)
4.3   BEAR Floater Valuation—No Structure Value Assumption—
         6.60% Discount Rate
4.4   BEAR Floater Valuation—15 Basis Point Structure Value Assumption—
         6.45% Discount Rate

Schedule 1. Yield Curve 11/2/1992

Taxable Yield Curve Input Screen

Name of Yield Curve: Treasury
Term of Swap / Bond: 30 years
Target Short-Term Ratio (%): 74.00
Avg. Exp. Short-term rate: 5.81

Year	Full Coupon	Implied Zero	Implied Forward	Tax-Ex Forward	Year	Full Coupon	Implied Zero	Implied Forward	Tax-Ex Forward
1	3.730	3.730	3.73	2.76	16	7.360	7.770	9.21	6.82
2	4.500	4.527	5.33	3.94	17	7.430	7.893	9.89	7.32
3	5.120	5.176	6.49	4.80	18	7.500	8.025	10.28	7.61
4	5.730	5.837	7.85	5.81	19	7.550	8.116	9.78	7.23
5	6.020	6.147	7.39	5.47	20	7.600	8.216	10.13	7.50
6	6.340	6.512	8.36	6.18	21	7.610	8.212	8.13	6.01
7	6.540	6.738	8.10	6.00	22	7.620	8.213	8.24	6.10
8	6.770	7.019	9.01	6.67	23	7.630	8.217	8.31	6.15
9	6.850	7.100	7.75	5.73	24	7.640	8.224	8.39	6.21
10	6.940	7.206	8.17	6.04	25	7.650	8.234	8.48	6.27
11	7.080	7.397	9.33	6.90	26	7.660	8.247	8.57	6.34
12	7.160	7.499	8.62	6.38	27	7.670	8.263	8.67	6.42
13	7.200	7.539	8.03	5.94	28	7.680	8.281	8.78	6.50
14	7.250	7.604	8.45	6.26	29	7.690	8.303	8.90	6.59
15	7.300	7.674	8.66	6.41	30	7.700	8.327	9.03	6.68

Implied SWAP Rates

3 year	3.80%	10 year	5.18%
5 year	4.48%	20 year	5.73%
7 year	4.88%	30 year	5.81%

Schedule 2.1 Yield Curve 11/2/1992 (7-Year Swap Value of 4.878%)

Taxable Yield Curve Input Screen

Name of Yield Curve:	Treasury			Target Short-Term Ratio (%):	74.00		
Term of Swap / Bond:	7 years			Avg. Exp. Short-term rate:	4.88		

Year	Full Coupon	Implied Zero	Implied Forward	Tax-Ex Forward	Year	Full Coupon	Implied Zero	Implied Forward	Tax-Ex Forward
1	3.730	3.730	3.73	2.76	16	7.360	7.770	9.21	6.82
2	4.500	4.527	5.33	3.94	17	7.430	7.893	9.89	7.32
3	5.120	5.176	6.49	4.80	18	7.500	8.025	10.28	7.63
4	5.730	5.837	7.85	5.81	19	7.550	8.116	9.78	7.23
5	6.020	6.147	7.39	5.47	20	7.600	8.216	10.13	7.50
6	6.340	6.512	8.36	6.18	21	7.610	8.212	8.13	6.01
7	6.540	6.738	8.10	6.00	22	7.620	8.213	8.24	6.10
8	6.770	7.019	9.01	6.67	23	7.630	8.217	8.31	6.15
9	6.850	7.100	7.75	5.73	24	7.640	8.224	8.39	6.21
10	6.940	7.206	8.17	6.04	25	7.650	8.234	8.48	6.27
11	7.080	7.397	9.33	6.90	26	7.660	8.247	8.57	6.34
12	7.160	7.499	8.62	6.38	27	7.670	8.263	8.67	6.42
13	7.200	7.539	8.03	5.94	28	7.680	8.281	8.78	6.50
14	7.250	7.604	8.45	6.26	29	7.690	8.303	8.90	6.59
15	7.300	7.674	8.66	6.41	30	7.700	8.327	9.03	6.68

Implied SWAP Rates

3 year	3.80%	10 year	5.18%
5 year	4.48%	20 year	5.73%
7 year	4.88%	30 year	5.81%

Schedule 2.2 Option Pricing Schedule 11/2/1992 (10.85% Cap Value of 0.01%)

Name of Bond:	Cap Bond		Volatility:	8.00%
Type of Index:	Kenny		Term of Option:	7 years
Cap Strike Price:	10.85%		Cap Value:	0.010%
Floor Strike Price:	0.00%		Floor Value:	0.000%

Year	CAP	FLOOR	Year	CAP	FLOOR	Year	CAP	FLOOR
0.5	0.000%	0.000%	7.5	0.012%	0.000%	19.0	0.224%	0.000%
1.0	0.000%	0.000%	8.0	0.015%	0.000%	20.0	0.270%	0.000%
1.5	0.000%	0.000%	8.5	0.015%	0.000%	21.0	0.282%	0.000%
2.0	0.000%	0.000%	9.0	0.015%	0.000%	22.0	0.295%	0.000%
2.5	0.000%	0.000%	9.5	0.016%	0.000%	23.0	0.308%	0.000%
3.0	0.000%	0.000%	10.0	0.018%	0.000%	24.0	0.323%	0.000%
3.5	0.000%	0.000%	11.0	0.033%	0.000%	25.0	0.339%	0.000%
4.0	0.000%	0.000%	12.0	0.041%	0.000%	26.0	0.355%	0.000%
4.5	0.000%	0.000%	13.0	0.046%	0.000%	27.0	0.372%	0.000%
5.0	0.000%	0.000%	14.0	0.055%	0.000%	28.0	0.390%	0.000%
5.5	0.002%	0.000%	15.0	0.068%	0.000%	29.0	0.409%	0.000%
6.0	0.006%	0.000%	16.0	0.091%	0.000%	30.0	0.428%	0.000%
6.5	0.010%	0.000%	17.0	0.133%	0.000%			
7.0	0.010%	0.000%	18.0	0.187%	0.000%			

Schedule 2.3   Inverse Floater Valuation
No Structure Value Assumption—6.70% Discount Rate

BULL\BEAR I n p u t S c r e e n	
Name of Bond: Inverse Floater	
BULL or BEAR Floater (Press Enter to Change)	BULL
Trade Settlement Date	11/02/1992
Link Coupon	6.150
Specified (Swap) Rate	4.700
Number of Implied Swaps	1
Conversion Date	08/15/1999
Maturity Date	08/15/2012
First Option Redemption Date	08/15/2002
First Par Opt. Red. Date	08/15/2004
Initial Optional Call Price	102.0
Purchase Price	93.439
Current Kenny Rate	3.000
Muni Market Term Swap Rate	4.878
Exp. Kenny Short-Term Rate	4.878
Investors Required Full-Coupon Bond Rate	6.700
(Kenny) Cap Rate	10.850
(Kenny) Floor Rate	0.010

Output Screen		
	BULL Floater	BEAR Floater
Current Kenny Rate 3.000%		3.000%
Current Coupon 7.850%		4.450%
Current Yield to Maturity 7.693%		5.894%
Exp. Kenny Short-Term Rate 4.878%		4.878%
Exp. Avg. Coupon (to Conversion Date) . .5.972%		6.328%
Exp. Avg. Yield to Maturity 6.664%		6.852%

BULL Floater Bond Prices:	Maturity	Price to . . . First Call	First Par Call
Value of Bond 94.007%		97.136%	95.554%
Value of Swap(s) . . . .-0.579%		-0.579%	-0.579%
Value of Cap(s) 0.010%		0.010%	0.010%
Value of Floor(s) 0.000%		0.000%	0.000%
Total Value of BULL Floater (SAP) 93.439%		96.567%	94.986%
Implied Structure Cost 0.000%		-3.128%	-1.547%

**Schedule 2.4   Inverse Floater Valuation
15 Basis Point Structure Value Assumption—
6.55% Discount Rate**

BULL/BEAR I n p u t S c r e e n	
Name of Bond: Inverse Floater	
BULL or BEAR Floater (Press Enter to Change)	BULL
Trade Settlement Date	11/02/1992
Link Coupon	6.150
Specified (SWAP) Rate	4.700
Number of Implied Swaps	1
Conversion Date	08/15/1999
Maturity Date	08/15/2012
First Optional Redemption Date	08/15/2002
First Par Opt. Red. Date	08/15/2004
Initial Optional Call Price	102.0
Purchase Price	95.019
Current Kenny Rate	3.000
Muni Market Term Swap Rate	4.878
Exp. Kenny Short-Term Rate	4.878
Investors Required Full-Coupon Bond Rate	6.550
(Kenny) Cap Rate	10.850
(Kenny) Floor Rate	0.010

Output Screen		
	BULL Floater	*BEAR Floater*
Current Kenny Rate 3.000%	3.000%	
Current Coupon 7.850%	4.450%	
Current Yield to Maturity 7.524%	5.758%	
Exp. Kenny Short-Term Rate 4.878%	4.878%	
Exp. Avg. Coupon (to Conversion Date) . .5.972%	6.328%	
Exp. Avg. Yield to Maturity 6.514%	6.699%	

BULL Floater Bond Prices:	Maturity	Price to . . . First Call	First Par Call
Value of Bond 95.587%	98.106%	96.738%	
Value of Swap(s) . . . .−0.579%	−0.579%	−0.579%	
Value of Cap(s) 0.010%	0.010%	0.010%	
Value of Floor(s) 0.000%	0.000%	0.000%	
Total Value of BULL Floater (SAP) 95.019%	97.627%	96.170%	
Implied Structure Cost 0.000%	−2.608%	−1.151%	

Schedule 3.1   Option Pricing Schedule 11/2/1992 (3.5% Cap Value of 4.886%)

Name of Bond:	Cap Bond
Type of Index:	Kenny
Cap Strike Price:	3.50%
Floor Strike Price:	3.50%

Volatility:	8.00%
Term of Option:	5 years
Cap Value:	4.886%
Floor Value:	0.737%

Year	CAP	FLOOR	Year	CAP	FLOOR	Year	CAP	FLOOR
0.5	0.000%	0.365%	7.5	9.265%	0.742%	19.0	22.092%	0.772%
1.0	0.000%	0.723%	8.0	10.170%	0.742%	20.0	22.887%	0.774%
1.5	0.212%	0.727%	8.5	10.786%	0.744%	21.0	23.359%	0.783%
2.0	0.425%	0.736%	9.0	11.381%	0.745%	22.0	23.807%	0.791%
2.5	0.998%	0.736%	9.5	12.027%	0.746%	23.0	24.228%	0.799%
3.0	1.556%	0.737%	10.0	12.651%	0.748%	24.0	24.625%	0.807%
3.5	2.496%	0.737%	11.0	14.194%	0.749%	25.0	24.997%	0.815%
4.0	3.408%	0.737%	12.0	15.396%	0.751%	26.0	25.347%	0.821%
4.5	4.159%	0.737%	13.0	16.343%	0.756%	27.0	25.677%	0.828%
5.0	4.886%	0.737%	14.0	17.322%	0.760%	28.0	25.987%	0.834%
5.5	5.826%	0.737%	15.0	18.270%	0.764%	29.0	26.278%	0.840%
6.0	6.736%	0.739%	16.0	19.254%	0.767%	30.0	26.554%	0.845%
6.5	7.545%	0.740%	17.0	20.277%	0.768%			
7.0	8.328%	0.740%	18.0	21.271%	0.770%			

Schedule 3.2   Cap Bond Valuation
No Structure Value Assumption—7.15% Discount Rate

Capped Municipal Bonds			
Name of Bond: Cap Bond			
Trade Settlement Date		11/02/1992	
Maturity Date		10/01/2016	
First Optional Redemption Date		10/01/2002	
First Par Optional Redemption Date		10/01/2004	
Coupon (Linked B.E.Y.)		6.600	
Purchase Price		100.000 %	
Initial Optional Call Price		101.5	
Cap Term		5 years	
Cap Rate		3.500 %	
Discount Rate		7.150 %	

		Price to . . .	
	Maturity	*First Call*	*First Par Call*
Value of Bond	93.733%	96.881%	95.631%
Value of Cap	4.886%	4.886%	4.886%
Total Bond Value (SAP)	98.620%	101.767%	100.517%
Implied Structure Cost	1.380%	−1.767%	−0.517%

Schedule 3.3   Cap Bond Valuation
                 15 Basis Point Structure Value Assumption—
                 7.00% Discount Rate

Capped Municipal Bonds			
Name of Bond: Cap Bond			
Trade Settlement Date	11/02/1992		
Maturity Date	10/01/2016		
First Optional Redemption Date	10/01/2002		
First Par Optional Redemption Date	10/01/2004		
Coupon (Linked B.E.Y.)	6.600		
Purchase Price	100.000%		
Initial Optional Call Price	101.5		
Cap Term	5 years		
Cap Rate	3.500%		
Discount Rate	7.000%		

		Price to . . .	
	Maturity	First Call	First Par Call
Value of Bond	95.380%	97.925%	96.795%
Value of Cap	4.886%	4.886%	4.886%
Total Bond Value (SAP)	100.267%	102.812%	101.682%
Implied Structure Cost	−0.267%	−2.812%	−1.682%

Schedule 4.1   Yield Curve—11/2/1992 (10-Year Swap Value of 5.185%)

Taxable Yield Curve Input Screen

Name of Yield Curve:	Treasury	Target Short-Term Ratio (%):	74.00
Term of Swap / Bond:	10 years	Avg. Exp. Short-term rate:	5.18

Year	Full Coupon	Implied Zero	Implied Forward	Tax-Ex Forward	Year	Full Coupon	Implied Zero	Implied Forward	Tax-Ex Forward
1	3.730	3.730	3.73	2.76	16	7.360	7.770	9.21	6.82
2	4.500	4.527	5.33	3.94	17	7.430	7.893	9.89	7.32
3	5.120	5.176	6.49	4.80	18	7.500	8.025	10.28	7.61
4	5.730	5.837	7.85	5.81	19	7.550	8.116	9.78	7.23
5	6.020	6.147	7.39	5.47	20	7.600	8.216	10.13	7.50
6	6.340	6.512	8.36	6.18	21	7.610	8.212	8.13	6.01
7	6.540	6.738	8.10	6.00	22	7.620	8.213	8.24	6.10
8	6.770	7.019	9.01	6.67	23	7.630	8.217	8.31	6.15
9	6.850	7.100	7.75	5.73	24	7.640	8.224	8.39	6.21
10	6.940	7.206	8.17	6.04	25	7.650	8.234	8.48	6.27
11	7.080	7.397	9.33	6.90	26	7.660	8.247	8.57	6.34
12	7.160	7.499	8.62	6.38	27	7.670	8.263	8.67	6.42
13	7.200	7.539	8.03	5.94	28	7.680	8.281	8.78	6.50
14	7.250	7.604	8.45	6.26	29	7.690	8.303	8.90	6.59
15	7.300	7.674	8.66	6.41	30	7.700	8.327	9.03	6.68

Implied SWAP Rates

3 year	3.80%	10 year	5.18%
5 year	4.48%	20 year	5.73%
7 year	4.88%	30 year	5.81%

Schedule 4.2   Option Pricing Schedule 11/1/1992 (3.95% Floor Value of 1.333%, 6.05% Cap Value of 1.990%)

Name of Bond:	Cap Bond		Volatility:	8.00%
Type of Index:	Kenny		Term of Option:	10 years
Cap Strike Price:	6.05%		Cap Value:	1.990%
Floor Strike Price:	3.95%		Floor Value:	1.333%

Year	CAP	FLOOR	Year	CAP	FLOOR	Year	CAP	FLOOR
0.5	0.0000%	0.587%	7.5	1.223%	1.309%	19.0	5.310%	1.407%
1.0	0.0000%	1.162%	8.0	1.478%	1.310%	20.0	5.673%	1.412%
1.5	0.0000%	1.223%	8.5	1.587%	1.317%	21.0	5.829%	1.431%
2.0	0.0000%	1.289%	9.0	1.698%	1.323%	22.0	5.984%	1.449%
2.5	0.002%	1.292%	9.5	1.844%	1.328%	23.0	6.133%	1.466%
3.0	0.004%	1.297%	10.0	1.990%	1.333%	24.0	6.281%	1.482%
3.5	0.095%	1.298%	11.0	2.520%	1.337%	25.0	6.423%	1.497%
4.0	0.193%	1.298%	12.0	2.867%	1.345%	26.0	6.561%	1.510%
4.5	0.249%	1.300%	13.0	3.104%	1.362%	27.0	6.695%	1.523%
5.0	0.310%	1.303%	14.0	3.393%	1.374%	28.0	6.825%	1.535%
5.5	0.489%	1.304%	15.0	3.696%	1.385%	29.0	6.950%	1.546%
6.0	0.661%	1.305%	16.0	4.065%	1.392%	30.0	7.073%	1.556%
6.5	0.809%	1.306%	17.0	4.503%	1.397%			
7.0	0.951%	1.308%	18.0	4.957%	1.402%			

Schedule 4.3   BEAR Floater Valuation
No Structure Value Assumption—6.60% Discount Rate

BULL/BEAR I n p u t S c r e e n	
Name of Bond: Inverse Floater	
BULL or BEAR Floater (Press Enter to Change)	BEAR
Trade Settlement Date	11/02/1992
Link Coupon	6.100
Specified (SWAP) Rate	5.000
Number of Implied Swaps	2
Conversion Date	08/15/2002
Maturity Date	08/15/2022
First Optional Redemption Date	08/15/2002
First Par Opt. Red. Date	08/15/2004
Initial Optional Call Price	102.0
Purchase Price	93.847
Current Kenny Rate	3.950
Muni Market Term Swap Rate	5.185
Exp. Kenny Short-Term Rate	5.185
Investors Required Full-Coupon Bond Rate	6.600
(Kenny) Cap Rate	6.050
(Kenny) Floor Rate	3.950

Output Screen		
	BULL *Floater*	*BEAR* *Floater*
Current Kenny Rate	3.950%	3.950%
Current Coupon	8.200%	4.000%
Current Yield to Maturity	7.885%	5.436%
Exp. Kenny Short-Term Rate	5.185%	5.185%
Exp. Avg. Coupon (to Conversion Date) . .	5.730%	6.470%
Exp. Avg. Yield to Maturity	6.363%	6.792%

		Price to . . .	
BEAR Floater Bond Prices:	*Maturity*	*First Call*	*First Par Call*
Value of Bond	93.507%	97.485%	95.936%
Value of Swaps(s)	1.654%	1.654%	1.654%
Value of Cap(s)	-3.980%	-3.980%	-3.980%
Value of Floor(s)	2.666%	2.666%	2.666%
Total Value of BEAR Floater (SAP)	93.847%	97.824%	96.276%
Implied Structure Cost	0.000%	-3.977%	-2.429%

Schedule 4.4   BEAR Floater Valuation
15 Basis Point Structure Value Assumption—
6.45% Discount Rate

BULL/BEAR I n p u t S c r e e n	
Name of Bond: Inverse Floater	
BULL or BEAR Floater (Press Enter to Change)	BEAR
Trade Settlement Date	11/02/1992
Link Coupon	6.100
Specified (SWAP) Rate	5.000
Number of Implied Swaps	2
Conversion Date	08/15/2002
Maturity Date	08/15/2022
First Optional Redemption Date	08/15/2002
First Par Opt. Red Date	08/15/2004
Initial Optional Call Price	102.0
Purchase Price	95.720
Current Kenny Rate	3.950
Muni Market Term Swap Rate	5.185
Exp. Kenny Short-Term Rate	5.185
Investors Required Full-Coupon Bond Rate	6.450
(Kenny) Cap Rate	6.050
(Kenny) Floor Rate	3.950

Output Screen		
	BULL Floater	BEAR Floater
Current Kenny Rate	3.950%	3.950%
Current Coupon	8.200%	4.000%
Current Yield to Maturity	7.703%	5.312%
Exp. Kenny Short-Term Rate	5.185%	5.185%
Exp. Avg. Coupon (to Conversion Date) . .	5.730%	6.470%
Exp. Avg. Yield to Maturity	6.218%	6.637%

BEAR Floater Bond Prices:	Maturity	Price to . . . First Call	First Par Call
Value of Bond	95.381%	98.552%	97.130%
Value of Swap(s)	1.654%	1.654%	1.654%
Value of Cap(s)	-3.980%	-3.980%	-3.980
Value of Floor(s)	2.666%	2.666%	2.666%
Total Value of BEAR Floater (SAP)	95.720%	98.891%	97.469%
Implied Structure Cost	-0.000%	-3.171%	-1.749%

CHAPTER 7

Fixed-Income Hybrid and Synthetic Securities

Christopher J. Williams
Managing Principal
Melinda M. Twomey
Senior Vice President
Hasan Latif
Senior Vice President
Bruce M. Usher
Senior Vice President
Ming Jiao Hsia
Vice President
DiAnne Calabrisotto
Assistant Vice President

Williams Financial Markets, a division of Jefferies & Company

INTRODUCTION

The market for derivative-based hybrid securities, also known as "structured notes," has experienced rapid growth since it's infancy in 1990. The growth in this market has been largely in response to the growing needs of institutional investors during a protracted period of declining yields. These instruments, issued by corporations, banks, governmental or quasi-governmental entities, were created to enable investors to purchase customized securities that meet specific investment parameters. Not only do these securities meet the investor's guidelines with regard to credit quality and maturity, they also enable investors to gain access to a variety of markets in ways previously not possible. For example, through the purchase of structured notes, institutions are able to take investment positions based on currency exchange rate views, expected yield curve shifts, or the performance of virtually any market. The degree of exposure to market changes inherent in these securities can be structured in accordance with the investor's risk profile.

As the market for structured notes has recently grown at a rate greater than that for any other sector of the derivative market (particularly during the 1991-1993 period), so has the need for a more precise understanding of the performance and price sensitivity of these securities. Because the instruments described in this chapter are "synthetic" debt securities, they can be analyzed by exploring the bond and derivative components of each instrument. In this chapter, a variety of derivative-based securities are discussed with regard to their performance under a variety of market conditions.

RETURN AND PRICE SENSITIVITY OF STRUCTURED NOTES

Several factors have significant impact on price volatility and performance sensitivity of structured notes. These factors include: (1) leverage; (2) maturity of the security; and (3) investment basis risk (the degree to which the benchmark index of the note is correlated to the market benchmarks against which the investor's overall performance is measured).

Leverage

Leverage is often defined as the amount of exposure to changes in an index per unit of a security purchased. For example, a $10 million note may have a principal redemption that is indexed to four times the amount by which the exchange rate changes between two currencies. In other words, the market value impact of exchange rates on this leveraged investment is equivalent to the market value impact experienced on a $40 million investment. As leverage increases, so does the sensitivity of the return.

Maturity of the Security

Like traditional fixed-income securities, structured notes with long maturities are more price-sensitive to movements in interest rates than are similar notes with shorter maturities. Also, longer maturities make it less likely that the investor's market expectations over the life of the security will be realized due to the inaccuracy of long-term forecasts.

Investment Basis Risk

The risk incurred by an investor increases when the determinants of return on a security are unrelated to benchmarks used to measure the investor's overall portfolio performance. This basis risk can cause a structured note to dramatically outperform or underperform the overall market.

Following are discussions of several popular derivative-based investment structures. Each security is explored with regard to its overall structure, derivative components, and the hedges required to create the security.

INVERSE FLOATING-RATE NOTE

Description

One of the most widely used investment structures since the late 1980s has been a security that offers enhanced returns to investors with bullish views on the fixed-income markets. The security, referred to as an Inverse Floating-Rate Note (IFRN), pays a coupon that increases as the level of interest rates to which the coupon is indexed decreases. Like many derivative-based securities, IFRNs typically provide an immediate current coupon benefit to investors who are willing to take a position that is contrary to market expectations with regard to the direction of interest rates. IFRNs are most popular in economic environments with low inflation and steep positively shaped yield curves, which reflect the expectation of rising rates. IFRNs may also be indexed to interest rates in an inverted yield curve environment. In such cases, the interest rate view implied by an IFRN is in agreement with the forward market.

The coupon on an IFRN is typically determined pursuant to a formula that takes the form of a fixed-rate less a variable-rate index or a multiple of a variable-rate index. The coupon on the IFRN is subject to a minimum of zero percent or, in certain instances, a minimum coupon greater than zero percent is guaranteed. The type of IFRN issued in the corporate fixed-income market is analyzed in this chapter. It should be noted that these securities behave in a similar manner to, but are distinct from, the inverse floater class of securities included in many mortgage-related securities.

Exhibit 1 shows the terms of a typical IFRN with a table showing how movements in LIBOR would affect the coupon.

Exhibit 1.   IFRN Terms

Face Amount:	$100,000,000
Maturity:	2 years
Coupon on Note:	12.77% – 2 × LIBOR actual/360 day count basis
Variable Rate Index:	6-Month LIBOR
Current 6-Month LIBOR:	3.5%
Interest Rate Resets:	Semiannually
Initial Coupon:	5.77%
Minimum Coupon:	0%

Coupon Table	
USD LIBOR	Coupon
5.50%	1.77%
5.00%	2.77%
4.50%	3.77%
4.00%	4.77%
3.50%	5.77%
3.00%	6.77%
2.50%	7.77%
2.00%	8.77%
1.50%	9.77%

Issuer's Hedge of Note

Issuers of structured notes enter into hedges to eliminate exposure to the market view inherent in the notes. A typical hedge consists of a swap in which the issuer receives swap payments that completely offset the coupon that the issuer pays on the note. In return, the issuer pays a simple floating or fixed rate over the life of the note.

The party with whom the issuer of a structured note executes the hedge is a swap dealer, typically a highly rated financial institution. In order to provide a hedge for the issuer, the swap dealer must hedge it's own risk by entering into offsetting swaps as described below, or by purchasing and selling interest rate futures contracts. The dealer manages this hedge portfolio, consisting of swaps and securities, on an ongoing basis. For simplicity, the numerical examples below do not include bid/offer spreads that would be required by the dealer.

Exhibit 2. Transaction Cash Flows

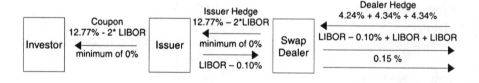

Exhibit 2 demonstrates the cash flow involved in an IFRN from the perspectives of the investor, the issuer, and the swap dealer.

A swap dealer supplying the hedge for this note must first offset the one leg of the swap in which it pays a fixed rate and receives LIBOR − 0.10 percent (the issuer funding target). In order to do so, the swap dealer pays LIBOR − 0.10 percent on a swap and receives a fixed rate of 4.24 percent actual/360 day count basis. The 4.24 percent rate is based on the assumption that the 2-year bid side swap rate (versus LIBOR flat) equals 4.34 percent on an actual/360 day count basis.

The swap dealer must also offset the coupon so that the issuer is fully hedged. When the investor receives a coupon 12.77 percent − 2 × LIBOR, the investor is essentially receiving 12.77 percent and paying 2 × LIBOR. In order to hedge this cash flow, the dealer pays LIBOR twice and receives two fixed rates of 4.34 percent each. The two rates plus 4.34 percent for the first swap total 12.92 percent. (The 12.92 percent rate is higher than the 12.77 percent fixed component of the coupon mentioned earlier. The 0.15 percent difference is discussed below.)

Because the coupon of the note is limited to minimum of 0 percent, the dealer purchases an interest rate cap on LIBOR at an interest rate of 6.385 percent (referred to as the cap strike). The 6.385 percent cap strike is equal to 12.77 percent divided by 2. By purchasing a cap on twice the face amount of the note, the dealer is able to guard against a rise in LIBOR over the prescribed rate. The cost of this cap accounts for the missing 0.15 percent (see Exhibit 3).

Exhibit 3. Summary of Cash Flows on Dealer Hedge

Receive Fixed versus LIBOR on Swap	1 × 4.24% (fixed)
Pay Floating Rate	1 × LIBOR – 0.10% floating
Receive Fixed versus LIBOR on Swap	2 × 4.34% (fixed)
Pay Floating Rate	2 × LIBOR
Pay Cap Premium	0.15% per annum
Payment Summary	■ Fixed 4.24% + 4.34% + 4.34% – 0.15% = 12.77%
	■ Floating LIBOR – 0.10% + LIBOR + LIBOR
	■ Dealer Pays Coupon to Issuer 12.77% – 2 × LIBOR, subject to minimum of 0%
	■ Dealer Receives Coupon from Issuer LIBOR – 0.10%

Benefits and Risks

The IFRN described herein provides investors with a significant above-market initial coupon in a positively sloped yield curve environment. The above-market initial coupon is the result of receiving a multiple of the high fixed swap rate that a swap counterparty pays versus LIBOR, for a swap with a term equal to the maturity of the note. A multiple of LIBOR is subtracted from the fixed rate. By definition, the LIBOR level is lower than the longer term swap rate due to the positively sloped yield curve. The two times leverage in the structure provides the investor with coupon sensitivity that is twice that of the movement in LIBOR. In addition to coupon sensitivity resulting from the leverage, the notes are also price sensitive due to the extended duration created by the leverage. Although the maturity of the note is two years, the duration is actually 5.71 years, as shown below.

Duration of 2-year note with 4.34% coupon: 1.90 years (times two)
Duration of 2-year note with 4.24% coupon: 1.91 years
Total duration: <u>5.71</u> years

The long duration of this instrument increases its price sensitivity.

Variations

In addition to being indexed to LIBOR, IFRNs may be indexed to virtually any rates that can be hedged in the cash or derivative market. For example, investors may take advantage of a bullish view on short-, medium-, or long-term interest rate benchmarks (e.g., Prime, Fed Funds, five-year swap rates or ten-year Treasury rates or even a basket of different rates). The leverage may also vary to reflect the investor's risk profile with regard to desired volatility, and the fixed component of the formula may also step up or down over time in accordance with the investor's view on future interest rate movements. Investors with bullish views on foreign markets, but who are restricted from investing in foreign securities, may also purchase an inverse floating rate note that is indexed to foreign interest rates but paid in U.S. dollars.

For example, an investor with a bullish view on two-year Canadian rates may purchase an IFRN indexed to Canadian rates. The note would be reset semiannually, which would enable an investor to benefit from future declines in two-year Canadian rates.

INDEXED AMORTIZING NOTE

Description

The Indexed Amortizing Note (IAN) is an innovation of the hybrid securities market, which first experienced wide popularity in early 1992. Initially, buyers of these securities were traditional investors in Collateralized Mortgage Obligations (CMOs) and high-grade callable agency notes. The investor universe has grown to include corporate bond buyers as well.

IANs are fixed-rate debentures whose face amount may decline prior to the stated maturity, depending on the level of a specified interest rate, such as three-month LIBOR. As the specified rate declines, or even if it remains stable, the IAN will amortize prior to its stated maturity, which is usually between three and five years. Unlike CMOs with similar average life characteristics, IANs have very short stated maturities, beyond which the security cannot extend. Although an IAN may be the obligation of a corporation or bank, the vast majority of IANs which have been placed through 1993 are obligations of U.S. government agencies. Yields on these securities are significantly higher than yields on fixed-rate bonds of comparable credit quality. IANs also have characteristics, such as the short-stated maturity and well-defined amortization schedule, that make them preferable to CMOs for many investors. An IAN's amortization is determined based on reference to specific interest rate movements rather than measurements that are more difficult to define, such as mortgage prepayment speeds.

The issuer of an IAN is hedged to obtain simple LIBOR-based funding through a swap that mirrors the security's structure (see Exhibit 4). The swap used to hedge this structure is actually a series of options on swaps. The IAN structure is most attractive to investors (i.e., the fixed-rate coupon is highest relative to market rates) when swap option volatility is high and the yield curve is steep, as the options embedded in the IAN are the most valuable in such an environment.

Exhibit 4

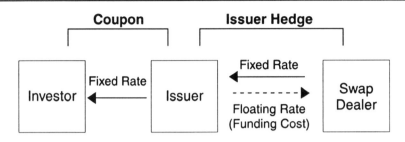

All issuer hedge terms, including any amortization, mirror the note terms.

Example

Face Amount of Note:	$100,000,000
Stated Maturity:	5 years
Coupon:	2-year Treasury + 0.90%
Interest Payments:	Monthly
Lock-out Period:	2 years
Reference Index:	3-month LIBOR, set 5 banking days prior to each payment date
Current 3-mo. LIBOR:	3.5%
Clean-up Call:	10%
Issuer:	U.S. Government Agency

Average Life Sensitivities

Reference Index LIBOR	Quarterly Amortization	Average Life Years
3.5%	100%	2
4.5%	100%	2
5.5%	18.30%	3
6.5%	6.40%	4
7.5%	0.00%	5

     The IAN, in the example described above, has a coupon equal to the two-year Treasury yield + 0.90 percent and will mature in two years as long as LIBOR is at or below 4.5 percent at the end of two years. If LIBOR rises above 4.5 percent, the final maturity and average life, will extend beyond two years. No amortization can occur prior to two years due to the lock-out provision. Amortization may occur on each of the subsequent payment dates according to the LIBOR settings, as shown above. If, for example, at the end of two years, LIBOR is set at 6.5 percent, 6.40 percent of principal will amortize on that quarterly reset date. If LIBOR were to remain at this level, the average life of the IAN would be four years, based on the amount of principal that amortized quarterly. The final maturity will not be beyond five years under any circumstances. Pursuant to the clean-up call provision, if less than 10 percent of the original principal amount is outstanding, the note will automatically mature.

Benefits and Risks

Investors have found IANs attractive for a number of reasons. Primary among them has been the high yield combined with relatively short-stated maturity. In addition, many investors prefer a bond with amortization tied directly to a specified interest rate rather than to mortgage prepayments, as in the case with CMOs. This characteristic allows the investor to know with absolute certainty how the bond will perform in any given interest rate environment. For added protection, most IANs have significant lock-out periods (often one to three years) during which no amortization can occur. Finally, as with the other hybrid securities described in this chapter, the characteristics of the IAN (average life, stated maturity, interest rate index, lock-out period, etc.) can be tailored to meet the investor's specific needs. As in the case with CMOs, IANs are subject to variations in average life, which may lower the security's return.

Exhibit 5 is an analysis of the variability of an IAN's maturity and a comparison of the total return of an IAN to that of a straight bullet security. The shaded rows compare the total return of an IAN, under several rate assumptions, to the total return of a Treasury note.

Variations

An IAN can vary in stated maturity and lock-out period from the one described above, with yield enhancement declining as the lock-out period approaches the maturity. In addition, the reference rate index may be a constant maturity Treasury rate or a swap rate. Most IANs to date have used LIBOR as the reference index because the swap market applies a higher option volatility to LIBOR than it does to longer rates. This high volatility in turn provides a higher yield to the investor. The bond described above has stable average life characteristics, as the note will not shorten to an average life of less than two years nor can it lengthen beyond its five-year stated maturity. The investor may choose a less stable bond (e.g., shortest average life of one year, longest average life of seven years) in exchange for receiving a higher yield. In addition, greater yield is also achievable if the investor accepts a lower quality credit such as a corporation or bank issuer rather than a governmental agency.

An innovation in this structure is to add a "knockout" feature to the IAN as added protection for the investor. If LIBOR is below the "knockout strike" (a specified interest rate) on the "knockout date" (generally 9 or 12 months after settlement), the IAN will mature on the lockout date. This feature was developed for investors who have the view that rates will stay low for 9-12 months but are much less comfortable taking a view on the level of interest rates at the end of two years.

Exhibit 5.   Total Return and Duration Analysis of Index Amortizing Note[1]

Projected 3-Month LIBOR Rate[2]	Average Life (Years)	Total Return at Maturity	Modified Duration	Constant Maturity Treasury		
				Modified Duration	Total Return	
3.2500%	2.00	4.75%	1.90			
3.5000%	2.00	4.75%	1.90			
3.7500%	2.00	4.75%	1.90			
4.0000%	2.00	4.75%	1.90			
4.2500%	2.00	4.75%	1.90			
4.5000%	2.00	4.75%	1.90	1.91	3.89%	2.00 year Treasury
4.7500%	2.06	4.75%	1.95			
5.0000%	2.17	4.89%	2.05			
5.2500%	2.39	5.02%	2.24			
5.5000%	3.02	5.08%	2.77	2.80	4.33%	3.00 year Treasury
5.7500%	3.19	5.16%	2.92			
6.0000%	3.41	5.21%	3.10			
6.2500%	3.68	5.24%	3.32			
6.5000%	4.00	5.22%	3.60	3.62	4.84%	4.00 year Treasury
6.6637%	4.14	5.22%	3.71			
6.7500%	4.21	5.22%	3.77			
7.0000%	4.44	5.19%	3.96			
7.2500%	4.71	5.13%	4.18			
7.5000%	5.00	5.03%	4.42	4.38	5.38%	5.00 year Treasury
8.0000%	5.00	5.06%	4.42			
8.5000%	5.00	5.08%	4.42			
9.0000%	5.00	5.18%	4.42			
Total Return and Duration Analysis Assuming Implied Market Forward Rates						
IAN	3.23	5.40%	2.945		Coupon: 4.82%	
2.00y Treasury	2.00	3.94%	1.915		Coupon: 3.92%	
5.00y Treasury	5.00	5.30%	4.378		Coupon: 5.20%	

(1) A to AA issuer.
(2) 3-month LIBOR rate at the end of second year.

SYNTHETIC CONVERTIBLE NOTE

Description

A synthetic convertible note (SCN) typically consists of a fixed-rate security and an option on the performance of an equity index or specific stock. As described herein, the SCN provides the investor with a low fixed-rate coupon and pays a minimum of par at maturity. In addition, the SCN offers the opportunity to earn more than par if the value of the stock or index (the "index") is above a predetermined level at maturity. The investor will receive greater than par at maturity only if the value of the index exceeds the strike. Regardless of the extent of any decline in the index value, the investor will receive a minimum of par.

Exhibit 6 shows the terms of an example SCN on a stock index.

Exhibit 6.   SCN Terms

Face Amount of Note:	$10,000,000
Maturity:	5 years
Coupon on Note:	2%
Option Strike:	1.1*MV Settlement
Principal Redemption Formula:	Par plus Par * $\frac{(\text{MV Mat.} - 1.1 \times \text{MV Settlement})}{\text{MV Settlement}}$
	Subject to a Minimum of Par
	(investor receives 100% of the amount by which the level of the index increases in excess of 10%)
Swap Dealer Pays Issuer:	2% semiannual coupon plus Principal Redemption Formula minus Par
Issuer Pays Swap Dealer:	LIBOR − 0.10%
Index Definition:	Broad Index of industrial stocks
MV Mat:	Market Value of Index at maturity
MV Settlement:	Market Value of Index at settlement

Hedge Assumptions

The issuer is hedged by receiving swap payments equal to the note coupons in addition to a payment at maturity that is equal to the amount of principal redemption in excess of par. The issuer pays LIBOR − 0.10 percent (the issuer's funding cost) in return. The swap dealer hedges itself by paying LIBOR − 0.10 percent and receiving a fixed rate of 2 percent on a swap that offsets its payment to the issuer. For discussion purposes, assume that the 2 percent interest rate received is approximately 4 percent per annum below the "at-the-market" swap rate that a dealer would normally receive in return for paying LIBOR − 0.10 percent. The 4 percent per annum swap rate differential is equal to a present value amount of approximately 17 percent. The swap dealer must therefore receive an up-front payment on the hedge, in an amount equal to the 17 percent present value figure, in order to be made whole when entering into this swap. This payment is therefore available to purchase call options on the desired market index (under the assumption that the investor pays par for the security even though the fixed-income component of the note is valued at 83 percent).

With the up-front payment, the dealer then buys a call option on the index for the benefit of the issuer. The option gives the dealer the right to buy the market index at a specific strike price at maturity. The option will expire worthless if, at maturity, the index value does not exceed the strike. In this instance, the investor will receive a minimum of par at maturity. If the index value exceeds the strike at maturity, the

Exhibit 7

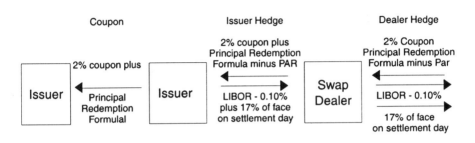

investor will receive more than par from the issuer. The amount received by the investor in excess of par is paid by the issuer from the proceeds of the exercise option (see Exhibit 7).

Summary of Dealer Hedge Cash Flows

Dealer Receives Fixed Rate versus LIBOR – 0.10% on swap:	2%
Up-front Payment to Dealer (based on off-market swap):	17%
Dealer pays for option:	(17%)
Payment Summary:	a) Dealer Pays to Issuer 2% and excess Principal Redemption
	b) Issuer Pays to Dealer LIBOR – 0.10% plus 17% of face amount

Principal Redemption Table

Basket Value	Principal Redemption	Annual IRR
–10%	100%	0%
0%	100%	0%
+10%	100%	0%
+20%	110%	3.85%
+50%	140%	8.72%
+100%	190%	15.27%

Benefits and Risks

Like a convertible fixed-income security, the SCN provides investors with a fixed coupon and additional upside if the value of a stock index rises above a specified level. Unlike a traditional convertible obligation that is convertible into the stock of the issuing company at a specific price and point in time, the SCN discussed herein pays an amount at maturity based on the increased value of the stock to which the principal amount is indexed. Whether the investor purchases an SCN or a traditional convertible note, the investor receives no upside if the value of the stock on the exercise date does not exceed the strike.

Variations

SCNs may be structured in a variety of ways to provide the investor with the flexibility to obtain principal upside based on the performance of an index, a specific stock, or a selected basket of stocks. In addition, the issuer can select the specific exercise strike desired, rather than being able to select only from available convertible notes.

INTEREST DIFFERENTIAL NOTES

Description

Interest Differential Notes (IDNs) are hybrid securities that are popular among investors who wish to establish a position referencing the differential between interest rates of two different countries. In the U.S., most differential notes are denominated in U.S. dollars and do not expose the investor to the risk of nondollar denomination. As with other indexed notes, variations of the interest differential notes exist. The first involves variable coupons and a fixed redemption amount. A second variation pays a fixed coupon and a principal redemption that varies in accordance with the level of reference interest rates. IDNs may also be indexed to rate differentials across currencies, or within one currency and across maturities in order to create a yield- curve trade.

Example: Deutsche Mark LIBOR versus U.S. Dollar LIBOR Differential Note

Maturity: 2 years
Coupon formula: (2 × DM LIBOR) minus (2 × USD LIBOR) minus 4.95%

The return of this note is linked to the spread between DM LIBOR and USD LIBOR. As the spread between the two interest rates widens, the coupon increases. Conversely, the coupon declines as the spread narrows.

This structure allows an investor to take advantage of the relationship of yield-curve slopes between different currencies. For example, the fact that the DM yield curve is inverted (downward sloping) and the U.S. yield curve is positive (upward sloping) implies that short-term DM rates are expected to fall while a rise in U.S. rates is expected. Combining the two yield curves in an Interest Differential Note allows an investor to avoid taking a position on the absolute level of rates in either country, and instead take a view on the relative levels of the interest rates in two countries. The Interest Differential Note permits the investor to earn a high yield in return for taking a view of future short-term U.S. and German interest rate movements that is contrary to the expectations implied in the yield curves of those countries.

To analyze an IDN, the investor should consider the note to be equivalent to a fixed-rate note plus a double indexation to the interest differential. The effect of the double indexation to the interest differential is to create two long positions in a two-year, U.S.-dollar, fixed-rate note and two short positions in a DM fixed-rate note. The short position in the DM note is such that the DM exchange rate risk is removed and the investor is exposed only to DM interest rate risk.

The issuer's swap hedge is composed of both U.S. dollar interest rate swaps and DM interest rate swaps. To provide for the structure outlined in Exhibit 8, the swap dealer will, in effect, take opposing (i.e., receiving fixed on one swap and paying fixed on the other swap) positions in DM and USD interest rate swaps. In addition, since the coupon may never fall below zero, the hedge incorporates an option on the spread between DM and USD LIBOR.

The table below is an analysis of the return of a DM-USD IDN under a variety of interest rate scenarios.

Exhibit 8

Coupon Formula:	(2 * DEM LIBOR - 2 * USD LIBOR) minus 4.95%
Current DEM LIBOR:	9.2500% Actual/360
Current USD LIBOR:	3.3750% Actual/360
Current LIBOR Rate Differential:	5.875% Actual/360
Initial Coupon:	6.8000% Actual/360
Current 2.0-yr Treasury:	4.20% S.A. 30/360
Yield spread over UST if LIBOR Differential remains constant:	2.69% S.A. 30/360
Assumed discount rate for PV Differentials:	4.50% S.A. 30/360

Per Annum Change in LIBOR Spread (bp per ann)	LIBOR Spread at Last Reset	P.V. Benefit versus UST	Per Annum Benefit versus UST
300	10.38%	13.57%	7.17%
250	9.63%	12.16%	6.43%
200	8.88%	10.75%	5.68%
150	8.13%	9.34%	4.93%
100	7.38%	7.92%	4.19%
50	6.63%	6.51%	3.44%
Unchanged 0	**5.88%**	**5.10%**	**2.69%**
-50	5.13%	3.69%	1.95%
-100	4.38%	2.27%	1.20%
-150	3.63%	0.86%	0.46%
Breakeven -180	**3.17%**	**0.00%**	**0.00%**
-250	2.13%	-1.64%	-0.87%
-300	1.38%	-2.35%	-1.24%
-350	0.63%	-2.98%	-1.57%

The exhibit shows that the Interest Differential Note offers a 269 bp p.a. yield pickup relative to the two-year U.S. Treasury note assuming that the differential between DEM LIBOR and USD LIBOR remains constant through the final coupon reset date. The table also highlights the significant increase in yield offered by the Note as the spread between the two indexes increases. Even if the differential were to tighten, the return of the Note exceeds that of the UST so long as the differential narrows at a rate less than 180 bp per annum.

Benefits and Risks

IDNs allow investors to take views on interest rates abroad without exposing themselves to currency risk in those countries. The U.S. dollar denomination of IDNs is attractive as relatively few investors are willing to expose their portfolios to currency fluctuations while implementing interest rate positions.

They may also be structured to provide exposure to any part of the yield curve. For example, the indexation may be structured based on the differential between 10-year rates in Germany and the U.S. A combination of maturities in the two currencies would also be possible. Finally, combinations of different maturities in the same currency may also be put together, allowing investors to take yield curve views in foreign or domestic bond markets. The securities often permit investors to earn potentially above-market yields on high credit quality securities in return for the market risk of the interest differential.

The basic risk of an IDN is that the interest differential could move in a direction opposite to that which would benefit the investor. For example, if in the case of the coupon indexed IDN the differential between DM LIBOR and USD LIBOR narrows, the coupon declines.

Variations

Principal Indexed Interest Differential Note

Maturity:	2 years
Coupon:	4% (Fixed)
Principal Redemption	
Formula:	100% + 15 × {0.70%–(FF swap rate – DM swap rate)}

This note pays a fixed coupon and pays a variable redemption amount at maturity that is indexed to the spread between seven-year French franc swap rates and seven-year Deutsche mark swap rates. If the spread widens above 70 bp, the redemption value is below par, and if the spread is less than 70 bp, the redemption value exceeds par. The degree to which the redemption value exceeds or is less than par is the result of a 15 times multiple of the change in the spread.

The principal indexed notes provide a means to take advantage of the expected convergence of long-term French franc and Deutsche mark rates. With the decline in inflation in France and the concurrent rise in German inflation during 1992 and 1993, investors began to expect French rates to fall below German rates. In anticipation of such an event an investor might purchase the bond described. By purchasing this note the investor is taking a view only on the interest rate spread without taking currency exposure to either the French franc or the Deutsche mark. The seven-year swap rates are used as proxies for long-term yields in the two currencies.

This note can be reconstructed and evaluated as a fixed-rate, two-year, U.S.-dollar-denominated note with indexation to forward swap rates. The exposure to the indexation is straightforward in that a 1 bp narrowing in the spread results in a 0.15 percent increase in the redemption value of the security. The trade is hedged by entering into a swap in which the dealer receives a fixed rate on a forward-starting French franc interest rate swap and pays the fixed rate on a forward-starting Deutsche mark interest rate swap.

Constant Maturity Treasury (CMT) Yield Curve Indexed Floater

Coupon: 4.95% + (CMT 2-yr – CMT 10-yr)
Maturity: 2 years

The CMT Curve Floater has a fixed redemption value at par and variable coupons indexed to the spread between two-year and 10-year U.S. Treasury yields. As the yield curve flattens (i.e., the spread narrows), the coupon of the note increases. Likewise, a steepening of the yield curve would result in a lower coupon. The coupons reset quarterly, enabling the investor to earn higher returns over time to the extent that the yield curve flattens.

Rising inflation expectations and the expectation of higher short-term rates relative to longer rates create an argument for a flattening of the yield curve. One way of capitalizing on such an expectation without taking actual long and short positions in the Treasury market is through the purchase of a note indexed to the yield differential between two-year and 10-year Treasuries.

The CMT Curve Floater enables the investor to take a view on the differential between two rates (in this case both within the same currency) rather than taking a view on the absolute level of rates. The structure can be viewed as a combination of a two-year, U.S.-dollar note and an indexation of each coupon to the shape of the yield curve. The note is hedged by taking long and short positions in Treasuries designed to create forward rates for each coupon reset date.

SUMMARY

The preceding discussion of structured notes is intended to provide an understanding of the hedge components required to create these securities. The principles used in structuring the securities described here have been applied to hundreds of other structured notes. Exhibit 9 summarizes several of the most popular structures in 1993. These include a variety of structures based on an historically steep U.S. dollar interest rate curve, and a group of structures based on high real foreign interest rates with coupons inversely tied to European, Japanese, or other foreign interest rates, but paid in U.S. dollars. These inverse floating rate notes allowed investors to take a view on falling international interest rates and at the same time eliminated the currency risk associated with buying non-dollar bonds.

Exhibit 9.   Popular Structures

Interest Rate Environment	Generic Structure Name	Coupon	Investor View
Steep U.S. $ interest rate curve	Yield Curve Notes	CMT minus LIBOR	Interest rate curve will not flatten as quickly as forwards imply.
Steep U.S. $ interest rate curve	Prime Notes	Prime minus LIBOR	Spread between Prime and LIBOR will not narrow as quickly as forwards imply.
Steep U.S. $ interest rate curve and high volatility	Range Notes/Accrual Notes	Above-market coupons paid every day LIBOR is within a pre-set range	Interest rates will remain steady to moderately higher.
Steep U.S. interest rate curve	SURF's/Deleveraged Floaters	50% CMT plus Spread	Interest rate curve will not flatten as quickly as forwards imply.
Steep U.S. $ interest rate curve	Ratchets/One-Way Floaters	LIBOR plus Spread-Coupon can increase a maximum of 25 bp/quarter, and can never decrease.	Interest rates will increase slowly and steadily.
High real European interest rates	Inverse floating rate note (IFRN)	Fixed rate minus DM LIBOR, paid in U.S. dollars.	Interest rates in Europe will decline faster than forwards imply.
High real Global interest rates	Basket Note	Fixed rate minus (Sum of Foreign interest rates), paid in U.S. dollars	Some interest rates may increase, but on average foreign rates will decline.

Continued innovation in the derivatives market will no doubt lead to increased diversity among the investment alternatives available to institutions.

Several different methods of evaluating the performance of these securities were used throughout this chapter. The appropriate means of analyzing and evaluating return is specific to each investor and is a function of the benchmarks against which each investor measures a security's performance.

CHAPTER 8

Opportunities for Hedging and Trading with Catastrophe Insurance Futures and Options

Joseph B. Cole
Managing Director
Richard L. Sandor
Chairman and Chief Executive Officer

Centre Financial Products Limited

INTRODUCTION

Not since the introduction of GNMA and T-Bill futures has the futures market traded such an innovative and exciting hedging and trading instrument as the Chicago Board of Trade's (CBOT) Catastrophe Insurance contract. This contract offers traders the opportunity to participate in the convergence of the financial and insurance markets through novel hedging and trading strategies. Moreover, this instrument represents a true "zero-beta" asset for investors and commodity funds managers for the purposes of portfolio diversification.

This chapter will begin with a brief description of the property reinsurance market. The subsequent section provides an overview of the CBOT contract specifications and illustrates the hedging and trading uses of this new instrument through several examples. This chapter concludes with a discussion of the "zero-beta" characteristics of catastrophe futures and options and describes the investment opportunities presented by this new asset class.

REINSURANCE

Reinsurance is utilized by insurers to reduce volatility in operating results, increase capacity, and provide financing. The relationship between insurance and reinsurance

Exhibit 1.   The Insurance, Reinsurance, and Retrocession Markets

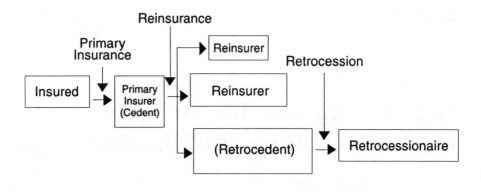

may be illustrated by the schematic in Exhibit 1. The primary insurance market is characterized by the sale of insurance policies, such as automobile or homeowner's policies, from a primary insurer to the insured. Primary insurers may "cede," or pass on, some or all of the insurance risk to another insurer, called the reinsurer. Reinsurers, in turn, may retrocede, or pass on portions of their reinsurance risk, to other insurers called retrocessionaires. Similar to "forward contracting," the market for reinsurance generally consists of bilateral contracts, which are negotiated individually between the reinsured and reinsurer and are sometimes facilitated by a reinsurance broker. The market for catastrophe reinsurance enables insurers to hedge against catastrophic losses and to manage their finances more effectively, thereby reducing earnings volatility and optimizing the use of capital.

Placement of reinsurance is usually done on a treaty or facultative basis. Treaty reinsurance for property risks can be written on either a proportional (pro-rata) or nonproportional (excess) basis. In either case, the ceding insurer and the reinsurer agree on what types of risks are covered by the reinsurance. In contrast, facultative reinsurance often involves one certain type of risk or one specific policy. Accordingly, catastrophe reinsurance is often provided on a treaty basis, since it is designed to provide the reinsured broad coverage against an accumulation of losses.

Nonproportional treaties have many characteristics that are similar to option hedging strategies. A "stop-loss" cover, for instance, provides a ceding company with protection above an agreed-upon dollar amount or ratio of losses and, thus, is similar to the purchase of a call option. An excess-of-loss treaty insures the reinsured for a stated amount of protection above an agreed-upon retention amount. For example, a $10 million excess of $30 million loss treaty would require the reinsurer to pay up to, but no more than, $10 million of additional losses beyond the initial $30 million in losses retained by the reinsured. Thus, an excess-of-loss policy is similar to a call option spread, where the reinsured is long a "$30 million/$40 million bull call option spread" relative to claims payments.

Although reinsurance treaties are written and purchased in order to control losses, they cannot prevent them. The severe catastrophic losses of the last four years have had a substantial impact on the earnings and surplus positions of many property insurers. Industries that experience a high degree of stress in the form of earnings volatility and increased risks often respond in three ways. First, since higher risks often mean higher rewards, new entrants are attracted to the industry through capital infusions or new start-up companies. Second, standardization and commoditization occur in the industry's products, increasing homogeneity, and the trading and transfer of risks. Third, efficient hedging mechanisms and risk management tools are developed.

The property reinsurance industry is currently exhibiting all three of these responses. During the twelve months following Hurricane Andrew, over $3.0 billion of new capital was raised for property insurance companies, mostly in the form of offshore reinsurance entities. Some evidence of reinsurance standardization may also be found in the increasing use of industry loss warranties that employ indexes or measures of industry catastrophic losses for the purposes of "double trigger" reinsurance treaties and other nontraditional covers. The third response, the development and use of efficient hedging mechanisms, is the topic of this paper.

THE FUTURES CONTRACT

Catastrophe Insurance Futures and Options contracts started trading on December 11, 1992, at the Chicago Board of Trade. Generally, a futures contract is a standardized agreement to buy or sell a financial instrument or commodity on an organized exchange at some time in the future for a price agreed upon today. The basis for the Catastrophe Insurance Futures is an index tracking the losses of approximately twenty-five (minimum of ten) property/casualty insurers who report their data to ISO Data, Inc. (Isodata), an independent data collection agency. Exhibit 2 presents the

---

Exhibit 2. The Board of Trade of the City of Chicago: Catastrophe Futures Included Insurers for Quarterly Contracts Covering Accident Quarters (Q1 '94–Q4 '94)

American Financial Group
AMICA Mutual Insurance Group
CIGNA Group
CNA Insurance Companies
Commercial Union Insurance
   Companies
Continental Insurance Companies
Employers Mutual Companies
Fireman's Fund Companies
General Accident Group
Hanover Insurance Group
ITT Hartford Group

Kemper Corporation/Group
   Kemper National Insurance
   Companies
Liberty Mutual Group
Lincoln National Group
Royal Insurance Group
Safeco Insurance Group
St. Paul Group
Transamerica Corporation Group
United States F&G Group
USAA Group
Westfield Companies
Zurich Insurance Group–U.S.

Source: CBOT

---

current composition of contributing insurers. Collectively, they represent about 23 percent of the U.S. property insurance industry.

As with other futures contracts, the Catastrophe Insurance futures contracts may be traded only by qualified Futures Commission Merchants (FCMs) on the floors of exchanges regulated by the Commodity Futures Trading Commission (CFTC). An initial margin must be posted; thereafter, each counterparty is responsible for a daily variation margin representing the change in value of the futures position, otherwise known as the "mark-to-market." The contract has a cash settlement because the underlying instrument, the index value, cannot be physically delivered. The Board of Trade Clearing Corporation (BOTCC) acts as the ultimate guarantor of all trades, ensuring the creditworthiness of the counterparties. Overall, these strict rules permit insurers and reinsurers to hedge the systematic risk component of their insurance liabilities as related to the index compiled by Isodata.

The primary purpose of using Catastrophe Insurance Futures and Options is to provide more effective risk management to insurers facing potentially large payouts in the property line of insurance. The Eastern, Midwestern, Western, and National Catastrophe Futures and Options contracts are now available and trading. Each contract's underlying index, as reported by Isodata, takes into account losses caused by the following: earthquake, flood, hail, riot, and wind across applicable lines, as shown in Exhibit 3.

Exhibit 3. Catastrophe Futures Contracts

Applicable Lines	Wind	Hail	Earthquake	Riot	Flood
Homeowners	♦	♦			
Earthquake			♦		
Fire	♦	♦		♦ (1)	
Allied	♦	♦		♦ (1)	
PP Auto Physical Damage	♦	♦	♦	♦	♦
Commercial Auto Physical Damage		♦	♦	♦	♦
Farmowners	♦	♦		♦	
Inland Marine	♦ (1)	♦ (1)	♦ (1)		♦
Commercial Multiple Peril	♦	♦		♦	

(1) Commercial Portion Only

Source: CBOT

As shown in Exhibit 4, the futures index value is calculated by multiplying the $25,000 unit of trading by the incurred catastrophic losses "standardized" by the earned property premium. Thus, the futures value represents, in essence, an industry loss ratio multiplied by $25,000 of "coverage." It is important to note that the changes in futures prices will be mostly due to unexpected catastrophic losses, since the premium is established, or fixed, in advance and, therefore, only the numerator is

---

**Exhibit 4.   Catastrophe Insurance Futures Index Value
(Unit of Trading)**

$= \$25,000 \times$ (Incurred Catastrophic Losses/Earned Property Premium)

Incurred Catastrophic Losses
Total losses reported as incurred at the end of the quarter following the catastrophe quarter

Earned Property Premium
Estimated quarterly premium based on the most recent statutory annual statements filed by the reporting companies

---

uncertain. Exhibit 5 presents the estimated quarterly premiums assumed for each of the four contract regions.

Exhibit 6 presents calculation and settlement methods for the Catastrophe Futures contracts.

Three important time periods occur during the trading cycle of a CBOT Catastrophe contract. The "loss period" encompasses the quarter one full quarter before the contract date. The "reporting period" spans the six-month period that includes the loss quarter and the quarter following the contract date. The "calculation period" comprises the three months and five calendar days following the reporting period. Cash settlement of the futures and options contract occurs at the end of the calculation period.

In the case of the March 1994 contract, trading began on October 6, 1993, and will continue until cash settlement on October 5, 1994. The loss period for this contract is the first quarter of 1994, or from January 1, 1994, through March 31, 1994. Isodata calculations employ losses that occur in this loss period and are reported for the six months including the loss period and three months following the contract date, in this case, January 1, 1994, through June 30, 1994. The reporting period spans six months

---

Exhibit 5.   Estimated Premiums of Catastrophe Futures Contract Regions

	1993 Contracts[1]	1994 Contracts[2]
National:	$12,242,060,112	$12,984,325,717
Eastern:	$5,718,769,160	$6,052,961,404
Midwestern:	$3,968,805,577	$4,237,619,841
Western:	$2,848,444,165	$3,006,003,081

For Settlement Value of CBOT Contracts

1   1993: March, June, September, December (March '94 Renamed)
2   1994: March, June, September, December

Source: Chicago Board of Trade

**Exhibit 6.   Catastrophe Futures Time-Line Calculations and
             Trading Schedule**

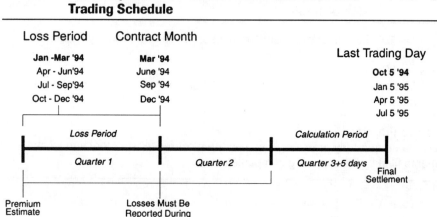

because of the time consumed filing claims and assessing damages. After losses are incurred during the loss period and filed during the reporting period, Isodata calculates, compiles, and issues the final settlement price three months and five calendar days after the month.

A FUTURES HEDGING EXAMPLE

Suppose an insurance company is interested in hedging third-quarter '93 catastrophic losses in the Eastern region. An effective way of doing so would be to purchase September Eastern Catastrophe Futures sometime in July. Details of this sample hedge are shown in Exhibit 7. The hedge would be undertaken to lessen the financial impact on the company during summer months when hurricanes frequently come ashore. Assume that the company has $28.5 million in Eastern region premiums for 0.5 percent market share. Actuarial estimates for the company's third-quarter losses are $10.0 million, while industry premium and loss estimates are $5.7 billion and $2.0 billion, respectively.

The September contract price in July may be calculated by dividing industry estimated, and reported, losses by the CBOT Eastern Catastrophe contract premium. Assuming 75 percent of the industry's $2.0 billion in losses is employed by Isodata to calculate the estimated settlement price, a hypothetical September Eastern futures price of $6,575 would result. In order to hedge $28.5 million of insurance premiums, the insurer would need to buy 1520 contracts.

Now, assume that on the last day of trading, April 5, 1994, the industry's reported losses equalled $3.0 billion and that 75 percent were reported and entered in the Isodata calculations. The final settlement price of the contract would thus be $9,875 ($25,000

Exhibit 7.   Company XX Hedging Strategy

♦   Limit the impact of catastrophic losses due to the frequency and severity of hurricanes, which commonly occur in August and September on the eastern seaborad.

♦   Early July: By September Eastern Catastrophe Futures

Actuarial Forecasts: Catastrophe Quarter July-September

	Company XX	*Industry*
Incurred Losses	$10.0 Million	$2.0 Billion
Premiums	$28.5 Million	$5.7 Billion
Losses Reported as % of Incurred by End September	75%	75%

Price of September Futures
(In July)¶

$25,000 × (Industry Estimated Loss/Industry Estimated Premium)

$25,000 × ([$2.0 Billion × 75%]/$5.7 Billion) = $6,575

Number of Contracts Company XX Needs to Buy

([Company Premium/Contract Size] × [Hedged Losses/% Reported])

([$28.5 Million/$25,000] × [1.00/0.75]) = 1,520 contracts

September Eastern Catastrophe Final Settlement Price
(In March)

$25,000 × (Industry Reported Losses/Industry Estimated Premium)
$25,000 × ([$3 Billion × 75%]/$5.7 Billion) = $9,875

Evaluating Company XX's Hedge

3rd Quarter Results	
Expected Incurred Results	$10,000,000
Actual Losses Incurred	$15,000,000
Increase in Losses:	$ 5,000,000
Futures Results	
Purchased September Futures @	$ 6,575
September Futures Settlement @	$ 9,875
Futures Gain per Contract:	$ 3,300
Contracts Purchased:	× 1,520
Total Futures Gain:	$ 5,016,000

× ([$3.0 billion × 75 percent]/$5.7 billion). Given the company's 0.5 percent market share, third-quarter property claims would be approximately $15.0 million. Upon evaluation of the hedge, it is evident that without the futures position, the company's actual incurred losses would have exceeded expected incurred losses by $5 million. The futures gain of $3,300 per contract would result in a total futures gain of $5,016,000, thereby offsetting unanticipated losses of $5 million by almost $16,000 for a small basis gain.

CALCULATING A HEDGING LAYER FOR SYNTHETIC REINSURANCE

The Catastrophe Insurance Options contracts at the Chicago Board of Trade (CBOT) may also be employed by insurers and reinsurers to create synthetic excess-of-loss reinsurance policies. The following example, summarized in Exhibits 8 and 9, illustrates the calculations and assumptions necessary for an insurer creating a synthetic excess-of-loss reinsurance policy.

The objective of the insurer is to hedge $40 million of loss exposure above $40 million in losses. In other words, the insurer wishes to hedge the $40 million to $80 million layer of potential underwriting losses. The insurer's book of insurance is assumed to be fairly similar (correlation of 100 percent) in terms of line and region to the CBOT National Catastrophe Futures contract. The insurer also has a 2 percent market share of industry.

Due to contract design and specifications, not all of the industry's ultimate loss for a catastrophe in a given quarter are "passed through" to the futures contract. As shown in Exhibit 9, quarterly industry losses are assumed to be incurred and reported at 75 percent of the ultimate industry loss. By dividing these reported losses by the National contract premium of $12.2 billion, a range of loss ratios given various

---

Exhibit 8. Calculating the Hedging Layer for a Synthetic Reinsurance Contract

---

Objective: An insurance (reinsurance) company wishes to hedge $40 million in exposure above $40 million in retaines losses

Assumptions: Company has 2% market share on National basis

                    Correlation between company and industry losses is 100%

                    75% of National incurred and reported losses impact settlement prices of CBOT Catastrophe Futures contracts

                    Normal or average quarterly losses at 5% influence CBOT Catastrophe Futures settlement prices

Solution: $40MM XS $40MM coverage is approximated by 17%/30% bull call option spread

---

Exhibit 9. Calculating the Hedging Layer for a Synthetic Reinsurance Contract

Industry	CBOT Catastrophe Futures			Company
Ultimate Loss ($Billions)	Reported Loss (× 0.75)	Reported Loss Ratio (/$12.2B)	CBOT Strike (+5%)	Market Share Losses ($MM)
1.00	0.75	6.1%	11.1%	20
2.00	1.50	12.3%	17.3% ⟷	40
3.00	2.25	18.4%	23.4%	60
4.00	3.00	24.6%	29.6% ⟷	80
5.00	3.75	30.7%	35.7%	100
6.00	4.50	36.9%	41.9%	120
7.00	5.25	43.0%	48.0%	140
8.00	6.00	49.2%	54.2%	160
9.00	6.75	55.3%	60.3%	180
10.00	7.50	61.5%	66.5%	200

quarterly catastrophe totals may be computed. This range is further adjusted upward by 5 percent, since the calculation procedure performed by Isodata for the CBOT settlement prices introduces normal quarterly losses of a like amount. This 5 percent "normal loss load" occurs because Isodata employs a calculation method that incorporates losses by state and line, which may include incidental losses not associated with large industry catastrophes as defined by Property Claim Services.

An examination of Exhibit 9 shows that an insurer with a 2 percent market share would experience $40 million in losses when the industry incurs $2 billion in losses. The appropriate "attachment points" for the company's $40 million to $80 million loss layer are approximately 17 percent and 30 percent. To hedge this layer, the insurer would simultaneously buy 17 percent strike call options and sell 30 percent strike call options. The 17 percent/30 percent bull call option spread would "mirror" industry losses of $2 to $4 billion and, by assumption, the company's $40 million of exposure above $40 million in retained losses.

CALCULATING EXPECTED WIN/LOSS RATIOS FOR 60/80 "HURRICANE" OPTION SPREADS

In addition to creating novel hedging strategies, the new Chicago Board of Trade's Insurance Futures and Options are providing unique trading opportunities. Recent trading activity in "Hurricane" option spreads is spurring additional study by speculators and traders. Specifically, the five-to-one risk/reward ratio of the Eastern September 60/80 bear call spread appears to offer substantial opportunities for profit with limited risk.

Exhibit 10. 60/80 "Hurricane" Bear Call Spread

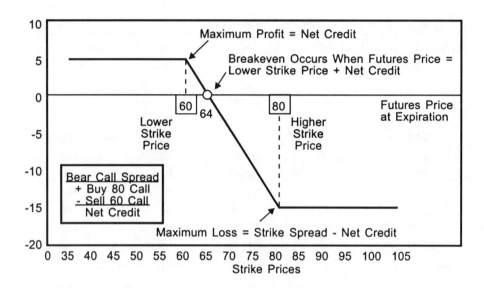

As discussed earlier, the CBOT's Catastrophe Insurance Futures contracts are designed to track quarterly catastrophic loss ratios for the property insurance industry. The September 1994 Eastern Catastrophe contract is based, for example, on insured losses incurred during July 1, 1994, through September 30, 1994, and reported from July 1, 1994, through December 31, 1994. These losses are divided by a predetermined quarterly industry premium and the result is the quarterly loss ratio. An Eastern futures value of 27.0 represents the expectation of a 27 percent loss ratio by the insurance industry for the Eastern region. Traders often refer to the Eastern September Catastrophe contract as the "Hurricane future," since the loss period encompasses the majority of seasonal hurricane activity.

Reflecting contract specifications, a 60/80 call spread represents a loss ratio range of 20 percent. This range approximates $4.8 to $6.5 billion in industry losses, assuming $6.1 billion in Eastern premium and a 75 percent reporting rate.[1] With the underlying September Eastern futures contract at 27.0, the lower leg of the spread is 122 percent out-of-the-money.[2]

The profit and loss potential of a 60/80 bear call spread priced at a 4.0 net credit is illustrated in Exhibit 10. This spread has a 5-to-1 risk/reward ratio with a $1,000 premium credit and $4,000 maximum loss since the contract multiplier equals

1 By assumption, the six-month reporting period for the CBOT settlement procedure captures 75 percent of total industry. Thus, a 60/0.75 futures index price represents $3.63 billion in incurred and reported losses and $4.8 billion (3.63/0.75) in total industry losses.
2 One hundred twenty-two percent is arrived at by calculating the quantity (60.0- 27.0)/27.0.

$25,000. Note that as long as the September futures remains below 64.0, representing $5.2 billion in reported and incurred losses, the spread writer earns a profit. The maximum loss is also represented in the graph and equals 16 points, or $4,000 per spread.

Since 1949, twenty-six intense hurricanes (Category 3 or higher) have hit the Eastern region, as illustrated in Exhibit 11. Two of the largest hurricanes, Hugo and Andrew, have occurred during the last four years. After adjusting the insured loss estimates for inflation, only Andrew, with a simulated loss ratio of 178.9, would have created a loss for the spread writer. Hugo, with a simulated loss ratio of 48.3, would still have returned 4.0 points in profit or $1,000, since the 60/80 spread would not have been hit.

Exhibit 12 presents a range of possible expected win/loss ratios by adjusting maximum loss and maximum return by probabilities of occurrence. Recent prices for the 60/80 Eastern September call spread are around 4 points, with 20 points of risk. Therefore, the market is pricing the spread at a five-to-one risk/reward ratio. As shown in Exhibit 12, the expected (probability-weighted) cost of the spread is 3.20, and equals 16 times the probability of loss (0.20). The expected (probability-weighted) profit is also 3.20 and equals 4.0 times the probability of no loss (0.80). Thus, the expected win/loss ratio is 0 percent as it should be, since the market prices all option spreads to an expected return of zero. In other words, equilibrium option pricing is a fair game and provides no probability of gain to either the seller or buyer.

Employing recent hurricane data from 1989 to date, historical odds of seven-to-one may be used to similarly value the potential expected win/loss ratio for the 60/80 call spread at 150 percent. If recent historical data suggesting fourteen-to-one odds are used to evaluate possibilities, the expected win/loss ratio for shorting the 60/80 Eastern September call spread exceeds 300 percent. Using inflation-adjusted hurricane data from 1949, the potential expected win/loss ratio of this short position approaches 600 percent, since out of 26 hurricanes only Hurricane Andrew would have created a loss.

The previous "odds" should also be adjusted for demographics as well as incorporating the inflation component. This expected win/loss ratio method of assessing the risk/return potential of a short 60/80 Eastern September Call Spread does, however, offer valuable insight into these exciting new futures and options contracts.

CATASTROPHE FUTURES AS ZERO-BETA ASSETS

Catastrophe-indexed securities, such as the CBOT Catastrophe Insurance Futures and Option contracts, may offer investors an effective way to diversify existing investment allocations while providing relatively high expected returns. Since returns on catastrophe-indexed securities are generally uncorrelated with the economy, these instruments will enhance portfolio performance so long as their expected return exceeds the risk-free rate.

Most investors maintain a diversified portfolio of traditional assets, including stocks, bonds, real estate, and cash. According to Modern Portfolio Theory, investors who manage their portfolios with respect to their risk and return preferences by shifting between assets achieve higher return with less risk. As a result, investors are constantly in search of combinations of assets defined by the "efficient frontier."

Exhibit 11. Intense Hurricanes, 1949–1992
       Category ≥ 3

Date	Hurricane	Class	Inches Pressure	Insured/PCS CPI-Adjusted	CBOT Simulated Setlmt. Ratios
31-Aug-49	SE FL	3	28.17	$53,386,611	
13-Oct-50	KING (SE FL)	3	28.20	$68,357,239	
25-Aug-54	CAROL	3	28.35	$780,534,645	
05-Oct-54	HAZEL	4	27.70	$700,185,490	
02-Sep-54	EDNA (NEW ENGLAND)	3	28.17	$66,001,091	
10-Sep-55	IONE	3	28.35	$25,922,427	
03-Aug-55	CONNIE	3	28.41	$145,165,591	
25-Jun-57	AUDREY	4	27.91	$179,003,630	
20-Sep-59	GRACIE	3	28.05	$69,213,159	
29-Aug-60	DONNA	4	27.46	$477,897,136	
03-Sep-61	CARLA	4	27.49	$518,155,319	
28-Sep-64	HILDA (CENTRAL LA)	3	28.05	$114,934,789	
26-Aug-65	BETSY	3	27.99	$2,345,979,793	
05-Sep-67	BUELAH	3	28.05	$150,345,496	
14-Aug-69	CAMILLE	5	26.84	$659,974,896	
30-Jul-70	CELIA	3	27.91	$1,168,557,920	
29-Aug-74	CARMEN (CENTRAL LA)	3	28.11	$45,188,545	
15-Sep-75	ELOISE	3	28.20	$326,379,398	
29-Aug-79	FREDERIC	3	27.94	$1,574,944,232	
31-Jul-80	ALLEN	3	27.91	$107,022,664	
15-Aug-83	ALICIA	3	28.41	$982,628,185	
08-Sep-84	DIANA	3	28.02	$50,454,278	
27-Aug-85	GLORIA	3	27.82	$564,092,038	
16-Sep-85	ELENA	3	28.32	$731,467,407	
10-Sep-89	HUGO	4	27.58	$4,939,159,757	48.3%
16-Aug-92	ANDREW	4	27.23	$15,949,500,000	178.9%

Sources: NOAA, Property Claim Services

Exhibit 12. Calculating Expected Win/Loss Ratios for Short 60/80 Call Spread

Eastern Sep 60 Call @ 16.0
Eastern Sep 80 Call @ 12.0
            4.0 pts credit
          20.0 pts risk

"Odds of Occurrence"	(1) Expected Loss (16) * Prob (Loss)	(2) Expected Return (4) * Prob (No Loss)	(2)/(1) Expected Win/Loss Ratios
Market (1:5) = 0.20	(3.20) = 16 * 0.20	3.20 = 4 * 0.80	0%
Recent (1:7) = 0.1429	(2.28) = 16 * 0.1429	3.43 = 4 * 0.8571	150% = 3.43/2.28
(1:14) = 0.0714	(1.14) = 16 * 0.0714	3.71 = 4 * 0.9286	325% = 3.71/1.14
Hurricane Data (1:26) = 0.0385	(0.61) = 16 * 0.0385	3.85 = 4 * 0.9615	631% = 3.85/0.61

The "efficient frontier" consists of all optimal combinations of minimum risk and highest return available to investors, as shown in Exhibit 13. Risk may be measured by standard deviation of return, with higher standard deviations representing higher risk. Return is measured by the total holding period return for the portfolio over a particular time period. Movements along the efficient frontier are accomplished by adding new assets that enhance the portfolio's risk/return trade-offs. Thus, assets with low correlation and high returns are quite valuable for both portfolio diversification and yield enhancement.

Catastrophe indexed securities may be considered "zero-beta" assets, since their payoffs are generally uncorrelated with the economy or almost any existing investment

Exhibit 13. Efficient Frontier
Risk-Return Trade-off Opportunities

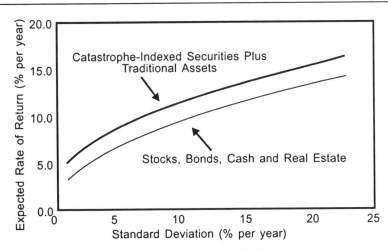

**Exhibit 14. Catastrophe Losses versus S&P 500
Comparison of Annual Percentage Changes**

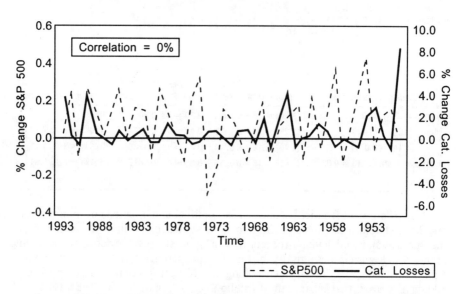

Source: Bloomberg Financial; Property Claim Services, Inc.

---

class. Indeed, little correlation exists between stocks and bonds and such catastrophic events as earthquakes, tornadoes, or hurricanes. In fact, the correlation of annual percentage changes of the S&P 500 Index and catastrophe losses, illustrated in Exhibit 14, is zero over the 1949 through 1992 period. Securities that have returns linked to catastrophic events may, therefore, be considered zero-beta assets.

The value of a high-yielding, zero-beta asset is especially apparent when diversification benefits are examined in terms of the Sharpe Ratio. Recall that the Sharpe Ratio is defined as the ratio of excess return (above the risk-free rate) to standard deviation. Generally speaking, alternative investments should be added to a portfolio if:

$$\begin{bmatrix} \text{Sharpe Ratio of} \\ \text{Alternative Asset} \end{bmatrix} \geq \begin{bmatrix} \text{Correlation Coefficient} \\ \text{of Alternative Asset} \end{bmatrix} \times \begin{bmatrix} \text{Sharpe Ratio} \\ \text{of Portfolio} \end{bmatrix}$$

Since a zero-beta asset, such as a synthetic reinsurance contract utilizing CBOT Catastrophe Options, is generally uncorrelated with the market, the right-hand side of the above equation reduces to zero. Thus, catastrophe-indexed instruments will enhance portfolio performance if their expected return exceeds the risk-free rate of interest.

CONCLUSION

This paper has reviewed several hedging and trading uses of the new CBOT Catastrophe Futures and Options contract. Although current trading activity is relatively low, many insurance and financial market participants are studying the new contracts and are initiating pilot programs. Regulatory impediments imposed by state insurance commissions in the United States are also being reduced or eliminated in states such as New York and California.

From a hedging perspective, the opportunity to employ a new risk management tool for property losses is quite timely. The last four years have been the costliest in terms of losses for the property insurance industry. As a result, reinsurance coverage is much more costly, tripling since 1990, and much more difficult to achieve due to capacity restrictions.

The difficulties of the reinsurance industry may be fortuitous, however, for investors and speculators. Given the well-defined features of the CBOT Catastrophe Insurance contracts, their overnight variation margining and their characteristics as a zero-beta asset, Catastrophe Insurance Futures and Options represent a tremendous opportunity for investors and commodity fund managers.

CHAPTER 9

The Derivative Products Company

Lisa M. Raiti
Managing Director
Centre Financial Products Limited

INTRODUCTION

The enhanced derivative products company (DPC), is one of the most important innovations in the over-the-counter (OTC) or off-exchange derivatives markets. The DPC is a subsidiary of a financial services firm that can be rated higher than its parent or sponsor. There are two main reasons this "enhanced" or higher rating is attainable by a DPC. First, the DPC does not depend on its parent's backing to meet financial obligations on its derivative contracts. Second, the DPC's capital is segregated in a separate subsidiary (see Exhibit 1). The first two 'AAA'-rated DPC "pioneers" were subsidiaries of U.S. securities firms: GS Financial Products International, L.P., and Merrill Lynch Derivative Products, Inc. (see Chapter 23: How Enhanced DPCs Are Rated 'AAA').

The enhanced DPC is one innovative solution for a dealer to access the credit-sensitive OTC derivatives market. OTC derivatives contracts are customized for and negotiated between two parties. Counterparty financial performance is based solely on credit quality. This OTC environment contrasts with that of the listed exchange, in which performance is often backed by the capital or performance guarantee of the exchange. The high premium the OTC market places on credit quality is simply based on the high cost of counterparty default. If a counterparty does not pay in accordance with the contract, the party who is hedging or neutralizing interest rate or foreign-exchange rate risk faces the very exposure the derivative contract had removed. A risk manager may reduce the likelihood of this adverse scenario by transacting with a counterparty with an 'AAA' financial capacity to honor its payment obligations under such derivative contracts. The enhanced DPC is one such counterparty.

This chapter is based on Standard & Poor's May 1992 publication, *Credit Sensitivity Spurs Enhanced DPC Growth*; however, the views expressed are those of the author and do not necessarily reflect the opinions of Standard & Poor's.

Exhibit 1. The Enhanced DPC

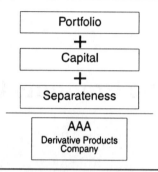

DPCs can best be understood in the context of the derivative products market, which is profiled below.

WHAT IS A DERIVATIVE PRODUCT?

A derivative product is an instrument that derives its value from the performance of another asset, security, rate, or index. For example, the value of an option on the S&P 500 depends on the level of that stock market index. As complex and diverse as they are, all derivative products contractually establish the structure of cash flow and accompanying value based on an "underlying" or specified asset, security, rate, or index.

DPCs engage in interest rate swaps, currency swaps, options, forwards, caps, floors, swap options, and similar products (see glossary on page 901). Capital market participants use these financial contracts in a wide array of business and portfolio strategies. Management of interest rate and exchange rate risk or enhancement of services to customers are among the multitude of derivative applications. Although these products can be utilized in speculative strategies, their application as risk management tools is more relevant to derivative products companies and their sponsors.

DRAMATIC GROWTH OF DERIVATIVES

The growth of the derivatives universe since the mid-1980s has been stratospheric. According to the International Swaps and Derivatives Association, Inc. (ISDA) interest rate and currency swaps alone grew in total notional principal value outstanding from an estimated $0.9 trillion in 1987 to over $4.7 trillion at year-end 1992. Three forces converged during the last decade to fuel activity in this market: globalization, innovation, and flexibility.

Globalization. Integration and globalization of operating and financing activities of capital market participants have provided opportunity and have introduced new risk over the last decade. Financial institutions now in the ordinary course of business lend, borrow, and underwrite overseas both as agents for their multinational customers and as principals. Financing activities now frequently span international markets, increasing capital-raising opportunities for derivative product end users but also introducing new elements of risk. One example is floating-rate debt tied to the London Interbank Offered Rate (LIBOR), which proliferated during the 1980s. An issuer of LIBOR-based debt can access a wider international investor base spanning U.S., European, and Pacific Rim markets.

However, this benefit of salability has a cost. The issuer of floating-rate debt with its coupon tied to LIBOR faces an uncapped variable interest rate on the debt liability that can increase over time. This is commonly called interest rate risk. A plain-vanilla interest rate swap directly counters interest rate risk. The issuer can enter into such a swap contract, promising to pay a fixed interest rate to the counterparty in exchange for LIBOR. The issuer simply applies the LIBOR interest receipt from the counterparty to the floating-rate LIBOR interest payment on the debt and, in effect, holds fixed-rate debt. The swap eliminates the interest rate risk, as long as the counterparty performs, and allows the issuer to realize the financial benefit of broader market access.

Another example of capital market activity that proliferated with globalization is financing by multinational entities in debt denominated in a foreign currency to currency-match an overseas business. Like the interest rate swap, the currency swap eliminates a risk in the transaction, exchange-rate risk in this case, while allowing the end user to realize the benefits of nondomestic funding. These examples show the synergy between globalized markets and derivative products.

Innovation. Globalization engendered innovation in the capital markets. Incorporation of derivative products into debt issuances such as those described above permits securities firms to engineer more cost-effective and innovative underwritings. Advances in quantitative techniques and computer technology allow risk monitoring and pricing of complex synthetic transactions involving derivative products. Whether a financial services firm acts directly as a principal or as an intermediary for its customers, it uses derivative products to increase market entree and neutralize risk while enhancing services to its clients.

Flexibility. Due to the combination of globalization and innovation, capital market participants demand more flexibility in capital-raising and risk-reduction activities. Derivative products provide this flexibility, in addition to cost reduction, return enhancement, and diversification. Increased volatility trends in interest rates and foreign-exchange rates have made derivative products important tools even in the most fundamental portfolio and business strategies.

THE RAISON D'ÊTRE FOR ENHANCED DPCs

What prompted the birth of enhanced derivative products companies? Enhanced DPCs are an innovative response to a credit-sensitive market, which became even more so with the negative trend in global credit quality that emerged in the late 1980s. The utility of derivative products in their myriad applications depends on one critical assumption: performance of the counterparty. This one simple principle puts top-tier credit quality at the nucleus of the OTC market (see Exhibit 2). The creators of enhanced derivative products companies are generally OTC participants that have seen market share decline as their credit ratings have fallen below the 'AAA' and 'AA' rating categories. One way in which financial firms can revitalize their roles in this credit-conscious sector is by conducting business through an 'AAA'-rated DPC.

Exhibit 2. The Science of Derivatives

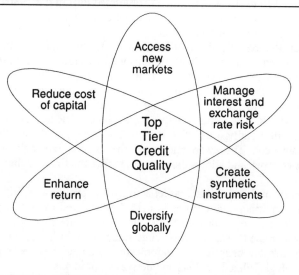

THE ESSENCE OF AN ENHANCED DPC

An enhanced DPC is a subsidiary of a financial services firm. It can be rated higher than its parent or sponsor because a DPC does not depend upon the parent's direct support to meet financial obligations on its derivative contracts, and its capital is segregated in a separate subsidiary. There are three building blocks in an enhanced DPC: portfolio, capital, and separateness (see Exhibit 1).

Portfolio is the set of derivative contracts, predominantly customized OTC products, that the DPC can buy and sell.

Capital is the excess of assets over liabilities, or net asset value, in the DPC. It provides credit support or protection for the DPC against credit risk, which is explained in the next section. Capital can be contributed by a parent, affiliate and/or third party, and can take any number of forms. Examples include paid-in capital such as common or preferred equity, subordinated debt, a letter of credit, a surety bond, or overcollateralization with additional portfolio assets.

Separateness is recognition and treatment of the DPC for legal, regulatory, and operational purposes as an entity separate and distinct from its often lower rated parent and affiliates.

CREDIT RISK IN A DPC

Capital covers credit risk in a DPC, but what is credit risk in a portfolio of swaps, options, and other derivative products with OTC counterparties? The enormous complexity of the answer stems from one unique characteristic: varying exposure (see Exhibit 3).

Exhibit 3.   Credit Risk in a DPC

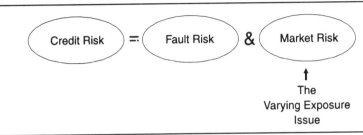

The
Varying Exposure
Issue

The implications of varying exposure can best be seen by first examining credit risk in a more traditional asset portfolio. Assume an investor holds a portfolio of 100 zero-coupon bonds to maturity, with each borrower owing the same amount. Furthermore, there is no trading, no buying or selling, and no recovery of principal after bond default. For simplicity, we define cash-flow losses purely from loss of principal, ignoring the time value of money. If ten borrowers default on their bonds, credit losses add up to 10 percent of total bond principal in portfolio.

Theoretically, if the bonds are replaced with derivative contracts, the credit-risk assessment should be similar. We have already assessed default risk by assuming that ten counterparties will not pay. But how much will the investor lose in each of these ten cases? Assume the investor holds a portfolio of U.S. dollar plain-vanilla interest rate swaps. In this basic type of swap, one counterparty makes fixed-rate interest payments to the other counterparty in exchange for floating-rate interest payments, most commonly based on LIBOR. In addition, we assume that only the differential between the two interest payments is exchanged and that the counterparties in the portfolio all owe LIBOR floating interest on identical swap agreements.

A portfolio that is receiving LIBOR and paying a fixed rate to each counterparty is in-the-money on a cash-flow and market-value basis when LIBOR exceeds the fixed rate. This means that the investor is entitled to a net receivable from the floating-rate payer and that the dollar interest rate swap is an asset. If ten counterparties default, the loss on each swap is the unpaid cash flow, or if the investor can replace the open position in a sufficiently liquid market, the replacement cost. The remaining question is defining the size of the loss. Unlike in the first example, the investor does not have a fixed bond principal cash-flow stream. This illustrates the varying exposure issue.

If the investor takes no action with respect to the open position, the loss is the unpaid cash flow over the remaining tenor or life of the swap, which varies with interest rate movements. If the investor chooses to replace the swap and close the position, the loss is the replacement cost. In both cases, credit risk or the amount of loss would vary, whether cash flow is lost or a replacement contract is purchased at market value. The size of the exposure will depend on the levels and volatility of spot and forward interest rates prevailing in the financial markets from and after the time of default.

The answer to the credit risk question is just as complicated when the investor's position is out-of-the-money, or in this example when the fixed rate exceeds LIBOR. The portfolio owes a net payable to that same counterparty. In this case, the investor needs to determine how to settle the varying out-of-the-money exposure with the defaulted counterparty.

Credit loss in a derivatives portfolio depends on default risk and on market risk in the relationship shown in Exhibit 3. This relatively simple example shows that risk can be accurately sized in a derivatives portfolio only by examining a wide range of market rate behaviors to estimate loss. Probability theory and statistical techniques are important tools for modeling risk and assessing the huge number of scenarios associated with a derivative portfolio's varying exposure. In its simplest form, the enhanced DPC combines capital sized to cover this particular variety of credit risk with a portfolio of predominantly investment-grade counterparties. The adequacy of that capital is a key consideration in the ultimate determination of the credit quality of the enhanced DPC.

THE ULTIMATE QUESTION

The most often asked question is how off-balance-sheet activities such as derivatives, and the related development of DPCs, have affected global systemic risk. Systemic risk in this context refers to a macro event with marketwide adverse impact. In the extreme "crash" scenario, chaotic conditions are present, with "fallout" in terms of market participants and the financial system as a whole. In order to answer this, we should separately address derivatives and DPCs.

There is no question that derivatives are products of markets characterized by increasing globalization, complexity, information, sophistication, technological advancements, and competition. Currency and interest rate markets are continually evolving. Interrelationships among markets and market variables, increasing volatility and increasing transaction velocity are only some examples of the material changes unfolding since the mid-1980s. The state of the financial market backdrop to derivative products brings to mind an example from the physical sciences, an oft-cited frame of reference for derivatives practitioners. Imagine a cylinder with a piston filled with a gas that has become subjected to increased pressure in the cylinder, all else equal. That pressure can be decreased and equalized to its original state, by moving the piston to expand the volume in the cylinder. This later state of equilibrium is representative of the derivatives' arena—expanded markets with new and different interactions among relevant variables, as represented by the gas particles. As such, the systemic risk function and the nature of certain events within the expanded container or derivatives-utilizing market universe has been altered.

In order to determine whether or not systemic risk has increased or decreased, however, one would also have to focus on the consequences of such events. Consequences and severity of effect are, in turn, a function of market response mechanisms and resilience, which this author believes have just as likely changed. Suffice it to say that change is the only definitely observable characteristic of the derivatives market universe.

As for how DPCs have affected global systemic risk, there are mainly three positive results of their development: (1) improved derivatives' portfolio credit quality due to higher volume with highly rated counterparties for the individual sponsor; (2) allocation of a specified amount of capital against the ongoing derivatives business by the individual sponsor; and (3) higher aggregate volume as well as potential liquidity in the derivatives market. In other words, the DPC fills and capitalizes a high credit quality niche while expanding market depth. On a microlevel, the DPC changes the anatomy and capital structure of the sponsor to enhance its own counterparty performance, portfolio of business, and risk quantification/capital allocation techniques. On a macrolevel, the DPC meets insatiable demand for 'AAA' credit.

More important than debating whether and to what degree risk has increased is how to manage evolving risk now, and protect against adverse scenarios, even if they cannot be predicted accurately. If we accept the market characteristics of expansion, less transparency, and altered systemic risk in the derivatives arena, risk management is the ultimate and most formidable challenge for DPCs and all counterparties.

There are three basic keys to circumspect risk management in the complex , highly engineered DPC and derivatives arena: measurement, matching, and management. There are no hard and fast rules, but there are aspects unique to derivatives to focus on.

Measurement

Measurement refers to the importance of prudently valuing and limiting the varying exposure described earlier. The idea is to increase transparency and obtain a realistic handle on such engineered positions. Exposure measurement should incorporate a set of assumptions for each relevant quantitative and qualitative variable. Some applicable variables include gross and net calculations of positions, different product liquidities, counterparty default risk and a wide range of stressed market behaviors. The most striking example of the importance of exposure measurement is the first. Assume incorrect allocation by a risk manager of capital on a net exposure basis when gross treatment governs close-out or settlement with a defaulting counterparty. It is easy to see the adverse consequences of a $500 million gross loss upon counterparty default, which had been carried and managed ats a $50 million net exposure.

Matching

Matching or hedging positions is the best protection against open exposure to index rate or price movements. Speculation and position-taking can be very risky propositions, even with traditional assets. Enhanced DPCs that must conserve segregated capital are largely matched, typically through "equal and opposite" transactions with the parent as counterparty. This means that mismatches, or "open positions," should be mainly involuntary, namely due to counterparty defaults.

Management

The challenge of running any derivatives business is to develop the necessary technology to solve a multivariate mathematical problem without creating a "black box." Maintaining communication between the highly technical quantitative side of the business and the more traditional portfolio management side of the business is the key to derivatives risk management.

Calculus and higher forms of mathematics aside, there is a right balance between using these valuable tools to deal with dynamic exposure, and applying traditional financial principles. If there is no "knowledge gap" between technology and tradition—e.g., the risk manager performs sensitivity analysis and reconciles output and expectations—accurate risk measurement and effective risk management are achievable.

In the end, the challenge for an enhanced DPC or any counterparty is to manage complex, dynamic derivative assets against finite capital while preserving top tier credit quality. Circumspect analysis of enhanced DPCs and their product markets recognizes two realities:

- Risk-reducing management is an important bridge between asset volatility and capital preservation.

- Derivative product markets are maturing, but are inherently complex, dynamic, and evolving with capital markets. Continuous observation of market events and behaviors is essential for any OTC participant.

PROSPECTS AND CHALLENGES

The 'AAA' DPC embodies the challenges ahead in the financial markets of the 1990s and beyond: Achieve more efficient allocation of capital, improve credit quality, and engage in ever more sophisticated global markets. The enhanced DPC is separately capitalized, and its business disciplined, yet it transacts in highly engineered, customized products. For the parent or sponsor, the DPC revitalizes its market share in derivative products, particularly with 'AAA' and 'AA' counterparties. For its counterparties, the DPC provides increased opportunities to do business with a 'AAA' credit. In the end, the enhanced DPC offers a solution to managing credit risk by expanding the universe of 'AAA' derivative product market participants.

It is expected that, *ceteris paribus*, and without material regulatory limitations, future growth of the DPC sector will be primarily driven by two factors. These are (1) activity in the underlying OTC derivative products market, and (2) OTC market demand for top-tier credit quality.

Activity in the underlying OTC derivative products market. Activity in the derivative products market experienced dramatic growth during the 1980s. In addition to expanded volume, standardization of documentation promoted evolution of a secondary market. Even as generic, relatively liquid products such as the plain-vanilla interest rate swap proliferate, it is expected that the OTC market will remain the breeding ground for customized products.

OTC market demand for top tier credit quality. As for the "high value added" of 'AAA' and 'AA' credit ratings in the OTC market, there appears to be no evidence that this will diminish. The prevailing forces in the derivatives markets are industry capital and credit constraints, ever changing underlying market behaviors, and opaque credit risks in more engineered OTC products. These systemic conditions should only enhance the value of credit strength in the off-exchange market.

Stimulated demand for both customized product and high credit quality in the OTC milieu will continue to be important factors in the cost-benefit equation for firms considering formation of a DPC. The potential costs arise mainly from the capital investment in the new company. The potential benefits arise from increased opportunities to transact higher volume with more highly rated counterparties. In the end, both benefits and costs can be substantial, and the decision to create a DPC will be a capital allocation decision unique to each firm.

PART TWO

APPLICATIONS: INVESTMENT AND TRADING

CHAPTER 10

Derivatives in Pension Plan Management

Thomas A. Szczesny
Senior Vice President and Manager
Investment Technology Division
The Bank of New York

THE PLAN SPONSOR AS INVESTMENT MANAGER

Investment Objectives

Knowledgeable U.S.-plan pension plan sponsors are aware of the tremendous growth of the derivative markets in the U.S. during the past few years and of the similar surge of derivative instruments that is occurring in the non-U.S. investment markets. They are aware that the derivative markets offer tremendous opportunity for creating more powerful, more complex, and more effective investment strategies, with better risk/return trade-offs. They are aware that there are tremendous pools of talent focused on the creation of new strategies and on the "selling" of these strategies. They are bombarded with proposals from new investment managers and with requests from their current portfolio managers to consider the use of derivative strategies in light of new developments. The ability of derivative instruments to alter risk/return trade-offs cuts to the core of the process of plan-level investment management.

The plan sponsor needs to create a process that identifies relevant candidate strategies, improves evaluation of strategies, and builds the necessary infrastructure for the effective management of these strategies. As in any strategic issue, a clear statement and understanding of objectives provides the necessary frame of reference. Pension plan investment objectives are formulated in the context of participant demographics, current funded status, capital market risk averseness, the legislative and regulatory framework, and the appropriate plan-level peer group identification as a touchstone for analysis of "prudence" or "reasonable investor" factors.

Investment Policy

The process of enunciating objectives, formulating policy, implementing strategic decisions, building a control process, and evaluating results in the context of appropriate benchmarks is multilevel and iterative. The levels are the plan, the asset class, and the portfolio. There are implications and applications of derivative strategies at each level.

Plan-level objectives will be reasonably stable. They are long-term in nature and are not likely to change from year to year. It is the process of policy formulation that links stable objectives to dynamic markets and the plethora of new derivative strategies. The policy formulation process is issue driven, and the investment policy document is a primary control tool. We are talking about a dynamic policy document that provides an effective communication vehicle to all involved participants. It contains a current statement of the investment objectives, risk posture, peer group, asset class definitions, asset allocation process, and overall portfolio management policy. Of particular importance at each level (plan, asset class, and portfolio) is clarity on the use of derivative instruments and derivative-based strategies.

An effective investment policy document is obviously not an end in itself. It is a manifestation of (and a tool used in) the ongoing policy reformulation required by capital market developments. Plan sponsors need to marshal the best thinking available in the industry concerning the appropriate use of derivative strategies within the context of their investment objectives and plan-level control process. The investment policy document is an excellent tool to focus the thinking and considerable resources available in the investment community on meeting the plan's objectives. It provides a frame of reference for productive, issue-oriented progress involving the board, the investment committee, current and potential portfolio managers, the actuary, outside consultants, custodian bank, and all vendors with a "better mousetrap" concerning the use of derivative strategies.

Asset Allocation as an Ongoing Process

As we all know, the asset allocation process, which forms the linkage between the plan level and the asset class level, is of crucial importance and will determine the bulk of a plan's investment results. Asset allocation is driven by perceptions of risk and expectations of return within and among asset classes. Derivatives can alter the risk/return dynamics. They offer easy cost-effective means of adjusting exposure to various asset classes and have implications on the required control infrastructure supporting an investment strategy.

It is important to remember that there are multiple participants in the asset management process. The plan sponsor retains ultimate responsibility for plan-level asset allocation. The responsibility of a portfolio manager may be within a single asset class or may span asset classes. The plan may also employ overlay managers to add value by managing the risk/return of an asset class or multiple-asset classes, primarily using derivatives.

The primary focus of asset allocation is at the plan level, and the very existence of derivative markets (futures, in particular) allows the plan sponsor extraordinary flexibility in managing plan exposure to various asset classes, independent of the actions of the asset class managers and the portfolio managers. A sponsor can increase exposure, hedge away risk, or even invest in new markets by using futures contracts or swap strategies. Changes in plan-level asset allocation can be made swiftly and cost effectively without hiring additional portfolio managers. Exposure changes to the markets can be managed while evaluating or implementing underlying manager shifts. Derivative strategies can be particularly useful when making a transition between managers.

The sponsor needs to develop investment policy and benchmarks for the total plan, for each asset class, and for each managed portfolio. Sometimes the plan asset allocation or selected risk parameters may stray beyond plan level guidelines. The sponsor can issue directives to the individual portfolio managers, or can use derivative instruments to alter plan-level characteristics without affecting the individual portfolio managers.

Implementation

The transition from the "white paper" stage to effective utilization of derivative instruments is a tremendous leap for many plan sponsors. Adequate infrastructure must exist so that the sponsor has confidence that controls are in place. This is particularly important when derivative strategies span multiple managers, as in asset class overlays, and even more so when the sponsor is taking plan-level actions to manage overall plan exposure.

Derivative-based, plan-level and asset class strategies spanning global markets significantly raise the level of service required from the custodian. This is not to say that the derivative strategy execution should be done at the custodian bank, but any strategy using derivatives to alter composite risks/exposures in a multimanager environment needs to be based on an ability to quantify accurately, quickly, and repeatedly just what these risks/exposures are. This can get quite complex, especially when managers of the underlying portfolios may be using derivative instruments themselves.

Performance Measurement

Performance measurement is done, of course, by security, sector, country ,and strategy within a portfolio, and by groups of portfolios within an asset class for the overlay management techniques and overall plan. Attribution assessment is done to quantify the impact of plan-level strategy, to assess the contribution of overlays, to evaluate active strategies versus passive management, or to identify the active management impact beyond the manager's "normal." But derivative strategies are used in a forward-oriented fashion to hedge against loss or maintain exposure to particular asset classes. Derivatives dramatically expand possibilities for multilayered delegation and control in pension plan management.

PLAN LEVEL

Asset Allocation Control

Asset class startups. When making major changes in allocation to an asset class, a futures contract can provide the desired exposure or hedging. In particular, when starting to invest in a new asset class, such as international equities, futures contracts can be used by a plan sponsor until specific active or passive individual portfolio managers are retained.

Manager changes. When terminating a manager or a group of managers, and hiring new managers within an asset class, overall plan-level exposure to the asset class can be held to the desired level with the coordinated use of derivative contracts.

Managed futures as an asset class. There are proponents of using managed futures as an additional asset class. The theory behind this argument is that the expected return is competitive with the other, more standard, asset classes, and the correlation of returns to the more standard asset classes is quite low.

Plan Terminations

The decision to terminate a plan is sometimes made because of the significant overfunding of a particular plan relative to the liabilities. Obviously, it is important that this apparent overfunding be realized in execution of the termination decision. Irrespective of the reason for termination, the lag between making the decision and liquidating the assets can be quite long relative to the possible moves of the market. The typical pension plan represents a sizeable pool of assets. Some of the positions can be over ten times the average trading volume in that security.

The well-coordinated use of futures contracts in applicable asset classes is a fundamental tool in managing the asset liquidation. Let's examine the case of the U.S. equity asset class. Several strategies are possible. One approach might be to use the overall equity position to determine the particular futures contract and the appropriate hedge ratio. A better approach might be to segregate the pool of equities into a group that can be sold as baskets of stock using the DOT System, and a second group that will be sold as individual stocks. The basket group could be hedged in a straightforward manner. The individual stock group would need more complex calculation of hedge ratios. The liquidation game plan would need to be set for each day. Coordinated elimination of the short futures contracts would need to be done. Calculation of actual hedging experience as well as liquidation progress would need to be monitored to recalibrate hedge ratios.

ASSET CLASS LEVEL

Swaps and Transformations

Within an asset class, such as fixed-income, interest rate swaps can be used to reconfigure the risk/return profile of the overall class versus one of the primary factors that drives valuation and return. Of even more interest, are techniques that can transform investment in one asset class into returns from another asset class. You can, quite readily, swap the returns of LIBOR for the returns of a customized basket of equity returns from any group of countries having viable equity derivative markets.

Overlays

FX. A number of pension plans are utilizing specialized managers to address the FX market aspect of their international equity commitment. This type of strategy can decouple the stock selection process from the FX concerns. It can also decouple the country selection process into equity considerations and FX considerations. Each can be addressed by organizations that demonstrate superior capabilities in their specialty.

Option overwrite. A second common strategy is to use an option overwrite manager in an asset class such as U.S. equities. This manager would execute an investment strategy using out-of-the-money options on one or more equity indexes in an attempt to add value over the portfolio managers for that asset class.

PORTFOLIO LEVEL

External/Internal Management

A variety of policy decisions and factors face the plan sponsor concerning use of derivatives at the portfolio level. A primary determinant is that of expertise. Many plans have some of the investment portfolios managed internally, rather than using a complete array of outside managers. This is particularly true of public pension plans, where the plan sponsor has long-term experience in managing fixed-income portfolios and addressing the operating needs of the state, county, or city.

Hedging

A typical request of a portfolio manager is that he or she be allowed to use derivatives to hedge the portfolio against adverse performance. A hedging situation may arise, for example, when the plan sponsor makes a significant cash contribution to the portfolio, which may take some time to fully deploy into individual purchases.

Risk/Reward Modification

Complex derivative strategies are possible, and some investment managers are well equipped to use these strategies. It becomes incumbent upon the plan sponsor to understand the dynamics of the group of strategies proposed by the manager in order to be able to decide if they are appropriate for use within the portfolio.

Arbitrage

Though its heyday is past, there still are investors employing arbitrage strategies using futures contracts and baskets of stocks to capture valuation anomalies between the markets.

EFFECTIVE CONTROL AT ALL LEVELS

Importance of Intent When Using Derivatives

Control, control, control. It is not simply a matter of having appropriate accounting systems in place that track the individual derivative instruments. It is crucial that the strategy intent that provides context to the derivative instrument is clear. Groups of traditional assets and derivatives are often combined to form a particular strategy. Whether that strategy is working or not (and if not, why not?) can only be evaluated in the context as a holistic entity comprised of all the components.

Benchmark Selection

As in any investment process, a clear definition of the objective is paramount. Having defined that objective, it is imperative that the appropriate, measurable benchmark be selected. For example, in an FX overlay strategy, the objective is often to "add value." But is this against an unhedged, a fully hedged, or a 50/50 hedged benchmark?

Exposure Management

Granularity. The tracking/control system must be able to account for and track all aspects of each derivative contract. Each relevant variation margin payment, collateral pledge, or mark-to-market is required to provide adequate control.

Linking of positions. All relevant positions that make up a strategy must be linked so that the daily or intraday evaluation of the total position relative to the strategy can be evaluated.

Side Effects and Surprises

The nightmare of side effects and surprises is the bane of any plan sponsor undertaking derivative strategies. No matter how many white papers, simulation models, or "historical" analyses are done, there is no guarantee that future market conditions will be patterned after history or that the simulations covered all possible contingencies.

Evaluation of "Value Added"

Correlation of risk and return and its trade-offs are the basis of investing. Derivative instruments can and do have a profound effect on these relationships and on the overall market dynamics. Each plan sponsor needs to be able to evaluate these relationships in order to make appropriate decisions.

A strong attribution analysis system that is able to handle the relevant factors addressing the derivative strategy needs to be in place. Let's not throw the baby out with the bath water if results are unfavorable. Learn and correct the process. Beware of unexpected windfalls also. They are an indication of potential trouble.

All cost factors need to be considered in using these strategies. Before and after fee results need to be evaluated. Understand your objectives. Have the control systems in place to monitor your progress. Take swift and appropriate action to keep the process in control.

CHAPTER 11

Industry Trends and Evolution in Managed Futures

Lois B. Peltz
Managing Editor and Vice President
Managed Accounts Report Inc.

The first commodity fund, Futures Inc., was developed in 1949, but was dissolved in 1975.[1] The modern history of the industry did not begin until the mid-1970s, when a few funds and advisors emerged. By 1979, Managed Account Reports (MAR) was tracking eight futures funds, five private pools, and 19 trading advisors. Over the last twenty years, tremendous growth has occurred.

PARTICIPANTS

Early Participants

General Partners

The major participants in the managed futures industry include the general partner, who puts together the legal structure and the disclosure document and who is responsible for the operations of the funds; trading managers, who select, allocate, and monitor the trading advisors; trading advisors, who actually manage the assets; and the investors.

Early general partners were the brokerage firms developing the early products such as A.G. Edwards, Conti Commodities, Clayton Brokerage, and Heinold.[2] Reallocation of assets among trading advisors was generally infrequent.

---

1 Tom Northcote, "Major Events in the History of Managed Futures Industry," 1993.
2 Ibid.

Trading Advisors

At the end of 1979, MAR tracked 19 trading advisors, including such names as Millburn, Nelson Chang, Campbell & Co., Dinesh Desai, Trendview Management, and Dunn Capital Management. Generally, these trading advisors were technical trend-followers who sold their services directly to individual investors who had been referred by another investor or the commodity broker who was earning commission on a managed account.

Investors

Individual investors were the initial market for managed accounts and futures funds, since these products proved to be more profitable than individuals speculating on their own. In addition to professional management, investors were attracted by increased portfolio diversification, enhanced returns, reduced portfolio volatility, participation in rising and declining markets, and access to global markets.

Managed futures offer potential for increased portfolio diversification because they are noncorrelated to traditional investments such as stocks and bonds. Historical data show that the periods of greatest negative correlation occur when the stock market experiences the most severe declines, e.g., October 1987 (see Exhibit 1).

Exhibit 1.   Crash of 1987: S&P versus MAR Fund/Pool Index

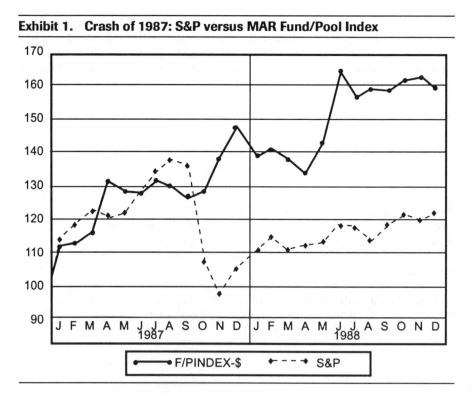

A number of studies indicate that a portfolio that includes managed futures can yield an appreciably higher and more stable return over a period of time than a portfolio that includes only stocks and bonds. Evidence indicates this can be achieved without added risk.

By increasing the percentage of managed futures with a stock and bond portfolio, overall returns may be enhanced for the overall portfolio. Harvard Business School professor John E. Lintner found that including futures in an investment portfolio reduced volatility while enhancing return and that such portfolios have substantially less risk at every possible level of return than portfolios of stocks, or stocks and bonds. Lintner found that the correlation between the returns on futures portfolios and those in the stock and bond portfolios was surprisingly low and sometimes negative. This paper helped legitimize futures and promoted the use of futures as an asset class. The data suggested that the use of futures for 10 to 20 percent of a diversified portfolio was prudent because it increased overall returns while reducing risk. In Carl Peters's book, *Managed Futures—Performance, Evaluation and Analysis of Commodity Funds, Pools and Accounts,* included over 18 academic studies; many updated Lintner's work.

Investors can participate and profit in rising/declining markets. During periods of hyperinflation, hard commodities (gold, metals, oil, grains) do well. During deflation, trading advisors can profit because they can sell the contracts initially.

Managed futures also provide access to global markets. The tremendous expansion of futures markets encompassing stock indexes, debt instruments, currencies, and options, has created new categories of profit opportunities that can be traded on a global basis.

Current Participants

General Partners

In the United States and Europe, more banks are entering the market as general partners/sponsors. Since banks have significant experience trading derivatives and cash markets and in managing portfolios, tremendous trading talent, large amounts of capital, market knowledge, and extensive client access, they are natural participants in the managed futures industry. In 1989, Banque Indosuez was the first European bank to develop and sell a fund—Galaxy Fund. Later that year, Chase Manhattan created the first open-ended currency fund for non-U.S. investors. By 1992, Chemical, Continental, Societe Generale, and Citibank were also active.

Chase Manhattan Bank, actively involved in managed futures since 1989, had raised over $200 million in eight private placements by the end of 1992. The Chase products are diversified private placements targeting qualified high-net-worth clients outside the U.S., and institutions, especially in Japan. In the United States, clients include institutions.

Chemical Bank has a currency fund for offshore clients that has been trading since July 1991. The First Chicago subsidiary also plans to raise money for an offshore currency fund. This bank focuses on high-net-worth clients and uses the managed account approach rather than a fund approach.[3]

Trading Managers

Trading managers, as a separate entity from the general partner, began to emerge in the mid-1980s as the number and quality of trading advisors increased, multiadvisor funds became more acceptable, trading methodologies became more diverse, and the environment became more competitive as more funds were set up. A subset of trading managers emerged that focused solely on pension fund business.

Trading Advisors

Today, about 400 global trading advisors and their programs are tracked by MAR. Of these, 33 trade over $100 million, while 9 handle over $500 million.[4] Over half the programs are diversified, with the remainder distributed as follows (see Exhibits 2 and 3):

Financial	19.1%
Currencies	15.2%
Energy	6.9%
Other	6.2%

In 1993, the "typical" trading advisor had:

- $40.3 million under management
- A track record of 6.4 years
- Five employees
- 87 percent located in U.S.; 13 percent located outside U.S.
- 2/3 technical trend-following; 1/3 discretionary
- 23 percent had prior experience in physical commodities; 19 percent worked in brokerage firms as traders, account executives, analysts; 6 percent were scientists; 5 percent were floor traders; and 5 percent have always been futures traders. Other miscellaneous categories included: computer programmers, 4.1 percent; accountants, 3.6 percent; economists, 3.1 percent; manufacturing, 2.6 percent; medicine, 2.6 percent; legal, 2.1 percent.

According to its year-end 1993 survey, MAR found that 45 percent of the U.S.-based trading advisors did not trade markets outside the U.S. However, that percentage was expected to fall to 30 percent in 1994. On the other hand, only one

3 "Europe's Banks Propelling Industry Growth . . . And More U.S. Banks Are Entering Fray," *Managed Account Reports,* 165 (November 1992), pp. 10–11.
4 "Trading Advisor With Assets Over $75 Million," *Managed Account Reports,* 169 (Sept. 1993), p. 6.

Exhibit 2.   Prior Experience of Traders

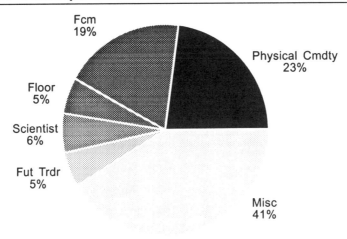

Exhibit 3.   Program Type

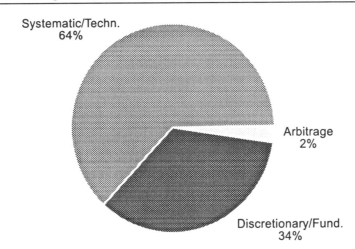

third of the U.S. trading advisors traded interbank markets and that percentage was not expected to change in 1994.

The most actively traded non-U.S. market was interest rates, followed by stock indexes and metals. All the respondents acknowledged LIFFE as the most-often traded non-U.S. exchange.

Some traders who had experience handling institutional accounts in other investment areas found opportunities in managed futures in the early to mid-1990s.

These included firms such as BEA Associates, Chancellor Capital Management, and FX Concepts. Henderson Administration, a British pension and institutional fund manager, acquired a 25 percent stake in Sabre Fund Management, a British trading advisor, reflecting growing European institutional interest in managed futures.

Select banks and brokerage houses started developing their own internal trading advisors, relying on in-house talent and their previous experience in managed futures.

Investors

While individual investors remain the primary investor group, institutional investors are appearing in greater frequency. Growing numbers of corporate and institutional investors have allocated a portion of their total portfolio assets to specially designed and professionally managed futures trading programs.

In 1986, Detroit Policemen and Firemen became the first pension fund to invest in managed futures. The initial commitment was $5 million, which by 1994 had grown to over $75 million. Meanwhile, Detroit General Retirement System's portfolio was about $25 million.

Since the stock market crash of 1987, an increasing number of large companies have been looking for alternatives to stocks and bonds, as they were rudely awakened to the necessity of portfolio diversification. Until then, institutional investors had taken a rather passive view of the statistical studies that suggested futures funds tended to perform well when stocks did not. In the fourth quarter of 1987, the MAR Fund/Pool Index was up 16.5 percent, while the S&P fell 30 percent.

In 1987, Eastman Kodak, the first Fortune 500 pension fund, made a $50 million investment. By 1994, that allocation was believed to be $300 million. In May 1991, the Virginia Retirement System allocated $100 million to be traded in managed futures from its $12.5 billion fund, making it one of the largest amounts ever committed to futures by a public employee pension fund. By December 1993, VRS decided to increase its 1 percent allocation to 4 percent, i.e., $650 million. Following this watershed event, other pension funds acknowledged their interest such as Conrail, Federal Express, San Diego County Employees' Retirement Association, Illinois Teachers' Retirement System.[5]

Table 1, which appeared in the March 1994 issue of MAR, lists some of the institutions involved in managed futures.

MAR estimates institutional participation in managed futures at about $2 billion today, about 9 percent of the managed futures industry assets.[6] However, because an institution could enter managed futures with a large chunk of assets, that percentage could change quite rapidly.

Institutions take a long-term view on performance. For example, John McClaren of Virginia Retirement System says that VRS uses a four-year performance evaluation

---

5 "The Road to Managed Futures—The Traditional Perspective," *Managed Account Reports*, 181 (March 1994) pp. 1, 12, 13.
6 Ibid.

Table 1.   The Big Money Gives Futures a Whirl

Pension Plan	Pension Plan
Alcoa	Libby Owens Ford Corp.
AMP Inc.	Mass. Bay Transit Authority Ret. Fund
Baptist Health Systems	Memphis Light, Gas & Water Division
British Columbia Hydro	Pa. Public School Employees Ret.
City of Montreal	System
Conrail (pending)	San Diego County Employees'
Detroit Police and Firemen	Retirement
Retirement System	Savannah Foods & Industry
Detroit Gen. Retirement System	Toyota
Eastman Kodak	University of British Columbia Staff
Echlin Inc.	Pension Fund
Federal Express	Virginia Public Employees Ret. System
H.J. Heinz	Weyerhauser
Illinois Teachers' Retirement System	World Bank
Intel Corp.	

time frame.[7] Institutional fee structures also differ significantly from retail fees. For example, for the registered investment manager (trading manager) in VRS's program, there are no management fees, but there is a hurdle incentive fee.

For the trading advisors, management fees range from 0 to 3 percent, while incentive fees range from 15 to 20 percent. In addition to the low management fees, interest income is not included in the incentive fee calculation.

PRODUCTS

Early Products

Managed Accounts

The investors who opened managed accounts in the late 1970s and early 1980s were primarily individual investors seeking profit opportunities from futures trading, who did not want the responsibility and demands of trading their own accounts. These investors wanted professional trading advisor expertise. The single investor and the

---

7 "18-Month Trading Results Meeting Virginia Retirement System's Objectives," *Managed Account Reports,* 166 (December 1992), pp. 7–9.

trading advisor agreed that in return for certain fees, the trading advisor would trade the investor's money.

Public Funds

A public fund consists of pooled investments of more than 35 unaccredited investors filing under registration requirements of the SEC and CFTC. Public funds allow even the smallest investor to participate in the futures market with professional management. Investors receive monthly statements reporting the performance of the fund and may generally redeem their units at month-end.

The oldest continuous public fund is Illinois Commodity Fund, launched by Heinold Commodities in January 1978. In 1979, the year MAR started to track the industry, only eight public funds existed. With the offering of funds to the public in the form of limited partnership units, participation in managed futures was suddenly made available to the public at large. The limited partnership structure was important since it limited a partner's risk exposure to the amount of the investment. It appealed to those investors who had previously shied away from managed accounts because of margin calls and unlimited downside. The shift gradually occurred from managed speculative accounts into funds and pools in the mid-1980s.

A large breakthrough in growing widespread acceptance for public funds was the brokerage houses' use of traditional stock and bond salespeople in addition to commodity brokers to sell the products. The public at large came to realize that futures funds could augment their traditional investments.

Most of the funds offered during the early 1980s were single-advisor funds. The funds were sold on the merits of the trading advisor's track record. Funds tended to be diversified, i.e., several diverse sectors were traded, including energy, agriculture, metals, etc.

While the first multiadvisor funds began to appear in 1978 with Thompson McKinnon's Futures Fund, multiadvisor funds became most popular in the mid-1980s. In 1986, the first $100 million multiadvisor fund was offered—Merrill Lynch's Futures Dimension Fund. After that time, the largest fund offering was $530 million for Dean Witter's Principal Guaranteed Fund. However, $280 millon had to be returned to clients since the offering was limited to $250 million. With multiadvisor funds, greater focus was placed on lowering the risk profile. These funds were sold on a much smoother historical pro-forma track record of the combined group of trading advisors, i.e., diversified trading methods lead to less volatility. The disadvantage of multiadvisor funds was that if the fund has too many advisors, losses from one advisor could offset gains of another advisor. Too much offsetting of trading methods could lead to relatively flat performance.

Guaranteed funds first appeared in 1986, with a Mint offshore guaranteed fund and Shearson's Futures 1000 Fund, the first guaranteed public offering. In 1990, over $600 million was raised through guaranteed funds. In 1991, another $400 million was raised. Guaranteed funds/pools currently represent about 10 percent of the funds tracked by MAR. The guarantee was provided in a variety of ways—by surety bond, letter of credit, zero coupons, leverage, etc. Investors were provided with a minimum return on their initial investment after a specified time period, if they remained in the fund for the specified time period.

The main advantage of a guaranteed fund was that investors felt more comfortable: their concerns were alleviated about poor performance, market volatility, etc.

A disadvantage of the guaranteed fund was that if an investor redeemed prior to the end of the specified period, he or she was not provided the guarantee. Furthermore, a sharp decline in net asset value early on in the markets could hurt performance for the longer term.

In public funds, commissions were generally charged on a round-turn basis, usually 80 percent of retail brokerage rates. Most funds paid advisors a 6 percent management fee and a 20 percent incentive fee.

Private Pools

A private pool commingles money from several investors, with the minimum investment usually starting at $25,000. The main advantage is the economies of scale that can be achieved by middle-sized investors. Because of lower administrative and marketing costs, private pools have historically performed better than public funds.

In 1979, five private pools existed in the MAR database. Campbell Fund, which started in 1972, is the oldest private pool still in existence.

Offshore Funds

The first offshore fund appeared in 1984; these funds are open only to non-U.S. investors.

Current Products

Managed Accounts

The bulk of individual investors no longer place their assets in managed accounts because of the benefits provided by limited partnerships. Only a few large trading advisors still use managed accounts as their primary vehicle. One such example is Colorado Commodities Management, which has more than 1500 individually managed accounts. According to Tom Kellerhals, vice president of marketing, the greatest percentage of those accounts started with $30,000.[8] With managed accounts, investors receive more personal communication from their financial consultant; clients receive reports on each trade and have liquidity and personal control.

Increasingly, institutional investors and high-net-worth individuals are opening individual accounts. These accounts require a substantial capital investment so that the trading advisor is able to diversify trading among a large number of market positions. An individual account enables the institutional investor to customize the account to his or her own specifications, e.g., certain markets are emphasized or excluded.

---

8 "Two Trading Advisors Expound on the Virtues of Differing Product Structures," *Managed Account Reports,* 169 (March 1992), p. 11.

Public Funds

At year-end 1993, MAR tracked 195 public futures funds. Currently, the emphasis is on more specialized funds—currencies, financials, and other international futures, which have generally been more profitable recently. This is particularly true for larger trading advisors who find greater liquidity in financial futures with much higher position limits or in the currency interbank market where there are no limits. Specialized funds have the advantage of allowing investors to focus on those markets that they believe have the most profit potential.

Another popular product is the sector-type fund. Each trading advisor in a multiadvisor fund focuses on the specific sector in which he or she achieved significant profits in the past. This sector approach represents a potentially valuable refinement of multiadvisor funds, in which trading advisors trade largely overlapping diversifying portfolios.

In 1993, 41.5 percent of the funds/pools were multiadvisor, while 58.5 percent were single-advisor. The trend is developing toward fewer advisors. The belief is that with many advisors trading all sectors, losses by some advisors cancel the gains of others, resulting in flat performance.

There is also a growing realization of the advantages and disadvantages of guaranteed funds. In early 1992, when the industry was undergoing difficult performance, two guaranteed funds ran into trouble. As a result, sponsors are now offering the investor the choice of whether or not to guarantee the product. The jury is still out: Credit Lyonnaise Rouse raised $18 million in its CLR Select Fund in 1992, in which investors had a choice of guaranteed or not; 85 percent selected nonguaranteed while 15 percent selected guaranteed. In Merrill Lynch's SECTOR Strategy Fund IV, in which about $90M was raised, 85 percent selected guaranteed, while 15 percent did not.[9]

In 1992 and 1993, there was some success with funds not being guaranteed: Dean Witter's Global Perspective Fund raised $69 million, its Diversified Fund raised $65 million, its Select Futures Fund raised $200 million.

The average size of the 88 funds raised in 1993 was about $13 million. Today, there is a wide range of commission charged to accommodate faster-trading discretionary traders. Many funds now charge commissions as a fixed percentage of assets managed rather than as a roundturn. Front-end loads are no longer common (see Exhibit 4).

Private Pools

Today, 197 private pools are tracked by MAR. Many of the longer-term best performing trading advisors have developed private pools as their sole trading vehicles for administrative reasons (see Exhibit 5).

In a recent study, MAR compared the performance returns of private pools, offshore funds and public funds. For the period 1990 through 1993, the median return was significantly higher for private pools at 46.5 percent compared with 33.5 percent for offshore funds and 23.6 percent for public funds. Similarly the Sharpe ratio, a

9 "Fund Business Picks Up," *Managed Account Reports,* 165 (November 1992), p. 2.

Exhibit 4.   Growth of Public Futures Funds (Number)

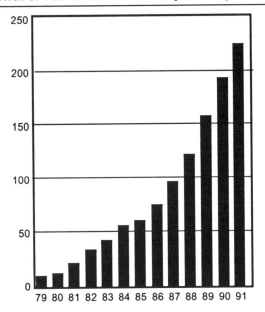

Exhibit 5.   Growth of Private Pools (Number)

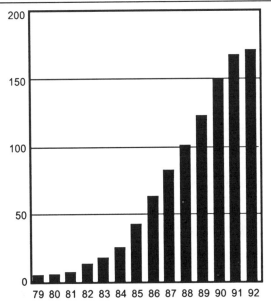

return-relative-to-risk measure, was higher as well. Possible explanations for the better performance is that they often are single-advisor funds representing the best performing advisors who have rolled-up activity into one vehicle. They also do not have the degree of administrative, custodian, legal, and regulatory fees as public funds.[10]

Offshore Products

More money is being raised offshore because of the attraction of offshore products—no k-1s; reduced regulatory and disclosure burdens; reduced taxation; improved access to an expanded pool of eligible trading advisors, derivative instruments, cash securities, hybrids, and markets; and the growing demand from both U.S. and non-U.S. investors. At the end of 1993, MAR tracked 104 such funds.

GROWTH

Global managed futures assets grew from $500M in 1980 to $12B in 1990. By the end of 1991, assets had grown to $21 billion. At 1992 year-end, the size of the global managed futures industry stayed relatively flat (see Exhibit 6). This global estimate includes futures traded by registered commodity pool operators who are not necessarily registered commodity trading advisors such as hedge fund managers Michael Steinhardt, Julian Robertson, etc.[11]

MAR estimated the size of the primary—i.e., purely speculative—managed futures industry at $23 billion in 1992 versus $11.4 billion in 1991.

A CFTC study in 1989 indicated that managed futures accounted for 10 percent of the volume on U.S. exchanges. Today, MAR estimates that managed futures account for 15 percent of exchange volume. As a result, exchanges have a growing awareness of the importance of managed futures trading to their overall volume. Several recent exchange developments occurred showing this: the average pricing system and order quantity system were introduced, and some speculative limits were increased or even eliminated.

Europe

The managed futures industry in Europe has emerged from an institutional background favoring financial markets over commodities and has spawned traders from interbank trading rooms rather than exchange trading floors. In this environment, many banks have come to the forefront of activity in Europe and have been instrumental in introducing futures money management to a clientele of cautious institutions and private individuals. European banks that have raised money recently include Citibank Private Banking Group, Credit Agricole, Credit Lyonnaise, Hypo Bank, and Banque Indosuez's subsidiary Carr Asset Mgt. The European network helped the bank reach institutional investors seeking a managed futures product.

---

10 "Private Pool Performance Outpaces That of Offshore and Public Funds," *Managed Account Reports,* 180 (Feb. 1994), p. 9.
11 "Industry Needs to Refocus on Investors, Lower Its Fees and Change Perceptions," *Managed Account Reports,* 168 (February 1993), p. 7.

Exhibit 6.   Growth of Managed Futures-Primary Market Share of Total

---

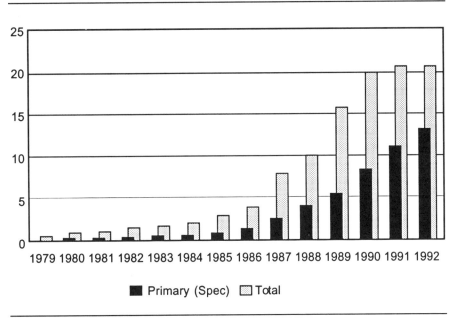

While Sabre Fund Management was established in 1981 in the United Kingdom, it was not until 1988 that other European trading advisors emerged. In 1990, the European Managed Futures Trading Association was formed. MAR currently tracks 67 European trading advisors and their programs.

Japan

In April 1992, Japan's Commodity Fund Law came into force. Before the law became effective, a number of funds had already been raised by leasing companies, trading firms, and Japanese brokerage houses. In 1988, Mitsubishi Corp. offered the first futures fund in Japan, raising $80 million. That same year, Dean Witter and General Leasing offered the first futures fund sponsored by a leasing company.

In 1989, Commodities Corp sold a 30 percent interest to ORIX of Japan for $80 million. Orix, later that year, launched its first Japanese fund.

In 1990, Dean Witter and Nikko Securities did the first Ministry of Finance-regulated futures fund in Japan. Later that year, Dean Witter teamed up with Shin-Ni-hon Shoken for the second Ministry of Finance-regulated futures fund in Japan.

In 1991, a huge amount of money was raised in Japan in 29 futures funds—about ¥75.2 billion. 1992 was much slower: 18 funds raised ¥32.4 billion. Nineteen funds were launched in 1993 with assets reaching ¥46.2 billion.

According to Masaaki Takahashi, owner of Synergy Development Management Inc. in Tokyo, several reasons exist for recent disappointing money-raising efforts: The recession; the drawdown of the equity markets reducing Japanese financial institutions' "hidden assets," which permit risk-taking investments. Reluctance of insurance companies to take risks and are trying to shift money from high-risk products, even traditional ones like real estate, equity, and foreign investment (fixed-income denominated in domestic currency). Sales force eagerness at securities firms had waned, scandals had occurred, and investors were losing confidence and were very cautious about securities firms' marketing people as well as any risk-related products they recommend. The regulatory environment had made marketing difficult as well—a unit of ¥100 million is too large a purchase under the current circumstances, since many people want to experiment with the funds first. Due to the decline in interest rates, the gold cash forward portion to securitize the principal increased, and therefore, the managed futures portion of fund share is only 20 to 30 percent. Marketing became more difficult and fund size grew smaller, it was difficult to structure funds, especially preferred multiadvisor funds.[12]

Yoshitake Kobayashi adds a different perspective, citing mediocre performance results which have been aggravated by high fees and choppy markets.[13]

Takahashi continues that long-term signs are optimistic—the companies that have applied to be commodity investment selling companies will help find new investors. The securities firms' losing profitable operations, are forced to seek new products that can earn marginal fees. The issue for the securities firms is whether commodity funds will be an acceptable product for their existing clients. Securities firms would like to sell funds by public offering. Some have asked the Ministry of Finance whether it would be acceptable to sell commodity funds in public, which means one unit will be an acceptable size for individual investors.

Banks will have to consider what securities business they can do and what subsidiaries must be set up. Life insurance companies are also beginning to examine commodity funds.[14]

Australia

In 1992, ANZ McCaughan Futures (subsidiary of ANZ Bank) announced the formation of the first Australian futures fund with an independent trading manager. Late that year, the Asia Pacific Managed Futures Association was formed.

CURRENT TRENDS

New Products

In Europe, several creative fund structures emerged in 1992. In Credit Lyonnaise Rouse's Select Futures Fund, investors have the opportunity to select a fund or a combination of funds that suits their needs. As many as 15 different share classes can be chosen, with the options including a guarantee or not; denomination in U.S. dollars, French francs, or German deutsche marks; portfolio composition of currencies, financials, or diversified. Investors can switch between sub-funds up to four times a

---

12 Ibid., pp. 8–10.
13 "Asset-Raising Activity Improves in 1993," *Managed Account Reports*, 179, (Jan. 1994) p. 9.
14 Ibid., pp. 8–10.

year without charge. This structure is useful to the investor because he or she can customize the fund to meet his or her own needs. And the structure is also useful to the fund sponsor, since it is easier and cheaper to bring out new shares under the same umbrella.[15]

In December 1992, Greystone Partners also offered an umbrella fund with five single advisor sub-funds—each managed exclusively by one of the five trading advisors chosen by the firm. Investors can place their investment in one or more of the funds and switch between the funds as desired.[16]

Stock market tracker funds also emerged with John Govett and Fidelity Investments. The bull funds are designed to track stock indexes in the United Kingdom, Europe, Japan, and the U.S. The corresponding bear funds are designed to perform in reverse by investing in contracts to sell the index. The funds are also designed to allow rapid switching between markets.

The Search for High Quality Advisors

The managed futures industry has enormous growth potential, but only as long as a commensurate trading advisor and fund management capacity is developed simultaneously. A few companies have been allocating capital to developing trading advisors for a while, and several new programs came into existence in 1992 to meet this need. These programs include in-house development programs, seed money funds, small allocations from an established fund, and development support programs.

In the in-house development programs, a few companies provide proprietary assets to a number of traders for several years. The idea of the program is to make the traders comfortable handling proprietary funds and to gain necessary experience with proprietary money before they start handling client money.

Other companies provide seed money to outside traders who are viewed as having good potential. In some cases, the funds are open to clients, while in others it is proprietary capital. The company works very closely with the trading advisors to develop their programs successfully. The relationship extends into the future as the trading advisors move out of the program as full-fledged advisors into the professional market. The ultimate aim is to bring advisors to the point where they will pass scrutiny by the leading professional asset allocators.

Given limited capital and their desire to invest with as many interesting new advisors as possible, some companies give the emerging trading advisor the smallest account possible that will provide the same trading and level of diversification as their own clients get. The test account rationale is to see, understand, and get comfortable with the performance characteristics that will be attained with a large client account.

Other companies provide a mentor, research and trading facilities, salary and benefits, and a profit share on individual performance.

Some trading managers allocate a small percentage of a larger fund, probably 10 to 20 percent, to emerging traders.

---

15 "New Funds Attract Investors," *Managed Account Reports,* 161 (July 1992), p. 2.
16 "Ex-Geldermann CEO's New Firm Tries Fund," *Managed Account Reports,* 166 (December 1992), p. 3.

Two European firms jointly launched a program to support development of European trading advisors in the initial stages of development. The program's objective is to identify, record, and verify emerging traders' skills as well as exposing them to standard industry practices regarding performance reporting and accounting.[17]

Whatever the method used to find and nurture emerging trading advisors, the benefits are immense:

- New trading talent is developed globally.

- The emerging trader benefits from the sponsors' facilities, administrative/regulatory work, suggestions on program design, etc.

- The emerging trader is exposed to standard industry practices regarding performance reporting and accounting.

- Companies nurturing these traders will develop early and possibly long-lasting access.

- The selection process weeds out many contenders, thus increasing the probability that the project will be successful.

In the case of in-house development programs, additional benefits exist:

- Vertical integration occurs. A company is able to control more of its fund business. Brokerage houses and banks can develop the funds, provide the advisors, do the brokerage, etc.

- In-house talent is usually available. Because banks and brokerage houses have been involved in the managed futures industry for a while, a pool of people exists who are familiar with trading as well as managed futures.

Despite these benefits, obstacles must be overcome:

- Significant proprietary capital is required to fund emerging traders with a meaningful amount of money.

- It is not easy to raise client funds for inexperienced traders.

- Depending on the sales positioning of a fund, investors may think the goal of an emerging advisor fund is to find the next great "megatrader." As a result, investors' expectations may be too high. In actuality, that is not the objective of most of the programs.

- A "seed" money fund for investors could be quite risky for the inexperienced investor if it is his or her only managed futures investment. While an investor is encouraged to have approximately 10 percent of his or her overall portfolio in managed futures, 10 percent in an emerging advisor fund could be too risky and volatile, since many of these traders do not have proven track records.

---

17 "Finding and Developing Emerging Traders," *Managed Account Reports*, 165 (November 1992), pp. 6–8.

- Because no exclusive arrangement exists, competitors may eventually develop a relationship with the trading advisors.

- The programs are expensive to run in terms of management costs. Fees may not cover the real cost. The payoff comes only if successful trading advisors emerge.

- A great deal of time is required to bring on new trading advisors, i.e., they need help in designing programs, they must be monitored extensively, and they need general hand-holding.

- Requirements for disclosure in the U.S. may be inconvenient and thus a hindrance.

And in the case of in-house development programs, additional negatives include:

- Keeping a good trader as an employee. If a trader is superior, he or she may prefer to be independent.

- Reluctance of other trading managers to use an advisor who is part of another brokerage house or bank.

- Conflict of interest may be seen if brokerage and trading advisors are provided. In fact, some institutional clients demand a separation of the functions.[18]

Overall, the benefits outweigh the obstacles. It will be instructive to see the "success ratio" for the different programs in the next few years.

Increased Participation from Europe

More and more U.S. trading advisors and trading managers are setting up offices in Europe. Recent names fitting the bill are Grenville Craig, Louis Bacon, Bruce Kovner, and Richard Dennis. In 1993, Commodities Corp. set up a new subsidiary located in Geneva to focus on marketing. According to Roch Hillenbrand, senior vice president of Commodities Corp. (USA), "The best way to develop investor relationships is to have a local office that allows direct contact with European institutional clients." Hillenbrand also added that the physical presence in Europe will also allow a point of contact for European traders. Tudor Investment Corp. also set up a proprietary trading office in London. Several European sources report Moore Capital recently raised over $1 billion in a guaranteed offering, primarily to European institutions.[19]

One reason why some American trading advisors and fund sponsors are looking to Europe is less stringent regulation. An advisor based in Europe has the ability to trade more types of investments—securities, cash instruments, etc. Furthermore, huge disclosure documents are not required. Some trading advisors note that it is difficult to trade European markets at midday from the U.S. Often, economic reports and speeches occur in the morning in Europe and U.S.-based traders miss opportunities.[20]

Meanwhile, the number of European traders is growing, as European traders have the benefit of a good time zone, which makes it easier to trade on 24-hour basis;

---

18 Ibid.
19 "Expansion into Europe Accelerates," *Managed Account Reports,* 169 (March 1993), p. 9.
20 Ibid.

they have greater trading opportunities, and it is more natural for them to trade non-U.S. markets, forward and options markets, allowing a more global orientation, trade .

Declining Fees

At MAR's fourteenth Annual Conference on Futures Money Management in January 1993 in San Diego, one of the recurring themes was: Fees must come down. Several speakers examined the current wide spread for different types of investment managers. Trading advisors receive management fees of 2 to 4 percent while hedge fund managers get 1 percent and equity managers get 40 to 100 basis points. Bundling fees in funds yield a 8-10 percent range. While this percentage has come down quite a bit, it is much higher than in bonds and stocks.[21]

One of the reasons for the high costs is the misperception by brokerage house sales forces that the products are risky and difficult to sell. At one large brokerage house, the production credit is an upfront 5 to 6 percent, with a 2 percent trail starting in the twelfth month after the sale. This compares to mutual funds with a 3 to 5 percent production credit and a 0-50 basis point-trail.[22]

Alternative incentive fees are being offered increasingly to institutional clients. In the case of Virginia Retirement System, an incentive fee hurdle has been structured. In order to receive an incentive fee, 8 1/2 percent performance must be attained. Between 8 1/2 percent and 25 percent, the incentive fee is 20 percent. Over 25 percent performance, the incentive fee is 30 percent.

Vertical Integration

An increasing number of banks and brokerage houses that have been acting as sponsor have developed their own in-house trading advisors for managed futures because they believe they have a natural body of trading talent. Several banks registered as CTAs in 1992 and 1993.

Trading advisors are also branching into other areas. In 1992, Trout Trading Fund Ltd. bought the Chicago futures operations of Gerald Inc. This marked the first time that a commodity pool operator owned its own clearing firm. Rand Financial Services Inc. became a new futures commission merchant by taking over Gerald's Chicago operations, including clearing functions and members at the Chicago exchanges. According to some industry sources, this move could push fund fees lower.

FURTHER DOWN THE ROAD—FUTURE TRENDS

Composite Track Record for Fund Sponsors

No uniform method exists to compare fund sponsors' performance. Clients want and need to see a composite track record. If the fund sponsor has a few funds, it is relatively

---

21 "Industry Needs to Refocus on Investors, Lower Its Fees and Change Perceptions," *Managed Account Reports,* 168 (February 1993) pp. 1, 7.
22 Ibid.

easy to examine those in detail. But if a fund sponsor has many funds—a few have well over 15—it is difficult for an investor to fathom. The client will not know if the fund presented by the fund sponsor as most representative is in fact just the best performer.

Of course, funds may have different objectives. In those cases, it may not make sense to put together a composite track record. However, if the fund sponsor has a cluster of different types of funds, it does make sense to put together a composite of each, e.g., a composite of guaranteed funds, a composite of nonguaranteed funds, a composite of single-advisor funds, a composite of multiadvisor funds, etc.

Many of the large fund sponsors have offered several series of funds, each with the same objective. A composite track record of these funds, which are similar in structure and which have the same objective, would also make sense.

There is another benefit: When a fund sponsor does a new deal, it does not have to include the performance tables on each fund—just the composite performance table—thus saving space and providing investors with a more meaningful track record.

Fund sponsors need to show the value-added functions and responsibilities they provide, including trading advisor database management, due diligence, trading advisor negotiations, performance monitoring, asset allocation, and portfolio rebalancing. Added value does not come from the historical track record of the trading advisors selected for the fund, but rather from the fund sponsors' track records. The fund sponsors' track records will illustrate their performance in selecting, monitoring, replacing, and rebalancing trading advisors.

Some fund sponsors may argue that they have too many funds and it would be too time-consuming to put together a composite. Yet, the average successful trading advisor has more than 50 accounts and they manage to put together a composite track record. If the trading advisors have managed to comply, fund sponsors should be willing to provide comparable information as well to the investor. In fact, many of the large institutional clients, through questionnaires, frequently ask for such a track record. As a result, many fund sponsors have such a track record already in place.

Overall, the benefits gained from a fund sponsor composite track record seem to outweigh the inconveniences. It would provide meaningful information for the investor, allowing for comparison of results, an accurate reflection of added value provided by the fund sponsor and fewer pages devoted to track records in prospectuses. Further, since institutional clients are increasingly requesting and receiving composite track records, they should be made available to all clients. Over time, fund sponsor track records may become the norm rather than the exception.[23]

More Diverse Products

In the managed futures industry, common categories include high return, yield enhancement, guaranteed product, and sector products. In some categories, the number of funds is quite small. In terms of its 195 public futures funds, managed futures is currently where mutual funds stood in the 1960s.

It is necessary to further distinguish funds by type and category. All funds are not alike; neither are investors' objectives. Some funds are high return/high volatility,

---

23 "Track Records Needed for Fund Sponsors," *Managed Account Reports*, 164 (Oct. 1992) p. 8.

others provide yield enhancement. These types and categories must continue to be used, understood, and accepted to help the investor distinguish among different objectives.

More Products with Mutual Fund-Type Characteristics

Further exploration is needed of equity features that traditional investors enjoy, such as the exchange privilege, the "family of funds" concept, offshore funds, and dividends. While a few funds offer these features, they tend to be the exception, not the rule.

Further Refinement of the Guaranteed Product

More products are needed that provide comfort rather than scare investors. A yield-enhancing "money market" type of product needs to be developed that is easy for clients to understand. Such a product could help speed the educational process.

While the guaranteed futures fund has done a great deal to alleviate investor concerns, guaranteed products have to be refined and further developed so that problems are alleviated (e.g., there is a several-year wait to get the initial investment back; trading may stop if a sharp decline occurs, this is exagerated even further in a low interest rate environment; difficulty exists in explaining and understanding the concept).

More Hybrid Products

The top tier of trading advisors who are long-term consistent performers are trading hedge funds; we would expect other trading advisors to do the same over time. Hedge funds can best be described as a category of potpourri since it has no precise legal definition. Common characteristic include: a private limited partnership that is free from government restriction regarding public disclosure of investments, registration and reporting requirements; fewer than 99 investors; and ability to redeem only quarterly or annually. The vehicles often engage in active trading of equities, government securities, commodities, financial futures, options, currencies, arbitrage and merger, and acquisition activities.[24]

---

24 "The Long and Winding Road from Trading Advisor to Hedge Fund Manager," *Managed Account Reports*, 177 (Nov. 1993) p. 8.

CHAPTER 12

Using Managed Futures as a Profit Center within a Conventional Portfolio

Jeff Reckseit
Director/Institutional Sales
Campbell & Company

HISTORY OF THE FUTURES MARKETS

The year is approximately 4000 B.C. The Pharaoh sits upon his golden throne in the Old Kingdom and, perusing reports on papyrus prepared by his faithful scribes, surveys the land. The Nile has yielded a bountiful harvest of wheat and the royal granaries are full. This is good. He summons the Royal CFO to contemplate flour sales to the people. "With so much wheat on hand, flour prices could plummet," he is told. This is bad. His sagacious advisor inquires, "What if you held the wheat and sold flour for future delivery?" The Pharaoh makes a market! In the early mists of time-out-of-mind, the first futures contract is incubated. This is good. Very good.

Cuneiform tablets dating back to the fourth century B.C. actually record, in stone, the price of wheat! These are generally regarded to be the earliest existing written commodities contracts. We're not talking about mere tradition. This is the history of civilization.

Fast forward with me to the Middle Ages. As early as A.D. 1114, in the Champagne region of what is now France, huge market fairs were held to accommodate trade between northern Italy and Flanders, as well as traders from England and Russia. They exchanged everything from rare metals, spices, and wool, to wine, fish, and salt. At the end of each fair, disputes often arose over the settling of accounts. A medieval code of mercantile law was developed, and this was the first use of forward contracts in Europe.[1]

---

[1] Richard J. Teweles, Charles V. Harlow, and Herbert L. Stone, *The Commodity Futures Game. Who Wins? Who Loses? Why?* (New York: McGraw-Hill, Inc., 1974) p. 6.

In 1570, the Royal Exchange opened in London, where traders could buy and sell commodities and manufactured goods. But it was in Japan, in the 1600s, where the first organized futures trading took place. These "rice tickets" were acceptable as currency in the form of a warehouse receipt for rice in storage. The rice was actually rent money that the peasants paid to their feudal lords as their share of the harvest. The nobility didn't like having their steady cash flow subject to the eccentricity of market fluctuation, so a mechanism was born to manage the risk of pricing rice. Today, rice still trades on the Osaka Exchange.[2]

In the United States, in the late 1700s and into the early 1800s, agricultural commerce could best be described as chaotic. Once a year farmers brought grain and livestock to town and, more often than not, the oversupply was dumped into the street after millers and packers had satisfied their short-term needs. Transportation and storage facilities were hopelessly inadequate, adding to the confusion. Then, there were the occasional shortages when prices were bid beyond affordability and people went hungry.[3]

In 1848, in an attempt to alleviate these serious problems, the Chicago Board of Trade was established, formalizing the practice of forward contracting. With the introduction of futures contracts a few years later, producers and users could now manage the price risk associated with their operations, and the speculator could take the other side of the trade in the hopes of making a profit. This accurately describes the function of the futures exchanges today.

FUNCTION OF THE FUTURES MARKETS

As mentioned, the primary function of the futures markets is to provide the bona fide hedgers, the producers and users of the actual commodities, with a means of protecting themselves against price fluctuation. The example usually given here is that of the primary food producer or farmer. Since this chapter is geared to the financial investment community, let's choose an example a bit more pertinent to your experience.

Within the last 15 years, foreign currencies, interest rates, and stock indexes have become widely traded futures markets. The dollar, the long bond, and the S&P 500 are commodities. Their corresponding contracts on the futures exchanges are used to manage risk, just like the more traditional agricultural contracts. Here's how it works. Let's say you're a portfolio manager for an employee benefit retirement plan of a U.S. corporation. You own a wide array of domestic equities in your portfolio, which provide returns that will help to fund employees' benefits upon their retirement. You decide to sell some stock because of a perceived weakness in the market. You don't wish to sell all of it, you just want to "lighten up" a bit and protect your assets. Actually, you'd prefer not to sell at all, since your long-term investment strategy is basically to buy and hold. You call in the "Royal CFO," or the like equivalent, and you are advised to sell an appropriate number of S&P 500 futures contracts against your long position. These will provide profits in your account should the market

2 Ibid., p. 8.
3 Chicago Board of Trade, *Commodity Trading Manual* (Chicago: Board of Trade of the City of Chicago, 1976) p. 3.

decline as anticipated. You then cover your short position on these instruments when appropriate, thereby effectively hedging market risk. Now, certainly, market timing is everything when considering the use of these full or partial hedges, but there are those who are in the business of designing and implementing these strategies, and their use has proven to be very successful in many cases.

A second function of the futures markets is not quite as obvious but extremely important nevertheless. It is referred to as "price discovery." Depth and liquidity in many of the futures markets has become so extensive that the buyers and sellers of the "actuals" or the cash commodities, refer to the trading on the exchanges to fix their prices. Examples of this are the price of West Texas intermediate crude oil, which is traded in New York, and the U.S. 30-year Treasury bond, which is traded in Chicago. During market hours those *are* the prices for these commodities, and oil companies and banks around the world recognize them as such and conduct their business accordingly.

Brief mention has been made of the speculator who bears the risk by taking the other side of the trade. In this endeavor, he or she has paved the way for what we know today as managed futures.

DESCRIPTION AND HISTORY OF MANAGED FUTURES

Managed futures is an investment strategy that uses the futures markets to generate a positive stream of return. It is a subset of the larger category of *derivatives,* which are used to manage risk in a stock, bond, or currency portfolio. The important distinction to be made is that, unlike derivatives used for hedging, managed futures operates as a stand-alone profit-center. A managed futures manager or Commodity Trading Advisor is used for profit much in the way an equities manager is used—to make money.

I use the phrase "investment strategy" as distinguished from "asset class." There is much discussion as to whether managed futures is an asset class at all. Although it's been in existence for over 20 years, managed futures is still a relatively new industry compared to the history of the stock and bond markets. Also, by some definitions, an asset class must have at least $100 billion in it to be defined as such. So I use "investment strategy" or "investment category" to describe managed futures.

The speculator uses the futures markets to endeavor to make a profit. He or she is called a speculator because there is leverage involved. The leverage is there so that the hedger (in our example, the portfolio manager) can use the futures markets to manage his risk without a substantial outlay of capital. Stock investors use the stock market to endeavor to make a profit also. If they bought stocks on margin they, too, might be classified as speculators. The similarity between them is that they are both using their respective markets with profit as the goal.

When stock investors elect to use professional management to achieve this goal, they may use an equity manager. Many equities managers organize their investment programs in the form of a mutual fund. When investors in the futures markets elect to use professional management, they may use a managed futures manager or commodity trading advisor (CTA). Both the equities manager and the futures manager use diversification and capital management to control risk. Furthermore, the futures manager controls the amount of leverage that he or she has available by keeping most of the equity under management, in cash. He or she can "de-leverage" and manage risk according to guidelines established by the client.

The first commodity fund was formed in 1949 by Richard Donchian at Hayden Stone. The oldest commodity fund still trading is the Campbell Fund which began in 1972. The first CTA to have $100 million under management was Millburn Partners in 1980. In 1983 Dr. John Lintner of Harvard University presented a research paper which substantiated the benefits of using managed futures in a stock and bond portfolio. Paul Tudor Jones and Monroe Trout both began trading in September of 1984. The first U.S. pension fund to invest in managed futures was the Detroit Policemen and Firemen Retirement System in 1986. They were followed by Kodak in 1987. In 1988, Dean Witter, in the most successful public fund offering ever, raised $531 million for investment in managed futures on the first day. Mint Investment Management exceeded $1 billion under management in 1990. And in 1991, The State of Virginia Retirement System invested $100 million in managed futures as a test account.[4] In 1993, Virginia committed to increase its managed futures allocation to $640 million, or 3.9 percent of its $16.4 billion total assets.

The total of assets under management in managed futures has grown from $500 million in 1980 to $25 billion today, with over one-third of it accurately defined as institutional, including off-shore. Again, while the numbers are considerably less than those associated with the more traditional asset classes of equities and fixed-income instruments, the rate of growth necessitates contemplation. From this point on, significant growth will require increased participation by public and private pension plans, as well as unions, endowments, and foundations. Presuming that the "if it ain't broke, don't fix it" mentality applies, then it's not hard to see why there hasn't been a rush by the institutions to embrace this alternative investment strategy. With stocks and bonds returning well above their historic averages for the past 15 years, there has been no strong motivation to change. More about this, later.

METHODS THAT FUTURES MANAGERS (CTAs) USE TO CAPTURE RETURNS

The methods that commodities trading advisors use to generate a positive stream of return from the futures markets can be categorized into two broad classifications: technical and fundamental. Purely technical, or "systems," traders rely only on analysis of prices for their investment decisions. Fundamental, or "discretionary," traders are primarily concerned with the factors directly affecting the supply and demand of the markets. Sometimes these two methods overlap.

Of the more than 3000 CTAs managing money today, the overwhelming majority of them, over 70 percent, use some form of technical trend-following system. The reason for this is very simple. A fundamental trader must analyze and constantly update all the news and data affecting all of the markets in which he or she trades. These can be as varied as domestic and international government reports which may

---

4 Darrell R. Jobman, "How Managed Money Became a Major Area of the Industry," *Futures Magazine*, July 1992, p. 52.

have an impact on the world stock, bond, and currency markets. They can be geopolitical events that may disrupt the supply of oil, for example. Or they can be weather-related occurrences, which could affect the prices of agricultural commodities. To organize all this information into a form that enables one to consistently trade these markets profitably requires genius by definition. This is why successful fundamentalists remain in the minority. There is only so much genius to go around.

This fact is emphasized by the following story: A man went to see a neurologist and said, "Doc, you've gotta help me. I can't concentrate at work; things are bad at home; I can't even write a check. There's something wrong with my brain." The doctor said, "Have you considered a brain transplant?" Upon asking if this was possible, the man was informed that he could have any kind of brain that he wanted, by profession. The brain surgeon took him into a large, cool room and closed the huge refrigerator door, and there in the brightly lit, white-tiled hall were row upon row of shelves, all lined with bell jars. Each jar held a brain suspended in a clear fluid and each was clearly marked with a profession. "How about this one?" the doctor asked the man. "The brain of a lawyer. I can let you have it for $3,500. Installed." "I don't think so," said the patient. "What else have you got?" "You can be a brain surgeon like me," offered the doctor, showing another brain. "I make a good living and I like my work. You can have this brain for $5,000." "Not for me," said the man. "What else?" "Follow me," the neurologist said. "This just came in." Back in the corner all by itself was a brain in a bell jar labeled "CTA." "CTA? What's that?" asked the patient. "Commodities Trading Advisor," said the doctor. "They invest their clients' money and make huge profits for them." "That sounds interesting," said the man. "How much for that?" "This brain will cost you $75,000," said the doctor. "$75,000?" screamed the man. "It was $3,500 for the brain of an attorney and $5,000 for the brain of a neurologist. Why is this one so expensive?" The doctor shouted back, "Do you know how many CTAs I had to put together just to make this one brain?"

The point of the story is this: we're not geniuses. Much of the mystery surrounding the role of the CTA is eliminated when the process is understood. Once the trading system is fully developed, implementation requires mostly good old-fashioned hard work. A successful CTA is no smarter than any other successful businessman in any other field. And as in other businesses, the geniuses are the exception, not the rule. Significant amounts of money, in any business, are made slowly and consistently, through hard work, persistence, and determination.

While the so-called fundamental or "value approach" might make more sense to the stock investor, the technical approach is probably easier to understand. Most technical traders use mechanical trend-following systems, which are based on the price histories of the various markets in which they invest. The premise is that a price trend, once established, will continue until its conclusion. The challenge of the successful trend-following system is to identify the trend once it's begun, and to recognize when it has exhausted itself. The more sophisticated systems have "filters," or indicators that measure volatility and momentum. These may be adjusted from time to time to allow for the dynamics of the markets. The development and refinement of these additional risk-management tools are usually a luxury afforded the advisory firm whose skill at money management has resulted in longevity of business and a large capital base. It takes money to hire research staff and time to back-test proprietary models. The computer-based technology is incredibly expensive as well.

All of this leads to the sensitive subject of fees. The proactive management style of this particular investment strategy is best described as a *skill class*. The skill of a successful fundamental trader is evident. A technical trader's systems, developed over the years, which lead to consistent profits and management of risk, are correctly identified as a skill class as well. The system may be mechanical, but one is still relying on manager skill for profits. It is both arrogant and wrong for a futures manager to justify high fees in terms of net performance. The fact is that making money in managed futures is more expensive than in traditional asset classes. Passive fixed-income with comparatively little management is at one end of the scale. Active stock selection moves up in the fee structure. Managed futures is at or near the top end, in terms of fee/equity ratio.

BENEFITS OF USING MANAGED FUTURES

One of the key tenets of modern portfolio theory is that more efficient portfolios may be created by combining investment categories that do not correlate. Managed futures has a low correlation with all asset classes, conventional as well as alternative.

When a component of managed futures is added to a conventional portfolio of stocks, stocks and bonds, or stocks, bonds, and property, this low correlation results in a reduction of volatility in the combined portfolio. This statement of fact has been substantiated through exhaustive academic research, beginning with the previously mentioned Lintner study in 1983. The most comprehensive collection to date, of studies done on this topic, may be found in a book edited in 1992 by Dr. Carl C. Peters, entitled *Managed Futures.*[5] Also recommended is *Managed Futures in the Institutional Portfolio,* edited by Charles B. Epstein.[6]

Exhibit 1 illustrates the low correlation that managed futures enjoys when compared to other benchmarks. The benchmark used for managed futures is the widely accepted MAR Trading Advisor Qualified Universe Index. MAR, or Managed Account Reports[7] is a publishing service that tracks the performance of over 450 CTAs and programs. The Index is dollar-weighted, net of all fees, and is described in more detail under the section entitled "Benchmarks for Managed Futures." The NCREIF is the Frank Russell Property Index. SLGC is the Shearson Government and Corporate Bond Index. The S&P 500 is with dividends reinvested. EAFE is the Morgan Stanley international equities index.

It is important to know that the low correlation attributed to managed futures comes almost entirely from the proactive management style, or the ability to go short as well as long. The variety of markets traded is a factor, but if you eliminate the less liquid markets and trade long and short just the markets with good volume, such as the S&P 500, the bonds, and the foreign currencies, you still achieve the phenomenon of low correlation. This benefit comes from the ability to profit in declining as well as rising markets, thereby enabling the successful CTA to make money in all market environments—inflationary or deflationary.

5   Dr. Carl C. Peters, *Managed Futures* (Chicago: Probus Publishing Co., 1992).
6   Charles B. Epstein, *Managed Futures in the Institutional Portfolio* (New York: Wiley, 1992).
7   Managed Account Reports, 220 Fifth Ave., New York, NY 10001 (212) 213–6202.

Exhibit 1. Correlation of Managed Futures with Other Benchmarks (1980–1990)

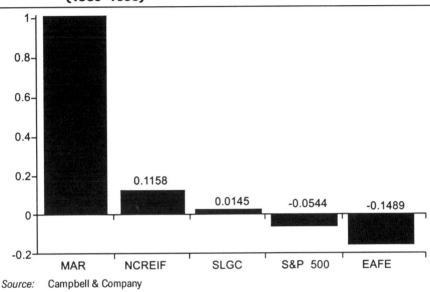

Source: Campbell & Company

Having established the low correlation, or covariance, of managed futures with other asset classes, we now observe what happens to a conventional portfolio when various percentages of managed futures are introduced. Standard deviation or volatility is reduced and, since returns for managed futures have been superior during the time period under analysis, we see that returns are increased in the blended portfolio also. As measured by MAR, managed futures from 1980 to 1990 have had an annual compound rate of return of over 20 percent, net of all costs of doing business. Also, using the Sharpe ratio as a measure, managed futures have outperformed stocks, on a risk-adjusted basis as well.[8]

In this chart, the MAR Index again is used as a proxy for the investment strategy of managed futures. The S&P 500 with dividends reinvested, is used as a proxy for stocks. Studies have also been done using a blended stock and bond portfolio, and bonds alone. The curve has the same shape, which means that the resulting volatility reduction and yield enhancement remain in evidence when managed futures are added to any balance of stocks and bonds. The reader is again referred to the aforementioned compilation of studies gathered by Dr. Peters, as well as those edited by Mr. Epstein.

In Exhibit 2, point A, on the lowest part of the curve, represents returns for 100 percent stocks, and the corresponding risk as measured by standard deviation. The next point, point B, is 90 percent stocks, 10 percent managed futures. As the managed futures portion is introduced, notice how the coordinates move into the upper left

8 "Past performance is not necessarily indicative of future results." Disclaimer required by the NFA when referring to performance. National Futures Association, 200 West Madison Street, Chicago, IL 60606 (312) 781–1410.

Exhibit 2.   Efficient Frontier Chart (1980–1990)

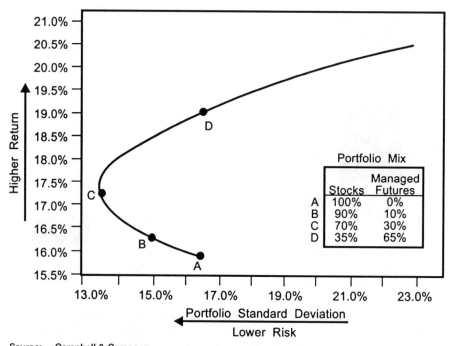

| | Portfolio Mix | |
	Stocks	Managed Futures
A	100%	0%
B	90%	10%
C	70%	30%
D	35%	65%

Portfolio Standard Deviation

Lower Risk

Source: Campbell & Company

quadrant of the efficient frontier, where low risk and high return reside. At point C—70 percent stocks, 30 percent managed futures—risk, or standard deviation, is reduced substantially, and there is a significant increase in return for the blended portfolio as well. Notice also that a portfolio comprised of fully 65 percent managed futures and 35 percent stocks (point D) is exposed to no more risk than that of 100 percent stocks.

It is fair to say that these figures may deviate as the variables change. The time period under analysis may be different. The compositions of the various benchmarks may change, as will their corresponding returns. But the premises demonstrated above will remain consistent: managed futures does not correlate with any other asset class; and consequently, introducing a component of managed futures into a conventional portfolio can reduce volatility and enhance return.[9]

---

9 "Past performance is not necessarily indicative of future results." Disclaimer required by the NFA when referring to performance. National Futures Association, 200 West Madison Street, Chicago, IL 60606 (312) 781–1410.

A DISCUSSION

The argument that managed futures adds diversification to a conventional portfolio is deserving of an analysis of the returns for conventional portfolios. Average annual total returns for U.S. common stocks have been around 15 percent for the last 15 years. Over the last 65 years, they've averaged around 10 percent. For the last 15 years, bonds have averaged almost 10.5 percent. They've averaged about 4 percent over the last 65 years. Clearly, for the last 15 years, returns for conventional portfolios have been above their historic averages. If you add in the returns for the S&P 500 in 1975 and 1976, of 37 percent and 24 percent, respectively, you've experienced a market that, except for a few "corrections," has known nothing but "up" since the establishment of ERISA in 1974. Perhaps these kinds of returns can continue indefinitely. However, a regression to the mean would imply less than stellar performance, sooner or later.

What about capacity? If plan sponsors develop an appetite for managed futures, can the markets and the industry handle the demand? The overwhelming majority of volume in the futures markets and in the managed futures industry today is in the financial markets—over 80 percent. Interest rate futures and stock indexes account for the bulk of it. And when foreign currencies traded in the interbank markets are included, they alone dwarf everything else in volume, including the New York Stock Exchange. So when one utilizes the systems-driven discipline of a futures manager who enjoys a successful long-term track record, and focuses his portfolio strategies and capital management skills toward markets with depth and liquidity, the capacity issue is eliminated. Most importantly, the key benefit of reduction of volatility due to low correlation remains. As mentioned earlier, it is the ability to go short as well as long that provides the diversification. I submit that the progressive development of the managed futures industry will be almost exclusively in currency management by the end of this decade. This will become widely accepted directly on the heels of the currency overlay programs, which have only just begun to be implemented within the past few years. Inclusion of stock indexes and interest rate futures will add still further diversification to the balanced managed futures portfolio, as well as precious metals and energies.[10]

But isn't managed futures a zero-sum game? An interesting answer to this important question was given at a conference on managed futures by a speaker representing one of the consulting firms. "Skilled active managers who are sensitive to loss control can extract return from trending markets. Although equity investing is a positive-sum game, active equity investing is a zero-sum game: if some managers beat 'the market portfolio,' others must underperform. The object of the game is to back the winners and avoid the losers. And many plan sponsors play this game."[11]

To summarize, the benefits of including managed futures as a profit center within a conventional portfolio are:

- Enhanced returns;

---

10 Jeff Reckseit, Campbell & Company, Baltimore, MD 21204 (410) 296-3301.

11 Robert Jaeger, Evaluation Associates, Inc., Norwalk, CT, *Defining the Institutional Market Conference*, New York, NY, April 9, 1992.

- Reduction of risk (due to the low correlation of managed futures with equities, fixed income, and all other asset classes);

- Diversification;

- Hedge against inflation/deflation (underperforming capital markets); and,

- Liquidity (usually within 24 hours).

BENCHMARKS FOR MANAGED FUTURES

There are at least two purposes served by industry benchmarks. One is to compare managers' performances within a given class. How do various equities managers compare to the S&P 500? How do various bond managers compare to the Salomon Bros. High-Grade Bond Index? How do various futures managers (CTAs) compare to the benchmarks that exist for managed futures?

A second purpose served by industry benchmarks is to compare performance *between* asset classes. For example, how do stocks compare (or correlate) with bonds? One might compare the S&P 500 to the Shearson Government and Corporate Bond Index. Or, how do international stocks compare (correlate) with property values? One might compare the Morgan Stanley Capital International Europe, Australia, Far East Index with the Frank Russell National Council of Real Estate Investment Fiduciaries Property Index (EAFE/NCREIF). We observe how all these asset classes correlate with each other. And finally, we can ask, how does managed futures correlate with any of them? For that, we would compare them to one of the benchmarks for managed futures.

The MAR Index has already been mentioned. There is one other widely accepted benchmark for managed futures, and that is the Barclay CTA Index. But before we discuss them, mention must be given to some other commodity-related indexes. Let me state unequivocally that these are not benchmarks for active futures managers, although they are pertinent to this topic. They are the CRB Index, the Goldman-Sachs Commodity Index, and the BARRA/MLM Index.

The CRB (Commodity Research Bureau) Index[12] is an unweighted geometric average of 21 nonfinancial commodity futures prices. There is no active management involved. It does have a high correlation with the Consumer Price Index (CPI) and therefore, may be viewed as an indicator of price inflation/deflation. Its use as a benchmark against which to measure the performance of a CTA, however, must be categorized as ineffective.

The Goldman-Sachs Commodity Index (GSCI)[13] is comprised of 20 commodities weighted by world production. Roughly half of it is in the oils or energy markets. It is a buy-and-hold, unleveraged, passive index. There is no manager skill involved. It too has a high correlation with inflation and commodities prices, and therefore, a low correlation with equities and fixed-income instruments. It may be perceived as a hedge against inflation. Because of the attractive way that Goldman-Sachs has made the GSCI available, it has generated quite a bit of interest. Some plan sponsors are

---

12 Commodity Research Bureau, 30 South Wacker Drive, Suite 1820, Chicago, IL 60606 (800) 621-5271.
13 Goldman, Sachs & Co., 85 Broad Street, New York, NY 10004 (212) 902-7850.

even considering holding the GSCI and using the CTAs' active management strategies as an overlay to add value.

The Barra/Mount Lucas Management Index[14] (MLM) tracks the cash price of the 25 largest, most active U.S. futures markets on an unleveraged basis. The monthly rate of return of the Index equals the risk-free rate plus the average of the individual markets' rates of return, depending on whether the market position is long or short. This is determined by the position of the market's asset value being above or below a 12-month moving average. The monthly rates of return are then compounded to compute the value of the Index. While there is no active manager skill involved, the BARRA/MLM Index demonstrates the returns potentially available to a futures investor and it is extremely useful in long-term correlation studies.

As mentioned, Managed Account Reports (MAR) is a reporting service that uses an index for measuring the performance of CTAs from 1980. They publish monthly and quarterly. The MAR Trading Advisor Qualified Universe Index shows the rate of return that the managed futures industry has been providing to the average investor. It is dollar-weighted and net of all fees. It is comprised of over 350 advisors managing over 450 programs. To be qualified, an advisor must have at least $500,000 under management and 12 months of trading client assets, or act as a trading advisor in public fund that is listed in MAR's fund table. To be free of survivor bias, the historic performance of the Index includes the performance of retired advisors for the period during which they were qualified.

The Barclay Institutional Report[15] is also a reporting service that publishes quarterly. Begun in 1980, the Barclay CTA Index measures the composite performance of approximately 200 CTA programs on an unweighted basis. Only those CTAs with at least four years of performance are included. Like MAR, it is reported net of all fees and commissions and it accurately reflects active management skill.

Barclay also publishes correlation tables comparing its managed futures index to the industry benchmarks of the S&P 500, the Lehman Government Bond Index, and the Lipper Growth Fund Index. It compares them all to each other for periods of one year, three years, five years, and ten years. It also has tables listing the top 30 CTAs ranked by compound annual return for the last quarter, 12 months, and 5 years. Other lists include the top 30 CTAs ranked by percentage of quarters in the top quartile for the last 3 years; the top 30 ranked by smallest worst decline; the top 30 by Sharpe ratio; the top 30 by Sterling ratio; the top 30 by equity under management; and several other tables.

The argument that makes MAR and Barclay qualified benchmarks by which to measure the performance of CTAs is that they're comparing "apples to apples." These two benchmarks are actually comprised of the active managers under consideration for hire. They show how they have done against their peers.

Both MAR and Barclay publish quarterly reports with extremely comprehensive performance measurements of over 350 CTAs. If one was interested in researching futures managers prior to contacting them directly for more information, and before visiting with them, MAR and Barclay constitute the most complete source of infor-

14 Mount Lucas Management Corp., 100 Palmer Square, Princeton, NJ 08542 (609) 924-8868.
15 Barclay Institutional Report, 508 N. 2nd Street, Fairfield, IA 52556 (800) 338-2827.

mation. Consequently, the benchmarks that these two companies have developed independently are the most accurate that the managed futures industry has at the present time.

PERFORMANCE MEASUREMENTS FOR MANAGED FUTURES

For those not intimately familiar with managed futures, the array of performance measurements available is surprising. MAR and Barclay, in their quarterly reports, list over 30 different measurement tools.

Measurement of returns for the CTA is consistent throughout the industry. The Commodities Futures Trading Commission (CFTC)[16] requires that every CTA must register a disclosure document with the CFTC accounting for every dollar of equity under management since the inception of the CTA's management programs. Data must be presented on at least a quarterly basis but is usually presented monthly. The columns include beginning and ending net assets; additions and withdrawals; net performance before and after all expenses, including management and incentive fees and brokerage; and the rate of return net of all costs of doing business. You will see exactly what the manager has done in the markets on a net basis. Fees and expenses are no longer an issue at this point. You have the ability to evaluate and compare manager skill using just the disclosure document. You as a buyer also have the ability, using these numbers, to strip away all fees and "proforma-ize" returns so that one manager may be compared to another, using the same "overlaid" fee structure. Disclosure documents must be updated every six months.

The monthly and annual returns are also expressed uniformly throughout the industry on a compounded basis. The last column in most disclosure documents is called the "VAMI." This stands for Value-Added Monthly Index, or the value of an initial $1,000 investment. It is computed from inception of the program so one can calculate exactly how much a discrete amount of money, invested at any time, has grown, with profits and interest reinvested. It is calculated exactly like a Net Asset Value (NAV). Again, this is net of all costs, fees, and expenses. Performance graphs for a managed futures program are usually charted using monthly returns calculated in the above fashion.

The "first cut" in measuring risk in a managed futures program is to look at the largest decline, or cumulative loss of equity from a peak to a valley over a specified period of time. This used to be known by the arcane and outdated term of "drawdown." "Largest decline" is more precise. Monthly "VAMI" numbers are used to calculate declines.

Standard deviation is another helpful measurement of risk. It is the degree to which each monthly return clusters about the mean. In a normal distribution, 68 percent of the months will be within one standard deviation of the mean, and 95 percent will be within two standard deviations. After computing the monthly standard deviation, it is annualized. Again, all these tools enable the analyst to compare managers to one another, and to the benchmarks for managed futures, as well as to other asset classes.

---

16   Commodity Futures Trading Commission, 2033 "K" Street, Washington, DC 20581 (202) 254-6387.

The Sharpe Ratio is the compound annual rate of return minus the T-bill return, divided by the annualized monthly standard deviation. This is one of the key risk/reward ratios used by the industry. A higher number is more favorable.

The Sterling Ratio is the average annual rate of return for the last three years, divided by the average of the maximum annual decline in each of those three years, plus 10 percent. Both the Sharpe and Sterling Ratios are used to compare the rate of reward from an investment with the risk incurred in gaining that reward.

Time windows are rolling time periods of varying lengths. They summarize the best, worst, and average performance for a CTA over varying periods. They are usually a minimum of three months, but they can go all the way out to rolling three-year windows for CTAs with sufficiently long track records.

The efficiency index is the annual return divided by the annualized monthly standard deviation. This answers the question, "Can I get from point A to point B without experiencing excessive volatility?"

The average recovery time is the average amount of time for an equity decline, measured from previous peak to new peak. It tells how long it took the investor to achieve recovery of principal after a decline. This is a very important measure of risk, especially when comparing those CTAs who have been successful at managing risk to benchmarks for equities. The difference in average recovery time, as well as for the longest recovery times, is astonishing. During the 1970s it took the Lipper Growth Fund Index 27 quarters (Dec.'72-Sept.'79) to get back to the same level. Average recovery time for some of the best CTAs can be as short as three months.

The relative volatility measure evaluates the probability of losing various specific percentages of one's investment. This is one of the most rigorous measures of risk. MAR reports for each CTA, the probability of losing 20 percent of one's capital, 30 percent of one's capital, or 50 percent of one's capital.

The distribution of monthly returns measures monthly frequency distribution probabilities. It displays, in a bar chart, the number of months a CTA's monthly performance historically falls within varying performance increments. This is a good measure of consistency.

The margin-to-equity ratio measures the amount of *leverage* used. Again, this is one of the most important methods CTAs use to manage risk. Some are more aggressive. Some are more conservative. There seems to be anecdotal evidence of a rather loose relationship between the time a CTA has been in business, the amount of equity he or she has under management, and the degree of risk to which he or she is unwilling to expose clients.

R squared measures the relationship between a CTA's performance and a benchmark. You may have noticed that many of the tools used to measure the performance of managed futures may be found in the more traditional investment classes as well.

The benchmarks for managed futures can be useful in comparing a futures manager (CTA) to the *average* of all CTAs. It is probably more useful to use the benchmarks to compare managed futures to other asset classes. In this way, the low correlation of managed futures to all other asset classes, both conventional and alternative, is confirmed, and the key benefit of reduction of risk, in the portfolio to which it is added, is therefore established.

Having substantiated that benefit as a reason to proceed, the next logical step is to choose the very best futures managers available. This is where the performance measurements are useful. Whether this is done "in-house" using the MAR and Barclay Reports, or with a consultant, it all amounts to a manager search. A benchmark is just that—a point of reference; a place to begin.

IMPLEMENTATION

In addition to the "in-house" method, and the use of the consultant, there is a relatively new industry that has appeared over the last seven or eight years. These companies are referred to as "trading managers." Their job is to select and monitor the vendors (CTAs) as a service to the buyers (pension plans). The extra expense is usually passed along to the CTAs and should not be viewed by the buyer as a deterrent. Since the trading managers are operating as managers of managers, you may frequently hear them alluded to as "moms" (MoMs).

Just as diversification among asset classes may result in a more efficient portfolio, so may diversification among managers within a class result in similar benefits. It has been shown in theory and, more importantly, experienced in practice, that combining carefully chosen CTAs can reduce volatility in a well-constructed managed futures program. This is best achieved when the managers in the group do not have a high correlation with one another. Varying styles and markets may account for this.

The trading managers have become very sophisticated at using all the above-mentioned performance measurements to screen and organize the CTAs in every imaginable way. They can create managed futures portfolios tailored to the buyer's specific criteria. After the strategic allocation is made, their role becomes even more critical. They are responsible for reconciliation, which means that they review with the custodian all of the activity in the account to make sure everything is correct. This is done on a daily basis. To avoid a perceived conflict of interest with regard to trading activity, CTAs usually are not brokers, and must execute their trades through a brokerage firm. Therefore, the trading manager must monitor the investment style of the CTA for consistency, as well as the clearing and execution of trading at the brokerage firm(s). Most plan sponsors would agree that this is a far more efficient use of their plans' time and staff, rather than to try and do everything internally.

The consulting industry is very important in this process too, because many potential buyers are looking toward the consultant for guidance and information. Responding to these inquiries, several of the consulting firms have published academic studies on managed futures, with many others working on them. The Callan Report, released in the spring of 1992, states, "An argument can be made that there is a positive expected long-run rate of return to a well-run managed futures investment program. Based on index performance before fees, a commitment of 2 to 3 percent to managed futures would have resulted in a fairly substantial reduction in standard deviation in a well-diversified institutional portfolio over the past 12.25 years."[17] The Cambridge Report, published the same year, also presents a very comprehensive analysis of

17 Greg Allen, Callan Associates, Inc., 71 Stevenson Street, San Francisco, CA 94105 (415) 974-5060.

managed futures, but its findings are proprietary. Interestingly, it includes an extensive section on implementation, which details over 20 trading managers.[18]

As an alternative to dealing directly with the CTA or the brokerage firm, both the consultant and the trading manager provide an extra level of insulation and objectivity. Either way, the buyer has an obligation to exercise due diligence, fiduciary responsibility, and prudence. Managed futures is clearly an alternative investment, so a determination should be made as to the time/cost effectiveness of the "in-house" approach versus some combination of the above choices. The larger plans seem to want to have more control over the selection process. It's strictly a personal decision.

CONCLUSION

With regard to timing a strategic allocation into managed futures, some mention has already been made about market conditions. Another issue has been raised from time to time concerning the "life cycle" of the investment. Apparently, some buyers perceive alternative investments as products that have clearly definable phases of development, growth, and maturation. This may have been demonstrated to be true in the past, but I have some questions about the application of this theory to managed futures.

These are free markets, governed only by supply and demand. Leaving the capacity issue aside, let's concentrate on foreign currencies, domestic equities, and U.S. interest rates. The prices of these markets are going to trade at their fair value regardless of whether or not CTAs are an active force. The causes and effects of the supply/demand equation may take many forms, but in the end they are all that matter. To insinuate that the participation for profit in the trends of these free markets has a life cycle of some sort is to indulge in the projection of another experience that may or may not be closely related.

I ask you to consider the following: As the increasingly connected global economy expands and contracts, all asset classes can be seen to generally advance and decline together over time, when a long-term horizon is examined. This is so because they are all interest-sensitive and it is the cost of money that, to a large extent, drives the economic cycle. Managed futures has been shown to have a low correlation with all asset classes because of its proactive management style and the ability to profit in declining as well as rising markets. The resulting reduction of volatility and enhancement of return in the combined portfolio has also been examined.

A pension fund's primary objective is preservation and accumulation of wealth, so that the security of retirees is guaranteed to the largest extent possible. There is a balance sheet consisting of assets and liabilities. The assets are the plan's investments and the liabilities are the employee benefits, both at retirement and for health and well-being during employment. There are assumptions made to address and answer these liabilities. They may be, for example, 7 percent. In many instances, over the past 10 or 15 years, plans have found themselves overfunded as the capital markets have produced generous returns. This could change. Funds can dry up quickly. Thoughtful

---

18 Ian Kennedy, Cambridge Associates, 4301 N. Fairfax Drive, Arlington, VA 22203 (703) 525-6800.

portfolio managers are aware of this. Some have taken action. Many are contemplating. Some will be forced into action by market conditions. These are tough choices.

> Divide your portion into seven or eight, because you never know what misfortune may occur upon the earth.

> — King Solomon

CHAPTER 13

A Technician's Approach to Option Trading

Jay J. Shartsis
Director of Options Trading
R.F. Lafferty & Co., Inc.

A New York writer of liberal disposition, decided to take a flutter on the stock market. He bought a prestigious stock that immediately went into a free fall. "There is only one rule," he writes, "buy low, sell high. All the rest is double talk." His broker told him that it was going to be a "difficult earnings quarter," and consoled him that the market was "shedding its downside risk." "Uh-huh, I said, understanding nothing, so I bought more." What has he learned from all this? Chiefly, that the stock market is the greatest game imaginable. "I have played board games seriously since I was twelve. Nothing matches the grand terror and wicked joy of trading. I'm not up against dice, or my PC's blips; I'm up against the entire known universe. Out there is every dollar since 1776 and every sharpie since Beelzebub, and here I am waiting for another opening bell."

> Doing Well and Doing Good
> Richard John Lewis

Terror and joy, indeed. Wait until he discovers the option market!

HOW TO MAKE A MILLION (ALMOST) IN NINE WEEKS

Early in 1993, one of our clients performed a feat that all of us at R. F. Lafferty will long remember—literally the stuff that option dreams are made of. The client I refer to is a 30-year-old physician who's been playing the option game for seven or eight years—experiencing the usual ups and downs (mainly downs)—employing a rather eclectic method of stock selection that encompasses chart reading, put/call ratios, sentiment sensing, guru querying, and strangely, some fundamental input. I say "strangely" to the fundamental analysts, since fundamentals and technicals are not usually mixed. (Also, I'm strictly from the Joe Granville school of hermetically sealed technicians. He defines himself as "a pure technician—unblemished by even a speck of fundamentalism.")

On December 17, 1992, our doctor friend bought 265 Philip Morris January 75 puts at 1 1/16. The bill came to $29,000, a sum that represented all the money in his account at the time—not at all an unusual move for our client—he thrives on taking risks that would turn nearly anyone into a quivering bowl of Jell-O®. The Morris puts dropped to 3/8 a few days later and, as Tom Cochran, who wrote about this story in his "Striking Price" column in *Barron's* (March 15, 1993), said, "that must have been a defining moment."

I remember quoting the puts on that day. They were 3/8 bid—7/16 asked, and I briefly considered buying some for myself. I didn't—a move I would soon regret. Our client's account on this late December day was worth just $8,500. From here the great liftoff would begin. Morris started to fall. Three weeks later, the puts were sold for 3 3/8. Most people would have probably sold them out at 1 1/8 or 1 1/4 just for the relief after feeling the excruciating pain of seeing them at 3/8. (If you trade, you know how powerful these emotions are). Not our guy. He knows how to let a profit run—just like the investment books tell you to. The next day he took all the chips and bought 700 GM February 35 calls at 1 1/8. Our medic noticed that GM had traced out a head-and-shoulders bottom and had stopped descending on bad news—a good sign. Seventeen days later, he sold them for 3 1/8. I asked him how he was able to sleep at night with such a large position. He said that he felt the position was correct and didn't doubt its successful resolution. How did he refrain from selling on the way up at 2 1/4—a neat double and a cool $70,000 profit? Same answer. Why did he sell at 3 1/8? The stock experienced a two-day reversal on heavy volume and it looked like the run in GM was over. It wasn't. The stock had a few more points on the upside, but one can't always hit it perfectly.

Observing the generally high levels of put buying and high put premiums in mid-February, our friend indulged his therefore contrarily bullish opinion the next day by purchasing 900 OEX March 410 calls at 2 1/8, with the OEX index just over the 400 level. That's a nearly $200,000 investment (did I say investment?). These calls didn't take off right away. In fact, I recall them going down to 1 13/16 a few days later, but they were holding very well in a retreating market—a bullish omen. The slide was short-lived and the market started rallying smartly. In a few more days the OEX calls were sold at 4 1/2 and 4 5/8. The account now stood at over $400,000. This was option leverage heaven and there was more to come.

Wasting no time, our man got up early the next day and went back to his old friend, the Philip Morris puts. Two fast trades yielded another $250,000 profit—not bad work. Hardly worth mentioning was a series of small gains and losses in Borland, Kodak, Coke, Motorola, and a few others. The good doctor then finished the market off with a Digital Equipment/IBM call knockout combination that brought the account value to over $750,000 by the end of February—elapsed time: two months nine days.

From \$8,500 to over \$750,000—an option trader's dream come true. Making this run even more fabulous was the fact that he employed both puts *and* calls without prejudice and had no outstanding luck such as holding puts in a crash or calls in a takeover! This is not to say that lady luck didn't smile broadly on our friend. He would be the first to admit she did. Keeping those gains, alas, is another tale. As an old associate of mine used to say, "If it was easy, everybody'd be doing it."

Of course, trading options is anything but easy. Most people lose, but that doesn't seem to stop them from trying. Attempting to duplicate our M.D.'s results probably costs the American public billions every year.

Some professionals believe that at least 30 percent, if not 60 percent, of all NYSE transactions are now option-related. If this figure is even close to the truth, the importance of options can hardly be overstated. Do you think it a coincidence that the last two significant peaks in the stock market came on option expiration days—August 1987 and July 1990? So whether you trade options or not, you should be aware that their impact is vast. Knowledge of the inner workings of the option market can offer valuable clues to overall market direction.

Since options are the focus of so much raw emotion, it is in the sentiment area that they offer particular insight.

PUT/CALL VOLUME RATIO

The most common measure of sentiment provided by the option market is the put/call ratio. It simply relates the volume of puts traded to calls traded. One looks for extremes of put buying to signify market bottoms and heavy-call buying to denote tops. Since option buyers are reliably wrong at market turns, it usually works just that way. A reading of 60 to 65 (or lower) puts traded on the CBOE (Chicago Board Options Exchange) for every 100 calls is a high level of optimism often seen at market tops (use a five-day average). A high level of pessimism is acknowledged by a reading of about 85 puts (or higher) for every 100 calls and often signals a buying opportunity.

The put/call ratio does have a pretty good record as an indicator, but some fine-tuning can make it even better. I have learned to adjust my perception of the put/call ratio by comparing it to the market's actual movement. For instance, if the market has a very sharp upmove, it is entirely normal for there to be heavy call trading as compared to put trading. This is due to the fact that option players, like most traders, tend to be trend followers and are just doing what comes naturally. A more unusual, but more predictive, condition obtains when in a flat or only moderately rising market one observes a high level of call volume. This is abnormal behavior in that it is not in response to rising prices and can therefore be termed "anticipatory" buying. It is quite likely to be proven wrong by a sell-off.

Incidentally, one should keep in mind that these parameters are reflective of the extraordinary bull market that has been in force for many years. They are very likely to change, perhaps substantially, in the next bear market. For example, we may find that stocks will keep right on declining with CBOE volume ratios in the '90s and will require several days of readings over 100 before a rally starts. We'll have to see what works at the time. All the other indicators we will be discussing may require adjustment too, when the bear returns.

An interesting exception to the normal put/call parameters happened in the great crash of October 19, 1987. Unexpectedly, the readings showed very heavy *call* volume, not *put* volume. I thought at the time that the data reported by the exchanges was wrong, since one would have expected an avalanche of put trading. With all the turmoil going on, reporting errors seemed entirely possible. However, it turned out that the data wascorrect—many more calls than puts were trading. What happened was that prices dropped so precipitously, so quickly, that lower-strike-price puts were not yet available for trading. It took about two days to introduce them. So in the crash and its immediate aftermath, only very deep-in-the-money, and expensive, puts were in existence. If the lower-strike-price puts had been listed, hundreds of thousands (millions?) of them would have traded, and this would easily have resulted in a record put/call ratio never to be seen again—perhaps for thousands of years (there'll always be an option market).

As with any indicator, one cannot always have blind faith in what it is saying. A little common sense is sometimes helpful. If the volume-based put/call figures reported for October 19, 1987, were taken at face value, another multi-hundred-point decline was suggested. However, other option-related indicators, such as the put/call *premium* ratio, were correctly reflecting the ferocious fear engendered by the crash and pointing to the wonderful buying opportunity that it turned out to be.

DOLLAR-WEIGHTED PUT/CALL RATIO

There is another, less well-known sentiment indicator derived from the option market that can be very helpful. Developed a number of years ago by the late Perry Wysong, it is sometimes referred to as the Wysong ratio. Perry used to edit the "Consensus of Insiders" newsletter. The ratio reveals the dollar value of puts traded versus that of calls. The idea here is that market bottoms see heavy dollar flows into puts, and tops are evidenced by calls getting the attention.

On the morning of October 5, 1992, the market plunged by about 106 Dow points during the first two hours. The dollar-weighted put/call ratio skyrocketed to over $8.00 in puts for every $1.00 in calls traded—a nearly unprecedented level. Sure enough, this figure, which represented an orgy of put buying, marked a terrific buying opportunity. October 5, 1992, was the start of a powerful rally. The reading of $8.00 was extraordinary, but one need not wait for such a number to turn bullish. A CBOE reading of about $1.50 to $2.00 usually does the trick (use a three-day average). Warning signals of an impending downturn are flashed when one sees about 25 cents, or less, in puts for every $1.00 in calls traded. A flat market can be expected to produce a CBOE reading of 50 to 60 cents in puts for every dollar in calls.

Incidentally, one needs a computer system to accurately calculate the dollar-weighted put/call ratio. Interestingly, Wysong used to hand figure the ratio by taking just the most active options and multiplying the price by the volume—still a valuable figure.

Personally, I like this indicator better than the more common volume-based put/call ratio because it has much more dramatic swings—so its signals are clearer.

MIRROR-IMAGE PREMIUM RATIO

When speculators get very bearish, they not only buy a lot of puts, but they are willing to pay a lot more to own them. The same, of course, is true for calls when the mood is bullish. The relative pricing between puts and calls is referred to as the premium ratio and can offer valuable input to the sentiment equation. For example, in early January 1991, just prior to the Gulf War, the S&P 100 (OEX) stood at about 295. The February 310 call was trading at 2 1/2 while its mirror-image put, the February 280, was trading at 7 1/2. The put and the call were each 15 points from the 295 level, hence the term "mirror-image." A more "normal" price for those puts would have been about 4 1/2. This overpricing reflected the very bearish mood that prevailed at that time. Most traders thought that the outbreak of hostilities would result in a sharp market sell-off, so they were heavily on the put side. This intense manifestation of bearishness was indeed a contrarian's delight, as the market shortly exploded upward in a historic advance. My rule of thumb is to look 10 or 15 points up from the current OEX level to the call price and an equal distance down to the put price and compare their premiums. I examine the current expiration month and if I find the puts priced more than 2 1/2 times their mirror-image calls, I get bullish. If I find that the calls are nearly the same price as the puts (within about 1/4 point) I get bearish. That's a sign of too much complacency. Incidentally, many people wonder why, in recent years, puts on the OEX always seem to be more expensive than the calls. The answer, I believe, can be traced to the crash of 1987. Prior to that watershed event, the theory of portfolio insurance encompassed the strategy of selling stock index futures to protect portfolios. This methodology was largely discredited in the crash because prices dropped too fast to allow effective sales of futures. Many portfolio insurers have since turned their attention to the S&P 100 puts to provide downside protection. So now there seems to be a significant contingent of players who are *always* in the market buying these OEX puts as insurance against a break in the market. Apparently, their demand keeps the price of the puts at permanently elevated levels vis-à-vis the calls.

MESSAGES FROM THE OEX

Many people express surprise when on occasion the OEX moves up a couple of points and the OEX calls that they're holding don't participate—or even worse, go down. How can that be? This is because the pricing mechanism for the OEX options is *not* the OEX itself but the S&P 500 futures contract. The OEX has no futures contract associated with it; therefore, its closest relative (S&P 500 future) serves as proxy. So when the OEX goes up one or two points and the S&P future is up only slightly, or not at all, it is entirely logical that the OEX calls won't rise (and puts won't fall). This leads us to another, more subtle, but very important phenomenon. On occasion, the OEX options will part company with the S&P futures themselves. For instance, if the near-term future contract moves up two points (my minimum benchmark movement for this observation is 1 1/2 points), we would expect, with the OEX at 413, that a one-month out 415 call might move from 3 to about 3 3/4. What if under such circumstances it is only 3 1/8 or 3 bid? Watch out! This is a highly reliable indication that a downturn is imminent. The most likely explanation for this situation is that major players are aware of sizable sell orders waiting in the wings and they are front-running these orders by effecting naked-call sales. Their actions keep a lid on the call prices. An even stronger signal would be flashing if these calls were priced at 2 7/8 or 2 3/4—down 1/8 or 1/4 for the day, and the 410 or 405 puts were actually up for the day—quite a rare development.

In other words, always check to see that the OEX options are validating the move in the S&P 500 futures—they almost always do. When they don't, they are calling your attention to as sure a bet as the market offers.

BUY OR SELL OPTIONS?

Should one be a buyer or seller of options? It is believed that as many as 80 percent of options expire worthless. If this is true, wouldn't it be logical to be on the sell side of the equation? Famed trader Blair Hull, in his interview for *The New Market Wizards,* states that speculators are usually on the buy side of options and that this bias imparts an edge to the seller. My observation from seventeen years on R. F. Lafferty's Option Desk bears this out. In fact, a fair proportion of option traders, especially newcomers, aren't even aware of the sell side. Not that selling of options is an easy road to riches. It isn't. I remind the reader of Option Principle #1: "If it were easy, everybody'd be doing it."

If one embraces the concept that selling is the superior approach, how does one go about it? Should we sell options with fat premiums—those that are overpriced? Indeed, there is a good-sized cottage industry of software vendors whose programs are designed to ferret out "overvalued" options. Most of these systems are based on the famous Black-Scholes option pricing model, the industry standard.

If the computer identifies a $3 call that "should be" trading at 1 1/2, can you safely sell it? Maybe we should first consider why the calls are so overpriced. In *The Geometry of Stock Market Profits,* Mike Jenkins says "Option premiums will always reflect inside information that is not available to the general public." He suggests looking for options that *are ridiculously expensive* with the intent of *buying* not selling them.

He says that in the short run, it is almost guaranteed that a large option premium will attract buyers. This is due to the impact of multibillion-dollar players such as large insurance companies, who are passive investors geared to collect dividends and do buy-writes. Their approach forces them to buy hundreds of thousands of shares in companies whose options have unusually large premiums. This buying will push up the stock. The stock going up will expand the option premium, and the process will feed on itself until all players who do buy writes have exhausted their pool of money and have their positions.

A very high premium may also hint at a coming takeover. Blair Hull speaks of some traders employing indicators called "wolf detectors"—a jump in implied volatility for the out-of-the-money options. Such an occurrence could warn of a "wolf"— perhaps a party looking to make a takeover bid for the company. How do call sellers protect themselves from getting crushed in a takeover? Hull suggests playing the high-capitalization stocks, which "tend to have information that is already in the marketplace. You tend to get far fewer sudden moves when trading the high-capitalization stocks."

I remember an incident back in 1979 when a broker friend of mine called to tell me that he was selling out-of-the-money Bally Manufacturing calls naked. The options were priced at 1 and were *very* far from the strike price. It looked pretty safe. The stock was about $35 and he was selling the 3-month out 50s (In those days, stocks were on a three-month expiration cycle). This "easy money" expedition turned into a catastrophe, as Bally skyrocketed and the calls were eventually repurchased at over $10. My friend wiped out quite a few of his clients as well as his own account. Now I'm not telling you these stories to discredit option selling as a strategy. Quite the contrary, I think it's the best approach. However, one should be aware that danger lurks everywhere in the option market. If you want to be completely safe, stay in T-bills. Speaking of safety, for quite a number of years prior to the crash of 1987, a lot of people thought that selling out-of-the-money puts was a pretty safe strategy. It was . . .

One of our biggest clients had for several years been buying calls and selling naked puts on the Value Line #1 rated stocks. He would call me every Monday and I would read him the Value Line selections (he lived in Canada and the report wouldn't reach him for several more days because of the mail delay). This strategy worked beautifully for him (and for us too—very nice commissions and easy business since he invariably traded "at the market" like a pro, never fooling around with unrealistic limit orders.) He'd been in the market a lifetime and was then nearly 80 years old. His account had grown from about $250K—$300K in 1984 to about $750K in August of 1987 using the aforementioned strategy. Six weeks later, the account was completely decimated in the crash as puts soared and had to be repurchased at prices that were unthinkable just days (or hours) before. The experience of the crash has had several other long-lived effects on the option market—more on that later.

Enough horror stories. Now I'm going to tell you about a man who lost several hundred thousand dollars selling naked calls and thereby proved what a good strategy it is. What?

The gentleman I speak of is in his early sixties—a retired horticulturalist (of all things) who now spends nearly all his time playing cards at the casinos in Las Vegas. On every option expiration day, he emerges to sell out-of-the-money calls on 10 to 15 stocks. He generally chooses high volatility OTC stocks whose options always sport high premiums. Card Man tells me that early in his investment career, he was influenced by a book that examined myriad investment techniques. It was found that the very best approach, over time, was the systematic selling of out-of-the-money calls.

Starting with $300K in the spring of 1990, his account was down to about $100K in early 1993. This is success? It is when you factor in the nearly unprecedented rise that the market has enjoyed during the past three years.

During this period, our client has suffered particularly sharp losses in the powerful Gulf War rally of Jan–Mar '91 and the Oct '92–Feb '93 advance. But, remarkably, he fights on every month, convinced of his eventual vindication. He has sound reason to think so because a number of years ago he used the same strategy to turn $50K into $500K in six years. I must say I admire his cool persistence in the face of devastating losing streaks. Most people would have lost heart and quit or altered their approach a long time ago. Not this man. He has a perfect temperament for the option game. Iron nerves, unfortunately, is not a commodity for sale. If it was, I'd buy it. When the market inevitably cools off, I have every confidence that Card Man will make a lot of money.

THE CENTERGROUND STRATEGY

Here's an option selling strategy that incorporates several of the elements we have discussed thus far. It involves naked sales of both puts and calls, often simultaneously, on the S&P 100 (OEX) Index. The objective is to collect as much premium as possible while modulating the inherent risks through an inter-option valuation analysis. It also contains an automatic stop-loss feature to guard against, as much as possible, the disasters that can obliterate naked-option sellers. Keep in mind that stop-loss orders won't help naked put sellers if the market decides to open down 300 points. Remember Option Theorem #2: "If you want to be completely safe, stay in T-bills."

The strategy is a derivative of the put/call premium ratio (see prior discussion). The first order of business is to identify whether the market is overvalued, undervalued, or neutral. This is determined by the relative valuations of mirror-image options, which I will shortly explain. If the market is found to be in neutral (CenterGround) condition, we will sell both puts and calls. The market, incidentally, spends most of its time in this state. In an overvalued market, only calls will be sold, and in an undervalued market, only puts will be sold.

An example will illustrate how we determine the valuation mode of the market. February 19, 1993, was an option expiration day. The OEX closed at 400.20. At the end of the day, the price of the March 410 call was 1 1/4. Its mirror-image put, the March 390, was 2 3/4. According to our formula, this placed the market in a "CenterGround" condition, and we therefore sold *both* calls and puts 15 points away from the OEX level (see Exhibit 1). We would sell the 415 call and the 385 put. Note that our valuation test is 10 points from the current market, while our sale candidates

---

Exhibit 1

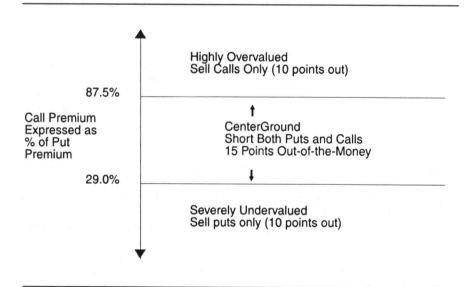

are 15 points away. If the market is in overvalued or undervalued mode, we sell only 10 points from current market, since perceived risk is lower and more premium would be captured.

If the put had been priced at 4 3/8 or higher, with the call still at 1 1/4 (29 percent of put premium), we would have considered the market undervalued (and the puts overvalued) and would have sold only puts. If the call had been priced at 2 7/16 or higher (87.5 percent of put premium), we would have considered the market (and these calls) overvalued and would have sold only calls. In other words, if we thought the market overvalued and therefore subject to a decline, we would not want to be short puts, since they would rise in a market decline.

To protect each position, a GTC buy stop order is entered at twice the entry price of each sale. The calls were sold at 1 1/4 so the buy stop is placed at 2 1/2 GTC. The puts were sold at 2 3/4, so the buy stop for them is placed at 5 1/2 GTC.

There are several subtle attractions attendant to the CenterGround strategy. For instance, if one is stopped out on the call position, then, by definition, the market has moved up, leaving the short-put position safer—unlikely to also be stopped out, since its strike price is further from the current market. So, in practice, if one side is bought back, the loss is very likely offset, at least partially, by the profit on the other side. To have to buy back both sides is fairly rare, though, of course, it will happen sometimes. The big profits come when both the puts and the calls expire worthless.

Another advantage of CenterGround relates to margin rules. When selling short *both* puts and calls on the same instrument (like OEX), one need margin only *one* side, *not* both. By the way, I told you that the crash of 1987 had "several other long-lived effects." Before that ghastly day, the exchange minimum margin requirement for the naked selling of index options was only 5 percent of the value of the index. It was raised to 10 percent shortly thereafter, and then later to its current level of 15 percent. Keep in mind that these are *minimums* set by the exchanges. Individual firms may, and often do, set higher house requirements. This stems from naked put calamities that happened in the 1987 crash (I think one major firm was hit for $23 million). Some firms were so frightened that they won't accept this sort of business anymore, at any price. A fine example of locking the barn after the horse is gone, since another crash even approaching the magnitude of October 19, 1987, would seem to be a very remote statistical probability, at least for a generation or so. A posting of 15 percent margin guards against a decline of 510 points from a Dow level of 3400.

I had a discussion about this situation several years ago with some pooh-bahs at the Amex and they told me that they were considering lowering this requirement (to 10 percent?) but nothing has happened. This would have a substantial impact upon any naked selling strategy. If the OEX is at 400 and you sold ten 400 calls naked, you now need to post a margin of about $60,000. If only 10 percent were required, $40,000 would be enough—a big difference in leverage. This situation has impact beyond the realm of the naked-option seller. Higher margin requirements mean fewer sellers writing fewer contracts. If you negatively impact the sell side of the equation, that means option premiums will be higher and spreads wider (less liquidity)—not good for option buyers either. If the brokerage firms want to be safe, why don't they go into the casino business?

EXPIRATION EXPLANATION

In the past six years the stock market has gone down on the Monday following option expiration day nearly twice as often as up. How come?

This phenomenon is very likely another legacy of the dark days of October 1987. The public has been haunted by the Crash and has often loaded up on puts looking for a re-crash. Mike Jenkins, in his aforementioned book, suggests that the market makers who sell all these puts are sometimes "naked" but more often hedge by going short the underlying stock. The speculators who bought these puts have no intention of exercising them, but hope to sell the puts at a profit as expiration approaches.

When the speculators begin selling their puts, they trigger a chain reaction: First, the market makers buy back the puts and consequently no longer need to be short the underlying stock. They then cover, which starts prices rising. This panics other put holders to sell, which creates more buying-in of stock. The rally attracts new call buyers who, in turn, force market makers to buy stock and sell calls to them. As you see, this can be quite explosive.

So in recent years, the public's bearish inclination has often helped force the market higher during option expiration week. At the close of business on Friday, the puts expire (few people have bought the next month yet, since they are quite expensive with at least four weeks to go) and this mechanism is no longer operative. Hence the market opens with a down gap on Monday.

There's another factor that contributes to the down-Monday-following-expiration syndrome. Because of a peculiarity in the margin rules, many option players are taking a "free ride" over the expiration weekend. On Friday, if the holder of an IBM call expects the stock to rise on the following Monday, he exercises the call into a long stock position. Provided he sells out the IBM stock by Monday's close, the speculator will not get a margin call at many firms, since it is considered a day trade.

This activity isn't lost on market makers and other smart cookies who have every incentive to start a drive to lower bids and sink prices. The undercapitalized option players are usually forced out on Monday's first dip—or by the close, at any rate, providing cheap stock to the waiting hands.

Moral: Wait for the Tuesday or Wednesday following expiration day to go long.

SUMMARY

The big mistake most option players make is coming into the game with unrealistic expectations. Such expectations can only be realized by taking extraordinary risks, which usually results in extraordinary losses. They buy out-of-the-money options in the expiring month. There's no law against buying in-the-money options with several months to run. Or better yet, as we have discussed, how about selling options as a strategy, which may not be as exciting but will probably work out better in the long run.

If you need to get the juices flowing every day, play the horses. It is much cheaper over time than having your head handed to you every month in the option market. Good luck!

Oh, about that liberal New York writer . . .

He has learned "that no one knows what's going to happen—not next quarter or next uptick. No one remembers what happened either; the market has no memory or loyalty and, scariest of all, no more self-preservation than a typhoon." In sum: "I've learned not to be somber about capitalism. Bear market, bull market, technical bounce, blow-off; how can anyone who talks like this be anything but irony writ large?"

CHAPTER 14

Market Neutral Investing— A Primer

Jeff Landle
Managing Director
Twenty-First Securities Corporation

INTRODUCTION

Market neutral investing is a style that has evolved as a result of a number of forces that have had a significant influence on both markets and investors in general. Increasingly sophisticated investors, supported by technology, are spawning complex strategies and instruments on a daily basis. Mortgage-backed securities (MBS), such as the interest only (IO) and principal only (PO) components of stripped MBS and various securitized versions of derivative-based investments, are some examples of these. In addition, Wall Street has provided a number of market neutral opportunities in less esoteric securities because of institutional biases. For example, the inefficiencies in the marketplace that allow short sellers to prosper have been a major contributor to the popularity of the most widely accepted form of market neutral investing, which involves long and short equity positions.

This chapter will define market neutral investing and provide coverage of current applications. Implementation of market neutral strategies—including trading, custody, and other mechanical considerations—will be discussed. The advantages and disadvantages of the style, and its implications for an asset allocation program, will also be covered. Finally, extensions to the concept will be touched on, with an emphasis on the inherent flexibility of the strategy.

STRATEGY DESCRIPTIONS

In a capital asset pricing model framework, market neutral investing might best be described as "zero-beta" investing. These strategies and programs strive to produce returns independent of the movements of a benchmark index. This section will profile several different implementations of market neutral investing.

Long/Short Equities

As the name implies, this strategy involves offsetting portfolios of long and short positions designed to eliminate the influence of the general market. An investor with an especially well-honed stock selection ability might prefer to take advantage of that talent by purchasing attractive issues in such a manner that a portfolio of selections mimicked the Standard and Poor's 500 or some other equity index, and thereby offsetting the equity risk by selling short futures contracts on the base index chosen. The resulting returns would bear little resemblance to those of the equity universe. Instead, performance would be a function of the "alpha," or unsystematic returns, generated by the stock selection methodology and the implied repo rate of the futures contracts sold. While the instruments employed to generate gains would be equity based (what will be designated hereafter as the "functional instrument"), a low or negative correlation with equity returns is the general result.

The vast majority of equity managers focus only on the long or "attractive" side of the market. While there are some dedicated short sellers, the "unattractive" stocks are more likely to fade from consciousness than receive notoriety for their poor performances. This is evidenced by the large ratio of research analyst buy recommendations to sell recommendations. Long/short equity strategies are designed to allow investors to benefit from variances from fair value on both sides—overvalued and undervalued. These equity programs make more efficient use of the information that securities analysts or quantitative models are supplying. Instead of making only partial use of the overvalued outputs (not purchasing or selling long positions), long/short equity managers try to actively benefit by selling overvalued stocks short. In its basic form, long and short portfolios with similar betas, or systematic risks, are formed. These offsetting portfolios may or may not be of equal dollar value, and may encompass a number of other risk factors besides systematic risk.

Programs that employ pairs trading (offsetting long and short positions in similar stocks—Ford versus General Motors, for example), can be implemented in a number of different ways. These include the utilization of options position, which is intended to benefit from poor valuation of the underlying as well as mispricing of the options. Some practitioners augment the returns profile of the low risk pairs strategy by employing less risk-averse strategies as part of an overall portfolio. An example of this would be a combination of market neutral, market and industry neutral, and options portfolios. Because of the low correlation between the three styles, returns may be increased with little in the way of increased volatility.

There are many variations of this strategy that can be envisioned. The number of modifications is a function of the different types of risk that can be classified and measured in the functional instrument. For example, there are numerous academic studies that focus on the relative importance of market and industry effects on equities.[1] If desired, the above market neutral equity strategy could be extended to

---

1 Benjamin King, "Market and Industry Factors in Stock Price Behavior," *Journal of Business* (January 1966), pp. 139–191.

being market and industry neutral. One way to accomplish this would be to purchase an attractive stock(s) in a given industry, while selling short an unattractive stock(s) in the same industry. This "pairs trading" is an extension of the practice of switching in and out of various stocks in the same industry based upon relative price movements. The resulting portfolio should be immune to the forces of both the general equity market and industry specific factors. Returns would be a function solely of stock selection, not related to industry or sector forces. Market neutrality implies only a beta of zero, but not necessarily a freedom from other risk factors. The generic capital asset pricing model was extended to the arbitrage pricing theory (APT) by Ross and Roll.[2] Applying the concept of APT to the above example would involve factor neutrality rather than industry neutrality. Zero-beta investing then becomes zero-factor investing, in which case both risks and returns should be further diminished.

PRIMEs and SCOREs

To this point, the focus has been exclusively on equity securities. It is quite feasible to structure a market neutral program using various combinations of other securities. For example, in the early 1980s Americus Trust Units were formed out of the shares of common stock of over 20 large corporations.[3] These units consisted of two underlying pieces, a PRIME and a SCORE. The PRIME component conferred upon the holder the right to all price appreciation on the common stock up to a certain price (the "termination value") and all dividend income (less a small administration fee). The PRIME was the equivalent of a covered call position (long the stock, short a call with a strike price equal to the termination value). The SCORE gave its owner the benefit of all price appreciation above the termination value. The two pieces could be reunited and exchanged for a share of common in the underlying company at any time prior to the fixed expiration date, at which time the trusts themselves would terminate. Upon termination, shares of stock would be distributed to the holders of the combined units.

Since there were no restrictions on combining the units into a share of common, arbitrage opportunities among the three should have been rare. However, because long-term options on individual company common stock were not readily available, the SCORE components were frequently expensive relative to their theoretical values. It follows that the PRIME component was frequently underpriced, which was also observed. Consequently, it was possible to construct a "delta neutral" hedge utilizing listed options to offset the price movements of the PRIMEs and allow the hedger to capture both an attractive dividend yield and the overpricing of the SCOREs. Given the arcane nature of the securities involved, along with a demand-induced structural mispricing, shrewd investors were able to attain a large positive alpha with little risk.

The successors to PRIMEs have a multitude of monikers, including PERCs, DECs and PRIDEs. The major difference between the current generation and their Americus Trust predecessors is that the companies themselves are issuing the securi-

---

2 Richard Roll and Stephen A. Ross, "An Empirical Investigation of the Arbitrage Pricing Theory," *Journal of Finance* (December 1980), pp. 1073–1103.
3 Robert Jarrow and Maureen O'Hara, "Primes and Scores: An Essay on Market Imperfections," *Journal of Finance* (December 1989), pp. 1263–1288.

ties (PERCS), or they are issued by financial institutions (DECS, PRIDES, etc.). This structure circumvents the tax issues that doomed the PRIMEs and SCOREs. The availability of listed long-term options (LEAPS) on most stocks underlying these issues and a more developed over-the-counter market obviate the need for an analogous SCORE component. What was possible with PRIMEs and SCOREs might also be attainable with this new breed of packaged securities. Risk/reward structures that are attractive to investors and issuers, and the opportunities they present, will generally persist over time despite legislative and regulatory impediments.

Convertible Arbitrage

Convertible arbitrage is another form of market neutral investing that has taken advantage of the complex nature of the securities involved. Convertible bonds and convertible preferred stock are hybrid securities that possess the characteristics of both a bond or preferred stock and an option on the common stock of the issuing company. This option and the yield advantage over the common that a convertible usually enjoys, when combined with the leverage that is generally employed by practitioners, result in a combination that can produce very attractive returns, with little or no sensitivity to the direction of the equity market or interest rates.

Consider the scenario depicted in Exhibit 1, which is typical of how such a program is structured. While two-to-one leverage is employed in this example, it is possible for some entities to increase returns dramatically through the use of five- or six-to-one leverage. Convertible arbitrage is often employed by broker/dealer firms for their own accounts because they are able to utilize a more heavily margined structure.

Volatility and interest rate risk are key hedging variables in a convertible arbitrage program. The value of the convertible security is very sensitive to the volatility of the underlying stock price because of the embedded call option in the convertible. The "delta" (sensitivity of the price of the convertible to changes in the price of the common) of the convertible is generally less than one; hence it is not necessary to hedge a long position on a dollar-for-dollar basis. As the price of the underlying common changes, the nature of the convertible and the hedge ratio will change. In situations where the prices of the two securities rise, the convertible will trade more like the underlying common, and the hedge ratio will increase. When values decline, so will the hedge ratio, as the convertible becomes more bondlike in nature.

The interest rate component of the strategy should also be hedged. There are two different risks that need to be addressed. First, since convertible securities have a fixed-income component, a rise in interest rates can have a negative effect on the value of this portion of the portfolio that may not be mirrored by a move in the underlying equity. Second, depending upon the amount of leverage employed, the financing costs of the strategy may also be large enough to impact returns if rates were to rise substantially. The interest rate risk is bifurcated in a convertible arbitrage strategy, and includes short-term and long-term components. Each must be quantified and offset on an individual basis.

Hedging a market neutral convertible arbitrage program is a very dynamic process. There are a number of "Greek" risks beyond delta that accompany the option component of convertible securities. In a discontinuous market, it is possible that the

Exhibit 1

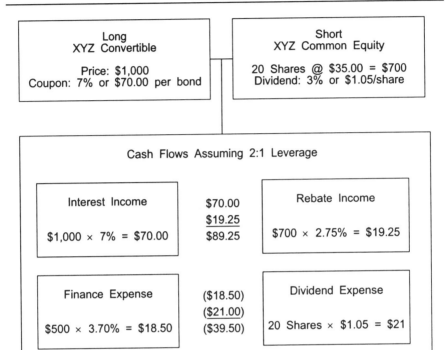

Long
XYZ Convertible

Price: $1,000
Coupon: 7% or $70.00 per bond

Short
XYZ Common Equity

20 Shares @ $35.00 = $700
Dividend: 3% or $1.05/share

Cash Flows Assuming 2:1 Leverage

Interest Income

$1,000 × 7% = $70.00

$70.00
$19.25
$89.25

Rebate Income

$700 × 2.75% = $19.25

Finance Expense

$500 × 3.70% = $18.50

($18.50)
($21.00)
($39.50)

Dividend Expense

20 Shares × $1.05 = $21

Net Cash Flow = $89.25 − $39.50 = $49.75
Invested Capital = $500
Rate of Return = $49.75/$500 = 9.95%

hedge may be difficult to adjust. Despite this fact, these programs are designed to be profitable in all market environments, and have generally rewarded patient and savvy investors.

High-Yield Bonds

A relatively new form of market neutral program is one that involves high-yield corporate bonds and common equity. The methodology in this case involves purchasing high-yield bonds and hedging the risk of holding them by selling short the common stock of the debt issuer. Once again, the ability to decompose returns into various pieces is essential to the implementation of the strategy. The holder of a corporate bond can be viewed as being long the value of the firm, and short a call with a strike price of the face value of the debt. A stockholder can be viewed as being long the call sold by the debt holder. Consider the following example. Firm XYZ has $200 in assets, debt of $100, and equity of $100. In this case, the equity holders are long a call with a strike price of $100. The value of their call would rise/fall with any increase/decrease in the asset value of the firm above the $100 that is owed to the debt holders.

In order to determine the relative values of the various components, it is necessary to measure the degree of credit risk assumed by the holder of the debt. This credit risk is analogous to the degree that the call written is in or out of the money. There are a couple of ways to approach this task. The first involves a factor model, which measures the interrelationship between certain firm characteristics and price movements of a firm's debt securities. Factors that have been shown to possess strong predictive ability include leverage (based on the market value of a firm's equity), debt maturity, the risk-free rate and equity volatility.[4]

A second procedure for measuring the value of the credit component of a corporate bond utilizes option-adjusted spread analysis. This model, originally developed by Ho and Lee,[5] and later extended by Jarrow[6] and others, provides an arbitrage-free methodology for valuing bonds based on the Treasury curve. It also takes into account the value of options, such as put and call features, that may be embedded in a bond's structure. Utilizing this framework, it is possible to turn a risky corporate bond into a "Treasury equivalent" and measure the difference between the actual bond and the analogous risk-free bond. This difference is the compensation for the credit risk assumed by the holder of the corporate debt.

The objective in measuring the credit component or yield premium necessary for investors to purchase risky debt is to determine a hedge ratio to mitigate that risk. The idea of a composite hedge was first promulgated by Richard Bookstaber,[7] but was limited to a theoretical framework, and not extended to measurement of individual hedge ratios. A composite hedge framework has been implemented, in a number of instances, on a portfolio basis utilizing market futures contracts to hedge credit risk with little success. More robust are programs that focus on individual issues. A portfolio of highly leveraged companies' stocks does not closely track or resemble any of the major indexes that have exchange-traded derivatives. This necessitates the focus on individual issues, rather than being able to hedge on a clustered basis.

The general goal of high-yield programs is to produce a return that approximates the current yield on the bonds at the time of purchase. The hedge is intended to immunize the position against changes in credit risk and interest rates. Exhibit 2 illustrates the relationship between a company's common stock and its debt securities. As a firm's credit quality improves, its sensitivity to equity decreases and its sensitivity to debt increases; conversely, deteriorating credit quality is correlated with increased sensitivity to equity and decreased sensitivity to debt.

These hedges require frequent adjustment in response to changes in the prices of the underlying securities, and are difficult to measure with a high degree of precision. Poor hedge rebalancing can be very detrimental to a program's performance.

4 Safe Harbor Capital Management, "Hedging the Risk of High Yield Bonds," May 1990.
5 Thomas S.Y. Ho and Sang Bin Lee, "Term Structure Movements and the Pricing of Interest Rate Contingent Claims," *Journal of Finance* (December 1986), pp. 1101–1130.
6 David Heath, Robert Jarrow, and Andrew Morton, "Bond Pricing and the Term Structure of Interest Rates: A Discrete Time Approximation," *Journal of Financial and Quantitative Analysis* (December 1990), pp. 419–440.
7 Richard Bookstaber and David Jacob, "The Composite Hedge: Controlling the Credit Risk of High Yield Bonds," *Financial Analysts Journal* (March/April 1986), pp. 25–36.

Exhibit 2.   The Sensitivity of High-Yield Bonds to Equity and Debt

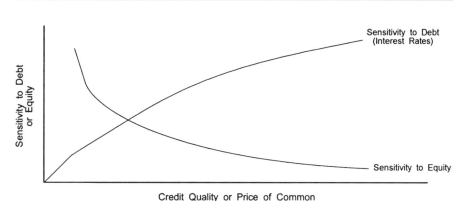

Experience and cost analysis can be very helpful in determining the optimal course. In a high-yield hedge, as with other market neutral investment programs, a diversified portfolio is a major risk reduction tool. There is a great deal of company-specific risk—which could result in a discontinuous market—that must be dispersed. The most effective risk reduction technique is adequate diversification.

Mortgage-Backed Securities

Mentioned briefly in the introduction, mortgage-backed securities are excellent vehicles with which to create a market neutral program. To this point, we have focused on equity and equity-related securities. Fixed-income instruments are in many cases more complicated in structure and therefore, more difficult to understand and price properly. Mortgage-backed securities are perhaps the most complex of all fixed-income securities, because they are primarily influenced by the speed of mortgage prepayments. Interest rates are an important component of prepayment rates, but the linkage is less than direct. Attempts to model prepayment speeds have been complicated by the lack of historical data and the importance of psychological factors that are difficult to quantify.

Collateralized mortgage obligations can be stripped or divided into different pay structure tranches. The result of these engineering feats includes such difficult to model and understand constructs as Planned Amortization Classes (PACs). PACs pay principal under a specified payment schedule, and have an almost certain yield and maturity as long as prepayment speeds remain within a predetermined band. Targeted Amortization Classes (TACs) differ from PACs by offering protection only in declining interest rate (faster prepayment rate) environments. Floating-rate CMOs pay coupons based on the spread over an index, and are backed by adjustable-rate mortgages. Inverse Floating Rate CMOs are bonds whose coupon increases as rates decline and vice versa, and whose price movements are highly volatile. Principal Only stripped CMOs (POs) are sold at a discount and benefit from declining rate environments. Interest Only stripped CMOs (IOs) return no principal and amortize to zero. IOs are desirable during rising rate (lower prepayment) environments.

These engineered securities offer significant opportunities for hedging risk. Since several of the above securities have an inverse sensitivity to interest rate changes relative to most fixed-income instruments (negative duration), it is possible to construct a portfolio that is market neutral (zero duration) without short sales. This allows a manager to assemble a portfolio that does not have the negative cash flows (interest or dividend payments) or the operational difficulties normally associated with short sales.

The ability to more accurately analyze CMOs and a very liquid and deep market has allowed managers to produce very attractive returns with little or no market risk. Prepayment risk is minimized, but not eliminated entirely, because prepayment speed is generally the variable relied upon to generate the overvalued and undervalued judgments relied upon to generate returns. Market neutral (zero duration) mortgage-backed security programs are predicated on the manager's ability to model and predict prepayment speeds better than the competition, just as a long/short equity manager's performance is based on the ability to select stocks better than the competition.

Futures Contracts

Somewhat illiquid or poorly designed futures contracts are excellent candidates for an arbitrage approach. For example, programs designed to take advantage of the poor design of the Commodity Research Bureau (CRB) inflation index have produced unusually large returns. The relationship between the index itself and the individual components is skewed in favor of the arbitrageur because geometric indexes, such as the CRB index, have inherent flaws. These include a downward bias, which favors purchasing the underlying commodities and shorting the index. Other index opportunities result from equal-weighted (versus capitalization-weighted) indexes that can be easily manipulated through the purchase of some of the smaller, less liquid components. The Nikkei 225 is a very good example of this.

Tax Arbitrage

Another market neutral strategy that deserves some mention is what might best be described as "tax arbitrage." This broad category is more transaction oriented than the above programs, and attempts to exploit opportunities that derive from differing tax treatments across borders or investment structures. For example, Germany recently amended its securities laws to discourage a number of dividend-related trades, in which tax-advantaged domestic entities would "strip" the dividends from equities held by other institutions with less favorable tax situations. For example, a U.S. entity holding German equities would enter into buy and sell agreements with a German corporation on a dividend paying German stock that straddled the stock's ex-dividend date. This arrangement allowed both to benefit. Holding period restrictions and limitations on the ability to transact with certain entities around dividend dates were instituted to make these strategies much more risky and deter participation.

In general, domestic arbitrage opportunities are few and far between, and they are becoming more uncommon as investors aided by improved technology wring every last basis point from low-risk trades. There does exist an arena where risk-averse investors can receive unusual rewards with minimal danger—cross-border arbitrage. These opportunities are generally more frequent for taxable than for nontaxable entities, but quirks and oddities resulting from different conventions present opportunities for all. These are not simple transactions, and they generally involve the ability to execute various legs simultaneously in separate markets. For the sophisticated and nimble, they offer returns that can be several times money market rates with similar risk profiles.

Examples of the differing practices that can spawn such strategies include tax rates, withholding schedules, trading practices, and regulatory inefficiency. Of special interest may be the arcane and anomalous tax structures that can distort a cash flow depending upon the tax status of the investor. One such example is the 12.5 percent withholding tax on Italian government bonds. This is an especially attractive area because of its size and liquidity (the market is the third largest in the world, behind the United States and Japan) and the active futures and options market that exists on these instruments (contacts of various types are traded on the LIFFE, the MATIF, and the Milan Exchange).

In order to gain a better understanding of how such an arbitrage might work, let's focus on the 10-year Buoni Del Tesoro Poliennali, or BTPs as they are commonly referred to. Under certain conditions, it is possible for taxable investors to utilize a combination of these bonds, BTP futures, and currency forwards to lock in double-digit annualized returns while hedging all price and currency risk. The reason for this is the unusual manner in which the bonds trade—net of the 12.5 percent tax withheld. When an investor purchases or sells a BTP, the accrued interest that must be paid or received is only 87.5 percent of the coupon rate. The same is true of the coupon payments, and occurs regardless of the tax status of the purchaser.

The pricing of the futures contract, on the other hand, reflects the tax status of the marginal buyer or seller, i.e., the least tax efficient investor. This creates an opportunity for investors, who can retrieve all or a portion of the withheld tax. The net result of this is a structural mispricing of the contract for the more favorably positioned investor.

In order to exploit this anomaly, an investor with the ability to recoup the withheld tax would purchase the bonds, while simultaneously (1) selling futures contracts to protect against price and credit/issuer risk and (2) entering into forward contracts to provide a hedge against currency movements. It is possible to leverage this trade by financing the purchase of the bonds. Through the use of repo financing, annualized returns on the order of 20 percent or more have been achieved.

Cross-border arbitrage becomes more difficult as countries and their markets become more interrelated. The increased focus of investors on international investments has led to increased standardization of trading rules and standards, while tax treaties have lessened other cross-border differences. These factors have made these trades more difficult. New hedging instruments and markets have the opposite effect. As new contracts and formats are introduced, new opportunities are born. The dearth of domestic anomalies as a result of increasingly efficient markets has not yet spread to the international arena. Cross-border strategies offer a fertile ground for the investor able to understand and execute complicated strategies.

Cross-border arbitrages involving sovereign and corporate obligations are also possible because of differing national regulations. The availability of numerous hedging instruments—including futures, forwards, options and various combinations of the three—provide the necessary risk-reduction tools that allow risk-averse investors to profit from these anomalies.

IMPLEMENTATION

The implementation of a market neutral program can range from slightly complex to extremely complex. In the case of a long/short equity program there are relatively few major obstacles, while in some of the tax arbitrage transactions, there are a number of hurdles that must be understood and overcome in order to achieve the desired results. The next section will provide an overview of how these programs are structured from an operational perspective.

Liquidity

Since a number of market neutral programs attempt to take advantage of arcane or poorly understood securities, liquidity is a prime consideration. Illiquidity has a cost that is not factored into most theoretical frameworks, and opportunities that appear attractive on paper may disappear when the market impact of a trade is included in the analysis. In the case of long/short equities, overvalued and undervalued stocks may converge rapidly toward fair value when buy and sell orders are entered. Many of the securities involved in market neutral programs are not exchange-traded, or if so, are very thinly traded. High-yield bonds, for example, are generally more liquid in the dealer market.

Some market neutral programs are able to produce spectacular returns with relatively small amounts of money, but cannot be expanded because of liquidity limitations. The previously mentioned CRB index arbitrage is a good example of strategies that encounter this restriction. Market impact costs can have a significant effect on most implementations, and must be monitored carefully to ensure that goals are met.

Short Sales

Short sales are an integral component of most market neutral programs. There are two implications to this. One is related to the ability to borrow the instrument to be sold. The other concerns custodial arrangements. In order to sell a stock or bond short, it is necessary to borrow the instrument first. Securities lending is a well-developed business and a method for holders to boost returns. In spite of this, there may be difficulty in borrowing a security for a number of reasons. One is related to taxes. When an entity lends a security that pays an income stream (dividends or interest), the income that the lender receives is from the borrower, not the institution that issued the security. Because of this, the nature of the income may be different. For example, the holder of a tax-exempt municipal bond or closed-end municipal bond mutual fund is unlikely to lend those securities, because the "in lieu of" payment the lender would receive from the borrower would be considered taxable income versus the tax-free payment that would have been received if the securities had not been lent. This ability to change the nature of income received and paid is central to a number of "tax arbitrage" strategies. While it is a detriment in some cases, it is an essential element in others.

Other difficulties related to short sales and borrowing stem from internal limitations placed on entities limiting the ability to lend securities. These include a desire on the part of the lender to retain the voting rights attached to a given security. There are also cases where an entity is restricted from selling securities it does not own. These situations are generally vestiges from an era when hedging was not nearly as well developed a science as it is currently. Mutual funds, for instance, are not allowed to exploit fully hedging techniques available to most of the general public because of regulatory restrictions on short sales. The maximum amount that a mutual fund is currently able to devote to short stock positions (whether speculative or defensive in nature) is currently one-third of the portfolio value, and this short position must be collateralized with cash. The effect of this is to penalize a fund employing short sales as a hedge by not permitting a portion of its assets (the segregated cash) to be allocated to an effective risk-reducing technique.

Custodial difficulties can also create some interference with short sales. In general, the broker that clears the short sale of a security will want some sort of collateral. In the case of a traditional long/short equity strategy, this collateral is generally supplied by the long stock positions—since equity is usually 50 percent marginable. If the long and short positions are not held by the same institution, the situation becomes more complicated. For example, in the case of a mutual fund, where the long positions would likely be held by a custodial bank and the shorts by the executing broker/dealer, agreement must be reached between the two regarding the rights of the various parties to the securities held. In general, a three-party custodial agreement giving the broker/dealer access to the securities held by the bank is sufficient to satisfy the margin requirements of the brokerage firm.

A third difficulty related to short sales is a "short squeeze." In these situations the price of a security moves up sharply, and short sellers are forced to cover their positions to stem their losses. Short squeezes can feed upon themselves as the buying pressure from the short coverers forces more short sellers out. A rising price can also create problems for borrowers, as some lenders may call in their shares to sell them as the price rises.

Trading

Trading a market neutral program is as much art as it is science. Given the complexity of many of these strategies, it is important to be able to judge the implementation risks involved. In most cases, the various hedging transactions that comprise a hedged position are not executable simultaneously—the trades must be "legged." It is usually advisable to deal with the more difficult-to-transact portion of the strategy first, and leave the easier portion for the end. For a long/short equity strategy, this implies executing the short sale first, since for listed stocks either a zero-plus tick or an up-tick is necessary before a short sale can be effected. The long purchase is usually a fairly simple matter.

In other instances, all portions of the trade are not easily executed. In the case of the high-yield bond hedging program mentioned earlier, the purchase or sale of a junk bond is not necessarily a simple matter. The market is fragmented and positions must be shopped extensively to ensure the best price. The equity securities of a highly leveraged firm are generally not especially liquid. Locating shares to borrow, liquidity constraints, and up-tick difficulties all serve to complicate this strategy.

There are risks associated with this method of transacting. The most obvious is that the relationships among the various legs can change after or more components have been completed, with the positive return expectations no longer reasonable. Transaction costs and market impact costs can also combine to derail profit expectations in cases where large trades are impractical. In many cases, it is advantageous to incorporate an electronic trading system, which can facilitate simultaneous entry and execution of a large number of orders with the appropriate constraints.

Rebalancing

Rebalancing the hedge in a market neutral program can be a difficult function to master. In a long/short equity strategy and most others, the primary concerns are liquidity, the ability to short, and transaction costs. The proper method for minimizing the impact of these risks must be tailored to the program.

Establishment of volatility bands for each individual hedge is an important component of any rebalancing strategy. These bands can be fairly simple in construct, such as standard errors from a regression analysis, or much more sophisticated in derivation such as a neural network analysis. The importance of these bands cannot be overstated from profit maximization and risk reduction standpoints. If the bands are too wide, positions will be under- or overhedged and unexpected risk will be borne by the investor. Conversely, unnecessary rebalancing will lead to lower than expected returns, as transaction costs are generated not by any risk-reducing activity, but simply by the noise inherent in short-term price swings.

Dynamic hedging, such as is necessary in the high-yield bond program described earlier, requires constant vigilance and well-designed guidelines to prevent a strategy with a high turnover rate from having its returns eroded by unnecessary transactions. Market neutral programs as a whole are more transaction intensive than more traditional strategies. This results from the hedging requirements, the desire to produce returns from a bevy of smaller successful trades versus one or two big winners, and the two-sided nature of a hedged position (for example, being long and short a single security for each dollar invested). The importance of rebalancing in as efficient a manner as possible cannot be overstated.

Custody and Operational Issues

Custody and other operational issues are most often encountered when dealing with short sales. The Federal Reserve Board governs the way short sales must be handled by brokerage firms. Current regulations require that short sales be effected in a margin account at a brokerage firm. This can create difficulties, since the securities needed for collateral may be held in custody away from the broker. Most brokers and custodians will work together to produce an arrangement that satisfies regulatory and safety considerations. There are instances, though, where custodians will charge for the additional expense of accounting for shorts not held by them.

Other operational considerations include the tax implications of short sales for tax-exempt institutions. The IRS has not publicly ruled, but is expected to do so shortly, on whether short sales, and specifically short rebate interest, give rise to unrelated business taxable income (UBTI). There have been private rulings where this issue has been addressed, and the UBTI issue dismissed. This is not, however, a closed issue. Finally, the viability of these programs under ERISA must also be addressed by institutions interested in market neutral strategies.

ADVANTAGES AND DISADVANTAGES

There are a number of advantages to incorporating market neutral programs into an overall investment strategy. First and foremost is the risk reduction and return enhancement that a diversifying asset class can add to a portfolio. Basic mean/variance portfolio optimization exercises show that adding an asset class with a low correlation to the existing assets in a portfolio results in higher returns with the same level of risk. This analysis is, of course, contingent upon the returns of the market neutral programs being lognormally distributed. While this is difficult to measure because of limited returns histories, experience with some of the longer-lived programs has shown this to approximate reality. Some strategies would clearly violate the preceding assumption, and are not intended to be part of this discussion. They include the majority of the tax arbitrage strategies because of the predictability of their returns. It should be noted that the truncated and unusual distributions associated with these strategies can have a desirable effect on portfolio risk/reward characteristics.

Table 1 illustrates the low to negative correlations between several market neutral programs and more traditional asset classes. In the parlance of modern portfolio theory, the "efficient frontier" is raised as more of these asset classes are combined.

Table 1.   Correlation Table

	T-BILL	SHCM	CONST	S&P 500	BNDS	STFA
T-BILL	1.00					
SHCM	0.40	1.00				
CONST	0.17	0.07	1.00			
S&P 500	-0.03	0.18	0.23	1.00		
BNDS	0.10	0.03	0.44	0.43	1.00	
STFA	0.07	0.16	-0.07	0.07	-0.05	1.00

The above table covers the period 6/91–7/93, and includes 90-day Treasury bills, Safe Harbor Capital Management's High Yield Bond Hedging Strategy, Wharton Management Group's Constellation Convertibles L.P. Convertible Arbitrage Partnership, the S&P 500, the Merrill Lynch Government Corporate Master Bond Index, and Stovall/Twenty-First Adviser's Competitive Hedge Program.

A second advantage of market neutral programs is their flexibility. The alpha earned by most market neutral managers can be attached to almost any other asset class through derivative overlays. For example, an investor with a desire for exposure to equities could engage a long/short equity manager whose expected return is 400 basis points over Treasury bills and purchase S&P 500 futures contracts. The net result would be a portfolio returning approximately 400 basis points over the S&P 500 (assuming the manager was able to produce the expected results). In this instance, the cost of carry on the futures contracts would be offset by the short interest rebate from the market neutral portfolio. Exposure to virtually any asset can be effected in this manner, and usually with minimal costs or market impact. In addition, shifting exposure between and among different assets, selling S&P 500 futures and purchasing Treasury bond futures, for example, can usually be accomplished more easily and cheaply through the futures markets. Changes in asset allocations are facilitated through this type of structure.

An ancillary benefit to utilizing futures overlays to accomplish asset allocation goals is that the tax implications of foreign investing become much less of an issue. Withholding tax structures can distort the benefits of overseas investing, depending on whether an entity is tax exempt or taxable domestically. For example, should XYZ pension fund purchase the stock of a British company, its return would be lower than that of a taxable entity because it would have no means to recover the portion of the dividend income withheld by the British government. The taxable entity, in contrast, would be able to claim credit for the taxes paid on its U.S. income tax returns. If the same pension plan were to get exposure to the same company via a listed or over-the-counter derivatives transaction tied to the total return of the same stock, the tax disadvantage would not be a concern.

Just as it is advantageous to diversify across asset classes, it is also more efficient to integrate different management styles within an asset class. Typically, equity managers have styles that reflect their investment philosophies. Some focus or tilt their portfolios toward growth stocks, others toward value stocks. The alphas or excess returns from these managers are not highly correlated, which is why different managers with different styles are combined in most programs. Since the alphas generated by most market neutral managers will have little or no correlation with those produced by the majority of managers employing more simplistic approaches, the inclusion of these programs with a futures overlay should benefit most investment programs.

A third benefit of market neutral programs is their use of methods and structures that are not usual or part of mainstream investing. Opportunities generally lie not where the majority of investors are active, but where there are fewer participants. For long/short equity managers, the more fertile fields are usually on the short side of the market. For others, arcane tax rules or complex security structures are the areas that are less efficient. It may be easier for market neutral managers to produce excess returns because of the markets and structures they utilize.

While complex strategies and unusual structures provide many of the opportunities for market neutral managers, they are also responsible for many of the risks. Difficulty in quantifying and understanding the hazards of many of these strategies is a serious concern for investors. For example, in the previously described high-yield bond hedging program it is necessary to measure and separate credit and interest rate risk for companies and securities with a variety of maturities, different seniorities, and put and call features. Sophisticated modeling techniques and some assumptions are required to accomplish this. The requirements in terms of personnel and technology can be significantly higher for these more sophisticated programs than for a less intricate strategy.

PERFORMANCE MEASUREMENT

Measuring the performance and defining benchmarks for market neutral managers is an area that has yet to evolve past the nascent stage. The difficulty with these programs is that they are quite heterogeneous, with substantial differences in risk levels, functional instruments, and investment approaches. Should a long/short equity manager be compared to a market neutral CMO manager? The answer is not an easy one, because rational arguments can be made for yes and no answers. On one hand, the goals of both programs are similar. On the other hand, they employ different instruments and have very different risk factors. Aside from the more basic problems of using a manager universe as a benchmark (such as investibility, specificity, and measurability), the biggest challenge with trying to gauge relative performance for a homogeneous group of managers is that the categories in many cases would end up having only one or two members. This might not be a problem with long/short equity programs, of which there are a large number of practitioners, but market neutral mortgage-backed managers are a very rare breed.

What is the appropriate benchmark for market neutral managers? There is no accepted standard for these programs, such as the S&P 500 or some other index might be for equity managers. This lack of structure has generally led managers to either compare results with a number of other asset classes or provide no benchmark at all. Market neutral managers, in many cases, view their strategies as being "cash alternatives," and prefer to use some form of premium over Treasury bills as the standard by which they should be measured. Intuitively this makes sense. Many of these programs involve some sort of short sale, which should generate some return linked to the level of short-term interest rates. Long/short equity managers, for example, generate rebate interest from selling short stock that should very closely track short rates. It is the magnitude of the premium that an investor should expect over the base rate that has generated some debate. Given the sometimes very different levels of risk associated with different managers, special care must be taken when establishing a benchmark. In addition, the limited track records of many market neutral programs provide very limited perspective from a risk standpoint.

Having a benchmark pegged to Treasury bills seems appropriate for those programs with some portion of their returns tied to a similar interest rate, but there are a large number of strategies that are more difficult to categorize. In many cases, managers provide an expected return, which can be arrived at in a number of different ways. One method is to extrapolate from historical returns data. This can lead to unrealistic expectations because of changing market conditions or other outside influences. Other approaches involve "slotting" volatility. For example, a program with a standard deviation between 10-year corporate bonds and equities might be compared to some combination of the two. There are a number of characteristics that an appropriate benchmark should exhibit, including similar risk exposure, liquidity, investibility, and a high correlation with the managed portfolio. In the instance of market neutral programs, indexes or composites with these properties are not available.

As a result of the difficulties involved in the creation of acceptable benchmarks, most market neutral managers are judged on a very subjective basis. The process of arriving at an adequate expected return is usually client specific. Some might feel that an absolute performance standard is appropriate, while others are more comfortable with an incremental increase over some variable interest rate. The ultimate solution will be more clear as market neutral investing becomes more pervasive. In the interim, a common sense approach to benchmark selection appears warranted: applying an incremental return bogey to those programs with a variable interest rate exposure, such as long/short equities, and a static benchmark to the others such as mortgage-backed programs.

FUTURE DEVELOPMENTS

The question of how the genre of market neutral investing will evolve is a difficult one to answer. To do so, it is helpful to have some perspective. The concept of market neutral investing has existed for quite some time (some managers have track records of nearly 20 years), but only recently has the strategy begun to mushroom in popularity. Some of the approaches discussed above have track records measured in months, not years. There remains an institutional bias against some of the underpinnings of these programs, such as short sales. It is evident through their growing acceptance that this approach is gaining adherents very quickly. Long/short equity managers' assets now aggregate over 1 billion dollars, with the bulk of that growth taking place over the last three to five years.

While these programs are becoming more acceptable to the institutional community, retail investors remain left out. It is this area that will likely see the most radical transformation. Regulatory restrictions limit the accessibility of most esoteric strategies. Mutual funds are generally limited in the types and amounts of such techniques they may use as short sales and leverage, as well as the options and other derivative instruments they may employ. There remains a fundamental lack of understanding on the part of most regulatory bodies of the intents and implications of most hedging techniques. For example, it is acceptable for a mutual fund to hedge a long portfolio using index futures or options. It is not permitted to sell short a portfolio of stocks against such a portfolio without significant collateral restrictions. Until these differentials are resolved, it appears that the public, and by extension, market neutral strategies will not benefit from each other to any great degree. It is probable, though, that this regulatory ignorance will dissipate and that new retail oriented structures will make these attractive alternative investments available to a broader spectrum of investors.

An area that does appear to have great near-term potential to surmount some of the major barriers to acceptance for these strategies is securitization. It is interesting that one of the trends so important to the development of many of these programs would also be so helpful in their distribution. By decomposing the returns of many market neutral strategies into different strata, investors might be able to pick and choose from a varied menu of different reward profiles. "Tranches" ranging from enhanced Treasury bills to those employing a high degree of leverage are possible. The natural issuers of these securities are highly rated financial institutions that have the necessary expertise to understand the risks that accompany market neutral programs and the financial strength to attract safety conscious investors. This method of leveraging off a debt rating is not widely accepted or understood, but will likely become more pervasive as more potential issuers become comfortable with market neutral opportunities.

The packaging of these programs into securities also facilitates the use of market neutral strategies by institutions that may be restricted because of internal policies that prohibit some of the underlying instruments these programs use (in many cases, the restrictive guidelines are and were targeted at speculative investments, and were not intended to address the hedging opportunities). This parallels the use of similar instruments to provide some investors with exposure to markets and other structures that may not be explicitly allowed. A restriction on buying Spanish stocks, the purpose of which was to protect against loss of principal, might not apply to a note worth par at maturity whose return was tied to the return on the Spanish stock market. One is deemed an equity investment, while the other is considered a fixed-income investment. This type of arbitrary distinction has fostered the rapid pace of financial engineering which in turn has provided such attractive opportunities for market neutral managers.

National differences and market restrictions have retarded the growth of some market neutral strategies overseas. Poorly developed security lending systems and unusual settlement procedures have made implementing those programs involving short sales difficult or impossible in many international markets. As mentioned earlier, the increased homogenization of the world's securities markets, accounting rules, and tax structures will benefit market neutral strategies because new securities will become available. The drawback to this is that greater efficiency will lessen the opportunities presented.

Finally, technology will continue to play a more and more important role in the development of market neutral strategies. Neural networks, genetic algorithms, fuzzy logic, and "chaos" theory are all being employed with various degrees of success in order to allow managers to find the increasingly difficult relationships that make many of the valuation-based programs possible. The theoretical advances in hardware and software, as well as the infusion of quantitative-based talent from other disciplines, such as physics and engineering, provide the fodder for increased competition among managers and less performance dispersion. Recent statistical studies that incorporate theories that are based on the physical sciences (especially nonlinear structures) have added new and valuable insights into the nature of securities returns. Information will become an even more valuable commodity as volume increases and communication enhancements combine to make markets more efficient.

Market neutral investing has gained respectability and many converts. The advantages that accompany its inclusion into an investment are many and significant. New forms and structures will be engendered by the product wizards at security firms around the world. While it is unlikely to become as accepted an asset class as equities or bonds, market neutral investing is the leading edge of the blurring of the distinctions among various asset classes, and its continued acceptance will only enhance its importance for investors.

CHAPTER 15

Through the Looking Glass: Cash, the "Other Side" of Derivatives

Jacob Navon
Senior Vice President
The Boston Company Asset Management Inc.

INTRODUCTION

The cash markets play an important role in derivatives. Short-term rates, for example, feature in the valuation of options, forwards, and futures contracts. Many swaps transactions, moreover, are executed with LIBOR as one side of the agreement between the counterparties. LIBOR stands for the London Interbank Offered Rate. It is the rate that banks charge each other for deposits in the largely unregulated Eurodollar market. It represents, therefore, the "purest" money market rate benchmark. Finally, many derivative applications require the investor to manage a portfolio of cash as part of the overall strategy.

This chapter will explore all of these factors in turn. It will briefly exemplify some valuation methodologies. These will illustrate the critical role short-term rates assume in pricing derivatives. The chapter will then explore various simple swaps transactions to demonstrate the same. It will examine more complex swaps. It will show how these, in turn, can be broken down into constituent simple swaps executed against LIBOR. The chapter will then describe a number of derivative investment applications.

Derivatives allow practitioners to achieve a given investment objective utilizing several alternative strategies. A perfectly efficient world would require an investor to be indifferent to the strategy used. The investment return would be identical. The real world, however, presents different investors with differing accounting treatments, taxes, laws, regulations, and borrowing costs. These differentiate between the possible investment approaches for a given player.

The optimal investment solution should utilize the lowest actual cost application. This often requires using derivatives as part of the strategy. Investors, consequently, need to invest a cash portfolio in conjunction with the derivative positions. This chapter will explore a variety of enhanced cash management techniques that lead to higher returns on cash. The higher returns achieved help lower the cost of the overall strategy. The chapter will finish our description of the role of cash in derivatives by giving specific examples showing how these strategic alternatives are being used today by sophisticated investors.

This chapter is meant to be a practical "user's guide." It will not provide a rigorous academic treatment of theory. That can be found elsewhere in this book. Also, it is written from an investor's perspective. As such, we deal with "assets": whether on balance sheet (corporate cash, for example) or off balance sheet (pension plan applications). All the concepts developed here can be applied by the treasury function of a corporation seeking to optimize the liability side of the balance sheet.

THE ROLE OF SHORT-TERM RATES IN VALUING DERIVATIVES

In order to understand the critical role that the cash markets play in derivatives, we need only exemplify how some common derivatives are valued. As we shall see, almost every derivative instrument incorporates a short-term interest rate as part of the methodology by which its price is determined. Valuation theorists have traditionally minimized the role of this rate to be some "risk-free" rate available to all market participants. This proved to be a useful simplification. In the "real" world, however, short-term rates are not identical for all players at all times. We will demonstrate later that this reality leads to some practical considerations that elevate one's understanding of short-term rates specifically, and the cash markets in general, to a central role in understanding, evaluating, and using derivative-based investment strategies.

Forward Agreements

A forward agreement represents one of the simplest derivative instruments in use today. Currency forwards are the most commonly used derivatives, if usage is measured by the total aggregated market value of outstanding positions at any given time. A currency forward merely represents an agreement struck today, between two consenting counterparties, to exchange a set quantity of one currency for a given amount of another at some predetermined future date. There is no standardized contract for this transaction. Nor does a formal marketplace (such as the New York Stock Exchange for U.S. equities) exist where these transactions occur. Rather, participants transact "over-the-counter" directly with one another. To facilitate transactions, several market information services, such as Reuters and Telerate, provide computerized screens where traders can advertise their quotes more widely. To a limited extent, some trading can occur directly on these screens. How should one determine at what price to conduct a particular transaction?

Suppose we needed to obtain $10 million U.S. worth of deutsche marks (DM) in 90 days. How many DM should we be content to receive? We really have three alternative strategies by which to obtain DM in the future. We could purchase them forward, using the aforementioned currency forward agreement; we could purchase DM at today's spot price and invest the DM position for 90 days; or we could invest the dollars for 90 days and only then convert them into DM at the then prevailing spot exchange rate.

Suppose today's spot exchange rate for these two currencies is 1.600 DM per dollar. Suppose further that short-term DM interest rates are at 8 percent and short term U.S. interest rates are at 3 percent. If we converted the dollars today, we would have 16,000,000 DM today. Investing for 90 days at 8 percent would yield us 16,320,000 DM in the future. (16,000,000 * (1+0.08 * 90/360)). Conversely, if we invested the dollars for 90 days at 3 percent, we would have $10,075,000 to convert into DM at the then prevailing exchange rate. Absent any prescient knowledge of the future level of foreign exchange rates, we would be indifferent to the two strategies if the future exchange rate were to be 16,320,000/10,075,000, or 1.6199 DM per dollar. One strategy yields 16,320,000 DM in 90 days. The other results in $10,075,000. Exchanging these future dollars into DM at a rate of 1.6199 would also result in 16,320,000 DM. This rate, then, should be the forward rate that we would be willing to set today, in order to exchange dollars for DM in the future. In fact, any player that could borrow and lend in both currencies would be able to lock in risk-free profits if the forward rate was struck at any other price. This arbitrage possibility ensures that currency forwards transact at prices determined purely by the *difference* in *short-term rates* prevailing in the two currencies. The arbitrage condition that determines currency forwards prices is called *interest rate parity*. Later in this section we will generalize the concept to gain deeper insight into more-complex derivative-based strategies. We turn next to futures contracts.

Futures Contracts

Futures contracts resemble forwards. Yet they differ in a number of key respects. Like forwards, they represent an agreement between counterparties to exchange goods at some future date but at a predetermined price struck today. Unlike forwards, they are transacted on the "floor" of a formal exchange market (such as the Chicago Board of Trade). More importantly, futures contracts represent highly standardized contracts that trade to an intricate set of rules and specifications that govern all aspects of the transaction, including: times when the contract can trade, maximum and minimum price changes that can occur, date of expiration, mode of delivery, what constitutes acceptable delivery, where delivery can take place, etc. These standardized rules contrast with the more "free form" nature of forwards agreements, where all these matters are subject to negotiation at the time of transaction. Yet we value futures contracts in a very similar fashion to forwards.

The price of a deutsche mark futures contract, for example, might be expected to be identical to the currency forward struck to the same date as expiration of the contract. In practice it is. In theory, prices should differ very slightly due to margin requirements on futures. These effects are negligible, however. Other futures must incorporate additional physical considerations such as storage costs. We can illustrate using gold futures.

Let us suppose that gold is trading at $375 per ounce in the spot market today. Let us further suppose that we wish to "go long" gold futures 60 days before expiration of the contract. This would obligate us to accept delivery of 100 troy ounces of gold per contract at expiration unless we closed the position some time before expiration.

If short-term rates in the U.S. are still at 3 percent, what is the appropriate futures price? Let us consider an alternative strategy we might deploy.

Instead of transacting gold futures, we might borrow money instead. We could then buy gold today at $375 per ounce, transport, insure, and store it for the next 60 days. We would be indifferent between the two strategies if gold futures traded at a price that would compensate us for the additional expenses of storing the gold, insuring it, transporting it, and financing the loan. If storage, delivery, and insurance amount to $5 dollars, the acceptable futures price would be $(375 * (1 + 0.03 * 60/360) + 5)$. That is, the amount borrowed, plus financing cost, plus $5. The correct price is $381.875 in total. If the futures price were different, then risk-free arbitrage would again be possible. The cost of insurance, transportation, and storage does not change very much with time. Gold futures prices, therefore, critically depend on today's spot price and the prevailing short-term interest rates.

What if we knew that a major new gold discovery had been made but the new mine would not begin to extract gold for a couple of months? Would the gold futures price not be depressed relative to today's spot price by the anticipated additional supply? No. Today's spot prices would be depressed too, exactly by the possibility of arbitrage. In this manner we can distinguish between two types of futures contracts. Cash-and-carry contracts versus price discovery markets. Gold futures and currency futures exemplify pure cash-and-carry markets, where information about future supply and demand is irrelevant to determining the appropriate futures price. And where, by the above examples, prevailing short-term interest rates critically determine the futures price. Supply/demand information in cash-and-carry markets does figure critically to determine today's spot prices, however. Price discovery contracts exist only where the commodity to be delivered against the contract does not exist today, or is sufficiently perishable that it could not survive the alternative strategy of buying it, storing it, insuring it, and delivering it against the contract. Winter wheat represents a good example of such a pure price discovery futures contract. Clearly we could not buy winter wheat in the summer in order to deliver it against the contract. Consequently, short-term interest rates do not feature in the contract's valuation. Only information about the likely future supply/demand situation is incorporated into pricing. As a corollary statement, pure price discovery markets can exist only for future goods and services that *have no spot price today.*

Additional complexities, moreover, arise from the various rules associated with the delivery mechanism of any particular contract. We will illustrate this point using bond futures. These differ from currencies in that more than one item can be delivered against the contract at its expiration. There is a range of securities that constitute permissible delivery. Once again, intricate rules govern the delivery mechanism to ensure that delivery of any particular bond "equates" to delivery of any other. In practice, however, there is always one particular security that will be "cheapest-to-deliver" (CTD) against the contract. Not surprisingly, the contract price usually tracks the price of the ctd bond quite closely. As interest rates rise or fall, the bond that is cheapest to deliver can change. When the ctd bond changes, one finds that the futures prices begin to track the new ctd bond. The party that is short the contract possesses an interesting option.

Trading in the bond contract ceases sometime before actual delivery takes place. The party that is short the contract, and that has to make delivery, can wait and decide which bond to purchase and deliver until after they know precisely how many bonds they need and what price they will receive for each bond that is in the deliverable set. This delivery option can be quite valuable. A precise derivation of the value of this option is beyond the scope of this chapter. Suffice it to say that it, too, depends on prevailing short-term interest rates. Suffice it further to say, that the bond futures contract price can be decomposed into two components: The first component comprises a cash-and-carry determination. Before expiration we determine which is the ctd bond and evaluate how much it would cost to purchase now on borrowed money and hold till expiration. This component of the bond futures price is analogous to the gold and currency contracts detailed above. The second component comprises an evaluation of the delivery option. The actual price of the contract is the sum of the two. The delivery option is quite complex to value; we next turn to evaluating some simpler options.

Options

Options differ from futures and forwards in the following key respect: While forwards and futures *obligate* the counterparties to the transaction (to deliver and receive the asset at the predetermined price), options merely convey to the option owner *the right* to receive the asset from the seller (call option) or deliver the asset to the seller (put option) at the predetermined price. The transaction occurs purely at the discretion of the option owner. In other key respects, options resemble forwards and futures. Some options trade over-the-counter to nonstandard specifications. Others trade on exchanges to strictly stylized contracts. Options valuation shares the following traits with futures and forwards: First, the price paid today depends in part on prevailing short-term interest rates. Second, valuation is achieved by considering equivalent strategies, and backing out a price.

Let us consider a simplified and highly artificial example. Let us assume that the stock of ABC Corporation (stock ticker is S) trades at a price of $100 per share today. Let us further suppose that exactly one year from today the price can be either $110 or $90 per share. Suppose we wish to purchase two call options on this stock, each with an exercise price of 100 and expiration date of one year. How would we value the options? Consider that each option at expiration is worth either $10 per share or zero. Each would be worth 10 if the underlying stock were trading at 110. They would be worth zero if S were trading at 90. Let us assume, further, that one-year rates are now 5 percent. Could we find an equivalent strategy that would have an identical payout as the options position?

Remember that we are buying two calls. Our entire position, therefore, will be worth either $20 or nothing at the end of one year. Suppose we could purchase one share of stock today at 100 and finance the purchase by borrowing $85.71. Our out-of-pocket expense for this strategy, therefore, is $14.29 (100 - 85.71). At the end of the year, we would owe 85.71 * 1.05, or $90. Our one share is worth either $110 or $90. One year from now, therefore, we would sell the stock and either have $20 left after we paid off the loan, or nothing. We have created a strategy with an equivalent payout as buying two options on S. What would we be willing to pay for each option today? If we paid any price other than 7.145 (14.29/2) risk-free arbitrage would be possible.

Note that in this example the option price is determined solely by the prevailing short-term interest rate. We borrow that amount of dollars today that would require $90 dollars to be paid in the future. If short-term rates doubled to 10 percent, we would still purchase one share of S, but borrow only $81.82 (81.82 * 1.1 = 90). The price we would be willing to pay for each option would increase to $9.09 ((100 – 81.82)/2).

The above example is highly artificial. Yet the methodology used underlies most option pricing theories. The limiting case, where we let the period shrink from one year to an infinitesimally small trading period; where we let the difference in prices at the end of each period shrink to be infinitesimally small as well; and where we assume a log-normal distribution of future equity prices; yields the most famous options pricing formula: the Black-Scholes model, summarized here:

The Black-Scholes option pricing formula:

$$C = e(-rT) * [S\ \varphi\ (d) - K\ \varphi\ (d - \sigma\sqrt{T})],$$
$$d = (\ln(S/K) + 1/2\ \sigma * \sigma\ T)/\sigma\sqrt{T}$$

where

C	=	Price of call option
S	=	Price of stock
K	=	Strike price of option
φ	=	Normal distribution
r	=	**prevailing short-term interest rate**
T	=	time to expiration of contract
σ	=	standard deviation of the difference between the log of prices

While this formula shows that options prices depend on several other factors, note that it retains the feature that short-term rates affect prices directly. In today's market one can transact some extremely exotic options. Not all lend themselves to a direct valuation using a derived formula. Some options can only be priced using numerical methods and a powerful computer. In these cases too, however, the methodologies used involve modeling short-term rates in order to achieve an adequate valuation.

Summary

This section examined three commonly used derivative instruments and demonstrated that valuation methodologies share the following traits: First, prevailing short-term interest rates, the cash markets, feature critically in valuing derivatives. Second, in all cases we assumed a single common short-term rate. Third, in order to value the derivative, we look for alternative strategies that utilize the underlying asset and borrowing or lending cash at the single short-term rate, and that result in an equivalent position at the investment horizon. By comparing the strategies we can infer the price of the derivative.

In the case of currency forwards we call the condition that equates the alternative positions "interest rate parity." We would like to generalize from this condition and define the term *objective parity*. We will utilize this term in the rest of the chapter to compare alternative strategies that share a common investment objective. Objective parity is the "real world" application of theoretical arbitrage-free conditions. It accommodates practical limitations imposed upon different market participants. Objective parity holds investors indifferent to any set of investment strategies that could be expected to yield an identical investment return. In the real world, however, alternative strategies rarely result in an identical return. Given the above discussion, for example, short-term rates are rarely the same for all investors. Different investors experience differing accounting treatments, laws, taxes, and regulations. Objective parity would require that in order to optimize investment returns, market participants should compare alternative strategies that would be expected to result in identical returns (if these types of friction did not exist) and deploy that particular strategy that either minimizes cost or maximizes return *for them!*

The proliferation of derivatives and synthetic products in the past decade or so has generated a concomitant proliferation of alternative investment strategies that can be designed to achieve common objectives. For example, an investor wishing to be exposed to gold as an asset no longer needs to buy the metal. He or she could invest the cash in short-term instruments and go long gold futures (by the above example). Alternatively, he or she might enter into a "gold index swap" in conjunction with the cash portfolio. The next section of this chapter will examine various swaps transactions. It will demonstrate again the critical role that short-term rates play in these important and vibrant derivatives markets. Additional sections will explore the ramifications of objective parity. As we shall see, one way to optimize investment returns relies on maximizing the returns from a short-term portfolio of cash and near-cash instruments, and projecting that enhanced return on cash onto other, more desirable, asset classes using derivatives.

THE ROLE OF LIBOR IN VALUING SWAPS

Interest Rate Swaps

The derivatives market changed profoundly in the early 1980s, with the advent of swaps agreements. The first swaps introduced were interest rate swaps. An interest rate swap calls for two counterparties to agree to swap cash flows tied to different interest rates at prespecified dates on a prespecified "notional" principal amount for an agreed-upon period of time (tenor). A typical example would require counterparty A to pay a fixed amount, say 7 percent per year on a semiannual schedule for five years, to counterparty B. B would simultaneously agree to pay A the floating rate of U.S.-dollar three-month LIBOR on a quarterly schedule for the same tenor. Suppose these parties agreed to make these payments on a notional amount of $100 million. Suppose further that LIBOR trades at 3 percent.

This swap agreement, therefore, simply obligates A to pay $3.5 million to B every six months for five years. B is obligated to pay A $750 thousand every three months for the same period, as long as LIBOR remains at 3 percent. B's payment will vary with LIBOR. Why would either agree to this silly sounding arrangement? In fact, the possible reasons are infinite. But let us suppose that A was convinced that short-term rates were going to rise over the period. While initially A would be disadvantaged to the tune of $4 million a year, she might end up receiving far more than she is paying, as rates increased. We do not have to predict a future change in interest rates, however, in order to understand the motivation for counterparties to agree to enter into such a swap.

Let us assume that A is a bank treasurer. A's bank naturally raises funds in the short-term deposit markets. Let us suppose further that the assets of A's bank constitute fixed-rate loans to small businesses. This bank is exposed to rising short-term rates. An interest rate swap might prove to be a beneficial hedging tool. As rates rise, A will receive a higher amount from the swap, to offset the increase in cost of funds. As rates fall, her cost of funds will fall in tandem with the lower amount received from B. Conversely, the fixed-rate business loans offset the fixed amount A guarantees to pay B. The swap does hedge A's exposure all around (see Exhibit 1). What should be the correct specifications for such a swap agreement? That is, what is the correct fixed rate that the counterparties should agree upon in exchange for the variable LIBOR rate?

Exhibit 1.   Simple Interest Rate Swap

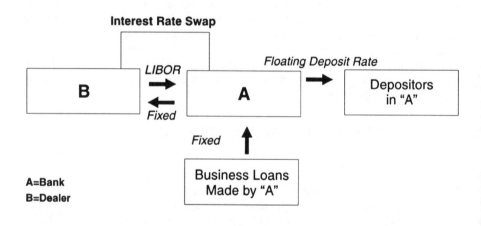

Let us suppose, further, that B represents a broker/dealer firm seeking to increase the flow of business from A. How would B price this hedging request? Remember that dealers are not necessarily in the business of taking a rate view in order to make money. Must B have the opinion that short-term rates will decline before he would accept the transaction? No. B could seek instead to hedge his exposure to A in other ways. There are vibrant futures and forwards markets for LIBOR. These markets price in the exact same manner explained in the preceding section. B could, consequently, short futures or forward contracts on LIBOR for the next five years to lock in the amount he would owe A at each quarterly payment period. Even though B has committed to pay an unknown quarterly amount to A, he could actually fix his payment stream using futures. The correct price for the swap, therefore, would be B's fixed payment plus some commission cost to make it worth his while.

In reality, swaps dealers usually seek to hedge themselves by entering into a mirror-image swap with another counterparty. While A in our example is a natural fixed-rate payer/floating receiver, other businesses have the opposite profile. For example let us suppose C is a corporate treasurer who has just funded the company by issuing cheap floating-rate paper. He might welcome entering into a mirror swap to receive floating/pay fixed, in order to lock in the company's funding cost. Absent B's ability to hedge himself in the forwards market, however, it would be very difficult to determine the correct terms of a simple interest rate swap transaction. In our example it would be proper to assume that the hedging calculation B would make allows him to conclude that 7 percent is the appropriate fixed rate against LIBOR. In order to highlight the valuation methodology, and the importance LIBOR and the forwards/futures markets for LIBOR play in determining terms, we have ignored other operational details of swaps, such as counterparty credit risk. These issues are detailed elsewhere in this book.

Compound Swaps

One is not limited to transacting interest swaps against LIBOR. We could, for example, enter into swaps agreements whereby we pay a fixed rate but receive a floating rate based on the then current two-year treasury rate. Or we could enter into a swap whereby we paid a floating rate based on the interest rate of the then current ten-year treasury and received a floating rate based on the prime rate, which banks charge for making loans to their best customers.

In all these cases we would use one of two valuation methodologies. We could seek appropriate forwards markets for the floating "leg" of the swap in order to hedge the unknown future cost in advance. This method was described above. Remember that the forwards prices themselves are determined by knowing short-term interest rates. Alternatively, we could break a complicated swap into simpler components against LIBOR. Consider, for example, a swap of fixed payments versus receipt of the constant maturity two-year government rate. This compound swap could be broken into two constituent parts: The first swap is a fixed for LIBOR swap, where we pay a fixed rate and receive LIBOR. The second swap is a LIBOR for the constant maturity two-year swap, where we pay LIBOR and receive the constant maturity two-year (see Exhibit 2).

The LIBOR payments cancel out and we are left with the desired compound swap. We would value each simple swap using the exact same methodology highlighted above. In all of these cases, LIBOR in particular, and short-term rates in general, are inherent in valuing swaps transactions.

Index Swaps

The swaps market began with the simple interest rate swaps depicted above, and the variations on the theme have since proliferated geometrically. Every young schoolboy in the U.S, and many a schoolgirl for that matter, is introduced to the joys of baseball card collecting. Other countries have their equivalents. Collections are enhanced by trading cards for which one has multiples, for other cards that one does not yet possess. In similar fashion, one can today find counterparties willing to swap almost any set of

Exhibit 2.   Compound Swap as the Sum of Two Simple Swaps

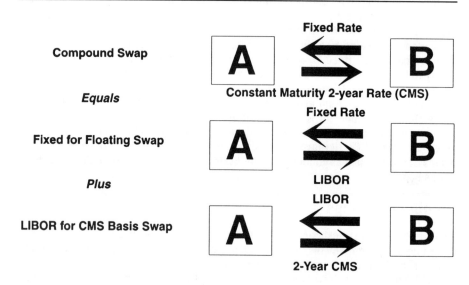

cash flows for almost any other set of cash flows. The counterparty either has a natural offsetting business exposure that makes him willing to enter into the swap, or he can find hedging vehicles by which to hedge his exposure to the swap. Each condition alone suffices.

Consider, for example, the case of a money management firm that specializes in managing portfolios that are indexed to the domestic U.S. equity market. Assume their typical benchmark is the S&P 500 Index. The manager would buy a portfolio of stocks comprising the S&P 500 stocks in the appropriate proportions, in order to achieve an index return. Suppose that one of their clients now wishes to invest in the French equity market and receive a return indexed to the CAC 40 French equity index. Suppose further that rather than lose the business to a competitor overseas, our money manager wishes to oblige the client.

Clearly, the manager could seek to purchase the CAC 40 stocks directly. This manager would build a portfolio constructed in a manner identical to a domestic S&P 500 indexed portfolio. This alternative presents complications, however. The French market trades at times when U.S. managers are typically asleep. There may be additional transaction costs involved. Examples of these include higher commissions, higher custodial fees, withholding taxes on dividends, and foreign exchange transaction costs. Could our money manager find an alternative strategy?

The manager could enter into an index swap, paying LIBOR and receiving the CAC 40 return plus/minus a spread. The manager could now convert a portion of the client's portfolio into U.S. dollar cash that generated a money market return. This return would presumably correlate very closely to LIBOR. In reality a portfolio of money market investments will most likely slightly underperform LIBOR over time. The reason why will be explored a little later. In exchange for the LIBOR payment, the manager would receive the CAC 40 index plus/minus the spread. In today's markets, when we net out all the payments, the manager would likely generate a return that is slightly less than the CAC 40. Should the manager execute this swap? Or should the manager investigate purchasing the stocks directly? Our concept of objective parity would obligate the manager to investigate both strategies and execute whichever is cheaper in the long run. Does the swap transaction that generates a return highly correlated to the CAC 40, but slightly less, outweigh buying the stocks directly but paying additional transaction costs?

This example might seem a little contrived, and yet we know of an actual transaction where a well-known index manager entered into a swap whereby he received the CAC 40 and paid the return of one U.S. stock. He contracted to pay the return on General Motors. Essentially, this transaction was a compound index swap. In one swap he received LIBOR and paid the return on GM. In another he paid LIBOR and received the CAC 40. From the manager's point of view, the transaction was highly logical. He generated the CAC 40 return perfectly, with no tracking error, by purchasing one stock—GM. Why would the counterparty, a well-known bank, agree to the transaction? Did they necessarily believe that the return on GM that they received was going to be higher over time than the return on the CAC 40 that they were paying? No. While we do not know their exact motivation for the trade, we could speculate, using objective parity. Consider how the bank might hedge their exposure. They could short GM and use the proceeds to buy a portfolio consisting of the CAC 40. They would need to borrow the GM stock against the short. Yet they could also lend the portfolio of CAC 40 stocks they own in the international securities lending markets. (A detailed explanation of securities lending transactions is beyond the scope of this chapter.)

Suffice it to say that to borrow GM stock, the bank has to post cash collateral, for which they would receive a money market return. To lend the CAC 40, this bank would receive cash collateral on which they would owe interest. The bank's profits would rely on how much they earned on the cash posted against the GM stock, less the interest paid on the cash received against the CAC 40. Note how the profits generated rely on cash market expertise, not on savvy equity investing. Regardless of the *actual* hedging strategy they used, we should infer they made money doing this transaction. We can infer how much money they *could* make by knowing the intricacies of securities lending, which is essentially a cash market activity.

Summary

In this section we have examined the swaps markets and some variations. As with futures, forwards, and options, valuation techniques in the swaps markets rely on an intimate knowledge of the cash markets in general and LIBOR in particular. This central thesis of the chapter has by now become repetitive. The last example of the CAC 40 for GM swap, however, serves to highlight the corollary part of our argument. Short-term rates are not the same for every player at all times! Different investment strategies that share a common investment objective will yield different returns for different players. Some investors benefit the most by buying the CAC 40 directly—the bank, for example. Others, such as the index manager, might more efficiently transact the CAC 40 for GM swap detailed above. Yet others might find they can extract the most value from a portfolio of cash and near-cash instruments to generate a return that dominates LIBOR. They could then swap LIBOR for the CAC 40 plus/minus a spread. Depending on how much they consistently beat LIBOR by, such investors might generate a superior return to the CAC 40 quite consistently. Objective parity requires investors to select that strategy that optimizes their own achievable return. Does this tenet conflict with efficient markets? Not necessarily—at least not with the weak and semi-strong versions of the theory. We will explore this further in the next section.

ENHANCED CASH MANAGEMENT TECHNIQUES

The Efficient Markets Hypothesis (EMH) was originally derived to explain the pricing of individual securities. The Capital Asset Pricing Model (CAPM) extended EMH to show how securities might be combined into portfolios. Objective parity relates to both these concepts. In a perfectly efficient world, EMH, CAPM, and objective parity would all require investors to be perfectly indifferent to which investment strategy they used to achieve a particular investment objective. If one could achieve a higher return from an alternative strategy, one must be assuming a greater risk. EMH and CAPM, however, were developed using some key simplifying assumptions. They assume, for example, that transaction costs are zero; there are no complications arising from differing accounting treatments, laws, and regulations; and borrowing and lending costs are both the same and equal for all market participants. Would that these conditions were so. We know, however, the "real" world to be quite different. To the extent that reality differs from these simplifying assumptions, there is a range of prices per security that might be considered "efficient." And different investment strategies that share a common objective would result in a range of "efficient" returns. These ranges are bounded by the economic impact of the variations of reality from the "efficiency" assumptions. That is why objective parity, under our definition, simply requires investors to choose that strategy that achieves a given investment objective most "efficiently" for them, from the set of all possible investment strategies that share that particular investment goal. The preceding section showed how one might use a "cash" portfolio to generate a LIBOR-type return and swap this return into another more desired market, the CAC 40 index of French equities, for instance.

Can we demonstrate techniques that allow us to generate returns from a cash portfolio that would be expected to dominate LIBOR over time? Are these superior returns derived merely from assuming more risk? If we could demonstrate that the answers to these questions are yes and no respectively, then we will have shown a very practical use for the derivatives and synthetic products highlighted elsewhere in this book. We will also have completed the thesis of this chapter, that knowledge of cash markets is key not only to valuing derivatives properly, but also to using them practically. The rest of this section discusses two of the many cash enhancement techniques that we have used at The Boston Company Asset Management, Inc. We will also attempt to prove that these techniques do not necessarily increase the risk profile of our clients' portfolios.

Maturity Extensions

The previous section on swaps showed that most such transactions are priced against LIBOR. We showed further that other swaps can always be broken into constituent simple swaps transacted against three-month LIBOR. Investing cash to generate three-month LIBOR can consequently form a key component of a derivatives based investment strategy. LIBOR turns out to be a highly elusive target practically, however. The reason is simple. LIBOR is the rate at which banks lend to each other in the London Interbank market. Presumably, these institutions can finance themselves at a lower rate, such as the rate on three-month time deposits. Time deposits, however, are illiquid investments. The rates on negotiable certificates of deposit (CDs) are lower still, to compensate for their additional liquidity. And the rates on bank CDs correlate very closely to the rates achievable by purchasing other negotiable money market investments, such as commercial paper, bankers acceptances, etc., assuming we are comparing issuing entities with very similar credit quality. Indeed, the money market is perhaps the most "efficiently" priced market of all. A portfolio created entirely with money market investments, therefore, will always slightly underperform three-month LIBOR. To provide a return that is consistently superior to LIBOR, we need to understand the unique constraints imposed on money market portfolio managers.

The money market is dominated by fund managers that operate under very strict rules. The three main types of manager that price money market instruments at the margin are: money market mutual funds (MMFs), bank operated short-term investment funds (STIFs), and corporate and municipal operating funds (OFs). The Securities and Exchange Commission (SEC) rule 2a-7 restricts MMFs to investing in securities that mature at a maximum of 13 months. It further constrains these funds to an average maturity no longer than 90 days. In similar fashion the Office of the Comptroller of the Currency (OCC) issues guidelines that essentially constrain STIF managers to a maximum maturity of one year and an average maturity of 90 days or less. OF managers frequently operate under investment guidelines that are set by their investment committees and that mimic the above rules. The money market demand for securities, therefore, abruptly stops at approximately the one-year maturity area.

The bond market demand for securities does not really begin until the two-year maturity. This maturity barrier does not exist because of regulations. Rather, a more practical consideration creates it. Bond investors typically are not limited to any particular investment maturity, except for specific client restrictions or prospectus requirements. These generally restrict longer maturities, not shorter ones. Bond market participants, however, are constrained by the mere passage of time. They invest specific portfolios to maintain particular duration, and/or average maturity targets. As these bond portfolios age, the managers must constantly conduct extension trades, just to keep the portfolios on target. The most efficient extensions require such managers to sell securities with one to two years left to maturity and purchase ones further out on the maturity spectrum. Bond managers are consequently natural sellers of securities with maturities just longer than one year.

Yet, as explained before, money market managers cannot purchase them. Add to this "secondary" market supply of one- to two-year securities, the natural "primary" supply by corporate issuers as they seek to balance out their liabilities, and you can appreciate that the relative supply/demand balance for short bonds and notes changes drastically with maturity. Demand for these securities drops off as maturities extend beyond one year. It does not really pick up again until maturities extend beyond two years. The supply of these securities varies inversely with demand. Surely such supply/demand variations would affect pricing. Securities with maturities between one and two years should be priced attractively and could, therefore, create return enhancement opportunities. Can we find any empirical evidence for these observations? To examine the potential return enhancements available purely from duration extension, let us neutralize all other possible sources of return, such as credit risk. Exhibit 3 plots the ten-year annualized rates of return for three all treasury indices. U.S. treasury securities are commonly accepted to represent the risk-free investment vehicle for each maturity. We show the returns of the Merrill Lynch 91-day Treasury Bill Index compared to the returns for the Merrill Lynch one- to three-year Treasury Index and the Merrill Lynch Intermediate Treasury Note Index. We plot these returns against the duration of each index. Duration is a commonly used bond market risk measure.

Exhibit 3.   10-Year Rates of Return Various Treasury Indexes (by duration) 7/21/83–7/31/93

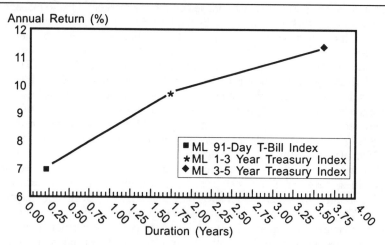

The period chosen, July 31, 1983, to July 31, 1993, represents a period of tremendous interest rate volatility. During certain subperiods, interest rates rose; during others, they fell. During yet others, they were quite stable. The term structure of rates also exhibited large shifts. At times the "yield curve" was positively sloped; at others, it inverted. It subsequently reverted back to a more usual positive shape. This decade, consequently, represents a period of several market cycles and subcycles. As can be seen, adding duration risk generally increased the long-term returns available. This can be expected from CAPM. But contrary to expectations, reward did not increase smoothly with risk. More of the return enhancement was obtained between the extension from below one year to between one and two. This return pattern appears to confirm our observation above. We find additional empirical evidence when we extend beyond Treasury securities.

Corporate obligations typically yield more than Treasuries of comparable maturity. This yield spread increases as a function of maturity, regardless of the underlying term structure of interest rates. We naturally would expect this condition, because the yield spread offered by corporate notes and bonds exists to compensate the holder for the additional credit risk associated with them. Credit risk itself is higher for longer securities. The question becomes, does the market compensate for credit risk as a smoothly increasing function with maturity? Contrary to expectations, again, we find an anomaly between one- and two-year maturities. Exhibit 4 shows the risk-adjusted spread to Treasuries of short corporate notes, plotted against maturity. We see that the maximum spread, on a risk-adjusted basis, occurs between one- and two-year maturities. These observations suggest that a strategy of purchasing short corporate notes with maturities longer than one year but shorter than two would consistently produce returns that dominate LIBOR. This has been our experience. One does not need to retain the additional duration risk inherent in this strategy either. We use a simple strategy called "asset-based swaps" to demonstrate.

Exhibit 4.   Risk Adjusted Spread to Treasuries of Short Corporate Notes

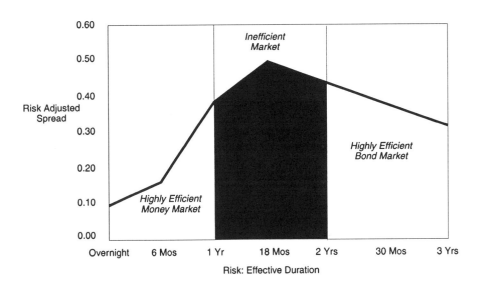

Managers can buy a fixed-rate note and simultaneously enter into a fixed for floating swap whereby they pay a fixed rate and receives a floating rate tied to LIBOR. Effectively, the manager has synthetically created a floating rate note (FRN). Corporate issuers, conversely, can issue FRNs directly. Many FRNs are permissible investments for MMFs and STIFs. Synthetic FRNs, however, are not. Can we find evidence, therefore, that synthetic FRNs yield more than regular FRNs? One recently could have purchased a permissible FRN issued by the Ford Motor Credit Company at a rate that reset quarterly at LIBOR plus 0.375 percent. Conversely, we could have created a synthetic FRN, using the same issuer, to result in a rate of LIBOR plus 0.75 percent. Twice the spread was obtainable by purchasing the note associated with less demand. And these two instruments exhibited exactly the same duration risk as three-month LIBOR itself.

To summarize, we could establish exposure to a given asset by holding a portfolio of cash invested in such FRNs and synthetic FRNs, and swap the LIBOR component into the index return via an index swap. Let us assume this particular index swap is priced at LIBOR flat. That means that every quarter we pay the counterparty the three-month LIBOR rate, and receive the index return for that quarter. To the extent that the FRNs and synthetic FRNs generate LIBOR plus 0.375 to 0.75 percent, we would be netted out the index return plus that spread. Did we add more risk? Not duration risk; the FRN portfolio has an equivalent duration to the LIBOR side of the swap. Nor credit risk; in both cases we had the same issuer. We might be considered to have added liquidity risk, however. The synthetic FRNs are less liquid than typical money market cash investments. But suppose our investment horizon was two years. If we purchased two-year notes to "fund" the swap, did we really add liquidity risk? No! The ability to project enhanced LIBOR investment returns onto other asset classes can have some profound implications on investment behavior.

Equity portfolio managers in the U.S. domestic pension arena have long been measured against the Standard and Poor's (S&P) 500 Index. Theory being that a manager must beat this "passive" index over time to demonstrate superior "active" management talents. But we have just shown that the S&P 500 index could be beaten by a portfolio of "near-cash" instruments, FRNs and synthetic FRNs, that is then swapped via an index swap. One of our clients has recently informed their equity managers that their relative return expectations have been increased by this possibility. The plan sponsor argued that since they themselves could "passively" generate returns superior to the S&P 500 index utilizing this strategy, their "active" equity managers had better demonstrate even higher returns over time or risk termination! This is the clearest example of objective parity, applied in a real situation, that we have seen to date. Note that the synthetic FRNs used, combine a fixed-rate note with an interest rate swap. This represents a fairly simple combination of a traditional security with derivatives, in order to produce superior cash returns. We next turn to a more complex example of how derivatives can be combined with traditional investments, in order to enhance returns.

Inverse Variable Rate Notes

This chapter was written at a time when an interesting investment opportunity existed to benefit from fundamental economic forces that could reasonably be expected to cause short-term rates in several European countries to fall. Short-term rates in Europe had been held high by German Bundesbank policies. These policies were a conse-quence of German reunification after the collapse of the Berlin Wall. Other European central banks were limited in their ability to lower their own domestic rates, else they would suffer the consequences of their currencies being thrown into turmoil versus the deutsche mark. The restrictive tight money policies that prevailed all over Europe served to slow their collective economies. This situation was not sustainable. Indeed, several countries had already removed themselves from the European Exchange Rate Mechanism (ERM) that governed currency rates and began lowering their short-term rates to stimulate domestic economic demand. Could we design an investment strategy that would benefit from a continuation of these short-term European rate declines? If so, could we properly apply this strategy to domestic U.S. cash portfolios in order to generate returns that would dominate LIBOR? In the following paragraphs we shall demonstrate the use of so-called Inverse Variable Rate Notes (IVRNs). We shall show that a portfolio of these instruments exposed to several European markets represents a truly diversified approach.

This latter point may sound surprising. Surely, by the above fundamental analysis, the central bank policies were shown to be linked. Currencies were linked via the ERM and via the desire by European governments eventually to establish a common European currency. While these statements were true, the empirical evidence summarized in Table 1 shows that several European short-term rates did move independently of one another. The table shows the variance/covariance matrix of short-term Interbank rates in several countries. Note the *lack of covariance* in short-term rates, even between France and Germany, where economic policies were the most closely linked. This empirical finding, suggested to us that a portfolio of securities, each designed to benefit from lower rates in a different country, would exhibit useful diversification benefits. How could we construct such securities?

Table 1.   Covariance Matrix of European LIBOR (Three-Month) Rates

	France	Germany	Italy	Spain	Sweden	U.K.	U.S.
France							
Germany	0.28						
Italy	0.17	0.24					
Spain	0.18	0.00	0.11				
Sweden	-0.20	0.15	0.00	-0.03			
U.K.	0.03	-0.08	0.16	0.00	-0.08		
U.S.	-0.07	0.04	0.14	-0.22	0.00	0.10	

IVRNs constituted a practical approach to execute our strategy. An IVRN represents a security that is paid for in dollars, generates variable-rate coupons that pay in dollars, and pays principal in dollars at maturity. The coupons vary, however, according to a formula whereby they increase as the foreign rate decreases. IVRNs, consequently, represent a U.S. dollar investment that benefits when foreign rates drop. There is no currency risk involved. A typical IVRN would be purchased at par, mature at par, yet pay coupons that vary according to the formula: 13 percent minus the Stockholm Interbank Offered Rate (STIBOR). This formula would clearly generate higher U.S. pay coupons as Swedish rates dropped. Exhibit 5 demonstrates how such a security might be created. Notice how the issuer nets out to have issued a note at

Exhibit 5.   STIBOR Inverse Variable Rate Note

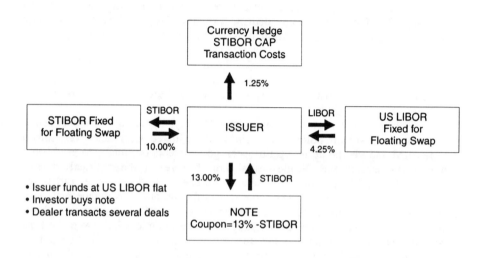

- Issuer funds at US LIBOR flat
- Investor buys note
- Dealer transacts several deals

U.S. LIBOR flat. A very attractive cost of funds for the issuer. The investor purchases the security described, which exposes him or her to falling Swedish rates. The broker/dealer gets to transact several swaps; gets a currency hedge and Swedish interest rate caps; and helps a corporate client fund itself in the process. The Swedish interest rate caps are necessary to ensure that the minimum coupon of this security is zero.

We did in fact create several portfolios of these securities. Our portfolios, further, included securities exposed to other fundamental opportunities as we perceived them. Our average coupon advantage to LIBOR varied anywhere from 0.5 percent to 1.25 percent, depending on the particular client portfolio. To satisfy ourselves that the resultant exposures reasonably could be expected to dominate LIBOR over time, we conducted extensive Monte Carlo simulations. We found that in 90 percent of the outcomes, our portfolios simulated enhanced returns over LIBOR. We believe that these results powerfully demonstrate how derivatives could be used to enhance the returns of cash portfolios. When we analyzed specific simulation scenarios, we found little correlation with the prevalent U.S. LIBOR level. That means that the level of enhancement did not relate to U.S. rates in any meaningful way. This fact is important. We have argued in this section that derivative-based strategies create returns that dominate LIBOR. They represent true alpha generation. A correlation between the alpha and LIBOR would invalidate this conclusion. Our results suggest that the alpha generated is independent of LIBOR. It can be relied upon in all market environments. That alpha can then be projected onto any asset class using index swaps.

CONCLUSION

This chapter presented a relatively simple thesis: Derivatives and synthetic products require an understanding of the cash markets in order to properly evaluate and execute transactions. We highlighted how short-term rates enter into the valuation of forwards, futures, and options. We further showed that short-term rates figure prominently in a variety of swaps agreements. We presented the idea that swaps in particular, and derivatives in general, allow us to create several means by which to achieve a given investment objective. Specifically, a portfolio of cash and near-cash instruments can be created to generate returns that dominate LIBOR. The LIBOR component of these returns can then be swapped, via index swaps, to project the enhanced return onto other asset classes.

This strategy represents a specific example of a more general concept that Myron Scholes has been using in recent presentations. We have heard him coin the "Hub and Spoke" concept of investing. Achieving enhanced returns, "alpha" to use CAPM terminology, can prove quite difficult. Managers with demonstrated ability to generate alpha in any given asset class should stick to their knitting. They can project their alpha using derivatives such as futures, or compound index-for-index swaps.

These concepts have found practical applications. One of our competitors, a well-known bond investment firm, has accepted equity management assignments utilizing exactly such a strategy. They manage a portfolio of short bonds designed to outperform LIBOR. They then project this alpha onto equities by going long S&P 500 futures contracts.

As mentioned in a previous section, one of our clients has changed their investment target, by which they evaluate their active equity managers. No longer do they tolerate such managers when they simply beat the S&P 500 benchmark. These managers now need to demonstrate a consistent ability to achieve returns higher than those generated by a portfolio of FRNs swapped into S&P 500 plus a spread. We have used derivative and synthetic products in order to achieve enhanced cash returns. Several of our clients have demanded returns superior to the yields generated by our own STIF. Derivative products have helped us achieve these clients' objectives. More recently, we have begun to "equitize" our clients' cash balances using index swaps. In one specific case we project our alpha onto international equities using a customized "near EAFE" index swap. EAFE stands for the Morgan Stanley Capital International Europe, Australasia, and the Far East equity index.

We believe that these trends will only continue as the derivatives markets generate new investment opportunities. Investment advisors, pension plan sponsors, and corporate liability managers increasingly will find that only their imagination will constrain their ability to perform their jobs better.

CHAPTER 16

Performance Measurement for Derivatives

Tanya Styblo Beder
President
Capital Market Advisors, Inc.

The derivatives market has reached trillions of dollars outstanding in notional principal amount. Market participants include a broad range of end users from borrowers and investors to hedgers, arbitrageurs, and intermediaries of risk. A common question posed is, "How well is a particular derivatives position performing?" The answer is sought not only by the holder of the position but also by senior management, the board of directors, credit or risk supervisors, regulators, accountants, lawyers, tax advisors, and others.

Portfolio managers have increased the focus on performance measurement due to historically frequent valuation policies and greater use of derivatives for asset allocation, hedging exposure, and improving total return. Dozens of derivatives-based funds have been launched successfully over the past twelve months. Pension plan sponsors as well seek to determine whether the derivative strategies of investment managers are adding value and protecting a plan from shortfalls and funding liabilities with as little money as possible. One drawback to more rapid derivatives growth has been the difficulty in assessing performance measurement. Index tracking and index benchmarking, while widely employed to measure performance in the bond, stock and commodity markets, are not readily available for the derivative markets. For example, in the bond markets the investor may select from a single-market index such as one for U.S. Governments or Gilts, and multimarket indexes are available such as Salomon Brothers' World Government Bond Index. In the stock markets, the investor may select from a single-market index such as the S&P 100, FT-SE 100, or Nikkei, and multimarket indexes are available, such as Morgan Stanley's Europe, Australasia, and the Far East (EAFE) Index. There are benchmark indexes published for GNMAs, gold, real estate, and loan prices. However, derivatives indexes are available only on a limited basis for many exchange-traded derivatives and only on a custom-tailored basis for OTC derivatives.(see Exhibit 1).

Exhibit 1. Measurement Options

	Single Market	Multimarket	Custom
Fixed Income	✔	✔	✔
Equity	✔	✔	✔
Real Estate	✔	✔	✔
Other	✔	✔	✔
Exchange Derivatives	✔	✔	✔
OTC Derivatives			✔

In addition to custom-tailored indexes, several methods are employed widely to measure performance for derivatives. Note that while each method is able to produce an answer as to how a derivative position is performing, the answers may differ significantly. It is crucial that users maintain an awareness that they are marking to "model" rather than "market." This is typically due to the embedded assumptions that are a necessary part of each model. Note that as increasingly complex optionality has been engineered into derivative products, the divergence of answers produced by the various methods has increased. Users are thus encouraged to use multiple models and to stress test results. Several common measurement methods are listed in Exhibit 2.

Exhibit 2. Common Measurements

- Discounted Cash Flow
- Dummy or Normal Portfolio
- Market Line Comparison
- Index or Benchmark (market or custom)
- Mark-to-Market
- Expected or Maximum Exposure
- Simulation
- Option-Adjusted Spread
- Other
- Catastrophic Probability and Other

Prior to employing one of the performance measurement techniques, several questions require answers. For example, what is the time frame for performance measurement? Will performance be measured for the current, single time period or for the remaining life of the derivative position? Will figures be on a cash or accrual basis? If *expected* cash flows are employed, how will they be generated? What is the potential for exposure or value to shift significantly? Can exposure shift enormously between evaluations? Are all factors included for which a small change can result in a large shift in value? Are all factors included that impact value and have a high probability of change?

Differing measurement goals provide additional "start-up" questions. For example, what is the purpose of the derivative application? If it is for hedging, what percentage of correlation will be deemed an *effective* hedge? How will diverse residual risks be compared? If the derivative is being used to transfer risk, how will disparate risks be quantified (for example, the exchange of interest rate risk for credit risk via an interest rate swap?) What will be the source of pricing, both initial and ongoing?

After such questions are analyzed, and all strategies to be measured are defined, one or more methods may be selected to measure performance. The selection of a performance measurement method often resides in the selection of the underlying assumptions and risks with which the user is most comfortable or best able to manage. A brief description of key assumptions for common performance measurements follows.

DISCOUNTED CASH FLOW

Under this model, the cash flows of the derivatives position are discounted to determine a current value. The quality of this model's output is dependent on (1) the certainty of the future cash flows; and (2) the selection of one or more appropriate discount rates. If a derivative's or derivative-linked security's cash flows have a high likelihood of varying from expected cash flows, the quality of this model's output may be poor (typically simulations are preferable in this case). Examples of such securities are mortgage-based securities with caps, or illiquid derivatives that require a terminal value due to the time horizon of the analysis. With respect to discount rate(s), it is often difficult to select the appropriate rate(s). One common practice is the use of a risk-adjusted, zero-based yield curve; however, a particular yield curve may not accurately reflect the range of investment alternatives available to a portfolio manager.

DUMMY OR NORMAL PORTFOLIO

Under this model, a hypothetical portfolio is constructed to which the derivatives-linked portfolio will be compared. The quality of this model is dependent upon the ability to construct an appropriate dummy portfolio and the ability to answer questions such as, "If the derivatives-linked portfolio underperforms the dummy portfolio, is it due to the underperformance of the manager or due to the overperformance of the dummy portfolio?" For derivatives that are difficult to dissect into liquid, cash-market components, the output of this method may be poor. An example might be viewing a ten-year interest rate swap as a series of forwards. For long-dated swaps, there is only a hypothetical cash market price for the implied forwards (for example, the forward rate on three-month LIBOR in nine years). Hence, extrapolation of known markets is required to establish the theoretical price of the dummy portfolio.

MARKET LINE COMPARISON

Under this model, the cash flows of the derivatives position are plotted versus the duration of the portfolio. The quality of this model's output is dependent on (1) the certainty of the future cash flows; and (2) the ability to determine the duration of the portfolio. Potential difficulties in forecasting cash flows and returns were discussed previously. With respect to duration, this can be difficult to determine for specific derivatives. Leveraged inverse floaters provide an example. Consider a floater that resets quarterly at 20 percent minus three times three-month LIBOR, subject to a minimum coupon of zero, with a maturity of two years. When the embedded cap is away from its strike (i.e., the yield on the floater is above zero) its price behavior is similar to that of a coupon-bearing security that matures in 18 years. When the cap is in effect, the duration changes significantly. Hence, for certain types of derivatives, the quality of this model's output may be poor (typically, option-adjusted spread models are employed but have other limitations).

INDEXES OR BENCHMARKS

Published or widely available indexes or benchmarks do not exist for most derivatives. However, custom indexes or benchmarks may be created. Under this approach, a set of derivatives and/or cash instruments are combined to which the derivatives-linked portfolio will be compared. The quality of this approach is dependent on (1) the ability to construct an appropriate index; and (2) the ability to obtain consistent pricing information for derivatives. In addition, the constructed index may not reflect the full range of investment alternatives available to the portfolio manager, making performance relative to the broader market difficult to assess.

MARK-TO-MARKET

Under this model, the market value of the derivatives-linked portfolio is determined dynamically or at stated intervals. The quality of this model's output is dependent on (1) the ability to establish prices; (2) the ability to achieve the mark-to-market prices upon sale or liquidation; and (3) the ability to interpret an ongoing stream of mark-to-market values. Consistent pricing information can be particularly difficult to obtain, especially in the case of options. Frequently, dealers employ different definitions of "in-" "out-of" and "at-the-money" and utilize different volatility models, thereby producing widely disparate prices for the same options. Further complicating the ability to compare derivatives prices are different practices by OTC derivatives dealers with respect to (1) use of bid, mid, and ask pricing; (2) generation of the yield curve and discount rates; (3) type of interpolation; (4) adjustments to price for illiquid or exotic products; and (5) methodology with respect to premiums and discounts.

　　　Mark-to-market is extremely popular as a measurement technique and has been widely adopted by regulators and accountants as well. It should be noted, however, that mark-to-market has limitations as a sole measure for performance or risk: Derivatives portfolios of vastly different size liquidity and risk components can have the same mark-to-market value. This is particularly important to be aware of in the case of derivatives that can change value quickly and significantly, for example, exotic or leveraged options.

EXPECTED OR MAXIMUM EXPOSURE

Typically combined with mark-to-market models, expected or maximum exposure measurement performs the same calculation in scenarios ranging from "most probable" to "worst-case." The quality of such measurement is dependent on the ability to select such scenarios. As experienced during the stock market crashes and the Gulf War, it is difficult to predict an item such as "maximum" volatility. The increasing complexity and optionality of many derivatives has made scenario selection considerably harder. Consider a portfolio of path-dependent options: Dozens of factors impact price and possible outcomes, making the ability to select "expected" or define "maximum" virtually impossible (see Exhibit 3 for an illustration of outcomes for a single path-dependent option).

Exhibit 3. Knock-Out Option
S&P 500

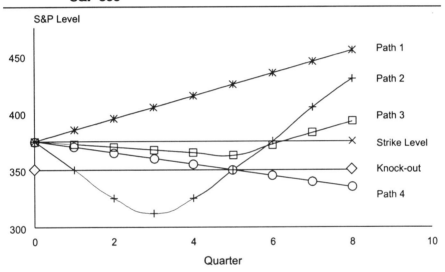

Terms	
Type:	Call Option on S&P 500
Maturity:	2 Years
Strike:	S&P 500 at 375
Knock-out:	S&P 500 at 350
Results	
PATH 1:	Triggered; S&P does not fall below knock-out.
PATH 2:	Not Triggered; S&P falls below knock-out level but matures above strike at maturity.
PATH 3:	Triggered; S&P does not fall below knock-out level and rises above strike at maturity.
PATH 4:	Not Triggered; S&P falls below knock-out level.

SIMULATION

Under this model, the performance of the derivative-linked security is analyzed under numerous hypothetical scenarios. The quality of this model's output is heavily dependent on (1) the selected probability approach (typically Monte Carlo or Binomial); (2) the ability to determine price, cash flows, and other returns under a specific market scenario; and (3) the ability to select appropriate scenarios. If a derivative's or derivative-linked security's cash flows have a high likelihood of varying from expected cash flows, or if catastrophic-type option results are possible, the quality of this model's output may be poor. A useful application of simulation models is to determine how a particular derivatives position or derivatives portfolio performs under stress conditions.

OPTION-ADJUSTED SPREAD MODELS

Option-adjusted spread models correct key limitations of the yield-to-maturity calculation, specifically, indeterminate cash flows are taken into consideration by incorporating the value of embedded options, and the shape of the yield curve is assumed not to be flat. The quality of the output of option-adjusted spread models depends on (1) whether shifts in the yield curve are somewhat parallel; (2) the probability-weight assigned to the embedded option; and (3) consistent default risk of the security. Given that dealers have varying methods for the generation of probability assumptions, interest rate paths, and forward risk-free rates, different option-adjusted spreads are frequently calculated for the same security. Accordingly, option-adjusted spread models are limited as a consistent gauge of relative value.

MEASUREMENT CHALLENGES

As summarized in Exhibit 4, there are numerous measurement challenges, no matter which model is selected. *Fallacy of composition* may occur when a compound derivative is separated into its pieces, with each piece separately priced or hedged: There is no guarantee that the pieces will behave as the combined whole, a lesson learned expensively by certain participants in the interest-only and principal-only mortgage-based securities markets. *Non-optimal data inputs* may result in incorrect model results and, therefore, inferior performance measurement. For example, an index that uses currency prices from Europe's close may be inappropriate as a benchmark for a U.S. fund pricing redemptions at the U.S. market's close. *Faulty portfolio assumptions* may also result in improper measurement. This is particularly true of illiquid derivatives for which the assumption "this behaves like . . ." is made. As learned in the case of commercial real estate and many other loans in bank portfolios, erroneous price assumptions can create significant problems.

Faulty grids may also create measurement problems. Examples are provided by the use of straight-line interpolation between five- and seven-year swap rates to establish six-year swap rates, and extrapolation of ten-year swap spreads to determine the level for longer-dated swaps. *Simulation bands* that are too narrow result in failure

---

Exhibit 4. Measurement Challenges

- Fallacy of composition
- Non-optimal data inputs
- Faulty portfolio assumptions
- Faulty interpolation grids or lack of benchmarks
- Simulation bands too narrow
- Unproven netting assumptions
- Yet-to-be-determined macro considerations

---

to establish proper measurement for many complex derivatives: During the currency crisis in Europe, some foreign exchange market participants discovered that their trading bands for currencies were too narrow and this produced unexpected losses.

Unproven netting assumptions provide one of the largest measurement challenges. Although the Bank for International Settlements has announced that it supports certain forms of netting, and industry groups such as the International Swaps and Derivatives Association support wider forms of netting, the international infrastructure is not in place in the event of a market dislocation or dispute. It has yet to be determined whether a long position in one country will be able to be liquidated at will against a short position in a second country with the blessing of the respective national regulators. Many other macro considerations have yet to be fully established. These are potential wildcards, as certain rulings or capital requirements have the ability to alter current market pricing significantly (see Exhibit 5).

Exhibit 5. Potential Wildcards

- Regulatory status
- Accounting status
- Tax status
- Legal status
- Bankruptcy status
- Cross-market relationships
- Market infrastructure discrepancies
- True market knowledge (e.g., size)

CONCLUSION

After selection of the performance measurement model, interpretations of the output should be made in the context of the required capital and risk. It is vital that comparisons be conducted within a risk-equivalent system: A less risky derivative producing the same return as a riskier derivative should be the preferred position. In addition, a derivative that places less capital at risk while producing the same return should be preferred.

The Group of Thirty recommendations on good risk management practice published in 1993 included several guidelines impacting performance measurement. Users are encouraged to mark positions to market using multiple models, to perform simulations to stress test positions, and to establish independent oversight. Subsequent to the Group of Thirty report, regulations or guidelines were published in the United States by the CFTC,[1] the OCC,[2] the NAIC,[3] and several politicians, notably Congressman Leach. Elsewhere, regulations or guidelines were also published by the Bank for International Settlements, as well as by regulatory authorities in England, Germany, Canada, Australia, and Japan.

Other key performance measurement changes include the introduction of the first volatility ratings by several rating agencies. Reflective of the fact that most losses in the derivatives market to date have been due to market risk rather than credit risk, managers, directors, regulators, accountants, and others are introducing such measures to capture the multi-dimensional aspects of performance measurement for derivatives.

---

1 Commodity Futures Trading Commission.
2 Office of the Comptroller of the Currency.
3 National Association of Insurance Commissioners.

PART THREE

RISK ANALYSIS AND MANAGEMENT

CHAPTER 17

A Credit Grade Risk Migration Utility (CGRMU)

Robert M. Mark
Partner
Coopers & Lybrand

The pricing of financial assets can be much improved if a credit grade risk migration utility (CGRMU) is used. It is a key input in determining the appropriate amount of risk-based capital and loss provision to be charged over the life of a financial asset. The CGRMU provides a new slant to an old problem. CGRMUs can also be used in grid pricing and as a directionally correct approach toward adjusting credit grades as a function of tenor.

For the purposes of this chapter, I assume that all assets have been appropriately credit graded and consequently, the chapter does not cover how to arrive at an obligor (or facility) credit grade.

To price an off-balance-sheet asset (like an FRA or swap) or an on-balance-sheet asset (such as a loan), a prespecified risk-adjusted return on risk-adjusted capital (RARORAC) must be achieved. Credit grade provisions and capital factors are two vital factors in this calculation. First, the basic chain of calculations (Exhibit 1) requires multiplication of a nominal exposure (say, $1,000) by a product weight (like 10 percent) to create a risk-adjusted asset ($100). The risk-adjusted asset is then multiplied by a provision factor (say 0.2 percent) to arrive at the provision ($0.20), and by a capital factor (say 2 percent) to get the capital ($2).

The product weight converts certain exposures into their loan equivalents before applying the provision and capital factors. Clearly, a $100 loan outstanding involves a different quality of risk than a $100 commercial letter of credit, a $100 unused facility, or a $100 swap. The risk-adjusted asset can be thought of as a means to translate all exposures into a common framework.

A second set of inputs requires knowledge of the projected credit grade (CG) migration path over the life of the asset. The CGRMU described below is a stand-

Exhibit 1.   Calculating Capital and Provision

ardized utility to adjust the current provision and capital factors to account for migration, and is used for pricing purposes.

If you could adjust pricing in time to cover credit losses (and other expenses), there would be a substantially reduced need for annual loan loss provisions or a loan loss reserve. The aggregate credit-risk premiums on all portfolio transactions must, over time, equal or exceed losses. This is the same as saying that each year we must set aside enough premiums to cover the average of the yearly expected losses (that is, an average loss over time).

If actual losses rise above the average for a sustained period, then you could easily consume the accumulated reserve. Therefore, a capital cushion sufficient to cover these peak loss periods is needed. These peaks, and the underlying volatility, are the basis behind the term "unexpected loss." How much cushion is required depends on the pattern of the losses—a more volatile loss pattern would require a bigger cushion. The size of the cushion also depends on the desired level of confidence (like 95 percent of the time) for the cushion to be sufficient.

The worse the risk grade, the higher the average losses sustained and, therefore, the bigger the annual loss provision needed to be built into pricing. Similarly, the worse the risk grade, the greater the volatility in loss patterns, and the greater the capital cushion required. That is why, in a pricing model and managerial reporting, lower quality credits should get hit not only by a greater loss provision but also by higher capital charges.

The measurement system should be set up so that the provision (expected loss) and capital (unexpected loss) factors apply only for a one-year time horizon. The amount of annual provision and capital required for a future time period (say, four years) is not the same as the normally published (one-year) numbers. The longer the maturity of the asset, the larger the ratio of the required factor to the one-year published factor. This ratio is greater than one, since there has been a tendency for downward credit-grade migration due to generic declining credit quality for longer-tenor assets and the holder's right to prepayment (which generally will be exercised should credit quality improve).

From a pricing perspective, you will want to recover more than the one-year published factors for any financial asset with a maturity greater than one year. The provision and capital charges are adjusted as the credit quality changes. This pay-as-you-go philosophy captures the appropriate charge over the life of the asset. The CGRMU proposed here adjusts for longer-tenor assets since the price of an asset depends on the projected credit-grade migration path.

A key principle is to separate the upcoming year's charge from the average future charge required for pricing. For example, a four-year swap or loan to a credit-grade 30 (CG30) customer should be priced differently from a one-year swap or loan to that same customer, but the risk-adjusted provision and capital charges over the upcoming year should be precisely the same for both maturities.

In arriving at credit-grade-specific loss provision and capital factors, it is crucial to choose a statistical sample of bonds that are deemed equivalent to internal risk buckets. Publicly listed bonds provide important information because the sufficiently broad, unbiased data on bank loans is unavailable. Internal risk buckets could be structured so that CG10 is assigned for a portfolio of AAA to AA, CG20 for a portfolio of AA to A. CG30 is for a portfolio of A+ to BBB+. CG+40 is for a portfolio of BBB+ to BBB, and so on. These credit grades, which map to overlapping bond ratings, could be further subdivided into 10 finer divisions (for example, CG10 running from CG10 to CG19) for a total of 100 expected losses. For each bucket, the expected loss is based on bond-default rates and assumed loss-given-default rates, while unexpected loss is based on the volatility of bond-credit spreads. The expected and unexpected loss statistics form the basis for the bucket. The bond-credit spread refers to the spread above duration-matched Treasuries that investors require to compensate for credit risk.

Care must be taken to adjust the credit-grade-specific capital factors for an individual asset to account for the portfolio effect within a credit grade. Since the capital factors are typically derived from analyzing a portfolio of assets within a credit grade, you need to adjust the portfolio capital factor to incorporate the specific risk of any individual asset within the credit grade. You must make adjustments to account for the fact that capital for any credit grade mostly reflects systematic risk. For example, if you have a $100 CG30 risk-adjusted asset and ten $10 CG30 risk-adjusted assets, then the unadjusted capital charge would be the same, but the larger number of loans should still obtain the benefit of portfolio diversification. Further, adding the capital for a portfolio of assets across credit grades results in more than is necessary. Adding capital across credit grades assumes a perfect correlation between each credit grade. For example, if you add the capital for a CG30 asset to the capital for a CG40 asset for two companies whose risk is uncorrelated, then the capital charge would be overstated.

Provision and capital factors adjust for the risk of actual loss of principal. But there are additional factors in a spread that need to be considered. For example, nonaccrual charges require revenue to be set aside to cover the cost of carrying nonaccrual assets. Liquidity charges also require revenue to be set aside to cover the costs of maintaining adequate access to funding throughout the life of the asset.

The next step is to determine the probabilities (conditional on the current credit grade) of migrating from one credit grade to another over a one-year period. You would apply the conditional probabilities over the life of the asset to arrive at a set of pricing factors that incorporate the expected average annual provisions and capital charges to be applied a s a function of tenor. There are two types of conditional probabilities: one is a stationary and stochastic Markov process; the other is nonstationary. A matrix multiplication technique is used in both cases to construct a CGRMU. Finally, the pricing factors would be adjusted in direct proportion to the confidence interval bands around the conditional probabilities used to describe the credit grade migration.

The confidence interval for a conditional probability (Q) is proportional to the square root of $Q-Q^2$. The largest confidence interval or poorest predictive quality occurs when Q equals 50 percent. The CGRMU shows both the expected yearly provision and expected capital charge as a function of maturity.

The CGRMU would need to be applied as a function of the type of financial product, special covenants, particular pricing characteristics, and so on. For example, nonamortizing financial assets would use one table, whereas amortizing assets would use another table. An asset that has special pricing adjustments requires a simple extension of the concepts outlined below.

Assume the charges per year for pricing nonamortizing assets are fixed for the entire duration of the contract. For example, as shown in Exhibit 2, pricing in capital for a $1,000 three-year risk-adjusted nonamortizing asset with a credit grade 40 is assumed to utilize $2.82 per year. Pricing in capital for the same asset for four years is assumed to use $2.91 for each of the four years.

Exhibit 2.   Credit Grade Capital Factors

Credit Grade		Tenor (1–10 Years)				
		1	2	3	4	10
10		C10.1	C10.2	–	–	C10.10
20		C20.1	C20.2	–	–	C20.10
30		C30.1	C30.2	–	–	C30.10
40		C40.1	C40.2	3.00	3.19	C40.10
50	Amortizing	C50.1	C50.2	–	–	C50.10
60	Asset	C60.1	C60.2	–	–	C60.10
70	Capital (%)	C70.1	C70.2	–	–	C70.10
80		C80.1	C80.2	–	–	C80.10
90		C90.1	C90.2	–	–	C90.10
100		C100.1	C100.2	–	–	C100.10
10		C10.1	C10.2	–	–	C10.10
20		C20.1	C20.2	–	–	C20.10
30		C30.1	C30.2	–	–	C30.10
40	Non-	C40.1	C40.2	2.82	2.91	C40.10
50	Amortizing	C50.1	C50.2	–	–	C50.10
60	Asset	C60.1	C60.2	–	–	C60.10
70	Capital (%)	C70.1	C70.2	–	–	C70.10
80		C80.1	C80.2	–	–	C80.10
90		C90.1	C90.2	–	–	C90.10
100		C100.1	C100.2	–	–	C100.10

Most credit grading systems only provide a single set of loss provision and capital factors for each credit grade (the shaded column of Exhibit 2). The charges for pricing amortizing assets are different from nonamortizing assets. Pricing in capital for a comparable amortizing asset would be $3.00 for a three-year average life and $3.19 for a four-year average life. Similar tables can be generated for credit grade loss provision factors.

There is general recognition that not all assets or products can be characterized by the same standardized credit-grade system. For example, capital market products are dealt with through computing loan equivalents called fractional exposures (FE). This is necessary since an asset that is marked to market (MTM) has a replacement cost risk less than its nominal amount.

The FE profile for a typical single cash-flow product is shown in Exhibit 3. The worst case (W) loss can be set at, say, the 2 standard deviation level (97.5 percent confidence level). The pricing of the MTM asset requires its expected MTM value (a fraction of the FE) to be forecast over its life and then used as a loan equivalent.

Exhibit 3. Fractional Exposure Profile for Single Cash-Flow Products

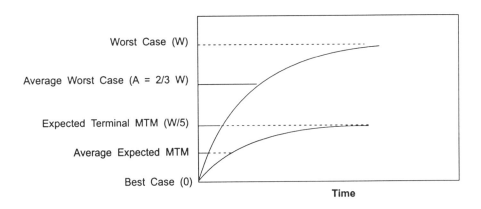

The expected or average worst case (A) for single cash-flow products whose risk grows as a function of the square root of time, can be shown to equal 2/3 × W, the expected terminal MTM equals W/5 (which corresponds to an at-the-money option terminal value), and the average expected MTM equals 2/3 × W/5. Observe that if W equals $3, then the average worst case euals $2. Similarly, the expected terminal MTM would equal $.60 and the average expected MTM would equal $.40. For example, the FE for a $1 million 3 × 6 FRA, where the FE is set at the 2 standard deviation level, has a worst case of $3,300 risk, an average worst loss of $2,200, and an expected terminal MTM of $650.

The provision and capital factors are based on a pay-as-you-go concept. Similar to MTM, the idea is that the factors can be applied to risk-adjusted assets in a portfolio to estimate the required provision and capital cushion needed for the next year. As soon as the risk grade of an asset in the portfolio changes, different provision and capital factors are applied to that asset.

For example, an asset that changes from a grade 30 to a grade 50 over three years would, under a pay-as-you-go system, be charged different annual premiums. Such a method is suited to the valuation of portfolios and the evaluation of business units.

However, the factors used in this system may be adjusted before they are appropriate for determining the risk components to be built into the pricing on a multiyear credit transaction. The adjustment is necessary because the pay-as-you-go factors have a one-year horizon, whereas the pricing on a multiyear credit transaction is likely to remain unchanged for several years. Further, there is a significant probability that any individual credit will, over time, migrate to other risk grades.

The credit grade migration path that a particular transaction will take is unknown. However, we can derive probabilities of the various paths, construct a matrix of those probabilities (Exhibit 4), and then use that matrix to derive factors for future years of a multiyear transaction.

Exhibit 4. Yearly Migration Probability Mix

Probability (%) that a credit starting from risk grade in far left column will be in grades in the columns on the right.

From Risk Grade	To Risk Grade After One Year						Total
	20	30	40	50	60	70	
30	2	**91**	5	2	0	0	100
40	0	3	89	6	2	0	100
50	0	0	4	87	7	2	100

As illustrated in Exhibit 5, this yearly matrix is applied repeatedly to derive the probability of the credit being in different grades during each year of the transaction. For example, there is an 83 percent probability that a CG30 today will stay a CG30 two years from today (the third year). Once we know the probabilities of a credit being in a given risk bucket or grade during a particular year of a multiyear transaction, we can derive a blended factor for that year by weighting the pay-as-you-go factor by the corresponding probability for each grade, and taking the sum. As illustrated in Exhibit 5, assume that in the second year there is a 2 percent chance of being a CG20, a 91 percent chance of being a CG30, a 5 percent chance of being a CG40, and a 2 percent chance of being a CG50. If we apply the respective pay-as-you-go credit grade provision factors (say W percent, X percent, Y percent, and Z percent—along the lines of Exhibit 2), then the weighted factors of W × 2 percent plus X × 91 percent plus Y × 5 percent plus Z × 2 percent provide a blended provision factor for the second year of K percent.

Exhibit 5. Probability of a Credit Changing Grades

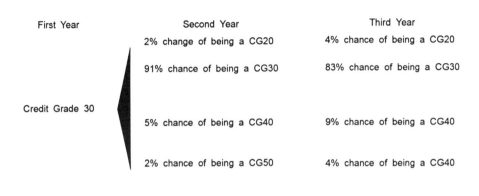

First Year	Second Year	Third Year
	2% change of being a CG20	4% chance of being a CG20
	91% chance of being a CG30	83% chance of being a CG30
Credit Grade 30	5% chance of being a CG40	9% chance of being a CG40
	2% chance of being a CG50	4% chance of being a CG40

The blended provision factor each year multiplied by the risk-adjusted asset for that year yields the projected provision in dollar terms for that year. The sum of these products is the total provision, over the life of the transaction, necessary to cover the expected losses given the migration probabilities. For example, in Exhibit 6, assume risk-adjusted assets in the first year are $10,000, $8,000 in the second year and $6,000 in the third. Further, assume the blended factors are respectively X percent, K percent, and L percent. Then the sum of X percent × $10,000 plus K percent × $8,000 plus L percent × $6,000 is the total provision over the life of the transaction.

Exhibit 6. Projected Provisions

The blended factor each year multiplied by the risk-adjusted asset yields the projected provision.

	Risk-Adjusted Assets ($)	Blended Factor (%)	Provision ($)
First Year	$10,000	0.12	12.00
Second Year	$8,000	0.14	11.20
Third Year	$6,000	0.19	11.40

Once we have the total provision over the life of the transaction, we need to derive that portion that is attributable at year one. As shown in Exhibit 6, the weighted average of the blended factor is the appropriate provision (0.14 percent in this case).

In summary, the CGRMU is a necessary pricing tool as well as an integral component of a pay-as-you-go credit charging methodology. My approach starts with the assumption that the current credit grade associated with the financial asset is correct, as defined by qualified credit experts.

CHAPTER 18

What Makes a Good OTC Counterparty?

Leslie Lynn Rahl
President
Leslie Rahl Associates

The OTC markets have become a core tool for managing risk and offer tremendous flexibility to corporate treasurers and investors. OTC swaps and derivatives are used to:

- Lower effective cost of debt
- Hedge market risks arising from new financings
- Manage existing assets and liabilities
- Offset options positions embedded in an institution's assets and liabilities
- Hedge transaction exposures
- Hedge translation exposures
- Enhance yield through arbitrage opportunities
- Manage interest rate and currency risk
- Allocate assets

There are many factors to consider when selecting a dealer for OTC swaps and derivatives:

- Creditworthiness
- Quality of their advice and education
- Structuring/financial engineering capabilities
- Price

- Willingness and ability to meet your servicing requirements (i.e., daily mark-to-markets)

- Willingness to terminate transactions before maturity at a fair market price

CREDIT

Credit has become one of the key issues facing the derivatives industry in the 1990s. During the 1980s very little emphasis was put on measuring and monitoring the creditworthiness of counterparties and little or no differentiation was made when pricing deals to counterparties of different credit quality. As the credit quality of counterparties has declined and the size of outstandings has increased, more and more emphasis has been placed on credit.

The credit focus of the 1990s has affected dealers in a variety of ways. Dealers without a top credit rating have felt the pressure:

- End users are sometimes not willing to deal with them.

- End users are demanding finer pricing from lesser-rated dealers than from top-rated dealers.

- There is reduced liquidity in the inter-dealer market. Many dealers are beginning to differentiate price by the credit quality of their counterparty.

All dealers, including those that are rated AAA, are facing increased pressure to include downgrade triggers in their documentation. The large amounts of credit lines that swaps and derivatives transactions—which average three to four years in maturity—consume, have made credit availability a constraint for even the best rated dealers. It is not unusual for a dealer to be "full up" on credit availability to another dealer, but this is often a temporary phenomenon that reverts when a deal matures or when other nonswaps transactions that sometimes share common lines (e.g., FX) expire.

Dealers are looking to a variety of techniques to enhance their creditworthiness:

- Creation of derivative product companies (DPCs)

- Surety bonds/letters of credit

- Clearinghouses

DERIVATIVE PRODUCT COMPANIES (DPCs)

Several major dealers have announced the creation of special purpose companies for their derivative products activities. An enhanced derivative products company (DPC) is a subsidiary of a financial services firm that can be rated higher than its parent because it does not depend on backing from its parent to meet the financial obligations on its derivative products. Several DPCs have been rated AAA, although their parents are securities firms with a senior unsecured debt rating of A+. The higher rating that these subsidiaries have been granted is due in part to the application of structured finance principles of credit-risk protection of the portfolio. One form of DPC credit support is excess assets over liabilities. This excess capital can be paid-in capital, subordinated debt, common or preferred equity, or overcollateralization with additional portfolio assets.

The building blocks of a AAA-rated DPC are the portfolio, capital, and separateness from its parent firm. Credit loss in a derivatives portfolio directly depends on both default risk and varying market risk. Sophisticated risk modeling and statistical tools are employed by the rating agencies to assess the market risk of a derivatives portfolio. The ultimate rating process, however, blends elements of structured and operating company analysis. Components of the ratings evaluation include:

- Portfolio credit quality

- Management and operating guidelines

- Parent-subsidiary relationship

- Capital adequacy and the risk model

One of the challenges of an enhanced DPC is to balance the different behaviors of dynamic derivative assets and often less volatile capital. Prudent management of the portfolio of derivative products is as critical as the quantity of capital.

Several dealers are actively considering creating enhanced DPCs, and it is expected that there will be more announcements soon. The first two vehicles (Merrill Lynch DPC and Goldman Sachs DPC) were heavily capitalized and restricted counterparties to AA- or better. Salomon's Swapco has taken another leap forward. The Swapco structure is unique in several ways:

- It allows for a full range of interest rate, currency, and equity derivatives.

- It allows Salomon to deal with all investment grade counterparties and to deal with nonrated counterparties on a case-by-case basis.

- It provides a unique termination structure where all deals are canceled at midpoint if Salomon fails to meet the capital requirements.

- It has dynamic capital requirements.

- If a counterparty is downgraded, it can stay in existing deals but not enter new agreements.

- Termination trigger events include not only a Sali bankruptcy, but also a deficit in Swapco's dynamic collateral requirements. A downgrade of Swapco to below A- is a termination trigger event, but a Sali downgrade is not.

Salomon did a survey of 50 global clients before deciding on their structure. Most of the clients surveyed preferred termination to continuation. They cited:

- Lack of sales force and trading capability to accommodate them if they want to restructure a contract.

- The worry that close-out or assignment would be at unattractive prices.

- Long-term monitoring expense.

The clients surveyed indicated a strong preference for termination, but this is obviously a controversial issue and it will take time before the market preferences settle out.

Although clearly a major breakthrough for the industry, these DPC companies are time-consuming and expensive to establish because of the significant capital that has been required by the rating agencies so far. Sali's dynamic capital approach has its pluses and minuses, and alternative capital structures are clearly being investigated by other dealers considering creating such vehicles.

SURETY BONDS/LETTERS OF CREDIT

The use of surety bonds /letters of credit either on individual transactions or as one of the layers of capital in DPC or clearing-type structures is in its infancy but is receiving increased focus. The most popular use of surety bonds/letters of credit to date in the swap market has been in the municipal swap market.

CLEARINGHOUSES

Several efforts are underway to create clearing mechanisms for swaps and derivative products. The obstacles to be overcome are enormous, but it appears that progress is being made. The development of a clearing mechanism would clearly have a profound effect on the market and, if properly done, could go a long way toward solving a lot of the credit constraints that are overhanging the swaps and derivatives market.

MARGIN SERVICE BUREAU

The creation of a margin service bureau to facilitate the operational aspects of using collateral for swaps and derivative products is perhaps a more realizable approach to reducing credit risk within the system than a full clearinghouse. A service bureau that administers the bilateral agreements entered into by participants without setting policies or taking credit risk has significant potential, especially if the capital requirements are reduced, as expected, by the regulators for collateralized transactions.

QUALITY OF THEIR ADVICE AND EDUCATION

The amount and quality of hand-holding that dealers provide varies considerably. Some dealers provide extensive support both before a transaction is entered into and during the life of the transaction. Others provide good support before you enter into the transaction but are less supportive on ongoing management. The complexity of your potential needs and the probability that you might want to terminate the transaction prior to maturity might impact the importance you place on selecting a dealer that is willing to give ongoing advice.

STRUCTURING/FINANCIAL ENGINEERING CAPABILITIES

Some dealers are better than others at providing competitive pricing on standard transactions. Some dealers excel at creating customized, highly financially engineered solutions to client problems. It is important to select a dealer with the expertise you require.

PRICE

Although price is an important issue, a survey that I recently completed for a client indicated that end users ranked price as the number 4 factor they consider when selecting a counterparty.

WILLINGNESS AND ABILITY TO MEET YOUR SERVICING REQUIREMENTS

Some dealers are more responsive than others at meeting your ongoing servicing requirements. The G30 study that was just released strongly suggests that end users:

- Mark their portfolios to market regularly
- Stress test their portfolios regularly
- Measure and monitor credit risk on an MTM plus future expected risk basis

Few end users are set up today to meet these recommendations independently. They require a significant level of assistance from their dealers. Some dealers are more responsive than others in providing regular mark-to-markets. Some dealers are willing to provide stress testing simulations of their client's portfolios; some are not. Some dealers are willing to share their methodologies for assessing potential credit exposure by transaction type; others are not. If this type of support is important to you, it is best to make sure *before* closing a transaction that the dealer is willing and able to meet your servicing requirements.

WILLINGNESS TO TERMINATE TRANSACTIONS BEFORE MATURITY AT A FAIR MARKET PRICE

Although the majority of swaps and derivatives transactions are held to maturity, it is becoming more and more common to terminate transactions before maturity. Some dealers are more responsive than others in accommodating an early termination. It is worthwhile to consider this potential eventuality *before* you enter into a transaction. Another factor to consider is the acceptability of your counterparty to other dealers should an assignment be necessary. If you decide to terminate a transaction before maturity and the termination price offered by your original dealer is unsatisfactory, the other alternative that you have is to assign the transaction to another dealer. This, of course, requires the consent of both your old and new dealer. Transactions that you would like to be able to assign should be entered into only with the most creditworthy dealers if you want to maintain the assignability option.

COUNTERPARTY EVALUATION

End users are increasingly focusing on what makes a good counterparty. When entering into a swap agreement or buying a cap or a floor, users have taken on the risk that their counterparty will perform for the life of the agreement. If a counterparty defaults on its obligations, at a time when the market has moved in the nondefaulting counterparty's favor and the defaulting counterparty is unable to pay the fair mark-to-market value of the remaining agreement, the nondefaulting party can be subject to a loss. If, on the other hand, the default comes at a time when the fair mark-to-market value of the agreement would require a payment from the nondefaulting counterparty to the defaulting counterparty, the nondefaulting counterparty will not sustain any losses as a result of the default. How should a user of these instruments think about the credit risk inherent in these agreements?

1. As in all credit-sensitive agreements, "Know your counterparty." There is no substitute for good, fundamental credit analysis and firsthand knowledge of the counterparty and its principals. If it is beyond the scope of the company's staff to track and monitor creditworthiness, they might consider subscribing to one of the credit advisory services offered by the major rating agencies.

2. The user should establish limits on the amount of risk he or she is willing to take with each counterparty. The creditworthiness of the counterparty as well as the diversification of counterparty credit exposure mix (commercial bank versus investment bank; U.S. versus foreign) should be considered.

3. The user should monitor exposure (mark-to-market value plus estimate of potential risk for remaining maturity) on a regular basis. One of the best ways to measure potential exposure is by measuring the mark-to-market value and then adding a factor that estimates the potential risk for the remaining maturity. The factors should probably be differentiated by transaction type and maturity. Obviously, the risk on a 10-year remaining life is higher than on a two-year remaining life, and the risk on a cross-currency swap or an equity swap is higher than on a U.S.-dollar interest rate swap.

4. The user should review limits on a regular basis and monitor the creditworthiness of all counterparties. Circumstances change. The amount of exposure that a company is comfortable with for a given counterparty can change for a variety of reasons. Perhaps a significant number of new transactions have been added that overweight exposure to Japanese banks or to French banks, for example, in aggregate and cause a change in appetite for additional exposure in that sector, even to a well-rated counterparty. The creditworthiness of a counterparty might deteriorate or improve, causing a reassessment of limits to that counterparty. The number of AAA counterparties might increase significantly, providing

increased liquidity and, therefore, possibly changing a company's appetite for lesser-rated credits.

5. The user should make sure that signed agreements are in place. Although the process has improved, it is not uncommon to have document negotiation drag on for months or years. Obviously, if a counterparty defaults, it strengthens a claim to have signed documents in place. If an agreement is not signed, at the very least make sure that there is a signed confirm.

6. The user should establish policies on actions to be taken if exposure exceeds the limits previously established. The best time to think through how to handle a problem is before the crisis occurs. If a sophisticated user has limits that fluctuate with market value, the limits can be passively exceeded if a larger market move than was built into the limits occurs (i.e., if a seven-standard-deviation move occurs and the limits were developed based on a 95 percent confidence level (two standard deviations). It is a good idea to think through in advance what to do in such a circumstance. Should the deal be terminated? Should an up-front adjustment be made to bring the deal closer to market and reduce the credit exposure? Should a pro rata portion of the deal be terminated to bring the exposure within the limit framework? Should the limit be revised?

7. The user should establish policies on what to do if the creditworthiness of a counterparty changes materially. If the creditworthiness of a counterparty improves, a company might want to consider increasing the limit to that counterparty and taking on new transactions. But what if the creditworthiness of a counterparty deteriorates? Should the deal be terminated? Should the deal be collateralized? Should an up-front payment be requested to bring the transaction to or close to the market and reduce exposure?

MEASURING CREDIT EXPOSURE

Credit exposure is a combination of several factors. The exposure is quite different on a two-year deal than it is on a 10-year deal. The potential credit exposure is also very different on a Nikkei swap than it is on a U.S.-dollar interest rate swap. Setting limits based on notional principal is a good first step, but that could lull a company into a false sense of security and leave it dangerously exposed in certain situations .

The credit exposure if a counterparty defaults and is unable to fulfill his or her obligations, is the cost or mark-to-market of going into the market and replacing the remaining portion of the transaction. This exposure fluctuates with the markets. If an interest rate swap was done three years ago with a counterparty who is paying a 9 percent fixed rate, the credit exposure to that counterparty grows every time interest rates decline and the swaps mark-to-market value increases. Unless the market value of transactions is monitored regularly, market moves can push exposure out of preset limits passively.

The credit equation must also include some measure of the changes in value that may occur during the future life of the swap. For example, the credit exposure of a seven-year swap done two years ago should be based on two factors: a measure of the swaps current mark-to-market and a measure of the risks involved in putting on a five-year swap today.

Another important factor is the complexity and liquidity of the structure. If the counterparty in a complex, customized swap structure goes bankrupt, it will cost much more to replace than a plain-vanilla swap. The new counterparty will be making a new bid/offer spread to cover his or her costs of hedging the transaction and fewer counterparties might be available to replace an exotic swap than a plain-vanilla one, potentially translating to higher costs.

Finally, credit exposure also depends on the nature of the underlying risk being hedged. Potential credit exposure is the likely amount it would cost to replace the swap if the counterparty defaulted. Because the mark-to-market value of a swap on a volatile underlying (i.e., an equity index) is likely to be larger than the mark-to-market value of a swap on a less volatile underlying (i.e., U.S.-dollar interest rates), the potential credit risk is greater.

The measurement of potential credit exposure depends on assumptions. Key determinants in evaluating potential credit exposure include:

- *Volatility of underlying instrument.* The more volatile the underlying instrument, the more likely that its value will be larger at the time of default. More volatile instruments, therefore, carry more credit risk. A commodity swap will have more credit risk than a U.S.-dollar interest rate swap, and a swap involving a highly volatile currency like the lira will have more credit risk than a yen swap.

- *Term of the transaction.* The longer the maturity of the transaction, the higher the credit risk. A 10-year swap obviously entails more credit risk than a two-year swap against the same index.

- *Liquidity of derivative and underlying markets.* The less liquid the transaction, the more credit risk is entailed. The cost of replacing the defaulted counterparty will be greater as a result of a larger bid/offer spread. In addition, if a counterparty for a highly structured, customized transaction with unique documents is being replaced, the choices might be more limited and the cost higher than anticipated.

- *Frequency of settlements/resets.* The more frequently the transaction is settled, the less the potential size of the accrued interest that will build up and, therefore, the lower the credit risk.

- *Ability to exercise options early.* The ability to exercise options early helps to reduce credit risk.

Calculating the credit risk for a given class of transactions is only one step. The other important step is to evaluate the likelihood that a counterparty will default. This is often done on a portfolio basis. Potential exposure is a function of the amount of risk and the likelihood of a loss.

Potential Credit Exposure = (Exposure) * (Probability of Default)

The expected exposure would be calculated using the current forward rates and current implied volatility. The maximum exposure would be calculated using extreme values for volatility and the slope of the forward curve.

WHAT MAKES A GOOD COUNTERPARTY?

Swaps involve a two-way extension of credit. End users are taking the risk that the dealer will perform its obligations throughout the life of the deal and, in turn, dealers are taking the risk that their counterparty will perform its obligations throughout the life of the deal. Factors that might influence a dealer's worthiness as a potential swap counterparty might include not only credit rating and price but such factors as relationship, service, quality of advice, and willingness to terminate transactions at fair market value before maturity.

Determining whether an end user is a good swap counterparty is usually done on a credit analysis basis. There are other counterparty risk factors that are also being evaluated by potential counterparties, rating agencies, and regulators, including:

- Does management understand the derivatives being used? Does senior management understand the derivative transactions that the firm has entered into and are they aware of the risks?

- Does the derivative trade make sense? Is there an underlying business purpose? Is the transaction a hedge? If so, is it a good hedge? If it is an arbitrage, what are the savings? Do they seem to adequately compensate for reduced liquidity and increased complexity?

- Are derivatives being used for hedging or for speculation? Derivatives are sometimes used to take a view on the direction of interest rates, the direction of currency movements, the shape of the yield curve, the direction of volatility, and basis relationships. This is not necessarily a bad thing, but speculation does have a negative aura. Understanding how derivatives are being used is an important prerequisite to getting comfortable that they are being used appropriately.

- Are hedges perfectly matched or do you have basis and/or maturity risk? Imperfect hedges are very common, but does the user understand the LIBOR-CP risk he or she is taking or the mismatch of reset dates and its implications?

- Are hedges held to maturity or are they "managed"? "Managing your positions" is becoming increasingly common. Users are extending and contracting maturities to take advantage of changes in the shape of the yield curve, converting caps into swaps and vice versa to take advantage of a changing rate environment, adding options to existing deals, etc. Responding to changes in the environment can be the sign of a well-managed user, but these types of more aggressive strategies need more internal risk management processes than hold to maturity hedging and arbitrage.

- How are these risks of derivatives analyzed, monitored, and controlled?
  - Market risk
  - Management risk

- Legal risk
- Regulatory risk
- Liquidity risk
- Credit risk

■ Have any losses been incurred from derivatives activity? The cause could be poor credit judgment, or it could be basis and/or market risk.

■ Are positions marked-to-market? How? How often? Regular mark-to-market of positions allows a user to monitor his credit exposure as well as to identify transactions that are either very far in-the-money or out-of-the-money and that might be candidates for "managing."

■ What is the role of internal and external auditors? How closely are derivatives activities being monitored?

■ How are duties segregated, e.g., dealing, analysis, confirmation, settlements, and monitoring? Is their adequate segregation of duties?

■ Are there signed documents in place on all transactions? Are there signed confirms? It is not unusual for documents to take months or years to complete. This obviously exposes both counterparties to greater risk.

■ What training does the staff have in the analysis and use of derivatives? This is a complex, ever changing field. Adequate training is key.

■ Who is authorized to execute trades? Is this documented? Formal procedures help provide a discipline.

■ How are counterparties selected? Are standards set by transaction type, by maturity? Is credit rating the only factor?

■ How is credit risk measured? Is notional principal used? Is mark-to-market calculated? Are add-ons used by transaction type? By maturity?

■ Are limits established by counterparty? How? How often are limits monitored?

■ Are there action plans laid out for what to do if the creditworthiness of a counterparty deteriorates? Advance planning on this contingency is a good idea, just as you would establish contingency plans for power blackouts, transportation strikes, etc.

■ Do they have their own pricing models to mark-to-market and evaluate proposals? This is probably not necessary for infrequent users, but active users should seriously consider an independent pricing capability not only to monitor risk, but also to allow them to evaluate the pricing in proposals they receive (especially when they are bundled transactions).

■ What is the process for approving a new derivative? A new counterparty? A new transaction? Unwinding an existing transaction? Written procedures and formal approval requirements are highly desirable.

■ Are there policies and procedures on what to do if limits are exceeded with a counterparty because of a market move?

GROUP OF 30

The Group of 30 Study that was just released contains recommendations toward good management practice for dealers and end users engaged in derivatives activities.
Recommendations for end users include:

1. End users should use derivatives in a manner consistent with the overall risk management and capital policies approved by the board of directors and reviewed as business and market circumstances change.

2. End users should adopt those valuation and market risk management practices recommended for dealers that are appropriate to the nature, size, and complexity of their derivatives activities. Specifically, end users should consider:

   a. Regularly marking-to-market their derivatives portfolios;
   b. Periodically forecasting the cash investment and funding requirements arising from their derivatives portfolios;
   c. Establishing a clearly independent and authoritative function to design and assure adherence to prudent risk limits.

3. End users are encouraged to implement performance assessment and control procedures.

4. End users should consider:

   a. Using a consistent method to measure market risk and comparing the result to risk limits;
   b. Performing simulation to determine how their portfolio would perform under stress conditions.

5. End users should measure credit exposure on derivatives on both a current exposure and a potential exposure basis.

6. Credit exposures on derivatives, and all other credit exposures to a counterparty, should be aggregated and regularly compared to credit limits.

7. End users should have a credit risk management function for all financial instruments with clear independence and authority, and with analytical capabilities in derivatives.

8. End users are encouraged to use one master agreement as widely as possible with each counterparty.

9. End users should assess the benefits of credit enhancement and related risk reduction arrangements against their cost.

10. Financial statements of end users should contain sufficient information about their use of derivatives to provide an understanding of the purposes for which transactions are undertaken, the extent of the transactions, the degree of risk involved and how the transactions are accounted for.

11. End users must insure that their derivatives activities are undertaken by professionals in sufficient number and with the appropriate experience, skill levels, and degree of specialization.

12. End users must insure that adequate systems for data capture, processing, settlement, and management reporting are in place so that derivatives transactions are conducted in an orderly and efficient manner in compliance with management policies.

13. Management of end users should designate who is authorized to commit their institutions to derivatives transactions.

CONCLUSIONS

Although there are many factors that affect counterparty selection, in the course of my consulting practice, credit is one of the key issues on clients' minds. Dealers are worried about enhancing their creditworthiness and about assessing the creditworthiness of their counterparties. Users are concerned about measuring and monitoring the creditworthiness of their counterparties. The 1990s swaps and derivatives business is very different from the business I became involved with in the early 1980s. Whereas innovation and growth characterized the first decade of the swaps and derivatives industry, "back to basics" seems to be the focus of the 1990s. The terms "credit," "risk management," and "strategy" are all popular today, but they were not high on the 1980s priority list.

CHAPTER 19

Exotic Options

Wendy L. Seward
Numerical Analyst
Ron S. Dembo
President

Algorithmics Incorporated

INTRODUCTION

When exotic options were first introduced, they appeared to be interesting academic exercises without much practical application but, over time, they have become widespread in practice. In fact, the range of exotics seems to be growing daily—different types of options are being developed and existing exotics are used in an ever wider range of structured products (see, for example, Kissane [1993] or Falloon [1993]). Papers in the academic finance literature and in practitioners' journals like *Risk Magazine* describe exotic options in terms of their payoff functions and give closed-form solutions for valuation when such formulas are possible. A number of summaries of these papers are available, for example, Rubinstein (1991b) or *Risk Magazine* (1992). The papers typically stop at the point of describing an option's value in terms of special functions like the normal distribution. What is often not addressed is the step to a computer implementation, which can be complicated by the restrictions of computer arithmetic.

We have chosen not to give the details of payoff and valuation formulas in this chapter. Instead, we explore two other aspects of exotic options—practical applications and valuation using computers, since exotic options used in practice generally are priced by computer programs. Our bibliography is by no means exhaustive but it is extensive enough to allow the reader to set off on his or her own study of valuation formulas for exotic options.

In the next section, we discuss some of the implications of computer arithmetic and explore numerical methods that can be used when closed-form solutions are not available. In the third section, we survey a range of types of exotic options and discuss their applications. Where the information was available to us, we give examples of actual offerings that have included exotic options. We found that information on uses of exotic options is considerably more difficult to obtain than mathematical formulas.

A closely related area of interest is the variety of exotic fixed-income products that is currently developing. We do not address this topic but our comments on computer arithmetic and numerical methods could be applied to the valuation of these products.

NUMERICAL METHODS IN OPTION VALUATION

As exotic options have become more popular in practice, a variety of methods have been applied to calculate their values. In many cases, closed-form solutions are available for pricing exotic options, particularly those with European exercise. In other cases, such formulas are not known or are not practical to apply, with the result that approaches based on approximate or numerical methods are used.

In fact, even the closed-form solutions use a numerical approach to calculate particular values. Consider the Black-Scholes formula for the fair value of a basic European call option:

$$V = SN(d_1) - Xe^{-r(T-t)} N(d_2) \tag{1}$$

Here, $N(d)$ refers to the cumulative normal distribution evaluated at d,

$$N(d) = \frac{1}{2\pi} \int_{-\infty}^{d} e^{(-x^2/2)} dx \tag{2}$$

To calculate the value of this integral given a value for d, it is necessary to use a numerical method. (Even looking up the value in a table involves using a numerical method indirectly, since the tables are constructed by such methods.)

The main approaches used to value options are as follows:

- *Closed-form solutions.* By a closed-form solution, we mean that a formula like Equation 1 for the value of the option can be derived.

- *Approximate analytic methods.* An approximate analytic method is a formula, like the Barone-Adesi and Whaley (1987) formula for the price of an American option, that approximates the fair value of the option. As in the Barone-Adesi and Whaley approximation, it may be necessary to use a numerical method to evaluate the formula.

- *Lattice methods.* Lattice methods are probably the best-known numerical methods used to value options. These methods have proved particularly useful in pricing fixed-income derivative securities.

- *Monte Carlo methods.* In a Monte Carlo method, the evolution of the price of the underlying security is simulated over time to the expiry of the option, and the final price is used to value the option at expiry. Since the history of the underlying price is available in the simulation, these methods are useful when intermediate quantities, like the maximum or minimum price of the underlying, affect the value of the option.

- *Quadrature methods.* When the value of an option can be expressed as an integral, a quadrature method can be applied to evaluate the integral numerically. This approach is useful when it is not possible to reduce the integral to a closed-form solution like Equation 1.

- *Finite difference methods.* A finite difference method is a method for solving the partial differential equation that describes the option value. These methods have the potential for a great deal of flexibility in pricing options but are typically more difficult to apply than the other methods that we have mentioned.

All of these approaches involve the use of numerical techniques to some degree and hence compute approximations to the "true" value of the option. When using such methods, it is important to be aware of the accuracy of the computation and also of the trade-off between accuracy and speed when implementing these methods on computers. In this paper, we survey the use of closed-form solutions, quadrature methods, and finite difference methods, with an emphasis on accuracy considerations in the numerical techniques.

One reason for the variety of methods that have been applied to the problem of option valuation is that each of the methods above is limited in its applicability. Some factors that influence the usefulness of a given method in valuing a particular option are:

- Type of exercise (European or American),

- Path-dependency, including testing conditions (like barriers) and calculating intermediate quantities (like maximum price of underlying or average price of underlying),

- Desire for discrete computation, e.g., the need to price a barrier option in which the barrier is tested at discrete intervals (daily, monthly).

In the next section, we discuss some of the basic ideas of accuracy and efficiency in numerical methods, and also briefly mention the effect of computer arithmetic. In the following three sections, we survey three of the methods from the list above, focussing on issues of accuracy and efficiency. Finally, we discuss the use of numerical methods in calculating sensitivities.

Accuracy and Efficiency in Numerical Methods

One of the main questions that should arise when applying a numerical method is, "How accurate is the computed result?" Even if a low accuracy is all that is required, it is important to be aware of the implications of using a particular method. In the low accuracy case, one might be doing more work than necessary to compute values.

There are two sources of inaccuracy when one implements a numerical technique as part of a computer program.

1. The numerical method is an approximation to the true value.

2. Computer arithmetic has certain inherent limitations. Hence, when the numerical method is programmed, the computed result will have an error due to computer arithmetic as well as the error due to the approximation. In general,

this computer arithmetic error, called rounding error, is not significant but it can, for example, influence the numerical calculation of option sensitivities.

When a numerical technique is presented, its accuracy is often described as part of the method. For example, Hull (1993) presents an approximation to the cumulative normal distribution that is accurate to four decimal places. A technique is accurate to p decimal places if the difference between true values and computed values is less than 0.5×10^{-p} in all calculations. If the accuracy of all numerical techniques could be described this simply, it would be straightforward to apply most methods. However, the accuracy of techniques like lattice or quadrature methods that can be applied to many different problems is usually dependent on the particular problem being solved. In this case, there are a number of different approaches that can be used to assess the accuracy of computed values.

The accuracy of a general numerical method usually depends on one or two parameters in the method. For example, as the time step in a binomial lattice applied to a European option is reduced, the value computed by the lattice approaches the solution of the Black-Scholes equation (Cox, Ross, and Rubinstein [1979]). One approach to assess the accuracy of a lattice computation is to solve the same problem with two different time steps, computing two results V_1 and V_2, and compare the two results. If the two values agree to p decimal places, that is,

$$|V_1 - V_2| \le 0.5 \times 10^{-p} \qquad (3)$$

then those p decimal places are probably correct.

This idea can be applied to most numerical techniques but it has the disadvantage that it requires a person to compare the two results. In many cases, it is possible to have the computer do this sort of analysis as part of the method. Such techniques are often called adaptive numerical methods and have the ability to calculate a result to a given accuracy in an efficient manner. In discussing quadrature and finite difference methods below, we will refer to adaptive numerical methods that have been developed in the computer science and engineering literature and can be applied to problems in finance.

One last concept that we require measures the accuracy of the arithmetic on a particular computer. The quantity called "machine epsilon" or "unit roundoff" can be roughly described as the largest machine-representable number ε such that $1 + \varepsilon = 1$ when the value $1 + \varepsilon$ is calculated on the computer. Sometimes, it is possible to increase the efficiency of calculations by cutting off computations if we can detect that the values that we are working with are, in fact, smaller than machine epsilon.

Closed-Form Solutions

In many cases of practical interest, the value of an option can be expressed in a closed form, possibly involving special functions such as the normal or multivariate normal distributions. Typically, such formulas are developed in the Black-Scholes framework (using the same assumptions about the behavior of the market) and hence can be applied when the return on the underlying is normally distributed and the option has European exercise. Closed-form solutions have been developed for many exotic option types, including barrier options, chooser options, binary options, lookback options, and currency-translated options. These formulas can be found in a series of papers by Rubinstein and others in *Risk Magazine*, 1991–1992, in Rubinstein (1991b) and in other papers in the finance literature.

All of the closed-form formulas mentioned above depend on evaluation of the cumulative normal distribution. Hull (1993) suggests two approximations to the distribution, one accurate to four decimal places and the other to six places. (These and other polynomial approximations to the normal distribution can be found in Abramowitz and Stegun [1972].)

As noted earlier, "accurate to four decimal places" means that when a value for the normal distribution is calculated, the difference between it and the true value will be less than 0.00005. If the calculated value is, say, 0.5847, then 0.00005 is a small error, but if the value that has been calculated is 0.0002394, then 0.00005 could be a significant source of error. In practice, these polynomial approximations seem to be sufficiently accurate for pricing "plain vanilla" options, where the normal distribution occurs only twice in the formula. For exotic options, where the normal distribution may be used repeatedly in the formulas (eight times in an up-and-in barrier call option, for example), the approximations could be a source of error.

More accurate formulas to evaluate the normal distribution are available in the numerical analysis literature, for example, the approximation due to Cody (1969). Cody's paper develops a method that approximates the normal distribution to at least 18 decimal places in theory. The accuracy achieved on a particular computer depends on the arithmetic system, the compiler, the computer's built-in functions, and proper selection of some machine-dependent constants. The paper explains how to choose these constants. Cody's formula gives as much accuracy as is useful on most computers that are used in practice for option valuation.

The cost of this additional accuracy is in the computer time needed to evaluate the formula. We compared Cody's formula to the four-digit polynomial approximation. On a SUN IPX workstation, Cody's formula took 1.2 seconds to evaluate the cumulative normal distribution 20,000 times, while the polynomial approximation took only 0.4 second. Hence, the polynomial method was three times faster, but both methods are so fast that it is probably worthwhile to use the more accurate function in general.

The question of efficiency versus accuracy is less clear when considering options whose closed-form solutions depend on higher-order normal distributions. For example, a best-of option (an option to receive the more expensive of two underlyings) can be expressed as the sum of three evaluations of the bivariate normal distribution, plus other terms (Rubinstein [1991b]). To evaluate the bivariate normal distribution requires the integration of a two-dimensional infinite integral. As for the univariate normal distribution, there are inexpensive low-accuracy methods available. For example, Hull (1993) quotes a method due to Drezner (1978), which is essentially a simple Gauss quadrature scheme, accurate to four decimal places. (Gauss quadrature is a popular method for numerical integration—see, for example, Kahaner, Moler, and Nash [1989].) The question then arises, if Drezner's scheme is sufficiently accurate to evaluate the bivariate normal distribution, why not apply it directly to the underlying integral that describes the option price? This direct approach would save two evaluations of a two-dimensional integral, but the effect on the accuracy of the calculated value is unclear.

This question leads us to consider the use of various quadrature methods in option pricing.

Quadrature

In the Black-Scholes framework, we can express the present value V of an option as the discounted value of its expected payoff

$$V = e^{-r(T-t)} \cdot E \, [payoff] \tag{4}$$

where r is the risk-neutral rate of return and $E \, [\, . . . \,]$ is the expected value in a risk-neutral world. Let $g \, (S)$ denote the probability distribution of the random variable S underlying the expected payoff. Then Equation 4 can be written in integral form as

$$V = e^{-r(T-t)} \cdot \int_{-\infty}^{\infty} (payoff \cdot g \, (S) \,) \, ds \tag{5}$$

Typically, the payoff function can be expressed in mathematical terms. For example, the payoff of a floating lookback call is $max \, (S - S_{min}, \, 0)$ where S_{min} is the minimum price of the underlying observed in the lifetime of the option. If the probability distribution $g \, (S)$ can also be expressed in closed form, as is the case for the lognormal distribution, then the integral can be evaluated numerically.

Quadrature, or numerical integration, methods replace an integral like Equation 5 by a finite sum of values that can be calculated by computer. The general form of a quadrature method is

$$\int f(x) \, dx = \sum_i w_i \cdot f(x_i) \tag{6}$$

where the w_i are called quadrature weights and the x_i are points where the function $f(x)$ is to be evaluated. The simplest quadrature methods, such as the trapezium rule or Simpson's rule, use equally spaced points x_i. Gauss quadrature methods, which are popular in practice, choose both the points x_i and the weights w_i according to more complicated rules; the return for this extra complication is that the methods are generally more accurate for the same amount of work. The points and weights for Gauss quadrature can be found in many references, such as Abramowitz and Stegun (1972).

From Equation 6 it can be seen that, to use a quadrature method to value an option, the integrand in Equation 5 must be of a form that can be evaluated at the quadrature points x_i. Some path-dependent options can be expressed in this form. The value of a barrier option, for example, can be expressed in terms of a number of different cases, where each case can be expressed in integral form (see, for example, Rubinstein [1991b]). Where intermediate quantities affect the value of an option, quadrature methods can be used if the distribution of that intermediate quantity is known. American exercise generally precludes the use of quadrature methods, since the option value cannot be expressed in the form of Equation 4, that is, as the present value of the expected payoff.

Given that we have fast and efficient methods for evaluating the cumulative normal distribution, there seems to be little point in using a quadrature method to value a basic European option, or an exotic option that can be expressed in similar form. However, there are exotic options that can be written in the form of Equation 5, but not reduced to closed-form solutions. In such cases, a quadrature method is one possible approach. For example, Nelken (1993) discusses the use of quadrature methods to price complex chooser options and compound options.

A quadrature method computes an approximation to the integral that represents the option value. When using such a method, one has to decide how accurate that approximation should be. To increase the accuracy of a method, it is necessary to use more points x_i in the formula, which means that it will take more computer time to evaluate the option. Ideally, the method should be as efficient as possible given a particular accuracy requirement. This idea can be automated by using an adaptive quadrature method, in which the method itself decides how many points to use to achieve a particular accuracy. Nelken (1993) discusses the use of a Gauss-Kronrod rule applied to the pricing of the complex chooser and compound options. General discussion of adaptive quadrature methods can be found in any basic book on numerical methods, for example, Mathews (1987) or Kahaner, Moler and Nash (1989).

One of the difficulties in applying any quadrature method, adaptive or not, to option valuation is that the integral (Equation 5) has an infinite limit. We need to replace that value with some finite limit. A general approach is to replace infinity with a value X such that for $x > X$, the value of the integrand is less than *machine epsilon* × *maximum value of the integrand*. After some manipulation, Equation 5 and related integrals can usually be expressed in terms of the standard normal density function (see, for example, Nelken [1993]). We know that the maximum value of this function is 1 and it usually straightforward to estimate the maximum value of other terms and, hence, to choose an appropriate value of X. Since the normal distribution decays very quickly away from its mean of zero, it turns out that it is often sufficiently accurate to replace infinity with some small finite value like 5, representing a range of 5 standard deviations. An additional way to assess the choice of X is to graph typical values of the integrand and observe their behavior. While this graphical approach is certainly not rigorous, it can give a good understanding of the behavior of a function. Any choice to replace "infinity" with a finite limit should be tested thoroughly when implementing a method for general-purpose use.

Options on multiple underlyings are more complicated to value than options on a single underlying. Rubinstein (1991b) discusses these options and develops closed-form solutions for a number of cases. Consider the case of a call option on the maximum of two risky assets, sometimes called a best-of option. The payoff of this option is

$$max [0, max (S_1, S_2) - K] \tag{7}$$

The value of the call, in integral form, is

$$C = e^{-r (T-t)} \iint max\left[0, max \left(S_1 (t) e^x, S_2(t) e^y \right) - K\right] f(x, y) \, dx dy \tag{8}$$

where

$$x = \ln (S_1/S_1(t)) \quad y = \ln (S_2/S_2(t)) \tag{9}$$

$S_i(t)$ denotes the price of underlying i at time t, S_i is its price at expiry and $f(x,y)$ is the joint probability distribution of the returns of the two underlyings, with correlation ρ. There is a closed-form solution to Equation 8, which involves two evaluations of the univariate normal distribution and three evaluations of the bivariate normal distribution. Given that evaluating the bivariate normal distribution requires the numerical integration of an integral similar to Equation 8, is it more accurate and efficient to use the closed-form solution or to use quadrature to evaluate Equation 8 directly?

The quadrature methods that we will discuss in the remainder of this section could be applied to computation of the bivariate normal distribution or to Equation 8 itself. As Rubinstein (1991b) points out, apparently simple generalizations of the best-of option do not have closed-form solutions. One such option is the spread option, for which the call has the payoff

$$max\ [0, (S_2 - S_1) - K] \tag{10}$$

In this case, a quadrature method would have to be applied to the expected value integral directly.

A number of different quadrature methods have been proposed for use in evaluating options on multiple underlyings. In mathematical terms, each underlying adds another dimension to the integrand. The most obvious method of multidimensional numerical integration is to use a one-dimensional quadrature rule in each dimension. The expense of this approach increases exponentially with the number of underlyings. If one uses a 100-point quadrature rule in one dimension, then two-dimensional integration based on the same rule uses 10,000 points, and a three-dimensional problem takes a million points. For problems in four dimensions or higher, more efficient methods than this obvious approach are available.

Rubinstein (1991b) develops a one-dimensional quadrature method specifically for use in option valuation, by using a lattice approach to pick the quadrature points and weights. This approach approximates the bivariate normal density with a discrete bivariate binomial density. In this case, the quadrature is independent of the option payoff but does depend on the correlation. It is necessary to compute a new set of quadrature points and weights for any correlation but once the points and weights have been computed, they can be stored and reused. Rubinstein suggests the use of a 100-point one-dimensional rule, that is, 100 points in each of x and y, where x and y are defined in Equation 9, which requires roughly 10,000 evaluations of the integrand. The paper states that this method was found to be more computationally efficient than Gauss quadrature.

The main disadvantage of these two approaches is that it is not simple to decide how many points to use. The correlation in options on multiple underlyings has a significant impact on how easy it is to evaluate the integral numerically. Consider the case of a spread call option (Equation 10) on two underlyings. If the correlation is 0 (the two underlyings are uncorrelated) then the integrand has the regular shape shown in Exhibit 1.

Exhibit 1 shows the value of the integrand for x and y lying in the interval $[-1, 1]$, where $S_1 = S_2 = 50$, $K = 1$, the risk-free rate is 10 percent, the volatilities of the two underlyings are 20 percent and 25 percent respectively, and the time to expiry is 0.5

Exhibit 1.   Spread Option Integrand—Correlation 0

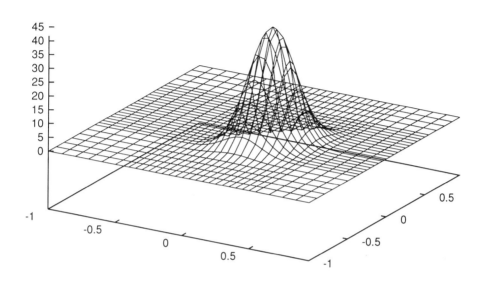

years. As the correlation approaches either 1 or –1, the integrand elongates and rotates toward the line

$$\frac{x - \mu_1 (T - t)}{\sigma_1} = sign (\rho) \frac{y - \mu_2 (T - t)}{\sigma_2} \tag{11}$$

where σ is the volatility of the ith underlying and

$$\mu_i = r - \frac{(\sigma_i)^2}{2} \tag{12}$$

Examples of the integrand for different correlations are shown in Exhibits 2, 3, and 4. If we simply use a quadrature method with points distributed over a fixed area, then for high correlations, we will need to use many points to integrate the elongated shape accurately. This observation brings us back to the idea of using an adaptive quadrature method. Such a method will essentially find the shape of the integrand automatically and place the quadrature points appropriately. One possible method is described in the paper by Berntsen, Espelid, and Genz (1991). Their method extends the type of approach described by Nelken (1993) to higher dimensions.

The method of Berntsen et al. would be useful for options on two, three, or possibly four underlyings but for higher dimensions, alternative approaches must be considered. The most common approach to higher-dimensional numerical integration is to use a Monte Carlo method. Monte Carlo methods for numerical integration are based on the same idea of generating random samples as Monte Carlo methods for option valuation. In numerical integration, one contains the integrand in an n-dimen-

Exhibit 2.   Spread Option Integrand—Correlation 0.5

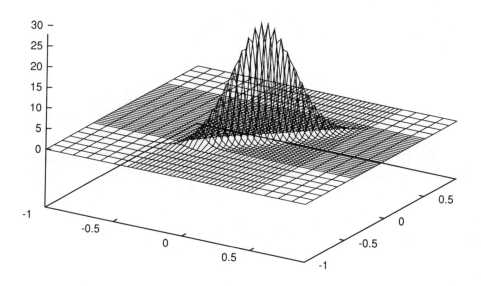

Exhibit 3.   Spread Option Integrand—Correlation 0.9

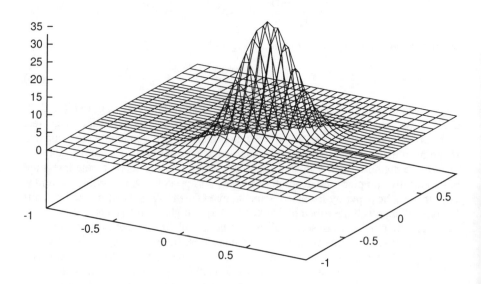

Exhibit 4.   Spread Option Integrand—Correlation −0.9

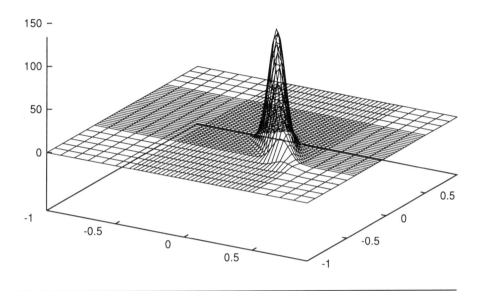

sional hypercube whose integral is known. One then generates random points in the hypercube and counts the number that land on the integrand. (For further information, see Kahaner, Moler, and Nash [1989]).

Barrett, Moore, and Wilmott (1992) suggest an alternative to Monte Carlo integration methods for valuing options on multiple underlyings. Their approach is based on a method due to Haselgrove (1961) and has elements of both standard quadrature rules and Monte Carlo methods. The authors claim that it is "far superior" to Monte Carlo integration. The paper includes a comparison of the Haselgrove method to Boyle's (1988) lattice method for pricing a best-of option, which shows that their approach produces a solution of comparable accuracy in a reasonable amount of computer time, on an IBM workstation. They note that the superiority of the method is more obvious in greater than two dimensions. Since the user does have to choose the number of quadrature points a priori in this method, it seems reasonable to use an adaptive quadrature scheme for options on two or three underlyings and consider the approach of Barrett et al. for problems in higher dimensions.

Solving the Partial Differential Equation

One possible approach to option valuation is to apply a numerical method directly to the partial differential equation (PDE) that describes the option value. This approach has been discussed by a number of authors, for example, Brennan and Schwartz (1978), Courtadon (1990), and Hull and White (1990). The method is often called the "finite difference" approach. Recently, Dewynne and Wilmott (1993) showed that the method can be quite general—it is possible to accumulate intermediate quantities like averages and to model American exercise of exotic options. The PDE formulation used by Dewynne and Wilmott is

$$\frac{\partial}{\partial t}V + f(S,t)\frac{\partial}{\partial I}V + (rS - D(S,I,t))\frac{\partial}{\partial S}V - rV + \frac{S^2\sigma^2}{2}\frac{\partial^2 V}{\partial S^2} = 0 \qquad (13)$$

where V is the value of the option, S is the price of the underlying, r is the risk-free rate of return, and σ is the volatility. The additional terms in Equation 13 give it the increased flexibility necessary to model a range of exotic options. Here, I represents an intermediate quantity, such as a maximum or average value of the underlying, and satisfies

$$I = \int_0^t f(S,\tau)\, d\tau \qquad (14)$$

The quantity $D(S,I,t)$ is used to model both discretely paid and continuously paid dividends. This generalized approach is described in detail in the book by Wilmott, Dewynne, and Howison (1993).

In general, Equation 13 will have to be solved using some sort of numerical method. The trade-off for the increased flexibility offered by this formulation is that it is more difficult to apply a numerical method to this model than, say, to apply a quadrature method to an integral. Dewynne and Wilmott note that PDEs having the same form as Equation 13 have been studied for 150 years and that, hence, there is a large body of theory that can be applied to the analysis of the equation. The same holds true for numerical methods—similar PDEs have been solved by computer for almost as long as computers have been around.

The finite difference method for solving Equation 13 is described by Hull (1993) and Courtadon (1990), among others. Very briefly, a finite difference method replaces the partial derivatives in Equation 13 by differences, which allows the solution of the PDE to be computed at discrete points in the (S,t) plane. In the most basic finite difference method, these discrete points are spaced at equal intervals in the plane, and the intervals are chosen before the problem is solved. This is similar to choosing a single quadrature rule with a fixed number of points to approximate an integral and suffers from the same drawback that it is difficult to know how to space the points. One may end up doing either too much work and achieving much more accuracy than is needed, or not enough work, with the result that the approximate solution is not sufficiently accurate. As for quadrature methods, adaptive methods for solving PDEs have been developed and are widely used in science and engineering. These methods can move the discrete points around in the plane as the numerical solution is being computed. The description of such methods is beyond the scope of this paper—we refer interested readers to any modern textbook on numerical methods for PDEs.

An additional similarity of the quadrature approach and the PDE approach is that one has to deal with "infinity" in both cases. The PDE (Equation 13) is defined for all values of S between 0 and ∞. To apply a numerical method, it is necessary to replace "infinity" by some finite value of S. A bad choice of that replacement can degrade the accuracy of the computed solution. As Dewynne and Wilmott observe, for a basic European option, the option value V approaches S as S becomes large.

Similar observations can be made for other option types and give some guidance as to finite values that can be used to replace infinity. This difficulty has been encountered in PDE problems in science and engineering and references can be found in the literature.

Computing Sensitivities

The sensitivities, *delta, gamma, theta,* etc., are as important in option trading and risk management as the option value itself. For European options, closed-form solutions are available for these sensitivities. For exotic options, even if a closed-form solution is available for the option value, it may not be possible to find closed-form expressions for the sensitivities. In other cases, the formulas for the sensitivities may be so involved that it is desirable to use a numerical method instead. The code needed to compute an approximation can be considerably simpler and hence stands a better chance of being correct.

The sensitivities are, in fact, partial derivatives of the option value with respect to various quantities. For example, *delta* is the derivative with respect to the price of the underlying. That is

$$delta = \frac{\partial V}{\partial S} \tag{15}$$

We can approximate *delta* by the centered difference

$$delta \cong \frac{V(S + \Delta S) - V(S - \Delta S)}{2\Delta S} \tag{16}$$

As with any numerical method, we have to decide how to compute *delta* accurately. In this case, the choice of the increment ΔS controls the accuracy. If we make ΔS too large, the approximation to *delta* will be poor. Unfortunately, if we make it too small, the approximation can be equally bad. This degradation in quality of the approximation as ΔS becomes very small is due to rounding error, the fact that the computer can only represent numbers to a limited precision.

For European options, the value of the option is well-behaved as a function of *S,* resulting in a smooth value of *delta,* as shown in Exhibit 5. Even a relatively large value of ΔS will result in a reasonable approximation to *delta.*

This smoothness is also characteristic of many exotic options, except that there may be points where the option value changes discontinuously as a function of *S.* Exhibit 6 shows value and *delta* for a down-and-in barrier call option for various values of *S.* It can be seen that the curve has a sharp bend at the barrier of 1.1; *delta* changes abruptly from a positive value to a negative value as *S* crosses the barrier. In this case, it is important to ensure that the difference (Equation 16) does not cross the barrier. It may be more accurate to use a one-sided difference formula close to the barrier. Either

$$delta \cong \frac{V(S + \Delta S) - V(S)}{\Delta S} \tag{17}$$

Exhibit 5.   Value and Delta for European Call Option

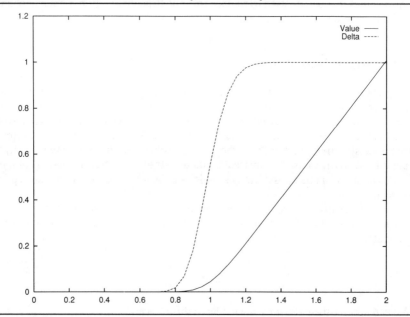

Exhibit 6.   Value and Delta for a Down-and-in Barrier Call Option

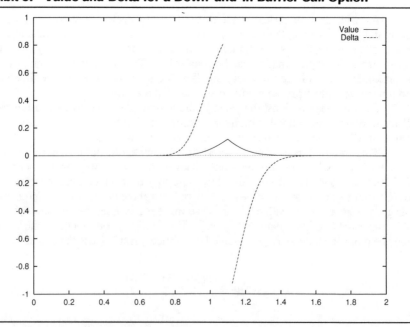

or

$$delta \cong \frac{V(S) - V(S - \Delta S)}{\Delta S} \tag{18}$$

could be used, depending on which side of the barrier S lies. Away from the barrier, the option value curve is smooth and it will be straightforward to compute *delta* using Equation 16.

If it is necessary to calculate an accurate numerical approximation to a sensitivity, one possible approach is to use a method called Richardson extrapolation. This method will compute the approximation as accurately as possible given the particular computer arithmetic system being using. Since the method is simple to describe, we will outline it here for the computation of *delta*. It starts by using Equation 16 to compute an approximate value of *delta*, using a reasonably large stepsize ΔS, say, $\Delta S = 0.01 \cdot S$. Let us call this initial approximation $D_{0,0}$. One then computes a second approximation, $D_{1,0}$, using a stepsize $(\Delta S)/2$. From these two values, one computes an "extrapolated" value

$$D_{1,1} = \frac{4D_{1,0} - D_{0,0}}{3} \tag{19}$$

It turns out that $D_{1,1}$ is significantly more accurate than $D_{0,0}$ or $D_{1,0}$, even though it is cheap to compute. Successive approximations are calculated in a similar fashion. The value $D_{j,0}$ is computed using Equation 16 with a stepsize $(\Delta S)/2^j$. Then the extrapolated values $D_{j,k}$, $k = 1, \ldots, j$ are calculated according to the formula

$$D_{j,k} = \frac{4^k D_{j,k-1} - D_{(j-1),(k-1)}}{4^k - 1} \tag{20}$$

The accuracy of the successive estimates can be estimated by comparing $D_{j,j}$ and $D_{(j-1),(j-1)}$. If the difference between the two values is sufficiently small, then the extrapolation process stops. It is also necessary to check if the difference is larger than the difference between $D_{(j-1),(j-1)}$ and $D_{(j-2),(j-2)}$. If this behavior is observed, then the effect of rounding error has corrupted the calculation, and the extrapolation process should stop, accepting $D_{(j-1),(j-1)}$ as the most accurate value that can be computed.

Table 1 compares the results of calculating *delta* for a European call option, using Equation 16 with $\Delta S = 0.01 \cdot S$, with $\Delta S = 0.001 \cdot S$, and using Richardson extrapolation. The other parameters to this option are: strike price $K = 1$, risk-free rate $r = 0.04$, volatility $\sigma = 0.20$, and option lifetime, 90 days. The solution computed using Richardson extrapolation is accurate in all the shown figures. It can be seen that using $\Delta S = 0.01 \cdot S$ leads to a solution accurate to three decimal places in this example. The solution computed using $\Delta S = 0.001 \cdot S$ is accurate to five to six decimal places in most cases, which is probably enough. The advantage of using Richardson extrapolation is that one knows how accurately the approximation has been computed. It is not necessary to compute a solution to nine places using Richardson extrapolation—the procedure can be set up to compute to as many places as are needed, limited only by the precision of the particular computer arithmetic.

Table 1.   Calculation of European Delta

Spot Price S	Using $\Delta S = 0.01 \cdot S$	Using $\Delta S = 0.001 \cdot S$	Richardson Extrapolation
0.60	0.000 000 306	0.000 000 293	0.000 000 293
0.80	0.018 106 818	0.017 959 085	0.017 957 593
1.00	0.559 018 446	0.559 196 783	0.559 198 491
1.20	0.976 219 817	0.976 414 007	0.976 415 966
1.40	0.999 793 066	0.999 797 754	0.999 797 801

Table 2 shows the results of calculating *delta* for a down-and-out barrier call option, using Equation 16 and Richardson extrapolation. The other parameters for this call option are: strike price $K = 1.55$, volatility $\sigma = 0.13$, a barrier of 1.6150 and no rebate. The original option was in fact a currency option and both domestic and foreign rates were equal. The poor approximation to *delta* when $S = 1.625$ and $\Delta S = 0.01 \cdot S$ arises because Equation 16 crosses the barrier in this case. Except for this case, the approximations computed with $\Delta S = 0.01 \cdot S$ are quite accurate but, having seen the two approximations, one might have preferred to use $\Delta S = 0.001 \cdot S$. Using Richardson extrapolation with an accuracy requirement of four decimal places would lead to the use of a stepsize near $0.001 \cdot S$ automatically.

Table 2.   Calculation of Down-and-Out Barrier Call Delta

Underlying price S	Using $\Delta S = 0.01 \cdot S$	Using $\Delta S = 0.001 \cdot S$	Richardson Extrapolation
1.625	0.990 869 897	1.227 141 513	1.227 143 902
1.650	1.223 891 389	1.224 112 086	1.224 114 317
1.675	1.217 820 478	1.218 017 249	1.218 019 237

Richardson extrapolation can be applied to any sensitivity that is approximated using the centered difference formula (Equation 16). The formulation that we have described here can also be applied to the difference formula that is commonly used to calculate gamma,

$$gamma \cong \frac{V(S + \Delta S) - 2V(S) + V(S - \Delta S)}{\Delta S^2} \qquad (21)$$

The process has to be modified slightly if it is to be used with one of the one-sided difference formulas, Equation 17 or Equation 18. The theory underlying Richardson extrapolation can be found in any basic book on numerical methods, for example, Mathews (1987).

APPLICATIONS

In the following sections we describe a number of different types of exotic options and their uses. In general, we have used the terminology of Rubinstein (1991b) and Fitzgerald (1993). Barrier options, average options, and currency-translated options seem to be most popular in practice, particularly as hedging instruments, and we give more detailed examples of the use of each of these types of options.

Packages or Hybrid Options

Rubinstein (1991b) defines a package as an option that is equivalent to a portfolio containing only standard European calls and possibly cash and the asset itself. For example, a European put can be expressed in this form, using put-call parity. Other examples of packages include collars, range forwards (also known as flexible forwards, cylinder options, option fences, minimax options, or forward bands), break forwards (also known as Boston options, forwards with optional exit, or cancellable forwards) and portfolio insurance. These options are described in detail in Rubinstein (1985) and Cox and Rubinstein (1985).

It is possible to construct a package that has an arbitrary piecewise linear payoff function. That is, these options can be used to tailor specific risk profiles. According to Fitzgerald (1993), hybrid options are typically American or pseudo-American (exercisable at particular times in the option lifetime) and often involve some sort of cap on total profit and/or loss.

Fitzgerald (1993) also describes time-dependent hybrid options, in which characteristics of the option, such as its strike price or exercise opportunities, are tailored to the needs of the investor and change over time. A typical application of such an option is to create a long-term insurance program at minimum cost.

A third type of hybrid option is described by Fitzgerald (1993) as a "complete investment instrument." These options combine some sort of capital guarantee with a geared investment in a specific asset such as a bond or a stock market index. GROI (guaranteed return on investment) notes are an example of this type of hybrid.

Forward Start Options

The purchaser of a forward start option will receive a regular call or put, which is at the money when issued, at some specified time in the future. Rubinstein (1991b) cites corporate incentive stock options as an example of forward start options. Further details can be found in Rubinstein (1991e).

Compound Options

A compound option is an option on an option: a call on a call, a call on a put, a put on a call, or a put on a put. As noted by Fitzgerald (1993), these options allow greater flexibility of timing in the market, for example, to hedge uncertain future cash flows. Additional references are found in Rubinstein (1991a), Geske (1979), and Nelken (1993).

Chooser Options

The holder of a regular chooser option will choose to receive either a call or a put at the choice date, where both the call and the put have the same strike price and time to expiry. In the case of a complex chooser option, the holder chooses between a call and a put that have different strike prices and times to expiry. Like the compound options, these chooser options are intended to allow flexibility in market timing. Fitzgerald (1993) notes that they give some of the advantages of straddle positions at a lower cost than a standard straddle.

Barrier Options

A barrier option has a payoff that depends on the final price of the underlying asset and whether or not the spot price of that asset has crossed some "barrier" price during the option lifetime. As indicated by Fitzgerald (1993), these options are intermediate between European and American options, since they exploit intermediate values of the underlying asset, but do not require the holder to make a decision. The term "barrier option" is used to denote a variety of option types, many of which are also known by different names.

1. *Lock Options*
   Fitzgerald (1993) describes lock options, in which the payoff amount is capped but the payoff is guaranteed if the cap is reached. These options typically pay at expiry. They reduce regret, where the option goes into the money then expires worthless, without costing as much as a lookback option (see below).

2. *Threshold Options and Ladder Options*
   Threshold options (Fitzgerald [1993]) are similar to lock options, but the option continues in effect after the threshold is reached and some specific return is · locked in. This formulation gives the possibility of additional profit without risking the return that has already been achieved.

   A ladder option has a number of thresholds, each locking in a higher return, generally with some ultimate cap on return. Ladder options are relatively common in the French market, often embedded in other structures. Kissane (1993) gives an example of such a structure. In 1991/92, Credit Foncier offered an equity-linked Eurobond issue, where the redemption of the eight-year zero was linked to the CAC-40 index. The ladder consisted of six thresholds rising from 125 percent of the initial value of the index to 250 percent in 25 percent intervals. Whenever the opening level of the CAC-40 reaches one of the thresholds, the gain is locked in.

3. *Trigger or Knock-In Options*
   A down-and-in option gives its holder a European option that comes into effect if the spot price falls below the barrier during the option lifetime. If the barrier is not reached, the down-and-in option expires, possibly paying a fixed rebate at expiry. Similarly, in an up-and-in option, a European option comes into effect if the spot price rises above the barrier during the option lifetime.

Both down-and-in puts and up-and-in calls are used as portfolio insurance, providing a reasonable measure of protection at a cheaper price than standard European or American options.

4. *Knock-Out Options*
The holder of a down-and-out option owns a European option that will expire immediately if the spot price falls below the barrier during the option lifetime. The option may pay a fixed rebate if the barrier is touched; otherwise it has the standard European payoff at expiry. Similarly, an up-and-out option expires immediately if the spot price rises above the barrier during the lifetime of the barrier option.

Like knock-in options, these options are useful in exploiting timing in the market and as portfolio insurance. According to Fitzgerald (1993), prior to the collapse of the Japanese stock market, up-and-out puts were often embedded in Nikkei-linked bond issues.

Since barrier options seem to be among the exotic types used most often in practice, we will describe their use in portfolio insurance in more detail. The following example shows how a down-and-out call could be used to hedge a currency transaction. Consider the U.S. company that will need to buy Deutsche marks in six months. To hedge exchange rate risk, the company could buy a European call option. Suppose that an option with the attributes shown in Table 3 could be purchased.

Table 3.   Currency Option Attributes

Attribute	Value
Spot exchange rate	0.5934
$U.S. risk-free rate	3.4%
DM rate	5%
Volatility	21%
Strike exchange	0.5934

An option to purchase 1 million DM would cost the company $U.S. 31,900. The cost of the corresponding down-and-out barrier call option will depend on where the barrier is set. With a barrier of 0.56 and no rebate, a down-and-out call on 1 million DM will cost $U.S. 21,900. If the exchange rate stays above the barrier over the next six months, the option will provide exactly the same protection as the European option at a reduced cost. If the rate falls below the barrier, the option expires immediately. The danger in this case is that the exchange rate then rises back above the strike price. The holder of the option would like to set the barrier as low as possible, but reducing the barrier level increases the price of the option, since it becomes less likely that the option will hit the barrier. With a barrier of 0.483 (or any lower barrier), the price of the down-and-out call would be $U.S. 31,900, the same as the European option. If the option holder believes that once the exchange rate falls to a certain level, it will stay at that level or at least below the strike price, then the down-and-out call is a reasonable approach to reduce the cost of the hedge.

Many references describe barrier options and their valuation, including Rubinstein (1991b), Rubinstein and Reiner (1991a), Cox and Rubinstein (1985), and Benson and Daniel (1991).

Binary Options

Unlike standard options, in which the payoff at expiry depends on the level of the underlying asset, binary options (also known as digital options) essentially pay either a fixed quantity or nothing, depending only on whether the spot price is above or below the strike. The simplest options of this type are path-independent. Examples of these options include cash-or-nothing options, which are also known as all-or-nothing options (Rubinstein [1991b], Rubinstein and Reiner [1991b], Hudson [1991]), asset-or-nothing options (Rubinstein [1991b], Cox and Rubinstein [1985]), gap options (Turnbull [1992]), and supershares (Hakansson [1976]). Rubinstein and Reiner (1991b) define 28 types of path-dependent binary options, with 44 different formulas (see also Rubinstein [1991b]).

Rubinstein (1991b) points out that cash-or-nothing and asset-or-nothing options can be combined to create arbitrary piecewise linear payoff patterns. Unlike packages, these payoff patterns can be discontinuous.

Lookback Options

A floating lookback option pays the difference between the spot price at expiry and the minimum (call) or maximum (put) price observed over the lifetime of the option, or some portion of it. In the Black-Scholes environment, it is assumed that the minimum or maximum is observed continuously; in practice, the minimum or maximum may be taken over discrete intervals. A fixed lookback (or look forward) option pays the difference between the strike price and the maximum (call) or minimum (put) price. These options reduce regret, since they are guaranteed to pay out if the option is in the money at any point in its lifetime. The cost for this guarantee makes lookback options more expensive than standard options. They can also be regarded as optimizing market timing—a call option gives the best timing when awaiting an upturn in the asset price while the put gives the best timing to enter the market on a downturn (Turnbull [1993]).

Variants of lookback options might take the minimum or maximum price over a discrete set of time points (e.g., weekly closing prices), or use some fraction (e.g. 90 percent) of the extreme value. Fitzgerald (1993) describes a range option, which is formed by combining calls and puts to obtain a payoff that depends on the difference between the maximum and minimum prices over a period. Such options represent a play on volatility, since they will pay off when extreme movements in the underlying asset price occur.

Mitsubishi Finance offered lookback call and put warrants on Japanese government bond futures in 1989.

Valuation formulas and further information can be found in Goldman, Sosin, and Gatto (1979), Garman (1989), and Conze and Viswanathan (1991), among others.

Asian or Average Options

Asian options are options whose value depends on the average price of the underlying over the lifetime (or some portion of the lifetime) of the option. In practice, arithmetic average options are of most interest; geometric average options arise mainly because they have closed-form solutions that can be used in pricing arithmetic average options. The average may be computed daily, monthly, or on any other discrete basis. Some pricing formulas assume that the average is computed continuously. Average price options pay the difference between the average price and a fixed strike price while average strike options pay the difference between the spot price at expiry and the average price.

Like barrier options, average options are among the exotics used most often in practice. They are typically cheaper than standard options; how much cheaper depends on the length of the averaging period. If the average is taken over a relatively short period near expiry, the option's price will be close to that of a standard European option, but the holder will be protected from fluctuations in the spot price (market squeeze) near expiry.

These options are often described as being useful in the commodities and foreign exchange markets, to hedge a series of known cash flows. An American aluminum company uses arithmetic average options to hedge its forward sales of aluminum. The company sells 15-month forward contracts on aluminum on a daily basis, to lock in a floor price for its production. However, the spot price in 15 months could be higher than the forward price and the company would like to profit from any such increase. To do so, it wishes to buy a call option to hedge each forward contract. The company could buy a European call option for each contract, each with a different strike price related to the forward price. Instead, it chooses to use an arithmetic average price option with the average computed over the last (fifteenth) month of the contract. Instead of buying roughly 20 different European options each month, the company buys 20 units of the average option, for a slightly lower cost. It resets its desired strike price on a monthly basis rather than daily.

Valuing arithmetic average options is difficult since the arithmetic average of a lognormally distributed random variable is not itself lognormally distributed. Monte Carlo methods, as described by Kemna and Vorst (1990) and approximate methods (Turnbull and Wakeman [1991], Levy [1992], Levy and Turnbull [1992]) are commonly used in valuation. Carverhill and Clewlow (1990) suggested another possible approach to pricing these options.

Exchange Options

The payoff of an exchange option has the form

$$V = max \, [0, S_2 - S_1] \qquad (22)$$

That is, the option pays off the difference between two assets—it is often described as a relative performance option. It can be interpreted as a call on asset 2 with a strike price equal to the price of asset 1, or as a put on asset 1 with strike price equal to the price of asset 2.

Fitzgerald (1993) describes a number of uses in the market: options on the relative outperformance of a stock against a stock market index, on two bond markets or on a yield curve spread (e.g., Treasury bond futures versus Treasury bill futures).

The term "exchange option" is sometimes used to include some of the options on two underlyings that we describe under the name "rainbow options" (see below). Further information can be found in Rubinstein (1991c) and Margrabe (1978).

Currency-Translated Options

Currency-translated options provide their holders with varying degrees of protection against adverse moves in exchange rates as well as equity prices. Like rainbow options (see below), these options are often used in asset allocation strategies.

Following Reiner (1992), we describe some of these options below, in order of increasing protection against exchange rate moves. All payoffs are expressed in terms of the domestic currency. We let r_E denote exchange rate, that is, the price in the domestic currency of one unit of the foreign currency. Prices in the foreign currency are indicated by a subscript F.

1. Foreign equity option struck in a foreign currency.
   This option provides no protection against moves in the exchange rate—it is a straightforward option in which the payoff is exchanged into the domestic currency. The payoff of a call option is

$$Call = r_E \cdot max \, [0, S_F - K_F] \tag{23}$$

2. Foreign equity option struck in domestic currency.
   This option allows the holder to hedge against the product of the foreign equity price and the exchange rate; hence, it provides some protection against moves in the exchange rate. The payoff of the call is

$$C = max \, [0, r_E \cdot S_F - K] \tag{24}$$

3. Fixed exchange rate foreign equity option.
   These options, also known as quanto options, hedge away all exchange rate risk by fixing the exchange rate as r_{FE}. Quanto options are traded over-the-counter and on the American Stock Exchange. Fitzgerald (1993) describes a "bi-currency protected size" option, which allows its holder to hedge away all adverse exchange rate effect, or to keep the effect if it is in the holder's favor.

   The basic quanto call option has payoff

$$Call = r_{FE} \cdot max \, [0, S_F - K_F] = max \, [0, r_{FE} \cdot S_F - K] \tag{25}$$

4. Equity-linked foreign exchange option.
   This option combines an equity forward with a currency option. It provides no protection against foreign equity exposure but places a floor or ceiling on exchange rate risk. The payoff of a call is

$$Call = S_F \cdot max \, [0, r_E - r_K] \tag{26}$$

where r_K is the strike exchange rate. Related options are discussed by Marcus and Modest (1986).

Like barrier and average options, currency-translated options are quite popular in practice and we give an example of their use. A Brazilian bank wanted to issue an option on the Bovespa index that would attract foreign investment. An option denominated in cruzeiros typically would be issued with a strike price that apparently sets the option far out of the money. In fact, the expectation that such an option would be close to the money at expiry is high, due to the high inflation rate in Brazil. This circumstance may not be clear to foreign investors, and an option denominated in U.S. dollars would probably be more attractive anyway. This led the bank to consider two currency-translated options, the foreign-domestic option (item 2 in the above list) and the quanto option (item 3 above).

A case study of a foreign-domestic call on the Bovespa index over a period of 133 days was made. At the start of the study, the option was defined by the values shown in Table 4.

Table 4.   Foreign-Domestic Option Attributes

Attribute	Value
Bovespa spot	9285 cruzeiros
Exchange rate	0.06277
Cruzeiro risk-free rate	460%
Bovespa volatility	58%
Strike price	$U.S. 582.81
$U.S. risk-free rate	4.1%
$U.S. volatility	1%
Correlation between Bovespa index and $U.S.	0

The price of the foreign-domestic call was $U.S. 84.80. At expiry, 133 days later, the spot price of the Bovespa index was 72,740 cruzeiros and the exchange rate was 0.01237. The option expired in the money, paying $U.S. 316.88.

A similar European option denominated in cruzeiros would be issued with a strike price of roughly 47,120 cruzeiros. Such an option would cost 1,506 cruzeiros and pay 25,620 cruzeiros; both amounts are close to the $U.S. amounts above, translated at the appropriate exchange rates. It is clear that an option issued with a strike price of 47,120 when the spot price of the underlying is 9,285 would not immediately appear to be an attractive investment alternative.

To price a quanto call option in the same circumstances, one needs to know the forward exchange rate. Using an interest rate parity argument and the values given in Table 4, the forward exchange rate in 133 days should be 0.01214. If this value is taken as the fixed exchange rate, the price of the quanto call is $U.S. 91.20, and the final payoff is $U.S. 300.29.

The Brazilian bank chose the foreign-domestic option to avoid the problem of setting the fixed exchange rate required by the quanto call. Since the exchange rate generally increases in the current Brazilian environment, it was felt that there was little need for the additional protection of the fixed exchange rate.

Rainbow or Multi-Asset Options

Rubinstein (1991b) describes multi-asset options as options on two or more underlying assets that cannot be valued as if they were options on a single asset (as, for example, was done by Margrabe [1978] to value exchange options). These options are closely tied to asset allocation procedures, as noted by Fitzgerald (1993).

The options in this class are mostly easily described by giving their payoff functions in the case of two underlying assets. Particular options include the following:

1. Best of two assets and cash (receive best option).

$$Payoff = max\ [S_1,\ S_2,\ K] \tag{27}$$

2. Worst of two assets and cash (receive worst option).

$$Payoff = min\ [S_1, S_2, K] \tag{28}$$

3. Option on the maximum of two risky assets and cash (best of option).

$$Call = max\ [0,\ max\ (S_1,\ S_2) - K] \tag{29}$$

4. Option on the minimum of two risky assets and cash (worst of option).

$$Call = max[0,\ min\ (S_1,\ S_2) - K] \tag{30}$$

5. *Spread options.*
   A spread option pays the difference between the outperformance of two assets and a fixed strike price. That is, a call has the payoff

$$Call = max\ [0, (S_2 - S_1) - K] \tag{31}$$

Bankers Trust International issued "Bond over Stock" warrants on the spread of a U.S. Treasury bond over the S&P 500 index in 1991. Mitsubishi Finance has offered a number of different spread warrants, including warrants on the spread between OAT and Bund futures, on the implied yield spread between U.S. Treasury long bond futures and Treasury bill futures and on the Deutsche mark/U.S. dollar three-month LIBOR interest differential.

A leading oil company has used an option on the spread between jet fuel (product) and gas oil prices to hedge the risk of the two prices diverging (*Financial Times* [1993]).

6. *Portfolio options.*
   The payoff of a portfolio option is

$$Call = max\ [0, (n_1 \cdot S_1 + n_2 \cdot S_2) - K] \tag{32}$$

where n_i is the number of units of the ith asset in the portfolio.

7. *Dual-strike options.*
A dual-strike call option has payoff

$$Call = max\,[0, S_1 - K_1, S_2 - K_2] \tag{33}$$

Further information can be found in Rubinstein (1991f), Stulz (1982), Johnson (1987), Boyle, Evnine, and Gibbs (1989), Boyle and Tse (1990), and Barrett, Moore, and Wilmott (1992).

Basket Options

A basket option is an option on a portfolio of instruments, often equities or currencies. It is typically cheaper to buy an option on a basket than options on the individual instruments, since the volatility of the basket will be dampened. These options can be useful in portfolio insurance. For example, in the wake of the European Exchange Rate Mechanism crisis, basket options have become a popular way to hedge a particular currency against a group of European currencies (*Financial Times* [1993]). These options are described by Gentle (1993) and Dembo and Patel (1990).

Structured Products

In many cases, exotic options occur as part of structured products, as described by Kissane (1993). For example, equity-indexed bond products have involved look forward, lookback, barrier, average, and spread options, as well as standard options.

Some examples of these structured products that have been offered in practice include the following:

1. A family of Yen Floating Rate Nikkei-Linked Notes were issued by Unibank (Denmark) in 1990. These notes paid off an amount dependent on the Nikkei Stock Average, with a cap on the payoff.

2. Societe Generale has offered capped lookback warrants with ladders every centime.

3. In 1989, Skandia offered a bond with performance linked to the FT-SE 100 index. The bond guaranteed a minimum return and offered a geared return on the index.

4. In 1992, Caisse des Depots et Consignations offered an eight-year zero-coupon bond with redemption at par plus the sum of the annual performances of the CAC-40 stock index. The strike price is reset each year and annual performance is capped at 35 percent.

5. Falloon (1993) describes accrual notes and swaps with embedded digital options that generate either a specified payout or zero over a series of time intervals.

ACKNOWLEDGMENTS

The second author wishes to thank Prof. P. Keast, Dalhousie University, Halifax, NS, for helpful advice on multidimensional integration and for pointing out the existence of an adaptive multidimensional quadrature method.

REFERENCES

Abramowitz, M., and I. Stegun. *Handbook of Mathematical Functions.* New York: Dover Publications, 1972.

Barone-Adesi, G., and R. Whaley. "Efficient Analytic Approximation of American Option Values." *J. Finance* 42, No. 2 (1987), 301–320.

Barrett, J., G. Moore, and P. Wilmott. "Inelegant Efficiency." *Risk Magazine* 5, No. 9 (Oct. 1992), 82–83.

Benson, R., and N. Daniel. "Up, Over and Out." *Risk Magazine* 4, No. 6 (June 1991), 17–19.

Berntsen, J., T. Espelid, and A.C. Genz. "Algorithm 698: DCUHRE—An Adaptive Multidimensional Integration Routine for a Vector of Integrals." *ACM Trans Math Software* 17 (1991), 452–456.

Boyle, P. "A Lattice Framework for Option Pricing With Two State Variables." *J. Financial and Quantitative Analysis* 23 (1988), 1–12.

Boyle, P., J. Evnine, and S. Gibbs. "Numerical Evaluation of Multivariate Contingent Claims." *Review of Financial Studies* 2 (1988), 241–250.

Boyle, P., and Y.K. Tse. "An Algorithm for Computing Values of Options on the Maximum or Minimum of Several Assets." *J. Financial and Quantitative Analysis* 25 (1990), 215–227.

Brennan, M., and E. Schwartz. "Finite Difference Methods and Jump Processes Arising in the Pricing of Contingent Claims: A Synthesis." *J. Financial and Quantitative Analysis* 13 (1978), 462–474.

Carverhill, A., and L. Clewlow. "Flexible Convolution." *Risk Magazine,* 3, No. 4 (Apr. 1990), 25–29.

Cody, W.J. "Rational Chebyshev Approximations for the Error Function." *Math. Comp.* 23 (1969), 631–638.

Conze, A., and Viswanathan. "Path Dependent Options: The Case of Lookback Options." *J. Finance* 46 (1991), No. 5, 1893–1907.

Courtadon, G. (1990). "An Introduction to Numerical Methods in Option Pricing." In *Financial Options: From Theory to Practice,* S. Figlewski, W. Silber, and M. Subrahmanyam, eds., Irwin, 1990, 538–573.

Cox, J., S. Ross, and M. Rubinstein. "Option Pricing: A Simplified Approach." *J. Financial Economics* 7 (1979), 229–263.

Cox, J., and M. Rubinstein. *Options Markets.* Englewood Cliffs, N.J.: Prentice-Hall, 1985.

Dembo, R., and P. Patel. "Protective Basket." *Risk Magazine* 3, No. 2 (Feb 1990), 25–28.

Dewynne, J., and P. Wilmott. "Partial to the Exotic." *Risk Magazine* 6, No. 3 (Mar. 1993), 38–46.

Drezner, Z. "Computation of the Bivariate Normal Integral." *Math. Comp.* 32 (1978), 277–279.

Falloon, W. "Fairway to Heaven." *Risk Magazine* 6, No. 12 (Dec. 1993), 21–27.

Financial Times. "Derivatives, A Financial Times Survey." Wed., Oct. 20, 1993.

Fitzgerald, M.D. "A Taxonomy of Exotics." *Proceedings of the Advanced Exotic Options Course, Euromoney Training,* London, Feb. 1993.

Garman, M. "Recollection in Tranquility." *Risk Magazine* 2, No. 3 (Mar. 1989), 16–19.

Gentle, D. "Basket Weaving." *Risk Magazine* 6, No. 6 (June 1993), 51–52.

Geske, R. "The Valuation of Compound Options." *J. Financial Economics* 7 (1979), 63–81.

Goldman, B., H. Sosin, and M. Gatto. "Path Dependent Options: Buy at the Low, Sell at the High." *J. Finance* 34 (1979), No. 5, 1111–1127.

Hakansson, N. "The Purchasing Power Fund: A New Kind of Financial Intermediary." *Financial Analysts Journal,* Nov./Dec. 1976.

Haselgrove, C. "A Method for Numerical Integration." *Mathematics of Computation* 15 (1961), 323–337.

Hudson, M. "The Value in Going Out." *Risk Magazine* 4, No. 3 (Mar. 1991), 29–33.

Hull, J. *Options, Futures and Other Derivative Securities,* 2d ed. Englewood Cliffs, N.J.: Prentice-Hall, 1993.

Hull, J., and A. White. "Valuing Derivative Securities Using the Explicit Finite Difference Method." *J. Financial and Quantitative Analysis* 25 (1990), 87–100.

Johnson, H. "Options on the Maximum or the Minimum of Several Assets." *J. Financial and Quantitative Analysis* 22 (1987), 227–283.

Kahaner, D., C. Moler, and S. Nash, S. *Numerical Methods and Software.* Englewood Cliffs, N.J.: Prentice-Hall, 1989.

Kemna, A.G.Z., and A.C.F. Vorst, A.C.F. "A Pricing Method for Options Based on Average Asset Values." *J. Banking and Finance* 14 (1990), 113–129.

Kissane, D. "Using Exotics in Structured Products." *Proceedings of the Advanced Exotic Options Course, Euromoney Training,* London, Feb. 1993.

Levy, E. "Pricing European Average Rate Currency Options." *J. International Money and Finance* 11 (1992), 474–491.

Levy, E., and S. Turnbull. "Average Intelligence." *Risk Magazine* 5, No. 2 (Feb. 1992), 53–59.

Marcus, A., and D. Modest. "The Valuation of a Random Number of Put Options: An Application to Agricultural Price Supports." *J. Financial and Quantitative Analysis* 21 (1986), 73–86.

Margrabe, W. "The Value of an Option to Exchange One Asset for Another." *J. Finance* 33 (1978), No. 1, 177–186.

Mathews, J. *Numerical Methods for Computer Science, Engineering and Mathematics.* Englewood Cliff, N.J.: Prentice-Hall, 1987.

Nelken, I. "Square deals." *Risk Magazine* 6, No. 4 (Apr. 1993), 56–59.

Reiner, E. "Quanto Mechanics." *Risk Magazine* 5, No. 3 (Mar. 1992), 59–63.

Risk Magazine. From Black-Scholes to Black Holes (a collection of *Risk Magazine* articles). London: *Risk Magazine,* 1992.

Rubinstein, M. "Alternative Paths to Portfolio Insurance." *Financial Analysts Journal,* July/August 1985.

Rubinstein, M. "Double Trouble." *Risk Magazine* 5 (1991), No. 1 (Dec. 91/Jan. 92), 73.

Rubinstein, M. "Exotic Options." Finance Working Paper No. 220 (1991), Walter A. Haas School of Business, University of California at Berkeley, Berkeley, CA.

Rubinstein, M. "One for Another." *Risk Magazine* 4 (1991), No. 7 (Jul/Aug 91), 30–32.

Rubinstein, M. "Options for the Undecided." *Risk Magazine* 4, No. 4 (Apr. 1991).

Rubinstein, M. "Pay Now, Choose Later." *Risk Magazine* 4, No. 4 (Apr. 1991).

Rubinstein, M. "Somewhere Over the Rainbow." *Risk Magazine* 4, No 10 (Nov. 1991), 63–66.

Rubinstein, M., and E. Reiner. "Breaking Down the Barriers." *Risk Magazine* 4, No. 8 (Sep. 1991), 28–35.

Rubinstein, M., and E. Reiner, "Unscrambling the Binary Code." *Risk Magazine* 4, No 9 (Oct. 1991), 75–83.

Stulz, R. "Options on the Minimum or the Maximum of Two Risky Assets." *J. Financial Economics* 10 (1982), 161–185.

Turnbull, S. "The Price Is Right." *Risk Magazine* 5, No 4 (Apr. 1991), 56–57.

Turnbull, S. "Valuing and Hedging Path-Dependent Options." *Proceedings of the Advanced Exotic Options Course, Euromoney Training,* London, Feb. 1993.

Turnbull, S.M., and L.M. Wakeman, "A Quick Algorithm for Pricing European Average Options." *J. Financial and Quantitative Analysis* 26 (1991), 377–389.

Wilmott, P., J. Dewynne, and S. Howison. *Option Pricing: Mathematical Models and Computation.* Oxford, England: Oxford Financial Press, 1993.

CHAPTER 20

Option's Risk Measurement Units

Robert M. Mark
Partner
Coopers & Lybrand

INTRODUCTION

Risks for option products are model-dependent and can be calculated utilizing a Risk Measurement Unit (RMU) approach. The approach presented here extends option risk management technology beyond the flawed traditional, partial derivative risk-factor-type sensitivity controls. RMUs provide a more accurate and comprehensible interpretation of option risk recognizable within a Dollars-at-Risk (DAR) framework.

REVIEW OF THE RMU CONCEPT

The basic RMU concept expresses a single transaction's risk in terms of an Instrument-level Risk Measurement Unit (IRMU) and adds up risk across a portfolio of transactions to compute a portfolio RMU. The rationale behind an RMU-based DAR system is straightforward and consistent with Modern Portfolio Theory (MPT). One RMU (set at, say $1,000) is the basic measure of risk such that actual losses will exceed the number of RMUs a preset percentage of the time (set at, say, on only one day out of 40). For example, if a position's DAR equals 10 RMUs then only 2.5 per cent of the time will the losses exceed $10,000.

The RMU and MPT analytics are fully explained in other published articles. Examples associated with a portfolio of three currencies purchased or sold against the U.S. dollar explicitly demonstrate the features of the RMU system. Example one consists of a portfolio of $5M long AUD$, $10M short the SFr and $5M long D-Mark. Example two assumes the $10M short SFr position in example one is closed due to a stop loss order placed in a passed book. Example three deals solely with a $10M SFr/D-mark cross. Assume that two times the one-day rate change volatility (two standard deviations) of AUD$ equals to 1.87 per cent. Similarly, two times the volatility of SFr and D-mark equals 1.56 and 1.54 percent, respectively. The correlation between SFr and D-Mark equals .97. Similarly, the correlation between D-mark and AUD$ equals .08, and the correlation between AUD$ and SFr equals .06.

In example one, the IRMUs for the AUD$ position is computed by multiplying 1.87 percent times $5M, which equals $93,500 or 93.5 RMUs. Similarly, the IRMUs for SFr and D-Mark are respectively 1.56 percent × $10M and 1.54 percent × $5M. The gross RMU is simply the sum of the IRMUs (326.5 equals 93.5 plus 156 plus 77). The position DAR is 122.9 RMUs. The DAR computation is consistent with MPT and is based on an RMU portfolio volatility algorithm that allows offsets between currencies based on their correlation.

The $10M gross position in example two is less than the $20M in example one. Nevertheless, the DAR in example two (125.8 RMUs) is higher than that in example one (122.9 RMUs). Consider next the SFr/D-Mark cross in example three. The gross position in example three ($20M) is higher than that in example two ($10M) yet the DAR in example three (44 RMUs) is lower. The DAR in example two (125.8 RMUs) is about the same as if we did a cross between AUD$ and D-mark or were short both AUD$ and D-Mark. Observe that neither gross nor net notional amount by itself is a good indicator of market risk.

The RMU system is easily understood at the trader level without the need for significant analytical insight or complex algorithms. RMUs cut across all levels of the organization and can be summarized vertically or horizontally to provide total portfolio risk. The RMU approach clearly measures the DAR at risk, whereas other commonly used approaches, such as risk equivalents, fail to adequately measure true risk. Finally, the RMU system can be used to construct optimal hedges.

REVIEW OF OPTION BASICS

It is well known that the major determinants of an option's price include the underlying price, volatility, time to expiration, discount rate, and strike price. This is clearly influenced by the type of option (i.e., American or European).

The major option price sensitivities are typically calculated through key risk-factor measures derived from first and second partial derivatives of the appropriate option pricing model. The standard partials are delta, gamma, vega, theta, rho, and kappa. Delta is the change in value of the option (Δo) divided by the change in the underlying (Δu). Gamma is the change in delta ($\Delta delta$) divided by the change in the underlying. Gamma ($\Delta delta/\Delta u$) is normally expressed in terms of the second partial derivative with respect to the underlying price. An analogy with physics is often drawn ... if delta is equated to volatility then gamma can be equated to acceleration. Vega is the Δo divided by the change in volatility (Δv). Theta, rho, and kappa are the Δo due respectively to the change in time ($\Delta o/\Delta t$), change in risk-free rate ($\Delta o/\Delta r$), and change in strike ($\Delta o/\Delta k$). The utility of these standard measures depends strongly on selecting the appropriate model from which the partials are derived.

MODEL RISK

It is self-evident that in order to properly compute the RMU of an option one must first have an appropriate model to evaluate an option's price. The literature is filled with increasingly sophisticated and robust option pricing models that allow one to introduce more complex option products (e.g., lookback options). Further, certain models allow one to consider sensitivities (e.g., transaction costs) ignored in the early models.

Option models range from the classic Black-Scholes model (for equity no dividend) to modified versions of Black-Scholes. A separate Black model is used for futures. Further, duration-adjusted volatility models force volatility to zero in order to capture a bonds price convergence to par (the "pull-to-par" effect). Options on Treasury bonds need to incorporate the cost of financing such as the repo rate. There is an increasing degree of complexity as one moves from options on short-term futures to options on note/bond futures with their futures cheapest-to-deliver feature. A binomial model is typically used to adjust for American-style options. We also have a variety of one-factor (advanced fixed income) as well as two-factor (more advanced fixed income) models, and so on.

The selection of the appropriate option model is clearly an important first step in properly measuring risk. Simple bond option models are often appropriate where the time to expiration of the option divided by the maturity of the bond is a small fraction. The closer the fraction is to zero the more one can use modified Blacks-Scholes to price a bond option. For example, the value of a six month American-style call option (C) on a five-year bond (B) might typically reveal the pattern shown in Table 1. The value of a three-year American call option (C) on a five-year bond (B) would typically show the pattern outlined in Table 2.

Table 1.   One to Ten Ratio

	6-Month Option		
Bond Price (B)	95	100	105
Two-Factor Model (C)	.82	2.58	5.72
Duration Adjusted (C)	.90	2.55	5.72
Black-Scholes (C)	.90	2.70	5.82

Table 2.   Six to Ten Ratio

	3-Year Option		
Two-Factor Model (C)	2.48	4.36	7.10
Duration Adjusted (C)	2.39	4.33	7.07
Black-Scholes (C)	3.63	5.65	8.27
Ratios:			
Two-Factor/Black-Scholes	.68	.77	.86
Duration Adj./Black-Scholes	.66	.77	.85

The difference between an American- and a European-style option's price is illustrated in Exhibit 1. If one utilizes the Black model to price European-style Eurodollar futures, the percentage difference is minor for all but deep in-the-money

---

Exhibit 1.   Percentage of Price Difference (A-E)/E

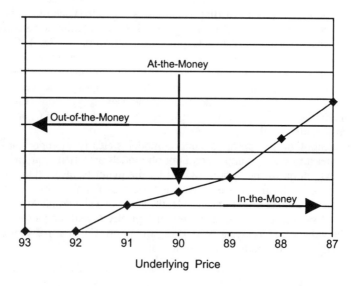

---

options. For example, the at-the-money Eurodollar put option value associated with an implied volatility of 15 percent, a 10 percent risk-free rate, a 90 strike, and one year to expiration is 54.1 ticks for a European-style option and 55.7 ticks for an American-style option. If the future price moves from 90 to 87, then the European-style option is worth 274 ticks, whereas the American-style option is worth 300 ticks.

To avoid model risk, one also needs to be aware of market conventions. For example, if options on futures are based on a payment up-front, such as an IMM-type option, then one needs to plug a risk-free rate into the Black model. If the payment occurs at exercise time, such as with a LIFFE-type option, then the risk-free rate in the Black model is set to zero. Comparison of LIFFE and IMM options for at-the-money options is shown in Table 3. The example makes the assumption that the risk-free rate equals 100 minus the underlying futures price.

Table 3.   Comparison of LIFFE and IMM Options

Risk-Free Rate %	Time to Expiration (Months)	LIFFE	IMM
10	12	59.8	54.1
10	6	42.5	40.4
5	12	29.9	28.4
5	6	21.2	20.7

Observe, in our example, that the call value equals the put value for at-the-money options. Observe also that the European IMM at-the-money put option in the first row of Table 3 is the same value (i.e., 54.1) as referenced earlier in creating Exhibit 1.

Certain option pricing models, such as the average price option or lookback option, change the classic interpretation of the standard partial derivatives. The average price option (sometimes called the Asian option) provides the holder with a tailor-made payoff, which depends on the average value of the underlying. The call option payoff is such that the call equals the max $(O, U_A - k)$ and the put payoff equals max $(0, k - U_A)$ where U_A is the arithmetic average of the underlying asset prices experienced over some portion , if not all, of the life of the option and k is the option strike price of the option. The average process compresses the vega or volatility-based distribution of terminal prices and therefore the premiums are cheaper than the standard option pricing equivalent.

The lookback option, also referred to as the "no regret" option, allows the holder to buy at the low or to sell at the high. This model requires one to compute kappa risk. Kappa for a lookback option is a meaningful risk. The call equals the max $(O, U_E - \text{MIN} \{U_N\})$ and the put equals max $(O, \max \{U_N\} - U_E)$, where U_N covers all of the underlying asset's prices experienced over the life of the option and U_E represents the underlying asset price at the expiration of the option. The key is the adjustment to the strike. At expiration the holder always receives the most favorable underlying asset value ever experienced. Further, lookbacks never get out-of-the-money since the strike is continually reset to the lowest value ever achieved.

Clearly, the choice of a model matters in pricing. There is a need to closely examine model assumptions versus market reality. Ultimately, the degree of complexity necessary will drive model selection. Somewhere between simple and complex is the appropriate model. In order to make meaningful applications of an option's partials (i.e., delta, gamma, . . .) one needs to ensure that the option model is appropriate for the option being offered. In short, not one model fits all.

MANAGING RISK PARAMETERS SIMULTANEOUSLY

In order to meaningfully measure option pricing risk one needs to translate option sensitivities into RMUs. One also needs to simultaneously manage all the option pricing sensitivities for large movements in the parameters that drive option price value.

The key is to manage these factors simultaneously, as conceptually illustrated in Exhibit 2 for sufficiently large movements. The RMU approach defines "large" as a movement beyond two standard deviations.

The evolution toward an option's RMU approach can be depicted as in Exhibit 3. This parallels the evolutionary path from nominal to RMUs as described earlier.

The option's RMU evolutionary path indicates that a system based on delta equivalents is not good enough. One needs more information than delta. We turn to the futures markets to demonstrate the dangers of a delta neutral position. The RMU approach determines the degree to which one's position has negative gamma. Our fourth example (Table 4) looks at a call option on the first Eurodollar future contract. Assume the strike price is 96, a 3 7/8 percent risk-free rate, an implied volatility equal to 19.3 percent, and 27 days to expiration. Plugging the underlying futures price into

---

Exhibit 2.   Simultaneous Management of Risk Parameters

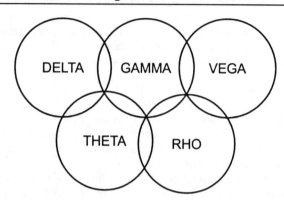

---

the Black model reveals a .74 delta. If one writes one hundred option contracts with an original 17 tick price and the new price (rates up) goes to 8 ticks then the gain is $22,500 (a 9 tick gain × $25 per tick × 100 contracts). Observe that the implied volatility was held constant at 19.3 percent. Similarly, if one originally purchased 74 futures contracts at 96.14 and the new price declines to 96.00, then one would lose $25,900 (equal to 14 × $25 × 74). Observe that a delta neutral hedge "doesn't do it" since the delta neutral position would lose $3,400. We will later show how RMUs will quantify the amount of risk taken for this illustrative delta neutral position.

Exhibit 3.   Option Risk Measurement Evolution

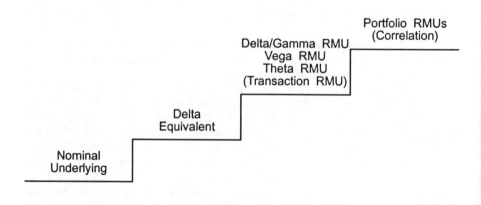

Table 4.   Example 4: 1st Contract

	Position	Original Price	New Price (Rates Up)	Change
Option	−100	17	8	22500
Future	74	96.14	96.00	(25900)
	Delta = .74	Strike = 96.0	–	(3400)
	Position Delta = 0	Vol = 19.3%	Vol = 19.3	

One can illustrate the dangers of both negative gamma and vega through analyzing options on the second futures contract. Assume the original option price is 15 based on an implied volatility equal to 21.6 percent, a 3 15/16 percent risk-free rate, a 96 strike, 118 days to expiration, and the future at 95.90. If one writes one hundred option contracts, with a .39 delta, then buying 39 futures leads to a zero position delta. If the futures price declines to 95.65 and the implied volatility rises to 22.4 percent then the option price would decline to 8. The written option is up $17,500 and the futures position is down $24,375.

Table 5.   Example 5: 2nd Contract

	Position	Original Price	New Price (Rates Up)	Change
Option	−100	15	8	17500
Future	39	95.90	95.65	(24375)
	Delta = .39	Strike = 96.0	–	(6875)
	Position Delta = 0	Vol = 21.6%	Vol = 22.4%	

As illustrated in Exhibit 4, one often observes that the implied volatility rises as the underlying price moves away from the strike. This phenomenon is sometimes called the "smile effect." One would generally find that the longer the time to expiration of the option the less pronounced the smile effect. The implied volatility pattern can be quite complicated as the underlying price moves away from the strike. For example, sometimes the pattern looks more like a smirk than a smile. To illustrate, recall that the option on the second future contract with a strike of 96 had an implied volatility of 21.6 percent. If the price of the second contract were to decline to say 95.65 then its implied volatility would rise to 22.4 percent.

Exhibit 4.   Effect of Price on Implied Volatility

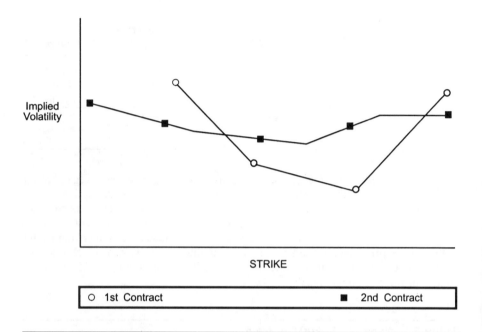

RMUs FOR OPTIONS

The general idea is to analyze delta/gamma, vega, and theta risk simultaneously and then add these risks together by analytically finding an internally consistent worst case scenario. The necessary analytics are beyond the scope of this chapter but the concepts embedded in the analytics will be intuitively explained. One should think of an option's RMU in terms of a set of analytics that efficiently finds the worst case risk. Computing the delta/gamma RMU requires one to analytically find an internally consistent worst case scenario. In other words, one should think of an option's RMU in terms of a set of analytics that efficiently finds the worst case risk.

In order to compute the delta/gamma RMU requires one to analytically couple together several scenarios. One can intuitively think of the analytics as testing a single option's profitability (or a portfolio of options) at multiple separate states to formulate its delta/gamma risk. The delta/gamma risk would be computed for each option within a prespecified section or maturity bucket of the yield curve. One would next add the delta/gamma risk for each maturity bucket, using the underlying change in yield correlations between buckets. Similarly, in order to add the vega RMU to the delta/gamma RMU, one would analytically test profitability with a combination of implied volatility and underlying positions. If one wanted to compile the vega risk alone then one would add up individual bucket vega risks by correlation between the implied volatilities. Theta requires one to age the portfolio by one business day and calculate the change in the value of the portfolio.

Let's take an illustrative example to demonstrate intuitively how the total options' RMU can be determined by analytically arriving at an internally consistent worst case scenario. Assume a purchased puts delta/gamma for a plus two standard deviation movement result in 100 RMUs. Further, assume the upward movement is also accompanied by a simultaneous decline in volatility. If one had solely purchased a put, then the vega risk would result in, say, an incremental risk of 50 RMUs. The incremental 50 RMUs caused by a simultaneous decline in volatility is arrived at by simply computing the incremental effect on the option value for a change in the implied volatility at the plus two standard deviation point.

The key word is "incremental," since the 50 RMU vega risk would be added to the 100 delta/gamma RMU risks, which assumed a constant implied volatility. In practice, one would need to compute the joint probability of the combined delta/gamma and vega worst case risks to maintain a DAR at the 2.5 percent level. The joint probability can be constructed via well-defined robust analytical techniques or through a Monte Carlo simulation. As shown in the shaded region of Table 6, adding the 10 RMU theta risk to the 150 RMUs would result in a total risk of 160 RMUs. The standard partial derivative approach is flawed, since it does not account for the interaction between the delta/gamma, vega, and the theta factor sensitivities.

Table 6.   Components of an Option RMU

Risk Measures		Underlying		
		+ 2 StD	Unchanged	–2 StD
Delta/Gamma		–100	0	+100
Vega	| – 2 Std	–50	–30	–75
	|Unchanged	0	0	0
	| + 2 std	+50	+30	+75
Theta		–10	–10	–10
Total RMU		–160	–40	15
RMU of Position is 160 RMUs (= MIN (–160, –40, 15)				

Let's next illustrate how one calculates RMUs through extending this intuition to our two specific examples. As pointed out above, a call option on the nearby future (the first contract) is worth 17 ticks, or $425, per contract (the put is worth only 3 ticks). As also pointed out above, the out-of-the-money call on the next nearby (the second contract) is worth 15 ticks (the put is worth 25 ticks). For illustrative purposes, assume that we ignore the smile effect and that the standard deviation of the underlying Eurodollar future is ten basis points and the standard deviation of implied volatility is 1 percent. In practice, one would consider the smile and smirk implied volatility effects.

Recall that in Example 4 we were short one hundred June 96 calls and long 74 futures contracts. Assuming that the implied volatility is held constant at 19.3 percent, observe that a downward (rates up) two standard deviation move in the underlying would lead to a 5.75 option price. Accordingly, the gain for the call writer would equal $28,125. Similarly, an upward two standard deviation move in the underlying leads to a 34.3 option price with a loss equal to $43,250. A downward two standard deviation move in the futures price to 95.94 (= 96.14 − 0.20) would result in a $37,000 (= 20 × 25 × 74) loss, whereas an upward two standard deviation change to 96.34 (= 96.14 + 0.20) would provide a gain of $37,000. Accordingly, the worst case delta/gamma risk arising from a 20 bp decline in the futures price is $8,875 (= 37,000 − 28,125). Observe that a 20 bp increase in the futures price would result in a $6,250 combined position loss, which is less than the $8,875 loss.

Next, in order to compute the vega risk, assume one holds the underlying futures price constant at 96.14. The option's writer gets hurt from a rise in the implied volatility. Observe that the call price would decline from 17 to 16.3 due to a two standard deviation decline in the implied volatility. This decline leads to a $1,750 (= 0.7 × 25 × 100) gain for the option's writer. Conversely, the call price resulting from an upward two standard deviation rise in the implied volatility equals 17.7 with a loss equal to $1,750. Accordingly, the vega risk is $1,750. In order to compute theta risk, assume the underlying futures price and options volatility are held constant. Accordingly, observe that the call price changes from 17 to 16.9 one day later. The position gains $250 and therefore the theta RMU equals 0.

Example 6 assumes a straddle is created through a simultaneous purchase long of one hundred 96 calls and long one hundred 96 puts on the second futures contract whose price is 95.90. Assuming one holds the volatility constant, if the price for the call moved from 15 to 8.6 based on a downward two standard deviation move, then the call one would lose $16,000. An upward two standard deviation move would lead to a 24.4 call price with a $23,500 gain. Similarly, if the futures price declined two standard deviations then the put whose value is 25 would rise to 38.2 for a $33,000 gain. Conversely, if the futures price rises two standard deviations then the put would fall to 14.5 for $26,250 loss. The net is equal to a $17,000 (= 33,000 − 16,000) gain for a downward 20 bp move and a loss of $2,750 (= 26,250 − 23,500) for an upward 20 bp move. Accordingly, the delta/gamma risk equals $2,750. Observe in Table 7 that the delta/gamma risk for the downward move is zero, since the combined two option portfolio earned money.

The buyer of an option gets hurt from a decline in the implied volatility. The call vega is computed by observing that the price changes from 15 to 13.2 for a downward two standard deviation move in volatility with a loss equal to $4,500 (1.8 × 25 × 100). Observe that an upward two standard deviation move in volatility would push the call value to 16.8 with gain equal to $4,500. Similarly, puts valued at 25 would move to 23.1 for downward two standard deviation move in volatility with a vega RMU or loss equal to $4,750. Observe that an upward two standard deviation change in volatility would move the puts to 26.7 with a gain equal to $4,250. Analogous to gamma, one can also observe the Δvega/Δ to assist in a complete risk analysis. The respective net equals a loss of $9,250 (4,500 + 4,750) and a gain of $8,750. The call theta is gotten from taking the original price of 15 and observing that one day later its value equals 14.90 with a $250 loss. The puts valued at 25 one day later would equal 24.8 with a $250 loss of $500. Accordingly, the theta risk equals for no change in the underlying to $750.

Observe in Table 7 that the RMU calculation for Example 4 would be associated with a negative two standard deviation move in the underlying. The $8,875 delta/gamma risk, $2,000 vega risk and 0 theta risk are shown in Column 1. In summary, the worst case RMU assumes the futures price declines from 96.14 to 95.94 to 20 bp (two standard deviations) and the implied volatility rises 2 percent. Accordingly, the portfolio RMU equals 10.9 RMUs. If one wanted to be less conservative then one could let the $250 gain due to theta reduce the worst case risk to 10.6 RMVs. In Example 6, the RMU is 10 since the RMUs are 8, 10, and 3 for respective changes of minus two, zero, and plus two standard deviations.

Also observe in Example 4, Table 7, that the option writer gets hurt less on vega as we move from in-the-money (–$500) through at-the-money (–$1,750) to out-of-the-money (–$2,000). The $2,000 vega-related loss is the incremental amount over the delta/gamma loss arising from a minus two standard deviation move in the underlying. Further observe in Example 6 that the worst case vega risk occurs where there is no change in the underlying. The put for Example 6 is slightly in-the-money with a delta equal to .6 and the call is slightly out-of-the-money. A key point to note is that one does not sum the individual worst case risk. The worst delta/gamma risk (–$2,750) occurs when the market moves up two standard deviations. The worst vega and theta occurs when there is no change in the underlying. The portfolio RMU is set at 10 RMUs which is different from summing the worst case (i.e., $12,750 equals $2,750 plus $9,250 plus $750) for each category of risk. In other words, the total RMU is not the sum of the individual delta/gamma plus vega and theta RMUs, since their individual values were determined while holding the others constant.

Table 7.   Portfolio RMU

Ex:	RMU	–2 StD. Devs.	No Change	+ 2 StD. Devs.
4	Delta/Gamma	–8875	0	–6250
	Vega	–2000	–1750	–500
	Theta	0	0	0
	Portfolio	10.9 (= –10875)	1.8 (= –1750)	6.6 (= –6750)
6	Delta/Gamma	0	0	–2750
	Vega	–7500	–9250	0
	Theta	–500	–750	–250
	Portfolio	8 (= 8000)	10 (= –10000)	3 (= –3000)

CONCLUSION

This report provides an analytical approach on how to evaluate the RMU risk of an option portfolio. The option RMU approach provides an explicit DAR measure. The approach works for any option pricing model. Further, the RMU approach does not suffer from the failure of the standard risk-factor sensitivity approaches to supply anything more than the classic partial derivative risk measures, which at best, can be useful only for small movements in the underlying market variable.

CHAPTER 21

Derivatives in Currency Management: Theory and Practice

Charles J. Freifeld
Vice President
Senior Quantitative Analyst
The Boston Company

INTRODUCTION

Institutional investors diversify their investment portfolios to raise returns and lower risk. Domestic investors have therefore allocated increasing portions of their portfolios to foreign stock and bond markets over the last 20 years. Domestic corporations engaged in international trade often accumulate large cash positions in foreign currencies. The growing liquidity of global markets has further encouraged increased international exposure.

Although the currency markets are the most liquid markets in the world, relatively little institutional money has been assigned to currency management strategies. This is unfortunate for two reasons: currency price volatility can have a substantial effect on the net performance of portfolios of foreign stocks, bonds, and cash; and the returns from currency management are uncorrelated with those from traditional investment classes.

This chapter presents the results of work done during the past 15 years on the theory and practice of currency management. It begins by placing currency investment in context by describing the evolution of modern investment management.[1] It then shows how the derivatives markets allow the institutional investor to capture the value

---

1 There is a large body of literature on the theory and practice of modern investment management. The work done by F. Black [3], [5], T. Cover [6], S. Taylor [12] and E. Thorp [14], [15], confirms our own research results, and was used by the author in designing the portfolio management system described in this chapter.

added by a manager's strategy without having to adjust the portfolio's capital allocation. This in turn creates the ability to design portfolios for maximum efficiency, and
the demand for more flexible investment strategies.

Next, currency hedging is examined, and is given a precise statement of its
purpose. Turning to the practice of hedging, several hedging strategies are compared
in the contexts of foreign cash, bond, and stock portfolios, and we show how to
construct a dynamic currency hedging system that can reduce the cost of hedging the
currency exposure of stocks, bonds, and cash to zero. The section on hedging is closed
by addressing the issue of choosing a performance benchmark.

Finally, currency management as a separate investment category is examined.
It is a valuable addition to institutional portfolios for two primary reasons: (1) currency
management can generate returns of over 20 percent annually, with risk levels
comparable to those of traditional investment categories; and (2) currency management returns are uncorrelated with returns from the investments usually held in
institutional portfolios. Once again, the section is closed with a discussion of performance benchmarks.

The chapter is concluded with two appendices whose contents provide the bases
for much of what is described in this chapter. The first delineates the fundamental
relationship between forward currency exchange rates and interest rate differentials,
known as "covered interest rate parity," and the second outlines the methodology we
use for constructing our currency portfolio management system.

BACKGROUND

The goal of investment management is to maximize the compounded rate of growth
of capital (the "geometric"[2] rate of return) over the long run. In practice, uncertainties
in forecasts, discontinuities in price movements, and modeling difficulties lead investors to focus on maximizing the compounded return of their portfolios without
exceeding acceptable risk levels.

Before the advent of Modern Portfolio Theory, investors generally avoided the
variance (risk) in investment returns by focusing on markets where returns were as
certain as possible. Funds were primarily invested in the fixed-income markets.
Modern Portfolio Theory (H. Markowitz, [9], W. Sharpe, [11]) showed investors how
to add return to their portfolios and control the risk through diversification. The rapid
growth of investment in the (domestic) stock market, foreign stocks, real estate, and
venture capital followed.

Two difficulties remained. First of all, because Markowitz mean/variance
analysis is essentially a "linear" technique, basing its recommendations on estimates
of the mean return (and correlations), it often recommends very unbalanced portfolios,
which must either be ignored or greatly modified at the discretion of the investor
(Black and Litterman, [5]). Secondly, since mean and variance estimates change over
time, the investor must deal with the high cost of frequent portfolio changes.

---

2 The term *geometric* is derived from the fact that a series of compounded returns is equivalent to the
geometric mean of the series raised to a power. See R. Vince [16], E. Thorp [14], [15].

The rapid growth of the markets for futures, options, and other derivatives in recent years has set the stage for the next step in the evolution of investment management: the design of efficient portfolios to achieve return and risk goals. Since using derivatives generally does not require much capital outlay, investors can now reallocate positions and exposures rapidly when their mean/variance estimates change.

For example, a pension plan concerned with increasing volatility in the stock market can sell futures contracts on the S&P 500 Index, thereby reducing exposure to the stock market, without disturbing the activity of any of its portfolio managers. Several major pension plans are now using such active asset allocation strategies. Similarly, a currency hedging strategy can be employed to mitigate exposure to currency risk in a foreign bond portfolio, without having to liquidate portions of the portfolio, because holding portfolios of currency forwards and futures does not require the outlay of significant capital.

The freedom to restructure portfolios rapidly at little cost using derivatives has in turn generated the first major change in investment management practice: the separation of a manager's "alpha" (value added) from the underlying capital allocation decision.

As an illustration, consider the case of a large pension fund that has decided to index a portion of its equity portfolio, and would also like to use the services of a cash manager who has been able to generate excess short-term returns. Instead of having to choose between allocating capital to indexing versus enhanced cash management, it can use the futures market to generate exposure to the S&P 500 Index's return while allocating the cash to the cash manager. The pension fund has now captured the cash manager's alpha, or value added, without forgoing its indexing strategy.

This ability to separate investment returns from the underlying capital has focused investor attention on designing portfolios to maximize the return/risk ratio on a continuous basis. Designing and revising portfolios on a continuous basis leads to the second change brought about by the derivatives markets: the heavy use of nonlinear payoff structures. Examples of this are: strategies using options; dynamic asset allocation strategies (A. Perold and W. Sharpe, [10]); nonlinear autocorrelation models, such as the GARCH volatility models (S. Taylor, [12]); and the dynamic hedging and currency management systems described in this chapter.

Investment strategies that respond dynamically to market movement can generate the desired return/risk characteristics more efficiently than the more static linear models. For example, in contrast to traditional linear hedging techniques, which sacrifice return in order to reduce risk, dynamic hedging strategies in the currency markets make it possible to reduce the cost of hedging to zero, or, in some cases, to a negative "cost," in which the user actually *gains* return while hedging.

In this chapter, we present the theory and practice of modern currency management in the institutional investment portfolio. Our underlying assumption is that the institution already holds a portfolio of assets and/or liabilities, denominated either in the domestic currency or in various foreign currencies, whose return and risk are subject to uncertainty. We further assume that the investor's goal is to maximize the compounded rate of return achieved on capital over the course of time. We first examine methods of hedging foreign currency exposure and then turn to currency management as a separate investment category, and investigate its "alpha."

CURRENCY HEDGING

Purpose of Hedging

The essential difference between a hedger and an investor is that the hedger begins with a given portfolio of assets and/or liabilities, while an investor usually begins with investment cash. Hedgers cannot arbitrarily alter the composition of their portfolios because they must by definition hold certain assets or liabilities, usually as a result of their business or investment activities. Typical examples of hedgers are corporations that hold (or owe) portfolios of foreign currencies as a result of international business activities and institutional investors with foreign bonds or stocks in their portfolios.

In general, the hedger seeks to alter the portfolio so as to improve its return/risk characteristics without abandoning the original positions. The term "hedging" refers to the strategies used to accomplish this. Most often, the goal is further constrained to require that the risk of the new portfolio be no higher than that of the original portfolio. Hedging may be viewed as a generalized form of insurance, which protects against excessive risk and/or improves the overall return of the portfolios being held.

In the specific context of currency hedging, the goal is to offset the effects of downside currency volatility on the portfolio. By downside volatility we mean the losses accruing to the foreign portfolio as a result of adverse currency movements.

A good currency hedging strategy will produce returns that are negatively correlated with the currency returns of the portfolio being hedged. That is, when the underlying currencies are performing poorly, the hedge will add positive returns, and when the underlying currencies are doing well, the hedge will attempt to be neutral or at least not to lose too much. In this way, the average return will be higher. Furthermore, all returns will be more uniform (have lower volatility) and so compound at a higher rate.

Referring to Exhibit 1, we will compare some of the many strategies that may be used for hedging. The diagram illustrates the payoffs from various strategies used to hedge a portfolio holding assets denominated in a foreign currency. The horizontal axis represents the movement in the currency price, and the vertical axis the profit or loss from the strategy, given the movement in the currency.

To begin, we distinguish between "static" and "dynamic" hedging strategies. A static hedging strategy is one in which the hedging decision is made once, and not changed, while a dynamic strategy may make frequent changes in the portfolio.

The decision not to hedge at all (the "No Hedge" strategy) is a static hedging strategy, as is the decision to hedge the entire exposure at all times (the "Full Hedge" strategy). As Exhibit 1 shows, the No Hedge strategy payoff is linear with respect to movements in the underlying currency. That is, it gains and loses in direct proportion to the appreciation and depreciation of the currency. The Full Hedge strategy payoff is constant: It is the same no matter how the currency moves. In general, there is a cost to avoiding the effect of currency volatility, so the Full Hedge payoff line is in the negative return area of Exhibit 1.

Let's look at these static hedging strategies and the reasons for choosing them. In later sections, we will compare these strategies with a dynamic hedging strategy in the specific contexts of cash, bond, and stock portfolios.

Citing empirical evidence, some researchers maintain that currencies have an expected return of zero over the long run. An investor holding this view with a portfolio

Exhibit 1.   Hedge Strategy Payoff Diagrams (Short Hedge)

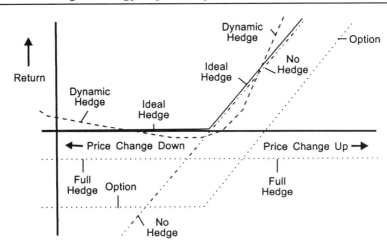

of currencies, foreign bonds, or stocks might choose the No Hedge strategy, if his or her investment return horizon were long enough. Many international equity managers adopt this strategy by concentrating on choosing foreign stocks with attractive expected returns while assuming that the currency price movement will either have no net effect on their portfolios or will deliver some benefit. This is an illustration of the separation of alpha mentioned in the introduction to this chapter: The equity manager wants to focus on his or her particular expertise, which is the added value of foreign stock portfolios, while the currency hedger focuses on adding value by managing the currency exposure.

Now consider a company whose business activities regularly require it to make payments in foreign currencies. Even if it held the opinion that the long-term net return from currency price movement is zero, it might want to avoid the dangers of short-term volatility, which could seriously affect each year's net income, by choosing to adopt a Full Hedge policy. Reducing the volatility of exposure is generally of great value to corporate competitiveness because low volatility means reduced need for capital, which is one of the major costs for many companies.

A Full Hedge strategy, which attempts to eliminate currency exposure entirely, usually sacrifices return to achieve the reduced risk. Can some hedging strategies *increase* return while they reduce risk? To understand how currency hedging can actually improve portfolio return, note that the compounded rate of return (the geometric rate of return G) squared is approximately equal to the square of the arithmetic return (expected return A) minus the variance V (the standard deviation squared):[3]

$$G^2 \cong A^2 - V$$

---

3 R. Vince, [16], pp. 45–46.

Thus, the compounded rate of return is a nonlinear function of both the expected (arithmetic) return and the variance of the return. The greater the volatility, the greater the average return must be to achieve the same geometric return.

If a portfolio is left unhedged, it will achieve large gains when the currencies move in the right direction, and large losses when they don't. A good hedging strategy tends to produce returns that are negatively correlated with the returns from the underlying portfolio. Therefore, the large (unhedged) gains will tend to be made smaller by hedging, and the large losses will also be diminished. That is, the variability of the returns will be smaller, while the average will remain approximately unchanged. The formula above shows that this will improve the return/risk of the portfolio and increase the compounded rate of return.

Therefore, if a company found that exposure to foreign currencies increased the variance of its returns without a corresponding increase in its overall returns, it would be wise to eliminate all exposure to the currencies by using the Full Hedge strategy.

Alternative static strategies, such as those using options, are generally similar to the Full Hedge strategy. Option strategies are nonlinear in their payoffs. They result in a constant payoff when the currency moves against the position, and produce a positive linear payoff function when the currency moves favorably (see Exhibit 1). The nonlinear characteristics of option strategies make them attractive when they can be executed at reasonable cost.

There are also Partial Hedge strategies, in which a portion of the currency exposure is hedged. For example, the company may choose to hedge only those currencies with lower than average yields. The less hedge coverage chosen, the greater the exposure to currency volatility.

Although static strategies may sometimes be desirable for institutional portfolios, they have certain shortcomings. With the No Hedge choice, the portfolio benefits from favorable changes in the underlying currency prices. However, it is damaged in direct proportion to the size of unfavorable movements in the currency prices. For the Full Hedge strategy, the portfolio is generally unaffected by adverse movements in the currency prices. Unfortunately, it does not benefit from favorable movements either. In addition, the Full Hedge strategy usually costs enough in sacrificed return to make it unattractive for many situations.

The ideal hedging strategy would produce compensating gains for the portfolio when the underlying currencies were generating losses, and would have no net effect when those currencies were either unchanged or were delivering profits to the portfolio. This is precisely what an option is designed to do, or, more generally, what insurance does.

Options cost money (the "premium") because some other party is taking on the risk of the adverse price movement. We have described them as a form of Full Hedge because the premium paid typically offsets any gains from favorable price movements.

The ideal hedging strategy would have an option-like payoff structure, and wouldn't cost anything. In Exhibit 1, the ideal hedge is shown as parallel to an option's payoff structure, but with a positive payoff in all circumstances. Dynamic hedging strategies attempt to approximate this ideal by reproducing an option's payoff structure. They are nonlinear in their output, but, in contrast to an option's payoff, they may not be piecewise linear. We have illustrated one possible payoff curve for a dynamic hedging strategy in Exhibit 1.

Now suppose that an institutional portfolio held assets denominated in foreign currencies worth $U.S. 100 million today. How can we create an option-like payoff structure for this portfolio without knowing what the future holds in store for the underlying currencies?

The solution is to use a statistically weighted allocation process. That is, sell forward currency contracts at any given time in proportion to the probability of a downward move in the underlying currency. To do this successfully, we need two things: a method for deciding when a (downward) movement is starting and a way of calculating the weight to be given to that movement (probability of success). We describe the principles and methods we used to construct such a dynamic hedging model in Appendix II and in the section Currency Portfolio Management in this chapter.

The key to the strategy is the development of a model of currency price movement, based on the nonrandomness of the currency markets. The model must be able to capture the price movement to a degree sufficient to generate profits comparable to the losses from downward movements in the corresponding currencies, while at the same time not produce too much of a loss when the currencies move favorably. The author has constructed one such model and used it to design the portfolio management and dynamic hedging systems described in this chapter.

Several recent studies have confirmed our own research showing that autocorrelations exist in the currency markets of a size sufficient to permit the design of profitable investment models. For example, Exhibit 2 shows the nonrandom distribution of autocorrelations in certain currency markets at lags of between one and thirty

Exhibit 2. Autocorrelations and Trends
Table of Autocorrelations for Returns*

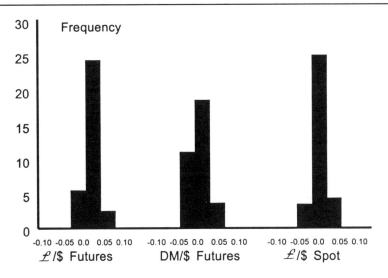

* Pg. 148 "Modelling Financial Time Series," Stephen Taylor, Wiley & Sons, 1986.

days.[4] Other investment systems can be designed using the same principles (S. Taylor [13], E. Thorp [14]).

We will show that dynamic hedging strategies are a very attractive alternative to the more traditional static strategies. By responding flexibly to currency price movements, they can deliver the excess returns available while simultaneously reducing the risk.

In order to convey a sense of the value of dynamic hedging strategies, before examining the design of these systems, we present a comparison of the results for various hedging strategies as applied to foreign cash, bond, and stock portfolios. Although there are many similarities among the three areas, we will treat each application as a separate, complete unit for the convenience of readers with specific areas of interest. Throughout the rest of this chapter, the dynamic hedging system being referred to is the one developed by the author and currently in use at The Boston Company Asset Management, Inc.

Hedging Foreign Cash Portfolios

Consider a U.S. manufacturer who sells its products to non-U.S. consumers. Payments made to the company in local currencies create inventories of foreign currencies, which the U.S. company can then deposit into foreign currency denominated short-term interest rate instruments. Since the company is based in the U.S., it is ultimately concerned with the U.S.-dollar returns it will receive for these investments. In fact, FASB accounting rules require the company to value its income and expenses on a current market basis, taking into account actual currency exchange rates.

The actual U.S.-dollar returns on these foreign currency instruments will of course depend on the prevailing foreign yields and the fluctuations in the underlying currency prices. The company can choose to hedge the currency exposure statically by selling contracts for the future delivery of the currencies, known as "forward" currency contracts. If these forward contracts cover the entire amount of the currencies being accumulated, the U.S. company will no longer have any exposure to foreign currencies. It will have converted its foreign currency inventory into a portfolio of U.S.-dollar short-term instruments, at prevailing U.S. money market yields (see Appendix I).

In the early 1980s, the U.S. dollar was strong relative to the other major currencies. Furthermore, U.S. interest rates were higher than foreign rates. As a result, there wasn't much interest in holding foreign debt instruments. However, the situation has changed in the last several years: Short-term interest rates in many countries are now higher than those in the U.S.

Assuming the company regularly accumulates large holdings of foreign currencies, would it be possible to take advantage of these higher yields? Since the volatility of currency price movements can easily overwhelm the interest rate advantage, resulting in net returns below U.S. levels, the company must choose a hedging strategy. We will compare three hedging strategies: No Hedge, Full Hedge, and Dynamic Hedge.

---

4   Further details on the statistical theory underlying the design of some of these models can be found in S. Taylor's book ([12]).

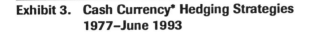

**Exhibit 3. Cash Currency* Hedging Strategies
1977–June 1993**

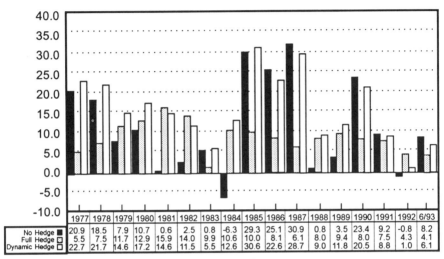

	1977	1978	1979	1980	1981	1982	1983	1984	1985	1986	1987	1988	1989	1990	1991	1992	6/93
No Hedge ■	20.9	18.5	7.9	10.7	0.6	2.5	0.8	-6.3	29.3	25.1	30.9	0.8	3.5	23.4	9.2	-0.8	8.2
Full Hedge ▥	5.5	7.5	11.7	12.9	15.9	14.0	9.9	10.6	10.0	8.1	6.1	8.0	9.4	8.0	7.5	4.3	4.1
Dynamic Hedge ☐	22.7	21.7	14.6	17.2	14.6	11.5	5.5	12.6	30.6	22.6	28.7	9.0	11.8	20.5	8.8	1.0	6.1

Annual Returns

* U.K., Canada, Germany, Japan, Switzerland, equally weighted.

As we have already noted, the Full Hedge strategy is equivalent to converting the portfolio into a portfolio of U.S.-dollar investments, with corresponding U.S.-dollar rates of return. The No Hedge strategy means holding the foreign cash investments and being fully exposed to the currency fluctuations. The Dynamic Hedge refers to using the hedging model developed by the author and described in Appendix II.

Exhibit 3 compares the results of these three hedging strategies over a period of 16.5 years, assuming the company had equal exposure to each of five major currencies at the start of each year: the British pound, Canadian dollar, German mark, Swiss franc, and Japanese yen. It shows that a portfolio of these five major currencies invested in one year LIBOR[5] notes returned 10.9 percent per year (average) in U.S. dollars between 1977 and June 1993. A portfolio of one-year U.S.-dollar LIBOR notes returned 9.0 percent per year over the same period. The excess return of the foreign portfolio was accompanied by volatility approximately three and one-half times that of the U.S. portfolio, making it unattractive to most companies because yearly returns would be too variable. When the Dynamic Hedge was applied, the return was *increased*

---

5 LIBOR is an acronym for the London Interbank Offered Rate, the most common short-term rate benchmark.

by over 4 percent per year, the volatility was *reduced,* and the Sharpe ratio[6] was comparable to that of the Full Hedge portfolio. Note also that the Dynamic Hedge produced large added returns between 1981 and 1984, when the U.S. dollar was strong, and did not cost very much in 1986 and 1987, when the U.S. dollar was weak. Based on these results, the company could have cut its exposure to foreign currencies by 30 percent and still have received the original unhedged return of almost 11 percent per year, with a risk not much higher than that of holding U.S.-dollar instruments.

Note that in this study, we assumed that the company accumulated foreign currencies and invested them in short-term interest-bearing instruments denominated in the respective currencies, regardless of the yield differentials between U.S. rates and those of the given countries. As the 10.9 percent annual return shows, this was not necessarily a bad idea, even in those years when foreign rates were below U.S. rates, because currency appreciation often contributed more than enough to the total return to compensate for the lower yield.

On the other hand, concentrating investment in the high-yielding currencies can backfire when those currencies depreciate rapidly against the U.S. dollar. For example, at the beginning of 1992, British one-year government yields were 10.81 percent, while Japanese one-year yields were 5.53 percent. A U.S. company that decided to buy only British paper (with No Hedge) instead of Japanese notes would have experienced a negative return in 1992, because the British pound depreciated by 18.88 percent against the U.S. dollar! The holder of yen notes would have earned approximately 6 percent, since the yen was essentially unchanged against the U.S. dollar in 1992. Even if the company used a dynamic hedging strategy designed to capture the benefit of appreciation and protect against depreciation, it is unlikely that it would have been able to offset completely the effect of such a rapid depreciation.

Since a dynamic hedging strategy can produce positive added returns by correctly weighting its tactical positions, an appropriate level of overall hedging needs to be chosen. For example, if the volatility of the foreign cash portfolio is 11.6 percent, and the dynamic hedge is negatively correlated with the cash portfolio, one might be tempted to add the hedge at a level that maximizes return without exceeding a volatility of 11.6 percent. However, this would not be in keeping with the ultimate purpose of the currency hedge, which is to offset the negative effects of the currency exposure. In choosing our dynamic hedging level, we measured the downside volatility of the underlying currency markets and set our hedging level to match that volatility.

The Dynamic Hedge system can also be applied to other foreign cash management needs. For example, the Dynamic Hedge could be used to enhance the return and reduce the volatility of a domestic money market mutual fund that invested in foreign cash instruments. Similarly, a company that had foreign currency liability exposure could use the Dynamic Hedge to protect and enhance its profitability. For example, a

---

6 The Sharpe ratio for an investment strategy refers to the mean return divided by the volatility (standard deviation). The riskless rate of return (Treasury bill rate) is usually subtracted from the mean return before dividing by the standard deviation, since the riskless rate would have been earned if the money had not been put into the investment being considered. In our case, since using forwards does not require actual outlay of money, the riskless rate can be assumed to be earned in addition to the return generated by the hedging process. The Sharpe ratio may be viewed as measuring the amount of return being earned per unit of risk, and can therefore be used to compare the attractiveness of portfolios having different risk levels.

company that regularly buys foreign products would owe payments in foreign currencies. The Dynamic Hedge will systematically cover these liabilities by buying forwards ("long hedge") when the currencies are appreciating. Comparison of static and
dynamic strategies yields results similar to those given above for hedging foreign cash
portfolios.

Hedging Foreign Bond Portfolios

The international fixed-income markets have grown rapidly in recent years, reaching
a size of over $15 trillion (U.S.) by the middle of 1993. At present, bonds denominated
in currencies other than the U.S. dollar account for over half of that amount. Most of
these foreign bonds are government issued, since the markets for corporate and
mortgage bonds are not so well developed outside the United States.

U.S. investors have been attracted to foreign bond markets by the higher yields
they have carried in the last several years (see Exhibit 4). Typical examples of investors
holding substantial foreign bond positions are pension funds and mutual funds.
Furthermore, as the top half of Table 1 shows, international bond returns, when viewed
in their local currencies, are not highly correlated, so that adequate diversification can
be achieved using a relatively small number of countries, provided that currency
effects cancel each other. Correlations are somewhat higher when the returns are
viewed in U.S.-dollar terms (bottom of Table 1). This means that attention should be
paid to the currency movements if diversification is to be achieved by U.S. portfolio
holders.

If we leave aside issues of credit quality, holding a portfolio of foreign government bonds, whether they be of short or long maturity, means receiving future cash
flows in a foreign currency, which is similar to holding a portfolio of forwards in the
underlying currencies. This shows immediately that holding a foreign bond portfolio
exposes the investor to currency risk. Are there hedging strategies that can mitigate
this risk?

We will again consider several hedging strategies: (a) No Hedge, (b) Full Hedge,
(c) Partial Hedge, and (d) Dynamic Hedge. The first three strategies are static. Over
the past several years, various studies have come to widely differing conclusions about
the value of static hedging for foreign bond portfolios (F. Black [4], [5]; M. Leibowitz
et al. [8]). Appendix I to this chapter shows why this should not be surprising. Our
approach here is entirely empirical: We will compare the outcomes of the various
hedging strategies over the last several years.

In the No Hedge decision, the investor exposes the portfolio to the currency risk.
The strategy is based on the belief that a diversified portfolio of currencies has an
expected return of zero over the long run, so that no damage will be done by not
hedging at all. For example, the U.S. dollar depreciated by about 2.5 percent per year
against an equally weighted portfolio of major currencies between 1977 and June 1993,
so that an investor in foreign bonds with a very long time horizon gained the benefits
of diversification without having to hedge. Unfortunately, currency fluctuations added
considerable volatility to yearly returns over most relevant time horizons, as we will
show shortly.

In the Full Hedge strategy, the investor sells an equivalent amount of currency
forwards against the bonds held. The effects of this strategy depend on the maturities

Exhibit 4. Foreign Bond Yield Spreads*

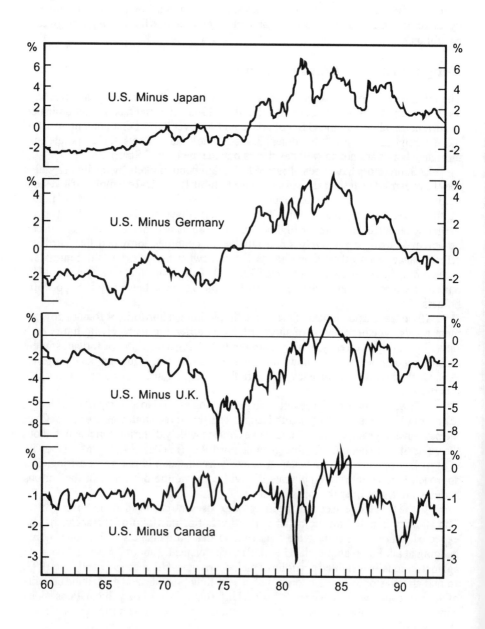

* 10-year government notes.
Source: Bank Credit Analyst

Table 1. Correlations of Returns for the Salomon Bond Index* (Local Currency) January 1985–September 1991

	Australia	Canada	France	Germany	Japan	Nether-lands	Switzer-land	U.K.	U.S.
Australia	**5.899**								
Canada	0.015	**6.828**							
France	0.112	0.488	**4.765**						
Germany	0.209	0.536	0.631	**3.699**					
Japan	0.103	0.461	0.489	0.617	**4.994**				
Netherlands	0.211	0.545	0.655	0.904	0.561	**3.177**			
Switzerland	0.170	0.376	0.417	0.592	0.485	0.654	**2.702**		
U.K.	0.188	0.477	0.439	0.540	0.568	0.436	0.367	**7.509**	
U.S.	0.063	0.817	0.533	0.525	0.485	0.526	0.451	0.418	**5.549**

Correlations of Returns for the Salomon Bond Index* (U.S. Dollars) January 1985–September 1991

	Australia	Canada	France	Germany	Japan	Nether-lands	Switzer-land	U.K.	U.S.
Australia	**15.882**								
Canada	0.165	**8.815**							
France	0.123	0.324	**13.543**						
Germany	0.124	0.291	0.956	**14.906**					
Japan	0.097	0.213	0.747	0.751	**15.976**				
Netherlands	0.132	0.294	0.956	0.994	0.743	**14.367**			
Switzerland	0.087	0.220	0.902	0.938	0.760	0.941	**14.883**		
U.K.	0.249	0.362	0.696	0.695	0.680	0.697	0.682	**17.704**	
U.S.	0.040	0.684	0.361	0.314	0.257	0.303	0.259	0.265	**11.098**

* Annualized Standard Deviation of Return shown on the diagonal.
Source: BARRA

chosen for the forward contracts. By covered interest rate parity, the yield differentials for each currency will be exactly offset by the discount (or premium) of the forward contract used to hedge, so that full hedging of foreign bonds by matching future cash flows with forward currency transactions will convert the foreign bond portfolio into a portfolio of domestic government bonds (see Appendix I). Hedging by mismatching the maturities will convert the exposure to foreign bonds into exposure to relative yield curve movements (Appendix I, Section 4). The results will now depend on correct forecasts of the relative yield curve changes. A Partial Hedge strategy, in which some portion of the currency exposure is sold forward, will produce results in between those of the No Hedge and Full Hedge.

In the Dynamic Hedge strategy, the level of hedging varies as conditions change. At The Boston Company Asset Management, Inc., we use a dynamic hedging strategy that was constructed from the currency management algorithms described in Appendix II, which exploit persistent inefficiencies in currency price movement in a statistical way to signal when to place hedges and when to lift them. It is this dynamic strategy whose results we describe below.

As we indicated in the previous section on foreign cash portfolios, choosing a dynamic hedging strategy requires choosing an appropriate hedging level. The goal of currency hedging is to offset the adverse effects of currency exposure on the returns realized from holding the foreign portfolio. We attempt to do this by setting the volatility of our Dynamic Hedge equal to the downside volatility of the underlying currency markets.

Exhibit 5 presents the results of applying our dynamic hedging model to an equally weighted portfolio of British, Canadian, German, Japanese, and French government bonds, where we have applied hedging in five currencies: British pound, Canadian dollar, German mark, Swiss franc, and Japanese yen.[7] (We relied on the high correlation between the French franc and Swiss franc currency movements to hedge in the more liquid forward Swiss market.)

Between 1986 and June 1993, the foreign bond portfolio had a compounded annual return (CARR) of 14.3 percent per year, in U.S. dollars. This is the No Hedge strategy. For the last few years, yields in these countries (excluding Japan) have been higher than in the U.S. Nevertheless, much of the 14.3 percent return was earned in 1987, when currency appreciation outweighed the lower yields on the bonds.

At the start of 1992, ten-year government bond yields in the U.K. stood at 9.79 percent, while yields in Japan were 5.62 percent. Yields declined in both markets throughout the year, as both countries' economies stayed weak. For 1992 U.K. government bonds (JP Morgan Index) returned 18.84 percent and Japanese government bonds returned 11.31 percent in their local currencies, respectively. However, in U.S.-dollar terms, the U.K. bonds *lost* 3.94 percent and the Japanese bonds gained 11.26 percent, because the British pound depreciated 18.88 percent while the yen remained stable against the U.S. dollar. As we saw in the previous section on foreign

---

7 The JP Morgan Government Bond Index was used to represent each country's government bond portfolio. This index is the average of a broad collection of each country's government bonds of durations and maturities similar to those of the U.S. government bonds in the Lehman and Salomon Bond Indexes.

**Exhibit 5.   Foreign Bond* Hedging Strategies
1986–June 1993**

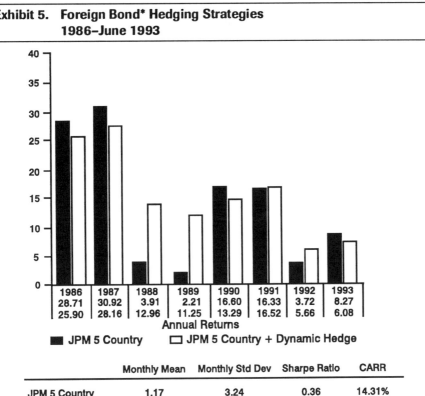

	1986	1987	1988	1989	1990	1991	1992	1993
	28.71	30.92	3.91	2.21	16.60	16.33	3.72	8.27
	25.90	28.16	12.96	11.25	13.29	16.52	5.66	6.08

Annual Returns

■ JPM 5 Country   □ JPM 5 Country + Dynamic Hedge

	Monthly Mean	Monthly Std Dev	Sharpe Ratio	CARR
JPM 5 Country	1.17	3.24	0.36	14.31%
JPM 5 Country + Dynamic Hedge	1.26	2.70	0.47	15.78%

*   JP Morgan Index: U.K., Canada, Germany, Japan, France, equally weighted.

cash portfolios, it is not necessarily rewarding to avoid the lower yielding foreign markets, because currency movements can have a dramatic effect on the return.

Between 1986 and June 1993, a portfolio of U.S.-dollar bonds, as represented by the Lehman Aggregate Bond Index, returned 10.6 percent per year (CARR), almost 4 percent less than the foreign bonds. However, the foreign bond portfolio had almost two and one-half times the volatility of the U.S. portfolio. This volatility was caused by the movement of the underlying currencies rather than the inherent bond return variation. In fact, when the foreign bond portfolio is viewed in local currency terms, its volatility is lower than that of the U.S. bond portfolio. This suggests that a hedging strategy that can offset adverse currency movements would be beneficial. Exhibit 5 shows that applying our dynamic hedge added 1.5 percent per year to the returns of the foreign bond portfolio, while it simultaneously reduced volatility. Note how the dynamic hedge added substantially to the returns in years in which the U.S. dollar was strong, such as 1988 and 1989, and did not sacrifice much return in years in which the U.S. dollar was weak, such as 1986 and 1987.

How did a Full Hedge strategy perform? Recall that if the cash currency flows are entirely hedged by selling forwards, the bond portfolio is transformed into a U.S.-dollar bond portfolio of similar maturity, whose returns we already know to be approximately 10.6 percent per year, depending on the relative levels of each country's yield curves (Appendix I). A commonly used variation of the Full Hedge strategy is to sell one-month currency forwards against the bond positions, mismatching cash flow durations. Table 2 shows that for the entire period, this Full Hedge strategy cost over 5 percent per year in return, while the Dynamic Hedge added approximately 1.5 percent per year. The full JP Morgan Index of non-U.S.-dollar bonds was used for this study, rather than an equally weighted portfolio of five major currency bonds, because the hedging data was more readily available.

Table 2.   Hedging the JP Morgan Bond Index

(1) No Hedge (1986–Jun. 1993):

Monthly Mean: 1.11%

Monthly Std Dev: 3.60%

Sharpe Ratio: 0.31

Compound Annual Return: 13.30%

(2) Full Hedge (1986–Jun.1993):

Monthly Mean: 0.64%

Monthly Std Dev: 1.14%

Sharpe Ratio: 0.56

Compound Annual Return: 7.89%

(3) Dynamic Hedge (1986–Jun 1993):

Monthly Mean: 1.20%

Monthly Std Dev: 2.98%

Sharpe Ratio: 0.40

Compound Annual Return: 14.82%

Of course, while the basket of currencies generally appreciated during the period, there were subperiods during which the U.S. dollar rose sharply against the basket, or was unchanged in value. What happened to the various strategies during those periods? Tables 3a., b., and c., show the results for three shorter time intervals, during which the U.S. dollar either rose sharply, depreciated sharply, or remained unchanged. Even during these short time periods, the Dynamic Hedge generally outperformed the Full Hedge.[8] As would be expected, when the U.S. dollar remained stable, both the Full Hedge and the Dynamic Hedge gave up return in comparison with No Hedge.

Table 3a. Hedging the JP Morgan Bond Index: Strong Dollar

(1)	No Hedge (1988–Jun.1989) U.S. Dollar Up 20%:	
	Monthly Mean:	−0.42%
	Monthly Std Dev:	3.43%
	Sharpe Ratio:	−0.12
	Compound Annual Return:	−5.57%
(2)	Full Hedge (1988–Jun. 1989) U.S. Dollar Up 20%:	
	Monthly Mean:	0.63%
	Monthly Std Dev:	0.83%
	Sharpe Ratio:	0.76
	Compound Annual Return:	7.84%
(3)	Dynamic Hedge (1988–Jun. 1989) U.S. Dollar Up 20%:	
	Monthly Mean:	0.51%
	Monthly Std Dev:	2.26%
	Sharpe Ratio:	0.22
	Compound Annual Return:	5.96%

Consider the period between 1988 and June 1989, when the U.S. dollar rose by approximately 20 percent against a broad basket of major currencies, or 13 percent annually. Since the No Hedge strategy lost 5.6 percent annually, there must have been a bond return (in the local currencies) of approximately 7.5 percent annually to the JP Morgan Index holder. Consistent with this, we see that the Full Hedge returned 7.8

8 Remember that the exact outcome of this Full Hedge strategy depends on the relative movement in yield curves, because cash flows are mismatched (Appendix I).

Table 3b.   Hedging the JP Morgan Bond Index: Weak Dollar

---

(1)   No Hedge (Jun. 1989–Dec. 1990), U.S. Dollar Down 19%:

    Monthly Mean: 1.30%

    Monthly Std Dev: 3.17%

    Sharpe Ratio: 0.41

    Compound Annual Return: 16.08%

(2)   Full Hedge (Jun. 1989–Dec. 1990), U.S. Dollar Down 19%:

    Monthly Mean: 0.28%

    Monthly Std Dev: 1.34%

    Sharpe Ratio: 0.21

    Compound Annual Return: 3.32%

(3)   Dynamic Hedge (Jun. 1989–Dec. 1990), U.S. Dollar Down 19%:

    Monthly Mean: 1.12%

    Monthly Std Dev: 2.88%

    Sharpe Ratio: 0.39

    Compound Annual Return: 13.71%

---

percent annually over the period, capturing the bond return in spite of the foreign currency depreciation. The Dynamic Hedge was also able to capture most of the local currency bond return, even though there was a very sharp move in the dollar.

During a short period of rapid depreciation of the U.S. dollar (June 1989 through December 1990), the No Hedge strategy performed better than the Dynamic Hedge, as would be expected. However, the Dynamic Hedge was much more effective than the Full Hedge. In the December 1990 through June 1992 period, when foreign yields were higher than U.S. yields, and the U.S. dollar was essentially stable, the Dynamic Hedge continued to perform better than the Full Hedge, although it gave up return versus the No Hedge as it attempted to hedge in the swings of what proved to be a sideways market.

In summary, when dynamic hedging is used in a consistent manner, it does not require giving up return in exchange for protection against currency exposure. In contrast to static hedging strategies, it can actually add return to the overall portfolio over the long run.

Table 3c.   Hedging the JP Morgan Bond Index: Stable Dollar

(1)	No Hedge (Dec. 1990–Jun. 1992), U.S. Dollar Up 1%:	
	Monthly Mean:	1.11%
	Monthly Std Dev:	3.54%
	Sharpe Ratio:	0.31
	Compound Annual Return:	13.33%
(2)	Full Hedge (Dec. 1990–Jun. 1992), U.S. Dollar Up 1%:	
	Monthly Mean:	0.68%
	Monthly Std Dev:	0.77%
	Sharpe Ratio:	0.88
	Compound Annual Return:	8.39%
(3)	Dynamic Hedge (Dec. 1990–Jun. 1992), U.S. Dollar Up 1%:	
	Monthly Mean:	0.91%
	Monthly Std Dev:	2.88%
	Sharpe Ratio:	0.32
	Compound Annual Return:	10.98%

Hedging Foreign Stock Portfolios

Institutional investors have added increasing amounts of foreign stock exposure to their portfolios in recent years, both to diversify and to capture attractive returns. In contrast to the situation with foreign bonds, where currency price movements can easily negate the yield advantage, most studies have concluded that static hedging of foreign equity portfolios can be valuable (F. Black [3], [4]). This is not surprising, since static hedging of currency exposure sacrifices (or captures) the yield differentials accruing to foreign currencies in exchange for eliminating currency exposure (Appendix I), while allowing the incremental stock returns to be captured. Because stock returns usually exceed interest rate differentials by a wide margin, the added return (alpha) provided by the investment passes through, albeit in a somewhat modified form.

As is the case for foreign bonds, the investor can choose among a number of equity hedging strategies: (a) No Hedge, (b) Full Hedge, (c) Partial Hedge, and (d)

Exhibit 6. Hedging Foreign Stocks*
1977–June 1993

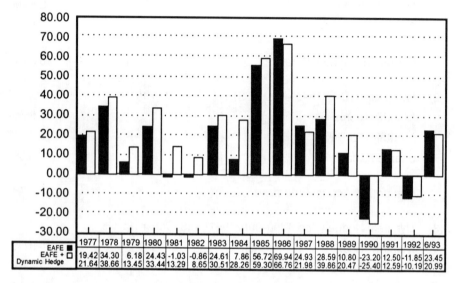

	1977	1978	1979	1980	1981	1982	1983	1984	1985	1986	1987	1988	1989	1990	1991	1992	6/93
EAFE ■	19.42	34.30	6.18	24.43	-1.03	-0.86	24.61	7.86	56.72	69.94	24.93	28.59	10.80	-23.20	12.50	-11.85	23.45
EAFE + □ Dynamic Hedge	21.64	38.66	13.45	33.44	13.29	8.65	30.51	28.26	59.30	66.76	21.98	39.86	20.47	-25.40	12.59	-10.19	20.99

Annual Returns

* EAFE Index

Dynamic Hedge. Once again, we are using our own dynamic hedging model to create the Dynamic Hedge. We chose the level of dynamic hedging employed in accordance with the discussion on hedging levels as presented previously.

A portfolio of foreign stocks (EAFE Index[9]) returned 16.5 percent per year between 1977 and June 1993. U.S. stocks, as represented by the S&P 500 Index with dividends reinvested, returned 13.8 percent per year over the same period. The foreign stock portfolio had 1.3 times the volatility. In contrast to the situation in the bond markets, domestic stock investors normally experience a relatively high level of return volatility, so that adding foreign stocks without hedging may be attractive to institutional investors. Note that the U.S. dollar declined by approximately 2.5 percent per year against a basket of major currencies between 1977 and June 1993, implying that foreign equities, viewed in their local currencies, returned about as much as U.S.

9 The Morgan Stanley EAFE Index is a capitalization weighted price index of the stocks of major companies in Europe, Australasia, and the Far East.

equities over this long time period. This supports the view that foreign stocks are a good diversification for domestic equity portfolios, provided that currency effects are small, or can be avoided.

An investor who thought that the U.S. dollar was going to continue to depreciate over the long run might be tempted to hold a foreign equity portfolio without currency hedging. Exhibit 6 shows that this would have produced volatile yearly (U.S. dollar) returns between 1977 and June 1993. Applying the dynamic hedging system added nearly 5.5 percent per year to the returns, and reduced the volatility at the same time, producing a higher Sharpe ratio. As Exhibit 6 shows, the hedge worked well, adding return when the strong dollar wiped out foreign stock returns in 1981, 1982, and 1984, and not costing very much when the weak U.S. dollar boosted foreign stock returns in 1986 and 1987.

Table 4 summarizes the situation from 1980 through June 1993. The EAFE portfolio returned 15.9 percent, the S&P 500 returned 15.7 percent, and the U.S. dollar declined by approximately 1.5 percent per year over this period. The Dynamic Hedge added 5.5 percent per year to the return and reduced the volatility, again raising the Sharpe ratio.

Table 4.   Hedging the EAFE Index: 1980–June 1993

(1)	No Hedge:	
	Monthly Mean:	1.42%
	Monthly Std Dev:	6.20%
	Sharpe Ratio:	0.23
	Compound Annual Return:	15.9%
(2)	Dynamic Hedge:	
	Monthly Mean:	1.80%
	Monthly Std Dev:	5.88%
	Sharpe Ratio:	0.31
	Compound Annual Return:	21.4%

To evaluate the Full Hedge strategy for foreign stocks, we chose one commonly used hedging process: selling one-month currency forwards. Table 5 shows that for the period 1986 through June 1993 (for which Full Hedge data was available), the Dynamic Hedge strategy had superior return to both the No Hedge and Full Hedge strategies. Once again, the higher Sharpe ratio for the Dynamic Hedge shows that it also provided a more efficient portfolio than either the No Hedge or Full Hedge strategy.

A basket of major currencies appreciated by about 5 percent per year against the U.S. dollar between 1986 and June 1993, and the Full Hedge strategy sacrificed the substantial benefit from this appreciation in exchange for the removal of exposure to

---

Table 5.   Hedging the EAFE Index: 1986–June 1993

---

(1)   No Hedge EAFE Index:
      Monthly Mean: 1.35%
      Monthly Std Dev: 6.06%
      Sharpe Ratio: 0.22

      Compound Annual Return: 15.0%

(2)   Full Hedge FT Actuaries:*
      Monthly Mean: 0.72%
      Monthly Std Dev: 5.21%
      Sharpe Ratio: 0.14

      Compound Annual Return: 7.2%

(3)   Dynamic Hedge EAFE Index:
      Monthly Mean: 1.44%
      Monthly Std Dev: 5.79%
      Sharpe Ratio: 0.25

      Compound Annual Return: 16.4%

---

*   The FT Actuaries Index is a composite price index of the stocks of major companies throughout the world. It was used here because the hedging data was more readily available to the author. The EAFE Index would have given similar results.

---

the currency fluctuations. Nevertheless, the volatility of the Full Hedge portfolio was almost as high as that of the No Hedge. Note also that in spite of the fact that the currencies appreciated, the Dynamic Hedge did not cost return, and actually added excess return by protecting the portfolio during downswings in the currencies.

We can also compare hedging strategies during several subperiods, to see what effect short-term movements in the underlying currencies would have had on the results. Table 6 shows that the Dynamic Hedge outperformed the Full Hedge in all cases. Note that for these shorter time periods, both hedging strategies cost return when the U.S. dollar was weak or unchanged. Nevertheless, the Sharpe ratios (not shown) remained stable, as was the case with foreign bonds. An important point to note here is the significant contrast with the world of foreign bonds. Foreign equities performed better when the U.S. dollar was strong than when it was weak! This again demonstrates that currency movements generally have a smaller effect on foreign equity returns than they have on foreign bond returns.

Table 6.   Hedging the EAFE Index: Selected Time Periods

	No Hedge	Full Hedge	Dynamic Hedge
Dollar Strong (12/87–6/89)	13.6%	29.6%	38.8%
Dollar Weak (6/89–12/90)	–6.6	–13.8	–9.1
Dollar Unchanged (12/90–6/92)	1.0	–6.2	–3.3

Performance Benchmarks

Traditional investment classes such as equities and bonds have a natural performance benchmark: Simply track what a passive investment in a diversified portfolio of assets in the class would have returned. Strategies based on the use of derivatives, such as currency hedging with forwards, do not usually have a natural benchmark. This is because the value added by buying or selling derivatives is a result of the expertise of the investment manager. There is no inherent return to holding a derivative instrument.

Because strategies using derivatives form a rapidly increasing part of investment portfolios, agreeing on an appropriate performance benchmark has become very important. How can the investor choose an appropriate hedging benchmark? To answer this, we must understand the purpose of investing in foreign markets: to receive the returns generated by the foreign investments, *regardless* of currency movement.

We repeat this important point: All U.S. investors who purchase foreign assets desire to receive the local currency return of those assets, *denominated in U.S. dollars.* More precisely, investors who purchase foreign notes, bonds, and stocks seek to avoid being affected by adverse currency price movements. For example, if an investor holds U.K. bonds, and the local currency return (in British pounds) of U.K. bonds in a given year is 18.8 percent, that is the return the U.S. investor wants to capture. If the investor's actual U.S.-dollar return is less than 18.8 percent, the currency hedging program was the reason.

This is the ideal performance benchmark.[10] In practice, the investor may not have access to a hedging strategy that can deliver protection at no cost. In this case, the costs of the best passive strategies will be compared, and the least expensive one will be used as a benchmark for the performance of the portfolio when a currency manager is hired.

As an illustration of this process, let's look at an institution holding foreign bonds or foreign stocks at the beginning of 1993. If it is willing to accept the volatility coming from currency exposure, it will not hire a currency manager at all. This implies

10 This is really a "minimum" ideal benchmark. Most investors would prefer to have currency *gains* unaffected by the hedge strategy, so that the U.S. dollar return of the foreign portfolio benefits from currency appreciation, *and* is not hurt by depreciation (see Exhibit 1, Hedge Strategy Payoff Diagrams, Ideal Hedge). Static hedging strategies cannot accomplish this; the dynamic strategy described in the text does deliver this ideal payoff, over the long run.

that the institution believes currency movement will have little effect on the U.S. dollar return of its holdings, or perhaps will be of benefit.

If it chooses to use a currency manager, it will calculate the costs of a Full Hedge and of buying options. At the start of 1993, foreign yields were higher than U.S. yields, and a Full Hedge strategy might cost approximately 3 percent. Buying options would probably cost about 5 percent, given the volatility of the currency markets. Note that the higher cost of the options is consistent with the fact that options allow the investor to benefit if the currencies appreciate against the U.S. dollar, while the Full Hedge eliminates exposure to the currencies entirely. Assuming the institution does not have access to dynamic hedge management, it will choose the least costly passive hedge, unless it has a strong opinion about the future course of currency prices.

As a result, its performance benchmark will not reflect the desired goal: the local currency return, in U.S. dollars. Access to a Dynamic Hedge strategy, such as the one we use at The Boston Company Asset Management, Inc., raises the possibility of achieving this desired benchmark return. Once again, the availability of dynamic hedging products that can deliver protection at no cost (over the long run) means that institutions can begin to capture the return that is really sought when foreign investment is made: the local market return, taken as a *U.S.-dollar* return.

A different benchmark might be appropriate if, for example, a foreign bond portfolio is being held as part of a U.S. fixed-income portfolio ("foreign bond" sector). In this case, the investor wants to add foreign bonds to a domestic portfolio to help outperform a domestic index. Therefore, the domestic index would provide the benchmark. This is broadly similar to using a Full Hedge strategy benchmark, by covered interest rate parity (Appendix I).

To summarize: The decision to invest in foreign markets should be viewed as a cash, fixed-income, or equity investment without regard to currency fluctuations; the currency hedging strategy should be viewed as insurance against the currency exposure; and the benchmark should be the local currency return achieved by the foreign investment, counted as a U.S. dollar return.

Summary

- The goal of currency hedging is to offset the effect of downside currency volatility.

- The No Hedge strategy exposes the portfolio fully to currency price volatility, which can be dangerous.

- The Full Hedge strategy eliminates exposure to currency volatility, and can be costly.

- Buying options is similar to the Full Hedge strategy, and usually costs as much.

- A Dynamic Hedge strategy can achieve higher returns while simultaneously lowering risk.

- The level of Dynamic Hedge to employ should be that for which the expected performance will best offset the underlying downside currency volatility.

- Over the long run, the Dynamic Hedge outperforms both the No Hedge and Full Hedge strategies, based on historical returns. Over short periods of time, No Hedge and Full Hedge may outperform Dynamic Hedge.

- The decision to invest in assets denominated in foreign currencies should be made without regard to currency fluctuations; the currency hedging strategy should be viewed as insurance against the currency exposure; the cost of this insurance should be used to determine the appropriate performance benchmark.

CURRENCY PORTFOLIO MANAGEMENT

In the previous sections, we showed how an institutional investor or a corporation having asset or liability exposure to foreign currency fluctuations could choose among several hedging strategies. As we stated in those sections, the purpose of currency hedging is to permit the investor to capture the returns generated by the foreign investments, without regard to the currency fluctuations.

Assume now that an institution holds a diversified portfolio of investments whose currency exposure has been satisfactorily hedged. The fact that dynamic hedging strategies can be constructed using the inefficiencies in the currency markets leads to a natural question: Is there any value in adding currency investment as an additional "asset class"? That is, can return be added to a diversified institutional portfolio by means of currency management strategies used as a separate investment class?

In traditional diversification strategies, capital is allocated to new investment opportunities when they offer the possibility of added returns. It is preferable for these new investments to be uncorrelated with those already in the portfolio.

While currency returns are usually uncorrelated with those from traditional investments, it is far from certain that the expected return from holding currencies is positive. Indeed, some argue that the expected return from holding currencies is zero, and that therefore, currencies do not constitute an "asset class," and should not be added to institutional portfolios. Others cite empirical studies showing the positive benefits from diversification through currency exposure in an institutional portfolio. These issues are explored more fully in the literature cited in the bibliography at the end of this chapter (G. Allen [1], A. Herbst [7], S. Taylor [13], F. Black [3]).

Since modern investment practice separates capital allocation decisions from the value added by investment strategies, we can approach currency management by asking whether there are currency investment strategies that produce added value for investment portfolios. For regardless of how an institutional portfolio has allocated its capital, it may use currency management strategies if these strategies improve the return/risk profile of the overall portfolio.

The relevant question therefore is not whether currencies (or any other investment categories) have an inherent return, but rather whether there are currency management strategies that can be reliably demonstrated to have positive return, and, of course, whether these positive returns improve the overall portfolio return/risk.

Furthermore, since the returns from currency management strategies tend to be uncorrelated with those from traditional investment categories, an institutional portfolio can expect to gain return and reduce volatility *simultaneously* by adding currency

---

**Exhibit 7. Efficient Frontier: 45% Bonds/45% S&P/10%
EAFE + Currencies***
1977–1992

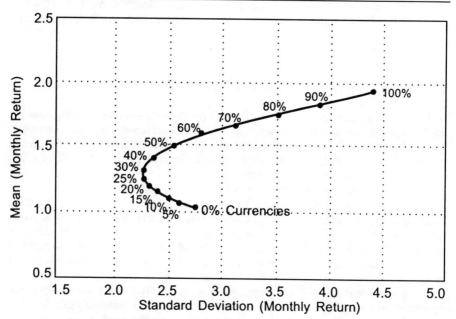

* For each percentage allocation to currencies, the remaining amount is allocated 45%/45%/10% to
U.S. bonds/U.S. stocks/EAFE.

---

management. Exhibit 7 shows the effect of adding our currency management system
(described below and in Appendix II) to a diversified portfolio consisting of bonds
and U.S. and foreign stocks, having an allocation similar to what is found in many
pension plans and endowment funds. Note the simultaneous reduction in risk and
increase in return at several allocation levels. Other currency management systems
would generate similar graphs. In the following sections, we will use our own currency
management system to describe how these investment strategies can be designed.

Discretionary and Algorithmic Methods

All investment strategies can be broadly divided into two camps: "discretionary" and
"algorithmic." A discretionary method relies on the decisions made by an investment
manager, using whatever investment techniques or factors he or she may choose to
emphasize at the time. In this context, by definition, it would be impossible to test the
validity of a discretionary method by simulating its performance over history.

 For example, a discretionary strategy in the fixed-income market might seek to
outperform the Lehman Government/Corporate Bond Index by buying mispriced
corporate bonds based on the investment manager's case-by-case analysis of company
prospects. The success of this strategy depends on the continued availability of

mispriced securities, and on the accuracy of the manager's analysis of corporate prospects. Since historical simulation of this method cannot be done, the decision to use this investment strategy is usually based on review of actual performance records and/or the plausibility of the underlying strategy. Currently popular strategies of investing in emerging markets around the world also belong in this category because lack of liquidity in the past would have prevented execution of the programs.

Algorithmic methods are those in which precisely defined investment procedures are used to exploit *systematic* inefficiencies in markets. Statistical methods are applied to verify that the inefficiencies are persistent. Algorithmic strategies are conveniently coded as software on a computer. Historical simulations are then performed, and the success of the method depends on finding profitable opportunities that continually reoccur, or, at worst, change very slowly over time. In the section Currency Hedging above, we described the basis for believing that these inefficiencies exist in the currency markets.

The major advantage of discretionary strategies is the ease with which they can be adapted to changing circumstances. Major disadvantages are the difficulty of determining effective risk allocations and the ease with which a disciplined investment approach can be abandoned under the pressures of the moment.

Similarly, the major advantages of algorithmic strategies are their ability to quantify risk, permitting more precise risk allocations, and the ease with which they can be applied in an unemotional, disciplined way. A major disadvantage is their general inability to incorporate new factors quickly.

A common misconception about algorithmic systems is that they are "black boxes": mysterious computer-driven mathematical models whose output must be accepted on faith. This ignores the fact that human beings must ultimately design and test the rules to be used. The computer merely performs a large number of systematic calculations rapidly. For example, the mathematical calculation of optimal risk capital allocations plays an important and often overlooked role in the performance of investment strategies. Without computers, such calculations would probably be impossible.

From this point of view, discretionary strategies are more like black boxes than are computerized methods, since by definition, for a discretionary strategy, the exact action that will be taken depends on which factors the investor chooses to give importance to at the time. In this chapter, we will focus primarily on algorithmic currency portfolio management systems. Nevertheless, much of what we say applies to all investment strategies.

In 1977, the author began to investigate the design of profitable algorithmic investment strategies in the futures markets. Early results were promising, showing that small inefficiencies in the markets existed, and could be exploited in a diversified portfolio that would yield significant returns without excessive risk. The first diversified portfolio management system was built and tested between 1980 and 1982.

Since that time, our model has been further developed and refined. It has also been used on a real-time basis for the last 12 years. In addition, over the past ten years, a (rapidly growing) body of literature has appeared confirming the existence of systematic inefficiencies in financial markets (S. Taylor [12], [13], E. Thorp [14]). There are now several companies offering investment management services based on computerized portfolio management systems.

The Currency Management System

Currency price fluctuations are the result of the interaction of major fundamental economic factors. These macroeconomic variables are difficult to observe, and their relative significance changes over time. Their influence is further obscured by the impact of randomly distributed short-term events ("noise").

Nevertheless, a small fraction of the movement generated by these large forces can be modeled. Moreover, our research shows that there is nonrandomness in the structure of the patterns generated, and that these patterns change very slowly, so that statistically robust investment methods can be designed.[11] These strategies generate returns that can overcome the costs of execution.

All investment management systems must have two components: rules for buying and selling and rules for risk allocation.[12] The rules for buying and selling used by our currency management system must satisfy several general requirements: (a) stability or robustness of the statistical patterns; (b) universal validity of patterns; (c) small number of exogenous variables; and (d) mathematically plausible underlying models.

We must have stability, since we want the model to continue to perform in the future as it has in the past. We have much greater confidence in patterns that are valid for many different markets, rather than those that apply only to special cases. Similarly, using a small number of variables avoids the risk of overdetermining ("fitting") the model, and thereby reducing its future reliability. Finally, we want to have the comfort of knowing that our model is consistent with accepted mathematical and economic theory.

The second part of investment system design concerns risk allocation. Historically, this component of portfolio construction has been given little attention. However, the fact that derivative securities can be used without the allocation of capital, and therefore with almost unlimited leverage, has forced the modern investor to examine portfolio risk, which can often be a dominant factor in investment return. To repeat, if no capital is required to gain exposure to a market, the investor is forced to address the question of optimal allocation of exposure, under conditions of almost no restraint on the degree of exposure that can be taken.

We will illustrate this by describing the mechanics of using our currency management system. Suppose that an institutional investor has decided, after analysis of alternative return/risk outputs, to apply our currency management system to $25 million of its funds. Because our system will operate in the forward or futures markets, little or no capital will be required to engage in the buying and selling activity specified by the system.[13]

---

11 A well-known example of inefficiency in the currency markets is provided by the large-scale intervention of central banks, usually for political or economic reasons, such as occurred in Europe between April and September 1992.

12 Usually these two aspects are intertwined because most buying and selling algorithms are tested with risk parameters already in place.

13 Small "margin" levels are set by exchanges as collateral for holding futures positions. These monies may be held in the form of interest-bearing Treasury securities. If forwards are used, dealers will usually accept a line of credit from a large institution in lieu of posting of funds.

We have designed our currency management system so that there will be a very small probability that the maximum downward swing (maximum "drawdown") in value will exceed 20 percent. The institution may choose to set aside $5 million to cover this maximum expected downswing, and these funds can be invested in any manner desired, so long as they remain available for quick use. For example, they could be placed in a short-term money market fund, or placed with an "enhanced" cash manager.

No other funds need to be set aside. Nevertheless, the return and risk delivered by our currency system will be based on the full $25 million since position size will be calculated on the full amount assigned to the system. Thus, using the currency system does not require major reallocation of assets in the institutional portfolio.

In this environment of minimal capital outlay, risk is clearly the central concern. Since maximizing the geometric or compounded rate of return is the ultimate goal of the investor, the relationship between risk and geometric return rates is crucial to the investment decision.

There is a nonlinear relationship between risk and compounded rate of return, in contrast to the linear (Markowitz) relationship between expected return and risk. A graph of this relationship would look like the curve shown in Exhibit 8 (R. Vince [16], E. Thorp [15]), where the vertical axis represents the multiple of original capital attained at the end of repeated investment, and the horizontal axis denotes the

Exhibit 8. Relationship between Return and Risk

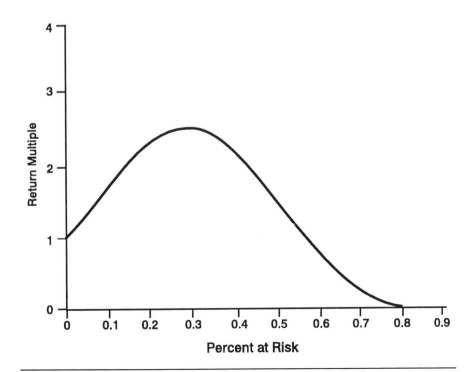

percentage of capital being exposed to loss at each investment opportunity. In theory, there is an optimal location on the risk axis that will produce a maximum geometric rate of return. If enough risk is taken beyond that optimal amount, the capital will be driven down to zero over the long run. The goal of successful portfolio construction is to place the risk of the portfolio at an appropriate point to the left of the maximum.

Note that the risk is purposely not set at a level corresponding to the maximum rate of return. Setting risk too close to this optimal point must be avoided, since uncertainties in the return estimates, discontinuities of price movement, and execution slippage could mean that the portfolio actually had greater risk than planned. Appendix II describes the method for setting risk in our currency management system in more detail.

When we set the volatility of our currency management system at a conservative level, below that experienced by most stock mutual funds, the historical returns produced were 20.6 percent per year compounded, for the period 1978–1992.[14] Table 7 shows the yearly returns and maximum drawdown.

Table 7.   Currency System Yearly Performance 1978–1992

1978	21.20%
1979	20.01%
1980	20.86%
1981	29.79%
1982	16.30%
1983	1.58%
1984	36.75%
1985	19.49%
1986	7.09%
1987	40.07%
1988	20.61%
1989	21.95%
1990	23.31%
1991	21.97%
1992	14.09%

Compounded Annual Rate of Return:	20.63%
Maximum Drawdown:	13.28%

---

14 Returns are net of all brokerage commissions, but not net of management fees. No earned interest has been added to the returns.

Table 8.   Correlations (Monthly Returns)*

1977–June 1993	Currency	U.S. Bonds	Foreign Bonds	S&P	EAFE
Currency	4.365				
U.S. Bonds	-0.116	2.081			
Foreign Bonds					
S&P	-0.012	0.330	-0.037	4.433	
EAFE	-0.012	0.167	0.390	0.389	5.791

1986–June 1993	Currency	U.S. Bonds	Foreign Bonds	S&P	EAFE
Currency	4.195				
U.S. Bonds	0.042	1.372			
Foreign Bonds	0.096	0.352	3.600		
S&P	0.142	0.271	-0.052	4.798	
EAFE	0.040	0.172	0.563	0.441	6.058

*   Monthly standard deviations shown on diagonals.

Table 8 shows the correlations (monthly returns) between the various investment categories, and confirms that our currency management returns are generally not correlated with equity or bond returns. The monthly standard deviations for each investment category have been placed along the diagonals. As we stated earlier, we chose a conservative risk level for our currency system, and the table shows that the volatility of the currency system was less than that of either domestic or foreign stocks.

Referring again to Exhibit 7, which shows the effect of adding the currency management system to a portfolio of stocks and bonds, we see that the Sharpe ratio is improved by the addition of currency management at allocations up to as much as 40 percent of the overall portfolio size. For example, adding currency management at a 30 percent allocation level increases monthly returns by 26 percent (from 1.04 percent to 1.31 percent) and reduces monthly volatility from 2.77 percent to 2.28 percent at the same time.

Table 9 gives the yearly returns that would have been achieved if our currency management system had been added to a diversified portfolio of bonds and stocks (including foreign stocks), at various allocation percentages, between 1977 and 1992.

Performance Benchmarks

For currency management programs used as a separate investment class, the choice of a benchmark is somewhat more difficult than it is for fixed income and equity investment, where well-known passive indexes exist. As we stated above, currency management is a special case of the use of derivatives to alter the investment allocation of a portfolio. It does not require the actual transfer of cash out of other investment

Table 9. Results of Adding Currency Management to a Diversified Portfolio of Stocks and Bonds* between 1977 and 1992

Percentage Allocation Currencies	Yearly Mean	Yearly Standard Deviation	Sharpe Ratio	Compounded Annual Rate of Return
0%	13.1%	9.2%	1.4	12.7%
5%	13.7%	8.4%	1.6	13.4%
10%	14.3%	7.6%	1.9	14.0%
15%	14.9%	7.0%	2.1	14.7%
20%	15.5%	6.5%	2.4	15.3%
25%	16.1%	6.3%	2.6	16.0%
30%	16.8%	6.3%	2.7	16.6%
40%	18.1%	7.2%	2.5	17.9%
50%	19.4%	9.1%	2.1	19.1%
60%	20.7%	11.5%	1.8	20.3%
70%	22.1%	14.4%	1.5	21.4%
80%	23.5%	17.6%	1.3	22.6%
90%	25.0%	21.1%	1.2	23.7%
100%	26.5%	24.7%	1.1	24.8%

*   For each percentage allocation to currencies, the remaining amount is allocated 45%:45%:10% among U.S. Bonds:S&P 500:EAFE.

assets because it uses the forward exchange market. Therefore, one appropriate benchmark is a zero return. That is, if the currency investment program generates a positive return, it has succeeded in delivering excess return, provided, of course, that it does not increase risk. In general, the investor may choose to use a currency management system if it improves the return/risk characteristics of the portfolio.

For derivative-based strategies such as currency management, a variety of other benchmarks can also be used. For example, if some cash is set aside against the currency positions, then the appropriate benchmark can be modified to include the interest earned on the cash. Or, if the investor knows of an acceptable passive currency investment strategy that has historically yielded a positive return, the benchmark can be the return generated by that passive strategy. Here, the passive strategy serves as a proxy for the traditional expected return from owning bonds or equities. The essential goal in setting a benchmark is to be able to compare the performance of the currency strategy with the investment return available to the investor via a feasible passive strategy.

Summary

■ Currency portfolio management strategies can be constructed to yield significant positive returns with acceptable risk levels.

- Returns from currency investment strategies are uncorrelated with traditional investment returns.

- Performance benchmarks should compare currency investment returns with available passive currency investment strategies.

- Currency management is a valuable addition to institutional investment portfolios.

APPENDIX I

Covered Interest Rate Parity

Covered Interest Rate Parity refers to the fact that the price *today* of the forward exchange rate (or futures contract) for a foreign currency is determined by the relative interest rate levels of the countries. In the following discussion, we show why this should be the case and illustrate how this principle is applied in practice.

1. DETERMINING CURRENCY FORWARD EXCHANGE RATES

Suppose that a one-year government note is available in the U.S., and that it yields 3.5 percent; suppose further that a one-year German government note is also available, and that it yields 6.5 percent.

The U.S. note will return $103.50 for every $100 invested, over a one-year period. Alternatively, a U.S. investor can exchange U.S. dollars for deutsche marks (DM) and then invest in the German note, for which he or she will receive 106.5 DM for every 100 DM invested, after one year. Since the U.S. investor must ultimately convert the deutsche marks back into U.S. dollars, the actual return from the German note will depend on the value of the DM in one year.

To avoid this uncertainty, the investor can enter into a contract today to sell the deutsche marks to be received in one year. This is known as selling the DM forward (one year). Since both the U.S.-dollar return and the DM return are certain (government-backed notes), the fair market quote today for the future 106.5 deutsche marks to be received must equal $103.50, the future quantity of U.S. dollars to be received. That is, 106.5 times the one-year forward DM rate must equal $U.S. 103.50. If this were not the case, a riskless arbitrage profit would be available. Therefore, the one-year forward exchange rate (in $U.S.) for the deutsche mark must satisfy

$$\text{1-year forward} = 103.5/106.5 \times \text{spot DM.}$$

Thus, today's forward exchange rate is completely determined by the interest rates in the U.S. and Germany.

2. FULL HEDGING AND COVERED INTEREST RATE PARITY

The principle of Covered Interest Rate Parity has important consequences for hedging strategies in the fixed-income markets. For example, it implies that a Full Hedge, in which cash flows are matched exactly by forward currency sales, converts a foreign fixed-income instrument into a U.S. fixed-income security, with no currency risk. The precise U.S. security that results from this hedge will depend on the relative yield curves of the two countries.

We illustrate this with an example using two-year notes. Everything described below can be applied equally well to variations on this example, such as coupon bonds with 10-year maturities, corporate bonds, mortgage bonds, short-term LIBOR-based notes, etc.

To make the example concrete, we will use actual yields and prices as of August 18, 1993. Assume that an investor buys a two-year government note denominated in deutsche marks, with face value of 1 million DM and coupon of 5.826 percent, interest paid annually. The annual coupon payment means the investor will receive two cash flows: 58,260 DM at the end of the first year and 1,058,260 DM at the end of the second year.

If these DM flows are fully hedged in order to avoid exposure to the DM exchange rate, one-year and two-year forwards will be sold in amounts equal to the DM receipts. By Covered Interest Rate Parity, the forward exchange rates will be determined by the relative yields at maturities of one and two years. On the above date, the one-year U.S. yield was 3.384 percent, the one-year DM yield was 5.962 percent (the DM yield curve was inverted between one and two years) and the DM was worth $0.5951. Therefore, one-year forward DM was worth $1.03384/1.0592 \times 0.5951 = \$0.5809$, by Section 1 above. So the 58,260 DM will be worth $33,840.

The two-year forward DM is worth $(1.03963)^2/(1.05826)^2 \times 0.5951 = \$0.5743$, since two-year yields in the U.S. and Germany are 3.963 percent and 5.826 percent, respectively. Therefore, the DM income of 1,058,260 at the end of year two will be worth $607,792. The total income from the fully hedged DM note is therefore $607,792 + \$33,840 = \$641,632$.

If, instead of buying the DM note, the investor buys a U.S. two-year note, the income would have been earned on $595,100 (equal to 1 million DM), at a yield of 3.963 percent. This comes to $23,584 + \$618,684 = \$642,268$. Thus, in spite of the fact that DM yields were higher than U.S. yields, the fully hedged DM note yields roughly what the U.S. note does, the difference being dependent on the term structure of yields. (We have ignored transaction costs in these computations.)

We used yields appearing on our quote screens to illustrate the calculation of forwards in the above example. If actual market quotes had been used, the results might have been slightly different. In any case, the important point to note is that the higher DM local currency yields are converted to U.S. market yields by the Full Hedge, so that the higher DM yields are lost in exchange for removal of currency risk.

3.   VARIATIONS ON FULL HEDGING

With recent German yields considerably higher than U.S. yields, we sometimes read that fixed-income managers are buying German bonds for the extra yield, and "hedging" away the currency risk. What are these managers actually doing? As we demonstrated in Section 2 above, strict, matched maturity hedging of a DM bond would convert the position into U.S. Bonds, with correspondingly lower yields. Hedging away the currency risk in this manner would not achieve the desired higher returns.

Rather, these managers are using one of two variations of hedging. First of all, suppose that in the example above, the manager hedged against currency risk by selling one-month forward DM rather than one- and two-year forwards. This mismatching of flows is a type of Full Hedge—as we stated in the chapter under Hedging Foreign Bond Portfolios—because essentially all of the currency risk is avoided.

This strategy will be successful if the shape of the German yield curve changes favorably, namely if it gets "flatter" (i.e., one- and two-year rates decline relative to one-month rates) relative to the shape of the U.S. yield curve. This is because the investor is basically long one- and two-year forwards (receiving DM cash flow at the ends of year one and two) and short the one-month forward (the hedge), and the forward prices will rise relative to spot DM if DM rates decline relative to U.S. rates, and decline if DM rates go up relative to U.S. rates, no matter what the spot currency does. So this kind of hedging is really a yield curve movement strategy. (It is similar to taking a "spread" position in the forward currency markets.) We give a more detailed example of this in Section 4 below.

Over the long run, if there are enough countries for which long-term rates decline while short-term rates stay about the same, this kind of hedging will produce positive results so long as the U.S. yield curve doesn't change much. For example, this strategy was used successfully in the European bond market in 1991 and 1992 as European economies were weak, while central banks continued to keep short-term rates high because of the ERM agreement.

The other hedging technique is to buy the DM note when the investor thinks the DM will remain stable in price or rise relative to the U.S. dollar, and then to use discretion (the advice of a good currency trader) to hedge whenever the DM looks weak. This dynamic hedging strategy, if successful, will provide the full (or partial) capture of the returns available from the foreign fixed-income securities.

The currency management model described in this chapter, and used at The Boston Company Asset Management, Inc., is an example of a completely automated dynamic hedging strategy that historically has provided full capture of the foreign market returns (see sections on Hedging of Cash and Fixed-Income Portfolios).

4.   FULL HEDGING WITH MISMATCHED DURATIONS

In this section, we provide an analysis of the behavior of the Full Hedge variation described in Section 3 above. As we said, this kind of hedge was used profitably with French and German bonds between 1991 and 1992, because there was a relative flattening of the foreign yield curves.

To make things concrete, let's assume that a U.S. investor believes that Australian long yields are going to fall relative to Australian short yields, because the Australian government is going to try to support its currency by raising or holding steady the short-term interest rates, while the weak economic outlook favors lower long-term rates. In addition, the investor expects the U.S. yield curve to remain the same, or not flatten much. The investor wants to earn the higher returns from holding the Australian notes, but wants to avoid exposure to the fluctuations of the Australian dollar.

In September 1992, the one year U.S.-dollar government note rate was 3.13 percent, the two-year U.S. rate was 3.83 percent, and the three-year rate was 4.35 percent. For Australia, the one-year rate was 5.90 percent, the two-year was 7.18 percent, and the three-year was 7.58 percent. Note that the difference, or slope of the yield curve between three-year and one-year, was 1.22 percent for the U.S. and 1.68 percent for Australia. In general, the greater the slope for Australia, the greater the potential gain from this strategy.

We will look at what happens when the investor buys $1 million U.S. worth of three-year Australian-dollar government notes and hedges this by selling one-year forward Australian dollars. We will assume, for the sake of simplicity, that the notes are sold on a discounted basis.

At the time, $A 1 was worth $U.S. 0.7282, or 72.82 cents, so that $U.S. 1 would be exchanged for $A 1/0.7282 = $A 1.3732491. Therefore, $U.S. 1 million will exchange for $A 1,373,249, so the portfolio manager will buy notes whose value at maturity will be $A 1.0758 × 1.0758 × 1.0758 × 1,373,249 = $A 1,709,794, since the three-year yield in Australia was 7.58 percent.

One-year rates in Australia were 5.90 percent and the one-year U.S. rate was 3.13 percent, so the one-year forward $A would be quoted at 1.0313/1.0590 × $U.S. 0.7282 = $U.S. 0.7092 at that time, by covered interest rate parity. The value of the note is expected to appreciate by 5.90 percent the first year, so 1.059 × 1,373,249 = $A 1,454,243 are hedged (sold) one year forward at $U.S. 0.7092 per Australian dollar.

As this is being written, one year later, the $A is worth $U.S. 0.6760. The one-year forward position will therefore have made a profit of (0.7092 − 0.6760) × 1,454,243 = $U.S. 48,281.

After one year, the note will be worth $A 1,709,794 in two years, so it must be worth $A 1,709,794/(1.0536 × 1.0536) = $A 1,540,254 now, since the two-year Australian yield has declined to 5.36 percent. $A 1,540,254 = $U.S. 1,041,212. Therefore, the net received in one year is $U.S. 1,089,493, or 8.95 percent on the invested capital. This return should be compared to the return of 6.71 percent that would have been earned on an investment in a U.S. three-year note yielding 4.35 percent. The strategy of mismatching the hedge maturity worked as planned: the investor avoided the risk of currency depreciation while benefiting from the relative steepening of the Australian yield curve resulting from the lower long-term Australian yields.

A variant of this strategy would have been to buy three-year Australian-dollar forwards and sell one-year forwards, while keeping the $1 million in a U.S. note. The results would have been similar to what was obtained in the example. In general, mismatched hedging protects against currency volatility because the investor is both long and short the forwards.

APPENDIX II

The Currency Management System

Our portfolio management system has two components:

1. Signal algorithms, and

2. Portfolio optimization.

SIGNAL ALGORITHMS

An algorithm is a set of precise rules providing for the purchase and sale of investment interests. In our case, these rules are applied in the futures and forward markets for currencies.

We currently use five (proprietary) signal algorithms:

1. A "relative strength" algorithm that signals action upon the detection of increased strength or weakness of a given futures or forward market relative to its past behavior;

2. A statistically based "break-out" algorithm that acts upon detection of statistically determined deviation from prevailing price distribution;

3. A "locally overbought/oversold" algorithm that measures the trend and then attempts to enter when it determines that the given market has reacted to a level from which it is likely to move in the direction of the trend;

4. A trend-following algorithm that continuously recalculates its entry and exit levels on the basis of measured market movement; and

5. An "expert system" algorithm that acts when certain patterns appear indicating imminent market reversal.

All signal algorithms have precise entry and exit rules, and include precise levels for closing out the position should it not be successful. This permits statistical computation of the risk associated with each signal.

These signal algorithms were designed over the course of 40 man-years of experience and research in the futures markets, and have been used in the markets on a real-time basis for the past 15 years.

Performance Metrics

Knowing the risk and return expected from each algorithm permits the analysis of optimal risk exposure bands. As stated at the beginning of this chapter, practical and theoretical limitations lead to consideration of maximizing return/risk locally. To accomplish this, we calculate performance metrics for each signal algorithm.

The metrics are constructed by measuring the daily return generated by the signals and calculating

a. its mean, a measure of the signal's profitability; and

b. its standard deviation, a measure of its risk.

These statistics are combined and calculated for the entire algorithm. Certain of the parameters are then adjusted in a statistically robust manner to produce the signal algorithm with the best performance metrics.

A further adjustment is then made to the risk of each signal using a proprietary model of volatility (see S. Taylor [12]). These risks are fed to the portfolio optimization process described in the next section.

PORTFOLIO OPTIMIZATION

A statistical study is made to decide the optimal signal algorithms for each account size. The larger the account, the greater the number of signal algorithms that can be used without decreasing the performance metrics.

Risk control in a portfolio is based on diversification across markets and algorithms. Once a set of signal algorithms is chosen, modern portfolio theory attempts to maximize the mean return with respect to a given standard deviation ("risk") for the portfolio of algorithms.

Generalizing the ideas in E. Thorp's paper ([14]) and subsequent research along those lines, we seek instead to maximize the compounded rate of return subject to a predetermined maximum expected drawdown. Recent academic research indicates that this latter portfolio will dominate those of modern portfolio theory in most utility function spaces (E. Thorp [14], [15], R. Bell and T. Cover [2]).

The problem is posed as one of finding the maximum of a function of many variables along the subspace defined by the drawdown. We use proprietary computer search techniques to solve this.

The resulting diversified portfolio allocates weights to each signal algorithm for each currency market in a manner that optimizes the overall performance metrics for the whole portfolio. "Blind" studies and statistical measures are then applied to verify the robustness of the final portfolio. This leads to a statistical estimate of the future returns possible with the portfolio. Table 7 in this chapter presents the historical computer-generated record for the currency management system presently in use at The Boston Company Asset Management, Inc.

Ongoing research is designed to develop new signal algorithms for further diversification and flexibility and to apply the techniques of portfolio construction theory to these algorithms.

BIBLIOGRAPHY

[1] Allen, Gregory C., "Managed Futures, an Institutional Investor's Primer," Callan Associates Inc., May 1992.

[2] Bell, Richard, and Thomas Cover, "Competitive Optimality of Logarithmic Investment," Math. of O. R., vol. 5, no. 2, May 1980, pp. 161–166.

[3] Black, Fischer, "Universal Hedging: Optimizing Currency Risk and Reward in International Equity Portfolios," *Financial Analysts Journal*, 45, 1989.

[4] Black, Fischer, "Global Reach," *Risk Magazine,* December 1992, pp. 27–31.

[5] Black, Fischer, and Robert Litterman, "Global Portfolio Optimization," *Financial Analysts Journal,* September–October 1992, pp. 28–43.

[6] Cover, Thomas M., "Universal Portfolios," Technical Report No. 66, Department of Statistics, Stanford University, July 1988.

[7] Herbst, Anthony F., and Joseph P. McCormack, "An Examination of the Risk/Return Characteristics of Portfolios Combining Commodity Futures Contracts with Common Stocks," *The Journal of Futures Markets,* Fall 1987, pp. 416–427.

[8] Leibowitz, Martin L., Lawrence N. Bader, and Stanley Kogelman, "Global Fixed-Income Investing: The Impact of the Currency Hedge," *Salomon Bros. Research Report,* December 1992.

[9] Markowitz, Harry, "Portfolio Selection," *Journal of Finance,* volume VIII, no. 1, March 1952, pp. 77–91.

[10] Perold, Andre F., and William F. Sharpe, "Dynamic Strategies for Asset Allocation," *Financial Analysts Journal,* January–February 1988, pp. 16–27.

[11] Sharpe, William F., "Capital Asset Prices: A Theory of Market Equilibrium Under Conditions of Risk," *Journal of Finance,* 19 (4), September 1964, pp. 425–442.

[12] Taylor, Stephen J., Modelling Financial Time Series (New York: John Wiley, 1986).

[13] Taylor, Stephen J., "Rewards Available to Currency Futures Speculators: Compensation for Risk or Evidence of Inefficient Pricing?" *Economic Record: Proceedings of the International Conference on Futures Markets, December 1990,* 1991.

[14] Thorp, Edward, "Portfolio Choice and the Kelly Criterion," *Proc. Amer. Stat. Assoc.,* pp. 215–224, 1971.

[15] Thorp, Edward O., and Louis M. Rotando, "The Kelly Criterion and the Stock Market," *Bulletin of the American Mathematical Society,* December 1992, pp. 922–931.

[16] Vince, Ralph, *The Mathematics of Money Management,* (New York: John Wiley, 1992).

CHAPTER 22

Hedging in Markets That Gap

Ron S. Dembo
President
Algorithmics Incorporated

INTRODUCTION

Dynamic hedging strategies based on Black-Scholes replication are well-suited to portfolio replication in efficient, frictionless markets that operate in a continuous fashion. Even the most efficient, liquid markets in practice exhibit jumps where the execution of such strategies becomes costly if not impossible. The sources of such jumps may be numerous, such as jumps in volatility, jumps in price, jumps in correlation measures, etc. Similarly, even in markets that exhibit smooth behavior, replication of instruments with discontinuous characteristics, such as certain exotic options, cannot be done effectively with methods that presuppose continuity. Just as serious is the fact that the cost of implementing dynamic hedging strategies under real conditions in real markets is not known or controllable. In this chapter we describe a patented portfolio replication technique, which we have pioneered and used for a number of years with great success. It is able to provide protection without rebalancing for reasonably contained market gaps. With this technique, it is possible to create a spectrum of replications/hedges in which one may trade off cost and expected tracking error, as well as the range of protection, thereby allowing trading institutions to measure, price, and control their risk profile.

Classical hedging methodology is based on a number of strong and often invalid assumptions about the behavior of the underlying instrument being hedged. Typical assumptions are:

- The price of the underlying is a continuous random variable.

- It follows an Ito process with future returns normally distributed.

- Volatility of price movements is fixed or is a known function of time.

- Discount rates are fixed or are known functions of time.

- There are no transaction costs (frictionless trading).
- The market is liquid, complete, efficient and arbitrage-free.

With these assumptions, Black and Scholes [1973] were able to develop a dynamic trading strategy that could perfectly replicate the payoff function of a European option. Their motivation was to derive a closed-form pricing formula. The beauty of their derivation, however, is that it is constructive. It not only provides a simple formula for European options, it also explicitly shows how the payoff of such an option may be replicated by trading a portfolio of cash and the underlying, provided of course that the above assumptions are valid. Such replication is the basis for the vast majority of hedging done today.

Unfortunately, the markets we operate in are not continuous, nor is trading frictionless. Real markets gap frequently and often severely. Gaps can and do occur. They occur in price changes, volatility changes, correlation and interest rate movements. Returns often are far from normal. Liquidity varies from instant to instant and often quite radically.

Consider some recent examples of severe gapping:

- The DAX market dropped close to 10 percent in the first half hour of trading during the day of the recent attempted coup in the former Soviet Union.
- The one-month implied volatility of sterling/deutsche mark options jumped almost instantaneously from a relatively stable value of 4-7 percent to 35 percent during the September 1992 ERM currency crisis.
- The U.K. short-term rate gapped three times in one day during the same crisis, each gap exceeding 200 basis points.
- West-Texas crude prices dropped over 30 percent on the day hostilities broke out in the Gulf War (January 1991), simultaneously, volatility dropped 40 percent.

There have been many attempts to try and remedy these shortcomings in the original model. They have resulted in extensions to Black-Scholes pricing theory but follow the same methodology using different processes to describe the underlying, such as a Poisson jump process to model market gapping. However, the primary failure of such extensions is that they do not have the same constructive nature as the Black-Scholes theory. That is, even if these extensions were to provide pricing that more accurately reflected true market prices, there is no way to infer from the theory what an appropriate hedge might be. They do not provide a practical means for hedging gaps even when the assumptions behind the derivations are valid. Thus, they lose the essential beauty of Black-Scholes.

Dynamic replication based on Black-Scholes theory is the primary means used to hedge options positions in practice. This practice is often referred to as D hedging. It is precisely when hedging is most needed that such hedges fail, since the principal assumptions upon which they are based do not hold in turbulent markets. It is unreasonable to expect that one can use continuous-time mathematics to derive a *constructive* approach to hedging in a fundamentally discrete setting. An explicit account of the discrete nature of all of the underlying stochastic parameters is needed, and to do so involves the use of discrete mathematics. This is the subject of the next section.

MULTISCENARIO REPLICATION

Assume, for the moment, that we operate in a market in which there are a finite number, N, of instruments available, each of which can only be traded in finite amounts without affecting price (finite liquidity). Furthermore, assume that there is a single period and that there are a fixed, finite number of possible outcomes/events/states/scenarios, S, that may occur over this period. Exactly one of these events will occur at the end of the period, but our perspective is assumed to be at the start of the period, where there is uncertainty as to which event will occur.

Each agent, i, in this market is characterized by his or her preferences, as manifested by the probability vector, p^i in R^S, whose components are the (subjective) probabilities of a future state occurring. Given any target portfolio, our objective is to find a replicating portfolio that behaves identically to the target *for all possible future states of the world*. Such a portfolio is called a perfect replication. Clearly, a perfect replication will produce a perfect hedge for the target portfolio. That is, a short position in the replicating portfolio coupled with a long position in the target portfolio will result in no-net exposure.

Let $(q_1, q_2, \ldots, q_N)$ be the known price of the replicating instruments at the start of the period. Let $(d_{i1}, d_{i2}, \ldots, d_{iN})$ be the value of the replicating instruments at the end of the period, if scenario i (i = 1, 2, . . ., S) were to occur. The notation d_i will be used to denote the N dimensional column vector with entries $(d_{i1}, d_{i2}, \ldots, d_{iN})$. A superscript T will be used to denote the transpose of a vector or matrix. The N by S dimensional matrix D has as its columns the vectors d_i (i = 1, . . ., S). Similarly, q will be used to denote the N dimensional column vector with entries $(q_1, q_2, \ldots, q_N)$. The portfolio of replicating instruments will be denoted by the column vector x. We assume the target is bought at the beginning of the period for c and is sold for $(t_1, t_2, \ldots, t_S)$, depending on which scenario actually occurs. As before, t will denote the column vector with entries $(t_1, t_2, \ldots, t_S)$.

For a perfect replication, therefore, we seek a portfolio that satisfies:

$$\sum_j d_{ij} x_j = t_i; \, (i = 1 \ldots, S) ; \tag{1}$$

or in matrix form:

$$D^T x = t. \tag{2}$$

This begs the question; when does such a replicating portfolio exist? Also, if such a portfolio does not exist, is there a rational way in which one should create the "best," albeit imperfect, replication? (see Exhibit 1.)

To answer these questions we need to introduce some concepts.

A *complete market* is one in which there always exists a portfolio x that perfectly replicates an arbitrary target portfolio. In other words, there always exists an x satisfying Equation 2 for arbitrary t. Such situations arise when the market is sufficiently rich so that there are always more "independent" instruments than scenarios. Unfortunately, real markets are incomplete. In the above terminology, it is not always possible to find a replicating portfolio x that satisfies Equation 2 for an arbitrary target portfolio t.

Exhibit 1. One-Period Replication

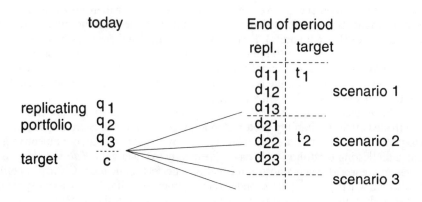

Scenario Optimization, Dembo [1991], provides an interesting framework for dealing with such situations. Let E(.) denote the expectation operator. Following Dembo [1991] and Dembo and King [1992], we introduce the *Regret* function, R, defined as:

$$R = E \left(\| D^T x - t \| \right). \qquad (3)$$

Thus, Regret measures the expected difference between the value of a given portfolio, x, and the target portfolio at maturity. *It measures what one can achieve with a given decision today against what one could achieve with perfect information,* since with perfect information the possible scenarios and their corresponding probability distribution are known at the start of the period. A replicating portfolio with zero Regret will perfectly match the target under all possible outcomes. Another interpretation of Regret that proves to be useful is as the value of residual or known risk in the replicating portfolio.

In what follows it is sometimes appropriate to use the notion of *Downside Regret*, defined as:

$$DR = E \left(\| (D^T x - t)_- \| \right), \qquad (4)$$

in which only negative deviations from the target are considered.

In complete markets it is always possible to find a portfolio, x, such that Regret is zero for an arbitrary, given target and distribution of scenarios. In cases where zero Regret is not achievable, it is natural to attempt to obtain a replicating portfolio that is as close as possible to zero Regret. This motivates the definition of the *Minimum Regret* function, MR, as:

$$MR = \text{Minimize}_x \ldots E \left(\| D^T x - t \| \right). \qquad (5)$$

Similarly, we may define *Minimum Downside Regret* as:

$$MDR = \text{Minimize}_x \ldots E \left(\| (D^T x - t)_- \| \right). \qquad (6)$$

Complete markets are therefore characterized by MR = 0 for all t. Incomplete markets have MR $\geq$ 0. Thus one may interpret the *Minimum Regret portfolio*, x^*, as the portfolio with the smallest possible residual risk that can be obtained under uncertainty. In the sense of the Regret function, x^* is the optimal replicating portfolio, since it minimizes residual risk. Recall that in discrete, incomplete markets there is seldom a perfect hedge and therefore a long position in the target and short position in x^* (or vice versa) is the best available hedge in the face of uncertainty.

We have said nothing about the cost of the hedge, just as in the same way such issues are ignored when doing D hedging using dynamic replication as derived by Black-Scholes. In fact, *the trade-off between the cost of a hedge and the quality of protection it offers should be the principal focus of any hedging methodology*. The cost of a hedge over the life of a deal in Black-Scholes theory is its fair market price. But this assumes many things are true (see the Introduction to this chapter). In practice, the assumptions required by Black-Scholes are far from true and hence *the cost of a hedge may be far from what the theory would predict*. In fact, in cases such as those we have described, where the market gaps, D hedging may be extremely costly, wiping out all possible profits from a trade. In extreme cases the cost of a D hedge may be enough to erase the entire annual profits of a trading operation. Such situations arise often enough to warrant the search for improved hedging techniques.

In the next section we show how the "cost-quality" trade-off may be computed for a multiscenario hedge.

HEDGING: THE TRADE-OFF BETWEEN RISK (QUALITY) AND RETURN

The cost of a hedge may be determined in a number of ways. For example, it could be computed as the initial cost of purchasing the replicating portfolio, q^Tx. This does not account for the value of the portfolio at the horizon. Possibly a better measure, therefore, is based on the expected profit or loss over the life of the hedge. This may be computed as follows:

Consider an issuer who sells the target short at the start of the period and covers the position with a multiscenario hedge obtained by replication. The position is then closed out at the end of the period. The accounting for this transaction would be as follows:

Start of period:

- c from selling the target

- $-q^Tx$ for purchasing the replicating portfolio

End of the period:

- $E(D^Tx)$ expected payoff from selling the replicating portfolio

- $-E(t)$ expected cost of purchasing the target to close out the deal

The *expected profit* from the deal is: $r^{-1}E(D^Tx - t) + (c - q^Tx)$ in today's terms, where r is 1 + the interest rate for the period.

This motivates the following parametric optimization formulation, which captures the "risk/reward" trade-off.

$$MR(K) = \text{Minimize}_x \dots r^{-1} E(\| D^T x - t \|) \tag{7}$$

$$\text{Subject to: } r^{-1} E (D^T x - t) + (c - q^T x) \geq K. \tag{8}$$

Equation 8 states that the deal should be expected to make at least K dollars (K could be positive or negative). Since MR(K) is an implicit function, which is monotonic nonincreasing in K, we may conclude that the more the expected profit we require from the deal the higher the residual risk (Minimum Regret).

Just what is the optimal value of K?

The issuer makes an expected profit of K, assuming a risk of MR(K). His or her *risk-adjusted profit* is therefore:

$$K - MR (K). \tag{9}$$

A natural criterion will therefore be to *maximize risk-adjusted profit,* that is:

$$\text{Maximize}_K \dots K - MR (K). \tag{10}$$

The solution to this problem is at K^*, which occurs at $\lambda = 1$, where λ is the shadow price of the profit constraint. This is shown graphically in Exhibits 2, 3, 4, and 5. The tangent to the curve MR(K) at K^* is the shadow price of the cost constraint and has a slope of 1. Viewed graphically in this way, it is easy to see that this is the point at which the difference $K - MR(K)$ is maximized. It is worth noting that, in the one-norm case, MR(K) is piece-wise linear and hence not differentiable at the breakpoints. In this case, the necessary condition for optimality is that 1 be in the subdifferential of $MR(K^*)$.

There are a number of distinct cases that are of interest. First, we need to define the notion of *arbitrage* in this context, since it helps interpret these various cases.

An arbitrage is a portfolio x with $(c - q^T x) > 0$ and $(D^T x - t) \geq 0$ or $(c - q^T x) \geq 0$ and $(D^T x - t) > 0$. That is, one can sell the target and buy a hedge at a profit today and, *for each and every possible scenario in the future,* liquidate the portfolio with no loss.

A system of /S/ constraints that would *preclude arbitrage* is therefore:

$$r^{-1} (D^T x - t) + (c - q^T x) = 0; \tag{11}$$

since $(c - q^T x) > 0$ would imply $(D^T x - t) < 0$ and $(c - q^T x) \geq 0$ would imply $(D^T x - t) \leq 0$ if Equation 11 were satisfied. Note that Equation 11 could be replaced by a less than or equal to constraint.

An *expected arbitrage* is a portfolio x with $(c - q^T x) > 0$ and $E (D^T x - t) \geq 0$ or $(c - q^T x) \geq 0$ and $E (D^T x - t) > 0$. That is, one can sell the target and buy a hedge at a profit today and *expect* to liquidate the portfolio with no loss. A single constraint that would preclude expected arbitrage is therefore:

$$r^{-1} E (D^T x - t) + (c - q^T x) = 0. \tag{12}$$

Clearly, no arbitrage implies no expected arbitrage. Also, because of its relationship to the profit constraint Equation 8, we sometimes refer to this condition as the zero profit condition.

There are four distinct cases of interest, shown in Exhibits 2–5.

Case 1: MR(0) = 0; MR(K) > 0 for all K > 0

This is the case one would observe in a *complete market with no arbitrage*. That is, a perfect replication under a no-arbitrage constraint and the need to assume some risk if there is nonzero expected profit. In this situation we would expect investors to seek a portfolio with an expected payoff of K^* and assume a positive risk of $MR(K^*)$.

Notice that in a complete market with no arbitrage, using Equation 11, we have:

$$c = q^T x^*; \tag{13}$$

where x^* is the Minimum (zero) Regret portfolio. That is, the cost of the target must be equal to the price of the (perfect) replicating portfolio.

Exhibit 2. The Risk versus Reward Trade-Off: Case 1

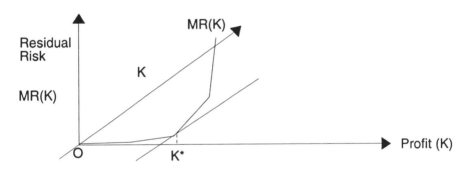

Case 2: MR(0) > 0

This case arises in situations in which there is no arbitrage and the market is *incomplete*.

Exhibit 3. The Risk versus Reward Trade-Off: Case 2

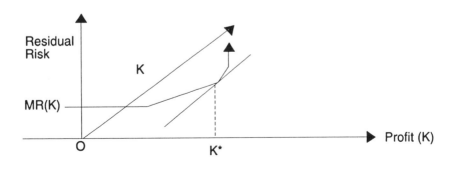

Case 3: MR(K) > K for all K

In this case there is no arbitrage and the deal always yields a risk-adjusted loss, i.e., K
− MR(K) < 0 for all K. A rational issuer would never undertake such a deal.

Exhibit 4. The Risk versus Reward Trade-Off: Case 3

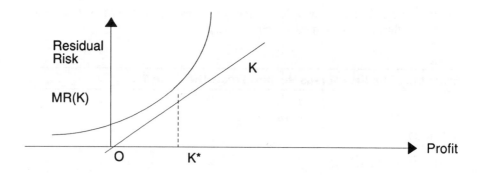

Case 4: MR(K) = 0 for K = 0 to K = Kₐ > 0

This occurs in a (possibly complete) market where arbitrage is possible.

It is interesting that even in this case it is optimal, under the assumption the issuer
wishes to maximize risk-adjusted profit, to seek a profit of $K^* > K_a$ which bears a risk
of $MR(K^*) > 0$ rather than take a riskless profit of K_a.

Exhibit 5. The Risk versus Reward Trade-Off: Case 4

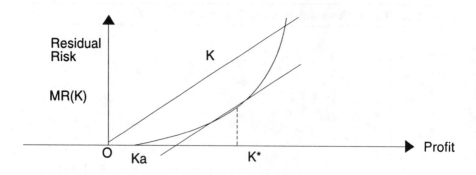

ISSUES ARISING IN PRACTICE

The theoretical basis for multiscenario (MS) hedging that we have described so far provides a good framework for a practical implementation, but clearly there are many more issues that need to be dealt with in a real-world setting.

An MS hedge will usually involve trading a portfolio of options and futures contracts to create the synthetic. This is more complicated than simply calculating a single number (the D of the portfolio) and holding the appropriate ratio of underlying to cash to create an instantaneous hedge. Some of the added complications associated with MS hedging are:

- Choosing scenarios

- Multiperiod hedging and the risks at rollover

- Liquidity and the lack of a diverse set of instruments with which to hedge

- The synthetic will be sensitive to more complicated combinations of risk factors, e.g.,

  —calendar spread risk

  —volatility smile risk

  —yield curve shifts

  —cost-of-carry shifts and others

This makes software for MS hedging far more complicated and places a higher burden on the trader implementing the hedge. The benefits, however, almost always far outweigh the complications.

Choosing Scenarios

Our experience indicates that first-time users of MS hedging usually focus on this as the number one difficulty. In practice, very simple choices for the scenarios go a long way toward creating hedges that are a vast improvement over instantaneous replication. We have found that simple choices work well and may always be refined as one's expertise in such hedging technology develops. For example, the following gross simplification works well as a rule.

- For the underlying, choose a uniform distribution over the range to be hedged.

- For volatility, choose three scenarios: an upward, downward, and unchanged shift in the volatility smile with a distribution skewed as desired.

- For yield curves and cost-of-carry curves, pick an arbitrary selection of curves (scenarios) that span the range of possible curve shifts around the spot curve; choose probabilities to reflect your perceptions of the likelihood of such shifts.

- Always choose scenarios that span the range of possibilities for market moves over the period being hedged, *even if these might seem highly unlikely.*

In certain cases, such as when multiscenario replication is used to price a new issue, model generated scenarios may be preferable to those generated subjectively by a user. For these cases, as an example, yield curve scenarios may be generated from an arbitrage-free lattice process. The only concern is that the number of scenarios be kept within reason, since the computation time for MS replication depends heavily on the number of scenarios generated. To cut down on computation time, in such cases one often resorts to statistical sampling.

There are many situations, particularly when hedging, for which user-defined subjective scenarios are often preferable. Hedging is an attempt to buy insurance against unforeseen market moves. Similarly, directional hedging is an attempt to orient a portfolio in a direction of perceived market movement. In both cases, MS replication offers the possibility to trade off a bet on a move in the predicted direction with one in a move in a different direction. By always including contrarian scenarios or scenarios that in some way span the direction of possible market movements, one may understand the cost-benefit trade-off by adjusting the likelihood (probabilities) of these scenarios.

To place this in context, using traditional hedging methods, based on continuous models, one hedges against a *single predicted outcome* (scenario). That is, one computes a D hedge that will instantaneously replicate the target perfectly only if the assumed values for yield, volatility, cost-of-carry, etc., are achieved. In MS hedging one bets on a *distribution of possible outcomes (scenarios)*. So, for example, this allows one to protect against downside movements and orient toward the benefit of upside movements simultaneously. In addition, it is possible to generate a risk/reward profile so as to maximize the risk-adjusted value of the hedge.

Multiperiod Hedging and Rollover Risk

Cost of Rebalancing

Often one needs to hedge a long-dated instrument using a portfolio of instruments of shorter maturity. This implies that the hedge portfolio will need to be rolled over a number of times over the life of the target. It is important, therefore, to know what risks are likely to be assumed at rollover.

Perhaps the best way to understand this is to compare D hedging and MS hedging for the most basic situation, namely one where the only random variable is the price of the underlying, assumed to evolve over time according to a binomial lattice process.

Consider the following binomial lattice, which describes the price evolution of the underlying. (If the binomial lattice were to be replaced by a much more complicated discrete process, the exact same discussion would apply.) In such a world, the market can be measured and action taken only at discrete points in time. A market gap in this world may be represented by a sequence of successive time periods in between which the market participant is unable to measure or act. In effect, the market participant is blindfolded for a few time steps and is not allowed to observe the market until the blindfold has been removed. At this point the market has a finite probability of having moved to values beyond those possible in a single time step (see Exhibit 6).

This model quite accurately reflects practical situations. For example, over weekends or trading holidays, when significant news might appear that could affect

Exhibit 6

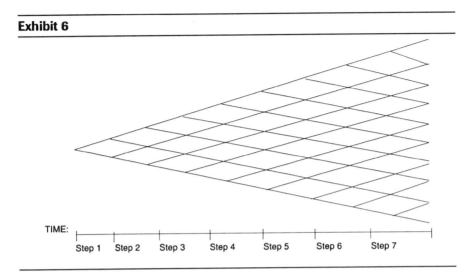

TIME:

Step 1   Step 2   Step 3   Step 4   Step 5   Step 6   Step 7

prices and the pressure of this news is allowed to build up with no trade occurring. Also, during normal trading days in which unusually severe market moves occur (e.g., the crash of '87), it can be impossible to trade and execution prices are not known. Over such periods, the market moves beyond a range that is normally anticipated. D, or instantaneous, hedging, in this context, corresponds to computing a perfect hedge for a single time step. That is, a combination of cash and underlying perfectly replicates the two possible outcomes over any given single time step. However, if the market gaps, the instantaneous hedge no longer matches the set of all possible outcomes. As the severity of the gap (as measured by the number of periods over which the participant remains "blindfolded") increases, so does the expected cost of rebalancing.

An MS hedge is capable of matching the outcomes, including path dependency, for more than one consecutive time step. The number of time steps for which the MS hedge remains perfectly valid depends on the nature of the set of possible replicating instruments. The richer the set, the more scenarios may be replicated perfectly. For example, in a binomial lattice it would require as much as 2^{n-1} independent instruments to perfectly replicate all possible paths over n periods. To perfectly replicate terminal values, such as in the case of a European option, only $n + 1$ independent instruments would be required.

In Exhibit 7 a perfect MS hedge, spanning five periods and replicating all path dependency, may be created with 20 independent instruments. It can withstand shocks equivalent to four upward movements and four downward movements beyond the validity of an instantaneous (D) hedge. It is also clear from the diagram that the larger the shock, the smaller will be the probability that an instantaneous hedge will remain valid. For MS hedging the trade-off lies in the complexity of the hedge versus the degree of gap protection desired. In the example, in Exhibit 7, a gap amounting to the equivalent of six time steps would still have a very small probability that rebalancing would be required.

One of the principles behind Black-Scholes/Cox-Ross-Rubenstein pricing is that, in frictionless markets, the riskless hedge may be rolled over until the maturity

---

Exhibit 7. Validity of Instantaneous (Delta) versus Multiscenario Hedging

---

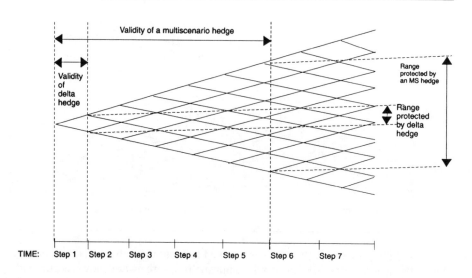

of the target at zero cost. Thus, the cost of financing the replication over the life of the hedge, discounted appropriately, becomes the fair market value of the hedge. Viewed in this way, MS hedging could be regarded as an extension of Black-Scholes (BS)/Cox-Ross-Rubenstein (CRR). The MS replication in a frictionless market may be rolled over at each time step at zero cost, until the maturity of the target. The cost of financing this replication, appropriately discounted, should be equal to the fair market value of the target. Consequently, in frictionless markets without gapping, the cost of the two strategies should be the same.

In markets where there are transaction costs, the difference between these strategies becomes apparent. Firstly, the cost of putting on a single MS hedge is likely to be greater than a BS/CRR hedge since it will involve more trading. However, the MS hedge will require fewer rebalancings. If we were assured that gapping would never extend above a certain known limit, then in principle we may implement an appropriate MS hedge at the beginning of the period and never have to rebalance. In such a case the BS hedge would be cheaper to initialize but would have to be rebalanced, perhaps frequently, each time incurring a cost that depended on the severity of the gap. The BS/CRR price, therefore, will underestimate the cost of the hedge, whereas the MS hedge will (perhaps) overestimate the cost if the hedge is "overinsured." If more details are known about the jump process, it is possible to design an MS hedge that is optimal and will replicate at minimum cost.

Note that in such situations, MS hedging retains much of the beauty of BS pricing. It is constructive in that the cost of the hedge and the portfolio needed to protect it are determined by the same model.

Thus, in practice, the cost of rebalancing is a trade-off between the expected cost of the replication (which depends on the degree of insurance required) and the quality of protection, as measured by the total rollover cost over the life of the target. An optimal strategy will depend on the amount and severity of gapping.

Liquidity Risk at Rebalancing

This is by far the most serious risk, since it cannot be controlled by the hedger. Liquidity can change at any time without warning. A mitigating factor is that in MS hedging there is more time to effect a rollover, since rollovers need not be done at each time step. Thus, in illiquid markets, MS replication allows one to operate effectively at higher than market liquidity levels because of the added time allowed for a rollover.

A major advantage of MS hedging over D or other instantaneous hedges is that, because MS hedges will be valid over larger market moves, one is not forced to rebalance every time the market moves by a small amount as one would have to do with a D hedge. Buying this time between rollovers is probably the most important feature of MS hedging. It allows traders to wait for opportunities that may arise rather than react to every market move.

Lack of a Diverse Set of Instruments with Which to Hedge

This is often the case in emerging markets. There are few option contracts traded and those that are are fairly illiquid. There is no restriction, however, on the use of OTC instruments within an MS hedge. In these markets some ingenuity is necessary, but the principles are the same. If it is cost-effective, any relevant available instruments may be used. Most importantly, in such markets the opportunities to exploit mispricing are significant, particularly if one can set up an MS hedge.

Modeling Liquidity Risk

Liquidity constraints may be added to the Minimum Regret model (Equations 7 and 8) by placing upper and lower bounds on the amount of an instrument that may be traded as follows:

$$l \leq x \leq u. \tag{14}$$

When a function relating trading cost and size of trade is known, this may also be modeled within the mathematical program MR(K). Unfortunately, whereas in principle this is straightforward, in practice in some markets it is never possible to measure the amount that may be traded at a given price without attempting the trade. In illiquid markets we usually plan a strategy for implementing an MS hedge by starting with a D hedge and slowly adjusting it over time to cover the desired range of protection.

The Sensitivity of the Hedge to Combinations of Risk Factors

The essence of MS hedging is to keep hedges as simple as possible (an example of this is given in the next section). A good analogy is multiple regression. In regression analysis the art is to find a model with as few independent variables as possible. The same is true for MS hedging. A naive implementation of the MS replication model will find a hedge that contains many replicating instruments. Naturally, there will be a high cost to implementing such a trade. With some additional modifications and careful weeding out of replicating instruments, one can usually find a much simplified replication. Just as in multiple regression, this is more art than science.

The primary purpose of simplification is to limit the possible complex sensitivities to risk factors. For example, by having options with many different maturities in a replicating portfolio, one is exposed to calendar spread risks as well as to different points on the yield or carry curve. By having options with many different strikes, one is exposed to volatility smile risk. By replicating with options near expiry, one is exposed to time decay risk. By using options on different, even if related, underlyings, one is exposed to basis risk. By using a fixed correlation to relate underlyings, one is exposed to correlation risk, etc.

Sometimes one has no choice but to assume such risks and to trade them off with the risk of being unhedged. By appropriate choice of Regret function, many of these risks are easy to measure and include in the trade-off. Wherever possible one should still simplify the hedge. Most importantly, one needs appropriate software to be able to measure the exposure associated with this type of hedge. This, however, is true for any portfolio approach to options.

PRACTICAL EXPERIENCE WITH MULTISCENARIO HEDGING

We have had over five years of experience with MS hedging, which we developed in 1986-1988; both in backtesting trials in various markets and in actual trading and issuing of synthetics; in commodities; equities, fixed income, mortgage-backed securities, and foreign exchange. Prior to this date there had been some work at Drexel Burnham on option replication using options, based essentially on least squares curve fitting. Whereas at first glance the MS approach might seem similar, it is significantly different; in particular, the Regret function is far more general than a least-squares objective, and the additional features allow for the computation of the risk/reward trade-off.

In all cases in which we have used MS hedging in live trading situations, it has outperformed any *a priori* performance estimates by a significant margin. Our best explanation for this has been that it affords the luxury of sitting and waiting for market opportunities. Unlike D hedging, one does not have to react to market movements as they arise. It works particularly well after a shock in the market, when there is usually a distortion of some kind that may be traded for profit. To illustrate this, consider two typical cases in which we have used this software in practice.

Hedging a Long-Dated Option on a Basket of Gold Stocks

Customized options on a basket of stocks, currencies, or commodities have become popular in the market. They offer tailored protection/exposure for clients and have the advantage of a possible significant reduction in cost over hedging/replicating the contents of the basket individually. This is largely because of the reduction of volatility due to diversification.

Creating and hedging a basket option is complicated by the fact that one needs to relate the contents of the basket via correlation measures. These measures vary randomly. Multiscenario replication may be used to hedge correlation risk, but in the case we describe below, correlation was assumed to be constant.

In November 1989, Algorithmics, together with an investment bank, issued two-year call warrants on a basket of gold stocks. These warrants had the following characteristics:

■ Each basket contained the following stocks:

—1 Placer Dome

—1 Corona

—1 American Barrick

—1 LAC Minerals

—1 Battle Mountain Gold

■ The value of the basket on the date of issue (November 22, 1989) was $101.17.

The performance of this warrant over the period November 22, 1989, to January 16, 1990, the first rollover date, is shown Exhibit 8. It is important to realize that over this period gold and gold stocks were quite volatile and that this hedge was entirely static; that is, there was no trading involved to maintain the hedge over this period. Despite this, the hedge tracks extremely well. A D hedge over the same period would have required frequent rebalancing.

Exhibit 8. Performance of the Gold Basket Warrant over the First Hedging Period

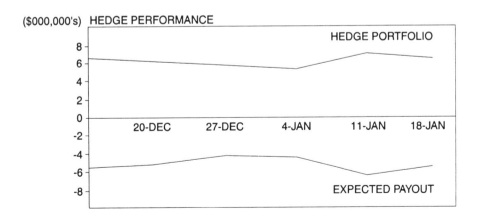

The performance of the warrant over the first replication period is shown in Table 1.

Table 1.   Gold Basket Warrant—Hedge Performance

8-DEC-89		
	■ Basket Value	$106.61
	■ Proceeds from Sale	$35.65/basket
	■ Cost of SBO	$31.06/basket
	■ Margin	$4.51/basket
"FIRST ROLLOVER"		
16-JAN-90		
	■ Basket Value	$112.14
	■ Proceeds from SBO	$44.46/basket
	■ Cost of new "no risk" SBO	$39.76/basket
	■ Cost of new "risky" SBO	$37.49/basket

Trading off risk and reward in this real case is evident in the possibilities faced at the first rollover. The hedge portfolio was worth $44.46 per basket at rollover and the cost of a multiscenario hedge was $39.76 per basket for an extremely good replication (see Exhibit 9) or $37.49 per basket for a replication that involved substantially more risk (see Exhibit 10). Thus, for an additional margin of approximately $2 per basket, we could have rebalanced with the hedge shown in Exhibit 10. A drop of 10 percent in the basket price, without rebalancing, would have resulted in an expected loss of over 1.3 million dollars in this case; whereas by forgoing the $2 additional margin, an instantaneous drop of 10 percent in the basket price would have resulted in an expected loss of approximately only $300,000. For jumps upward in price the hedge is almost perfect. This is representative of the kinds of trade-offs one

Exhibit 9.   Tracking of the Multiscenario Replication to Target Portfolio—Case 1

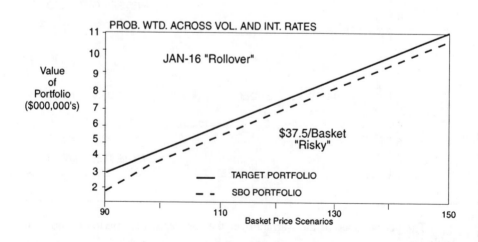

Exhibit 10. Tracking of the Multiscenario Replication to Target Portfolio—Case 2

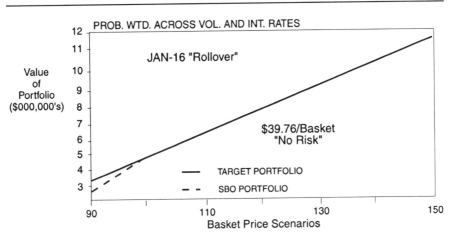

has to make in real situations. The advantage of multiscenario hedging is that these trade-offs are explicitly quantified by the model. Thus, a market maker has an entire spectrum of hedges available, depending on his or her appetite for risk. In addition, the nature of the risk profile assumed may be tailored to reduce specific risks, such as price risk, gamma risk, etc.

Another aspect to notice regarding the first rollover is the significant margin between an excellent replication and the market price of the basket option. This is indicative of a market with significant expected arbitrage, which was typical of the long-dated warrant market at that time.

Whereas in this case no trading was done between rollovers, in practice many opportunities arise during the hedging period. An extremely beneficial fact from a trader's point of view is that with multiscenario hedging one does not have to react as often or as quickly as with a D hedge. This allows for better market timing to take advantage of price distortions, which may generate expected arbitrage opportunities. D hedgers are forced to react to relatively small market movements. In addition, all traders hedging the same market must react in unison, thereby distorting the market even further. A good example of this was the crash of 1987, in which portfolio insurers were accused of distorting the S&P futures market.

How well do such hedges perform over multiple rollovers? Typically, they perform very well even in extreme situations as is shown in the next case study.

Hedging a Long-Dated Index-Linked S&P Note

Index-linked notes have been, and continue to be, a very popular investment vehicle. They offer a simple way in which an investor can buy exposure to some domestic or foreign index. In addition, they offer downside protection, often guaranteed by high credit. They are the appropriate vehicle for selling portfolio insurance, where the floor

Table 2.   The Performance of the Replicating and Target Portfolios—S&P-Linked Note

| | 03/13/89 to 03/03/90   COUPON: 1% | | MULTIPLE 102.5% | |
| | Monthly | | Cumulative | |
Date	Portfolio	S&P 500	Portfolio	S&P 500
04/10/87	-0.25%	0.90%	-0.25%	0.90%
07/10/87	1.14%	2.24%	2.68%	6.37%
10/09/87	-2.87%	-3.39%	2.98%	7.31%
12/11/87	-2.43%	-4.20%	-4.34%	-18.82%
01/08/88	1.62%	3.43%	-2.80%	-16.04%
04/08/88	2.51%	1.69%	4.58%	-7.06%
07/08/88	0.68%	-0.46%	3.69%	6.85%
11/14/88	-0.69%	-2.82%	2.07%	-7.65%
02/10/89	2.26%	2.87%	6.73%	0.73%
06/09/89	4.6%	4.09%	18.37%	12.69%
10/13/89	-0.01%	-4.33%	25.66%	15.10%
12/08/89	2.33%	2.83%	26.88%	20.28%

Portfolio Total Increase 22.94%   Portfolio Excess Value $5,961,782
S&P 500 at 102.5% of Increase 16.99%   Effective Increase 138%

is protected by a bond. In essence, they are a zero-coupon bond combined with a long-dated option on an index.

In this case study, for the period March 13, 1987, to March 3, 1990, we consider a multiscenario replication whose goal is to hedge or, if possible, outperform an index-linked note with the following characteristics:

- 3-year term

- coupon of 1 percent

- 102.5 percent of the *increase* in the S&P

To create the replicating portfolio, we used traded options and futures on the S&P with a maturity of three months or more. The replicating portfolio was held, without further trading, and rolled over into a new portfolio every three months until the maturity of the note.

The replicating portfolio was chosen to outperform a three-year call option on the S&P. Because we were able to detect a significant degree of expected arbitrage, on most rollovers the hedge outperformed the target. This is interesting since the S&P is one of the most efficient markets in the world. Also, presumably we could have improved the performance of the hedge by more active trading.

The period of this case study included the crash of October 1987, during which it became impossible to execute dynamic (D) hedging strategies and where portfolio insurance executed in this manner earned a dirty name. This was a good example of a discrete market. A smaller, but nevertheless significant, discrete jump occurred in October 1989. So, this period definitely favored multiscenario hedging.

The results of the hedge are shown in Exhibit 10 and in Table 2.

As can be seen from Table 2, the replicating portfolio outperforms the target by a significant margin, yielding an excess of just under 6 percent of the underlying. Assuming a $100 million note, the excess hedging profits were $5,961,782. It is particularly interesting to examine the behavior of the portfolios over the crashes, where it can be seen that the multiscenario hedge, without trading, offers significant protection. We did not predict the crash, nor were there adequate scenarios generated prior to the crash to reflect the extreme nature of the events that were to follow. That is, even better protection could have been obtained if more extreme scenario variations would have been used in the construction of the hedge. Yet despite this, the hedges performed quite adequately (see Exhibit 11).

Exhibit 11. Tracking of Hedge and Target Portfolios

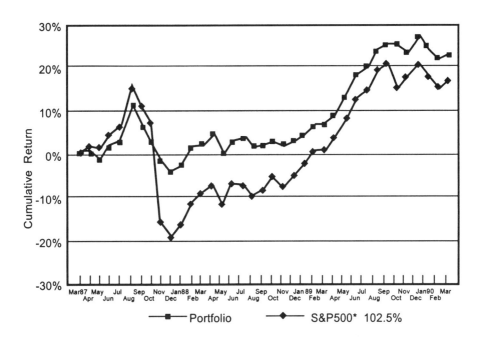

CONCLUSIONS

Multiscenario hedging is significantly more complicated than D hedging. Once understood and with the proper software support, it offers many advantages over D hedging and can protect against discrete market moves without trading. It buys time, over D hedging, during which market opportunities may be exploited. Most importantly, it permits one to trade off the cost of a hedge versus the quality of protection it offers.

REFERENCES

Black, F., and M. Scholes, "The Pricing of Options and Corporate Liabilities," *Journal of Political Economy*, Vol. 81, 637–654 [1973].

Dembo, R. S., "Scenario Optimization," *Annals of Operations Research,* Vol. 30, 63–80 [1991].

Dembo, R. S., and A. J. King, "Tracking Models and the Optimal Regret Distribution in Asset Allocation," *Applied Stochastic Models and Data Analysis,* Vol. 8, 151–157 [1992].

Information on the patent for multi-scenario hedging may be obtained from Algorithmics Incorporated, 822 Richmond Street West, Toronto, Ontario M6J 1C9 CANADA.

CHAPTER 23

How Enhanced DPCs Are Rated 'AAA'

Lisa M. Raiti
Managing Director
Centre Financial Products Limited

INTRODUCTION

The enhanced derivative product company (DPC) has three fundamental characteristics:

1. It is a separate subsidiary of a financial services firm that can be rated higher than its parent or sponsor.

2. It is backed by segregated capital that serves as credit support.

3. It recaptures the top tier 'AAA' and 'AA' ratings that over-the-counter (OTC) derivatives market participants value so highly. The enhanced DPC is one way for a bank or securities firm to revitalize its role in a credit-conscious market (see Chapter 9, The Derivative Products Company).

This chapter will answer the question, "How is an enhanced DPC rated 'AAA'?" from the vantage point of the rating agency Standard & Poor's Corporation (S&P). S&P also rates 'AAA' derivative product companies that are guaranteed or directly supported by 'AAA-' rated parent firms, such as insurance companies. The enhanced or separately capitalized DPC focused on here, however, can be rated higher than its parent.

S&P's rating on a DPC is a financial programs rating. Although analogous to a senior unsecured debt rating, the financial programs rating addresses the capacity of a DPC to meet its financial obligations as a counterparty on its derivative product contracts.

This chapter is based on Standard & Poor's May 1992 publication, Credit Sensitivity Spurs Enhanced DPC Growth; however, the views expressed are those of the author and do not necessarily reflect the opinions of Standard & Poor's.

RATING PERSPECTIVE

S&P's rating of a separately capitalized DPC combines elements of structured and operating company analysis. This "blended" or "hybrid" rating approach directly parallels the nature of an enhanced DPC. Its rating can be enhanced above the parent's rating with segregated capital in a separate subsidiary—a familiar concept in structured transactions, such as mortgage-backed and asset-backed securities. At the same time, however, a DPC is an operating entity that will originate new business and expand its portfolio. S&P applies principles of structured finance in assessing capital adequacy and in examining protection of an enhanced DPC from its parent's financial condition. S&P applies principles of fundamental analysis in assessing changing portfolios, which can include different mixes of derivative products. S&P evaluates operating guidelines, capital ratios, maintenance tests, as well as management's risk aversion, monitoring systems, and controls applying both structured finance and fundamental analysis.

It is important to note that the ratings of the DPC and its parent are not entirely independent. A DPC is different from most structured issuers in that it is an operating entity. Although separately capitalized, a DPC will originate new business and manage a dynamic portfolio. Because the DPC is an active entity, it is important that its parent operate it in a manner consistent with its status as a separate legal entity. S&P's rating, therefore, takes into account such legal issues as separateness and nonconsolidation in bankruptcy common in structured transactions, but in the context of the rating "spread" or difference between a DPC and its lower-rated parent. These structural protections allow for the positive rating spread between DPC and parent by loosening, but not completely eliminating, the link between them.

S&P's rating approach to DPCs has four main components (see Exhibit 1).

Exhibit 1. Blended Rating Approach

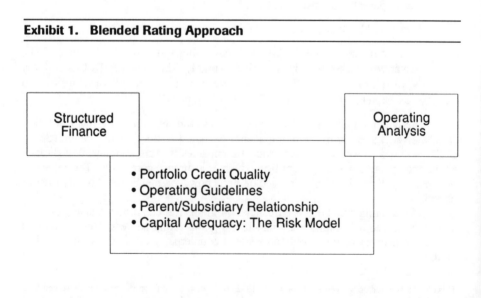

- Portfolio Credit Quality
- Operating Guidelines
- Parent/Subsidiary Relationship
- Capital Adequacy: The Risk Model

1. Portfolio Credit Quality

2. Operating Guidelines

3. Parent/Subsidiary Relationship

4. Capital Adequacy: The Risk Model

Portfolio credit quality. The DPC's portfolio credit quality is based on the credit quality of its counterparties. To evaluate default risk, S&P designs capital stress tests assuming various default probabilities based on each counterparty's S&P senior unsecured debt rating. S&P's analysis is based on empirical studies of default experience and on a DPC's credit quality criteria. DPCs limit counterparty defaults to low-frequency events by transacting with highly rated investment-grade counterparties (see Exhibit 2).

Exhibit 2. Portfolio Credit Qualtiy

- Counterparty S&P Rating
- Default Probability

Operating guidelines. Operating guidelines cover a wide range of tests, ratios, triggers, and limits on DPC activities. In effect, they are risk controls, which target three objectives (see Exhibit 3):

1. Limit credit exposure

2. Limit market exposure

3. Maintain capital

■ *Limit credit exposure.* Classical portfolio theory taught us that diversification is a powerful tool for controlling risk and limiting exposure to loss achieving the so-called "portfolio effect." The DPC can diversify, and thus lower severity or cost of default through its credit exposure limits on counterparties, industries, and countries. For example, the DPC may have net exposure limits of U.S.$50 million per 'A-' rated counterparty. Alternatively, the DPC may require that all eligible counterparties must be rated at least 'AA-', with no single country exposure exceeding the amount of capital..

■ *Limit market exposure.* Operating guidelines requiring matching or offsetting positions protect the DPC against fluctuations in the underlying rate, index, or asset price. Typically, DPCs have achieved matching through "equal and opposite" or "mirror" transactions with the parent. As a result, the DPC portfolio is

---

Exhibit 3. Operating Guidelines

- • Limit Credit Exposure
- • Limit Market Exposure
- • Maintain Capital

---

hedged against market risk, as long as no counterparty—parent or third party—defaults.

Because of the potential for counterparty default risk, DPC managers do need to protect against the accompanying market mismatches they may face involuntarily. For example, the DPC may limit exposure to its parent on the matching transactions, and/or require posting of collateral to protect itself from market risk in the event of a parent default. In addition, the DPC may have "basket" limits such as 5 percent of net market value or of notional principal in relatively illiquid or exotic products to mitigate post-default market risk.

As noted above, DPC portfolios assessed to date have been matched or hedged via the parent. To the extent that matching transactions are conducted with a DPC parent or other affiliates, the benefits of hedging must be weighed against the cost of exposure to the lower-rated parent. Operating guidelines of future DPCs may well implement independent dynamic hedging strategies, at least with respect to generic products.

■ *Maintain capital.* Operating guidelines can help preserve capital and cash needed in the event of counterparty defaults. For example, the DPC may commit to maintaining capital at four times its largest BBB exposure on a replacement cost basis, and/or at least its largest non-'AAA' exposure.

Capital maintenance also includes prudent investment of paid-in or accumulated capital in highly rated instruments with sufficient liquidity to meet cash flow needs. For example, the DPC may require that its capital investments be rated 'AAA', and that 50 percent of capital consist of cash equivalents or 'A-1+' rated liquid assets maturing within 30 days.

In general, operating guidelines relate changing exposure to capital. Exposure measurement is behind all these operating guidelines, which inevitably brings up the netting question: Does net exposure measurement and coverage apply? Put another way, can the replacement cost of positions with defaulted counterparties be netted across contracts with that same counterparty? Netting, or close-out netting, simply means offsetting all of a counterparty's payables and receivables against one another to settle the positions when terminating with a bankrupt or insolvent counterparty. Generally, netting treatment and capital maintenance against smaller net exposures is permitted if S&P obtains sufficient legal and regulatory comfort with respect to the governing jurisdiction of the defaulted counterparty. Otherwise, gross exposure limits and tests are more relevant, and S&P recommends them in any case to prudently monitor capital and temper concentration risk.

There are different legal and regulatory positions across the globe on close-out netting, although the outlook for resolution through regulatory and trade initiatives is positive. The U.S. is the only country that has codified netting treatment in its Bankruptcy Code and its banking regulations. However, the momentum continues with respect to resolution of this all-important risk exposure issue in the Group of Seven and other industrialized active derivatives market sectors. Encouraging developments include the revised 1992 International Swaps and Derivatives Association, Inc. (ISDA) master agreement that provides for netting treatment across a broader product line. In addition, the 1993 Bank for International Settlements (BIS) stated that netting can be used as the basis for a bank's capital adequacy calculations for transactions under a master derivatives agreement that specifies and achieves legally valid, binding, and enforceable netting treatment in the applicable jurisdiction.

Parent/subsidiary relationship. S&P's main concern is separateness of an enhanced DPC and insulation of capital from a legal, operational, and regulatory standpoint. The reason is the positive spread between the 'AAA' rating on the DPC subsidiary and the often lower rating on the parent. These separateness and capital insulation issues are familiar in the context of structured financings and special-purpose vehicles.

As noted earlier, a DPC differs from most structured issuers in that it is an active, operating entity. Because of the DPC's operating nature, S&P applies the blended rating approach. The focus is to evaluate whether or not the structural protections agreed to by the DPC subsidiary and its parent are sufficient to support the DPC's separateness and its 'AAA' financial programs rating. The backdrop to S&P's rating analysis is the spread or difference between the ratings of DPC and parent, which can be significant. S&P views the benefits to a parent that can act as an intermediary through an 'AAA' rated DPC subsidiary as a powerful economic incentive for the parent to preserve the capital and financial strength of its enhanced DPC subsidiary.

In the first three 'AAA-' rated DPCs, this spread was initially two rating categories. All three were subsidiaries of U.S. securities firms with senior unsecured debt ratings in the general 'A' category (see the section below on the enhanced DPC universe). Although there are no hard and fast rules, it is not anticipated that below 'BBB-' rated or noninvestment-grade sponsors will become active issuers of 'AAA' DPCs. This is because of the loosening but not complete elimination of the link between DPC and parent discussed earlier. In addition, it is anticipated that the substantial commitment of capital associated with 'AAA' DPCs, and the profile of major global participants in the OTC derivatives markets, will have a "gatekeeper" effect.

There are three main areas of the parent/subsidiary relationship, outlined below. These also form the basis for S&P's legal analysis (see Exhibit 4).

Exhibit 4.   Parent/Subsidiary Relationship

---

* Legal Issues: Indicia of Separateness
* Regulatory Issues
* Dividend & Corporate Governance Policies

■ *Legal issues.* The most important legal issue is separateness of the DPC. The DPC is set up as a legal entity separate from the parent and its affiliates in order to protect the DPC's assets in the event of the insolvency or bankruptcy of the parent or any of its affiliates. This separateness is achieved by the presence of so-called "indicia of corporate separateness." These include procedures and practices by the DPC subsidiary to make it separate and distinct from its parent and affiliates. Examples include independent board interest in the form of outside directors or officers; segregation of assets, funds, and accounts; and dedicated office space. Intercompany transactions, servicing, or contractual arrangements should be conducted on an "arms'-length" basis. Since the DPC is an operating entity, it is important that these indicia of legal separateness not only be in its bylaws or corporate charter, but actually maintained over the life of the DPC. To this end, the DPC and its parent should agree to operate the DPC in a manner consistent with the DPC's treatment as a separate legal entity.

There are a host of other relevant legal issues. Depending on the corporate structure of a DPC and the nature of its protection from the parent, legal analysis can include issues familiar in structured financing vehicles. Examples include true sale, fraudulent conveyance, preference, and first-perfected security interest in collateral. In addition, legal issues unique to the derivative product contracts and their terms are relevant, including netting, termination events, seniority, guarantees, and enforceability.

■ *Regulatory issues.* Regulatory comfort should be obtained on the same above issues on which legal comfort is obtained. Viability, separateness, and insulation of capital as well as all relevant legal protections in an enhanced DPC need to be achieved from the vantage point of the appropriate regulator(s).

■ *Dividend and corporate governance policies.* Dividend and corporate governance policies are also important to protect a DPC's assets and capital from the parent and affiliates. In general, with respect to dividends, only "truly excess capital" should be upstreamed to the parent.

The presence in the DPC of independent board interest in the form of outside directors or officers is a key indicia of corporate separateness. This representation of outside interests, or even outside equity ownership, acts to balance the parent or affiliate interest in the DPC. The outside directors should

Exhibit 5.   Capital Adequacy: The Risk Model

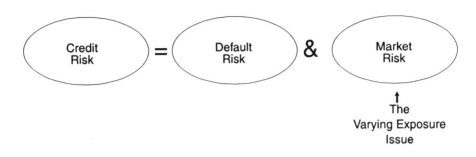

be included in the required voting block to decide material issues, such as dividends, investments, business lines, or a bankruptcy petition filing.

Capital adequacy: the risk model. A key focus of the S&P rating is the adequacy of capital in covering the unique brand of derivatives credit risk. The DPC risk model is the main tool for combining the effects of default and market risk in the credit risk relationship (see Exhibit 5).

The first part of the credit risk relationship—default risk—should be the same in any portfolio. The question is "To what extent will counterparties default in the applicable time horizon?" (See the section on Portfolio Credit Quality.)

The second part of the relationship—market risk—is where derivative instruments' singular property of varying exposure introduces much complexity. The question is "How much loss and capital consumption will occur when counterparties default?" In a derivatives portfolio, the amount of loss will depend on the underlying spot and forward prices, foreign exchange rates, or interest rates, in terms of levels, volatilities and correlations prevailing in the financial markets at the time of counterparty default. Credit risk can only be accurately sized in the DPC's portfolio by applying probability theory and quantitative techniques across a wide range of market behaviors. Mathematical and statistical applications in complex and sophisticated probabilistic risk models become indispensable means to assessing capital adequacy.

Capital adequacy should be measured through a robust probabilistic model that conservatively analyzes a broad range of potential exposures. Of course, complexity is unavoidable here—we do have a large multivariate problem. However, the risk model is an important means of examining the dynamic derivatives portfolio under myriad counterparty defaults and dynamic market conditions. S&P evaluates capital stress scenarios to assess capital adequacy, sensitivity and the risk model's conservatism in its calculation of varying exposures. Some of the relevant variables are counterparty default probability by S&P rating category, behavior of the underlying market determinants of the derivative portfolio value, recovery on defaulted contracts and derivative product liquidity. Probabilistic risk models analyze capital adequacy in DPCs, taking into account varying exposure, the multivariate nature of a derivative products portfolio, and capital volatility.

In the end, the risk model should aid in determining that the 'AAA' DPC has an extremely high probability of meeting its financial obligations as a counterparty (see the section on DPC Risk Modeling Techniques in the Appendix to this chapter).

ENHANCED DPC UNIVERSE

The birth of the enhanced DPC could be considered the launch of Merrill Lynch & Co., Inc.'s vehicle in November 1991. The first three 'AAA-' rated enhanced DPCs were all subsidiaries of U.S. securities firms (see Exhibit 6). GS Financial Products International, L.P., Merrill Lynch Derivative Products, Inc., and Salomon Swapco Inc., comprise this universe. A brief synopsis of each follows.

Exhibit 6. Initial Enhanced DPC Universe

	Financial Programs Rating	Capital	Structure
GS Financial Products International, L.P.	AAA	Dynamic	Continuation
Merrill Lynch Derivative Products, Inc.	AAA	Fixed	Continuation
Salomon Swapco Inc.	AAAt	Dynamic	Termination

GS Financial Products International, L.P. S&P assigned a 'AAA' financial programs rating to GS Financial Products International, L.P. (GSFPI), the Goldman Sachs Group, L.P.'s enhanced DPC. The 45-billion-yen portfolio initially consisted of European options on the Nikkei 225 Japanese stock index, all with highly rated A or better counterparties. Approximately 9.3 billion yen, or 20 percent of the portfolio's fair market value in capital, was in the dynamic form of excess asset value from in-the-money option contracts. S&P also assigned an 'AAA' rating to 30 billion yen in notes issued by GSFPI to fund its purchase of the initial portfolio from an affiliate. GSFPI's DPC is therefore unique in that it was a securitization of derivative contracts into notes. GSFPI's portfolio, substantially hedged or immunized from index movements through affiliate transactions, withstood the strongly bearish message the Japanese equity markets sent it during 1992, its first year of existence.

Merrill Lynch Derivative Products, Inc. S&P assigned a 'AAA' financial programs rating to Merrill Lynch Derivative Products, Inc. (MLDP), Merrill Lynch & Co., Inc.'s enhanced DPC. MLDP was designed to engage primarily in interest rate swaps, currency swaps, and related options with counterparties rated "AA-" or better. MLDP acts as direct intermediary between Merrill Lynch Capital Services and third-party counterparties. The U.S.$350 million in initial capital was in the fixed form of $300 million of common equity purchased by Merrill Lynch, and $50 million of outside preferred equity. Dynamic collateral neutralized the varying exposure of MLDP to its parent, Merrill Lynch, who acts as counterparty on matching transactions.

Note that Exhibit 6 categorizes both the Goldman Sachs and Merrill Lynch DPCs as "continuation" structures. This means that the DPC is designed and capitalized to honor its financial contracts to final maturity, even if the DPC parent or affiliate becomes bankrupt or insolvent. The 'AAA' financial programs rating in these cases addresses the capacity of GS Financial Products International, L.P. and Merrill Lynch Derivative Products, Inc. capacity to make payments on financial contracts in accordance with their original terms. This is in contrast to the DPC that incorporates a "termination" structure, as explained below.

Salomon Swapco Inc. S&P assigned the first of its kind 'AAAt' financial programs rating to Salomon Swapco Inc. (Swapco) Salomon Brothers Holding Company's enhanced DPC. The suffix "t" indicates that Swapco represents a "termination" structure. This means that the DPC's financial contracts could be terminated prior to maturity as a result of nonstandard events, such as failure to maintain capital, collateral, or liquidity, or bankruptcy of the parent or certain affiliates. The 'AAAt' addresses Swapco's capacity to make cash settlement at a specified price, or termination amount. This amount represents Swapco's determination of the mid-market value of all transactions between Swapco and each counterparty. Capital is in the fixed form of U.S.$175 million initially paid in, and in a dynamic form to increase with exposures in the derivatives portfolio. Dynamic collateral neutralizes the varying exposure of Swapco to its parent Salomon Brothers Holding Co., who acts as counterparty on matching transactions.

CONCLUSION

To summarize, whether a continuation or termination structure, four aspects of DPCs add up to the enhanced 'AAA' rating:

1. High portfolio credit quality

2. Operating guidelines that act as effective risk controls

3. Separation of the DPC entity from its parent and affiliates

4. Capital adequacy analyzed through the risk model

The assignment of the 'AAA' financial programs rating is only the beginning of the DPC's intermediation in the OTC market. S&P actively monitors these same four aspects of the DPC, recognizing the dynamism of the DPC's business, its credit risk, its capital adequacy, and its market environment. While S&P focuses on documentation governing the DPC, it also takes into account management's risk appetite and strategy .

The challenge for an enhanced DPC is to manage the different behaviors of dynamic, potentially volatile derivative assets while conserving a finite amount of capital.

APPENDIX

DPC RISK-MODELING TECHNIQUES

Determination of capital adequacy for an enhanced derivative products company (DPC) involves both qualitative and quantitative elements. S&P's analysis of quantitative factors includes the evaluation of a DPC's risk model, which provides a base level of required capital for the vehicle. The techniques that can be used to support capital modeling of enhanced DPCs are discussed below, and many of the specialized terms used are defined in the accompanying glossary (see glossary on page 445).

ELEMENTS OF A DPC MODEL

In theory, modeling a derivatives portfolio should be no different than modeling a portfolio of any other kind of assets. The nature of the assets that is, asset-payment behavior, liability behavior, and the priority of payments, needs to be determined. Asset cash flow is then applied to the liabilities. Any shortfall of payment on any security, which represents debt to the transaction, creates a default. This allows analysis of the credit and liquidity requirements of a transaction for any given rating category.

In reality, the creation of a DPC risk model is more difficult because normal structured financing cash-flow models tend to be deterministic. Asset payment behaviors—such as the severity and timing of default and delinquency frequency and the severity and timing of prepayment frequency—and the terms of the payment of the assets and liabilities are preset. Economic variables are generally held constant for defined periods of time. Finally, the stresses used to test the vehicle are relatively straightforward. When trying to understand the nature of these static variables, testing involves other deterministic tests to look at the sensitivity of default vis-à-vis discrete changes to some or all of the variables.

In DPC modeling, the high volatility of asset values implies a fluctuating and highly volatile equity base if risk-control mechanisms are not put in place. Additionally, the dynamic nature of the vehicle's portfolio may make it impossible to determine a worst-case stress test for a given rating category. Issuers will be forced into the realm of stochastic modeling.

Probabilistic models require an adjustment to S&P's methods of analysis. Input and output variables must be evaluated as a known or assumed distribution of possible events. In looking at a DPC model, it must be recognized that the number of variables proliferates very quickly. S&P must determine what worst-case combination of these remote events is less likely than the default of an 'AAA' rated security.

GENERAL METHODOLOGY

Derivative products, such as swaps and options, have contract terms relating to amount, maturity, and in some cases prematurity cash flows, such as interest or dividends. They also have terms related to execution of various actions by one or both of the parties involved in the contract. Examining some of these contractual terms will help clarify the need for a different type of modeling.

Claims under most of these contracts are contingent in that the amount and timing of the obligation can vary. The value of the contract is determined by the difference in some index value and a static value set at the time of sale of the derivative. Another factor that makes these obligations difficult to model is the credit quality of the obligors or counterparties. Because a frequent use of these instruments is risk transfer, the credit quality demanded in the market is very high. Professional risk intermediators must, by market convention, be rated in the 'AA' category, which is a positive factor for portfolio credit quality. However, the paucity of investment-grade defaults and the relatively limited number of players in the intermediary market adds a layer of complexity because the default curve is not as smooth and predictable as for noninvestment-grade credits.

Any general model to test the credit quality for a DPC should make allowances for these peculiarities. The general model to test sufficiency of cash flow in a DPC may include the following features:

- Random number generator

- Monte Carlo simulation software

- Modeling capacity to define the underlying index

- Logical variable to model defaults (a logical variable takes only two values, e.g., 0 or 1).

Random number generator. A random number generator (RNG) generates a stream of random numbers, taking either discrete values (0 through 9) or continuous values (0.0 through 1.0). In either case, the underlying distribution must be uniform, and the generated numbers at different drawings must be completely uncorrelated. In theory, using a computer to generate such a sequence of random events is impossible. However, using certain programming methods, it is possible to create a pseudo-random number generator that will provide outputs that are random enough to pass statistical tests that determine if the generator is good enough for use in a particular application.

Monte Carlo simulation software. Monte Carlo simulators are software packages that simply run a huge number of paths using an RNG to simulate the behavior of an underlying group of variables, then compute an outcome based on those variables in a static financial model. Each individual path is deterministic, but repeating path creation provides a distribution of outcomes, which, if the stochastic behaviors are well-defined, should give a reasonable estimate of the potential range and likelihood of any particular outcome occurring. The problem with such a simulator is specifying how many runs are sufficient to get the desired level of confidence so that a distribution represents all outcomes at their "true" frequency of occurrence. This requires specifying an acceptable level of tolerance for error and a level of confidence in that tolerance. The tolerance itself is composed of two parts: tolerance to statistical error (how far away the simulated distribution is from the real distribution) and tolerance to the nonrandomness of the RNG.

Modeling capacity to define the underlying index. Modeling the behavior of an underlying index can be viewed as a balance between two extremes. The index behavior may be considered completely random or be completely determinable, but neither of these extremes is a tenable argument. Two approaches are normally made. The first is the standard approach to modeling a structured transaction. A range of values that the variables can take on is established. From the nature of the assets and liabilities, several worst-case scenarios of the variables are created and tested to establish if the transaction can survive material stress. Unfortunately, this approach is inappropriate in a portfolio where some asset terms are contingent because the blend of the assets and liabilities can cause the transaction to be at risk at any level of the index. The second approach is the method that is used in DPC transactions. The behavior of the index is modeled in some way and a large number of index paths are run to test the transaction through a range of potential values.

This method simplifies the rating process in several regards. First, the analyst does not have the impossible job of determining the definitive worst case. Second, if the model is good, the analyst will have a fair idea of the likelihood of any potential outcome. The problem with this approach is the qualification inherent in the second simplification: Is the model good?

In order to answer that question, two assumptions need to be made. First, the modeling of the index is possible. Second, the means of predicting the level or the relationship of the variable being modeled will not change or the change in that variable can be modeled.

Validating the first assumption is accomplished by looking at empirical work. Is there any predictability in the index? There are certain things one can say about indexes. Empirical work has been done to suggest that stock indexes, as well as interest and exchange rates, have predictable distributions. An assumption can be made that the indexes cannot go below zero and that either the level of the index or the changes in the value of the index are normally distributed.

The second assumption, that the means of predicting the level or the relationship of the variable being modeled will not change or that the change in the modeled variable may itself be modeled, may not be as difficult as it first seems. It must be remembered that a key attribute that varies is the volatility of the index. The volatility of the index can be increased or decreased. The analyst will still have the opportunity to specify a path that S&P wants tested by bypassing the simulation stage of the index path and substituting a specific path for the index to take.

Logical variables to model defaults. The final element of the models is the method of simulating defaults. Two methods are suggested, one of which may be accomplished in two ways.

The first method is to simulate defaults by the use of two-staged variables. Although this is not the technical term for the variable, it serves as a description. The variable is divided into two parts: the first is an indicator of default; the second gives the likelihood of default in the period in question. The RNG then provides a random number that is compared to the likelihood of default. If the value of the random number is less than or equal to that likelihood, a default has occurred in the transaction. This method can be accomplished in a second fashion. Instead of a single probability of default, a table is created, giving the likelihood of change in a rating over a period of time. An example of this would be the probability of an A rating changing to a BBB rating in a year. All ratings are included in the table, and a rating that has defaulted during the period has a 100 percent certainty of remaining defaulted in all successive periods.

The second method of determining the effects of defaults is to calculate the probability of all the possible default combinations with their corresponding exposures. A table is then constructed displaying the different levels of exposure and their probabilities.

The techniques described are the key elements of DPC risk models, which differ from standard financial modeling techniques used throughout the structured finance community. They provide enhancements that are necessary for understanding how the need for capital can vary when analyzing the risks involved in managing an enhanced DPC's portfolio.

DPC RISK MODELING: A GLOSSARY

Correlation: The covariation of two numerical variables with each other. The degree of linear association between two variables is often measured with the correlation coefficient, which takes values ranging from -1 to +1. A negative value indicates a tendency for the two variables to move in opposite directions, and a positive value indicates a tendency for the two to move in the same direction.

Deterministic model: A model in which all the determining variables are nonrandom. Within such a model, the behavior of the variables of interest is assumed not to be influenced by any chance-dependent factor.

Lognormal distribution: If the natural logarithm of a random variable follows a normal distribution, the random variable has a lognormal distribution. The natural logarithm is an ordinary logarithm with base "e", where "e" is approximately 2.7183.

Normal distribution: A bell-shaped probability distribution of a random variable that is symmetrical around its mean. It assigns a probability of about .68 for the random variable to fall within one standard deviation from the mean, and over .95 to fall within two standard deviations from the mean and about .99 to fall within three standard deviations from the mean.

Stochastic model: A model in which at least one of the variables influencing the behavior of the variables of interest is chance-dependent and behaves randomly.

Uniform distribution: A probability distribution of a continuous random variable, defined over a finite interval, that assigns equal probabilities for the random variable to take values within subintervals of equal size.

The author wishes to acknowledge Thomas C. Kitto and Reza Bahar of Standard & Poor's Corp. for this appendix.

PART FOUR

THE GLOBAL MARKET
FOR SYNTHETIC AND
DERIVATIVE PRODUCTS

CHAPTER 24

Derivatives and Global Tactical Asset Allocation

Richard A. Crowell
President and Chief Investment Officer
PanAgora Asset Management, Inc.

INTRODUCTION

Global Tactical Asset Allocation (GTAA) is an investment strategy that shifts assets among equity, bond, cash, and currency markets around the world. GTAA earns extra returns by overweighting attractive markets and underweighting markets that are richly priced. GTAA is an exciting development because it represents the culmination of extensive work in several different investment fields. It is a systematic worldwide approach to the management of several asset classes simultaneously. As the name suggests, Global Tactical Asset Allocation developed from U.S. Tactical Asset Allocation (US TAA), which shifts assets between U.S. stocks, bonds, and cash reserves. GTAA is the logical extension of successful U.S. Tactical Asset Allocation concepts to the world markets.

WHY GLOBAL TACTICAL ASSET ALLOCATION

GTAA is growing rapidly for several reasons. First, it is now widely recognized that asset allocation is the single most important investment decision. As much as 50 percent of an individual stock return can be attributed to market performance. For diversified portfolios, the impact of the overall market is even more important, often exceeding 98 percent. For example, Sharpe found that 97.3 percent of the variation in returns of the popular Fidelity Magellan Fund could be explained by the appropriate passive returns. (William F. Sharpe, "Asset Allocation: Management Style and Performance Measurement," *Journal of Portfolio Management,* Winter 1992, Vol. 18, No. 2, p. 13.) Thus, getting the market decision right is critical for all investors.

Second, GTAA is growing because US TAA has a proven track record over more than a decade. This success in the U.S. capital markets makes Global TAA a plausible investment concept. If disciplined tactical asset allocation works in the highly efficient U.S. markets, it follows that it should work in global markets as well.

Third, there has been an explosion in international databases in computer-sensible form. By sitting at a personal computer anywhere in the world that has reliable telephone service, investment managers can access current and historical data on companies, industries, country economies, etc. High-quality, on-line international databases are now available, many at very reasonable costs. (Even as I write this sentence, my computer is receiving stock, bond, and futures prices in the background.)

Fourth, there continues to be high growth in international investing. U.S. pension funds, for example, realize that their traditional focus on U.S. investments is parochial. They have often missed major investment opportunities in international markets. Greenwich Associates, a pension consulting firm, expects international investment by U.S. pension funds to grow from $50 billion in 1987 to $280 billion in 1995. Other experts foresee even more rapid growth. This trend to international investing is amplified by investor concern about the high level of the U.S. equity market (at this writing). Better investment opportunities are available around the world.

Fifth, traditional active strategies have been disappointing in global investing. Many traditional investment managers have underperformed their international and global benchmarks over long time periods. Frank Russell Company's performance database indicates that for the 10 years ending December 31, 1992, the median international manager earned a return of 16.7 percent per year versus 17.4 percent for the EAFE index. This represents a deficit of 0.70 percent per year for a decade.

Some international managers have outperformed for a time by taking major risks, often making large bets in single countries. For example, from 1989 to 1992, it was easy to beat EAFE simply by underweighting Japan. However, some of the managers who avoided the bear market in Japan had sold so early that they missed most of the gains in the 1980s. Astute clients perceive these large bets as risky and many clients view temporary superior performance as lucky and not repeatable.

Finally, the growth in derivatives is crucial to GTAA. The growth in derivatives means that global asset allocation decisions can be implemented quickly, effectively, and efficiently. This is vital in global investing because international transaction costs are notoriously high. Derivatives trading dramatically reduces the cost of implementation and makes GTAA feasible. Exhibit 1 lists the major derivatives currently available on global markets. However, the CFTC has not, as yet, approved some of these derivatives for U.S. investors. In those markets not available to U.S. investors, alternatives range from using cash securities to arranging synthetics with brokers who can, in turn, take the corresponding futures positions for their own account.

THEORETICAL FRAMEWORK FOR GLOBAL TACTICAL ASSET ALLOCATION

All tactical asset allocation strategies are based on the assumption that markets are inefficient in the short term but efficient in the long term. This means that markets can be mispriced today, allowing investors to take positions in undervalued markets and sell overvalued markets. Long-term efficiency means that short-term misvaluations

Exhibit 1. Global Derivative Markets

Country	Equity Futures	Bond Futures
Australia	ALL ORDINARIES FUTURE	
Austria	ATX INDEX FUTURE*	
Belgium	BEL-20 INDEX FUTURE*	
Brazil	BVSP INDEX FUTURE*	
Canada	TORONTO 35 FUTURE	CAD TREAS 10-YR FUTURE
Chile	ISPA INDEX FUTURE*	
Denmark	KFX INDEX*	
Finland	FOX INDEX FUTURE*	
France	CAC-40 INDEX FUTURE	FRF OAT 10-YR FUTURE
Germany	DAX INDEX FUTURE*	GER TREAS 10-YR FUTURE
Hong Kong	MSCI HONG KONG FUT*	
Italy		ITL GOVT BOND FUTURE
Japan	NIKKEI 225 INDEX FUTURE	JPN TREAS 10-YR FUTURE
"	TOPIX INDEX FUTURE	
Netherlands	EOE 20 INDEX FUTURE*	
New Zealand	NZSE 40 INDEX FUTURES*	
Norway	OBX INDEX FUTURE*	
Spain	IBEX 35 SPAIN FUTURE*	ESP GOVT BOND FUTURE
Sweden	OMX SWEDEN FUTURE*	
Switzerland	SWISS MARKET FUTURE*	
United Kingdom	FTSE INDEX FUTURE	UK GILT BOND FUTURE
USA	S&P 500 INDEX FUTURE	US TREAS 10-YR FUTURE
"	S&P MIDCAP INDEX FUTURE	
Other	EUROTOP FUTURE	

* Not CFTC Approved for U.S. Investors

are eventually recognized and markets return to fair value. Thus, investors can profit from mispricing. There is no profit in holding an undervalued asset that is never recognized as undervalued.

Market inefficiencies are caused by biases in human decision making. The most obvious bias in international investing is the parochial nature of many investors. They know a lot about investing in their own local market but are not familiar with other "foreign" markets. They are efficient at allocating assets to their local markets but are prone to ignore major mispricing in other markets. They are comfortable with the local market. But, in investing, comfort often means little opportunity for return.

The second aspect of market inefficiency is based on cognitive bias. Most investment theories assume that investors are rational profit maximizers (or utility maximizers). This is based on the old economic concept of "the rational economic man," who always does the right thing in economic or financial terms. In reality, none of us are rational about investing. We all exhibit cognitive bias. For example, people tend to give too much importance to recent events and not enough to longer-term trends. People tend to jump to conclusions based on a few characteristics of an individual situation and not pay sufficient attention to long-term probabilities. Also, people tend to be unduly impressed by visual, graphic images at the expense of overlooking objective facts. This is why we are impressed with "stories" about individual investment opportunities and are willing to discard proven investment principles if the story rings true.

The third aspect of market inefficiency is human emotions. There are numerous examples of human emotions, including fear and greed, that dominate investment decisions. No one is exempt from these emotions. The waves of fear and greed lead to excessive market panics and rallies. Each market panic or rally is a potential market inefficiency that can provide return opportunities.

In depending on market mispricing, GTAA is no different from any other active investment strategy. For example, stock selection strategies assume that specific stocks can be mispriced today, allowing investors to establish positions. But this stock mispricing is eventually recognized, allowing investors to realize profits.

The largest and most exploitable inefficiencies are across markets and between asset classes. Exhibit 2 shows the range of returns in major world equity markets over the last several years. There are huge disparities between the best- and worst-performing markets. The range from the best to worst country can vary from 60 percent to 160 percent in a single year.

There is also diversity of performance across markets. The same countries do not stay at the top or bottom of the list. The legendary long-term growth of the Japanese stock market (up to 1989) was achieved while Japan was only once at the top of the performance list (1987). Japan also made the bottom of the list as the worst performer in 1979.

In general, the U.S. equity market, as measured by the S&P 500 Stock Index, has not been the best global investment. In fact, international equity markets, as measured by the Morgan Stanley Capital International Index for Europe, Australasia, and the Far East (EAFE), usually beat the S&P 500 Stock Index. The period from 1989 to 1991 was a notable exception.

Exhibit 2 illustrates only the major equity markets. When the smaller equity markets as well as bond and currency markets are considered, the differences are even more pronounced. GTAA is designed to take advantage of these opportunities.

GTAA adds value because it is unbiased and is inherently contrarian. GTAA is based on objective measures of valuation and economic conditions which knowledgeable people agree should be the basis for investment decisions. GTAA's advantage is that it acts on these factors while traditional approaches often allow cognitive bias to interfere. GTAA provides the discipline required to be a successful contrarian investor.

Exhibit 2. Country Allocation Is Important—Annual Performance in U.S. Dollars

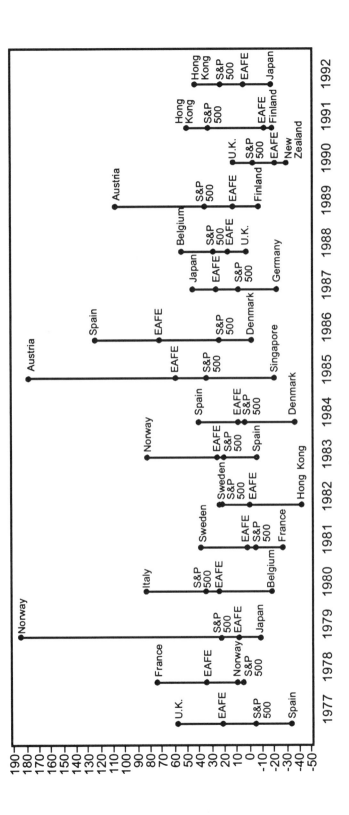

TRANSACTION COSTS

Much of the underperformance of traditional management strategies is due to leakage from transaction costs. Transaction costs can destroy whatever value-added might be available from skillful investment management. This is especially true of international and global portfolios because trading costs for international security portfolios are high. In fact, U.S. investors are often surprised at the extent of international transaction costs.

Transaction costs include high trading commissions, market impact, and significant taxes. In Japan, by far the largest equity market outside the U.S., there is a 0.35 percent stamp tax on all sales. In the U.K., the stamp tax is 0.50 percent on all purchases. Until 1993, Sweden had a 1 percent tax on both purchases and sales. Investors in the Swedish market faced a 2 percent round-trip Swedish tax in addition to commissions and market impact!

GTAA adds value by keeping transaction costs to a minimum. This is accomplished in several ways. GTAA very carefully balances risk and return. In this way, GTAA minimizes turnover by keeping diversification high and making small bets where value can best be added. Another way GTAA minimizes transaction costs is package or basket trading. Often a set of stocks representing a market index can be traded for lower costs. One reason for this is that often the trade is "crossed" with another institutional investor going in the opposite direction.

Derivatives are a great advantage in international investing because of their substantially lower transaction costs. In some cases, derivatives trades are exempt from local stamp taxes. Exhibit 3 compares transaction costs for stocks versus futures on major international equity markets. Note the dramatic savings! U.S. transaction costs drop from 0.75 percent to 0.11 percent; U.K. transaction costs drop from 1.15 percent to 0.12 percent; Japan drops from 1.30 percent to 0.11 percent. These savings accrue directly to investment performance.

GTAA INVESTMENT DECISIONS

GTAA investments are based on decisions for allocations to world equity markets, world bond markets, and currency and cash equivalent markets. These decisions can be made in a variety of ways. In general, there are three steps: (1) return forecasting, (2) risk analysis and portfolio optimization, and (3) implementation. These steps are depicted in Exhibit 4.

Return Forecasting

The core of the GTAA investment process is a set of country equity, bond, and currency valuation models covering the major world markets. We require all return forecasting models to be based on concepts that are both sensible and reliable. Each input factor considered in a return forecast must be sensible. There must be a logical a priori reason that the factor should affect return. For example, equity returns can be projected based on relative valuations to bond and cash markets, current economic conditions reflecting the stage of the business cycle, monetary policy, trends in currency markets,

Exhibit 3. Estimated Round-Trip Transaction Costs as a Percentage of Amount Invested*

	U.S.	Japan	U.K.	France	Germany
Stocks					
Commissions	0.20%	0.20%	0.20%	0.10%	0.10%
Market Imp**	0.55	0.80	0.45	0.55	0.50
Taxes	0.00	0.30	0.50	0.00	0.00
Total	0.75%	1.30%	1.15%	0.65%	0.60%
Avg Stock Price*** in US dollars	39.10	27.3	7.73	158.60	385.65
Futures					
Commissions****	0.01%	0.06%	0.02%	0.04%	0.03%
Market Imp**	0.10	0.05	0.10	0.10	0.05
Taxes	0.00	0.00	0.00	0.00	0.00
Total	0.11%	0.11%	0.12%	0.14%	0.08%

*   Assumes a $25 million cap-weighted indexed portfolio executed as agent, does not include settlement and custody fees, as of 11/92.
**   Trader estimate.
***   Local index: S&P 500, Nikkei 225, FT-SE 100, CAC-40, DAX.
**** All contracts are quarterly except for the CAC-40.

Source: Goldman Sachs

Exhibit 4. Global Tactical Asset Allocation Investment Process

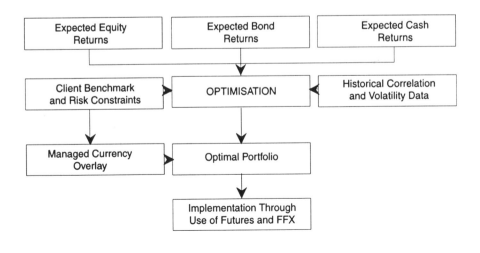

political conditions, and so forth. All these factors make sense, as an experienced investor would agree that they should be important to return.

The factors must also be reliable. They must consistently affect returns over many market cycles. This brings up a number of statistical issues. It is easy to fit a model to any particular subsample of the data. It is much harder to create a model that comes close to the *true* structural form, the true relationship underlying the data. This true structural form, however, is the only relationship that is likely to be stable over time. From a forecasting perspective, only a stable relationship will have any lasting value. As a result, model stability is a key issue throughout the entire model development process.

We employ a number of tests to assure stability. First, we limit our consideration to independent variables, which should, intuitively, be correlated with our dependent variable. Thus, we exclude relationships like the famous "Super Bowl" phenomena, which, however compelling historically, are not likely to be truly causal, and are therefore not likely to be stable. By focusing on variables that are likely to be causal, we have more a priori confidence that the same relationships that held historically will persist in the future.

Second, we extensively test the stability of those relationships that we deem compelling. We test for stability over time, over economic policy regimes such as stages of the business cycle, and over political regimes, to name but a few. For example, a model that works well over recent history as a whole but performs poorly in recessions is in danger of making systematically poor forecasts in a recession.

We employ a battery of tests to evaluate the stability of forecasting models, including Chow tests, Wald tests, CUSUM tests, and ARCH-type tests. Only a model that we can have confidence in for the future, irrespective of policy regime or economic conditions, is implemented.

The following is a brief description of some of the statistical tests for stability:

Chow test: Tests the joint stability of the estimated coefficients over relevant subsamples of the estimation interval. These subsamples may be defined either over time or across regimes.

Wald test: As Chow test, but tests an individual coefficient's stability over relevant subsamples. This is important if a model passes a general Chow test but one suspects an individual coefficient of being unstable.

CUSUM test: Tests for a statistically significant "breakpoint" in the residuals of a model. Helps determine when there is a structural change in the model.

ARCH-type tests: A family of tests for evaluating time dependency in the squared residuals (variance) from a model. Useful in determining if the confidence interval around the forecast is growing, shrinking, or constant. (Stands for AutoRegressive Conditional Heteroskedasticity—the family of tests also includes GARCH, E-GARCH, ARCH-M, etc.)

A variety of factors meet the dual tests of sensible and reliable. For example, the price of oil is important in Italy. This makes sense because Italy is a major importer of oil. In the U.K., the foreign exchange rate is important as a measure of industrial competitiveness. The German stock market is sensitive to interest rates since the German central bank is a powerful advocate of anti-inflationary policies. In most countries, the relationship between equity valuations, as measured by dividend yield or P/E ratios, and local interest rates is important. The slope of the local yield curve is another powerful measure.

For individual world bond markets, the valuation models are based on an appropriate set of sensible and reliable factors for bonds. These factors include relative value, monetary policy, volatility, economic strength, and market psychology.

Currency markets are forecast in a similar manner. However, the currency models reflect the nature of the currency markets. Currency is a zero-sum game. The long-term trend of equity markets is up. Bond markets earn interest every day. The equity and bond markets are a positive sum game. But there is no reason to expect net long-term trends in currencies. The gains of one country are offset by the losses of others. However, there are distinct short-term trends in currencies. Therefore, in forecasting currencies, momentum plays an important role. In addition, purchasing power parity and relative interest rates affect currency returns.

Models of this nature are used to project returns for equity, bond, and currency markets based on factors that are both sensible and reliable.

Risk Analysis and Portfolio Optimization

Risk is a key element of GTAA. Volatility is typically used as a measure of the investment risk of individual markets (individual assets), although other measures are worth investigating. Risk reduction through diversification is especially important in global investing. It is well known that international markets have low correlation with each other. This is the source of the risk-reducing feature of international investing. International markets do not always move up and down together.

GTAA also provides the opportunity to control risk relative to the client's benchmark. Many clients select benchmarks such as 60 percent global equities and 40 percent global bonds. Or, they may have targets or limits on individual countries or regions of the world. This allows GTAA to take risks versus the benchmark where return opportunities are the greatest. Thus, GTAA carefully manages risk relative to the client's investment needs.

Return and risk are balanced using standard portfolio optimization techniques. This enables GTAA to take specific risks only where extra return is available. This assures efficiency in portfolio management. The result of portfolio optimization is a recommended set of allocations to global equity, bond, and currency markets.

Portfolio Implementation

Given the optimal portfolio, GTAA is now prepared for the final step of implementation. Facing the high level of international transaction costs, efficient and effective implementation is critical. Transaction costs can easily eat up the value-added from active management.

In this context, derivatives are critical. The variety of derivatives available on world equity and bond markets provide choices to minimize transaction costs. In fact, these low transaction costs available through derivatives make GTAA viable.

IMPLEMENTATION: BALANCED BENCHMARKS

Clients typically select benchmarks that reflect global balanced portfolios. These benchmarks allocate a portfolio to global equities and a portion to global bonds. They may also state whether the benchmark is in local currencies or hedged into the client's currency, e.g., U.S. dollars, etc.

Balanced GTAA benchmarks result in implementations that make great use of derivatives. However, in some countries with no liquid derivatives (or none available to U.S. investors), baskets of securities are used to effectively capture the local market return.

Exhibit 5 is an example of a typical balanced GTAA portfolio. Note that Exhibit 5 is not dated, as its purpose is illustration only. The portfolio manager must decide on the most efficient implementation strategy for each market. Note that securities are used where derivatives are not available.

Exhibit 5. Sample Balanced GTAA Portfolio

Position	Number of Futures	Equivalent Market Value	Percent of Portfolio
Bonds			
Canadian 10-Year Sep 93	7	$626,095	4.3
FRF Notionnel Bond Future	1	$117,807	0.8
Germany 10-Year Sep 93	6	$1,466,833	10.2
US 10-Year T-Note Sep 93	12	$1,386,375	9.6
Total Bonds		$3,597,110	25.0
Equities			
AUD All Ordinaries Sep 93	4	$523,488	3.6
Belgium Stocks*		$312,900	2.2
CAC-40 Sep 93	1	$74,903	0.5
DAX Sep 93	9	$1,019,577	7.1
Italy Stocks*		$192,500	1.3
MSCI Hong Kong Index Future	9	$594,096	4.1
Spain Index Sep 93	629	$1,577,353	10.9
Swiss Market Index Future	15	$1,252,875	8.7
S&P 500 Index Sep 93	18	$4,148,100	28.8
TOPIX Sep 93	7	$1,116,795	7.8
Total Equities		$10,812,587	75.0
Total		$14,409,697	100.0

Cash equivalent positions not shown.
* Cash securities used where futures not available.

IMPLEMENTATION: GLOBAL MARKET NEUTRAL STRATEGIES

GTAA readily adapts to market neutral strategies. In fact, we expect to see rapid growth in this form of implementation. Exhibit 6 shows an example of a GTAA market neutral portfolio implemented using index futures and FFX contracts. Exhibit 6 is not dated, as its purpose is only to illustrate the structure of a market neutral portfolio.

Exhibit 6. Sample Market Neutral GTAA Portfolio

Position	Number of Futures	Equivalent Market Value	Percent of Portfolio
Bonds			
Canadian 10-Year Sep 93	-22	($1,967,727)	-4.9
Germany 10-Year Sep 93	18	$4,400,498	11.0
Japan Treasury 10 Year Sep 93	-4	$4,289,694	10.7
U.K. Gilt Sep 93	-39	($4,223,650)	-10.6
U.S. 10-Year T-Note Sep 93	37	$4,274,656	10.7
Total Bonds		$6,773,471	16.9
Equities			
AUD All Ordinaries Sep 93	-36	($4,711,393)	-11.8
CAC 40 Sep 93	-33	($2,471,799)	-6.2
LIFFE FTSE 100 Sep 93	41	$4,718,022	11.8
S&P 500 Index Sep 93	19	$4,378,550	10.9
TOPIX Sep 93	-28	($4,467,179)	-11.2
TSE 35 Sep 93	53	$4,150,436	10.4
Total Equities		$1,596,637	4.0
Currencies			
DEM		($9,132,562)	-22.8
GBP		($7,435,622)	-18.6
JPY		$8,364,893	20.9
Total Currencies		($8,203,291)	-20.5
Net Long: Bonds + Equities + Currencies		$166,817	0.4
Total Notional Value		$40,000,000	100.0

Cash equivalent positions not shown.

Market neutral strategies require that the net equity position be zero (or nearly zero). That is, long equity positions must be offset by short equity positions in alternative equity markets. Similarly, long bond positions must be offset by short positions in other bond markets. Similar statements apply to currency positions.

Market neutral strategies are equivalent to naming cash or Treasury bills as the benchmark. Usually, the client is willing to accept a modest degree of tracking risk relative to the benchmark, such as a tracking risk standard deviation of 3 percent per year. Given this small degree of tracking risk, GTAA can be expected to add meaningful value over time.

Also, a market neutral strategy with a Treasury bill benchmark can be leveraged, taking extra risk to seek extra return. One popular approach is to increase risk to levels commensurate with bonds or equities. This enables investors to seek bond-like and equity-like returns, or even superior returns, with little correlation with the bond or equity market.

As a technical note, given a Treasury bill benchmark with modest tracking risk, it is not necessary to be *exactly* market neutral in *both* equities and bonds. The optimization techniques can maintain the tracking risk, allowing slight net long positions in one asset class offset by equivalent net short positions in the other. That is, the net positions of stocks plus bonds plus currencies are zero.

GTAA market neutral strategies are most effectively implemented using derivatives for stock and bond markets (and forward foreign exchange contracts for currencies). Derivatives allow the implementation of long and short positions with equal ease. And, derivatives can be used to implement a leveraged position if that is appropriate for the client.

CONCLUSION

Global Tactical Asset Allocation is a relatively recent investment concept developed from U.S. Tactical Asset Allocation. It is based on the premise that markets are inefficient in the short term but efficient in the long term. Interest in GTAA is growing rapidly, as GTAA provides an effective and efficient approach to value-added active investing. By concentrating on the asset class and markets decision, it focuses on the most important element of return. In addition, by minimizing transaction costs through extensive use of derivatives, GTAA reduces the transaction cost leakage from investment portfolios, making it easier to add value.

CHAPTER 25

Global Synthetic Index Funds

Anne B. Eisenberg
Vice President

Brian R. Bruce
Vice President

State Street Bank and Trust Company

Synthetic index funds based on the U.S. equity markets have been available to investors since the introduction of the S&P 500 futures contract in 1982. A more recent development is the ability of investors to get exposure to the non-U.S. equity markets through the use of derivatives. Exchanges worldwide have begun offering futures contracts on their respective country equity indexes. The result of these developments is that, for the first time, investors can use derivatives to construct synthetic index funds, which provide liquid, low-cost exposure to global equity markets.

MARKETS

Worldwide trading in the derivatives markets is becoming an increasingly popular means of acquiring equity exposure. In many markets, including the U.S., the average daily trading volume on the futures exchanges exceeds that on the stock exchanges. Contracts are offered on 16 of the 22 markets covered by the MSCl World Index and cover more than 95 percent of the index's capitalization.

1991 saw the launch of several pan-European derivative instruments such as LIFFE's FT-SE Eurotrack 100 and Amsterdam's Eurotop 100 indexes. Both contracts have not been well received by the investing public and have experienced low trading volumes. One possible explanation for the marked lack of enthusiasm may be a preference on the part of investors to trade individual markets rather than global regions. Country-specific contracts provide a cost-effective, convenient means of trading within regions.

The latest development in European derivatives is the FT-SE 100 futures contract offered by the Chicago Mercantile Exchange. This contract is very similar to the LIFFE contract with a few notable exceptions. First, the CME contract is dollar-based, so U.S. investors will not be exposed to currency market risk. For these investors, a dollar-based contract eliminates the need of trading forward contracts to offset the currency exposure inherent in the LIFFE contract. Second, U.S. investors may find the CME contract more convenient to trade than the LIFFE contract because its trading hours correspond with regular U.S. business and stock exchange hours.

CONSTRUCTION

Synthetic index funds can be constructed on individual country indexes. Alternatively, global or "umbrella" synthetic index funds can replicate the returns of indexes such as the MSCI EAFE Index.

The use of separate country funds *within* a global synthetic index fund gives investors considerable flexibility in structuring international portfolios. While the existence of an umbrella fund allows investors to purchase overall global exposure—for example, the MSCI World Index—separate country funds allow investors to pick and choose in which of the fund's markets they wish to invest. For example, an investor may want an EAFE ex-Japan portfolio, or may desire only U.K. exposure, or may wish to invest in all the available markets but use customized country weights. Not only do synthetic index funds allow investors to accomplish these goals, but the ease and low costs of trading derivatives permit synthetic index funds to open every day for cash flows. The operational and administrative issues involved in trading actual equities make it difficult for traditional international equity funds to offer daily liquidity.

BENEFITS

Using derivatives instead of stocks to get equity exposure offers several benefits to investors. The three most significant advantages involve lower transaction costs, liquidity, and convenience.

TRANSACTION COSTS

Table 1 (expressed in bid/ask spreads as a percentage of the underlying stocks/indexes) shows that the market impact cost is smaller when executing in the futures market. The round-trip cost comparisons are between futures contracts and a basket of stocks of similar size.

Table 2 compares round-trip commission costs between a basket of stocks and a basket of stocks under futures contracts.

The above numbers must be adjusted to reflect individual investor and country cost structures; however, it is obvious that derivatives provide an extremely cost-effective means of getting exposure to equity markets.

Table 1

	Cash	Futures	Ratio
Japan	0.80%	0.04%	20 to 1
France	1.10%	0.04%	28 to 1
United Kingdom	1.30%	0.08%	16 to 1
United States	0.60%	0.03%	20 to 1

Source: Paine Webber, *Derivative Products Research*, Index Derivatives Monitor, May 1, 1992.

Table 2

	Cash	Futures	Ratio
United States	0.20%	0.01%	20 to 1
Japan	0.20%	0.01%	20 to 1
United Kingdom	0.10%	0.02%	5 to 1
France	0.3%	0.04%	8 to 1

Source: Paine Webber, *Derivative Products Research*, Index Derivatives Monitor, May 1, 1992.

Even though synthetic funds can cover a significant portion of a global index, there is inevitably going to be a certain amount of expected tracking error because it is usually not practical for such funds to cover every market in the benchmark index. Also, the local market indexes are not necessarily those that are included in the benchmark index. However, an optimizer or quadratic program can be used to minimize tracking differences relative to the benchmark, and the liquidity and cost savings benefits derived from trading derivatives must be weighed against the disadvantages of increased tracking error.

Table 3 shows the expected annual tracking of a global synthetic index fund, which invests in five of the largest MSCI EAFE markets relative to the local market indexes. This fund would expect annual tracking of approximately 2.0 percent. However, over one-half of this tracking (if the tracking is negative) is offset by trading cost savings.

Table 3

Country	Index	Estimated Annual Tracking versus MSCI	Estimated Round-trip Trading Cost Savings (Futures versus Stocks)
France	CAC-40	2.97%	1.95%
Germany	DAX 30	1.88	1.05
United Kingdom	FT-SE 100	1.37	1.80
Japan	TOPIX	3.45	1.25
Australia	All Ordinary	2.56	1.87
Fund Total:		2.16%	1.47%

In addition, the use of completion portfolios can significantly reduce the expected tracking of synthetic index funds. Owning a few well-chosen securities in each market can dramatically improve relative performance.

The use of derivatives allows global investors to avoid many other expenses normally associated with equity trading. For example, participants in index funds that invest in foreign securities pay a withholding tax on dividends. While taxable organizations may sometimes be able to recoup this expense with a credit against their domestic taxes, tax-exempt investors cannot. Synthetic index funds do not own stock and, therefore, the participants do not pay any withholding tax. This can result in significant savings for tax-exempt investors.

Also, with an ordinary foreign stock trade, it is not unusual—because of the size and the liquidity of the names involved—for a trade to be only partially executed by the time the market closes. Since the derivatives markets are very liquid, in most cases synthetic index funds allow investors to avoid the potential opportunity costs and potential shortfall associated with unexecuted trades.

LIQUIDITY

The derivatives markets in the U.S. are extremely liquid. The most heavily traded index futures contract is the S&P 500 contract. This contract accounts for over 80 percent of all equity index futures trading in the U.S. and is, by far, the most liquid of all the domestic index futures. The average daily dollar trading volume of the S&P 500 futures contract is approximately 135 percent of the NYSE average volume and an average of 45,000 contracts trade per day.

Other derivatives markets, while usually not as liquid as those in the U.S., are still liquid enough to accommodate most trading needs. The FT-SE 100 contract has an average daily volume of approximately 8,000 contracts (or 650 million USD). The Osaka Nikkei 225 Japanese contract trades over 60,000 contracts daily for a USD value of more than $14 billion. The average daily trading volume for the German DAX contract is roughly 2,000 contracts—or slightly under 200 million USD. The French CAC-40 contract has daily volume of 5,000 contracts for a USD value of $375 million.

The trading volume for the French contract should increase in the future because the contract was just recently approved for U.S. investors.

Many index funds are open for contributions and redemptions only once a week or even once a month. Recently some funds have begun opening on a daily basis. However, trading costs can prevent investors from taking full advantage of the daily liquidity offered by an index fund. Fund participants and managers adjust their exposure as infrequently as possible in order to keep costs down. The low costs of trading derivatives allows synthetic index funds to offer all the cost benefits of a commingled investment vehicle as well as provide a cost-effective means of adjusting equity exposure and, therefore, provide investors with a more practical or usable daily liquidity.

CONVENIENCE

A contribution to a traditional equity index fund necessitates the purchase of multiple securities—often the full number of securities in the benchmark index. Futures contracts, on the other hand, provide immediate access to broad equity markets through a single purchase. As a result, custody expenses are kept to a minimum.

As investors increase their exposure to international equities, they must understand the mechanisms and costs of trading equities in markets other than their own. For example, in the U.K., trading is conducted by a quote-driven, screen-based system. Competing market makers display their best bids and offers; however, large transactions may not be reported until after a 90-minute delay. Because there is neither a centralized marketplace nor a DOT-like execution system, trading baskets of securities can be a difficult process. Equity transactions are assessed a stamp duty of 0.5 percent and foreign investors may be subject to dividend withholding taxes. Equity settlement is not done on a rolling basis (i.e., settlement within five business days), but on an account settlement basis. For all the above reasons, the use of futures contracts simplifies the trading process.

Global synthetic index funds offer several additional advantages relative to traditional stock funds:

> In addition to being a cost-effective means of getting equity exposure, synthetic index funds make excellent "cash sweep" vehicles. Investors can remain 100 percent exposed to the equity markets—and avoid cash drag in up markets—by sweeping accruing income and cash receipts every day into a synthetic equity fund rather than into a cash account. In the U.S., investors have the option of sweeping their cash into daily synthetic equity funds, but many global investors have, until now, had no option except to put dividend income into cash accounts.

Synthetic index funds can also be used as hedging tools. Instead of having to wait for the day that an index fund accepts contributions and redemptions, or waiting until a new manager is hired, synthetic funds provide investors with immediate equity exposure and eliminate the risk of participating in, or missing, a significant move in the market.

Synthetic index funds can be used to efficiently implement country allocation shifts. The use of separate country funds gives investors the ability to switch between markets with differing equity settlement periods. This is an important development for international investors who, until now, have been bound by the settlement constraints of different countries. For example, if an investor wants to move out of the U.K. market and into the Japanese market, it would normally take two weeks to settle the U.K. stock trades. This long settlement period means a delay before the investor can achieve his or her Japanese exposure. For the first time, the use of derivatives allows investors to make country switches in a timely manner.

CONCLUSION

Global stock index futures can be used in many of the same ways that domestic derivatives have been used in the U.S. for years. In the future, it seems logical that the growth of global derivatives will parallel the growth experienced by domestic derivatives in recent years. Synthetic index funds are but one example of how stock index futures can be used by investors to achieve their investment goals.

CHAPTER 26

Derivatives on Emerging Market Sovereign Debt Instruments

Varun Gosain
Head of Emerging Market Fixed-Income Derivatives
Paribas Capital Markets

INTRODUCTION

The last five years have seen explosive growth in the interest in and trading volumes of emerging market sovereign debt instruments. Emerging market sovereign debt includes the following categories of debt instruments:

External Debt Instruments

- Commercial bank loans made directly to sovereigns or with sovereign guarantees.
- Bonds issued as a result of the restructuring of commercial bank loans. Brady bonds are the largest type of such bond.
- Eurobonds and Yankee bonds issued directly to investors by emerging market issuers.

Domestic Debt Instruments

- Dollar-denominated domestic instruments, e.g., Bonex in Argentina, Ministry of Finance bonds in Russia.
- Local-currency-denominated domestic debt instruments, e.g., Cetes in Mexico and T-bills in Poland and Bulgaria.

The scope of derivatives is as wide as the market for different types of debt instruments. This chapter focuses on one part of the market, namely, derivatives on external debt instruments, particularly loans and Brady bonds. This is the most liquid part of the market for sovereign debt instruments and also the most active sector of the market for derivatives.

Exhibit 1 shows the growth in trading volumes over the last six years for emerging market external debt instruments.

**Exhibit 1.   Emerging Market External Debt
                    Trading Volume Estimate ($U.S. billions)**

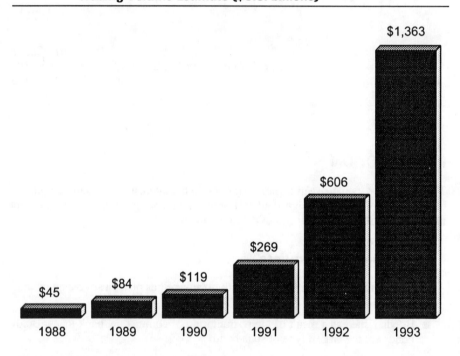

Source: Latin Finance

TYPES OF DERIVATIVES ACTIVITY

Derivatives activity in the external debt market can broadly be classified into the following categories:

- When and If Issued Contracts
- Options
- Structured Notes

WHEN AND IF ISSUED CONTRACTS

The When and If (W&If) Issued contract is an instrument that has developed in response to the peculiar circumstances and requirements of trading and investing in emerging market external debt.

It is typically considered to be more a part of the cash market than the derivatives market for these instruments. It is, however, perhaps the most important and interesting derivative instrument for emerging market external debt. It has developed to meet the unique needs of the market and is probably the most different from derivative instruments commonly used in other markets.

The When and If Issued contract specifies a contract between a buyer and a seller to transact:

■ At a specified price.

■ On the issuance of the bonds.

■ If and only if the bonds are indeed issued on or prior to a specified date, called the "drop-dead" date.

These contracts are therefore contingent contracts, with the contingency being the completion of a restructuring and issuance of the bonds on or prior to the drop-dead date.

These contracts arose in response to typical Brady plan restructurings, which are characterized by some of the following circumstances:

■ An agreement between a country and its commercial bank creditors to an exchange of loans into one or more instruments.

■ A freeze on assignments of loans prior to the exchange completion date. The period of the freeze can sometimes extend for up to a year, as in the case of the Brazilian Brady plan.

■ The presence of conditions for the completion of the restructuring and issuance of the bonds. One of the most significant conditions is typically an agreement with the IMF, which in turn often hinges upon budgetary adjustment and other economic reforms by the country in question.

■ Uncertainty as to the final date for the issuance of the bonds.

■ Uncertainty about the final mix of bonds or the exchange terms available to holders of the loans. This is because Brady packages are based on the principle of voluntary choice on a creditor level together with requirements of a balanced mix of options on an aggregate level. The incompatibility of the result of individual choices with desired target levels for a balanced mix often results in mandatory restrictions on choices between different bonds and forced allocations.

The W&If Issued contract can be valued:

■ Relative to other bonds of the same sovereign or, where no such bonds exist, relative to similar bonds issued by other obligors.

- Relative to the loans that will be converted into the bonds that are the underlying instrument of the contract.

Given the lack of easily comparable benchmarks and the nature of the uncertainties involved, the pricing of the contract requires a good deal of judgment.

The factors affecting the price of a When and If Issued contract relative to the loans to be exchanged for the bonds are:

- *Deal risk:* The probability of the completion of the Brady deal prior to the drop-dead date and the consequences of the deal not being completed by the drop-dead date. Typically, the drop-dead dates are initially set to allow plenty of time for completion of the deal for reasons other than a collapse of the agreement. However, as a result of delays, it is possible for the risk inherent in the contract to go from a collapse of the basic agreement to the risk of an inability to issue the bonds before the drop-dead date for reasons of a technical nature.

- *Reallocation risk:* The risk that the mix of bonds issued in exchange for the loans is changed. Such changes are typically the result of forced allocations of an inferior mix of bonds, though in some circumstances improvements are also possible.

- *Cost of carry to an uncertain date:* The value of the contract is affected by the net cost of carrying the loans to an uncertain issuance date. The loans typically accrue interest, some or all of which is paid in cash, while the unpaid interest is typically exchanged for other bonds.

One way to represent the W&If Issued contract relative to the loans to be converted into the bonds that are the underlying instrument of the contract would be as shown below:

$$W = L(1 + r - y)^{t_e} + \left[L(1 + r - y)^{t_e} - V_{ND} \right] \frac{(1 - P)}{P} + R$$

W	=	W&If Issued price
L	=	Current loan price (appropriately adjusted if the exchange ratio into bonds is different from 1:1)
p	=	Probability of completion of deal by drop-dead date
V_{ND}	=	Value of loans in a no-deal scenario
R	=	Risk-adjusted premium required to take on reallocation risk.
r	=	Risk-free rate
y	=	Income on the loan as a percentage of the price of the loan, including both cash payments and the market value of unpaid interest accruals
t_e	=	Expected time to issuance

- Once all the uncertainty about deal completion and reallocation risk is eliminated and the time of issuance is known with certainty, the W&If Issued contract is just a simple forward contract and priced as such.

- Once the deal risk and reallocation risk are insignificant, the W&If Issued contract becomes a forward contract with some uncertainty about settlement date. At this time, since assignment of loans is still not possible, the trading in the W&If becomes the dominant means for risk transfer and price discovery in the market and the pricing for the underlying loans is done relative to the W&If Issued contracts.

■ During the time that the probability of deal completion, reallocation risk, value in a no-deal scenario, and likely time of issuance are uncertain, the W&If Issued contract remains a unique and very interesting contract. When there are few traded bonds with which the W&If Issued contrct bonds can be compared, the dominant instrument for risk transfer and price discovery remains the loans with participations between counterparts, since assignment are not permitted. The pricing of the W&If Issued contract is typically done relative to the loans, with transactions reflecting the different assessments by market participants of the factors affecting the value of the W&If Issued contracts.

TRADING EXPERIENCE OF W&IF ISSUED CONTRACTS

The When and If Issued contract initially developed as a response to the following situation:

■ The prices of Brady bonds implied by the trading levels of loans to be exchanged for these bonds seemed very attractive to some potential buyers.

■ The buyers were either prohibited from buying the loans or unwilling to take on the risk that the proposed deal may fail.

■ Dealers stepped in to take on the deal risk at levels that they felt adequately compensated them for the risk of the deal falling apart.

The Mexico Brady plan saw the use of the first few W&If Issued contracts. The Venezuelan Brady plan more so. Then came the Brady restructuring in Argentina. Initially, deal risk was a factor in the pricing of these contracts. It did not take too long for the perceived deal risk to drop to insignificant levels. At the same time, because of complicated reconciliations required before issuance of the bonds, there was a long period of time between the stop of assignments of the loans and the issuance of the bonds. During this period it was possible to transfer economic interests in the loans through loan participations. However, because of easier settlement for W&If Issued contracts over loan participations, the W&If Issued contract became the primary means of transfer of risk and price discovery.

Assignments of Brazilian Loans stopped in March 1993 and as of the writing of this chapter, the expected date for issuance of the bonds is April 15, 1994. The deal risk is still considered significant and is a very important factor affecting the prices of the W&IF Issued contracts for the different bonds. Prices of W&IF Issued contracts on some of the Brazilian bonds as well as prices of loans that will be exchanged into these bonds adjusted for exchange terms are shown in Table 1.

In the case of Argentina, some W&If Issued contracts did not settle because of technical disputes regarding drop-dead dates. A number of contracts specified the drop-dead date with respect to the settlement date, which in turn was to be as soon as possible after issuance of the bonds.

Table 1

	Loan		W&If	
	Bid	Offer	Bid	Offer
Capitalization	68	69	73 3/4	74 3/4
Par	56 3/4	57 3/4	61 1/4	62 1/4
Discount	47 1/2	48 1/2	50	51

Prices as of Feb. 23, 1994

The bonds issued in exchange for past-due interest claims on Argentine loans (FRBs) were initially issued into escrow on March 31, 1993 as the agents were unable to reconcile the ownership of these bonds by different counterparts. The bonds were released from escrow on October 29, 1993. The most common drop-dead date used by the market for W&If Issued FRB contracts was June 30, 1993. Almost all the market participants agreed to honor these contracts by accepting that the intent of the contracts was satisfied by issuance into escrow. However, some contracts did indeed drop dead, as a small number of parties held out that they were entitled to let the contracts drop dead.

In the case of Brazil, IDU bonds were issued in exchange for interest arrears that had accrued on the loans prior to December 31,1990. Some of the earlier W&IF Issued contracts on the IDU bonds did indeed drop dead, as the final issuance of the bonds took much longer than originally anticipated. The IDU bonds were finally issued on November 20, 1992, and a very large number of W&If Issued contracts were consummated.

The perceived risk of noncompletion of the Brazilian Brady deal is probably higher than for any previous Brady deal. Trading in the Brazilian loans and W&If Issued contracts reflects this and permits participants to express views on deal completion risk by trading between the loans and W&If issued bonds.

Exhibit 2 shows the prices for loans committed to be exchanged for capitalization bonds and W&IF Issued contracts for the same capitalization bonds.

Many more countries—including Bulgaria, Panama, Ecuador, Poland, Peru, and Russia—are in the process of or may go through a restructuring of the Brady type, and the W&If Issued contract is likely to be seen in many of these situations.

OPTIONS ON EMERGING MARKET DEBT INSTRUMENTS

Size

There is an active OTC market in options on emerging market debt instruments. Volume has been growing significantly over the last two years, as shown in Exhibit 3.

This is a reflection of the growing interest in the market as a whole, as also reflected in rapid growth in volumes in the cash market. Also as a result of the good liquidity characteristics of the underlying instruments, it has become easier to hedge options on these instruments. On the demand side, it is no surprise that as the market has grown more sophisticated, many of the derivative contracts, such as options and structured notes, have been used increasingly by investors and trading houses.

Exhibit 2.   Brazilian W&If and Cash "C" Bond Prices

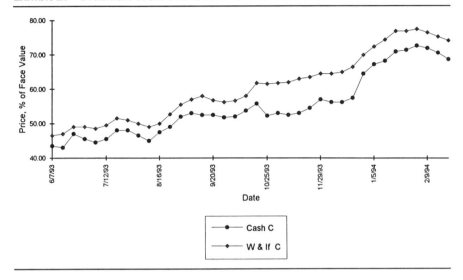

**Exhibit 3.   Emerging Market Debt Options
                Trading Volume ($U.S. billions)**

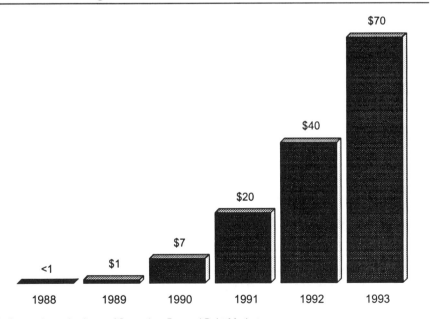

Paribas estimated volume of Secondary External Debt Market.

Participants

The participants in the market for options on external debt include

- Commercial bank holders of loans and bonds
- Trading houses
- Mutual funds
- Hedge funds
- High-net-worth individuals

The differences in risk/return preferences, transaction costs, regulatory constraints, and tax and accounting motivations drive the different entities active in this market just as is the case in other options markets. One feature that is a particularly important factor is the very large difference in the cost of funds faced by local Mexican, Argentine, and Brazilian institutions active in the market and their American and European counterparts. This makes the local institutions better buyers of call options and the European and American institutions better sellers.

Table 2 shows the characteristics of the typical options traded in the OTC market.

Table 2.   OTC Options in Emerging Market Debt

	Liquid	*Less Liquid*
Underlying	■ Argentine Par, Discount, FRB	■ Morocco Loans
		■ Brazil MYDFA, W/If C
Instruments	■ Brazil, IDU	■ Nigeria Par
	■ Mexico Par, Discount	■ Ecuador
	■ Venezuela Par, DCB	■ Peru
	■ Poland DDRA	■ Bulgaria
Notional Amount	$5 MM	
Bid/Ask	1/2% to 3/4% of Notional	
Maturity	1 month to 1 year	
Documentation	Nonstandard	
Option Type	American	

Exhibits 4 to 6 give the historical price and volatility for some of the instruments on which options are traded in the OTC market. Exhibits 7 and 8 show historical price and volatility of the Mexican Par bond and the 30-year U.S. Treasury bond. The Mexican Par bond is one of the most actively traded emerging market debt instruments

Exhibit 4.   Argentina Par: Price and 3-Month Volatility

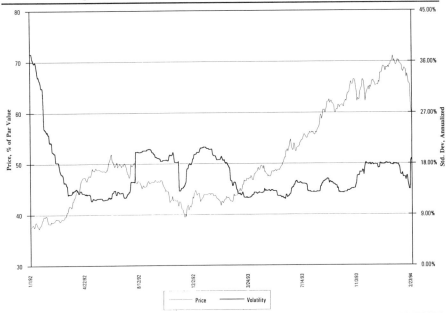

Exhibit 5.   Venezuela Par: Price and 3-Month Volatility

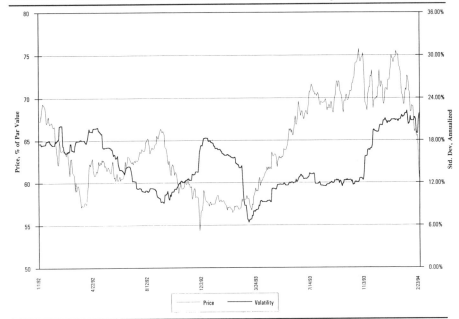

Exhibit 6.   Nigeria Par: Price and 3-Month Volatility

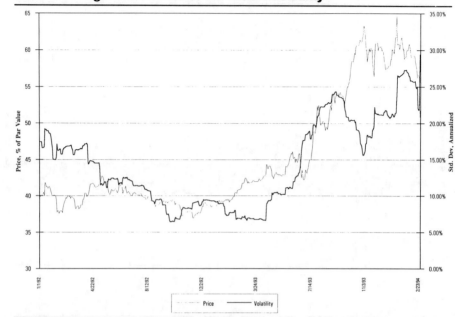

Exhibit 7.   US 30-Y Bond and Mexico Par Price

Exhibit 8.   US 30-Y Bond and Mexico Par Price Volatility

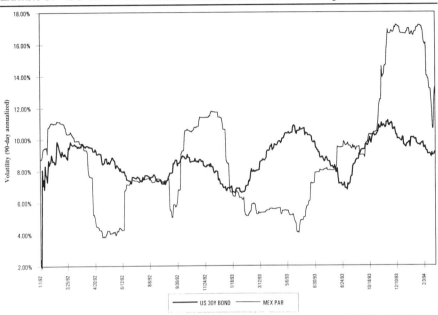

and it is interesting to see the relationship between the movements in the Mexican Par bond and the U.S. 30-year bond.

The volatilities of emerging market debt instruments are higher than developed country fixed-income instruments but are lower than those for equities in developed markets and much lower than for equities in emerging markets.

Table 3 gives prices of options on some of the commonly traded issues.

Pricing options on emerging market debt is not very different from pricing options in other markets, and the following discussion focuses on the points of difference resulting from the conventions and characteristics of the market for the underlying instruments.

IMPACT OF RESTRUCTURINGS

For loans that have the prospect of being restructured during the term of the option, it is important to clearly address some of the following issues.

■ Will the option survive the restructuring? OTC options are typically structured to survive the restructuring with appropriate modifications. Some contracts, however, require the option buyer to exercise within some period of the announcement of a restructuring or the option expires.

■ Who gets to choose between restructuring alternatives? Generally, the buyer of the option has the right to specify what elections to make on the underlying loan, subject to all the restrictions imposed at different stages of the restructuring. This

Table 3.   Option Prices on Some Instruments*

		Spot Price		Prices for 90-Day Options		Implied Volatility(%)
				Bid	Offer	
Argentina	Par	65.50	Calls	1.50	1.90	13–16
			Puts	1.90	2.35	
Mexico	Par	78.50	Calls	1.65	1.95	13–15
			Puts	2.30	2.70	
Brazil	IDU	83.625	Calls	1.40	1.70	9.5–11.5
			Puts	1.75	2.25	
Venezuela	DCB	65.0	Calls	2.75	3.20	23.5–27
			Puts	3.20	3.65	
Poland	DDRA	45.50	Calls	2.50	2.80	28–31
			Puts	2.50	2.80	

*   As of February 23, 1994.

is not a universal practice, and it is important to address this issue up front to avoid potential conflicts in the future.

3. How are the underlying instrument and strike price adjusted by the restructuring?

Change in Nominal Principal

Frequently, the exchange ratio for conversion of loans into bonds is different from 1:1. This is easy to adjust for by multiplying the nominal amount of the principal by the exchange ratio, e.g., if $60 of bonds are issued for $100 of loans (exchange ratio 0.60) then an option on $100 of loans at a strike price of 50 would transform into an option on $60 (100*0.60) of the bonds at a strike price of 80.33 (50/0.6).

Treatment of Past-Due Interest

Many loans trade together with past-due interest, e.g., Poland, Peru, Panama, Ecuador, Bulgaria, and Russia. In the case of Poland DDRA, the strike price is expressed as a percentage of the total of the principal plus past-due interest. In the case of the other loans, the strike price is generally expressed as a percentage of the principal amount of the loan and the past-due interest transfers to the buyer free of additional payment (Interest for free).

It is important to clearly define if the buyer of the option has the right to the cash and bonds issued in exchange for the past-due interest, and if the buyer does, whether the strike price payable is affected by this amount.

Treatment of Interest on Past-Due Interest

In restructurings, holders of loans get cash and bond payments in exchange for interest accrued on past-due interest as well. The rights to these claims as well as any corresponding adjustments to the strike price have to be addressed.

Conceptually, the impact of exchange of past-due interest for cash and/or bonds is similar to the payment of cash and stock dividends and can be handled in a similar manner for purposes of valuation.

ISSUES IN FORWARD PRICE CALCULATIONS FOR EMERGING MARKET DEBT INSTRUMENTS

The characteristics of different emerging market debt instruments and their trading conventions have an impact on the calculation of forward prices for these instruments. This in turn has an important impact on the valuation of options on these instruments. For purposes of forward price calculations, the different instruments can be considered among the following categories:

- Bonds with interest guarantees covering all coupon payments prior to the maturity of the option, e.g., Mexico Par, Venezuela Par. Here the present value of the coupon payments can be calculated using the risk-free rate.

- Bonds without interest guarantees, e.g., Brazil IDUs, Argentina FRBs. Here the appropriate methodology is to value the coupon adjusting for the risk inherent in the obligation of the issuer. A good alternative is to use the discount rate appropriate for a cash flow of that obligor with the same maturity as the coupon payment.

- Non-performing loans trading with past-due interest
  - Pay for principal and past due interest, e.g., Poland DDRA. The price of the asset is quoted as a percentage of the total amount of principal plus past-due interest. Since the past-due interest is increasing over time, the yield on such an asset is not zero but equal to the rate of accrual of interest multiplied by the forward price of the asset.
  - Pay for principal only with past-due interest transferred for free, e.g., Peru, Ecuador. Here the yield is zero and the forward price calculation is the spot price plus the carrying cost at the risk-free rate.

BORROWING COSTS AND IMPACT ON OPTION PRICES

Emerging market debt instruments can often be very expensive to borrow. It can cost 1 to 1.5 percent per annum of face value to borrow loans and even bonds. This translates to 1.5 percent to 3 percent of market value for borrowing and can sometimes distort relative pricing of calls and puts (making puts more expensive). Over time, as the market develops, these borrowing costs should come down and reduce these distortions.

WARRANTS

A number of warrants on individual issues as well as baskets of issues have been brought to market. These warrants have typically had a maturity of 9 to 18 months and have been oriented particularly to offshore retail investors who are not able to access the OTC options market. Warrants on loans and baskets of loans have also been particularly important in allowing many investors to gain exposure to loans without having to deal with the problems related to transacting in loans such as legal infrastructure for closing loan transactions as well as high assignment costs. These warrants (often called pre-Brady warrants) made it possible for many investors to make a play on the restructuring of these loans with relatively low transaction and other access costs.

STRUCTURED NOTES

Structured notes linked to emerging market instruments have become increasingly popular. With the considerable growth in the OTC options market it has become possible to provide an enormous range of customized payoffs linked to emerging market debt instruments through structured notes. The structured notes linked to emerging market debt instruments have been used to create payoffs linked to the absolute or relative movements in prices or yields of one or more instruments. Some degree of leverage and/or some limitation on the maximum loss that can be suffered has typically been incorporated into the structured notes.

CONCLUSION

The last five years have seen explosive interest in emerging market debt instruments and substantial growth in activity in both the cash and derivatives markets for these instruments.

This chapter outlines the types of derivatives available on loans and Brady bonds, which constitute the largest segment of this market. The focus of the chapter is to give the reader an idea of the types of derivative products available as well as a sense of the extent to which the nature, conventions, and nuances of the underlying instruments make these products different from standard derivative products.

CHAPTER 27

Managed Futures and Emerging Markets

Michael Keppler
President
Keppler Asset Management, Inc.

INTRODUCTION

Managed Derivatives have certain asset class-specific characteristics that make them a unique diversifier for a global equity portfolio: expectation of high return combined with low to negative covariability.

DESCRIPTION OF INVESTMENT VEHICLES

The returns used for Managed Derivatives are based on the monthly net asset values of a Cayman Islands exempt corporation, limited by shares, that commenced trading in March 1987. The corporation was sponsored by one of the leading derivatives companies in the United States. Shareholder equity has grown exclusively through retained profits. The returns are considered to be representative of the Managed Derivatives asset class. They are based on "real" returns after transaction costs, management and incentive fees, adjusted for the current cost structure of the product, which was changed in 1993. The investment vehicles include leveraged trading of cash, futures, and forward markets worldwide.[1]

The author thanks Xing-Hong Xue for his valuable computer assistance.

---

1 For regulatory reasons, the name of the product and the sponsor cannot be disclosed.

The returns shown for passive global equities (major markets) are based on monthly total returns of the Morgan Stanley Capital International (MSCI) World Index with net dividends reinvested.[2] No deductions were made for transaction costs or management and incentive fees.

Passive emerging markets equities returns are based on monthly total returns of the International Finance Corporation's Composite Investable Index of emerging markets equities.[3] This index takes into account liquidity and foreign ownership constraints. No deductions were made for transaction costs or management and incentive fees.

The active global and active emerging markets equities returns used for this study are based on the "Top Value" investment strategies developed by Keppler Asset Management Inc., New York. While actively managed public mutual funds following these strategies are available to non-U.S. investors, the history of these funds is not long enough to be considered for purposes of this chapter.[4] Therefore, the returns shown are pro forma returns after transaction costs and management and incentive fees—estimated at 2 percent annually for the major equity markets and 5 percent annually for the emerging markets equities.

CORRELATION MATRIX

One characteristic that makes Managed Derivatives so attractive as diversifiers for global equity portfolios is their low to negative correlation with alternative investments. During the 4 3/4-year period ending September 1993 (see Table 1), total returns of Managed Derivatives had correlation coefficients of –0.21, 0.17, –0.19, and –0.30, with the total returns of the MSCI World Index, the Major Markets Top Value Strategy, the IFCI Composite Index, and the Emerging Markets Top Value Strategy, respectively. The 4 3/4-year period covers the entire history of the IFCI-Composite Index, which goes back to the end of 1988. Before that time, no representative global index was available for investable emerging markets equities.

MANAGED DERIVATIVES COMBINED WITH MAJOR MARKETS EQUITIES

The 4 3/4-year study period ending September 1993 was characterized by below-average returns for both Managed Derivatives and major markets equities. While the former have expected long-term annual rates of return exceeding 20 percent, the pro

---

2 See monthly editions of the *Morgan Stanley Capital International Perspective*, published by Morgan Stanley, New York, NY 10020.

3 See *Monthly Update on Emerging Markets*, International Finance Corporation, Central Capital Markets Department, Washington, DC 20433.

4 During 1993, State Street Bank and Trust Co., Boston, under the Global Advantage Funds umbrella, has launched both a Major Markets High Value Subfund and an Emerging Markets High Value Subfund in Luxembourg for European investors. The investment strategies implemented in those funds are developed in cooperation with Keppler Asset Management, Inc., New York.

Table 1.   Correlation Coefficients of Total Returns in U.S. Dollars December 1988–September 1993

	MSCI World Index	Major Markets Top Value Strategy	IFCI Composite Index	Emerging Markets Top Value Strategy	Managed Derivatives Portfolio
MSCI World Index	1.00				
Major Markets Top Value Strategy	0.41	1.00			
IFCI Composite Index	0.48	0.11	1.00		
Emerging Markets Top Value Strategy	0.54	0.21	0.78	1.00	
Managed Derivatives Portfolio	−0.21	0.17	−0.19	−0.30	1.00

Note: All active strategies are after transaction costs and management and incentive fees.

forma compound annual returns of our Managed Derivatives portfolio reached 19.05 percent. This compares with a total compound annual return of only 5.81 percent for the MSCI World Index, which fell well below the long-term average return of global equities. An investment of $100 in Managed Derivatives grew to $229 during the 4 3/4-year test period. During the same time, $100 invested in the MSCI World Index grew to $131 with net dividends reinvested (see Exhibit 1 and Table 2).

The standard deviation of monthly returns of 4.77 percent for the Managed Derivatives (standard deviation of the MSCI World Index: 4.38 percent) may lead to the assumption that Managed Derivatives were riskier than major markets equities. This is confirmed by a slightly higher average loss during losing months (3.21 percent versus 3.15 percent) and a longest losing streak of five months, compared with only four months for the major equity markets. However, other important risk measures— such as the number of losing months and the probability of a monthly loss, the expectation of a monthly loss, and the largest drawdown from a previous high—favor the Managed Derivatives portfolio as the less risky one.

**Exhibit 1.   MSCI World Index and Managed Derivatives Portfolio
(in U.S. Dollars) December 1988–September 1993**

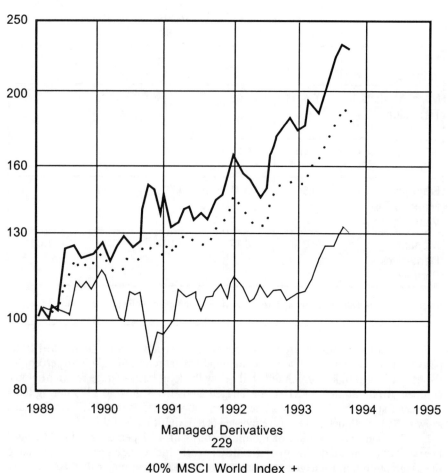

Managed Derivatives
229
_____

40% MSCI World Index +
60% Managed Derivatives: 189
· · · · · · · ·
MSCI World Index
131
_____

Note: All active strategies are after transaction costs and management and incentive fees.

Table 2. Asset Allocation between MSCI World Index and Managed Derivatives Portfolio December 1988–September 1993 (in U.S. Dollars)

MSCI World Index	100%	90%	80%	70%	60%	50%	40%	30%	20%	10%	0%
Managed Derivatives Portfolio	**0%**	**10%**	**20%**	**30%**	**40%**	**50%**	**60%**	**70%**	**80%**	**90%**	**100%**
Compound Annual Return (%)	5.81	7.36	8.86	10.31	11.71	13.07	14.37	15.62	16.82	17.96	19.05
Average Monthly Return (%)	0.57	0.67	0.77	0.87	0.97	1.07	1.17	1.27	1.37	1.47	1.57
Highest Monthly Return (%)	11.30	10.19	9.09	8.06	8.34	8.61	8.88	9.33	10.63	11.94	13.24
Lowest Monthly Return (%)	−10.57	−8.95	−7.33	−5.71	−4.33	−4.66	−5.26	−5.85	−6.45	−7.46	−8.69
Probability of Gain (%)	54.39	54.39	63.16	57.89	54.39	64.91	63.16	63.16	64.91	63.16	63.16
Average Gain in Winning Months (%)	3.68	3.45	2.84	3.02	3.20	2.75	3.01	3.27	3.49	3.96	4.37
Expectation of Monthly Gain (%)	2.00	1.87	1.79	1.75	1.74	1.78	1.90	2.07	2.27	2.50	2.76
Standard Deviation of Monthly Returns (%)	4.38	3.89	3.46	3.13	2.95	2.92	3.06	3.35	3.75	4.23	4.77
Probability of Monthly Loss (%)	45.61	45.61	36.84	42.11	45.61	35.09	36.84	36.84	35.09	36.84	36.84
Average Loss in Losing Months (%)	3.15	2.65	2.78	2.09	1.68	2.03	1.97	2.16	2.55	2.80	3.21
Expectation of Monthly Loss (%)	1.44	1.21	1.03	0.88	0.77	0.71	0.73	0.79	0.89	1.03	1.18
Longest Losing Streak (# Months)	4	4	4	4	4	4	5	5	5	5	5
Largest Drawdown from Previous High (%)	24.34	20.41	16.38	12.25	8.96	9.47	10.10	11.23	12.35	13.46	14.57
Risk-Adjusted Return (Keppler Ratio):											
– Return per Unit of Expectation of Loss	0.40	0.55	0.75	0.99	1.26	1.50	1.61	1.60	1.54	1.43	1.33
Volatility-Adjusted Return (Sharpe Ratio):											
– Return per Unit of Standard Deviation	0.13	0.17	0.22	0.28	0.33	0.37	0.38	0.38	0.37	0.35	0.33
Number of Periods (Months)	57	57	57	57	57	57	57	57	57	57	57
Number of Losing Months	26	26	21	24	26	20	21	21	20	21	21
Number of Winning Months	31	31	36	33	31	37	36	36	37	36	36

Note: All active strategies are after transaction costs and management and incentive fees.

The expectation of a monthly loss was significantly lower for the Managed Derivatives (1.18 percent) than for the MSCI World Index (1.44 percent), while the relationship of the standard deviations of returns of both investments was exactly the opposite: standard deviation was higher for the Managed Derivatives. This indicates that the return distribution of the Managed Derivatives may be skewed positively. Volatility risk measures, such as the standard deviation of returns, become irrelevant for nonsymmetrical return distributions. The Sharpe ratio, which indicates the return per unit of standard deviation, cannot be used in these cases. The other risk measures shown in Table 2—i.e., the probability of a monthly loss, the average loss in losing months, the expectation of a monthly loss, the longest losing streak, and the largest drawdown from a previous high—can be applied to both parametric and nonparametric return distributions, regardless of their shape. In the author's opinion, the expectation of a monthly loss, which combines both the magnitude and the probability of investment losses, is the most reliable statistical risk measure for performance measurement purposes.

During the 4 3/4-year test period, the highest risk-adjusted return was achieved with a 60/40 mix in favor of Managed Derivatives. This 60/40 combination would have resulted in a 2.5 times higher compound annual return (14.37 percent) with half the risk (as measured by the expectation of a monthly loss) compared to an investment in the MSCI World Index (see Exhibit 2 and Table 2).

Exhibit 2. Asset Allocation between MSCI World Index and Managed Derivatives Portfolio (in U.S. Dollars) December 1988–September 1993

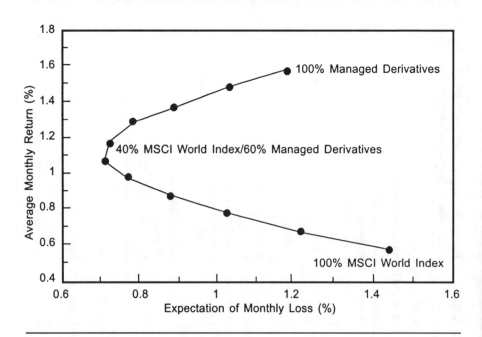

A combination of Managed Derivatives with an active global equity strategy—e.g., the Major Markets Top Value Strategy—yields even higher performance advantages. As shown in Table 3, a 50/50 mix results in a maximum drawdown reduction to 26.8 percent of the maximum drawdown of a global equity portfolio invested exclusively according to the Major Markets Top Value strategy. In addition, all other risk measures shown are significantly lower for the 50/50 mix. At the same time, the return for the combined portfolio was 16.87 percent, compared to 12.97 percent for the Major Markets Top Value Strategy (see Table 3 and Exhibits 3 and 4).

MANAGED DERIVATIVES COMBINED WITH EMERGING MARKETS EQUITIES

As indicated by the negative correlation coefficient of –0.19, Managed Derivatives are also an excellent diversification tool for emerging markets equities, as measured by the IFCI Composite Index. Both the volatility- and risk-adjusted returns suggest that a 50/50 mix offers the most attractive returns for risk-averse investors. The 50/50 portfolio shows a striking reduction of the average loss in losing months to 44 percent, compared with an investment in the IFCI Composite Index. Since there also is one less losing month in the 50/50 mix, the expectation of a monthly loss was even further reduced to 42 percent of the expectation of a loss for the IFCI Composite Index. The largest drawdown in the 50/50 mix amounts to only 38 percent of the drawdown for the emerging markets equity-only portfolio (see Table 4 and Exhibits 5 and 6).

Finally, the author analyzed the diversification benefits of combining Managed Derivatives with the Emerging Markets Top Value Strategy, an active emerging markets equity strategy. Based on the negative correlation coefficient of -0.30, the expectations for risk reduction and return enhancement again are very high—and rightly so. A 30 percent Managed Derivatives component cuts the drawdown almost in half and, at the same time, considerably reduces volatility, magnitude of losses, and expectation of losses. The risk-adjusted return rises from 5.92 for the portfolio consisting of the active emerging markets equities to 6.84 for the 30/70 mix—an extremely high reward-to-risk ratio compared to alternative investments (see Table 5 and Exhibits 7 and 8).

SUMMARY AND PRACTICAL IMPLICATIONS

The 4 3/4-year test period from the beginning of 1988 through September 1993 is not long enough to confirm statistically significant relationships between the returns of the presented asset classes: Managed Derivatives, passive/active global equities, and passive/active emerging markets equities. This was a difficult period for many derivatives managers. Further, the period is characterized by below-average returns for the major markets equities, as measured by the MSCI World Index, and above-average returns for the emerging markets equities, as measured by the IFCI Composite Index. Therefore, the relationships described in this chapter can be classified as time-specific only. More research on future returns of the various asset classes is required.

Table 3. Asset Allocation between Major Markets Top Value Strategy and Managed Derivatives Portfolio December 1988–September 1993 (in U.S. Dollars)

Major Markets Top Value Strategy	100%	90%	80%	70%	60%	50%	40%	30%	20%	10%	0%
Managed Derivatives Portfolio	0%	10%	20%	30%	40%	50%	60%	70%	80%	90%	100%
Compound Annual Return (%)	12.97	13.89	14.74	15.52	16.23	16.87	17.44	17.95	18.38	18.75	19.05
Average Monthly Return (%)	1.11	1.16	1.20	1.25	1.30	1.34	1.39	1.44	1.48	1.53	1.57
Highest Monthly Return (%)	10.88	10.01	9.13	8.26	7.69	8.07	8.45	8.83	9.65	11.44	13.24
Lowest Monthly Return (%)	-10.16	-8.58	-7.00	-5.43	-3.85	-4.36	-5.02	-5.68	-6.33	-7.46	-8.69
Probability of Gain (%)	61.40	66.67	68.42	68.42	64.91	66.67	66.67	64.91	63.16	63.16	63.16
Average Gain in Winning Months (%)	3.72	3.18	2.88	2.71	2.85	2.88	3.00	3.25	3.64	4.00	4.37
Expectation of Monthly Gain (%)	2.29	2.12	1.97	1.85	1.85	1.92	2.00	2.11	2.30	2.52	2.76
Standard Deviation of Monthly Returns (%)	4.23	3.70	3.23	2.88	2.68	2.68	2.86	3.20	3.66	4.19	4.77
Probability of Monthly Loss (%)	38.60	33.33	31.58	31.58	35.09	33.33	33.33	35.09	36.84	36.84	36.84
Average Loss in Losing Months (%)	3.04	2.89	2.42	1.91	1.59	1.73	1.83	1.92	2.22	2.70	3.21
Expectation of Monthly Loss (%)	1.17	0.96	0.76	0.60	0.56	0.58	0.61	0.67	0.82	1.00	1.18
Longest Losing Streak (# Months)	5	5	2	2	4	4	4	5	5	5	5
Largest Drawdown from Previous High (%)	18.54	15.12	11.64	8.19	5.85	4.97	6.34	8.06	10.26	12.44	14.57
Risk-Adjusted Return (Keppler Ratio):											
– Return per Unit of Expectation of Loss	0.95	1.20	1.58	2.07	2.33	2.33	2.28	2.13	1.81	1.53	1.33
Volatility-Adjusted Return (Sharpe Ratio):											
– Return per Unit of Standard Deviation	0.26	0.31	0.37	0.43	0.48	0.50	0.49	0.45	0.41	0.36	0.33
Number of Periods (Months)	57	57	57	57	57	57	57	57	57	57	57
Number of Losing Months	22	19	18	18	20	19	19	20	21	21	21
Number of Winning Months	35	38	39	39	37	38	38	37	36	36	36

Note: All active strategies are after transaction costs and management and incentive fees.

**Exhibit 3.   Major Markets Top Value and Managed Derivatives Portfolio
(in U.S. Dollars) December 1988–September 1993**

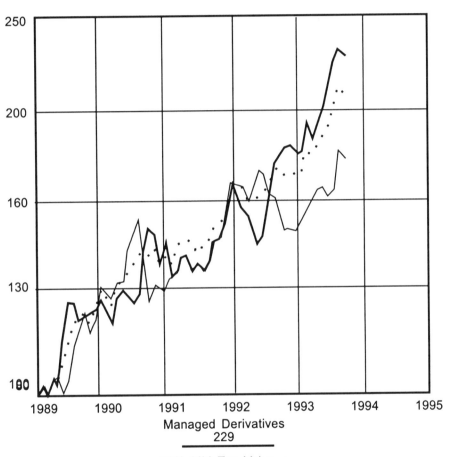

Managed Derivatives
229

50% MM Top Value +
50% Managed Derivatives: 210

MM Top Value Strategy
179

Note: All active strategies are after transaction costs and management and incentive fees.

Exhibit 4.   Asset Allocation between Major Markets Top Value Strategy and Managed Derivatives Portfolio (in U.S. Dollars) December 1988–September 1993

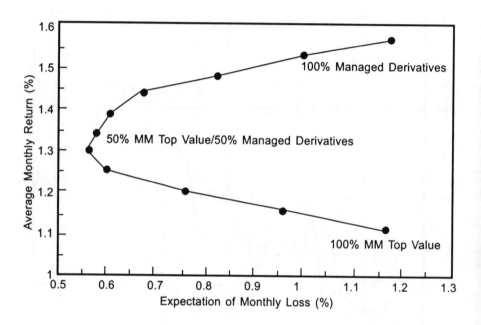

Nevertheless, and on a more optimistic note, it is possible to make a projection based on the long-term consistent and excellent real-time results of the manager of the Managed Derivatives portfolio and on the author's own experience in the global major and emerging equity markets. That projection leads to the conclusion that the basic results—in terms of risk-return relationships, not absolute returns—of a similar five-year ex-post facto study, undertaken in 1998 and using currently available real-time portfolios, may not be substantially different from the results presented here.

Table 4. Asset Allocation between IFCI Composite Index and Managed Derivatives Portfolio December 1988–September 1993 (in U.S. Dollars)

IFCI Composite Index	100%	90%	80%	70%	60%	50%	40%	30%	20%	10%	0%
Managed Derivatives Portfolio	**0%**	**10%**	**20%**	**30%**	**40%**	**50%**	**60%**	**70%**	**80%**	**90%**	**100%**
Compound Annual Return (%)	26.22	25.92	25.52	25.02	24.43	23.74	22.97	22.12	21.17	20.15	19.05
Average Monthly Return (%)	2.11	2.06	2.01	1.95	1.90	1.84	1.79	1.74	1.68	1.63	1.57
Highest Monthly Return (%)	18.26	16.54	14.83	13.12	11.40	10.31	10.24	10.17	10.76	11.90	13.24
Lowest Monthly Return (%)	-11.64	-9.49	-7.81	-6.34	-5.91	-6.20	-6.49	-6.78	-7.07	-7.75	-8.69
Probability of Gain (%)	64.91	64.91	63.16	64.91	64.91	66.67	66.67	70.18	68.42	63.16	63.16
Average Gain in Winning Months (%)	5.04	4.69	4.49	4.08	3.79	3.50	3.47	3.35	3.54	4.08	4.37
Expectation of Monthly Gain (%)	3.27	3.04	2.84	2.65	2.46	2.33	2.32	2.35	2.42	2.58	2.76
Standard Deviation of Monthly Returns (%)	5.60	4.97	4.39	3.89	3.51	3.28	3.25	3.42	3.75	4.21	4.77
Probability of Monthly Loss (%)	35.09	35.09	36.84	35.09	35.09	33.33	33.33	29.82	31.58	36.84	36.84
Average Loss in Losing Months (%)	3.30	2.80	2.25	1.98	1.60	1.46	1.58	2.05	2.34	2.57	3.21
Expectation of Monthly Loss (%)	1.16	0.98	0.83	0.69	0.56	0.49	0.53	0.61	0.74	0.95	1.18
Longest Losing Streak (# Months)	5	4	4	4	4	5	5	5	5	5	5
Largest Drawdown from Previous High (%)	25.31	22.20	19.04	15.85	12.61	9.64	8.92	8.93	9.95	11.90	14.57
Risk-Adjusted Return (Keppler Ratio):											
– Return per Unit of Expectation of Loss	1.82	2.10	2.42	2.81	3.38	3.79	3.40	2.83	2.28	1.72	1.33
Volatility-Adjusted Return (Sharpe Ratio):											
– Return per Unit of Standard Deviation	0.38	0.41	0.46	0.50	0.54	0.56	0.55	0.51	0.45	0.39	0.33
Number of Periods (Months)	57	57	57	57	57	57	57	57	57	57	57
Number of Losing Months	20	20	21	20	20	19	19	17	18	21	21
Number of Winning Months	37	37	36	37	37	38	38	40	39	36	36

Note: All active strategies are after transaction costs and management and incentives fees.

**Exhibit 5.   Emerging Markets and Managed Derivatives Portfolio
(in U.S. Dollars) December 1988–September 1993**

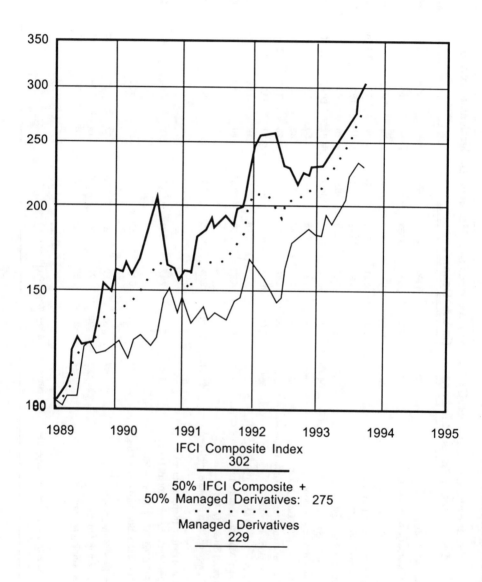

IFCI Composite Index
302
———————

50% IFCI Composite +
50% Managed Derivatives: 275
· · · · · · · ·

Managed Derivatives
229
———————

Note: All active strategies are after transaction costs and management and incentive fees.

Exhibit 6. Asset Allocation between IFCI Composite Index and Managed Derivatives Portfolio (in U.S. Dollars) December 1988–September 1993

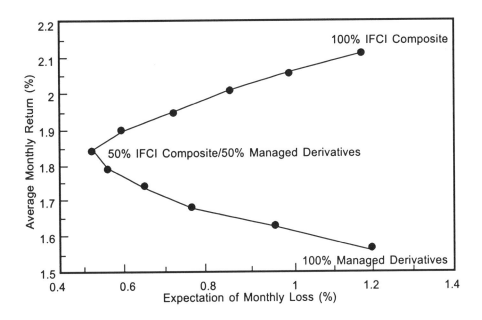

Table 5. Asset Allocation between Emerging Markets Top Value Strategy and Managed Derivatives Portfolio December 1988–September 1993 (in U.S. Dollars)

Emerging Markets Top Value Strategy	100%	90%	80%	70%	60%	50%	40%	30%	20%	10%	0%
Managed Derivatives Portfolio	0%	10%	20%	30%	40%	50%	60%	70%	80%	90%	100%
Compound Annual Return (%)	78.23	71.88	65.61	59.44	53.35	47.37	41.48	35.71	30.04	24.48	19.05
Average Monthly Return (%)	5.23	4.87	4.50	4.13	3.77	3.40	3.04	2.67	2.31	1.94	1.57
Highest Monthly Return (%)	32.42	29.96	27.51	25.05	22.60	20.15	17.69	15.24	13.07	13.06	13.24
Lowest Monthly Return (%)	-10.38	-9.72	-9.06	-8.40	-7.75	-7.09	-6.43	-5.77	-5.11	-6.71	-8.69
Probability of Gain (%)	78.95	78.95	77.19	77.19	77.19	71.93	70.18	70.18	63.16	63.16	63.16
Average Gain in Winning Months (%)	7.74	7.13	6.70	6.14	5.61	5.48	5.10	4.66	4.80	4.54	4.37
Expectation of Monthly Gain (%)	6.11	5.63	5.17	4.74	4.33	3.94	3.58	3.27	3.03	2.87	2.76
Standard Deviation of Monthly Returns (%)	8.07	7.36	6.68	6.06	5.50	5.02	4.66	4.45	4.39	4.50	4.77
Probability of Monthly Loss (%)	21.05	21.05	22.81	22.81	22.81	28.07	29.82	29.82	36.84	36.84	36.84
Average Loss in Losing Months (%)	4.20	3.64	2.96	2.65	2.46	1.92	1.83	2.01	1.97	2.53	3.21
Expectation of Monthly Loss (%)	0.88	0.77	0.67	0.60	0.56	0.54	0.54	0.60	0.73	0.93	1.18
Longest Losing Streak (# Months)	3	3	3	3	3	3	3	3	5	5	5
Largest Drawdown from Previous High (%)	19.18	15.45	12.55	10.52	8.46	7.09	6.52	7.83	9.62	12.12	14.57
Risk-Adjusted Return (Keppler Ratio):											
- Return per Unit of Expectation of Loss	5.92	6.35	6.67	6.84	6.73	6.30	5.58	4.46	3.18	2.08	1.33
Volatility-Adjusted Return (Sharpe Ratio):											
- Return per Unit of Standard Deviation	0.65	0.66	0.67	0.68	0.69	0.68	0.65	0.60	0.53	0.43	0.33
Number of Periods (Months)	57	57	57	57	57	57	57	57	57	57	57
Number of Losing Months	12	12	13	13	13	16	17	17	21	21	21
Number of Winning Months	45	45	44	44	44	41	40	40	36	36	36

Note: All active strategies are after transaction costs and management and incentive fees.

Exhibit 7. Emerging Markets Top Value and Managed Derivatives Portfolio (in U.S. Dollars) December 1988–September 1993

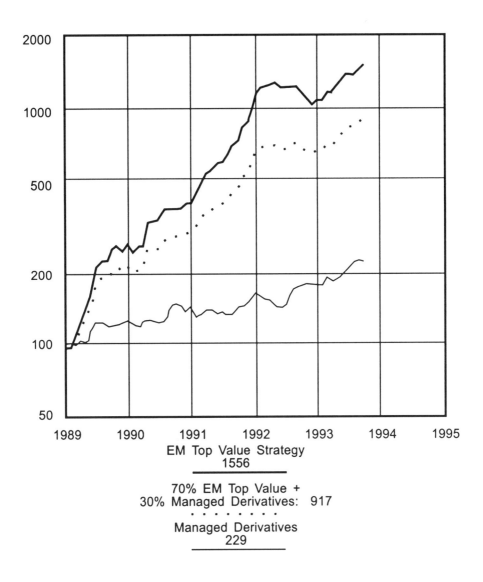

EM Top Value Strategy
1556

70% EM Top Value +
30% Managed Derivatives: 917
· · · · · · · ·
Managed Derivatives
229

Note: All active strategies are after transaction costs and management and incentive fees.

**Exhibit 8. Asset Allocation between Emergining Markets Top Value
Strategy and Managed Derivatives Portfolio (in U.S. Dollars)
December 1988–September 1993**

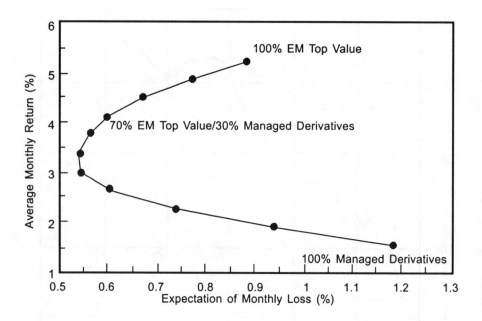

CHAPTER 28

Derivatives in the Spanish Market

Juan-Antonio Ketterer
Deputy General Manager
MEFF Renta Fija

INTRODUCTION

The year 1987 was a turning point for the financial markets in Spain. In that year a new securities law was issued and several other changes took place. The two most important were the creation of the Book Entry System for Government Debt and the electronic linkage of the four regional stock exchanges. Nineteen eighty-seven also saw the creation of the *Comisión Nacional del Mercado de Valores,* the Spanish equivalent of the U.S. Securities and Exchange Commission and the Commodity Futures Trade Commission, all in one.

All these developments produced the necessary infrastructure to begin a new era in the Spanish financial system.

In 1989 the derivatives exchanges began trading their first contracts, which were futures and options on government debt. These first contracts paved the way to a full array of derivatives, which are currently traded in Spain. Nowadays, the Spanish financial markets have obtained a highly prominent position within the world's leading securities markets.

THE SPANISH FINANCIAL MARKETS

Government Debt

The Spanish Treasury issues three types of securities: three-month and one-year bills *(Letras del Tesoro),* three- and five-year notes *(Bonos del Tesoro),* and ten-year bonds *(Obligaciones del Tesoro).*

The Spanish treasuries market is an over-the-counter market supported by a *book entry system.* This facility, introduced in 1987, was set up and organized by the Bank of Spain. The system is run and is regulated by the central bank, with an extreme degree of efficiency. In practice, the book entry system becomes a full-fledged, stated-owned, clearinghouse. This is because the central bank guarantees de facto all transactions and heavily penalizes any hint of insolvency.

Other measures adopted were the creation of a broad range of instruments issued by auction at regular intervals; the issue of tranches of medium- and long-term instruments that add up to large issues, hence achieving high liquidity; new tax treatment of coupon payments for nonresident investors; the creation of a system of market makers; the introduction of screen-based inter-dealer broker systems; and the creation of futures and options exchanges.

Instruments

Treasury Bills *(Letras del Tesoro)*. Treasury bills were issued for the first time in June 1987. Treasury bills have a nominal value of pta one million and are issued at a discount for a period of one year, three and six months. Treasury bills are issued every 15 days, using a system of competitive auctions.

Secondary market transactions can be spot, forward, or repurchase agreements. Clearing and settlement of spot transactions are carried out on the same day as the trade is reported.

Treasury Notes and Bonds *(Bonos y Obligaciones)*. Three types of securities are issued: Three- and five-year notes *(Bonos)* and ten-year bonds *(Obligaciones)*.

All these fixed-income securities bear a fixed annual coupon, and redemption is at par. (The coupon on issues prior to March 1990 was semiannual.) These three instruments are issued regularly in monthly auctions. If a minimum volume of approximately pta 400 billion is not reached in the first three tranches, additional tranches of the same issue are usually auctioned until that volume is issued.

Market Structure

Trading figures have grown substantially since 1990, largely due to the increase in the outstanding balance of issues, the active involvement of nonresidents in the market, and the expansion of domestic institutional investors. The most common type of transactions are spot, forward, and repo.

Bonds are quoted in clean prices and the average trade size ranges between pta 500 million and pta one billion. Bid-offer spreads are between five and ten basis points in the most liquid issues. The development of the repo market in bonds has greatly helped to invigorate the cash market and it provides a link between the cash and futures markets. Most cash trades have a value date within seven days, in line with general Euromarket practices, although settlement can be made on the same day or on another value date up to a maximum of seven days.

The access to the government debt "professional" market is restricted to financial institutions holding securities and cash accounts at the central book-entry office at the Bank of Spain. There are two types of members:

■ *Account-holder entities.* These can only trade on their own account and hold securities accounts in their own name.

- *Registered dealers.* These can hold securities and trade for their own and for third-party accounts.

There are also brokers, acting only as intermediaries. These brokers operate via telephone in the traditional way, or some of them operate through screen-based systems with firm quotes (these are the so-called blind brokers).

Clearing and Settlement System

Transactions between a registered dealer and a third party nonmarket member are cleared by the registered dealer, which records the security's transfer between its own account and the third-party account. Securities are registered the same day that the funds are received. For nonresidents working from the Euromarket, Euroclear and Cedel have a third-party account at a registered dealer within the book-entry office. However, transactions between nonresidents, taking place through Euroclear or Cedel, are not recorded by the book-entry office.

Tax Treatment

In accordance with Spanish legislation as of January 1, 1991, coupon payments and capital gains on Treasury securities held by nonresident investors are not subject to taxes in Spain. This special tax regime does not apply to residents of tax havens. It does not apply either to investments made by Spanish branches of a nonresident institution.

Money Markets

Parallel to the government debt market, there is a market for time deposits. Banks and other credit institutions use this market mainly to adjust the reserve coefficients. The overnight market is the most active segment. However, the longer-term tranches—30 and 90 days—are also fairly active.

The central bank's monetary policy has increasingly become market-oriented, particularly since 1982, when the Bank of Spain targeted Spanish money supply tightly to control credit growth and inflation. The key mechanism that the Bank of Spain currently uses consists of auctions of 10-day "monetary regulation loan certificates." Those can be used by banks only to meet their reserve requirements, but they are not tradable. The central bank operates revolving 10-day reserve periods for the banking system, during which 4.5 percent of eligible liabilities must be deposited. The Spanish market has discount houses that intermediate between banks and the central bank to funnel the system's daily liquidity needs.

Daily volume in the MIBOR (Madrid Interbank Offered Rate) deposit market has been steady at between pta 1000 billion and pta 1500 billion for the past year. Almost 90 percent of the market's volume is overnight. Banks short of liquidity may also seek overnight funds from the discount houses, who intermediate between the banking system and the Bank of Spain.

The Stock Market

Market Structure

There are four stock exchanges in Spain: Barcelona, Bilbao, Madrid, and Valencia. Madrid is the main exchange, accounting for 84 percent of trading activity. Spain's "big bang" took place in 1989 with the termination of the traditional open-outcry trading process and the introduction of the Computer Assisted Trading System (CATS). This is an electronic trading system that links the four exchanges. Most of the trading on stocks takes place in the electronic system.

Another significant measure of the reform was the suppression of the monopoly status of the stock jobbers. These were the only ones authorized for trading in stocks, and they operated with a system of fixed fees. Nowadays there are two types of stock intermediaries: stock brokers *(Agencias de Valores)* and stock dealers *(Sociedades de Valores)*. Both have to be incorporated, with a minimum capital of 150 million pesetas for the former and 750 million for the latter. *Agencias* can act only as pure intermediaries, and *Sociedades* can also trade for their own account.

As of May 1993, the stock market capitalization was 11 trillion pesetas. Thirty-five percent of stocks are held by individual investors, seven percent are held by institutional investors, and 11 percent belong to foreign investors.

One of the cornerstones of Spanish equity market reforms in recent years has been the determination to improve the quality of reporting and accounting from Spanish-listed companies. It is the obligation for issuers of listed securities to send quarterly and half-yearly public information to the *Comisión Nacional del Mercado de Valores* (CNMV). Listed securities in Spain must now inform the public, as any factor may significantly influence share prices.

Stock Indexes

For 1993 the Madrid Stock Exchange General Index was made up of 96 companies, two more than in 1992. This represented 84.4 percent of the market capitalization, excluding foreign stocks. Since 1992 a new index, the IBEX-35, has been the official index of the continuous market. It is made up of the 35 stocks that are most actively traded.

The IBEX-35 covers 74 percent of total market capitalization and 78 percent of volume traded. It correlates at the 98 percent level with the Madrid Stock Exchange General Index. The IBEX-35 is calculated and managed by the four stock exchanges. Every six months an independent committee revises the composition of the index. This committee has executive powers to substitute the stocks comprising the index. It is not adjusted for dividend payments but it is adjusted for new issues of existing stock.

The Over-the-Counter Derivatives Markets

Since 1987, the OTC markets for derivatives on interest rates and on currencies have grown at a fast pace.

The OTC markets on government securities and interbank deposits are somewhat regulated by the central bank. The infrastructure of the Book Entry System for

Government Debt is used for clearing and settlement of OTCs on government bonds. The repo market also benefits from that facility. The OTC derivatives markets are organized around a network of telephone brokers that interconnect the participant financial institutions that participate in it. The most important OTC derivatives traded in Spain are FRAs, forwards on government debt, repos, and currency and interest rate SWAPS.

The growing success of the OTC derivatives and increasing investors demand led to the creation of full-fledged exchanges to trade interest rates and equity products.

THE DERIVATIVES EXCHANGES

At present, in Spain there are two "twin" derivatives exchanges, one located in Madrid and the other in Barcelona. Each of the exchanges has its own membership and its own clearinghouse. Both exchanges are fully owned by a holding corporation called *MEFF Sociedad Holding de Productos Financieros Derivados, S.A.* (MEFF Holding Corporation of Financial Derivatives). This holding company has two subsidiaries: *MEFF Renta Fija* (MEFF Fixed-Income Derivatives) in Barcelona and *MEFF Renta Variable* (MEFF Equity Derivatives) in Madrid. Membership and the ownership of the exchanges are two separate things. An institution can become a member of the exchange without having to become a stockholder. Therefore, exchange membership is nontradeable or transferable.

MEFF Renta Fija trades and clears interest rate derivative products and *MEFF Renta Variable* trades and clears stock index derivatives and stock options. Both exchanges share the same trading and clearing technologies and the same rules and regulations. Of course, some operating procedures are different, since the instruments traded are of a different nature.

Regulatory Environment

Derivative exchanges are regulated and overseen by the *Comisión Nacional del Mercado de Valores* (CNMV), which is a government agency that supervises the securities markets in Spain. The CNMV is the Spanish equivalent of the U.S. SEC and CFTC together. The exchanges and the CNMV have worked very closely together to develop the current regulatory framework for derivatives trading in Spain.

In 1991 there were major changes in the financial futures and options markets. These changes affected both the legal framework and the organization of the financial derivatives markets. The legal framework was modified by the adoption of new general regulations governing organized futures and options markets. These previously operated under provisional rules (Article 77 of the Securities Markets Law and the Resolution of March 21, 1989, of the *Dirección General del Tesoro y Política Financiera*). The new regulations are set out in the Royal Decree 1814/1991, of December 20, 1991.

The CNMV is in charge of supervision, inspection, and discipline of these markets. It is empowered to order the suspension of trading in a contract, not only at its own initiative or at the request of the pertinent governing board, but also at the request of the governing boards of markets in which assets underlying the futures and options contracts are traded. This is due to the relation existing between futures and options and their underlying assets.

Exchanges and Clearinghouses

The structure of the exchange-clearinghouse in Spain is somewhat different from the Anglo-Saxon model. *MEFF Renta Fija* is a single corporation, the purpose of which is to organize trading as well as the clearing and settlement of the contracts. Both *MEFF Renta Fija* and *MEFF Renta Variable* act in the twofold capacity of exchanges and clearinghouses.

The rules and regulations of *MEFF Renta Fija* and *MEFF Renta Variable* allow for three types of membership:

■ Custodian clearing members can trade and clear for their own account, for other members (clearing members and nonclearing members), and on behalf of their own clients. They custody the margins posted by the clearing members.

■ Clearing members can trade and clear for their own account, for other members (clearing members and nonclearing members), and on behalf of their own clients. They have to post initial and variation margin with one or several custodian clearing members.

■ Nonclearing members act as pure intermediaries. They can trade for their own account and on behalf of clients, but they have to clear through a clearing member.

Furthermore, for each one of the contracts traded, there can be a set of designated market makers. They form the core of the market. Their function is to maintain the supply of bids and offers open to all market participants and to provide the market with liquidity.

The requirements for membership are:

CUSTODIAN CLEARING MEMBER

1. To be an *Agencia* or a *Sociedad de Valores* (securities broker or dealer), a bank, a savings bank, or any of the other classes of organization indicated in parts a), b), and c) of Article 76 of the Securities Markets Act.

2. To be a Government Debt Book-Entry Institution member with full powers to hold accounts for third parties. The general conditions of each futures or options contract may modify this requirement.

3. To hold a contract with *MEFF Renta Fija,* accepting its rules and regulations.

4. To post an initial margin with *MEFF Renta Fija* for guaranteeing at all times the satisfaction of its obligations with relation to the posting and maintenance of margins for open positions.

5. To be specifically authorized by the CNMV.

NONCLEARING MEMBER

1. To be a securities dealer *(Sociedad de Valores)* or securities broker *(Agencia de Valores)*, bank, savings bank, or any of the other classes of organization indicated in parts a), b), and c) of Article 76 of the Securities Markets Act *(Ley del Mercado de Valores)*.

2. To hold a clearing contract with a clearing member. A nonclearing member may hold contracts of this type with several clearing members.

3. To hold a contract with *MEFF Renta Fija,* accepting its rules and regulations.

4. To post an initial margin with *MEFF Renta Fija* for guaranteeing at all times the satisfaction of its obligations with relation to the posting and maintenance of margins for open positions.

CLEARING MEMBER

1. To be a securities dealer *(Sociedad de Valores)* or securities broker *(Agencia de Valores)*, bank, savings bank, or any of the other classes of organization indicated in parts a), b), and c) of Article 76 of the Securities Markets Act *(Ley del Mercado de Valores)*.

2. To hold a contract with *MEFF Renta Fija,* accepting its rules and regulations.

3. To hold a contract with a custodian clearing member, where it will post the margins. A clearing member may hold contracts of this type with several custodian clearing members.

4. To post an initial margin with *MEFF Renta Fija* for guaranteeing at all times the satisfaction of its obligations with relation to the posting and maintenance of margins for open positions.

5. To be specifically authorized by the CNMV.

Clearinghouse Guarantee

An important characteristic of the guarantee provided by the clearinghouses, both in *MEFF Renta Variable* and *MEFF Renta Fija,* is that it applies also to the clients of the members. This means that in the event of a member defaulting, the clearinghouse would make good on any of the claims of this member's clients. That is equivalent, from a practical point of view, to having clients' monies in segregated accounts from members. The implication of that practice in the risk management of the clearinghouse is that margin deposits have to be collected on a "gross basis"—that is, without netting the overall position of the member bringing together its own and its clients' positions. This is a very distinct characteristic of the MEFF clearinghouses that provides their users with an extra degree of safety.

Risk Management

Membership in *MEFF Renta Fija* and *MEFF Renta Variable* is separate. However, most institutions are members of both.

MEFF Renta Variable and *MEFF Renta Fija* have a highly sophisticated risk management facility. Its most important feature is that it allows real-time risk monitoring. The clearinghouse is able to know at any moment during the trading session the margin requirement and the profit and losses that are incurred by any of its members and clients. The risk monitoring facility is also used by the members to follow up the risk positions of their clients.

MEFF Renta Fija and *MEFF Renta Variable,* in their role of clearinghouses, have implemented all the standard safety mechanisms. These include a state-of-the-art margining system, flexible limits to daily price fluctuations, real-time surveillance of open interest, and audits to member firms.

The margining system is analogous to those used by the major clearinghouses around the world. It belongs to the so-called class of risk-based margining systems. The system is, then, able to cross-margin between futures and options on the same underlying. The risk parameters of the margining system are continuously updated to reflect current market conditions of volatility and to capture other factors affecting the clearinghouse counterparty risk. For example, MEFF has daily fluctuation limits for some of its futures contracts. These limits are reviewed and updated according to market volatility.

Currently, the limits are the following:

- 3-year government bond futures: 100 basis points
- 10-year government bond futures: 130 basis points
- MIBOR-90 Futures: 40 basis points

The limits have a "stop and go" character. That is, when markets hit a limit, the clearinghouse can make the corresponding margin calls to its members and hence continuing trading. Several times, exchange limits have been reached, but there was not a single time that trading had to be halted for more than 10 minutes. On the other hand, MEFF, giving notification to the CNMV, may decide to totally or partially suspend the market for whatever period of time it deems appropriate. The CNMV may force MEFF to lift this suspension. The suspension of the market shall in no event suppose any limitation on either the right of *MEFF Renta Fija* to require margins or on the obligation of members and clients to post them.

Trading System

MEFF Renta Fija and *MEFF Renta Variable* are both fully electronic exchanges. Members issue their orders from computer terminals located in their dealing rooms. The orders travel through high-speed telephone lines to a central processing unit. This unit receives, matches, and executes the orders, or stores them for later execution. The choice of an electronic, rather than an open-outcry, trading system was based on five reasons:

1. Setting up an electronic exchange requires a much lower investment than what is needed for a floor trading exchange. This is so from the point of view of the exchange and from the perspective of the members.

2. The operating costs are also cheaper for an electronic exchange than for a pit-trading one.

3. There is a general tendency in exchange-traded products to move into electronic networks. The same applies for "organized" OTC trading.

4. Auditing and surveillance are much easier to conduct whenever there is an electronic register of each step involved in the trading operation.

5. Electronic exchanges generate an output that can be cleared and margined in real time. This reduces the possibility of intraday failure.

MEFF Renta Fija: Fixed-Income and Interest Rate Products

The first contract traded in *MEFF Renta Fija* was launched in March 1990. It was aimed to provide an interest rate risk management tool for the three-year-maturity segment in the government bond market. This was the issuance range for which the Spanish Treasury used to show a preference at that time.

The three-year government bond futures contract is very similar to those traded in other exchanges. It settles upon delivery of a basket of bonds, adjusting the prices by a set of predefined conversion factors.

On October 19, 1990, the exchange was granted regulatory approval to trade short-term interest rate futures. The chosen underlying asset was a time deposit referenced to the 90-day MIBOR (Madrid Interbank Offered Rate). The MIBOR is fixed following a procedure very much like the one used to determine the LIBOR. Indeed, its reliability—and wide acceptance—is proven, since it is used to settle the FRAs traded in the OTC market. All other aspects of the contract follow international standards, such as cash settlement.

In April 1992, following the issuance policy of the Spanish Treasury, a 10-year government bond future was launched. This contract provided the investors with a hedging tool for the domestic market. As well, it was meant to achieve spread trading against other European government bond contracts. Spread trading is the most efficient way to state a view on the EEC convergence process. Risk arbitrage on interest and exchange rate can be instrumented in a very flexible way by using the 10-year contract. The characteristics of this contract are similar to those traded in all major European exchanges.

After launching a full range of futures contracts and having the market consolidated, the next logical step was to introduce options on the futures. There were several reasons for choosing options on futures over options on the underlying cash instruments:

1. The futures markets are usually more liquid than the markets for the cash assets.

2. There is an unlimited supply of futures contracts. Thus, options can be exercised in optimal conditions.

3. Options on futures and the underlying futures are traded on the same exchange, and under the same clearinghouse. This allows a benefit from an efficient cross-margining system. It also reduces the costs of coordination involved in the process of exercising options.

4. Arbitrage between the option and its underlying can be fully exploited, since there are no short-selling restrictions on the futures markets.

The options on bond futures and on 90-day interest rate futures are both American-style. The former expire two weeks before the settlement date of the underlying futures contract, and the latter ones expire the same day.

MEFF Renta Variable: Equity Derivatives

In 1992 the first stock index derivative was launched in Spain: a futures contract on the IBEX-35 index. In fact, this index was especially designed to be the underlying for derivative products. A basic characteristic of this index is its high correlation with domestic investment portfolios of institutional as well as individual investors.

The specifications of the futures contracts, similarly to those traded in *MEFF Renta Fija,* follow international standards.

At the same time, options on the index were introduced. These are European-style options on the cash index, rather than on futures. But since both the futures and the options expire the same day, and the options are European, it is equivalent options on the cash index or options on futures.

Stock options on Spanish leading corporations were launched in 1993. In February trading began on *Telefónica* and *Endesa,* and in May on *Banco Bilbao-Vizcaya* and REPSOL. In the near future, *MEFF Renta Variable* intends to extend options trading to include 10 Spanish blue chip corporations listed on the stock exchange.

The stock options are American-style options and are settled upon delivery of the underlying shares of stock.

APPENDIX I

Contract Specifications

3-Year Treasury Note Futures

UNDERLYING ASSET:	Government bond, 3-year maturity and 7 percent coupon
CONTRACT SIZE:	Pta 10 million
CONTRACT MONTHS:	March, June, September, and December
EXPIRATION DATE:	Third Wednesday of the contract month
LAST TRADING DAY:	Two business days prior to the expiration date
MINIMUM PRICE CHANGE (TICK):	One basis point (equal to pta 1000)
SETTLEMENT DAY:	At delivery
DELIVERY PROCEDURES:	Physical delivery
CONTRACT LAUNCH DATE:	March 16, 1990

10-Year Government Bond Futures

UNDERLYING ASSET:	Government bond, 10-year maturity and 9 percent coupon
CONTRACT SIZE:	Pta 10 million
CONTRACT MONTHS:	March, June, September, and December
EXPIRATION DATE:	Third Wednesday of the contract month
LAST TRADING DAY:	Two business days prior to the expiration date
MINIMUM PRICE CHANGE (TICK):	One basis point (equal to pta 1000)
SETTLEMENT DAY:	At delivery
DELIVERY PROCEDURES:	Physical delivery
CONTRACT LAUNCH DATE:	April 10, 1992

MIBOR-90 Futures

UNDERLYING ASSET:	Interest rate on a 90-day interbank deposit
CONTRACT SIZE:	Pta 10 million
CONTRACT MONTHS:	Eight months in the March, June, September, and December quarterly cycle
EXPIRATION DATE:	Third Wednesday of the contract month
LAST TRADING DAY:	The last business day prior to the expiration date
QUOTATION METHOD:	Index base 100 Where 100 × Futures Price—implicit interest rate
MINIMUM PRICE CHANGE (TICK):	One index point (equal to pta 250)
SETTLEMENT AT MATURITY:	Cash settlement on the basis of differences
CONTRACT LAUNCH DATE:	October 22, 1990

Interest Rate Options: Main Characteristics

UNDERLYING ASSETS:	3-year Treasury note, 10-year government bond, and MIBOR-90 Futures
CONTRACT SIZE:	One 3-year, 10-year, or MIBOR-90 contract in each case
OPTION TYPE:	American-style
OPTIONS TRADED:	Those with underlying asset are the first and second closest months to the March, June, September, and December cycle
EXPIRATION:	First Wednesday for the 3-year Treasury note and 10-year government bond, and third Wednesday for the MIBOR-90 of the underlying futures contract month

Index IBEX-35 Futures

UNDERLYING ASSET:	Index IBEX-35
MULTIPLIER:	Pta 100
CONTRACT SIZE:	The value of the index times the multiplier
CONTRACT MONTHS:	Next three months
QUOTATION:	Index points
MINIMUM PRICE CHANGE (TICKS):	One point of index equal to pta 100
MAXIMUM DAILY FLUCTUATION:	None
LAST TRADING DATE:	Third Friday of the maturity month
SETTLEMENT DATE:	Third working day after maturity date
SETTLEMENT PROCEDURE:	Cash settlement

Option on IBEX-35 Index

UNDERLYING ASSET:	Index IBEX-35
MULTIPLIER:	Pta 100
CONTRACT SIZE:	The value of the index times the multiplier
CONTRACT MONTHS:	Next three months
OPTION TYPE:	European
QUOTATION:	Points of index
MINIMUM PRICE FLUCTUATION:	One point of index (pta 100)
DAILY MAXIMUM FLUCTUATION:	None
EXPIRATION DATE:	Third Friday of the maturity month
EXERCISE:	Automatic for options in-the-money
SETTLEMENT DATE:	Third working day after maturity date
LAST TRADING DAY:	Maturity date
EXERCISE PRICE:	In full points of index finishing by 50 or exact 100

Stock Options Contract Specifications

UNDERLYING ASSET: Originally shares of *Endesa, Telefónica, Banco Bilbao Vizcaya,* and REPSOL

CONTRACT SIZE: 100 shares per contract

OPTION STYLE: American

EXPIRATION: Every month. At least the closest expiration and two others in the March, June, September, and December cycle shall be traded at all times

EXPIRATION DATE: The third Friday of the expiration month

EXERCISE DATE: Any business day until the expiration date, inclusive

SETTLEMENT DATE: On the first business day following the exercise date the shares shall be sold, the payment for which shall be settled in the corresponding period

EXERCISE: The exercise can be communicated to *MEFF Renta Variable* any working day, including the expiration date, before 18:00 hours. Exercised options will be assigned randomly and the assigned party will be informed before 11:00 hours of the day when the stock transaction must take place

LAST TRADING DAY: Expiration date

QUOTATION: In ESP per share, with minimum fluctuation of ESP 1

MAXIMUM FLUCTUATION: None

APPENDIX II

THE IBEX-35 INDEX

During 1989 and 1990, *MEFF Renta Variable* completed a survey of the Spanish stock investment industry and a series of studies to create the IBEX-35 index, which would act as the underlying instrument for stock index derivatives to be traded in Spain.

The IBEX-35 was designed to satisfy three requirements:

1. To be an aggregate market indicator

2. To be difficult to manipulate

3. To be calculated and published continuously for each new transaction

The IBEX-35 is a capitalization-weighted index composed of the 35 most liquid Spanish stocks.

The base date for the index is December 29, 1989. At this date the index was given the value of 3,000.00.

The IBEX-35 stock index has been designated to be an accurate substitute for a diversified portfolio of Spanish stocks.

It covers over 74.12 percent of the total market capitalization, and over 77.85 percent of the total market turnover, with less than 10 percent of the stocks traded on the Madrid Stock Exchange.

The small number of stocks that compose the index make the IBEX-35 an easy one to replicate. At the same time, due to the high liquidity of the component stocks, it is manipulation-free.

In order to ensure that the 35 stocks that form the IBEX-35 are the most liquid ones, the index is revised every six months, in January and July.

The IBEX-35 and the Madrid General Index, designed to represent the stock market as a whole, have shown a very close correlation (0.98) since January 1990.

The IBEX-35 has been designated by independent consultants with the help of experts on indexes on the Spanish stock market.

The real-time production of the index as well as the necessary adjustments and modifications are carried out by the Index Manager. The index manager is *Sociedad de Bolsas,* S.A.

Modifications to the index, when necessary, will be proposed by the index manager but will only be implemented after being approved by the Committee of Experts, which is composed as follows:

■ One person representing the Spanish stock markets, who acts as president

■ One person representing the index manager

■ One person representing *MEFF Renta Variable*

■ Two prestigious finance professors

How the IBEX-35 Is Calculated

1. Stocks composing the index. The index manager publishes the 35 component stocks and the number of shares used in the index calculation. Changes in either the stocks or the number of shares used in the index calculation are announced prior to its implementation.

2. Weighting of component stocks. IBEX-35 is a capitalization-weighted index; therefore, the weight of each one of the stocks is calculated by the relative proportion of its capitalization over the total index capitalization.

   The weight of each component stock varies whenever one of the two variables used for calculating the capitalization (i.e., price and number of shares) varies. Hence, its weight varies as the price of that particular stock fluctuates throughout the day, and whenever the number of shares is adjusted.

3. The equation. The IBEX-35 at time (t) is calculated by dividing the total index capitalization at time (t) by the total index capitalization at time (t-1) and then multiplying the resulting ratio by the index value at time (t-1).

   It can also be expressed by the following equation:

$$\text{Index}_{(t)} = \text{Index}_{(t-1)} \times (\text{SumCap}_{(t)} / \text{SumCap}_{(t-1)} + J_{(t)})$$

Where,

s	=	Stock; $s = 1, \ldots, 35$
t	=	Time
$Shares_{(s,t)}$	=	Number of shares for s at t
$Price_{(s,t)}$	=	Last paid price for s at t
$CapVal_{(s,t)}$	=	Capitalized value, $shares_{(s,t)} \times price_{(s,t)}$
$SumCap_{(t)}$	=	Sum over s of $CapVal_{(s,t)}$
$Index_{(t)}$	=	Index value at t
$J_{(t)}$	=	Adjustment added when stock issue takes place to the pre-issue capitalization

4. Sectorial weight. Certain sectors represent a large share of the IBEX-35. These sectors and their approximate weight are as follows:[1]

   ■ Banking: 27.83 percent. *Banco Bilbao Vizcaya, Banco Central Hispanoamericano, Banco Santander, Banco Popular, Banesto,* and *Bankinter.*

   ■ Utilities: 28.22 percent. *Endesa, Iberdrola, Fecsa, Unión Fenosa, Sevillana, Cantábrico, Gas Natural,* and *Aguas Barcelona.*

   ■ Communications: 17.04 percent. *Telefónica, Acesa* and *Aumar.*

---

1 Based on the list of June 11, 1993.

Then follows these sectors:

- Real estate
- Food and beverages
- Metallurgy
- Construction
- Chemical and textile
- Other

APPENDIX III

Delivery Procedures for the Government Bond Futures Contracts

The procedure for the delivery of bonds at the expiration of futures contracts on the 3-and 10-year government bonds is carried out in accordance with the following time schedule:

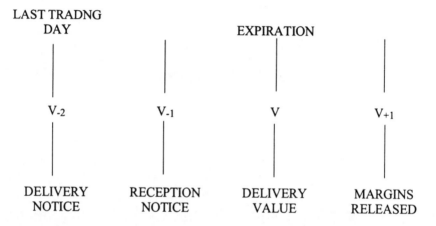

Delivery is initiated by the short side at the end of the last trading day (V_{-2}) by sending a Delivery Notice to *MEFF Renta Fija*.

On receiving the delivery notice, *MEFF Renta Fija* will proceed to:

1. Confirm reception to the issuing member

2. Allocate the deliverable securities notified to the oldest positions (FIFO criterion), notifying the securities allocated to each account

3. Notify the agent bank and the Bank of Spain as to the characteristics of the deliveries to be made by each member in accordance with the notices received, the list of bonds to be received by each member, and the corresponding cash amounts

MEFF Renta Fija will proceed with the above notices no later than 10:00 a.m. on the day following the delivery notice date (V_{-1}).

Deliveries will be made by the clearing members before 12:00 on the second business day following the delivery notice date, i.e., the expiration day (V).

Deliveries and receptions of bonds will be made through a purchase/sale with the agent bank, in accordance with the procedures stipulated in the *Reglamento de la Central de Anotaciones del Banco de España* (Regulations of the Book Entry Office of the Bank of Spain).

The margins corresponding to bonds delivered and received will be released on the business day following the expiration day (V_{+1}).

CHAPTER 29

DTB: The German Futures and Options Exchange

Jörg Franke
Chief Executive Officer
DTB Deutsche Terminbörse

The Deutsche Terminbörse (DTB), the German Futures and Options Exchange, opened for trading on January 26, 1990. Designed as a computerized exchange, DTB not only marked the beginning of a new era in German exchange trading, but it also paved the way for innovative developments on the international scene.

DTB operates a centralized order book, matching supply and demand in an orderly and transparent form via its nationwide network. DTB thus helps to prevent market fragmentation and ensures a high degree of liquidity. Another of the system's merits is that it provides uniform and immediate market access for all investors—no matter where they are based. And last but not least, the fully electronic, integrated clearing system provides for efficient settlement.

SUCCESSFUL START

Meanwhile, DTB has become an institution in the financial services marketplace. In German finance, options and futures are here to stay. Rising volumes and the continual expansion of a product portfolio geared to investor and market needs attest to DTB's increasing appeal among investors worldwide.

Step by step, DTB has launched new futures and options contracts, and now offers a broad spectrum of financial derivatives that are commonly traded on international markets (see Table 1 for the products that are traded at DTB as of March 18, 1994).

Table 1.	DTB Products	
	Based on Stocks	*Based on Interest Rates*
Options	Stock options DAX options Options on DAX futures	Options on Bobl futures Options on Bund futures
Futures	DAX futures	FIBOR futures (futures on three-month Frankfurt Interbank offered rate) Bobl futures (futures on German government bonds with 3.5 to 5 years remaining maturity) Bund futures (futures on German government bonds with 8.5 to 10 years remaining maturity) Buxl futures (futures on German government bonds with 15 to 30 years remaining maturity)

Using this variety of innovative products, investors can put together a range of efficient portfolio management strategies. Attractive strategies are available to institutional and private investors for hedging risk, improving returns, or speculating to enhance performance.

Unlike its individual stock options on 16 German blue chips, DTB's options and futures based on the German stock index DAX are geared to the direction of the German market as a whole, making it possible to hedge against the risk of adverse developments in a single transaction. Conversely, investors pursuing an aggressive strategy can speculate on the overall trend in the German stock market without assuming the risks associated with individual stocks.

DTB's interest rate futures and options offer the investor the possibility not only to hedge against fluctuations in the German interest rates, but also to take advantage of such movements and increase asset performance. The range of product covers the entire yield curve: The FIBOR futures in the short-term segment, the Bobl, Bund, and Buxl futures cover the medium- to long-term part.

Heavier trading at DTB reflects the success of DTB's concept and the increased demand on the part of investors for its products. In 1991, total turnover reached 15.4 million contracts, more than double the 6.4 million contracts traded in 1990, the exchange's inaugural year. In 1993, total turnover reached 50.2 million contracts, after 34.8 million contracts in 1992. This exceptional growth has been continuing so far in 1994.

LEADING OPTIONS EXCHANGE

DTB has bolstered its competitive position on the international scene as well. It has headed the list of European options exchanges since June 1991, and was the fastest growing European exchange in 1993 with a 44 percent increase in turnover to over 50 million contracts. But DTB has a favorable record in futures trading as well. In 1992, DTB gained considerable ground on LIFFE in the Bund futures market, and now handles about one-third of total Bund futures trading. What is more, contrary to all of the gloomy predictions at the start, LIFFE's introduction of a Bobl futures contract has not been successful.

The fact that DTB is attracting the lion's share of Bobl futures business to its own market is a success for DTB; and there is an obvious reason for this: Bobl futures were being traded at DTB for more than a year before LIFFE got into the market for this product on January 15, 1993. So DTB had a definite advantage in this case. In the meantime, international investors have grown accustomed to trading this product at DTB, and they are staying at DTB because it is efficient. And that is all that matters to investors today. They are looking for efficient markets, regardless of whether they involve an open-outcry system or a computerized exchange.

Another sign of DTB's growing international appeal is the higher proportion of foreign-based members. Non-German institutions now make up more than 40 percent of DTB's membership, compared with one-fifth in January 1990.

CURRENT DTB STRATEGY

DTB has no intention of resting on its laurels. It plans to meet the toughening international competition of the 1990s by continuing to expand its fully electronic trading facilities. This strategy is geared to maintaining the exchange's "leading-edge" technology. However, DTB's customer focus will also be further enhanced by an expanded range of services. The introduction of an order-routing system is one example. This service interfaces in-house order-processing workloads of DTB's member institutions with the DTB system—an advantage, incidentally, that also works especially to the benefit of private investors. Most recently, DTB integrated a give-up function into its system. Give-up trades allow end users added flexibility, since they can place their buy and sell orders with different DTB market participants but can clear them through a single institution.

DTB is also reaching for further market internationalization in the years ahead. The expansion of its electronic trading system to other European markets will make a significant contribution to that effort. The first step is to set up trading monitors outside Germany at the branches of DTB's current 88 members. The first of these "Euroterminals" was put into operation in Amsterdam in May 1993. It will be followed by the installation of further DTB trading screens, not only in Amsterdam, but also in other European financial centers such as London, Paris, or Zurich. The second step is aimed at providing immediate and direct access to European brokerages.

In December 1993 the DTB signed a cooperation agreement with the French options and futures exchange known as MATIF. The objective is to give the participants on both exchanges the possibility to trade selected instruments on each other's exchange. In the initial stage, participants on the MATIF exchange are to be given direct access to the DTB system through the installation of terminals in France. The second stage envisages the installation of the DTB software in the French options and futures exchange. Selected MATIF instruments can then be traded by computer and also be made available to participants on the DTB exchange.

CHANGING LEGAL ENVIRONMENT

Internationally, DTB's attractiveness depends to a great extent on Germany's status as a financial center. Forging a competitive capital market over the medium and long term requires a clearly defined legal framework. A model worked out by the German government is worthy of broad-based support. Under the government's proposal, legislative measures would be taken to restructure and expand the supervisory and regulatory mechanisms for German stock markets and securities trading.

In addition to the passage of an insider-trading law that meets international standards, an important part of the government's proposal is the establishment of a centralized public watchdog authority that would be vested with all necessary supervisory and enforcement powers and would co-operate with foreign securities regulatory agencies. Effective, unbureaucratic market supervision is integral to a liberal financial market. In this spirit, German policy makers are working in tandem with the business and financial community to improve the legal framework in order to heighten the attractiveness of Germany as a financial marketplace.

CHAPTER 30

The MATIF: The French Derivatives Market

Gérard Pfauwadel
Chairman
MATIF

INTRODUCTION

The Act of July 13, 1985, created the MATIF. This Act was initiated by the French Treasury Department so as to modernize the French financial market as well as the government security market—sale by public auction, the mechanism of allotment, the introduction of the status of primary dealers and correspondents in Treasury securities facilitated the emergence of an efficient futures and options market.

Originally a financial futures and options market (Marché à Terme d'Instruments Financiers), the MATIF was henceforth to be called the Marché à Terme International de France, regrouping financial and commodities contracts, which were already traded in France as early as the nineteenth century, under the aegis of the Bourse du Commerce. This merger, anticipated by the Act of December 31, 1987, has been implemented progressively by the Conseil du Marché à Terme and MATIF SA.

The Marché à Terme International de France (MATIF) is a regulated market on which standardized futures contracts on financial instruments or commodities are traded.

The MATIF currently offers a total of nine financial products: five interest rate futures contracts, options on three of those products, and one equity future contract. Since 1988, when it merged with the French commodities exchange, it has also been trading futures on white sugar and potatoes.

The MATIF operates on an open-outcry system during trading hours (8:30 a.m.–5:00 p.m.). In addition, as the first non-U.S. member of GLOBEX, the 24-hour screen-based futures trading system developed jointly by the Chicago Mercantile Exchange, the Chicago Board of Trade, and Reuters, the MATIF offers its members the opportunity for after-hours electronic trading.

The MATIF's mission is to provide a complete line of risk management instruments for financial professionals faced with fluctuations in interest rates and stock and commodities prices. The exchange offers professionals a secure market as well as fair and open pricing.

In seven years, the MATIF has grown beyond its original role as a domestic exchange to become an international financial futures marketplace that offers a diversified product base to global investors.

THE INSTITUTIONS AND THE MATIF

The Supervisory Authorities

The Ministry of Economy

The Ministry of Economy is represented by the Treasury. The Ministry's supervision is exercised in the following ways:

- Sanction by the minister of the general market regulations

- The appointment of two members of the Conseil du Marché à Terme (CMT)

- Designation of a government Commissioner to the CMT

This administrative body played a significant role in the setting up of the MATIF in 1986. It is responsible for the ratification of the General Rules & Regulations of the Futures and Options Market.

Banque de France

Within the scope of its general role as a supervisory body of capital markets and banking institutions, the Banque de France has specific prerogatives regarding the MATIF:

- A representative of the Banque de France acts as censor on the Board of Directors of MATIF SA, the managing body of the market.

- It ensures supervision of institutions subject to banking law.

- Finally, it puts forward an opinion regarding contracts in money-market instruments.

In addition, the Banque de France is consulted in connection with general regulations as well as on the establishment or abolition of certain contracts.

Furthermore, the bank is the supervisory authority of the two financial institutions responsible for clearing.

The Commission des Opérations de Bourse (COB)

The COB has the following duties:

- Protecting savings

■ Checking information given to investors

■ Monitoring proper operation of all securities markets, for listed financial instruments and markets for negotiable futures

As a public market, the MATIF falls under the supervision of the COB, which is responsible for the protection of savings and the information of investors. The COB gives an opinion regarding the General Rules & Regulations of the Futures and Options Market, prior to ratification by the Ministry of Finance, as well as all new contracts.

The COB is to issue an opinion concerning the general market regulations. It is also consulted in connection with establishment or abolition of contracts.

The Market Authority

The Conseil du Marché à Terme (CMT; Futures Market Board)

The Conseil du Marché à Terme, consisting of members representing the various professions concerned (stock brokers, banks, treasurers, etc.), is responsible for overseeing proper operation of the futures and options market.

In particular, it carries out the following tasks:

■ Determination of market operating rules

■ Laying down conditions for market access and the framework within which brokers act

■ Determination of participants' ethical obligations

■ Exercising disciplinary powers

MATIF SA, the Managing Body

A specialized financial institution falling under the jurisdiction of banking law, MATIF SA is the operational managing body of the MATIF. Shares of MATIF SA are distributed in thirds among the Société des Bourses Françaises, the banks and financial institutions, and insurance companies. Furthermore, members hold investment certificates issued by MATIF SA.

The Role of MATIF SA

The tasks entrusted to MATIF SA by the parliament are very extensive. In effect, the clearinghouse MATIF SA is also responsible for organizing the trading of contracts.

As a trading organizer, its duties are to:

■ Organize the confrontation of bids and asks according to a procedure accepted by the CMT

■ Determine the trading calendar and the official trading hours

■ Record and publishes prices

■ Oversee compliance with Trading Rules & Regulations

As a clearinghouse, its role is to:

- Ratify members who have been given clearing access
- Record every operation and act as a counterpart in all transactions
- Guarantee that the recorded transactions are successfully concluded
- Set the level of initial margins
- Calculate and call the margins and the initial margins on a daily basis
- Monitor the positions of market participants
- Calculate open interest after having balanced a participant's long and short positions
- Automatically close out the positions of defaulting members
- Organize delivery upon maturity of the contracts

Within the scope of the execution of its assignments, MATIF SA ensures supervision of compliance to trading rules:

- It supervises trading on the trading pits of the different contracts through the presence of exchange supervisors.
- It monitors the compliance of operations via active surveillance during trading as well as via examination of documents in the offices of the exchange members on the authority of the CMT.
- It keeps track of customer's consolidated positions of customers by centralizing risks.

Being at the service of market participants, Matif SA also plays an equally significant role in the development of the futures and options market in France: promotion of the exchange and its products, creation of new contracts, and the training of direct or indirect investors are activities implemented by the managing body.

Because of the inherent riskiness of the MATIF as a futures market, regulations grant an essential role to the market and the clearinghouse concerning operations security through either market management, position monitoring, or guarantee of transactions. In the interest of market security, the MATIF demands initial margins and calls up daily variation margins.

Finally, brokers are subject to ethical obligations, their violation entails heavy penalties.

MATIF MEMBERS: THE MARKET PROFESSIONALS

MATIF's members constitute a vital distribution network between the exchange and its end-users. This dynamic group of professionals plays a crucial part in the smooth functioning and sustained growth of the exchange. As such, it has been largely responsible for the success of the MATIF. Members of MATIF are organized into an association of futures markets professionals—Aprim. Created in 1987 by 12 members, the association serves as a link between the exchange and its members and provides a forum where issues of mutual interest and proposals can be put forward and discussed. A liaison committee has been set up to discuss strategic matters in quarterly meetings; joint working groups deal with more technical topics.

Exchange Member Categories

On April 6, 1988, the Futures Market Board (CMT) adopted a major reform concerning the status of MATIF membership, which led to the creation of the distinct statuses of general clearing member (GCM), individual clearing member (ICM), negotiating broker (NEC), and local (NIP). These reforms led to a real distinction between the two different activities of clearing and trading.

Market members are thus defined as traders or as clearning members. As set forth in Article 8 of the amended Act of March 28, 1985, their status is determined by the activities available to them: For all the contracts traded on the MATIF, they can on the one hand place orders on the market, and on the other, participate in the clearning of the resulting transactions. Excepted from this are the NIPs who can only trade on futures contracts with no possibility of direct activity on options.

Clearing Members

Clearing members (legal persons) can belong to one of the categories cited in Article 8 of the amended Act of March 28, 1985, i.e.:

- A stockbroker
- A credit institution as defined in Article 1 of the Act of January 24, 1984, the so-called Bank Act
- A securities house (Article 18 of the Bank Act)
- An interbank market agent (Article 69 of the aforementioned act)
- An authorized commission agent, an authorized broker under oath, or an authorized commodity trader
- As well as the Caisse des Dépôts et Consignations.

Clearing members of MATIF SA have the monopoly on clearing all operations transacted on the MATIF.

A clearing member submits the positions taken for his or her clients' accounts to the clearinghouse and reevaluates them on a daily basis (mark to market).

All market operations must be carried out by the clearing members, who thus are the only legal and financial contracting parties with the clearinghouse.

- Individual clearing members must have a net worth of 200 million French francs, or a minimum of 50 million French francs plus a bank guarantee. An individual clearing member is authorized to trade and clear trades for his or her own account and for its clients.
- In addition to the privileges enjoyed, individual clearing members are authorized to appoint negotiating brokers and clear their trades. They can also clear the trades of locals whom they sponsor. The net worth required for this status is 750 million French francs, or 375 million French francs plus a bank guarantee.

■ A negotiating broker handles transactions for clients only. With 7.5 million French francs in net worth, a member in this category must clear trades through the general clearing member who appoints him or her.

■ A fourth category, the local, was introduced in January 1989 to allow operators to trade for their own account. Sponsored by a general or an individual clearing member, with whom they have deposited a minimum of 100,000 French francs, locals base their activity on their expectations and take advantage of price differentials. Their transactions thus add liquidity to the market. In 1992, locals effected 10 percent of all transactions carried out on the MATIF.

The year 1992 was a year of renewal for MATIF's membership, with a total of eight seats changing hands. MATIF's new membership has further enhanced its international profile, since six out of the eight new members are controlled by nonresidents. Nonresident ownership thus grew to 37 percent in 1992 compared with 33 percent in 1991 (see Exhibit 1).

Exhibit 1.   An International Membership

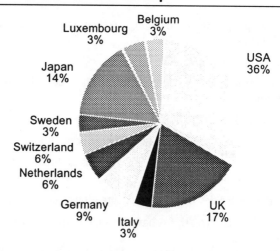

At the beginning of 1993, MATIF counted 12 general clearing members (GCM), 73 individual clearing members (ICM) and 12 negotiating brokers (NEC). Moreover, 60 locals (NIP), up from 50 at the end of 1991, trade for their own account on the MATIF floor, in the Notional and the CAC 40 contracts, and increasingly in the ECU bond and the PIBOR contracts.

PRODUCTS AND OPERATIONS

Futures and options contracts on financial instruments and on commodities are traded on the MATIF.

A WIDE RANGE OF FINANCIAL PRODUCTS

MATIF offers a wide range of products for financial operators: the 3-Month PIBOR and its option, the French-Medium Term futures, the NOTIONAL Bond futures and its option, the French Treasury Bond, and an ECU Bond futures and its option as well as a contract based on the CAC 40 stock index.

Definitions That Are Common to All Contracts

Underlying Products

The term "underlying product" refers to the product on which the future or the option bears. Firm futures bear either on financial instruments or on commodities. For options listed on the futures and options market, the underlying product is generally a firm future.

The Price

The contract price is determined continuously on the market by means of multilateral matching up of bids and asks. This price is reported at all times on computer screens, both within the market and on the premises of subscribers to the main electronic information systems.

    The option price is generally called the premium.

    The settlement price is the price at the end of the daily session and is generally called the premium. It is used as the price on which margins calls are based.

    The closing price or liquidation price is the closing price of the contract at the expiration of a delivery month.

Price Variation

Prices of futures contracts change depending on market supply and demand.

    The minimum price movement on the MATIF is called the "tick."

Delivery Dates

At the expiration of fixed delivery months, operations tendering takes place.

    Only certain months of the year (delivery months) are selected in the interest of standardization, a fact that ensures better market liquidity. In reality, deliveries are unusual, because the majority of operators settle their positions by way of an operation in the other direction before the expiration date.

    However, the possibility of delivery contributes to maintaining a link between the futures price and the spot price, which converge at the time of contract expiration.

    The delivery date of an option is also called the "expiration date."

Marketmakers and Specialists

The terms "market maker" and "specialist" are equivalent and designate members who act as counterparts at any time in connection with options contracts.

Delivery

Upon expiration, the seller must carry out actual delivery of the product (bonds, Treasury bills, commodities, etc.). It is also possible, and this is the general rule, for participants to settle their contract by taking an identical position but in the opposite direction to their original position before expiration. They then receive the corresponding profit or pay out the loss. In the case of certain contracts (3-month PIBOR contract, CAC 40 stock index futures) cash settlement takes place of securities delivery.

Liquidation

The term "liquidation" is reserved for automatic liquidation of a position, i.e., at the initiative of the clearinghouse or of a market member.

Contracts Traded on the MATIF

Financial Instruments

The MATIF approach is set on an innovation continuity. As of June 17, 1993, MATIF is the first European futures market to offer the full range of instruments covering the whole of the French yield curve.

Those instruments fall into two categories:

1. Interest rate contracts: the underlying product is the interest rate paid on a category of securities. In particular, the following are traded :

   - Long-term interest rate contracts (contract on the 15-year and over French Treasury bond, the 10-Year notional bond and option)
   - A medium-term interest rate contract (3- to 5-year French medium-term futures contract)
   - A short-term interest rate contract (3-Month PIBOR and option)
   - A long-term interest rate ECU Bond futures (6- to 10-year bond)

   These contracts make it possible to hedge the effect of rate variations on a bond portfolio, a loan, or borrowing. This protection is all the more effective when the portfolio, the loan, or borrowing is closer to having characteristics of the listed contract.

2. Stock index contracts: the underlying product is the average of the prices of a sample of shares, known as the "index" (CAC 40).

   Proper use of stock index futures makes it possible to limit the risk inherent in stock transactions. We draw your attention to the following points:

   - Market stock index contracts may be used to hedge the risk of a decline in the value of a diversified share portfolio close to the sample of issues constituting the index. In practice, however, it is difficult to acquire the same shares and in the same proportions as the ones represented in the index.

- The stock index contracts may be used to hedge the market, i.e., the risk that general factors influencing the market as a whole may have the same effect as on these shares.

However, the effectiveness of hedging on one or several shares by means of stock index futures depends on the sensitivity of each share to the general factors influencing the market.

THE PRODUCTS: RISK-MANAGEMENT TOOLS

The ECU Bond Futures Contract and Its Option

Table 1.   ECU Bond Futures Contract Specifications

Underlying Instrument	6- to 10-year fictitious ECU Bond, redeemable at maturity, 10% coupon
Trading Unit	ECU 100,000
Price Quotation	Percentage of nominal value with 2 decimals
Tick Size	2 basis points, i.e., ECU 20
Delivery Months	Two successive delivery months among March, June, September, December
Last Trading Day	Four business days preceding the last business day of delivery month
Delivery	6- to 10-year eligible bonds denominated in ECU, issued by sovereign states or supranational organizations, fixed coupon, redeemable at maturity
Daily Price Fluctuation Limit	+/– 250 basis points of prior clearing price
Initial Margin	Regular: ECU 3,000 Straddle: ECU 750 Spot month: ECU 6,000
Trading Hours	Open-outcry hours: 9:00 a.m. – 4:30 p.m. GLOBEX®* HOURS**: 4:30 p.m. – 9:00 a.m.

*   Globex® is a registered trademark of the Globex® Joint Venture L.P.
**   On Friday (or the day before a nonworking day), MATIF GLOBEX trading stops at 10:00 p.m. Paris time and resumes on Monday (or the day after a nonworking day) at 7:00 a.m. Paris time for all contracts (in Chicago, trading on MATIF contracts stops at 8:00 p.m. on Friday and resumes at 12:00 a.m. on Monday).

Table 2.   Option on ECU Bond Futures Specifications

Underlying Instrument	ECU Bond Futures
Trading Unit	One ECU Bond Futures
Price Quotation	Percentage of nominal value with 2 decimals
Strike Price	Integer multiples of 50 basis points, at least 9 closest-to-the money
Price Quotation	Premium in percentage of nominal value with 2 decimals
Tick Size	1 basis point, i.e., ECU 10
Delivery Month	2 Successive delivery months among March, June, September, December
Last Trading Day	Last business Thursday of the month preceding the ECU Bond Futures delivery month
Delivery	ECU Bond Futures contract
Initial Margin	Cross-margining of futures and options positions
Trading Hours	Open outcry hours: 9:00 a.m. – 4:30 p.m. GLOBEX® HOURS*: 4:30 p.m. – 9:00 a.m.

*   On Friday (or the day before a nonworking day), MATIF GLOBEX trading stops at 10:00 p.m. Paris time and resumes on Monday (or the day after a nonworking day) at 7:00 a.m. Paris time for all contracts (in Chicago, trading on MATIF contracts stops at 8:00 p.m. on Friday and resumes at 12:00 a.m. on Monday).

Background

In 1992, the MATIF's ECU bond futures contract (see Tables 1 and 2) demonstrated its effectiveness as a hedging instrument during periods of financial uncertainty despite the extent of the crisis in the underlying ECU cash market. During the year, 1.3 million contracts were traded, for a daily average of 5,400 contracts and an average open interest of 13,200 lots at the end of 1992. The total volume on the futures contract grew by almost 150 percent.

With liquidity on the ECU bond futures contract firmly established, options on the contract began open-outcry trading on May 5, 1992. With five market makers operating on this new product, approximately 83,000 contracts were traded during the year.

The underlying ECU cash market achieved unprecedented growth in 1990 and 1991, with several large issues coming to market and serving as extremely liquid benchmarks. As such, they have contributed to the success of the ECU bond futures contract. During the first six months of 1993, the MATIF's ECU bond futures contract broke a number of volume and open interest records, it culminated on June 17, when, for the first time, its trading volume on the contract exceeded that on the PIBOR and CAC 40 futures contracts.

Later in the year, the negative Danish vote on ratification of the Maastricht Treaty led to a momentary halt in primary and secondary ECU hard cash markets and temporarily slowed futures contract trading. Volume declined to 3,000 contracts a day by the end of the year, as compared with 5,000 to 10,000 a day during the summer. (See Exhibits 2-5.)

The 3-Month PIBOR Futures Contract and Its Option

Table 3. The 3-Month PIBOR Futures Contract Specifications

Underlying Instrument	3-Month Pibor
Trading Unit	FRF 5,000,000
Price Quotation	100 minus 3-Month Pibor with decimals
Tick Size	1 basis point, i.e., FRF 125
Delivery Months	8 successive quarterly delivery months (March, June, September, December)
Last Trading Day	Second business day preceding the third Wednesday of delivery month at 11:00 a.m. (Paris time)
Delivery	Cash settlement
Daily Price Fluctuation Limit	80 basis points of prior clearing price
Initial Margin	Regular: FRF 12,500 Straddle: FRF 6,250
Trading Hours	Open-outcry hours: 8:30 a.m. – 4:00 p.m. GLOBEX® HOURS*: 4:00 p.m. – 8:30 a.m.

* On Friday (or the day before a nonworking day), MATIF GLOBEX trading stops at 10:00 p.m. Paris time and resumes on Monday (or the day after a nonworking day) at 7:00 a.m. Paris time for all contracts (in Chicago, trading on MATIF contracts stops at 8:00 p.m. on Friday and resumes at 12:00 a.m. on Monday).

Exhibit 2.   ECU Bond Contract—Average Volume and Open Interest

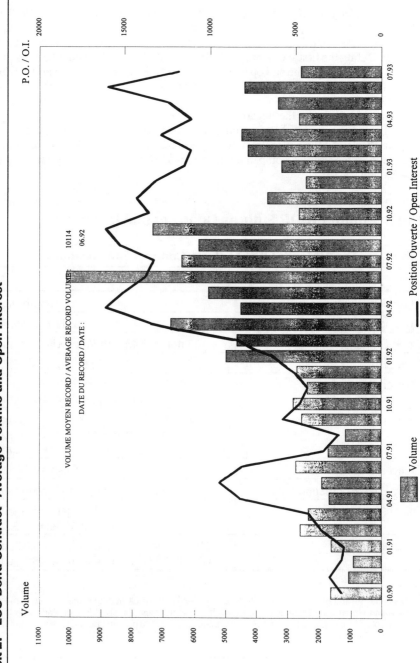

MATIF - STATISTIQUES

Exhibit 3. Option on ECU Bond Contract—Average Volume and Open Interest

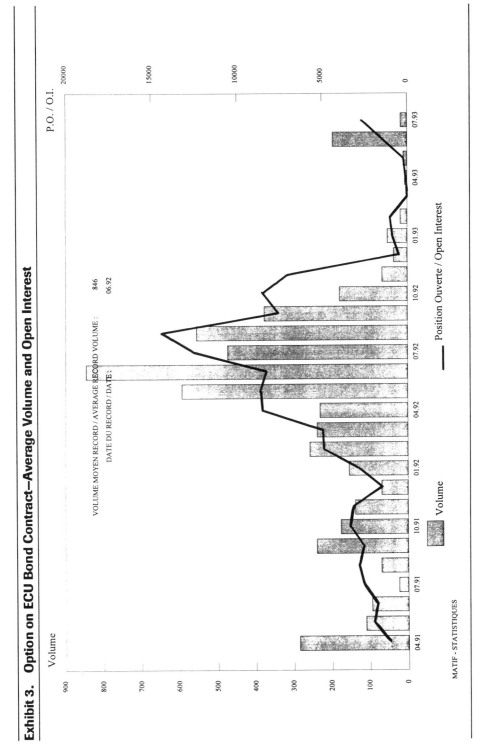

Exhibit 4. Settlement Price on ECU Long-Term Contract—Since October 18, 1990

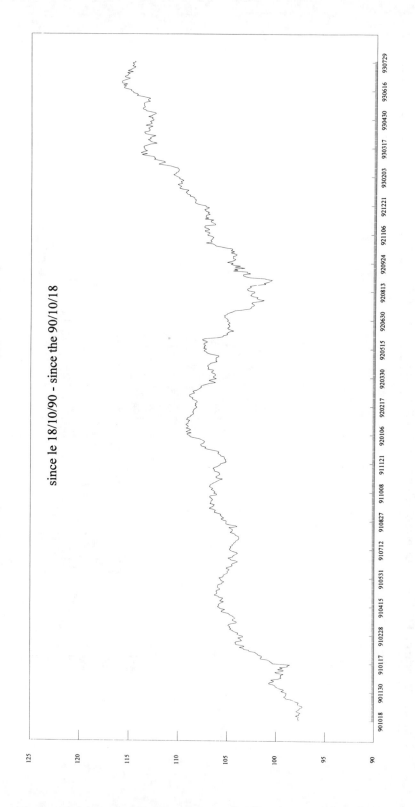

since le 18/10/90 - since the 90/10/18

Exhibit 5. Settlement Volatility on Option on ECU Bond Contract—Since April 22, 1991

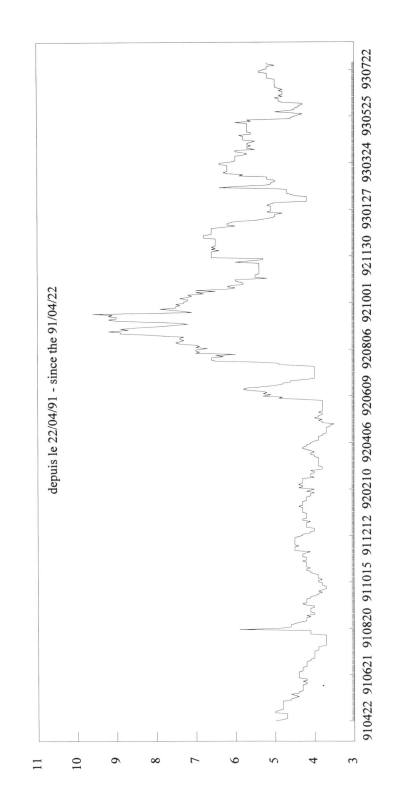

depuis le 22/04/91 - since the 91/04/22

Table 4.   Option on 3-Month PIBOR Futures Specifications

Underlying Instrument	3-Month PIBOR Futures
Trading Unit	One 3-Month PIBOR Futures
Price Quotation	Percentage of nominal value with 3 decimals
Strike Price	Integer multiples of 10 basis points, at least 15 closest-to-the money
Tick Size	1/2 basis point, i.e., FRF 62,5
Delivery Month	March, June, September, December
Last Trading Day	Second business day preceding the third Wednesday of delivery month at 11:00 a.m.
Delivery	3-Month PIBOR Futures contract
Initial Margin	Cross-margining of futures and options positions
Trading Hours	Open-outcry hours: 8:30 a.m. – 4:00 p.m. GLOBEX® HOURS*: 4:00 p.m. – 8:30 a.m.

*   On Friday (or the day before a nonworking day), MATIF GLOBEX trading stops at 10:00 p.m. Paris time and resumes on Monday (or the day after a nonworking day) at 7:00 a.m. Paris time for all contracts (in Chicago, trading on MATIF contracts stops at 8:00 p.m. on Friday and resumes at 12:00 a.m. on Monday).

Background

Clearly, 1992 was the "Year of the PIBOR" on the MATIF. Almost 6.5 million PIBOR futures contracts (see Table 3) were traded during the year, an increase of 114 percent over 1991. Introduced in September 1988, the 3-month PIBOR futures traded its 10 millionth contract in July 1992. Activity was especially steady during the months of September and November, with 900,000 and 780,000 contracts traded, respectively, reflecting currency concerns and significant interest rate movements. Trading by non-French participants alone accounted for nearly 50 percent of this volume (see Exhibits 6–9).

On February 21, 1992, the MATIF increased the number of contract maturities available on the PIBOR futures contract from four to eight. This two-year extension in the PIBOR quotation horizon thus brought the contract in line with short-term contracts proposed by foreign markets reference. Liquidity on these back month maturities continues to grow, demonstrating the real need that prompted the change.

The corresponding option contract on the PIBOR (see Table 4) evolved on a parallel track, with underlying movements in the PIBOR futures contract generating increased positions in the option. The option-to-futures contract ratio is maintained at approximately 40 percent.

Exhibit 6. 3–Month PIBOR Contract—Average Volume and Open Interest—Since Opening

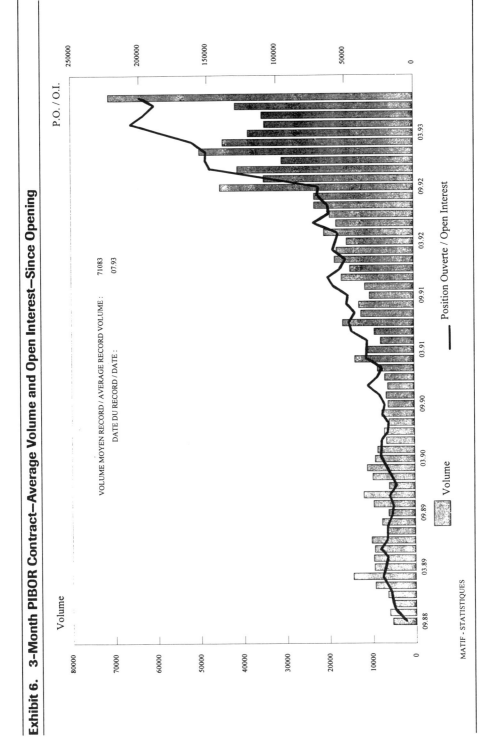

VOLUME MOYEN RECORD / AVERAGE RECORD VOLUME :   71083

DATE DU RECORD / DATE :   07.93

MATIF - STATISTIQUES

Exhibit 7. Option on 3-Month PIBOR Contract—Average Volume and Open Interest

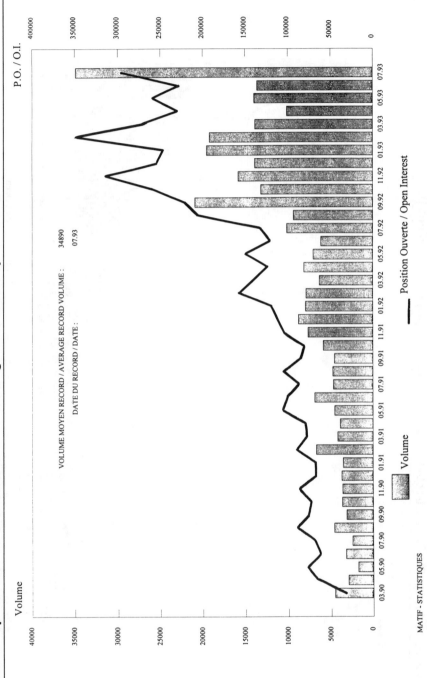

VOLUME MOYEN RECORD / AVERAGE RECORD VOLUME :   34890

DATE DU RECORD / DATE :   07.93

Volume

P.O. / O.I.

MATIF - STATISTIQUES

Volume   Position Ouverte / Open Interest

Exhibit 8. Settlement Price on PIBOR Contract—Since September 8, 1988

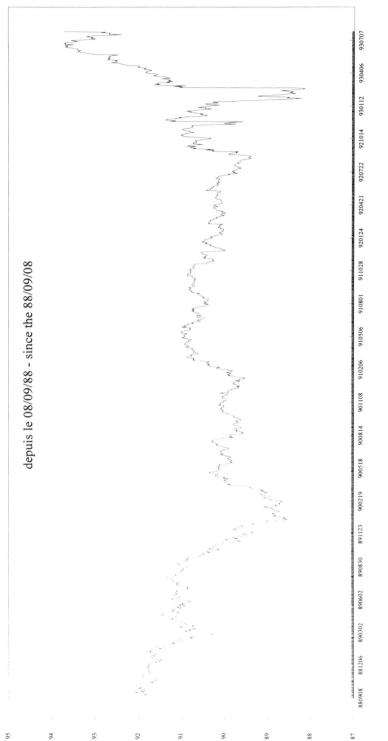

depuis le 08/09/88 - since the 88/09/08

Exhibit 9.   Settlement Volatility on Option on PIBOR Contract—Since March 1, 1990

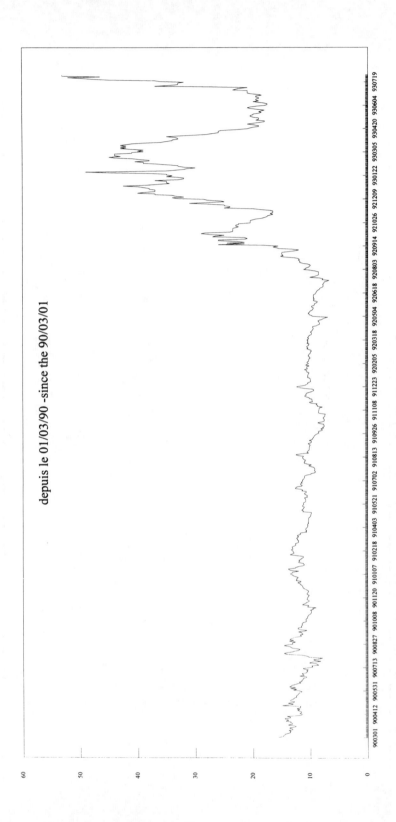

depuis le 01/03/90 -since the 90/03/01

The French Medium-Term Futures

Table 5.   The French Medium-Term Futures Specifications

Underlying Instrument	3- to 5-year notional French government securities, denominated in FRF, redeemable at maturity, 6% coupon
Trading Unit	FRF 500,000
Price Quotation	Percentage of nominal value with 2 decimals
Tick Size	1 basis point, i.e., FRF 50
Delivery Months	Four successive quarterly delivery months: March, June, September, December
Last Trading Day	Second business day preceding the third Wednesday of delivery month at 11:00 a.m.
Delivery	Securities are selected by the seller from an official list of 3- to 5-year BTANs and OATs, redeemable at maturity, based on settlement price
Daily Price Fluctuation Limit	+/– 150 basis points of prior clearing price
Initial Margin	Regular: FRF 10,000 Straddle: FRF 2,500 Spot Month: FRF 20,000
Trading Hours	Open-outcry hours: 9:00 a.m. – 4:30 p.m. GLOBEX® HOURS*: 4:00 p.m. – 8:30 a.m.

*   On Friday (or the day before a nonworking day), MATIF GLOBEX trading stops at 10:00 p.m. Paris time and resumes on Monday (or the day after a nonworking day) at 7:00 a.m. Paris time for all contracts (in Chicago, trading on MATIF contracts stops at 8:00 p.m. on Friday and resumes at 12:00 a.m. on Monday).

Background

On June, 17 1993, MATIF SA launched a new futures contract based on French Treasury securities (BTAN and OAT). (See Table 5 and Exhibits 10 and 11.) Their maturities are set between three and five years, thus completing the product line based on the French franc yield curve.

From now on, MATIF will offer its clientele the opportunity to hedge their risk on the medium-term segment of the curve as well as the other sectors of the French yield curve with:

■ the 3-Month PIBOR contract and its option

Exhibit 10. French Medium-Term Futures
Average Volume and Open Interest, Since Opening

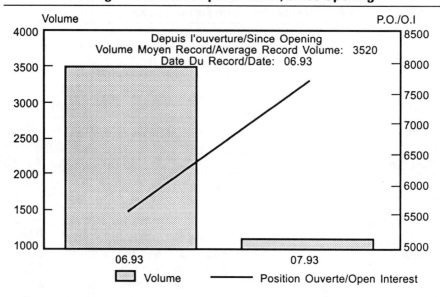

Depuis l'ouverture/Since Opening
Volume Moyen Record/Average Record Volume: 3520
Date Du Record/Date: 06.93

☐ Volume   ——— Position Ouverte/Open Interest

Exhibit 11. Settlement Price on French Medium Treasury Bond
Since June 17, 1993

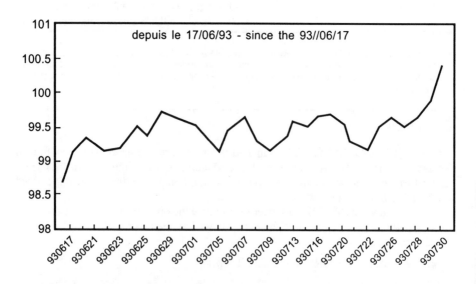

depuis le 17/06/93 - since the 93//06/17

■ the NOTIONAL (7- to 10-year) contract and its option

■ the French Treasury bond (15 years and over)

The French medium-term futures not only offers the usual hedging opportunities but also the possibility to spread the French yield curve, and intermarket spread and cash versus futures arbitrage.

The Notional Bond Futures Contract and Its Option

Table 6.   The Notional Bond Futures Contract Specifications

Underlying Instrument	7- to 10-year fictitious French government bond, 10% coupon, redeemable at maturity
Trading Unit	FRF 500,000
Price Quotation	Percentage of nominal value with 2 decimals
Tick Size	2 basis points, i.e., FRF 100
Delivery Months	March, June, September, December
Last Trading Day	Four business days preceding the last business day of delivery month
Delivery	7- to 10-year eligible French government bonds, redeemable at maturity
Daily Price Fluctuation Limit	+/– 250 basis points of prior clearing price
Initial Margin	Regular: FRF 15,000 Straddle: FRF 3,750 Spot month: FRF 30,000
Trading Hours	Open-outcry hours: 9:00 a.m. – 4:30 p.m. GLOBEX® HOURS*: 4:30 p.m. – 9:00 a.m.

*   On Friday (or the day before a nonworking day), MATIF GLOBEX trading stops at 10:00 p.m. Paris time and resumes on Monday (or the day after a nonworking day) at 7:00 a.m. Paris time for all contracts (in Chicago, trading on MATIF contracts stops at 8:00 p.m. on Friday and resumes at 12:00 a.m. on Monday).

Table 7.   Optional on Notional Bond Futures Specifications

Underlying Instrument	NOTIONAL Bond Futures
Trading Unit	One NOTIONAL Bond Futures
Price Quotation	Percentage of nominal value with 2 decimals
Strike Price	Integer multiples of 100 basis points, at least 9 closest-to-the money
Price Quotation	Premium in percentage of nominal value with 2 decimals
Tick Size	1 basis point, i.e., FRF 50
Delivery Month	March, June, September, December
Last Trading Day	Last Thursday of the month preceding the business NOTIONAL Bond Futures delivery month
Delivery	NOTIONAL Bond Futures contract
Initial Margin	Cross-margining of futures and options positions
Trading Hours	Open-outcry hours: 9:05 a.m. – 4:30 p.m. GLOBEX® HOURS*: 4:30 p.m. – 9:05 a.m.

*   On Friday (or the day before a nonworking day), MATIF GLOBEX trading stops at 10:00 p.m. Paris time and resumes on Monday (or the day after a nonworking day) at 7:00 a.m. Paris time for all contracts (in Chicago, trading on MATIF contracts stops at 8:00 p.m. on Friday and resumes at 12:00 a.m. on Monday).

Background

Year after year, the Notional futures contract (see Tables 6 and 7) has continued to establish its leadership position among European futures products. As one of the principal futures contracts in the world, its 1992 volume of 31 million contracts was nearly three times greater than that of all other long-term contracts in Europe, and was 47 percent higher than in 1991. Approximately 31 percent of this volume was generated by foreign participants. In a period of uncertainty and tension over currencies and interest rates, the Notional traded its 100 millionth contract on September 18, 1992. This milestone occurred just two days after the contract set a one-day volume record, with more than 346,000 contracts traded. The Notional attained its highest price for the year—112.56—on December 30, at the time when traders anticipated a lowering of interest rates.

In addition, the volume of the option on the Notional contract increased by 19 percent in 1992, reaching 10 million contracts traded during the year—or an average of 40,000 contracts per day (see Exhibits 12-15).

Exhibit 12. Notional Bond Contract—Average Volume and Open Interest—Since Opening

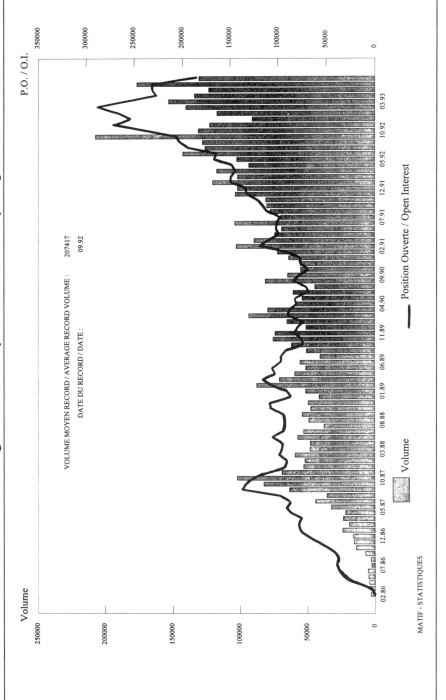

VOLUME MOYEN RECORD / AVERAGE RECORD VOLUME :   207417

DATE DU RECORD / DATE :   09.92

P.O. / O.I.

Volume

— Position Ouverte / Open Interest

Volume

MATIF - STATISTIQUES

Exhibit 13. Option on Notional Bond Contract—Average Volume and Open Interest—Since Opening

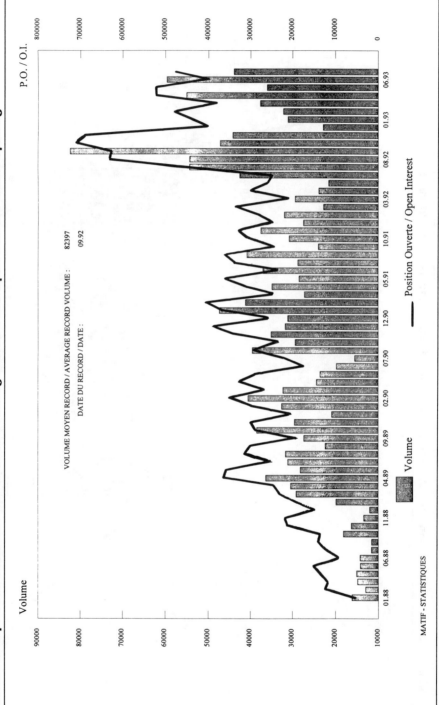

VOLUME MOYEN RECORD / AVERAGE RECORD VOLUME :   82397

DATE DU RECORD / DATE :   09.92

Volume

Position Ouverte / Open Interest

MATIF - STATISTIQUES

Exhibit 14. Settlement Price on Notional Contract—Since February 20, 1986

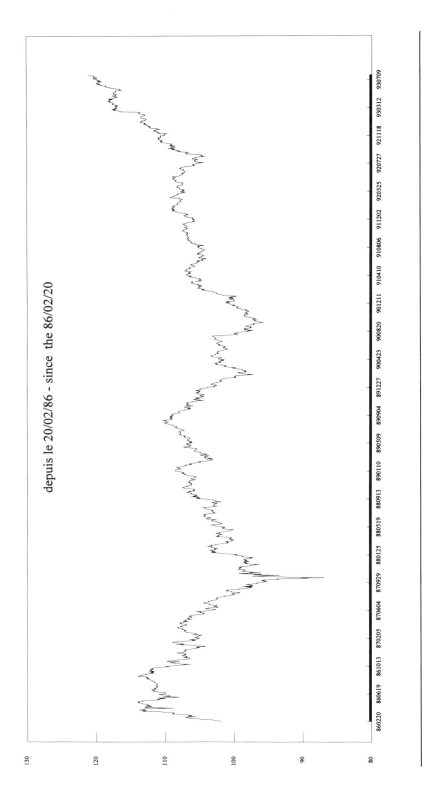

depuis le 20/02/86 - since the 86/02/20

Exhibit 15. Settlement Volatility on Option on Notional Contract—Since January 14, 1988

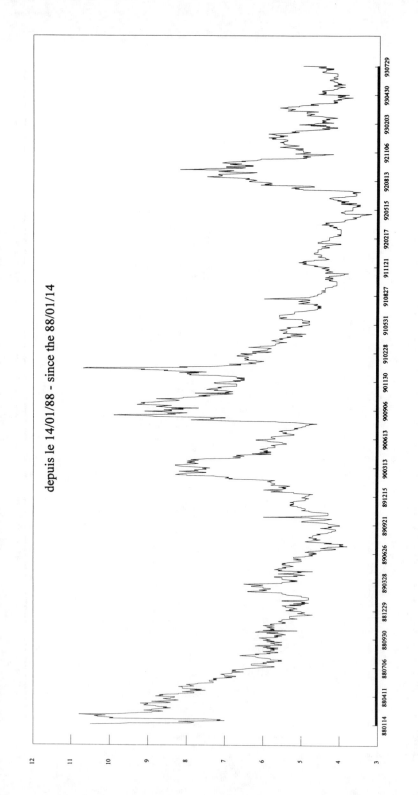

depuis le 14/01/88 - since the 88/01/14

On November 27, monthly maturities set up between the existing quarterly maturities were introduced on the options. This enhancement has offered market participants options with lesser time value and a better opportunity to trade very short-term volatility.

The French Treasury Bond Futures Contract

Table 8.   The French Treasury Bond Futures Contract Specifications

Underlying Instrument	15-year and over fictitious French government bond, redeemable at maturity, 8% coupon
Trading Unit	FRF 500,000
Price Quotation	Percentage of nominal value with 2 decimals
Tick Size	2 basis points, i.e., FRF 100
Delivery Months	March, June, September, December
Last Trading Day	Four business days preceding the last business day of delivery month
Delivery	Bonds are selected by the seller from an official list of 15-year and over eligible French government bonds, redeemable at maturity, based on settlement price
Daily Price Fluctuation Limit	+/– 400 basis points of prior clearing price
Initial Margin	Regular: FRF 20,000 Straddle: FRF 5,000 Spot Month: FRF 40,000
Trading Hours	Open-outcry hours: 9:00 a.m. – 4:30 p.m.

Background

Launched for trading on the MATIF on January 29, 1993, the French Treasury bond futures contract (see Table 8) provides international market participants with a new alternative to the Chicago Board of Trade's contract on the 30-year U.S. Treasury bond. The deliverable pool of bonds underlying this contract is a compilation of four 8.5 percent French Treasury bonds, maturing in 2008, 2012, 2019, and 2023. The total outstanding value of these securities approached 180 billion French francs January 1993 (see Exhibits 16 and 17).

Exhibit 16. French Treasury Bond
Average Volume and Open Interest, Since Opening

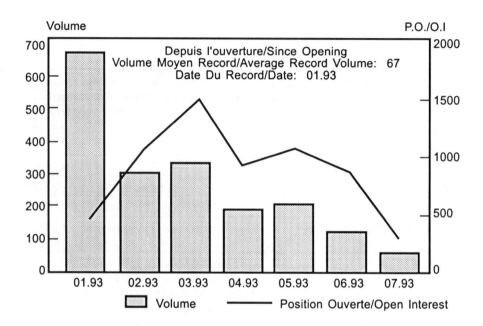

With the introduction of this contract, the MATIF provides market participants with an extension of the maturity of French Treasury debt, an important underlying market created just a few years ago. There is an increasing need for this type of contract, as all of the monthly issues since 1990 contained at least one long-term French Treasury bond. As a result, investors of these securities have been requesting a hedging instrument suited to the longer maturities.

Exhibit 17. Settlement Price on French Treasury Bond—Since January 28, 1993

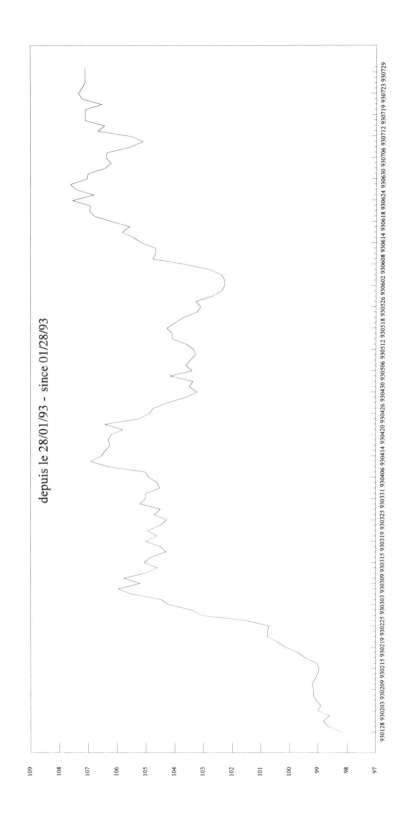

depuis le 28/01/93 - since 01/28/93

The CAC 40 Stock Index Futures Contract

Table 9.   The CAC 40 Stock Index Futures Contract Specifications

Underlying Instrument	CAC 40 Index
Trading Unit	Contract valued at FRF 200 times the futures quoted Index
Price Quotation	Index with 1 decimal
Tick Size	0.5 index points, i.e., FRF 100
Delivery Months	3 spot months and 3 quarterly delivery months
Last Trading Day	Last business day of the month at 4:00 p.m.
Delivery	Cash settlement
Daily Price Fluctuation Limit	+/– 120 index points of prior clearing price
Initial Margin	Regular: FRF 30,000 Straddle: FRF 12,000
Trading Hours	Open-outcry hours: 10:00 a.m. – 5:00 p.m. GLOBEX® HOURS*: 5:00 p.m. 10:00 a.m.

*   On Friday (or the day before a nonworking day), MATIF GLOBEX trading stops at 10:00 p.m. Paris time and resumes on Monday (or the day after a nonworking day) at 7:00 a.m. Paris time for all contracts (in Chicago, trading on MATIF contracts stops at 8:00 p.m. on Friday and resumes at 12:00 a.m. on Monday).

Table 10.   The CAC 40 Index—August 31, 1993

NUMBER OF SHARES, WEIGHT, AND ADJUSTMENT FACTOR			
Mnemonic	Shares	Number of Shares	% Weight
AC	ACCOR	24.729.536	1,19
AI	AIR LIQUIDE	58.202.933	3,31
CGE	ALCATEL-ALSTHOM	143.023.310	7,93
CS	AXA	31.320.391	3,67
CB	BANCAIRE (Compagnie)	23.816.108	1
EN	BOUYGUES	19.657.233	1,04
BN	BSN	64.944.224	4,39
AN	CANAL+	20.939.749	1,98
CAP	CAP GEMINI	42.309.942	0,67

NUMBER OF SHARES, WEIGHT, AND ADJUSTMENT FACTOR			
Mnemonic	Shares	Number of Shares	% Weight
CAR	CARREFOUR	12.812.916	2,85
CO	CASINO	56.132.020	0,65
CCF	CCF	60.422.748	1,13
CW	CGIP	5.894.530	0,54
CR	CHARGEURS	6.907.601	0,56
CU	CLUB MED.	10.956.742	0,35
FF	CREDIT FONCIER	10.112.009	0,88
EX	EAUX (Gle des)	25.283.924	4,62
AQ	ELF-AQUITAINE	251.649.774	8,23
SO	ELF-SANOFI	22.075.451	1,61
EDL	EURODISNEY	170.007.997	0,75
AJ	HAVAS	45.165.505	1,56
LG	LAFARGE	60.405.791	1,9
LR	LEGRAND	2.140.624	0,77
MC	LVMH	15.770.536	4,96
LY	LYONNAISE-DUMEZ	48.198.251	1,89
LH	MATRA-HACHETTE	93.815.548	1,11
ML	MICHELIN	106.246.364	1,53
OR	OREAL (L')	58.164.183	5,01
PM	PARIBAS	92.596.920	3,43
RI	PERNOD	46.988.884	1,48
UG	PEUGEOT	49.999.560	2,46
RPP	RHONE POULENC	250.845.264	3,02
SGO	SAINT GOBAIN	72.421.132	3,08
RS	SAINT LOUIS	6.989.849	0,71
SE	SCHNEIDER	22.296.167	1,28
GLE	SOC. GENERALE	80.579.396	3,88
FS	SUEZ	150.771.848	3,94
HO	THOMSON	111.206.871	1,51
FP	TOTAL	218.531.630	5
UAP	UAP	86.520.000	4,12
Adjustment factor:		1,679 562 147 589 090	
Increase of the outstanding shares:			
OREAL (L') Avis n° 2435 du 27 août 1993			
SAINT GOBAIN Avis n° 2430 du 27 août 1993			

Background

Since its introduction in 1988, the CAC 40 stock index futures contract (see Tables 9 and 10 and Exhibits 18 and 19) has grown steadily. Its average daily volume was 2,000 contracts in 1989, 6,000 contracts in 1990, 9,000 contracts in 1991, and 14,000 contracts in 1992. The month of September was especially active with high activity and volatile prices, as with the other MATIF contracts. In 1992, open interest increased by 75 percent from 1991, demonstrating the continued maturity of the contract.

On October 22, 1992, in response to the needs of non-French participants, who represented 44 percent of the open interest at the end of the year, the MATIF added two quarterly maturities to the CAC 40 index's three monthly maturities and to the quarterly maturities already in existence. The change allows a 10- to 12-month maturity coverage period, rather than the previous 4- to 6-month period.

CHANGES IN THE DELIVERY CALENDARS OF FINANCIAL CONTRACTS

In order to comply with international practice, MATIF SA has decided to bring the delivery calendar of MATIF deliverable financial contracts in line with the calendar of its PIBOR futures contract. This modification was approved by the Conseil du Marché à Terme in May 1993.

Trading on deliverable financial contracts (Notional, French T-Bond, ECU Bond and the French medium-term) will close on the second business day preceding the third Wednesday of the delivery month at 11:00 a.m. (Paris time).

The new calendar will come into force in September 1993, and in June 1994 for all other contracts.

Thereafter, the opening of a new delivery month will take place the day after the expiry of the spot month.

So as to comply with by anticipation with this new rule, June 1994 will open on Friday June 25, 1993.

A COMPLEMENTARY TOOL: INTER-CONTRACT CROSS-MARGINING

Since July 23, 1993, MATIF SA has offered to the market professionals an inter-contract cross-margining system that is based on three governing principles:

■ Margin settlement on futures contracts

■ Immediate payment of the premium by the options buyer to the options writer

■ Futures/options, inter-maturity and inter-contract cross-margining

The common futures/options margin requirement system is compatible with the one that is applied to futures contracts alone, while at the same time taking into consideration the specific nature of options (particularly sensitivity of premium to underlying price fluctuations and to volatility). The method, used for a combination of options and futures contracts, induces a strict correlation between the initial margin

Exhibit 18. CAC 40 Index Contract—Average Volume and Open Interest—Since Opening

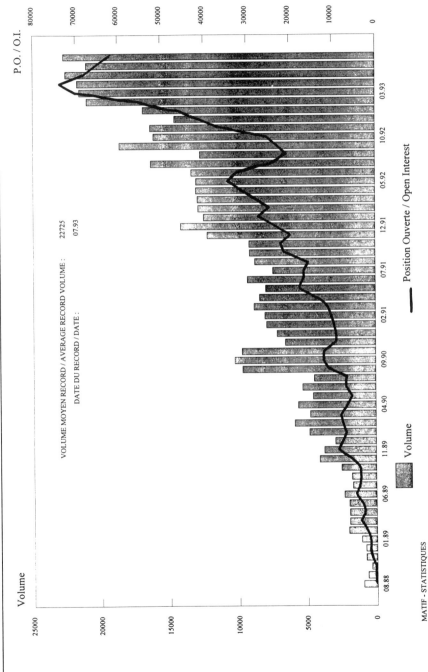

Volume

P.O. / O.I.

VOLUME MOYEN RECORD / AVERAGE RECORD VOLUME :   22725

DATE DU RECORD / DATE :   07.93

▬▬▬ Position Ouverte / Open Interest

▨ Volume

MATIF - STATISTIQUES

Exhibit 19. Settlement Price on CAC 40 Index Future—Since August 18, 1988

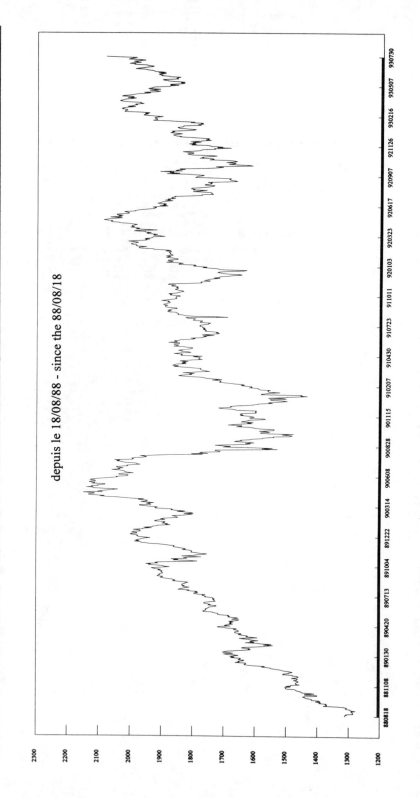

depuis le 18/08/88 - since the 88/08/18

and overall risk. It takes the reducing aspect of hedged positions on the futures contract and its corresponding option into consideration.

The initial margin corresponds to the liquidating value of a portfolio, determined according to the most unfavorable possible changes of the following parameters:

- Futures contract price varying within a range
- Inter-maturity differential of futures price
- Inter-contract differential of futures prices variations
- Volatility

The margin requirement system uses a portfolio valuation approach. Options that are bought (sold) consist of assets (liabilities) having positive (negative) liquidating value. The actual liquidating value is equivalent to the sum of the values of the repurchase and resale of the options at their closing price.

For each contract group by maturity, theoretical premiums are calculated for each options series for each reference price within the underlying fluctuation range. Futures/options positions are matched by adding the liquidation values of each options series and the variation of the futures contracts value for each reference price of the underlying instrument.

Inter-maturity cross-margining: the futures contract price variation range is divided into intervals of equal amplitude. Each interval comprises the same number of reference prices. For each maturity and each interval, the lowest of the values is kept. The liquidation balance of the interval is worth the sum of the lowest values of each maturity.

Inter-contract cross-margining: for each contracts group, the liquidation values are divided into new intervals. For each contracts group and each interval, the lowest of the liquidation values is kept. The initial margin of the futures/options and inter-contract match equals the balance of the most negative liquidation.

GLOBEX®

Background of GLOBEX®

June 1988: The Chicago Mercantile Exchange (CME) and Reuters decide to develop an internationally oriented automated trading system

February 1989: The Commodity Futures Trading Commission (CFTC) approves GLOBEX®.

March 1989: The MATIF announces its intention to join GLOBEX®.

November 1989: The MATIF formally joins GLOBEX®.

January 1990: The Futures Market Board (CMT) approves GLOBEX® in principle.

November 1991: Approval of the regulatory framework by the CMT, the French Exchange Trading Commission (COB), and the French Treasury.

April 1992: The CBOT joins GLOBEX® by signing an agreement with the CME and Reuters.

June 1992: CME and CBOT products begin trading on GLOBEX® in Chicago, New York and London.

March 1993: The 3-Month PIBOR, the ECU and their options are traded on GLOBEX®.

May 1993: The Notional and its option are traded on GLOBEX®.

June 1993: The CAC 40 stock index futures is traded on GLOBEX®.

The pre-eminence of an open-outcry trading system in no way excludes the possibility of developing a complementary electronic trading system.

GLOBEX® is an international automated trading system that allows trading on the contracts listed by a number of partner exchanges. A contract may be traded on GLOBEX® outside the hours of the trading session where it is quoted on its exchange of origin. The members of the contract's exchange of origin and, under certain conditions, the members of the other partner exchanges, have access to this method of trading.

Created in 1988, the GLOBEX® electronic screen-based trading system provides a decentralized global market on which the world's major futures and options contracts are traded. GLOBEX® was developed jointly by Reuters and the Chicago Mercantile Exchange (CME), combining the two organizations' respective expertise in computer networks and futures markets. Since then, the Chicago Board of Trade (CBOT) and the MATIF have joined the system. In 1992, volume on these three exchanges represented approximately 72 percent of the total volume traded by the seven largest futures markets in the world. Access to this crucial mass on GLOBEX® is an important feature of this truly global market.

By operating outside regular trading organizations' hours, GLOBEX® has been able to capture a portion of the market totaling 12 percent of the overall volume traded by the MATIF, or 6.7 million contracts in 1992.

QUOTE VENDORS

A large number of major international quote vendors carry MATIF prices. These are:

- Matif Diffusion
- ADP
- Bloomberg
- Bridge Data
- Chronobourse
- CMS
- CQG Ltd.
- Datastream
- DRI/McGraw-Hill
- Fides
- Fininfo

- Futrebd
- Futuresource
- GL Consultants
- ICV—Comstock
- K.R.U.
- Prominnofi
- Quotron
- Reuter IDN
- Reuter Monitor
- Servisen
- Telekurs
- Telerate
- Track Data
- Tradermade

Table 11. MATIF, Record Figures as of July 30, 1993

Contracts	Total		CRIEE Open-Outcry			T.H.S After Session			GLOBEX			Open Interest		Prices Open-Outcry Most Liquid Maturity			
	Volume	Date	Launching	Volume	Date	Launching	Volume	Date	Launching	Volume	Date	Lots	Date	High	Date	Low	Date
NOTIONAL	360,836	21-Sep-92	20-Feb-86	324,210	16-Sep-92	03-Feb-88	58,331	21-Apr-93	14-May-93	23,397	30-Jul-93	302,703	08-Mar-93	120.60	26-Jul-93	86.05	19-Oct-87
PIBOR	141,824	22-Jul-93	08-Sep-88	132,701	22-Jul-93	08-Sep-88	21,427	28-Jan-93	15-Mar-93	21,414	30-Jul-93	223,825	30-Jul-93	93.82	01-Jul-93	87.08	01-Feb-93
CAC 40	67,960	30-Jul-93	09-Nov-88	62,172	30-Jul-93	17-Aug-88	13,118	05-May-93	04-Jun-93	5,788	30-Jul-93	80,542	27-Apr-93	2153.0	09-May-90	1428.0	15-Jan-91
EURODEM	11,036	12-Feb-90	09-May-89	10,685	19-Apr-93	19-Apr-89	9,659	25-Apr-89				7,693	24-Nov-89	93.37	02-Aug-89	90.62	02-Mar-90
ECU	19,514	04-Jun-92	18-Oct-90	17,356	04-Jun-92	18-Oct-90	2,955	15-Jun-92	15-Mar-93	1,583	01-Jul-93	19,489	08-Jun-93	116.10	29-Jun-93	97.24	06-Nov-90
BTP	14,454	10-Sep-91	05-Sep-91	12,050	12-Sep-91	05-Sep-91	5,977	10-Sep-91				8,064	12-Sep-91	88.35	18-Mar-92	84.70	05-Sep-91
BTAN	2,294	18-Sep-89	01-Jun-89			14-Jun-90						10,342	22-Dec-89	98.58	02-Aug-89	90.06	20-Feb-90
FLT	1,241	11-Mar-93	28-Jan-93	1,241	11-Mar-93	28-Jan-93	395	08-Apr-93				1,846	04-Mar-93	107.90	29-Jun-93	97.90	28-Jan-93
FMT	6,803	17-Jun-93	17-Jun-93	6,693	17-Jun-93	17-Jun-93	1,279	21-Jun-93				8,439	22-Jul-93	99.90	29-Jun-93	98.50	17-Jun-93
OPTIONS NNN	155,066	18-Sep-92	14-Jan-88	145,977	16-Sep-92	26-Jul-89	47,311	26-Oct-92	14-May-93	9,500	01-Jun-93	799,353	25-Nov-92				
OPTIONS PIB	88,323	22-Jul-93	01-Mar-90	83,146	22-Jul-93	01-Mar-90	19,009	07-Mar-90	15-Mar-93	8,900	23-Jul-93	389,017	12-Mar-93				
OPTIONS EDM	11,110	22-Jun-90	05-Apr-90	11,110	22-Jun-90	05-Apr-90	7,667	11-Apr-90				37,692	11-Sep-90				
OPTIONS ECU	2,846	27-Aug-92	05-May-92	2,828	27-Aug-92	19-Apr-91	2,000	11-Feb-92	15-Mar-93	180	30-Jul-93	17,194	26-Aug-92				
OPTIONS BTP	300	18-Oct-91	18-Oct-91			18-Oct-91						595	28-Oct-91				
TOTAL	634,672	16-Sep-92									61,656	30-Jul-93	1,607,850	25-Nov-92				

Table 12. MATIF Yearly Activity Since the Beginning to July 30, 1993

CONTRACTS	1986	1987	1988	1989	1990	1991	1992	1993	TOTAL
Notional Bond	1,663,961	11,911,434	12,357,118	15,004,901	15,996,096	21,087,899	31,062,844	20,196,352	129,280,605
90-Day T-Bill	50,117	106,856	15,973						172,946
3-Month PIBOR			452,374	2,296,359	1,900,851	3,000,111	6,436,765	6,505,949	20,592,409
CAC 40 Index			64,688	581,473	1,641,398	2,311,196	3,601,476	3,035,832	11,236,063
3-Month Eurodem				613,748	393,850	285			1,007,883
4-Year BTAN				84,628	27,866				112,494
ECU Bond					56,292	546,273	1,354,012	517,241	2,473,818
Italian Bond						148,491	101		148,592
French Treasury Bond								25,923	25,923
French Medium Term								58,156	58,156
Financial Futures	1,714,078	12,018,290	12,890,153	18,581,109	20,016,353	27,094,255	42,455,198	30,339,453	165,108,889
Notional Option			3,430,915	7,149,559	7,410,305	8,411,903	10,047,391	6,120,751	42,570,824
PIBOR Option					709,736	1,373,567	2,659,534	2,579,403	7,322,240
Eurodem Option					109,445	400			109,845
ECU Option						21,179	82,820	6,387	110,386
BTP Option						890	0		890
Financial Options			3,430,915	7,149,559	8,229,486	9,807,939	12,789,745	8,706,541	50,114,185
Total Financial	1,714,078	12,018,290	16,321,068	25,730,668	28,245,839	36,902,194	55,244,943	39,045,994	215,223,074
Sugar FF			160,441	321,463	255,978	45			737,927
Sugar USD					46,930	199,368	218,250	159,931	624,479
Coffee			3,383	2,826	1,799	488	608	330	9,434
Cocoa			2,336	167					2,503
Potato 40 MM			700	606	23				1,329
Potato 50 MM			7,838	30,983	37,165	26,787	10,437	6,354	119,564
Total Commodities			174,698	356,045	341,895	226,688	229,295	166,615	1,495,236
TOTAL MATIF	1,714,078	12,018,290	16,495,766	26,086,713	28,587,734	37,128,882	55,474,238	39,212,609	216,718,310

Contracts Launching Dates

1986	1988	1989	1990	1991
NNN : 20.02 TES	ONN : 14.01 TES	EDM : 19.04 THS	OPI : 01.03 TES	OXU : 19.04 THS
BDT : 25.06 TES	NNN : 03.02 THS	EDM : 09.05 TES	OPI : 01.03 THS	BTP : 05.09 TES
	BDT : 04.02 THS	BTA : 01.06 TES	ODM : 05.04 TES	BTP : 06.09 THS
	CAC : 17.08 THS	ONN : 26.07 THS	ODM : 05.04 THS	OBT : 18.10 THS
	PIB : 08.09 TES		BTA : 14.06 THS	
	PIB : 08.09 THS		ECU : 18.10 TES	
	CAC : 09.11 TES		ECU : 18.10 THS	

1993	1993			
FLT : 28.01 TES	CAC : 04.06 GLO			
FLT : 28.01 THS	FMT : 17.06 TES			
PIB : 15.03 GLO	FMT : 17.06 THS			
ECU : 15.03 GLO				
OPI : 15.03 GLO				
OXU : 15.03 GLO				
NNN : 14.05 GLO				
ONN : 14.05 GLO				

Commodities statistics made by MATIF SA since July 1, 1988.

APPENDIX 1

BOARD OF DIRECTORS—as of July 6, 1993

Chairman
Gérard Pfauwadel

Members

Jacques-Antoine Allain	Société de Bourse Bacot-Allain-Farra SA
Bernard Darmayan	Crédit Lyonnais
Philippe Bordenave	Banque National de Paris
Olivier Colas	JP Morgan
Henri Daru	Union des Assurances de Paris International
Alain Ferri	Société de Bourse Ferri SA
Bertrand Gaffet	Caisse Centrale des Banques Populaires
Jean-Bernard Guillebert	Société Générale
Gérard de la Martiniére	AXA
Serge Sayan	Assurances Générales de France
Jean-François Théodore	Société des Bourses Françaises
Government Commissioner	Ministry of Economy
Serge Allain	

Censor

Robert Raymond   Represents the Banque de France

Statutory Auditors

HSD CASTEL JACQUET Ernst & Young International
SALUSTRO REYDEL

APPENDIX 2

LIST OF MATIF MEMBERS

BACOT ALLAIN SA
65, rue de Courcelles
75008 PARIS
Tél.: 48 88 30 30

BANKERS TRUST FUTURES (EUROPE) GIE
12/14, rond-point des Champs-Elysées
75386 PARIS CEDEX 08
Tél.: 42 99 30 00

BANQUE BRUXELLES LAMBERT FRANCE
Immeuble KUPKA-B
16, rue Hoche
92906 PARIS LA DEFENSE
Tél.: 41 26 70 00

BANQUE D'ESCOMPTE
13, boulevard Haussmann
75009 PARIS
Tél.: 48 24 85 44

BANQUE EUROPEENNE DE TOKYO
4-8 rue Sainte-Anne
75001 PARIS
Tél.: 49 26 49 80

BANQUE FEDERATIVE DU CREDIT MUTUEL
34 rue du Wacken
67000 STRASBOURG
Tél.: 16 88 14 88 14

BANQUE FRANCAISE DU COMMERCE EX-TERIEUR (BFCE)
21, boulevard Haussmann
75009 PARIS
Tél.: 48 00 48 00

BANQUE GENERALE DU PHENIX ET DU CREDIT CHIMIQUE
6, avenue Kléber
75116 PARIS
Tél.: 44 17 21 00

BANQUE INTERNATIONALE DE PLACE-MENT (BIP)
108 boulevard Haussmann
75008 PARIS
Tél.: 44 70 80 80

BANQUE LEHMAN BROTHERS
56, rue du Faubourg Saint-Honoré
75008 PARIS
Tél.: 44 56 41 00

BANQUE NATIONALE DE PARIS (BNP)
20, boulevard des Italiens
75009 PARIS
Tél.: 40 14 45 46

BANQUE NOMURA FRANCE
19-21, rue de Ponthieu
75008 PARIS
Tél.: 44 21 19 00

BANQUE PARIBAS
3, rue d'Antin
75002 PARIS
Tél.: 42 98 12 34

BANQUE REGIONALE D'ESCOMPTE ET DE DEPOTS (BRED)
18, quai de la Rapée
75012 PARIS
Tél.: 48 98 60 00

BANQUE SAN PAOLO
52, avenue Hoche
75008 PARIS
Tél.: 47 54 40 40

BNP FINANCE
9, boulevard des Italiens
75002 PARIS
Tél.: 40 14 16 01

BZW -SOCIETE DE BOURSE
21, boulevard de la Madeleine
75038 PARIS
Tél.: 44 58 32 32

CAISSE CENTRALE DES BANQUES POPU-LAIRES (CCBP)
115, rue Montmartre
75002 PARIS
40 39 30 00

CAISSE CENTRALE DE CREDIT COOP-ERATIF (CCCC)
Parc de la Défense / BP 211
33, rue des 3 Fontanot
92002 NANTERRE Cedex
Tél.: 47 24 85 00

CAISSE DES DEPOTS ET CONSIGNATIONS (CDC)
56, rue de Lille
75007 PARIS
Tél.: 40.49.56.78

CARDIF BANCAIRE TRANSACTION (CBT)
2, rue de la Trinité
75009 PARIS
Tél.: 47 38 83 00

CARGILL INVESTOR SERVICES SNC
46, rue Notre Dame des Victoires
75002 PARIS
Tél.: 44 82 31 60

CCF ELYSEES BOURSE
103, avenue des Champs-Elysées
75008 PARIS
Tél.: 40 70 70 40

CG L'LIONE
36, rue du Louvre
75001 PARIS
Tél.: 40 26 02 89

CHEUVREUX DE VIRIEU SA
44/46, rue de Courcelles
75008 PARIS
Tél.: 44 95 24 24

CHOLET DUPONT SA
3, rue de Gramont
75002 PARIS
Tél.: 44 77 15 15

CITIBANK SA
19, Parvis de la Défense
LA DEFENSE 7
92073 PARIS LA DEFENSE
Tél.: 49 06 10 10

COMPAGNIE PARISIENNE DE REESCOMPTE (CPR)
4, Cité de Londres
75009 PARIS
Tél.: 45 96 20 00

COURCOUX BOUVET SNC
5, rue Gaillon
75002 PARIS
Tél.: 40 17 50 00

CREDIT AGRICOLE FUTURES SNC
Immeuble Cotentin
90, boulevard Pasteur
75015 PARIS
Tél.: 43 23 52 02

CREDIT COMMERCIAL DE FRANCE (CCF)
103, avenue des Champs-Elysées
75008 PARIS
Tél.: 40 70 70 40

CREDIT LYONNAIS ROUSE (FRANCE) SNC
Boite courrier n°22, 31
6/8 rue Ménars
75002 PARIS
Tél.: 42 95 48 99

DAIWA EUROPE (FRANCE) SA
26, avenue des Champs-Elysées
75008 PARIS
Tél.: 44 35 56 00

DEUTSCHE BANK AG
3, avenue de Friedland
75008 PARIS
Tél.: 44 95 64 00

DIDIER PHILIPPE
12/14, rond-point des Champs-Elysées
75008 PARIS
Tél.: 42 99 29 00

DUPONT DENANT SA
42, rue Notre Dame des Victoires
75002 PARIS
Tél.: 42 21 25 25

FERRI SA
11, avenue Delcassé
75008 PARIS
Tél.: 40 76 08 49

FINACOR VENDOME
52, avenue Champs-Elysées
75008 PARIS
Tél.: 40 74 15 15

FINANCIERE DES MARCHES A TERME SNC (FIMAT)
32, rue de Trévise
75009 PARIS
Tél.: 44 79 20 20

FRANCE COMPENSATION FUTURES
34/36, avenue de Friedland
75008 PARIS
Tél.: 47 54 80 00

GIE INDOSUEZ CARR FUTURES
11, rue Marsollier
75002 PARIS
Tél.: 49 27 07 37

GIF FUTURES
10, rue du Faubourg Montmartre
75009 PARIS
Tél.: 47 70 41 47

GALFI FUTURES
103, avenue des Champs Elysées
75008 PARIS
Tél.: 40 70 70 40

GOLDMAN SACHS PARIS Inc. et Cie
6, rue Newton
75116 PARIS
Tél.: 49 52 10 10

HAYAUX DU TILLY et Cie
19, rue de Provence
75009 PARIS
Tél.: 42 46 82 76

IFITEC
49, avenue de l'Opéra
75002 PARIS
Tél.: 47 42 31 22

INTERNATIONAL FINANCE FUTURES SNC (IFF)
45, boulevard Haussmann
75009 PARIS
Tél.: 42 65 47 00

JEAN-PIERRE PINATTON SA
24, rue des Jeûneurs
75002 PARIS
Tél.: 44 82 14 14

JP MORGAN et Cie SA (Banque)
21, place du Marché St-Honoré
75001 PARIS
Tél.: 40 15 45 00

JP MORGAN SA (Société de Bourse)
27, boulevard des Capucines
75002 PARIS
Tél.: 40 15 48 00

LEVEN SA
63, rue Sainte-Anne
75002 PARIS
Tél.: 40 20 74 74

LOUIS DREYFUS FINANCE
87, avenue de la Grande Armée
75782 PARIS Cedex 16
Tél.: 40 66 11 11

LYONNAISE DE BANQUE
24, rue de la Banque
75002 PARIS
Tél.: 49 27 68 68

MERRILL LYNCH CAPITAL MARKETS (FRANCE) SA
96, avenue d'Iéna
75116 PARIS
Tél.: 40 69 15 00

MFK FUTURES
8, rue du Sentier
75002 PARIS
Tél.: 40 39 56 00

MORGAN STANLEY SA
12, rue d'Astorg
75008 PARIS
Tél.: 44 71 27 25

MR FUTURES SNC
16, boulevard Montmartre
75009 PARIS
Tél.: 42 46 72 64

NATWEST SELLIER
12, rue d'Uzès
75002 PARIS
Tél.: 44 76 50 00

NIKKO FRANCE SA
10, rue de la Paix
75002 PARIS
Tél.: 44 58 39 00

NORD FUTURES
6/8, boulevard Haussmann
75009 PARIS
Tél.: 40 22 43 10

ODDO FUTURE
12, boulevard de la Madeleine
75009 PARIS
Tél.: 44 51 85 00

PAINEWEBBER FRANCE SA
56, rue du Faubourg Saint-Honoré
75008 PARIS
Tél.: 42 66 54 54

PATRICE WARGNY SA
24, rue des Jeûneurs
75002 PARIS
Tél.: 44 82 14 14

PATRICK DU BOUZET SA
15, boulevard Poissonnière
75002 PARIS
Tél.: 40 22 19 92

REFCO SA
29, rue du Louvre
75002 PARIS
Tél.: 42 21 18 21

SALOMON BROTHERS SA
4, avenue Hoche
75008 PARIS
Tél.: 47 63 79 07

SBS-DERIVES GIE
112-114, avenue Kléber
75116 PARIS
Tél.: 44 34 80 00

SCHELCHER PRINCE SA
10, rue du Faubourg Montmartre
75009 PARIS
Tél.: 48 01 16 16

SECURITE FUTURES
12, rue Gaillon
75002 PARIS
Tél.: 49 24 00 65

SKANDINAVISKA ENSKILDA BANKEN— Succursale de Paris
69, boulevard Haussmann
75008 PARIS
Tél.: 44 71 92 00

SOCIETE DE TRANSACTIONS ET D'ARBITRAGE SUR FUTURS FINANCIERS (STAFF)
42, rue d'Anjou
75008 PARIS
Tél.: 47 42 70 20

TRANSOPTIONS COMPENSATION
26, rue de la Baume
75008 PARIS
Tél.: 40 75 62 62

TRIFUTURES
1, rue Méhul
75002 PARIS
Tél.: 42 61 55 98

TULLETT & TOKYO (FUTURES & TRADED OPTIONS) PARIS SA
12/14, rond-point des Champs-Elysées
75008 PARIS
Tél.: 40 76 09 12

UBS FUTURS ET OPTIONS SNC
69, boulevard Haussmann
75008 PARIS
Tél.: 44 56 45 45

UNION EUROPEENNE DE CIC
4, rue Gaillon
75002 PARIS
Tel.: 42 66 70 00

VIEL MONETAIRE FUTURS
42, rue d'Anjou
75008 PARIS
Tél.: 47 42 70 20

YAMAICHI FRANCE SA
51/53, avenue des Champs-Elysées
75008 PARIS
Tél.: 44 13 25 25

APPENDIX 3

For any additional information pertaining to the MATIF:

PUBLICATION

MATIF offers a variety of publications free of charge covering its contracts and their uses:
Contact: Tel (33-1)—40 28 80 53

EDUCATION

MATIF offers specific courses pertaining to the different contracts, conducted by market professionals:
Contact: Tel (33-1)—40 28 81 20

PRODUCTS

For any complimentary information about our contracts:
Contact: Tel (33-1)—40 28 81 06

MEMBERSHIP

For specific procedures pertaining to the membership:
Contact: Tel (33-1)—40 28 80 55

VENDOR

For information on quote vending:
Contact: Tel (33-1)—44 76 86 50

LEGAL MATTERS

For any information on specific legal matters: rules, taxes, etc.:
Contact: Tel (33-1)—40 28 82 36

GLOBEX® ASSOCIATE BROKER STATUS

For any information pertaining to this status:
Contact: Tel (33-1)—40 28 81 50

CHAPTER 31

Next Generation Trading System (NGTS) at the Oslo Stock Exchange

Jan Aaseth
Currency Broker
Den norske Bank

Roger Kristiansen
Director of Derivatives Securities
Oslo Stock Exchange

The Oslo Stock Exchange (OSE) in Norway is currently in the process of implementing a new electronic trading system, called Next Generation Trading System (NGTS), which is the first trading system to integrate trading in bonds, equities, and derivatives. Trading in options and futures will, in particular, be greatly enhanced with NGTS. The first section of this chapter will briefly discuss the general trends and attitudes in the global derivative markets with respect to automation. The second section will give a general description of the support functions of NGTS at the Oslo Stock Exchange, and finally, in the third section, specific system features relevant to the derivatives market, such as the execution of combination orders, will be described.

THE MARKET AT THE OSLO STOCK EXCHANGE

The Oslo Stock Exchange (OSE) in Norway is a relatively small securities market with a market capitalization approximately equal to $35 billion. The derivatives market was established in May 1990, and has experienced a remarkable growth since the introduction. Currently, options on the OBX Stock Index (25 most heavily traded stocks at the OSE) and six blue chip stocks are listed. After its second full year of operation, the options market turnover totalled 1,540,620 contracts, equivalent to around $3.3 billion in underlying values. This ranked the derivatives market at the OSE ninth out of 16 derivatives exchanges in Europe. In addition, futures on the OBX index and futures on 5- and 10-year government bonds are listed.

Until now, the derivatives trading has been telephone-based via the exchange block order desk. However, in order to position the exchange in a competitive market with increased investor demands, the OSE is now in the process of replacing its current electronic Trading Support System (TSS), installed in 1988. This system automated the trading for stocks and bonds, but after the introduction of the fast-growing derivatives market, a need for an electronic system comprising all three market segments has become imminent. The Next Generation Trading System (NGTS) is a fully integrated electronic trading system based on the latest available technology. The new system is designed to facilitate integrated and simultaneous trading in all three market segments—stocks, bonds, and derivatives—which will increase the efficiency and liquidity of the marketplace. Access to the marketplace will be greatly improved and market transparency will be enhanced due to the users' ability to design their own workstations and the quality of information dissemination provided by the system. The system, which is Windows-based and fully automated, will also provide specific improvements to the institutional investor's working conditions. More specifically, an investor can input combinations of dependent orders in all three segments, which can be processed by a single broker. Therefore, the system has capacity to meet the anticipated and eventual trend toward a "total broker" concept, in which the broker will operate in all segments of the market through enhanced workstations. Derivatives combinations and covered strategies can be executed by the system, and standard two-legged combinations will be updated automatically when prices in any of the legs are altered. No other system existing today provides this automatic link between and within market segments, enabling Windows-based point-and-click execution of combinations and single orders.

AUTOMATION TRENDS

A much debated topic at futures and options conferences around the world is whether screen-based trading is the future, and, if so, what kind of system is most suitable to meet investor and market demands. Market participants agree that efficiency is the key to derivatives trading in the future, and it is believed that a computer environment will provide the best conditions for adequate liquidity, efficient pricing, a high degree of transparency, and high-quality financial intermediation. Integration with the bonds and equities segments is also considered vital to an active derivative market. Therefore, many exchanges have now made a commitment to electronic trading systems, and some exchanges have already implemented electronic systems. We will now most likely see a change from pit- and telephone-based trading toward fully integrated and automated electronic trading systems.

The importance of automation is stressed worldwide, but large and small exchanges have different perceptions with respect to the degree of importance. Larger exchanges, such as the Chicago Mercantile Exchange (CME) and the Chicago Board of Trade (CBOT), view computerized trading as a supplement to the open-outcry systems, and not as a replacement for the traditional pits. Electronic trading systems are only regarded as after-hour trading systems and on-exchange systems for illiquid products. We believe, however, that electronic trading systems will take over all trading activities in the future.

Smaller exchanges, such as the Oslo Stock Exchange, view automation as the key to success and the only way to gain a competitive edge in the increasingly crowded global marketplace. The phrase "automate or die" can be heard more often in the investment community, and several smaller exchanges have taken measures to rebut the dramatic deterioration in their competitive position. The Dutch market is living proof that investors see no country borders but are merely concerned about price. The screen-based, quote-driven system at the London Stock Exchange, called SEAQ-International, has captured large numbers of investors from the Amsterdam Stock Exchange because of easy access to an efficient automated system, lower trading costs, and the ability to handle bigger volumes. The Oslo Stock Exchange faces the same problem. The trading in Norwegian securities on SEAQ-International constitutes a competitive threat to the OSE, but volumes have kept stable at relatively comfortable levels, where only three or four blue chip stocks have higher investor-based volumes in London than in Oslo. The OSE anticipates to regain market shares with the introduction of NGTS.

The attitude toward automated systems is also changing. A traditional trader with 20 years on the floor of a pit-based exchange swore that an electronic trading system would only serve as a supplement, and could never replace face-to-face trading. After three months with an electronic pit replication system, the same trader was found in front of the trading screens praising the system. In particular, the great improvement in information dissemination and the resulting market overview impressed the traditional trader. More and more traders adopt the same attitude, indicating that electronic trading more or less is a reflected image of what the users want.

Some problems have been encountered with existing order-matching systems. First, the response time has been relatively slow when it comes to the actual matching of bid and offer. Some systems, such as the DTB system at the German exchange, ran into complications when volumes increased. Second, the interface between the keyboard and the user could be sluggish causing traders to miss good trades. However, trading systems developed today have improved technical solutions, and the belief in automated efficiency is now widely shared.

NGTS–A GENERAL DESCRIPTION

The NGTS marketplace at the Oslo Stock Exchange consists of a single logically integrated exchange and settlement system for trading in equities, bonds, and derivatives. The exchange supports up to 40 member firms trading in approximately 2,000 instruments in total. The business concept behind NGTS envisages a fully electronic marketplace, customized for the Norwegian market and based on the experience gained in using the present Trading Support System (TSS) over the last few years. The main purpose of NGTS is to support a centralized and controlled marketplace for the trading in any instrument allowed by the Oslo Stock Exchange. A computerized system will enable members to submit buy and sell orders into electronic order books in the market or to report trades executed outside the computerized marketplace. Once orders are submitted, they will be executed either through an automatic matching process or accept mechanism. Exhibit 1 depicts the main components of NGTS and the different links between the central unit and the users.

NGTS supports trading in equities, bonds, options, and futures, and market making coexists with client-driven orders in an electronic marketplace. In the equity

Exhibit 1. Main Components of NGTS

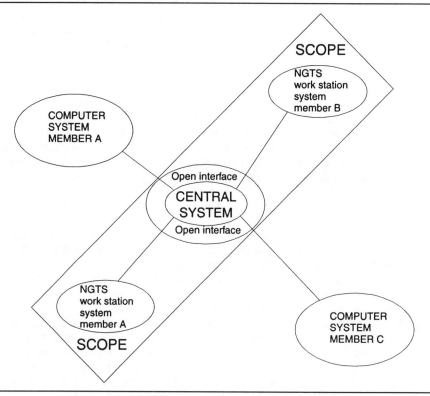

segment, spot trading is predominant. Trading in bonds will occur spot or forward. In the derivatives segment, trading in options on equity, indexes, and interest rates is supported. In NGTS, any option can be specified for trading either American- or European-style. OTC options are traded off-exchange, but reported via NGTS. In addition, trading in interest rate futures and OBX index futures is supported.

NGTS Features

The major features of the new NGTS marketplace are:

■ *Centralized trading on a single exchange.* The system supports links between instruments across the different market segments and maintains these links automatically. This provides improved trading control and increased trading opportunities for market participants. A trader can, for example, input a combination of dependent orders with legs in all three segments. Hence, it is possible to buy government-issued bonds and sell interest rate futures in the same operation, creating an instant hedge. Therefore, portfolio managers can, as a result of the link between market segments, easily and efficiently change exposure between financial instruments.

■ *Support for trading in foreign currencies.* Any instrument can be quoted and traded on NGTS in a foreign currency. This feature provides the OSE with the necessary flexibility to enable the exchange to easily list foreign products. Moreover, domestic stocks, such as Norsk Hydro, may be listed in currencies such as British pounds and U.S. dollars in addition to Norwegian crowns (NOK). Therefore, one specific issue may have many order books, one for each tradeable currency, because of different pricing characteristics. One cannot, however, match a stock order for Norsk Hydro in dollars with another placed in NOK, but NGTS ensures that links are maintained between each order book so that a broker can easily navigate on his or her workstation. Every order book has its own set of statistics.

It is believed that trading instruments in foreign currencies in NGTS could maintain and strengthen the competitiveness of the OSE toward foreign exchanges trading Norwegian stocks, such as London and New York. The NGTS will provide the needed effectiveness of trading, better pricing, and liquidity, which will ensure that the OSE remains the principal market for the trading of Norwegian financial instruments.

■ *Continuous trading.* During exchange hours, continuous trading takes place electronically through NGTS via centralized order books for each instrument. Any instrument can be traded using either the automatic matching process or the accept mechanism, but not both at the same time.

■ *Flexible order matching.* Orders can be matched in four different ways, depending on the instrument. First, orders may be automatched. This is the case for blue chip stocks, most bond issues, and derivatives. Automatching may, however, not always be suitable. An accept-method may then be applied. This means that the trader using the point-and-click method to trade must take the entire quantity of the order at the price displayed. Composed derivatives combinations, such as covered straddles and butterflies, are executed with the accept mechanism, and the broker must then take the entire quantity of each contract. The third way to match orders is via an order book, where orders are either firm and subject to the accept-method or merely indicated interests. Accept orders are identified by a star. The final alternative is a bulletin board, which is an electronic order book where indicative interests are displayed. This order book may be used for off-exchange trading and for trading in illiquid instruments. Hence, order matching facilities in NGTS provide great flexibility for investors.

Off-exchange trading is by negotiation. It can take place either after continuous trading has finished and automatic matching and accept functions are switched off, or when trades are negotiated in exchange hours and reported in NGTS. The OSE facilitates off-exchange trading through the electronic bulletin board. No rules are imposed stating that orders must be executed on NGTS, but for trades executed outside the system, members are obliged to report details to the exchange for publication. NGTS provides electronic fill-in forms for the reporting of trades in OTC options. This greatly reduces both the paperwork for the members and the time lag between the OTC trade and the dissemination of the trade information to the market.

■ *Best execution.* For instruments for which automatic matching is used, best execution is guaranteed by the system. Orders are processed on a strict "first come, first served" basis within each price. Therefore, brokers cannot pick and choose which specific order is to be executed against them. Any order that is visible in the order book is actually an order that cannot be matched with another in the same order book, since the automatic matching process is carried out only on receipt of each incoming order until possible trades have been generated. Orders displayed in the order books can be executed by brokers using the point-and-click method on their Windows-based trading screens.

■ *Exchange supervision and control functions.* Facilities are built into NGTS to protect the member from execution of orders at unrealistic prices. Furthermore, surveillance facilities in an organized legal framework are included to ensure that trading is carried out in a fair, visible, and orderly fashion. The market is subject to automatic controls, and NGTS will produce alerts and print activity reports when it suspects unfair market practices. The exchange may then decide to intervene.

■ *Support for both brokers and market makers.* NGTS provides electronic order books, where both broker and market maker orders may coexist. Brokers should notice that a market maker order with the same price as a broker's order may be given matching priority. This market maker privilege is provided on an instrument-by-instrument basis. The OSE believes that this should give members the incentive to provide liquidity in the Norwegian marketplace.

■ *Market visibility.* Nonmembers see supply and demand as aggregated volumes at each price level in an instrument. Licensed members can see every individual order in the order books. The OSE can enhance the transparency of the market to ensure greater market visibility. All trades are published in real time with both price and volume. Members have access to all data and news items published by the OSE.

■ *Enhanced workstations.* The market overview is also dramatically improved by the enhanced Windows-based workstations, which enable brokers to have all three market segments on the screen simultaneously. Users can define and tailor their screen layouts for each inquiry window to suit their specific needs. The screen may contain an unlimited number of windows, which will display real-time data and prices. The OSE defines specific data streams and data items for each stream so that brokers can choose what data is presented in a particular window and the sequence in which the data is to be shown. Hence, for one instrument the broker may choose to see high/low/last/volume, while for another the broker may choose to see last/aggregated volume.

The system allows the broker to maintain more than one trading profile, to be selected at will. Each trading profile contains window layouts, data selections, maximum update rates, definition of instruments in the group, and definition of confirmation levels of order entries. As a result, the workstation provides the broker with greatly enhanced flexibility, market control, and visibility. The number of screens needed will also be dramatically reduced. Exhibit 2 gives an example of a broker's flexible trading screen.

Exhibit 2. NGTS Trading Screen

Price Information - Derivatives

Instr	U.lying pr	Bid vol	Qty	Bid	Ask	Qty	Ask vol	Theo.pr	Last	Qty	Bid vol	Own Bid	Ask	Own Ask vol
X320H	332.02	17.56	210	13	15.5	50	22.28	15	14	100	17.56	13	16	24.30
X340H	332.02	18.02	20	3	4	30	21.48	3.57	3.5	20	17.11	2.5	4	21.48
X320T	332.02	22.90	330	2.25	2.5	180	24.01	1.61	2.5	140	21.82	2	2.5	24.01
X340T	332.02	16.12	90	9	12	80	26.42	10.1	10	50	16.12	9	12	26.42
B140I	147	28.52	100	11	13	30	39.5	11.26	12	80	28.52	11	14	41.32
B140U	147	36.28	60	4	6	80	46.84	2.56	4.5	70	36.28	4	6	46.84
N180L	189	17.24	260	18.5	22.5	140	30.00	23.02	20	120	--	--	22.5	30.00
N180X	189	21.88	90	4.5	6.5	60	24.09	6.86	5	20	--	--	6.5	24.09
N190X	189	23.75	120	8	10	50	28.22	10.80	9	100	--	--	10.5	29.96

Price Info - Stocks

Instr	Qty	Bid	Ask	Qty
NHY	10000	188	189	5000
BEB	5000	146	148	1500
SAG	7000	77.5	79	2000
KVI	1000	144	145.5	6000
HNA	2500	117	118	8000
UNS	10000	15.30	15.5	20000
ELK	5000	50.5	51	3000
AKE	3000	49	51	5000
SMT	500	81	82	2000

Combination Order Book

Id	Combination	Qty	Price	Mkt Bid	Mkt Ask
+ X320H, X320T	Buy straddle	100	17,5	15.25	18
+ H140I / H150I	Bullspread	50	5	4.5	6.5
...angle	...re...	200	18	16	19

Ticker

Instr	Qty	Price	Time
NHY	10000	189	10:22
NHY	5000	188.5	10:22
SAG	7000	78	10:22
X32H	100	14	10:23
N18L	120	20	10:23
S463L	100	118.69	10:24
S459	1000000	119.43	10:24
BEB	15000	147	10:24
SAG	5000	77.5	10:24

Indices & keys

Instr	Last	Chng
OBX	332.02	+ 4.62
TOTX	526.72	+ 5.84
BRIX	1632.55	+ 2.67
FTSE	2934.50	+ 16.7
DAX	1803.23	- 30.47
SFOX	1189.43	+ 14.32
DJI	3567.42	+ 8.30
USD	7.4570	+ 0.0005
DM	1.7405	- 0.0010
BRENT	16.85	- 0.05
NIBO-3	6.04	- 0.07

Input Offer

Options   Help

Instrument: [BEB140U]   Bergesen B 140 Sept Put

- No Condition (●)
- Minimum (○)
- Fill or Kill (○)
- Fill and Kill (○)
- Accept (○)

Quantity [50]
Minimum [ ]
Hidden [ ]

Price [6]

- No Condition (●)
- Stop Loss (○)
- On Stop (○)
- Disseminate (☒)

- National (○)
- International (○)
- Derivatives (●)

VPS A/C No [ ]
Reference [ ]

- Suspended (☒)
- Negotiable (☐)
- Expiry Time [ ]

[OK] [Cancel]   [Reset]   [Confirm]

- *Connection to vendors.* NGTS is designed to support the dissemination of information from other information vendors. The system can receive relevant information and data from vendors, such as Reuters and Telerate, which users of NGTS can use in calculations or simply as market information.

- *Open access.* The specific trading support functions available in the central workstation system are able to communicate with any third-party-developed systems via an open interface. Hence, members can use their own software and tailor solutions for the trading and settlement system, as depicted in Exhibit 1. This means, however, that system changes implemented by the exchange will have a greater impact, since members have to incorporate the system changes in their internal systems. Therefore, the exchange may only make system changes a certain number of times per year to allow members to revise their systems.

- *News functionality.* In Norway, all listed companies must submit price-sensitive information to the OSE. Therefore, NGTS gives priority to the news function to ease both the companies' reporting procedures and the market distribution of the submitted information. Hence, NGTS is designed to efficiently receive electronic information from fax, third-party systems, or manual input as free text. The information will consequently be distributed to the market via NGTS without delay.

- *General trading support functions.* The NGTS workstation system supports a number of general functions, which include report printing, transfer of trades to back office, and end-of-day processing. Message distribution is also facilitated. The OSE sends informational messages which are queued up and displayed on the screens one at a time. Alerts are also distributed in this manner. The broker may click the messages away immediately if he or she wishes.

- *Automatically updated database.* As an extra service, NGTS provides members with a database consisting of static data, which will always be updated. The data includes, for example, information about listed companies, instruments, members, other exchanges, and issuer inquiries. The database will make it easier to obtain information, and will enable brokers to provide their customers with improved service.

GENERAL SYSTEM FUNCTIONALITY

The general central system support functions are logically composed of four major subsystems: communications, processing of orders, trades, and inquiries. The communications system handles electronic connections between all users of the system, while the three processing subsystems provide trading support to brokers and market makers. Exhibit 3 gives an overview of the central system support functions.

The order processing function handles new orders, amendments, and deletions. When changes occur, the subsystem updates the appropriate order book and statistics. The system maintains an order book for each instrument for round lots, odd lots, or combinations, as appropriate for the instrument type. When an order is received, it is validated according to the current data in the system. If the order is accepted by the

Exhibit 3. The Four Subsystems of NGTS

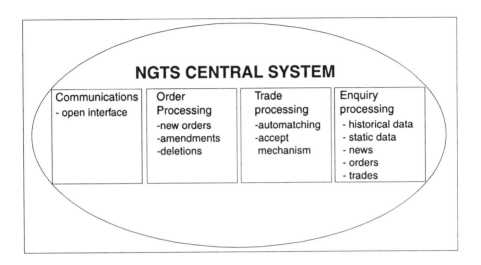

system, a confirmation is sent to the broker's screen and the order is submitted to the relevant order book. The order will then be subject to automatic matching, as is the case for derivatives and most stocks, or for display if automatic matching is off or not applicable. The system both validates volume (odd or round lot) and price (if it is acceptable). The order will then get a number and time stamp and best execution is guaranteed. If there is an amendment of critical information, such as an increase in order size, a new time stamp will be allocated to the order. A reduction of order size does not result in a loss of execution priority. The system guarantees that the time elapsed from when a new order or a reported trade is received by the central system to when the according update is sent to all connected system is a maximum of two seconds. This guarantee also includes an update of all central databases.

The trade processing subsystem contains the automatching process, which will generate and disseminate trades to all interested parties. This unit also processes off-exchange trades that are reported to the system. The automatching process attempts to generate trades between the incoming order and existing orders in the order book. The matcher will attempt to find orders for which the prices are equal or crossing and will establish the price and volume that can be traded. If the order cannot be matched, or if there is some quantity remaining after matching, the remainder of the order may be entered into the order book, depending on the incoming order specification.

Where a match can be found, a trade is generated. A price for the trade is established and the two matched orders are updated or deleted, as appropriate. A record of the trade is then created. The trade record will be related to the number of relevant orders. The last trade price information and other relevant statistics are then updated. Access to some or all of the information stored is consequently made available to the market. This entire process will occur in milliseconds. While the present trading system handles eight transactions per second, NGTS is designed to handle 70 transactions per second. This can be expanded as the hardware is improved. The system also guarantees a 99.9 percent availability rate which in practice means that it will not shut down during system trading hours.

The inquiry processing subsystem handles inquiries on orders, trades, news, and certain historical or static information. Information inquiries are filtered to safeguard private data. Information returned is restricted according to the information requested and from whom the request has come.

ORDER INPUT AND EXECUTION

A broker wishing to input an order must click on the specific stock, bond, futures, or option series on his or her trading screen. The broker will then be prompted with a window to specify conditions for price and volume. Exhibit 4 shows the input offer window, where a broker can input a selling order.

Orders without a price will be executed if possible at the best price currently available in the market. For instruments that are not automatched, orders without price are invalid. If a price is input, the order will be executed, if possible, at the same or better price than the price specified. Orders with price conditions may include trigger

Exhibit 4.   Order Execution Window

Input Offer		
Options Help		
Instrument	NHY190F	Norsk Hydro 190 June Call ▼

No Condition ○   Quantity [150]   Price [10.50 ⬍]
Minimum ○
Fill or Kill ●   Minimum [   ]   No Condition ●
Fill and Kill ○   Hidden [   ]   Stop Loss ○
Accept ○   On Stop ○
                                     Disseminate ☒

National ○   VPS A/C No [   ]   Suspended ☒
International ○   Reference [   ]   Negotiable ☐
Derivatives ●   Expiry Time [   ]

[OK]   [Cancel]   [Reset]   [Confirm]

orders, stop-loss, and on-stop orders. Trigger orders specify that the order should be activated and executed only if the market price on a specific instrument hits a prespecified level. Stop-loss orders will be activated automatically if the instrument hits a prespecified price. The system will then instantly sell or buy back the instrument. This also applies for on-stop orders. Orders with the above price conditions will not be seen by other market participants but will lie latent in the system.

In the round lot market, bids and offers cannot be entered with quantity restrictions such as all-or-nothing orders. Quantity conditions, such as hidden orders, fill-and-kill, and fill-or-kill orders may, however, be activated. Input of a hidden order allows the broker to hide the total volume on his or her bid or offer. The broker will then prevent influencing the market by showing large lots. The broker enters a total of 1000 hidden contracts, but will only show 100 at a time. Only 100 contracts will be shown in the relevant order book and hence, receive a time stamp. When the order is hit by the market, the system will immediately input another 100 contracts on the same price until the order is filled. The broker will only have priority for the 100 contracts that are actually displayed in the order book.

A fill-or-kill order is a type of all-or-nothing order. A broker wants to fill an order for 1000 contracts but only 500 are shown on the screen. He or she can then enter the order as fill-or-kill to find out whether any of the displayed orders have hidden volumes. If this is the case, the order will be filled. If not, it will be canceled. The market will not see this order unless it is filled.

A fill-and-kill order can also be entered if the broker wants to buy 1000 but only 500 is shown on the screen. He or she can then place the fill-and-kill order, which will then fill up shown volumes and any hidden volumes up to 1000 contracts. If 800 contracts are available, the 200 contracts left unfilled are canceled. If this had been an ordinary automatching order without price or volume conditions, the remaining 200 contracts would have been left in the order book.

NGTS AND THE DERIVATIVES SEGMENT

NGTS at the Oslo Stock Exchange is the first electronic trading system to integrate all three market segments in one single system. The derivatives segment has up to now been kept out of electronic trading systems around the world, either because the derivatives market is physically separated from the stock exchanges or because the present system works too well to give incentives for integration. The Oslo Stock Exchange is a relatively small exchange, with all three segments traded at a single location. Therefore, conditions are perfect for the implementation of an integrated trading system such as NGTS.

Combination Orders

The most important feature of NGTS with respect to derivative investors is that combination orders can be entered into the market. All combinations in the combination order book may be accepted for trading by brokers using the accept mechanism. All relevant prices from the main order book and the combination order book are checked and displayed to the broker as he or she performs combination order input. The broker may choose at a later time to convert his or her combination into a series of single limit orders, which are consequently executed one-by-one via automatching in the main order book with no connections between them. Exhibit 5 shows the combination order book in NGTS.

Exhibit 5.   The Combination Order Book

Id	Combination	Quantity	Price	Market Bid	Market Ask
+ X320H, X320T	Buy straddle	100	17,5	15.25	18
+ B140I/B150I	Bull spread	50	5	4.5	6.5
- N190L, N180X	Sell strangle	200	18	16	19
+ X320T/X340T	Bear spread	70	8,5	6.5	9.75

Combinations can be entered into the combination order book. The exchange will have predefined which combinations are standard and which are composed. Standard combinations are option and futures combinations with two legs, such as time spreads, bull spreads, bear spreads, strangles, and straddles. Ratios, with different volumes in each leg, are considered to be composed combinations and are not subject to automatching. Covered combinations containing separate legs in futures and options, such as simultaneous buying of futures and selling of calls, are considered standard and are automatically updated and matched.

The standard combinations, when entered into the order book, will automatically be dispatched to the appropriate legs. For example, if an investor wishes to buy a straddle, hence buy put and call with the same expiration and exercise price, he or she will enter the combination into the combination order book. The system, which will define the combination as standard, will then automatically input prices in the respective put and call order books derived from the existing market prices in those legs. If prices in any of the legs are altered, the derived price in the other leg will be automatically updated. The volume shown on the derived price will depend on the volume shown in the other leg. Time stamp and priority will also depend on the other leg. The combination will be executed if one leg that will satisfy the price condition is hit. The system will then automatically execute the corresponding leg and delete the combination from the combination order book. The information will then instantly be disseminated to the market over the ticker.

The combination can also be executed directly from the combination order book by a broker using the point-and-click method. The system will automatically establish prices within the bid-and-ask spreads in each leg that will satisfy the combination. The trade will instantly be shown on the ticker.

The combination order book also contains composed combination orders. These are orders consisting of more than two legs—such as butterflies, condors, and tabletops—or combinations with legs in different market segments—such as covered calls and covered straddles. The legs of these combinations will not be dispatched to the order books of the appropriate legs but can only be executed by the point-and-click method in the combination order book. Each leg may be executed at any price between the best bid and ask in the main order book. As long as the total price equals the combination limit price, both brokers will be happy with the outcome. Because of this "floating element" in the pricing of composed combinations, all resultant trades are marked as "Accepts" when shown on the ticker or trade inquiries. Brokers are thereby made aware that the prices on such trades are not relevant to the main market.

Combinations may be input with or without price or volume conditions. Brokers may also choose to convert the combination into a series of single limit orders. These will then be executed one-by-one via automatic matching in the main order book with no connections between them.

COMPETITIVE POSITIONING FOR THE FUTURE

The survival of small exchanges such as the Oslo Stock Exchange depends on their ability to position the exchange in the increasingly competitive environment. Automation of trading is definitely the single most important key to success. The NGTS was developed with this in mind. The OSE believes that a flexible, user-friendly, and cost-efficient trading system such as NGTS, where the link between market segments and other exchanges provides unique opportunities for simultaneous cross-market trading, will provide the OSE with the necessary competitive edge to satisfy the strict demands of the investment community. It is also important to us that the new trading system allows various flexible solutions to trading practices and trading rules. If a trading practice turns out to be unfavorable to market participants, the flexible system can be changed overnight. The unique trading features and flexibility of NGTS will ensure that the Oslo Stock Exchange will survive as an active exchange in the future.

CHAPTER 32

A Pan-European Stock Index Futures Contract: The Eurotop 100 Prospects and Outlook

R. McFall Lamm, Jr.
Vice President and Chief Economist
Coffee, Sugar & Cocoa Exchange

INTRODUCTION

International futures market activity over the last decade has been characterized by the emergence of a fundamentally new product: stock index futures contracts. A contract based on the Value Line Index was introduced in February 1982 by the Kansas City Board of Trade and was followed two months later by the S&P 500 Index futures contract, introduced by the Chicago Mercantile Exchange (CME). The S&P contract was immediately successful and became one of the most widely traded futures contracts in the world. Foreign equity futures contracts based on various indexes followed over the next few years: the FTSE 100, traded on the London International Financial Futures Exchange (LIFFE) in 1984; the CAC-40, traded on the Marche a Terme International de France (MATIF) in 1989; the DAX, traded on the Deutsche Terminbörse (DTB) in 1990; and importantly, the Nikkei 225, traded on the Osaka Stock Exchange (as well as the SIMEX and CME) in 1988.

The tremendous success of stock index futures contracts indicates that they satisfy obvious market needs. Specifically, index futures allow market participants to hedge against unanticipated changes in stock prices and also provide an effective trading vehicle for speculators with views on market direction. An important question, however, is why stock index futures contracts based on the U.S. and Japanese equity markets have been successful and, conversely, why no pan-European stock index futures contract has emerged.

This chapter was written when the author was Vice President and Chief Economist with the Commodity Exchange Inc.

This chapter provides a response by suggesting that three major factors have hindered the evolution of a pan-European stock index futures contract. First, the European equities market is fragmented, consisting of multiple exchanges, currencies, and regulatory regimes that inhibit the trading of "baskets" of equities. Second, a pan-European index future (or a proxy basket of indexes) is complex. Its fair value is not easy to compute. And finally, it is difficult to arbitrage a pan-European index. The major conclusion of this chapter is that structural changes now occurring in global securities and futures markets, as well as European economic union, will eliminate existing problems, making a pan-European stock index viable.

BACKGROUND

The impetus for a European stock index is the same as that for a U.S. or Japanese stock index: there is a need for a benchmark performance measure as a basis for evaluative comparison. But while the S&P 500 and Nikkei serve this purpose for the U.S. and Japan, there is limited consensus on the appropriate benchmark for the European stock market. Many U.S. pension fund managers use the European component of the Morgan Stanley Capital International (MSCI) Index, while European managers tend to use the Financial Times Actuaries (FTA) Index as a benchmark. Typically, these indexes are used to review the performance of active money managers hired to manage equity funds or to provide a basis for constructing a portfolio of stocks that provides the same return as the index.

A major constraint in using the MSCI and FTA indexes to construct model portfolios is that they are not entirely tradeable. Both indexes contain equities that may not be owned by foreigners, less-liquid stocks and equities traded in smaller-country markets. This differs from the S&P 500 and the Nikkei 225, in which all stocks may be purchased and the indexes fully replicated (even though a subset strategy is sometimes employed). Consequently, both the MSCI and FTA fail to meet the "tradeability" criterion necessary for an index to serve as a basis for a futures contract.

Recognizing this problem, the European Options Exchange (EOE) in Amsterdam and the London Stock Exchange (LSE) created tradeable pan-European stock indexes in 1989 and 1990, respectively. The EOE's effort was driven by leadership within the exchange itself, while the LSE index was the result of a collaborative effort led by a team put together by Goldman Sachs and the LSE. Each organization developed a pan-European stock index with the objective of trading derivative financial products (futures and options) based on the index.

The EOE index product, named the Eurotop 100 Index, is denominated in ECUs and consists of a basket of the 100 most actively traded blue chip equities on nine European exchanges. The index is capitalization- and GDP-weighted by country, with individual stocks selected on the basis of the last three years' sales (to include only the most liquid and largest traded value stocks). No country's weight is allowed to exceed 22 percent of the total index, to minimize the dominance of U.K. stocks that occurs in pure capitalization-weighted indexes such as the MSCI and FTA.

The LSE products, the Eurotrack 100 and 200 Indexes, consist of 100 continental stocks, and a basket of 200 stocks obtained by combining the Eurotrack 100 with the FTSE 100. The Eurotrack indexes, although capitalization-weighted, are calculated based on the average of bid and ask prices quoted on the London SEAQ system.

Consequently, these indexes fail to capture actual transaction prices on constituent European exchanges. Also, London SEAQ trades significantly less volume than the home exchanges on the Continent. Further, the Eurotrack includes more countries (14) than the Eurotop and is more complex as a result.

The EOE started trading options and futures on the Eurotop 100 in June of 1991; the LIFFE started trading futures on the Eurotrack 100 about one month later. The Swiss Options Exchange (SOFFEX) also began to trade options on a Swiss franc version of the Eurotop 100 at about the same time. Although the Eurotop 100 traded more volume than the Eurotrack, neither contract was highly liquid. One major reason was that the contracts did not appeal to European institutional investors. Few European institutions index a significant portion of their portfolios and those that do typically do not utilize futures contracts. Furthermore, the vast majority of European money managers are active managers who rarely hedge.

A second reason why neither pan-European index emerged as a highly successful product was that neither LIFFE nor EOE received approval from the CFTC and SEC to market their contracts to U.S. institutions. In contrast to their European counterparts, U.S. institutions typically view Europe as a single geographic entity for asset allocation purposes and are obvious potential users of such contracts. In addition, U.S. pension funds and money managers are familiar with stock index futures and use these contracts to equitize cash and rebalance their portfolios. As such, they are the natural buyers and sellers of European index products.

MARKET PARTICIPANTS

Pension funds, trusts, and other institutional investors, as well as the money managers employed by these organizations, use stock index futures contracts to perform three primary functions. First, they create synthetic portfolios by continuously purchasing and rolling over stock index futures contracts. This minimizes transaction costs by avoiding the need to purchase hundreds of stocks simultaneously when the same objective can be accomplished by carrying out one futures transaction. In particular, institutions will buy futures contracts when they trade "cheap" to fair value as a substitute for actually owning stocks. Institutions then can remain continuously "long" stocks by owning futures contracts and experiencing the same gains and losses as if they owned the underlying stocks.

Second, institutional investors use stock index futures contracts to obtain immediate exposure (or to reduce exposure) to equities when cash is received (or must be paid out). This is advantageous because the time lag between receiving or paying out funds and purchasing or selling stocks can be significant. By using stock index futures contracts, institutions can avoid missing a major market move due to the delay. Futures, therefore, allow firms to "equitize cash" immediately.

Finally, many U.S. institutions use futures contracts to "rebalance" their portfolios to maintain specific exposure targets by asset class. For example, 60 percent stocks—20 percent of which are in international issues—and 40 percent bonds is a typical balance. As stock prices change relative to bonds, actual allocations diverge from targets. To rebalance the portfolio, the most efficient method is simply to buy or sell equity and bond futures contracts. This allows an institution to maintain a fixed-asset allocation without having to reshuffle funds from one manager to another, or to buy or sell stocks and bonds constantly. Also, institutions often use futures contracts to implement changes in asset allocation immediately when a reallocation decision is made.

In the first two applications—holding synthetic portfolios and equitizing cash—institutions would be natural market "longs." That is, they would be buyers of stock index futures contracts. In the last application—rebalancing portfolios—institutions could be either natural longs or "shorts," depending on the directional movement of stock and bond prices.

Another class of market participant—index arbitragers—may be either long or short in futures. As the price of a futures contract exceeds its fair value, these firms will sell futures and buy stocks. Alternatively, if the price of a futures contract falls below its fair value, arbitragers will buy the futures and sell stocks. Brokerage houses and firms engaged in stock market making activities are in the best position to arbitrage, since they have the lowest transaction costs.

The interaction of arbitragers with other natural longs and shorts creates the basic demand and supply for stock index futures contracts. The magnitude of trading volume of the S&P 500 and Nikkei 225 futures contracts indicates natural demand, and supply is sufficient to create viable futures markets for these indexes. Because the European equities market is nearly as large as that of the U.S. and Japan, anecdotal evidence suggests an analogous need for a viable futures contract market for European stocks. For example, survey data published by Greenwich Associates show that U.S. institutions continue to increase their international equity exposure, with forecasts of a doubling in foreign equity assets within three years, while other surveys show increased institutional use of futures.

THE EUROTOP 100 INDEX AND FUTURES CONTRACT

To be useful, any equity index must meet a number of criteria: it must be tradeable; it must be representative of the general market; and it must be relatively fixed in composition with respect to both country and component stock selection.

The Eurotop 100 contains Europe's most liquid equity issues. Countries represented in the index are members of the Organization for Economic Cooperation and Development (OECD) with the highest exchange capitalizations. Base weights for each country component are calculated as a function of their relative stock market capitalization and gross domestic product (Table 1). Individual stocks are selected from the most actively traded issues within each country.

The index is computed and disseminated by the European Options Exchange (EOE) in Amsterdam. It is continually calculated using the latest stock prices and foreign exchange quotes. Prices are based on actual transactions in the home exchange, while foreign exchange rates used are current ask rates for local currency in European Currency Units (ECUs). The EOE disseminates the Eurotop 100 index every 15 seconds between 9:30 a.m. and 5:30 p.m. central European time through Telerate, Reuters, Comstock, Bloomberg, and other third-party on-line data vendors.

Country composition is reviewed in even-numbered years. This ensures that the Eurotop 100 index includes countries with the highest exchange capitalizations. Changes in the stocks included in the index are minimized and are made only when country weights change or there are mergers. Any changes in the individual composition of stocks are announced six months in advance, except in the case where a stock has permanently ceased trading due to a merger or acquisition.

Table 1.   Country/Industry Weightings

Country	Weight	Sector	Weight
	—%—		—%—
United Kingdom	22	Consumer goods	16
France	15	Industrials	7
Germany	15	Tel & utilities	10
Italy	10	Electronics	10
Switzerland	10	Energy	9
Netherlands	8	Conglomerates	9
Spain	8	Automobiles	8
Sweden	8	Chemicals	6
Belgium	4	Financial	22
		Business services	4

Source: European Options Exchange

RELATIONSHIP WITH OTHER INDEXES

Table 2 presents the correlation coefficients between the Eurotop 100 index and other country and benchmark indexes. The results show that the Eurotop is highly colinear with most tradeable European indexes. The FTSE, DAX, and CAC-40, the accepted indexes now reflecting price movements in European stocks, show the highest levels of correlation. In contrast, the Eurotop is not highly correlated with Nikkei 225 and the S&P 500 indexes, illustrating the benefit of globally diversifying a portfolio. With respect to the Morgan Stanley Capital International (MSCI) index of 13 European countries, the Eurotop is essentially perfectly correlated.

In addition to near-perfect correlation, the Eurotop follows the MSCI with a tracking error of only 1.51 percent. This is considered, by most standards, an extremely acceptable level. The fact that there is a difference is due, in large part, to the differences in the country composition of the two indexes. The MSCI contains almost double the weighting of U.K. stocks compared to the Eurotop. The European Options Exchange (EOE), as compiler and disseminator of the Eurotop, limits any country composition to twice an equal weighting of all the countries in the index. This permits the Eurotop 100 to provide a better indication of pan-European equity activity. In their own independent study of the Eurotop 100 and MSCI index returns, Barra International, a leading international investment consultant, concludes that "The beta of the portfolio and the level of (residual) risk suggests that the Eurotop 100 approximates the MSCI-Europe quite well."

Table 2.   Eurotop 100 Index Correlation with Individual Equity Indexes

Indexes	Correlation with Eurotop 100
Financial Times 100 (U.K.)	0.93
DAX 100 (Germany)	0.90
CAC-40 (France)	0.87
SMI (Switzerland)	0.95
EOE (Netherlands)	0.80
OMX (Sweden)	0.90
Nikkei 225 (Japan)	0.16
S&P 500 (U.S.)	0.65
Morgan Stanley-EUR 13	0.99

Daily correlation from March 1989 to March 1992

EUROTOP 100 CONTRACT SPECIFICATIONS

The contract design for the Eurotop is based largely on the format used for other U.S. futures contracts such as the S&P 500 and the Nikkei 225. All three contracts are cash-settled for delivery during the end-of-quarter calendar months of March, June, September, and December. Because the Eurotop 100 contract is priced in dollars directly from the ECU-denominated cash index, a futures position in the Eurotop is insensitive to currency movements between the European Currency Unit and the U.S. dollar.

INDEX ARBITRAGE

A major reason for the existence of futures contracts on stock indexes is that they provide an efficient method of realizing gains (or losses) in the value of a basket of stocks. For example, the transaction cost of purchasing 10 S&P 500 futures contracts is a little more than $100. This gives the buyer exposure to appreciation or depreciation in a basket of 500 stocks valued at about $2 million. If the stocks are purchased directly, brokerage charges would total thousands of dollars, making the transaction costs of purchasing the stock basket much higher relative to buying futures contracts.

The Eurotop 100 futures contract offers similar arbitrage opportunities. First, at the beginning of the trading day, the futures contract is directly arbitrageable against the constituent stocks of the index as traded on the home exchanges. (The appendix to this chapter lists the underlying stocks in the Eurotop index.)

Alternatively, the Eurotop futures contract can be arbitraged against other futures contracts traded in Europe. This is done by adjusting for relative index weights and futures contract values in a basket of the six available European futures contracts. A study carried out by EOE indicates the correlation of the Eurotop 100 with the six-futures basket is 0.992, with a beta of 0.93. The volatility of the index is 16.8

Table 3.   Eurotop 100 Futures Contract Specifications

Item	Futures Contract	Options Contract
Unit of Trading	$100 per point of the Eurotop 100 Index	One Eurotop 100 Index futures contract
Delivery months	March, June, September, and December	Same as futures plus two near months
Delivery	Cash settlement	Cash settlement for end-of-quarter months, otherwise book transfer of futures contract
Last trading day	Third Friday of the delivery month until 7:00 a.m.	Same
Minimum price movement	0.1 index point $10 per contract	0.05 index point $5 per contract
Trading hours	5:30 a.m. to 11:30 a.m. (NY)	5:30 a.m. to 11:30 a.m.(NY)
Price quotation	Index points	Index points
Exercise	N/A	Permitted at any time prior to expiration
Strike price intervals	N/A	10 index points

percent versus 15.8 percent for the basket (Table 4). Alternatively, a basket of the FTSE 100, DAX, CAC-40, and TOP 5 has a beta of 1.03 versus the Eurotop 100, a correlation of 0.988, and volatility of 17.5 percent.

A third way to arbitrage the Eurotop 100 index is to replicate the index, using ADRs traded in the U.S. For example, there are 41 stocks traded on the NYSE, AMEX, and NASDAQ markets that are included in the Eurotop Index. Based on research conducted by the EOE, the correlation between a basket of the 41 ADRs and the index itself is 0.98, with a beta of 1.11. This is very high given that the U.K. and Sweden are overrepresented in ADRs, whereas Germany and Switzerland are underrepresented (Table 5). Also, the data used compare closing Eurotop 100 index values at 11:00 a.m. ET with ADR values at 4:00 p.m. ET.

Yet another way to arbitrage the Eurotop 100 futures is through the use of Eurotop 100 index options. By purchasing an at-the-money call and selling an at-the-money put, the market participant can effectively create a synthetically long futures position. An arbitrage opportunity exists between the pricing of the futures contract and the effective price of entering into the options transaction. When pricing favors the synthetic, arbitrage activity will generate changes in the futures and options pricing so that the put/call spread of the at-the-money options will fall in line with the futures prices. When pricing favors the purchase of the futures, the opposite transaction will occur.

Table 4.   Hypothetical Arbitrage of the Eurotop 100 Index with Futures Contracts

Futures Contract	Market	Relative Weight	Futures Value	Number of Contracts
		−%−	-000 ECU-	−#−
FTSE 100	U.K.	28	81.5	0.34
DAX	Germany	19	87.5	0.22
CAC-40	France	19	57.3	0.34
SMI	Switzerland	13	48.4	0.26
TOP 5	Netherlands	10	53.3	0.19
OMX	Sweden	10	11.1	0.92
Eurotop	9 Countries	100	99.2	1.00

Source: European Options Exchange

Table 5.   Country Weights in the Eurotop 100 Index versus Available ADRs

Country	Index	ADRs	Country	Index	ADRs
U.K.	22%	43%	Sweden	8%	14%
Germany	15%	2%	Spain	8%	9%
France	15%	9%	Switzerland	10%	2%
Italy	10%	8%	Belgium	4%	0%
Netherlands	8%	12%			

Source: European Options Exchange

FAIR VALUE OF THE EUROTOP 100 FUTURES CONTRACT

For index arbitrage to be profitable, the price of the futures contract must be different from its "fair" value. Fair value is the current index value, adjusted for the number of days until the futures contract expires, stock dividends not received, and interest received by depositing bonds as initial margin. In theory, selling futures above and purchasing futures below fair value and taking the opposite position in equities results in profits. However, differences in interest rates, and to a lesser extent transaction costs, will impose an upper and a lower limit on fair value, creating a range within which price arbitrage is unlikely to occur. This is often called the "no-arbitrage" band.

In comparing the Eurotop 100 no-arbitrage band against that of the S&P 500 futures, several points are clear (Table 6). First, it is apparent that the Eurotop has a slightly wider relative band than that of the S&P 500. This is primarily due to the lower prices of the underlying securities in the Eurotop. These lower prices require more shares to be purchased, raising transaction costs.

Second, the index multiple for the Eurotop 100 produces a higher hedge ratio, hence higher futures commissions costs when compared to the S&P 500. While this may be offset to some extent by lower bid/ask spreads on the futures, the overall transaction costs expressed in index points are higher for the Eurotop compared to the S&P 500. Clearly, market participants with lower transaction costs and bid/ask spreads would have a distinct advantage in buying and selling profitably outside a narrower trading band.

The no-arbitrage band is most sensitive to changes in the yield spread between the marginal borrowing and lending rates. At any given level of this spread, the relative arbitrage band width, as measured by the width of the band divided by the index value, increases linearly over time. In fact, the narrower this interest rate differential, the narrower the no-arbitrage band at any given time.

MARKET OUTLOOK

A number of factors are working to make the Eurotop futures contract a more essential tool for managing portfolio risk. First, U.S. institutions are investing more funds in European equities. Many studies show institutional investment in Europe doubling in three years. Some institutions already hold up to 30 percent of their equities in international stocks. Second, U.S. institutions are using more international index funds. These are designed to deliver an indexed return based on indexes such as the Eurotop. Studies show passive indexers outperform active managers more than 1 percent per year. Third, U.S. institutions are increasingly using futures to equitize cash, to carry long positions in equities (especially when futures trade cheap to fair value) and to accomplish asset reallocation efficiently. The continuation of this process can only serve to increase demand for the Eurotop futures contract among U.S. institutions.

With respect to European institutional participation, the use of futures contracts remains in its infancy. Like their American counterparts, European institutions will eventually increase their use of futures contracts and utilize more passive index managers. In addition, they will invest more beyond their borders. Now many European institutions invest virtually entirely in real estate and domestic securities. This will change as the benefits of diversification are realized. In addition, European countries are just beginning to put into place funded pension programs that will require establishing managed investment portfolios. All these factors will stimulate European demand for Eurotop futures.

On the supply side, increased sophistication of arbitragers will generate volume in the Eurotop. Development of software and systems to trade the Eurotop will take time, given its complexity compared with other single-country indexes such as the S&P 500 and the Nikkei 225 futures contracts. A particular challenge for the Eurotop is conducting stock purchases and sales simultaneously on nine exchanges in nine currencies. As arbitrager sophistication increases, market liquidity will be enhanced, eventually assuring the contract will be traded near fair value.

Table 6.   Fair Value and No-Arbitrage Band Worksheet

Arbitrage cost	S&P 500	Eurotop 100
Spot index value (#)	400	825
Size of portfolio ($mil)	10	10
Average share price ($)	65	25
Number of shares (000's)	154	400
Commission per share ($)	0.015	0.015
Total commissions ($)	4,615	12,000
Bid/ask spread per stock ($)	0.125	0.125
Total bid/ask cost ($)	19,231	50,000
Required futures contracts (#)	50	121
Commission per round turn ($)	12	12
Total futures commissions ($)	600	1,455
Bid/ask spread per futures ($)	0.05	0.10
Total futures bid/ask cost ($)	1,250	1,210
Total commissions and bid/ask costs($)	25,696	64,665
Total costs in index points	1.1	5.3
Corporate borrowing rate	5.0%	5.0%
Corporate lending rate	4.5%	4.5%
Dividend rate	3.5%	3.5%
Days to expiration	30	30
Upper bound	401.6	831.3
Lower bound	399.3	820.4
Arbitrage range	2.3	10.9
Range/spot index value	0.6%	1.3%
Days to expiration	60	60
Upper bound	402.1	832.3
Lower bound	399.6	821.1
Arbitrage range	2.5	11.3
Range/spot index value	0.6%	1.4%

CONCLUSION

Many U.S. institutions—including pension funds, money managers, managed futures funds, and mutual funds—already use baskets of European futures contracts to equitize cash, reallocate assets, create synthetic long portfolios, and to hedge. The Eurotop 100 futures contract provides a more efficient means of accomplishing these objectives through a single transaction.

In addition, industry management trends suggest that demand for the contract will continue to increase in the future. In particular, increased automation, greater international portfolio diversification, increased funds managed under pension programs, more indexation of institutional funds, and increased sophistication of market participants in using futures will be the key driving forces. In this regard, the Eurotop 100 contract, although more complex than traditional index products, represents a significant financial market innovation.

APPENDIX

Eurotop 100 Stock Weightings the Number of Shares of Each Stock Represented in the Index Effective 4/19/93

Great Britain		Sweden		Dresdner Bank AG	1.80
				Commerzbank AG	2.40
Glaxo Holdings	218	Ericsson B free	88	Schering AG	0.90
British Petroleum Co.	378	Astra A free	18		
British Tele	280	Electrolux B free	41	***Italy***	
British Gas	277	Skandia Group free	78		
BAT Industries	93	Asea AB free Series B	13	Fiat SpA	533
Shell Transport	142	Volvo AB Class B free	15	Generali	88
Grand Metropolitan	191	SKF B free	68	Montedison SpA	1,297
Imperial Chemical Inc.	68	Investor B free	38	Banca Comm Italiana	324
Hanson	337			Stet	529
Guiness Plc	150	***Netherlands***		Mediobanca SpA	87
Barclays Bank Group	171			SIP	638
Cable & Wireless Plc	91	Royal Dutch	32.0	Olivetti & Co SpA	476
Smithkline Beecham A	156	Unilever NV	14.0	IFI Priv	64
BTR Plc	105	Phillips Electronics NV	83.0	CIR	620
Natl Westminster Bank	135	Intl Netherlands Group	32.0		
General Electric Plc	182	Akzo NV	10.1	***Switzerland***	
Tesco Plc	235	ABN/AMRO Holdings NV	25.0		
Marks & Spencer Plc	152	Elsevier NV	9.0	Roche Holdings	1.20
Allied-Lyons	95	DSM	13.0	UBS (Bearer)	3.90
Reuters Holdings	37			Nestle SA (Bearer)	2.30
Vodafone Group	124	***Belgium***		BBC Brown Boveri A (Bearer)	0.60
RTZ (BR)	71	Petrofina SA	6.0	C S Holdings (Bearer)	0.95
		Electrabel	6.0	SBC (Bearer)	3.80
France		Delhaize	31.1	Sandoz (PC)	0.40
		Solvay et Cie Class A	1.7	Ciba-Geigy (Bearer)	1.70
Alcatel-Alsthom	18.0			Alusuisse-Lonza (Bearer)	1.90
Elf Acquitaine SA	26.0	***Germany***		Swiss Reinsurance (PC)	1.20
Eaux	3.5	Siemens AG	7.00		
BSN	7.6	Daimier Benz AG	7.50	***Spain***	
Peugeot SA	12.5	Deutsche Bank AG	6.00		
Total Energy	35.0	Volkswagen AG	8.00	Banco Central Hispano	57.0
Suez	22.0	Veba AG	4.40	Telefónica de Español	142.0
LVMH-Louis Vuitton	1.8	Bayer AG	6.00	Repsol	45.0
Saint Gobain	11.0	Allianz Holdings AG	0.56	Iberdrola 1	186.0
Societe Generale	7.0	Mannesmann AG	4.00	Banco Santander	22.0
Paribas	10.0	BASF AG	4.00	Banco Bilbao Vizcaya	28.0
Lafarge Coppee	11.0	Hoechst AG	3.50	Banco Popular Español	5.5
Lyonnaise des Eaux D	9.0	Thyssen AG	4.50	Union Electrica-Fenosa	163.0
Air Liquide	5.0	RWE AG	2.00		
Eurotunnel	93.0				

REFERENCES

Bruce, B., and A. Eisenberg, "Global Synthetic Index Funds," *The Journal of Investing,* Vol. 1, No. 2, Fall 1992, pp. 45-47.

Barra International, "Tracking Error: The Eurotop 100 Versus the Eurotrack," unpublished paper prepared for the European Options Exchange, 1992.

European Options Exchange, *Eurotop 100 Index Specifications,* Amsterdam, 1992.

Kawaller, I., "Determining the Relevant Fair Values of S&P 500 Futures: A Case Study Approach," *The Journal of Futures,* Vol. II, No. 4, 1991, pp. 453-60.

Lakonishok, J., A. Shleifer, and R. Vishry, "The Structure and Performance of the Money Management Industry," *Brookings Papers: Microeconomics,* 1992, pp. 339-91.

Makin, C., "Eurobonanza? What Eurobonanza?" *Institutional Investor*, April 1992, pp. 50-56.

Morgan, N., "Investing in Europe: Investment Portfolio for the Changing European Market," *The Journal of Investing,* Vol. 1, No. 1, Summer 1992, pp. 51-55.

CHAPTER 33

The Development of Derivatives Markets in the Asia-Pacific Region

Andrew Parry
Assistant Manager/Public Relations
Sydney Futures Exchange Limited

INTRODUCTION

While Asian financial markets are relatively less developed than those in the U.S. and Europe, the Asia-Pacific region has experienced phenomenal growth over recent years. This growth has attracted an enormous inflow of capital as fund managers begin to recognize the region's potential. It is expected that Asia-Pacific markets will continue to expand during the 1990s and represent a larger share of world markets.

This chapter takes a brief look at financial derivative markets in the Asia-Pacific region (excluding Japan, which is covered in Chapter 35).

FINANCIAL MARKETS IN ASIA-PACIFIC (EXCLUDING JAPAN)

Major markets

- Australia
- Hong Kong
- Singapore

Developing markets

- Indonesia
- Malaysia
- New Zealand
- South Korea
- Taiwan
- Thailand
- Philippines

Potential future markets

- China
- Vietnam

THE REGION'S EXPANSION

The four economic "tigers" of Asia, which have brought about the fastest industrial revolutions the world has seen, are South Korea, Taiwan, Singapore, and Hong Kong. Another four that are currently experiencing enormous reformation and growth are Thailand, Malaysia, Indonesia, and China. These countries are regarded as the "emerging tigers" of the region.

Together, these eight economies are defying the downturn that Europe, the United States, and Japan have experienced and are boosting the overall growth of the region. The Asia Development Bank predicts average growth of around 7 percent for its 25 developing member nations. Meanwhile the International Monetary Fund has lowered its forecast for world growth from 3.1 percent to 2.3 percent for 1993.

This spectacular level of growth for the region over recent years and high investment yields has attracted a wave of funds from U.S., European, and Japanese fund managers chasing a higher return on their investments. And if the current level of optimism is any indication, funds invested in the Asia-Pacific region (excluding Japan) could double over the next five years.

The largest economy of the region is Australia, with a GDP of nearly US$300 million in 1991 (see Exhibit 1). The country also has the lowest inflation rate among OECD nations and a revised GDP growth of nearly 4 percent. Although the country is experiencing a near record level of unemployment, prospects for a strong upturn in the economy and expansion of the private sector are improving.

ASIA-PACIFIC EQUITY MARKETS

Given the rapid growth of foreign institutions investing in the Asia-Pacific region, attention has focused on indexes of the region.

Exhibit 1. 1991 GDP—Selected Asia-Pacific Nations

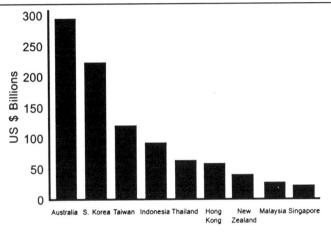

Table 1 is a list of individual equity markets of the region.

Table 1

	Market Capitalization $U.S. Billion (Est)	Index	Price/ Earnings ratio	Estimate 1993 GDP growth	Inflation %
Australia	$150	All Ordinaries	19	3.9	0.3
Hong Kong	$180	Hang Seng	15	6.0	10.0
Indonesia	$12	Jakarta Composite	16	5.5	7.5
Malaysia	$78	Malaysian Composite	18	8.5	4.5
New Zealand	$16	NZSE-40 Capital	15	2.4	2.3
Philippines	$17	Manila Composite	12	4.5	9.5
South Korea	$92	Seoul Composite	16	7.0	9.5
Singapore	$83	Straits Times	16	6.5	2.3
Taiwan	$134	Taipei Weighted Index	29	7.2	4.0
Thailand	$43	SET Index	12	7.0	4.4

ASIA-PACIFIC CAPITAL MARKETS

Capital markets of the region are highly developed, with a variety of government, semigovernment, and private debt securities traded (see Table 2).

Table 2

	Debt Securities
Australia	Highly developed capital market and the largest in Asia-Pacific region excluding Japan. Securities include: Commonwealth government bonds; semigovernment securities; bank transferable certificates of deposit; securitized mortgage-backed bonds; company debentures; and/or unsecured notes.
Hong Kong	Most of the bonds traded in Hong Kong are issued by foreign companies. Debt securities issued by Hong Kong companies are relatively insignificant. Trading in locally issued debt instruments is thin.
Indonesia	There are three listed companies that have issued bonds, to the total of Rp.404,718 million.
Malaysia	A private debt securities market has seen rapid growth, especially the fixed- and floating-rate promissory notes issued by prime corporations and statutory bodies. The more established government bond market saw an increase in net funds raised from M$2,458.9 million in 1989 to M$3,797.6 million in 1990.
New Zealand	Deregulation of the financial system has resulted in a sophisticated bond market with the following securities: State-owned enterprise bonds Local authority bonds Corporate bonds
Philippines	NA
Singapore	Private debt securities market
South Korea	Public bond issues occur, although the capital markets are dominated by corporate bond issues.
Taiwan	Government bonds, corporate bonds, and financial debentures. Corporate bonds are issued by limited companies, while financial debentures are issued by financial institutions.
Thailand	Bonds issued by the government or government agencies and debentures issued by private corporations.

Source: "Securities Markets in Asia and Oceania"

INCREASED DEMAND FOR DERIVATIVES

Derivative markets in the Asia-Pacific region have grown substantially over recent years in response to the demand for effective methods of hedging and risk management. But the growth can also be attributed to fund managers who are using derivatives markets, such as futures and options, to gain an exposure to a country or a region without any underlying exposure to physical equities, fixed-interest instruments, or currency risks.

Stock index futures are becoming an increasingly popular means of gaining an exposure to a country's equity market, while interest rate contracts of the region have attracted interest as they generally have a low correlation with major interest rate contracts in the U.S. and U.K. The stock index and interest rate futures contracts of the region are listed in Table 3.

Table 3

Country	Share index futures	Interest rate futures	Exchange
Australia	Share Price Index	90-day bills 3-year bonds 10-year bonds	Sydney Futures Exchange
New Zealand	Forty Index	90-day bank bills 5-year government stock 10-year government stock	New Zealand Futures and Options Exchange
Hong Kong	Hang Seng Index	3-month HIBOR	Hong Kong Futures Exchange
Singapore	Nikkei Index (Japan)	Eurodollar Euromark Euroyen	SIMEX

FUTURES EXCHANGES OF THE ASIA-PACIFIC REGION (EXCLUDING JAPAN)

- Sydney Futures Exchange (SFE)
- New Zealand Futures and Options Exchange (NZFOE)
- Singapore International Monetary Exchange (SIMEX)
- Hong Kong Futures Exchange (HKFE)
- Kuala Lumpur Commodities Exchange (KLCE)
- Manila International Futures Exchange (MIFE)

SYDNEY FUTURES EXCHANGE (SFE)

The oldest futures exchange in the Asia-Pacific region, the Sydney Futures Exchange (SFE) was established in 1960 as the Sydney Greasy Wool Futures Exchange to provide a hedging facility for Australia's largest export industry at the time—merino wool.

SFE has grown to become the largest open-outcry futures exchange in the region (see Exhibit 2) and offers a wide range of financial and agricultural futures and options contracts. Volumes at the exchange have surged in recent years to reach a record annual turnover of 21.4 million contracts in 1993.

**Exhibit 2. Asia-Pacific Futures Exchanges (Excluding Japan)
Total Volumes for 1992**

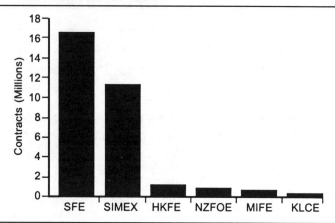

Recognized as highly innovative, SFE was the first futures exchange outside the U.S. to trade financial futures and the first exchange to introduce an after-hours screen-dealing system called SYCOM (Sydney Computerized Overnight Market). SFE has also been acclaimed as having one of the most complete and technologically advanced trading floors in the world. In recent years, SFE has seen a surge in interest from overseas investors, particularly from the U.S. and the U.K.

NEW ZEALAND FUTURES AND OPTIONS EXCHANGE (NZFOE)

NZFOE was established (as the New Zealand Futures Exchange) in January 1985. The first futures contract launched was based on the $U.S./$NZ exchange rate. The second contract, introduced a few months later in May 1985, was the highly successful prime commercial paper (PCP) contract, an interest-rate contact based on the local 90-day commercial bill. A 5-year government bond contract began trading in February 1986, while other contracts include wool and the Forty Index futures share-price index.

NZFOE was officially sold to a subsidiary of Sydney Futures Exchange at the end of 1992 and while the business is now a wholly owned subsidiary of SFE, it will continue to be known as the New Zealand Futures and Options Exchange.

SINGAPORE INTERNATIONAL MONETARY EXCHANGE (SIMEX)

SIMEX was established in 1984, when the government foresaw that Singapore's development as a regional center depended on, amongst other things, the ability to provide sophisticated risk management services to international investors. SIMEX was the first futures exchange in Asia to trade gold, interest rate, and currency futures.

Without a large captive domestic market, SIMEX has had to ensure that it was sufficiently competitive and innovative. Of the exchange's 71 corporate members, 21 are from Japan, 18 from the U.S., and 13 from Europe.

SIMEX now trades a range of commodity, currency, and stock-index futures, while most trading at SIMEX occurs in the exchange's Eurodollar, Euroyen, and Nikkei contracts. Total volumes at SIMEX during 1992 were 12.1 million contracts, compared to 6.1 million contracts the previous year.

HONG KONG FUTURES EXCHANGE (HKFE)

Established in its present form in 1985, the Hong Kong Futures Exchange gained immediate recognition with the launch of its successful stock-index contract based on the Hang Seng Index in May 1986. The October 1987 crash, however, led to a four-day closure of the exchange and revealed a number of weaknesses in the market. In December 1987, the HKFE issued a package of reforms aimed at counteracting these weaknesses, including a new clearing system.

Self-regulation of Hong Kong's financial markets ended in 1989 with the creation of the Securities and Futures Commission, a body with broad powers to enforce new rules and regulations following the crash of 1987.

Today the exchange trades stock index, interest rate, and commodity futures. Most of the activity is in the Hang Seng Index and the sugar contract.

KUALA LUMPUR COMMODITIES EXCHANGE (KLCE)

KLCE was established in 1980 and currently trades crude palm oil, rubber, and tin. The exchange is studying the possibility for introducing financial futures in 1993. The Kuala Lumpur Options and Financial Futures Exchange (KLOFFE) was recently established by a group of Malaysian companies and broking firms to offer futures and options not provided by the Kuala Lumpur Commodities Exchange (KLCE) or the Kuala Lumpur Stock Exchange. KLOFFE plans to list a stock-index futures contract by the middle of 1993.

MANILA INTERNATIONAL FUTURES EXCHANGE (MIFE)

Trading at the Manila International Futures Exchange (MIFE) began in October 1986. MIFE claims a very diverse range of futures contracts, including interest rate, currencies, and commodities such as coffee and soybeans. The exchange is also the only futures exchange in the world to trade copra and U.S. dollar/peso futures.

FIRST MANAGED FUTURES ASSOCIATION FOR THE ASIA-PACIFIC REGION

Complementing the growth of the futures markets in the Asia-Pacific region, a new association entitled the Asia-Pacific Managed Futures Association (APMFA) was recently formed. The first body of its kind in the region, APMFA was formed to represent managed futures throughout Asia, Australia, and New Zealand.

The association's main objectives are to promote managed futures funds as a viable investment alternative, to heighten awareness of managed futures funds among a variety of investors, and to promote and campaign for changes to laws or regulations prevailing within the Asia-Pacific region that will facilitate the establishment, management, and investment in managed futures funds.

FUTURE DEVELOPMENTS

Asia-Pacific economies and financial markets are some of the fastest growing in the world (see Exhibit 3). The region boasts a broad and sophisticated range of equity, capital, over-the-counter, and exchange-traded futures and options products that have developed to satisfy the demand for efficient risk management and investment exposure to countries in the region.

Futures exchanges of the region, in particular, have a diverse and highly liquid range of products, including interest rate, equity, and commodity futures and options contracts.

**Exhibit 3.   The Global Futures Industry
Percentage of Total Volume Traded**

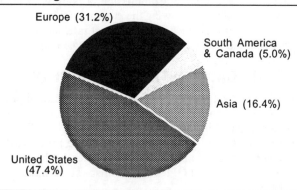

Europe (31.2%)

South America
& Canada (5.0%)

Asia (16.4%)

United States
(47.4%)

CHAPTER 34

The Development of a Financial Futures and Options Market in Tokyo

Planning and Coordination Section
The Tokyo International Financial Futures Exchange

BIRTH OF THE DERIVATIVES MARKET IN JAPAN

The deregulation and internationalization of Japan's financial market has fostered development of new financial instruments with floating interest rates, and also generated a surge in yen-denominated assets and liabilities in and out of Japan.

The era of financial futures and options in Japan was ushered in with the listing of 10-year government bond futures on the Tokyo Stock Exchange (TSE) in October 1985. This was followed by the launch of the Stock Futures 50, a basket of the nation's 50 leading stocks, on the Osaka Securities Exchange (OSE) in June 1987.

Prior to the enactment of the Revised Securities and Exchange Law and the Financial Futures Trading Law in May 1988, Japanese investors were prohibited from trading in any product not backed by the physical asset. The lifting of this restriction prompted the introduction of TOPIX futures and Nikkei 225 Stock Index futures on the TSE and OSE, respectively, in September 1988. This was followed, in 1989, by listing of options on stock price index at Japan's three major stock exchanges—the TSE, the OSE, and the Nagoya Stock Exchange—and the start of an over-the-counter options market on government bonds. Finally, the TSE initiated trading in options on 10-year government bond futures in 1990. Thus, Japan saw a full-fledged futures and options market emerge from nothing in the space of just five years.

ESTABLISHMENT OF TIFFE AND BEYOND

The Financial Futures Trading Law was promulgated in May of 1988, and the Tokyo International Financial Futures Exchange (TIFFE) was established in April 1989, based on this law, and began trading in June 1989.

Growing Market Scale

TIFFE has become one of the world's largest futures and options exchanges in just under four years. The 1992 annual trading volume was over 15.5 million contracts. Average daily volume stood at 62,663 contracts, while open interest increased to a record high of 664,492 on December 14. The trading volume put TIFFE in the world's top ten exchanges listing futures and options contracts.

Table 1.   Trading Volume of Financial Futures Contracts

	Products	1992	1991
1	U.S. Treasury Bond Futures Chicago Board of Trade	70,003,894	67,887,497
2	Three-Month Eurodollar Futures Chicago Mercantile Exchange	60,531,066	37,244,223
3	Notional Bond Futures Marché à Terme International de France	31,062,844	21,987,899
4	Three-Month Euroyen Futures Tokyo International Financial Futures Exchange	14,959,373	14,665,521
5	Cruzeiro Interest Rate Futures Bolsa de Mercadorias & Futuros	14,072,749	2,607,741
6	German Government Bond Futures London International Financial Futures and Options Exchange	13,604,523	10,112,305
7	S&P 500 Stock Index Futures Chicago Mercantile Exchange	12,414,157	12,340,380
8	Three-Month Euromark Futures London International Financial Futures and Options Exchange	12,173,431	4,783,649
9	Nikkei 225 Stock Index Futures Osaka Securities Exchange	11,927,329	21,643,085
10	10-year Japanese Government Bond Futures Tokyo Stock Exchange	11,868,127	12,822,414

*   Except options contracts.

Three-Month Euroyen Interest Rate Futures

In 1992, the trading volume of three-month Euroyen interest rate futures recorded 14.9 million contracts and ranked as the fourth largest financial futures contract in the world (see Table 1). This is also reflected in the entire money market in Japan. The scale of the Euroyen futures market almost equals that of the cash market (see Table 2).

Table 2.   Amounts Outstanding in Money Markets in Japan (in $U.S. 100 million)

End of Year	Call Money and Bills	CD	Bonds with Repurchase Agreement	CP	Treasury Bills	JOM Yen- Denominated	3- Month Euroyen Futures
1988	2,678	1,269	584	738	181	1,904	–
1989	3,155	1,470	440	911	349	3,143	1,046
1990	3,032	1,393	485	1,164	584	2,734	2,286
1991	4,138	1,381	483	990	690	3,762	2,018
1992	4,819	1,332	710	979	892	3,933	3,524

Source: TIFFE
Notes: 1.   The figures of TB are the amount at the end of fiscal year, ended March 31,
       2.   Amounts outstanding are converted into U.S. dollars in terms of the $U.S./yen spot rate at the end of each year.

Generally, liquidity and volatility are said to be the key factors of successful futures and options markets. Concerning the Euroyen futures, the Japanese official discount rate was raised four times in the 14 months after the listing, and then it was reduced six times to date. It was a period of fluctuating short-term interest rates. The deregulation and internationalization of finance, and global use of the yen have been advancing rapidly to meet the needs of investors in and out of Japan, so the market has become very active in a short period.

Euroyen futures contracts are considered an effective means of hedging against fluctuation of interest rates as well as an innovative means of investment.

Recent trends in trading of three-month Euroyen interest rate futures include significantly increased activity among foreign concerns and an extension in trading activity from front months (the two latest contract months) to back months (the six contract months after the front months). Such developments point to an expanding user base and growing investor familiarity with the diverse applications of this product (see Exhibit 1).

Options on Three-Month Euroyen Futures

Options on three-month Euroyen futures contract is a relatively new contract, listed in July 1991. TIFFE introduced market makers for options contracts on July 1, 1992

Exhibit 1.   Front Months and Back Months

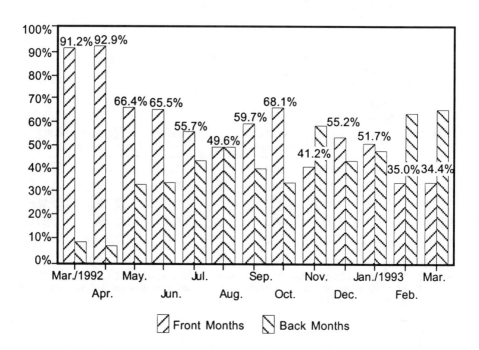

Front Months   Back Months

---

to stimulate the market further. Since then, the market has been expanding rapidly. Trading volume in the second half of 1992 showed an increase of 78 percent, compared with the first half, before the introduction of the market makers.

The liquidity of the market has been secured and bid/ask spreads are tighter than when options trading opened. As a result, it is easier for investors to trade options. The number of participants in the options market has also greatly increased since July of 1992.

The value of turnover in TIFFE's options on three-month Euroyen futures in the period before introduction of the market makers was equivalent to between 2 percent and 3 percent of transactions underlying Euroyen interest rate futures. The figure has since increased to between 5 percent and 6 percent. Compared with other countries, however, this ratio remains lower than is the case with other equivalent contracts, such as options on Eurodollar futures at CME (listed in March 1985) and options on three-month sterling futures at LIFFE (listed in November 1987), where turnover in the options markets is around 20 percent of that in the underlying market.

One of the reasons is because the option contract was a relatively new financial transaction, and many investors at home were not accustomed to using them effectively. However, as the three-month Euroyen interest rate futures contract, which is the underlying asset of the options, is already traded worldwide and has one of the most active markets, the market for options on three-month Euroyen futures promises to attract growing demand and will be much more active in the near future.

One-Year Euroyen Interest Rate Futures

TIFFE diversified its lineup of interest rate futures with the launch of the one-year Euroyen interest rate futures contract in July 1992 in response to the needs to hedge against the fluctuation of medium- to long-term interest rates. Although this product is not traded briskly so far, we are convinced that there is substantial untapped demand for it as a hedging and arbitrage tool for use in combination with interest rate swaps. To stimulate this demand and boost trading levels, we are implementing educational and publicity programs to broaden awareness and understanding of the contract's advantages.

TIFFE CREDIBILITY

One reason why the TIFFE market has become so large is the high credibility of the clearinghouse, as well as the changes in the economy and finance described above. Investors benefit from a clearing system under which TIFFE guarantees settlement of transactions in the market.

Membership

There are 215 members—109 clearing members and 106 general (nonclearing) members—consisting of banks, security houses, insurance companies, money brokers, and futures brokers.

A recent feature of TIFFE is the increasing transactions of overseas investors. Trading by foreign members has become active. At present, although the number of foreign members is 19, less than 10 percent of the total, their trading share in 1992 was more than 20 percent of the total. They have been increasing brokerage transactions as well as house-account transactions and they can be said to be the leading players in the TIFFE market. This tendency reflects the increasing need of overseas investors to hedge against fluctuation of interest rate on yen-denominated assets.

Fully Automated Computer Trading System (FACTS)

TIFFE has used electronic trading from the start. Factors in favor of automated trading include market fairness and transparency, accurate trading records, quick order execution, and real-time market information. At first, it was a semiautomated system whereby orders were placed over the telephone to exchange operators, who input them into a computer. In February, 1991, TIFFE switched over to a fully automated system so that members could trade directly via terminals in their offices. As a result, order processing time was reduced effectively; orders are registered in the host computer and matched automatically within seconds. Members can now respond to market fluctuations even more easily.

FACTS is a highly reliable system and it is an indispensable element in maintaining a fair market. Since its inception, the system has run smoothly, with no breakdowns or stoppages.

Introduction of After-Hours Trading Session

TIFFE extended its trading hours in December, 1991 (called the after-hours trading session), to respond to the needs of investors in and out of Japan. Previously, TIFFE trading hours were from 09:00 to 12:00 and 13:30 to 15:30 (JST). The extra after-hours trading session is from 16:00 to 18:00. As a result, investors can easily catch the interest rate fluctuations that might occur after the close of market at 15:30. Also, the after-hours trading session overlaps with the trading hours in key European markets so that overseas investors can participate in the Tokyo market more easily. Today, the after-hours trading session is very active. The trading volume in the after-hours trading session is more than 10 percent of the total.

NEW TENDENCIES OF THE MARKET

The financial market in Tokyo has become one of the world's largest markets. Recently, the market is showing new tendencies.

Diversity of Market Participants

When TIFFE started trading in 1989, most transactions were members' house accounts. However, recently, transactions by customers' accounts—i.e., institutional investors and corporations in and out of Japan—have been increasing along with the increased transactions by foreign members. The stratum of investors can be said to be actually growing because the percentage of customers' transactions increased to 23.6 percent in 1992, from 9.93 percent in 1989.

THE FUTURE OF TIFFE

Less than four years since its inception, TIFFE has become one of the largest markets in the world. The needs for futures and options will be higher from now on as financial deregulation and internationalization, including the likely lifting of restrictions on the use of forward-rate agreements (FRAs) in Japan, progress. In such an environment, TIFFE is aiming to provide investors around the globe with cost-effective services that facilitate their risk management by consolidating the financial footing, fine-tuning its operations to bring them even more closely in line with international norms. Regarding tie-ups with exchanges overseas, TIFFE is providing the Singapore International Monetary Exchange with the final settlement prices for three-month Euroyen futures. And in the future, we wish to find various ways in which we can cooperate and strengthen linkages with other exchanges to offer better services to meet the needs of investors in and out of Japan.

CHAPTER 35

Exchange Alliances and Linkages

David Courtney
Marketing Director
OMLX, The London Securities and Derivatives Exchange

INTRODUCTION

Alliances between derivatives exchanges are by no means a new phenomenon. One of the most successful and well documented, and one that works as well today as it did when it was launched, is the mutual offset arrangement between the IMM and SIMEX for Eurodollar futures. This was a direct response by the two exchanges to protect the contract, which had become the subject of competition following the inauguration of LIFFE in 1982. It was interesting that LIFFE, being placed at a competitive disadvantage to the IMM/SIMEX alliance, responded by forming a similar alliance with the Sydney Futures Exchange (SFE), which also had ambitions toward greater international product coverage.

There have been a number of other examples of alliances involving exchanges on each of the continents. But whereas the names and, indeed, the mechanisms have increased in number, the principles and motives have remained constant. In an increasingly competitive world, exchanges have been obliged to assess their activities and assimilate them with an ever-changing landscape. For many, isolation is not only unenviable as a means of countering competitive pressures, but in certain instances it could well prove to be fatal. Exchange alliances, in whatever guise, have been seen in the past (and increasingly so today) as an efficient and effective means of product distribution to counter competitive threats.

Although this trend can be documented quite distinctly, the emphasis has undoubtedly changed. The earlier examples were focused on "global access," following naturally on the perceived move at the time toward the transition to a fully global marketplace for many products. The IMM/SIMEX link is a perfect example of the importance attached to global coverage. More recently however, globalization is less of an issue. Instead, exchange alliances are more localized, involving exchanges located on the same continent. Closer cooperation and alliances are being formed between U.S. exchanges, such as the plan for the Chicago and New York exchanges to develop and deploy a single clearing model. Elsewhere, the SFE and its neighbor the New Zealand Futures Exchange (NZFE) are linking their exchanges to improve market liquidity and efficiency. Although much activity can be identified on a worldwide scale, perhaps the most important recent examples are being witnessed in Europe—and for very good reason.

EXCHANGE ALLIANCES

Since 1978, when derivatives trading was first introduced to Europe by the EOE-Optiebeurs in Amsterdam and the London Traded Options Market (LTOM), derivatives exchanges have mushroomed to the extent that today no fewer than 14 European countries have at least one derivatives exchange of their own, with at least one other exchange—in Portugal—scheduled to appear in the near future. Set against a background of closer economic, political, and monetary cooperation, with the intention of it leading eventually to a single European currency, the possibility is that the proliferation of derivatives exchanges during the '80s will lead to a consolidation in their number during the '90s. In this context, only the most efficient and forward-thinking exchanges will survive. Not surprisingly, this has led many exchanges to the conclusion that cooperation is one of the most effective means of competing against other exchanges in order to ensure survival in the longer term. Strategic alliances between a number of exchanges have been formed to provide the basis for precisely these reasons.

The two most obvious examples are the First European Exchanges (FEX) alliance, which was created in 1992 between the EOE; OM Stockholm; OMLX, The London Securities and Derivatives Exchange; SOFFEX; and, through a bilateral arrangement with SOFFEX, Otob, the Austrian exchange. A linked marketplace between OM Stockholm and OMLX, The London Securities and Derivatives Exchange, has been working with great success since December 1989, but the first manifestation of the new FEX alliance was inaugurated on January 29, 1993, between the London-based exchange once more and the EOE in Amsterdam.

Meanwhile, a Franco-German alliance was formed between the Matif and the DTB. This was motivated by a single common objective: to provide a viable and powerful alternative to LIFFE, which is Europe's most international and largest derivatives exchange. By combining forces, the MATIF/DTB alliance aims to increase their collective competitiveness to wrestle back existing contracts from LIFFE and to improve their prospects in the united Europe of the future.

BLUEPRINTS FOR SUCCESS

Recognizing the idiosyncrasies of different exchanges, their operations, products, and organizations, means that no single blueprint for exchange alliances exists. However, these alliances are becoming more formal, involving linkage and product distribution as axial criteria. Already a number of different blueprints have appeared.

For instance, the EOE/OMLX exchange link is one involving an open-outcry exchange in the former case, and a fully electronic exchange in the latter case. This obviously introduces a number of problems, which dilutes the efficiency of the link. In effect, members of the EOE wishing to access the OMLX exchange can do so via terminals located in Amsterdam, but transactions in the reverse direction still involve the use of floor members in Amsterdam executing trades by normal procedures.

However, clearing is conducted on a local level, using a specific clearing vehicle between the two exchanges. As such, members of each exchange clear business on their opposite exchange locally—the local exchanges' clearinghouses being responsible for guarantee and administrative functions for its members.

Despite some of the difficulties of trading EOE products from London, the concept of the link is very sound, and the link performs many of the tasks expected of it. Liquidity is combined and enhanced, leading to increased turnover in the contracts included on the link.

Insofar as the MATIF trades by means of open outcry and the DTB is fully electronic, the MATIF/DTB link faces many of the same problems. However, the MATIF has decided that it should not only create a local network for its members in Paris to access DTB products, but at a subsequent point in time it will transfer certain contracts presently traded on the exchange floor to the electronic system so that DTB members can gain access in return. This is a logical and important step forward.

The only limiting factor is in the clearing environment. Rather than localize the clearing arrangements as in the case of the EOE/OMLX exchange link, the MATIF/DTB arrangement, at least in the first instance, provides for a centralized clearing regime in that all contracts traded on the MATIF in its products will be cleared by the MATIF and vice versa. This means that while members of either exchange can trade freely in one another's products, they will have to appoint a local clearing agent and pay commissions for clearing and settlement in the normal way. Those who have membership on both exchanges, however, would be exempted from having to do this, but at the same time they will have to run two separate operations in order to qualify for the benefits. This does not necessarily produce optimum results in either eventuality.

Optimization is arguably a combination of the aforementioned cases. This is perfectly illustrated in the link between OM Stockholm and the OMLX exchange in London. In this instance, trading is fully automated, such that trading access is granted to members of both exchanges on an equal basis, while clearing is conducted locally between the exchanges and their respective members. This maximizes the efficiencies of both the trading and clearing environments.

This is, perhaps, one of the greatest challenges that exchanges face in the linkage projects. Creating common systems and operations with partner exchanges, in order to maximize the efficiencies as detailed above, and carrying this out in a way that does not compromise the autonomy and individuality of the exchanges concerned, approaches a very fine dividing line that is difficult to define. Nonetheless, it is important that exchanges be able to build on their strengths and successes, recognizing the dynamics of the marketplaces in which they operate, but reconciled with the advantages of harmonized trading and clearing routines.

Given that 11 of the 14 European derivative exchanges are fully electronic, future linkages will most likely involve exchanges that are able to link fully electronically as a matter of course, and the overwhelming logic of local clearing should ensure that it is conducted as efficiently as the trades in the first place.

BENEFITS

Linking exchanges is a strategy that extends a number of benefits to the three major parties concerned. Whether from the perspective of the exchange itself, the members of the exchange, or the ultimate customers of the exchange's products, very clear advantages can be identified.

EXCHANGES

There are two main elements that benefit the exchanges. The first may be considered to be protection from external competition; the second, diversification.

Taking each in turn, linkages provide exchanges with a clear ability to counter competitive threats by means of protecting existing contracts. Exchange linkages will improve liquidity by allowing greater and more widespread access to the exchange, which in turn, will increase the efficiency of the market and therefore, improve the chances of the exchanges to consolidate and improve their contracts over the longer term. It must be pointed out, however, that electronic linkage is not the sole means of improving either liquidity or efficiency, but taken within a list of alternatives, it is certainly one of the strongest contenders for implementation.

Improving or increasing the size of the international marketplace for certain contracts is one thing, but even if exchanges have very strong contracts of their own, linkages can often be the only route available for them to diversify and internationalize their product portfolios. Given the level of competition, which encourages closer inspection of linkages in the first instance, there is tremendous difficulty in internationalizing products, as many exchanges, even to the size of the MATIF, have recognized. As exchange linkages involve mutual access to products, the effect is that for many exchanges a process of internationalization can be secured at the same time as protecting existing generic contracts. Over the longer term, this will represent the basis of ongoing growth and success that would otherwise be unavailable.

MEMBERS

Members of exchanges also gain tremendous advantages from linkages. Membership on exchanges can be expensive and represent a significant investment. As such, the more contracts that are available the greater the opportunities to participate and the greater the corresponding value of the membership rights received. For many traditional exchanges, which issue shares from which trading rights are accorded, this would theoretically result in a significant increase in the value of those shares. But members of those exchanges that charge initial and annual membership fees also benefit insofar as they are extended a greater variety of contracts from which to generate revenue.

CUSTOMERS

Customers of the exchanges, meanwhile, benefit in two ways. First an improvement in the liquidity should result in tighter bid/offer spreads and more contracts available at each price, which reduces the direct costs of dealing. In some markets, this is of considerable value. But equally, as the costs of intermediation fall as direct access is achieved by members rather than indirect access through further intermediaries, so too should commissions fall. By reducing the distribution chain and increasing the efficiency of market access, there is a very real prospect that efficiency gains can be passed on to customers without any erosion in margins or profits for the members concerned.

POTENTIAL OBSTACLES

So far, everything appears to be straightforward and there are huge benefits for all parties. If this were the absolute case, then many more linkages would probably exist today. Evidently, certain obstacles exist, but they are by no means insurmountable.

Perhaps the first obstacle is regulation. Exchanges are, in the first instance, regulated in their country of incorporation. More recently, and particularly so in Europe as a result of the Investment Services Directive (ISD) and the move toward closer integration, the regulatory framework in which exchanges operate is being harmonized. However, there remain a number of countries that need to improve, increase, or reconstruct their regulatory environments to satisfy more international demands.

Linking exchanges demands that regulatory approval be granted before trading can take place. And regulators must be completely satisfied that the foreign exchange is adequately regulated and protects investor interests to a standard equal to or greater than the domestic market. If not, the regulators may withhold permission and insist that the regulatory conditions in the foreign market be improved before linkage may progress.

Another barrier involves the trading interface itself. Obviously, linking an open-outcry exchange with an automated exchange is fraught with problems, but even linking two computerized exchanges can take significant time and money. Exchanges may use different systems architecture and equipment and different software with radically different capabilities. Linking the two systems can involve considerable investment and the deployment of a great deal of human resources. Only if the exchanges share significant characteristics is the process simple, but even then capacities would have to be reviewed and alterations made.

Clearing can also exacerbate the situation. Today's clearing systems can be highly sophisticated models employing risk analysis of portfolios as a means of determining the appropriate level of margin. Others are rather more simple, applying straight initial and variation margin amounts to positions without offset. This disparity may also introduce certain obstacles that take time and money to overcome. This is even more problematical as new contracts delivered by means of the link are, almost by definition, denominated in a different base currency to that in the domestic exchange.

The sum total is that new clearing techniques have to be adopted, new banking arrangements have to be organized, and settlement and delivery of the underlying securities—where appropriate—have to be arranged as well.

At the same time, certain interests have to be acknowledged. From an exchange perspective it is important that fees, both in terms of access and on a per-transaction basis, are consistent between the two exchanges involved in the linkage. Unless fee equalization is achieved, an unwelcome result could be a migration of members from an "expensive" exchange to a "cheap" exchange, where access can be gained in equal measure, but would be carried out in a way that could undermine the continued existence of either exchange. Evidently, this is quite the antithesis of the principles supporting linkage and so equalizing the operational environment is a wholly neces- sary exercise. Failure to do so could result in an unwanted shift of business away from the domestic market, if the foreign exchange involved in the linkage provides access to the same contracts, but at a cheaper cost.

Yet, the interests of the exchange are not the only ones that need to be understood and respected. Members' interests, particularly those of brokers, also need to be acknowledged. While linkages provide an excellent means for many exchange mem- bers to access new and liquid contracts at little or marginal cost, many brokers are concerned that the short-term impact on their revenues and profits will be negative. The reason for this is that certain of their existing customers may well be able to dispense with their services when links are established, but that the compensating volume of business and income from the linkage products will take time to develop. This can be a particularly sensitive issue, but is one that principally affects the brokerage community. Other exchange members such as market makers, proprietary traders, or locals would not witness any deterioration in income as they are not reliant upon third parties.

ALTERNATIVES TO LINKAGES

In certain instances, exchanges may investigate other avenues. Electronic linkage is by no means the only method of protecting contracts from the possibility that competing exchanges will list a similar or identical contract, but it is perhaps one of the few ways in which an extension to an exchange's contract range may be achieved in the process.

One alternative is to dispense with the pursuit of gaining access to new contracts and concentrate on protecting existing contracts. This can be pursued in any one of a number of ways, but one that has been gaining in popularity is to seek greater numbers of members across a wider geographical base. This principally involves electronic exchanges, which are not constrained by the presence of a centralized exchange trading floor. Access to an electronic exchange may be gained from virtually any location, subject to adequate telecommunications and regulatory approvals. External members and the siting of terminals in foreign countries becomes a viable alternative.

However, while the benefits of creating a broader membership base, thereby achieving improved product distribution channels, can be identified, the process also involves some time and investment and assumes that there are organizations elsewhere who would be prepared to take up membership from a remote location. This involves additional cost to them and is certainly a much less attractive proposition than gaining access as an extension to an existing membership. A further complicating factor is the time needed to obtain regulatory approvals in order to pursue this strategy.

At the same time, it could be argued that this is an even less interesting and attractive package for existing members, particularly brokerage concerns. For not only does this introduce the prospect of their losing clients as foreign houses take up membership of their own, but there is no compensating benefit in terms of access to other contracts. If exchanges pursued unilateral strategies of this nature in favor of exchange linkages, the members of each exchange would also have to face the reality of having to join other exchanges themselves at great cost, to gain the access that otherwise would have been free.

Alternatively, exchanges may decide to participate in GLOBEX or investigate a means to reproduce the benefits of GLOBEX, but carried out via an alternative network provider. Again, the motivation would be to extend product distribution, but the drawback is simply that as GLOBEX is widely considered an after-hours trading system; the additional liquidity would theoretically originate from wider geographical sources and in periods during which the principal and underlying domestic markets are closed. As such, and as has been witnessed so far in the experience of GLOBEX, success would have to rely upon a spread of liquidity well outside normal market hours. This is an entirely different proposition, however, and for many exchanges membership in GLOBEX or something similar may be an unreliable basis upon which to gain greater product distribution.

Only by running the trading of products concurrently on GLOBEX in a way that would extend distribution would any real benefits accrue. This implies either the external siting of terminals or the extension of access to members of other exchanges who are themselves GLOBEX partners. This, sadly, is something of an irony. For, what this would in effect produce, would be a duplication of an exchange linkage by other means. As such, rather than becoming involved in a global trading system that only delivers real benefits if trading is carried out in normal exchange hours, it may well be simpler and more expedient to enter into more localized, less elaborate linkages in the first place.

Given that global demand for many contracts is as yet unproven, even mechanisms, such as mutual offset arrangements, are unavailable. There would be little point in extending distribution to areas where demand did not exist or was insufficient to ensure a consistent and liquid market.

Apart from the aforementioned, there are few realistic alternatives that spring readily to mind. But faced with real problems and increased competition, a policy of no action will surely not prove to be an acceptable course to take.

CONCLUSION

Competition is endemic in today's financial markets and is increasing as the rewards and stakes increase. As derivatives trading is now an intrinsic, if not an integral, part of the world's financial machinery, it is very much at the forefront of developments. Exchanges are under increasing pressure to protect their contracts from competitors and thereby secure an ongoing presence in the marketplace. But they must act decisively if they are to succeed and excel. Exchange linkage, and a linkage that is established with an electronic platform at its foundation, is perhaps the most efficient and effective way of accomplishing this strategic goal.

Perhaps the perception of linkages will improve as time passes and alternative solutions are deleted from the drawing board. There is only one really effective linkage that may be taken as a working blueprint—the one that exists between London and Stockholm. The success of this linkage is phenomenal and is a lesson on what may be achieved with time and commitment.

As in any major trend, success will breed success. The more exchanges that enter into linkages will encourage still greater numbers in the future. No single entity can afford to be isolated whether by choice or by design. Isolationism is retrogressive. The world is progressive. Denying progress could prove to be calamitous to all but the strongest and most efficient of markets and exchanges.

PART FIVE

TECHNOLOGY FOR SYNTHETIC AND DERIVATIVE PRODUCTS

CHAPTER 36

The Building Blocks of Derivatives Technology

Peter Harris
Editorial Director
Waters Information Services

THE TECHNOLOGY JUNGLE

Today, it is not unusual for major financial institutions to spend millions of pounds building new dealing rooms. Quite apart from the building infrastructure—including fail-safe electrical systems, lighting and air conditioning systems—the cost of supplying the requisite information and technology that allow dealers, if they are good, to make money is staggering.

When all the elements have been accounted for, including real-time and historical information services, telephone and intra-dealing room voice communications equipment, on-line trading networks, systems for information display, systems for entry of trades and position monitoring, and decision support systems for analysis of information, the cost per dealer position can easily reach £50,000 or more.

Moreover, unlike the building or the infrastructure services, which are likely to be adequate for decades, dealing room technology has a comparatively short lifetime. Advances in technology, the ever-increasing demands of dealers, and changes in the financial markets combine to make the average life of a dealing room no more than five years.

A SOLUTION LOOKING FOR A PROBLEM

The introduction of technology into dealing rooms has to some extent been driven by the increasing availability of financial information. The introduction of real-time price services from the likes of Reuters—which revolutionized the foreign exchange business in 1973 through the launch of its Monitor service—has changed the business of financial trading from a collection of localized gentlemen's clubs into a global industry, where one's right to compete is measured by balance sheet strength and where the availability of financial information is the facilitator. And, increasingly so, the use of technology is the factor that governs success.

Economic and political events, and regulatory changes, also act as catalysts for rapid technological change. In the run-up to deregulation in the U.K. in 1986—the so-called "Big Bang" era—banks spent fortunes on acquiring local trading firms and equipping them with the very latest technology, often without any firm idea of what benefits it would bring.

In recent years, many financial institutions have installed technology in the belief that it will reduce information services costs. Others believe that by providing dealers with decision support tools, and with risk-management systems, they will trade more profitably and expose their employer to less risk. But today, the jury is still out on whether these benefits have been uniformly achieved. In markets such as foreign exchange and equities, the instinct of an experienced dealer is likely to be a more effective weapon than a host of computer systems.

But in one area for certain—in the trading of derivatives—the value of technology is unquestionable. The pricing of derivative products would be laborious without the use of high-power PCs and workstations on which to implement Black-Scholes, Cox Ross Rubinstein, and other algorithms. Swaps trading would be an administrative nightmare if settlement systems didn't keep track of the resulting cash flows. And the back-testing of new trading methodologies would be impossible without the high-performance database engines that are now accepted as essential tools of the trade by the rocket scientists that head up specialized derivatives boutiques.

So it is this enabling technology—PCs, workstations, operating systems, databases, graphical user interfaces, and object-oriented programming—that the rest of this chapter will cover.

POWER TO THE PEOPLE: PCs, WORKSTATIONS, AND NETWORKS

Computers have been used by financial institutions for a couple of decades or more. But, in common with other industries, the cost, the physical size, complexity, and support requirements of early mainframe or minicomputer systems meant that they had to be operated by a specialized and usually centralized data processing (aka information technology or management information systems) department.

While computers were successfully introduced early on to deal with typical administrative tasks—e.g., payroll, accounts—and into settlement departments, their use by dealers in the support of trading operations was usually extremely limited.

During the late 1970s and early 1980s, the introduction of cheap and relatively easy-to-use personal microcomputers from the likes of Apple, Tandy, and Commodore began to provide opportunities for trading departments to implement systems for themselves. Citibank was an early enthusiast—implementing its Cititrader position-keeping system on Apple II hardware.

The arrival in 1980 of the IBM PC acted as a catalyst for the use of personal computers. Not only did IBM's entry into the market legitimize their use as a serious business tool, but IBM's decision to publish the specifications of the computer encouraged a host of software companies to write business programs—word processors, spreadsheets, and programming languages—to run on it.

Since 1980, the power provided by PCs has increased by several orders of magnitude. This power is typically measured by the speed at which the PC can execute programs and the amount of memory available for programs. Other measures—the size of hard-disk memory and the ability to attach peripherals—may also be used.

The sheer processing power of a PC is affected by two key criteria: the speed of the internal "clock" that determines how fast the PC's central processing unit (CPU, otherwise known as the microprocessor or "chip") executes individual instructions, and the size (or width) of the data channel employed by the PC to communicate between the CPU, the memory, and other components.

The original IBM PC—employing an Intel 8088 chip—ran at a clock speed of 4.77 megahertz and employed an eight-bit (binary digit) data channel. The later IBM PC AT ran at six and eight megahertz and used the 16-bit Intel 80286 microproccesor. PCs available today are likely to employ the Intel 80486 Pentium chips, which feature a 32-bit data channel. Clock speeds in excess of 50 megahertz are common. Overall, today's high-performance PC typically runs 100 times faster than the original PCs.

To some extent, the increasing performance of PCs has been driven by competition from what has been dubbed the workstation market. Unlike PCs, which grew up from the home computer market, workstations very much evolved by the continual downsizing of professional computers. The giant mainframe computers of the 1970s spawned departmental minicomputers during the 1980s and, now, the personal workstation of the 1990s.

During their early evolution, workstations could be differentiated from PCs in a number of ways. They typically did not utilize the Intel microprocessor, instead utilizing more powerful chips from the likes of Motorola. Also, they featured more memory than their PC counterparts, and superior graphics display capabilities.

In recent years, the increasing performance of PCs has caused them to overlap in power and functionality with many workstations. But the fastest workstations today still outperform PCs.

The development during the late 1980s of RISC—Reduced Instruction Set Computer—microprocessors gave a boost to the workstation market. The theory of RISC is that by making the microprocessor simpler—restricting the number of different basic instructions that it can perform—it is possible to execute individual instructions much faster than traditional (or CISC—Complex Instruction Set Computer) microprocessors.

RISC developments, such as the SPARC chip from Sun Microsystems or the Alpha from Digital Equipment Corp. (DEC), have enabled workstations to provide computer power hitherto available only from machines in the supercomputer bracket.

Today, the majority of financial information providers—including Reuters, Telerate, and Knight-Ridder—use PCs to deliver their services. PCs are commonplace in dealing rooms, while many of the newer rooms also feature workstations from Sun, DEC, Hewlett-Packard, or other manufacturers.

In many cases, these PCs and workstations do not operate in isolation. It is increasingly the case that they are linked together to provide a so-called distributed computing environment. The most common method of interlinking PCs and workstations is by the Local Area Network or LAN.

A LAN is a mechanism for linking computers via a very fast data communications channel. Data transmission speeds of 10 million bits per second are typical for inexpensive twisted-pair or coaxial LANs. Speeds of 10 times that figure can be achieved with fiber-optic LANs. One drawback of achieving these high speeds is that the networks cannot be geographically dispersed (hence their name). In general, LANs provide data communications within departments, or perhaps buildings.

The two most common type of LANs found in dealing rooms are Ethernet and Token Ring. An Ethernet LAN consists of a single wire, to which all computers are connected. A special adaptor, which fits into each PC or workstation, is used to connect to the Ethernet. Thus, Ethernet provides a simple method of linking computers, and it provides relatively high data transfer speeds.

Token Ring, which is common in IBM environments, provides similar functionality. With Token Ring, all computers are daisy-chained together, with the last computer connected to the first, so as to form a ring. While physically implementing a Token Ring network is more difficult than for Ethernet, Token Ring generally copes better with high volumes of data traffic, and is more resilient to cable breaks, when compared to Ethernet.

LANs enable PCs (or workstations) to access data stored on one another and to pass messages from one PC to another or to a group of other PCs. In many cases, LANs are used to provide access to common resources, such as a computer with large disk capacity that acts as a repository for data files. These so-called file servers—and other servers that provide networked, multi-user, access to applications or peripherals (such as printers)—are essential components of dealing room LANs.

Typical dealing room applications for LANs include: the distribution of real-time financial information, where a server might receive a feed of prices and distribute them to PCs; the capture of deals, where deals might be entered by dealers into individual PCs for transfer to and storage on a file server; and access to central applications, such as an options pricing tool.

LEVERAGING PC POWER: OPERATING SYSTEMS AND GUIs

As PCs and workstations have evolved, so too have the key software components that run on them. This so-called operating software has grown in complexity—sometimes lagging, sometimes leading the development of hardware. This increasing complexity has been directed toward a number of goals: the ability to effectively utilize large amounts of memory; the ability to run several applications at one time; the ability to operate within network environments; and the ease with which users, who may not be computer literate, can operate the computer.

The most fundamental software component of any computer is the main control program, or operating system. The operating system is responsible for managing the computer's resources and provides a means by which a user can control and make use of them.

In the world of PCs and workstations, two operating systems have dominated: Microsoft's DOS, which has become the standard for PCs; and Unix, an operating system invented at AT&T's Bell Labs, which has been adopted by just about all of the workstation manufacturers.

When IBM introduced the IBM PC, it provided DOS as an operating system. Written by Microsoft, DOS was also made available for manufacturers that built IBM PC clones. Because it was easy to implement, and at the time provided reasonable functionality, DOS established itself as a standard for PCs, quickly defeating other hopefuls, such as Digital Research's CP/M.

DOS provides fairly basic facilities, and to be honest, no longer on its own adequately makes efficient use of the facilities provided by high-power PCs (80386-based and later). Its main user interface is still command-based—e.g., typing "dir" displays a list of files on the hard disk—and its ability to use the large amounts of memory available on newer PCs is also limited. Moreover it does not provide multitasking facilities—i.e., it may run only one program at a time.

Recent versions of DOS have improved its functionality—a menu-driven command interface (that can be controlled with a mouse pointing device as well as a keyboard) was introduced in Version 4, while Version 6 added facilities designed to utilize memory in a more efficient manner.

The trend over the last couple of years has been to extend DOS by running Microsoft's Windows program in conjunction with it. Windows provides basic multitasking facilities, makes use of all available memory, and has an easy to use Graphical User Interface (GUI).

As well as Windows, another DOS-compatible operating system—OS/2—has also been introduced. Originally developed by Microsoft in conjunction with IBM, OS/2 extends DOS by providing similar features to Windows. Because of OS/2's overlap with Windows, Microsoft pulled out of the project and the two products now compete with each other. But despite being universally recognized as a technically sound product, OS/2 hasn't sold nearly as well as Windows.

While DOS was becoming the standard for PCs, so Unix was carving out the same status for itself in the workstation market. Unix's acceptance was to a large extent due to the generous licensing terms available from its owner—AT&T. But it was also easy to adapt to run on different computers. Only a small portion of Unix—the kernel—is written in the machine code of an individual machine. The rest of it is written in a high-level language, known as "C." Thus to adapt —or port—Unix to a new computer requires a minimum of effort. To computer companies with a principal expertise in hardware, not software, the availability of Unix was most welcome.

One major drawback of Unix, however, is that over the years, many different versions of it have evolved. During the late 1980s the two key versions were AT&T's System V and the Berkeley Standard Distribution V4.2. Many workstation manufacturers, and other software developers, took these basic offerings and added to them. The result in the 1990s is a host of different versions of Unix.

While Unix pundits continue to promote Unix as a standard operating system, the availability of different versions does little to support that claim. And while there have been efforts to develop standard versions of Unix, these have been thwarted by vested commercial interests. The formation a few years ago of the Open Software Foundation (OSF), comprising IBM, DEC, and H-P to build a standard Unix was countered by the formation of Unix International, led by Sun Microsystems. Today, it looks as though the existence of these two bodies will result in there being at least two versions of Unix for some time to come.

Unix has also been criticized as difficult to use. Like DOS it features a command-driven user interface. Unlike DOS, Unix commands are often arcane, giving rise to the accusation that entering virtually any combination of three letters will cause Unix to perform some function.

Despite these shortcomings, Unix's multitasking and memory facilities, and the compatibility of its design with RISC-based processors, has made it the operating system of choice for the workstation market.

Microsoft's recently announced Windows NT (for New Technology) operating system aims to knock Unix from its leading position. Featuring the same level of multitasking, networking, and memory management features as Unix, and offering a user interface identical to Windows, NT is certain to provide serious competition to Unix.

Both DOS and Unix suffered initially from poor user interfaces. But the emergence of GUIs have made PCs and workstations much simpler to use. GUIs typically allow commands to be executed by presenting users with either a menu of options or perhaps an icon, which graphically illustrates the function required. And the physical computer screen can be split into multiple windows, each one controlling a single application. User commands are entered typically via a mouse,with the keyboard reserved for text input.

As with operating systems, a number of different GUIs have developed. For DOS, Windows is by far the market leader. OS/2 has its own GUI, known as Program Manager, which is very similar to Windows.

In the Unix environment, most GUIs have adopted a common windowing program—X Windows—as their base. X Windows was developed at Massachusetts Institute of Technology in 1984 and provides basic window display and control facilities that applications can make use of.

Of particular value is that X Windows handles the vagaries of different types of screen hardware, so that applications programs need not be concerned with the hardware environment in which they run. Another important feature is that X Windows operates in a network environment, so that an application on one computer can control a display on a screen attached to another computer.

But while X Windows provides windowing facilities—the ability to open and close windows, to move them, and to copy data from one to another—it does not define the actual "look and feel" or layout of the screen, or the actions to be performed by user commands. So it is not in itself a GUI. Instead, it is the GUIs that are based on X Windows that provide these features.

As with Unix, the rival OSF and Unix International camps have competed in the development of GUIs, although the OSF's Motif GUI has effectively won the battle against OpenLook from Unix International. In particular, Sun's new Solaris version of Unix has adopted Motif as its GUI.

BRINGING IT ALL TOGETHER: DEALING ROOM NETWORKS

The advent of PCs, workstations, LANs, operating systems, and GUIs has had a tremendous impact on systems installed in dealing rooms. In particular, the rise of so-called digital distribution systems based on this technology has caused a revolution

Exhibit 1.   Video Service Delivery

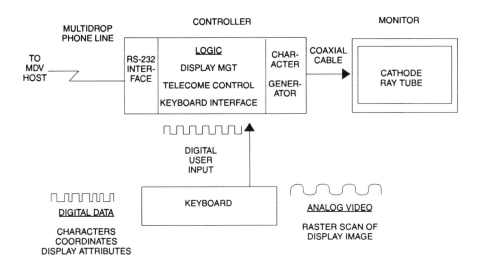

in the supply of financial information, and has enabled such information to be integrated into application developments.

Before the availability of digital distribution systems, dealing rooms received financial information via stand-alone video terminals provided by the information vendors. Exhibit 1 shows a typical stand-alone video terminal setup, where information is supplied via a communication line to a terminal controller, which supports one or more terminals, each consisting of a screen and a keyboard.

These terminals typically provided basic page display capabilities, allowing dealers to view information that was formatted by the information vendor. No facilities to manipulate or reformat the information were available. And each terminal required its own keyboard and operated according to its own set of commands. For dealers requiring access to several information services, the physical number of screens and keyboards that ate into desk space and the requirement to learn how to use different services were major obstacles to overcome.

The terminal clutter—known in the U.S. as desktop real estate—problem was partially overcome by the invention of the video switch, which acts as a front end to information service terminal controllers, allowing a single keyboard to be switched between multiple information services. As well as switching the keyboard, video switches also allow the screens of information service terminals to be switched between one of a number of general-purpose screens mounted at each dealer position. Thus, a dealer could choose to place Reuters information on screen one, Telerate on screen two, and so forth.

Exhibit 2.   Video Switch Installation

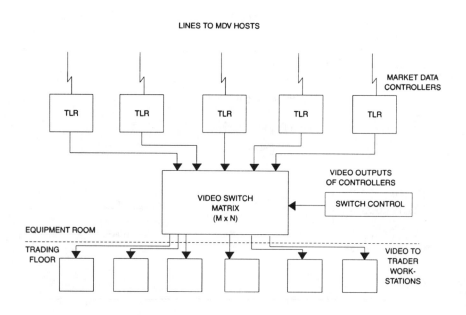

Exhibit 2 shows a typical video switch installation. During the early 1980s, video switch manufacturers - Micrognosis Inc. and Rich Inc. in the U.S. and International Data Media in the U.K.—grew rapidly as financial service companies attempted to rationalize the delivery of information to their dealers. Rich was acquired by Reuters in 1985.

While video switches go some way toward solving the information management problem, they do not allow information to be manipulated or reformatted. And they don't solve the problem of different command structures. Thus, the digital data distribution system was born.

Digital data distribution systems can solve both problems—and the terminal clutter issue—by receiving information in its raw form and distributing it via a LAN to PCs and workstations. Rather than installing terminal controllers, the information vendor provides a datafeed of information that may be fed directly into a user's computer, which typically forms part of the data distribution system (usually known as the datafeed gateway or server).

Over the last few years, many information vendors have begun to offer digital datafeeds. Reuters offers its Selectfeed and Marketfeed 2000 services; Telerate has its Telerate Digital Page Feed (TDPF); and Knight-Ridder has its Digital Data Feed (DDF).

Exhibit 3.   Digital Distribution System at Bankers Trust, London

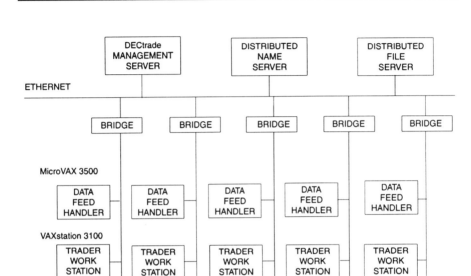

Typically, a digital data distribution system will connect to several digital datafeeds, as shown in Exhibit 3. As well as datafeed gateways, the system will also likely include servers providing value-added functions, such as composite paging, or perhaps an options pricing facility.

Users access information and value-added servers via workstations and PCs. Sometimes a digital distribution system is accessed via a video switch (see Exhibit 4). This arrangement allows services that are available only in video format, such as Reuters Dealing 2000 or Bloomberg, to be displayed alongside digitally delivered services.

Today, many companies provide digital data distribution systems, although only a few can be considered as worthy global players. These include Reuters, with Triarch 2000; Teknekron Software Systems' Teknekron Information Bus; and DEC's DEC-trade.

But digital data distribution systems allow much more than just the display of information. The *raison d'être* for such systems is that they allow computer processing to be carried out on financial data. Applications—provided either by the distribution

Exhibit 4. Digital/Video Hybrid Distribution

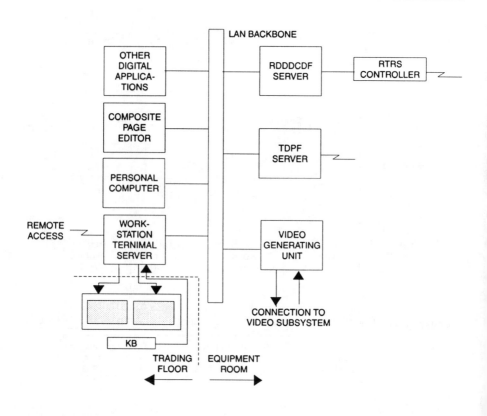

system vendor, by a third-party software house, or by user firms—access raw data by making use of an applications programming interface (API).

The APIs provided by distribution systems vendors differ in detail, although they all offer the same basic facilities: the ability to receive financial information in real time and the ability to provide information to other applications. Applications that receive information are often referred to as Consumer or Sink applications, while those that provide information are termed Providers, Publishers, or Sources. Reuters adopts the Source and Sink terminology for its API, which it calls its Source/Sink Library (SSL).

Typical uses of an API might include: a supplier of a charting package might adapt it to use the Sink element of Reuters' SSL so that it can make use of any data carried on Reuters' Triarch; a real-time spreadsheet might use the Sink features to receive real-time data to calculate foreign exchange cross rates, and then might use the Source facility to make those rates available to other applications; and an information provider might use the Source API to build an interface between its digital feed and Triarch.

KEEPING INFORMATION IN ITS PLACE: DATABASES

More often than not, some form of database application will make use of an API allowing it to be integrated within a digital data distribution system. A database is an organized collection of items of data. An address book is a simple example. A computer-based employee database is likely to be found at most companies, for payroll processing.

Within dealing room environments, databases are used for several purposes, and the types of database vary accordingly. Perhaps the most common form of database is known as a historical or time-series database. These are used to store a historical sequence of price data—maybe including individual trade prices or high/low prices for each day—and are used as the basis for technical analysis and for back-testing of trading models.

Although information vendors offer services that include technical analysis—offerings from Reuters, Telerate, Knight-Ridder, FutureSource, CQG, and many others are common sights in the dealing room—the drawback of these services is that users are limited to the analyses provided by the vendor. There is usually no—or very limited—ability for users to develop their own trading strategies. Also they are expensive, compared to straightforward information services.

Since digital data distribution systems receive data in real time, it makes sense for them to store that data so that it may be reused in a manner required by the user, and with no extra cost.

Another use for databases in the dealing room is for storing post-trade information, which forms the basis of risk-management systems. Typically, the data stored will include an instrument identifier, a counterparty name, a trade price, and a trade size. And databases may also be used for storing client information—for example, to support a bank in the sales and marketing of services to corporations.

Because of the large volumes of data and the high transaction rates involved in handling real-time information—Reuters' Marketfeed 2000 peaks at over 200 updates per second—the design of databases used for dealing room applications has historically been bespoke. By designing a database for a specific function, and by making use of specific characteristics of microprocessors, operating systems, and hardware (especially disk memory), it has been possible to build databases optimized for speed.

During the last few years, however, commercial general-purpose database packages have increased their presence in the dealing room. Their infiltration has owed as much to the increased processing speed of workstation hardware as it has to any specific dealing room functionality or efficiency enhancements.

Database offerings like Sybase, Oracle, and Informix are now commonly used to underpin risk-management systems development. These databases are so-called relational databases. In a relational database, information is organized into tables, with each column representing one element of data. The database enables relationships to be established between tables, allowing information to be extracted or combined.

Access to relational databases is via a query language, with one in particular—Structured Query Language (SQL) being a de facto standard. The benefits of installing a database compatible with SQL are numerous. Database independence is one—if two databases both adhere to SQL as a query language, data may be transferred between them with ease, or one database can be replaced by the other should that be required.

Network transparency is also a feature of SQL. When a workstation-based application issues SQL queries to a database, it need not know where the database physically resides. It could be present on the same workstation, or it could be on a file server, or even a mainframe computer. Moreover, SQL-compatible databases are generally built to conform to a Client/Server model, which means that search queries are actually processed by the computer that hosts the database, minimizing network traffic.

Data source transparency is a feature of another database concept—the data dictionary. Data dictionaries provide a naming mechanism for items of data or other objects, which includes data held in databases, applications, or other system resources.

Within a data dictionary, an object name is given a definition of where the object is located and how it should be accessed and used. These definitions may be set up and amended with ease, decoupling applications from the physical sources of data.

An example of this might be the price of a spot foreign exchange rate. "Cable"— the U.S. dollar/sterling spot rate could be defined as being derived from a Reuters datafeed. An application, when retrieving the rate, would specify "Cable" as the name of the item in its API call. The data dictionary would map that name onto the physical source, and retrieve the data from Reuters. If it is decided to change the source of the data—to Knight-Ridder, for example—it is only necessary to amend the data diction- ary definition. The application requires no modification.

MAKING IT EASY: TOOL KITS AND OBJECT ORIENTATION

The API concept introduced earlier in this chapter goes some way toward making it easy for applications to gain access to data, whether it be real-time or from databases. However, many distribution system vendors also provide tools that make the devel- opment of applications even easier.

These so-called tool-kit applications—which include data dictionaries—offer a wide variety of facilities, including those listed below.

Page shredders are applications that are used to extract individual data items from formatted pages supplied by information vendors. Since much of the data supplied by vendors—even via digital feeds—is in a formatted form suitable for viewing, individual items need to be extracted before they can be used in applications or referenced by a data dictionary.

A page shredder uses X-Y page coordinates to extract prices and often performs some initial processing so as to provide data in a normalized form. For example, the same bid/ask price of an instrument might be shown on a page in various forms: "1.5125/1.5135" or "1.5125/35" or "1.5125-35." Typically, it is the page shredder that will parse the text within the page and extract the two individual prices.

A time-series database is another commonly included tool, and allows users to define which instruments they wish to be held in the database, the frequency of update (tick-by-tick, every minute, every hour, etc.) and whether end-of-day highs/lows should be calculated. Archiving instructions might also be specified.

The real-time spreadsheet is another common tool-kit application, and is either a proprietary spreadsheet built by the distribution system vendor or a third-party product to which real-time links have been added. Reuters offers its own real-time spreadsheet as part of Triarch, although it also provides links to other products, such as Informix' Wingz or Leading Market Technologies' Expo.

All of these applications may be used in conjunction with user-developed programs. While they might not always offer absolutely ideal functionality, their availability makes the rapid development of applications by users all the more possible.

Rapid development of applications—and their ease of modification—is the goal of another programming methodology, known as Object Oriented Programming (OOP).

OOP is perhaps the current state of the art in software development. The concept of OOP is simple. Complex programs are broken down into modules of code known as objects, each of which performs a well-defined function and has the ability to interface with other objects via an equally well-defined interface.

Programs are built by combining objects. Individual objects may be used in more than one program, so that once a few programs have been written, the process of writing another can be speeded up by reusing objects previously defined.

Objects can either be relatively simple—perhaps controlling the display of a dialog box on a user input screen—or complex, such an object to price a swap. Once defined, the swap-pricing object can be used in as many applications as necessary.

While the concept of OOP is simple, the practice—today—is not. To write efficient OOP applications requires developers to design their programs in a different way than they would for traditional programming methodologies. Subsequently, there is a learning curve—put at around six months—for most developers when they first adopt OOP. Thereafter, however, development timescales can be reduced significantly by using OOP techniques.

Derivatives software suppliers and end users have embraced OOP because it offers fast development timescales. Since new derivative instruments can be created quickly and often have a short "shelf life," the ability of technology to match the business timescales is an important benefit.

A number of systems suppliers, such as Infinity International Financial Technology and Renaissance Software, have developed their systems using OOP techniques, and actively promote OOP as being relevant to the derivatives trading business.

CHAPTER 37

Operational Challenges of Derivative Products

Steven A. Babus
Vice President and
Head of Internal Management Consulting
Union Bank of Switzerland North America Region

MARKET PARTICIPANTS

The financial markets have traditionally classified derivatives market (futures/options) participants as either hedgers or speculators. These categories are also applicable to the broader over-the-counter derivatives markets. However, two additional categories of participants are integral to the market—those buying instruments to minimize their costs of funds, tax liabilities, or associated clearance and settlement costs; and those engineering the products to facilitate these objectives (see Exhibit 1).

As in other markets, hedgers are largely engaged in controlling downside risk of assets under management or in filling gaps in the match between assets and liabilities. These gaps may be of either term or currency. Speculators take positions in anticipation of market movements or to take advantage of pricing irregularities.

The additional market participants are better understood by examining examples of their business objectives.

Obtaining Cheap Funds

An example of this first objective is a chief financial officer or corporate treasurer issuing a floating-rate and foreign-denominated fixed-income instrument and simultaneously entering into a swap agreement with the underwriter, resulting in fixed U.S.-dollar payments lower than if a fixed-rate U.S.-dollar fixed-income instrument had been originally issued. In this case the interest rate swap is providing a vehicle to take advantage of market inefficiencies and coincidentally smooth out these inefficiencies by providing intermarket liquidity.

Exhibit 1.   OTC Derivative Market Participants

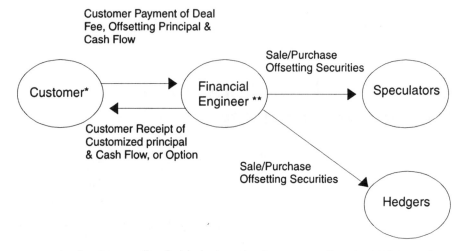

Customer Payment of Deal
Fee, Offsetting Principal &
Cash Flow

Sale/Purchase
Offsetting Securities

Customer*

Financial
Engineer **

Speculators

Customer Receipt of
Customized principal
& Cash Flow, or Option

Sale/Purchase
Offsetting Securities

Hedgers

*   Minimizing costs of funds, tax liabilities, or associated clearance and settlement costs.
**   Operate as market intermediaries; improving overall market efficiency, taking a spread, and
      according to their models, remaining essentially flat.

Minimizing Tax Obligations

The second objective, minimizing tax obligations, often entails a hedging strategy to defer realizing gains on security positions that are no longer deemed appropriate or desirable holdings. Rather than liquidating a position and incurring taxes on realized gains, a synthetic security can be purchased to meet the new investment strategy and/or protect existing holdings from downside risk. Other times, synthetic securities are purchased or sold to take advantage of the differing tax policies and treatments applied to different legal structures in the various countries in which a business entity may conduct business.

Avoiding Transaction Costs

An example of the third objective is a fund manager who wishes to rebalance his or her portfolio holdings and rather than incurring the transaction costs of selling the securities, enters into an equity floor for this period of anticipated poor market performance, whereby payments are triggered if and when the market or custom index penetrates the defined floor index value. The anticipated transaction costs are normally just a component in the decision to enter into such a hedge transaction.

"Rocket Scientists"

The last group of market participants, the financial engineers, are to many the most interesting. These "rocket scientists," or quantitative analysts, create derivative or synthetic security instruments with special performance characteristics. These instruments may be developed to satisfy a specific customer need or may result from creative "deal" structuring by the analysts and derivative sales groups. The instrument characteristics are typically related to some "unique" funding, hedging, or investment strategy. By engineering instruments that satisfy these strategies, a fee or premium is captured, usually in the form of some basis point spread. This is effectively compensation for the product manufacturing service and for taking the risk of providing "liquidity" between markets. The size of the premium is normally related to the risk and inefficiencies of the quoted markets as calculated by the engineer's model, adjusted for competitive factors. The size of the spread has historically been larger for unique instruments and declines as the form of derivative instrument reaches maturity in the marketplace.

These predictive models do fail in their predictive capabilities, transforming these sophisticated hedgers into somewhat unprepared speculators. This is because most models rely on past performance to project likely future occurrences. The performance of portfolio insurance strategies in the 1987 crash is a classic example of model failure.

The nature of an organization's derivatives market participation largely determines both the types of operational and system problems encountered, and the appropriate treatment for measuring derivative instrument performance.

ACCOUNTING GUIDELINES

Before we discuss the operational, system, and performance measurement issues related to trading and investing in derivative instruments, it is appropriate to touch upon some of the accounting guidelines developed to handle these instruments. This discussion, however, is in no way intended to be a comprehensive treatment of these guidelines.

FASB (Financial Accounting Standards Board) 105 requires the disclosure of concentrations in credit risk associated with off-balance-sheet instruments. This includes concentration both by product type and by counterparty.

Credit risk is defined as the maximum potential loss the company faces due to possible nonperformance by obligors and counterparties. This represents the maximum loss or replacement cost of in-the-money financial instruments.

FASB 80 enables the profit and loss associated with a futures contract entered into as a hedge to be accrued over the life of the associated asset or liability, rather than being included as an adjusted value to the asset or liability.

The FASB Emerging Issues Task Force made the following recommendations to address complex options strategies:

- *90-17*—Hedge accounting should be used for purchased foreign currency options with little or no intrinsic value at the time they are designated a hedge.

- *91-4*—Hedge accounting should also be used for financial instruments other than purchased options with little or no intrinsic value at the time they are designated a hedge.

These recommendations were responded to with the following:

■ *SEC Opinion Letter*—You cannot defer realized or unrealized gains or losses arising from complex options or similar transactions with respect to anticipated transactions.

FASB 39 provides the legal right to offset assets and liabilities with a particular counterparty for balance sheet reporting. This requires that a legal agreement exist between the two counterparties that supports this netting (e.g., ISDA agreement). This netting must be consistently applied to be an acceptable practice.

FASB 115 requires that dealers in securities (broadly defined to include most derivatives) use mark-to-market accounting. Financial institutions that practice the amortized cost method for investments need to segregate their security holdings into three categories: held to maturity (HTM), trading securities, and available-for-sale securities (AFS). Unrealized gains in HTM must be amortized into P&L, trading securities must be marked to market directly into P&L, and AFS unrealized gains and losses are excluded from earnings and reported as a net amount in shareholders' equity until realized. All dividends and interest, and amortization of premium and discount arising at acquisition, are included in earnings.

FASB 107 requires the disclosure of fair value of all financial instruments on financial statements. This required valuation of derivative instruments is a challenge to all market participants and is discussed in the following section.

PRICING THE INSTRUMENTS

To determine this fair market value, two alternatives are available: external pricing sources and internal estimation techniques.

External Pricing Sources

External pricing sources come in a variety of forms, varying from public exchange markets (CBOE, AMEX, CBT), and quotation services (Reuters, Telerate, Bloomberg) to pricing services (S&P) and valuation specialists/appraisers (Big Six accounting firms). Listed options and futures securities can be readily priced using publicly disseminated market data. Less liquid securities that are available on quotation service pricing pages should be priced utilizing these prices either as a control check for independently developed pricing models or in their absence, as a reasonable indicator of the current market value.

PRICING MODELS

The least liquid securities are far more difficult to price and require special pricing models. These models vary a great deal in sophistication, which is normally related to the role of the market participant. Active product originators, or market makers, will tend to have the most sophisticated models. However, sophisticated asset managers who actively purchase derivative securities also commonly maintain highly engineered pricing models. Less-active market participants usually calculate security valuations through less-sophisticated analytics resident in spreadsheet models.

Almost any model will require significant modifications to produce a market value for more tailored and customized instruments. Those institutions in the business of derivative product origination, trading, and marketing are more likely to have the necessary in-house resources to allocate to this activity on an ongoing basis. These resources include dedicated quantitative analysts, extremely flexible analytical software, and a robust technology and data infrastructure.

The major internal estimation techniques and model types fall into three basic categories: the application of matrix pricing techniques, the calculation of the net present value of an instrument's expected cash flows, and a variety of option pricing models. Both net present value and option pricing techniques require methods for calculating market or security volatilities, and/or projecting zero yield curves under various interest rate scenarios.

Matrix Pricing Models

Matrix pricing models utilize a set of security characteristics (e.g., duration, yield to call, credit rating) to calculate a basis spread from a series of selected benchmark securities. These are either actively quoted standard benchmark securities (available on Bloomberg, Telerate, or Reuters) or a set of internally held and quoted comparable securities. In major broker dealers these benchmarks are priced on a daily basis by the traders on the appropriate trading desk. Other institutions call around the street and receive prices for their benchmarks surreptitiously or as part of ongoing customer service from the broker/dealer market makers.

Net Present Value Models

Net present value models are also fairly straightforward in concept. A zero-based yield curve (one per currency under consideration) is constructed, using current market prices. The front part of the yield curve is generated using money market rates; the middle part of the curve (generally 3 months to 2 1/2 years) using rate futures; and the later part of the curve (out to 30 years) is generated using the current market swap rates. Once the zero curve is created, it is used for calculating expected cash flows for floating-rate, fixed-income instruments or sides of swap contracts. For equity derivatives these flows also reflect the anticipated dividend stream of the component securities within the index. These cash flows are then discounted to a net present value and totaled to determine a market value of the instrument or swap side.

Option Pricing Models

Option pricing models come in many different forms. Some of the more common are: Modified Black-Scholes; Modified Cox, Ross, and Rubenstein; binomial models; differential equations; and Monte Carlo simulations. The most frequent modifications—but certainly not only modifications to Black-Scholes or Cox, Ross, and

Rubenstein—are attempts to adjust volatility and or adapt the models to other types of options, such as European (exercisable only on expiration date) or Asian (average value over life of contract) options. Detailed descriptions of these models are inappropriate here, as the mathematical underpinning required is a significantly different discussion than the one intended. Option pricing models typically contain three components: the construction of a volatility, or simulated movement, of the underlying index or interest rate over the life of the security; calculation of the remaining time value of the security; and determination of the securities' current and projected in-the-money values, discounted to the present.

PRICING VALIDATION OF UNREALIZED P&L

Periodic External Pricing

A pricing alternative often used for control purposes is to have a pricing service or valuation specialist periodically (quarterly or annually, depending on control needs) mark to market your holdings. This is normally done to provide some assurance to executive management that the prices used for calculating unrealized P&L or portfolio performance are not significantly different from those produced by the standard in-house pricing methodology.

Daily Independent Pricing

Although uncommon, some organizations have their derivative portfolios independently marked to market on a daily basis. This can be accomplished through the use of off-the-shelf vendor software run in-house or by applying an independently developed or maintained pricing model. This model may be provided by an external vendor (e.g., a Big Six accounting firm) or, as mentioned, may be part of a commercially available software package supported within the treasury, controller, or internal audit function. Unfortunately, recently engineered derivatives will probably not be supported by either alternative.

Consortium Pricing/Model Assessment

A somewhat different approach is to participate in consortiums organized by the Big Six, where each member of the consortium applies its analytical model(s) to a small set of deals contributed by each consortium participant. The results are distributed to participants without identifying the consortium member associated with each set of pricing results. This provides a good mechanism to check for the overall reasonableness of each member's pricing models. The identities associated with the pricing results are not known—to ensure consortium participation and to prevent participants from utilizing this information for competitive advantage.

Prior Release of In-house Model

Another alternative for control pricing is to keep a copy of the last formally released production analytical pricing model and to utilize its pricing output as a control mechanism to ensure that recent model modifications have not corrupted its pricing logic. This is a sensible approach, as pricing models are frequently changed "on the fly" in support of engineering new financial instruments or in support of a unique deal. This rapid and frequent code modification, although necessary to support the financial engineering process, has an associated high degree of risk in introducing unintended software changes that could affect security pricing. This is less of a concern in object-oriented software environments.

External Benchmark/Portfolio Pricing

A number of sizable "buy-side" customers contract with major broker dealers to run their portfolios through the broker's analytical models for purposes of marking to market. The downside to this approach is that the models used to engineer many of the instruments are the same ones used later to mark them to market. Another alternative used is to select a set of benchmark securities and to call around the street to receive a current bid price for structuring a similar deal. These prices are then compared to those produced by the in-house analytical model for control purposes. Consistent pricing differences are less suspect than erratic pricing outcomes. Other institutions periodically obtain market bid prices for their highly illiquid and/or custom engineered security instruments. These quotes usually represent the liquidation price, and as such provide only an indication of market value for instruments to be held to maturity.

Table 1 summarizes the strengths and weaknesses of these methods of assessing unrealized P&L.

PERFORMANCE MEASUREMENT OF DERIVATIVE INSTRUMENTS

It is extremely important to establish performance objectives for a portfolio or portfolio component that will be using derivative instruments for hedging or performance enhancement purposes. This is necessary to supply a benchmark for measuring the rate of return, both including and excluding these hedging or performance enhancement programs. The cost of these hedging and indexing programs (but not performance enhancement) are often calculated separately and excluded from the basis for calculating rates of return for the other portfolio components that may be effectively using these hedges.

The performance of securities purchased for hedging purposes is not a significant consideration because these are often written down to zero at purchase and are liquidated only if there is a significant change in strategy or the hedge must be activated and the gain realized. As long as the hedging instruments are meeting their desired hedging or asset/liability matching objectives it is not a concern if they are out-of-the-money. It is important that the credit risk associated with counterparty default for in-the-money securities be quantified through periodic quotes for security replacement from other broker-dealers.

Calculating portfolio performance, including exotic securities, requires a mechanism for pricing these instruments. We have just completed a fairly detailed discussion of approaches to pricing these securities. However, the following is worth

Table 1.   Methods of Assessing Unrealized P&L

Methods of Assessing Unrealized P&L	Strengths	Weaknesses
Periodic external pricing	Standard and cost-effective operating approach	Quarterly assessment may miss model flaw and significant market move
Daily independent pricing	Provides true independent marking	Additional software license and operating environment necessary. Will not price latest and greatest derivatives
Consortium pricing/ model assessment	Provides validation of pricing model vs. industry and its "best practices"	Only prices small number of deals on an infrequent basis. Overhead incurred pricing industry deal suite
Prior release of in-house model	Detects corruption of existing pricing model components	Requires duplicate production environment to run last release of software
External bench-mark/portfolio pricing	Daily pricing quickly identifies model discrepancies	Pricing broker may use same model that engineered product

mentioning: Obtaining external quotes is often the most viable approach for pricing illiquid instruments, unless you have access to sophisticated pricing models. Quotes should be obtained from multiple sources, if at all possible. A reasonableness check should be applied to these prices before applying them for performance calculations. Quotes obtained from security issuers are likely to represent their buy-back price and as such, accurately reflect a liquidation price. This price is likely to be deemed too low for "true" mark to market, especially if the securities will be held to maturity.

Bifurcated or hybrid securities (securities having characteristics of two or more basic security types (e.g., fixed-income and option) are most easily priced by partitioning these complex instruments into their components. This is especially true for in-house pricing purposes. Each component is priced independently using the appropriate pricing vehicle and models. The core or fundamental component of the instrument can usually be priced using matrices of comparables, whereas the conversion, indexing, or barrier features must be modeled separately. An example of a security well-suited to this pricing approach is a fixed-income instrument paying a fixed rate unless the current yield of some benchmark (e.g., 90-day LIBOR) exceeds a threshold (barrier). At that time the yield increases according to a predefined ratio. Here the fixed-income core component could be priced versus a matrix of comparably rated, yielding, and duration fixed-income instruments. The option against LIBOR should be priced separately by an in-house option pricing model. One must be careful when applying this approach because in certain circumstances, the values of the components may offset each other, making the value of the sum of the parts greater than the whole.

Other points that should be kept in mind are:

- The present value of cash flows should also be adjusted to reflect the current collateral used to enhance creditworthiness and the current credit rating of the counterparty (or issues).

- Special security features that were engineered for the security buyer have an associated high purchase cost, which should be determined and retained at the time of purchase (spread over vanilla).

- Incremental feature costs have a time value, which decays as the instrument approaches maturity or expiration and should be amortized over the life of the instrument. This applies for both in- and out-of-the-money security features. In addition, instruments with in-the-money features should be priced to reflect their current market redemption price or replacement values.

STRATEGY PRICING

Riskless arbitrage investment strategies using derivative instruments pose a different problem. Standard accounting principles require a mark to market of both sides of the "riskless" and fully hedged strategy. Over the life of the strategy, this can result in wide monthly shifts in the unrealized P&L, when in fact the positions are essentially flat. Trading management normally chooses to avoid acknowledging the unrealized gains but is not in a position to do this for occurrences of monthly unrealized losses. This is more than a management reporting problem because the monthly "gains" result in additional cost of carry, and the monthly "losses" result in senior management unnecessarily allocating capital as loss reserves.

SYSTEM SUPPORT ISSUES

The more recently engineered the financial instrument, the less likely the in-house developed or commercially available operational support software will be able to clearly accommodate the instrument. This lag time in system support often exceeds a year for those instruments embraced by the marketplace (e.g., swaptions, equity index swaps). For those newly engineered derivatives that gain no market acceptance, system support in most cases is never forthcoming.

The lag in some portfolio management and back office processing systems often extends out to two or three years. This is the root cause of many operational problems as securities are "force processed" through the operational stream to the firm's books and records (e.g., swaps or CMOs being entered as loans and deposits). At times, dummy security numbers, or cusips, are used. In many cases the system changes ultimately incorporated are not flexible enough to handle variations of the instruments due to overall limitations of the software environment. This occurs more commonly in older, less-structured, non-table-driven software.

This lag time varies considerably, based on the software's flexibility, the development organization's responsiveness and overall backlog of enhancement requests. In the case of service bureaus and software package vendors, the responsiveness depends on the pressure exerted by potential and existing customers in satisfying marketwide requirements (e.g., complying with new regulations), or the willingness of an individual customer to bear the full costs of the required enhancements. Release schedules are often planned well in advance, making it difficult for software vendors with large installed bases to respond to individual firm requests in a timely manner.

The software's data structures normally have trouble accepting and storing "peculiar" security characteristics, especially in a manner that will enable it to utilize the information in its core operational, pricing, or accounting functions (e.g., accruing interest). In many cases, these core functions require significant software modifications to handle new variations on accretion or amortization, indexes, triggers, step functions, barriers and ladders, resets, and principal repayment.

PC Spreadsheet/Workstation Tracking

As a result, these instruments are frequently carried and tracked on PC spreadsheets or workstation models. This creates a whole set of control, support, and reconciliation issues. Daily backups and rigorous off-site storage is required, as is the tight control of system access. Nightly downloads or uploads from the firm's core systems may be required to facilitate daily reconciliations. Regular journal entries may be necessary to adjust for differences in interest accruals or principal repayment, or to book the prior day's activity. These inter-system reconciliations can take many forms, from reconciling the in-house SWAP operational system to the asset/liability matching facility, to reconciling the portfolio management system to the accounting or external custodian system.

Control Issues

The inability of core operational systems to maintain derivative securities with adequate data integrity creates other control issues. Credit and risk management are being strongly focused upon by virtually every financial institution worldwide. The desire to be able to centrally monitor firm-wide counterparty, FX, basis, country, or market risk across all products and geographical locations is universal. What most of the projects currently under way to achieve this objective fail to address is that the very products containing the greatest amount of uncertainty and risk are those products most recently engineered. These products are likely to contain characteristics or calculations that cannot be readily accommodated by these planned risk management facilities.

Another critical "nonoperational" control issue is monitoring position limits and the unrealized P&L of open derivative positions. As we have already discussed, there is a significant challenge in valuing open positions in highly customized and illiquid securities. However, it is worth mentioning that an extremely large number of financial institutions have had to absorb significant losses on derivative positions (IOs, POs, swaptions) because they were kept outside the normal processing stream. A discussion of suitable risk management practices and control procedures is outside the scope of this chapter.

Instrument Maturity

It is important to understand that the window of greatest market opportunity in a newly engineered product depends to a large extent on the inability of the market to accurately price the said securities. This allows the product engineers to capture a wide spread based on the performance characteristics projected by the models and used to engineer the product, and overall market inefficiency and illiquidity. Once the product is readily available from multiple market participants, the spread on the new product has already narrowed. By the time commercially available software can price the product, it has become a commodity with extremely narrow spreads. The market has reached an improved and more mature level of efficiency and liquidity.

INSTRUMENT SPECIFIC OPERATIONAL ISSUES

CMOs (Collateralized Mortgage Obligations)

Although CMOs are normally classified as a form of mortgage back and not a derivative per se, they are a form of synthetic security with customized cash and principal flows. This section touches upon some of the key operating considerations in originating, maintaining, and purchasing these securities.

The greatest challenge in deal structuring is to match the WAC (weighted average coupon) and WAM (weighted average maturity) of the pools so that they meet the obligations set out in the prospectus. Until 48 hours before the settlement date of the TBAs (agency securities) purchased to comprise the CMO, one does not know for sure whether the collateral and cash flows will be satisfactory because of permitted variances in security characteristics for delivery. If all of the required pools are not in the box (in possession), other pools must be substituted and the resulting financial characteristics rechecked. If further bonds must be purchased, the TBA trader buys in extra securities. The "final" CMO collateral is than delivered to FNMA, FHLMC, or a custodian. Outside accountants than review the financial characteristics and produce comfort letters as an external verification and control.

CMO maintenance is normally conducted by a custodian and requires that the principal and interest payments received from the underlying pool of mortgage-backed securities or whole loans (on a monthly basis) is properly allocated to each tranche of the CMO according to its payment schedule. The sequencing of principal paydowns to each CMO tranche is detailed in the prospectus. Any remaining principal, after the tranche principal allocations, is allotted to the residual tranche.

Purchasing or selling CMOs has one difference from other securities. On nonagency deals the factor is not known until after settlement date (except if settlement date coincides with factor date). The original settlement transaction has to be adjusted for the factor difference, and the cash payment made. The original transaction also has to be adjusted or canceled and rebooked to reflect the actual announced factor.

IO/POs

IOs (interest onlys), and POs (principal onlys) are purchased on the new-issue market on a yield maintenance basis, which is based on an estimated WAC and WAM and PSA (Public Securities Association) prepayment speed. On settlement date the original purchase price must be adjusted to reflect changes in the WAC and WAM. This must be recalculated in-house using a matrix model of comparable securities.

In addition, the confirm sent to the counterparty must contain special wording concerning this settlement adjustment characteristic. Maintenance of IOs and POs from the custodial perspective does not differ from CMOs except for the total allocation of the principal and interest to different securities.

A frequent operational problem encountered in processing residuals and IO/POs is that the effective interest rates for accruals may exceed the processing system's capabilities, resulting in the need for manual workarounds.

Securitized Receivables

The operational burden for purchasers of these securities in the secondary market is equivalent to mortgage backs. This entails the correct application of principal and interest factors after they are released, and pricing the instruments. In these security types the primary operational responsibilities and associated complexity of tasks falls on the trustee and is largely outside the scope of this discussion. A brief description of the basic structures and characteristics of the instruments is presented here because it will assist in understanding the pricing of the securities.

Investors can track performance of their asset-backed holdings by monitoring the performance of the underlying pool of assets through reports provided by S&P, Moody's, and Fitch. These are retrievable via Bloomberg, or through direct issuer statistics reported on Telerate. In addition, both the issuer's and issuee's credit rating should be monitored.

Issues differ largely in whether there is a discrete (security specific) or master (group of assets with multiple securities) trust, in the credit enhancement mechanism, in the trancheing or subordination of classes (if any), and of course in the details of the principal repayment and interest payment structures.

Credit enhancement mechanisms include: Excess servicing; where the deal is structured so that finance charge collections remain after the payment covering the investor coupon, servicing fees, and any losses; subordinated tranches to provide priority claim to the senior tranche on cash flows; overcollateralization, whereby additional assets are placed in trust to service the security; letters of credit; and cash collateral accounts.

Revolving credit-card, wholesale auto loans, and revolving home equity loans pay out principal through either controlled amortization or as a bullet payment. In controlled amortization, principal payments are typically reinvested in new assets, followed by a period in which equal monthly principal payments are made to the buyer until they are fully repaid. Bullets pay out principal on predefined dates but come in three forms: Soft bullets which may pay, depending on cash flow, at a later date than specified, without default; hard bullets, which provide date guarantees; and titanium bullets, which utilize a master trust structure to allow principal collections from other series (securities) in the trust, but do not guarantee the payment date. If the performance of the portfolio of the issuer deteriorates or the issuer enters bankruptcy, principal collections will be passed directly through to the owner of securities as early amortizations.

In term receivables, such as retail auto loans and closed-end home equity loans, principal collections are passed through to investors rather than being reinvested in additional assets. There are two methods of allocating cash flows: pass-throughs and pay-throughs. Pay-throughs allow the issuer to manage the amount and timing of distributions, whereas pass-throughs do not. An additional structure called Turbo provides for accelerated principal repayment from excess finance charges.

Prefunded issues contain assets whose value is lower than the face of the securities, with the difference being in cash in a prefunding account. These funds are then used for investment in eligible investments, but during the period as cash, reduce the overall rate of return of the asset.

Asset-backed securities consist of four primary types: credit-card receivables, retail auto loans, wholesale auto loans, and home equity loans.

Credit-Card Receivables

Credit-card receivable portfolios are normally evaluated based on the following: yield of finance charges and fees, the age and extent of delinquencies, losses, payment (principal repayment) rate, coupon or weighted average coupon of each series contained in the trust, the geographical concentration of the receivables, the weighted average age or seasoning of the portfolio (for projecting losses), and most importantly, its excess servicing (revenues minus expenses).

There are two forms of trust for credit-card receivables: discrete trust and master trust. The discrete trust contains a single pool of assets, whereas the master trust enables the issuer to have one pool of assets support multiple issues. Master trusts typically contain greater diversification and enable the issuer to add new accounts with high yields and seasoned accounts, which are very stable. Investors in master trusts' structured securities may be affected by future issuance as the cash distribution may change. This depends on the cash flow allocation method, which is commonly based on coupon or issue size.

Tranche structures for card securities include: single tranche, with an associated cash collateral account or letter of credit; traditional senior/subordinated tranches, with the latter's payment claims junior to the former and the senior tranche having a credit enhancing facility; and 94/6 senior/subordinated, in which the credit enhancement facility covers both tranches.

Retail Auto Loans

Retail auto loans differ from credit-card lines in that they are secured loans with specified payment schedules and maturities of generally five years and younger. Grantor trusts operate as pass-throughs with cash flows paid directly to the investors based on their pro rata share. Owner trusts enable the trustee to manage the cash flows of the assets in the trust. Typically, several tranches are involved, with different maturity and credit characteristics. Purchasers of senior tranches usually are receiving a debt obligation of the trust, whereas buyers of the subordinated tranche are purchasing equity interests.

Key evaluation criteria for retail loan securities include: the weighted average annual percentage rate (APR), or yield; coupon; weighted average remaining term of the portfolio; and the loss history, which normally follows a predictable curve. Other factors include payment history (weighted average seasoning), recourse for default recapture from dealers, new versus old cars, and geographical concentrations.

Credit enhancement is usually provided through a combination of a subordinated class, which is purchased by the issuer, and a spread or reserve account. Spread accounts provide additional liquidity, whereas reserve accounts also provide credit support.

The ABS prepayment rate is the monthly number of loans expected to prepay as a percentage of the original number of loans in the pool. Prepayment of auto loans is typically stable because of a lack of financing alternatives.

Interest rates are calculated in three ways: precomputed actuarial loans, where fixed-dollar payments reduce the principal balance by a predetermined amount each month; simple interest, where the amount of the payment used to pay down principal depends on the number of days passed since previous payment; and rule of 78s, where payments are split into predetermined principal and interest according to a specific formula.

Wholesale Auto Loans

Wholesale auto loans are floating-rate loans provided to car dealers to fund inventory. These are sold to master trusts who package the securities using both a subordinated class and a reserve account to provide credit enhancement. As these are floating-rate instruments, they require basis risk protection in the form of a swap or floor. Because car sales and related repayments are so seasonal, cash collected from liquidated assets is collected and placed in an account (excess funding account) to provide additional loans. If cash exceeds a specified percentage of total trust assets, distributions will be made to certificate owners (asset composition event).

Home Equity Loans

Home equity loans consist of two types: closed-end second mortgages and revolving home equity loans. Both are secured by a lien on the borrower's residence and experience significantly lower losses than credit-card receivables.

CPR, or constant prepayment rate, is the most common measure of loan prepayments. It is the percentage of the receivables balance that is expected to prepay in a given period based on the outstanding balance of the receivables at the beginning of the period. This is expressed on an annual basis.

In addition, these issues are evaluated based upon the combined loan to collateral value (CLTV) which is the first and second mortgage as percentage of appraised value, and the principal allocation basis. This allocation basis comes in three basic forms: on a fixed percentage; on a floating basis, which is based on the pro rata interest in the receivables at the end of the revolving period; or FIFO, where investors are entitled to 100 percent principal collections regardless of additional borrowings against the line of credit.

Home equity loan securities are issued out of REMIC or credit-card-type trusts and take all forms, from a single class pass-through to multiple tranche pay-throughs. Issues have used the range of credit enhancement features including subordination, reserve accounts, and third-party credit enhancement. Floating-rate portfolios with fixed-rate tranches also normally have some form of basis risk protection.

Interest Rate Agreements

Interest rate agreements have a host of unique operational requirements. As a result, most dealers have a separate middle office providing operational support that reports directly to the trading desk. Institutional investors need to conduct the same activities except for on a smaller number of deals.

Effective swap operations have the following characteristics:

- Accurate, complete, and timely counterparty and deal documentation information

- Adequate control processes to validate trade information

- Maintenance of counterparty exposure data

- Detailed procedures for credit approval and establishment of credit and collateral limits

- Accurate monitoring of deal and counterparty collateral

- Detailed calculations marking interest rate agreements to market

- Accurate payment schedules, maintenance, and rate information

- Timely delivery of bills to insure payment delivery and receipt

- Maintenance of accounting procedures and chart of account in accordance with GAAP

One of the most significant operational activities is the preparation of deal confirmations and the correct recording of all deal characteristics. This is critical for all downstream deal processing. This information includes: notional amounts, currencies, notional amortizations, stub periods, up-front and back-end payments, cap or floor strikes, lockout period, knockout features, cleanup provisions; rate resetting information, including index, rate-reset date, first compounding date, reset frequency, reset variance, reset weekday, holiday calendars, before and after conventions, reset compounding frequency rounding conventions.

Over-the-counter security contracts must specify the calendar convention (e.g., U.S. or U.K. holidays) for use in rate resets and interest accruals or amortizations. Similar to holiday calendars, before and after conventions specify the method for conducting payment calculations should month-end or reset date fall on a weekend with or without an abutting holiday on Friday or Monday.

Master agreements must be put in place with each counterparty. These are structured around ISDA (International Swap Dealers Association) standards by legal counsel and specify legal obligations vis-à-vis interest rate agreements. Some of these agreements contain provisions in case of counterparty credit downgrades.

Obtaining initial or revised credit approval, and monitoring the credit utilization for counterparties, is critical for counterparty risk management. This requires the tracking of all deal activity per counterparty and ongoing calculations of limit utilization. In more primitive risk-management environments, this constitutes tracking of gross notional amounts. In more sophisticated environments, this reflects an adjusted (plus some percentage) net mark to market of counterparty positions.

The calculation of payment notices is an extremely critical task. Proper compliance with the various deal characteristics including rate reset conventions, holiday calendars, and before and after conventions is required. Although these are normally calculated by a support system, in most environments they are verified and rechecked by hand. This is done prior to the issuance of payment notices and before the generation of payments resulting from the receipt of a payment notice.

Bank activity control requires the preparation of payment schedules and the monitoring of all payments and disbursements, especially those resulting from deal resets and associated payment notices.

In a previous section we discussed the problems in monitoring price marks for deals held in inventory. However, all open deals on the books must be priced to determine projected unrealized P&L, and to monitor firm risk. In addition, other hedging transactions (i.e., Treasuries, futures) must be priced along with any deal or counterparty credit enhancing collateral. This collateral must be monitored and compared to the specified collateral requirements on a regular (at least weekly) basis.

Other required operational activities include: maintaining FX rates; calculating index and reference rates; monitoring customer and counterparty credit ratings; processing deal terminations, assignments, reversals, and restructurings; activating spread locks and exercising swaptions; confirming notional amount resets and handling irregular payments.

Equity Derivatives

The operational issues surrounding equity derivatives do not differ significantly from those discussed in the proceeding section on interest rate agreements. The difference is the additional complexity surrounding the treatment of the dividend stream associated with the index (e.g., S&P 500 or FTSE 100). This requires that these additional characteristics are specified as part of the deal terms and are correctly captured and confirmed. The index can be extremely customized, down to an industry sector or specific list of weighted or unweighted stocks (basket). Many exotic deal structures require additional deal information capture that is not supported on standard confirm forms. This is especially true as the equity derivative market is not a mature market and at times the confirms can run up to 20 pages. Because of this, it is extremely important that the terms and conditions specified in the confirm are thorough and do not leave anything open to interpretation.

In addition to correctly capturing clearly agreed upon deal terms, systems and operational support must calculate the resets which requires correctly calculating and applying the dividend stream. The dividend stream may be invested at a fixed or variable rate of return or reinvested in the index, effectively increasing the "notional" amount. The dividends may also be applied on either an ex-dividend or payment date basis.

Over-the-Counter Options

These options really fall into two categories: those based on the terms of listed options but being of either longer tenor (time period) or of size sufficient enough to significantly move the market if brought to the exchange floor, and exotic or customized options. The former do not really provide significant operation challenges, whereas the latter require the same kind of detailed recording of the terms and conditions of the transaction, in a manner that is not open to interpretation. This is especially true of barrier and ladder options, because issues can arise about whether a barrier or ladder rung was really touched or penetrated, activating the associated option characteristics. These discussions sometimes result from bad prints on the tape (erroneously reported trade prices). Purchasers or writers of these exotic options typically have a model to monitor their exercisability and in-the-money value. Although the trader, hedger, or portfolio manager has true responsibility for this activity, operations areas will typically also monitor these positions and, as appropriate, create tickler files to take actions.

PRIMARY OPERATIONAL CHALLENGES FOR DERIVATIVES
Cause of Operational Difficulties

In summary, operational problems for derivative securities are largely a result of three causes:

- Inability of the key processing system to handle unique security characteristics or calculations (different accrual basis or payment frequency)

- Two or more systems processing the securities applying different logic (e.g., rounding convention for interest accrual) or base data (e.g., FX rates for forwards)

- Extensive manual effort required to calculate and or confirm interest accruals, principal adjustments, rate resets, and security values

These causes result in an incredible variety of operational difficulties, which can be grouped as follows:

Confirmation Processing

The more complex and uncommon the instrument, the greater the requirement for more detailed written confirmations. In many financial institutions significant losses have resulted from recording incorrect deal conditions, even including the wrong side of the over-the-counter instrument.

Interest Accrual and Principal Adjustments

Problems frequently occur due to system limitations and the complex terms of the instruments. In addition to problems handling the correct amortization of purchase premiums and accretion of discounts (especially with changing or accelerated prepayments), anything goes in the required terms for calculating interest accruals. This includes things such as resets in arrears and resets based on index values differences between periods or against a specific range or value. Difficulties arise in handling principal paydowns for certain CMO- and asset-backed instruments because they are not available on a timely basis, resulting in back value adjustments and reaccruals.

Rate Reset, Trigger, and Barrier Monitoring

Floating-rate notes, options, swaps, and other instruments that utilize nonstandard indexes may create operational burdens because the underlying data and logic required to calculate these index reset, trigger, or barrier values may not be available on an automated basis. It is highly unlikely that the core processing system can support the calculations required for monitoring exotics; one must apply the analytical system or the spreadsheet originally used in creating or evaluating the deal. In many institutions current payment calculations are recalculated by hand (spreadsheet) prior to issuing payment notices or wiring funds.

Valuation

Issues in valuation have been covered in detail in a previous section, but can be summarized by the following statement: The more exotic the instrument, the more dependent you are in applying an in-house pricing model, which is likely to be the same one used in evaluating the pricing of the original deal.

Reconciliations and Journal Entries

As a result of derivative instruments' unique security characteristics and the inability of the core processing and accounting systems to accommodate them, significant efforts are required to correctly post adjustments and accounting entries to the firm's books and records.

Credit and Collateral Monitoring

This last category, although related to the previously stated causes of operational problems, largely results from the inability of institutions to integrate complicated system environments. It is separately mentioned here because of the heightened attention paid to these activities in the derivative product markets.

CHAPTER 38

Systems to Support Derivative Products

Colin Southall
Senior Consultant
BRAXXON Technology, Limited

INTRODUCTION

Derivative products are becoming ever more complicated, regulatory reporting requirements are increasing, more comprehensive corporate risk management information is required, and new technologies are being introduced into an already complex environment.

The time taken to develop applications and install the systems required to trade, settle, and manage the risk associated with new products is a critical factor in an organization's ability to stay in the market and to reduce the cost-per-trade. The increasing integration of business units in order to make best use of hedging opportunities, and hence the need for systems to communicate effectively, has made systems development more complex.

These issues are being faced in some form by all organizations that actively trade derivative products. Short-term benefits can be obtained by applying technology on a case-by-case basis. However, in the longer term, this leads to increasing constraints on the firm as system integration issues come to dominate discussion on how business activities can be organized.

The alternative approach is to establish an architecture for system and application development that can provide guidance for individual projects and that ensures that these systems can be integrated, as required, to meet business needs.

This architecture will be dependent on:

■ The characteristics of the business. For example, the number of business units that exist and the degree of collaboration required to trade and manage a particular product.

- The characteristics of the products traded. For example, the data requirements for the pricing algorithms that are used.

- The characteristics of the technologies that the firm has the skills to adopt and manage or that are deemed to provide key functionality for the business.

The base technologies and approaches to systems design and implementation have been described in the preceding chapters. Here we will review the characteristics of the business and products and then describe three system configurations that can be adopted as the basis for the systems architecture. Choosing an appropriate configuration requires some analysis, and we describe an approach that takes into account both business organization and product characteristics.

BUSINESS ORGANIZATION

The organization of the business places constraints on the range of system solutions that will satisfy the needs of business users. As with the product definitions given below, we must define the business environment in order to be able to perform the analysis of system options.

There are three aspects of the business that need to be considered:

1. The business units that perform some part of the work required to trade and settle the products handled.

2. The activities that are performed in processing these products.

3. The degree of collaboration that is required in order to process these products and manage risk.

Business Units

For the sake of the analysis we assume that the organization has three business units that are involved in trading and settlement:

- *Traders*. Traders are responsible for analyzing market opportunities, performing product pricing, and closing deals with counterparties.

- *Front office staff*. Front office staff are responsible for inputting and validating contract and transaction information, generating confirmation telexes, and handling the exercise and expiry of options.

- *Back office staff*. Back office staff are responsible for validating deal information and obtaining contract documentation, validating payments and controlling the generation of payment instructions, fixing rates, and controlling the generation of fixing messages.

Product Life Cycle

The main activities performed by traders and operations staff when dealing with these products, as shown in Exhibit 1, are:

- *Analytics.* Traders make use of position and pricing information in order to identify or confirm the details of trades that they may wish to execute.

- *Deal input.* Once a trade has been executed, a deal ticket is written out and passed to the front office staff, who input the deal contract, transaction, and cash-flow information into the system.

- *Validation.* The deal information is then printed out and passed to the trader for validation. Amendments are passed back to the front office staff for input. The deal is then validated by back office staff, who check the transaction, cash-flow, and accounting records and also check the confirmation telex details against the contract.

- *Position update.* Following validation, the deal information is used to update the position database. This information is distributed to traders during the course of the day.

   At the end of the day all positions are recalculated after carrying out end-of-day processing, such as removing matured contracts. The updated position information is made available to traders for the start of the following day's trading.

- *Payments and fixings.* Payments and fixings are handled by the back office staff, who update the system to reflect the receipt of payments or the fixing rate used. Journal entries are generated as a result of this activity and sent to the accounting system.

- *Option exercise/expiry.* An option may either expire on the final exercise date or be exercised. Options can be exercised either by creating the underlying deal or by cash settlement. This is handled by front office staff.

   These events can be divided into two groups: (1) those that occur prior to or as a result of a committed deal being entered into the system, and (2) those events that occur following the initial deal entry.

   The events that follow the initial deal entry are either triggered by some unplanned external event—for example, a modification to the contract—or are planned—for example, a fixing. The planned events should occur on a specific date or within a specific period that was defined when the deal was made. Special processing is required to handle the case when a planned event fails to occur—for example, a fixing is missed.

Collaboration between Business Units

The nature of the work performed by traders and operations staff can be analyzed along three dimensions to identify the degree of collaboration required to perform each task:

- The number of people who must work together in order to perform a task. Using a spreadsheet macro to calculate a price on deal information input by a trader does not require any collaboration, whereas product settlement requires that many people work together to complete the task.

Exhibit 1.   Product Life Cycle

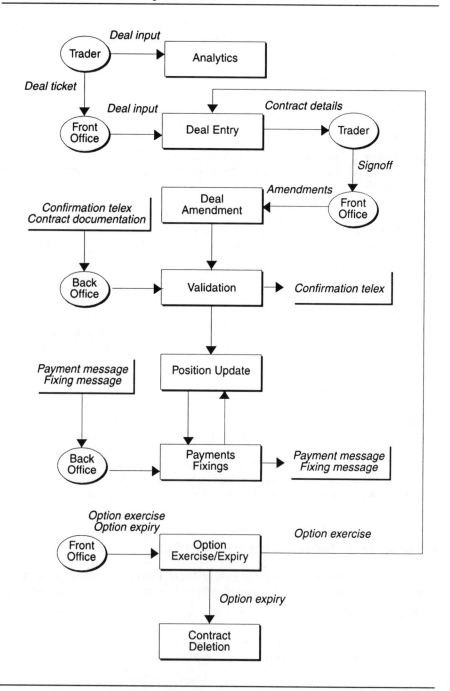

- The number of people who must work on a task simultaneously. Some tasks can be performed in a sequence of steps each of which requires only one person's input, e.g., deal input. Other tasks, such as structuring a trade, often require many people to be involved at the same time.

- The location of the people who must work on the task must also be considered. People who work in the same office can meet to discuss issues, whereas people who are in other offices must use other means to obtain the information required to perform the task.

The most demanding situation is where many people must collaborate simultaneously across many geographical locations in order to complete the specified task. This is the case for organizations that have adopted a global book approach to trading and risk management of derivative products.

If we assume that the organization has two offices, one in London and the other in New York, and that there is a common back office, which is located in London, we have five information flows to consider, as shown in Exhibit 2.

- High-priority flows within each location supporting traders' deal input and position-keeping functions.

- High-priority flows of deal information between locations to maintain the global book in a consistent state at all times.

- High-priority flows between systems supporting differing product groups at each location and between locations to provide effective risk management.

Exhibit 2. Information Flows

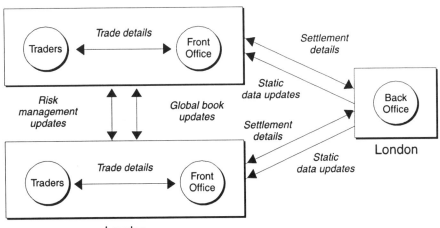

- Low-priority flows between front and back office required to support settlement, accounting, and end-of-day reporting.

- Low-priority flows between locations to maintain consistency of static information, such as counterparty details.

PRODUCT REPRESENTATION

There are many ways of representing products and the associated trades within a computer system. We need to define the product structure here in order to provide the basis for comparison of system options discussed later in this chapter. Different product structures will lead to slightly different results from the analysis. However, this does not invalidate the analysis process.

First we present a product structure, and then we show how a range of derivative products can be represented using this structure.

Product Structure

One way to define the product structure is to view a product as consisting of a contract that consists of a number of transactions that in turn consist of a number of cash flows, as shown in Exhibit 3.

Exhibit 3.   Product Structure

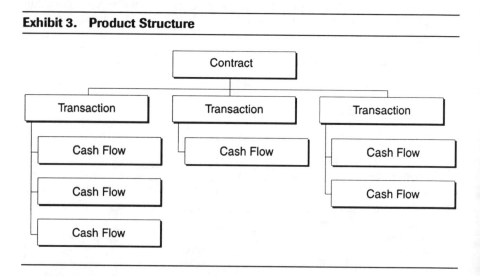

Each of these records has some internal structure, such as the counterparty name or a fixing date, which is required in order to capture the full definition of the product.

Contract Data

Contract data includes counterparty name and address, bank account details, the status of the contract documentation, and other details about the counterparty.

Each trade has a single contract record, which has links to all the transaction records that are associated with the contract.

Transaction Data

There is a transaction record for each of the different aspects of a product:

- Fixed-rate or conditional fixed-rate transaction
- Floating-rate or conditional floating-rate transaction
- Commission
- Option premium
- Option cash settlement details

Each transaction record contains some information about the specific transaction and links to the associated cash-flow records.

Cash-Flow Data

There are two classes of cash-flow record:

- Principal cash flows. Principal cash-flow records contain information on the amount, the currency, and the date on which the payment is due. This information is normally defined at the time that the deal is agreed.
- Interest cash flows. Interest cash-flow records can be either for a fixed amount or for a floating amount:
  - *Fixed-interest cash flows.* A fixed-interest cash flow record contains a definition of the interest rate that will be used in calculating the interest due on the outstanding principal on a specified date. The amounts involved can be calculated at the time that the deal is agreed.
  - *Floating-interest cash flows.* A floating-interest cash flow contains information about the reference rate to be used for the interest calculation, the dates when the reference rate will be fixed, whether the interest will be calculated on a compounding or noncompounding basis, and the date on which payment will be made. The amounts involved cannot be calculated at the time that the deal is made.

Product Representation

Using the product elements described above, we are now in a position to define the representation of a trade for a number of basic derivative products.

Swaps

Swaps involve the exchange of future interest cash flows between two counterparties with or without an exchange of principal. The cash flows can be in the same or differing currencies and can have either fixed or floating bases for calculating the interest amounts involved.

A fix-float interest rate swap with two fixed-interest payments, a single floating-interest payment and a commission payment would have the transaction and cash flow records shown in Exhibit 4.

Exhibit 4. Fix-Float Interest Rate Swap

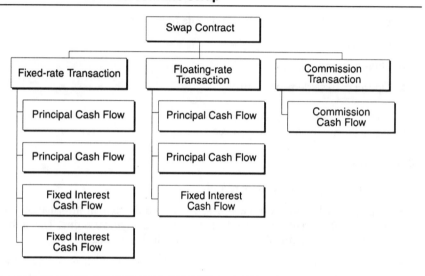

Swaptions

A swaption gives the buyer the option to purchase a swap at some future time. The buyer must specify which leg of the swap he or she has the option to buy. The option can be exercised either by creating the underlying swap or by cash settlement. The option can also expire without being exercised.

A premium is charged for the option and the trader can charge a commission for arranging the deal. The transaction and cash-flow records for an option on a fix-float interest rate swap are shown in Exhibit 5.

SYSTEM CONFIGURATIONS

In order to provide a basis for the analysis, it is necessary to define the system components that can be used to build distributed systems. A common view of the main components in a distributed systems environment is shown in Exhibit 6.

These components perform the following functions:

■ *Site database.* The site database holds corporate data, which is created, accessed, and updated by applications. Applications do not update the data directly but use the database access component to perform these functions on their behalf.

Exhibit 5.   Option on Fix-Float Interest Rate Swap

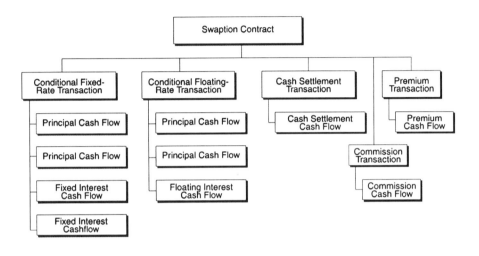

The site database is normally managed by a proprietary system such as Oracle, Sybase, or Ingres.

■ *Database access.* Applications access the site database using the database access component, which handles any communications and performs system error detection and recovery. Application (data) errors are handled by the application algorithm component.

The database access component provides an interface for the application algorithm component. This interface is usually based on SQL, often embedded in user-written code, which forms part of the application algorithm component.

Exhibit 6.   Distributed System Components

The database access component may provide local caching of data in order to improve performance or provide resilience. The caching is transparent to the application algorithm component.

■ *Application algorithm.* The application algorithm constructs database queries and performs processing on the data that is obtained from the database or from users.

The application algorithm component is written by the customer and reflects the business rules processing that the system is designed to support. The application algorithm component uses the database access component to request data from the database and uses the user interface component to handle user interaction.

The application algorithm component may choose to cache data or to store data locally in order to improve performance or to provide resilience. User applications may also need access to local data.

■ *User interface.* This is the component that defines the format and positioning of data on the screen. It defines the menu commands that are available and the user actions that are required in order to trigger business rules processing, which is performed by the application algorithm component.

The system developer will determine what functions will be provided, how requests are made, and how results will be displayed to the user. The user interface component sends commands and data to the display system component and receives user input from the display system component. It interprets this data in order to identify and initiate the required action in the application algorithm component.

■ *Display system.* The display system component is responsible for the management of the screen display. It performs the processing required to display data on the screen in response to requests from the user interface component and to capture user input, which is passed back to the user interface component for interpretation.

The display system component is normally provided by a proprietary package such as Microsoft Windows or an X Windows server.

There are a number of ways in which these components can be combined to form distributed systems. In each case the grouping results in different physical interfaces and different volumes of data transfer and processing requirements, which will provide a mix of benefits and constraints for business users.

The following common component configurations are described below:

■ Workstations connected to a central database

■ Local compute server

■ Local terminal server

Workstation

In the workstation configuration, shown in Exhibit 7, all processing required to handle user requests is performed on a workstation at the user's desk. The workstation is connected to the central database and will obtain information from the database using the database access component, which runs on the workstation.

Exhibit 7. Workstation Configuration

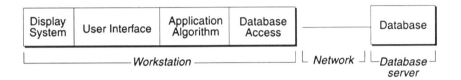

The benefits of this configuration are:

■ Processing power is dedicated to handling the user's requirements. The addition of new users will not degrade the performance of the workstation (but may affect the provision of data to the workstation).

■ The workstation can function independently of the database. Provided that local caching of data is performed on the workstation, it may be possible to provide adequate levels of service to the user for extended periods in the event of a database server failure.

■ Workstations can be remotely sited from the database server.

■ It will be possible for the user to run local applications on the workstation, which makes use of either local data or data obtained from the database.

The disadvantages of this configuration are:

■ It is expensive to provide workstations for all users. The workstations will need to be configured to cope with the peak processing loads and data storage requirements that are expected.

■ There may be a need to transfer large amounts of data from the database to the workstation, depending on the particular application that is being run.

■ The system is not easily scalable, since the database must support each workstation directly. The addition of a new workstation is likely to result in some degradation in database performance, which will impact all existing users. Increasing the capacity of the database is unlikely to be very cost effective and may, in extreme cases, be impossible.

Compute Server

In the compute server configuration shown in Exhibit 8, the user workstation is responsible for handling the user interface and the management of the screen display. All application processing is performed on a local compute server which is, in turn, connected to the database server.

Exhibit 8.   Compute Server Configuration

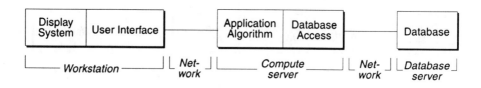

The advantages of this configuration are:

■ The workstation costs are lower, since the compute server handles the application processing.

■ The database server will need to support only a limited number of compute servers and so should be able to provide a better level of service than the workstation configuration.

■ It will be possible to remotely site both the compute server and the user workstations.

■ The system is more scalable than the workstation configuration, since the addition of a new user workstation will affect only the limited number of other users who are connected to the same compute server. The addition of a new compute server will affect all users but, as the number of compute servers will be lower than the number of directly connected workstations in the workstation option, there will be less impact on database server performance.

The disadvantages of this configuration are:

■ The compute server will have to be configured to handle the peak processing loads and data storage volumes that are expected. The addition of a new user workstation may require that a new compute server be provided, leading to a relatively high marginal cost for the increase in the number of users supported.

■ Users are now dependent on the compute server to perform the main business processing that they require. Failure of a compute server will affect several users. However, failure of the database server will have the same impact as for the workstation configuration, provided that the compute server performs local caching of data.

■ The user may not be able to run local applications on the workstation. Local applications, if run on the workstation, will need to access the compute server in order to read corporate data from the database and, possibly, to store local data.

Terminal Server

The terminal server configuration is shown in Exhibit 9. This configuration reduces the amount of processing that is performed on the user's desk to a minimum. The local terminal server is responsible for all application processing, with only the information display being handled by the terminal. The terminal server handles all access to the database server.

Exhibit 9.   Terminal Server Configuration

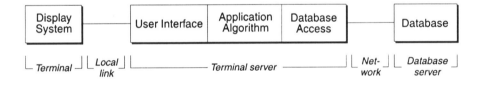

The advantages of this configuration are:

■ The user terminal is relatively inexpensive.

■ The local terminal server will probably support fewer terminals than the compute server will support workstations and so the impact of system failure will be reduced.

The disadvantages of this configuration are:

■ There may be no local processing capability on the terminal and so all processing will need to be performed on the terminal server. If user applications can be run on the terminal, then they will require access to the terminal server in order to obtain corporate data from the database server and, possibly, to store local data.

■ It may not be possible to have the terminals remotely sited from the terminal server as the bandwidth requirements (to handle expected data volumes and satisfy user response needs) are likely to be high.

■ The database server performance will be affected more than in the case of the compute server configuration, as more terminal servers will be required to support the same user population.

CHOOSING AN APPROPRIATE CONFIGURATION

Using the business organization and product representation described above, we are now in a position to analyze different system configurations and assess their suitability for the particular business.

The analysis is performed in three stages:

1. Specification of the physical system configuration.

2. Allocation of processing responsibilities across the available processors.

3. Identification of the volumes of data and the processing loads that will have to be catered to by each processor.

Physical Configuration

Given the organization structure shown in Exhibit 2, we can define a physical system configuration that provides workstations for each of the traders and terminal servers that provide terminals for each of the front and back office staff.

This configuration has been chosen because it provides a cost-effective way of meeting the compute needs of the traders while keeping front and back office costs to a minimum. Other configurations are, of course, possible but they will not be covered here.

Assuming that there are five traders, two front office staff and two back office staff, then the resulting physical configuration is shown in Exhibit 10.

In order to keep the example to a manageable size, no allowances have been made for equipment failure, network and communications link failure, or disaster recovery in this configuration. A comprehensive contingency planning exercise would need to be carried out in order to identify the main business risks and the cost of the associated risk reduction measures and disaster recovery actions.

Processing Responsibilities

The processing steps that are performed during the product life cycle were shown in Exhibit 1. Having defined the physical configuration, we must now allocate these processing steps to physical processors, as shown in Table 1.

Most operations are performed on the terminal servers, as they are used by front office and back office staff. Most of these operations are not very complex, as they are handling only one deal at a time. The analytics, position update, and fixings operations are more complex, as they handle multiple deals and/or are using involved mathematics.

Exhibit 10. Physical Configuraiton

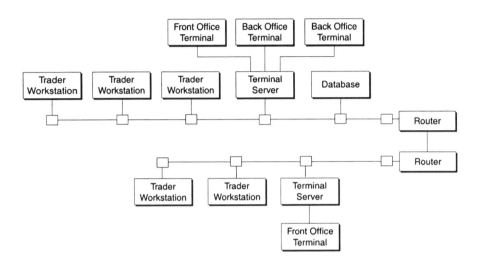

Table 1.   Processing Responsibilities

Processing Step	Processor
Analytics	Trader workstation
Deal entry	Terminal server
Deal amendment	Terminal server
Validation	Terminal server
Position update	Terminal server
Payments and fixings	Terminal server
Option exercise/expiry	Terminal server
Contract deletion	Terminal server

Data Volumes and Processing Loads

Business activity will vary depending on the time of day and the state of the market. The system must be able to cope with expected peak loads as well as being able to handle the total volume of business that is performed during the day.

For the sake of the analysis we will define the total volume of business activity to be as shown in Table 2. The peak load is assumed to be half these volumes performed over a one-hour period.

Table 2.   Business Activity

Processing Step	Number of Events/Day
Analytics	100
Deal entry	5
Deal amendment	10
Validation	5
Position update	40
Payments and fixings	10
Option exercise/expiry	5
Contract deletion	1

In order to identify the data volumes and processing loads, we must ascertain the data and processing requirements for each of the business processes. Assuming that the business is solely concerned with trading swaps and swaptions, that the deal representations shown in Exhibit 4 and Exhibit 5 each require 3,000 bytes of storage, and that only one deal is involved in each operation then the resulting data flows and processing load characteristics are shown in Table 3.

Table 3.   Data Volumes and Processing Loads

	Volume of Data (bytes)		
Processing Step	Input	Output	Processing Load
Analytics	300,000	–	High
Deal entry	–	15,000	Low
Deal amendment	30,000	30,000	Low
Validation	15,000	15,000	Low
Position update	120,000	120,000	High
Payments and fixings	30,000	30,000	High
Option exercise/expiry	15,000	15,000	Low
Contract deletion	3,000	–	Low

Given these assumptions, it is clear that the system data flows can be easily catered for using standard network technology. However, it will be necessary to size the terminal servers carefully as they have a range of processing operations to perform, some of which are compute intensive.

CONCLUSION

In order to choose an appropriate system configuration it is necessary to have a clear understanding of the business organization, the product representation, and the processing that must be performed. Different physical configurations can be compared by reviewing the processing responsibilities, data volumes, and processing loads that result in each case and the associated implementation and operating costs.

Examples of possible system configurations have been described and one configuration has been analyzed using assumptions for data volumes and processing loads. This analytical approach can be used to select an appropriate systems architecture which meets business organization and processing needs.

PART SIX

LEGAL AND
REGULATORY ISSUES

CHAPTER 39

Regulation of Exchange-Traded Options

Brandon Becker
Director, Division of Market Regulation
Securities and Exchange Commission

Jeffrey P. Burns
Associate
Gordon Altman Butowsky Weitzen Shalov & Wein

THE REGULATION OF EXCHANGE-TRADED SECURITIES OPTIONS MARKETS

The options exchange markets are a valuable national asset that provide important hedging and investment opportunities for investors.[1] Indeed, the United States has

---

[1] The seller of any option is known as the "writer" of the option contract and is said to be "short" the option. The buyer is the holder of the option and is said to be "long" the option. Generally, a stock option gives the holder either the right to buy or sell a specified number of shares at a specified price (called the "strike price") of a designated underlying stock during the life of the option. For this right, the holder of the option pays the writer an amount of money called the "option premium." An option giving the holder the right to buy the underlying stock is known as a "call option," while an option giving the holder the right to sell the underlying stock is known as a "put option." Equity options, if exercised, require the delivery of the underlying security, while equity index options are settled in cash. Standardized options may be offset by entering into an opposite transaction. Put and call standardized options are categorized as either American-style or European-style. An American-style option is one that may be exercised by the holder at any time after it is purchased until it expires, while a European-style option is one that may be exercised only during a specified period prior to expiration. Therefore, the standardization and fungibility of the option contract on U.S. securities exchanges has provided the necessary mechanism to enable secondary trading in options to flourish for the benefit of U.S. capital markets.

This article was written while Mr. Burns was employed by the Securities and Exchange Commission, Division of Market Regulation, Branch of Derivatives Regulation. As a matter of policy, the Commission disclaims responsibility for any private publication or statement by any of its employees. The views expressed in the article do not necessarily reflect the views of the Commission or of Messrs. Becker's or Burns' colleagues on the staff of the Commission.

been the leader in developing new and innovative financial products. At the same time, due to the complex nature of many options trading strategies and the leverage inherent in options trading, a special regulatory regime has been developed for options. These rules are designed to protect investors and maintain fair and orderly markets while still facilitating the development of new products as well as market competition and efficiency.

This chapter briefly summarizes the regulation and oversight of the standardized options market in the United States.[2] We have not attempted to address the burgeoning development of the over-the-counter (OTC) derivatives markets (i.e., OTC options, synthetics, swaps, etc.). We only note that these OTC markets raise many similar questions regarding sales practices, credit quality, and interactions between cash and derivatives markets.

HISTORY

Since its creation, the Securities and Exchange Commission (SEC) has been responsible for the oversight and regulation of stock options and other securities-based derivative products. Hearings conducted by Congress after the 1929 stock market crash focused on stock market regulation and practices.[3] The Pecora Commission[4] in its report in 1934 concluded that "[t]hrough the medium of options, manipulators of every sort are enabled to carry on large-scale operations with a minimum of financial

---

2 Standardized options are defined in Rule 9b-1 under the Securities Exchange Act of 1934 (1934 Act) as option contracts either trading on a national securities exchange, or an automated quotation system of a registered securities association [i.e., the National Association of Securities Dealers, Inc. (NASD) Automated Quotation (NASDAQ) system], or a foreign securities exchange, which contract terms are limited to specific expiration dates and exercise prices. In addition, the SEC may designate other securities as "standardized options" determined to be consistent with the 1934 Act. For purposes of this chapter, the terms "standardized options" and "listed options" are interchangeable.

3 Stock Exchange Regulation: Hearings on H.R. 7852 and H.R. 8720 Before the House Committee on Interstate and Foreign Commerce, 73rd Cong., 2d Sess. 457-58; Stock Exchange Practices, Report of the Senate Committee on Banking and Currency Pursuant to S.Res. 84 (72nd Cong.) and S.Res. 56 and S.Res. 97 (73rd Cong.) S.Rep. No. 1455, 73rd Cong., 2nd Sess. 1 (1934)["Report on Stock Exchange Practice"].

4 The Senate Committee on Banking and Currency, which was authorized by various Congressional resolutions to investigate stock exchange and securities practices, was aptly referred to as the "Pecora Commission" after the committee's lead counsel, Ferdinand Pecora. On March 2, 1932, the Pecora Commission, through the Committee on Banking and Currency, was authorized to make a thorough and complete investigation of securities practices such as the buying and selling and the borrowing and lending of listed securities on the various stock exchanges, the values of such securities, and the effect of such practices upon interstate banking and foreign commerce, upon the operation of the national banking system and the Federal Reserve System, and upon the market for securities of the United States government, and the desirability of the exercise of the taxing power of the United States with respect to such securities. See Report on Stock Exchange Practices, supra, note 3 at 1.

risk."[5] Although the Pecora Commission viewed the manipulative schemes and devices relating to options in the context of pools or syndicates[6] on a stock exchange, such options-related manipulative activity was not limited solely to such pools but also was employed by NYSE members on listed NYSE stock.[7]

The congressional investigations noted above initially recommended that all options trading should be banned to eliminate the manipulative abuses of pools and other syndicates.[8] Nevertheless, put and call dealers in New York City argued against complete prohibition, identifying the legitimate purposes of options trading, i.e., hedging, price protection, and market stabilization.[9] As a result, Congress did not ban exchange trading in stock options in the 1934 Act but instead required the SEC to specifically approve such options trading through rule making under Section 9 of the 1934 Act.

Section 9 of the 1934 Act gives the SEC authority to set the terms and conditions of exchange trading of options on equity securities. The SEC did not use its authority under Section 9 of the 1934 Act to permit exchange options trading until the creation of the Chicago Board Options Exchange, Inc. (CBOE) in 1973. Prior to 1973, securities options were traded exclusively OTC (known as "conventional options"), and generally were the subject of negotiation between a customer and an options dealer. Upon consummation of a trade, a contract was executed containing the details of the option bought or sold.[10]

---

5 Report on Stock Exchange Practices, supra note 3 at 45. Options trading during this period was executed between members of the organized exchanges, but was not performed on the exchanges themselves. From the period January 1, 1929, to August 31, 1933, there were 286 option contracts executed involving stock listed on the New York Stock Exchange, Inc. (NYSE) of not less than 10,000 shares each. The member firms of the NYSE that participated in these options totaled 78, with 25 partners of the member firms also participating. The total NYSE shares involved in the 286 option contracts was approximately 17.4 million.

6 A pool or syndicate is an agreement between several people to actively trade in a single security. The purpose of a pool was to raise the price of a security by concerted activity of the pool members, enabling the members to unload their holdings at a profit upon public buying interest. The use of a pool or syndicate in this manner is viewed as incompatible with the maintenance of a free and open market, and as a result, Congress in Section 9 of the 1934 Act attempted to prohibit this type of manipulative activity for securities listed on a national securities exchange.

7 Id. at 45.

8 Stock Exchange Regulation: Hearings on H.R. 7852 before the House Committee on Interstate and Foreign Commerce, 73rd Cong., 2nd Sess. 17-18 (1934).

9 Hearings on S.Res. 84 (72nd Cong.) and S.Res. 56 and S.Res. 97 (73rd Cong.) before the Senate Committee on Banking and Currency, 73rd Cong., 1st Sess. Part 15 at 7063 ["Stock Exchange Practice Hearings"]. These hearings described the legitimate business practice of options trading as follows:

These contracts [puts and calls] have been developed and sanctioned by business practice over a period of 2 to 3 centuries. Undoubtedly, they had their origin in transactions involving the merchandising of commodities, and in this respect are closely akin to the future contract system now in vogue and such an indispensable part of the marketing of all great staple commodities. As a matter of fact, the future contract system was devised entirely for the purpose of insurance against injurious price changes. The put and call system is in the same category, for it insures the investor in securities against violent fluctuations due to unexpected developments.

10 Specifically, these option contracts included: the date; the name of the security on which the contract was written; the price at which the security could be bought or sold; the length of the contract; actual date of expiration; and endorsement by a member firm of the NYSE guaranteeing the terms of the contract.

Due to the absence of standardization, secondary trading in conventional put and call options was both costly and difficult. First, since the option was an individually tailored, private contract between the holder and options dealer, such a contract was required to be presented to the writer for exercise. Second, in order to ensure performance, option holders were required to affirmatively exercise, otherwise the option expired worthless.[11] Third, option holders who wanted to liquidate their positions prior to expiration were required to deal with put-call options dealers.[12] Accordingly, liquidating an OTC options position was both expensive and lacked transparency due to the absence of a continuous, liquid options market.

The CBOE commenced trading in 1973.[13] Listing and trading standardized option contracts in an auction market, such as the CBOE, provides enhanced liquidity and virtually eliminates counterparty risk through the presence of a financially strong contractual intermediary, such as the Options Clearing Corporation (OCC), to guarantee contracts.[14] Other stock exchanges, such as the American Stock Exchange, Inc. (AMEX) and the Philadelphia Stock Exchange, Inc. (PHLX), followed the CBOE's lead and started trading standardized options in 1975.[15] One year later, the Pacific Stock Exchange, Inc. (PSE) commenced their options trading program while the NYSE waited until 1985 to implement standardized options trading comparable to the other exchanges.[16]

---

11 Today, the options exchanges have developed automatic exercise procedures that will automatically exercise an option at expiration if "in-the-money."

12 This intermediary matched buyers and sellers of options profiting on the spread between what buyers would pay and sellers receive. During those times where the dealer could not find a buyer for the option to be sold, the dealer would effectively "make a market" by exercising the option for his or her own account and purchasing or selling the underlying stock.

13 See Securities Exchange Act Release No. 9985 (February 1, 1973), 1973 SEC LEXIS 3257.

14 If a holder of an option wishes to liquidate or close out his or her position, he or she may do so by selling an identical option to the one bought, thereby cancelling out the obligation and realizing the profits or losses. In the case of a writer of an option, closeout of the position will occur by simply making an offsetting buy transaction. OCC (a clearing agency regulated by the SEC), which was established to issue the options contracts and to guarantee clearance, settlement, and performance, is the primary reason why convenient liquidation can occur in the options markets. Specifically, an option buyer looks to OCC rather than to any particular option writer for performance. Similarly, the obligations of option writers are owed to OCC rather than to any particular buyer. The obligations of options writers to OCC are guaranteed by "clearing members" that carry the accounts of writers of their brokers. Clearing members are required to meet special financial requirements and must provide OCC with margin or other collateral for the writers' positions that they carry and must contribute to stock and nonequity clearing funds, which protect OCC against a clearing member's failure. The financial strength of OCC's clearing members, the collateral that they deposit, and the clearing funds together make up OCC's backup system.

15 See Securities Exchange Act Release Nos. 11144 (December 19, 1974), 1074 SEC LEXIS 2108 (AMEX) and 11423 (May 15, 1975), 1975 SEC LEXIS 1605 (PHLX).

16 See Securities Exchange Act Release Nos. 12283 (March 30, 1976), 41 FR 14454 (PSE) and 21759 (February 14, 1985), 50 FR 7250 (NYSE).

SPLIT JURISDICTION

The Commodity Futures Trading Commission (CFTC) was created in 1974 by the enactment of the Commodity Futures Trading Commission Act of 1974 (CFTC Act).[17] The CFTC Act amended the Commodity Exchange Act (CEA) and established the CFTC as an independent regulatory agency, vesting it with exclusive jurisdiction over futures and commodity options trading.[18] The 1974 amendments to the CEA expanded the definition of "commodity" to include "all goods . . . and all services, rights, and interests in which contracts for future delivery are presently or in the future dealt in."[19]

In the early 1980s a jurisdictional controversy arose between the SEC and CFTC regarding the trading of Government National Mortgage Association (GNMA) options by the CBOE.[20] The Seventh Circuit Court of Appeals in that case held that the CFTC had exclusive jurisdiction over the GNMA options; and that even apart from the CFTC's exclusive jurisdiction, the SEC lacked jurisdiction to permit the trading of options on GNMAs. The court reasoned that options on exempt securities, such as GNMAs, were commodities within the purview of the CEA, and therefore under the jurisdiction of the CFTC.[21] The underlying theme of the Seventh Circuit's decision concerned the apparent legislative bifurcation of regulatory powers between the CFTC and SEC. As a result of the GNMA case and the regulatory problems it revealed, the chairmen of the SEC and CFTC discerned a need to specify each agency's jurisdiction in the area of options and futures regulation. The agencies worked together to reach a jurisdictional compromise in 1982 ("Johnson-Shad Accord"), which subsequently was enacted into law by Congress in 1982.[22]

The Johnson-Shad Accord delineates the jurisdictional reach of the securities laws and the CEA, for purposes of options regulation, based on the underlying

---

17 Pub. L. No. 93-463, 88 Stat. 1389 (1974).
18 The legislative history of the CFTC Act described the purpose of the Act as follows:

[The CFTC Act] makes extensive changes in the Commodity Exchange Act, brings under federal regulation all agricultural and other commodities, goods, and services traded on exchanges, and otherwise strengthens the regulation of the Nation's $500 billion commodity futures trading industry. The bill is designed to further the fundamental purpose of the Commodity Exchange Act in insuring fair practice and honest dealing of the commodity exchanges and providing a measure of control over those forms of speculative activity which often demoralize the markets to the injury of producers, consumers, and the exchanges themselves.

S.Rep. No. 1131, 93rd Cong., 2d Sess. 19 (1974).
19 See 7 U.S.C. Section 2 (1992)[Section 2(a)(1)(A) of the CEA].
20 *Board of Trade of the City of Chicago v. Securities and Exchange Commission,* 677 F.2d 1137 (7th Cir. 1982), *vacated as moot, Chicago Board Options Exchange, Inc. v. Board of Trade of the City of Chicago,* 459 U.S. 1026, 103 S.Ct. 434 (1982). This case arose out of SEC approval of options trading on GNMA securities, which was challenged by the Chicago Board of Trade (CBOT). See Securities Exchange Act Release No. 17577 (February 26, 1981), 46 FR 15242.
21 The Court considered that the only substantive grant of authority to the SEC over options is contained in Section 9 of the 1934 Act, that the SEC consistently relied on Section 9 for its authority over exchange-traded options, and that Section 9(f) explicitly provides that the provisions of Section 9 do not apply to an exempted security. *CBOT v. SEC,* 677 F.2d at 1159–60.
22 This compromise jurisdictional agreement was passed by Congress as part of both the Securities Act Amendments of 1982 and the Futures Trading Act of 1982. See Public Law Nos. 97- 303, 96 Stat. 1409 (1982) and 97–444, 96 Stat. 2294 (1982).

instrument involved. Specifically, the jurisdiction of the SEC reaches options on securities, certificates of deposit, foreign currency if traded on a national securities exchange, exempted securities, and stock groups or indexes. The CFTC's jurisdiction extends to futures contracts and options on futures contracts on exempted securities (except municipal securities), certificates of deposit, and broad-based groups or indexes of securities, as well as options on foreign currency not traded on a national securities exchange. In addition, futures or options on futures on individual nonexempt securities and municipal securities are not permitted.[23]

Although the statutory bifurcation of the SEC and CFTC's jurisdiction has remained unchanged since the Johnson-Shad Accord in 1982, judicial interpretations subsequently have addressed these issues. Specifically, in the area of new product development, a national securities exchange may be prevented from listing and trading an instrument having the attributes of both a security and a futures contract.[24] On October 28, 1992, The Futures Trading Practices Act of 1992 (FTPA) was enacted into law.[25] The legislation bolsters CFTC regulation of the futures exchanges. As part of this revision to the CEA, Title V of the FTPA provides the CFTC with exemptive authority over certain hybrid products, swaps, and other derivative products.[26] After the passage of the FTPA, the CFTC adopted rules establishing procedures for exempting certain hybrid securities and banking products and swaps from the CEA.[27] Accordingly, certain derivative instruments that meet the requirements of the CFTC's

---

23 Congress, upon passing the Johnson-Shad Accord into law, also added a provision providing the SEC with a special consultative and concurrent role in the approval process concerning stock index futures contracts. In particular, the SEC must find that the specific stock index futures contract is cash-settled, is not readily susceptible to manipulation, and reflects a substantial segment of the underlying cash market.

24 See *CME v. SEC*, 883 F.2d 537 (7th Cir. 1989), *cert. denied*, 110 S.Ct. 3214 (1989)("IPs Decision"). Index Participations (IPs) are products based on the current value of an index of stocks, are of infinite duration, and entitle the holders to receive on a quarterly basis cash payments equivalent to a proportionate share of any regular cash dividends declared on the component stocks of the underlying index. On April 11, 1989, the SEC approved rules permitting the Amex, Phlx and CBOE to list IPs for trading. See Securities Exchange Act Release No. 26709 (April 11, 1989), 54 FR 15280. IPs began trading on May 12, 1989. On August 18, 1989, however, the U.S. Court of Appeals for the Seventh Circuit held that IPs were subject to the CFTC's exclusive jurisdiction. Even though the instrument lacked bilateral obligations, a traditional attribute of a futures contract, the court found that IPs contained an element of futurity, which rendered CFTC jurisdiction exclusive. As a result of the decision, IPs have ceased trading anywhere in the U.S.

25 Pub. L. No. 102-546, 106 Stat. 3590 (1992).

26 Congress in enacting the FTPA discerned a need on the part of the CFTC to be able to exempt certain derivative instruments from the "exchange-trading" requirement of Section 4(a). The legislative history states that the purpose of this broad exemptive authority is to provide the CFTC with a means of providing certainty and stability to existing and emerging markets so that financial innovation and market development can proceed in an effective and competitive manner. See H.R. Conf. Rep. No. 978, 102nd Cong., 2d Sess. 77 (1992).

27 See 17 CFR Part 35, Exemption for Certain Swap Agreements, 58 FR 5587, dated January 22, 1993, and 17 CFR Part 34, Regulation of Hybrid Instruments, 58 FR 5580, dated January 22, 1993.

exemptive rules may be traded off-exchange, while the CEA's antifraud and antimanipulation provisions may continue to be applicable to some such transactions.[28]

EXCHANGE LISTING

Section 19(b) of the 1934 Act

Section 19(b) of the 1934 Act confers broad statutory authority on the SEC to approve or deny any rule change proposed by a self-regulatory organization (SRO), including rules relating to the trading of derivative products. As a result, the SEC must approve SRO proposals to trade new derivative products, provided these products are within the SEC's jurisdiction.[29] SEC approval requires a finding that the proposed rule is consistent with the requirements of the 1934 Act and relevant rules and regulations thereunder. Further, certain procedural requirements calling for public comment and timely review must be complied with by the SEC during the review process.[30]

The SEC will consider the merits of the proposal with respect to various requirements of the 1934 Act found in Section 6. Specifically, Sections 6(b)(1), (5) and (8) mandate that exchange rules meet the following requirements:

(1) Such exchange is so organized and has the capacity . . . to enforce compliance by its members and persons associated with its members, with the provisions of this title, the rules and regulations thereunder, and the rules of the exchange;

(5) The rules of the exchange are designed to prevent fraudulent and manipulative acts and practices, to promote just and equitable principles of trade, to foster cooperation and coordination with persons engaged in regulating, clearing, settling, processing information with respect to, and facilitating transactions in securities, to remove impediments to and perfect the mechanism of a free and open market and a national market system, and, in general, to protect investors and the public interest; and are not designed to permit unfair discrimination between customers, issuers, brokers, or dealers, or to regulate by virtue of any authority conferred by this title matters not related to the purposes of this title or the administration of the exchange; and

(8) The rules of the exchange do not impose any burden on competition not necessary or appropriate in furtherance of the purposes of this title.[31]

---

28 In addition, the exemptive authority granted to the CFTC did not in any way affect the Johnson-Shad Accord pertaining to the jurisdiction of the SEC and CFTC. Cf. Exemption for Certain Contracts Involving Energy Producers, 58 FR 21286 (April 20, 1993)(CFTC order exempting certain energy contracts from the provisions of the CEA including the anti-fraud provision.

29 SROs are the principal means contemplated by the federal securities laws for the enforcement of fair, ethical, and efficient practices in the securities industry. The SROs include the national securities exchanges, the National Association of Securities Dealers, Inc. (NASD), and the Municipal Securities Rulemaking Board (MSRB).

30 See 15 U.S.C. section 78s (b) (1) (1982).

31 15 U.S.C. Section 78f(b) (1), (5), (8) (1982).

Where relevant, the SEC also must conclude that an exchange proposal is consistent with the other provisions of the 1934 Act and the rules and regulations thereunder. These requirements must be satisfied in connection with SRO proposals relating to the trading of new derivative products.[32]

Listed Derivative Products

U.S. securities exchanges and the NASD have standards that must be met in order for stocks, bonds, options, and/or warrants to be traded on such exchanges.[33] In the case of standardized equity options, the listing and maintenance standards for securities underlying the options are as follows:[34]

1. A minimum of 7 and 6.3 million shares outstanding, respectively, which are owned by persons other than "insiders" as defined in Section 16 of the 1934 Act;

2. A minimum of 2,000 and 1,600 shareholders, respectively;

3. Trading volume of at least 2.4 and 1.8 million shares, respectively, during the past 12 months;

4. For original listings, the market price per share of the underlying security must have closed at or above $7.50 during the majority of business days over the preceding three months. To maintain its listing, the market price per share of the underlying security must have closed at or above $5 during the majority of business days over the preceding six months;[35]

5. The security must be duly listed on a national securities exchange or designated as a NASDAQ/National Market System (NMS) security; and

6. The issuer must be in compliance with applicable reporting requirements under the Exchange Act.[36]

---

32 A finding that a new derivative product is consistent with the 1934 Act would be difficult with respect to a new derivative product that served no hedging or other economic function, because any benefits that might be derived by market participants likely would be outweighed by the potential for manipulation, diminished public confidence in the integrity of the markets, and other valid regulatory concerns.

33 See, e.g., Amex *Company Guide,* NYSE Listed Company Manual, and NASD Manual.

34 There are no uniform listing standards for stock index options. See, e.g., Amex Rules Section 11 (Stock Index Options), Rules 900C et al., and CBOE Rules, Chapter XXIV (Index Options).

35 The SEC has approved amendments by the options exchanges that lowers the stock price maintenance standard for certain low-priced securities. Specifically, these amendments provide that an equity option can remain listed if the price of the underlying security falls below $5.00 if: (1) the aggregate market value of the underlying company equals or exceeds $50 million; (2) customer open interest in the option equals or exceeds 4,000 contracts; and (3) the trading volume in the underlying security equals or exceeds 2.4 million shares during the preceding 12 months. In addition, a "step up" procedure exists whereby the market price of the underlying security must increase to comply with the $5 stock price maintenance standard by the end of a one-year period. See Securities Exchange Act Release No. 33257 (December 7, 1993), 58 FR 64416.

36 Securities Exchange Act Release No. 29628 (August 29, 1991), 56 FR 43949. See, e.g., Amex Rules 915 and 916 and CBOE Rules 5.3 and 5.4.

In the case of stock index warrants and currency warrants traded on a national securities exchange, there are no uniform standards for issuance eligibility. The various standards imposed by each trading market or exchange, however, are designed to ensure that the issuer can meet its obligations under the warrants and that the market for the warrants will be fair and orderly. For example, the AMEX requires issuers seeking to list stock index and/or currency warrants to: (1) have assets in excess of $100 million and (2) substantially exceed the exchange's listing criteria. In addition, each warrant issue must satisfy the following requirements: (1) a minimum public distribution of 1 million warrants; (2) 400 public holders; and (3) an aggregate market value of $4 million.[37]

During the past several years, the national securities exchanges have added provisions to their listing standards to accommodate securities that could not be readily categorized under traditional listing guidelines for, among other instruments, common and preferred stock, bonds, debentures, and warrants.[38] The driving force behind these amendments to the listing standards is that issuers and underwriters increasingly are creating and proposing to list innovative new securities products. These securities often possess attributes or features of more than one category of currently listed securities (e.g., fixed face amount debt securities incorporating an opportunity, at maturity, to receive an amount in excess of par based upon the performance of an index or group of securities or some other financial instrument; debt securities whose interest or coupon payments are linked to the performance of some other financial instrument or instruments; equity securities whose dividend payments are linked to the performance of some other financial instrument or instruments; warrants to purchase debt securities; and "put" rights issued by an affiliate of a listed company, which allow holders to put their common shares back to the issuer at the initial public offering price on a specific date after the initial public offering). Accordingly, because these securities combine different features of various securities, they are commonly referred to as "hybrid" securities. Typically, such securities are designed to achieve more than one objective and, as a consequence, such securities may take a variety of forms, depending on the particular objective or objectives being sought as well as general market conditions.

The hybrid listing standards established by the securities exchanges and approved by the SEC are not uniform. Specifically, the NYSE standards found in Section 703.19 of its Listed Company Manual require issues to have: (1) a minimum public distribution of one million securities; (2) a minimum of 400 shareholders; (3) a minimum duration of one year; (4) at least a $4 million market value; and (5) otherwise

---

37 Securities Exchange Act Release No. 26152 (October 3, 1988), 53 FR 39832.
38 For example, the AMEX *Company Guide* sets forth specialized listing criteria in Sections 102, 103, 104, 105, and 106 for equity issues, preferred stock, bonds, warrants, and currency and index warrants. In addition, Section 107 provides additional listing criteria for those securities that are not otherwise covered by Sections 101 through 106 of the *Company Guide* (i.e., hybrid instruments).

comply with the NYSE's initial listing criteria.[39] In addition, the NYSE continues to monitor each hybrid issuance to verify that it complies with the Exchange's continued listing criteria.[40]

The NASD's standards for listing hybrid securities on NASDAQ/NMS provide that (1) issuers have assets in excess of $100 million and stockholders' equity of at least $10 million; (2) issuers have pretax income of at least $750,000 in the last fiscal year or in two of the three prior fiscal years; (3) a minimum public distribution of 1 million trading units, including a minimum of 400 holders; (4) a principal amount or aggregate market value of not less than $20 million; and (5) cash settlement in U.S. dollars.[41] These standards are designed to ensure sufficient float and shareholder base for a hybrid security so that fair and efficient markets may be maintained, while also providing acceptable flexibility to accommodate new issues without the regulatory burden of adding additional listing criteria for each new hybrid instrument.[42]

SALES PRACTICES

Account Opening Procedures

The national securities exchanges and the NASD require that in order to engage in options trading, a customer's account must be specifically approved for such trading.[43] Accordingly, prior to opening an account, a broker/dealer must exercise due diligence to learn the essential facts regarding the customer, his or her investment objectives, and financial situation. Account approval must be in writing and can be made only by

---

39 The hybrid listing standards in Section 703.19 of the NYSE's Listed Company Manual are intended to accommodate listed companies in good standing, their subsidiaries and affiliates, and nonlisted equities that meet the Exchange's original listing standards. Domestic issuers must also meet the earnings and net tangible assets criteria set forth in Sections 102.01 and 102.02 of the NYSE's Listed Company Manual. Specifically, the minimum original listing criteria requires that issuers have: (1) 2,000 holders holding 100 shares or more or have 2,200 holders with an average monthly trading volume of 100,000 shares; (2) a public float of 1.1 million shares; (3) an aggregate public market value of $18 million or total net tangible assets of $18 million; and (4) earnings before taxes of $2.5 million in the latest fiscal year and earnings before taxes of $2 million in each of the preceding two fiscal years, or earnings before taxes of $6.5 million in the aggregate for the last three fiscal years with a $4.5 million minimum in the most recent fiscal year (all three years are required to be profitable). See e.g., Global Telecommunications Market Index Target-Term Securities [Securities Exchange Act Release No. 32840 (September 2, 1993), 58 FR 4785].

40 See Section 802 of the NYSE's Listed Company Manual.

41 See Section 2 of Part III of Schedule D to the NASD's By-Laws.

42 See also Section 107 of the Amex *Company Guide*. These listing guidelines under Section 107 provide that (1) issues must have a minimum public distribution of one million trading units with a minimum of 400 holders, an aggregate market value of $20 million, and, where applicable, cash settlement in U.S. dollars and a redemption price of at least $3; and (2) the issuers of such securities must have assets of $100 million, stockholders' equity of $10 million, and pretax income of at least $750,000 in the last fiscal year or in two of the three prior fiscal years. Those issuers not meeting the earnings criteria may in the alternative have assets in excess of $200 million and stockholders' equity of $10 million, or assets in excess of $100 million and stockholders' equity of $20 million.

43 See Amex Rule 921; CBOE Rule 9.7; NASD Section 16 of Appendix E to Article III of the Rules of Fair Practice; NYSE Rule 721; Phlx Rule 1024(b); and PSE Rule 9.18(b).

a Senior Registered Options Principal (SROP) or a Registered Options Principal (ROP).[44]

Suitability

The complexity of and degree of leverage obtainable through derivative products, such as standardized options, poses significant risks for investors, therefore, the trading of these products requires unique supervisory systems within broker-dealers. Adequate supervision of derivative and hybrid products requires brokerage firms to actively and continuously ensure that knowledgeable supervisory personnel oversee the activities of registered representatives, that registered representatives are adequately trained and that they transact business only with those investors who can appreciate and bear the risks that derivative products trading entails. Accordingly, the account opening, suitability, and disclosure rules applicable to the trading of standardized options generally are more stringent than those applicable to the trading of the underlying securities.

The options exchanges and the NASD have uniform rules in place to ensure that brokers make suitable options recommendations to their customers.[45] Under the options suitability rule, every person associated with a member broker-dealer who recommends an options transaction to a customer must have reasonable grounds for believing that the recommendation is not unsuitable for such customer, based on information provided by the customer, reasonable inquiry, and other information obtained by the broker. In addition, the broker must believe, at the time of making the recommendation, that the customer has such knowledge and experience in financial matters, and that he or she is reasonably capable of evaluating and bearing the risks of the recommended transaction.[46] The SROs also have suitability rules applicable to recommendations in nonoptions transactions.[47] In addition, the SEC together with the securities exchanges have required heightened suitability on a case-by-case basis with regard to non-option leveraged products, such as warrants and other hybrid instruments.

Risk Disclosure

The federal securities laws and the rules of the SROs require that options investors receive an Options Disclosure Document (ODD) at or before the time his or her account is approved for options trading. With respect to options products, the ODD discloses, among other things, the unique features of the products, their risks and purposes.

Form S-20 under the Securities Act of 1933 (1933 Act) and Rule 9b-1 under the 1934 Act establish a disclosure framework specifically tailored to the informational

---

44 Id.
45 See, e.g., CBOE Rule 9.9 and Section 19 of Appendix E to Article III of the NASD's Rules of Fair Practice.
46 Id.
47 See, e.g., AMEX Rule 411; Article III, Section 2 of the NASD's Rules of Fair Practice; and NYSE Rule 405.

needs of investors in standardized options.[48] Under this options disclosure system, the exchange(s) on which standardized options are listed and traded are required to prepare an Options Disclosure Document (ODD) describing the uses, mechanics, and risks of options trading and other matters in language that can be easily understood by the general investing public. The disclosure document is filed pursuant to the 1934 Act and is subject to review by the SEC. Broker-dealers must provide a copy of the ODD to each customer at or prior to the approval of the customer's account for trading in any standardized option. The issuer of a "standardized option" is able to use Form S-20 in conjunction with the ODD. The content of the abbreviated S-20 registration statement generally is limited to information related to the registrant (i.e., OCC) and the securities to be registered. Broker-dealers must distribute any amendment to the ODD to all accounts approved for trading in options.

Under Rule 9b-1, use of the ODD is limited to "standardized options" for which there is an effective registration statement on Form S-20 under the 1933 Act. Standardized options are defined in the Rule as:

> [O]ptions contracts trading on a national securities exchange, an automated quotation system of a registered securities association, or a foreign securities exchange which relate to options classes the terms of which are limited to specific expiration dates and exercise prices, or such other securities as the Commission may, by order, designate.

The SEC has reserved for itself authority to designate other options as standardized in order to permit the use of Rule 9b-1 for new investment vehicles that may not meet the technical terms of the rule. The SEC has used this authority sparingly.[49]

Sales Literature

The rules of the options exchanges and the NASD establish detailed standards concerning the content and manner of options advertisements and sales literature.[50] All advertisements and sales literature pertaining to options must be approved in advance by the firm's Compliance ROP and be retained by the firm in an accessible place for examination by the Exchange for a three-year period. In addition, the broker-dealer firm is required to submit all sales literature to the options exchanges and NASD for approval prior to use.[51]

---

48 See Securities Exchange Act Release No. 19055 and Securities Act Release No. 6426 (September 16, 1982), 47 FR 41950. The SEC recently approved amendments to the ODD reflecting changes to the options markets, which, among other things, includes disclosures regarding cash/spot foreign currency options, capped-style index options, FLEX options, and cross-rate currency options. See Securities Exchange Act Release No. 33582 (February 4, 1994), 59 FR 6661.

49 The SEC has used its authority to designate a particular product as a "standardized option" in the case of the Chicago Board Options Exchange, Inc. (CBOE) Flexible Exchange Options (FLEX options) and in conjunction with the approval of the listing and trading on national securities exchanges of Index Participations (IPs). See Securities Exchange Act Release Nos. 31910 (February 23, 1993), 58 FR 12286 (FLEX Options 9b-1 order) and 26709 (April 11, 1989), 54 FR 15280 (IPs approval order).

50 See Securities Exchange Act Release No. 29682 (September 13, 1991), 56 FR 47973.

51 See, e.g., CBOE Rule 9.21.

Discretionary Authority

The options exchanges further require prior written authorization by the customer to the firm's ROP in order for discretionary account trading to occur.[52] A SROP or ROP is required to approve and initial a discretionary options trade on the day it is executed. In addition, the SROP reviews the acceptance of each discretionary account to determine that the ROP had a reasonable basis to believe that the customer was able to understand and bear the risks of the proposed transaction, thus ensuring that investors will be offered an explanation of the special characteristics and rules applicable to the trading of options.

TRADING RULES

Margin

The authority to review margins for stock and stock index options was delegated by the Federal Reserve Board to the SEC in 1983.[53] In 1985, the options exchanges and the NASD, in conjunction with the SEC, established a premium-based customer margin system for "short" options positions.[54] Under this uniform system, the options exchanges and the NASD, with regulatory review and oversight by the SEC, set appropriate margin levels consistent with market conditions. Presently, the margin requirements for options are as follows.

First, the margin requirement for all long options positions, regardless of the underlying instrument, is 100 percent of the option premium. Second, for equity and narrow-based index options the margin requirement is 100 percent of the option premium plus 20 percent of the underlying product value, less any out-of-the-money amount, with a minimum of premium plus 10 percent of the underlying product value. Third, in the case of broad-based index options, the margin requirement is 100 percent of the option premium plus 15 percent of the underlying aggregate index value, less any out-of-the-money amount, with a minimum requirement of the option premium plus 10 percent of the underlying index value. Fourth, the margin requirement for all foreign currency options, except options on the Canadian dollar, is 100 percent of the option premium plus 4 percent of the value of the underlying instrument, less any out-of-the-money amount, with a minimum of premium plus 0.75 percent. For Canadian dollar options, the margin requirement is 100 percent of the option premium plus 1 percent of the value of the underlying instrument, less any out-of-the-money amount, with a minimum of premium plus 0.50 percent. Lastly, stock index warrants and currency warrants are margined in the same manner as straight stock, i.e., 50 percent of the underlying value on the long side and 150 percent of the underlying value on the short side.

---

52 See, e.g., Amex Rule 924 and CBOE Rule 9.10.
53 See Credit by Brokers and Dealers; Complete Revision and Simplification of Regulation T, 48 FR 23161 (Federal Reserve System 1983).
54 See Securities Exchange Act Release No. 22469 (September 26, 1985), 50 FR 40633.

Position and Exercise Limits

Position limits restrict the number of stock or stock index options contracts that an investor, or group of investors acting in concert, may own or control. Similarly, exercise limits prohibit the exercise of more than a specified number of puts or calls on a particular instrument within five consecutive business days. The principal purposes of position and exercise limits are: (1) minimizing the potential for mini-manipulations,[55] as well as other forms of market manipulation; (2) imposing a ceiling on the position that an investor with inside corporate or market information can establish; and (3) reducing the possibility of disruption in the options and cash markets.

The position limit applicable to a particular equity option is determined by the trading volume in the underlying security and is limited to positions of 10,500, 7,500, and 4,500 contracts. Position limits for narrow-based stock indexes have a similar three-tiered structure, i.e., 10,500, 7,500, and 5,500 contracts. The applicable position limit for a narrow-based index is determined by the percentage capitalization of a single stock or specified group of stocks within the index.

In addition, the options exchanges have been operating under a pilot program for equity options that provides for an automatic exemption from position limits for accounts that have established one of the four most commonly used hedged positions on a limited one-for-one basis (i.e., 100 shares of stock for one option contract). The exempted hedged positions are: (1) long stock and short calls; (2) long stock and long puts; (3) short stock and long calls; and (4) short stock and short puts. The maximum position limit (hedged and unhedged combined) held pursuant to the exchanges' pilot programs may not exceed twice the normal position limit.[56]

The options exchanges have been operating under a pilot program for broad-based stock index options that provides public customers with the ability to apply for a "hedge exemption" from position limits. Under the pilot programs, the exchanges may exempt from their position limits any positions held by public customers, provided they are hedged against qualified portfolios of stock that are approved by the relevant exchange. To be qualified, a portfolio must: (1) be net long (or short) in each component stock (or security readily convertible to common stock); (2) include at least four industry groups; (3) be comprised of at least 20 stocks (or their equivalents), no one of which constitutes more than 15 percent of the portfolio value; and (4) be carried by a member firm of the relevant exchange. The maximum position limit (hedged and unhedged combined) held pursuant to the exchanges' pilot programs for broad-based index options may not exceed three times the normal position limit.[57]

The only hedge position limit exemption program currently available for narrow-based index options is in the PHLX's Utility Index (UTY) option. Under this pilot program, if public customers hold a stock portfolio consisting of 10 UTY-component stocks, no one of which accounts for more than 15 percent of the portfolio, then they may apply to the PHLX for a position limit exemption of up to 16,000 contracts (hedged and unhedged combined), twice the normal limit.[58]

---

55 Mini-manipulation is an attempt to influence, over a relatively small range, the price movement in a stock to benefit a previously established derivatives position.

56 See, e.g., Securities Exchange Act Release No. 25738 (May 24, 1988), 53 FR 20204.

57 See, e.g., Securities Exchange Act Release No. 27322 (September 29, 1989), 54 FR 41889.

58 See Securities Exchange Act Release No. 27486 (November 30, 1989), 54 FR 50675.

Due to diversification, larger positions are permitted with regard to broad-based stock index options than in individual equity options.[59]

For example, on July 21, 1992, the SEC approved a CBOE proposal to: (1) raise position and exercise limits for European-style, SPX options that settle based on the opening prices of its component securities; (2) expand the existing hedge exemption from position limits; and (3) permit a facilitation exemption from position limits for money managers that control or manage several accounts. The basis for authorizing the increased SPX position limits and expanded exemptions from SPX position limits is the switch from closing to opening price settlement for the SPX option, as well as the institutional nature of this index option versus others such as the OEX.[60] These new higher positiion limits are detailed as follows: Position limits for the SPX option are 45,000 (approximately $2.0 billion) contracts on the same side of the market without the telescoping provision for near-month positions. In addition, hedge exemptions from position limits of up to 150,000 contracts may be granted to certain investors, and certain money managers may hold up to 250,000 contracts (approximately $10 billion) on the same side of the market in aggregate accounts, or 135,000 contracts (approximately $6 billion) on the same side of the market in a single account under its control. Lastly, member firms may obtain a position limit exemption of up to 100,000 (approximately $4 billion) SPX contracts on the same side of the market in order to facilitate large customer orders.

A new type of OEX option and SPX option has been developed by the CBOE, which expires on the first business day of the month following the end of each calendar quarter and is aptly named a Quarterly Index Expiration Option or QIX.[61] Previously, exchange-traded index options expired only on the Saturday immediately following the third Friday of the expiration month.[62] For position and exercise limit purposes, positions in SPX QIXs are aggregated with positions in a.m.-settled SPX options (45,000 contract limit) and positions in OEX QIX options are aggregated with positions in OEX options (25,000 contract limit).

---

59 For purposes of describing the SEC's position limit regulatory framework, the requirements for broad-based index options that are currently applicable to the CBOE's Standard & Poor's Corporation (S&P) 100 (OEX) and 500 (SPX) Index option contracts will be discussed in the following text. Similar position limits apply to the Amex's Major Market (XMI) and Institutional (XII) Index option contracts. See Securities Exchange Act Release Nos. 29798 (October 8, 1991), 56 FR 51956 and 31844 (February 9, 1993), 58 FR 8796. Index option position limits were originally based on the dollar value of the positions ($300 million). As a result of the fluctuating values of the OEX, SPX, XII and XMI indexes, however, position limits are now based on the number of contracts held.

60 See Securities Exchange Act Release No. 30944 (July 21, 1992), 57 FR 33376 [CBOE Rule 24.4(b)].

61 See Securities Exchange Act Release No. 31800 (February 1, 1993), 58 FR 7274. The SEC has also approved an Amex proposal to trade QIX Options based on the XMI, XII, and S&P MidCap 400 (MID) Indexes. See Securities Exchange Act Release No. 31844 (February 9, 1993), 58 FR 8796. The exercise settlement values for QIXs are based on the closing prices of the component securities on the last trading day prior to expiration.

62 For many money managers, institutional investors, and other market participants, options expiring at the end of a calendar quarter are preferable to the regular cycle expiration because the performance of these investors typically is judged on a quarterly basis. Accordingly, with QIX options, investors have more flexibility to tailor their hedges to coincide with relevant performance appraisal dates.

Similarly, the CBOE has also developed an OTC-type stock index option.[63] Flexible Exchange Options or FLEX Options are large-sized, customized index options based on certain SEC-approved Indexes. FLEX options were developed in response to the growing OTC market for index options.[64] As with OTC index options, large institutions will be able to establish positions in customized options to meet their hedging needs.[65] Each opening transaction in a FLEX option must have a minimum value of $10 million, with the term of the contract not exceeding five years. With regard to position and exercise limits, the CBOE has set a limit of 200,000 contracts for FLEX options.[66]

The PHLX is currently the only national securities exchange trading foreign currency options.[67] The established position limits for these options are 100,000 put or call option contracts on the same side of the market relating to the same underlying currency, with an exercise limit of 100,000 contracts within five consecutive business days. In addition, the PHLX also trades cross-rate currency options.[68] Cross-rate currency options are identical to U.S.-dollar-denominated foreign currency options except that the "trading" currency is a foreign currency, not U.S. dollars. For example, the exercise price in the case of the British pound/Japanese yen cross-rate is expressed as a certain number of yen per pound and premiums are quoted and paid in yen. The yen is the trading currency and the pound is the underlying currency. As in the case of traditional foreign currency options, position limits for cross-rate foreign currency

---

63 See Securities Exchange Act Release No. 31920 (February 24, 1993), 58 FR 12280. The original FLEX Options approval order permitted the CBOE to list and trade FLEX Options based on the OEX and SPX Indexes. The SEC has subsequently approved an additional CBOE filing to trade FLEX Options based on the Russell 2000 Index. See Securities Exchange Act Release No. 32694 (August 5, 1993), 58 FR 41814.

64 The SEC has also approved similar FLEX options proposals submitted by the AMEX based on the XMI, XII, and MID Indexes. See Securities Exchange Act Release No. 32781 (August 20, 1993), 58 FR 45360, as well as the Japan Index. See Securities Exchange Act Release No. 33262 (December 8, 1993), 58 FR 64622.

65 Specifically, with FLEX options, investors will be able to determine through exchange auction the following contract terms: (1) strike prices; (2) exercise type (i.e., European or American); (3) expiration date; and (4) method of settlement (a.m.- or p.m.-settled).

66 This is a maximum limit on a given underlying index without aggregation for other contracts on the same index. One exception to the 200,000 limit does exist at expiration. Specifically, at the close of business two days prior to the last day of trading of the calendar quarter, positions in p.m.-settled FLEX options and comparable QIX positions must be aggregated, and may not exceed the QIX position limits of 25,000 contracts for OEX and 45,000 contracts for SPX. See supra note 61.

67 The PHLX initially commenced the trading of foreign currency options on December 10, 1982, with the introduction of options on the British pound, Canadian dollar, Japanese yen, German mark and Swiss franc. See Securities Exchange Act Release No. 19133 (October 14, 1982), 47 FR 46946. The Exchange subsequently expanded its foreign currency options program to include three other foreign currencies: the French franc, European Currency Unit, and Australian dollar. See Securities Exchange Act Release Nos. 10822 (April 4, 1984), 49 FR 14611 (French franc); 22853 (February 3, 1986), 51 FR 5129 (European Currency Unit); and 23945 (December 30, 1986), 52 FR 633 (Australian dollar). All of these foreign currency options are based on the U.S. dollar. With a U.S.-dollar-denominated foreign currency option, an option holder receives the right to purchase or sell a stated amount of a particular foreign currency at a predetermined price (i.e., exercise price) that is denominated in U.S. dollars. The currency in which the option premium and exercise price are denominated, in this case the U.S. dollar, is referred to as the "trading" currency, while the other currency is referred to as the "underlying" currency.

68 See Securities Exchange Act Release No. 29919 (November 7, 1991), 56 FR 58109.

options are 100,000 contracts on the same side of the market.[69] A recent PHLX innovation approved by the SEC is the cash/spot foreign currency option.[70]

Surveillance

The 1934 Act requires an exchange to have rules designed to prevent fraudulent and manipulative acts and practices and to promote just and equitable principles of trade.[71] In addition, the 1934 Act also requires an exchange to have the capacity to comply with, and enforce compliance by its members with, the provisions of the 1934 Act, the rules thereunder, and the rules of the exchange. Therefore, each exchange is obligated to have in place a comprehensive surveillance program designed to detect manipulation and other improper trading activities.[72]

The options exchanges, as required by the SEC, have developed extensive surveillance systems in order to detect fraudulent and manipulative practices, engineered through the use of equity options, index options, and/or warrants. The linkage between the underlying cash or equity market and the derivative market creates a possibility for manipulation. Specifically, the options exchanges currently have extensive surveillance procedures to detect a variety of fraudulent practices including mini-manipulation, frontrunning, capping/pegging,[73] insider trading, improper quote dissemination, marking-the-close and pre-arranged trading. The SEC continues to work closely with all exchanges that trade derivative products, in order to enhance the surveillance systems presently in place.

---

69 The SEC originally approved position and exercise limits of 7,500 contracts for cross-rate foreign currency options due to the large contract sizes at that time. See Securities Exchange Act Release No. 29919 (November 7, 1991), 56 FR 58109. The PHLX subsequently reduced by 1/16 the cross-rate currency option contract size in order for these contracts to equal the level of its traditional foreign currency options contract. See Securities Exchange Act Release No. 30905 (July 9, 1992), 57 FR 31549.

70 A cash/spot foreign currency option is a cash-settled, European-style option issued by the OCC that allows holders to receive U.S. dollars representing the difference between the current foreign exchange spot price and the exercise price of the cash/spot foreign currency option. These options will have the same contract size as existing foreign currency options and will trade in one-week and two-week expirations. Positions will be aggregated with existing contracts on the same underlying currency for position limit purposes. The PHLX will originally trade a DM cash/spot option. See Securities Exchange Act No. 33732 (March 8, 1994), 59 FR 12023.

71 The antifraud provision of the 1934 Act, Section 10(b), and Rule 10b-5 thereunder, are applicable to the sales practices and trading activities of broker-dealers. The regulation of derivative products by the SEC renders the 1934 Act's prohibitions against manipulative and deceptive devices found in Rule 10b-5 binding on those individuals marketing and trading these new financial instruments.

72 U.S. exchanges and many foreign stock and options exchanges are members of the Intermarket Surveillance Group (ISG). Membership in ISG permits the free exchange of surveillance information with respect to the underlying cash market in the case of equity index options or other transactions in derivative instruments.

73 Capping is the process whereby stock transactions are effected shortly prior to an options expiration date in order to depress or prevent a rise in the price of a stock so that previously written call options will expire worthless and the premium received therefrom will be protected. Pegging, on the other hand, uses stock transactions to prevent a decline in the price of the stock so that previously written put options will expire worthless, thus protecting the premiums received. See supra note 55 (definition of mini-manipulation).

Frontrunning

Frontrunning is the practice of effecting an options transaction or transactions in other derivative instruments based upon nonpublic information regarding an impending block transaction in the stock market, in order to obtain a profit when the options or other derivative market adjusts to the price at which the block trades. Specifically, in the context of stock equity and index options, an exchange member or associated person who is in possession of material nonpublic market information concerning a transaction in a single stock or component stock of an index, and trades options on that stock or index to its advantage before information concerning the stock transaction has been made publicly available, may be in violation of the frontrunning prohibition.[74] The SROs have issued circulars clarifying their intermarket frontrunning prohibitions and policies.[75]

Disclosure

Rule 10b-10 under the 1934 Act requires broker-dealers to send written confirmations to customers at or before the completion of each securities transaction. In particular, the broker-dealer must disclose whether he or she acted as principal or agent in the transaction, specify the date and time of the transaction (or indicate that the time will be furnished upon request) and identify the price and number of shares or units (or principal amount) of the security purchased or sold.[76] For options transactions, the exchanges require a written confirmation of each transaction, showing the underlying security, the type of option, expiration month, exercise price, number of contracts, premium, commissions, transaction and settlement dates, whether the transaction was a purchase or sale, and whether the broker-dealer acted as principal or agent.[77]

FINANCIAL RESPONSIBILITY RULES

All registered broker-dealers are subject to SEC rules governing financial responsibility that are designed to protect their integrity and financial stability. These rules include recordkeeping and reporting rules and the net capital rule. The net capital rule, in

---

74 In addition, the anti-fraud prohibitions of Section 10(b) and Rule 106-5 under the 1934 Act would presumably apply to those cases where a floor trader, market-maker, or specialist, at an options exchange, unduly takes advantage of non-public information obtained in dealings with customers to the detriment of such customer and the market. "Trading ahead of one's customer," "scalping," and other fradulent or manipulative-type activity would likely be deemed a violation of "just and equitable principles of trade" found in exchange and NASD rules. See e.g., SEC, Division of Market Regulation, Market 2000: An Examination of Current Equity Market Developments (January 1994).

75 See Securities Exchange Act Release No. 25233 (December 10, 1987), 53 FR 296 (SR-AMEX-87-28; SR-CBOE-87-52; SR-NYSE-87-36; SR-PSE-87-26; SR-PHLX-87-29; and SR-NASD-87-45).

76 The rules of the national securities exchanges impose similar confirmation requirements.

77 See, e.g., CBOE Rule 9.11.

particular, plays a significant role in the maintenance of fair and orderly markets in the U.S. by ensuring that broker-dealers maintain sufficient net, liquid assets to enable them to satisfy promptly their obligations to customers and other broker-dealers. These assets also provide a cushion against potential market and credit risks.

The net capital rule applies solely to the broker-dealer itself, and does not cover, affiliated entities (*i.e.*, Derivative Product Subsidiaries). The SEC, does however, collect information from registered broker-dealers concerning the activities of affiliated entities in order to permit an evaluation of risk management systems.[78]

In the context of exchange-traded options, there are two different capital treatments under the net capital rule.[79] In the first method, it is assumed that the option will be held to expiration, so that capital charges are based on the market value of the underlying security. Conversely, the second method assumes that the options are frequently traded, requiring capital charges (or haircuts) based on the market value of the option, not the underlying security. Under both approaches, a minimum charge is assessed for "naked" options positions as well as for recognized options strategies, to account for potential price movements not reflected in the option's current value. In sum, the first approach affects the net capital of a broker-dealer who has actual proprietary positions in options which reflects actual market risk, while the second approach affects the net capital of a broker-dealer that guarantees or carries the account of an exempt market-maker in options which reflects the underlying credit risk.

In addition to specific financial requirements imposed on broker-dealers trading options, systems have also been established to ensure the efficient and accurate clearance and settlement of trades. Options transactions effected on a national securities exchange are cleared and settled in a continuous net settlement system operated by the Options Clearing Corporation ("OCC"). This system significantly reduces counterparty risk through the presence of a financially stable contractual intermediary that interposes itself as the contra party to both sides of the transaction.

CONCLUSION

In sum, the regulatory framework instituted by the options exchanges and the NASD with SEC oversight has had as its primary purpose the protection of investors and the maintenance of fair and orderly markets consistent with encouraging market competition and efficiency. For the future, we hope that a balanced regulatory approach will allow the U.S. to maintain and enhance its leadership role in the derivatives markets.

---

78 The SEC was provided with the authority to obtain holding company risk assessment information from affiliates of broker-dealers pursuant to the Market Reform Act of 1990. See Pub. L. No. 101-432, 104 Stat. 978 (1990). Under this legislative mandate, the SEC has adopted temporary risk assessment rules. See 17 C.F.R. Sections 240.17h-1T and 240.17h-2T [Securities Exchange Act Release No. 30929 (July 16, 1992), 57 FR 32159].

79 The SEC has proposed amendments to the net capital rule that would allow broker-dealers to use a theoretical pricing model (such as the Cox-Ross-Rubinstein model) when calculating capital charges for listed options and related positions. "Haircuts" for these options and related positions, when computed using this model, would more accurately reflect the risk inherent in broker-dealers' options. See Securities Exchange Act Release No. 33761 (March 15, 1994), 59 FR 13275; see also Theoretical Pricing Haircuts, SEC No-Action Letter, Fed. Sec. L. Rep. (CCH) ¶76,835 at 78,425 (March 15, 1994).

CHAPTER 40

Regulatory Issues Presented by the Growth of OTC Derivatives: Why Off-Exchange Is No Longer Off-Limits

Sheila C. Bair
Commissioner
Commodity Futures Trading Commission

INTRODUCTION

Prior to my appointment to the Commodity Futures Trading Commission in 1991, I embarked on a crash course in futures regulation in order to equip myself with the knowledge necessary to assume my new responsibilities as commissioner of the CFTC. Coming from a securities background, I found the most intriguing aspect of futures regulation to be the "exchange trading requirement," sometimes less charitably referred to as the "contract market monopoly," which served as the centerpiece of futures regulation.[1] That is, I discovered that unlike securities law (where there has always been both recognition *and* regulation of off-exchange products), commodities regulation was built on the premise that futures could be legally traded only on contract markets designated as such under the Commodity Exchange Act. Attempts to play off the organized markets in over-the-counter trading were viewed as nefarious "bucketing" and were completely and totally banned.

Once I became a CFTC commissioner, I soon discovered that this "exchange trading requirement" had become a historical anachronism that was presenting the most vexing of policy issues for the agency. The problem was simply this: Beginning

---

1 Commodity Exchange Act § 4(a), 7 U.S.C. § 6 (1982).

The author is a member of the Commodity Futures Trading Commission. The views expressed in this chapter are those of the author and do not necessarily reflect those of the Commodity Futures Trading Commission.

in the 1970s, financial innovation had given birth to a number of OTC markets in a wide variety of risk-shifting instruments, some of which closely resembled futures contracts in design and which were virtually identical in terms of economic function. Far from the notorious bucket shops of the early 1900s, which Congress sought to eradicate through the exchange trading requirement, these were legitimate markets dominated by institutional users and serving bona fide economic needs. Most problematic was the development of swaps—agreements between two parties to exchange periodic payment flows over a period of time based on a "notional amount," which is generally not exchanged between the parties. (For instance, with the plain-vanilla interest rate swap, one party agrees to make payments based on a floating rate and the other agrees to make payments based on a fixed rate.) Swap transactions are widely used by financial institutions and others to hedge interest rate and currency risk. They are also used to hedge price risk on commodities as diverse as energy products, precious metals, and grains.

The CFTC's initial response to the development of these markets was to take a hands-off approach. However, with their increased popularity and rapid growth, by the late 1980s, the "problem" became too big to ignore. In 1987, the agency launched an investigation into Chase Manhattan Bank's activities as a dealer in commodity swaps, a highly controversial action that effectively suspended most domestic commodity swap activity and forced the business overseas. Bowing to the firestorm of criticism precipitated by its enforcement action, the agency shifted gears and in late 1989 issued a policy statement designed to provide a safe harbor to most swaps activity from CEA regulation, including the exchange trading requirement.[2]

In a related action, that same year, the CFTC issued a statutory interpretation designed to provide regulatory certainty for novel "hybrid instruments" which, while possessing elements of futures or commodity options subject to CEA jurisdiction, were predominantly securities or depository instruments.[3] Such instruments were coming under increasing use as a means of combining capital-raising and risk-shifting functions into a single instrument, frequently allowing issuers to obtain capital at a lower cost. For instance, an oil company might issue debt repayment linked to the price of oil. This would allow the company to create a better "fit" between its repayment obligations and its specific risk profile.

---

2 CFTC Policy Statement Concerning Swap Transactions, 54 Fed. Reg. 30694 (July 21, 1989). The policy interpretation expressed the view that "at this time most swap transactions, although possessing elements of futures or options contracts, are not appropriately regulated." It then went on to list criteria that it stated, if met, would make CEA regulation "unnecessary." These criteria were:
   —the transaction had to be individually tailored as to its material terms;
   —it could be terminable only with the consent of the counterparty (that is, there was no "exchange-style" or automatic right to offset);
   —it had to be connected to the party's line of business;
   —it could not be marketed to the general public.
   The policy interpretation also required that the swaps could not be guaranteed by a clearing organization or supported by a mark-to-market margin and settlement system. This particular requirement precluded safe harbor treatment for clearing and settlement systems that were essentially indistinguishable from regulated exchange clearing systems. However, critics pointed out that it also created disincentives to the creation of multilateral clearing systems that would reduce counterparty risk.
3 CFTC Statutory Interpretation Regarding Hybrid Instruments, 54 Fed. Reg. 1128, 1139 (Jan. 11, 1989).

For a time, these CFTC regulatory actions, successfully headed off serious legal challenges to the enforceability of swaps and other off-exchange derivatives. However, as those markets and the number of participants grew, so did concerns about counterparty risk and the possibility that a defaulting counterparty would attempt to avoid liability by claiming that such transactions were illegal off-exchange futures contracts. Those concerns were heightened when, in 1990, another OTC market—that in Brent Oil forward contracts—suffered a major disruption as a result of a federal district court holding that those contracts were unenforceable futures.[4] The CFTC promptly issued yet another regulatory interpretation seeking to give legal sanction to such contracts.[5] However, many U.S. participants in the Brent Oil market complained that foreign firms remained reluctant to deal with them.

The issue of OTC markets surfaced with a vengeance in 1990, during congressional consideration of the CFTC's reauthorization legislation. Faced with the increasingly difficult task of finding ways to reconcile the exchange trading requirement with the rapid growth of legitimate off-exchange risk-shifting instruments, the CFTC sought statutory clarification of the status of swaps and other OTC instruments. The Senate was the first to respond by passing a package of jurisdictional amendments contained in Title III of its bill S. 207. Title III included a specific statutory exemption for swaps as well as a general grant of discretionary authority to the CFTC to exempt OTC transactions from the CEA's off-exchange trading ban if they were entered into exclusively by institutions for business reasons, and the exemption was otherwise consistent with the public interest and the CEA.

Title III, however, became highly controversial and ran into stiff opposition in the House of Representatives. Regulated exchanges felt that the mandatory swaps exemption was overly broad and would create too much of an uneven playing field between OTC products and exchange-traded instruments. In the end, Congress decided to drop the special mandatory exemption for swaps, but did give the CFTC general discretionary authority to grant exemptions from any or all provisions of the CEA, except the Johnson-Shad accord.[6] This general grant of exemptive authority, however, was not without conditions.

First, the new law required that the Commission make a determination, before providing any exemption from a CEA provision, that such action was consistent with the public interest. In addition, any exemption from the exchange trading requirement had to be accompanied by specific findings that the Commission's action was consistent with the purposes of the Act, including the "maintenance of the integrity and soundness of markets and market participants,"[7] and that it would not interfere with the ability of the Commission or any contract market to discharge its regulatory or self-regulatory responsibilities. The law also directed that no exemption from the

---

4 *Transnor (Bermuda) Limited v. BP North America Petroleum*, 783 F. Supp. 1472 (S.D.N.Y. 1990).
5 CFTC Statutory Interpretation Concerning Forward Transactions, 55 Fed. Reg. 39188 (Sept. 25, 1990).
6 The so-called Johnson-Shad accord of 1982 (named, respectively, for the then-Chairmen of the CFTC and SEC) was a jurisdictional accord granting the CFTC exclusive jurisdiction over futures and options on futures based on broad-based stock indexes, while reserving to the SEC jurisdiction over options on stock indexes. The accord also gave the SEC a consultative role and veto power over CFTC approval of stock index futures products. The accord also bans futures on narrow-based stock indexes or individual stocks. See Commodity Exchange Act, § 2s(a) (1) (B).
7 H.R. Rep. No. 978, 102d Cong., 2d. Sess. 78 (1992).

exchange trading requirement could be granted unless the exempted transaction would be entered into solely between "appropriate persons." The law generally defined "appropriate persons" as restricted to institutional participants or trading professionals, but also included "[s]uch other persons that the Commission determines to be appropriate in light of their financial or other qualifications, or the applicability of appropriate regulatory protections."[8]

In the Conference Report accompanying the legislation, Congress gave somewhat conflicting guidance as to how it wanted the CFTC to use this new authority. At one point, the Conference Report stated that "the goal of providing the Commission with broad exemptive authority is not to prompt a wide-scale deregulation of markets falling within the ambit of the Act. Rather, it is to give the Commission a means of providing certainty and stability to existing and emerging markets so that financial innovation and market development can proceed in an effective and competitive manner."[9]

However, the Report also instructed that:

"... [T]he granting of general exemptive authority is intended to promote responsible economic and financial innovation and fair competition ... [T]he Commission, in considering fair competition, will implement this provision in a fair and even-handed manner to products and systems sponsored by exchanges and non-exchanges alike."[10]

In other words, Congress asked the Commission to (1) provide legal certainty to the existing OTC markets in such a way as to permit them to develop without (2) giving undue competitive advantages to these instruments, while (3) not commencing a wide-scale deregulation of the futures markets. Not an easy task! The new law also directed the Commission to "promptly ... exercise the exemptive authority" with regard to "classes of hybrid instruments that are predominantly securities or depository instruments" and "classes of swap agreements that are not part of a fungible class of agreements that are standardized as to their material economic terms."[11] The Conference Report also requested that the Commission "review the situation" regarding the Brent Crude Oil market and "determine whether exemptive or other action should be taken."[12] Responding to these congressional directives, in January of 1993, the Commission finalized rules relating to swaps and hybrids, and in April of 1993, approved an order designed to exempt the Brent Oil market and certain other energy markets and products from CEA jurisdiction. Each action is discussed in more detail below.

THE SWAPS EXEMPTION

The swaps exemption approved by the Commission was patterned after the mandatory swaps exemption originally contained in Title III of S. 207, referenced above, with certain changes. Like Title III, the CFTC rule adopted the relatively broad definition

---

8 Commodity Exchange Act, § 4(c) (3) (K), 7 U.S.C. § 6(c) (3) (K) (1992).
9 H.R. Rep. No. 978, at 78.
10 Id.
11 Commodity Exchange Act, § 4(c) (4), 7 U.S.C. § 6(c) (4) (1992).
12 H.R. Rep. 978, at 82.

of "swap agreement" utilized in the Bankruptcy Code.[13] The CFTC rule also limited the exemption to swaps transactions entered into between certain classes of investors (though it set somewhat more restrictive standards than the statute.) These included:

- Regulated financial institutions, such as a bank or trust, savings association, credit union, or insurance company;

- An investment company regulated under the Investment Company Act of 1940;

- A commodity pool regulated under the CEA, with total assets exceeding $5 million;

- A business entity with total assets exceeding $10 million, or with net assets exceeding $1 million, but that is entering into the swap to offset a risk incurred in the conduct of its business;

- A pension plan subject to ERISA with total assets exceeding $5 million;

- A broker-dealer subject to regulation under the Securities Exchange Act or a futures commission merchant, floor broker, or floor trader subject to regulation under the CEA; and

- A natural person with total assets exceeding $10 million.

The rule included three other requirements intended to provide a policy basis for distinguishing exempt swap transactions from traditional futures contracts subject to the CEA. First, exempt swap agreements could not be part of a fungible class of agreements that are standardized as to their material economic terms. Second, the creditworthiness of any party had to be a material consideration in entering into, or determining the terms of, the swap agreement. Finally, the rule provided that the swap agreement could not be entered into or traded on a "multilateral transaction execution facility," described in the preamble to the rule as a "physical or electronic facility in which all market makers and other participants that are members simultaneously have the ability to execute transactions and bind both parties by accepting offers which are made by one member and open to all members of the facility."[14]

Not surprisingly, the CFTC's rule making on swaps was no more popular with the regulated futures exchanges than had been the original Title III of S. 207. In a comment letter jointly filed by the Chicago Board of Trade, Chicago Mercantile Exchange, and Commodity Exchange, the exchanges challenged both the policy grounds and legal basis for the exemption.[15] Their primary legal challenge focused on

---

13 11 U.S.C. § 101(55). **Swap Transaction** means (A) an agreement (including terms and conditions incorporated by reference therein) which is a rate swap agreement, basis swap, forward rate agreement, commodity swap, interest rate option, forward foreign exchange agreement, rate cap agreement, rate floor agreement, rate collar agreement, currency swap agreement, cross-currency rate swap agreement currency option, any other similar agreement (including any option to enter into any of the foregoing); (B) any combination of the foregoing; or (C) a master agreement for any of the foregoing together with all supplements.

14 58 Fed. Reg. 5591.

15 Letter from Thomas R. Donovan, President and Chief Executive Officer, CBT; William J. Brodsky, President and Chief Executive Officer, CME; David Halperin, President, COMEX to Jean Webb, Secretary to the CFTC, pp. 2–4 (Dec. 28, 1992).

the Commission's failure to make specific findings that swaps were futures contracts, arguing that under the plain meaning of the statute, the CFTC could only "exempt any agreement, contract, or transaction (or class thereof) that [was] otherwise subject" to the CEA.[16] They also challenged whether the Commission had adequately addressed the required statutory determinations discussed above. But the heart of their challenge was that the rule created an uneven playing field for regulated products. They proposed that, at a minimum, the Commission should condition relief on the establishment of a self-regulatory organization (SRO) for swaps, and should expressly retain certain fundamental regulatory requirements such as the CEA's prohibitions against fraud and manipulation.

The Commission did make certain changes before finalizing the rule in an effort to be responsive to legitimate exchange concerns (though these changes did not go nearly so far as to ameliorate the exchange's strong opposition to the final rule.) Perhaps the most significant of these changes concerned the final rule's treatment of multilateral clearing facilities.

As originally proposed, the preamble to the swaps rule suggested that clearing systems, other than those that "mutualize risk" or "novate" payment obligations, would qualify for the exemption under the rule. The exchanges pointed out (rightly, to my mind) that this arbitrarily disadvantaged futures style clearing, while appearing to permit other types of centralized clearing systems that might guarantee payment obligations through letters of credit or third-party insurance. It was also unpopular with the Federal Reserve Board, which argued in its comment letter that the exemption should permit the development of any "appropriately structured multilateral payment netting and settlement facilities."[17]

In an effort to respond to these concerns, the Commission, in its final rule, sought to distinguish the types of netting arrangements that would be permissible on a bilateral and multilateral basis. For bilateral arrangements, the rule and preamble made clear that all forms of netting, including netting of payment obligations, as well as collateral and mark-to-market margining arrangements, were permissible. This was a significant expansion from the 1989 policy interpretation, which did not permit such credit enhancement measures, even on a bilateral basis. With regard to multilateral arrangements, however, the Commission's final swap exemption was redrafted to permit bookkeeping and processing functions for the multilateral netting of payments, but stopped short of permitting systems that would allow a centralized counterparty to assume legally binding net obligations of swap participants. As the preamble to the final rule explained, multilateral netting arrangements would only be permitted

---

16 However, the Conference Report indicates that "The Conferees do not intend that the exercise of exemptive authority by the Commission would require any determination before-hand that the agreement, instrument, or transaction for which an excmption is sought is subject the Act." H.R. Rep. 978, at 82–83.

17 Letter from William W. Wiles, Secretary to the Board of Governors of the Federal Reserve System, to Jean Webb, Secretary to the CFTC, regarding 17 CFR Part 35 Exemption for Certain Swap Agreements, p. 2 (Jan. 28, 1992).

"provided that the underlying gross obligations among the parties are not extinguished until all netted obligations are fully performed."[18]

The Commission also added a proviso to the rule to make clear that it would accept applications for exemptions for any type of clearing arrangement or facility, and act on them, subject to any terms or conditions that might be appropriate, taking into account the applicability of other regulatory regimes. The preamble to the final rule expressed the Commission's desire to give maximum latitude to market participants in developing multilateral mechanisms to control credit and settlement risk.

To my mind, these changes in the final rule's treatment of clearing were extremely important, given the clear governmental interest in the swap market relating to the reduction of systemic risk. It is imperative for the CFTC to facilitate and encourage the development of the most efficient and effective types of clearing facilities, without disadvantaging any particular type of facility or arrangement. At the same time, given potential pitfalls in the development of centralized clearing systems for swaps and other OTC derivatives, the CFTC's caution in using a case-by-case application approach is justified. As was stated in the "Report of the Committee on Interbank Netting Schemes of the Central Banks of the Group of Ten Countries" (the "Lamfalussy" Report),

> Even when legally effective in producing net exposures, multilateral netting systems also have the potential to increase systemic risks because they concentrate risks on the central counterparty. If a system is able to manage and contain prudently its exposures to the participants, and to the extent that in the event of one participant's default, it is able to continue to satisfy its obligations to the others, then the system's operation will increase the likelihood that the credit or liquidity problems of one market participant will suddenly and negatively affect the condition of others. Moreover, the concentration of risks on the central counterparty exposes all participants to the risk the central counterparty itself may fall.

The Commission made two other important changes to its final swaps rule. First, it decided to retain the applicability of the CEA's general antifraud provisions to those transactions that would otherwise be subject to the CFTC's jurisdiction under the Commodity Exchange Act. This change, I believe, was necessary in order to balance the need to provide exemptive relief to the swap market with the need to preserve protections that lie at the core of the CEA and to guard against abuse by those who might try to misuse the exemption as a shield against fraudulent activities. It is becoming increasingly difficult to craft "bright line" legal distinctions between the growing number of legitimate OTC derivative products from the traditional, illegal off-exchange boiler room operations. Thus, in my view, it is imperative that we retain residual antifraud authority as a "fail-safe" to ensure that the OTC exemptive process does not in any way undermine our enforcement program. Regrettably, as discussed below, the Commission did not retain antifraud authority in providing exemptive relief for certain energy contracts.

---

18 58 Fed. Reg. 5591.

The Commission also clarified that it was retaining authority to enforce antimanipulation requirements against any attempt to manipulate cash commodity or futures
prices by any person. Again, this change was viewed as necessary to ensure that core
CEA protections against price manipulation were not in any way compromised. This
was a noncontroversial change, one that was also adopted in the Commission's energy
exemptive order, and I would assume, one which will be a standard part of any future
OTC exemptions granted by the Commission.

THE HYBRID RULE

At the same time the Commission approved its swaps rule, it also finalized exemptive
relief for certain "hybrid" instruments that combine equity or debt securities or
depository instruments with features of either commodity futures, options, or both.
Under the rule approved by the Commission, an economic test would be applied to
such instruments to determine their "predominant" nature. Those hybrid instruments
in which the commodity interest did not predominate would be exempt from CEA
regulation.[19]
    The Commission's hybrid rule making presented fundamentally different policy
issues than the swaps exemption, as well as the Commission's energy order, discussed
below. With swaps and energy contracts, it is unclear that any system of federal
financial regulation would apply absent CEA requirements, but for hybrids the
question really was not *whether* there should be federal regulation but rather, *which*
system should apply. In writing its hybrid test, the Commission sought to make the
determination of which system should apply based on the predominant characteristics
of a given instrument. But constructing a test to express the concept of predominance
in regard to financial instruments that include elements of futures and/or commodity
options turned out to be a difficult and complex task, one which precipitated a number
of comment letters,[20] and produced an end product with which probably no one was
completely satisfied. It may be impossible to know whether the CFTC's final hybrid
rule is an effective one until it has been in operation for a while and we have a chance
to see how it works. In this regard, I think it will be imperative for the CFTC to
coordinate with other regulators to remain apprised of the types of instruments that
are offered in reliance on the rule.
    The difficulties the CFTC faced in constructing a workable rule that assigned
responsibility for oversight of hybrid instruments to the "proper" regulator perhaps
underscores why there has been an increasing interest in moving toward a unified
system of financial regulation. To be sure, in these times of strained resources, one
has to ask whether it is really profitable for the Commission and other financial

---

19 58 Fed. Reg. 5580.
20 Commenters expressed a wide variety of views on the Commission's proposed predominance test.
    Some commenters tempered their support with "suggestions to modify or clarify certain aspects of the
    rule . . ." Others suggested "the use of alternative . . . ways to value the option components of the
    instrument when applying the test." Several said "the technique used to establish predominance is
    flawed because the test uses a volatility-sensitive measure of exposure for futures-like com-
    ponents . . ." Also, the test is flawed because it treats "the return on the performance bond deposit as
    if it were part of the return on the customer's investment."

regulators to spend substantial amounts of time and resources grappling with whether an instrument is predominantly a future, commodity option, security, or banking instrument, when perhaps the more important inquiry is whether the instrument should be regulated, and if so, how should it be regulated? The Commission discussed this issue in its October 1993 report on OTC Derivative Markets and Their Regulation. The report, requested in the Conference Report to the CFTC's 1992 reauthorization bill, analyzed the idea of a single regulator for futures options, swaps, derivatives, and securities. The Commission concluded that, at present, cross-market concerns about these products could best be addressed by the establishment of an interagency council composed of the CFTC, the SEC, and bank regulators which would supplement the agencies' current efforts at cooperation, information sharing, and harmonization of regulatory efforts. The Commission offered the Working Group on Financial Markets established in March 1988 as an example of the type of interagency council that it envisioned.[21] The Working Group is composed of the Secretary of the Treasury, who acts as Chairman, the Chairman of the CFTC, the Chairman of the SEC, and the Chairman of the Board of Governors of the Federal Reserve System. Consistent with the CFTC's recommendation, on January 3, 1994, Secretary of the Treasury Lloyd Bentsen wrote to the heads of the CFTC, SEC, and the Federal Reserve Board requesting that the Working Group consider the issues raised by the growth of the OTC derivatives market.

THE ENERGY EXEMPTION

On April 13, 1993, the Commission, on a divided vote, approved an order exempting contracts for the deferred purchase or sale of specified energy products. The order stemmed from an application for exemptive relief filed by a group of producers, processors, merchandisers and others engaged in commercial businesses related to crude oil, natural gas, or their products. As approved, the order would apply to contracts for the deferred purchase or sale of crude oil, condensates, natural gas liquids, or their derivatives, which are used primarily as an energy source. To qualify, transactions would have to be between "commercial participants" who "incur risks, in addition to price risk, related to the underlying commodities" and "have a demonstrable capacity or ability . . . to make or take delivery." The participants would also have to fall within certain defined categories of "appropriate persons."

Though the ostensible purpose of the order was to provide commercial participants in existing "forward-like" energy markets such as the Brent Oil market with exemptive relief, in my view, the order, by its terms, went far beyond what was necessary. The problem of overbreadth was compounded by the Commission's failure to retain basic antifraud authority. As a result, I voted against the order, viewing it as a serious misapplication of our new exemptive authority and as setting a dangerous precedent.

Clearly, the proposed order went far beyond the traditional forward contract exclusion recognized under the CEA. Indeed, the only arguable distinguishing feature I could see between exempt transactions under the order and the typical gasoline boiler

---

21 OTC Report at 126, n. 146.

room operation was the requirement that participants be "commercial entities." However, this "commerciality" requirement in the order was by and large undefined. Indeed, it was arguable that an entity, simply by entering into an exempt transaction, could become a "commercial," by its willingness to assume delivery risk.[22] In any event, the Commission had never before recognized an exception to its jurisdiction based solely on the "commerciality" of the participants, nor could I see any valid policy reason why commercial firms engaging in futures transactions should not be covered by basic antifraud protections, just as they are in the regulated markets.

One argument set forth in the preamble to the order for the antifraud exemption was that because participants in exempt energy transactions would be only so-called "sophisticated" institutional users or entities of high net worth; they would not "need" CFTC antifraud protections.

However, if this were a valid rationale for exemptions from antifraud and other components of our regulatory scheme, the CFTC might as well close its doors tomorrow, because approximately 98 percent of users of regulated, exchange-traded futures would meet the relatively low eligibility requirements of the exemptive order. (To be eligible to participate in an exempt transaction, a business entity must have a net worth exceeding $1 million, or total assets exceeding $5 million, *or* be guaranteed by an entity meeting those requirements. No net worth or asset requirements would apply to a participating bank, trust company, broker-dealer, or futures commission merchant.)

Moreover, large firms are defrauded—the CFTC has brought a number of enforcement actions where the victims have been so-called institutional or sophisticated investors. This argument also missed the mark because the preamble to the order expressly recognized the opportunity for indirect *public* participation in these markets through collective investment vehicles, such as commodity pools.

In opposing CFTC retention of antifraud authority, the energy companies applying for exemptive relief argued that antifraud protections would place an onerous burden on market participants, and in particular, put U.S. participants in the Brent Oil market at a competitive disadvantage. I found this latter argument to be particularly unpersuasive, given the fact that the United Kingdom, under the Financial Services Act, subjects many participants in the Brent Oil market to a quite extensive regulatory structure, including antifraud prohibitions. These markets are also subject to state antifraud laws (which, given conflicts in state law, are probably more onerous than the federal forums and remedies provided under the CEA) without any apparent "chilling" effect. Finally, participants in these markets had always run the risk that their transactions could be deemed "futures" and subject to the whole plethora of CEA requirements, not just antifraud. Thus, it did not seem to me to impose much of a burden on market participants for the Commission to retain a sliver of authority regarding fraudulent conduct.

I also felt that the precedent set by the energy order was a dangerous one. I could see no valid policy reason for retaining antifraud authority in our swaps rule, yet declining to do so with energy contracts. I was very concerned that we would inevitably raise the expectations of other potential applicants for exemptive relief that they would also be able to escape basic antifraud provisions. Moreover, it was unnecessary for us

---

22 See, 58 Fed. Reg. 28690.

to paint ourselves into that kind of corner. The main reason why the CFTC sought general exemptive authority was to have the flexibility to craft appropriately tailored exemptive relief based on public policy considerations, instead of having to deal with the CEA's former rigid regulatory structure. Unfortunately, in approving the energy order, the Commission opted for the "all or nothing" approach of the past, when in my view, we should have more carefully weighed individual aspects of our regulations and made a reasoned determination as to which requirements should and should not apply.

FUTURE ISSUES TO BE ADDRESSED BY THE COMMISSION

Futures-Style Clearing for OTC Derivatives

Federal regulatory concerns regarding OTC derivatives markets—particularly swaps—have focused to a large extent on systemic risks related to the default of one or more major participants. Among the first to articulate this concern publicly was then-Federal Reserve Bank of New York President E. Gerald Corrigan, in a January 1992 speech to the New York State Bankers Association. In this speech Corrigan issued a "warning" to bankers to examine more closely their off-balance-sheet activities related to OTC derivatives, stating that the interest rate swap market, in particular, could be "introducing new elements of risk" into the marketplace, including "possible distortions to the balance sheets and income statements of financial and nonfinancial institutions alike."

In November 1990, the Bank for International Settlements published the Lamfalussy Report, which concluded that netting schemes for OTC derivatives could have the potential to reduce systemic risk, provided that certain conditions were met. In reaching its conclusion, the Report specifically analyzed what it called the "centralized" systems, utilized by futures and options clearinghouses, whereby all risks are borne and managed by the clearinghouse acting as central counterparty, which in turn, requires participants to post collateral or margin to secure the system's exposure to risk in the event of default by one or more participants. The Report found that this type of system, as well as more "decentralized" systems,[23] should, if properly constructed, "provide credit and liquidity safeguards that would ensure the system's ability to manage exposures and complete settlements."[24]

Former CFTC Chairman Susan Phillips, now a member of the Board of Governors of the Federal Reserve System, has also spoken to the growing interest in developing a clearinghouse for swaps and other OTC derivatives. In a speech to the Conference on Regulation of Derivative Products before the Institute for International Research in March of 1993, she encouraged OTC market participants to explore the

---

23 The Lamfalussy Report described a "decentralized" system as one whereby "[m]ultilateral netting would be used to produce legally binding net positions. But in the event of a participant's default, credit losses associated with its net position vis-à-vis the central counterparty would then be allocated on a pro-rata basis among the surviving participants based on their bilateral dealings with the defaulter."

24 Lamfalussy Report at 3.

benefits of a clearinghouse, stating that "[m]ultilateral netting is a potentially powerful tool for reducing counterparty credit exposures." Phillips recognized that "While some highly creditworthy swap dealers may fear that the creation of a clearinghouse would harm their competitive position, it is not clear to me why a clearinghouse that served the dealer community would in any way erode the advantage that highly rated dealers have in competing for the business of end user." She concluded that "Such end users still would have incentives to deal with the most creditworthy dealers, while the clearinghouse would allow such dealers to reduce credit exposures and related capital changes in the interdealer market." In a later interview,[25] Phillips called the futures exchanges' clearinghouses "the very piece of their operations that may be the most economically attractive" to swap market participants.

As discussed above, the Commission, in the preamble to its final swaps rule, also encouraged the development of clearing facilities for OTC derivatives, recognizing the potential importance of such facilities in reducing systemic risk, and invited applications for appropriate exemptive relief. Moreover, in my view, this is clearly an area where futures exchanges can and should play a role, given the overwhelming success of the U.S. futures clearing system in controlling risks related to regulated futures and commodity options. Promoting and encouraging the development of clearing systems for OTC derivatives would not only help facilitate reduction of risk in OTC markets, but reduce the danger of "flow-back" risk in the regulated exchange markets as well. OTC market participants frequently hold offsetting positions in regulated futures and options markets, yet exchange clearinghouses are unable to access information about market participants positions and exposures in unregulated, off-exchange markets. As a result, these risks cannot be taken into account by the clearinghouse in setting its risk management requirements, making regulated clearing systems also potentially vulnerable in the event of a major default in the OTC markets.[26]

In evaluating issues related to the development of OTC clearing systems, I think it will be important for the CFTC to consult with other interested regulators and to draw on their experiences in setting standards for such facilities. Certainly, the minimum standards for netting systems set forth in the Lamfalussy Report would, I believe, provide a useful basis for analysis. These standards, as stated in the Report, are:

- Netting schemes should have a well-founded legal basis under all relevant jurisdictions.

- Netting scheme participants should have a clear understanding of the impact of the particular scheme on each of the financial risks affected by the netting process.

- Multilateral netting systems should have clearly defined procedures for the management of credit risks and liquidity risks, which specify the respective responsibilities of the netting provider and the participants. These procedures

---

25 *Knight-Ridder Financial News*, "Phillips Sees Swaps Products Potentially Offered by Exchanges" (April 28, 1993).
26 See, e.g., "Report of the Bachmann Task Force on Clearance and Settlement Reform in the U.S. Securities Markets" (May 1992) pp. 9–10.

should also ensure that all parties have both the incentives and the capabilities to manage and contain each of the risks they bear and that limits are placed on the maximum level of credit exposure that can be produced by each participant.

■ Multilateral netting systems should, at a minimum, be capable of ensuring the timely completion of daily settlements in the event of an inability to settle by the participant with the largest single net-debit position.

■ Multilateral netting systems should have objective and publicly disclosed criteria for admission, which permit fair and open access.

■ All netting schemes should ensure the operational reliability of technical systems and the availability of backup facilities capable of completing daily processing requirements.[27]

In addition, the degree to which institutions participating in any proposed clearing facility or arrangement would be subject to oversight by the Federal Reserve Board, the Securities Exchange Commission, or another regulator, would be an important factor for the CFTC to consider in crafting appropriate exemptive relief. Finally, the CFTC's own experiences in overseeing futures clearing systems will be extremely important, given the promise of adapting futures-style clearing facilities to OTC derivatives markets.

Exchange Competitiveness Issues

As previously discussed, in explaining how Congress intended the CFTC to use its new exemptive authority, the Conference Report to the 1992 reauthorization directed that the Commission "in considering fair competition, will implement this provision in a fair and even-handed manner to products and systems sponsored by exchanges and nonexchanges alike."[28] The Conferees also stated, however, that the Commission "may make distinctions between exchanges and other markets, taking into account the particular facts and circumstances involved, consistent with the public interest and the purposes of this Act, where such distinctions are not arbitrary and capricious."[29] In addition, the Conferees admonished that "The goal of providing the Commission with broad exemptive powers is not to prompt a wide-scale deregulation of markets falling within the ambit of this Act."[30]

Notwithstanding these potentially conflicting directives, it seems clear that Congress did contemplate that exemptive authority could be applied to exchange-traded products, as well as OTC instruments, where such action would promote a "level playing field," so long as it was consistent with the public interest and purposes of the CEA, and would not result in a "wide-scale deregulation" of futures markets.

It also seems clear that the rapid growth of OTC derivatives has created new competitive challenges for regulated exchanges (although there is also significant evidence that the growth of OTC markets has created business for the exchanges

---

27 Lamfalussy Report at 26.
28 H.R. Rep. 978, *Supra*, at 78.
29 Id. at 78.
30 Id. at 81.

through OTC dealers laying off their risks in the regulated markets). And there may well be aspects of the CEA and implementing regulations that were designed more for the protection of small users, emanating from the origins of the futures markets in agriculture futures and the desire to protect small producers. Not all components of our customer protection rules may be appropriate for all contract markets, which today are dominated by financial instruments, many of which are used almost exclusively by sophisticated institutional users and trading professionals.

The Commission has already demonstrated a willingness to ease particular regulatory requirements related to customer protection based on the notion of the "sophisticated investor." For instance, in 1992, the Commission exempted commodity pools, which are marketed exclusively to institutional or high net worth investors, from most reporting and disclosure requirements.

At the same time, it should be emphasized that the goal of the CEA and implementing regulations is not simply to protect small retail customers; rather, it is also to protect the integrity of open, competitive trading and the price discovery process, as well as to preserve the financial integrity of the system. Moreover, it would seem that institutional customers benefit from these latter components of CEA regulation, at least as much as the so-called "small investor." Audit trail standards, trade surveillance, and trade practice rules were all mentioned as important by representatives of institutional investors during a discussion on this topic at a March 12, 1992, meeting of the CFTC's Financial Products Advisory Committee. These types of requirements, as well as capital standards, net worth, and other financial requirements on market participants may be particularly important to regulated investment vehicles, such as pension funds, investment companies, and insurance companies, whose own regulators may be less willing to allow them to participate in contracts traded on futures exchanges if there are exemptions from such requirements.

In considering possible exemptions or easing of regulations pertaining to market and financial integrity, both from a business and a regulatory perspective, caution would seem to be in order. The nation's two largest futures exchanges, however, have decided to take a separate tack. On April 7, 1993, the Chicago Mercantile Exchange filed the first exchange application for exemptive relief, on its "rolling spot" foreign currency contracts. These contracts, which have already received approval from the CFTC to trade as regulated futures and options on futures, seek to replicate certain transactions in the foreign currency forward and swap markets. Similarly, on June 30, 1993, the Chicago Board of Trade submitted a petition seeking a "professional trading market exemption" to apply to trading in any instrument on the CBOT or any other board of trade, including those previously designated by the Commission. In their applications, the CME and CBOT have sought relief from all CEA requirements, except antimanipulation and antifraud, arguing that they should receive relief coextensive with that provided by the CFTC's swaps exemption. Both exchanges would limit access to trading to those broad categories of investors qualified to engage in exempt transactions under the CFTC's swaps rule.[31] On August 16, 1993, the Commission sought public comment on the exchange petitions. The Commission's staff is

---

31 For a good overview of policy issues presented by application of the CFTC's new exemptive authority to exchange-traded products and systems, see Kevin M. Foley, "Exchanges Enter Two-Tiered Market," *Futures Magazine*, (March/April 1993).

reviewing these comments and is expected to make recommendations to the Commission in the first half of 1994.[32]

CONCLUSION

Finding the right balance between the need to help regulated futures exchanges remain competitive in the face of burgeoning OTC markets and the need to maintain core regulatory protections fundamental to the CEA may be the primary challenge confronting the CFTC for the next several years. Questions pertaining to the regulation of OTC markets will also continue to arise. In this regard, major studies of OTC derivatives markets by the Commission and the Group of Thirty have been completed. Another by the General Accounting Office is expected to be completed by June 1994.

It seems certain that Congress will want to revisit issues related to the growth of OTC markets and exchange competitiveness when it takes up the CFTC's next reauthorization in 1994. At this point, it appears that the future trend among Washington policy makers may well be increased regulatory interest and oversight of OTC markets—as trading in them becomes more standardized and participation becomes more widespread, particularly among smaller, less creditworthy participants. On the other hand, as regulated exchanges seek to compete with OTC markets with the development of more customized products marketed to highly capitalized institutional users, less regulatory oversight of such products and the development of a "two-tiered" regulatory system may be in order.

---

32 58 Fed. Reg. 43414 (Aug. 16, 1993).

CHAPTER 41

Legal Issues Associated with Derivative Municipal Securities Created in the Secondary Market

George G. Wolf
Partner
Gary A. Herrmann
Partner
Adam W. Glass
Partner

Orrick, Herrington & Sutcliffe

INTRODUCTION

This chapter summarizes the principal legal issues under federal law associated with municipal derivatives created in the secondary market.[1] By secondary market transactions, we mean transactions in which tax-exempt obligations (whether newly issued or outstanding for some time) already exist and are repackaged in some form. "Secondary market" stands in contrast to "primary market" transactions, in which the arrangements for the payments of interest are established directly pursuant to the terms of the bonds. Two of the principal attributes of municipal securities are their exemption from registration under the federal securities laws and the exclusion from federal income taxation of their interest income. Because the benefit of the securities law exemption attaches only to the municipal obligation itself, a fundamental issue with respect to municipal derivatives in the secondary market is to ensure that no "separate

---

1 This chapter addresses many of the issues connected with common structures associated with municipal derivatives as of the time of this writing. Particular structures in the market have varied as the market has developed over the past several years. While many of the issues addressed will arise in connection with any structure, new structures may pose additional issues or involve different considerations. In the tax area, for example, the IRS has not issued any pronouncements specifically addressed to municipal derivatives for a number of years.

security" is created. Similarly, the benefit of the income tax exclusion flows only to the owner of the municipal security for federal income tax purposes; so the other fundamental issue with respect to municipal derivatives in the secondary market is to ensure that tax ownership of the underlying security "flows through" the derivative structure to the beneficial owner of the interest.

One common type of municipal derivative is synthetic floating-rate municipal bonds—a structure that mimics an obligation putable by the holder every seven days to a liquidity provider, usually a bank. Obligations of this type are often acquired by tax-exempt money-market mutual funds. In general, this type of investment consists of the acquisition of a bundle of assets consisting of (1) a fixed-rate municipal bond, (2) a right to put the bond at par on seven days notice, (3) a remarketing arrangement to determine the lowest rate that would permit the bond to be remarketed at par, taking into account the put right, and (4) an obligation to pay to a third party the difference between the coupon on the bond (or some amount related to the coupon) and the remarketing rate.

Another common type of municipal derivative is the synthetic primary and residual floating-rate structure, or floater/inverse floater. In this type of structure, ownership of the bonds is divided between primary investors and residual investors. The primary investor may receive a floating rate determined by a "Dutch auction" procedure, usually every 28 days, or the arrangement may include a put option or tender right and a remarketing agreement that determines the primary floating interest rate on a seven-day or similar basis. The inverse floater investor receives the remainder of the interest on the underlying bonds, after expenses of the arrangement (such as the auction agent fee and custodial fees). In the Dutch auction structures, the floater and inverse floater interests will usually each represent an interest in 50 percent of the principal amount of the bonds. As in the structures involving puts, the primary investor is afforded significant protection against market movements, as the interest rate on its interest resets frequently to a market rate. However, because the investor has no put, he or she is subject to greater market risk in the event interest rates trend quickly upward toward the maximum rate available to the primary investors. In the seven-day put structures, the primary floater's interest in the bonds may be 50 percent, 90 percent, or even 99 percent, affording differing levels of protection against interest rate movements within the structure itself, but ultimately relying on the put to provide both liquidity and price protection.

These types of investments raise federal securities and income tax issues, as well as fund accounting (other than tax) questions. The fundamental securities law issues raised by such products are (1) the securities law exemption, if any, of the underlying assets of the arrangement, (2) whether the arrangement creates a "separate security," which will in turn determine whether it may be publicly offered without securities law registration or must be privately placed, and (3) whether the arrangement creates an "investment company" (which will also be affected by issue (2) above). The fundamental federal income tax issues raised by such products are: (1) the tax-exempt status of the underlying municipal bond, (2) the "flow-through" character of distributions on the underlying bonds to investors as retaining their tax-exempt character (which is lost if the structure creates a separate taxable entity), and (3) the status of the investor as the owner of the investment package, and therefore as the recipient of tax-exempt interest.

STRUCTURES

Synthetic floating-rate municipal bonds have a variety of structural features, not all of which are present in every type of transaction. Some of the structural features are clearly alternatives. Individual sponsors of these investment products tend to group these structural features in their own particular manner, depending in part on the particular marketing emphasis that the sponsor desires and to some extent by the particular emphasis of the sponsor's counsel. Broadly speaking, it probably cannot be said that any single combination of features is "best" in the sense of having the least amount of risk. Every structure must be analyzed on its own merits.

Custody Agreement and Trust

In virtually all cases the bonds themselves are held by a bank, either as custodian under a custody agreement or as trustee under a trust agreement. The custodian or trustee will also be the holder of legal title to any other specific assets, such as an interest rate swap, if any.

In all likelihood there is no tax advantage of one form over the other, although some counsel believe that the custody agreement presents a stronger case on the trust classification issue (see the section "Tax Issues" later in this chapter).

Credit Enhanced Versus Unenhanced

Occasionally, in connection with creating the synthetic floating-rate bond, the sponsor will also add credit enhancement. This will usually be in the form of bond insurance, but could also take the form of a bank letter of credit. The credit enhancement can be an additional asset of the custody arrangement or the trust estate, or can be the subject matter of a second custody agreement or trust agreement. The second, or double trust structure, is probably preferable because it simplifies breaking up the floating-rate trust while retaining the credit enhancement.

The addition of credit enhancement weakens somewhat the tax position on ownership.

Explicit Swap Plus Put and Put with Variable Fee

One standard structure combines a fixed-rate bond with an explicit interest rate swap contract. If the fixed-rate bond is trading at par, the swap will provide that the investor pays to the counterparty the coupon rate on the bond and receives a variable rate determined by the remarketed rate on the package. The remarketing arrangement and the par put right are with respect to the package of the bond and the swap. If the bonds are trading at a premium, the fixed rate on the swap may be set at the current market and the premium on the bonds reflected in the offering price and an adjusting put price. Because the swap is a very good hedge of the bonds, the package of the bond and the swap will usually be valued at very close to par. Accordingly, there is a relatively nominal fee for the put.

The second major type of structure consists of the fixed-rate bond with a par put directly on the bond, but with a variable fee paid for the put. The amount of the fee paid for the put is the excess of the coupon on the bond over the remarketed rate on the bond.

There is probably no significant tax difference between these two structures, although the explicit swap structure has an easier tax analysis when dealing with premium bonds, as well as the deductibility of net expenses (see "Tax Issues," later in the chapter). In the explicit swap structure it is also possible that the floating rate will rise above the fixed rate, thus potentially generating some taxable income. This is not possible in the variable put fee structure, because the variable rate is capped at the bond coupon.

It should also be noted that in both of these structures it is typical for the swap expense or the variable put fee, as the case may be, to be fully recourse but only against the principal amount of the bond. This enhances the tax conclusion that these investments do not involve variable coupon strips. On the other hand, some fund accountants have worried about whether they must account for the cash flows on the investment on a gross basis (i.e., reporting the full amount of the coupon interest on the bond as income for accounting purposes and the full amount of the swap expense or put fee as an expense for accounting purposes) rather than on a net basis.

Put Features

Fixed or Variable Put Periods

For most of the synthetic products offered to money market funds, the investment package can be put at par to a bank or other institution writing the put on seven days' notice, and the interest rate is accordingly determined by reference to such seven-day period. Many of these products do not permit the seven-day put and interest period to be changed without unwinding the transaction and starting over. Some of these investment products, however, permit the put period to be changed at the discretion of the sponsor, with adequate notice to holders, in a manner substantially similar to issuer-based floating-rate bonds with "multimode" tender option features. Some counsel believe that the variable put period weakens the tax conclusion that the investor is the tax owner of the bonds.

Extraordinary Termination

Virtually all of these investment products provide that the put right will be lost in the event of a monetary default on the bonds. Another common, but by no means universal, feature is the termination of the put right upon a downgrade in the credit rating of the underlying bonds; this would usually occur only on a reduction of at least two rating categories. Another very common feature is termination of the put right in the event the underlying bonds are determined to be taxable (note that the termination is not triggered by a determination that the synthetic structure is tax defective).

Other extraordinary termination provisions may be present in the structures of particular sponsors. In general, from the tax perspective, the more situations in which the put right can be terminated, the stronger the conclusion on tax ownership. On the other hand, there is a strong competing bias on the business side in favor of providing the maximum protection to investors on this issue. The rating agencies generally try to keep the extraordinary termination events to a minimum, but every sponsor's product should be analyzed carefully. In addition, the investor should institute and maintain procedures to protect its position prior to the termination of the put right.

Termination Provisions

Free Opt-Outs

Many synthetic structures have points at which the investment arrangement automatically terminates, or the investor can elect to terminate the arrangement without paying any negative value associated with the variable expense on the swap or put. Most common is the back-end termination of the arrangement (with one final put right) at a point where there remains at least 20 percent of the expected term of the bond (as measured from the date that the original package was put together). Another feature that is seen in some of these products is the periodic (e.g., at five-year intervals) option to cancel the arrangement and take the bond free of the variable expense. Finally, for synthetic floaters packaged at the time of original issuance of the bonds (but where the issuer is not itself a party to the arrangement), some bond counsel require an initial period, typically 60 days, in which the investor has the option to cancel the arrangement without paying the termination value of the variable expense (but may be required to pay the accrued expense to the date of cancellation).[2]

Market Value Unwinds

In addition, or sometimes as an alternative, to the free termination provisions described above, many investment products give the investor, or the primary floating investor in a floater/inverse floater structure, a right to terminate the arrangement and capture all or part of the increase in the value of the bonds or other assets in the arrangement. This right may be accompanied by an obligation to pay the negative value associated with an explicit swap or the implicit swap in a variable put fee structure, as the case may be. In these types of arrangements, the investor can request the sponsor to provide quotes, sometimes on a daily basis, for the current market value of the bond and, if applicable, the current unwind or termination price of the swap or variable put. In situations where the value of the bond alone or the combined value of the bond and the swap is above the par put price, as the case may be, the investor can elect to unwind the arrangement and realize a profit. These unwind rights will often be subject to blackout periods and threshold requirements and are not available at all in Dutch auction structures. This is always in addition to any right to put the entire primary investment at par, provided the put right has not terminated as discussed above.

In floater/inverse floater structures, the inverse floater will usually have the option of purchasing the primary floating piece at par, plus (except in the Dutch auction structures) a share of the market appreciation in the bond. This right also may be subject to blackout periods. In explicit swap-based and variable fee put structures, the swap or put provider will often have the right to terminate the swap or the put, subject to paying or receiving its unwind value. Again, the primary investor would always have the right to put its entire interest, provide the put right has not terminated.

---

2 The purpose of this front-end opt-out is to help demonstrate that the synthetic arrangement is a true secondary-market transaction. This may be especially important for bonds with yield restricted proceeds, such as advance refunding bonds or single-family mortgage revenue bonds.

Sponsors of synthetic products that use the swap unwind mechanism to enhance the tax ownership conclusion have conducted studies that show that there is enough difference in the bond market and the related-term swap market to produce regular opportunities for arbitrage profit in the 25 to 50 basis point range for the primary investor. Some of these products have in fact unwound to produce such profits.

Any feature that tends to give the primary floating investor more opportunity for gain on the underlying bond enhances the tax ownership position. In any of these unwind scenarios (including the free opt-outs described above), the investor has the opportunity to sell the package to another investor that can perform the unwind, so that investors (e.g., certain money market funds) who do not want to hold long-term bonds even for an instant, can nonetheless realize market value in respect of the underlying bonds.

The underlying theory is that most investors will act rationally to maximize total income, so that the optional termination provisions will be utilized at least occasionally to maximize profit where the market value of the bond is higher than the put price. Even for tax-exempt money market funds, at least in general, realization of such a profit is not out of the question, either to enhance overall performance or to offset realized capital losses (permitting capital gains to be realized essentially tax free).

SECURITIES ISSUES

A synthetic floating-rate municipal bond will often be structured to retain the exemption from registration under the Securities Act of 1933, as amended (the 1933 Act), attaching to the underlying municipal obligation, on the basis that it creates no separate security.[3] If exempt status is retained, the arrangement under which the synthetic investment is issued will also not be an "investment company" required to register under the Investment Company Act of 1940, as amended (the 1940 Act).[4]

This section discusses (1) structuring municipal derivative transactions to create no separate security, and (2) structuring such transactions to create a separate security, which is privately placed under the 1933 Act and the 1940 Act. It then analyzes 1940 Act exemptions other than the private placement exemption, with an emphasis on Rule 3a-7. It concludes by discussing the possibilities and problems inherent in developing a new frontier: 1933 Act-registered, publicly offered municipal derivative products that are exempt from 1940 Act registration under Rule 3a-7.

---

3 If the synthetic investment is deemed to create a "separate security," then a sale without registration or exemption will violate Section 5 of the 1993 Act, entitling each purchaser to require the "issuer" and any "underwriter" of the security to repurchase it at the purchase price paid by the investor, with interest, under Section 12 of the 1993 Act.

4 If the issuance arrangement is deemed to constitute an "investment company", it will be required to register under the 1940 Act and will become subject (together with its sponsor) to a host of substantive requirements, including prohibitions on dealings with affiliates, annual financial reporting to the Securities and Exchange Commission (SEC), special requirements for custodianship of owned securities, management by a board of directors, regular audit-type supervision by the SEC, investor voting requirements, leverage restrictions, limitation to no more than one class of senior securities, strict limits on the ability of mutual funds to purchase its securities, and daily calculation of the net asset value of securities owned according to detailed procedures mandated by the SEC.

No Separate Security

A municipal bond is exempt from 1933 Act registration under Section 3(a)(2), which exempts any security issued by a state or political subdivision. Similarly, Section 2(b) of the 1940 Act provides that the 1940 Act does not apply to any state or political subdivision. Interests that "mirror" an underlying municipal obligation are said not to create any "separate security," which would be subject to the securities laws in a way that the underlying obligation is not.

Derivative products that rely on the "mirror security" approach are usually styled as "receipts," consistent with the notion that no new security is created and that the receipt is a mere device for evidencing ownership, like a baggage claim check, that creates no substantial rights separate from the property interest in the underlying obligation (or baggage) whose ownership it represents.

The conclusion that no separate security has been created depends on a closely reasoned analysis of nine factors first set forth in a Securities and Exchange Commission (SEC) no-action letter, *Merrill Lynch Pierce, Fenner & Smith Incorporated* (available September 26, 1990), in light of the facts of the particular transaction. The nine factors have been applied in at least two favorable no-action letters since the Merrill Lynch no-action letter. See *CRT Government Securities, Ltd.* (available November 24, 1992) (applying *Merrill Lynch* nine factors to custody receipt program); *Bear Stearns & Co. Inc.* (available January 28, 1992) (same). See also *Apfel & Company, Inc.* (available July 18, 1991) (dicta).

Underlying Securities Exemption

As discussed later in the chapter under "Tax Issues," secondary market structures by their nature are based on existing municipal bonds. If the underlying security in a custody arrangement is not itself exempt from the securities laws, the fact that no separate security is created in remarketing it as a derivative product will not change this fundamental flaw. Sponsor's counsel in a "mirror security" offering will not reconfirm the conclusion that the original municipal obligation was exempt. Instead, it will assume the exempt status of the original obligation and examine the facts of the derivative transaction in light of the nine factors set forth below.

Nine Factors

For a receipt to be recognized by the SEC staff as creating no separate security, the following nine factors must be present:

Factor 1: The receipt holders will have all the rights and privileges of owners of the underlying municipal securities.

Factor 2: Each receipt holder, as a real party in interest, will have the right, upon default of the underlying municipal securities, to proceed directly and individually against the issuer of those securities.

Factor 3: The receipt holder will not be required to act in concert with other receipt holders or the custodian, and an opinion is rendered to this effect, and to the effect set forth in 1 and 2 above.

Factors 1, 2, and 3 depend on an analysis of the structure in light of the governing state law chosen in the custody agreement, which will typically be New York law.

Counsel must analyze the legal relationship under that state's law between the custodian and the receipt holders, which may be an agent and principal relationship, a trustee and beneficiary relationship, a bailee and bailor relationship, or a relationship containing some elements of each type without wholly fitting within any one category, depending on the precise terms of the particular custody agreement. Factors 2 and 3 can generally be favorably resolved by the insertion of appropriate language in the custody agreement, together with analysis of the issues referred to above under the governing state law. Some counsel derive comfort if the custody agreement permits the receipt holder to remove the underlying bond on presentation of a receipt (or a combination of different types of receipts, as applicable) evidencing ownership thereof, and payment of any applicable fees; other counsel consider this feature less important. A provision in the underlying indenture or bond resolution to the effect that the issuer need recognize only the registered holder of the bond as the person entitled to vote, receive notifications, and otherwise exercise all the rights and powers of an owner should not preclude giving the required opinion. The municipal issuer will usually have the right to recognize only the registered holder under Section 8-207(1) of the Uniform Commercial Code in any event. Since this type of provision applies equally to a receipt holder and any owner of a bond issued through the book-entry system of the Depository Trust Company (DTC), for example, in which case DTC is the only registered holder, it cannot have any significance in determining whether a custody receipt is a "separate security" for 1933 Act and 1940 Act purposes.

Factor 4: Each receipt represents the entire interest in a discrete, identified interest payment or principal payment on the underlying municipal security.

This factor presents the principal functional limitation on structuring derivative products to create no separate security, since it limits the interests that can be sold to an entire interest payment or an entire principal payment on a single bond, or any combination of these basic building blocks (including an interest in all the principal and interest on a single bond). See *CRT Government Securities, Ltd.* (available November 24, 1992) (receipts on combinations of components of Treasury obligations). This factor is generally thought to preclude (1) stripping a fixed number of basis points off a bond and selling such "stripped coupon" separately from the bond principal (and the remaining "unstripped" interest on the bond), and (2) selling fractional interests in a bond (i.e, subdividing the bond in an amount that is less than the minimum denomination, or which otherwise fails to correspond to any authorized denomination [or an interest payment thereon]).

While the need for this factor appears unconvincing to some, it has been given great weight by the SEC staff.

Factor 5: The custodian bank performs only clerical or ministerial services.

Factor 6: Neither the custodian nor the sponsor additionally will guarantee or otherwise enhance the creditworthiness of the underlying municipal security or the stripped-coupon security.

Factors 5 and 6 will prevent the custodian and the sponsor from providing credit enhancements that might otherwise be permissible from a tax point of view. While some counsel apparently take the view that these factors would not prevent the corporate trust department of a bank from acting as custodian while its commercial side provided a letter of credit, as of June 1993 the SEC staff adhered strongly to the opposite view. The staff is not convinced by arguments that these different arms of the bank are separate legal entities or are acting in distinct legal capacities. Nor do they accept the argument that transactions permissible under the *Financial Security Assurance Inc.* (FSA) (available March 30, 1988) no-action letter and the Financial Guaranty Insurance Company (FGIC) (available February 15, 1989) no action letter, discussed below, need not comply with the "nine factors" applied in later letters.

On the question of credit enhancement in particular, staff of the SEC have expressed the view in conversations with the author that the FSA and FGIC letters prohibit the custodian from providing credit enhancement. The staff bases this view on the fact that the FSA and FGIC requests both represented that the functions of the custodian would be purely ministerial. This factor was noted as being particularly important in the staff's favorable responses to both letters. Moreover, even if these letters can be interpreted not to prohibit provision of credit enhancement by a custodian, the staff's current position is reflected in its later letters, which explicitly prohibit this role for the custodian (including its "commercial side").

Based on these conversations, it is the author's view that all receipt programs intended to create no separate security should be structured to meet all nine factors set forth in the *Merrill Lynch* letter, *including* the requirements for legal opinions that the receipt holders will be the real parties in interest with direct enforcement rights against the underlying issuer and that the bonds deposited will not be assets of the sponsor or the custodian.

While some counsel apparently take the view that the letters applying the "nine factors" apply only to their specific factual contexts (i.e., stripped-coupon/stripped-bond receipts on municipal securities, "bundling" of stripped interest and stripped principal Treasury components, receipts on Small Business Administration origination fees, and FNMA master notes) and programs that are directly analogous, in the author's view this approach gives the nine factors a much narrower application than that intended by the SEC staff. To be comfortable that a no-action letter would be obtainable for any receipt program offered today, sponsors should take care to ensure that all nine factors are met.

Factor 7: The custodian undertakes to notify receipt holders in the event of a default, and to forward to receipt holders copies of all communications from the issuer of the underlying municipal security to the bondholders.

Factor 8: An opinion of counsel is provided indicating that the underlying municipal securities will not be considered assets of either the sponsoring firm or the custodian bank (the so-called "true sale" opinion). (A previous version of this factor—that the receipt holders not be affected by bankruptcy or insolvency proceedings against the custodian—was cited in the FSA request as a principal criterion for determining whether a separate security existed, although the staff did not single this factor out as being of particular importance in its response.)

Factor 8, while uncontroversial in receipt transactions that simply involve separating the coupons from a fixed-rate bond and selling them at a discount as individual zero-coupon obligations (for example, Merrill Lynch M-TIGRS, Goldman Sachs Municipal Receipts, and PaineWebber M-Strips), will require careful analysis in most synthetic floating-rate bond transactions. Typically, the liquidity bank will wish to lay off its exposure to market risk on the underlying bond to a third party. It will generally look to the investment bank sponsoring the transaction to make it whole if it is required to repurchase a receipt under the liquidity arrangement. Because the bank usually only "fronts" the market risk on the bond instead of ultimately bearing it, the provider of the true sale opinion will have to cope with the market risk ultimately retained by the sponsor as an adverse fact in making the facts-and-circumstances-based determination that a "true sale" of the bonds has occurred. If a true sale has occurred, in the event of the bankruptcy of the sponsor, the bonds would not constitute part of the sponsor's bankruptcy estate. (This conclusion is generally much easier with respect to the custodian.) With respect to the sponsor, such factors as the termination of the liquidity arrangement upon a downgrade in the credit rating of the underlying bond (see the earlier section "Structures,") or the ability of the receipt holder to take the bond out of the custodial arrangement either through a "free opt-out," (see "Structures") or an optional termination provision under which the holder pays a termination fee (see "Structures"), may give counsel a sufficient basis, especially in light of other facts of the transaction that suggest that an absolute sale rather than a secured borrowing has occurred, to render the required opinion.

Factor 9: Other factors are not present, such as remarketing agreements, that would require the investors in the stripped-coupon securities to rely on the sponsor to obtain the benefit of their investment.

Factor 9 is generally understood not to prohibit the presence of remarketing agreements that are unconditionally backed by an obligation of a bank to purchase the receipt if it cannot be remarketed. The theory is that even if the remarketing agent is obligated to attempt to remarket the receipt prior to tendering it to the bank, the remarketing is done on behalf of the bank, not the receipt holder, who relies only on the performance of the bank to obtain the benefit of the receipt's "put" feature.

The nine factors were discussed more recently in *Apfel & Company, Inc.* (available July 18, 1991), *Bear Stearns & Co. Inc.* (available January 28, 1992), and *CRT Government Securities, Ltd.* (available November 24, 1992), demonstrating the SEC staff's continuing commitment to the Merrill Lynch approach. Given the significant body of no-action letters in which the factors listed in Merrill Lynch were developed (see, e.g., FSA and FGIC, supra, and the letters cited therein), their continuing use in the more recent letters cited above, and the tenor of the author's recent conversations with the SEC staff, this approach to "separate security" analysis appears to represent a well-established SEC position that is unlikely to change in the near future.

Application to Synthetic Floating-Rate Municipal Bonds

The *Merrill Lynch* letter was obtained in connection with the Merrill Lynch Municipal Tax-Exempt Investment Growth Receipts (Municipal TIGR) program for selling, as separate zero-coupon instruments, entire interest coupons and the remaining principal payment on fixed-rate municipal bonds. Because Municipal TIGRs are not synthetic floating-rate municipal bonds, they lack the following characteristics of this type of instrument: (1) a right to put the bond at par on seven days' notice, (2) a remarketing arrangement to determine the lowest rate that would permit the bond to be remarketed at par, and (3) an obligation to pay to a third party the difference between the coupon on the bond and the remarketing rate (see "Introduction").

However, in *Merritt Forbes & Company Incorporated* (available October 30, 1985), the staff analyzed an arrangement in which a municipal bond was sold together with a put to an insurance company and determined that no separate security was created,[5] on the theory that the indemnity bond that constituted the put was an exempt insurance policy under Section 3(a)(8), and its attachment to the exempt underlying municipal bond created no "separate security" requiring registration.

It is also noteworthy that the staff of the SEC's Division of Investment Management has taken a no-action position on a primary market tender option program substantially similar to synthetic floating-rate municipal bonds, in that both transactions involve the placement of a tender option on a fixed-rate tax-exempt bond, the payment to the purchaser of a portion of the fixed interest payment made by the issuer of the bond determined by reference to a short-term market rate not in excess of such fixed payment, and the payment to the tender option provider of the difference between such fixed payment and the interest paid to the owner as a tender option fee. The staff found the tender option bonds eligible for purchase by money market funds under 1940 Act Rule 2a-7, provided certain conditions are met, while expressing no opinion on the status of third-party option agreements under the 1933 Act (Nuveen Advisory Corp. (available September 4, 1990)).

Credit enhancement may also be added to a municipal bond in the secondary market (though it may not be provided by the sponsor or the custodian, see above) without creating a separate security.[6] (See FSA and FGIC, cited above.)

Reasoning from the no-action positions taken in the no-action letters discussed above and in other no-action letters, counsel have taken the position that municipal bonds may be repackaged with credit enhancement and liquidity features so long as there is favorable authority for determining that each separate element of the "package"—the municipal bond, the "put," and the credit enhancement—retains its status as an exempt security.

Variable Put Fee. It is important for securities law analysis, as for tax, that the receipt holder be recognized as the owner of the underlying municipal bond. For securities purposes, any payments to third parties (for example, put fees or credit enhancement fees) must be properly characterized as fees paid by the receipt holder from the interest on the underlying bond for services rendered by the put provider or credit enhancer.

---

5   An affiliate of Merritt Forbes proposed to purchase fixed-rate municipal bonds exempt from registration under the 1993 Act in the secondary market and to offer each bond with a tender option, giving the owner the right to tender the bond for purchase on a specified date at a price (the "strike price") established by Merritt Forbes at the time the bonds and the tender option were sold. The obligation to pay the Strike Price was a limited obligation of Merritt Forbes, payable solely from an indemnity bond issued by an insurance company in favor of the tender agent for the benefit of the bond owners, who had the right to enforce the insurance policy directly against the insurer. The Merritt Forbes obligation was necessitated by state law requirements that, to be valid, surety insurance must guaranty obligations, contractual or otherwise, of a principal (i.e., Merritt Forbes). It was made clear in the letter that Merritt Forbes' credit was in no way relevant to the ultimate investment decision, and that, therefore, the "economic realities" of the transaction dictated that the only "issuer" of securities was the insurance company. The staff agreed to take no action under the 1933 Act.

6   If the seller of the receipts is a "Section 20" subsidiary of a bank holding company and the underlying municipal obligation is not "bank eligible" (e.g., an industrial revenue bond), additional limits may apply to prevent either the bank holding company of any bank subsidiary from providing credit enhancement, liquidity, or any other facility that tends to enhance the marketability of a security sold by the Section 20 subsidiary.

Otherwise it may be difficult to establish that the receipt holder owns "the entire interest in a discrete, identified interest payment" on the underlying municipal obligation, as required by *Merrill Lynch*.

Tax and securities law concerns differ somewhat in that stripping a portion of the coupon off the underlying bond and selling it to a third party would not itself interfere with the conclusion that the receipt holder was the tax owner of the remaining stripped bond entitled to the balance of the tax-exempt interest thereon. Under the *Merrill Lynch* approach, however, such a coupon strip would create an impermissible equity interest or "profit participation" in the underlying bond for securities purposes, resulting in two separate securities (the "stripped-coupon" and the "stripped-bond"), neither of which is exempt from registration. This difference between the securities and tax analysis tends to surface when the underlying municipal obligations to be deposited in custody are premium bonds.

Some counsel have expressed the view that even the variable put fee paid in the typical secondary-market synthetic floating-rate municipal bond transaction could be viewed as a disguised "profit participation," raising separate security concerns. However, given the large volume of primary market single-family housing bonds issued with bank puts in which the banks earned an arm's-length variable put fee calculated in the same manner as in the secondary-market programs, there is ample support for the view that the put fee is an arm's-length, "market-based" fee for services and not a disguised equity interest. Moreover, the SEC staff is familiar with the structure of floating-rate municipal "put" bonds, which were before it in the Nuveen no-action request in the context of 1940 Act Rule 2a-7.

Swap Agreements

Swap agreements have generally not been packaged with municipal bonds for resale to the public on an exempt basis, notwithstanding that the counterparty that pays the floating rate to the municipal derivative investor in privately placed transactions is often a bank. Until recently, swap agreements entered into in connection with municipal bond repackaging relied on the Policy Statement Concerning Swap Transactions of the Commodity Futures Trading Commission (CFTC), 54 Fed. Reg. 30694-01 (July 21, 1989), for exemption from regulation by the CFTC as futures or commodity option transactions under the Commodity Exchange Act (CEA). The Policy Statement creates a safe harbor from CFTC regulation for swaps, which requires that (1) the swap agreement have individually tailored terms; (2) the swap agreement not contain any exchange-style offset; (3) the swap agreement not be supported by the credit of a clearing organization or a margin system; (4) the transaction be undertaken in conjunction with a line of business (including financial intermediation services); and (5) the swap transaction not be marketed to the public. Since the Policy Statement requires that the swap agreements not be marketed to the public, municipal derivative transactions that packaged swap agreements with municipal bonds were done as private placements, an approach also suggested in part by 1933 Act "separate security" concerns.

Effective February 22, 1993, with retroactivity to October 23, 1974, the CFTC adopted an exemption for certain swap agreements (the Swap Exemption) that exempts covered agreements from all provisions of the CEA (with certain exceptions not relevant here) provided that, among other things, the swap agreement is entered into solely between "eligible swap participants" who have that status at the time of entering into the agreement (17 C.F.R. Part 35). An "eligible swap participant" is defined to include, among other things, a trust, not formed solely for the specific purpose of constituting an eligible swap participant, which has total assets exceeding $10 million. The Swap Exemption thus permits the offering of municipal bonds packaged with a swap in a trust meeting the requirements of an "eligible swap participant." In most circumstances the CFTC will not "look through" eligible swap participants to their investors, so long as the entity was not formed solely for the specific purpose of constituting an eligible swap participant.

Because the SEC has in general taken a pragmatic approach to collective investment vehicles and has not hesitated to "look through" a trust that is the nominal issuer of a security to the underlying obligor,[7] it may be possible to structure a municipal derivative offering containing a bond packaged with a swap that may be publicly offered under applicable SEC no-action letters because it creates no separate security, but that fits within the Swap Exemption because the swap agreement is between the trust and the bank or other swap counterparty, and is not deemed to be between the trust's investors and such swap counterparty.

Purchase by Tax-Exempt Money Market Funds: Rule 2a-7

Pursuant to Rule 2a-7 under the 1940 Act, as amended in May 1991, a registered investment company cannot call itself a money market fund unless, among other things, it has not purchased any instrument (other than a United States government security) with a remaining maturity in excess of 397 days (Rule 2a-7(b), 2a-7(c)(2)(i)). A money market fund must also maintain a dollar-weighted average portfolio maturity of 90 days or less (Rule 2a-7(c)(2)(iii)). A "variable-rate instrument," however, if subject to a "demand feature," is deemed to mature on the next interest rate adjustment date or the next "put" exercise date, whichever is later (Rule 2a-7(d)(3)).

In *Nuveen Advisory Corp.* (available September 4, 1990), the staff agreed that a "tender option bond"[8] may be treated as a variable-rate instrument with a demand feature, provided certain conditions are met.

To obtain the shorter maturity treatment, at purchase and at each tender opportunity, the fund adviser must reasonably expect that, prior to the next tender opportunity:

■ Short-term tax-exempt rates will not exceed the interest rate on the underlying bonds, and

---

7 See, e.g., *National Cooperative Services Corporation* (available November 25, 1988); *National Cooperative Services Corporation* (available April 3, 1986); *American Airlines, Inc.* (available July 18, 1983); *World Airways, Inc.* (available August 12, 1977).

8 A "tender option bond" was defined as a long-term bond coupled with the agreement of a third-party financial institution to purchase the bond at par at periodic intervals, in exchange for a tender fee equal to the difference between the bond's fixed-coupon rate and the rate (determined by a remarketing agent) that would cause the bonds to trade at par on the date of such determination.

■ The events that would relieve the tender option provider of its obligation to purchase the bond (e.g., a substantial downgrading of the bonds, a nonfinancial default on the bonds, or a determination that interest on the bonds is no longer tax-exempt) will not occur.

The SEC position described above apparently relates to primary market transactions, but there appears to be no reason why the same rule should not apply to secondary market "tender option bonds."

In *Morgan Keegan & Company, Inc.* (available July 24, 1992), the SEC staff examined whether variable-rate certificates guaranteed by the Small Business Administration (SBA), which had final maturities of greater than 13 months and which did not have demand features, were eligible for purchase by money market funds.[9] The staff found that the certificates could be purchased under Rule 2a-7(d)(1), which applies to United States government securities on which the variable rate of interest is readjusted no less frequently than every 762 days, noting that its conclusion was based on the assumption that upon reset of the interest rate, the certificates could reasonably be expected to have a market value that approximates their par value. In other words, money market funds relying on Rule 2a-7(d)(1) are precluded from purchasing instruments with variable rates that may not rise above a preset cap.

Morgan Keegan has apparently been interpreted by some fund counsel as preventing the purchase of synthetic floating-rate municipal bonds because the floating rate is subject to a cap consisting of the fixed rate on the underlying municipal bond (less any applicable trustee, credit enhancement, or other service fee). *Morgan Keegan* applies only to United States government securities and other "capped floaters" without demand features, however, and has no effect on the validity of the staff position in Nuveen permitting money market funds to purchase synthetic floating-rate municipal bonds under Rule 2a-7(d)(3). This view was confirmed in a letter dated June 16, 1993, from Robert E. Plaze, Assistant Director of the Division of Investment Management, to the Investment Company Institute, which was subsequently circulated by the Investment Company Institute.[10]

On December 17, 1993, the Commission proposed significant amendments to Rule 2a-7 for the purpose, among other things, of (i) tightening the risk-limiting conditions imposed on tax-exempt money market funds, (ii) imposing new requirements on investments in asset-backed securities for taxable and tax-exempt money funds, (iii) tightening procedures for determining that fund investments present minimal credit risk, and (iv) requiring that more information be available on municipal bonds underlying synthetic securities.

---

9 The SBA guarantee is backed by the full faith and credit of the United States.

10 In a subsequent letter to the Investment Company Institute dated June 25, 1993, the staff explained that *Morgan Keegan* was intended to have two consequences. First, money market funds may not purchase long-term capped floaters without demand features. Second, funds must measure the maturities of short-term capped floaters (those with final maturities of 397 days or less) by reference to their final maturities. The staff stated that this interpretation would become effective September 1, 1993. Since both of the consequences explained in the June 25, 1993, letter do not apply to synthetic floating-rate municipal bonds with demand features, the letter does not change the analysis set forth in the text above.

The proposing release is notable for its acknowledgment of the dominant role played by instruments subject to demand features, including synthetic floating-rate municipal bonds, in tax-exempt money funds. According to the release, approximately 60 percent of the assets held by single state funds, and 70 percent of the assets held by national funds, consist of primary market variable rate demand notes and similar "synthetic" short-term tax-exempt instruments. However, certain of the proposed amendments could make it harder for tax-exempt funds to buy synthetic securities. These include:

1. Requiring actual ratings rather than a determination of comparable quality for the synthetic security.

2. Limiting national fund investment in synthetic securities with a common sponsor or depositor to 5 percent of total assets.

3. Limiting fund investment in instruments subject to puts from the same institution to 10 percent of total assets.

4. Limiting permissible conditions on the exercisability of puts to payment default on the underlying security, insolvency of the issuer of the underlying security or a guarantor, a downgrading of the underlying security or a guarantor by two full rating categories, and a determination of taxability.

5. Requiring, with respect to synthetic floating-rate municipal bonds, that funds have written procedures requiring on-going review of the continued minimal credit risk of the underlying municipal bond.

6. Requiring, in connection with item (5) above, that financial data for the issuer of such underlying bond be either publicly available or available to the fund under the terms of the underlying bond's governing documentation. (Such information is generally not now available to the public or bondholders as of right for most municipal issuers.)

These amendments have generated considerable discussion and comment by money funds and sponsors of asset-backed and synthetic securities. In response, the Commission extended the public comment period by 30 days to May 6, 1994. While the volume of public comment suggests that significant changes may be made to the proposed amendments and even that the rule may be issued again in proposed form, allowing further comment, Rule 2a-7 as ultimately revised is almost certain to significantly affect market practices for synthetic floating-rate municipal bonds.

Marginability

Regulation T. Section 7(c) of the Securities Exchange Act of 1934, as amended (the Exchange Act) makes it unlawful for a broker-dealer "directly or indirectly to extend or maintain credit or arrange for the extension of credit to or for any customer" on any nonexempted security in contravention of the rules promulgated by the Board of Governors of the Federal Reserve System (FRB). The FRB has implemented this authority by adopting Regulation T. Exempt securities (including municipal securities) are accorded "good faith" margin treatment under Regulation T (12 CFR 220.18(b)).

The staff of the FRB has confirmed in a published interpretation that custodial receipts for U.S. government securities qualify for the good faith margin treatment accorded exempt securities. (See FRB Staff Opinion 5-628.24, August 11, 1992, 3 Fed. Banking L. Rep. (CCH) ¶ 32,794, at 15,551-4.) Based on this interpretation and conversations with FRB staff, the author believes that custodial receipts on municipal securities structured in accordance with the Merrill Lynch "nine factors" should also be accorded "good faith" margin treatment under Regulation T.

Section 11(d)(1). Moreover, municipal custodial receipts are probably also considered "exempted securities" for purposes of Exchange Act Section 11(d)(1). Section 11(d)(1) of the Exchange Act makes it unlawful for a person who is both a broker and a dealer to extend, maintain, or arrange for credit "to or for a customer on any security *(other than an exempted security)* which was part of a new issue in the distribution of which he participated as a member of a selling syndicate or group within thirty days prior to such transaction." (Emphasis added.) While SEC staff have not addressed the question whether custodial receipts on municipal securities qualify as exempted securities for purposes of Section 11(d)(1), SEC staff have indicated in conversations that they would be inclined to act favorably on a no-action request.

These favorable positions on margin questions for custodial receipts stand in contrast to an earlier, more conservative position taken by FRB staff in connection with certain certificates of accrual on U.S. Treasury securities (CATS) (see FRB Staff Opinion 5-628.13 (December 13, 1984), 3 Fed. Banking L. Rep. (CCH) ¶ 32,794, at 15,551-2) and to the New York Stock Exchange's current position that CATS are not exempted securities for purposes of NYSE Rule 431 (see NYSE, Interpretation Handbook, at 4303).

Separate Security That Is Privately Placed

Municipal derivative products that fail to satisfy the "no separate security" criteria set forth above will not retain the securities exemptions applicable to the underlying municipal obligation, and a separate basis for exemption must be found. Such interests are usually offered as interests in an arrangement constituting a trust under applicable state law (although it may be considered either a grantor trust or a partnership under federal income tax law), and are often denominated as "trust certificates," reflecting their status as certificates of undivided beneficial ownership interest in the assets of the trust.

Private Placement Under the 1933 Act: Section 4(2)

Under the 1933 Act, a registration requirement applies to all offers and sales of securities unless specifically exempted. Section 4(2) provides an exemption for transactions by an issuer not involving any public offering. To qualify, the securities must be offered and sold to a limited number of investors who take the investment for their own account and not with a view to any distribution. However, whether the offerees are of a type requiring the protection of 1933 Act registration is more important than their absolute number. Furthermore, resale to an unlimited number of Rule 144A "qualified institutional buyers"[11] is permitted in accordance with Rule 144A.

The issuer, which for this purpose is the *trust* issuing the certificates, *not* the municipal issuer of the underlying obligation, will usually obtain investment representation letters from its purchasers; the trust documents will state that resale of the trust certificates will be restricted; and the trust certificates will bear a legend describing the restriction. Any resales of the certificates must also be made as private placements, relying on the so-called "Section 4(1 1/2)" exemption for resales to investors who could have purchased in the original private placement. This exemption is based on SEC lore and widespread practice, but is not derived from any specific 1933 Act section.

Unlike the receipts described earlier, which must meet the "nine factors" in order to avoid creating a separate security, trust certificates are admittedly separate securities and can be structured with any features desired, as long as the material aspects are adequately disclosed. The private placement exemption depends on the way in which the certificates are sold rather than on the characteristics of the certificates.

Offerings to High-Net-Worth Individuals. Typically, given high minimum denominations and an institutional investor base, most municipal derivative offerings make straightforward private placements and raise no significant issues. However, sales to high-net-worth individuals (HNWI) structured as private placements can be more problematic. There will be more offerees and purchasers, and it will be necessary to determine that all HNWI had the proper qualifications to be offerees. If after the fact a purchaser were determined to be a person needing the protection afforded by 1933 Act registration, the exemption would be lost as to all offerees and purchasers, not just the purchaser who failed to qualify. In addition, where sales are made to HNWI, more care may need to be taken to ensure that the manner of contacting the individuals did not cross the line into "general advertising and solicitation" incompatible with the private placement exemption.

State Securities Laws. In private placements, state securities laws must also be reviewed. State laws generally exempt sales to institutional investors, but are much more stringent when individuals are the offerees. To avoid giving the purchaser an unintended "put," or rescission right, a state-by-state blue-sky review is necessary, covering every state where offers or sales are to be made. Often, regulation or qualification *will be necessary* if sales to individuals are contemplated.

Private Placement Under the 1940 Act: Section 3(c)(1)

The 1940 Act will also affect trust certificate offerings. It applies to issuers that are engaged primarily in investing in securities. This includes a trust or custodial arrange-

---

11 Generally, a "qualified institutional buyer" is an entity, acting for its own account or the accounts of other qualified institutional buyers, that owns and invests on a discretionary basis at least $100 million in securities of nonaffiliated issuers.

ment created to hold municipal bonds in connection with the issuance of a derivative product.

Section 3(c)(1) provides an exemption for issuers who are not making and do not propose to make any public offering, and whose securities, other than commercial paper, are beneficially owned by less than 100 persons.[12] (The general portion of the following discussion [*i.e.,* the portion not relating specifically to municipal derivatives] comes largely from Lemke & Lins, *Private Investment Companies Under Section 3(c)(1) of the Investment Company Act of 1940*, 44 Bus. Law. 401 (1989), published in 1989 and still the best article available on Section 3(c)(1).)

Attribution Rule (the "first 10 percent test"). If a company owns more than 10 percent of the voting securities of an issuer, then the company's beneficial owners are counted for purposes of determining whether there are more than 100 beneficial owners of the issuer's securities.

Exception to the Attribution Rule (the "second 10 percent test"). If the company's investment in the issuer, together with its investment in certain similar companies, is less than 10 percent of the company's assets, then the attribution rules do not apply (and the company is counted as *one* beneficial owner).

The practical significance of these provisions is that an issuer relying on Section 3(c)(1) of the 1940 Act must have a way of tracking the number of its investors, and preventing transfers from occurring if the transfer would cause beneficial owners to exceed 100.[13] Freedom from this requirement is one of the principal advantages of relying on the alternative exemption created by new Rule 3a-7, discussed below, in transactions that are treated as private placements for 1933 Act purposes.

Voting Securities. Because a single purchaser with multiple shareholders could conceivably count as hundreds or even thousands of beneficial owners if it owns more than 10 percent of the issuer's voting securities, the issuer should also take steps to assure itself that the purchaser will be counted as one owner. The most effective way to accomplish this is to eliminate purchaser voting rights. If the issuer has no voting securities, than no investor can trigger the first 10 percent test (which requires ownership of more than 10 percent of the voting securities). See *Meuse, Rinker, Chapman, Endres & Brooks* (available May 1, 1989); *Alpha Cash Management* (available July 2, 1986). Not only is the attribution rule (or "first 10 percent test") inapplicable, but the issuer will not be treated as an investment company even for purposes of 1940 Act Section 12(d)(1), making it easier for mutual funds to buy greater amounts of the product.

Voting rights means any explicit voting rights; the right to appoint, dismiss, approve, or replace, the managing partner or trustee (see *CMS Communications Fund*

---

12 Any SEC-registered offering will be considered a public offering, even if offered and sold to only one person. LOX Group (August 15, 1988), cited in Lemke & Lins, *supra*, at 429 & n.98.

13 For example, the operative documents should provide, and the certificates should be legended to the effect, that no transfer will be permitted to occur if, in the judgment of the program sponsor, after such transfer the beneficial owners of the certificates, together with the beneficial owners of certificates issued in other programs of the same program sponsor that would be required to be "integrated" with the certificates, would be greater than 100.

[available March 18, 1987]; *Kohlberg Kravis Roberts & Co.* [available August 9, 1985]; Lemke & Lins, "Private Investment Companies Under Section 3(c)(1) of the Investment Company Act of 1940," 44 *Bus. Law.* 401, 415 & n.54 (1989); the right to terminate the trust, custodial or partnership arrangement; the right to restrict the election of a new general partner; actual taking part by certificate holders in the management or control of the trust; the right to approve or veto certain general partner or trustee actions, see *Horsley Keogh* [available March 28, 1988]); and the holding of limited partnership interests conferring sufficient ability to exercise control through economic power over a partnership so that limited partnership interests are equivalent to voting securities (see *Nautilus Trust* [available February 1, 1982]; *Engelberger Partnership* [available December 7, 1981]; *Pierce, Lewis & Dolan* [available March 17, 1972]).

Voting rights do not include (1) the right of a supermajority of holders to direct the trustee to sell any or all of the bonds in the trust (see *Meuse, Rinker,* supra); (2) the right of a limited partner to dispose of its limited partnership interest under certain limited circumstances; (3) the right of limited partners to elect a liquidator to oversee the dissolution of the partnership in the event of bankruptcy or withdrawal from the partnership of the general partner; or (4) the right of trust beneficiaries to petition a court to remove a trustee for cause under applicable state law. (See *Alpha Cash Management,* supra; Sarofim Trust Co. [August 26, 1982]).

Voting rights are less likely to be found in the context of passive municipal derivative trust vehicles than for actively managed investment partnerships, where effective control through economic influence (and therefore voting rights) may be more common.

Investor Representations. If it is not possible to structure the transaction so that investors have no voting rights, each purchaser in the initial offering, and each subsequent transferee, should represent that it will be treated as "one person" for purposes of Section 3(c)(1)(A), either because it owns less than 10 percent of the certificates, or because its investment in the certificates, together with its investment in all other Section 3(c)(1) issuers, is less than 10 percent of its assets.

For investors that are direct or indirect subsidiaries of other corporations, in general, the SEC staff would look to the attributed percentage ownership of the ultimate parent corporation. (See Lemke & Lins, supra, at 421–22.)

Integration. Integration is an SEC staff-created rule for treating 3(c)(1) companies that are nominally independent but share the same fundamental investment attributes, as the same 3(c)(1) company for purposes of the 100-investor limit under Section 3(c)(1) (see *Lemke & Lins,* supra, at 424-28; *PBT Covered Option Fund* [available January 18, 1979]).

Generally, the SEC staff will require two different municipal derivative offerings with the same program sponsor to be treated as the same *unless* the securities issued would be perceived as materially different by an investor qualified to purchase both securities. See *Rogers, Casey & Associates, Inc.* (June 16, 1989) (two funds with (1) the same investment objectives, (2) substantially the same portfolios, and (3) similar portfolio risk/return characteristics, and which were designed for one group of investors with similar investment profiles, would be integrated). The no-action letters suggest that the difference must be one of *kind,* not of *degree.* See *Equitable Capital*

Management Corporation (available January 6, 1992) (request letter stating that because "materially different" analysis is subjective and heavily dependent on facts, no assurance that funds will not be integrated unless they have "wildly different" risk/return characteristics, i.e., they are tailored for different groups of investors). If two offerings are integrated, the combined "integrated" program will likely have more total investors than either program treated separately, increasing the likelihood that each offering will lose the private placement exemption.

Trusts that contain bonds from different specialty states (that is, states with a state income tax), or from a specialty state and a nonspecialty state, will not be integrated. Other trusts, however, are likely to be integrated unless either the underlying bonds or the allocation of cash flows to derivative holders (and therefore the risk/return characteristics and expected investment performance for the securities) are so different from other trusts that the trusts appear to have been designed to appeal to different groups of investors.[14]

To date, the practical effect of this limitation for municipal derivatives offerings has probably been small. It is quite possible, and even likely, that there are currently fewer than 100 institutional buyers of privately placed municipal derivative products in the entire country. However, as this market becomes broader, both by expanding the number of institutional buyers and by selling to HNWI, the 100-investor limit will become more onerous, making reliance on the alternative exemption set forth in Rule 3a-7 more desirable.

The secondary market Dutch auction floater/inverse floater structures, FLOATS/RITES, RIBS/SAVERS, etc., pose a special problem because while the universe of investors is small, sales of certificates are made on a regular basis (every 28 or 35 days), posing a much greater risk, theoretically at least, that the number of investors will inadvertently be exceeded and the exemption lost. This risk is addressed in practice by requiring that all transfers in auctions be made through specified broker-dealers, and requiring those broker-dealers not to make any sales except to a purchaser who has filed a "master purchaser" letter with the broker-dealer in which

---

14 The SEC staff has found that the following Section 3 (c) (1) companies did *not* need to be integrated:

(1) A partnership for tax-exempt investors and a partnership for taxable investors, see *Oppenheimer Arbitrage Partners* (available December 26, 1985); (2) a diversified "growth" fund and an undiversified, riskier "special situations" fund, see *Meadow Lane Associates* (available May 24, 1989); (3) a fund offered to pension funds and a fund for non-pension-fund investors, see *C & S Investment Funds* (available February 17, 1977); and (4) separate, individually negotiated collateralized bond obligation (CBO) offerings with a common sponsor/manager, see *Equitable Capital Management Corporation* (available January 6, 1992). See also *Pasadena Investment Trust* (available January 22, 1993) (staff would not integrate a non-United States investment company ("offshore fund") and a registered investment company whose securities comprised substantially all of the assets of the offshore fund where differing tax laws created materially different investment opportunities for foreign and United States investors).

The SEC staff would apparently integrate the following: (1) a "large capitalization" equity mutual fund, a "small capitalization" equity mutual fund, and a "balanced" equity income fund, see *Frontier Capital* (available July 13, 1988); and (2) two funds that had a common investment objective with respect to 80 percent of their contributed funds, see *Monument Capital* (available July 12, 1990).

the purchaser represents, among other things, that it is a single beneficial owner for 1940 Act purposes.

Other 1940 Act Exemptions—Especially Rule 3a-7

Before describing Rule 3a-7, which was adopted in November 1992 and has the potential to make reliance on Section 3(c)(1) obsolete for many municipal derivative offerings, it is worthwhile to spend a moment on other exemptions that have been used in the municipal derivative area, but which are likely to see less use after the adoption of Rule 3a-7.

Sales Finance Exemption: Section 3(c)(5)(A)

Section 3(c)(5)(A) of the 1940 Act creates an exemption, in pertinent part, for entities not engaged in the business of issuing redeemable securities who are primarily engaged in acquiring notes and other obligations representing part or all of the sales price of merchandise. This exemption was relied on in tax-exempt lease grantor trust transactions offered by affiliates of IBM, GE, and Unisys. Because the municipalities had acquired computers and other equipment under finance leases or installment payment agreements that were being repackaged, the receivables from these leases or agreements were qualifying "sales finance receivables" for purposes of the exemption.

Mortgage Exemption: Section 3(c)(5)(C)

Municipal derivative transactions backed by mortgage bonds have also attempted to rely on the mortgage exemption, Section 3(c)(5)(C), which applies, in pertinent part, to entities purchasing or otherwise acquiring mortgages and other liens on and interests in real estate. Unfortunately, applicable SEC no-action letters interpret interests in less than all of the indebtedness secured by a mortgage as not qualifying as a "mortgage" unless the holder of the lesser interest (or "participation") has the right to foreclose the mortgage. See, e.g., *Northwestern Ohio Building and Construction Trades Council* (available May 21, 1984). Thus, if less than the entire issue of an issue of bonds is being deposited in the derivative transaction, it is likely that the transaction will not be able to rely on Section 3(c)(5)(C).

Asset Securitization Exemption: Rule 3a-7

Requirements of the Rule. Rule 3a-7 applies to any issuer who is engaged in the business of purchasing, or otherwise acquiring, and holding eligible assets (and in activities related or incidental thereto), and who does not issue redeemable securities, provided that, in pertinent part, all the following requirements are met:

    Fixed-Income Securities. The issuer issues fixed-income securities or other securities that entitle their holders to receive payments that depend primarily on the cash flow from eligible assets.

    Investment-Grade Rating. Securities sold by the issuer or any underwriter thereof are fixed-income securities rated, at the time of initial sale, in one of the four highest categories by at least one nationally recognized statistical rating organization (except that (1) any fixed-income securities may be sold to accredited institutional investors; and (2) any securities may be sold to qualified institutional buyers as defined in Rule 144A).

Limitations on Acquisition and Disposition of Assets. The issuer acquires additional eligible assets, or disposes of eligible assets, only if: (1) the assets are acquired or disposed of in accordance with the terms and conditions set forth in the agreements, indentures, or other instruments pursuant to which the issuer's securities are issued; (2) the acquisition or disposition of the assets does not result in a downgrading in the rating of the issuer's outstanding fixed-income securities; and (3) the assets are not acquired or disposed of for the primary purpose of recognizing gains or decreasing losses resulting from market value change.

Trustee Requirements: Perfected Security Interest or Ownership Interest. If the issuer issues any securities other than § 3(a)(3) commercial paper, the issuer: (1) appoints a trustee that meets the requirements of Section 26(a)(1) of the 1940 Act and that is not affiliated with the issuer or with any person involved in the organization or operation of the issuer, that does not offer or provide credit or credit enhancement to the issuer, and that executes an agreement or instrument concerning the issuer's securities containing provisions to the effect that it will not resign until a qualified successor trustee has been appointed; (2) takes reasonable steps to cause the trustee to have a perfected security interest or ownership interest valid against third parties in those eligible assets that principally generate the cash flow needed to pay the fixed-income securities holders, provided that such assets otherwise required to be held by the trustee may be released to the extent needed at the time for the operation of the issuer; and (3) takes actions necessary for the cash flows derived from eligible assets for the benefit of the holders of fixed-income securities to be deposited periodically in a segregated account that is maintained or controlled by the trustee consistent with the rating of the outstanding fixed-income securities.

Definitions. For purposes of Rule 3a-7, "eligible assets" means financial assets, either fixed or revolving, that by their terms convert into cash within a finite time period plus any rights or other assets designed to assure the servicing or timely distribution of proceeds to security holders. "Fixed-income securities" means any securities that entitle the holder to receive: (1) a stated principal amount; or (2) interest on a principal amount (which may be a notional principal amount) calculated by reference to a fixed rate or to a standard or formula that does not reference any change in the market value or fair value of eligible assets; or (3) interest on a principal amount (which may be a notional principal amount) calculated by reference to auctions among holders and prospective holders, or through remarketing of the security; or (4) an amount equal to specified fixed or variable portions of the interest received on the assets held by the issuer; or (5) any combination of amounts described in (1), (2), (3), and (4) above, provided that substantially all of the payments to which the holders of such securities are entitled consist of the foregoing amounts.

Application to Municipal Derivative Transactions. In general, municipal derivative transactions will not have trouble meeting the requirements of Rule 3a-7, since they fall within the scope of its provisions aimed at essentially passive investment vehicles. The SEC staff has expressed the view in comment letters that floater/inverse floater vehicles may be issuing "redeemable securities," as discussed below. Otherwise, any securities issued are likely to be "fixed-income securities," since the holder will receive either a stated principal amount, interest on a principal amount (including a notional amount) calculated by reference to auctions among holders and prospective holders or by remarketing, a variable portion of the interest received on the assets held by the issuer, or some combination of these amounts. The municipal derivative securities will not always be rated, but as fixed-income securities they may be sold to accredited institutional investors (by far the lion's share of the market at present) without a rating.

The limitations on acquisition of eligible assets would not pose difficulties for any of the existing structures, which generally do not contemplate asset acquisitions after issuance for any reason. Dispositions of assets may be made under the existing structures, but generally only at the holder's initiative, and in no circumstances under conditions that could be interpreted as being for the primary purpose of recognizing gains or decreasing losses for investors resulting from market value changes.

Finally, fixed-rate municipal bonds are "financial assets" that "by their terms convert into cash within a finite time period," as are interest rate swap agreements.

Redeemable Securities

Tender Option Receipts. Synthetic floating-rate municipal tender option bonds are not "redeemable securities," based on three no-action letters under Section 3(c)(5), *La Quinta Motor Inns, Inc.* (available January 4, 1989), *Shearson Lehman/American Express, Inc.* (available May 20, 1985), and *McDonald & Company Securities, Inc.* (available December 14, 1983). The rationale supporting this no-action position is that the tender option is not exercisable against the trust (or the custodian in a custody arrangement) or anyone designated by the trust acting on its behalf, but is exercisable solely against the bank. Also, upon exercise of the tender option, the holder does not receive a proportionate share of the issuer's "current net assets." It instead receives the unpaid principal amount of the synthetic floating-rate bond, plus accrued interest thereon.

Note that for certain types of securities where the underlying obligation is itself a floating-rate instrument whose market value can be expected to approximate its par amount, the fact that the receipt holder receives par plus accrued upon exercise of the tender option gives less comfort, since this amount will be approximately equal to a proportionate share of the issuer's "current net assets." However, synthetic floating-rate municipal tender option bonds generally (although not always) use fixed-rate bonds rather than floating-rate bonds as the underlying obligation, in which event establishing that they are not "redeemable securities" is straightforward.

Because synthetic floating-rate municipal tender option bonds are not redeemable securities, they will qualify for the Rule 3a-7 exemption if the other Rule 3a-7 requirements (principally investment-grade rating for securities sold to persons other than institutional accredited investors and use of an independent trustee) are met. While relying on Rule 3a-7 provides an independent basis for 1940 Act exemption in addition to the no-action letter precedents in the "no separate security" area, an exemption from registration under the 1933 Act is still necessary. For this reason, Rule 3a-7 does not appear to significantly facilitate the offering of such tender option bonds.

Floater/Inverse Floater Certificates

The SEC staff has expressed concern in comment letters and telephone conversations that trusts created by sponsors of Dutch auction floater/inverse floater municipal derivative programs (and sought to be registered on Form S-3 as described below) are issuers of "redeemable securities." The staff's concern appears to be based on the ability of the holder of an inverse floater security to "link" his security with an equal principal amount of a "floater" security and create a "linked floater/inverse floater" security that can be exchanged for the underlying bond. In the author's view, this concern is misplaced.

1. *Basis for Withdrawal Rights.* The reason for permitting holders of inverse floaters to require the mandatory tender of primary floaters is that inverse floaters are expected to be relatively illiquid, and their market value is expected to be extremely volatile. The primary floaters, on the other hand, are generally expected through the auction process to maintain a par value (provided the interest rate cap is not met) and to be quite liquid.

   To provide the inverse floater holder an effective mechanism to liquidate its investment, privately placed secondary market programs have given such holder the ability to obtain corresponding floaters (to create whole interests) and then to withdraw whole bonds corresponding to its whole interests. The whole bonds can then be sold in the secondary bond market, which is a significantly deeper market than the market for inverse floaters.

   Acquisition of the primary floaters generally occurs as part of the normal auction process; only in the relatively unusual situation where floater holders submit hold orders in sufficient numbers to preclude inverse floater holders from buying at the minimum possible rate would it be necessary for the inverse floater holders to exercise their option to require a sale of floaters (chosen randomly) to create whole interests. The floater holders, in turn, should be relatively indifferent to having floaters "called away" inasmuch as the call at par plus accrued interest should in virtually all circumstances be substantially equal to the value of the floaters.

2. *Analysis under Rule 3(a)(7).* Under Section 2(a)(32) of the 1940 Act, "redeemable security" means: Any security, other than short-term paper, under the terms of which the holder, *upon its presentation to the issuer* or to a person designated by the issuer, is entitled (whether absolutely or only out of surplus) to receive approximately his proportionate share of the issuer's current net assets, or the cash equivalent thereof. (Emphasis added).

   The mechanism described above that permits inverse floater holders to obtain the underlying bonds related to their inverse floater certificates cannot be exercised "upon [the inverse floater investor's] presentation [of its inverse floaters] to the issuer" as required by Section 2(a)(32). Instead, it is a precondition to the exercise of its withdrawal privilege that the inverse floater holder obtain, through participation in the auction or by exercise of its right to call floaters, an equivalent amount of primary floater certificates. Doing so will require the inverse floater holder to pay the floater holder whose floaters are purchased or called away a purchase price equal to the par amount of such floater certificate plus any accrued interest at the floater rate.

The SEC staff appears deaf to arguments that since neither the floater nor the inverse floater standing alone is redeemable, and the "linked floater/inverse floater" is not a security in its own right, but merely a mechanical device for indicating which floater holders also hold inverse floaters, the arrangement is not issuing any redeemable securities. In fairness to the staff, the floater/inverse floater registration statements that have been filed were based on secondary-market private placement transactions, which do appear to treat the "linked floater/inverse floater" as a security that has its own CUSIP number and is issued separately through DTC—a circumstance which may have colored the SEC's analysis of the "redeemable security" issue. The current impasse could probably be resolved, however, by changing the structure in one of two different ways to respond to SEC concerns.

The problem is that the SEC views the linked floater/inverse floater as a redeemable security issued by the trust. If the linked floater/inverse floater were treated as a separate security and *registered under the 1933 Act,* and the underlying bonds could no longer be "taken out" of the program, there would no longer be anything even colorably resembling a redeemable security associated with the floater/inverse floater program. The liquidity desired by investors would be obtained by the SEC-registered character of the linked floater/inverse floater, which would permit it to be publicly traded.

Alternatively, the concept of "taking the bond out" could remain, but the concept of "linking" would disappear. Under this approach, there would be no such thing as a "linked floater/inverse floater certificate." Instead, the floater certificate would carry with it the right to receive an equal face amount of the underlying bonds, upon presentation of the floater and a matching inverse floater. Similarly, the inverse floater certificate would have, as one of its terms, the ability to obtain the corresponding underlying bond upon presentation of the inverse floater to the trustee together with a matching floater certificate. This approach would not change the economics of the floater/inverse floater program significantly. It would, however, dispose of any argument that the "linked floater/inverse floater certificate" is a redeemable security by striking from the documents the "linked floater/inverse floater certificate" concept. This may make it easier for the SEC to accept that neither the floater nor the inverse floater by itself constitutes a redeemable security under Section 2(a)(32), and since the issuer is not issuing any other securities, it is not issuing any "redeemable securities" under Rule 3a-7.

However, the staff in a recent no-action letter appeared to take a contrary view, finding that a structured financing program issuing two types of securities that were not redeemable alone, but which gave investors direct withdrawal rights if combined, was issuing a "combined security" of which the program was the obligor, and such "combined security" was a "redeemable security." Brown & Wood (available February 24, 1994).

SEC-Registered Municipal Derivative Securities: The Future?

Form S-3

Form S-3 may be used for registration of securities involving (1) investment-grade asset-backed securities, and (2) nonconvertible securities of majority-owned subsidiaries of so-called "seasoned" companies currently subject to the reporting requirements of the 1934 Act.

Form S-3 is the shorter, easier form of registration statement, allowing for incorporation by reference of other SEC-filed documents and allowing for "shelf" offerings (see below). Until recently, registrant and transaction requirements had to be satisfied in order for the registrant to use Form S-3. However, the potential availability of Form S-3 for use in municipal derivative transactions was increased significantly by amendments to the Form S-3 rules adopted in November 1992.

These amendments largely eliminate the registrant requirements of "public float" and reporting history for investment-grade asset-backed securities meeting specified transaction requirements. Note that for purposes of the 1933 Act, the depositor to an asset-backed trust ordinarily will be the "registrant" for purposes of the registration statement.

Investment Grade Asset-Backed Securities. Asset-backed securities to be offered for cash may be offered on Form S-3, provided the securities are rated "investment grade" (typically, in one of the four highest rating categories) by a nationally recognized statistical rating organization.

"Asset-backed security" means a security that is primarily serviced by the cash flows of a discrete pool of receivables or other financial assets, either fixed or revolving, that by their terms convert into cash within a finite time period, plus any rights or other assets designed to assure the servicing or timely distribution of proceeds to the security holders.

In general, any municipal derivative security of an issuer that qualifies for the Rule 3a-7 exemption will also be an "asset-backed security" for purposes of Form S-3.

The type or category of asset to be securitized must be fully described in the registration statement at the time of effectiveness. A registration statement may not merely identify several alternative types of assets that may be securitized. What this means in the context of registered municipal derivative offerings is not yet clear. The SEC staff initially took the position in comment letters that this means the registration statement may include only one type of asset. The better view is probably that multiple types of assets that fit within a broad category may be registered on a single registration statement as long as the SEC has had the opportunity to review and approve specimen disclosure for each specific type of asset. Based on a recent telephone conversation with the SEC staff, the staff has apparently moved in this direction by permitting alternative types of assets (the staff used the example of credit card and auto loan receivables) to be registered on a single Form S-3 registration statement as long as the registration statement contains a "core prospectus" for each alternative asset type.

Single Obligor Limitation. No formal asset concentration limit has been imposed, but if a significant amount of the asset pool represents obligations of a single obligor or related obligors, financial information and other disclosure about the obligor(s) may be required. Similarly, asset-backed offerings with significant asset concentration may involve one or more co-issuers under 1933 Act Rule 140, in which case such co-issuers would be required to sign the registration statement. Finally, although an asset concentration test has not been included, the adopting release for the Form S-3 amendments states that the definition does not encompass securities issued in structured financings for a single obligor (or group of related obligors).

The inclusion of a municipal bond issued by a single state or local obligor as the sole asset of a trust would obviously cause the securities issued by the trust to be backed by the obligations of a single obligor (although it is not clear that such an offering should be considered a structured financing "for one obligor" if the municipal obligor was not a party to, and did not initiate, the structuring). The single obligor requirement is contained only in the Release adopting the Form S-3 amendments and not in the actual text of the amendments. The author believes the SEC staff has the power to interpret the Form S-3 amendments to permit use of Form S-3 for single-obligor structured financings where appropriate in the public interest. The staff's position on this issue is evolving and is being determined in the context of repackagings of corporate bonds as well as municipal obligations. The staff's current view appears to be that they will entertain proposals for single-obligor Form S-3 offerings if a proposal for adequate disclosure about the underlying municipal issuer is made and if the acquisition of the underlying bonds occurred in a secondary-market transaction. Based on a recent conversation with the SEC, if the municipal issuer's credit is material to the transaction, the Form S-3 registration statement must include the same information that would be required if the municipality itself were registering an offering of its securities on Form S-1. Merely attaching an Official Statement for the underlying bonds to the municipal asset-backed prospectus is not sufficient (or even encouraged). What else the requirement for "Form S-1-type information" for a municipality might mean, given the obvious differences between municipalities and the corporate issuers that more typically use Form S-1, would have to be worked out by studying Form S-1's requirements for financial and other information and attempting to apply them to the municipality in a practical manner, most probably in active consultation with the SEC staff.

The only written statement of the staff's view of which the author is aware is contained in materials presented by Linda C. Quinn, the Director of the Commission's Division of Corporate Finance, at a seminar in early 1994. This statement is set forth in its entirety below.

The offering of asset-backed securities supported by pools of municipal bonds where asset concentration exists; in general, requires that financial statements and other information relating to the underlying municipal issuer be provided. This information must be included directly in the prospectus, must be current, and must otherwise satisfy fully the disclosure requirements under the federal securities regulations. While the Official Statement ("OS") utilized in connection with the initial distribution of the municipal securities may be attached to or delivered with the prospectus, the OS may not serve as a surrogate for a complete prospectus.

While there may be instances where financial statements of the municipal issuer are not material to be investor in the asset-backed security, such instances would appear to be rare and the staff will require appropriate legal opinions and other documentation necessary to support the conclusion that financial and other information relating to the municipal issuer is not material to investors.

To the author's knowledge, although several municipal asset-backed registration statements on Form S-3 have been filed with the Commission, only one, which is limited to single-family housing bonds where no single municipal obligor represents more than 10 percent of the pooled assets, has been declared effective.

Majority-Owned Subsidiary

For this type of Form S-3 offering, the registrant (or its parent company, if the registrant is a majority-owned subsidiary, as will be typical for asset-backed offerings not falling under the "investment-grade asset-backed securities" provisions of Form S-3) must be all of the following: (1) a domestic company, organized under U.S. or state law, with principal business operations in the U.S. (certain foreign issuers may also qualify); (2) a reporting company under the 1934 Act; (3) a company subject to the requirements of Section 12 or Section 15, which has filed all material required by Section 13, Section 14 or Section 15(d) of the Act for at least 12 calendar months prior to filing of registration statement; (4) a company that has filed in a timely manner all reports required during the prior 12 calendar months and any portion of a month immediately preceding filing of the registration statement; (5) the company and its subsidiaries have not, since end of last fiscal year for which certified financial statements were included in any report filed pursuant to Section 13(a) or Section 15(d), failed to pay any dividend or sinking fund installment, or defaulted on any installment on indebtedness or rental on any long-term lease, which defaults in the aggregate are material to the issuer's financial position.[15]

The transaction must also meet specified transactional requirements. The offering must be one of four types, only one of which has practical application to securitized offerings, namely, nonconvertible securities offered for cash by or on behalf of the issuer, provided that such securities are rated as "investment grade" by at least one rating agency.

This is potentially useful for securitized offerings that fail to qualify as asset-backed securities because, among other things, the assets securitized are obligations of a single obligor. It used to refer to nonconvertible debt or preferred securities, and was revised in 1992 to clarify that Form S-3 is available to register securities other than traditional debt securities. However, it is not clear whether this provision would be available where the majority-owned subsidiary is the depositor to a municipal derivatives trust, but the subsidiary's credit does not stand behind the securities issued.

If the issuer is a majority-owned subsidiary (such as a special-purpose corporation), one of the following additional requirements must be met: (1) the issuer itself

---

15 Requirements (a) and (e) are also technically applicable to offering of investment-grade asset-backed securities, but will usually have no practical impact.

meets the registrant and transaction requirements listed above (highly unlikely in an asset securitization), (2) the parent of the issuer meets the registrant requirements, and the issuer is making a primary offering of nonconvertible investment-grade securities (most likely in an asset securitization), or (3) the parent of the issuer meets the registrant and transaction requirements and fully guarantees securities being registered as to principal and interest (in this case, the guarantee is considered a separate security that must be registered separately on the same registration statement).

Form S-1

Finally, Form S-1 is used for the registration of publicly offered securities that do not qualify for use of Form S-3. The timing of use of Form S-1, which will usually require at least two months for SEC review between finalizing an offering document and being able to offer and sell securities, will preclude its use in most municipal derivative offerings. However, for certain types of offerings this timing, and the uncertainty imposed by the SEC review process, may be acceptable.

Form S-1 has no registrant or transaction requirements. There must be full disclosure regarding the issuer and the offering and no incorporation by reference to other materials is permitted.

TAX ISSUES

The three most important tax issues presented by an investment in a synthetic floating-rate municipal bond are (1) that interest on the underlying municipal bond is tax-exempt; (2) that the structure does not create a separate taxable entity that will trap the exempt interest on the bond; and (3) that the investor will be treated as the tax owner of the investment package.

Underlying Tax Exemption

Secondary-market structures, by their very nature, are based on existing municipal bonds. In the event of any defect in the underlying bonds that would cause the interest on them to be taxable, none of the interest received by investors in the secondary-market product would be tax-exempt. In none of the synthetic investments does the sponsor's counsel review or reconfirm the tax exemption opinion rendered by bond counsel on the original issuance of the underlying bond. Instead, sponsor's counsel will merely rely upon the original opinion given by bond counsel or special tax counsel given in connection with the original issuance of the bonds.

If the underlying bonds are specified private activity bonds so that interest is included in alternative minimum taxable income, that characterization will also flow through the synthetic structure to the same extent that the characterization as tax-exempt interest flows through.

Flow-Through Treatment

An entity in which the investors are treated as the owners of the assets of the entity for tax purposes or the income of the entity assets otherwise flows through with character retention is essential for achieving the objective of synthetic floating-rate municipal bonds. For structures providing the primary investor with a put, this is most commonly accomplished by means of a grantor trust, subject to the provisions of Section 671 et seq. of the Internal Revenue Code of 1986 (the Code).[16] The investment structure may be treated as a grantor trust for federal income tax purposes whether or not it employs an explicit trust or merely a custody agreement.[17]

An alternative approach is to treat the entity as a partnership for federal income tax purposes even though the arrangement is not documented as a partnership for state law purposes.[18] Partnership structures are increasingly utilized for structures involving puts, and are the predominant structure for primary/residual floater products. An unincorporated investment arrangement that does not qualify as a grantor trust or as a partnership for federal income tax purposes generally will be an association taxable as a corporation. Distributions made by such an entity generally would be ordinary dividends to the extent of the earnings of the arrangement.

Grantor Trust

For a trust or custody arrangement to qualify as a flow-through trust for tax purposes, the documentation establishing the arrangement must satisfy two tests. (See Treas. Reg. § 1.7701-4(c).) First, the investments in the trust must be established at the outset of the trust, and there must be no power on the part of the trust fiduciary to vary the trust's investments. In other words, there can be virtually no management of trust assets, and only ministerial servicing is permitted. Very little leeway is allowed for regularizing the stream of payments. This is commonly known as a fixed-investment trust.

Second, the trust cannot have more than one class of beneficial interest, unless the creation of an additional class is merely incidental to the creation of the trust and is to facilitate direct investment in the underlying assets. The prohibition against multiple classes of beneficial ownership in a trust is not violated where trust income or assets are paid to third-party service providers. Thus, reasonable compensation for services actually rendered will not violate the grantor trust rules. Fixed fees for traditional services, such as trustee's fees, are almost certainly permitted. Variable fees, particularly those paid to the sponsor of the program, require more justification.[19] The variable fees for the interest rate swap or the put fee are often explicitly justified by the sponsor by reference to the current market for interest rate swaps. There is virtually no authority on the application of this particular rule, however, so there is

---

16 Revenue Ruling 77-349, 1977-2 C.B. 20, was the seminal ruling in which the Internal Revenue Service concluded that grantor trust analysis applied to a pass-through mortgage certificate.

17 Some counsel believe that the custody arrangement provides a somewhat stronger case for flow-through treatment, because no explicit trust is created and therefore no risk of creating a "bad" grantor trust. This is believed to be a minority view.

18 In a series of private letter rulings involving so called "hub and spoke" arrangements for regulated investment companies, the IRS has confirmed that an arrangement documented as a trust may nonetheless qualify as a partnership for federal income tax purposes. See, e.g., PLR 9122007 (June 18, 1990).

19 A variable fee that cannot be justified as reasonable compensation risks classification as a variable interest coupon strip. Although not expressly prohibited by the trust classification regulations, there is also no favorable authority permitting such transactions, and counsel are generally reluctant to approve variable coupon stripping transactions in the absence of permissive regulations, most likely under Section 1286 of the Code. See "Coupon Stripping Rules—Floater/Inverse Floaters," below.

some risk that the Internal Revenue Service (IRS) might challenge the trust status of these arrangements.

In investment products of this type, the sponsor should make an explicit representation that the fees charged, particularly the variable fees, represent arm's-length compensation for services and are justified by reference to the market for similar transactions. Potential investors should carefully review the strength of the opinion of sponsor's counsel on this issue.

Floater/inverse floater structures generally are not structured so as to qualify as grantor trusts for federal income tax purposes.

Partnership Analysis

Most floater/inverse floater structures, and a small number of synthetic floating-rate put structures, rely on classifying the investment entity as a partnership rather than as a trust. The hope is to qualify the residual interest, which is classified as swap income or put fee income in the grantor trust analysis, instead as tax-exempt interest income to the recipient. In the put structures, this approach to the entity classification is more risky, primarily due to the uncertain character of the investor's interest bearing the put right being classified as equity in the partnership. The characterization of the primary investor's interest as debt or equity is discussed below under "Equity Classification."

Partnership Classification. Secondary-market put and Dutch auction products generally are documented as a custody arrangement or trust in which a specified party, usually the sponsor, holds a 1 percent interest. This may consist of a pro rata interest in the underlying bonds or of an interest in one class constituting an interest in profits of 1 percent or more. Structures that do not require a 1 percent interest may make the four-factor analysis described below more difficult. Either the sponsor will expressly assume any liabilities of the investment vehicle, or the investment vehicle will be structured so as not to insulate investors from liabilities it may incur.

Four-Factor Analysis. Treasury Regulations § 301.7701-2 set out four factors that determine whether an entity (whether or not a partnership for state law purposes) will be classified as a partnership or as an association taxable as a corporation for federal income tax purposes. These factors are (1) whether the entity possesses the corporate characteristic of limited liability; (2) whether the entity possesses the corporate characteristic of continuity of life; (3) whether the entity possesses the corporate characteristic of centralized management; and (4) whether the entity possesses the corporate characteristic of free transferability of interests. Under the Regulations, an entity will avoid characterization as a corporation if it lacks two or more of these characteristics. These characteristics are discussed below. For most secondary-market floater/inverse floater products, the crucial two characteristics are limited liability and continuity of life.

Continuity of life. Treasury Regulations § 301.7701-2(b)(1) provide that an entity will lack continuity of life if the bankruptcy, resignation, or retirement of the general partner of a limited partnership will cause a dissolution of the organization, unless the remaining general partners agree to continue the partnership or unless all remaining limited partners agree to continue the partnership. In this type of arrangement, the sponsor generally will hold a 1 percent interest in the partnership, and the sponsor's bankruptcy or withdrawal will cause a termination of the arrangement (i.e., sale of the bonds and distribution of proceeds to the investors). Thus, the arrangement is generally thought to lack the corporate characteristic of continuity of life. Structures not requiring a 1 percent interest-holder may have more difficulty establishing that continuity of life is lacking.

Limited liability. Treasury Regulations § 301.7701-2(d) provide that an organization possesses limited liability if under local law there is no member who is personally liable for the debts of or claims against the organization. Some floater/inverse floater products are structured so that all owners are liable for claims against the organization (i.e., the arrangement under which the underlying bonds are held). Synthetic floating-rate structures that intend to rely on partnership classification will generally be documented as a custody arrangement so that the investment vehicle itself provides no protection from liability for investors. That is, purchasers of interests in the synthetic investment generally take on "general partner" type liability. These entities will lack the corporate characteristic of limited liability. Other products are structured so that only the sponsor is liable for claims against the arrangement. These arrangements, too, are generally thought to lack limited liability, provided that the sponsor has substantial assets or is not a mere "dummy" of the other members.

The Regulations provide that the person who is personally liable cannot merely be a "dummy" of the members and must possess substantial assets. Under the current IRS ruling guidelines on classification as a partnership, a corporate general partner generally must have on a continuing basis a net worth equal to at least 10 percent of the total contributions to the entity in order for the entity to be treated as not possessing limited liability. See Rev. Proc. 89-12, 1989-1 C.B. 798. In rendering opinions on this issue, many tax counsel focus on whether the net worth of the entity with unlimited liability (e.g., the sponsor) is substantial in an absolute sense and relative to the liability that it may encounter as general partner, rather than rigidly adhering to the 10 percent test.

In addition, the IRS guidelines require that the general partners of a partnership maintain a substantial stake in the partnership. The guidelines generally require that the general partners continually maintain an interest of at least 1 percent in all material items of partnership income, gain, loss, deduction, or credit. The guidelines also generally require that the general partners continually maintain minimum capital account balances in the partnership of the lesser of 1 percent of the aggregate positive capital account balances of the members of the partnership or $500,000. However, if the aggregate amount of contributions to the partnership exceeds $50 million, the 1 percent interest is reduced in the ratio that the $50 million bears to the aggregate contributions, with a minimum percentage interest of 0.2 percent. This 1 percent guideline is the basis for the requirement of a 1 percent sponsor interest.

Another IRS ruling guideline for limited partnerships with a sole corporate general partner requires that the limited partners not own a 20 percent or greater interest in the general partner. This guideline generally does not pose any issues for the secondary-market products.

Free transferability of interests. The partnership classification regulations provide that an entity has free transferability of interests if its members have the power, without the consent of other members, to transfer all of the attributes of their interest. The investment entities are usually structured so that the transfer of some or all investors' interests (often the holders of the inverse floater interests) is subject to the sole and discretionary consent of the sponsor. Because investors may not accept such restrictions, some products are structured such that it is merely the voting rights associated with the underlying bonds that cannot be transferred by an investor without the consent of the sponsor. The classification regulations indicate that free transferability of interests does not exist where a member can assign all of its economic rights in the organization but cannot assign its right to participate in management without the consent of other members. Although the restriction on transfer of voting rights with respect to the underlying bonds should negate the corporate characteristic of free transferability of interests, it is not certain that the restriction is sufficient for this purpose.

An organization will possess free transferability of interests if "substantially all" of its members can freely transfer their interests. The IRS ruling guidelines take the position that a transfer restriction applicable to 20 percent of the interests is sufficient to satisfy this requirement. Thus, in cases where the transferability restriction applies only to the residual interests, they generally should constitute at least 20 percent of the interests in the organization. Because of uncertainties in the application of these rules, in some cases the conclusion of tax counsel as to the lack of free transferability of interest may be more qualified than its conclusion as to continuity of life and limited liability.

Centralized management. The partnership classification regulations provide that centralized management is a concentration of authority to make business decisions on behalf of the entity that do not require ratification by the members of the organizations. The arrangements in these cases require very little in the way of management other than the actions normally permitted to be taken by a trustee, custodian, or agent with respect to passive trusts or custodial accounts. Some products are structured so that any voting rights with respect to the bonds remain in the hands of investors. It is unclear whether this feature is sufficient to avoid the characteristic of centralized management.

Properly documented, therefore, the arrangement should be able to be classified as a partnership for federal income tax purposes, thus providing flow-through characterization for tax-exempt interest income as well as asset flow-through treatment. (See generally GCM 39207 (December 14, 1983).) This conclusion does not by itself, however, solve the equity classification issue referred to immediately above.

Publicly Traded Partnerships. Section 7704 of the Code provides that, with certain exceptions, a publicly traded partnership shall be treated as a corporation. A publicly traded partnership is a partnership the interests in which are traded on an established securities market or are readily tradeable on a secondary market. In Notice 88-75, 1988-2 C.B. 386, the Internal Revenue Service provided safe harbor exemptions from classification as a publicly traded partnership. Under one such exemption, a partnership will not be classified as readily tradeable on a secondary market if (1) all interests in such partnership were issued in a transaction that was not registered under the Securities Act of 1933, and (2) either (A) the partnership does not have more than five hundred partners, or (B) the initial offering price of each unit of partnership interest is at least $20,000 and the partnership agreement provides that no unit of partnership interest may be subdivided for resale into units smaller than a unit the initial offering price of which would have been at least $20,000. Most of the synthetic investments intended to qualify as partnerships have been designed to qualify for this exemption.

With the advent of Rule 3a-7 and the possibility of SEC registration of many of these synthetic investment products (see "Securities Issues" and "SEC Registered Municipal Derivative Securities: The Future?" above), another basis to avoid publicly traded partnership status becomes available. Under Section 7704(c), a publicly traded partnership will not be treated as a corporation if 90 percent or more of its gross income for each taxable year of its existence consists of qualifying income, which includes interest income.[20] This exception is not available, however, to any partnership that could qualify as a regulated investment company under Section 851 of the Code, which in turn treats any company as a regulated investment company if it is required to be registered under the 1940 Act. Hence, new Rule 3a-7, which affords exemption for a broad new class of passive investment vehicle from registration under the 1940 Act, will similarly permit avoidance of qualification as a regulated investment company under the Internal Revenue Code, hence permitting reliance upon the qualifying income exception to publicly traded partnership status notwithstanding registration and public offering of the partnership's securities under the 1933 Act. The much more limited exception to investment company treatment afforded by the sales finance exemption (see "Securities," above) has permitted certain publicly registered and offered partnership transactions to be accomplished without adverse tax consequences even prior to the promulgation of Rule 3a-7.

Taxable Mortgage Pools. Yet another potential impediment to flow-through tax treatment is Section 7701(i) of the Code, which treats a taxable mortgage pool as a corporation. Sometimes referred to as the REMIC exclusivity rule, a taxable mortgage pool is any entity or part of an entity if (1) substantially all of its assets consist of debt obligations and more than 50 percent of those debt obligations consists of real estate mortgages, (2) the entity or portion thereof is the obligor under debt obligations with two or more maturities, and (3) payments on the entity's liability debt obligations bear a relationship to the payments on the entity's asset debt obligations. The statute further empowers the Treasury to provide in regulations that equity interests of varying classes that correspond to maturity classes of debt shall be treated as debt for purposes of these rules. In proposed Treasury Regulations § 301.7701(i)-1(g)(1), the Treasury appears to have exercised its regulatory authority to the maximum permissible extent under this last provision.

Under the taxable mortgage pool rules, any entity intending to be classified as a partnership for tax purposes whose principal assets consist of real estate mortgages and having differing maturities of debt and/or equity classes should carefully consider the ramifications under the taxable mortgage pool rules. This statutory provision first became effective, however, only in 1992, and the proposed regulations do include some favorable transition relief.

---

20 There is little doubt that qualifying interest income for this purpose includes interest on municipal obligations, even though such interest may be excluded from gross income for regular income tax purposes. There has been some suggestion that a partnership intending to rely upon the qualifying income exception to publicly traded partnership status should include a token amount of taxable interest income to avoid any question on this issue.

Section 761 Election. Section 761(a) of the Code permits an election to be made to be excluded from the provisions of the Code that govern the taxation of partnerships generally (but not out of partnership classification). The principal purpose of the election is to avoid the necessity of filing partnership information returns and sending schedules K-1 to individual partners. Other purposes of some sponsors are to avoid the complications of partnership accounting.

Sponsors of synthetic floating-rate investments intended to qualify as tax partnerships typically plan to make the Section 761 election out of partnership tax rules. One of the advantages of the election for synthetic floating-rate investments is that it permits the tax-exempt income of the arrangement to flow through to investors as earned, rather than at the end of the partnership's taxable year.[21] The authority for making this election is not altogether clear. If the election is not properly made, the income and expense items of investors could be shifted into different taxable years. In addition, individual investors could be liable for certain penalties under the Code, none of which are terribly large.[22]

Equity Classification

Put Structures. The primary floating investor's interest in the "partnership" would be the primary floating-rate instrument with the seven-day put right and the seven-day interest period. There is some risk, however, that such an instrument would not be classified as an equity interest in the partnership but instead as a form of debt in the partnership, particularly if the put right is to a person that directly or indirectly bears the economic benefits and burdens of the inverse floater.[23] This issue is very closely related to, but analytically distinguishable from, the tax ownership issued addressed below.

In Revenue Ruling 90-27, 1990-1 C.B. 50, the Internal Revenue Service held that Dutch auction preferred stock constituted an equity interest in the corporation. One of the enumerated factors in reaching that conclusion, however, was that there

---

21 Under the regular partnership tax rules, the tax items of a partnership flow through to investors in the investor's taxable year that includes the last day of the partnership's taxable year. See Section 706(a) of the Code.

22 The principal penalty that might be assessed is under Section 6698 of the Code, for failing to file a partnership return, which is $50.00 per month up to five months multiplied by the total number of partners in the partnership during the taxable year. Each partner is individually liable for that penalty to the extent liable for partnership debts generally. The penalty might be avoided on a showing of reasonable cause.

23 If the investment product is structured so that the inverse floater investor is a member of the partnership, and the economic burden of the put right is borne by that investor, the risk is that the structure might be recharacterized as ownership of the underlying bonds by the inverse floater investor, with its position financed by a demand loan from the primary floater investor. Such characterization would result in loss of tax exemption for the interest paid to the primary floater investor. If the put right is to a person who does not have an interest in the underlying bonds, it is more difficult to characterize that person as the owner of the bonds prior to exercise of the put right, since that person has no claim to ownership of the bonds at that time.

was no expressed or implied right to cause any person to purchase the preferred stock under any circumstances. Having such a right to compel someone to purchase the partnership interest, especially in as short a period as seven days, raises the degree of concern on equity classification. It is generally believed that the investor's diminished exposure to the burdens of ownership (i.e., risk of loss) must be counterbalanced by providing it with greater potential for gain.

If the primary floating-rate interest were not classified as equity in the partnership, income in respect of that interest would not be treated as exempt from federal income tax.

Dutch Auction Floater/Inverse Floaters. For income received from the partnership to be tax-exempt, the fund investor's interest in the partnership must be treated for federal income tax purposes as an equity interest, rather than a form of debt of the partnership. As mentioned, in Revenue Ruling 90-27 the Internal Revenue Service held that Dutch auction preferred stock in a corporation, where the investor had no express or implied right to require any person to purchase the preferred stock, constituted an equity interest in the corporation. This ruling provides solid support for the conclusion that the Dutch auction floating-rate interest in a secondary-market program constitutes an equity interest in the partnership. In this respect, these programs are stronger from the tax perspective than programs that give the investors a seven-day or other short-term right to put their interests to another party, such as a bank.

Some program variants attempt to give the primary floating-rate investors protection in the event of significant movements in interest rates or the credit quality of the bonds by providing the floating-rate owners with a preference over the residual owners. For example, the program may require a sale of the bonds and a distribution of sale proceeds to investors, with the floating-rate holders receiving their investment and the excess being distributed to the residual holders, upon a specified number of failed auctions or upon the value of the bonds held by the program decreasing to a specified percentage of the investment of the floating-rate investors. Because these features diminish the risk faced by floating-rate investors and provide rights similar to a right to put the interest, these features must be examined carefully to determine the degree to which they threaten the conclusion that the floating-rate instruments represent equity rather than debt of the partnership. There are no bright-line standards separating debt from equity in this context. Many counsel believe that a greater degree of insulation from possible losses remains consistent with equity classification if coupled with a greater potential for profit.

Ownership

Tax ownership in synthetic floating-rate investments involving puts is a somewhat more difficult analysis than the entity classification issue described above. This is because ownership is an analysis based on all facts and circumstances. It is essential that sponsor's counsel address the ownership question and give a suitably strong opinion that investors in the arrangement will be treated as tax owners of the bonds or the arrangement.

Benefits/Burdens Test; Risk Concentration

By far the most important factors in determining tax ownership of property are to determine who has the risk of loss and the opportunity for gain.

If the risk of loss, either through default or changes in market value, on the underlying bonds is transferred to the investor, then the investor is much more likely to be viewed as the owner of the bond for tax purposes. Failure to acquire credit or market risk, or both, will not be fatal to tax ownership in the investor, but will put greater emphasis on other factors, principally the opportunity for gain. Virtually all synthetic floating-rate structures eliminate the investor's market risk through the par put right; some also diminish or eliminate the investor's credit or default risk on the underlying bond, through bond insurance or a bank letter of credit. In transactions in which default risk and market risk are shifted away from the investor, these two risks will usually be borne by two different parties. Some counsel view separation of these risks as an important feature of any such arrangement, in order to avoid too much risk concentration in a single party. In the Dutch auction floater/inverse floater structure, the primary floater, having no put right, has significant risk of loss, so there is little doubt on ownership in that case.

It is important for the investor's tax ownership that it have meaningful opportunity for gain in respect of the underlying bond. Any of the structures described above that have periodic free opt-outs or a termination at the 20 percent point are generally thought to provide such opportunity. Likewise, the structures that rely on a swap unwind pricing mechanism, as giving the investor an opportunity for market arbitrage profit in respect of the bond and the related variable fee, are generally believed to provide such opportunity for market gain. The puttable partnership structures usually give even more opportunity for gain. The more such opportunities exist, the stronger the investor's case for tax ownership.

To have a meaningful opportunity for gain, it is also important that the bond be sold to the investor at a price that does not exceed its fair market value. This is to avoid an economically compelled put.

Numerous other factors can be taken into account in determining tax ownership, including the form of the transaction, loan-type covenants, indemnification, fixed sale price, and a pattern of dealing between the parties. The form, of course, will always be consistent with investor ownership. The other factors are likely to be somewhat ambiguous. Finally, the investor should strive to maintain a pattern of exploiting its ownership of the underlying bond whenever possible; this obviously can be tempered by cash flow and regulatory considerations.

Revenue Ruling 82-144

In Revenue Ruling 74-27, 1974-1 C.B. 24, the Internal Revenue Service held that an investor who acquires both a bond and a contract to tender the bond back to the seller for a fixed price at a fixed date would not be treated as the owner of the bond, and would be treated as receiving taxable rather than tax-exempt interest. This ruling was based on a series of cases that disregarded formal ownership when another person had contracted to bear the risk of both increases and decreases in market value of the bonds.[24] However, where the formal owner had an option (but not an obligation by law or by practice) to tender his bond back to the seller, and where the purpose of the tender option was to provide liquidity, it was held that the form of the transaction would be respected.[25] In response to a series of requests for private letter rulings, the IRS published Revenue Ruling 82-144, 1982-2 C.B. 34, addressing the tax ownership of a bond coupled with a put right. The relevant facts in Revenue Ruling 82-144 are (1) the bond was purchased from a dealer; (2) the put was purchased from the same dealer; (3) the bond was purchased for fair market value; (4) an additional price was paid for the put; (5) the put was at a fixed price; (6) the term of the put was substantially less than the remaining term of the bond (establishing the 20 percent tail); (7) the put was nonassignable; (8) the put would terminate on disposition of the bond; (9) there were no restrictions on the sale of the bond; (10) the bond was not callable by the dealer or by any other person; (11) the dealer would not be soliciting buyers for the bond while it was held by the investor; and (xii) the bond was acquired for the investor's own account and not as security for a loan to the dealer.

In reaching the conclusion that the investor and not the dealer was the tax owner of the bonds, the IRS relied on distinguishing the facts in the described transaction from the pattern of cases involving so-called repurchase agreements. The principal distinctions were that there was a separate arm's-length price paid for the put, the purpose of the put was to provide liquidity to the investor, and the term of the put was shorter than the remaining term of the bonds.

The synthetic floating-rate structures have fact patterns very similar to those in Rev. Rul. 82-144. The principal distinctions are with respect to items (7) (these puts are assignable) and (8) (the put does not terminate on disposition of the bonds). In addition, some of the structures, principally the explicit swap structures, have no specific tail on the put right, which can extend through the remaining maturity of the bonds; however, because the put can be canceled by the investor at any time, it is thought that the intent of this factor is substantially met.

Shortly after issuing Rev. Rul. 82-144, the IRS issued Revenue Procedure 83-55, 1983-2 C.B. 572, in which it announced that it would not issue advance rulings or determination letters as to who is the true owner of property in cases of the sale of securities where the purchaser has the contractual right to cause the security to be purchased by either the seller or a third party.

Because of the high degree of similarity between most of the synthetic floating-rate products and the facts set forth in Rev. Rul. 82-144, most counsel feel fairly comfortable that investors in such products will be treated as the tax owners thereof. Nevertheless, because there are some distinctions in the fact patterns, as well as the no-ruling posture announced by the IRS, opinions on this issue are always qualified to some degree.

---

24 See e.g., *First National Bank of Nashville v. United States*, 467 F.2d 1098 (6th Cir. 1972); *Union Planters National Bank of Memphis v. United States*, 426 F.2d (6th Cir. 1970); *American National Bank of Austin v. United States*, 421 F.2d 442 (5th Cir. 1970).
25 *Citizens National Bank of Waco v. United States*, 551 F.2d 832 (Ct. Cl. 1977).

Typical Features

Different sponsors' products will mix the ownership factors in slightly different ways. On default risk, true default risk may lie with the investor or may be shifted to a third party through credit enhancement. Some additional credit risk may be assigned to the investor through the put termination on a two-rating-category downgrade; this feature may be absent, however, particularly with prerefunded bonds and mortgage revenue bonds where the default risk is or is thought to be small in any event.

All of the investment programs eliminate market downside risk to the investor through the mechanism of the par put right (unless the put right is terminated through default or other event described above).

Every investment product of this type gives some mechanism to the investor to realize market upside with respect to the bond. This will come about through a swaplike unwind, through periodic or back-end (or occasionally front-end) free termination features, or through a specific right to some percentage in the market appreciation in the bond.

Each investment product must be examined on its own merits. Stronger market upside with respect to a particular product may justify lesser market or credit risk for that product.

Coupon Stripping Rules—Floater/Inverse Floaters

The provisions of the Code relating to stripping interest and principal components of a tax-exempt bond require the purchaser of a stripped principal or interest component to treat it as a bond issued with original issue discount equal to the difference between its purchase price and its stated redemption price at maturity. The investor's original issue discount is tax-exempt only to the extent the investor's yield, determined at the date of purchase, does not exceed the original yield on the underlying bonds.

If a trust or custodial arrangement is employed to effectuate a coupon stripping transaction, Treasury Regulation § 301.7701-4(c) provides that the arrangement will be treated as a grantor trust providing flow-through tax treatment only if the purpose of multiple classes of interest in the trust is to facilitate direct investment in the assets of the trust. If the purpose of multiple classes of interests is not to facilitate direct investment, the arrangement is analyzed as a partnership or association taxable as a corporation under the four-factor analysis outlined above. Although transactions in which a fixed rate of interest or a fixed percentage of the interest on a bond is stripped satisfy the "facilitation-of-direct-investment" restriction, the situation is not clear for "variable-rate strips," in which an amount that is a varying percentage of the interest on the underlying bonds is stripped. Under a coupon stripping analysis, the maximum tax-exempt yield on each of the primary floating-rate interest and the inverse floating-rate interest would be capped at the original yield on the bonds; any excess yield would constitute taxable discount income. I.R.C. Sec. 1286(d). Under current market conditions, this limitation would be of greater concern for holders of inverse floating-rate instruments. Because IRS representatives previously have made statements to the effect that variable-rate stripping transactions would not satisfy the grantor trust rule described above, it is generally thought to be highly unlikely that the IRS would take the position on a retroactive basis that the secondary market floater/inverse floater products *must* be analyzed under the coupon stripping rules and would be subject to the cap described above on the amount of interest that is tax-exempt. The IRS is presently working on rules to govern variable coupon strips under Section 1286 of the Code, however, so this issue may be changing in the future.

State Taxes

In addition to the federal income tax consequences described above, an investor must consider various state tax issues. These include: (1) whether the underlying bond is exempt from tax under the laws of a particular state; (2) whether the structure employed complies with state law requirements to pass through exempt interest to investors; and (3) whether there are any additional state or local taxes imposed on investments (such as an intangibles tax) held through intermediaries rather than held directly.

Opinions

As mentioned in the above discussion, it is essential that opinions from knowledgeable and reputable counsel be obtained on the three major issues: (1) the tax exemption on the underlying bond (given by original bond counsel or special tax counsel), which should be the standard form of unqualified opinion; (2) the entity classification issue (given by sponsor's counsel), which should be a "would hold" or "will" opinion; and (3) the tax ownership issue (given by sponsor's counsel), which should also be a "would hold" or "will" opinion. Each of the latter two opinions will typically contain some amount of disclosure, that is, they will be qualified to some extent. Depending on the level of qualification, that has become standard in the market.

Other Tax Issues

Bond Premium/Discount

In any of the structures of this type, the investor must pay a purchase price for the investment package that represents the fair market value of the underlying bond. If that purchase price is higher than the principal amount of the bond payable at maturity, bond premium will result, which is required to be amortized pursuant to Section 171 of the Code. Amortizable bond premium on a tax-exempt bond is not deductible for tax purposes, but does reduce the holder's basis in the bond.

If the purchase price of the bond is less than the principal amount of the bond payable at maturity, bond discount will result. If such discount arises in connection with the original issuance of the bond, the discount will be "original issue discount," which accrues as additional tax-exempt interest income on the bond. If such discount arises after original issuance, it will result in taxable "market discount," which may be avoidable through capitalization of all or part of the put fee, if any. In a floater/inverse floater partnership structure, market discount will usually be allocated to the inverse floater investor.

Put Fees; Married Put Rule

Amounts paid for a put (i.e., an option to sell property, usually at a fixed price) are generally treated as capital expenditures. If the put is exercised, the amount paid for the put is treated as an adjustment to the gain on the sale of the property. If the put lapses without exercise, the price paid therefor will generally be treated as a capital loss. An exception to this rule applies to a put acquired on the same day on which the property identified as intended to be used in exercising such put is acquired (a so-called "married put"). I.R.C. Sec. 1233(c).

In synthetic floating-rate bond transactions with an expected duration longer than one year, where the put is written as a one-year put that is renewed annually, a question arises as to whether the put right for the entire expected duration of the investment is subject to the married put rule or, on the other hand, the put is viewed as a series of one-year puts with only the first subject to the married put rule. The authorities on this point are at best ambiguous, but there is at least a good reporting position, perhaps a more likely than not legal position, that the put should be treated as a single put throughout the life of the investment, all subject to the married put rule.

Swap Income, Expense

Notional Principal Contract Regulations. On October 8, 1993, the Internal Revenue Service published final Regulations on the accounting treatment for so-called notional principal contracts, that is, interest rate and similar swap contracts. Under those Regulations, swap expense and income should be accounted for in the year in which it accrues under the swap contract. Net swap expense for a year is thought to give rise to a deductible expense, possibly subject to disallowance under Section 265 (relating to expenses incurred in connection with tax-exempt income). The Regulations do not specify whether the expense is capital or ordinary, but most tax practitioners believe that such expense is ordinary.

Any net income realized in respect of a termination of the swap will be includible in income for the taxable year of termination. Any such gain or loss will be capital gain or loss. Such a termination could occur on a deemed disposition of the swap resulting from a transfer by the swap counterparty of its position in the swap.

Amortization of Swap Premium. Some synthetic structures utilizing explicit swaps in connection with premium bonds sell the package at par. For tax purposes, this is treated as a sale of the bond at its fair market value (i.e., at a market premium) together with a payment by the swap counterparty of a premium for entering into an "off-the-market" swap, with the swap premium being used by the investor to pay the bond premium. Under the final swap Regulations, the swap premium is not included in the investor's income, but is instead amortized over the term of the swap agreement. Under the Regulations, the swap premium can be amortized either under the so-called Black-Scholes option pricing model or on a bond yield to maturity basis. In addition, the amortized premium allocable to any particular period is first netted against any other swap income or expense to determine aggregate net swap income or expense for the period. Thus, the amortized swap premium would be an additional item to be taken into account each year in determining whether there is net swap income or net swap expense for the year.

The amortizing swap premium also effectively lowers the tax-exempt ceiling on premium tax-exempt bonds. For example, a 9 percent bond in a 7 percent market will generate 9 percent of tax-exempt interest income even though, on a yield basis, the total income on the bond is only 7 percent. In such a market, a 9 percent bond purchased as part of a synthetic floating-rate package with a 9 percent swap will, because of the amortization of the swap premium, generate taxable income whenever the floating rate on the swap goes above a rate that is equal to 7 percent over the life of the bonds, but because of the yield to maturity amortization of the swap premium is higher in the early years and lower in the later years. The sponsor of individual investments can provide detailed numbers.

CONCLUSION

A substantial amount of these transactions, in terms of both numbers of deals and dollar volumes, have been consummated, with opinions given by a number of different law firms. Most of the large investment banking firms and some large commercial banks have programs involving synthetic floating-rate investments. These instruments have received a substantial amount of attention from both the banking and the legal communities, as well as the Investment Company Institute, the SEC, and the IRS. With respect to the IRS, in particular, several different market participants, including the authors, have explained these transactions to the relevant authorities on several different occasions, and have received varying levels of comfort to the effect that these investments violate no specific tax policy and are not presently intended to be the subject of any tax enforcement action. That is not to say that any Treasury Department or IRS personnel, officially or unofficially, directly or indirectly, has stated that these investment structures in general, or any one in particular, is safe from IRS challenge. But it is upwards of four years now since the IRS was made directly aware of these investment structures (which actually date back to the early 1980s, in their most rudimentary forms), and no enforcement action has in fact been taken.

Investment in these types of transactions is not entirely risk-free. In general, however, with proper structuring, the authors believe they present only a small amount of tax and securities regulatory risk.

PART SEVEN

TAX AND ACCOUNTING ISSUES

CHAPTER 42

U.S. Tax Considerations for Institutional Investors Acquiring Derivative Products: A Methodology for Evaluating Tax Risks

Steven D. Conlon
Vincent M. Aquilino

Chapman and Cutler

This chapter provides an overview of the U.S. federal income tax rules that apply to various types of derivative financial products acquired by investors. The chapter is intended to assist investors in developing a working approach for analyzing the federal income tax consequences of these products by discussing the principal tax rules that apply, and identifying collateral tax rules that may be relevant. The federal income tax treatment of options, futures contracts, and interest rate swaps is discussed in detail. The chapter describes those tax rules that apply to financial products having derivative-like features, such as embedded swap and embedded cap bonds. Noting that current federal income tax rules do not permit global integration of hedging transactions for tax purposes, the chapter provides examples of cases where the tax law may "bifurcate" or "deconstruct" financial products into their various components, which are subject to separate tax analysis. Also as a practical aid to the investor, the Appendix to this chapter provides a list of "Ten Basic Tax Questions that an Investor Acquiring a Derivative Product Should Consider."

The authors gratefully acknowledge the substantial assistance of Suzanne M. Russell, the assistance of Alan L. Kennard, and the insightful review and comments of L.G. "Chip" Harter, III and Richard M. Hervey.

INTRODUCTION

What Is a Derivative?

The term *derivative* refers to financial contracts such as options, forward contracts, swaps, caps, floors, and similar devices that provide value measurements by reference to movements in debt, interest rate, currency, equity, or commodity markets. While these financial products derive their value from fluctuations in their referenced markets, they do not require direct participation in those markets. Some market participants may consider financial products that fall outside this definition as derivatives.

Derivative products can be, and are regularly, used as tools for hedging market risk. As a result, other products that achieve this hedging result are often categorized as derivatives. Similarly, innovative debt securities may incorporate features that have derivative-like characteristics. For this reason, these types of debt securities are frequently categorized as derivatives (or are treated as including a derivative-like component). Moreover, the products, and their permutations, continually evolve as financial engineers look for more cost-effective products or products that reap micro-market arbitrage benefits. The term *derivative financial product* has a different meaning depending on one's market perspective, so it is quite difficult to be precise about which financial products are properly classified as "derivatives." Any attempt to be limiting in one's view of the term is to ignore the constant evolution of the products, which is a most apparent fact in analyzing the subject.

This chapter addresses the United States federal income tax issues that institutional investors should consider in acquiring certain derivative products. Special tax considerations for dealers and market makers are not discussed. Investors should carefully consider whether they are treated as "dealers" for federal income tax purposes because new "mark-to-market" rules applicable to dealers in financial products and derivative financial products were enacted in 1993.[1] These rules may apply to taxpayers who would not otherwise generally consider themselves dealers and, if a taxpayer is a dealer, may subject portfolio investments of the dealer that are not part of its dealer inventories to the mark-to-market rule unless the investments are properly identified.[2] The tax rules applicable to dealers are in many cases very different from the tax rules discussed in this chapter.

In addition, providing the ideal kind of straightforward "black and white" textbook guidance is significantly hampered by several factors. First, as duly noted, the market has differing views of which financial products are truly "derivative." Second, the products and their uses continue to change. Third, the development of the law governing these products significantly lags behind market development. We have nonetheless attempted to provide an overview of a number of different federal income

---

1 These rules are contained in Section 475 of the Internal Revenue Code (the "Code") which was enacted as part of *The Revenue Reconciliation Act of 1993*, Pub. L. No. 103-66, § 13223(a) (1993). Unless otherwise indicated, all references to Sections shall refer to the Code.

2 *See* Section 475(b)(2). *See generally* Letter to Leslie B. Samuels, Assistant Secretary for Tax Policy, Department of the Treasury, from John Shivers, President-Elect, Independent Bankers Ass'n of America, dated November 4, 1993, *reprinted in* HIGHLIGHTS & DOCUMENTS, November 19, 1993, at 2851 (opposing the potential application of Section 475 to community banks).

tax rules that apply to derivative products with the express desire of not only answering some of the more basic tax questions, but pointing out the tax issues that will need to be addressed to assure the ongoing assessment of new derivative products which may be of interest to investors.

How Important Are Tax Considerations?

Financial products are designed to satisfy specific financial objectives. The delivery of desired return on investment, achieving lower cost sources of funds, or protection against a variety of market risks associated with asset and liability management are but a few of the objectives frequently mentioned. It is the delivery of the specific financial objective that dominates the evaluation of the product—requiring a thorough understanding of credit, market, and structural risks such as contract enforceability and bankruptcy. Tax considerations often do not receive the attention they deserve. It is obvious that unexpected tax consequences can do severe damage to a derivative product's usefulness as a financial tool.

Tax considerations relating to derivative products should not be overlooked because the imposition of undesirable tax treatment is an economic cost that can adversely affect the benefits obtained from the financial product. Many financial products place the burden of any tax liabilities associated with the product on the investor. Thus, an unanticipated tax cost may partially or totally negate the anticipated economic benefit to be obtained by the investor. Moreover, as discussed below regarding global or integrated transactions, it may not be possible to "net" transactions involving derivatives for tax purposes in the same manner that such transactions may be netted for financial purposes. As a result, an investor may incur tax liabilities that are inconsistent with the net economic consequences of a transaction. This could be a result of potential limitations on losses, discussed in the section of this chapter entitled "The Importance of the Tax Character of Income and Losses." Also, the development of products that minimize undesirable tax risks or that take advantage of desirable tax characteristics (such as products in the tax-exempt municipal market, for example) by definition, places greater emphasis on the ability to deliver the desired tax treatment. These types of products, because of their focus on tax results relating to the product, require special attention in evaluating the risks associated with their ability to deliver the desired tax benefits.

CONSIDER THE BASIC TAX RULES THAT APPLY

Understanding Which Set or Sets of Basic Rules Apply

Federal income tax law does not provide a single set of tax rules that apply to all financial products. Thus, financial products must first be classified into basic categories, with tax rules applying on the basis of the product's classification, although the categories overlap one another to some extent. As indicated below, because these rules vary widely, financial products that are classified differently may have very different federal income tax consequences to investors.

Current tax law may classify derivative financial products into the following categories: (1) debt, (2) stock, (3) "pass-through" equity, (4) options or forward contracts, (5) "mark-to-market" contracts, and (6) "notional principal contracts." A general discussion of the basic tax rules relating to these different categories follows. A more detailed discussion of the tax rules relating to notional principal contracts such as swaps, caps, and floors is provided in a later section of this chapter.

In addition, a financial product may be "bifurcated" or broken down into several different products for tax purposes, and each product would be subject to separate tax analysis. Bifurcation further complicates the tax analysis and is discussed separately in a later section of this chapter.

"Global" or "Integrated" Transactions

Hedging transactions can be structured to hedge specific risks associated with a particular asset or liability. These types of hedges are sometimes referred to as *microhedges*. Hedging transactions can also be structured to hedge an investor's risks associated with a number of assets or liabilities. For example, a company that conducts business in a foreign country may enter into hedging transactions that are intended to address all of the company's foreign currency risks associated with its business operations in the foreign country, rather than conduct a number of hedging transactions that individually hedge each of the company's discrete foreign currency risks associated with particular assets and liabilities. These types of hedges are sometimes referred to as *global hedges*.

Similarly, a series of financial transactions can be entered into that, taken as a whole, produce essentially the same economic result that can be obtained through the acquisition of a single financial product. For example, an investor could acquire a fixed interest rate debt instrument that permits the investor to convert the debt instrument into common stock of the issuer of the debt instrument on its scheduled maturity date and at a specified conversion price. Alternatively, the investor could acquire a fixed interest rate debt instrument that does not provide for conversion and a separate option to purchase stock on the debt instrument's maturity date at a specified price. Because the acquisition of a debt instrument and an option to acquire stock produces the same economic consequences as the acquisition of a single financial product—convertible debt—an investor may analyze this series of transactions (the acquisition of debt and the option) by focusing on their overall economic effect. A series of transactions may, thus, be treated as "integrated."

Unfortunately, except in very limited instances the federal income tax law does not currently analyze the tax consequences of separate financial products on a global or integrated basis.[3] An important exception to the general rule in the derivative products area relates to the federal income tax rules permitting the integration of certain

---

3 However, under Section 269B, certain entities and ownership interests are deemed to be "stapled." Moreover, under the "step transaction doctrine," the various segments of a transaction are analyzed as a whole in determining the tax effects. *See generally* 1 BORIS I. BITTKER & LAWRENCE LOKKEN, FEDERAL TAXATION OF INCOME, ESTATES AND GIFTS ¶4.3.5 (2d ed. 1989). Note that the preamble to the Final Swap Regulations (as defined below) indicates that the IRS is still evaluating the possibility of integrated treatment for notional principal contracts and other derivative financial instruments. 58 Fed. Reg. 53, 126 (October 14, 1993).

foreign currency hedging transactions for tax purposes.[4] Another important exception to the general rule relates to so-called hedging transactions governed by proposed and temporary regulations issued in 1993.[5] As a result of the limited availability of integrated tax treatment, the federal income tax treatment may differ significantly from the manner in which a market participant generally views global or integrated transactions (as an economic matter, for accounting purposes or otherwise).

How Should an Investor Approach These Issues?

Many derivative products such as swaps, caps, and floors are sold privately. In many cases, disclosure documents discussing the nature and risks associated with the product are either not provided or lack substantive discussion of the tax risks. As a result, investors are often on their own in the task of assessing and evaluating the risks, including tax risks, associated with the products.

In connection with the sale of some debt securities with derivative-like features and some pass-through equity securities with derivative-like features, an investor may receive a private placement memorandum or other form of offering document. These offering documents will typically include a discussion of federal income tax risks associated with the product (which often indicates that it is not complete or exhaustive) and investors should consider the disclosed risks therein relative to their own standards of comfort with tax risks.

State Law Form Versus Tax Law Substance

It is important to note that the state law classification of a financial product or an entity that issues a financial contract is not necessarily determinative of its federal income tax classification. Thus, instruments labeled and qualifying as "debt" for state law purposes may be recharacterized as "equity" or "stock" for federal income tax purposes.[6]

---

4 *See* Treas. Reg. Section 1.988-5. This rule is discussed in more detail in a later section of this chapter.
5 Three different sets of regulations were released by the IRS on October 18, 1993 (a temporary regulation addressing the character of "hedging transactions;" a proposed regulation addressing special identification requirements applicable to certain types of hedges; and a timing regulation addressing the timing of income and expense recognition with respect to both the hedged property and the related hedge). *See* 58 Fed. Reg. 54,037 (October 20, 1993); 58 Fed. Reg. 54,075 (October 20, 1993); 58 Fed. Reg. 54,077 (October 20, 1993). However, these new hedging rules will not, as a general matter, apply to investment activities because they only apply if the hedge relates to "ordinary property" which cannot produce capital gain in any circumstance. Temp. Treas. Reg. Section 1.1221-2T(b)(2). Ordinarily, the disposition of investment property may generate capital gain or loss. As a result, a hedge of investment property would ordinarily not be subject to these rules. Moreover, as a technical matter, the rules do not require "integration" of the hedged property and the related hedge for federal income tax purposes, but rather, simply consistent character and timing treatment of the related hedged with the hedged property. *See* Preamble to Prop. Reg. Section 1.446-4, 58 Fed. Reg. 54,079. It is expected that final regulations will be issued in the near future. Finally, it is possible that similar rules may be applied to hedges relating to investment property at some point in the future.
6 These instruments might, for example, lack certain of the tax indicia of debt such as a fixed maturity date, set interest rate, and creditors' remedies.

Similarly, an entity formed as a trust under state law may be classified as a partnership for federal income tax purposes.[7] Conversely, the taxation of a transaction for federal income tax purposes does not necessarily control its taxation for state tax purposes.

Basic Tax Rules for Notional Principal Contracts

While a detailed discussion of the taxation of swaps is presented in a later section of this chapter, this section provides a general overview for purposes of contrasting the taxation of interest rate swaps, caps, floors, and similar types of contracts with the taxation of other financial products.

Historically, controversy surrounded the federal income taxation of interest rate swaps, caps, floors, and similar contracts, even though the size of the market for such contracts had dramatically increased over the years.[8] In response to the need for guidance in this market, the Internal Revenue Service (IRS) issued proposed regulations (the Proposed Swap Regulations) in 1991 and final regulations (the Final Swap Regulations) in 1993 regarding "notional principal contracts" (NPCs).[9]

The Final Swap Regulations address the timing of income and expense recognition with respect to "notional principal contracts," the technical term that covers many types of derivative products such as swaps, caps, and floors.[10] The Final Swap Regulations generally require the amortization of payment obligations (including both lump-sum and ongoing payments) on the swap, cap, or floor over its term, determined on a "net" basis.[11]

There are several aspects of the Final Swap Regulations that merit special attention, including the "embedded loan" rules (which recharacterize payments as if

7 *See, e.g.,* Rev. Rul. 88-79, 1988-2 C.B. 361 (organization formed as a business trust under Missouri law is classified as a partnership for federal income tax purposes); Rev. Rul. 88-76, 1988-2 C.B. 360 (a Wyoming limited liability company is classified as a partnership for federal income tax purposes); Priv. Ltr. Rul. 9233046, dated May 21, 1992; Priv. Ltr. Rul. 9318029, dated February 8, 1992.
8 Kevin M. Keyes, Mikol S. Neilson, Peter J. Connors, Glenn N. Eichen & Stanley Smilack, Committee on Financial Transactions Task Force of the Interest Rate Agreements Subcommittee, Section of Taxation, American Bar Association, *Report on Selected Aspects of Interest Rate Caps, Floors, and Collars,* 44 TAX LAW. 1075 (Summer 1991).
9 56 Fed. Reg. 31,350 (July 10, 1991)(the Proposed Swap Regulations); 58 Fed. Reg. 53,125 (October 14, 1993) (the Final Swap Regulations).
10 A notional principal contract is defined by Treas. Reg. Section 1.446-3(c)(1)(i) as "a financial instrument that provides for the payment of amounts by one party to another at specified intervals calculated by reference to a specified index upon a notional principal amount in exchange for specified consideration or a promise to pay similar amounts." Treas. Reg. Section 1.446-3(c)(3) defines a "notional principal amount" as "any specified amount of money or property that, when multiplied by a specified index, measures a party's rights and obligations under the contract, but is not borrowed or loaned between the parties as part of the contract." Swaps, caps, floors, and collars are generally included within the definition of notional principal contract. *See* Treas. Reg. Section 1.446-3(c)(1)(i). The Final Swap Regulations are generally effective for notional principal contracts entered into on or after December 13, 1993. Treas. Reg. Section 1.446-3(j). An important exception to this general rule relates to the application of Treas. Reg. Section 1.1092(d)-1, which treats notional principal contracts as personal property of a type that is actively traded if similar contracts are actively traded and which may trigger the application of the "straddle rules" of Section 1092. This rule generally applies for positions entered on or after July 8, 1991. Treas. Reg. Section 1.1092(d)-1(d).
11 Treas. Reg. Section 1.446-3(d).

the contract includes a loan for tax purposes if the amount of any payments made with respect to a swap, cap, or floor that do not qualify as periodic payments is "significant").[12] Under these rules, certain financial instruments may be treated as comprised of two distinct assets for tax purposes: an "at market" notional principal contract and an embedded loan. An investor would need to account for the distinct tax characteristics of each component of a derivative subject to the embedded loan rule. It should be noted that the embedded loan rule was controversial, as evidenced by the number of comments received by the IRS on the rule set forth in the Proposed Swap Regulations.[13] In addition, the Proposed Swap Regulations treated the assignment by one party of its rights and obligations with respect to a notional principal contract to a third party as a "termination event" *triggering the recognition of gain or loss with respect to the nonassigning party.*[14] Fortunately, this rule was revised in the Final Swap Regulations so that an assignment is only treated as triggering a taxable event to the nonassigning party if the transaction constituted a "deemed exchange . . . and realization event under section 1001" of the contract.[15]

There are several tax accounting issues under the Final Swap Regulations that should be considered by investors. First, nonperiodic payments (the terms *periodic payment* and *nonperiodic payment* are defined in the more detailed discussion of these rules set forth later in this chapter) that are not recharacterized as embedded loans must be amortized in a manner that reflects the economic substance of the contract and cannot be amortized on a straight-line basis.[16] In the case of swaps, "economic substance" requires amortization by reference to the values of a series of cash-settled forward contracts that reflect the specified index and the notional principal amount.[17] Nonperiodic payments with respect to caps and floors are amortized in accordance with the values of a series of cash-settled option contracts that reflect the specified index and notional principal amount.[18] Moreover, the Final Swap Regulations permit

---

12 Treas. Reg. Section 1.446-3(g)(3) and (g)(4). Unfortunately, the Final Swap Regulations do not provide any safe harbor or bright line test with respect to swaps. Instead, they merely include two examples (an example treating the swap premium as an embedded loan involving a premium equal to 66.7 percent of the net present value of the fixed payments on the swap and an example that does not reclassify the swap premium as an embedded loan involving a premium equal to 9.1 percent of the present value of the fixed payments on the swap). The Proposed Swap Regulations were criticized in this regard. *See* Comment Letter to the IRS, Vincent M. Aquilino & Steven D. Conlon of Chapman and Cutler, dated September 20, 1991 (available as Document 91-8187, 91 TNT 203-35 from Tax Analysts). The Final Swap Regulations do not include final rules for determining whether a cap or floor includes an embedded loan. Instead, the embedded loan rules applicable to caps and floors have been retained in proposed form. The Proposed Swap Regulations do include a safe harbor regarding the determination of whether amounts paid with respect to a cap or floor are significant. Prop. Reg. Section 1.446-3(e)(4)(iv).

13 *See* Daniel P. Breen, Steven D. Conlon, Peter J. Connors, Glenn N. Eichen, L.G. "Chip" Harter & Mikol S. Neilson, Committee on Financial Transactions, Section of Taxation, American Bar Association, *Comments Regarding Prop. Reg. §§1.446-3, 1.446-4, 1.512(b)-1(a)(1), and 1.1092(d)-1, Proposed Regulations Regarding Accounting for Notional Principal Contracts* (1992) (available as Document 92-6255, 92 TNT 150-35 from Tax Analysts) (hereinafter *ABA Swap Regulations Report*).

14 Prop. Reg. Section 1.446-3(e)(6).

15 Treas. Reg. Section 1.446-3(h)(1). Note that it may be difficult to determine whether an assignment triggers a taxable exchange under Section 1001 of the Code.

16 Treas. Section 1.446-3(f)(2)(i) and (f)(2)(iv).

17 Treas. Reg. Section 1.446-3(f)(2)(ii).

18 Treas. Reg. Section 1.446-3(f)(2)(iv).

a nonperiodic payment with respect to swaps, caps, and floors to be amortized under a level payment method.[19] The Final Swap Regulations also permit the IRS to issue revenue procedures or revenue rulings that could include alternative methods of amortizing nonperiodic payments.[20] Although the Final Swap Regulations permit the use of the level payment method of amortization in a number of cases, the basic methods permitted by regulations are complex and may prove difficult for many investors to fully implement. Second, ongoing periodic payments with respect to a notional principal contract must be accounted for on a daily basis.[21] Special rules apply, requiring adjustments in the subsequent tax year, if the amount of a periodic payment is not determinable at the end of the taxpayer's tax year.[22] Third, special rules apply with respect to the termination of a notional principal contract (or the deemed termination of a notional principal contract, as previously discussed) and with respect to termination payments.[23] Fourth, Treas. Reg. Section 1.1092(d)-1, which addresses the extent to which a notional principal contract constitutes property of a type that is actively traded, may trigger the application of the straddle rules of Section 1092 (discussed separately later in this chapter).[24] Finally, it should be noted that the Final Swap Regulations do not directly address the character of items as ordinary or capital (although as discussed later in this chapter, they attempt to classify certain NPCs as straddles, which would have character implications).[25]

Basic Tax Rules for Options and Forwards

There is no clear, comprehensive set of rules in the Internal Revenue Code specifically relating to the taxation of options and forward contracts despite the fact that options and forward contracts have been an important component of the financial markets for a long time. As a result, the taxation of these products has been addressed in an ad hoc fashion throughout the years by Congress under various Code sections, the IRS (in the form of published revenue rulings and private letter rulings) and the courts, on an issue-by-issue basis.

Moreover, given the manner in which the law has developed in this area, the basic rules have not yet been overhauled (except with respect to "mark-to-market" contracts, as discussed below), as have rules relating to the taxation of other types of financial products (such as the original issue discount rules applicable to debt instruments). In this regard, some commentators have criticized the current rules generally

---

19 Treas. Reg. Section 1.446-3(f)(2)(iii) and (f)(2)(v). Note the special rules contained therein regarding this optional method and limitations on its availability set forth in Treas. Reg. Section 1.446-3(g)(2).

20 Treas. Reg. Section 1.446-3(f)(2)(vi). The preamble to the Proposed Swap Regulations also included a proposed form of revenue procedure that would have included a table that investors could have used to amortize cap and floor premiums. Preamble to the Proposed Swap Regulations, 56 Fed. Reg. 31,352-31,353. The adequacy of the table was criticized. *See ABA Swap Regulations Report, supra* note 13.

21 Treas. Reg. Section 1.446-3(e)(2).

22 Treas. Reg. Section 1.446-3(e)(2)(ii).

23 Treas. Reg. Section 1.446-3(h).

24 Note that the Proposed Swap Regulations were criticized in this regard. *See ABA Swap Regulations Report, supra* note 13.

25 Except to the extent the embedded loan rules apply. *See* Preamble to the Proposed Swap Regulations, 56 Fed. Reg. 31,351.

applicable to options and forward contracts and have suggested that those rules be completely rewritten.[26]

In order to discuss the taxation of options, certain terms must be defined.[27] A "holder" of an option has the right to exercise the option, while a "writer" of the option typically receives an initial premium (or payments over time) in exchange for its obligations on the option to the holder (either directly or to an exchange). A "put" gives the holder the right (but not the obligation) to sell property (stock, securities, etc.) at a specified price. A "call" gives the holder the right to acquire property at a specified price.

Timing of Income and Deductions

Two critical features of the taxation of puts and calls are that premiums *paid* by a holder are capitalizable, *not deductible,* and premiums *received* are not immediately treated as income to the writer.[28]

Rev. Rul. 78-182, 1978-1 C.B. 265 addressed certain tax issues for holders and writers of puts and calls traded on the Chicago Board Options Exchange. The revenue ruling provides that a holder's cost of acquiring a call is a nondeductible capital expenditure, not an expense (either immediately deductible or amortizable over time). If the holder sells the call, the cost is taken into account in computing gain or loss on sale.[29] If the call expires without exercise, the expiration is treated as a sale or exchange, resulting in a capital loss.[30] If the call is exercised, its cost is added to the holder's basis in the property acquired. Similarly, a holder's cost of acquiring a put is a nondeductible capital expenditure. If the holder sells the put, the cost is taken into account in computing gain or loss on sale.[31] If the put expires without exercise, the expiration is treated as a sale or exchange, resulting in a capital loss.[32] If the put is exercised, its cost reduces the amount realized upon the sale of the property to which the put relates.

The premium received by the writer of a call is not included in the writer's taxable income at the time of receipt but is instead carried in a deferred account until (1) the writer's obligation under the call expires, (2) the call is exercised by the holder, or (3) the writer engages in an offsetting closing transaction. The premium received by the writer of a put is also not included in the writer's taxable income at the time of receipt but is instead carried in a deferred account until (1) the writer's obligation under the put expires, (2) the put is exercised by the holder, or (3) the writer engages in an

---

26 *See* Letter to Harry L. Gutman, Chief of Staff, Joint Comm. on Taxation, from David C. Garlock, dated January 29, 1992 (available as Document 92-1590, 92 TNT 38-42 from Tax Analysts).

27 The definitions employed here are simplistic, relative to the actual workings of the markets, but are adequate for our purposes.

28 *See* Rev. Rul. 71-521, 1971-2 C.B. 313.

29 *See also* Section 1234.

30 *Id.*

31 *Id.*

32 *Id.* However, in the case of a "married put" where the option to sell the property is acquired on the same day the property is acquired this rule does not apply. Instead, the cost of the option is added to the basis of the property to which the option relates. *See* Section 1233(c).

offsetting closing transaction.[33] Rev. Rul. 78-182 also addresses holding period issues relating to the identified transactions involving puts and calls.

In spite of these basic timing rules, investors must consider whether other rules override the treatment discussed above. For example, the "short sale rules" of Section 1233 of the Code affect both the character of gains (as short-term) and the holding period of property. Also, the mark-to-market rules (which are discussed immediately hereafter) generally override the rules discussed above in the case of "Section 1256 contracts." In addition, the "straddle" rules of Section 1092 of the Code may defer all or a portion of the loss that would otherwise be recognized under the rules discussed above.

Character of Income

An important consideration relating to the tax treatment of puts and calls concerns whether gains or losses recognized will be characterized as capital gains or losses, and if so, whether such gains or losses will be "long-term" or "short-term."[34] In the case of corporations, capital losses are only deductible to the extent of capital gains.[35] In the case of other taxpayers, only $3,000 of capital losses in excess of capital gains can generally be deducted against ordinary income in any tax year.[36] Capital losses that cannot be deducted or offset against capital gains can be carried back or carried forward to other tax years.[37]

There are two special provisions (the *straddle rules* and the *wash sale rules*) that may apply in connection with puts and calls that can affect whether capital gain or loss is long-term or short-term, including whether capital gain or loss on the disposition of property to which the put or call relates is long-term or short-term.[38] These rules are discussed in a later section of this chapter.

Basic Tax Rules for "Mark-to-Market" Contracts

Section 1256 of the Code sets forth special rules that require the recognition of gain or loss for "Section 1256 contracts" as of the last day of the tax year for a taxpayer by

---

33 If the writer of the put is the issuer of the stock to which the put relates, special rules apply. Rev. Rul. 88-31, 1988-1 C.B. 302. Moreover, in the case of the writer of any option (including both puts and calls) relating to stock, securities or commodities, such writer's gain, if any, is generally characterized as short-term capital gain, except in the case of a dealer or market maker. *See* Section 1234(b)(1) and (b)(3).

34 Section 1234 sets forth the basic rules regarding the character of gain or loss attributable to the sale or exchange of, or loss attributable to exercise of, an option. Special rules apply if the option is a "married put" (*i.e.*,for an option to sell property at a fixed price acquired on the same day on which the property identified as intended to be used in exercising such option is acquired and which, if exercised, is exercised through the sale of the property so identified). Section 1233(c). Capital gains or losses are short-term if the property is "held" for one year or less prior to disposition and long-term if the property is held for more than one year prior to disposition. Section 1222. There are a number of rules in the Code that may need to be taken into account in determining how long property has been held (its "holding period") for these purposes; however, the basic rules are set forth in Section 1223.

35 Section 1211(a).

36 Section 1211(b).

37 Section 1212.

38 Sections 1092 and 1091.

treating each such contract as if it were sold at a price equal to its fair market value as of such date.[39] Section 1256 contracts include (1) any regulated futures contract, (2) any foreign currency contract, (3) any "nonequity option" (this definition is discussed in more detail below), and (4) any "dealer equity option" (this definition is also discussed in more detail below). Regulated futures contracts, which are included in the definition of a "Section 1256 contract,"[40] are subject to a "mark-to-market" system under which a daily valuation system for such contracts is maintained by the board of trade or exchange and is used to establish minimum deposit or margin requirements for participants that enter into contracts under the board or exchange. Because the tax rules set forth in Section 1256 apply to regulated futures contracts, these special rules are generally referred to as the "mark-to-market" rules (even though the rules apply to the other categories of contracts listed above). Because a taxpayer recognizes gain or loss with respect to a Section 1256 contract based on the contract's fair market value as of the end of such taxpayer's tax year, these rules essentially require a taxpayer to "mark-to-market" its tax gain or loss with respect to such securities as of the close of its tax year.

Contracts Subject to Section 1256 Rules

As indicated above, four basic types of contracts are treated as Section 1256 contracts (regulated futures contracts, foreign currency contracts, nonequity options, and dealer equity options). The definition of a regulated futures contract was described above. A foreign currency contract is a contract (1) that requires delivery or settlement based on the value of foreign currency positions that are traded through regulated futures contracts, (2) that is traded in the "interbank market," and (3) that is entered into at arm's length at a price determined by reference to the interbank market.[41] The definition of a foreign currency contract, because it focuses on contracts that are traded in the interbank market, subjects currency contracts for major world currencies to the mark-to-market rules. Foreign currency swaps are not presently treated as foreign currency contracts and therefore are not currently considered to be covered by the mark-to-market rules.[42]

A "nonequity option" is any "listed option" which is not an "equity option."[43] A *listed option* is any option (other than a right to acquire stock from the issuer of the

---

39 Section 1256(a)(1).

40 Section 1256(b)(1).

41 Section 1256(g)(2)(A). *See* Priv. Ltr. Rul. 8818010, dated February 4, 1988 (certain currency swap agreements were not foreign currency contracts). For background on the meaning of the term "interbank market," *see generally* S. REP. No. 592, 97th Cong., 2d Sess. 26 (1982) (indicating that bank forward contracts, which are economically comparable to regulated futures contracts, are traded in the interbank market). Note that Section 1256(g)(2)(B) give the IRS power to issue regulations to exclude or include contracts from the definition of a "foreign currency contract" as is appropriate to carry out the purpose of Section 1256.

42 *See* Priv. Ltr. Rul. 8818010, dated February 4, 1988.

43 Section 1256(g)(3).

stock) that is traded on (or subject to the rules of) a qualified board or exchange.[44] An *equity option* means any option to buy or sell stock, or any option the value of which is determined directly or indirectly by reference to any stock (or group of stocks) or stock index, except for certain options with respect to a group of stocks or a stock index if (1) there is a designation by the Commodity Futures Trading Commission (CFTC) of a contract market for a contract based on such group of stocks or stock index or (2) the IRS determines that the option meets the requirements of law for such a designation.[45] Because of the exclusion of equity options other than those relating to a group of stocks or an index designated by the CFTC, "broad-based" stock indexed options are typically subject to the mark-to-market rules while other equity options are not.

A *dealer equity option* means, with respect to an "options dealer," any listed option that (1) is an equity option, (2) is purchased or granted by such options dealer in the normal course of his or her activity of dealing in options, and (3) is listed on the qualified board or exchange on which such options dealer is registered.[46] An "options dealer" is any person registered with an appropriate national securities exchange as a market maker or specialist in listed options or any person whom the IRS determines performs functions similar to those performed by an exchange-registered market maker or specialist in listed options.[47]

What Are the Consequences of These Rules?

There are three basic rules that generally apply to Section 1256 contracts (the Basic Rules).[48] First, as discussed above, the principal consequence of the "mark-to-market" rules is the recognition of gain (or loss) with respect to such contracts at the end of the taxpayer's tax year without regard to whether such contracts have in fact been sold by the holder thereof. Second, in subsequent years, including the disposition of the Section 1256 contract, the taxpayer must make appropriate adjustments in order to avoid incorrectly recognizing gain or loss that had previously been recognized in a prior tax year of the taxpayer and taken into account at that time under the mark-to-market regime.[49] Third, gain or loss recognized under the mark-to-market regime is generally characterized as capital gain or loss (not ordinary) and automatically treated as 40 percent short-term capital gain or loss and 60 percent long-term capital gain or loss.[50] The Basic Rules also apply if a Section 1256 contract is terminated or

---

44 Section 1256(g)(5). A "qualified board or exchange" is defined by Section 1256(g)(7) as (1) a national securities exchange which is registered with the Securities and Exchange Commission, (2) a domestic board of trade designated as a contract market by the Commodity Futures Trading Commission, or (3) any other exchange, board of trade, or other market which the IRS determines has rules adequate to carry out the purposes of Section 1256.
45 Section 1256(g)(6).
46 Section 1256(g)(4).
47 Section 1256(g)(8).
48 Sections 1256(a)(1), (a)(2) and (a)(3).
49 Section 1256(a)(2).
50 Section 1256(a)(3). Note that this rule does not apply if the gains or losses would otherwise be characterized as ordinary, rather than capital. *See* Section 1256(f)(2).

transferred, regardless of the manner in which the contract is terminated or transferred.[51]

If all the offsetting positions of any "straddle" consist of Section 1256 contracts (and such straddle is not part of a larger straddle), the straddle rules of Sections 1092 and 263(g) of the Code do not apply.[52]

Special Rules and Exceptions

There are a number of important exceptions and special rules that apply in various circumstances. First, Section 1256(d) provides for a *mixed straddle* election. If this election is made, Section 1256 contracts that are part of a mixed straddle are not subject to the Basic Rules.[53]

A *straddle* is generally defined by Section 1092(c) as "offsetting positions with respect to personal property" where there is a substantial diminution of risk of loss from holding any position with respect to personal property by reason of holding one or more other positions with respect to personal property.[54] A straddle is a *mixed straddle* if at least one (but not all) of the positions comprising the straddle are Section 1256 contracts (that is why it is referred to as a mixed straddle) and each position comprising the straddle is clearly identified before the close of the day on which the first Section 1256 contract forming a part of the straddle is acquired (or such earlier date as the IRS may prescribe).[55] As discussed above, the tax rules normally applicable to Section 1256 contracts are based on an annual mark-to-market method, while the tax rules applicable to other types of options and contracts that are used as hedges are not.[56] Given this difference in tax treatment, the recognition of gain or loss on the Section 1256 contract portion of a mixed straddle on a mark-to-market basis would be distortive (since gain or loss on the non-Section 1256 contract components of the mixed straddle would not be recognized on a mark-to-market basis). A mixed straddle election permits taxpayers to avoid this result. It should be noted that the election, once made, applies for the entire tax year and all subsequent tax years, unless the IRS consents to revocation of the election.[57] Accordingly, investors should carefully consider the merits and consequences prior to making the mixed straddle election.

The other important exception to the mark-to-market rules applies to *hedging transactions.*[58] A hedging transaction is any transaction if (1) it is entered into in the normal course of the taxpayer's trade or business primarily to reduce risk of price

---

51 Section 1256(c)(1) makes it clear that this "termination rule" applies regardless of whether the contract is terminated (or transformed) by entering into offsetting positions, by taking or making delivery of the property to which the contract relates, by exercise, by assignment or being assigned, by lapse or otherwise.

52 Section 1256(a)(4).

53 Section 1256(d)(1).

54 Section 1092(c). "Personal property" for these purposes means any personal property of a type which is actively traded. Section 1092(d)(1).

55 Section 1256(d)(4).

56 Section 1256(e)(1).

57 Section 1256(d)(3). Although the election is irrevocable without IRS consent, only mixed straddles which are timely identified are subject to the rule. Thus, by failing to timely identify certain mixed straddles, taxpayers can effectively choose which mixed straddles will be subject to the rule.

58 Section 1256(e)(1).

change or currency fluctuations with respect to property held (or to be held) by the taxpayer or to reduce risk of interest rate or price changes or currency fluctuations with respect to borrowings or obligations (including future borrowings or obligations) of the taxpayer, (2) the gain or loss on such transactions is treated as ordinary income or loss and (3) the taxpayer clearly identifies the transaction as a hedging transaction before the close of the day on which such transaction was entered into.[59] The hedging transaction exception does not apply in the case of transactions entered into by syndicates.[60] More importantly, the Supreme Court's decision in *Arkansas Best Corp. v. Commissioner*[61] had raised an issue regarding the extent to which the hedging transaction exception is ordinarily available, because of concerns regarding whether the "ordinary income or loss" requirement can be satisfied. In response, the IRS issued the Hedging Regulations, which along with *Arkansas Best* and the ordinary character of income or loss on hedging transactions, are discussed separately later in this chapter.

Section 1256(e)(4) provides a special rule that limits the deductibility of losses from hedging transactions in the case of "limited partners" and "limited entrepreneurs" (as defined in Section 464(e)(2)).[62] Gains on hedging transactions are treated as ordinary income, not capital gain.[63]

Basic Tax Rules for Debt

In general, interest paid on debt is taxable as ordinary income to the investor as it accrues or when it is paid, depending upon the investor's method of tax accounting (cash or accrual).[64] Interest expense is ordinarily deductible by the payor.[65]

Special tax rules relating to original issue discount (OID) apply to debt that is issued at a discount or that provides for interest payment delays, differing rates of interest, contingent interest payments, variable interest rates, or prepayments based on other prepayable debt.[66] These rules generally require the inclusion of income by an investor on a constant yield, daily accrual basis regardless of the investor's method of tax accounting and regardless of the specified accrual terms of the debt instrument.[67] Thus, because the application of the OID rules can affect the timing and amount of income recognized, it is important for investors to consider whether the OID rules

---

59 Section 1256(e)(2).
60 Section 1256(e)(3)(A).
61 485 U.S. 212 (1988).
62 This rule is modified for hedging transactions relating to property other than stock or securities. Section 1256(e)(4)(C). It is also modified for any hedging loss to the extent such loss exceeds the aggregate unrecognized gains from hedging transactions as of the close of the taxable year attributable to the trade or business in which the hedging transactions were entered into. Section 1256(e)(4)(B).
63 Section 1256(f)(1).
64 Sections 61(a)(4) and 446.
65 Section 163(a).
66 Sections 1271 through 1275.
67 Section 1272.

apply. Unfortunately, the rules are complex, and final, comprehensive regulations regarding their application have not yet been issued by the Internal Revenue Service.[68]

If a debt instrument provides for a high interest rate (a rate in excess of five percentage points above the applicable federal rate as of the time the debt was issued), has OID and a term in excess of five years, special *high yield discount obligation* (HYDO) rules may apply.[69] If the yield is in excess of six percentage points above the applicable federal rate, these rules may recharacterize a portion of the investor's return as dividends, rather than interest.

The characterization of payments on a financial contract as "interest" for federal income tax purposes can be significant for a number of special reasons. For example, interest on debt issued by states and political subdivisions of states, which is received by an investor, is excludible from gross income, *i.e.*, "tax-exempt" (although it may be subject to the alternative minimum tax), provided that certain special tests in the Code are satisfied.[70] In addition, interest on debt that is received by non-U.S. persons can generally qualify for a special exemption from U.S. taxation and U.S. withholding taxes (this exemption is referred to as the "portfolio interest exemption") provided that certain relationship and investor certification requirements are satisfied.[71] And as previously mentioned, interest expense is generally deductible by the payor.

Contrasting Convertible and Callable Debt with the Tax Treatment of Separate Equivalent Options

In many cases, debt instruments provide for rights *(call rights)* that permit the issuer to redeem or "call" the debt instruments from the holder before their final stated maturity date *(callable debt)*. The precise form of call rights—such as the date on which the call may be exercised; whether the call may be exercised at the sole discretion of the issuer; or the conditions that must be satisfied in order to permit the issuer to exercise the call and the amount the issuer must pay (the *call price*) to the holder of the debt instrument upon exercise of the call—vary substantially from debt instrument to debt instrument and are often influenced heavily by the particular market in which the debt instrument is sold.

Similarly, certain debt instruments provide that the issuer or the holder (depending upon the precise terms of the instrument) may exchange the debt instrument for stock of the issuer or stock of a third party *(convertible debt)*. As is the case with

---

68 Final regulations were issued in 1994 (59 Fed. Reg. 4799 (February 2, 1994)). Proposed regulations were issued in 1986 (51 Fed. Reg. 12,022 (April 8, 1986)) and in 1992 (57 Fed. Reg. 60,750 (December 22, 1992)). *See generally* DAVID C. GARLOCK, A PRACTICAL GUIDE TO THE ORIGINAL ISSUE DISCOUNT REGULATIONS (1990); Steven D. Conlon & Mary Sue Butch, *New OID Proposed Regulations Provide More Flexibility, But Additional Guidance Is Required*, 79 J. TAX'N 116 (1993); David C. Garlock, *A Primer on the New Proposed (Almost) Regulations for Contingent Debt Instruments*, TAX NOTES, March 1, 1993 at 1225; David P. Hariton, *Significant Changes in the Original Issue Discount Rules*, 58 TAX NOTES 347 (January 18, 1993); Lawrence Lokken, *The Time Value of Money Rules*, 42 TAX L. REV. 1 (1986). Although final regulations regarding the basic rules were recently issued, rules for debt subject to anticipated prepayments (Section 1272(a)(6)), contingent debt, and other important aspects of these provisions have not yet been finalized.

69 Section 163(e)(5).

70 Sections 103, 141-150.

71 Sections 871(h), 881(c).

callable debt, the precise conversion rights of convertible debt differ greatly from debt instrument to debt instrument (such as the date on which the call may be exercised, the amount of stock received in exchange for the outstanding debt obligation, and the type of stock and the issuer of the stock that is received upon conversion) and often such terms depend greatly upon the current state of the market in which the debt instrument is issued.

As an economic matter, both callable debt and convertible debt can be viewed as equivalent to noncallable debt, coupled with either a call option or a stock option. Accordingly, the separate value of the "noncallable debt" feature and the "option" feature of callable debt and convertible debt can be analyzed separately, and as a general matter, an independent value for each of these two components can be established.

A confusing aspect of existing federal income tax law relates to the fundamentally different tax treatment of convertible and callable debt as compared to the tax treatment of the ownership of economically equivalent noncallable debt and an option. If an investor acquires both a noncallable debt instrument and an option, the investor will be taxed on the debt instrument under the rules relating to debt instruments and the investor will be taxed on the option under the applicable tax rules relating to options. However, if the investor acquires convertible debt or callable debt, it is generally treated as holding a single debt instrument for federal income tax purposes, and the call feature or conversion feature is analyzed as an integral component of the debt instrument in determining the debt instrument's tax treatment under the basic tax rules applicable to debt.[72]

Embedded Swap and Cap Bonds and Contingent Payments

As mentioned at the outset of this chapter, debt instruments are being created that have certain derivative-like characteristics. The derivative-like characteristic is typically impressed into the fabric of the debt instrument in one of four ways: (1) it is embedded into the interest rate formula for the debt instrument; (2) it is included as an additional, "contingent" interest payment the amount of which is dependent upon the changes in value of the referenced property; (3) it is taken into account in adjusting the amount of principal payable on the debt instrument; or (4) it is included as part of the terms of a conversion right integrated into the debt instrument. In addition, an investor could purchase a so-called investment unit comprised of two separate assets: (1) a debt instrument and (2) a separate stock warrant, swap, commodity option, or other type of derivative. However, the components of an investment unit are separately analyzed under the set of basic rules that apply to each of the components. One important issue with investment units is determining the investor's purchase price for the investment unit, which is allocable to the debt instrument and the property right. Depending upon the allocation, the debt instrument could be treated as issued with OID that the investor would need to include in income on an accrual basis.[73]

---

72 A discussion of the full ramifications of this inconsistent treatment, its historical development and the applicable case law is beyond the scope of this chapter and has been intentionally omitted. However, *see* Treas. Reg. Sections 1.1272-1(e) and 1.1273-2(h) and (j).

73 *See* Conlon & Butch, *supra* note 68, at 120.

Debt instruments that include embedded derivative-like characteristics should be carefully analyzed by investors. Often, the derivative-like characteristics have been embedded on the assumption that this will permit the tax treatment of the derivative-like rights to be analyzed under the tax rules applicable to debt rather than under one or more of the other sets of rules that would normally apply to an economically comparable derivative right that was not embedded in a debt instrument. However, there may be a variety of non-tax business reasons for embedding derivative-like characteristics in debt.

The key tax question for debt with certain derivative-like characteristics is: Will the derivative-like payments be treated as an integral part of the debt instrument for federal income tax purposes and analyzed as either interest or principal, or will the derivative be characterized as a separate property right distinct from the debt instrument? This complex question is discussed later in this chapter in the section regarding bifurcation. An investor should carefully consider the consequences if such debt is bifurcated and the embedded swap or cap or other type of contingent payment right is treated as a separate swap or cap or separate property right. For example, to the extent such payments are not treated as interest, they could not qualify as tax-exempt interest (if the bond was a tax-exempt bond) and the payments may not qualify for withholding tax exemptions (if the bond was held by a non-U.S. investor and U.S. withholding tax otherwise applied).

Basic Tax Rules for Stock

Distributions received by an investor on stock ordinarily fall into one of three categories: (1) "dividends" (which are taxable as ordinary income); (2) a return of investor tax "basis" (*i.e.,* generally the amount paid by the investor for the stock); and (3) other amounts received that are taxable as capital gains.[74] Whether amounts received are treated as dividends depends upon the paying corporation's current and accumulated "earnings and profits."[75] The basic tax theory is that amounts distributed to a shareholder that represent a corporation's economic earnings should be taxed as income at the shareholder level. However, the distributing corporation is itself a taxpayer and must pay federal income tax on its taxable income.[76] It is important to note that the paying corporation is not generally entitled to a deduction for dividends paid.[77] Because both the corporation and its shareholders are separately taxed on the corporation's income (corporations pay federal income tax and shareholders treat distributions that are classified as dividends as taxable ordinary income), the U.S. taxation scheme for corporations and their shareholders is commonly referred to as one of "double taxation."

---

74 Section 301(c).
75 Sections 301(c) and 316(a).
76 Section 11. There are certain exceptions; *see, e.g.,* Section 501 (certain organizations and trusts); Section 115 (states and municipalities, etc.); Section 1361 *et seq.* (S corporation flow-through treatment); Section 401 (qualified pensions, profit-sharing and stock bonus plans).
77 Except for certain types of corporations such as regulated investment companies and real estate investment trusts, and for taxes applicable to personal holding companies and foreign personal holding companies. *See generally* Sections 561, 562, 852, and 857.

Because corporate earnings are generally subject to double taxation, if a corporation received dividends from another corporation, such earnings could effectively be taxed at least *three times* (once at the paying corporation level, once at the receiving corporation level, and again when the receiving corporation pays dividends to its investors). As partial relief, the Code provides a "dividends received deduction" (DRD), available only to corporations for dividends they receive.[78] The dividends received deduction is expressed as a specified percentage of the dividends received and depends upon the investing corporation's percentage ownership of the paying corporation (a 70 percent DRD generally applies). A corporation is required to hold the stock paying the dividends for at least 46 days in order to qualify for the DRD. Section 246(c)(4) imposes special tests that focus on whether the stock holding corporation has retained sufficient risk of loss relating to the stock owned in determining whether the 46-day holding period requirement has been met.[79]

As a result of the DRD, a corporation's net-after-tax return on dividends can be significantly greater than with respect to other forms of investment with comparable return/risk characteristics. However, the use of various forms of hedging devices, which act to protect the investor from risks of loss associated with the stock, could result in the inability to satisfy the 46-day holding period requirement, preventing an investor from being entitled to the DRD.

Special rules apply to corporations that qualify as "regulated investment companies" (RICs) or "real estate investment trusts" (REITs), which generally permit such entities to deduct dividends paid (thereby minimizing or eliminating double taxation concerns for such entities).[80] Dividends paid by regulated investment companies can qualify for treatment as "capital gain dividends" or "exempt-interest dividends" under prescribed circumstances and be treated by the recipients as capital gains and tax-exempt income, respectively. Dividends, unlike interest (which can qualify for the portfolio interest exemption previously discussed), are generally subject to U.S. withholding tax if paid to non-U.S. persons (although an applicable tax treaty may reduce the withholding tax rate but will not generally eliminate U.S. withholding tax).[81]

Distinguishing Stock from Debt

As discussed above, the basic tax rules applicable to debt are very different from the basic tax rules applicable to stock. Thus, it is important to consider whether a particular

---

78 Section 243. A dividends received deduction was previously available to individuals under former Section 116 of the Code, but it was repealed in 1986.

79 Proposed regulations were released in 1993 relating to when a taxpayer is required to reduce its holding period of stock for purposes of the DRD because it has diminished its risk of loss by holding a position in substantially similar or related property. 58 Fed. Reg. 30, 727 (May 27, 1993).

80 Sections 561, 562, 852, and 857.

81 Sections 1441, 1442. Legislative proposals have been introduced from time to time to permit certain dividends paid by regulated investment companies to their shareholders to qualify for an exemption from U.S. withholding tax in the same fashion that a portion of dividends paid by a regulated investment company can be characterized as tax-exempt interest or long-term capital gains pursuant to Sections 852(b)(5) and 852(b)(3) of the Code. Capital gain dividends paid by a regulated investment company (which would not include short-term capital gains) are exempt from U.S. withholding tax. *See* Rev. Rul. 69-244, 1969-1 C.B. 215.

investment will be classified as debt or stock for federal income tax purposes. Unfortunately, the determination of whether an investment constitutes debt or stock for federal income tax purposes has proven inherently difficult under existing law. Section 385 of the Code was enacted to permit the IRS to issue regulations addressing this issue but the question has proven so difficult and the regulations that were issued were so controversial that the IRS withdrew its regulations under Section 385 over 10 years ago and has not issued new regulations since that time.[82] The IRS has announced that it will not generally issue private letter rulings regarding this question.[83] Section 385(c) was added to the Code in 1992 and provides that the issuer's treatment of an interest as stock or debt is binding on it and all holders (except for holders that properly disclose in their tax returns any inconsistent treatment). Investors should, therefore, seek assurances from the issuer of any security regarding the position the issuer intends to take regarding the tax classification as debt or stock of such security.

Because the IRS has withdrawn its regulations, leaving investors with little guidance or certainty on the debt-equity issue, investors often require legal opinions addressing the status of a particular security as stock or debt. In this regard, the opinions should be carefully reviewed to make certain that the investor understands counsel's *level* of comfort (that is, does counsel believe that the investment "should" or "will" be characterized as stock or debt and is their opinion subject to reasonable doubt) and the assumptions (if any) that counsel is relying on in rendering their opinion.[84]

Basic Tax Rules for "Pass-Through" Equity

An investment may be characterized as an interest in a partnership or a grantor trust. Neither partnerships nor grantor trusts are subject to entity-level federal income taxation. Instead, the partners in the partnership or holders of beneficial interests in the trust are taxed on the income received by the partnership or trust as if it was received directly by such partners or holders. Because of this basic tax characteristic, these types of entities are typically referred to as "pass-through" entities (because the character and taxation of such an entity's income "passes through" from the entity to its investors). The analysis of pass-through interests is essentially a three-step process.

---

82 Proposed and final regulations issued under Section 385 were withdrawn approximately eleven years ago. *See* Prop. Reg. Sections 1.385-1 through 1.385-8, 47 Fed. Reg. 164 (January 5, 1982) and Treas. Reg. Sections 1.385-1 through 1.385-10, 45 Fed. Reg. 86,438 (December 31, 1980).

83 Rev. Proc. 94-3, 1994-1 I.R.B. 79, 87 (Section 4.02(1)). Section 1936(a) of H.R. 776, 102d Cong., 2d Sess. 268 (enacted as Pub. L. No. 102-486, *The Energy Policy Act of 1992*), amended Section 385 by (i) providing that the characterization of an interest in a corporation by the issuer as stock or debt as of the time of issuance is binding, (ii) requiring notification of inconsistent treatment, and (iii) authorizing the promulgation of related regulations.

84 *See generally* William T. Plumb, Jr., *The Federal Income Tax Significance of Corporate Debt: A Critical Analysis and a Proposal*, 26 TAX L. REV. 369 (1971).

Entity Classification

First, it must be determined that the entity satisfies the rules necessary to qualify as a partnership or grantor trust.[85] If the entity doesn't satisfy the rules, the entity could be classified as an association taxable as a corporation, subject to entity-level federal corporate income tax. Distributions to investors could be recharacterized as dividends and would not be deductible by the entity in computing its taxable income. This could adversely affect the availability of cash available for distribution to investors and could adversely affect the character of distributions received by investors.[86] Investors in financial contracts are normally not indemnified against tax risks; thus they should consider whether they are comfortable with this risk. This risk is typically addressed by the receipt of a legal opinion that provides that the entity is properly classified as a partnership or grantor trust (as the case may be), rather than as an association taxable as a corporation.[87]

Equity Classification

Second, it must be determined that the investment contract is an "equity" type interest in the pass-through interest rather than some other type of interest (such as a debt instrument, option, etc.) that would be subject to different tax rules. This determination can be difficult, because there is little applicable law. Often tax advisers resort to analyzing the proper tax treatment of the investment contract under the debt/equity rules applicable to stock. As discussed above, those rules are complex and unclear in many ways. Investors should request a legal opinion regarding the proper tax classification of their investment contract (as a partnership interest or grantor trust interest, for example). Unfortunately, because of the difficulties in making this determination, counsel may not be able to provide investors with a high level of comfort on this issue, depending upon the particulars of the investment.

Operating Rules

If an investment contract is characterized as an equity interest in a pass-through entity like a partnership, certain consequences must be considered. First, the federal income

---

85 The rules which apply for determining whether an entity qualifies as a partnership are set forth in Treas. Reg. Section 301.7701-2. The rules applicable for determining whether an entity is treated as a trust are set forth in Treas. Reg. Section 301.7701-4—if the entity is classified as a trust, grantor trust classification is determined by reference to Subpart E of Subchapter J of the Internal Revenue Code (Sections 671-679) and a number of published revenue rulings issued by the IRS (*see, e.g.*, Rev. Rul. 70-544, 1970-2 C.B. 6; Rev. Rul. 70-545, 1970-2 C.B. 7 and Rev. Rul. 84-10, 1984-1 C.B. 155).

86 For example, distributions of tax-exempt income by partnerships and grantor trusts essentially retain their tax-exempt character when received by investors, while dividends paid by corporations (other than regulated investment companies that must satisfy a number of special tests) are taxable *even if they relate to tax-exempt income received by the corporation* because tax-exempt interest is included in the computation of a corporation's earnings and profits pursuant to Treas. Reg. Section 1.312-6(b) and dividends paid to a corporation's shareholders are taxable as ordinary income to the extent of the corporation's current and accumulated earnings and profits pursuant to Section 301.

87 As indicated above, an investor should carefully review the legal opinion received, in order to determine just how much comfort is really being provided.

taxation of partners and partnerships is governed by Subchapter K of the Code (Sections 701-761), which includes special rules regarding the taxation of partners and partnerships.[88] For example, a partner typically recognizes its share of partnership income as of the close of the partnership's tax year regardless of whether such amounts are distributed.[89] As a result, unless the partner's tax year coincides with the partnership's tax year, this rule could result in a deferral of income or loss recognition, which may have unanticipated consequences to the investing partner.[90]

Investors in grantor trusts are treated as directly acquiring and owning a pro rata interest in each asset of the trust.[91] Thus, sales of assets to generate cash for one investor in a grantor trust may result in taxable gains that must be recognized by other investors, even though the other investors do not receive cash.

Moreover, the type of tax information an investor will receive with respect to an investment (if any) depends upon how the investor's investment contract is classified. Partners typically receive an IRS Form 1065 K-1, while investors in grantor trusts will typically receive a Form 1099 for each of the various reportable types of income distributed by the trust. However, if a partnership meets certain tests, its partners may be able to make a so-called 761 election, which permits the partners to elect to avoid the imposition of the tax rules normally applicable to partnerships.[92]

BIFURCATION CONCERNS

A number of innovative financial products have been developed with hybrid characteristics so that they resemble part-debt and part-option, or part-debt and part-equity.[93] Recently, both Congress and the IRS have developed rules that divide a financial product into several components for purposes of federal income tax analysis. This section briefly outlines those rules.

High-Yield Discount Obligations

Section 163(e)(5) of the Code contains the so-called high-yield discount obligation or HYDO, rules of the Code. These rules apply to a debt instrument that has three basic characteristics: (1) it has a yield greater than five percentage points over the long-term "applicable federal rate" (which is an IRS published rate based on a blended yield of U.S. Treasury securities of specified maturities) determined at the time the instrument

---

88 Section 704 includes special rules that govern the allocation of income among partners, Section 721 governs the tax consequences of contributions to a partnership, Section 731 governs the tax consequences of distributions by a partnership to its partners, Section 708 may result in deemed terminations of partnerships (which may have tax consequences to partners), and Section 752 governs the tax consequences to partners of debt incurred by a partnership.

89 *See* Section 706.

90 For example, the amount of income recognized by a partner for its tax year may affect the character of distributions by the partner to its investors.

91 *See* Section 671.

92 *See* Section 761 and related regulations regarding the requirements that must be satisfied in order to make the election and the manner in which the election is made.

93 *See* Lee A. Sheppard, *Things That Go Bump In the Portfolio*, 60 TAX NOTES 1423 (September 13, 1993).

is issued, (2) it has a term of more than five years, and (3) it is issued with "significant original issue discount."[94] If this rule applies, the issuer cannot deduct the disqualified portion of the original issue discount until paid.[95] Moreover, if the yield on the debt instrument exceeds *six* percentage points over the long-term applicable federal rate, the excess is essentially treated by the investor as dividends eligible for the dividends received deduction.[96] Thus, the HYDO rule may treat amounts received by an investor on a debt instrument as part interest and part dividends under certain circumstances.

Debt/Equity Classification

Section 385 of the Code provides the IRS with the authority to issue regulations addressing the character of an interest in a corporation as debt or equity (regulations were issued and withdrawn under this section over ten years ago and no new regulations have been issued). Section 385(a) was amended in 1989 to permit the IRS to issue regulations treating an interest in a corporation as part-debt and part-equity. The IRS has not yet issued regulations under this grant of authority.

Foreign Currency Gains and Losses

Section 988 of the Code addresses the taxation of currency gains and losses that are with respect to a currency other than the taxpayer's "functional currency" (*i.e.*, either the U.S. dollar or the currency in which a qualified business unit conducts its activities and maintains its books and records). As a general rule, foreign currency gains and losses attributable to any financial instrument are broken out from the gain or other income recognized and separately treated under special rules set forth in Section 988. Thus, foreign currency gains and losses may be bifurcated for tax purposes. The Section 988 rules are discussed in more detail later in this chapter.

Capital Gain Conversion Transactions

Section 1258 of the Code recharacterizes gain from certain financial transactions from capital gain to ordinary income. The section was added to the Code in 1993 in connection with an increase in tax rates that resulted in a noticeable differential between the maximum stated tax rate applicable to capital gains (28 percent) and the maximum stated tax rate applicable to ordinary income (39.6 percent). Section 1258 identifies an "imputed income amount" based on 120 percent of the applicable rate (which is also based on U.S. Treasury rates for debt with maturities similar to the term of the transaction). Thus, this rule may effectively bifurcate gains from certain transactions into part capital gain, part ordinary income. A more detailed discussion of this provision is included later in this chapter in the section relating to the character of income and losses.

---

94 Section 163(i).
95 Section 163(e)(5)(A).
96 Section 163(e)(5)(B).

Market Discount

Section 1276 of the Code provides that "accrued market discount" arising from the purchase of a debt instrument at a price below its stated principal amount (or below its "revised issue price" if it was issued at an original issue discount) is taxable as ordinary income. Thus, the sale of a debt instrument acquired at a market discount can result in the recognition of ordinary income (based on the amount of accrued but not previously recognized market discount as of the date of sale) and capital gain (if the instrument is sold at a gain that is greater than the amount of accrued market discount).

Stripped Tax-Exempt Bonds

Section 1286 of the Code addresses the tax consequences of "stripping" a debt instrument (separating and selling some or all of the interest or principal payments on the debt instrument). Section 1286(d) of the Code addresses the extent to which stripped interests in a tax-exempt bond are treated as tax-exempt. This rule essentially provides that an investor can treat the return on the stripped interest as tax-exempt only to the extent that the investor's yield on the stripped interest does not exceed the "coupon rate" (or the bond's original yield, if the taxpayer so elects) on the underlying tax-exempt bond. If the investor's yield exceeds the coupon rate, the investor's return is bifurcated into a taxable and tax-exempt component and the investor must accrue both taxable and tax-exempt original issue discount on the stripped investment.[97]

Stripped Preferred Stock

Section 305 of the Code was also amended in 1993 to provide for rules governing the inclusion of income if preferred stock is "stripped" (*i.e.*, the right to receive dividends is separated from the other ownership rights associated with the stock).[98] These rules merely require the current inclusion of income as ordinary income and do not address a number of related issues that appear relevant (such as the extent to which any party to such a transaction is entitled to the DRD with respect to dividends paid on the stripped preferred stock).[99]

Notional Principal Contracts/Embedded Loans

With respect to interest rate swaps and other types of notional principal contracts, the Final Swap Regulations may bifurcate certain contracts into a separate "at-market" contract and an "embedded loan" (this concern was discussed above in the section regarding swaps, caps, and floors). Although the rules are likely to be revised for caps and floors, it is anticipated that the IRS will continue to explore the development of

---

97 Section 1286(d)(1)(A).
98 Section 305(e).
99 The legislative history accompanying the enactment of Section 305(e) makes it clear that various issues relating to the DRD are yet to be resolved. *See, e.g.*, H.R. CONF. REP. No. 213, 103d Cong., 1st Sess. 81-82 (1993).

rules that may bifurcate a financial product into its "component" tax elements for purposes of analyzing the taxation of the product.[100]

Contingent Debt/U.S. Withholding Tax

In 1993, Sections 871(h) and 881(c) of the Code were amended to provide that contingent payments on a debt instrument that were based on the issuer's profits, cash flow, sales, or income were ineligible for the so-called portfolio interest exemption from U.S. withholding taxes upon payment of such amounts to non-U.S. persons.[101]

Also, as discussed above in the section on the basic tax rules applicable to debt, the IRS has issued complex regulations relating to the tax treatment of contingent debt under the original issue discount rules of the Code.[102] These special rules may be particularly relevant in analyzing debt with derivative-like features. Under certain circumstances, a debt instrument may be bifurcated under these rules and treated as part-debt and part-property. This could have adverse consequences if the characterization of the derivative-like payments as interest is important.

THE IMPORTANCE OF THE TAX CHARACTER OF INCOME AND LOSSES

Why Character Is Important

The tax character of gains and losses can be important for a number of reasons. As discussed above, a taxpayer's ability to deduct capital losses is limited (corporations, for example, can only use capital losses to offset capital gains and cannot use capital losses to offset ordinary income). Long-term capital gains are subject to a lower maximum stated rate of taxation than ordinary income.[103] Moreover, the changes in tax rates enacted in 1993 have increased the tax rate advantage that long-term capital gains enjoy by increasing the differential between the maximum stated rate that ordinary income is taxed at (35 percent in the case of corporations and 39.6 percent in the case of individuals) and the maximum stated rate at which long-term capital gains are taxed (28 percent).

In light of the favorable tax rates that long-term capital gains enjoy and the disadvantageous limitations on a taxpayer's ability to utilize capital losses, it is not surprising that taxpayers often attempt to manage their affairs in a manner that

---

100 Lee A. Sheppard, *Financial Products: The Switchboard Approach*, 60 TAX NOTES 942 (August 16, 1993). *See also* Steven D. Conlon & Suzanne M. Russell, *Final Swap Regulations Leave Embedded Loan Concerns Unanswered,* 80 J TAX'N 202 (April, 1994).
101 Revenue Reconciliation Act of 1993, Pub. L. No. 103-66, §13237 (1993).
102 *See* Prop. Reg. Section 1.1275-4(g), 56 Fed. Reg. 8308 (February 28, 1991); Prop. Reg. Section 1.1275-4 (issued on January 19, 1993 and withdrawn on January 22, 1993); *see generally* Steven D. Conlon, Peter J. Connors & Mary Sue Butch, *Contingent Debt Instruments Are "Divided and Conquered" Under the New OID Proposed Regs.,* 75 J. TAX'N 46 (July, 1991); David C. Garlock, *A Primer on the New Proposed (Almost) Regulations for Contingent Debt Instruments,* 58 TAX NOTES 1225 (March 1, 1993); David P. Hariton, *Contingent Debt: Putting the Pieces Together,* 58 TAX NOTES 1231 (March 1, 1993).
103 Section 1(h).

maximizes long-term capital gains and minimizes capital losses. This section discusses some of the rules that restrict a taxpayer's ability to achieve favorable tax character for the income and losses it generates.

It should be noted that the character of income for tax purposes can be important for other reasons. For example, as discussed above, interest income may qualify for an exemption from U.S. withholding taxes if paid to a non-U.S. person, while dividend income typically does not. Thus, depending upon a particular taxpayer's situation, character of income may be an important issue for reasons besides the benefits and disadvantages of capital gains and capital losses just discussed.

Arkansas Best and Business Hedging Losses

Businesses hedge the various risks associated with their operations, inventory, borrowings, plant, and investments in a number of ways. As discussed above, the character of any losses associated with the hedges that are employed is important. If the hedging losses are ordinary, they can offset the ordinary income generated by the business. However, if the hedging losses are characterized as capital losses, they can generally only offset capital gains generated by the business. As a result, taxpayers often take the position that hedging losses should be categorized as ordinary losses.

Arkansas Best

In 1988, the U.S. Supreme Court rendered its opinion in the landmark case *Arkansas Best Corp. v. Commissioner*.[104] In *Arkansas Best* the Supreme Court held that a taxpayer's motive for entering into business hedging transactions was irrelevant in determining whether losses relating to such transactions were ordinary rather than capital in nature. Prior to this decision, taxpayers, the courts, and the IRS had broadly construed the Supreme Court's 1955 decision in *Corn Products Refining Co. v. Commissioner*[105] as permitting ordinary loss treatment for hedging transactions entered into in connection with a taxpayer's business activities. More importantly, in *Arkansas Best* the Supreme Court indicated that its decision in *Corn Products* had been misinterpreted and merely stood for the more limited position that hedging transactions that were an integral part of a taxpayer's inventory purchase system were sufficiently linked to the inventory such that they were excepted out of the definition of a capital asset and therefore, resulted in ordinary, rather than capital, loss.

The Supreme Court's position in *Arkansas Best* served as a major impediment to the hedging activities of taxpayers, since it had the effect of increasing the likelihood that such activities will result in capital rather than ordinary losses because many legitimate hedging activities of businesses relate to hedging of asset and liability risk that does not relate to inventory purchase systems.

Arkansas Best raised fundamental issues regarding the proper character of hedging transactions. For example, some commentators have raised concerns regarding the viability of the Section 1256(e) hedging rules, given that they presume a hedging match that appears broader than the apparent scope of the "inventory hedging"

104   485 U.S. 212 (1988).
105   350 U.S. 46 (1955).

holding of *Arkansas Best* (note that Section 1256 was enacted during a time when the IRS, taxpayers, and Congress believed expansive business hedging was permitted).[106] Moreover, the IRS had been unwilling to issue regulations that affect similar types of character issues because of this decision.

FNMA

Prior to the recently decided Tax Court case, *Federal National Mortgage Association v. Commissioner*[107] *(FNMA)* involving hedging transactions entered into by FNMA in connection with interest rate risk associated with its acquisition of mortgage loans and borrowings to finance such acquisitions, many commentators believed that the Tax Court would attempt to reinstate the "business purpose hedging rule" and its related ordinary loss characterization of business hedging losses that had been shut down by *Arkansas Best*. The Tax Court followed the Supreme Court's analysis in *Arkansas Best* that a hedge that related to property that is not a capital asset under Section 1221 of the Code avoids capital asset (and therefore capital loss) characterization. Because the Tax Court found in favor of the taxpayer on this basis, the Tax Court indicated that it did not need to consider additional arguments raised by the taxpayer in favor of ordinary loss treatment.

FNMA expands the Supreme Court's reasoning in *Arkansas Best* in two important respects. First, the Tax Court expressed the view that the Supreme Court's interpretation of the *Corn Products* case to the effect that hedging transactions that were an integral part of a taxpayer's inventory purchase system were sufficiently linked to the inventory that they were excepted out of the definition of a capital asset (since inventory is not a capital asset) extends to hedges that are integrally related to *any other exception from the Section 1221 definition of a capital asset.* Second, the Tax Court noted that although a taxpayer's business purpose for entering into a hedge does not, by itself, permit ordinary loss treatment, business purpose is nonetheless relevant for purposes of determining whether a hedging transaction is integrally related to an asset or transaction that is not a capital asset. Thus, a taxpayer's business purpose is relevant for purposes of determining whether a hedge is linked to a noncapital transaction, which in turn will determine whether losses generated by the hedge are ordinary rather than capital.

In *FNMA,* the Tax Court concluded that FNMA's hedging of its mortgage loan portfolio and of its interest rate risk on debt issued by it to finance its portfolio were integrally related and that its mortgage loan portfolio constituted "notes receivable, acquired in the ordinary course of [its] trade or business for services rendered." Such notes receivable are explicitly excluded from the definition of a capital asset by Section 1221(4) of the Code. Because the Tax Court concluded that FNMA's hedging activities were an integral part of the system by which FNMA purchased and held mortgages and that such mortgages were not treated as capital assets, the Tax Court held that FNMA's hedging losses were entitled to ordinary loss treatment.

---

106   *See generally* Letter to Dana Trier, Tax Legislative Council, Office of the Assistant Secretary of the Treasury for Tax Policy, Dept. of the Treasury, from Anthony J. Cetta, President, Wall Street Tax Ass'n, Inc., dated April 17, 1989 (available as Document 89-3587, 89 TNT 98-42 from Tax Analysts).
107   100 T.C. No. 36 (June 17, 1993).

Impact of FNMA on Others

Because the Tax Court in *FNMA* did not simply permit a business purpose exception for hedging transactions, other taxpayers must consider whether their particular hedging activities are integrally related to one of the limited categories of assets that do not qualify as capital assets. Unfortunately, many hedging activities will relate to hedging of legitimate business risks that do not clearly fall within one of these narrow categories. In addition, the IRS and taxpayers are continuing to litigate the character of hedging losses. Accordingly, because the courts will continue to examine these issues, the ultimate development of the law in this area is unclear.

The Temporary and Proposed Hedging Regulations

Because of the burdens on taxpayers and the IRS of extensive litigation on business hedging, business groups have been seeking revisions of the law in this area for some time. For these reasons, the IRS issued temporary and proposed regulations regarding the character and timing of income and loss associated with business hedging transactions in October of 1993 (the *Hedging Regulations*).[108]

However, the Hedging Regulations do not apply to hedging transactions if the property to which the hedge relates can produce capital gain or loss under any circumstance.[109] Accordingly, because investment assets can generate capital gains or losses under various circumstances, the Hedging Regulations would not apply to hedges relating to investment assets. However, the Hedging Regulations *could recharacterize* transactions where derivatives are being used to hedge noninvestment assets that cannot generate capital gain or loss. Thus, if a derivative is being used as a hedge for business property that cannot generate capital gain or loss and the hedge is subject to the Hedging Regulations, then gain or loss on the derivative that would otherwise be capital gain or loss would be recharacterized as ordinary.[110]

The tax treatment of business hedges has received significant attention in the business community. Prior to the release of the Hedging Regulations, some business groups had proposed changing the law to clearly provide that business hedging transactions generated ordinary losses.[111] It is presently unclear whether the Hedging Regulations will satisfy taxpayers' concerns. However, given the importance of this area in light of the growing use by business managers of hedging devices to manage various business risks, new developments are likely to continue to occur for some time.

---

108 *See supra* note 5. Each set of proposed regulations is generally effective with respect to transactions entered into on or after 60 days after the publication of final regulations. The temporary regulations generally apply to all open tax years, except for the identification requirements contained therein that apply to transactions entered into on or after January 1, 1994, and to transactions that were entered into before January 1, 1994 and that remain in existence on March 31, 1994.

109 Temp. Treas. Reg. Section 1.1221-2T(b)(2).

110 *See* Preamble to the Proposed Regulations, 58 Fed. Reg. 54,077 (October 20, 1993).

111 *See, e.g., Business Coalition Continues to Push for Legislative Solution to Arkansas Best,* DAILY TAX REPORT (BNA), August 25, 1993, at G-4; *Coalition Proposes Legislative Solution to Arkansas Best* (Release Date: June 30, 1993) (available as Document 93-7701, 93 TNT 148-27 from Tax Analysts).

The Straddle Rules

The straddle rules of Section 1092 of the Code were enacted because taxpayers would use hedged positions in options and stock or equity to generate capital losses to offset capital gains or to effectively transform short-term capital gains into long-term capital gains while using the hedge to insulate themselves from the economic risks typically associated with holding the loss- or gain-generating asset. Section 1092 limits a taxpayer's ability to recognize losses at a particular time and affects a taxpayer's holding period in property, which is intended to prevent the conversion of short-term gains into favorably taxed long-term capital gains.[112] The straddle rules are very complex and there is considerable concern regarding their precise application in many contexts. The discussion set forth below focuses on the definition of a straddle, the consequences of these rules, and the special rules and exceptions that may apply.

What Is a "Straddle"?

A *straddle* is defined by Section 1092(c) as "offsetting positions with respect to personal property" where there is a substantial diminution of risk of loss from holding any position with respect to personal property by reason of holding one of the other positions with respect to personal property.[113] If one or more positions offset only a portion of one or more other positions, the IRS is authorized to issue regulations prescribing the manner for determining the portion of such other positions that is to be taken into account under the straddle rules.[114]

There are certain presumptions that generally apply for purposes of determining whether positions are "offsetting." Positions are presumed to be offsetting if (1) the positions are in the same personal property (whether directly or pursuant to a contract that references such property); (2) the positions are in the same personal property, even though the property may be in a substantially altered form; (3) the positions are in debt of a similar maturity (or other debt instruments described in the regulations); (4) the positions are sold or marketed as offsetting positions (whether or not such positions are referred to as "straddles," "spreads," "butterflies," or any similar name); (5) the aggregate margin requirement for such positions is lower than the sum of the margin requirements for each such position (if held separately); or (6) there are such other factors (or other tests established in the regulations that are satisfied) such that the IRS, in regulations, treats such positions as offsetting.[115]

As indicated, a straddle exists if there are offsetting positions with respect to *personal property* where there is a substantial diminution of risk of loss from holding

---

112 This chapter does not discuss the transitional rules regarding Section 1092 or any of the extensive litigation involving straddles that arose under prior law.
113 "Personal property" for these purposes means any personal property of a type which is actively traded. Section 1092(d)(1). Section 1092(c)(4) excludes from the definition of a straddle certain straddles consisting of one or more qualified covered call options and the stock to be purchased from the taxpayer under such options.
114 Section 1092(c)(2)(B). Moreover, positions which are not part of an "identified straddle" within the meaning of Section 1092(a)(2)(B) are not treated as an offsetting position with respect to an identified straddle. Section 1092(c)(2)(C).
115 Section 1092(c)(3)(A). The presumption may be rebutted by the taxpayer. Section 1092(c)(3)(B).

any position with respect to personal property by reason of holding one of the other positions with respect to *personal property*. Because a straddle must involve "personal property," it is important to consider the definition of this term. Section 1092(d)(1) provides that personal property "means any personal property of a type which is actively traded." In light of this definition, there has been considerable focus regarding whether property should be considered "actively traded." This issue will be discussed in the next section of this chapter regarding swaps.

A "position" is defined as an interest (including a futures or forward contract or option) in personal property.[116]

An important exception is that, in general, stock is not considered personal property (and therefore is not subject to the straddle rules).[117] However, this exception is not available if at least one offsetting position with respect to such stock is (1) an option with respect to such stock or substantially identical stock or securities or (2) pursuant to IRS regulations, a position with respect to substantially similar or related property (other than stock).[118] This exception is also not available with respect to stock of a corporation formed or availed of to take positions in personal property that offset positions taken by any shareholder.[119] Moreover, a taxpayer must not simply look to its own conduct, but rather, it must take into account positions in personal property held by *any related person*.[120] "Related persons" include the spouse of the taxpayer, any member of a consolidated group, and certain flow-through entities such as partnerships or trusts.[121]

What Are the Consequences of the Straddle Rules?

Deferral of losses. The fundamental consequence of the straddle rules is that they prevent a taxpayer from immediately recognizing a loss for federal income tax purposes that might otherwise be available in connection with closing out one of the positions in personal property comprising a part of the straddle. Instead, all or a portion of the loss may be *deferred* until a subsequent period when the offsetting positions are closed out. Section 1092(a)(1) provides that "[a]ny loss with respect to [one] or more positions shall be taken into account for any taxable year only to the extent that the amount of such loss exceeds the unrecognized gain (if any) with respect to [one] or more positions which were offsetting positions with respect to [one] or more positions from which the loss arose." Any loss that is subject to deferral under this rule is carried forward and, subject to the application of the same basic loss deferral rule in the subsequent year, shall be taken into account in a later year.[122]

Impact on character of gains and losses. Section 1092(b)(1) grants to the IRS the authority to issue regulations regarding gains and losses on positions with respect to straddles as appropriate to carry out the purposes of the straddle rules. Pursuant to this

---

116 Section 1092(d)(2).
117 Section 1092(d)(3)(A).
118 Section 1092(d)(3)(B)(i).
119 Section 1092(d)(3)(B)(ii).
120 Section 1092(d)(4)(A).
121 Section 1092(d)(4)(B) and (C).
122 Section 1092(a)(1)(B).

grant of authority, the IRS has issued regulations regarding the determination of holding periods and losses with respect to straddle positions.[123] Under the general rule of the regulations, the holding period of any position that is part of a straddle does not begin earlier than the date the taxpayer no longer holds directly or indirectly (including through related persons or flow-through entities) an offsetting position with respect to that position.[124] However, if property constituting a position of a straddle had been held by a taxpayer for the long-term capital gain holding period (or longer) before a straddle that includes such position is established, the general rule does not apply and that portion of the straddle that previously qualified for long-term capital gain treatment retains its long-term gain eligible holding period.[125] Because property must be held for at least one year prior to disposition in order for gain or loss with respect to such property to be treated as long-term gain or loss,[126] the general rule makes it likely that the disposition of positions of property that comprised a straddle will generate short-term capital gains and makes it more difficult to obtain long-term gain characterization except in the case of positions in property that were eligible for long-term capital gain treatment before a straddle that included such positions was established.

The regulations include a *loss character rule,* under which losses with respect to positions of property comprising a straddle are treated as long-term losses if (1) on the date the loss-generating property was acquired, the taxpayer directly or indirectly held one or more offsetting positions, and (2) all gain or loss with respect to one or more positions in the straddle would be treated as long-term capital gain or loss if such positions were disposed of on the day the loss position was entered into.[127] Note that this rule, because it focuses on whether the disposition of *any* position would be eligible for long-term capital gain or loss, may recharacterize losses recognized on other positions in the straddle as long-term, which may be disadvantageous. Special rules regarding losses that apply to "mixed straddles" are discussed below.

The regulations provide that these special holding periods and loss rules do not apply to positions that (1) constitute parts of hedging transactions (within the meaning of Section 1256(e)), (2) are included in straddles comprised only of Section 1256 contracts, or (3) are included in a mixed straddle account.[128] Moreover, the regulations include a special rule for regulated investment companies that are intended to avoid potential disqualification of such companies under the so-called short-short or 30 percent test, which they must meet in order to maintain qualifying status as regulated investment companies.[129]

Section 1092(f) provides that the holding period of stock is suspended (*i.e.,* the holding period of such stock for purposes of determining whether gain or loss relating to the sale or other disposition of the stock is characterized as long-term or short-term gain or loss does not include any period during which the holder is a grantor of an

---

123 *See* Temp. Treas. Reg. Section 1.1092(b)-2T.
124 Temp. Treas. Reg. Section 1.1092(b)-2T(a)(1).
125 Temp. Treas. Reg. Section 1.1092(b)-2T(a)(2).
126 Sections 1222(3) and (4).
127 Temp. Treas. Reg. Section 1.1092(b)-2T(b)(1).
128 Temp. Treas. Reg. Section 1.1092(b)-2T(c)(1).
129 *See* Temp. Treas. Reg. Section 1.1092(b)-2T(d).

option and this rule applies) with respect to a holder of stock who grants a qualified covered call option to purchase such stock with a strike price less than the "applicable stock price" and any loss recognized with respect to such option shall be treated as long-term capital loss (if at the time such loss is realized, gain on the sale or exchange of the stock would be treated as long-term capital gain).

Capitalization of interest and carrying costs. In addition to rules that defer the recognition of losses and that may affect the character of gains or losses recognized with respect to positions of a straddle, Section 263(g) prevents a taxpayer from deducting on an ongoing basis interest and carrying charges that are allocable to the personal property that constitutes positions of a straddle. "Interest and carrying charges" for this purpose is defined as interest incurred or continued to purchase or carry the personal property and all other amounts, including charges to insure, store, or transport the personal property, paid or incurred to carry the personal property, reduced by various specified items of ordinary income that may be generated by the property.[130]

Section 263(g) requires that such items must be capitalized as part of the cost of the personal property to which such items relate. As a result, a taxpayer will recognize these items when gain or loss is recognized upon disposition of the related property constituting a portion of a straddle and because they are capitalized as part of the cost of such property, such amounts will merely affect the amount of capital gain or loss recognized and will not result in deductions that can be used to reduce ordinary taxable income.

This provision does not apply in the case of Section 1256(e) hedging transactions and is applied after other restrictions on interest expense deductions for short sales, market discount, and short-term debt instruments are taken into account.[131]

Special Rules and Exceptions

Identified straddles and interaction with Section 1256. Section 1092 includes a number of special rules that should be considered. First, it provides rules that apply to "identified straddles." Section 1092(a)(2)(B) defines an identified straddle as any straddle that is clearly identified on the taxpayer's records as such before the earlier of (1) the close of the day on which the straddle is acquired, or (2) such time as prescribed by IRS regulations. Because the straddle must generally be identified on the day it is entered into and a straddle is defined as "offsetting positions" it would appear that *all* of the offsetting positions of the straddle must be identified. In addition, all of the original positions of the straddle must be acquired on the same day and either (1) all of the positions must have been disposed of on the same day during the tax year or (2) none of the positions comprising the straddle must have been disposed of during the tax year.[132] Moreover, the identified straddle must not be part of a larger straddle.[133]

---

130 Section 263(g)(2).
131 Sections 263(g)(3) and (4).
132 Section 1092(a)(2)(B)(ii).
133 Section 1092(a)(2)(B)(iii).

As a result, this rule has been criticized because it does not accommodate transactions that are part of a "macro-hedging" strategy.

Temporary Regulations include rules for identified mixed straddles covered by Section 1092(b)(2). If a taxpayer satisfies the identification requirements with respect to an identified mixed straddle, the general loss limitation rule discussed above (which only limits the recognition of losses to the extent of unrecognized gains with respect to any of the offsetting positions of the straddle) does not apply and no loss is recognized until the day on which all of the positions making up the straddle are disposed of.[134] Moreover, the loss character rule of the regulations does not apply to an identified mixed straddle.[135] A benefit of identifying a mixed straddle that qualifies under this rule is that the IRS regulations provide that gain or loss recognized with respect to the offsetting positions is netted.[136] Another important aspect of the identified mixed straddle rule is that none of the offsetting positions comprising the identified mixed straddle are considered "offsetting positions" for any other position in personal property that the taxpayer may have.[137]

Interaction of the straddle rules with the mark-to-market rules. Given the broad definition of a straddle, it must be considered how the straddle rules interact with the mark-to-market rules that would otherwise ordinarily apply to positions of a straddle. First, if not all of the positions of a straddle are subject to the mark-to-market rules of Section 1256, Section 1092(d)(5)(A) provides that the straddle rules apply to any Section 1256 contract and any other position making up a straddle, even if one of the positions comprising such straddle is a Section 1256 contract (which would normally only be subject to the Section 1256 rules). Second, if all of the positions of a straddle are subject to the mark-to-market rules, the straddle rules do not apply.[138] However, in the case of identified straddles that include positions in property that are ordinarily subject to the mark-to-market rules (*identified mixed straddles*), the special rules discussed above regarding identified straddles apply and the Section 1256 contracts comprising such identified mixed straddles are subject to special rules.[139]

Mixed straddle account. An important aspect of the straddle rules is the rules for so-called "mixed straddles." As discussed above in the section regarding the mark-to-market rules, a straddle is a mixed straddle if one or more (but not all) of the positions comprising the straddle are Section 1256 contracts and each position comprising the straddle is clearly identified before the close of the day on which the first Section 1256 contract forming a part of the straddle is acquired.[140] Given the difference in tax treatment between Section 1256 contracts (which are generally subject to the mark-to-market rules) and other types of options and forward contracts, the recognition of gain or loss on the Section 1256 contract portion of a mixed straddle

---

134 Section 1092(a)(2)(A).
135 Temp. Treas. Reg. Section 1.1092(b)-2T(c)(2).
136 Temp. Treas. Reg. Section 1.1092(b)-3T.
137 Section 1092(c)(2)(C).
138 Section 1256(a)(4).
139 *See* Section 1092(d)(5)(A) and Temp. Treas. Reg. Section 1.1092(b)-3T(b)(2) and (b)(4).
140 Section 1256(d)(4).

on a mark-to-market basis would be distortive (since gain or loss on the non-Section 1256 contract components of the mixed straddle would not be recognized on a mark-to-market basis).

A confusing aspect of the straddle rules and the mark-to-market rules is that they each contain different rules for mixed straddles. Section 1256(d) permits a taxpayer to elect to avoid the application of the mark-to-market rules to the positions of a mixed straddle that are ordinarily subject to the mark-to-market rules (a *Section 1256(d) election*). Section 1092(b)(2) permits a taxpayer to elect to establish and maintain a mixed straddle account for its mixed straddles (a *mixed straddle account election*).

A taxpayer may account for mixed straddles by establishing and maintaining one or more "mixed straddle accounts."[141] Regulations providing guidance regarding the accounting for mixed straddles through the establishment of a mixed straddle account by the taxpayer have been issued.[142]

By making a mixed straddle election, a taxpayer is permitted to net offsetting positions before the application of the mark-to-market rules of Section 1256, and the 40 percent short-term/60 percent long-term rule will apply only to net gain or net loss attributable to Section 1256 contracts.[143] In addition the "long-term loss character rule" of Section 1233(d), which applies to short sales where the taxpayer holds on the date of such short sale substantially identical property that had been held for more than one year, shall not apply to mixed straddles.[144] Finally, there are limits on the maximum amount of gain or loss from a mixed straddle account that can be characterized as long-term or short-term. Section 1092(b)(2)(B) provides that not more than 50 percent of net gain from a mixed straddle account for any tax year may be treated as long-term capital gain and not more than 40 percent of net loss from a mixed straddle account for any tax year may be treated as short-term capital loss.

Taxpayers should carefully consult their advisors regarding the appropriateness of making a mixed straddle election and maintaining a mixed straddle account. Although the election to utilize a mixed straddle account may be beneficial, once made it is irrevocable as to the year for which the election was made and for subsequent years unless IRS consent to revoke the election is obtained.[145]

Reporting of unrecognized gains. Section 1092(a)(3)(B) generally requires taxpayers to disclose to the IRS each position of a straddle with respect to which there is unrecognized gain (as of the close of the taxpayer's tax year) and the amount of such unrecognized gain.[146] Consistent with this requirement, a taxpayer must report straddle transactions on a separate IRS form (Form 6781).[147]

---

141 Section 1092(b)(2)(A)(i)(II). Separate mixed straddle accounts must be maintained for each separate designated class of activities of a taxpayer. Temp. Treas. Reg. Section 1.1092(b)-4T(b)(1).
142 *See* Temp. Treas. Reg. Section 1.1092(b)-4T.
143 Section 1092(b)(2)(A)(ii).
144 Section 1092(b)(2)(A)(iii).
145 Temp. Treas. Reg. Section 1.1092(b)-4T(f)(4).
146 This rule does not apply in the case of identified straddles, inventory, depreciable property used in the taxpayer's trade or business, positions in property which are part of a Section 1256(e) hedging transaction, or if no loss has been recognized. Section 1092(a)(3)(B)(ii).
147 Treas. Reg. Section 1.1092(b)-4T(f)(2).

The Wash Sale Rules

Section 1091 disallows the recognition of losses in the case of so-called "wash sales." This rule applies if a taxpayer recognizes a loss from the sale or disposition of stock or securities and, within a period beginning 30 days before the date of such sale or disposition and ending 30 days after such date, the taxpayer has acquired, or has entered into a contract or option to acquire, "substantially identical stock or securities."[148] If a lesser amount of substantially identical stock or securities is acquired compared to the amount sold, then only a portion of securities sold shall be taken into account in applying the wash sale rule and only a portion of the loss recognized will be disallowed.[149] To the extent the wash sale rule applies, the basis of the stock or securities acquired is adjusted to account for the basis of the stock or securities disposed of.[150] Because the basis in the stock or securities acquired is adjusted, the rule merely defers the recognition of loss until the newly acquired stock or securities are disposed of (assuming that the loss recognized upon disposition of the newly acquired stock or securities is not further subject to deferral on account of a wash sale).

Although the wash sale rule's application must be carefully evaluated, it perhaps could be viewed as having limited vitality. First, it applies only to stock or securities. It is unclear whether certain financial contracts such as swaps, caps, floors or similar contracts fall within the intended definition of "securities."[151] Second, it applies only if the newly acquired stock or securities are "substantially identical." The applicable case law interpreting this rule has defined this standard as requiring "economic correspondence exclusive of differentiations so slight as to be unreflected in the acquisitive and proprietary habits of holders of stocks and securities."[152] This standard has proven easy to avoid because bonds of different issuers, or the same issuer but with substantially different payment terms, interest rates, or maturity dates are not generally considered "substantially identical."[153]

Finally, the interaction of the wash sale rule and the straddle rules must be considered. IRS regulations provide that the wash sale rule, which provides for a total disallowance of losses if applicable, is applied before the straddle rule.[154]

The Capital Gain Conversion Rule

Section 1258 of the Code was added by the Revenue Reconciliation Act of 1993. The rule was intended to prevent taxpayers from entering into transactions that were intended to transform ordinary income into capital gains, given the increased beneficial tax rate differential applicable to long-term capital gains. The provision applies to "conversion transactions" and recharacterizes capital gains as ordinary income to

---

148 This rule does not apply if the taxpayer is a dealer in stock or securities and the loss is sustained in the ordinary course of business. Section 1091(a).
149 Treas. Reg. Section 1.1091-1(c).
150 Section 1091(d).
151 However, it should be noted that pursuant to Section 1091(a), except as provided in regulations, "stock or securities" include contracts or options to acquire or sell stock or securities.
152 Hanlin v. Commissioner, 108 F.2d 429 (3d Cir. 1939).
153 *See generally* Rev. Rul. 76-346, 1976-2 C.B. 247; Rev. Rul. 58-211, 1958-1 C.B. 529; and *Hanlin, id.*
154 Temp. Treas. Reg. Section 1.1092(b)-1T(a)(1).

the extent such gain does not exceed the "applicable imputed income amount."[155] The applicable imputed income amount is based on the amount of interest that would have accrued on the taxpayer's net investment at 120 percent of the applicable rate (which is based on U.S. Treasury borrowing rates).[156] In order for a transaction to be treated as a conversion transaction subject to this rule a two-part test must be met: (1) substantially all of the taxpayer's expected return from the transaction must be attributable to the time value of the taxpayer's net investment in the transaction; and (2) the transaction must be (A) the holding of property and the entering into a contract to sell such property (or substantially identical property) at a price determined in accordance with the contract, provided that such contract must be entered into on a substantially contemporaneous basis, (B) an applicable straddle (which means any transaction that would constitute a straddle under the straddle rules of Section 1092, including transactions that would constitute a straddle if stock were treated as personal property for purposes of the straddle rules), (C) any other transaction that is marketed or sold as producing capital gains, or (D) any other transaction specified in IRS regulations.[157]

Because the provision is relatively new, it is unclear how often it will apply. However, because it includes any transaction that would constitute a straddle under a broad definition of the test and any other transaction that is marketed or sold as producing capital gains, practitioners have been concerned that it may potentially apply in a number of unanticipated circumstances.

TAX RULES APPLICABLE TO SWAPS, CAPS, AND FLOORS

IRS Guidance Is Not Yet Comprehensive

As mentioned in an earlier section, there was a substantial period of time during the development and growth of the interest rate swap market when there was no guidance from the IRS regarding a number of basic tax issues relating to these products. In fact, the IRS did not issue proposed regulations addressing a number of basic tax issues relating to these products until 1991, over ten years after the interest rate swap market began. Moreover, even though final regulations relating to tax accounting for these contracts were issued in 1993, the IRS guidance issued to date has not been comprehensive. In other words, there are tax issues relating to these products that the IRS has not yet addressed. For example, in light of ongoing concerns regarding the character of gains and losses in light of *Arkansas Best* and the lower tax rates applicable to capital gains, the IRS has not yet addressed the character of income from swaps, caps, and floors, even though the character of payments made or payments received is of fundamental tax importance to investors. Thus, investors should monitor or consult with their tax advisors regarding the state of the tax law relating to these products on an ongoing basis.

---

155 Section 1258(a).
156 Section 1258(b).
157 Section 1258(c).

Important IRS Guidance Issued to Date

IRS Notices

In 1987 the IRS began issuing guidance relating to swaps, caps, and floors on an issue-by-issue basis. Notice 87-4 gave comfort to the market concerning U.S. with-holding tax risk. The Notice addressed the sourcing of income and expense attributable to U.S.-dollar-denominated interest rate swaps.[158] In Notice 89-21 the IRS provided that the inclusion in a single tax year of the entire amount of a payment received on an interest rate swap, cap, or floor that relates to the obligation to make payments in other tax years does not clearly reflect income and is an impermissible method of accounting.[159] Notice 89-21 was issued in response to transactions in which taxpayers characterized front-loaded swap and cap payments received as income recognized in the year of receipt to "soak up" unused net operating losses that were ready to expire or would become subject to restrictions due to change in ownership of the business, which the IRS viewed as abusive (the subsequent payment obligations on such contracts would generate expense deductions in future years that could offset taxable income generated after the net operating losses would have expired). Whether the rule of the notice or *Schlude v. Commissioner*, 372 U.S. 128 (1963) (a Supreme Court case requiring the immediate inclusion in income of lump sum payments received) will ultimately prevail with respect to such payments has not yet been tested by the courts. Notice 89-90 sets forth rules regarding the treatment for purposes of the foreign personal holding company income rules of Section 954(c)(1)(E) of the Code of income attributable to an interest rate swap, cap, or floor that is denominated in the functional currency of a qualified business unit (as defined in Section 989(a) of the Code).[160]

IRS Regulations

Treas. Reg. Section 1.863-7 (the *Swap Sourcing Regulation*) sets forth the rules for determining whether income or expenses relating to interest rate swaps, caps, or floors

---

158 Notice 87-4, 1987-1 C.B. 416. The notice provided that swap income was sourced to the residence of the recipient of such income unless the swap income was attributable to a U.S. trade or business (in which case the income would be sourced as U.S. and characterized as effectively connected to the U.S. trade or business). Because only U.S. source income is subject to withholding, this "sourcing rule" essentially eliminated the U.S. withholding tax concern. The notice has been replaced by Treas. Reg. Section 1.863-7 (which is referenced later in this chapter).

159 Notice 89-21, 1989-1 C.B. 651. The notice provides that the rule of *Schlude v. Commissioner*, 372 U.S. 128 (1963), and *American Automobile Association v. United States*, 367 U.S. 687 (1961), does not apply to such contracts. The notice requires the amortization of such amounts over the life of the contract under some reasonable method, provides specific guidance regarding change in accounting considerations, and provides limited guidance on the possibly retroactive effect of subsequent regulations. The rule of Notice 89-21 has been incorporated into Treas. Reg. Section 1.446-3 (discussed below).

160 Notice 89-90, 1989-2 C.B. 407. The Notice provides that income from such an NPC is generally treated as interest (*i.e.*, foreign personal holding company income) for these purposes. Notice 89-90 notes that its rule is different from the rule set forth in Temp. Treas. Reg. Section 1.954-2T(h)(1). The Notice also contains several exceptions to this general interest characterization rule. The rule of the Notice is effective for all items of income received or accrued on or after its publication date.

are treated as "U.S. sourced income" or "foreign sourced income."[161] It also provides guidance regarding the character of such income in certain cases. The Swap Sourcing Regulation follows the rule of Notice 87-4 by sourcing income by reference to the taxpayer's residence.[162] The regulation provides exceptions to this sourcing rule for foreign qualified business units of U.S. taxpayers and for income that arises in connection with the conduct of a U.S. trade or business of a foreign taxpayer.[163]

In 1991, the IRS published the *Proposed Swap Regulations* and in 1993 the IRS published the *Final Swap Regulations*. These regulations principally address the timing of income and expense recognition with respect to these products (it should be noted that both the Proposed Swap Regulations and Final Swap Regulations provide that they apply to "notional principal contracts"; this term of art is defined differently for purposes of the swap regulations than under the Swap Sourcing Regulation and covers many types of derivative products such as swaps, caps, and floors).[164]

In July 1992, final regulations were issued that explicitly treat "income from notional principal contracts (as defined in Treasury Regulations 26 CFR 1.863-7 or regulations issued under Section 446)" as investment income excludible from the definition of unrelated business taxable income for tax-exempt organizations such as "not-for-profit" organizations.[165]

Key Aspects of the Final Swap Regulations and Other IRS Guidance Issued to Date

Defining a "Notional Principal Contract"

While the Final Swap Regulations provide guidance for "notional principal contracts" (NPCs), certain contracts may not qualify as NPCs and thus, may not technically be covered by the Regulations. An NPC is defined by Treas. Reg. Section 1.446-3(c)(1)(i)

---

161 The Swap Sourcing Regulation does not apply to income from a Section 988 transaction within the meaning of Section 988 of the Code. The Swap Sourcing Regulation is generally effective for interest rate swap, cap, or floor income includible in taxable income on or after February 13, 1991. *See* Treas. Reg. Section 1.863-7(a)(2).

162 Residence is determined under the rules of Section 988(a)(3)(B)(i) of the Code. Treas. Reg. Section 1.863-7(b)(1).

163 Treas. Reg. Section 1.863-7(b)(2) and (b)(3).

164 Treas. Reg. Section 1.446-3; Temp. Treas. Reg. Section 1.988-2T(h); and Treas. Reg. Section 1.1092(d)-1, 56 Fed. Reg. 31,350 (July 10, 1991). The Final Swap Regulations are generally effective for notional principal contracts entered into on or after December 13, 1993. Treas. Reg. Section 1.446-3(j). An important exception to this general rule relates to the application of Treas. Reg. Section 1.1092(d)-1, which treats notional principal contracts as personal property of a type that is actively traded if similar contracts are actively traded and which may trigger the application of the "straddle rules" of Section 1092. This rule generally applies for positions entered on or after July 8, 1991. Treas. Reg. Section 1.1092(d)-1(d). For a general discussion of the Final Swap Regulations, *see* Conlon & Russell, *supra* note 100.

165 Treas. Reg. Section 1.512(b)-1(a)(1). Note that the final regulations are a substantial improvement over the proposed regulations that were published by the IRS on September 3, 1991 (the "Proposed UBTI Regulations"). 56 Fed. Reg. 43,571 (September 3, 1991). The preamble to the Proposed UBTI Regulations included a proposed form of published revenue ruling that addressed the UBTI consequences of interest rate and currency swap transactions. For a discussion of concerns raised under the Proposed UBTI Regulations, *see ABA Swap Regulations Report, supra* note 13, at 17-18.

as "a financial instrument that provides for the payment of amounts by one party to another at specified intervals calculated by reference to a specified index upon a notional principal amount in exchange for specified consideration or a promise to pay similar amounts" and the regulations define a "notional principal amount" as "any specified amount of money or property that, when multiplied by a specified index, measures a party's rights and obligations under the contract, but is not borrowed or loaned between the parties as part of the contract." The notional principal amount serves only as a reference for determining the amount of payments to be made under the contract and is not actually borrowed or loaned between the parties. A key aspect of the Final Swap Regulations is that the notional principal amount referenced in the contract may vary over its term, provided certain conditions are met.[166] Swaps, caps, floors, and collars are generally included within the definition of an NPC.[167]

What Contracts Do Not Fall Within the Definition of an NPC?

It should be noted that certain types of swaps, caps, and floors may not fall within the NPC definition. For example, the applicable rate under the contract may not constitute a "specified index" under the Final Swap Regulations.[168] Although the Final Swap Regulations broadly define this term, certain contracts may rely on indices or permit changes in the notional principal amount that cause the contract to fail to qualify as an NPC. For example, a contract that provides for payments based on the unique circumstances of one of the parties (such as the value of its stock, its profits, or its dividends) would not qualify as an NPC.[169]

Contracts between a taxpayer and qualified business units (as defined in Section 989(a) of the Code) are not treated as NPCs "because a taxpayer cannot enter into a contract with itself."[170] Section 1256 contracts, futures contracts, forward contracts, options, and debt instruments are not notional principal contracts and therefore, are not subject to these rules.[171]

In addition, the Final Swap Regulations provide that each contract entered into pursuant to a master agreement is treated as a separate NPC.[172] Options or forward contracts to enter into, extend, cancel, or change the terms of an NPC are not NPCs (although NPCs may subsequently come into existence pursuant to such contracts).[173] Note that this rule results in a difference between the tax treatment of forward swaps and their business law analysis. A forward swap is generally viewed as a business law matter as a swap contract today that merely provides for payments that begin at a later date. However, the Final Swap Regulations treat such contracts as forward contracts to enter into an NPC that begins on the date payments begin. Collars are treated as two or more separate NPCs but can treated as a single NPC under the regulations.[174]

---

166 Treas. Reg. Section 1.446-3(c)(3).
167 *See* Treas. Reg. Section 1.446-3(c)(1)(i).
168 *See* Treas. Reg. Section 1.446-3(c)(2) and (c)(4)(ii).
169 Treas. Reg. Section 1.446-3(c)(4)(ii).
170 Treas. Reg. Section 1.446-3(c)(1)(i).
171 Treas. Reg. Section 1.446-3(c)(1)(ii).
172 Treas. Reg. Section 1.446-3(c)(1)(i).
173 Treas. Reg. Section 1.446-3(c)(1)(ii).
174 Treas. Reg. Section 1.446-3(c)(1)(i).

Netting of Payments

The Final Swap Regulations adopt a "netting" approach, permitting a taxpayer to take into account its share of ongoing periodic payments, nonperiodic payments, and termination payments in determining its income or loss for the tax year from the NPC.[175] Note that consistent with the Proposed Swap Regulations, the Final Swap Regulations do not address the character of income or loss generated pursuant to an NPC (except to the extent the "embedded loan" rules apply, as discussed below).[176]

Periodic Payments

Periodic payments are defined as payments that are generally payable at periodic intervals of one year or less during the entire term of an NPC and that are based on either a single notional principal amount or a notional principal amount that varies over the term of the contract in the same proportion as the notional principal amount that measures the other party's payments.[177] Regardless of the taxpayer's method of tax accounting, a taxpayer must take into account the ratable daily portion of periodic payments for the applicable tax year under the netting rule referenced above.[178] If the applicable rate (and therefore the daily portion) of a periodic payment is not determinable at the end of the taxpayer's tax year, the daily portions are determined based on the applicable rate as of the close of such tax year unless the taxpayer believes that such rate does not provide a reasonable estimate of the specified index that will apply when the payment becomes fixed, in which case the taxpayer may use a reasonable estimate, provided that it (and any related party) uses the same method each year and uses the method for financial and creditor reporting purposes (and adjustments for any differences between the actual rate and end-of-the-tax-year rate are made in subsequent tax years).[179]

Nonperiodic Payments

The Final Swap Regulations define a "nonperiodic payment" as "any payment made or received pursuant to a notional principal contract that is not a periodic payment . . . or a termination payment."[180] Cap and floor premiums (even if paid in installments), yield adjustment fees or swap premiums for off-market interest rate swaps and the premium paid for an option to enter into a swap (if and when the option is exercised) are all examples of nonperiodic payments.[181]

Under the Final Swap Regulations, taxpayers must recognize their ratable daily portion of any nonperiodic payments in the related tax year, regardless of their method

---

175 Treas. Reg. Section 1.446-3(d).

176 *See* Preamble to the Proposed Swap Regulations, 56 Fed. Reg. 31,350, at 31,351 (July 10, 1991).

177 Treas. Reg. Section 1.446-3(e)(1). Appropriate adjustments must be made for the length of the intervals between payments. *Id.*

178 Treas. Reg. Section 1.446-3(e)(2)(i).

179 Treas. Reg. Section 1.446-3(e)(2)(ii). Similar adjustments are required if the notional principal amount is not fixed throughout the term of the contract and is determined in arrears. *See* Treas. Reg. Section 1.446-3(e)(2)(iii).

180 Treas. Reg. Section 1.446-3(f)(1).

181 *Id.*

of tax accounting, and a taxpayer's ratable daily portion must be determined in a manner that "reflects the economic substance of the contract."[182]

Thus, consistent with Notice 89-21, the Final Swap Regulations require the amortization of nonperiodic payments (referred to as premiums in the Notice). Unlike the Notice, both the proposed and final regulations are clear that the appropriate method is not straight-line.[183] In the case of swaps, nonperiodic payments are generally amortized in accordance with the values of a series of cash-settled forward contracts that reflect the applicable index and notional principal amount of the NPC.[184] In the case of caps and floors, nonperiodic payments are generally amortized in accordance with the values of a series of cash-settled option contracts that reflect the applicable index and the notional principal amount.[185] The option pricing used by the parties to calculate the premium will be respected, if reasonable.[186] Nonperiodic payments made with respect to interest rate swaps and caps and floors that hedge debt instruments may be eligible for amortization under various optional "level payment methods."[187] The Final Swap Regulations also permit the IRS to issue revenue procedures or revenue rulings providing for alternate methods of amortizing nonperiodic payments.[188] Although a collar is treated as comprised of two separate NPCs (a cap and a floor) under the regulations, a special rule permits a taxpayer to treat it as a single contract for purposes of amortizing any nonperiodic payments with respect to the collar.[189]

Embedded Loans

The Final Swap Regulations retain the concept of the "embedded loan" that had been introduced by the Proposed Swap Regulations.[190] If the amount of any payments made with respect to a swap, cap, or floor that do not qualify as periodic payments are "significant," an embedded loan is deemed to exist.[191] Thus, certain derivative products may be treated under the Final Swap Regulations as comprised of two distinct

---

182 Treas. Reg. Section 1.446-3(f)(2)(i).
183 See e.g., the last sentence of Prop. Reg. Section 1.446-3(e)(3)(ii)(C) and Treas. Reg. Section 1.446-3(f)(2)(iv).
184 Treas. Reg. Section 1.446-3(f)(2)(ii).
185 Treas. Reg. Section 1.446-3(f)(2)(iv).
186 Id.
187 Treas. Reg. Section 1.446-3(f)(iii) and (f)(v). Note also that these methods may not be available in certain cases. See Treas. Reg. Section 1.446-3(g)(2).
188 Treas. Reg. Section 1.446-3(f)(2)(vi). The preamble to the Proposed Swap Regulations included a proposed form of revenue procedure that included tables that taxpayers other than dealers and traders could have used to compute amortization of cap and floor premiums with respect to certain types of caps and floors. Preamble to the Proposed Swap Regulations. 56 Fed. Reg. 31,350, at 31,351-31,353 (July 10, 1991); the utility and correctness of the tables had been questioned and the tables were not included in the Final Swap Regulations. For commentary regarding the tables, see, e.g., ABA Swap Regulations Report, supra note 13, at 35-38; Comment Letter to the IRS, Edward I. O'Brien of the Securities Industry Association, dated September 20, 1991 (available as Document 91-8429, 91 TNT 209-58 from Tax Analysts); Comment Letter to the IRS, Saul M. Rosen of Salomon Brothers, dated December 6, 1991 (available as Document 91-10469, 91 TNT 255-37 from Tax Analysts).
189 See Treas. Reg. Sections 1.446-3(c)(1)(i) and (f)(2)(v)(C).
190 See Treas. Reg. Section 1.446-3(g)(4). See Prop. Reg. Section 1.446-3(e)(4)(iii) and (iv).
191 The Proposed Swap Regulations had been criticized in this regard. See Comment Letter to the IRS, Vincent M. Aquilino & Steven D. Conlon of Chapman and Cutler, dated September 20, 1991 (available as Document 91-8187, 91 TNT 203-35 from Tax Analysts).

assets for tax purposes: an "at market" notional principal contract and an embedded loan. A taxpayer will need to account for the distinct tax characteristics of each component of a derivative subject to the embedded loan rule. Although the Final Swap Regulations include embedded loan rules for swaps, the embedded loan rules for caps and floors remain in proposed form.[192]

Unfortunately, the Final Swap Regulations do not provide any "safe harbor" or "bright line test" for purposes of determining whether an embedded loan exists under a contract with respect to interest rate swaps.[193] Instead, the Final Swap Regulations merely include two examples (an example treating the swap premium as an embedded loan involving a premium equal to 66.7 percent of the net present value of the fixed payments on the swap, and an example that does not reclassify the swap premium as an embedded loan involving a premium equal to 9.1 percent of the present value of the fixed payments on the swap).[194] The Proposed Swap Regulations included a safe harbor regarding the determination of whether amounts paid with respect to a cap or floor are significant.[195]

Termination Payments

A termination payment (for all parties to an NPC) is defined as "a payment made or received to extinguish or assign all or a proportionate part of the rights and obligations of any party under a notional principal contract . . ." and includes "a payment made between the original parties to the contract (an extinguishment), a payment made between one party to the contract and a third party (an assignment), and any gain or loss realized on the exchange of one notional principal contract for another."[196] Except as otherwise provided under the Code (for example under the installment sales rules of Section 453 of the Code or the straddle rules of Section 1092 of the Code), termination payments are recognized in the year of extinguishment, assignment, or exchange.[197] In addition, payments that have been made or received but that have not yet been recognized because of the daily ratable portion rules applicable to periodic payments and nonperiodic payments are recognized in the year of extinguishment or assignment.[198]

A controversial aspect of the termination payment rules under the Proposed Swap Regulations was that they resulted in a deemed termination to a nonassigning counterparty to an NPC when the other counterparty assigned its interest in the NPC to a third party.[199] However, the Final Swap Regulations do not include this controversial rule. Instead, the termination payment rules of the Final Swap Regulations

---

192 *See* Preamble to the Final Swap Regulations. 58 Fed. Reg. 53,125, at 53,127 (October 14, 1993).
193 *See* Prop. Reg. Section 1.446-3(e)(4)(iii). The ABA Swap Regulations Report had recommended that a safe harbor be added for swaps but the Final Swap Regulations essentially retain the embedded loan rules for swaps that had been included in the Proposed Swap Regulations and do not include a safe harbor. *See ABA Swap Regulations Report, supra* note 13, at 6.
194 Treas. Reg. Section 1.446-3(g)(6)), Examples (2) and (3).
195 Prop. Reg. Section 1.446-3(e)(4)(iv). As discussed earlier, these rules remain in proposed form and the Final Swap Regulations do not include an embedded loan rule for caps and floors.
196 Treas. Reg. Section 1.446-3(h)(1).
197 Treas. Reg. Section 1.446-3(h)(2).
198 *Id.*
199 *See* Prop. Reg. Section 1.446-3(e)(6)(ii). *See ABA Swap Regulations Report, supra* note 13, at 49-60.

trigger a deemed termination to the nonassigning party if the assignment is a deemed exchange of contracts and is treated as a realization event under Section 1001 of the Code.[200]

Treatment of NPCs as Actively Traded Property for Purposes of the Straddle Rules

Treas. Reg. Section 1.1092(d)-1 provides that an NPC is treated as "actively traded property" for purposes of the straddle rules of Section 1092 "if contracts based on the same or substantially similar specified indices are purchased, sold, or entered into on an established financial market . . ." as defined elsewhere in the regulations.[201] To the extent the straddle rules apply, losses may be deferred and income, gain, or loss may be recharacterized as short-term or long-term capital gain.[202] Although the IRS's attempt to treat NPCs as subject to the straddle rules is understandable (because of the straddle rules' recharacterization and deferral principles), there are a number of technical concerns regarding whether many NPCs are actively traded.[203] It is important to note that the Final Swap Regulations provide that this rule applies to NPCs entered into on or after July 8, 1991.[204]

Anti-Abuse Rule

The Final Swap Regulations include an anti-abuse rule, which permits the IRS to exercise discretion to depart from the rules of the final regulations as necessary to reflect the appropriate timing of income and deductions from the transaction if a taxpayer enters into a transaction with a principal purpose of applying the rules of the regulations to produce a material distortion of income.[205] The Final Swap Regulations also permit the IRS to recharacterize all or part of a transaction (or series of transactions) if the effect of the transaction (or series) is to avoid the application of the regulations.[206]

Investor Concerns Regarding the Final Swap Regulations

Overall, the amortization rules and embedded loan rules of the Final Swap Regulations adopt approaches that track the underlying economics of derivative products. Unfor-

---

200 Treas. Reg. Section 1.446-3(h)(1). Although the determination of whether a deemed termination is triggered for a non-assigning party may remain an issue, given the lack of exhaustive guidance under Section 1001 of the Code, at least the rule of the Final Swap Regulations is consistent with the general realization rules of Section 1001 of the Code.
201 Treas. Reg. Section 1.1092(d)-1(c)(1). An "established financial market" is defined in Treas. Reg. Section 1.1092(d)-1(b).
202 Sections 1092(a) and 1234A of the Code.
203 *See ABA Swap Regulations Report, supra* note 13, at 68-69.
204 Treas. Reg. Section 1.1092(d)-1(d).
205 Treas. Reg. Section 1.446-3(i).
206 Treas. Reg. Section 1.446-3(g)(1).

tunately, these rules are inherently complex (which is contrary to the IRS's general objective of simplicity) and require information regarding derivative product pricing that many market participants view as proprietary, and that may be arbitrary or nonexistent. However, it is believed that the alternative amortization methods permitted under the regulations will generally permit the use of more simplified methods of amortizing nonperiodic payments and will simplify taxpayer compliance.

Moreover, the possible treatment of NPCs as actively traded property, potentially subjecting a taxpayer's NPC position (and the asset or liability to which it relates) to Section 1234A and the straddle rules, which could affect the timing and character of income or loss, is a major concern.

Special Concerns for Equity Swaps

In addition to financial contracts that measure payment obligations by reference to interest rate and foreign currency rate movements, market participants have developed similar contracts that measure payment obligations by reference to changes in the value of specifically identified property. Depending upon whether the property is stock (or a basket of stocks) or a commodity (or basket of commodities), these products are commonly referred to as "equity swaps," "equity index swaps," "commodity swaps," or "commodity index swaps."

Except with respect to NPCs linked to the stock, profits, or dividends of a single issuer, it appears clear that the Final Swap Regulations apply to these types of contracts (although it is necessary to consider the technical definition of an NPC in concluding whether a particular contract is covered by the regulations). However, the preamble to the Final Swap Regulations also indicates that the IRS "is considering whether notional principal contracts involving certain specified indices (*e.g.,* one issuer's stock) should be excluded from the general sourcing rules of Sections 861 through 865 and whether contracts involving other specified indices (*e.g.,* United States real property) are subject to section 897."[207]

The IRS has focused on the proper treatment of equity swaps and equity index swaps for sourcing and U.S. withholding tax purposes because certain payments that may be made pursuant to these types of contracts may economically resemble payments of dividends on stock. As discussed below under the section "U.S. Withholding Tax Considerations," dividends paid on stock of U.S. companies to non-U.S. persons are generally subject to U.S. withholding tax. Because payments on an equity swap or equity index swap can be designed to replicate the consequences of stock ownership, including payment of dividends, the IRS may be concerned that these types of contracts permit the avoidance of U.S. withholding tax liabilities that would be applicable if the counterparty to the swap owned the stock directly or if payments made to the counterparty were actual payments of dividends on stock.[208] However, there are

---

207 58 Fed. Reg. 53,126.
208 *See* Lee A. Sheppard, *To Withhold or Not to Withhold on Equity Swaps,* 55 TAX NOTES 1719 (June 29, 1992).

a number of reasons why it would appear inappropriate to treat payments made pursuant to equity swap and equity index swap contracts as subject to U.S. withholding tax.[209] Although a discussion of this issue and the reasons supporting the treatment of equity swap payments as exempt from U.S. withholding tax is beyond the scope of this chapter, this is an important issue that an equity swap participant should consider, and this area should be carefully monitored for possible future developments in the applicable law. Moreover, because equity swaps replicate the consequences of owning stock or receiving dividends on stock, it must be considered the extent to which other income character rules applicable to stock ownership (including eligibility for the dividends received deduction, and character of gains and losses recognized in connection with dispositions of stock) should apply to participants in these types of contracts.

CERTAIN ADDITIONAL SPECIAL CONSIDERATIONS

This section of the chapter addresses certain key additional federal income tax considerations relating to derivative products. Given the wide range of additional issues that may arise, depending upon the specifics of the derivative product or the particular tax situation of the investor, it is not possible to identify or discuss every possible tax concern that may arise.

Foreign Currency Rules

Section 988 imposes special rules for certain foreign currency transactions (*i.e.,* transactions relating to the receipt or payment of amounts that are denominated in or determined by reference to one or more currencies other than the taxpayer's "functional currency").[210] Financial transactions potentially subject to these rules include the disposition of foreign currency and transactions relating to foreign currency linked debt instruments, payables and receivables, forwards, futures contracts, options, or similar contracts and swaps, caps, floors, collars, etc.[211] It is important to note that regulated futures contracts and nonequity options subject to the mark-to-market rules of Section 1256 are not subject to Section 988 unless the taxpayer so elects.[212]

---

209 *See id.* at 1721; *ABA Swap Regulations Report, supra* note 13, at 69-72.
210 *See* Sections 985 and 988(c)(1). Note that it is not necessary that payments actually be made in a foreign currency as long as any amount is determined by reference to foreign currencies. *See* Treas. Reg. Section 1.988-1(a)(1).
211 *See* Treas. Reg. Section 1.988-1(a)(1)(i) and (2)(i), (ii), (iii) and (iii)(B).
212 Treas. Reg. Section 1.988-1(a)(7).

As indicated above under the section regarding bifurcation, the general rules of Section 988 provide that foreign currency gains and losses are separately accounted for and are characterized as ordinary income or loss.[213] As part of this separate accounting treatment, foreign currency gains and losses are generally not treated as interest.[214] The amount of any foreign currency gains or losses recognized with respect to a transaction subject to Section 988 cannot exceed the total amount of gain or loss recognized by the taxpayer with respect to the transaction.[215] The Section 988 rules have differing applications, depending on the type of transaction under consideration and, due to their complexity, not all of the aspects of these rules are discussed herein.[216]

In the case of debt instruments (assuming the investor is an accrual basis taxpayer), foreign currency gain or loss must generally be determined in connection with the accrual of interest income (the average exchange rate for the relevant accrual period is used, unless the investor elects to use the spot rate).[217] The same rules apply with respect to accruals of original issue discount.[218] Special rules address the treatment of bond premium and market discount.[219] Foreign currency gain or loss must also be taken into account with respect to actual payments of interest and principal, based upon the spot rate of exchange.[220] Certificates of deposit and demand or time

---

213 Section 988(a)(1)(A). Note that a taxpayer may be able to elect to treat foreign currency gains or losses attributable to a forward contract, futures contract or certain options as capital gains or losses pursuant to Section 988(a)(1)(B). *See* Treas. Reg. Section 1.988-3(b), which imposes various requirements that must be met in order to make this election. Section 988(c)(1)(D) effectively excludes regulated futures contracts or nonequity options subject to the mark-to-market rule of Section 1256 from the Section 988 rules unless the taxpayer otherwise elects to subject such contracts to the Section 988 election (Section 988(c)(1)(D)(ii)). In general, gains or losses relating to contracts subject to Section 1256 are treated as capital gain or loss (40 percent short-term and 60 percent long-term) and are recognized at the close of the taxpayer's tax year on a marked-to-market basis. Section 988(c)(1)(E)(iv)(II) provides that, in the case of a partnership that constitutes a "qualified fund," 100 percent of any gains or losses relating to any bank forward contract, foreign currency futures contract traded on a foreign exchange or as otherwise provided by regulation shall be treated as short-term capital gain or loss under the Section 1256 rules. Treas. Reg. Section 1.988-1(a)(10) provides that Section 988 does not apply to certain intra-taxpayer transfers. Also, in certain cases foreign currency gains or losses may be "integrated" as discussed *infra* at text accompanying notes 228 through 230. *See* Section 988(d).
214 *But see* Section 988(a)(2).
215 *See generally* Section 988(b).
216 For more information, *see* Marylouise Dionne & Stephen Orme, *Foreign Currency Transactions Under the Section 988 Regulations*, 70 TAXES 532 (August 1992); David P. Hariton, *New Foreign Currency Debt Regulations—An Analysis and a Recommendation*, 56 TAX NOTES 1201 (August 31, 1992).
217 *See generally* Treas. Reg. Section 1.988-2(b)(2)(ii)(C), (iii)(A) and (iii)(B).
218 Note the parenthetical reference in Treas. Reg. Section 1.988-2(b)(2)(ii)(C).
219 *See* Treas. Reg. Section 1.988-2(b)(10) and (b)(11).
220 *See* Treas. Reg. Section 1.988-2(b)(3) and (b)(5). Note that each of these provisions includes a parenthetical clause which specifically provides that a material modification of a debt instrument that constitutes a Section 1001 event also triggers the recognition of foreign currency gain or loss under these rules. Foreign currency gain or loss is also recognized in connection with the exchange of foreign currency denominated or linked debt for the obligor's stock. Treas. Reg. Section 1.988-2(b)(13). Special payment ordering rules set forth in Treas. Reg. Section 1.988-2(b)(7) must be considered. Foreign currency loss recognized in connection with a tax-exempt bond is treated as a reduction of tax-exempt income, thereby denying the investor a deductible loss. *See* Treas. Reg. Sections 1.988-2(b)(12) and 1.988-3(c)(2).

deposits are subject to special rules.[221] Foreign currency gains or losses with respect to forwards, futures, and option contracts are generally recognized in accordance with the ordinary rules for income recognition with respect to such contracts.[222] The timing of income recognition with respect to a notional principal contract is governed by Section 446 and the Final Swap Regulations.[223] Consistent with the general federal income tax concept that separate transactions are not ordinarily "integrated," the regulations generally provide that foreign currency gain or loss is not recognized solely because a transaction is offset by another transaction.[224]

In early 1992, proposed amendments to the regulations relating to Section 988 were published (the *Proposed 988 Regulations*).[225] Two controversial aspects of the Proposed 988 Regulations are: (1) the parallel bifurcated treatment for Section 988 purposes of a debt instrument into a debt instrument and a separate property right under the original issue discount rules discussed above, and (2) the bifurcation of so-called dual currency and multiple currency debt instruments into two or more separate, single currency debt instruments for purposes of applying the Section 988 rules.[226] Because each of the hypothetical, separate debt instruments will have an interest component as a result of the application of the OID rules, foreign currency gain or loss relating to the ongoing accrual of OID will be recognized prior to the maturity of the debt instrument.[227] Thus, these rules will impact the timing and complexity of compliance. Moreover, they may in many cases accelerate the recognition of foreign currency gain or loss.

Foreign Currency Transaction Integration

A key method of avoiding the burdensome complexities and potentially undesirable effects of the Section 988 rules is to "integrate" financial transactions that would otherwise be subject to these rules as part of a "hedging transaction."[228] For example, an investor might buy a foreign currency denominated bond and simultaneously enter into a foreign currency swap that would effectively hedge the entire foreign currency risk to the investor, providing the investor on a net basis with a U.S.-denominated debt instrument (because the foreign currency risk has been hedged). If a taxpayer is able to properly structure a "qualified hedging transaction" (as defined under the regula-

---

221 *See, e.g.*, Treas. Reg. Section 1.988-2(a)(1)(iii)(B), (C), (D) and (E); Treas. Reg. Section 1.988-2(b)(1).
222 *See* Treas. Reg. Section 1.988-2(d)(2)(i).
223 *See supra* notes 9–25 and accompanying text. The preamble to the Final Swap Regulations makes it clear that a currency swap can qualify as an NPC. *See* 58 Fed. Reg. 53,126. Note that there are special rules for currency swaps and off-market swaps. Treas. Reg. Section 1.988-2(e)(2) and (e)(3).
224 Treas. Reg. Section 1.988-2(d)(2)(ii).
225 57 Fed. Reg. 9217 (March 17, 1992). The Proposed 988 Regulations also include special rules for so-called "hyperinflationary" contracts and swaps, apply the "significant nonperiodic payment" rule of Prop. Reg. Section 1.446-3(e)(4)(iii) of the Proposed Swap Regulations (now contained in Treas. Reg. Section 1.446-3(g)(4) of the Final Swap Regulations), discussed *supra* at note 12 and accompanying text, and include additional hedging rules. Prop. Reg. Sections 1.988-2(d)(5), (e)(3)(iv), (e)(7) and 1.988-5(d).
226 Prop. Reg. Section 1.988-1(a)(3), (a)(4) and (a)(5).
227 *See generally* Prop. Reg. Section 1.988-1(a)(4)(ii)(A), (B) and (a)(5)(ii); Hariton, *supra* note 216, at 1210-13; Robert Feldgarden (Letter to the Editor, dated September 23, 1992), *Don't Abandon the Bifurcation Approach for Dual Currency Obligations*, 57 TAX NOTES 283 (October 12, 1992).
228 *See* Section 988(d) and the related implementing regulation, Treas. Reg. Section 1.988-5.

tions) that effectively eliminates foreign currency exchange risk, no foreign currency exchange gain or loss is recognized.[229] There are special considerations beyond the scope of this chapter that must be taken into account in determining whether a transaction is part of a qualified hedging transaction.[230] However, investors should carefully note that one of the applicable requirements for qualified hedging transaction treatment is a designation requirement that must be satisfied at the time the transaction is entered into. Investors should take this requirement into consideration in planning their hedging activities.

In summary, foreign currency transactions raise a host of considerations for investors, both in terms of their tax impact under Section 988 and the investors' abilities to properly account for such transactions in light of the complexities. Foreign currency issues are likely to arise in connection with derivative financial products such as options, swaps, caps, and floors. They will also arise in connection with "derivative-like" investments in dual or multiple currency debt instruments.

Securities Lending Transactions and Deemed Sales of Securities

As a general matter, dealers or other market makers often continuously offer to buy and sell the particular securities in which they make a market. Due to the dynamic nature of the markets, from time to time dealers and market makers have a need to acquire securities from others that they can use to satisfy the dealer or market maker's commitments to sell securities to third parties that are made in the ordinary course of its business.

In order to satisfy this need, dealers and other market makers often enter into "securities lending transactions" whereby they obtain securities from a party that has holdings in those securities needed by the particular dealer or market maker to satisfy third-party purchaser demands. Typically, the "provider" or "lender" of the securities is a mutual fund or pension fund or other "long" investor who has substantial securities holdings. The provider or lender does not intend to sell outright the securities it "lends" to the dealer or market maker. Instead, the provider or lender is motivated by the receipt of a fee from the "borrowing" dealer or market maker. In exchange for the fee, the provider or lender transfers the "loaned" securities to the dealer or market maker. Later, the dealer or market maker will transfer substantially identical securities back to the provider or lender.

It is important to note that the securities that are transferred back to the provider or lender are typically not the same securities that were originally lent by the provider or lender. The original securities were sold by the dealer or market maker to satisfy its obligations to third parties, and the securities that are transferred back to the provider or lender may be from the same series of securities issued by the particular entity bearing the same dividend or interest payment rate, but are merely substantially identical.

---

229 Treas. Reg. Section 1.988-5(a)(1).
230 *See* Treas. Reg. Section 1.988-5; *see generally* Dionne & Orme, *supra* note 216, at 544-49; Hariton, *supra* note 216, at 1210-13.

Securities lending transactions facilitate the functioning of the markets by providing a mechanism for the delivery of securities by dealers or market makers to third-party investors. However, because the provider or lender does not receive the same securities back when the "loan" is repaid, it must be considered whether the transaction really constitutes a loan of the securities for federal income tax purposes or whether it constitutes a sale of securities followed by a subsequent repurchase of substantially identical securities.

The tax characterization of the transaction as a sale and repurchase rather than a loan has fundamental consequences to the parties. First, if the transaction is treated as a sale, the provider or lender may be forced to recognize taxable gain. Taxable gain or loss is not generally recognized when property is lent rather than sold. Moreover, although gain may be recognized if the transaction is recharacterized as a sale, the subsequent "purchase" of substantially identical securities may trigger the application of the straddle or wash sale rules, which would prevent the provider or lender from recognizing tax loss. Second, the character of payments made by the dealer or market maker to the provider or lender may be affected. If the transaction is a loan rather than a sale, the "fee" may be characterized as interest for federal income tax purposes. If it is characterized as a sale, the fee may be characterized in some other fashion. Moreover, if the dealer or market maker receives any payments, such as dividends or interest on the securities prior to their resale, such payments received by the dealer or market maker may be treated as interest payments (if the transaction is characterized as a loan) or may retain their tax character upon receipt by the dealer or market maker. As indicated earlier, the character of payments may have important income and expense recognition timing and withholding tax consequences that the parties to a securities lending transaction should consider.[231]

The recognition of taxable gain from the transfer of securities by a provider or lender was considered particularly troubling because the provider or lender was not motivated to enter into the transaction due to a desire to sell the securities. Instead, the provider or lender considered itself simply to be assisting in the ongoing functioning of the markets in exchange for fee income.

Cottage Savings

A recent Supreme Court decision, *Cottage Savings Association v. Commissioner,*[232] raises additional concerns regarding whether various transactions involving the trans-

---

231 Note that the IRS has indicated that it will not ordinarily issue private letter rulings regarding the sourcing of payments made pursuant to securities lending transactions, their character or whether such payments constitute a specific type of income for U.S. tax treaty purposes. Rev. Proc. 94-7, 1994-1 I.R.B. 174, 175 (Section 4.01(20)).

232 111 S. Ct. 1503 (1991). On December 1, 1992, the IRS issued Prop. Reg. Section 1.1001-3 which addresses when a modification to the terms of a debt instrument triggers a taxable exchange. 57 Fed. Reg. 57,033 (December 2, 1992). The preamble to the proposed regulations indicates that it is based on the Supreme Court's analysis in *Cottage Savings*. The proposed regulations have been subject to substantial criticism. *See generally* Richard L. Bacon & Harold L. Adrion, *Taxable Events: The Aftermath of* Cottage Savings, 59 TAX NOTES 1227 (May 31, 1993) (Part I), 59 TAX NOTES 1385 (June 7, 1993) (Part II).

fer of securities constitutes a taxable sale rather than some sort of tax-free transfer. *Cottage Savings* addressed whether a savings and loan could recognize tax losses on exchanges of mortgage pools. The exchanges were principally motivated by these tax losses and were structured to prevent their recognition for regulatory accounting purposes. The IRS disallowed the savings and loan's tax losses. A significant number of these transactions were entered into by a number of taxpayers. Accordingly, the Supreme Court's decision to permit the taxpayer to recognize its taxable loss on the exchange was an important victory to the savings and loan industry and the Resolution Trust Company.

In order to comply with regulatory accounting rules that permitted the savings and loan to avoid the recognition of losses for financial statement purposes, a long list of key characteristics relating to the exchanged mortgage loans had to be identical or substantially similar, including identical maturities and stated interest rates on the mortgage loans, approximately identical principal balances, and similar fair market values, etc. Also, the mortgage loans were exchanged in pools, and, as an economic matter, were analyzed in the aggregate.

Given the similarities of the mortgage loans exchanged, the IRS principally argued that the exchange did not constitute a taxable exchange, and, therefore, a tax loss could not be recognized. The Court's decision essentially provides that the exchange of otherwise identical debt instruments issued by different issuers is clearly a taxable event, thereby permitting the recognition of gain or loss. In particular, the Court noted that the exchanged mortgage loans represented distinct "legal entitlements" from the mortgage loans exchanged.

In the context of securities lending transactions, *Cottage Savings* means that an investor cannot avoid the recognition of gain or loss if property is exchanged that is economically identical. Instead, an investor must focus on whether the exchanged property embodies different "legal entitlements" and if it does, a taxable gain or loss must be recognized even if the exchanged property is economically identical.

Qualified Securities Lending

In order to provide providers or lenders in securities lending transactions comfort that the transfer of securities in these transactions would not trigger the recognition of taxable gain for federal income tax purposes, Section 1058 of the Code was enacted. Section 1058 provides that no gain or loss is recognized by a taxpayer who transfers securities (for this purpose, a security is defined as stock in any corporation, any form of debt, or any right to subscribe or purchase the foregoing) in a securities lending transaction made pursuant to a "qualifying securities lending agreement." In order for a securities lending agreement to qualify as a qualifying securities lending agreement, the agreement must be in writing and it must (1) provide for the return to the transferor of securities that are identical to those transferred (meaning that the securities returned must be of the same class and issue as the securities lent), (2) require that payments shall be made to the transferor of all interest, dividends, and other distributions which the owner of the securities is entitled to receive during the period the securities are lent, and (3) not reduce the risk of loss or opportunity for gain of the transferor with respect to the transferred securities (the agreement must provide that the lender can terminate the loan upon five days' notice).[233] Except with respect to recently issued proposed regulations regarding the income sourcing rules and withholding tax rules, which are discussed below regarding U.S. withholding tax concerns, the applicable regulations regarding qualified securities lending transactions provide that the provider or lender's tax basis in the returned securities is a carryover basis determined by reference to the basis of the securities lent, and that the income received for making the securities loan is taxable fee income (rather than interest, dividends, or otherwise) regardless of whether such fees are equivalent to interest or dividend payments.[234]

It is important to note that Section 1058 does not cover all types of securities lending transactions. Some may be pursuant to securities lending agreements that do not meet the requirements set forth above. In addition, some securities lending agreements may involve loans of inventory or dealer property, which is not covered by Section 1058.[235]

U.S. Withholding Tax Considerations

Sections 1441 and 1442 generally impose a 30 percent withholding tax obligation on payors that make payments of U.S.-sourced "fixed or determinable annual or periodical gains, profits, and income" (FDAP income) to nonresident alien individuals, foreign partnerships, and foreign corporations.[236]

Withholding does not apply if the payments are effectively connected with the payee's U.S. trade or business, provided proper certification (Form 4224) is received by the payor.[237] The statutory withholding tax rate of 30 percent may be reduced, possibly to zero, pursuant to the terms of an applicable tax treaty between the United States and the country in which the foreign resident is located, provided proper certification is received by the payor. U.S. withholding tax is an important concern for U.S. taxpayers because even though tax liability is triggered in connection with distributions of income to non-U.S. persons, *the U.S. payor is liable for the tax.*[238]

---

233 Section 1058(b); Prop. Reg. Section 1.1058-1(b).
234 Prop. Reg. Sections 1.1058-1(c) and (d). The fee income is not taxable to a tax-exempt organization as debt-financed income under the provisions of Section 514. *See* Section 514(c)(8). In addition, a regulated investment company will treat such income as dividends and interest, although it will not qualify for the dividends received exclusion or deduction when distributed to shareholders. *See generally* Sections 852, 854.
235 Section 1058 applies to "securities" as defined in Section 1236(c). Under Section 1236, "security" means "any share of stock in any corporation, note, bond, debenture or evidence of indebtedness, or any evidence of an interest in or right to subscribe to or purchase any of the foregoing."
236 Section 1445 imposes withholding tax obligations in connection with special federal income tax rules generally referred to as the "FIRPTA" rules that impose U.S. tax on sales of foreign-owned U.S. real estate. These rules are complex but should not generally be relevant in the case of derivative products unless the particular derivative constitutes an equity interest in real estate or an entity holding real estate. Section 1446 imposes withholding tax obligations in connection with partnerships that have foreign partners. These rules would be relevant if the derivative held by the foreign investor is structured to qualify as a partnership interest.
237 Section 1441(c)(1); Treas. Reg. Section 1.1441-4(a)(2).
238 Treas. Reg. Section 1.1441-6 and Prop. Reg. Section 1.1441-6.

When Is U.S. Withholding Tax an Issue?

If U.S. withholding tax applies to distributions made to an investor, the investor's return will be adversely affected. In many cases, investors are not indemnified against this risk and bear the entire risk themselves. Thus, the investor is often faced with the burden of determining itself whether there is a risk that U.S. withholding tax will be imposed.

Interest Rate Swaps, Caps, and Floors

Distributions to a foreign person on interest rate swaps, caps, floors, and other contracts that fall within the scope of the rule should not generally be subject to U.S. withholding tax because the income distributed on the contract will be sourced as non-U.S. income (since the Swap Sourcing Regulations provide that such income is sourced by reference to the residence of the taxpayer).[239] However, this sourcing rule does not apply in the case of qualified business units of U.S. taxpayers and for income that arises in connection with the conduct of a U.S. trade or business.[240] To the extent the sourcing rule is not available, an investor should consider whether it has provided the required certification to avoid U.S. withholding tax. Moreover, as discussed above in the section "The Tax Rules Applicable to Swaps, Caps, and Floors," investors should monitor potential developments concerning U.S. withholding tax issues relating to equity swaps.

Securities Lending Transactions

On January 8, 1992, the IRS issued proposed regulations regarding cross-border securities lending transactions.[241] The proposed regulations address the treatment of "substitute interest payments" and "substitute dividend payments" made to a provider or lender of securities in a securities lending transaction, as defined in Section 1058(a), or a substantially similar transaction. The proposed regulations treat substitute interest payments and substitute dividend payments as if they were direct payments to the provider or lender on the securities transferred to the dealer or market maker pursuant to the securities loan rather than payments from the dealer or market maker for purposes of the foreign income sourcing rules and the U.S. withholding tax rules.[242] As a result, if the rules of the proposed regulations are ultimately adopted as final regulations, U.S. sourced substitute dividend payments made to a non-U.S. person could become subject to U.S. withholding tax. In addition, U.S.-sourced substitute interest payments could be treated as payments of interest eligible for the portfolio interest exemption discussed below in connection with the U.S. withholding tax issues

---

239 Residence is determined under the rules of Section 988(a)(3)(B)(i). Treas. Reg. Section 1.863-7(b)(1).
240 Treas. Reg. Section 1.863-7(b)(2) and (b)(3).
241 57 Fed. Reg. 860 (January 9, 1992).
242 Prop. Reg. Sections 1.861-2(a)(7), 1.861-3(a)(6), 1.871-7(b)(2), 1.881-2(b)(2), 1.1441-2(a)(1). *See also* Prop. Reg. Section 1.894-1(c) for rules defining substitute payments as equivalent to interest or dividends for U.S. tax treaty purposes.

relating to debt.[243] Because the proposed regulations would result in U.S. withholding tax in the case of certain substitute dividend payments and could result in U.S. withholding tax in the case of interest payments for which the necessary withholding tax exemption certifications have not been provided, the proposed regulations have been criticized.[244] Investors should monitor developments in this area in order to assess potential U.S. withholding tax risks.

Forwards, Futures, and Options

U.S. withholding tax applies to FDAP income. FDAP income does not include gains and losses recognized in connection with forwards, futures, and options.[245] Moreover, income that is recognized on a "mark-to-market" basis does not involve a distribution or payment, and as a result, such income should similarly not be treated as FDAP income. For these reasons, income realized from forwards, futures, and options (regardless of whether such contracts are subject to the mark-to-market rules of Section 1256) should not ordinarily result in U.S. withholding tax risks.

Derivatives That Are Characterized as Debt

If the important exception from U.S. withholding tax discussed below does not apply, U.S. withholding tax risk *could* be an issue with respect to an investment in a derivative product that is characterized as *debt* for federal income tax purposes. Distributions to foreign investors with respect to such securities would likely constitute FDAP income, potentially subject to withholding tax (thereby making such securities undesirable to individual investors). A key withholding tax exemption that is relied on to avoid U.S. withholding tax liability with respect to such products is the so-called "portfolio interest exemption" provided for in Sections 871(h) and 881(c).[246] Although there are a number of technical issues that must be considered in connection with the portfolio interest exemption, the fundamental requirement is that the exemption applies only to payments of *interest*. As a result, the status of the product as a debt instrument and the determination that all payments thereon constitute either interest or principal (or otherwise qualify for an exemption from U.S. withholding tax) can be critical if the product is being sold to foreign investors. Note that distributions from a mutual fund

---

243 Note that it would be necessary to consider whether the certification requirements which must be satisfied in order to qualify for the portfolio interest exemption are satisfied.

244 New York State Bar Association Tax Section, *Report on Proposed Regulations on Certain Payments Made Pursuant to Securities Lending Transactions*, dated July 7, 1992, *reprinted in* HIGHLIGHTS & DOCUMENTS, July 27, 1992, at 1393.

245 For a discussion of income subject to withholding, *see generally* JEFFREY GILBERT BALKIN, U.S. INCOME TAX WITHHOLDING—FOREIGN PERSONS (341 T.M.P.) A-4 (Bureau of National Affairs 1991).

246 Section 1441(c)(9) provides the withholding tax exemption for portfolio interest.

are classified as "dividends" for federal income tax purposes rather than interest.[247] In addition, payments of interest to non-U.S. branches of foreign banks on loans made in the ordinary course of their trade or business and payments of interest to certain related persons are not eligible for the portfolio interest exemption.[248]

In 1993, the portfolio interest exemption was amended to provide that "contingent interest" does not qualify for the exemption. Contingent interest is defined for this purpose as any amount of interest that is determined by reference to (1) any receipts, sales, or other cash flow of the debtor or a related person, (2) any income or profits of the debtor or a related person, (3) any changes in value of any property of the debtor or a related person, or (4) any dividend, partnership distributions, or similar payments made by the debtor or a related person.[249] Thus, distributions of contingent interest would be subject to U.S. withholding tax unless some other exemption applies. As a result, investors should carefully consider whether a derivative product provides for the payment of amounts that could be classified as "contingent interest" subject to U.S. withholding tax risk.

Derivatives That Are Characterized as Stock or Pass-Through Equity

Dividends paid on stock are generally subject to U.S. withholding tax (unless the recipient is doing business in the U.S., although an applicable tax treaty may reduce, but not eliminate, the rate of withholding tax). Distributions with respect to a derivative product characterized as a partnership "equity" interest may be subject to U.S. withholding tax under Section 1446. Distributions with respect to a derivative product that is characterized as a pass-through "equity" interest in a grantor trust will be subject to U.S. withholding tax based on the nature of the underlying assets held by the trust.[250]

---

247 In order for a mutual fund to qualify as a regulated investment company, it must, among other things, be classified as a corporation for federal income tax purposes. Section 851(a) of the Code; Treas. Reg. Section 1.851-1(a). Although Section 9101 of the version of H.R. 11, passed by the Senate on September 29, 1992, contained an exemption from withholding for certain mutual fund dividends paid to foreign investors, this provision was not included in the Conference Bill (which was vetoed by former President Bush on November 4, 1992).

248 See Sections 881(c)(3)(A), 871(h)(3), 881(c)(3)(B) and 881(c)(3)(C).

249 Section 871(h)(4)(A). Contingent interest for this purpose does not include (i) any amount of interest solely by reason of the fact that the timing of any interest or principal payment is subject to a contingency, (ii) any amount of interest solely by reason of the fact that the interest is paid with respect to nonrecourse or limited recourse indebtedness, (iii) any amount of interest all or substantially all of which is determined by reference to any other amount of interest not described in Section 871(h)(4)(A) (or by reference to the principal amount of indebtedness on which such other interest amount is paid), (iv) any amount of interest solely by reason of the fact that the debtor or a related person enters into a hedging transaction to reduce the risk of interest rate or currency fluctuations with respect to such interest, (v) any amount of interest determined by reference to (A) changes in the value of property (including stock) that is actively traded (within the meaning of Section 1092(d)) other than property described in Section 897(c)(1) or (g), (B) the yield on property described in (A), other than a debt instrument that pays interest described in Section 871(h)(4)(A), or stock or other property that represents a beneficial interest in the debtor or a related person, or (C) changes in any index of the value of property described in (A) or of the yield of any property described in (B), and (vi) any other type of interest identified in IRS regulations. Section 871(h)(4)(C). There is a transitional rule for debt issued before April 8, 1993 or issued pursuant to a written binding contract in effect before April 8, 1993.

250 See Temp. Treas. Reg. Section 5f.163-1; Treas. Reg. Section 1.163-5.

Accordingly, any derivative product that is characterized as stock or pass-through equity may raise U.S. withholding tax concerns.

Bifurcation

Finally, each component of a bifurcated product should be analyzed to determine whether a U.S. withholding tax risk exists in connection with distributions made with respect to such a component.

Passive Foreign Investment Companies

In general, federal income tax law taxes income when it is *recognized*. Ordinarily, property must be sold or transferred or payments of income, such as interest, original issue discount, or dividends, must be accrued or received in order for a person to be subject to federal income tax with respect to such amounts.[251] Except with respect to property subject to the mark-to-market rules, a taxpayer does not ordinarily recognize income based on the mere appreciation in the value of the property it owns. Instead, the taxpayer must generally sell or otherwise dispose of the property in order to become subject to tax on the amount of any gain recognized.

Taxpayers took advantage of the concept of "recognition" with respect to non-U.S. investments by investing in financial products structured to avoid ongoing distributions to U.S. investors (which would have been subject to U.S. tax, since the receipt of such distributions would trigger income recognition for federal income tax purposes). Instead, the non-U.S. investments were designed so that current earnings were not distributed but were reinvested offshore. Thus, although the non-U.S. investments appreciated in value due to the reinvestment of current earnings, U.S. taxation was avoided because the income was never distributed to the investors. Because ongoing U.S. taxation was avoided, the amount available for reinvestment each year was larger (although such earnings may have been subject to applicable taxes of foreign countries) and therefore, the compounded effect of reinvesting a greater amount each year substantially increased the rate of appreciation of the investment. When the U.S. investor desired to recognize its gain, it would sell the investment. Thus, by developing structures that deferred current federal income taxation by delaying income distributions and therefore U.S. income tax liability, the investor's return was substantially enhanced.

Because this deferral technique resulted in the ongoing reinvestment of a U.S. investor's assets outside of the U.S. and beyond the reach of U.S. taxation, Congress ultimately considered the technique abusive and enacted the "passive foreign investment company" (PFIC) rules.

While the PFIC rules are complex, and a thorough discussion of them is beyond the scope of this chapter, this section provides a general understanding of when PFIC concerns may arise and the basic consequences of the PFIC rules. In the context of derivative products, the PFIC rules should be relevant only if a U.S. investor holds a

---

251 The mark-to-market rules discussed in an earlier section of this chapter are a notable exception to the normal income recognition rules. The original issue discount rules discussed earlier provide for the recognition of amounts which economically represent interest on debt as such income accrues.

derivative product that is characterized as "stock" in an entity that is a non-U.S. corporation.

An entity is considered a PFIC if it is a non-U.S. corporation that satisfies either an income test or an asset test.[252] The income test is satisfied if 75 percent or more of the gross income of the corporation for its tax year is "passive income."[253] The asset test is satisfied if the average percentage of the value of the corporation's assets held during the tax year that produce passive income or that are held for the production of passive income is at least 50 percent.[254] Passive income is defined for these purposes by reference to the definition of foreign personal holding company income, which includes dividends; interest; royalties; rents; the excess of gains over losses from sales or exchanges of certain income-generating property; interests in partnerships, trusts, or REMICs or property that does not give rise to income; any taxable income that consists of the excess of gains over losses from transactions (including futures, forwards, and similar transactions) in any commodities (but excluding gains or losses that arise out of bona fide hedging transactions reasonably necessary to the conduct of any business by a producer, processor, merchant, or handler of a commodity, in the manner in which such business is customarily and usually conducted by others); are active business gains or losses from the sale of commodities by an active producer, processor, merchant, or handler of commodities, or are foreign currency gains or losses attributable to Section 988 transactions; the excess of foreign currency gains over foreign currency losses (which is not excluded as described above); and income equivalent to interest.[255] The PFIC rules also include a "look-through" rule under which the assets of other foreign corporations in which a foreign corporation has an investment that exceeds 25 percent (in value) in such other corporations must be analyzed to see if the foreign corporation meets either the income test or the asset test.[256] The look-through rule is particularly troubling for two basic reasons—first, by looking at the assets of the entities in which the foreign corporation has investments it makes it more likely that the foreign corporation will be classified as a PFIC. Second, it is difficult for an investor to consider prospectively, since it may be difficult to obtain the information regarding the assets and income of the foreign corporation and the assets and income of each of the corporations in which it holds an investment interest, which is necessary to apply the income test and asset test for purposes of determining whether the foreign corporation is a PFIC.

---

252 Section 1296(a).
253 Section 1296(a)(1).
254 Section 1296(a)(2).
255 Section 1296(b)(1), which cross references Section 954(c). However, the following types of income are excluded from the definition of passive income: (1) income which is derived from the active conduct of a banking business by an institution licensed to do business as a bank in the U.S. (or any corporation, to the extent provided in regulations), (2) income which is derived in the active conduct of an insurance business and which would be subject to tax under Subchapter L of the Internal Revenue Code if it were a U.S. corporation, and (3) income which is interest, dividend, rent, or royalty, which is received or accrued from a related person (within the meaning of Section 954(d)(3)) to the extent such income is properly allocable (under IRS regulations) to income of such related person which is not passive income. Section 1296(b)(2).
256 Section 1296(c).

If a U.S. person holds stock in a PFIC, a complex set of rules applies that are intended to eliminate the tax benefit relating to the deferral of current taxation.[257] These rules are mechanical and are particularly complex. They may result in a substantial tax liability, since they are intended to fully negate any tax benefit associated with the reinvestment of earnings offshore. These rules are triggered upon the receipt of dividends or other distributions by the investor or the sale of stock.[258]

In order to avoid the imposition of these complex rules, a "qualified electing fund election" may be made.[259] The investor, rather than the PFIC, makes the election.[260] Once made, the election applies for subsequent years and cannot be revoked without IRS consent.[261] In addition, in the case of an investor who makes a qualified electing fund election with respect to stock in a PFIC, the investor can elect to recognize gain based on the value of its shares as of the first day of the tax year for which the election is made.[262] If an investor makes this election, the recognized gain is subject to tax under the PFIC rules referenced above and thereafter the investor recognizes income under the special rules applicable to qualified electing funds.

Because the qualified electing fund election is made on an investor-by-investor basis, a qualified electing fund is defined as any PFIC (1) with respect to which the investor has made the necessary election and (2) which complies with IRS requirements intended to assist in the determination of the PFIC's income and net capital gain by the investor and the IRS.[263]

If an investor makes a qualified electing fund election, the investor is taxed each year on its pro rata share of the ordinary earnings and net capital gains of the qualified electing fund, without regard to whether such income is distributed to the investor.[264] Thus, if an investor makes a qualified electing fund election, it becomes subject to current taxation with respect to the investor's pro rata share of the income and gains of the PFIC. The benefit of the election is that the investor does not need to apply the complex rules that are intended to eliminate the benefit of off-shore deferral and that would ordinarily apply if a qualified electing fund election were not made.[265]

In general, an investor should be careful to avoid investments in entities classified as PFICs, due to the potential tax liabilities associated therewith, unless a qualified electing fund election can be made. Because the election can be made only if the PFIC provides the information necessary to comply with IRS requirements referenced above, an investor should make certain that the entity can and will provide such information. Moreover, because the investor is taxed on its portion of income earned by the entity on an ongoing basis if the election is made, the investor should

---

257 Section 1291.
258 Section 1291(a)(1) and (2).
259 See Sections 1291(d)(1) and 1295.
260 Section 1295(a)(1). This is appropriate because the investor is a U.S. taxpayer, while it is presumed that the PFIC is not.
261 Section 1295(b)(1).
262 Section 1291(d)(2).
263 Section 1295(a).
264 Section 1293(a)(1), (b). Income from the qualified electing fund is determined based on the tax year of the shareholder in which or with which the tax year of the qualified electing fund ends. Section 1293(a)(2).
265 Section 1291(d)(1).

consider whether distributions will be received from the entity on an ongoing basis in an amount that will at least satisfy the resultant U.S. tax liabilities.

Tax-Exempt Derivatives

Derivative products are used by participants in the municipal markets. Interest rate swaps, caps, and floors can be used by issuers of and obligors on municipal bonds to manage the interest rate risks associated with issuing municipal bonds. Tax-exempt bonds with derivative-like interest rate terms can provide investors with tax-exempt income while also giving investors enhanced rates of return or hedging features. Investors that desire short-term tax-exempt securities may invest in "synthetic" tax-exempt securities that replicate the characteristics of conventional floating-rate demand bonds when the conventional bonds are in short supply. Each of these basic product types raises a number of potential issues.[266] For example, issuers must consider the impact of derivative products on the compliance with the arbitrage yield restriction and arbitrage rebate rules of Section 148 of the Code that must be satisfied in order for interest on the bonds to qualify as tax-exempt. Treas. Reg. Section 1.148-4(h) provides specific guidance in this regard. Investors must consider whether amounts received from these products are treated as taxable, rather than tax-exempt, interest. This analysis is complex, with little guidance provided by the IRS. Finally, synthetic products raise a question regarding whether the structures result in a taxable entity that could be subject to entity-level taxation that would adversely affect distributions to investors. A thorough discussion of the complexities regarding the taxation of municipal market tax-exempt derivative products is unfortunately beyond the scope of this chapter.[267]

Deductibility of Expenses

In connection with the acquisition or ongoing ownership of a derivative product, the potential cash flow available to the investor may be reduced by certain expenses. Depending upon the nature of the derivative (*i.e.,* stock, debt, option, etc.), the nature of the entity that issued the derivative (*e.g.,* the classification of the issuing entity as a trust, partnership, or corporation) and the nature of the expense, these expenses may not be deductible by the investor, and may result in so-called "phantom income" (*i.e.,* taxable income in excess of the amount of cash income distributed to the investor).

For example, Section 67 provides that an individual can deduct "miscellaneous itemized deductions" only to the extent that the total amount of such deductions for any tax year exceeds 2 percent of the individual's adjusted gross income for such year. Section 67(c) essentially provides that indirect deductions incurred by pass-through

---

266 *See generally* Steven D. Conlon, Vincent M. Aquilino & Dale S. Collinson, *Tax Law Fundamentals of Tax-Exempt Derivatives*, 55 TAX NOTES 381 (April 20, 1992); Steven D. Conlon, Vincent M. Aquilino, Dale S. Collinson, M. John Trofa & W. Scott Jardine, *Tax-Exempt Derivatives and Municipal Swaps: Special Considerations*, 1993 BOND ATTORNEYS' WORKSHOP (1993).

267 *See id.;* STEVEN D. CONLON & VINCENT M. AQUILINO, TAX-EXEMPT DERIVATIVES: A GUIDE TO LEGAL CONSIDERATIONS FOR LAWYERS, FINANCE PROFESSIONALS, AND MUNICIPAL ISSUERS (1994 American Bar Association Urban, State, and Local Government Law Section).

entities must be taken into account under these rules.[268] This rule effectively requires an individual investor to "gross up" the amount of income received from pass-through entities by the allocable amount of expenses incurred by the entity that would qualify as miscellaneous itemized deductions if incurred directly by the individual. Thus, Section 67 may have relevance to the extent that the derivative product provides for the ongoing payment of expenses and if the derivatives are sold to individuals (or pass-through entities, the interests of which are held by individuals). It is important to note that Section 67(c)(2) provides that the gross up rule does not apply with respect to "publicly offered regulated investment companies."[269]

Section 265 disallows deductions if an investor receives tax-exempt income. The scope of this disallowance depends upon the type of taxpayer and the nature of the deduction. If a derivative product generates tax-exempt income, an investor should consider the impact of Section 265. Of special concern to mutual funds is Section 265(a)(3), which imposes a special disallowance rule on regulated investment companies. This rule essentially subjects *all* expenses of a regulated investment to pro rata disallowance, based upon the relative proportion of tax-exempt income received by the regulated investment company to the total amount of income received by it (excluding capital gain net income).

As discussed above, Section 263(g) provides that certain interest and carrying charges relating to a position in a "straddle" (as defined in Section 1092(c)) cannot be deducted and must instead be capitalized.

Foreign Sourcing Issues

The "source" of income and expense items for federal income tax purposes can be very important for a number of reasons. For example, U.S.-source income that is paid to a non-U.S. investor may be subject to U.S. withholding tax, while foreign-source income is not subject to U.S. withholding tax.[270] In addition, the source of income and expense items may be important to U.S. investors that conduct their business in foreign countries. U.S. federal income tax law includes complex rules governing the U.S. taxation of foreign income, and the source of income and expense is of fundamental importance in applying those rules. The sourcing rules may be important to an investor because they will be used in the computation of foreign tax credit limitations, which may restrict the amount of foreign tax credits that the U.S. taxpayer can utilize to reduce its U.S. tax liabilities. The sourcing rules and their impact are beyond the scope of this chapter.[271] However, the sourcing of income and expenses associated with derivative products may be significant to certain investors and should be considered in such cases.

---

268 *See* Temp. Treas. Reg. Section 1.67-2T.
269 Many, but not all, mutual funds qualify for this special rule. Accordingly, the general concerns regarding the impact of Section 67(c) on the ownership of derivative products do not apply to mutual funds that invest in such securities, provided that such funds qualify as publicly offered regulated investment companies for purposes of the rule.
270 *See* the reference to "gross income from sources within the United States" set forth in Section 1441 of the Code.
271 The basic sourcing rules are contained in Sections 861 through 865.

Unrelated Business Tax

Tax-exempt organizations (which are generally exempt from federal income tax pursuant to Section 501) must nevertheless pay "unrelated business tax" on their "unrelated business taxable income."[272] Thus, an important consideration for tax-exempt organizations in evaluating a potential investment in a derivative product is whether the investment will result in unrelated business tax liability. Section 512(b) lists various categories of investment-type income that is excluded from the definition of unrelated business taxable income and therefore, is not generally subject to tax. However, there were originally concerns regarding whether income earned on interest rate swaps, caps, floors, and similar contracts would be subject to unrelated business tax because such income was not explicitly listed as a type of investment income excluded from the definition of unrelated business taxable income. In July 1992, final regulations were issued that explicitly treat "income from notional principal contracts (as defined in Treasury Regulations 26 CFR 1.863-7 or regulations issued under section 446)" as investment income excludible from the definition of unrelated business taxable income.[273]

Although investment income is not ordinarily subject to unrelated business tax, such income is subject to tax if the investment generating the income is considered "debt-financed property" within the meaning of Section 514.[274] Thus, tax-exempt organizations should consider whether income from their investments becomes subject to unrelated business tax as a result of the debt-financed property rule. Derivative products and related transactions should be reviewed by the investor for the existence of loans that could trigger the application of this rule.

CONCERNS FOR SPECIAL TYPES OF TAXPAYERS

There are a number of taxpayers—such as charitable organizations, pension and profit-sharing plans, mutual funds qualifying as "regulated investment companies" (RICs), real estate investment trusts (REITs), real estate mortgage investment conduits (REMICs), S corporations, different types of insurance companies, banks, savings and loans, and co-ops—that are subject to special federal income tax rules.[275] In addition, nonresident aliens and foreign corporations are subject to specific tax rules, and a number of types of corporations are subject to special taxes (personal holding companies, corporations subject to accumulated earnings tax, controlled foreign corpora-

---

272 *See* Sections 511 and 512.

273 Treas. Reg. Section 1.512(b)-1(a)(1). Note that the final regulations are a substantial improvement over the proposed regulations that were published by the IRS on September 3, 1991 (the "Proposed UBTI Regulations"). 56 Fed. Reg. 43,571 (September 3, 1991). The preamble to the Proposed UBTI Regulations included a proposed form of published revenue ruling that addressed the UBTI consequences of interest rate and currency swap transactions. For a discussion of concerns raised under the Proposed UBTI Regulations, *see ABA Swap Regulations Report, supra* note 13, at 17-18.

274 *See* Section 512(b)(4).

275 *See generally* Sections 401-424 (pension and profit-sharing plans); Sections 501-528 (exempt organizations); Sections 581-597 (banking institutions); Sections 801-848 (insurance companies); Sections 851-855 (regulated investment companies); Sections 860A-860G (real estate mortgage investment conduits); Sections 1361-1379 (S Corporations); and Sections 1381-1388 (cooperatives).

tions, and domestic international sales corporations).[276] Moreover, federal income tax law provides for an alternative minimum tax, which is computed differently from the way in which taxable income is ordinarily computed for federal income tax purposes. In particular, 75 percent of the "adjusted current earnings" of a corporation ("earnings" are a special federal income tax measure of economic income) that are not otherwise included in the taxable income of the corporation must be included in the computation of the corporation's alternative minimum tax liability.[277]

Given the diversity of rules that may govern particular taxpayers, it is not practical to discuss all of the special rules that apply to each type of entity or the concerns that may arise depending upon the specific derivative product that they may acquire. However, investors should make certain that they understand the tax rules that apply to them and should consider whether, because of special tax rules that may apply, the characterization and timing of income and expense recognition associated with a derivative transaction may have adverse consequences. For example, tax-exempt organizations are subject to tax on income with respect to "debt-financed property."[278] Depending upon how a derivative is characterized, this rule may apply. Similarly, a mutual fund must satisfy certain tests relating to the character of its income, the diversification of its assets, and the timing of income distributions to its shareholders in order to qualify as RIC and avoid double taxation.[279] Depending upon how a derivative is characterized, it may result in a mutual fund being unable to satisfy one of these tests.[280]

CONCLUSION

There is no uniform set of federal income tax rules applicable to derivative financial products. The products must be broken down into their tax components, of which there may be several. Derivative products with *identical* economic consequences may break down into different tax components, potentially resulting in significantly different tax consequences to the investor. Finally, different investors, because of their particular tax situation (*i.e.,* need to offset capital gains or losses, whether they are subject to the alternative minimum tax or whether they are a bank, mutual fund, tax-exempt organization, etc., subject to special federal income tax rules) should closely examine whether a particular derivative product, because of the investor's special tax considerations, results in adverse tax consequences that are not discernible by merely

---

276 *See generally* Sections 531-537 (accumulated earnings tax); Sections 541-547 (personal holding companies); Sections 551-558 (foreign personal holding companies); Sections 921-927 (foreign sales corporations); Sections 951-964 (controlled foreign corporations); and Sections 991-997 (domestic international sales corporations).
277 Section 56(g). It is important to note that certain types of corporations such as regulated investment companies, real estate investment trusts, S corporations, and real estate mortgage investment conduits are not subject to this adjustment. Section 56(g)(6).
278 *See* Section 514.
279 *See* Sections 851(b)(1), (b)(4) and 852(a).
280 *See* Steven D. Conlon & Suzanne M. Russell, *Tax Considerations for Mutual Funds Investing in Asset-Backed and Derivative Securities,* 71 TAXES 12 (January 1993). *See generally* RICHARD M. HERVEY, TAXATION OF REGULATED INVESTMENT COMPANIES (10 T.M.P.) (1987).

assuming that the "normal" tax treatment applies. Unfortunately, we have seen problems in this regard in a number of circumstances.

Our goal was to set forth the basic U.S. federal income tax rules that may be relevant to an investor in understanding the tax treatment of different derivative products. The lack of uniform rules and the diversity of the products has hampered our ability to provide short, direct guidance. Hopefully, this chapter will be helpful in analyzing and understanding the issues inherent in a tax analysis of derivative products. The Appendix to this chapter provides a list of ten questions that an investor should consider in analyzing the tax consequences of investing in a derivative financial product.

APPENDIX

Ten Basic Tax Questions That an Investor Acquiring a Derivative Product Should Consider

1. What is the tax characterization of the product?
   (Stock, debt, pass-through equity, option, swap, etc.)

2. Is there a risk of entity-level taxation relating to the financial product that could affect anticipated cash flows or the character of distributions?
   (A risk that the entity will be taxed as a corporation, including taxable mortgage pool and publicly traded partnership risks.)

3. What is the likelihood that taxable income will be recognized in a manner inconsistent with the timing of cash receipts on the investment?
   (Do special rules such as the "mark-to-market," OID, or option rules apply?)

4. Will special rules affect the character of, or disallow the deductibility of, expenses relating to the investment?
   (Do the straddle capitalization rules, option, tax-exempt bond expense, market discount, or other disallowance rules apply?)

5. What type of tax reporting information will be provided?

6. Will any of the following special rules apply?

   —original issue discount rules
   —mark-to-market rules
   —foreign currency rules
   —U.S. withholding tax rules
   —straddle rules
   —notional principal contract rules

7. What is the character of gains, losses, or income associated with the product?

8. Will special rules result in the disallowance or deferral of losses?
   (the straddle rules; the wash sale rules)

9. What is the level of comfort that counsel or the person marketing the product is providing to the buyer regarding these issues?

10. What are the state tax consequences relating to investing in the product?

    In addition, investors should always consider whether they are subject to special tax rules (such as banks, insurance companies, or mutual funds).

CHAPTER 43

Accounting and Financial Reporting for Derivatives and Synthetics

Robert H. Herz
Partner
Coopers & Lybrand

> Accounting is a system that feeds back information to organizations and individuals, which they can use to reshape their environment.[1]

INTRODUCTION

The accounting and financial reporting environment plays a critical role in designing new derivative and synthetic products, implementing new strategies with regard to these products, and evaluating the results of using these products. While accounting rule makers have been hard pressed to keep pace with the rapid development of new products, a number of pronouncements covering accounting for forwards, futures, and options exists. However, the authoritative literature represents a somewhat piecemeal, and often internally inconsistent, set of rules on the subject. Accordingly, the Financial Accounting Standards Board (FASB) continues to work on a major project on financial

---

1 Kieso, Donald E., and Jerry J. Weygandt, *Intermediate Accounting* New York: John Wiley & Sons, 1989, p. 4.

instruments[2] and off-balance-sheet financing, the goal of which is to develop a more comprehensive and consistent framework for accounting for all financial instruments, including derivatives and synthetics. Because of the complexity of the issues involved, specifically with regard to the recognition and measurement issues, the FASB decided that an interim step, improved disclosure about financial instruments, was necessary.

In this regard, two Statements of Financial Accounting Standards (SFAS), Nos. 105 and 107, have been issued. The application of these two pronouncements will be covered later. SFAS No. 105 and SFAS No. 107 did not alter the existing accounting practices; however, they did mandate much more extensive disclosure regarding financial instruments in general, and derivatives in particular. Moreover, as discussed at the end of this chapter, the FASB is currently considering further disclosure requirements relating to derivatives.

The primary goal of accounting is to produce relevant information that is reliable, neutral, and capable of being compared among different entities. Also, embedded in accounting theory is the belief that the costs of obtaining information should not exceed the benefits (broadly defined) of such information.[3] The "matching principle," under which gains and losses on related items should be recognized in the same period, is also important, as it underlies hedge accounting practices.

Accounting theory has traditionally been based on the notion of historical cost. Accountants have traditionally relied upon arms-length transactions to report the value of assets and liabilities. Lately, however, with the perceived increased riskiness of the investment portfolios of many financial institutions, there has been increasing pressure from regulators and Congress toward the use of fair value accounting for financial assets and liabilities. Moreover, advocates of mark-to-market or fair value accounting for financial instruments argue that this is more relevant to users of financial statements than measurements based on historical cost. Such mark-to-market accounting for financial instruments has traditionally been followed by broker-dealers, swap dealers, investment companies, hedge funds, and pension funds who generally report unrealized gains and losses on securities and financial instruments as part of the current period's earnings. Until recently, however, most other financial institutions such as banks, thrifts, and insurance companies, as well as commercial and industrial compa-

---

2 "Financial instruments" have been defined by the FASB in various pronouncements as follows: A financial instrument is cash, evidence of an ownership interest in an entity, or a contract that both:

a. Imposes on one entity a contractual obligation (1) to deliver cash or another financial instrument to a second entity or (2) to exchange other financial instruments on potentially unfavorable terms with the second entity

b. Conveys to that second entity a contractual right (1) to receive cash or another financial instrument from the first entity or (2) to exchange other financial instruments on potentially unfavorable terms with the first entity.

It should also be noted that although the thrust of the FASB's project has been directed toward financial instruments as defined above, similar accounting generally applies in the case of contracts that can be settled by delivery of physical commodities.

3 For example, see the discussion on SFAS No. 107. Under that pronouncement disclosures are to be made to the extent that the costs of computing "fair market value" are practicable, i.e., the costs do not exceed the benefits.

nies, generally carried most of their securities on a historical cost or lower of cost or market basis. However, the issuance by the FASB of Statement of Financial Accounting Standards (SFAS) No. 115, *Accounting for Certain Investments in Debt and Equity Securities*, in May 1993, dramatically changes this. As discussed later in this chapter, starting in 1994, even these "non mark-to-market" entities will now have to carry significant portions of their debt securities and all of their marketable equity portfolios on a market or fair value basis. This change is bound to have an impact, particularly on banks, thrifts, and insurance companies, both in reported earnings and capital and in the way they invest in, trade, and hedge their securities portfolios.

This chapter will cover the existing accounting and disclosure rules and practices applicable to investors in and users of derivatives and synthetics, as well as the FASB's ongoing efforts in this area and current SEC views on derivatives. The rules applicable to mark-to-market entities such as pension funds, mutual funds, hedge funds, broker-dealers, to financial institutions such as banks, thrifts, and insurance companies, and to industrial and commercial enterprises will be covered.

Transactions that are entered into to hedge the risks associated with other transactions and that meet specific requirements qualify for a special accounting treatment commonly referred to as "hedge accounting." Hedge accounting will be discussed in detail later in this chapter; briefly, though, accounting for a transaction as a hedge generally means that the gains or losses from the hedge position are recognized in the same period as losses or gains on the hedged item.

Increasingly, companies are using derivatives in connection with cash market positions to produce so called "synthetic instruments" that replicate the economic attributes of a single recognizable instrument. The key accounting issue is whether the individual instruments comprising the synthetic should be accounted for separately or as one combination based on the synthesis.

Another important issue that merits some discussion is the netting of positions. As "swap webs" become increasingly entangled, participants in the derivatives market are seeking to "net-out" their positions. For the accountant, a key issue emerges in presenting the financial statements and related footnote disclosures of the entity: should this netting of positions be done by product type, counterparty, duration, or otherwise, if at all?

The chapter will conclude with a discussion of the possible changes that loom on the horizon in the accounting and disclosure rules affecting derivatives and synthetics.

CURRENT AUTHORITATIVE GUIDELINES

Several sources of guidance on accounting for derivatives and synthetics exist. The Securities and Exchange Commission (SEC), under the authority of the Securities Act of 1933 and the Securities Exchange Act of 1934, has the power to set financial reporting guidelines for publicly traded companies. Although the SEC generally defers to the FASB and the Emerging Issues Task Force (EITF) of the FASB with regard to accounting treatment of new products, the Commission has taken a stand on certain hedging and disclosure issues related to derivatives and synthetics.

It is the FASB's mandate to narrow the range of alternative accounting principles and develop an underlying conceptual framework. As such, the Board has issued

Table 1. Key FASB Documents

Document	Title	Application
SFAS No. 52	*Foreign Currency Translation*	Hedge accounting with regard to foreign currency transactions including forwards and currency swaps
SFAS No. 80	*Accounting for Futures Contracts*	Establishes standards of accounting and reporting for futures contracts
SFAS No. 105	*Disclosure of Information about Financial Instruments with Off-Balance-Sheet Risk and Financial Instruments with Concentrations of Credit Risk*	Disclosures relating to financial instruments with off-balance-sheet exposure and concentrations of credit risk
SFAS No. 107	*Disclosures about Fair Value of Financial Instruments*	Requires disclosure of fair value of financial instruments
SFAS No. 115	*Accounting for Certain Investments in Debt and Equity Securities*	Accounting for debt and marketable equity securities
FIN No. 39	*Offsetting of Amounts Related to Certain Contracts*	Right of offset with regard to derivatives transactions executed with the same counterparty

several pronouncements that apply to derivative products, the most important of which are shown in Table 1.

As previously noted, SFAS No. 115 covers the accounting for debt securities and marketable equity securities (other than those accounted for under the equity method or as investment in consolidated subsidiaries), for enterprises in industries that do not have specialized accounting practices for these items. Therefore, it covers most commercial and industrial companies and financial institutions such as banks, thrifts, and insurance companies, but it does not apply to broker-dealers, swap dealers, pension and hedge funds, or investment companies.

The major requirements of SFAS No. 115 are discussed in the next section, "Overview of Industry Practices," because they impact not only on the accounting by the affected entities for their debt and marketable equity securities, but also on the accounting for the derivatives used in connection with hedging or yield enhancement of these securities.

SFAS Nos. 52 and 80 are discussed in the section on hedging. FASB Interpretation No. 39 (FIN No. 39) on netting of positions in the balance sheet is discussed later. The application of the two principal disclosure pronouncements, SFAS Nos. 105 and 107, also is detailed later in the chapter.

The American Institute of Certified Public Accountants (AICPA) offers practical guidance, although not authoritative pronouncements, to the profession with regard to accounting and financial reporting. The AICPA issues Statements of Position (SOPs) and industry accounting guides, which assist in the planning of audit engagements, the application of FASB pronouncements, and the dissemination of generally accepted industry accounting practices. The AICPA also publishes issues papers on accounting topics, one of which, Issues Paper No. 86-2, *Accounting for Options,* which although not recognized as authoritative, is often relied upon with regard to accounting for options and option strategies.

Finally, a very important source of guidance is the consensus opinions reached by the Emerging Issues Task Force of the FASB. In June 1984, the FASB established the EITF as part of its plan to provide timely guidance on implementation questions and emerging accounting issues. The 15-member Task Force includes representatives of major public accounting firms, smaller public accounting firms, the Financial Executive's Institute, the National Association of Accountants, and the Business Roundtable. The Chief Accountant of the SEC attends the Task Force meetings as an observer, and the FASB's Director of Research and Technical Activities is the Task Force's chairman. Consensus by the Task Force is intended to indicate that significant diversity in practice is not expected on a given issue (three dissenting votes precludes consensus on a given issue). Moreover, EITF consensuses are regarded as authoritative and as part of generally accepted accounting principles by auditors and by the staff of the SEC. It is noteworthy that over half of the issues dealt with by the EITF since its inception have related to financial instruments and new financial products, including many issues dealing specifically with derivatives and synthetics. See Table 2 for the most important EITF issues in this regard.

**Table 2.	Key EITF Documents**

Document	Title	Application
EITF No. 84-36	*Interest Rate Swap Transactions*	Provides guidance rather than authoritative rules on interest rate swaps
EITF No. 90-17	*Hedging Foreign Currency Risks with Purchased Options*	As described in title
EITF No. 91-1	*Hedging Intercompany Foreign Currency Risks*	As described in title
EITF No. 91-4	*Hedging Foreign Currency Risks with Complex Options and Similar Transactions*	As described in title

OVERVIEW OF INDUSTRY PRACTICES

The primary accounting distinction with regard to treatment of financial instruments, including derivatives and synthetics, is based on whether or not the entity utilizes market or fair value or historic cost when accounting for financial instruments. This varies by industry and, as discussed below for those entities covered by SFAS No. 115, it also depends on how a particular security is classified.

Brokers and dealers in securities, swap dealers, investment companies, hedge funds, and pension plans generally carry all of their investments at market or fair value. For the most part, the accounting treatment of financial instruments does not differ among these market value entities. Thus, the following excerpt from the *Audit of Brokers and Dealers in Securities* on accounting for options typifies the accounting by these market value entities:

> [market value entities] carry all securities at market or fair value, and it is appropriate that options positions also be reflected at market or fair value. The cost or proceeds from sales of options are subsequently adjusted to the current market (marked-to-market) or fair value of the options, and as in the case of other securities, any gain or loss is included in the results of operations. The current market value of exchange-traded options generally should be based on the quoted bid and offer prices. The fair value of unlisted options should be determined by the broker's or dealer's management which considers the price of the underlying securities, the liquidity of the market, and the time remaining to expiration date. The process of adjusting option positions to market or fair value gives appropriate accounting recognition to the option premium.[4]

This market/fair value applies to these entities whether the derivatives or synthetics are used for trading or speculative purposes, as part of a yield enhancement or arbitrage strategy, or even for longer-term investment purposes.

For most other entities, SFAS No. 115 is the key pronouncement covering the accounting for their financial assets. Some of the important requirements of this pronouncement include:

- Debt securities must be classified into three categories—held-to-maturity, trading, and available-for-sale—while marketable equity securities, including equity options, must be classified into two categories—trading and available-for-sale. Debt securities covered by SFAS No. 115 include mandatory redeemable preferred stocks, securitized loans, collateralized mortgage obligations (CMOs) and CMO residuals, interest-only and principal-only securities (I/Os and P/Os).

- Investments in debt securities classified as held-to-maturity are, consistent with prior practice, generally carried at amortized cost. However, the new rules under SFAS No. 115 make it more difficult to classify debt securities as held-to-maturity. Not only must the entity have the positive intent and ability to hold the debt securities to maturity, but SFAS No. 115 explicitly prohibits an entity from classifying such securities as held-to-maturity if they might be sold in response to changes in market interest rates, prepayment risk, the enterprise's liquidity needs, foreign exchange risk, tax planning strategies, or other similar factors.

---

4 *Audits of Brokers and Dealers in Securities* (New York: AICPA, 1985), pp. 84-5.

■ Trading securities (both debt and equity) are carried at market value with unrealized gains and losses included currently in income.

■ Any securities (both debt and equity) that are neither to be held-to-maturity nor acquired for trading purposes are classified as available-for-sale with unrealized gains and losses reported in a separate component of stockholders' equity until realized or until the security is judged to have suffered an "other-than-temporary" decline in value.

■ If the decline in fair value is judged to be other than temporary, the cost basis of the individual security should be written down to fair value with a charge to earnings, i.e., the writedown is accounted for as a realized loss.

■ Gains and losses, both realized and unrealized on qualifying hedges of securities positions should follow the accounting for the related security. For example, gains and losses on hedges of trading securities are included currently in income, while those relating to hedges of securities in the available-for-sale category are included in stockholders' equity.

As a general rule, the accounting treatment of derivatives by commercial and industrial companies or by banks, thrifts, and insurance companies depends mainly on the purpose and designation of their use in a particular transaction. If specific criteria are met, hedge accounting treatment results. In other cases, primarily with regard to interest rate swaps that are used to alter the interest flows on interest-bearing liabilities or assets, another form of accounting known by a variety of names such as "swap accounting," "settlement accounting," or "synthetic alteration accounting" results. In other, more complex situations, other forms of synthetic instrument accounting might apply. Failing these, the company would generally be presumed to be entering into a speculative transaction, and, therefore, mark-to-market accounting with recognition of all gains and losses in current period's earnings would result.

Valuation Sources

The determination of market or fair value[5] for accounting purposes warrants discussion, since for many entities it is their basis of accounting for investments in derivatives and synthetics, and, even for those entities that do not carry these items on this basis, fair value is now a required disclosure under SFAS No. 107. Fair value is considered by the FASB to be the dollar value for which a given instrument would be willingly exchanged in a situation other than forced sale or liquidation. For traditional financial instruments (equities and listed futures, for example) this is not a difficult concept to apply. However, for thinly traded, nontraded, and/or customized financial products, fair value is not as readily determined. At many organizations, the traders may be the only ones who know how to compute the value of a particular financial instrument; however, it is obvious that traders should not be the ones who are valuing their own portfolios for purposes of financial reporting. The following is a hierarchy of sources

---

5 Market value, one form of fair value, based upon published prices reported by public exchanges, is generally regarded as the best indicator of fair value for most purposes, including financial reporting.

Exhibit 1. Determining Fair Value of Selected Derivatives

	External Sources					Internal Estimates			
	Public Exchange Markets	Dealer Markets	Quotation Services	Pricing Services	Specialists/Appraisers	Market Comparables	Internal Comparables	Present Values	Option Pricing Models
Hedging Instruments									
Futures Contracts	◆								
Swaps		◆	◆	◆	◆	◆		◆	
Options	◆	◆			◆	◆			◆
Forward Exchange Contracts		◆			◆	◆		◆	◆

and methods for determining the value of a particular financial instrument (see Exhibit 1 for a graphic depiction of this information):

External Valuation Sources

Public exchange markets. When available, the quoted price of an instrument on a public market generally provides the most reliable measure of fair value. Many equity and debt securities as well as certain derivative products, such as options and futures, trade in exchange markets. When a financial instrument is traded in an active market, its fair value is normally determined by reference to the last trade price.

Dealer markets or quotation services. Dealers trade a plethora of financial instruments for their own account. Generally, these dealers provide the last bid and ask. The bid and asking prices should be used to estimate the fair value of assets (long positions) and liabilities (short positions), respectively.

Quotations services gather quotes from dealers and report them—either electronically or in hard copy form—to other dealers and investors. Dealer prices and quotation services are generally available for most interest rate swaps and related derivatives.

Pricing services and other valuation specialists. Pricing services and other valuation specialists use a variety of sources and techniques. Pricing models are often proprietary; therefore, it is necessary to gain comfort with the service providing the quote. These services value thinly traded products, such as warrants on foreign equity.

Market comparable. This is an empirical pricing technique based on factors that can be objectively confirmed, such as yield curves and prices of similar securities for which quotes can be obtained. For example, a petroleum derivative future may not be actively traded on a public exchange. By developing a price relationship between a base commodity, such as West Texas Intermediate and the less widely traded Dubai, long-dated forward prices can be derived.

Internal Valuation Methods

Internal comparable. This technique utilizes prices currently charged by the entity for similar products. Recent sales of similar securities can provide a reasonable estimate of market value.

Present value of expected cash flows. Often, accountants must estimate the value of a given security by examining the expected cash flows, discounted by an appropriate rate. The discount rate used to calculate the present value should take into account both the current interest rate levels and the creditworthiness of the counterparty. This technique has obvious applications with regard to swaps.

Pricing models. Most swap and derivative products dealers have internal models, usually based on variations of the better-known option pricing models, such as Black-Scholes or the binomial model, to value many of their derivatives. This valuation approach, sometimes referred to as "mark-to-model," is often necessary to value the more esoteric or customized instruments in a portfolio, for example, over-the-counter options with features different from those traded on public exchanges, "knock-out" options, and long-dated or highly structured interest rate and currency swaps.

As noted in the July 1993 study by the Group of Thirty entitled *Derivatives: Practices and Principles*, the precise valuation techniques used by different dealers vary. The study recommends that derivatives portfolios of dealers be valued based either on mid-market price levels less specific adjustments, or on appropriate bid or offer levels. Where the mid-market approach is used, valuation adjustments should allow for expected future costs related to the portfolio, such as unearned credit spread to reflect credit risk, close-out costs associated with unmatched or unhedged instruments, investing and funding costs during the life of an instrument, and the administrative costs that will be incurred to administer the portfolio. Obviously, the combination of the use of often complex mathematical models to value the instruments, together with the adjustment of such values for some or all of the costs described above, can make the valuation of a swap dealer's portfolio of derivatives a very complex exercise.

By utilizing the above sources, those engaged in the preparation and audit of financial statements can determine appropriate values for most derivatives and synthetics. Exhibit 1 summarizes the alternative valuation methods for some common derivatives.

HEDGE ACCOUNTING

While, as previously noted, the U.S. accounting rules have developed over time in a somewhat piecemeal fashion and are currently in a state of flux, the following general principles apply:

- Derivatives used for trading or speculative purposes are "marked to market" with the resulting unrealized gains and losses included currently in income, whereas,

- "Hedge accounting" applies where certain specific criteria are met. As discussed below, these hedging criteria can differ depending on the particular derivative (e.g., foreign currency forwards or swaps vs. futures vs. options) being used to effect the hedge. Accordingly, an understanding of the various hedging criteria applicable to different types of derivatives is critical to those seeking to qualify for hedge accounting treatment.

In practice, whether a transaction qualifies for hedge accounting should be determined on a case-by-case basis. Before the appropriate accounting can be determined, however, the economics and purpose of the transaction must be fully understood.

Accounting for a transaction as a hedge generally means that the gains or losses from the hedge position are recognized in the same period as losses or gains on the hedged item. For example, if unrealized changes in the hedged item are included in income, the changes in the hedge will also be recognized in income as they occur. Alternatively, when the hedged item is an asset carried at lower of cost or market (for example, inventory), changes in the hedge should be recorded as an adjustment of the carrying amount of the hedged item (however, the hedge accounting adjustment cannot result in the asset being carried at higher than market). The deferred gain or loss on the hedge becomes part of the carrying amount of the hedged item that will be recognized when the item being hedged is disposed of (e.g., when inventory is sold).

In other words, hedge accounting is an extension of the matching principle in the sense that since the hedge and the hedged item are economically linked, it is appropriate to recognize gains or losses on the hedge in the same accounting period that losses or gains on the hedged item are recognized.

Although there is no comprehensive authoritative pronouncement that addresses accounting for transactions involving hedges, there is general agreement that hedging transactions are frequently accounted for differently than transactions for other purposes and that certain criteria must be met to account for a transaction as a hedge. The authoritative pronouncements, SFAS No. 52 and SFAS No. 80, provide hedging criteria for foreign currency transactions and transactions involving non-foreign-currency futures contracts, respectively. In addition, EITF Issues 90-7, 91-1, and 91-4 address hedging of foreign currency risk with purchased options, intercompany foreign currency risks, and foreign currency risks with complex options, and similar types of instruments. Analogy to these pronouncements may be utilized for transactions not covered therein (including forwards, options, and swaps).

Hedge Accounting Criteria

Criteria for hedge accounting generally include the following:

- The item to be hedged exposes the enterprise (or separate entity for a foreign currency transaction) to price, currency, or interest rate risk.
- The hedge position reduces the exposure (e.g., there is high correlation between changes in the market value of the hedge position and the inverse changes in market value of the hedged item).
- The hedge position is designated as a hedge.

There must be risk. The first criterion concerning exposure to risk means that hedge accounting cannot be applied to situations where there is deemed to be no risk. The purpose of hedging is to reduce risk, so without risk, hedge accounting is inappropriate. In situations without risk, gains, or losses from positions in hedge-type instruments cannot be deferred.

In this regard, SFAS No. 80 describes risk as "the sensitivity of an enterprise's income for one or more future periods to changes in market prices or yields of existing assets, liabilities, firm commitments, or anticipated transactions." The Statement recognizes that the specific circumstances that create risk can and do vary significantly from company to company; the hedge recognition criteria for accounting purposes depend on whether the risk ultimately affects income. Not all situations expose an enterprise to price or interest rate risk. A footnote to SFAS No. 80 cites the following example:

> An interest-bearing financial instrument that an enterprise will retain to maturity does not, in and of itself, create interest rate risk if the instrument's interest rate is fixed. The amount of cash inflows or outflows is certain (assuming no default) and is not affected by changes in market interest rates. Notwithstanding that the cash flows associated with the instrument are fixed, the enterprise may be exposed to interest rate risk if it has funded its assets with instruments having earlier maturities or repricing dates. Futures contracts may qualify as a hedge of a fixed-rate financial instrument the enterprise intends to hold to maturity if the maturity or repricing characteristics of the instrument contribute to the enterprise's overall asset-liability mismatch.

Following this example, a financial institution that funds short-term variable-rate assets with floating-rate debt of similar maturity may not be exposed to interest rate risk.

SFAS No. 80, dealing with futures contracts, and the consensus of the EITF Issue 90-17, dealing with purchased options, differ from SFAS No. 52 as to how risk should be assessed. SFAS No. 80 and the EITF Issue 90-17 generally require that for hedging instruments to be accounted for as a hedge, a risk condition must be present on an enterprise perspective. Determining whether a company's income is at risk requires evaluating whether a potential risk condition at one location or operating center is mitigated by conditions at another location or operating center. For example, a parent company with several subsidiaries should apply SFAS No. 80, using a total enterprise perspective if relevant information to assess risk on that basis is available. However, realizing that many large companies manage risk on a decentralized basis by business unit, SFAS No. 80 also permits risk assessment on that basis (i.e., by business unit). SFAS No. 52, in contrast, permits hedge accounting based on assessing risk on a transaction basis. For example, a U.S. parent may hedge a foreign currency commitment with a forward exchange contract even though a foreign subsidiary whose functional currency is the U.S. dollar may have a foreign currency balance equal and opposite to the commitment exposure of the parent and even though the parent itself may have offsetting exposures in the foreign currency.

Hedge position reduces exposure. The second criterion for hedge accounting concerns the correlation between the hedge position and changes in market value of the hedged item. This means that changes in the market value of the hedging instrument must track the changes in the market value of the hedged item. Under SFAS No. 52, this is not normally an issue, since that statement generally limits hedge accounting to hedges denominated in the same currency as the exposure being hedged (i.e., it does not generally permit cross-currency hedges). In contrast, SFAS No. 80 permits cross-hedging, and, therefore, demonstrating the effectiveness of a hedge is essential because it is the basis for entering into the hedge transaction in the first place (i.e., that the gain or loss on the hedged item will be offset by the loss or gain on the hedge). When determining whether high correlation is likely, an enterprise is required to consider such factors as historical correlation and variations in correlation that could be expected.

While companies may use a variety of approaches to evaluate expected future correlation, regression analysis is the statistical method most commonly used to measure this relationship. Regression analysis techniques examine historical data relevant to each variable and calculate the expected value of one variable based on the value of the other. The result is a measurement of the expected sensitivity of the movement in one variable to movement in another variable (this is referred to as the correlation coefficient). Once the correlation coefficient has been calculated, statistical analysis must be used to verify its strength, since knowing the strength of this coefficient is critical to a successful hedging program.

The strength of the correlation coefficient is indicated by the R-square statistic. An R-square statistic of 1 (its maximum value) means that 100 percent of a change in one variable can be explained by a change in the other variable. For example, if a 1 percent change in the value of item A triggers a 0.5 percent change in the value of item B and there is an R-square statistic of 0.90, there is a 90 percent assurance that if the value of item A moves 1 percent, the value of item B will move 0.5 percent. The price movements would then be said to be highly correlated. In this situation, selling futures contracts on item B that are twice the value of hedged item A will be highly effective in offsetting the effects of price changes on item A.

The assessment of correlation requires judgments that must be made on a case-by-case basis. Although measurement and analysis of correlation is an evolving process, and it is difficult to establish precise guidelines, a hedging instrument that is 80 percent or more correlated with the hedged item (i.e., that has an R-square statistic of 0.80 or higher) is generally considered to meet the test of "high correlation."

Indirectly related to the criterion regarding correlation is another difference between SFAS No. 80 and SFAS No. 52. Cross-hedging is a strategy where the hedging instrument's underlying item is different from the item being hedged. SFAS No. 80 permits cross-hedging as long as the high correlation requirement is met and there is a clear economic relationship between the item underlying the futures contract and the item being hedged. SFAS No. 52 permits cross-hedging only when it is not practical or feasible to hedge in a transaction denominated in the identical currency. So, for example, even if a company can demonstrate that it was economically hedged by entering into a forward exchange contract for Australian dollars to hedge its British-pound-denominated debt, SFAS No. 52 does not permit hedge accounting for the forward exchange contract because British pound forward exchange contracts are available.

Designation as hedge. The third criterion for hedge accounting is the designation of the position, by the entity entering into the transaction, as a hedge of specific items. The hedge must be initially designated as such to recognize gains or losses from the hedging position in the same accounting period as the losses or gains of the hedged item. In other words, it is not appropriate to wait until it is determined that a loss has occurred in a position and then at that time decide to defer the loss—the hedge should be designated "up front."

Indirectly relating to the designation criterion is another difference between SFAS No. 52 and SFAS No. 80. SFAS No. 80 permits hedging of firm commitments as well as anticipated transactions if the significant characteristics and expected terms of the anticipated transaction are identified and it is probable that the anticipated transaction will occur. SFAS No. 52 permits hedging of firm commitments but not of anticipated transactions. An example of an anticipatory hedge is a financial institution that purchases Treasury note futures contracts to lock in the yield on a Treasury note it expects to purchase in three months when cash becomes available. The institution may be able to designate the futures contracts as a hedge and defer the gains and losses on the futures contract until the Treasury note is purchased (at which time the deferred gain or loss will become part of the carrying value of the Treasury note). However, if that same financial institution entered into a forward exchange contract to hedge an anticipated borrowing it had arranged in the European market, it would not qualify for hedge accounting (i.e., it could not defer the gains or losses on the forward exchange contract) because the anticipated borrowing would not be viewed as a firm commitment under SFAS No. 52 (e.g., usually a legally enforceable obligation).

The lack of authoritative literature and the differences between SFAS No. 52 and SFAS No. 80 make it difficult to apply specific criteria to many hedging transactions. As discussed later in this chapter, the FASB is currently reviewing all hedge accounting rules. However, in the meantime, companies entering into transactions involving hedging instruments, particularly those not specifically covered by SFAS No. 52 and SFAS No. 80, should consult with their accounting advisers to determine whether hedge accounting is appropriate in their particular circumstances.

Purchased Foreign Currency Options

EITF Issue No. 90-17 permits hedge accounting for purchased foreign currency options (with little or no intrinsic value at the date of purchase) used to hedge anticipated transactions, provided that the conditions in SFAS No. 80 are met.

In evaluating these conditions, SFAS No. 52 establishes the nature of foreign currency risk that may be hedged for accounting purposes—that is, risk associated with transactions and commitments in currencies other than the transacting entity's functional currency. In addition, the exposure to foreign currency risk from anticipated transactions should be evaluated on an "enterprise basis," as defined in paragraph 4(a) of SFAS No. 80.

For a purchased option to qualify for hedge accounting, it must be probable that a high correlation will exist between the currency underlying the option contract and the currency in which the anticipated transaction is denominated. This correlation must exist at the time that the option is designated as a hedge and throughout the hedge period (or life of the option contract, if shorter). These criteria also permit hedge accounting using purchased options in highly correlated tandem currencies.

Guidance in paragraph 9 of SFAS No. 80 should be followed for purposes of identifying significant characteristics and expected terms of the anticipated transaction and assessing the probability that the anticipated transaction will occur. Judgment is required in determining if these conditions are met and that the likelihood of meeting such criteria diminishes the further into the future the anticipated transaction is expected to occur.

In connection with Issue No. 90-17, the EITF also discussed the propriety of hedge accounting in certain specific situations using purchased foreign currency options with little or no intrinsic value.

One situation addressed an enterprise that estimated its minimum probable foreign sales for the next several years and would like to reduce its exposure to the related foreign exchange risk. In this case, the propriety of hedge accounting depends on an assessment of the transactions using the SFAS No. 80 criteria described above.

Another situation addressed hedging by a U.S. parent of the net income of its foreign subsidiary. The foreign subsidiary generates revenues and incurs costs denominated in its functional currency. In this case, hedge accounting would not be appropriate because (1) the parent would not have foreign currency risk, as defined in SFAS No. 52, for its subsidiary's transactions denominated in the subsidiary's functional currency and (2) future net income does not qualify as an anticipated transaction because it is the net result of many transactions and accounting allocations.

Hedge accounting would not be appropriate in situations where foreign currency options are purchased as a "strategic" or "competitive" hedge, where the gains on the options are intended to offset lost operating profits from increased competitive pressure associated with exchange rate changes that benefit competitors. To qualify for hedge accounting, the options must be designated and effective as a hedge of a net investment in a foreign entity, a firm foreign currency commitment, or an anticipated foreign currency transaction.

Complex and Combination Options

EITF Issue No. 91-4, "Hedging Foreign Currency Risks with Complex Options and Similar Transactions," addresses the use of hedge accounting for those option transactions that were specifically excluded from EITF 90-17, such as deep-in-the-money purchased options, written options, options purchased and written as a unit (combination options), and similar transactions, including synthetic forwards, range forwards, and participating forwards. EITF 90-17 addressed only foreign currency options with little or no intrinsic value (the amount of advantage, if any, that would be realized by exercise of an option equal to the difference between the exercise price and the spot rate of the underlying currency). EITF 91-4 is limited to combinations of foreign currency options that are established as contemplated integral transactions, where the components are entered into at or about the same time, are designated as a unit, and have the same expiration date.

At the March 19, 1992, EITF meeting, the Chief Accountant of the SEC indicated that the SEC will object to the deferral of gains and losses arising from complex options and other similar transactions with respect to anticipated foreign currency transactions. Additionally, the Chief Accountant noted that the SEC's staff will object to deferral of losses with respect to written options because they believe they do not reduce but increase risk. The SEC's staff will not, however, object to deferral of gains on purchased options having little or no intrinsic value, as addressed in EITF Issue No. 90-17. As a result of EITF Issues 90-17 and 91-4, combined with the prohibition in SFAS No. 52 on hedging anticipated (but not firmly committed) foreign currency transactions, those seeking to hedge such anticipated transactions and receive "hedge accounting" are forced to use simple purchased options, which are generally more expensive than forwards or combination options.

Intercompany Foreign Currency Risk

EITF Issue 91-1 provides that transactions or commitments among members of a consolidated group with different functional currencies (i.e., intercompany transactions) can present foreign currency risk that may be hedged for accounting purposes. The appropriate accounting guidance depends on the type of hedging instrument used. The provisions of SFAS No. 52 must be applied to forward exchange contracts, foreign currency futures, and agreements that are essentially the same as forward exchange contracts. When hedging foreign currency commitments, SFAS No. 52 requires that both of the following conditions exist:

1. The foreign currency transaction must be designated as, and effective as, a hedge of a foreign currency commitment.

2. The foreign currency commitment must be firm.

In connection with the second condition, an intercompany foreign currency commitment may be considered firm if there is a firm commitment to a third party obligating the affiliates to comply with the terms of the intercompany agreement.

In the event that a third-party commitment is not present, a firm commitment exists only if the agreement is legally enforceable and performance is probable due to sufficiently large disincentives for nonperformance. Examples of disincentives for nonperformance include minority interests, existing laws or regulations, and fiduciary responsibilities that result in significant economic penalties to the consolidated entity for nonperformance. The specific facts and circumstances surrounding each transaction need to be assessed in determining whether disincentives for nonperformance are sufficiently large.

The guidance set forth in EITF Issue 90-17, discussed above, is also appropriate for hedges of intercompany transactions using purchased foreign currency options.

Illustrations of Hedge Accounting

Assuming a transaction qualifies for hedge accounting, how are the hedge accounting concepts applied? The following illustrations and discussions apply the hedge accounting concepts to the basic hedging tools: futures, forwards, swaps, and options.

Futures Contracts

As discussed earlier, SFAS No. 80 describes the accounting for a futures contract. It requires all futures contracts to be marked to market and, if serving as a hedge, to defer the gain or loss until the loss or gain on the hedged item is recognized. Accounting for a futures contract that is hedging an anticipated borrowing is illustrated by the following hypothetical transaction.

Situation. On May 2, 19X1, a manufacturer expects to borrow $10 million on May 20, 19X1, for 90 days, with an interest rate tied to LIBOR (London Interbank Offered Rate), to finance the acquisition of inventory. The manufacturer expects to renew the loan for an additional 90 days, repay half the loan in November, and roll over the $5 million balance for another 90 days. Ninety days later, it will roll this $5 million over again. The manufacturer is exposed to risk because an increase in interest rates before the loan is incurred or rolled over will increase its financing costs.

Hedge strategy. To lock in the 9 percent interest rate in effect on May 2, 19X1, for a period of one year, the manufacturer sells a strip of Eurodollar futures contracts that coincide with the dates when it expects to borrow and roll over the debt:

- Ten* June** 19X1 Eurodollar contracts are sold to lock in the interest rate on the $10 million to be borrowed on May 20, 19X1.

- Ten* September** 19X1 Eurodollar contracts are sold to lock in the interest rate on the $10 million loan when it is rolled over on August 18, 19X1.

- Five* December** 19X1 Eurodollar contracts are sold to lock in the interest rate on the $5 million when it is rolled over on November 16, 19X1.

- Five* March** 19X2 Eurodollar contracts are sold to lock in the interest rate on the $5 million when it is rolled over on February 14, 19X2.

    *Eurodollar futures contracts are sold in units of $1 million, each of which represents a certificate of deposit with a major London bank maturing in 90 days. Therefore, 10 contracts are needed to cover each 90-day $10 million.

    **These months represent the nearest relevant settlement months for which Eurodollar futures contracts are available.

Contracts are closed as the debt is actually borrowed or rolled over. Eurodollar futures contracts are expected to reduce the manufacturer's risk of loss, since the price of these contracts and the interest expense associated with the loan are highly correlated.

Hedge results. The company's position in the futures contract is illustrated in Table 3.

Table 3.   Hedge Results

Date	Cash Position	Futures Position	Margin Initial	Margin Variations[3]
May 2, 19X1		Sell 10 June 19X1 Eurodollar contracts @ 91.00[1]	$30,000[2]	
		Sell 10 Sept. 19X1 Eurodollar contracts @ 90.86		
		Sell 5 Dec. 19X1 Eurodollar contracts @ 90.62		
		Sell 5 Mar. 19X2 Eurodollar contracts @ 90.42		
May 20, 19X1	Borrow $10,000,000 @ 9.25%	Buy 10 June 19X1 Eurodollar contracts @ 90.64		$ 9,000
		Market values:		
		· 10 Sept. contracts–90.39		11,750
		· 5 Dec. contracts–90.18		5,500
		· 5 Mar. contracts–89.94		6,000
				$32,250
Aug. 18, 19X1	Roll $10,000,000 @ 10.18%	Buy 10 Sept. 19X1 Eurodollar contracts @ 89.59		$20,000
		Market values:		
		· 5 Dec. contracts–89.18		12,500
		· 5 Mar. contracts–88.92		12,750
				$45,250
Nov. 16, 19X1	Roll $5,000,000 @ 9.87%	Buy 5 Dec. 19X1 Eurodollar contracts @ 89.94		($ 9,500)
		Market values:		
		· 5 Mar. contracts–89.54		(7,750)
				($17,250)
Feb. 14, 19X2	Roll $5,000,000 @ 10.00%	Buy 5 Mar. 19X2 Eurodollar contracts @ 89.84		($ 3,750)

1   Eurodollar contracts are quoted using an index of 100 minus the annualized LIBOR for 90-day deposits. A quotation of 91.00 means the annualized LIBOR is 9.00 percent. A price change of one basis point (0.01 percent) equals $25.00 ($1,000,000 x 0.0001 × 90/360).

2   A margin deposit of $1,000 per contract was deposited with the broker, as required by the futures exchange.

3   Changes in market value of futures contracts will result in the requirement for increased (decreased) margin to be posted.

Calculating gains and losses on futures contracts. Because interest rates changed during the period covered by the futures contracts, the company incurs gains and losses equal to the increases and decreases in variation margin shown in the hedge results. The gains and losses on the futures contracts are the decreases or increases in their market value. For example, the gain of $32,250 as of May 20 is calculated as shown in Table 4.

Table 4

	June Contracts	Sept. Contracts	Dec. Contracts	Mar. Contracts
Market value on May 2	91.00	90.86	90.62	90.42
Market value on May 20	90.64	90.39	90.18	89.94
Market value change (in basis points)	36	47	44	48
Value per basis point	× $25	× $25	× $25	× $25
Market value decrease per contract	$900	$1,175	$1,100	$1,200
Number of contracts sold	× 10	× 10	× 5	× 5
Total gain on contracts as of May 20	$9,000	$11,750	$5,500	$6,000

Calculating hedge effectiveness. The basis gain or loss on a particular contract determines the overall effectiveness of that contract. The futures contract results are compared with the additional interest incurred because of rate changes. For example, the effectiveness of hedging the first rollover period is calculated as follows:

Additional interest cost:

Principal	$10,000,000
Change in rate (9% to 10.18%)	× 1.18%
Cost for 360 days	$ 118,000
Cost for 90 days	$ 29,500

Gains on Sept. futures contracts:

Gain through May 20	$ 11,750
Gain for May 20 through Aug. 18	20,000
	$ 31,750
Net basis gain	$ 2,250

This calculation shows that high correlation was achieved; the gain on the futures contracts offset 108 percent of the increased borrowing costs. The effective interest rate for this period as a result of the hedge can be calculated as follows:

Principal	$10,000,000
Target interest for 90 days (9%)	$ 225,000
Less basis gain	(2,250)
	$ 222,750

Effective rate for quarter:

$$\frac{\$222,750}{\$10,000,000 \times 90/360} = 8.91\%$$

Summary. The net futures gains realized by the company reduced its overall borrowing cost from what would have resulted had the company not hedged. The impact of the hedge results can be summarized as shown in Table 5.

Table 5

	May 20– Aug. 18	Aug. 19– Nov. 16	Nov. 17– Feb. 14	Feb. 15– May 16	Cumulative
Target interest (9%)	$225,000	$225,000	$112,500	$112,500	$675,000
Additional interest cost because of rate increases	6,250	29,500	10,875	12,500	59,125
Total interest paid	231,250	254,500	123,375	125,000	734,125
Gain on futures contracts	(9,000)	(31,750)	(8,500)	(7,250)	(56,500)
Net final interest cost	$222,250	$222,750	$114,875	$117,750	$677,625
Target rate on May 2	9.00%	9.00%	9.00%	9.00%	9.00%
Hedged rate	8.89%	8.91%	9.19%	9.42%	9.04%

Forward Exchange Contracts

To illustrate the accounting for forward exchange contracts (see Table 6), assume a company enters into a forward exchange contract to hedge a 90-day currency risk on its foreign-denominated zero-coupon borrowing.

There may be differing ways to apply SFAS No. 52 rules to the hypothetical transaction. The author believes that the method chosen should be one that best reflects the economics of the integrated nature of the borrowing and the forward contract. This objective is achieved by distinguishing between the two elements of the 90-day note, namely, the principal portion (representing the face amount less the unamortized discount) and the unamortized discount portion (representing the future commitment to pay interest expense), and by treating the corresponding amounts of the forward contract as hedges of each of the elements of the 90-day note.

Table 6.   Accounting Entries

	Debit	Credit
May 2, 19X1		
Amount due from broker	$30,000	
Cash		$30,000
(To record initial margin deposit)		
May 20, 19X1		
Cash	$10,000,000	
Loan payable		$10,000,000
(To record 90-day borrowing)		
May 2–May 20, 19X1		
Amount due from broker	$32,250	
Deferred gain on futures contracts		$32,250
(To record deferral of cumulative gain on futures contracts)		
May 21–Aug. 18, 19X1		
Interest expense	$222,250	
Deferred gain on futures contracts	9,000	
Cash		$231,250
(To amortize cumulative deferred gain on June contracts over the hedge period, and to record interest expense on the $10,000,000 borrowing)		
Amount due from broker	$45,250	
Deferred gain on futures contracts		$45,250
(To record deferral of gain on futures contracts since May 20, 19X1)		
Aug. 19–Nov. 16, 19X1		
Interest expense	$222,750	
Deferred gain on futures contracts	31,750	
Cash		$254,500
(To amortize cumulative deferred gain on Sept. contracts over the hedge period, and to record interest expense on the $10,000,000 borrowing that was rolled over on Aug. 18, 19X1)		
Deferred gain on futures contracts	$17,250	
Amount due from broker		$17,250
(To record loss on futures contracts since Aug. 18, 19X1, as a reduction of the deferred gain account)		

Table 6.　(Continued)

	Debit	Credit
Nov.16, 19X1		
Loan payable	$5,000,000	
Cash		$5,000,000
(To record repayment of half the loan)		
Nov. 17, 19X1–Feb. 14, 19X2		
Interest expense	$114,875	
Deferred gain on futures contracts	8,500	
Cash		$123,375
(To amortize cumulative deferred gain on Dec. contracts over the hedge period, and to record interest expense on the $5,000,000 borrowing when it was rolled over on Nov. 16, 19X1)		
Deferred gain on futures contracts	$3,750	
Amount due from broker		$3,750
(To record loss on futures contracts since Nov. 16, 19X1, as a reduction of the deferred gain account)		
Cash	$86,500	
Amount due from broker		$86,500
(To record receipt of margin deposit when hedge is terminated on Feb. 14, 19X2)		
Feb. 15–May 16, 19X2		
Interest expense	$117,750	
Deferred gain on futures contracts	7,250	
Cash		$125,000
(To amortize cumulative deferred gain on Mar. contracts over the hedge period, and to record interest expense on the $5,000,000 borrowing when it was rolled over on Feb. 14, 19X2)		
May 16, 19X2		
Loan payable	$5,000,000	
Cash		$5,000,000
(To record final principal payment due on the $10,000,000 loan)		

Under this approach, the exchange gain or loss on the principal portion of the 90-day note (which results from a change in exchange rates between the date of the borrowing and the intervening balance-sheet date or settlement date) is included in income. Offsetting this is the exchange loss or gain on the forward contract hedging the principal amount.

The interest expense relating to the FC$ discount is the U.S. dollar value of the current period amortization determined on the effective interest method and translated at the average exchange rate for the period. The exchange gain or loss on the forward contract that hedges the unamortized discount portion (representing the future commitment to pay interest expense) is included in the measurement of the interest expense at the time of recording the amortization of the discount. As a result, the interest expense (the amortization of the discount on the note) is effectively fixed (based on the exchange rate at the date of issuance of the note) by the forward contract.

SFAS No. 52 also requires the premium or discount on a forward contract (i.e., the difference between the contract rate of the forward contract and the exchange rate at inception of the forward contract multiplied by the FC$ face amount of the forward contract) to be amortized over the life of the forward contract. Since the amortization method is not specified in SFAS No. 52, the straight-line method may be used. However, the author believes that the preferable method, given the circumstances under which the discount on the note is amortized, is the effective interest method.

Further, SFAS No. 52 is silent as to the specific expense or income account in which the premium or discount should be included. The author believes it is appropriate, given the financing nature of the hypothetical transaction, to reflect it as an adjustment of interest expense.

With respect to the balance sheet of the issuer, the foreign currency dollar face amount and the unamortized discount of the note are translated at the reporting period's current exchange rate. Additionally, any receivable or payable relating to the forward contract is reflected on the balance sheet. To the extent the transaction is material to the financial statements of the issuer, a description of the transaction is required to be disclosed in the notes to the financial statements.

The accounting treatment described above is illustrated below:

■ FC$ 90-Day Note:

- Issued at a discount rate of 15 percent per annum
- Face amount of FC$10,000,000
- Proceeds received by issuer of FC$9,625,000
- 90-day maturity

■ Forward Contract:

- Purchase FC$10,000,000
  - Hedge of principal of FC$9,625,000
  - Hedge of the commitment of FC$375,000 (interest)
- Fixed contract price of FC$1/U.S.$0.63
- Delivery date of the forward contract is the same as the maturity of the 90-day note

■ FC$/U.S.$ Exchange Rates:

- Inception date FC$1.00 = U.S.$0.65
- Reporting date (i.e., end of fiscal year)
  - End FC$1.00 = U.S.$0.68
  - Average FC$1.00 = U.S.$0.66
- Settlement date FC$1.00 = U.S.$0.70

The financial statement reporting date occurs 30 days into the term of the 90-day note.

The following represents the accounting journal entries (and related calculations) required to be made by the issuer of the 90-day note at the date of issuance and at the reporting date (Note: "BS" represents balance sheet accounts, and "IS" represents income statement accounts):

Issuance of 90-Day Note

1.	(BS) Cash (a)	$6,256,250	
	(BS) Discount on note payable	243,750	
	(BS) Note payable (b)		$6,500,000
	To record issuance of the note		
2.	No entry is required with respect to the forward contract.		

(a) FC$9,625,000 × U.S. $0.65.
(b) FC$10,000,000 × U.S. $0.65.

Reporting Date—90-Day Note

1.	(IS) Foreign currency transaction Loss (a)	$292,500	
	(BS) Discount on note payable (c)	7,500	
	(BS) Note payable (b)		$300,000
	To record the exchange loss on a foreign currency note		

Calculation of Exchange Gain (Loss)—90-Day Note

(a) Outstanding principal, beginning of period:

FC$9,625,000 × $0.65* =	U.S.$6,256,250

Current period amortization:

FC$125,000 × U.S.$0.65* =	U.S.$ 81,250
	U.S.$6,337,500

Outstanding principal, end of period:

FC$9,750,000 × U.S.$0.68** =	U.S.$ 6,630,000
	U.S.$ (292,500)

(b) FC$/U.S.$ exchange rate at inception date   U.S.$0.65
     FC$/U.S.$ exchange rate at reporting date   U.S.$0.68
     Difference   U.S.$0.03
     Multiplied by face amount   FC$ 10,000,000
                                                                 U.S.$ 300,000

(c) FC$/U.S.$ exchange rate at inception date   U.S.$0.65
     FC$/U.S.$ exchange rate at reporting date   U.S.$0.68
     Difference   U.S.$0.03
     Multiplied by the unamortized discount***   FC $250,000
                                                                 U.S.$ 7,500

*   Exchange rate at inception.
** Exchange rate at reporting date.
*** Beginning balance FC$375,000 less current period amortization FC$125,000.

Reporting Date—Forward Contract

1.   (BS) Forward contract receivable $359,100
          (IS) Foreign currency transaction gain (a) $292,500
          (IS) Interest expense (b)   66,600
     To record the exchange gain and
       amortization of the discount

(a) Calculation of gain on the forward contract relating to the hedge of the
     principal amount:
     FC$/U.S.$ exchange rate at reporting date   U.S.$0.68
     FC$/U.S.$ exchange rate at inception date   U.S.$0.65
     Difference   U.S.$0.03

     Multiplied by the principal amount*   FC$ 9,750,000
                                                                 U.S.$ 292,500

(b) Calculation of discount on the forward contract:
     FC$/U.S.$ exchange rate at inception date   U.S.$0.65
     FC$/U.S.$ exchange rate at contract rate   U.S.$0.63
     Difference   U.S.$0.02

     Multiplied by the FC$ contract amount   FC$10,000,000
     Discount amount   U.S.$200,000
     Current period amortization (30 days)   U.S.$ 66,600

---

* Represents the hedge of the principal of FC$9,625,000 at inception plus the current period
   amortization of the discount of FC$125,000.

2.	(BS) Discount on note payable	$1,250	
	(BS) Deferred gain (a)		$1,250
	To record the transaction gain on the forward contract that hedges the commitment		
3.	(BS) Deferred gain	$1,250	
	(IS) Interest expense		$1,250
	To include the transaction gain in the measurement of the commitment portion recognized		

Reporting Date—Income Taxes

1.	(BS) Income taxes receivable	$5,860	
	(IS) Provision for income taxes		$5,860
	To record the income tax benefit of the interest deduction (40% blended rate × $14,650)		

(a) Calculation of transaction gain on recognized portion of forward contract:

Current period amortization	FC$125,000
Multiplied by the difference in FC$/U.S.$ exchange rates:	
Average rate	U.S.$0.66
Inception rate	U.S.$0.65
	U.S.$0.01
	U.S.$1,250

The net effect of these entries as of the reporting date is as follows:

Income Statement

Interest expense, comprised of:

• Amortization of discount on 90-day note	$82,500*
• Adjustment relating to the hedged commitment	(1,250)
• Amortization of discount on the forward contract	(66,600)
	$14,650**

---

*   FC$125,000 x average rate 0.66 exchange rate.

** Interest expense for 30-day period approximates one-third of 90-day note fixed interest of $43,750.

Transaction (gain) loss, comprised of:
- Transaction loss on the 90-day note $292,500
- Transaction gain on the forward contract   (292,500)
                                                                         $ -0-

Provision for income taxes   ($5,860)

Balance Sheet

Note payable, comprised of:
- Face amount*   ($6,800,000)
- Less the unamortized discount**   170,000
                                                                         ($6,630,000)

Forward contract receivable, comprised of:
- Transaction gain on the forward contract $292,500
- Amortization of discount on the forward contract   66,600
                                                                         $359,100

Income taxes receivable $ 5,860

---

*   (FC$10,000,000 × U.S.$0.68).
** (FC$250,000 × U.S.$0.68).

Similar calculations would be made at each intervening reporting date and at the settlement date. In addition, at the settlement date the final entry to record the delivery of the forward contract and 90-day note would be made as follows:

(BS) Note payable (a)	$7,000,000	
(BS) Cash (b)		$6,300,000
(BS) Forward contract receivable		$ 700,000

The total net effect on income at maturity would be interest expense of $43,750 ($6,300,000 − $6,256,250), a transaction gain or loss of zero, and an income tax benefit of $17,500 (40% of $43,750).

(a)   FC$10,000,000 × U.S.$0.70 (exchange rate at settlement date).
(b)   FC$10,000,000 × U.S.$0.63 (forward contract rate).

Forwards Not Involving Foreign Currencies

As for forwards not involving foreign currencies, the FASB excluded forwards from SFAS No. 80; however, in paragraph 34, the Board states:

> Exclusion of forward contracts from the statement should not be construed as either acceptance or rejection by the Board of current practice for such

contracts, nor should the exclusion be interpreted as an indication that the general principles of this statement might not be appropriate in some circumstances for certain forward contracts, and it may address the conceptual aspects of accounting for executory contracts generally.

Accordingly, if it qualifies as a hedge, the forward would generally be carried at market value, and gains or losses would be deferred and included in the basis of the hedged item. In certain industries—for example, in the mining and other extractive industries—where commodity forwards are used to fix the price of future sales of production, common practice is to account for these as "synthetic" fixed price sales at the time the sales are recorded without any intervening marking to market and hedge accounting for the forwards.

Interest Rate Swaps

Currently, there is no U.S. authoritative literature that deals with accounting for interest rate swaps. In general, the accounting treatment for interest rate swaps should not be analogized to other situations because swap transactions have unique characteristics that may not be present in other transactions. However, accounting for interest rate swap transactions has generally been as follows:

- Since most swaps are entered into either as an integral part of a borrowing arrangement or to hedge interest rate exposure, it is generally inappropriate to recognize gain or loss related to changes in value of the swap contract except in instances in which the associated assets or liabilities are also being adjusted for changes in value (marked to market).

- Accordingly, interest expense should be adjusted for the net amount receivable or payable under the swap arrangement (i.e., interest expense should reflect the revised interest rate).

- The typical interest rate swap transaction provides a legal right of offset for amounts due under the arrangement. Accordingly, any receivable or payable related to such a transaction should be presented net in the balance sheet (i.e., the swap should not be presented broad by recording a gross receivable and payable).

- With the exception of certain specialized industry practices, fees received or paid for entering into the swap should be amortized over the life of the swap as yield adjustments. However, fees received by an intermediary for arranging a swap when there is no continuing involvement may be recognized in income.

- Unrealized gains and losses for changes in market value of speculative swaps should generally be recognized currently.

- Gains or losses on early termination of swaps accounted for as integral to a borrowing arrangement or as a hedge should be associated with the related debt and spread over the remaining original life of the swap. (This is consistent with an EITF consensus on accounting for termination of an interest rate swap.)

Currency Swaps

Currency swaps, on the other hand, are covered by authoritative literature. Paragraph 17 of SFAS No. 52 states: "Agreements that are, in substance, essentially the same as forward contracts, for example, currency swaps, shall be accounted for in a manner similar to the accounting for forward contracts."

Example. Company A issues a £1,000,000 bullet note that matures in five years and bears interest at a rate of 10 percent a year. Company A hedges this transaction by entering into a currency swap. The currency swap consists of three elements: (1) an initial exchange; (2) the intervening payments; and (3) the maturity exchange. The payment dates of the swap are matched to those of the foreign currency debt.

Exchange rates and LIBOR rates for the next two years are as follows:

Year	Rate	LIBOR
0	1.60	
1	1.65	11.0%
2	1.58	11.5%

Table 7 provides the pertinent cash-flow information. The journal entries for the first two years to record the transaction are shown in Table 8.

Table 7. Cash Flow Analysis for Currency Swap Example

	Debt		Currency Swap			
Year	Principal	Interest	Initial Exchange	Intervening Payments	Maturity Exchange	Total Cash Flow per Period
0	£1,000,000		£(1,000,000) $1,600,000			$1,600,000
1		£(100,000)		($LIBOR) £100,000		($LIBOR)
2		£(100,000)		($LIBOR) £100,000		($LIBOR)
3		£(100,000)		($LIBOR) £100,000		($LIBOR)
4		£(100,000)		($LIBOR) £100,000		($LIBOR)
5	£(1,000,000)	£(100,000)		($LIBOR) £100,000	£1,000,000 $(1,600,000)	($LIBOR) $(1,600,000)

Options (Other Than Foreign Currency Options)

As described earlier, nonauthoritative guidance on accounting for options is provided by AICPA Issues Paper 86-2, *Accounting for Options*, dated March 6, 1986. Also,

Table 8

Year	Description	Debit	Credit
0	Cash	$1,600,000	
	F/X debt		$1,600,000

(To record the issuance of the £-denominated debt. Note: no entry is made to record the currency swap.)

1	Interest expense	176,000	
	Accrued liability		176,000

(To record the net swap payment and the interest due on the debt [$1,600,000 × 11%].)

1	Transaction loss	50,000	
	F/X debt		50,000

(To record the unrealized F/X loss on the debt [$1.65 – $1.60 x £ 1,000,000].)

1	F/X contract receivable	50,000	
	Transaction gain		50,000

(To record the unrealized transaction gain on the currency swap.)

2	Interest expense	184,000	
	Accrued liability		184,000

(To record the net swap payment and the interest due on the debt [$1,600,000 × 11.5%].)

2	F/X debt	70,000	
	Transaction gain		70,000

(To record the unrealized F/X gain on the F/X debt [£1,000,000 x 1.58 – 1,650,000].)

2	Transaction loss	70,000	
	F/X contract receivable		50,000
	F/X contract payable		20,000

(To record the unrealized transaction loss on the currency swap.)

EITF issues 90-17 and 91-14 address the accounting for options that are intended to hedge foreign currency risk.

Accounting

In general, the accounting recommended in the issues paper is similar to the accounting for futures, that is:

- Options should generally be marked to market.

- For speculative options, the mark-to-market adjustment should be reflected immediately in income.

- For options that are hedges, the mark-to-market adjustment should be deferred and recorded as an adjustment of the carrying value of the item being hedged.

- Consistent with SFAS No. 80 provisions covering futures contracts, the dollar amount of commodities underlying the futures contract (into which the option is exercisable) is not included in the entity's balance sheet.

- The requirements for an option to qualify as a hedge are the same, i.e., risk reduction, high correlation, and designation, with one important exception that in the case of options (except for foreign currency options where the risk assessment is on an enterprise basis), the risk assessment can be made only on a transaction-by-transaction basis, and not on an overall enterprise basis as for futures contracts.

- When determining the probability of high correlation, the hedger should consider the correlation during relevant past periods *and also the correlation that could be expected at higher or lower price levels.* The option may be for an item different from the item to be hedged (i.e., a cross hedge) if there is a clear economic relationship between their prices and high correlation is probable.

- Written (sold) options can qualify as a hedge only to the extent of the premium received.

- Options can be used to hedge existing assets or liabilities, firm commitments, and anticipated transactions.

There are, however, some differences in the accounting that reflect the economic differences between a futures contract and an option. An option is a unilateral contract where the holder has a right, but no obligation, to take (call) or make (put) delivery of the property underlying the option contract, whereas a futures contract is two-sided. Since a futures contract is a legally binding bilateral agreement, the holder of a futures contract position will benefit or suffer 100 percent of the consequences of a change in price of the underlying commodity. With a purchased option, however, the holder has a right, not an obligation. Essentially, the long position pays a price, the premium, to cover risk of adverse price (interest rate, exchange rate) change.

Secondly, the accounting for that price, the premium, recognizes that it may contain two elements:

- Intrinsic value, based on the degree to which the option is in-the-money

■ Time value, representing the market's estimation of how likely it is that the option will become valuable (in-the-money) before it lapses

Only in-the-money options have intrinsic value; however, all options may have time value. The deeper out-of-the-money they are, the less likely they are to have any significant time value.

Recognizing that the premium paid for an option may include both these elements, the options issues paper requires the two elements to be separately accounted for by the option buyer in most cases. Essentially, it generally requires that the time value be amortized and recognized as expense over the life of the option since, in essence, the time value of an option is similar to an insurance premium. Any intrinsic value, however, is deferred and marked to market. This split accounting is illustrated in Example 1 below.

Example 1. BankCo buys a June $89.00 U.S. Treasury bond call in February when June U.S. Treasury bond futures are trading at $90.00. BankCo pays a premium of $2,800. BankCo carries its investments in U.S. Treasuries at cost. The option is $1,000 in-the-money, so it has a $1,000 intrinsic value, and the remaining $1,800 paid must be time value. The intrinsic value would be recorded as an asset and marked to market at the end of each accounting period. The $1,800 time value would be amortized over the next four months—the life of the call option.

In certain situations, the time and intrinsic values of a purchased option would not be split or accounted for separately; for example, in the case of a purchased option that qualifies for hedge accounting and hedges an asset, liability, or firm commitment carried or to be carried at market and where gains and losses on the hedged item are included in income as they arise.

If the time and intrinsic values of an option are not split, changes in the entire value of the option should be included in income as they occur. Example 2 below illustrates this.

Example 2. On September 1, Secure Securities (a broker-dealer) purchases 1,000 puts on Acme Manufacturing Corp. for a premium of $1,875 as hedge against a price decline on the 1,000 shares of Acme in its portfolio. The puts have a strike price of $22 and expire on December 31. As the current selling price of Acme stock equals $21, the option premium includes $1,000 of intrinsic value ([$22-$21] x 1,000) and $875 of time value ($1,875 - $1,000). The broker-dealer follows mark-to-market accounting, and, therefore, daily changes in portfolio value are included in income, and the time and intrinsic values of the option premium are not split and accounted for separately.

At the purchase date of the options, the following journal entries would be made:

| Options | 1,875 | |
| Cash | | 1,875 |

If the stock price rose to $23 and the market value of the options fell to $750, the following entries would be recorded:

Stock	2,000	
Gain on stock		2,000
Loss on options	1,125	
Options		1,125

If market prices were to rise, the entries similarly would record the change in value of both the options and the stock. This process continues until the options are exercised, closed out, or expire.[6]

As discussed earlier, an option that hedges a firm commitment or an anticipated transaction may qualify for hedge accounting. The portion of the time value of such an option that relates to the period before the related transaction occurs may be included in the measurement of the transaction or, alternatively, amortized to expense over that period.

When a purchased option that qualifies for hedge accounting is closed out, the difference between the unamortized balance of the time value and the time value received on closing out the option should be treated in the same manner as was the time value prior to the close-out. If the time value was being amortized to income, the difference should be recognized in income. If the time value was being deferred (e.g., in the case of a hedge of a firm commitment or anticipated transaction), the difference likewise should be deferred.

Written Options

The issues paper recognizes that written options can only provide an economic hedge to the extent of the premium received by the writer, and, therefore, any losses to the writer of an option beyond the amount of the premium he or she received must be charged to income.

Written options qualify as hedges if:

- The three criteria specified for purchased options are satisfied; and

- The option is so deep-in-the-money that it is reasonably assured that the option will remain in-the-money throughout its term.

The last condition would be met, for example, when: (1) a call option with a one-year exercise period is written on a bond with a $900 strike price, when the market value of the bond is $1,000 (i.e., the option is $100 in-the-money); (2) over recent one-year periods the bond's market value has not changed by more than $100; and (3) the volatility of the bond's market value is not expected to change significantly in the future. The time and intrinsic values may not be split for a written option qualifying for hedge accounting.

SYNTHETIC INSTRUMENTS

The accounting method previously described for interest rate swaps that are linked to borrowings or to interest-bearing assets is an example of what has become known as "synthetic instrument accounting." While the topic of synthetic instrument accounting cannot be found in the current authoritative accounting literature, there have been a

6 This example was adapted from *Accounting for Options,* Issues Paper 86-2 (New York: AICPA, 1986), pp. 177-78.

number of articles on the subject and recent FASB discussion documents[7] acknowledging its existence. As applied in practice, synthetic instrument accounting involves treating two or more distinct financial instruments as having synthetically created a single recognizable instrument and, accordingly, accounting for those multiple instruments as the single instrument that was created. Thus, floating-rate debt, together with a swap of the floating interest payments into fixed payments, is treated as fixed-rate debt. The same holds true for the reverse, where fixed-rate debt is swapped into floating, to basis swaps that modify the interest rate characteristics of debt, and to interest rate swaps combined with interest-bearing assets. In all cases, the swap is not accounted for separately in either the income statement or balance sheet, and only the net payments under the swap and the related debt or asset are treated as periodic interest expense or income.

While this seems logical and appropriate because of the absence of authoritative standards or guidelines on the subject, questions can and have arisen in practice, even in the case of simple interest rate swaps. For example, must the swap be entered into at the inception of the borrowing or lending transaction to be afforded the synthetic instrument accounting? Under current practice as it has evolved, the answer is generally no. The interest rate swap can be entered into after the related borrowing or lending transaction[8] and need not even be held through the maturity of the linked debt or asset to be afforded the synthetic treatment.

Other issues can arise in practice. For example, should synthetic treatment apply where either the debt or interest-bearing asset or the interest rate swap (or both) are zero-coupon instruments? Moreover, the extension of synthetic instrument accounting to other kinds of transactions, for example, to currency swaps linked with a foreign currency borrowing, raises a host of accounting issues. For example, should a deutsche mark borrowing whose principal has been effectively converted into U.S. dollars via a currency swap be accounted for as a single instrument, U.S.-dollar debt? Here the answer under current accounting rules is no. Under FASB Statement No. 52 on foreign currency translation, both the deutsche mark debt and the currency swap are marked to market with the resulting gains and losses included in the current period's earnings. Thus, to the extent the loss or gain on the swap offsets the gain or loss on the debt, earnings are unaffected. However, for balance sheet purposes the debt and the swap must be shown "broad," that is, in accordance with the consensus in EITF Issue No. 86-25, the current value of the swap must be shown separately and cannot be offset against the debt.[9] Accountants would argue that this treatment properly reflects the fact that the debt and the currency swap are with different counterparties. That notwithstanding, many accountants would acknowledge the synthesis and permit "as if" synthetic accounting for other purposes, for example, in the case of U.S.-dollar debt that has been swapped in deutsche marks, treating the combination as an effective

---

7 For example, see chapter 8 of the 1992 FASB Discussion Memorandum, *Recognition and Measurement of Financial Instruments,* and the FASB staff's June 1993 document on hedging and risk-adjusting activities, discussed later in this chapter.

8 However, as discussed later in this chapter, in its "tentative conclusions" the FASB would limit synthetic instrument accounting to situations where the interest rate swap is entered into at the inception of the related borrowing or lending transaction.

9 This assumes the debt and the swap are with different parties. When the debt and the swap are with the same party, balance sheet netting would be permitted provided there is a legal right of offset.

hedge under FASB Statement No. 52 of a firm commitment to receive deutsche marks or of a net investment in a German subsidiary.

Synthetics involving options and swaptions raise additional accounting issues due to the one-sided nature of these instruments. Take the example of synthetic noncallable fixed-rate debt that arises from the combination of issuing callable fixed-rate debt and selling a swaption against the embedded call.

Assume the entity issues five-year callable (after three years) fixed-rate debt while simultaneously writing a swaption excerciseable concurrently with the call date of debt. The swaption would be structured such that, if exercised, the issuer receives LIBOR and pays fixed during years four and five.

In this example, if interest rates have fallen at the call date in three years, the company will likely call the debt and refinance it short term with commercial paper. Similarly, the holder of the swaption will likely exercise it and enter into the two-year swap, paying the company LIBOR and receiving the fixed interest payment. If interest rates have risen, however, the company would not call the debt and the swaption holder would not exercise it. In either case, it is argued the company has effectively created noncallable five-year fixed-rate debt, with the up-front premium received on the swaption providing a reduction of the effective financing cost. It would therefore seem logical to treat this transaction as a single instrument, synthetic five-year fixed-rate debt and amortize the premium received on the swaption as a reduction of interest expense over the five years. However, this presumes the intended synthesis will occur and will be effective, which in turn presumes symmetry between the company's decision whether or not to call the debt in three years and the swaption holder's decision whether or not to exercise the swaption at that date. Such symmetry might not always exist, for example, when a call premium is involved or when, as in the above example, different floating rates are involved (e.g., refinancing by the company at commercial paper rates versus receipt of LIBOR on the swap), or when in three years, for whatever reason the company would be unable to refinance if it called the debt. Most accountants would therefore carefully assess the facts and circumstances surrounding a particular transaction of this kind before concluding on the propriety of using synthetic instrument accounting. Such facts and circumstances would include the company's financial condition and likely ability to refinance at the call date as well as the range of interest rates under which, given any call premium and/or differences in the floating-rate bases of the refinancing and the swap under the swaption, there might be asymmetry between the actions of the company and the swaption holder at the call date. Moreover, the longer the term of the debt and the farther out the call date—for example in the case of 20-year debt with a call at year 10—the more difficult it is to convince most accountants and auditors of the propriety of applying synthetic instrument accounting to this type of transaction.

In summary, at present there are no authoritative rules or guidelines governing the accounting for synthetics. In the absence of such guidance, accountants have generally only permitted synthetic instrument accounting in those cases where it is clear that the multiple instruments create another recognizable financial instrument and that there is a high probability that the company can achieve and maintain the intended synthesis. As discussed later in this chapter, however, the FASB has begun formally looking at the subject of synthetic instrument accounting and has reached certain tentative views on how and when it should be applied.

ACCOUNTING ISSUES RELATING TO INVESTMENTS IN MORTGAGE DERIVATIVES

For accounting purposes, mortgage derivatives—including CMO securities, CMO residuals, and mortgage-backed I/Os and P/Os—are generally considered to be debt securities. Thus, mark-to-market entities, such as broker-dealers, investment companies, and pension funds, generally carry investments in these securities at market or fair value, with any cash received and any changes in value reported as part of current-period income. For most other entities—including banks, thrifts, insurance companies, and commercial and industrial enterprises—SFAS No. 115 applies. Under SFAS No. 115, investments in these securities must be classified and accounted for as either held-to-maturity, available-for-sale, or trading in accordance with the previously discussed rules.

While the above accounting appears simple in concept, its application to some mortgage derivatives such as CMO residuals and I/Os is more complex and raises a number of issues. Many of these derivatives have little or no principal component and their value is dependent not only on interest rates but also on the effect of changes in interest rates on prepayment levels. They are often referred to as "high-risk mortgage securities" both in the accounting literature and by financial institutions regulators because of their often volatile nature and because they have the potential for loss of a significant portion of the original investment. A few of the important accounting issues raised for such securities include:

1. How to value them? If market or dealer quotations are available, they should be used to value these securities. If not, fair value should be estimated based on expected cash flows discounted at current market interest rates for similar securities. In estimating future cash flows, prepayment rates should be estimated based on current interest rate levels.

2. Can such securities qualify as held-to-maturity under SFAS No. 115, and if so, how is amortized cost determined? SFAS No. 115 does not specifically address classification of debt securities with uncertain maturity; however, it does not proscribe held-to-maturity classification of such securities.

   Although the EITF did not reach a consensus in Issue 94-4, the EITF did observe that due to the nature of I/Os, meeting the criteria under SFAS No. 115 for classification as held-to-maturity would be rare.

   If the security is classified as held-to-maturity, its amortized cost basis should be determined based on the guidance in EITF Issue No. 89-4. The investor should allocate total cash flows expected to be received over the estimated life of the investment between principal and interest, using the "prospective method" in the following manner. At the date of purchase, an effective yield is calculated based on the purchase price and anticipated future cash flows. In the initial accounting period, interest income is accrued using that rate. Cash received on the investment is first applied to accrued interest, with any excess reducing the recorded investment balance. At each reporting date, the effective yield is recalculated based upon the amortized cost of the investment and the then current estimate of future cash flows. The recalculated yield is then used to accrue interest income on the investment balance in the subsequent accounting period. This procedure continues until all cash flows from the investment have been received. In this manner, the amortized balance of the investment at the end of the period will equal the present value of the estimated future cash flows discounted at the newly calculated effective yield.

3. If under SFAS No. 115 these securities are classified as either held-to-maturity or available-for-sale, when should such securities be considered to be impaired, thereby requiring a writedown to fair value via an immediate charge to earnings?

Prior to SFAS No. 115, EITF Issue No. 89-4 specified that investors in high-risk CMO instruments should evaluate each instrument separately to determine whether expected future cash flows are adequate to recover the recorded investment balance. However, under the EITF guidelines, an impairment writedown was not required, provided the recorded balance for each investment exceeded the *undiscounted* estimated future cash flows, i.e., the effective yield was not negative.

SFAS No. 115 changes the method of measuring impairment in Issue No. 89-4 from one based on undiscounted cash flows to one based on fair value. In Issue No. 93-18, the EITF reached a consensus that when the present value of estimated future cash flows discounted at a risk-free rate is less than the amortized cost basis of the instrument, an impairment loss should be recognized. The excess of the amortized cost basis over the instrument's fair value should be recognized as a realized loss in the income statement.

In summary, the accounting for most mortgage derivatives is governed by SFAS No. 115 although its application to high-risk CMO instruments is complex and evolving.

THE NETTING OF POSITIONS

The rules for netting of positions are contained in FASB Interpretation No. 39, *Offsetting of Amounts Related to Certain Contracts,* which although issued in 1991, is not mandated for most entities until 1994. These rules dictate when amounts due from the same counterparty may be offset in the reporting entity's balance sheet and related footnote disclosures such as those under SFAS No. 105. Accountants have relied primarily upon the legal definition of the right of offset in determining whether financial positions should be netted. As such, the right of offset is defined as a debtor's legal right, by contract or otherwise, to discharge all or a portion of the debt owed to another party by applying against the debt an amount that the other party owes the debtor. The following conditions generally must be met in order to net positions with the same counterparty:

■ Each of the two parties owes the other determinable amounts.

- The reporting party has the right to set off the amount owed with the amount owed by the other party.

- The reporting party intends to set off.

- The right of setoff is enforceable at law.

These four conditions were contained in an earlier FASB Technical Bulletin (No. 88-2) on the subject and carried forward by FIN No. 39. The conditions have proven troublesome, particularly to entities, such as banks, investment banks, and derivatives product dealers, who regularly have numerous open positions of varying durations with various counterparties and across various product lines (e.g., swaps, options, and forwards). While industry practice among such entities has not been uniform, many such dealers have reported their entire position as a single mark-to-market receivable or payable, arguing that the criteria for Technical Bulletin No. 88-2 should not apply to them. Recognizing the special nature of these entities' activities, FIN No. 39 permits offsetting of positions with the same counterparty (but only with the same counterparty) provided:

1. The positions are covered by a valid master netting agreement between the two parties, and

2. The reporting party carries the positions at market or fair value.

In effect, for the swap and derivatives product dealers, FIN No. 39 represents a compromise between the existing practice of netting positions across counterparties and the accounting rules that, if literally applied, would permit offsetting of only those positions that will actually be settled on a net basis with a particular counterparty. By putting in place valid master netting agreements with each counterparty, these entities will be permitted by FIN No. 39 to net open positions across product lines by counterparty in their balance sheet and related footnote disclosures. This same treatment presumably also will apply to positions covered by master netting agreements held by mark-to-market investing entities such as pension funds, investment companies, and hedge funds.

Disclosure Requirements Relating to Derivatives and Synthetics

The current disclosure requirements relating to derivatives and their use are covered by a number of pronouncements including FASB Statements Nos. 52, 80, 105, and 107, and by EITF Issue No. 91-4. Moreover, at the time of writing (February 1994) the FASB is working on a project that could further expand and modify these requirements. Discussed below are the current and possible future requirements.

SFAS No. 52 requires disclosure of gains and losses from hedges and SFAS No. 80 requires disclosure of "(a) the nature of the assets, liabilities, firm commitments, or anticipated transactions that are hedged with futures contracts and (b) the method of accounting for the futures contracts." The EITF reached a consensus in Issue 91-4 that when using currency options, option combinations, and similar instruments to hedge, the following should be disclosed in the notes to the financial statements:

Exhibit 2.   Decision Flowchart for Statement 107

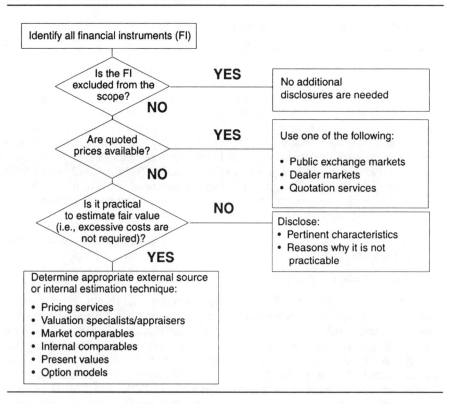

- ■ The method of accounting for those instruments, including a description of the events or transactions that result in recognition in income of changes in value

- ■ The nature of the anticipated transactions for which there is no firm commitment that are hedged by those instruments

- ■ The maximum number of years over which anticipated, but not firmly committed, foreign currency transactions are hedged by those instruments

- ■ The combined realized and unrealized net gain or loss deferred as of each balance sheet date on those instruments that are designated as hedges of anticipated transactions for which there is no firm commitment

SFAS No. 105

In March 1990, the FASB issued SFAS No. 105, *Disclosure of Information About Financial Instruments with Off-Balance Sheet Risk and Financial Instruments with Concentrations of Credit Risk.* This statement requires all entities to report the following information about financial instruments with off-balance-sheet risk of accounting loss:

- The face, contract, or notional principal amount

- The nature and terms of the instruments and a discussion of their credit and market risk, cash requirements, and related accounting policies

- An amount of the loss, at the balance sheet date and ignoring any collateral, the entity would incur if the counterparties to its off-balance-sheet financial instruments failed to perform

- The entity's policy for requiring collateral or other security and a description of the collateral on instruments presently held.

The statement also requires disclosure of information about significant concentrations of credit risk from an individual counterparty or group of counterparties for all financial instruments. An example of this disclosure from a major financial institution is included in Appendix I.

SFAS No. 107

In December 1991, SFAS No. 107, *Disclosures About Fair Value of Financial Instruments,* was issued, requiring all entities to disclose, when *practicable,* the fair value of a variety of on- and off-balance-sheet financial instruments (see Exhibit 2 for a decision flowchart useful for applying SFAS No. 107). These instruments include debt and equity securities, derivative products (e.g., swaps, options, forwards, and future contracts) asset-backed securities, financial guarantees, letters of credit, and commitments to extend credit.

Practicable means that an estimate of fair value can be made without incurring excessive cost. This concept is dynamic—what is impracticable one year may be practicable the next. If management determines that it is not practicable to estimate the fair value of a financial instrument, then this fact should be documented. The meaning of the term "fair value" is precise:

> For purposes of this statement, the fair value of a financial instrument is the amount at which the instrument could be exchanged in a current transaction between willing parties, other than in a forced or liquidation sale.[10]

Paragraph 10 of SFAS No. 107 requires that the method(s) and significant assumptions used to estimate the fair value of financial instruments be disclosed. Also, in some instances, an entity's management may decide to provide further information about the fair value of financial instruments to avoid misleading inferences. If it is not practicable to estimate the fair value of a financial instrument, paragraph 14 requires the disclosure of the following:

---

10 *Disclosures About Fair Value of Financial Instruments,* SFAS No. 107 (Norwalk, CT: FASB, 1991), ¶ 7.

- When it is not practicable, a statement in the notes to the financial statements that a reasonable estimate of fair value could not be made without excessive costs would generally be sufficient, and

- Information helpful in estimating the instrument's fair value (e.g., carrying amount, effective interest rate, maturity).

Appendix II of this chapter provides an example of a typical SFAS No. 107 disclosure for a large financial entity.

The Current FASB Project on Improving Disclosures on Derivatives and SEC Views on Derivatives Disclosures

The continued tremendous growth in the use of derivatives by entities of all types has led to widespread calls to further improve financial statement disclosures in this area. In July 1993, the Group of Thirty, an international association of bankers and former government officials chaired by Paul Volcker, published a study entitled *Derivatives: Practices and Principles,* containing recommendations for the management of derivatives activity including the need for improved and broader disclosures. Since then the business press, financial analysts, members of Congress, and various regulators, such as the Federal Reserve, the Comptroller of the Currency, and the SEC, have all expressed concerns regarding the risks associated with derivatives and with the perceived lack of adequate disclosures by companies on their use. Essentially, there seems to be a consensus that the current disclosures under Statements 105 and 107 are often ambiguous and do not clearly present the extent of an entity's involvement with derivatives, its sensitivity to interest rate and other market risks, and the extent and effect of its hedging policies. While at this time (February 1994) it is not possible to predict precisely how the current disclosure rules might be changed or expanded, the FASB is examining the following possibilities:

- Broadening the scope of SFAS 105 to require fair value disclosures for all financial instruments rather than only those that have off-balance-sheet risk of an accounting loss. Accordingly, the disclosure requirements would be expanded to include financial instruments such as purchased options, interest rate caps and floors held, fixed-rate loans and mortgage purchase commitments held, financial guarantees held, and any other derivative that subjects a company to potential economic loss, either credit or market.

- Eliminating some of the flexibility currently allowed by SFAS 107 by requiring a company to include all fair value information in one comprehensive footnote together with the comparable balance-sheet carrying amounts.

- Enhancing the reporting about a company's financial risk management and hedging activities by disclosing a company's hedge accounting policies and the nature of its risk management activities, providing an analysis of changes in deferred gains and losses on hedging instruments, estimating when deferred gains and losses on hedging instruments will be recognized in the income statement, and even disclosing the portion of a company's earnings derived from financial risk management activities.

It is also interesting to note that in regard to the above the Board is also considering requiring disaggregation of the disclosures by type of activity, i.e., dealer versus end user.

SEC Views on Derivatives Disclosures

For companies that are SEC registrants, it is important to note that the staff of the SEC publicly stated in January 1994 that it expects registrants to disclose as much about their derivatives activities and positions as they disclose about on-balance-sheet financial instruments. In this regard, the SEC staff has indicated that the types of disclosures it generally considers relevant for traders and dealers in derivatives would include:

- A description of the nature of the trading activities, including the business purpose for these activities, tolerable risk levels, and types of instruments traded; and

- The amount of trading income recognized in the income statement by each major type of financial instrument.

For registrants that use derivatives for asset/liability management purposes, the staff indicated that it considers the following types of disclosures to be meaningful:

- A disaggregated description of the outstanding derivative instruments, including a description of the type, amount, expected maturity, and fair value of these instruments

- A discussion of any risk being hedged and any limitations of the hedge

- A tabular presentation of (1) items being hedged and (2) the products used to hedge, setting forth for each the duration of the hedge or derivative and the maturity by year of the derivative

- A discussion of how management monitors the hedging activity and any modeling techniques utilized in determining the status of any hedging activity

- A reconciliation of the notional or contractual amounts from the beginning of the period to the end of the period, i.e., a summary of the change in notional or contractual amounts resulting from new, terminated, and matured or expired contracts

- Disclosure of the amount of deferred gains and losses from hedging or risk-adjusting activities and the expected amortization of such amount on a period-by-period basis

- The current period impact of derivative activities on either net interest income, if applicable (e.g., if the registrant is a financial institution), or income from continuing operations

With respect to anticipatory hedges, the staff indicated that registrants should consider disclosing:

- The dollar value of the anticipatory hedges

■ The period the anticipated transactions are expected to occur

■ The effect of closing hedges where the actual transactions did not occur

Clearly, there is an increasing and heightened focus on companies' derivatives activities and on the adequacy of their footnote and other disclosures related to these activities. Judgment is required to determine the extent of disclosures needed in a particular situation. Companies may be well served to inventory their derivatives activities and positions and discuss with their accounting advisers the effect these have on their present and future financial statement disclosures and their commentary in management's discussion and analysis.

WHAT'S AHEAD? THE FASB PROJECT ON HEDGING, DERIVATIVES, AND SYNTHETICS

As discussed at the outset of this chapter, the current set of accounting rules were developed in a piecemeal fashion; they provide somewhat inconsistent guidance and do not explicitly cover a number of today's hedging instruments and techniques. As part of its broader project on financial instruments, the FASB has begun formally reviewing the current rules on hedge accounting and accounting for derivative instruments. In September 1991, it issued a lengthy Research Report, *Hedge Accounting: An Exploratory Study of the Underlying Issues.* This was followed in November 1991 by a Discussion Memorandum, *Recognition and Measurement of Financial Instruments,* which contains some 80 issues, many relating to various derivative instruments, hedge accounting, and synthetic instrument accounting. In June 1993, the Board circulated an informal document entitled "A Report on Deliberations, Including Tentative Conclusions on Certain Issues Related to Accounting for Hedging and Other Risk-Adjusting Activities" ("Report on Deliberations").

The June 1993 Report was circulated to a limited group and served as the basis of discussion for two meetings the Board had with selected knowledgeable parties in September 1993. Since then the Board has continued its deliberations on this project. While any formal revisions to the current rules are probably at least a year away, the Board's discussions to date are important because a number of its tentative conclusions summarized in the June 1993 Report represent changes that could have far-reaching implications for companies engaged in hedging and financial risk-management programs.

There seems to be general agreement that hedge accounting should be permitted for hedges of existing assets, liabilities, or firm commitments provided (1) there is a clear economic relationship between the hedging instrument and the item(s) being hedged and (2) there is a reasonable expectation at the hedge's inception of high inverse correlation. Perhaps most notably, however, at least several Board members believe that hedge accounting should not be permitted for anticipated transactions that are not in the form of firm commitments (referred to as "forecasted transactions"). This would represent a significant rollback of the current rules, which permit the deferral of gains and losses on qualifying hedges involving interest rate and commodity futures (SFAS 80) and on purchased foreign currency options (EITF Issue No. 90-17) used to hedge anticipated transactions that are considered probable of occurring. This view reflects some FASB members' and SEC's Office of the Chief

Accountant's concerns over both the conceptual propriety of the current hedge accounting model, which permits the deferral of current gains and losses on instruments used to hedge future transactions, and the more practical concern over the ability to develop workable rules that prevent companies from deferring losses in situations where the expected transactions may never materialize. Changing the rules in this manner could have profound effects on companies that now engage in extensive hedging of interest rate risk, commodity price risk, or foreign currency risk associated with anticipated but not firmly committed future transactions. Continuing such hedging programs would mean using mark-to-market accounting on the hedge instruments, while discontinuing the hedging programs would expose them to unwanted price risks. At this point, FASB Board members are far from unanimous on this issue and could be swayed by the likely torrent of criticism the Board will receive on any formal proposed revision of the current rules along these lines.

The June 1993 Report also reflects a number of other potential changes in the current hedge accounting model. As previously discussed, the current rules contain a variety of tests relating to risk reduction and continuing high correlation between the hedge and the hedged item. As an alternative, the Report describes a "partial effectiveness method" under which only an expectation of high inverse correlation between the hedge and the hedged item will qualify the hedge for hedge accounting; however, if the partial effectiveness method is adopted, the hedge accounting model would be changed dramatically. Under this method a hedge would be considered effective to the extent that changes in the fair value of the hedging instrument do not exceed the (inverse) change in the fair value of the item being hedged. A change in the fair value of the hedging instrument that exceeds the (inverse) change in the fair value of the hedged item would be recognized currently in earnings. To illustrate, consider the following two situations involving the hedge by a metals company of its aluminum inventory through the sale of aluminum futures contracts. In the first case, if aluminum prices rise such that the value of the aluminum inventory rises by say $1 million while there is an unrealized loss on the futures contract of $900,000, the entire $900,000 loss would be deferred. On the other hand, if the inventory value rose by only $800,000, only that amount of the futures contract losses could be deferred, with the remaining $100,000 charged to current-period earnings. In contrast, under the current rules, the entire $900,000 loss could generally be deferred in both scenarios. On the other hand, the use of the partial effectiveness method would simplify and broaden the current rules by eliminating the often troublesome continuing high correlation requirement of SFAS 80 and would permit the greater use of hedge accounting for cross-currency hedges, which, under the current SFAS 52 rules, do not generally qualify for hedge accounting treatment. It would also expand the availability of hedge accounting to situations where a cash market position, instead of a derivative, is used to hedge interest rate or commodity price exposure.

Consistent with the approach under SFAS 80, assessment of risk under the Board's tentative conclusions described in the June 1993 Report would be determined at the level of the overall enterprise or for companies that operate in a decentralized manner at the business unit level. However, in contrast to the SFAS 80 rule, which requires only that such an assessment be conducted at the inception of the hedging transaction, an ongoing test of continued enterprise (or business unit) exposure to risk would be necessary for a transaction to continue to be afforded hedge accounting, a requirement that some commentators feel is not practical or feasible.

For financial institutions and other entities that manage net interest rate or currency risk of their overall asset/liability position, the June 1993 Report indicates that macro and dynamic hedging should be permitted under an alternative mark-to-market pool approach. Under this pool approach, all components of the dynamically managed portfolio (i.e., assets, liabilities, commitments, and related derivatives) would be measured at current market or fair value with the resulting gains and losses reported in current period earnings. Because this would be an available elective method, many are concerned that it would give rise to "cherry-picking" of gains by financial institutions seeking to boost reported income. It could also have the perhaps unintended effect of obviating the requirements of SFAS No. 115, which as previously discussed requires companies to value many of their debt and marketable equity positions at market or fair value. The "assets-only" approach in SFAS No. 115 was heavily criticized by many financial institutions that argued for similar treatment of the related liabilities funding such assets. As described, the proposed mark-to-market pool approach would accomplish this.

Finally, the June 1993 Report also discusses the area of synthetic instrument accounting, where derivatives are used in connection with borrowing or lending transactions to modify the structure of a transaction or to synthetically create a single "prototype" financial instrument. Under the approach being discussed, the company would combine and measure the separate instruments used in the synthesis as net proceeds received or paid. The company would report the combination of these instruments as the single prototype instrument being synthesized. For subsequent financial reporting periods, the company would recognize in current period earnings the difference between the changes in fair value of the synthesized instrument and the prototype instrument.

This approach as contemplated appears to restrict synthetic instrument accounting to situations where the swap or other derivative is entered into at the inception of a borrowing or lending transaction. Thus, for example, a company that borrowed on a floating-rate basis several years ago and that now, due to lower interest rates, locks in a fixed rate on the remaining term of the borrowing by entering into an interest rate swap would be precluded from using synthetic instrument accounting and would presumably have to carry the swap on a mark-to-market basis. This would represent a significant and, in the author's view, an inappropriate and unwarranted change from current practice under which mark-to-market accounting can usually be avoided for swaps that change the interest characteristics of existing debt or assets, even though the swap is entered into some time after the original borrowing or lending transaction. Further, the discussions to date have focused only on synthetics involving simple borrowing or lending transactions and have not encompassed the many other types of combination instrument techniques now in use.

In addition to the June 1993 Report, the Board is expected to consider other alternatives during its 1994 discussions on hedge accounting. One of the alternatives being evaluated includes an approach based on concepts in SFAS No. 115. Under this approach, all derivative instruments would be carried at fair value and classified as either trading or availabe-for-sale. Those used for risk management (i.e., both for risk reduction/hedging and risk selection) would be classified as available-for-sale and unrealized gains and losses would be recorded in equity. Realized gains and losses on risk management derivatives would be deferred to the extent they are offset by unrealized losses and gains on the related assets and liabilities. All other derivatives would be classified as trading and marked to market in the income statement.

The Board's deliberations on hedge accounting would continue in 1994; however, it has not indicated a formal timetable for issuing an exposure draft on this subject.

CONCLUSION

This chapter provided an overview of the current accounting and financial reporting rules and practices for derivatives and synthetics. As explained, these are incomplete and often inconsistent. However, the FASB is now focusing on this area in earnest and its proposals may significantly change the current rules and hopefully would provide a more comprehensive and consistent guidance on accounting for derivatives and synthetics. Further, expanded disclosure requirements relating to derivatives and their use are expected to be promulgated in the near future. In the meantime, those involved in using derivative instruments should be conversant with the current rules and should exercise care before initiating new transactions involving derivative instruments to ensure that the intended accounting results will be achieved, and should consult with their accounting professionals on both the current rules and the FASB's progress on developing new rules.

APPENDIX I*

Off-Balance-Sheet Financial Products and Credit Concentrations

As a global financial services institution, Citicorp enters into a variety of financial transactions with a diverse group of U.S. and foreign corporations, governments, institutional investors, and individual consumers. The various financial products used in these transactions were developed in response to the growing sophistication of the financial markets and are designed to provide customers with credit enhancements as well as flexible ways to manage liquidity needs, funding costs, and foreign exchange exposure. Many of these products do not necessarily entail present or future funded asset or liability positions but are instead in the nature of executory contracts.

Financial instrument transactions are subject to the full range of Citicorp's credit standards, financial controls, and risk-limiting and monitoring procedures. Collateral requirements are made on a case-by-case evaluation of each customer and product. Collateral held varies but may include cash, securities, receivables, real estate, and other assets.

As described in the Statement of Accounting Policies, credit risk on these products is taken into consideration in determining the allowance for credit losses. No portion of the allowance is specifically allocated to these products.

Following are discussions of certain significant products, with indications of gross volumes.

Loan Commitments

Citicorp and its subsidiaries had outstanding unused commitments to make or purchase loans, to purchase third-party receivables, to provide note issuance facilities or revolving underwriting facilities, to extend credit in the form of lease financing, or to extend check credit and related plans to consumers of $55.8 billion at December 31, 1992, and $57.4 billion at December 31, 1991. The majority of these commitments are at a floating interest rate. In addition, there were $64.7 billion and $58.0 billion of unused commitments to extend credit to consumers in the form of retail credit cards at December 31, 1992, and December 31, 1991, respectively. The majority of these commitments are contingent upon customers maintaining specific credit standards.

Commercial commitments generally have fixed expiration dates and may require payment of fees. Such fees (net of certain direct costs) are deferred and, upon exercise of the commitment, amortized over the life of the loan or, if exercise is deemed remote, amortized over the commitment period.

Loans Sold with Recourse

Citicorp and its subsidiaries are obligated under various recourse provisions related to the sales of loans or sales of participations in pools of loans. Total loans sold with recourse, except sales of participations in pools of credit card receivables and mortgage loans securitized under Government National Mortgage Association (GNMA) agree-

---

* From Citicorp's 1992 annual report. This is a sample SFAS No. 105 disclosure.

ments, which are described below, totaled $31.7 billion and $38.7 billion at December 31, 1992 and 1991, respectively. The maximum obligation under recourse provisions on these sold loans was approximately $9.0 billion and $12.5 billion at December 31, 1992 and 1991, respectively. Of these amounts, approximately 98% at December 31, 1992, and December 31, 1991 related to sales of residential mortgages. The net decrease in total loans sold with recourse during 1992 of $7.1 billion primarily represents an increase in the level of prepayments. Citicorp also has secondary recourse obligations under sale/servicing agreements with GNMA covering approximately $5.5 billion of residential mortgages at December 31, 1992, and $7.2 billion at December 31, 1991.

Certain Citicorp subsidiaries are also obligated under certain provisions related to the sale of participations in pools of credit card receivables of $25.6 billion at December 31, 1992, and $21.1 billion at December 31, 1991. Excess servicing fees are recognized over the life of each sale transaction. The excess servicing fee is based upon the difference between finance charges received from cardholders less the yield paid to investors, transaction costs, credit losses, and a normal servicing fee, which is also retained by certain Citicorp subsidiaries as servicers. As specified in each sale agreement, the excess servicing fee earned each month is deposited in an escrow account, up to a predetermined maximum amount, and is available to absorb additional credit losses over the remaining term of each sale transaction. When the escrow account reaches the predetermined amount, excess servicing fees are passed directly to the Citicorp subsidiary that sold the receivables. The amount available in the escrow account to absorb credit losses is included in other assets and was $772 million at December 1992, and $590 million at December 31, 1991.

Citicorp maintains reserves, outside of the allowance for credit losses, relating to asset securitization programs discussed above. These reserves totaled $544 million at December 31, 1992, and $412 million at December 31, 1991.

Standby letters of credit (see Table 1) are used in various transactions to enhance the credit standing of Citibank customers. Standby letters of credit are irrevocable assurances that Citibank will make payment in the event that a Citibank customer cannot perform its obligations to third parties.

Table 1.   Standby Letters of Credit

In Millions of Dollars at Year End	Expire within 1 Year	After 1 but within 5 Years	After 5 Years	Percentage Collater- alized	1992 Amount Out- standing	1991 Amount Out- standing
Type						
Bid Guarantee, Performance	$3,371	$1,349	$399	9.75%	$5,119	$6,981
Clean Payment	691	106	77	7.21%	874	1,044
Options, Purchased Securities, Escrow	1,125	32	33	23.10%	1,190	1,968
Insurance, Surety	7,370	740	400	43.48%	8,510	7,383
Backstop State, County, and Municipal Securities	290	248	101	–	639	1,481
All Other Debt Related	3,262	3,665	1,438	19.68%	8,365	10,209
Total	$16,109	$6,140	$2,448	24.99%	$24,697	$29,066

Citibank issues standby letters of credit on behalf of its customers for five primary purposes: to ensure contract performance and irrevocably assure payment by the customer under supply, service, and maintenance contracts or construction projects; to provide a payment mechanism for a customer's third-party obligations; to act as a substitute for an escrow account; to assure payment by a foreign reinsurer to a U.S. insurer; and to assure payment of specified financial obligations of a customer. Fees are recognized ratably over the term of the standby letter of credit.

Interest Rate and Foreign Exchange Products

Citicorp offers interest rate and foreign exchange futures, forwards, options, and swaps, which enable customers to transfer, modify, or reduce their interest rate and foreign exchange risks. Futures and forward contracts are commitments to buy or sell at a future date a financial instrument or currency at a contracted price, and may be settled in cash or through delivery. Swap contracts are commitments to settle in cash at a future date or dates, based on differentials between specified financial indices, as applied to a notional principal amount. Option contracts give the acquirer, for a fee, the right, but not the obligation, to buy or sell within a limited time a financial instrument or currency at a contracted price that may also be settled in cash, based on differentials between specified indices.

In most cases, Citicorp manages the exposures related to these products as part of its overall interest rate and foreign exchange trading activities, which include both funded (asset and liability) and nonfunded positions. For example, Citicorp may hold a security in its trading portfolio and, at the same time, have futures contracts to sell that security. The losses on one position may substantially offset gains on the other position. Citicorp also uses these products to reduce exposure outside the trading portfolios as hedges of interest rate and foreign exchange positions.

The price and credit risks inherent in traditional banking services are also present in these specialized financial products, as are the various operating risks that exist in all financial activities.

Price risk is the exposure created by fluctuations in interest and foreign exchange rates, and is a function of the type of product, the volume of the transaction, the tenor and terms of the agreement, and the volatility of the underlying interest rate or exchange rate. Price risk is affected by the mix of the aggregate portfolio and the extent to which positions have offsetting exposures. The price risk of an interest rate swap, for example, will be reduced by the presence of securities, financial futures, or other interest rate swap positions with offsetting exposure. Citicorp manages its trading activities in these specialized financial products on a market value basis that recognizes in earnings the gains or losses resulting from changes in market interest or exchange rates. Trading limits and monitoring procedures are used to control the overall exposure to price risk.

Citicorp uses a variety of techniques to measure and manage its risk exposure in interest and foreign exchange rates. While the complexity of Citicorp's operations necessitates customized risk-management techniques for the various businesses it engages in, the monitoring procedures generally entail an objective measurement system, various risk limits at appropriate control levels, and timely reports to line and senior management in accordance with prescribed policy. These comprehensive techniques enable Citicorp to prudently manage the maximum and probable impacts of price risk on its projected earnings based on historical and current implied interest and foreign exchange rate volatilities.

Credit risk is the exposure to loss in the event of nonperformance by the other party to a transaction and is a function of the ability of the counterparty to honor its obligations to Citicorp.

For these specialized financial products, the amount due from or due to the counterparty will change as a result of movement in market rates, and the amount subject to credit risk is limited to this fluctuating amount. Credit risk is controlled through credit approvals, limits, and monitoring procedures, and the recognition in earnings of unrealized gains on these transactions is dependent on management's assessment as to collectibility.

Citicorp has a significant presence in the interest rate and foreign exchange markets. Table 2 presents the aggregate notional principal amount of Citicorp's outstanding interest rate and foreign exchange contracts at December 31, 1992 and 1991:

Table 2

In Billions of Dollars at Year End	Interest Rate Products		Foreign Exchange Products	
	1992	1991	1992	1991
Futures Contracts	$91.2	$57.0	$0.1	$0.1
Forward Contracts	162.0	127.1	788.1	584.7
Swap Agreements	217.0	206.2	37.6	50.8
Purchased Options	79.9	53.7	43.1	40.7
Written Options	61.3	55.7	41.1	40.2

Notional principal amounts are often used to express the volume of these transactions and do not reflect the extent to which positions may offset one another. These amounts do not represent the much smaller amounts potentially subject to risk.

Citicorp's credit exposure related to interest rate and foreign exchange products included in the trading portfolio can be estimated by calculating the present value of the cost of replacing at current market rates all outstanding contracts; this estimate does not consider the impact that future changes in interest and foreign exchange rates would have on such costs. The gross aggregate unrealized gains based on current market values were $6.2 billion and $6.1 billion for all interest rate contracts and $23.3 billion and $23.2 billion for foreign exchange contracts at December 31, 1992, and December 31, 1991, respectively. Additionally, commitments to purchase when-is-sued securities were $0.9 billion and $0.1 billion at December 31, 1992 and 1991, respectively. Credit losses in 1992 related to these interest rate and foreign exchange products were higher than in prior years, reflecting commercial real estate related exposures. Apart from these, credit losses have not been material; however, there can be no assurance that this experience will continue in the future.

Concentrations of Credit Risk

Concentrations of credit risk exist when changes in economic, industry, or geographic factors similarly affect groups of counterparties whose aggregate credit exposure is material in relation to Citicorp's total credit exposure. Although Citicorp's portfolio of financial instruments is broadly diversified along industry and geographic lines, material transactions are completed with other financial institutions, particularly in the securities trading, interest rate, and foreign exchange business. Additionally, North America commercial real estate, U.S. mortgages, U.S. credit card receivables, leveraged acquisition finance, and the cross-border refinancing portfolios represent areas of significant credit exposures.

Appendix II*

Fair Values of Financial Instruments and Certain Nonfinancial Instruments

Statement of Financial Accounting Standards No. 107, *Disclosures About Fair Value of Financial Instruments* (FAS 107), requires the disclosure of estimated fair values of all asset, liability, and off-balance-sheet financial instruments. FAS 107 also allows the disclosure of estimated fair values of nonfinancial instruments. Fair value estimates under FAS 107 are determined as of a specific point in time, utilizing various assumptions and estimates. The use of assumptions and various valuation techniques, as well as the absence of secondary markets for certain financial instruments, will likely reduce the comparability of fair value disclosures between financial institutions.

Financial Instruments

The fair value estimates disclosed in Table 1 are based on existing on- and off-balance-sheet financial instruments and do not consider the value of future business. Other significant assets and liabilities, which are not considered financial assets or liabilities and for which fair values have not been estimated, include premises and equipment, goodwill and other intangibles, deferred tax assets and other liabilities. The estimated fair values of the corporation's financial instruments as of December 31 are set forth in Table 1 and explained below.

   The following methods and assumptions are used by the corporation in estimating its fair value disclosures for financial instruments.

Cash and cash equivalents. The carrying value of cash and cash equivalents approximates fair value due to the relatively short period of time between the origination of the instruments and their expected realization.

Trading account securities, investment securities, mortgage-backed securities, investment and mortgage-backed securities available for sale and student loans available for sale. Fair values of these financial instruments were estimated using quoted market prices, when available. If quoted market prices were not available, fair value was estimated using quoted market prices for similar assets.

Mortgages held for sale. Fair values of mortgages held for sale are stated at carrying value, which is the lower of aggregate cost or market.

Loans and leases. Fair values for loans are estimated based on contractual cash flows adjusted for prepayment assumptions, discounted using an investor yield. The investor yield is the rate that an investor would require to purchase an instrument with similar credit risk, maturity characteristics, and servicing cost. The assumed maturities of

---

*From Norwest's 1992 annual report. This exhibit shows a sample SFAS No. 107 disclosure.

Table 1

	1992		1991		1990	
	Carrying Amount	Fair Value	Carrying Amount	Fair Value	Carrying Amount	Fair Value
Financial assets:						
Cash and cash equivalents	$2,781.8	$2,781.8	3,035.2	3,035.2	4,633.5	4,633.5
Trading account securities	132.0	132.0	157.9	157.9	114.8	114.8
Investment securities	874.8	926.4	2,449.5	2,700.1	2,925.3	3,042.4
Mortgage-backed securities	–	–	9,892.0	10,179.9	6,198.1	6,246.9
Investment securities available for sale	1,393.9	1,632.9	–	–	–	–
Mortgage-backed securities available for sale	9,022.7	9,224.7	–	–	–	–
Student loans available for sale	1,158.6	1,170.9	–	–	–	–
Mortgages held for sale	4,727.8	4,727.8	3,007.7	3,007.7	1,842.4	1,842.4
Loans and leases, net	22,310.0	23,515.6	19,617.2	20,891.3	20,627.6	21,449.4
Interest receivable	285.8	285.8	283.8	283.8	332.8	332.8
Excess servicing rights receivable	9.0	20.7	3.0	3.0	7.0	7.0
Total financial assets	42,696.4	44,418.6	38,446.3	40,258.9	36,681.5	37,669.2
Financial liabilities:						
Nonmaturity deposits	17,595.1	17,595.1	15,960.0	15,960.0	14,999.6	14,999.6
Deposits with stated maturities	9,374.7	9,527.0	10,560.6	10,811.5	11,425.5	11,513.1
Short-term borrowings	8,575.4	8,575.4	5,785.5	5,785.5	6,095.5	6,095.5
Long-term debt	4,468.2	4,557.2	3,578.6	3,773.3	2,967.2	3,115.0
Interest payable	247.1	247.1	282.3	282.3	298.2	298.2
Total financial liabilities	40,260.5	40,501.8	36,167.0	36,612.6	35,786.0	36,021.4
Off-balance-sheet financial instruments:						
Forward delivery commitments	(35.7)	(35.7)	(122.7)	(122.7)	(39.6)	(39.6)
Interest rate swaps	0.7	(7.0)	0.7	18.0	(0.3)	3.3
Futures contracts	–	–	17.9	–	1.9	–
Interest rate caps/floors	23.4	36.3	10.7	55.1	6.3	9.0
Option contracts to sell	–	–	(3.8)	(11.5)	(3.5)	(7.5)
Total off-balance-sheet financial instruments	(11.6)	(6.4)	(97.2)	(61.1)	(35.2)	(34.8)
Net financial instruments	$ 2,424.3	3,910.4	2,182.1	3,585.2	860.3	1,613.0

credit card receivables is one year, based on actual historical repayment of such receivables. Market interest rate swap spreads are utilized to convert variable loan coupon rates to the equivalent fixed coupon interest rate for calculation purposes. The fair value of the corporation's consumer finance subsidiary's loans has been reported at book value, since the estimated life, assuming prepayments, is short-term in nature.

Interest receivable and payable. The carrying value of interest receivable and payable approximates fair value due to the relatively short period of time between accrual and expected realization.

Excess servicing rights receivable. Excess servicing rights receivable represents the present value using applicable investor yields of estimated future servicing revenues in excess of normal servicing revenues over the assumed life of the servicing portfolio.

Deposits. The fair value of fixed-maturity deposits is the present value of the contractual cash flows, including principal and interest, and servicing costs, discounted using an appropriate investor yield.

In accordance with FAS 107, the fair value of deposits with no stated maturity, such as demand deposit, savings, NOW, and money market accounts, are disclosed as the amount payable on demand.

Short-term borrowings. The carrying value of short-term borrowings approximates fair value due to the relatively short period of time between the origination of the instruments and their expected payment.

Long-term debt. The fair value of long-term debt is the present value of the contractual cash flows, discounted by the investor yield, which considers the corporation's credit rating.

Commitments to extend credit, standby letters of credit, and recourse obligations. The majority of the corporation's commitment agreements and letters of credit contain variable interest rates and counterparty credit deterioration clauses, and, therefore, the carrying value of the corporation's commitments to extend credit and letters of credit approximates fair value. The fair value of the corporation's recourse obligations are valued based on estimated cash flows associated with such obligations. As any potential liabilities under such recourse obligations are recognized on the corporation's balance sheet, the carrying value of such recourse obligations approximates fair value.

Forward delivery commitments, interest rate swaps, futures contracts, and interest rate caps and floors. The fair value of forward delivery commitments, interest rate caps, floors, swaps, and futures contracts is estimated, using dealer quotes, as the amount that the corporation would receive or pay to execute a new agreement with terms identical to those remaining on the current agreement, considering current interest rates.

Certain nonfinancial instruments. Supplemental fair value information for certain nonfinancial instruments as of December 31 are set forth in Table 2 and explained below.

The supplemental fair value information, combined with the total fair value of net financial instruments from Table 1, is presented below for information purposes. This combination is not necessarily indicative of the "franchise value" or the fair value of the corporation taken as a whole.

Table 2

	1992	1991	1990
Nonfinancial instrument, assets, and liabilities:			
Premises and equipment, net	$ 640.8	595.6	596.4
Other assets	1,219.9	1,251.4	1,328.9
Accrued expenses and other liabilities	(1,223.9)	(1,290.9)	(699.6)
Other values:			
Nonmaturity deposits	1,097.3	998.5	1,108.1
Consumer finance subsidiary loans	1,716.9	1,321.2	793.1
Credit card	84.6	109.2	31.0
Banking subsidiaries consumer loans	224.4	198.3	182.3
Mortgage servicing	187.2	69.7	16.3
Mortgage loan origination/wholesale network	277.4	140.0	54.1
Trust department	467.0	413.0	362.0
Net fair value of certain nonfinancial instruments	4,691.6	3,806.0	3,772.6
Fair value of financial instruments	3,910.4	3,585.2	1,613.0
Net stockholders' equity at the fair value of net financial instruments and certain nonfinancial instruments*	$8,602.0	7,391.2	5,385.6

*   Amounts do not include applicable deferred income taxes, if any.

The following methods and assumptions were used by the corporation in estimating the fair value of certain nonfinancial instruments.

Nonfinancial instrument assets and liabilities. The nonfinancial instrument assets and liabilities are stated at book value, which approximates fair value.

Nonmaturity deposits. Table 1 does not consider the benefit resulting from the low-cost funding provided by deposit liabilities as compared with wholesale funding rates. The fair value of nonmaturity deposits, considering these relational benefits, would be $16,497.8 million, $14,961.5 million, and $13,891.5 million at December 31, 1992, 1991, and 1990, respectively. Such amounts are based on a discounted cash flow analysis, assuming a constant balance over 10 years.

Consumer finance subsidiary loans. The fair value of the corporation's consumer finance subsidiary's loans has been reported at book value in Table 1. This approach to fair values of financial instruments excludes the fair value associated with expected future balances. The corporation estimates such fair value based on discounted cash flow analysis, assuming a constant replacement of current loan balances over a 10-year life, as $1,716.9 million, $1,321.2 million, and $793.1 million at December 31, 1992, 1991, and 1990, respectively.

Credit card. The fair value of financial instruments in Table 1 excludes the fair value attributed to the expected credit card balances in future years with the holders of such cards. The fair value of such future balances is estimated to exceed book value by $84.6 million, $109.2 million, and $31.0 million at December 31, 1992, 1991, and 1990, respectively. This represents the fair value related to such future balances of both securitized and on-balance-sheet credit card receivables, based on a discounted cash flow analysis, utilizing an investor yield on similar portfolio acquisitions.

Banking subsidiaries consumer loans. For purposes of Table 1, the fair value of the banking subsidiaries' consumer loans is based on the contractual balances and maturities of existing loans. The fair value of such financial instruments does not consider future loans with customers. The fair value related to such future balances is estimated to be $224.4 million, $198.3 million, and $182.3 million at December 31, 1992, 1991, and 1990, respectively. This fair value is estimated by cash flow analysis, discounted utilizing an investor yield. The expected balances for such purposes are estimated to extend 10 years at a constant rate of replacement.

Mortgage servicing. Mortgage servicing represents the present value of estimated future normal profit on servicing revenues. Based upon independent appraisal, the corporation estimates that the fair value of its mortgage servicing exceeds book values by $187.2 million, $69.7 million, and $16.3 million at December 31, 1992, 1991, and 1990, respectively.

Mortgage loan origination/wholesale network. The supplemental fair value table includes the fair value associated with the corporation's originations of mortgage loans, which is estimated to be $277.4 million, $140.0 million, and $54.1 million at December 31, 1992, 1991, and 1990, respectively. Such estimates are based on current price/earnings ratios for similar networks.

Trust department. The fair value associated with the corporation's management of trust assets is estimated to be $467 million, $413 million, and $362 million at December 31, 1992, 1991, and 1990, respectively. Such estimates are based on current trust revenues using an industry multiple.

APPENDIX

Index of Futures and Options Contracts

SOFTS

Cocoa Futures Contracts

Cocoa Futures Contracts (The Kuala Lumpur Commodity Exchange—*Trading hours:* 11:15–12:00, 15:00–19:00), 299

Cocoa Futures Contracts (London FOX—The Futures and Options Exchange—*Trading hours:* 09:30–12:58 call, 14:30–16:45 call), 428

Cocoa Futures Contracts (Coffee, Sugar & Cocoa Exchange, Inc.—*Trading hours:* 09:30–14:15), 496

Cocoa Beans Futures Contracts (MATIF-Marché à Terme International de France—*Trading hours:* 10:30–12:55; 15:00–17:55), 193

Cocoa Option Contracts

Cocoa Option Contracts (Coffee, Sugar & Cocoa Exchange, Inc.—*Trading hours:* 09:30–14:10, 14:10 closing call commences), 496

Cocoa Traded Option Contracts

Cocoa Traded Option Contracts (London FOX—The Futures and Options Exchange—*Trading hours:* 09:30–12:58, 14:30–16:45), 430

Coffee Futures Contracts

Brazil-Differential Coffee Futures Contracts (Coffee, Sugar & Cocoa Exchange, Inc.—*Trading hours:* 09:05–13:58), 494

Coffee Futures Contracts (Manila International Futures Exchange, Inc.—*Trading hours:* 09:30, 10:30, 13:30, 14:30), 344

The material in this appendix is extracted from *The Handbook of World Stock and Commodity Exchanges,* published by Blackwell Publishers. The editors wish to thank Herbert L. Skeete for granting permission to reprint this material.

Sugar Option Contracts

Sugar Traded Option Contracts

GRAINS AND OILSEEDS

Barley Futures Contracts

Barley Traded Option Contracts

Beans Futures Contracts

Red Beans Futures Contracts (Kanmon Commodity Exchange—*Trading hours:* Morning sessions: 09:00, 10:00, 11:00), 270

Red Beans Futures Contracts (Kobe Grain Exchange—*Trading hours:* Morning sessions: 09:00, 10:00, 11:00), 271

Red Beans Futures Contracts (Nagoya Grain and Sugar Exchange—*Trading hours:* Morning sessions: 09:00, 10:00, 11:00), 274

Red Beans Futures Contracts (Osaka Grain Exchange—*Trading hours:* Morning sessions: 09:00, 10:00, 11:10), 275

Red Beans Futures Contracts (Tokyo Grain Exchange—*Trading hours:* Morning sessions: 09:00, 10:00, 11:10), 282

White Beans Futures Contracts (Hokkaido Grain Exchange—*Trading hours:* November through April: (morning sessions) 09:00, 10:00, 11:00; (afternoon sessions) 13:00, 14:00, 15:00), 270

White Beans Futures Contracts (Nagoya Grain and Sugar Exchange—*Trading hours:* Morning sessions: 09:00, 10:00, 11:00), 274

Birdseed Futures Contracts

Birdseed Futures Contracts (Buenos Aires Cereal Exchange—*Trading hours:* 12:30–13:00. 16:00–16:30), 104

Canola Futures Contracts

Canola Futures Contracts (The Winnipeg Commodity Exchange—*Trading hours:* 09:30–13:15), 151

Canola Option Contracts

Canola Option Contracts (The Winnipeg Commodity Exchange—*Trading hours:* 09:30–13:20. On the last trading day of an expiring contract, trading in that contract closes at 12:00), 153

Corn Futures Contracts

Corn Futures Contracts (Rosario Stock Exchange—*Trading hours:* 12:15–12:50, 16:00–16:40), 101

Corn Futures Contracts (Buenos Aires Futures Market—*Trading hours:* 14:00–14:30), 102

Corn Futures Contracts (Buenos Aires Cereal Exchange—*Trading hours:* 12:30–13:00. 16:00–16:30), 103

Corn Futures Contracts (Budapest Commodity Exchange—*Trading hours:* Tuesdays and Thursdays, 11:30–13:00), 225

Corn Futures Contracts (Tokyo Grain Exchange—*Trading hours:* Morning sessions: 09:00, 11:10), 282

Corn Futures Contracts (Chicago Board of Trade—*Trading hours:* 09:30–13:15, except on the last trading day of an expiring contract, when trading closes at 12:00), 470

Corn Futures Contracts (MidAmerica Commodity Exchange—*Trading hours:* 09:30–13:30), 502

Yellow Corn Futures Contracts (Kanmon Commodity Exchange—*Trading hours:* Morning sessions: 09:00, 10:00, 11:00), 271

Corn Option Contracts

Corn Option Contracts (Buenos Aires Futures Market—*Trading hours:* 14:00–14:30), 102

Corn Option Contracts (Chicago Board of Trade—*Trading hours:* 09:30–13:15, except on the last trading day of an expiring contract, when trading closes at 12:00), 475

Oats Option Contracts

Oats Option Contracts (Chicago Board of Trade—*Trading hours:* 09:30–13:15, except on the last trading day of an expiring contract, when trading closes at 12:00), 476

Palm Oil Futures Contracts

Crude Palm Kernel Oil Futures Contracts (The Kuala Lumpur Commodity Exchange—*Trading hours:* 11:15–12:15, 15:45–18:30), 298

Crude Palm Oil Futures Contracts (The Kuala Lumpur Commodity Exchange—*Trading hours:* 11:00–12:30, 15:30–18:00), 298

RBD Palm Olein Futures Contracts (The Kuala Lumpur Commodity Exchange—*Trading hours:* 11:30–12:30, 15:30–18:00), 208

Potato Futures Contracts

Potato Starch Futures Contracts (Hokkaido Grain Exchange—*Trading hours:* November through April: (morning sessions) 09:00, 10:00, 11:00; (afternoon sessions) 13:00, 14:00, 15:00), 270

Potatoes Futures Contracts (Agricultural Futures Market Amsterdam [ATA]—*Trading hours:* 10:45–12:45, 14:00–16:00), 319

Potatoes Futures Contracts (London FOX—The Futures and Options Exchange—*Trading hours:* 11:00–12:30, 14:45–16:00), 429

Potatoes No. 1 Futures Contracts (Marché à Terme de la Pomme de Terre—*Trading hours:* 11:00–12:45; 15:00–16:30), 195

Sweet Potato Starch Futures Contracts (Nagoya Grain and Sugar Exchange—*Trading hours:* Morning sessions: 09:00, 10:00, 11:00), 274

Potatoes Traded Option Contracts

Potatoes Traded Option Contracts (London FOX—The Futures and Options Exchange—*Trading hours:* 11:00–12:30, 14:45–16:00), 431

Rice Futures Contracts

CRCE Rice Futures Contracts (MidAmerica Commodity Exchange—*Trading hours:* 09:15–13:30), 503

Rice Option Contracts

Rough Rice Option Contracts (MidAmerica Commodity Exchange—*Trading hours:* 09:15–13:30. On the last day of trading, expiring contracts close at 12:15.), 505

Rye Futures Contracts

Rye Futures Contracts (Buenos Aires Cereal Exchange—*Trading hours:* 12:30–13:00. 16:00–16:30), 104

Rye Futures Contracts (The Winnipeg Commodity Exchange—*Trading hours:* 09:30–13:15), 152

Sorghum Futures Contracts

Sorghum Futures Contracts (Rosario Stock Exchange—*Trading hours:* 12:15–12:50, 16:00–16:40), 101

Sorghum Futures Contracts (Buenos Aires Cereal Exchange—*Trading hours:* 12:30–13:00. 16:00–16:30), 103

Soybean Futures Contracts

Domestic Soybeans Futures Contracts (Hokkaido Grain Exchange—*Trading hours:* November through April: (morning sessions) 09:00, 10:00, 11:00; (afternoon sessions) 13:00, 14:00, 15:00), 270

Imported Soybeans Futures Contracts (Hokkaido Grain Exchange—*Trading hours:* November through April: (morning sessions) 09:00, 10:00, 11:00; (afternoon sessions) 13:00, 14:00, 15:00), 269

Imported Soybeans Futures Contracts (Kanmon Commodity Exchange—*Trading hours:* Morning sessions: 09:00, 10:00, 11:00), 271

Imported Soybeans Futures Contracts (Kobe Grain Exchange—*Trading hours:* Morning sessions: 09:00, 10:00, 11:00), 271

Imported Soybeans Futures Contracts (Osaka Grain Exchange—*Trading hours:* Morning sessions: 10:00, 11:10), 275

Soybean Meal Futures Contracts (London FOX—The Futures and Options Exchange—*Trading hours:* 10:30–12:00, 14:30–16:45), 429

Soybean Futures Contracts (Rosario Stock Exchange—*Trading hours:* 12:15–12:50, 16:00–16:40), 101

Soybean Futures Contracts (Buenos Aires Futures Market—*Trading hours:* 16:15–16:45), 102

Soybean Futures Contracts (Buenos Aires Cereal Exchange—*Trading hours:* 12:30–13:00. 16:00–16:30), 103

Soybean Meal Futures Contracts (Chicago Board of Trade—*Trading hours:* 09:30–13:15, except on the last trading day of an expiring contract, when trading closes at 12:00), 471

Soybean Meal Futures Contracts (MidAmerica Commodity Exchange—*Trading hours:* 09:30–13:30), 502

Soybean Oil Futures Contracts (Chicago Board of Trade—*Trading hours:* 09:30–13:15, except on the last trading day of an expiring contract, when trading closes at 12:00), 471

Soybeans Futures Contracts (Manila International Futures Exchange, Inc.—*Trading hours:* 09:45, 10:45, 13:45, 14:45), 345

Soybeans Futures Contracts (Chicago Board of Trade—*Trading hours:* 09:30–13:15, except on the last trading day of an expiring contract, when trading closes at 12:00), 471

Soybeans Futures Contracts (MidAmerica Commodity Exchange—*Trading hours:* 09:30–13:30), 502

U.S. Soybeans Futures Contracts (Tokyo Grain Exchange—*Trading hours:* Morning sessions: 10:00, 11:10), 281

Soybeans Option Contracts

Soybean Meal Option Contracts (Chicago Board of Trade—*Trading hours:* 09:30–13:15, except on the last trading day of an expiring contract, when trading closes at 12:00), 476

Soybean Oil Option Contracts (Chicago Board of Trade—*Trading hours:* 09:30–13:15, except on the last trading day of an expiring contract, when trading closes at 12:00), 477

Soybeans Option Contracts (Buenos Aires Futures Market—*Trading hours:* 15:15–16:45), 103

Soybeans Option Contracts (Chicago Board of Trade—*Trading hours:* 09:30–13:15, except on the last trading day of an expiring contract, when trading closes at 12:00), 476

Soybeans Option Contracts (MidAmerica Commodity Exchange—*Trading hours:* 09:30–13:30), 505

U.S. Soybeans Option Contracts (Tokyo Grain Exchange—*Trading hours:* Opening session: 10:00–10:30), 282

Tin Futures Contracts

Zinc Futures Contracts

PRECIOUS METALS

Gold Contracts

Gold Forward Contracts

Gold Futures Contracts

Gold Option Contracts

Silver Option Contracts

1,000–oz Silver Option Contracts (Chicago Board of Trade—*Trading hours:* 07:25–13:25), 479

Silver Option Contracts (Toronto Futures Exchange—*Trading hours:* 09:05–16:00), 150

Silver Option Contracts (Commodity Exchange, Inc. [COMEX]—*Trading hours:* 08:25–14:25), 499

Weekly Silver Option Contracts (Commodity Exchange, Inc. [COMEX]—*Trading hours:* 08:25–14:25), 500

FINANCIALS-CURRENCIES

Currency Futures Contracts

Australian Dollar Futures Contracts (Chicago Mercantile Exchange—*Trading hours:* 07:20–14:00, except on the last day of the expiring contract, when close is at 09:16), 481

Australian Dollar Futures Contracts (Philadelphia Board of Trade—*Trading hours:* 19:00–23:00 EDT [18:00–22:00 EST]), 517

British Pound Futures Contracts (Finnish Options Market—*Trading hours:* 10:00–16:00), 182

British Pound Futures Contracts (Singapore International Monetary Exchange Ltd. [SIMEX]—*Trading hours:* 08:25–17:15), 366

British Pound Futures Contracts (Chicago Mercantile Exchange—*Trading hours:* 07:20–14:00, except on the last day of the expiring contract, when close is at 09:16), 482

British Pound Futures Contracts (MidAmerica Commodity Exchange—*Trading hours:* 07:20–14:15), 504

British Pound Futures Contracts (Philadelphia Board of Trade—*Trading hours:* 19:00–23:00 EDT [18:00–22:00 EST]), 517

British Pound Futures Contracts (Twin Cities Board of Trade—*Trading hours:* 07:00–14:00), 518

Canadian Dollar Futures Contracts (Chicago Mercantile Exchange—*Trading hours:* 07:20–14:00, except the last day of the expiring contract, when close is at 09:16), 482

Canadian Dollar Futures Contracts (MidAmerica Commodity Exchange—*Trading hours:* 07:20–14:15), 504

Canadian Dollar Futures Contracts (Philadelphia Board of Trade—*Trading hours:* 03:30–14:30 EDT/EST), 517

DEM/FIM Currency Futures Contracts (Finnish Option Exchange Ltd.—*Trading hours:* Monday-Thursday: 10:00–16:30; Friday: 10:00–13:00), 186

Deutsche Mark Futures Contracts (Finnish Options Market—*Trading hours:* 10:00–16:00),183

Deutsche Mark Futures Contracts (Brazilian Futures Exchange—*Trading hours:* 10:00–16:30), 136

Deutsche Mark Futures Contracts (Singapore International Monetary Exchange Ltd. [SIMEX]—*Trading hours:* 08:20–17:10), 366

Deutsche Mark Futures Contracts (Chicago Mercantile Exchange—*Trading hours:* 07:20–14:00, except the last day of the expiring contract, when close is at 09:16), 482

Deutsche Mark Futures Contracts (MidAmerica Commodity Exchange—*Trading hours:* 18:00–21:30), 504

Deutsche Mark Futures Contracts (Philadelphia Board of Trade—*Trading hours:* 19:00–23:00 EDT [18:00–22:00 EST]), 517

Currency Option Contracts

FINANCIALS-INTEREST RATES

Bills Futures Contracts

90–Day Bank Accepted Bills Futures Contracts (New Zealand Futures & Options Exchange Ltd.—*Trading hours:* 08:00–17:00), 326

90–Day Bank-Accepted Bills Futures Contracts (The Sydney Futures Exchange—*Trading hours:* Floor: 08:30–12:30 EST. 14:00–16:30 EST), 108

Three-Month U.S. Treasury Bills Futures Contracts (Chicago Mercantile Exchange-Trading hours: 07:20–14:00, except on the last day of the expiring contract, when close is at 10:00), 483

Treasury Bills Futures Contracts (MidAmerica Commodity Exchange—*Trading hours:* 07:20–14:15), 504

Treasury-Bill-OMVX 180 Futures Contracts (The Swedish Futures and Options Market), 391

Bills Option Contracts

90–Day Bank Bill (BBO) Option Contracts (New Zealand Futures & Options Exchange Ltd.—*Trading hours:* 08:00–17:00), 329

90–Day Bank-Accepted Bills Option Contracts (The Sydney Futures Exchange—*Trading hours:* Floor: 08:30–12:30 EST. 14:00–16:30 EST), 110

Short-Term Interest Rate (IRX) Option Contracts (Chicago Board Options Exchange—*Trading hours:* 07:20–14:00), 468

Three-Month U.S. Treasury Bill Option Contracts (Chicago Mercantile Exchange—*Trading hours:* 07:20–14:00), 490

Bond Futures Contracts

9% 2022 Mortgage Credit Bond Futures Contracts (FUTOP[reg]-The Guarantee Fund for Danish Options and Futures—*Trading hours:* 09:00–15:30), 173

Belgian Government Bond Futures Contracts (Belgian Futures and Options Exchange (BEL-FOX)—*Trading hours:* 09:00–17:00), 125

CT2 Urban Mortgage Bank of Sweden Bond Futures Contracts (The Swedish Futures and Options Market), 392

CT5 Urban Mortgage Bank of Sweden Bond Futures Contracts (The Swedish Futures and Options Market), 392

Five-Year Interest Rate Swap Futures Contracts (Chicago Board of Trade—*Trading hours:* 07:20–14:00. On the last trading day of an expiring contract, trading in that contract closes at 09:30), 474

Five-Year Government Stock No. 2 Contract (GSC) Futures Contracts (New Zealand Futures & Options Exchange Ltd.—*Trading hours:* 08:00–17:00), 326

French Treasury Bond Futures Contracts (MATIF-Marché à Terme International de France—*Trading hours:* 09:00–16:30), 193

German Government Bond (Bund) Futures Contracts (The London International Financial Futures and Options Exchange [LIFFE]—*Trading hours:* 07:30–16:15), 433

Government of Canada Bond (CGB) Futures Contracts (The Montreal Exchange—*Trading hours:* 08:20–15:00), 146

Guilder Bond (FTO) Futures Contracts (Financial Futures Market Amsterdam [FTA]—*Trading hours:* 09:00–17:00), 321

Italian Government Bond (BTP) Futures Contracts (Italian Futures Market—*Trading hours:* 09:10–17:00), 254

Deposit Forwards Contracts

Deposit Futures Contracts

Deposit Option Contracts

Deposit Swap Contracts

Gilts Futures Contracts

Gilts Option Contracts

Notes Futures Contracts

Notes Option Contracts

FINANCIALS-INDEXES

Index Futures Contracts

Index Option Contracts

OTHER

Broiler Futures Contracts

Broiler Option Contracts

Chemicals Futures Contracts

Cocoons Futures Contracts

GLOSSARY

Lisa M. Raiti
Managing Director
Centre Financial Products Limited

American option: An option that may be exercised at any time before expiration.

At-the-money: An option that has no intrinsic value, with its strike price equal to the current market price or level of the underlying asset, security, rate, or index.

Call option: A contract under which the buyer acquires the right but not the obligation to purchase an asset, security, rate, or index at the strike price on or before a specified expiration date.

Cap: A multiperiod interest rate option that provides a cash payment to the option holder whenever the reference rate is greater than the contracted ceiling rate on a fixing date.

Counterparty: A principal to a swap or other derivative instrument, as opposed to an agent such as a broker.

Credit risk: Combined risk or exposure from default risk and market risk.

Currency swap: An agreement for the exchange of a future series of interest and principal payments in which one party pays in one currency and the other party pays in a different currency. The agreed-on exchange rate is fixed over the life of the swap.

Default risk: The risk that a counterparty to a contract, such as a swap, will be unable to fulfill its obligations due to bankruptcy or other cause.

End user: In the context of swaps, the final counterparty rather than intermediaries such as swap dealers.

European option: An option that may be exercised only on the expiration date.

Exchange rate risk: The risk that a future spot exchange rate will deviate from its current value.

Exercise: The process by which the holder of an option notifies the seller of its intention to take delivery of the underlying asset in the case of a call or, in the case of a put, to make delivery at the specified exercise price.

Fixing date: The date on which the reference rate is observed for purposes of calculating the cash payment or settlement amount due on an interest rate option such as a cap or floor.

Floor: A multiperiod interest rate option that provides a cash payment to the option holder whenever the reference rate is less than the contracted floor rate on a fixing date.

Forward contract: A contract under which the buyer is obligated to take delivery and the seller is obligated to make delivery of a fixed amount of a commodity, foreign currency, or other financial instrument at a predetermined price on a specified future date. Payment in full is due at the time of delivery.

Forward exchange rate: An exchange rate at which a currency seller or buyer is willing to sell or buy currency at a specified future date.

Forward interest rate: An interest rate at which a lender is willing to lend for a specified term at a specified future date.

Hedge: A position taken in order to offset the risk associated with some other position. Often the initial position is a cash position and the hedge position involves a risk-management instrument such as a swap.

Interest rate risk: The risk that a future interest rate will deviate from its current value.

Interest rate swap: An agreement between two parties to engage in a series of exchange of payments, based on two different interest rates, on the same notional principal denominated in the same currency.

In-the-money: An option that has an intrinsic value based on the strike price of the option and the current market price or level of the underlying asset, security, rate, or index.

Intrinsic value: The difference between the market price of the underlying asset, security, rate, or index and the strike price. Alternatively, the amount an option is in-the-money. Out-of-the-money or at-the-money options have an intrinsic value of zero.

Market risk: Risk or exposure arising from the behavior of a market indicator, e.g., a price, rate, index, or value.

Market value: The price, often estimated as replacement cost, at which buyers and sellers trade similar items in an open marketplace.

Netting: The reduction of risk exposures by offsetting payments under a master swap agreement on an ongoing basis and, potentially, when terminating positions with a counterparty.

Notional principal: The amount of principal on which the interest is calculated on a swap or related instrument. In the case of interest rate swaps, the principal is purely "notional" in that no exchange of principal ever takes place.

Option: A contract that grants the holder the right to purchase (call) or sell (put) a specified quantity of shares of an asset, security, rates, or index at a fixed price for a period of time.

Out-of-the-money: An option that has no intrinsic value based on the strike price of the option and the current market price or level of the underlying asset, security, rate, or index.

Over-the-counter: A dealer market in which transactions take place via telephone, telex, and other electronic forms of communication as opposed to trading on the floor of a formal exchange. Such markets allow for great flexibility in product design.

Plain-vanilla: The simplest form of a financial instrument. Often associated with the first manifestation of an instrument (e.g., a plain-vanilla swap).

Put option: A contract under which the buyer acquires the right but not the obligation to sell an asset, security, rate, or index at the strike price on or before a specified expiration date.

Reference rate: A designated rate such as six-month LIBOR or three-month T-bill on any cash settled interest rate option such as a cap or floor. It is the rate observed on the fixing date for purposes of determining the amount of any cash settlement.

Replacement cost: The cost incurred to replace in the market a contract that has terminated prematurely with an assumed identical contract. Replacement generally occurs when one of a pair of matched contracts has been terminated early.

Spot exchange rate: Exchange rate on currency for immediate delivery.

Spot interest rate: Interest rate fixed today on a loan that is made today.

Strike price: Price specified for calling (buying) or putting (selling) an asset, security, rate, or index underlying an option. Also known as exercise price.

Swap: An agreement providing for a series of exchange of two series of cash flow in the same currency (an interest rate swap) or in different currencies (a currency swap).

Swaption: An option on a swap. The swaption purchaser has the right to enter into a specific swap for a defined period of time.

Volatility: The degree to which the price of an underlying asset, security, rate, or index tends to fluctuate over time.

Zero-coupon swap curve: The implied spot yield curve for swaps. This curve is derived from the conventional yield curve for at-the-market swaps (swaps with current market rates and terms).

Index